Rendezvous with Destiny

RENDEZVOUS WITH DESTINY

Ronald Reagan and the Campaign

That Changed America

CRAIG SHIRLEY

002000393335

ISI
BOOKS

WILMINGTON, DELAWARE

Shirley, Craig.

      Rendezvous with destiny : Ronald Reagan and the campaign
      that changed America / Craig Shirley.

      p. cm.
      Includes bibliographical references and index.
      ISBN 978-1-933859-55-2 (cloth bound : alk. paper)

          1. Presidents—United States—Election—1980. 2. Reagan, Ronald. 3. United States—Politics and government—1977–1981. 4. Political campaigns—United States. I. Title.

E875.S46 2009
973.927092—dc22   2009029922

ISI Books
Intercollegiate Studies Institute
Wilmington, DE 19807-1938
www.isibooks.org

Manufactured in the United States of America

Most men are lucky to have one good woman in their lives.

I have been fortunate to have had several. To my mother, Barbara Shirley Eckert, who taught me about life and love; my friend Diana Banister, who taught me about loyalty; my sister, Rebecca Sirhal, who taught me about God's gift of forgiveness; and my daughter, Taylor, who taught me about miracles.

And to the most important men in my life, my dear departed father, Edward Bruce; and my sons, Matthew McGiveron, Andrew Abbott, and Mitchell Boman Reagan Shirley.

But most especially for my wife and best friend, Zorine, who taught me about what is really important in this world.

It is to her that this book, as with everything, is dedicated.

CONTENTS

Foreword

by George F. Will

L ooking back, as Americans are notoriously disinclined to do, it all seems
so inevitable. But it did not seem so—it did not *feel* so—at the time. And
in fact it was not so.

Looking only at the electoral-vote outcome—489–49—the victory of Ronald Reagan in the 1980 presidential election seems like a walk in the park, a play without drama. But looked at from the inside of the campaign, as Craig Shirley did at the time and now recollects in this exhilarating history, the drama was almost too abundant.

If we consider only the nation's retrospective affection for Ronald Reagan, and his extraordinary achievements in office—a demoralized nation revitalized, the Cold War concluded victoriously and peacefully—it is easy to assume that his victory over an incumbent president, Jimmy Carter, whose failures were manifold and manifest, was a foregone conclusion. It is easy, but wrong. Shirley demonstrates just how wrong in this worthy successor to his masterful chronicle of Reagan's unavailing quest for the 1976 Republican presidential nomination, *Reagan's Revolution: The Untold Story of the Campaign That Started It All*.

That volume and this one are antidotes to the intellectual error known as "presentism"—the fallacy of depicting, explaining, or interpreting the past from the perspective of current-day knowledge and understandings. Shirley rescues Reagan's victorious campaign from lazy presentism.

Reagan's rise to the White House began from the ashes of the 1976 Republican convention in Kansas City. Truth be told, it began from the podium of that convention, with Reagan's gracious—but fighting—concession speech. No one who knew the man and listened to him carefully could have mistaken that speech for a valedictory statement by someone taking his leave from national politics.

The path from that nadir to the triumph four years later was a rocky, uphill climb. It was achieved by a politician whose cheerfulness and amiability concealed a toughness and longheadedness that few have analyzed as meticulously as Shirley does here. As was the case with Winston Churchill, another politician spurned by his party and consigned to "wilderness years," the iron entered Reagan's soul after adversity. In a sense, therefore, his loss in 1976 was doubly fortunate: The Carter presidency made the country hungry for strong leadership, and the Reagan of 1980 was stronger and more ready to lead than was the Reagan of 1976.

This book is both a primer on practical politics and a meditation on the practicality of idealism. It arrives, serendipitously, at a moment when conservatives are much in need of an inspiriting examination of their finest hour.

Here it is.

Prologue

A NEW BEGINNING

*"I believe this generation of Americans today also
has a rendezvous with destiny."*

July 17, 1980

Ronald Reagan stood before the multitude of cheering Republicans in Detroit's Joe Louis Arena, at long last master of all he surveyed.

Millions of his fellow Americans watched on television. Most had little choice, as the three networks—ABC, NBC, and CBS—dominated the airwaves and promised gavel-to-gavel coverage. Cable was in its infancy. The upstart Cable News Network, only five weeks old, also was covering the Republican convention, but with its tiny audience and seemingly quixotic mission of providing twenty-four-hour news coverage, most political pros regarded CNN as Ted Turner's folly.

A tiny, hidden fan blew lightly on Reagan's face at the podium to keep him from sweltering. Several strands of his forelock wafted gently in the stirring air. Reagan, sixty-nine, was dressed handsomely and impeccably in a dark suit, every crease sharp. With his aging but still handsome movie star profile and aw-shucks grin, he appeared to be an oasis of cool in the oppressive summer heat.

Everybody on the floor, however, was sweating heavily. Convention planners failed to appreciate that the thousands of gesticulating, dancing, partying, delirious Republicans packed into the arena—far more than official capacity of twenty thousand allowed—would raise the temperature and overwhelm the airconditioning system unless the facility was precooled for hours ahead of time. A heat wave had ravaged the nation for three weeks; Detroit's daytime temperature had topped out at 97 degrees on the second day of the convention. Nobody on the floor seemed to mind the sticky conditions, though.

Fortunately, fashion had changed dramatically since the last time Republicans had gathered to nominate a president. Sensible summer suits for men in 1980 were made of breathable, lightweight cotton, wool, and poplin, more loosely tailored and with narrower lapels. They had replaced stifling, tightly woven polyester suits, with garish colors and wide lapels that made every man look like a John Travolta wannabe. Women, too, had gone from the suffocating and unflattering synthetic pant suits of 1976 to cooler, more comfortable natural-fiber dresses and skirts. Long hair had also gone out of style, for both men and women.

Times they were a changin' in both style and substance.

Conservatism in 1980 no longer meant a calcified status quo—it represented *change*. For the first time since Reagan's boyhood hero Franklin Roosevelt transformed the political landscape, conservatism posed a serious challenge to the reigning liberal orthodoxy. The conservative "movement," of which Reagan was the avatar, was changing the way Americans viewed their government and their world. Conservatism was leading the sprint away from the 1970s, one of the most dispiriting decades in the history of the American Republic. Reagan, the maverick populist, had wrought a fusion between the "Social Right" and the "Sociable Right," and the moderates in the party would have to get comfortable riding shotgun in the new GOP.

As the *Wall Street Journal* aptly put it, "What was extreme conservatism 16 years ago, now is politics with mainstream appeal."[1]

After two generations in which FDR's New Deal coalition dominated American politics, Reagan had emerged as the Republican answer to Roosevelt: a larger-than-life father figure who would bring his party out of the wilderness and demoralized Americans into the sunshine.

His opponent, President Jimmy Carter, was increasingly seen as a latter-day Herbert Hoover, a hapless incarnation of do-nothing incompetence. The great campaign biographer Theodore White said of Carter, "Approach him with pity. He has been caught up and crumpled by the hand of history more cruelly than any president since Herbert Hoover." Of Reagan, White said, "Approach him with self-protecting skepticism. He is the most instantly charming and likeable candidate for the presidency since John F. Kennedy."[2]

Reagan's new GOP had discarded "détente," the slow-motion surrender of the West to the Soviets. Tax cuts and reductions in the size and scope of government had replaced balanced budgets as the centerpiece of the party's economic policy. On social matters, Reagan espoused a muscular yet spiritual message: the power of parents over that of the "nanny state." It all emanated from Reagan's devotion to freedom as the organizing principle of his new Republican Party.

It was hard to believe that just four years earlier, in the wake of the Watergate scandals and the Republicans' devastating electoral losses, the punditocracy was giving last rites to the GOP.

The bloodbaths that had dominated Republican conventions for the past forty years were over, or at least masked over. Even the liberal Republican senator from New York, Jacob Javits, a chronic Reagan critic, was a Reagan delegate in Detroit.

Wall Street, too, was learning to love the populist Reagan. When he had announced his candidacy the previous November, the *Wall Street Journal* wrote in an editorial, "For political packaging, we do not need to turn to a 68-year-old man." The paper conceded eight months later that Reagan had "learned something."[3]

Now the man of the moment stood astride the new GOP, high above the convention floor. In large white letters below the nominee, across a blue half circle, the theme of the convention read, "TOGETHER . . . A NEW BEGINNING." Hundreds of red and white carnations adorned the rostrum.

On either side of Reagan across the large stage were the many and varied leaders of the revived Republicans. Congressman Jack Kemp of New York; party chairman Bill Brock; Senator Bob Dole of Kansas; Ambassador George Bush, Reagan's running mate; House Minority Leader John Rhodes of Arizona; and of course, according to homey political tradition, the Reagan and Bush families, including Barbara Bush, a bored-looking George W. Bush, and a beaming Nancy Reagan.

Unfortunately, the most important Reaganite of all, Senator Paul Laxalt of Nevada, the national chairman of Reagan's campaign, was missing. He had left the night before, after nominating his old friend Ron. Rumors held that Laxalt was dismayed over the last-minute choice of Bush, a Connecticut-bred Brahmin, for VP.

BY 1980 TELEVISION HAD become the nation's fully dominant cultural force. Network reporters were firmly affixed atop pedestals in American culture as paragons of knowledge—despite their frequent fatuity, as when rising star (and future tragic figure) Jessica Savitch of NBC asked a GOP operative later in the year how it was that the delegates at the Republican convention could then go to the Democratic convention and be just as enthusiastic.[4] Some complained that TV reporters were too intent on making news rather than simply reporting it, as in the case of the "co-presidency" debacle between Reagan and former president Gerald Ford the night before in Detroit. What had started as idle gossip—a Dream Ticket—had become a full-blown imbroglio, much of it fed by ill-informed TV correspondents.

Many print stories in 1980 were devoted to the reporters, the anchors, and the resources the networks invested in the national conventions. In addition, a new trend featuring network anchors interviewing network reporters about network coverage of conventions was inaugurated in 1980. Television reporters increasingly beheld themselves like Narcissus transfixed with his own image. This phenomenon would only accelerate in coming years.

Yet all of these trends were mere eddies in the face of the mighty political currents at work in Detroit in 1980. A tsunami was beginning to crest over America.

Jack Kemp—football star, college phys-ed major, self-taught historian and economist—understood this better at the time than almost everybody else. In speaking to the GOP convention two nights before Reagan's speech, Congressman Kemp had said, "There is a tidal wave coming. A political tidal wave as powerful as the one that hit in 1932."[5]

The 1932 election was one of the few profoundly meaningful elections in American history. Most elections are only breezes that gently buffet the ship of state. Several, though, have been torrential storms, dramatically changing America's course. The election of 1980 would prove, like those in 1800, 1860, and 1932, to be one of the most consequential in American history, radically altering the future and giving rise to a new generation of conservatism.

BILLY JOEL'S ALBUM *Glass Houses* topped the charts and his hit "It's Still Rock and Roll to Me" was the number-one single in the country. The number-four album in the country was the movie soundtrack to the *Star Wars* sequel, *The Empire Strikes Back*, a sentiment that could have been the theme for the resurgent Republicans this night.

The mood of the rest of the country, in contrast, was dark, brooding, and apprehensive. Americans faced the second-worst economic calamity in the nation's history, behind only the epochal Great Depression.

Gasoline—when it was available—had nearly doubled in cost over four years, rising from 77 cents to $1.30 per gallon and more.

Taxes, not including Social Security, had gone up 30 percent, but income had risen only 20 percent.

Unemployment was closing rapidly on 8 percent, but this statistic was deceptively low. Millions of despondent Americans who could not find work had simply dropped out of the job market. Some projections had joblessness rising to 9.4 percent by the end of the year.[6]

The economy was in negative growth, with factories shuttered across the country. But inflation continued, as it had for three years, in double digits—depending on the day and hour, 17 percent, 17.5 percent, 18 percent. A new word had been coined: "stagflation," meaning a combination of inflation and stagnating growth, a worst-of-both-worlds scenario that economic textbooks said could not exist.

Few places were as bad off as the city in which the Republicans were gathered. Detroit had become an economic basket case, spiraling downward after the 1967 race riots accelerated "white flight" to the suburbs. The anemic state of the auto industry contributed to the city's decay. Still, Detroit officials had done their best to put on the dog. Almost three dozen decrepit buildings were razed, another fifty painted or boarded up. Junk cars were towed away and thousands of trees and shrubs were planted to spruce things up. Even outdoor water fountains that had not operated for years were turned back on. Joe Louis Arena itself had been built just the year before, at a cost of $57 million. More than two thousand cops were patrolling the city's streets to ensure that nothing befell the Republicans. Meanwhile the Coast Guard was standing watch on the Detroit River, and hundreds of sheriffs, state troopers, and Secret Service agents were also on hand.[7]

Along with economic disaster, a spiritual depression was afoot in the land. For the first time in the national consciousness, parents did not believe their children's future would be brighter than it had been for them. Many didn't feel good about their country anymore.

A malaise had descended upon America.

Conditions were equally bleak in the international arena. The America of 1980 was confronting a so-called Cold War, but with 55,000 young Americans killed in Vietnam and another 33,000 killed in an earlier quagmire on the Korean Peninsula, it was difficult to see this "long twilight struggle," as JFK put it, as anything but a hot war.[8]

The Soviets were on the march after invading Afghanistan a year earlier and were arming anti-American guerrillas in Central America and Africa. The Soviet embassy in Washington was regarded as nothing more than a forward operating post for the KGB. America's military might was a thing of the past, and many GIs were on food stamps. The Eastern bloc was running amok and the West was losing. South Vietnam, Laos, Cambodia, and other countries had fallen to Communism. NATO was withering, and Italy in the '70s had come within a hairsbreadth of voting into power a Communist government.

Dominoes were falling across the globe.

Yet despite America's troubles, and despite the low esteem in which Jimmy Carter was held, the odds were stacked against Reagan. Americans did not like to kick presidents out of office. In twenty previous elections dating back to 1900, only twice—in 1912 and 1932—had the American people found sufficient reason to boot the elected incumbent. More presidents in the twentieth century had left the White House feet first than had been given their walking papers by the American voter.

THE ROAD AHEAD FOR Ronald Reagan would be rough, but the road behind had been strewn with many hazards. In 1980 he made his third try for the Republican Party's nomination. This was his last chance, after he lost in 1968 to Richard Nixon and again in 1976 to Gerald Ford. The defeat in 1976 was particularly bitter. His fight against President Ford had grown nasty and had been carried all the way to the Republican National Convention in Kansas City.

Awful things had been said and written about Reagan, and not just by liberal editorialists. Some of the worst had come from the GOP establishment and self-appointed conservative leaders. Reagan was in many ways a libertarian, distrustful of the abuses of governmental power—including abuses by overzealous conservatives, some of whom viewed government as a weapon to be used against those who dared oppose them. Many in the New Right had opposed this candidacy, supporting other, more malleable contenders. They remained wary of him.

So, too, did many on the left. David Lucey was the son of Pat Lucey, the Democratic governor of Wisconsin who became independent presidential candidate John Anderson's running mate in 1980. The younger Lucey recalled in an interview, "People on our side of the spectrum in 1980, we thought [Reagan] was a nutcase."[9]

Reagan's uphill climb, especially over the past four years, had been nothing short of remarkable. He had defied doubts about his age, his wisdom, his endurance, and his capacity—doubts not only from his political opponents but also from his own party and even top aides. He had also overcome a hostile media; a sometimes balky campaign operation; his own mistakes, gaffes, and indifference to the management of his last quest; and several bona fide heavyweight contenders for the 1980 GOP presidential nomination. His campaign had utterly collapsed seven months earlier after the disastrous loss in Iowa's caucuses to George Herbert Walker Bush. Only through sheer force of will did Reagan right himself and his campaign and turn it around to win the nomination.

Even in the past twenty-four hours Reagan had had to overcome big obstacles. He had picked Bush to be his running mate only at the very last moment. He so resisted the notion of choosing Bush, the obvious choice to some if not to the Reagans themselves, that the Gipper had seriously pursued the Dream Ticket with

Ford. Just a day earlier, the entire assemblage in Detroit—the media, the delegates, the hangers-on, the operatives—was convinced that the two men would go under the gun and marry at the political altar. Negotiations between Ford's and Reagan's representatives didn't break down for good until near midnight. Having exhausted all options, Reagan only reluctantly called Bush.

Henry Kissinger, Reagan's old nemesis, was the Machiavellian behind the "co-presidency" idea. In the end, his presence and demands helped torpedo the deal. One Reaganite had the last word on the role of Kissinger's obstinacy in the negotiations when he said, "For the first time in my life, I felt sorry for the North Vietnamese."[10] Kissinger, who had negotiated Nixon's "peace with honor" end to the American military presence in South Vietnam, was interested in maintaining his own proximity to power, insisting on a major foreign-policy portfolio in any Reagan-Ford administration. It was a self-serving, behind-the-scenes role Kissinger had played in the past. During the 1968 presidential race, he had hedged his bets by relaying sensitive information to both the Nixon and Humphrey camps.[11] Realpolitik, indeed.

If politics was the art of the compromise, the art of the possible, the unlikely ticket of Reagan and Bush proved it. Both had to get over their mutual dislike and make possible a "team of rivals"—something many considered unlikely, if not impossible. Two years earlier Reagan had campaigned against Bush's son George W. in a Republican congressional primary in Texas, prompting *U.S. News & World Report* to write, "A Ronald Reagan–George Bush ticket for the Republicans in 1980? Party leaders who like the idea now say personal animosity between the two all but rules it out."[12]

REAGAN WAS BORN IN 1911, only a few years after Teddy Roosevelt had used the presidential "bully pulpit" to exhort America. TR once said, "The only true conservative . . . sets his face toward the future."[13]

Yet, rather than the old Rough Rider, it was another Roosevelt, a Democrat named Franklin, who was Reagan's favorite president and inspiration. FDR unveiled a new phrase at the Democratic National Convention in June 1936. The theme of his speech to his fellow Democrats and all of America was that the country had a "rendezvous with destiny."

Roosevelt told the Democrats, "There is a mysterious cycle in human events. To some generations much is given. Of other generations, much is expected. This generation of Americans has a rendezvous with destiny."[14] Though the nation was still struggling in the depths of the Great Depression, FDR was giving his fellow countrymen hope. In telling Americans of their "rendezvous," he was revealing that they and their country had a future, something many did not believe possible.

FDR's words were prescient, as this "greatest generation" went on to defeat the Empire of Japan and Nazi Germany and then, with typical American magnanimity and generosity of spirit, rebuild those war-torn countries to get them back on their feet as prosperous democracies.

The phrase "rendezvous with destiny" had its roots in a poem about World War I by Alan Seeger, a young American who had volunteered to join the French Foreign Legion. His poem was entitled "I Have a Rendezvous with Death." That was unfortunately true, as Seeger was killed on July 4, 1916, during the battle of the Somme, at Belloy-en-Santerre, just days after his twenty-eighth birthday. His poem was published posthumously. John Kennedy so loved the romantic style of Seeger's poem that his wife, Jacqueline, memorized it and repeated it to him often.

Seeger's phrase "rendezvous with death" was adapted for FDR's convention speech by a member of Roosevelt's original "Brain Trust," the famous—or notorious, depending upon one's point of view—Tommy "The Cork" Corcoran. A New Dealer since day one, Corcoran was FDR's political fixer and had virtual run of the White House.[15] Corcoran was helping with Roosevelt's speech for the convention in Philadelphia when he paraphrased Seeger's poem, transforming it into "rendezvous with destiny." Years later Corcoran, bent and aged, told his tale to author and Bush confidant Vic Gold.[16]

Listening to FDR that night in June 1936 was a twenty-five-year-old radio broadcaster at WHO in Des Moines, Iowa, known to his audiences as Dutch Reagan. The young man fell in love with the phrase "rendezvous with destiny." To him there was something lyrical, something magical and heroic, about FDR's idiom.

At the time Reagan was a New Deal Democrat. He would not switch his registration to the GOP until much later in life, when he was fifty-one years old.[17] As he progressed in life and politics, he retained FDR's idealism and would use the expression in all his important speeches, even as he evolved from a "hemophiliac liberal," as he later put it, to a populist conservative.[18]

In October 1964, only two years after becoming a Republican, Reagan at the last minute was asked to give a nationally televised speech lauding the presidential candidacy of Senator Barry Goldwater. Toward the end of the speech, Reagan told his studio audience and millions of Americans, "You and I have a rendezvous with destiny. We can preserve for our children this, the last best hope of man on earth, or we will sentence them to take the first step into a thousand years of darkness."[19] Reagan's fiery remarks electrified conservatives everywhere. The speech was later released as an LP album entitled *Rendezvous with Destiny*.

But the GOP of 1964 was far different from the party of sixteen years later. The party in 1964—eastern-based and dominated by country clubs and corporate boardrooms—deemed Reagan's phrase unsophisticated and the man himself a vulgarian. Serious Republicans simply did not talk that way. It was tacky.

Reagan did not back away from the phrase. As the post-Nixon Republican Party struggled for relevance in early 1975, Reagan used it in a speech before the annual gathering of the Conservative Political Action Conference (CPAC) in Washington. The speech was widely regarded as one of Reagan's most important to the conservative movement, as it laid down critical ideological markers.[20]

Reagan turned to the phrase again in November 1979 when he announced his third and final attempt at the Republican Party's presidential nomination. This Reagan, more hopeful, also quoted his favorite political philosopher, Thomas Paine, telling the American people, "We have it in our power to begin the world over again."

SINCE THE TIME WHEN he was just a shirttail kid, Reagan had been infused with heroic dreams. He had read Horatio Alger's books as a youngster, books about poor but honest and brave boys who were rewarded in the end for their character. He had dreamt of being in the cavalry, leading the charge. He had come a long way from those small towns in the Midwest that novelist Sinclair Lewis derided.

Reagan sprang from those quintessentially small-town values that the worldly liberal Lewis mocked as parochial and philistine. Ronald Reagan was in fact born on "Main Street," in an apartment above the local bank building in Tampico, Illinois. His father, John Edward Reagan, was an alcoholic Irish-American who, when working, sold shoes. Reagan's mother, Nellie Wilson Reagan, was a devoted member of the Christian Church who worked with the needy, sometimes even inviting released convicts to stay at their home.[21]

Reagan and his brother, Neil, had a comfortable relationship with their parents, so much so that as children, they called their parents by their first names. In turn, the boys were always called "Moon" and "Dutch." As a baby, Reagan's father nicknamed him, exclaiming when his second son was born, "Why he looks just like a fat little Dutchman!" As the boy grew older, he refused to use his Christian name, Ronald, thinking it was sissified. After becoming president, residing in the upstairs quarters of the White House, Reagan would often joke that he was "living above the store again."[22]

It was from his mother that Reagan inherited his faith in the goodness of people. His humanitarian streak would surface throughout his life. Once in the 1950s he received a letter from a despondent woman, deeply worried about her young son, who was suffering from depression. Reagan was the little boy's hero. Reagan did not want to simply show up at the door, knock, and ask for the youngster, so he devised a plan to go through the boy's neighborhood, as if he were taking a survey for General Electric. He arrived, clipboard in hand, to interview the starstruck child. Reagan engaged him in conversation and gave him advice on life. The mother wept at Reagan's kindness. She and her son asked Reagan to stay in touch. He of course did.[23]

By 1980, that world had changed completely. The verities of pre-Vietnam America seemed to be a thing of the past. Cynicism was not only rampant—it was fashionable.

STANDING ON THE DAIS in Joe Louis Arena, Ronald Reagan gave his remarks accepting the nomination of the Republican Party for president of the United States. Reagan used strong sentences and powerful prose to make his case against Jimmy Carter, against big government, and for his conservative approach, whose centerpiece was "family, work, neighborhood, peace, and freedom." The nominee mentioned but three presidents: Lincoln and FDR warmly, Carter less so.

Reagan called on all his fellow countrymen, not just Republicans, to join his crusade. "I want to carry our message to every American, regardless of party affiliation, who is a member of this community of shared values."[24] He made an open appeal to the young, considered a Democratic constituency. "They expect you to tell your children that the American people no longer have the will to cope with their problems; that the future will be one of sacrifice and few opportunities."[25] He also appealed to labor and minorities. In reaching out to these groups, Reagan was asking for the support of staunch members of the Democratic Party's coalition who were being taken for granted by the incumbent Democrat; he was "breaking precedent," as he had quipped the night before.[26]

Like any good leader, Reagan knew that he needed to tell a story to make his case. As a Hollywood veteran, he realized that all good scripts contain three essential elements: introduction, conflict, and resolution. His landmark speech in 1980 reviewed the state of affairs in America—its awful conditions and his bold solutions.

Noting the thousands of Americans he had met on the campaign trail, Reagan observed, "They are concerned, yes; they are not frightened. They are disturbed, but not dismayed. They are the kind of men and women Tom Paine had in mind when he wrote—during the darkest days of the American Revolution—'We have it in our power to begin the world over again.'"

The former Democrat then returned to FDR, saying, "Nearly 150 years after

Tom Paine wrote those words, an American president told the generation of the Great Depression that it had a 'rendezvous with destiny.' I believe this generation of Americans today also has a rendezvous with destiny."[27]

Approaching his conclusion, Reagan told the assembled and those watching across America, "I ask you not simply to 'Trust me,' but to trust your values—our values—and to hold me responsible for living up to them. I ask you to trust that American spirit which knows no ethnic, religious, social, political, regional, or economic boundaries; the spirit that burned with zeal in the hearts of millions of immigrants from every corner of the Earth who came here in search of freedom."[28] Many of the delegates wept.

As Reagan neared the end of his speech, he hesitated, as if debating whether to continue. He went ahead, albeit haltingly. "I'll confess that I've been a little afraid to suggest what I'm going to suggest. I'm more afraid not to. Can we begin our crusade joined together in a moment of silent prayer?"[29]

More than twenty thousand people fell silent.

Solemnity covered Joe Louis Arena, and only the mechanical sound of the air conditioning could be heard faintly in the background. Several moments passed. Reagan then lifted his head, looked out at the GOP convention, and ended the proceedings by saying, in a voice husky with emotion, "God bless America. Thank you."[30]

A roar erupted from the Republican faithful. Reagan's apotheosis was complete; his conservative crusade was officially joined.

LIKE HIS POLITICAL HERO, Franklin Roosevelt, Ronald Reagan had a clear vision of what he wanted to do if he got the job of president. He, too, had a rendezvous with destiny.

Reagan's first job was in 1926, as a lifeguard at the Rock River in Lowell Park, near his home of Dixon, Illinois. "I saved 77 lives," Reagan proudly asserted many years later. The high school boy, tall, athletic, and good-looking, would notch a mark on a wooden log for every life he saved.[31]

His instincts as a lifeguard never left him. In 1967, at a poolside party, a little girl fell into the water and quickly sank to the bottom. No one noticed what happened except for Governor Reagan, who, while still in his suit, jumped into the pool and saved the child.[32]

Now the former lifeguard sought the challenge of a lifetime.

Ronald Reagan was out to save America.

1

Exit, Stage Right

"It was the worst I'd ever seen him."

August 20, 1976

Ronald Reagan was angry, frustrated, and disappointed.

He left the Republican Party's convention in Kansas City satisfied that he'd done all he could do to wrest the nomination away from President Gerald Ford, yet at the same time Reagan was disquieted that he'd lost to a man he deemed a political inferior. Reagan gave an impromptu, eloquent, and bittersweet address to the delegates on the last night of the convention, and those assembled thought this would be the last time they would ever see him. Many in Kemper Arena wept. They sent Reagan off with a resounding outpouring of affection.

He had attempted the extraordinary: seizing the nomination from an incumbent president, albeit an embattled one. He'd come astonishingly close. Ford won the nomination by only 57 votes more than the 1,130 he needed, beating Reagan by just a handful of delegates. Had Reagan prevented Ford from winning the nomination on the first ballot and forced a second balloting, he may well have won the GOP nomination. The delegates in North Carolina, Kentucky, and other states were mandated to vote for President Ford on the first ballot but would have been free to vote for Reagan a second time around, and he was their real preference. Reagan had certainly been welcomed more warmly than the incumbent by the seventeen thousand GOP faithful in Kemper Arena. A California state senator, H. L. Richardson, summed up the abilities of the two when he said, "Reagan could get a standing ovation in a graveyard. Ford puts you to sleep in the third paragraph."[1]

Lyn Nofziger, one of Reagan's closest aides, later confided, "To my surprise, Reagan, who is seldom bitter, went to California a bitter man, convinced that Ford had stolen the nomination from him."[2]

Of Reagan's conservative crusade, *Washington Post* reporter Lou Cannon presciently wrote, "But whether the Republicans win or not, it is also quite conceivable that Reagan's campaign this year and his impact on the Republican credo may lead Americans to conclude that the GOP, once again, really stands for something."[3]

"He almost certainly believed that his political career, in terms of any future candidacy, was at an end," Peter Hannaford wrote in *The Reagans*.[4]

So, too, did the rest of America.

Departing Kansas City on his way to the airport, Reagan passed a hand-painted sign in a bakery shop that read, "Goodbye, Republicans. You picked the wrong man."[5]

Reagan, as far as everybody was concerned, was finished as a prospective president. He had been around the track twice, and lost twice, and would be seventy years old by 1981. Political obituaries popped up in the mainstream press. *Newsweek* ran a small story on the end of Reagan with a headline that was characteristic: "Into the Sunset."[6]

Though many in Kansas City thought a "unity" ticket between Ford and Reagan was best for the GOP, neither man thought it was best for him. It was the only thing they agreed on. Reagan, and especially Mrs. Reagan, could barely be in the same room with the Fords. President Ford, for his part, utterly rejected the notion of Reagan as his running mate, saying, "Absolutely not. I don't want anything to do with that son of a bitch."[7] Ford ignored the pleas of his staff, including his young White House chief of staff, Richard Cheney, and his pollster, Bob Teeter, even after they came to Camp David several weeks before the convention armed with polling data showing that Ford's only chance against Jimmy Carter in the fall was with Reagan at his side. Cheney and Teeter understood Reagan's ability to connect with disaffected lunch-bucket Democrats in electoral-vote-rich states like New York, New Jersey, and Pennsylvania—voters who would eventually become known as "Reagan Democrats"—as well as Catholics and voters in Jimmy Carter's "Cotton South."[8]

Reagan's militant supporters were just as contemptuous of Ford. When asked what the Reaganites' "demeanor" should be toward the victorious Ford supporters, the irreverent Nofziger quipped, "Da meaner da better."[9] Reagan campaign staffers—now out of work—milled around, drinking, laughing, crying, and bitching about Ford and the convention, the real or perceived failures of Reagan campaign manager John Sears, and the various missed opportunities over the previous year. They, too, felt that despite all the discord and disorganization at the campaign committee, Citizens for Reagan, it had ultimately been luck, money, and naked power in the Ohio, New Jersey, Pennsylvania, and New York primaries, along with betrayal in Mississippi, that had cost their man the nomination.

SETTLING INTO HIS AIRPLANE seat for the flight back to California, Reagan looked quietly out the window, holding hands with Nancy. During the flight, Marty Anderson, the Gipper's key policy adviser, asked Reagan to sign his convention hall pass and Reagan wrote wistfully, "We dreamed—we fought and the dream is still with us."[10]

Peter Hannaford, Reagan's soft-spoken, talented aide, was also on the plane. "I was right behind the Reagans. The seat-belt sign went off and the governor stood and said, 'Well, fellas, I guess we've got to get back to work.' I said, 'Yes, sir, your first taping is two weeks from Wednesday and your column is due.'" Reagan looked at him and jokingly said, "You didn't think I'd win, did you?" Hannaford replied, "Yes, sir, but you always have to have a contingency plan!" Everybody laughed, especially Reagan.[11] Later, the Reagans walked up and down the aisles, Nancy hugging sobbing staffers, Reagan philosophically saying, "We do not know the reason, but someday we will." Michael Deaver, another young aide, said everyone was "devastated."[12] Frank Reynolds of ABC did a touching story that evening, closing with a shot of the Reagans' plane flying off into the western horizon as Reynolds was saying, "So long, Rawhide. See you later, Rainbow." "Rawhide" and "Rainbow" were of course their Secret Service code names.[13]

REAGAN WAS EXHAUSTED AFTER ten grueling months on the campaign trail. From the time of his announcement in November 1975 until the end of the convention in August, he had been on the road continuously, traveling perhaps one hundred thousand miles or more, eating on the run, sleeping in hotels, getting up early, going to bed late, shaking hands with thousands, giving innumerable interviews and speeches. He needed to recharge his batteries, and nothing did that for him like being at Rancho del Cielo—his "Ranch in the Sky"—with only Nancy and his horses for company. The ranch covered nearly seven hundred acres high in the Santa Ynez Mountains, thirty miles outside of Santa Barbara. There, for days on end, he woke early, rode, cut trees and underbrush, erected fences, rebuilt the 1,200-square-foot main building, tended the horses, soaked up the sun, and thought. At night, he'd relax with a book, write letters, go for long quiet walks with "Mommy"—Reagan's nickname for Nancy—and talk, as always, about the future.

He quickly set to work, however. As Hannaford had promised, Reagan needed to return to his nationally syndicated column, which King Features distributed to hundreds of newspapers twice a week. He also started recording five-minute radio commentaries that began broadcasting on September 20. The commentaries went to more than five hundred radio stations with a combined audience of around forty million people at any given time. One of Reagan's early radio segments touted the tax cuts in a bill offered by a young Republican backbencher in Congress, Jack Kemp of Buffalo. It was a revolutionary concept; tax cuts had been a Democratic issue, not a Republican one. John Kennedy had cut taxes, and the GOP was the balanced-budget, green-eyeshade party. Giving people back their money fit into Reagan's pro-growth optimism and evolving political framework. Tax cuts, which empowered individuals and lowered their dependence on government, were a critical part of the development of Reagan's new conservatism; his optimism involved much more than just a sunny personality.

In September, Reagan gathered the core of his defunct campaign staff, some members of his "Kitchen Cabinet"—a group of wealthy Californians who had advised him to run for governor back in 1964—and a handful of other friends and aides at his home in Pacific Palisades for a "seafood salad served on avocado wedges and a raspberry desert," and conversation.[14] Conspicuously absent from the meeting was the controversial John Sears, which was just fine with several of the attendees, especially Nofziger. They were still angry at Sears's missteps over the past year, which they believed had cost Reagan opportunities to overtake Ford.[15] Many blamed Sears at least in part for the "$90 billion" gaffe in late 1975. At Sears's direction Reagan had given a speech in which he made specific proposals for shifting responsibilities to the states without proposing how to fund them. The flap contributed to Reagan's losing the New Hampshire primary. (Some years later Sears did take responsibility for the "$90 billion" mayhem.)[16]

No one at the meeting talked about a 1980 Reagan campaign. It was just blue sky over the horizon. Still, Reagan was looking ahead. He decided to create a permanent political operation designed to assist candidates and campaign staffers of the Right in building for the future, spreading the word about Reagan's small-government approach to policy and politics, and keeping Reagan in front of the American people. The new organization would not be announced until after the election, however. Jimmy Carter was well ahead of Ford in the polls and few at the meeting thought the president would win; some Reaganites, in fact, were pulling for Ford to lose. But Reagan did not want to appear to be presumptuously dancing on the grave of Ford's presidency before Ford actually lost the election.

Although Reagan still felt wounded by the derision and ridicule that the Ford team and the GOP establishment had directed at him, he did agree to campaign for President Ford and his running mate, Senator Robert J. Dole of Kansas. Reagan also made a thirty-minute television appeal for the GOP, taping the entire speech in one take. It aired on Sunday, September 19, at 10:30 P.M. eastern time on NBC. The focus of the speech was not on Ford but on the differences between the Republican and Democratic platforms—an important issue for Reagan, since the GOP platform had his fingerprints all over it.[17] Later in the campaign, he made four commercials in Hollywood, promoting the platform and, finally, Ford. But as the *New York Times* noted, "It was duty more than heartfelt enthusiasm that produced the Reagan ads for the Ford campaign."[18]

Ford was lagging far behind Carter and needed desperately to shore up his base, but the president waited almost a month after the convention before actually calling Reagan and asking him to campaign. Even then, the Ford team did not make good use of the popular Reagan. Hannaford later recounted that "the Ford campaign had made few specific requests until near the end of the campaign, when they wanted [Reagan] in a place he could not get to one day without scrubbing several other long-promised appearances."[19]

In late October, by which point the polls had tightened, a leak from Ford aides to the *New York Times* said, "Former Gov. Ronald Reagan of California has refused a request by President Ford's top election strategists to campaign on the President's behalf in three key states in the final days of the Presidential race." The story made it appear as if Reagan wanted Ford to lose the election, when in fact Reagan was campaigning heavily for Ford and the GOP in California, which Ford needed if he was to have any chance of winning the election.[20] Reagan also campaigned in North Carolina, Texas, Louisiana, and the Midwest.[21] All told, he appeared in twenty-five states for the Republicans in the closing months of the 1976 campaign. Reagan was also asked to become the honorary chairman of the Ford campaign, but he took a pass.

Despite his campaigning for the Ford-Dole ticket, Reagan made it unmistakably clear at a joint appearance in Los Angeles that he wanted to be anywhere other than with Gerald Ford. "It was the worst I'd ever seen him," remembered Lou Cannon, who was covering the event for the *Washington Post*.[22] Reagan's body language and his refusal to address the president directly, much less talk up his chances against Carter, were lost on no one. "I can remember saying . . . to my editors, this is not much of an endorsement," said Cannon. "The words do not begin to convey how distant he was. I've never seen Reagan like that in my entire life."[23] The Ford children and the Reagan children stood at opposite sides of the room and simply glared at each other.[24] Cheney had previously gone to California on a "peace mission" to smooth the relationship between Ford and Reagan, but he met with little success; when he reached Mike Deaver on the phone, "he got a distinctly cool reception."[25]

Ford loathed Reagan, but he needed him. Reagan loathed Ford, but he needed to keep up appearances for the sake of any political future.

CARTER BEGAN TO DECLINE in the polls but it was not because the voters had discovered that they had fallen in love all of a sudden with the wallflower Republicans. Far from it. Doubts were being raised about Carter. Even the old crook Willie Sutton said, "I've never seen a bigger confidence man in my life, and I've been around some of the best in the business." Sutton knew his psychobabble. When a psychiatrist once tried to plumb his depths, asking why he robbed banks, Sutton famously replied, "Because that's where the money is."[26]

By Election Day 1976, Gerald Ford had battled back from a 30-point midsummer deficit in the polls, thanks in part to his so-called Rose Garden strategy, which amounted to staying in the White House and acting presidential. But in the end, Carter successfully ran out the clock on Ford. He won narrowly in the Electoral College, 297–240, and even more closely in the popular vote, defeating Ford by a hairsbreadth, 50–48 percent.

So it was that America ended up with this improbable president, James Earl Carter, the peanut farmer and former one-term Georgia governor. Carter, like Reagan, had grown up in an atmosphere of populism; also like Reagan, he had campaigned against the Washington buddy system. The beliefs of Carter and Reagan were based on cultural, religious, and moral values, though Carter was a distinctly more left-wing populist. But the media and the American people had a hard time figuring the Democrat out. "I was a conservative southern governor who believed in human rights . . . and a balanced budget," Carter recalled. "It was kind of a strange mixture."[27]

Some of Reagan's aides were delighted at the outcome of the election, because to them it proved that a conservative majority existed in America, outside the limited boundaries of a clannish, elitist GOP, which excluded Democrats and independents, but not outside the reach of Reagan, the conservative populist. They were convinced that had Reagan been the nominee, he would have made inroads into the South and won the election. They were also convinced that Reagan would have made mincemeat out of Carter in the debates, unlike Ford, who had made a hash of them.

Reagan himself remained publicly undecided about whether to take another shot at the GOP nomination and the White House. When a UPI reporter caught up with him on Election Day and asked him about his plans for the future, Reagan said frankly that he "'wouldn't rule out and wouldn't rule in' another try . . . in four years."[28]

POSTELECTION, PRESIDENT FORD SUMMONED Vice President Nelson Rockefeller, former Texas governor John Connally, and Reagan to discuss the future of the GOP. The time for the meeting was changed at the last minute and Reagan had to scramble to make it. He later confided in a letter to an old friend, former senator George Murphy of California, "Do you suppose they were hoping I wouldn't come?"[29]

One of the key issues involved the chairmanship of the Republican National Committee (RNC). Ford and Rockefeller were quietly supporting James A. Baker III, Ford's skillful delegate hunter in the spring and summer of 1976. Baker had done more than anyone in the Ford operation to secure Ford's nomination, thwarting Reagan. Reagan objected, saying that Baker would be unacceptable to Sun Belt conservatives. The meeting was inconclusive—except for the fact that when the old curmudgeon of the Republican Party, Mr. Sun Belt himself, Barry Goldwater, caught wind of the meeting, he pitched a fit for not having been invited, said it was an "insult," and vowed never to raise money for the party again.[30] By then, however, Ronald Reagan had eclipsed Goldwater as the conservative leader in America.

In mid-January, the GOP's state chairmen and national committee members gathered to vote for a new national chairman. It was the first time anyone could recall an RNC chairman being chosen in such a fashion. Prior, the chairman was either handpicked by an incumbent Republican president or chosen by party elders. Ford pushed Baker, perhaps too overtly, as it caused a number of the more conservative Republican committee members to support former Tennessee senator William Brock or Reagan's choice, the little-known Dick Richards of Utah. Baker quickly dropped out of contention and Richards did not engender much enthusiasm. Brock won on the third secret ballot.[31]

Brock was the Republicans' "third way": choosing him provided neither Reagan nor Ford with bragging rights. The choice was vitally important for the party, as Brock, despite his distaste for Reagan, would become one of the most effective chairmen in the GOP's history, credited with bringing it into the modern political world.

Such modernization was crucial for the fate of the Republican Party, for at that point the party's very survival was in doubt. "Back in the 19th century," the *Washington Post* noted in 1976, "a Minnesota legislator described a mule as a creature that has neither pride of ancestry nor hope of posterity. The legislator was talking about the Democratic Party of his day, but his definition would fully apply to the Republican Party."[32] The mule is, of course, the hybrid offspring of a donkey and a horse. Sterile at birth, it cannot create a breed of its own, so it literally has no past and no future. Much like the Republican Party, it seemed then.

Among voters less than thirty years of age, identification with the GOP stood at a humiliating 11 percent in 1977. The party was seen as corrupt and just plain worn-out. Despite the Republicans' famous "Southern Strategy," after the wipeouts of 1974 and 1976 the GOP controlled only 10 percent of the state legislative seats in the eleven states of the Old South.[33] Such was the ruinous political legacy of Richard Milhous Nixon.

In Reagan's view, the Republican Party could stage a comeback only if it made itself a home for conservatives and conservatism. To that end, in late January 1977 he formally announced his political action committee, Citizens for the Republic (CFTR), through which he would "promote conservative Republican candidates and promote conservative views."[34]

The CFTR headquarters was set up on the second floor of a nondescript office building in Santa Monica, California. Reagan tapped Lyn Nofziger to run the operation. One of Nofziger's first employees was Cindy Tapscott, a chatty young woman from Oklahoma. In her interview, Nofziger asked Tapscott two questions. "Do you smoke?" She did. "Do you drink?" She did. Tapscott was hired.[35] Nofziger himself was partial to a cigar and a dry martini—no olive, and no vermouth. Aide Jim Stockdale said the group around CFTR in those days resembled "adult juvenile delinquents. I don't think we took ourselves as seriously as the crowds that followed us."[36] A young follower, Fred Ryan, was a college student at nearby USC, and would frequently drop by the CFTR offices to pick up Reagan literature to pass out to his classmates.[37]

The operation was not slapdash, however. Some of Reagan's able aides, including Nofziger, Deaver, Hannaford, and Ed Meese, who was Governor Reagan's chief of staff, began meeting over coffee one day a week, usually on a Friday morning, at the Bicycle Club restaurant to coordinate matters. CFTR also had substantial funding, starting out with a budget of nearly $1.5 million left over from the 1976 campaign committee, Citizens for Reagan (though at year's end about $600,000 would be returned to the Federal Election Commission because it represented unused matching funds).[38]

As Reagan was the most in-demand conservative in America, Deaver and Hannaford expected the governor's personal income from his syndicated column, radio commentaries, and speaking fees to range between $400,000 and $750,000 per year. The demands kept Reagan perpetually in motion. His young aide Dennis LeBlanc recalled that as they flew together, Reagan was either reading or writing, making the most of his time. Nancy Reagan remembered the same: "But all the time he was writing. He would always fly first class. He'd sit by the window, and I'd sit in the aisle next to him. It didn't matter whether or not there was a movie being shown and all the lights were out—he'd turn on his reading lamp and would constantly be writing."[39]

JIMMY CARTER MOVED AHEAD quickly with his first address to the nation after becoming president, appearing on television less than two weeks after his inauguration. Dressed in a light-colored cardigan sweater in front of a roaring fire in the White House, Carter followed his populist instincts and took on the Washington establishment, vowing to bring the federal government to heel by freezing federal hiring and cutting regulatory red tape, and also the oil companies and utilities, calling on them to sacrifice.

Taking on the oil companies was easy. They were unpopular and were already a favorite whipping boy in Washington. Taking on the entrenched bureaucracy was quite another thing. Shrink government? Since when did any Democrat advocate this? Moreover, in telling the American people that their future would be one of scarcity and sacrifice, Carter was making himself and his party the skunks at the garden party. The Democrats had owned the future since 1932, being the party of hope, but now Carter was ceding the political battleground of the future. The sour speech set the tone for Carter's presidency.

Fittingly, the first movie aired in the Carter White House was *All the President's Men*. but Carter fundamentally misunderstood the consequences of Watergate. He made symbolic gestures, including taking limousines away from the White House staff, banning the playing of "Hail to the Chief," carrying his own suit bag slung over his shoulder (though rumors were rampant that the bag was empty), wearing dungarees, and other "depomping the presidency" efforts. He thought the American people wanted their next-door neighbor to be president.[40] Carter, like Ford before him, confused the dignity of the office with the character of the individual occupying it. The American people wanted somebody with a common touch, but they also wanted somebody with uncommon dignity. They didn't mind—indeed, actually liked—a little bit of pomp; what they objected to was pomposity.

A *New York Times* story three weeks after Carter had taken office reflected Americans' skepticism about the Carter emphasis on "showboat populism." "I want my President to have some class," one American complained. Carter "carrying his own suitcases" put another off. "That's going too far."[41] Even Carter worried in his diary that he'd gone too far with the whole "depomping" thing.[42]

Carter's peripatetic pollster, Pat Caddell, wrote, "We must devise a context that is neither traditionally liberal nor traditionally conservative, one that cuts across traditional ideology."[43] Carter's instincts were already in this direction, but he was governmentally tone-deaf.

REAGAN'S METHOD OF TAKING on the status quo was far different from Carter's. In the opening months of 1977, he addressed important conservative organizations to explain his vision for a "New Republican Party." First, in January, he addressed the annual dinner of the Intercollegiate Studies Institute, and then in early February he spoke at the Conservative Political Action Conference (CPAC). Reagan told his young listeners to look beyond the simple math of the two parties and instead focus on the disparity between self-identified conservatives and liberals. During his CPAC address he noted that "on January 5, 1977, by a 43–19 plurality those polled by Harris said they would 'prefer to see the country move in a more conservative direction than liberal one.'"[44]

Reagan called for bringing into the Republican fold those Democrats concerned with "social issues—law and order, abortion, busing, quota systems—[that] are usually associated with the blue-collar, ethnic, and religious groups."[45] In short, he proposed a fusion between those mercantile and economic interests long associated with the GOP, who were mostly concerned with government regulations, and social conservatives, who believed the fabric of society was also threatened by big, intrusive government.

He told the conservatives to join him in creating a "new, lasting majority. This will mean compromise. But not a compromise of basic principle. What will emerge will be something new, something open and vital and dynamic, something the great conservative majority will recognize as its own, because at the heart of this undertaking is principled politics."[46]

Then Reagan took on the GOP, telling his CPAC audience that the party "cannot be one limited to the country-club, big-business image that . . . it is burdened with today. The 'New Republican Party' I am speaking about is going to have room for the man and woman in the factories, for the farmer, for the cop on the beat."[47]

He closed his groundbreaking speech by telling the assembled conservatives:

Our task is not to sell a philosophy, but to make the majority of Americans, who already share that philosophy, see that modern conservatism offers them a political home. We are not a cult; we are members of a majority. Let's act and talk like it. The job is ours and the job must be done. If not by us, who? If not now, when? Our party must be the party of the individual. It must not sell out the individual to cater to the group. No greater challenge faces our society today than ensuring that each one of us can maintain his dignity and his identity in an increasingly complex, centralized society.

Extreme taxation, excessive controls, oppressive government competition with business, galloping inflation, frustrated minorities, and forgotten Americans are not the products of free enterprise. They are the residue of centralized bureaucracy, of government by a self-anointed elite.

Our party must be based on the kind of leadership that grows and takes its strength from the people. Any organization is in actuality only the lengthened shadowed of its members. A political party is a mechanical structure created to further a cause. The cause, not the mechanism, brings and holds the members together. And our cause must be to rediscover, reassert, and reapply America's spiritual heritage to our national affairs.

Then with God's help we shall indeed be as a city upon a hill, with the eyes of all people upon us.[48]

Reagan received a resounding ovation from the young conservatives gathered at CPAC. The "True Believers" understood Reagan's call. The former governor was not only taking on the established order in Washington, he was also continuing the fight against the dug-in and hostile interests inside the GOP. His followers understood that Reagan was distrustful of the concentration of governmental *or* corporate power. Reagan believed in a "natural aristocracy" of men who climbed to their highest ambitions without the heavy-handed aid of nobility or government connections. He was defining a new ideology of optimistic and enlightened conservatism that was unsettling to the powers-that-be that ran the Republican Party. They didn't understand it, so how could they possibly support it?

He showed off both his literate side and his sense of irony as he told the young listeners, "I have seen the conservative future and it works."[49] Of course, Reagan was paraphrasing Lincoln Steffens, a Communist sympathizer from America who uttered this line, minus the word "conservative," upon returning from the Soviet Union in 1919.

In the early days of 1977, the conservative movement was growing and extending its power and influence. These conservatives had aggressively explored a third-party option for the past several years, but now they concluded that the better option was to take over the feeble GOP. It was a practical decision: the two-party system was favored by the new federal campaign laws, which enhanced the ability of the two major parties to mail at lower rates than other political entities. It was at this CPAC where conservatives began to refer to themselves as "The Movement."

Though Reagan was energizing conservatives, he more and more had to contend with the burgeoning "age issue." American Conservative Union staffer Jim Roberts spoke for many when he told Lou Cannon of the *Post*, "If he was four years younger, we'd be off and running right now. . . . But there is a nagging feeling that he may be too old."[50]

If Reagan was too old, he certainly didn't show it. He appeared to be the picture of health, at least ten years younger than he really was. He was 6'1", tanned, and broad-shouldered, with a crinkly smile and a ready handshake. The only signs of age were the blemishes on the back of his hands, a few wisps of gray in his temples, and the fact that he was hard of hearing in his left ear. He drank moderately and exercised daily, not including the heavy outdoor work at the ranch. He had quit smoking years earlier, using jelly beans to replace his nicotine craving. He hadn't lost a step, and actually appeared much more self-confident when speaking about national and global affairs than he had been just a year earlier. The *Washington Post*'s David Broder described him as "inexhaustible."[51]

Reagan prepared better than most for his speeches, which he often wrote on his own. He was a perfectionist when it came to researching, writing, practicing, and delivering a speech. He was so superior in his speaking abilities that it was actually news when he turned in a poor performance.

Reagan had worn contact lenses in public and glasses in private for years, as he was extremely nearsighted. Before he gave a speech, he would pop out his right contact lens to read the text and keep the left one in so he could see his audience and their reaction to him. Deaver and Hannaford often asked the governor if he just wanted to show up, make his speech, and then leave, but Reagan rarely took them up on this option. He liked to settle in, have dinner, and observe the other speakers, but especially the crowd, to judge its mood and temperament. He also hated missing out on the after-dinner dessert. Years later, as president, he was quickly hustled out of a CPAC dinner speech and later complained to an aide that he didn't get to stay long enough to have the apple pie à la mode that was being served that evening.

As the conservative movement accelerated its upward trajectory, the "New Right" was developing new ideas on policy, politics, and, most especially, tactics.

What distinguished the New Right from its progenitors was an attitude, a belief in ideas, and a "take no prisoners" approach. These Young Turks became a formidable new force in American politics thanks to their impressive use of technology, such as direct mail, Quip machines (the precursor to the fax machine), telephones, and computers; their ability to raise money; and their sophisticated approach to public relations. Unlike previous conservatives, who despised the "liberal media" and thus shunned reporters and columnists or, even worse, denounced them, these conservatives courted the media, knowing controversy and action were two favorite topics of national political reporters.

No New Right meeting of the era would have been complete without the presence of Paul Weyrich, head of the awfully named Committee for the Survival of a Free Congress and one of the leading theoreticians in the New Right; direct-mail impresario Richard Viguerie, "Godfather of the New Right"; Howard Phillips of the Conservative Caucus; and Phyllis Schlafly, "First Lady of the Conservative Movement" and author of the groundbreaking bestseller *A Choice, Not an Echo*, published in the days leading up to Barry Goldwater's nomination in 1964.

Weyrich had come up through Wisconsin politics and radio, and ended up in Washington as a speechwriter for Senator Gordon Allott of Colorado. Seated next to him in the senator's office on Capitol Hill was a talented young conservative writer, George F. Will. In 1979 *Time* magazine selected Viguerie, who raised many millions of dollars for conservative causes, as one of the "Fifty Future Leaders of America." Others on the list were Bill Clinton, Ted Turner, and Jesse Jackson. He was more libertarian in his outlook than the others, and was known to enjoy a good game of poker and Jack Daniel's whiskey. Phillips was one of the original signers of the Sharon Statement, the founding document of Young Americans for Freedom, written at the Connecticut estate of William F. Buckley. Phillips had traveled a long ideological road; in 1960, when he was running for student council president at Harvard, one of his biggest supporters was a hyperkinetic liberal named Barney Frank.[52] Schlafly had gone back to college to get her law degree while still a homemaker raising children, and became a leading voice against what she called "radical feminism."

These New Right leaders began to flex their muscles, same as Reagan. They no longer feared rejection at the hands of the GOP establishment, because there was little of a GOP establishment to speak of anymore. They'd put up with a lot over the previous thirty years, from Wendell Willkie to Tom Dewey to Dwight Eisenhower, Nelson Rockefeller, and finally Richard Nixon and Gerald Ford. All, at one time or another, had insulted or ignored conservatives. These moderate Republicans were now gone and the party was an embarrassing shell of itself.

The conservative movement was far more consequential and important than the Republican Party itself. The conservatives would lead. They would dictate policy. They would bring the party to them rather than the other way around. Woe to the Republican officials who deviated from conservative orthodoxy, because the New Right delighted in making an example of them. In punishing heretics, the True Believers could be ruthless.

The New Right eschewed the traditional alliance between the GOP and big business. Congressman Jack Kemp, a rising star in national politics, told a seminar at Harvard that "the movement needs a visible break with big business. Big business has become the handmaiden of big government."[53]

Kemp was a trumpeted addition to the New Right's growing panoply of young and articulate leaders. He had movie-star good looks and had been a pro football quarterback, first with the San Diego Chargers and later for the Buffalo Bills. With his keen devotion to economic theory, he had become a close friend and devotee of the economic theories of *Wall Street Journal* columnist Jude Wanniski and economist Arthur Laffer. In 1976, impressed with their presentation on supply-side economics, Kemp introduced a "jobs-creation bill" providing for large cuts in income taxes across the board for all Americans, as an idea to jump-start the economy while producing greater revenue for the federal treasury.

Though Kemp had been a Ford delegate in Kansas City (mainly because of a personal relationship with Ford from their days together in Congress), Reagan did not hesitate to get behind the young congressman's tax-cut plan. After his initial radio commentary on Kemp's bill in the fall of 1976, Reagan did another five-minute broadcast endorsing Kemp's idea in late March 1977. It was a "tax plan based on common sense," Reagan said, reminding listeners of the success of the Kennedy tax cuts of the early 1960s.[54]

By the summer of 1977 Reagan had emerged as the most high-profile and vocal critic of the Carter administration, scoring it on policy and politics and hypocrisy.

In the month of June alone, Reagan made thirteen major policy speeches in New York, Washington, and other locations while keeping up with his daily radio commentaries and his twice-a-week column. He went after Carter over détente and his desire to recognize Vietnam, which Reagan charged with "holding an estimated nineteen million people in forced captivity, including some in concentration camps."[55]

He also hit Carter on the forthcoming Panama Canal treaties,[56] for which the Carter White House had scheduled a signing ceremony on September 7. During the 1976 primaries Reagan had come out strongly against any agreement that gave up U.S. control over the Panama Canal, decrying such a move as a "giveaway" of the canal to Omar Torrijos, the military strongman of Panama. In fact, Reagan's near-successful comeback against Gerald Ford had been due in large part to his exploitation of this issue. If Ford never heard again Reagan's refrain from 1976— "We built it! We paid for it! It's ours! And we're going to keep it!"[57]— it would be too soon. The Carter White House attempted to persuade Reagan to support the documents it had negotiated, but after considerable contemplation he demurred. He returned to the theme he had sounded during the campaign, citing his concern that the United States would surrender the "rights of sovereignty we acquired in the original treaty."[58]

Not every conservative sided with Reagan on the canal issue. Most notably, *National Review* editor William F. Buckley Jr. and actor John Wayne, both friends of Reagan's for many years, publicly supported the treaties. The fight over the canal came to define the resurgent conservatives and the growing New Right. Reagan talked about the issue so often, he opened up one radio broadcast by saying, "Would it shock & surprise you if I did a little talking about the Panama Canal? I hope not because that's what I'm going to do."[59] He called Carter's efforts to rally support "a medicine show, a wave of propaganda."[60] At the end of every commentary came his signature signoff, "This is Ronald Reagan. Thanks for listening."

Although the Panama Canal treaties would still need to receive the votes of two-thirds of the U.S. Senate—by no means a certain proposition—the Carter administration went ahead with an extravagant signing ceremony featuring Torrijos and Carter on the White House lawn. The media and the liberal establishment were startled to see large crowds of protesters mobilized that day on Capitol Hill and outside the White House.[61]

Conservative groups in Washington were meeting, often daily, to coordinate their grassroots lobbying, advertising, public relations, and direct-mail efforts to stop the treaties. Reagan gave a speech to the National Press Club in early September blasting Carter over the issue; he cut more radio commentaries on the subject; he also testified before the Senate outlining his opposition.[62]

Meanwhile, a letter went out under Reagan's signature on behalf of the RNC, asking for money to help stop Carter's initiative. "I'm convinced the only way to defeat the Carter negotiated treaty is to conduct a full-fledged campaign to alert citizens to the dangers Republicans see in this treaty," Reagan wrote. "Believe me, without your support, the canal is as good as gone. I've read this treaty carefully from cover to cover, and in my honest opinion, it's a line by line blueprint for potential disaster for our country." The mail response to Reagan was overwhelming and the RNC raised, by its estimate, more than $1 million.[63]

Problem was, RNC chairman Bill Brock had no intention of using a dime of the money to actually stop the treaties. Brock would not go against his old friend Gerald Ford, who remained a supporter of the documents. Nor did he want to create an uncomfortable situation for another old friend, Howard Baker, the minority leader of the U.S. Senate. Brock and Baker were former Senate colleagues, both from Tennessee, and Baker was equivocating his stance, one of the few remaining Republicans not to take a position on the matter. Reagan staffer Charlie Black recalled, "What Brock was really worried about was embarrassing his close friend Howard Baker."[64]

Reagan graciously issued a statement attempting to paper over the disagreement with Brock: "I am concerned that some reports have given the impression that [RNC] officials and I are in disagreement and that I have withdrawn my support of the party. This impression is mistaken. To the extent that there is any difference, it is limited to the ways and means by which to best oppose the proposed . . . treaties."[65]

Lyn Nofziger and Paul Laxalt, the national chairman of Reagan's 1976 presidential campaign, knew better. They would have liked to tie a millstone around Brock's neck and drop him in the nearest pond. Later that day Laxalt got into the act, as he announced that conservatives were going to the mattresses against Carter without Brock and the RNC, telling reporters that Brock's decision "reaffirms my feeling that if we are going to be effective as conservatives, it will have to be outside the RNC. It's obvious they're not sympathetic to our goals."[66]

After speaking with the fuming Laxalt and Nofziger, Reagan reversed his course a day later and told Brock in a letter that his name was not to be used in any more fundraising appeals for the RNC for any issue, especially the Panama Canal. In snapping tones, Reagan told Brock, "My credibility is involved in this. . . . Letters with my name on them have gone all across the country asking for money to help fight the treaties. Now we discover that money raised by the letters will not be used for that purpose. And worse than that, we discover that the national party has no plans to campaign against the treaties."[67] Brock ducked reporters' calls about the angry Reagan and a spokesman for the committee lamely said, "The party does not provide money for groups unaffiliated with the party except for cases approved by the party's national committee."[68]

It would not be the last run-in involving the antiestablishment, conservative populist Reagan and the moderate, toast-of-the-establishment scion of the candy company bearing his name, Brock.

In the midst of Ronald Reagan's very public crusade against Jimmy Carter and the Panama Canal treaties, he and his wife sat down for a long interview in Los

Angeles with Al Hunt of the *Wall Street Journal*. "Ronald Reagan's political juices are rising again," the respected journalist noted in his piece. But Hunt accepted at face value the argument that Reagan did not hunger for the White House, concluding that "many Reagan insiders think the farther he gets from his 1976 campaign, the less he may want to try again." Hunt quoted former Reagan aide David Keene to buttress his point: "He isn't all consumed by the desire to be President the way . . . Carter or . . . Nixon were."[69]

Both Hunt and Keene overlooked the obvious: While Nixon and Carter may have been obsessive, Reagan was nonetheless fiercely competitive and was ferociously articulating his future-orientated conservative philosophy in hundreds of newspapers twice a week, on five hundred radio stations daily, and in dozens of speeches across the country. Another run at the White House was never far from his mind.

On December 20, 1977, Reagan convened a very private dinner at his home with his most trusted former advisers. The topic was 1980. Attending were John Sears, Lyn Nofziger, Ed Meese, Peter Hannaford, Jim Lake, Marty Anderson, Dave Keene, and a few others. Several who were playing footsie with other candidates were surprised when both Reagans showed "more enthusiasm than most members of his inner circle," as the *Washington Post* later reported.[70]

It was unclear whether Sears would run Reagan's 1980 campaign—if there was one. He had accumulated a wealth of political enemies, many of them influential conservatives and Reaganites. Former Reagan press secretary Jim Lake said that some Reagan staffers had nicknamed Sears "John P. Satan."[71]

Reagan had many decisions to make, but it seemed that on the big question—whether to run again in 1980—he had already made up his mind, even if his closest advisers weren't yet on board.

2

RETURN OF THE REPUBLICANS

"Jimmy Carter will never have a nonturbulent year."

S itting in a comfortable chair in front of a crackling fire in the library of the White House, Jimmy Carter attempted in a twenty-two-minute nationally televised address to refute charges made by critics of the Panama Canal treaties. It was February 1, 1978, and Carter told the viewing audience that the treaties were of the "highest national interest of the United States."[1]

Then the leader of the Free World openly took on private citizen Ronald Reagan. Directly quoting Reagan's oft-repeated phrase "We bought it, we paid for it, it's ours," Carter intoned, "I must repeat a very important point. We do not own the Panama Canal Zone—we have never had sovereignty over it. We have only had the right to use it."[2]

The Gipper could not have been more thrilled. The president had singled him out for criticism and CBS offered the Californian unprecedented broadcast time to reply. Reagan responded to Carter's left jab with a right uppercut, telling *his* national audience that the president was being less than forthright with the American people by suggesting that the treaties were about protecting America's "permanent right to use the canal." Reagan said, "We have that permanent right—right now—but will we effectively have it if the Carter-Torrijos treaties are ratified? I have very serious doubts that we will." He suggested that President Carter had misled the American people, leaving "the mistaken impression that we acquired the Canal Zone by some underhanded means; that the Canal was somehow forced on Panama. Nothing could be further from the truth."[3]

Reagan would ultimately lose the fight. In the spring, the Senate finally (though barely) mustered the required two-thirds votes to pass the treaties. The first treaty, which affirmed that the United States could defend the canal against any interference with its continued neutral service to ships of all nations, was ratified on March 16 by a vote of 68–32;[4] the second, which turned the canal over to Panamanian control on December 31, 1999, was ratified on April 18, 67–33.[5] Reagan, in Japan on a lecture tour, issued a statement lamenting the loss: "Naturally, I am disappointed. . . . I feel this is a very extreme case of ignoring the sentiment of the people of our country. They were overwhelming in their disapproval of the treaties."[6] In private to aide Peter Hannaford, Reagan released a blast of invective and obscenities over the Senate votes.

But the long fight over the Panama Canal had boosted for a time Reagan's political capital—and drained Carter's. The president's unpopular campaign for the canal treaties, combined with the slowing economy and White House missteps, had dropped him in the polls. According to a new Harris survey for ABC News, Carter was losing in a trial heat against Gerald Ford, 48–43 percent, and to Reagan, 47–46 percent. Only two months before, he had bested Ford, 50–42. He was also getting trounced among Democratic voters by Senator Ted Kennedy, 60–35. The number of Americans who thought Carter was doing a good job had fallen to 29 percent.[7] "Jimmy Carter will never have a nonturbulent year," his White House consigliere, Hamilton Jordan, said.[8]

THE GREATEST POLITICAL UPHEAVAL of 1978 took place on June 6 in Reagan's California with the passage of Proposition 13. If it had been measured as an earthquake, Proposition 13 would have gone off the Richter scale and much of California's political establishment would have slid into the Pacific. This was "The Big One." Property taxes in California had been going up for years, and by June 1978, property owners had had enough. In some cases, unchecked property taxes had gone up more than 1,000 percent.[9] Suddenly, those who'd pooh-poohed tax cuts were in a headlong rush to prove they were for them and had been all along. The referendum didn't just pass; it passed in a rout, 65–35 percent.[10]

One of the most neck-straining turnarounds came from California governor Jerry Brown, who was contemplating his own 1980 challenge to Carter in the Democratic primaries. Brown switched sides within a matter of hours and on June 7 was championing Proposition 13, talking as if he'd invented it. Even Reagan, who had initially been lukewarm about the radical "Prop 13," was now embracing it.

The new law cut property taxes by 57 percent and compelled government programs to be cut across the board, as it immediately slashed $7 billion in annual revenue headed for Sacramento.[11] It was the first tax cut since 1970, when Governor Reagan refunded California's taxpayers $73 million.

The two leaders of Proposition 13 were Paul Gann, a sixty-five-year-old retired real estate agent and head of People's Advocate, a grassroots antigovernment pressure group, and Howard Jarvis, a seventy-four-year-old self-made millionaire who enjoyed large cigars. Jarvis was sui generis. He was short with a booming voice, a face and neck that looked like a California mudslide, and a knack for self-promotion. Jarvis became a household name in America and an instant folk hero.[12]

At once, tax-limitation propositions sprang up in sixteen other states and were described by the *Washington Post* as "sons of Proposition 13, California's gift to the tax rebellion."[13] States included were spread across the country and no region was left out. They ranged from the liberal Hawaii to the conservative Alabama. It was truly a nationwide populist uprising. Nearly all the initiatives and ballot referenda were a result of direct citizen action and not that of elected officials, most of whom were running for the tall grass, terrified of these newly empowered citizens' tax groups.

Because of Reagan, Congressman Jack Kemp, and celebrity economists such as Art Laffer, Jude Wanniski, and Milton Friedman, tax cuts had become a canon of the Republican Party in just two short years. Reagan and the fast-rising Kemp had star billing in the GOP, but Laffer and the others had developed their own cultish fan base as well. Laffer, a professor of economics at USC, talked a blue streak. The political columnists Rowland Evans and Robert Novak depicted the flamboyant Laffer "sipping wine on the patio of his $225,000 home in Palos Verdes . . . while a big green macaw perches on his shoulder."[14]

Laffer and Wanniski had attempted to sell their ideas to Dick Cheney and Donald Rumsfeld while Ford was in the White House, but the young aides had dismissed the radical approach out of hand. Kemp was the first politician to embrace Laffer and Wanniski's ideas. Laffer said they sold the concept to Kemp, whose middle name was "French," in part by telling him that he could be the next "JFK."[15]

Laffer also began meeting with Reagan—often over meals—to discuss economic theories. "He would bring in all sorts of stuff," Laffer recalled. Once, over lunch, they got into a hot-pepper-eating contest. Laffer ate one and thought his mouth was on fire. "I literally couldn't breathe." There was Reagan, "bright purple. And when we finally caught our breath he said, 'Okay, Art, you ready for another one?' And I said, 'Surrender, sir,' and he won the contest, because I don't know whether he was bluffing or not, but I sure as hell wasn't about to call him on it."[16]

The center of liberalism was collapsing and conservative thinkers and writers moved to fill the void. "The prevailing theory of liberalism, providing a common intellectual core of beliefs that many leaders in Washington could rally behind, has broken up," said William J. Baroody of the American Enterprise Institute.[17] Some argued that this was merely the manifestation of a "countervailing" force in that the "outs" always looked better than the "ins" to the American people, and indeed there was some truth in this. On the other hand, a populist, middle-class revolt was washing across the country. Referenda, the growth of the conservative movement and right-of-center think tanks, the growing popularity of conservative books, new lawsuits against affirmative action, the outpouring of opposition to the Panama Canal treaties and the Equal Rights Amendment—all were tangible evidence of creative revolt in the land. People were "mad as hell and not going to take it anymore."

The issues that Reagan had been warning about for years—excessive government spending and regulations, taxation, a drooping economy, a falling dollar, job stagnation, inflation, Soviet expansion, decaying moral standards, weak national leadership—were now on everybody's mind. And he and his fellow conservatives were offering concrete solutions, including a more aggressive foreign and national defense policy for the United States against Soviet adventurism.

But it was unclear, at least to the public, whether Reagan himself would attempt to lead conservatives into the White House. Like Ford, Reagan remained coy about whether he would actually run for president in 1980.

George Bush, meanwhile, was anything but coy. By the summer of 1978, the former congressman, United Nations ambassador, and CIA director was telling potential supporters, the media, and anyone else who would listen that he was going to make the race. He called his son Jeb, working in South America, and told him that he was going to run for president. The young man replied, "President of what?"[18]

Senate minority leader Howard Baker was also moving ahead. When pressed he had finally come out in support of the Panama Canal treaties, which had badly damaged his chances for the GOP nomination. In any case, though he was well known and well liked in Washington, he did not have a high profile outside the Beltway and had not acquired a signature issue on which to campaign for the presidency.[19]

Jack Kemp's stock was rising so quickly that his name was being mentioned as a possible contender in 1980 as well. He faced a potential pitfall: a news report said that some in the GOP considered him a "pushy upstart." The overly confident Kemp was unfazed by such criticism.[20]

Another young and articulate congressman looking at 1980 was Philip M. Crane of Illinois, whose father, "Dr. Crane," had been a nationally syndicated columnist for many years. Crane, the highly intelligent chairman of the American Conservative Union, was only forty-seven years old in 1978, with chiseled features that made women look twice. Elected in a 1969 special House election in Illinois to fill the unexpired term of another intelligent if brash young man, Donald Rumsfeld, who had gone into the Nixon administration, Crane, some conservatives were saying, was a "younger Reagan." Crane paid a courtesy call on Reagan and Paul Laxalt in late July 1978, when the governor was in Washington, to advise them of his intentions to run for the GOP nod. Reagan took it okay until Crane suggested that the Californian step aside and become a "senior statesman" in the party.[21] Crane had been a part of Citizens for Reagan in 1976, but he had heard from many people that Reagan was being too guarded, that he was too old, and that the detested John Sears would be back running Reagan's campaign.

Reagan was not happy about any of this. Earlier, Crane had as much as told Reagan's men that he would support Reagan again. Worse, Crane threatened to compromise Reagan's support among New Right leaders. Richard Viguerie, for example, joined Crane's direct-mail fundraising. Although Crane was nowhere in the polls, he had assets. The American Conservative Union claimed 300,000 members. He had written three books, including *Surrender in Panama*, and had a nationally syndicated column. He had seven attractive daughters and one young son, so he could count on a photogenic entourage.[22] Crane knew his chances for winning the 1980 nomination were slim, but if a moderate like Howard Baker or George Bush won the nomination, the candidate would need a conservative running mate to create a unified convention and party. And if Crane shaved off a few points from Reagan in the primaries and in so doing cost Reagan the nomination, well, *c'est la vie*.

Nor was Reagan pleased with the way Crane and many others focused on concerns about his age. Crane himself told reporters that Reagan's age could be "a potential problem" for the Gipper.[23] A Crane supporter would later describe his candidate as "Reagan without wrinkles."[24] Publicly, Reagan laughed off the issue, using self-deprecating humor with audiences. He sometimes said, "I can remember when a hot story broke and the reporters would run in yelling, 'Stop the chisels.'"[25] But privately, Reagan sometimes fumed over the age issue.

Faced with these new challenges, Reagan took off on a fall 1978 campaign swing through twenty-six states in support of Republican candidates. Keeping his options open, he did not limit his campaigning to only conservatives who had supported him in 1976. He also pitched in to help some people who couldn't stomach him in 1976, including liberal senator Chuck Percy of Illinois, who was in trouble with conservatives in his state over his support for the Panama Canal treaties.

Reagan also campaigned enthusiastically for Jim Baker in Texas, who was running for attorney general. Baker had been Ford's supremely competent delegate honcho in 1976, but Reagan and Baker genuinely liked each other. So much, in fact, that while Reagan was in the Lone Star State for Baker, he and Mike Deaver took Baker aside to inquire about his availability to run the Reagan for President operation—which struck Baker and his campaign manager, Frank Donatelli, as odd, since Baker was engaged in his own campaign that was looking very promising.[26]

Reagan's campaigning also brought him to his first private meeting with Gerald Ford since the Kansas City convention two years earlier. The meeting was held at Ford's new home in Palm Springs, where the two filmed unity commercials for the GOP as well as endorsement spots for Republicans running elsewhere in the country. They met with the media and were unfailingly polite toward each other, if a bit stiff. Still, the bad blood remained. As the *Washington Post* reported, "Republicans who have talked recently with former president Ford say he rarely fails to remark how old Ronald Reagan is looking."[27]

While Reagan was clearly gearing up for a possible run in 1980, he had to face continuing questions about John Sears. Sears was more and more on the mind of conservatives—and not happily. Since 1976 Reagan had been writing letters to people questioning his former campaign manager. "Don't worry about John Sears," he confided to one old friend. "He is a political technician, not an adviser on philosophy."[28] The matter came to a head when Reagan met with a group of disgruntled conservatives at the U.S. Capitol.[29] The second question Reagan was asked was about Sears's role in the 1980 campaign. Reagan assured them that "John Sears will not be managing my campaign."[30]

Senator Paul Laxalt, slated to be the Reagan campaign's grand pooh-bah once again, delivered the same message, telling Lou Cannon that "Sears will not be the campaign manager in 1980, but will have a role in the Northeast and as a strategist if he wants one."[31] To address the Sears problem, Reagan had approached the well-regarded Bill Timmons, Ford's former political aide, about running things for 1980, but their talks were inconclusive.[32] That fall, the Gipper put in fifty-six separate appearances, and over the previous two years, the Associated Press reported, Reagan had "made more than 300 speeches, held more than 200 news conferences and interviews, and delivered more than 700 radio broadcasts and newspaper columns."[33] Still, Reagan was trailing Ford among Republicans, 37–31, according to Gallup in August.[34]

IN SEPTEMBER, CARTER ENGINEERED the most significant foreign-policy agreement of his presidency with the signing of the Camp David Accords, a historic and durable agreement between Egypt and Israel. Through the sheer force of his own will, along with not-so-gentle cajoling, he brought the two old adversaries—going back to the Exodus and even before—to an agreement. It was an impressive achievement, one that had eluded every president before him, and he got a momentary bump of 11 percent in the polls.

Although Americans may have been pleased about the prospects for peace in the Middle East, what really kept them up at night were high taxes and the economy. Unemployment was creeping up, as was inflation. In June alone, almost 500,000 people lost their jobs. By the fall, Carter's numbers had dropped back to where they had been before the Camp David Accords; according to Harris, the president was at 48 percent approval. Voters disapproved of Carter's handling of the economy by a margin of 2–1.[35] These issues became the centerpiece of the Republicans' campaign efforts in the 1978 midterm elections.

Another issue emerged in California, where voters' attention centered on a new ballot proposition—Proposition 6, or the Briggs Amendment. Simply put, the Briggs Amendment would prohibit out-of-the-closet homosexuals or those advocating a gay lifestyle from being public-school teachers in California. State Senator John Briggs had seen what Anita Bryant was doing in Dade County, Florida, with the repeal of a gay-rights ordinance, and decided to do the same in California, mostly to boost his own political aspirations. The usual Hollywood suspects lined up in opposition to the Briggs Amendment.

One who was also opposed, and who shocked people when he did so—but should not have shocked them if they had studied the man—was Ronald Reagan. Reagan was taking on the Christian Right, an important and growing force in American politics that would hold great sway in the 1980 GOP primaries. Reagan didn't care. His attitude of benign neglect toward homosexuality surely came in part from his days in Hollywood, where gay men thrived and morals were rather casual, but for him this issue also involved a deeply felt principle about privacy and free speech.[36]

Not to say that he didn't have a sense of humor when it came to gays. Early in his governorship, a homosexual scandal threatened his new administration. When informed of the gays in his administration, Reagan deadpanned to Lyn Nofziger, "Well, none of them ever asked me for a date!"[37] He then joked that since Truman Capote was visiting the next week, maybe they ought to tie a rope around him and "troll him down the halls" to see what they could catch.[38]

On Election Day, Republicans picked up twelve seats in the House of Representatives—respectable, but nothing near the thirty-plus they had hoped for. They won six gubernatorial contests and managed a net pickup of more than three hundred state legislators. The best news of the night, though, was the addition of three new senators, which meant that Howard Baker and the Republicans had forty-one: enough now to mount a filibuster if necessary.[39] Senator Percy won reelection, helped by Reagan's eleventh-hour assistance, but Jim Baker lost the attorney general race in Texas.

Proposition 6 went down to a crashing defeat in California, and when John Briggs was asked for the reason why, he simply said, "Ronald Reagan."

ALTHOUGH THE GIPPER HAD a near mystical hold over grassroots conservatives, he was still not held in high regard by the power brokers in the GOP. In the spring of 1979, a survey of leading Republicans showed John Connally to be their first choice for GOP nominee in 1980, with 31.9 percent of the vote; Howard Baker came in second with almost 18 percent; Reagan was essentially tied with George Bush at 11 percent.[40]

Reagan had important work to do to shore up his chances for 1980. He began by romancing the cantankerous Barry Goldwater, who had supported Ford over Reagan in 1976. Goldwater had a love-hate relationship with Reagan. He owed Reagan many favors, but was envious of Reagan's abilities to connect with the American people. Nancy Reagan's parents, Dr. and Mrs. Loyal Davis of Phoenix, had been furious with their old friend Barry for supporting Ford over "Ronnie."[41]

As Reagan began laying groundwork for 1980, he made a tactical decision that would have a profound effect on his campaign: John Sears would come back for another tour as campaign manager, despite Reagan's promises to friends and conservatives that this would not be the case. There was never any meeting in which Sears and Reagan discussed his role; it just sort of happened, for two reasons. One, no one stepped forward to directly challenge Sears's authority, and two, Mrs. Reagan liked Sears. Another reason might have been that the old poker player ran a successful bluff: he told Reagan aide Mike Deaver that Senator Howard Baker was trying to hire him for his campaign. Like the Reagans, Deaver still believed in Sears; he later recalled the controversial campaign manager as "a brain for hire who wanted to play on a winning team."[42]

Distrusted by many Reaganites, Sears was popular among the national media. That was partly because he had no hobbies other than poker, smoking, drinking, and politics—interests that many national political reporters shared. He chain-smoked Viceroy cigarettes and liked a drink, though he seemed to have that under control now. He was also a devout Catholic who would excuse himself from a poker game to attend evening Mass. He had "the softening physique of a person seldom exposed to sun, wind or exercise," in the words of *Time* magazine.[43]

Sears was called "brilliant" by some and "erratic" by others. His first national campaign had been Richard Nixon's in 1968, and he viewed everything through the prism of that experience. He told reporters that the 1980 Reagan campaign would be one of "new ideas with Nixonian thoroughness."[44] That thoroughness involved thick briefing binders that provided answers to every probable question under the sun. Nixon was obsessed with paper and despised working with people; he needed the briefing books because he had no governing framework. Reagan loved to read, but he'd rather be with people than paper, and he had a governing framework based on freedom. Reagan was indifferent to the briefing books Sears had painstakingly prepared; Reagan staffers remember the yelling matches between the candidate and the campaign manager over the binders.[45]

One of Sears's first decisions in 1979 was to take Reagan off the road, where he had been almost constantly for thirty years. Reagan would travel little and say less. He was still doing his radio commentaries and writing his syndicated column, but the relentless public speaking came to an end. Sears regarded Reagan as the clear front-runner and adopted a strategy of risk avoidance: the only person who could beat Reagan was Reagan. To have Reagan say nothing and go to few places was safer than to have the candidate speak his mind, Sears concluded. His plan was to make clear that Reagan's nomination was "inevitable" and that he was the "mainstream" candidate.

Later that year, political columnists Jack Germond and Jules Witcover wrote a piece that clearly took the side of their old poker and drinking buddy Sears, and patronizingly talked about Reagan as if he were a product that was being repackaged for 1980: "The purpose . . . is to have the old model sound a lot newer—and better informed—when he is wheeled out of the showroom onto the campaign trail later this fall."[46]

But the "keep Reagan under wraps" strategy only encouraged reporters to begin speculating that Reagan was too old for one more try. Worse, it deprived the Reagan campaign of one of its great strengths—the candidate's public-speaking abilities, which had matured considerably. The Reagan of the 1960s was often angry—angry at student protesters, angry at college professors, angry at recalcitrant Democratic legislators in Sacramento. By 1979, he had developed a more hopeful and more optimistic message. He had been working on a new stump speech, one that was more upbeat: "We have to make our own successes by our own effort. . . . At the heart of that message should be five simple, familiar, everyday words. No big economic theories. No sermons on political philosophy. Just five short words. Family, Work, Neighborhood, Freedom, Peace." He said that Republicans needed to begin "looking at things in a new way."[47]

Sears's plan provided an opening for John Connally, who was even better than Reagan in a large setting. Connally formally announced his candidacy in January 1979. He had spent most of his life as a Democrat—as Texas governor he had been in the car in Dallas on November 22, 1963, when President Kennedy was assassinated, and had been severely wounded by one of Lee Harvey Oswald's bullets—but he changed parties in 1973 after he became Richard Nixon's treasury secretary. Many in Washington and corporate boardrooms expected "Big John," with his bravado and good press clippings, to be a formidable candidate who would fare much better against Carter than would Reagan.

It wasn't going to be easy for Connally, though. The dean of Washington columnists, James "Scotty" Reston of the *New York Times*, wrote that Connally was "denounced by the Democrats as a turncoat and resented by many Republicans as a presumptuous newcomer."[48] When the Texan made his first foray into New Hampshire, the *Manchester Union-Leader*, published by Reagan's number-one fan, William Loeb, blasted Connally as a "Born-Again Wheeler Dealer."[49]

Less noticed at the time, but detrimental to Connally's candidacy, was the fact that the governor of Texas, the position Connally held from 1963 to 1969, was a constitutionally weak role. In contrast, Reagan had been the governor of California, which had a constitutionally strong executive branch.

The Sears strategy also opened a door for George Bush, who actively campaigned despite not having formally announced his candidacy. Bush had already made repeated trips to Iowa, doing his utmost to replicate Carter's achievement in 1976; that year "Jimmy Who?" unexpectedly won the Democratic caucuses against a field of better-funded and better-known contenders, and became the nominee. While the Iowa caucuses had not received much emphasis from GOP activists up to that point, the situation would be very different in 1980. Bush campaigned everywhere in Iowa, spoke to everyone, and was unfailingly polite, as he wrote thousands of handwritten notes to people he had met. Handwritten notes had become passé by 1979 and struck some as slightly effeminate (a joke going around at the time: "Why do Junior Leaguers hate group sex? All those thank-you notes!"), but from Bush these were effective and became cherished keepsakes. Along with outhustling everyone else in the field, the athletic Bush was going to out-good-manner them as well.

Bush busily assembled a team of talented if eclectic political pros. Jim Baker came aboard as campaign chairman. Baker's assets included a very smooth relationship with the national media. He didn't play poker with them or drink with them like John Sears, but he always returned their phone calls and was a master at giving reporters much-needed background information.

Also signing on was Vic Gold as speechwriter, consultant, and body man, or personal assistant. Bush needed a peer whom he respected on the plane with him; Gold, an attorney, speechwriter, and novelist who had been Barry Goldwater's deputy press secretary in 1964 and Vice President Spiro Agnew's press secretary in the White House, filled the bill. Gold would have been more ideologically comfortable with Reagan, for whom he had worked in 1968. But the mercurial and hot-tempered Gold (Jim Wooten of ABC once said that the "working definition of insanity in Washington is Vic Gold") would never have meshed with John Sears. For a time a young political knockabout, Karl Rove, worked for Bush, but before the campaign got going, Bush fired him for leaking to the media, according to Dave Keene.[50]

Another addition for Bush was Keene himself, who had been Reagan's southern political director in 1976. Keene had done a commendable job winning delegates and primaries for the Gipper, and the media had grown to like him for his candor, humor, and blunt talk. Bringing a prominent Reaganite over constituted a coup for the Bush campaign and advanced the case that Bush was acceptable to conservatives. Keene had angled to be the Reagan campaign's chief spokesman, which made some sense given his relationship with the national media. But Sears had other ideas. Keene had been seen by many as Sears's protégé in 1976, but as the native Wisconsinite became more and more prominent in Washington, he emerged as a threat to Sears's authority and a competitor for the media's affection. Sears offered Keene jobs either as head of coalitions or as the campaign's liaison with Capitol Hill—both of which Keene considered "ghetto" positions.[51]

Sears then offered Keene up as tribute to some of the Californians around Reagan, who were suspicious of the campaign manager. But Keene had also run afoul of Mike Deaver by refusing to support Deaver's brief covert bid to replace Sears; this meant, by extension, that Keene was also in hot water with Mrs. Reagan.[52] Deaver, who had tried to take Sears out, then joined forces with Sears to take Keene out.

Keene was furious with Sears for selling him out. Jim Baker of the nascent Bush operation caught wind of this and offered him a position, but Keene's old friend Lyn Nofziger tried to keep him in the Reagan fold. Nofziger arranged for a private meeting with Reagan, Keene, and himself at the Madison Hotel the next time Reagan was in Washington. They met after work and had a couple of drinks, and Reagan told jokes, quipping to the two conservatives that, between marriages, he'd been pretty randy in Hollywood, "but I got so tired."[53] Reagan never asked Keene to remain with his campaign, however, even after Nofziger told him that Keene would stay only if Reagan directly asked him. Keene signed on shortly after that with Bush.[54]

While the Bush and Reagan teams were jockeying for staffers, Senator Bob Dole of Kansas entered the race for the Republican nomination in late February 1979.[55] In any other year, Dole would have been considered a more serious candidate. He was a wounded war hero who had struggled through years of painful therapy to regain partial use of his left arm and hand but virtually no use of his right. Dole worked his way through law school, was elected to the House and then the Senate, and had been Ford's running mate. He was well liked by both the media and conservatives. His voting record was conservative enough, without being off-putting to more moderate elements in the party.

But Dole was also a wisenheimer, leading some to conclude he was not serious. As a Kansan, Dole knew farm policy better than anyone else in the GOP. This should have made him more popular in rural states like Iowa and New Hampshire. Yet in Iowa he was only scoring 2 percent in the polls, tied with both Crane and Bush.[56]

ON MARCH 7, REAGAN filed his own campaign exploratory committee with the Federal Election Commission. The charade of the exploratory committee rather than a full-fledged campaign committee was chosen so Reagan could continue to earn income from his speeches, radio commentaries, and syndicated column.[57]

As in 1976, the plan was for Paul Laxalt to lead the campaign as chairman. Laxalt told reporters, "Reagan hasn't changed . . . but the country has. Not since General Eisenhower's first election almost 30 years ago has there been such a perfect fit between the man and the public mood as there is today with Gov. Reagan and the American people."[58]

Four years earlier, Laxalt had held a similar press conference, but only a ragtag group of individuals had been willing to be associated with Reagan's challenge to Ford. Now the list of Reagan supporters was impressive, including four former members of Ford's cabinet. Indeed, fully 25 percent of the people on the list had supported Ford in 1976, including Caspar Weinberger.[59]

As long as Reagan remained the front-runner, John Sears would be safe, especially given his close relationship with Mrs. Reagan and Mike Deaver. But he was quickly making enemies inside the Reagan operation. He and Nofziger had been engaged in a four-year feud; Sears had accused Nofziger of leaking against him to muckraking columnist Jack Anderson, while Nofziger accused Sears of trying to "moderate" Reagan. Sears was making clumsy and unpopular personnel decisions. He was insulating himself from critics and driving out perceived competitors. He was beginning to load up the Reagan campaign with people whom Reagan had never laid eyes on and whose names he was not familiar with. By mid-February, there would be seven Reagan staffers working in an office in Alexandria, Virginia, thirty-four in the Los Angeles offices, and another twenty-nine people working in the field—but very few people in New Hampshire, the site of the first primary just one year away.

At one point, Sears became angry with Reagan—so angry, in fact, that he refused to take his candidate's phone calls.[60] Nancy Reagan took note of the change in Sears and wondered what had happened to him since 1976. She thought he had "become arrogant and aloof."[61]

Moreover, as 1979 progressed, Sears's decision to put Reagan on ice was becoming a problem. Reagan's nonavailability became such an issue that Peter Hannaford was forced to produce a memo showing how many interviews the Gipper actually gave between January 1979 and the end of October. All told, Reagan did 101 interviews or media availabilities—almost nothing compared with what the other candidates were doing.[62] This monumental mistake, combined with Sears's fights with Reaganites and profligate spending, would nearly destroy Reagan's candidacy.

3

LE MALAISE

"No one is big enough for the job."

The decade of the 1970s was winding down, and not a moment too soon. The country's bicentennial in 1976 stood out as the only event in which America could take pride. Otherwise, it had been a miserable time of declinism, littered with lost jobs, lost national pride, lost dreams—and lost hope. It was one of the most uninspiring decades in the history of the American Republic. As 1980 approached, there was not much that seemed exceptional about America anymore.

The decade had begun with the sappy movie *Love Story*, acted woodenly by Ryan O'Neal and even more so by the pretty but maladroit Ali MacGraw. The poster for the movie carried the inane slogan "Love means never having to say you're sorry," which was, as the *New York Times Magazine* noted, a "glossy reflection of the urge to be free of guilt and responsibility to anyone outside the self."[1] How this new Age of Narcissism would finish was unknown, but anything would be better than having to watch that dreadful movie ever again.

Advertisers were in a mad race to the bottom to appeal to the lowest common denominator. No one had ever accused any advertising agency on Madison Avenue of trying to appeal to Mensa members, but the counterculture's "If it feels good, do it" ethos had reached ridiculous and often scary extremes. From "It's your face, let Schick love it" to "At McDonald's we do it all for you" to Burger King's "Have it your way," personal pronouns including "me," "my," and "I" had replaced the inclusive "we," "us," and "our" that had defined America for two hundred years. In the "Me Decade," as Tom Wolfe tagged it, everyone was out for himself. Vanity license plates began to flourish.

The sexual and cultural revolutions of the 1960s were codified by the 1970s; what began as heady rebellion became the status quo. The consequences were dark. Trends that seemed novel during the Summer of Love in 1967 now came off as tawdry. The country had spiraled downward from the debauchery of Woodstock to the decadence of disco, from "harmless" grass to dangerous cocaine, from sexual freedom to the same old licentiousness. Love must have been "free," because it seemed like everyone was giving it away. The aftermath was an American landscape littered with ruined marriages, broken homes, and drug addiction. The social fabric was in tatters.

A cultish faction sprang up in Los Angeles and on college campuses called the "human potential movement," but no one seemed to quite know what it was. Loss of trust in public institutions, politicians, and societal leaders had sent young Americans scurrying off to find their own slice of heathen. "We're afraid to believe too much in anything or, anyone," one undergraduate at American University whimpered.[2]

Reality seemed to touch these affluent brats only when inflation jacked the cost of their drugs. At the University of Michigan, an ounce of marijuana rose from twelve dollars to fifteen dollars, and at Boston University, Quaaludes went up from thirty cents per tablet to as much as three dollars.[3] Prescription drugs were readily available for stressed-out parents, and now they, too, wanted to "ask Alice" about the white rabbit. The era was not graceful, but it was slick. No-fault divorces came into vogue and Catholic priests found their parishioners coming to confession less and less for one simple reason: they no longer felt guilty.

College students of the late 1970s may have inherited the 1960s commitment to rutting, anonymous, casual sex, but they were, unlike their older brothers and sisters who marched in the 1960s, indifferent to politics and the world around them. With the Vietnam War lost and the draft over, students found new ways in which to occupy their leisure time. Rather than bomb ROTC buildings, male undergraduates at Wake Forest took turns fluff-drying themselves in coin-operated dryers. "It sounds kind of dumb," one said. "But after a few beers, it seems like an entirely reasonable thing to do."[4] Fewer than half of college students bothered to register to vote.[5] The eighteen-year-old vote had seemed so important just a few years earlier. Now no one could remember what the fuss was all about.

American women had gone in a few short years from "Earth Mother" to "Disco Mama." Hair care was back in style, as was personal hygiene. Indeed, as men's hair got shorter, women's seemed to get longer. Women also took to wearing makeup once again. As if to compensate for their older sisters' disdain for cosmetics, some of the disco women of the 1970s appeared to apply it with a trowel.

Young men were borrowing their mothers' blow driers and hair spray and nobody thought twice about it. Then they headed out to the discos in their double-knit leisure suits.

In those discos—which were little more than petri dishes for gratuitous sex and "recreational" drug use—young Americans did their bump-and-grind dance routines to the beat of "YMCA," a celebration of young homosexuals meeting in public bathhouses, and "Bad Girl," in which Donna Summer sang admiringly of prostitution. Virtually every song of the 1970s was about sex, sex, and more sex, as in the case of "Afternoon Delight" and "Shake Your Booty," which left little doubt as to their subject matter. People listened to it all on eight-track tapes, the bulky plastic cassettes that had become all the rage, and AM radio, which dominated not with political talk but with rock 'n' roll and "bubblegum" music. Meanwhile, the Rolling Stones began the first of their "farewell" tours. Thirty years later, the band was *still* on a farewell tour. "You get what you need"? You bet.

In 1973, the stock market topped out at 1,050 and then fell for the rest of the decade. No one in America was investing in the future anymore. Eat, drink, and be merry, for tomorrow there will be no tomorrow became the idealized philosophy of America in the 1970s.

In the spring of 1979, the famous Russian dissident and Nobel Prize–winning author Aleksandr Solzhenitsyn saw the decay of the West and eviscerated it in a commencement speech at Harvard. He deplored the "TV stupor" and "intolerable music" along with the "spiritual exhaustion" evident in America.[6] To be sure, he hated the Soviet Union, where he had been imprisoned and beaten, leading him to write the internationally acclaimed book *The Gulag Archipelago*, but Solzhenitsyn could not bring himself to call the culture of the West superior to that of the collectivist state he'd left behind. When a demonstrator in the crowd held up a sign that said, "You Can't Fight Stalinism with Fascism," Solzhenitsyn departed from his prepared text to angrily condemn the protester, saying that only those who had never been held captive in a Soviet labor camp could have the audacity to call him a Fascist.[7]

He was also booed for criticizing the anti-American protests during the Vietnam War. The peaceniks of the '60s and '70s, he said, "wound up being involved in the betrayal of Far Eastern nations, in a genocide and in the suffering today imposed on 30 million people there."[8] He hit the materialism of America especially hard, condemning the worldview that put "man as the center of everything that exists."[9] The world, according to Solzhenitsyn, was "at a major turning point."[10]

For pointing out the obvious problems plaguing America and the West, Solzhenitsyn was denounced as "dangerous" and a "zealot" by the *New York Times*.[11]

But the signs of decay were everywhere. America's cities had become burned-out shells. New York City was now a war zone. A record 1,733 New Yorkers were murdered in 1979. On New Year's Day 1980 alone, twelve people were slain, including a pregnant girl and her teenaged boyfriend, who got into a melee over seating arrangements in a disco.[12]

Detroit was suffering because it was turning out some of the worst cars imaginable: flimsy, gas-guzzling heaps that often began rusting within months of leaving the showroom. Japan's auto industry, exporting sporty, well-made, fuel-efficient, and economical cars to the United States, had nearly destroyed the domestic auto industry—and with it, Detroit.

The city of Cleveland was in worse shape. Teetering on the verge of bankruptcy, the "Mistake by the Lake" was in awful condition in every way imaginable. Even its sports teams stank, especially baseball's Indians and the Cavaliers of the NBA, who set records—for the most losses and the least fans. One-third of Cleveland's citizens said they wished they lived somewhere else. The city's mayor, a pint-sized thirty-two-year-old named Dennis Kucinich, was in over his head in every way imaginable, and he'd been photographed tottering embarrassingly behind a podium on several large phone books, struggling to reach the microphones.[13] The city had become the butt of jokes nationwide. A favorite was about a man who won a contest; first prize was one week in Cleveland, and second place—two weeks in Cleveland.

All in all, America was a crummy place for many Americans in the 1970s. Cultural, economic, political, and foreign Lilliputians had tied down the pitiful giant America.

THE GROWING SENSE IN America by the late spring of 1979 was that Jimmy Carter, though by reputation a nice guy, was not up to the task. One of his own "allies" in the House, Majority Leader Jim Wright of Texas, said bluntly of Carter's presidency, "No one is big enough for the job." He then coldly added, "So we have to settle for what we've got."[14]

The U.S. economy continued to founder. When the first-quarter results came in, they showed 0.7 percent growth in the gross national product, which was just ahead of a recession level. Inflation was also on the rise and housing starts plummeted.[15] The price of oil had risen from $1.80 a barrel in 1970 to $14.54 per barrel in 1979, an approximate 800 percent increase.[16]

The international scene was becoming more and more disturbing as well. Iran was the latest concern. Under the shah, a longtime U.S. ally for his anti-Communist and pro-West positions, the situation inside Iran had been deterio-

rating for several years. The shah infuriated Iran's powerful radical Muslim cler-
ics, who regarded him as a puppet of American imperialists and oil companies
and were outraged by his recognition of Israel and such western-style reforms as
granting suffrage to women. By the beginning of 1979 Iran had descended into
chaos as basic services vanished and widespread strikes crippled the country. The
Soviets exploited the unrest by broadcasting anti-American propaganda into the
country, fomenting revolution.

Carter, with his insistence on human rights, turned his back on the shah,
seeing the authoritarian ruler as a torturer and tyrant. Without the help of the
United States, the shah could do nothing to quell the growing tumult in his country, and in February 1979, he and his family fled the country. Jubilant Iranians
danced in the streets of Tehran and pulled down statues to celebrate the shah's
toppled regime.

The shah became an international pariah, as no country would allow him permanent residence. Although America's insistence that the shah "Westernize" his
country had contributed to his downfall, Carter shabbily opposed allowing the shah
to come to the United States; in a letter the president cited the "high probability" of
an outbreak of anti-American retaliation in Iran.[17] For a time, the U.S. intelligence
community hoped that Iran's new leader, the Ayatollah Ruhollah Khomeini, might
be an ally against the Soviets, but this turned out to be a delusion.

With even prominent Democrats questioning Carter, it became increasingly
clear that the president might face a challenge in 1980 from his own party. For
a time California governor Jerry Brown, who succeeded Reagan in 1974, had
seemed the kind of fresh face who could take on Carter. Brown, the son of former California governor Pat Brown, the man Reagan had defeated in 1966, had
entered a few presidential primaries in 1976 and shown astonishing strength,
but his late-starting campaign could not catch Carter. After a surprisingly strong
reelection for governor in the Republican year of 1978, Brown seemed ready to
take on Carter again. But by 1979 voters and journalists had grown tired of his
quirks and non sequiturs, his New Age "the Earth is your mother" utterances, and
his high-profile relationship with singer Linda Ronstadt, which struck many as
just plain weird. Chicago columnist Mike Royko bestowed the moniker "Governor Moonbeam" on Brown, and he never shook it.

A more likely, and prominent, Democratic opponent was Ted Kennedy.
Polls showed Kennedy swamping Carter in popularity contests; a survey in New
Hampshire, for instance, showed Kennedy beating the president by better than
2–1.[18] "Draft Kennedy" organizations were popping up around the country.

In full bravado mode, Carter told a group of Democrats when asked about a Kennedy challenge, "I'll whip his ass." Stunned to hear the president use such language, one of those present asked him to beg their pardon, but what did you say, Mr. President? Carter repeated the sentence, word for word.[19]

The president's pollster, Pat Caddell, saw a different picture. In the spring of 1979, his polling showed a precipitous drop in the president's numbers across the board, especially relating to Americans' confidence in the future. Caddell turned to First Lady Rosalynn Carter, the president's best friend and closest confidante. In an extended meeting with the first lady, the pollster laid out Carter's atrocious standing. Mrs. Carter immediately scheduled Caddell for a private breakfast with the president.

At their breakfast, Caddell reviewed the gloomy outlook and began to pass along to Carter books to read, including Christopher Lasch's *The Culture of Narcissism*. Caddell later gave Carter a 107-page memo analyzing the state of disrepair in his administration.[20]

IF RELATIONS WERE FROSTY between Carter and prominent Democrats, they were downright glacier-like between Ronald Reagan and Phil Crane. After Congressman Crane jumped into the campaign in August 1978, the former Reagan supporter had a few good months, but then he began making one stumbling mistake after another. Much of the problem was the meddling of the candidate's wife, Arlene, who could not bear being the candidate's wife; she wanted to be the candidate, the manager, the chief pollster, and the center of all attention. The *Washington Star* described her as "destructive" and a "cannonball rolling loose on the pitching deck."[21] (Mrs. Crane once told a reporter that raising seven daughters was easy: "You just put birth control pills in their cereal.") Many talented individuals, such as Paul Weyrich, walked away from the campaign because of her divisive ways.

William Loeb, the curmudgeonly publisher of the *Manchester Union-Leader* and a Reagan man through and through, used his statewide daily paper to denounce the candidate he saw as betraying the Gipper. Loeb published a flurry of stories and editorials charging Crane with serial infidelity and claiming that the congressman and his wife engaged in excessive partying. One anonymous source told the *Union-Leader* that Crane said it was his goal to "bed down 1,000 women."[22] A young female aide in the offices of Senator Gordon Humphrey, smitten with the handsome Crane, said her goal was to be "number 1,001." Crane probably wouldn't have seen the humor in the comment.

Crane's campaign blamed Reagan for putting Loeb up to it; Reagan was furious at Crane for making the unfounded charge. This was the first time that someone had accused Reagan of engaging in dirty politics and he did not like it one bit. It was an aspect of politics that Reagan despised.

Another Republican for whom Reagan had little regard announced his candidacy in early 1979. Senator Lowell P. Weicker of Connecticut, a liberal Republican, hated Reagan, and Reagan in his diaries later responded in kind, confiding that he thought Weicker was a "schmuck" and "a pompous no good fathead."[23] Indeed, Weicker had an ego that made Charles de Gaulle's look retiring by comparison. The senator stood 6'6" tall and he needed every inch of that frame to house his massive sense of self.

Weicker's affixed sobriquet was invariably "Maverick." He was a media hound who had had White House ambitions since he'd first run for Congress in the 1960s. It was said that the most dangerous place in Washington was between Weicker and a microphone. When he announced his presidential candidacy in Hartford, he blew a cold blast of rhetoric at his own party: the senator, born in Paris, raised on Park Avenue in Manhattan, and educated at the best New England prep schools before graduating from Yale, said that the GOP "excludes normal people."[24]

Weicker's campaign was over before it ever began; in mid-May, just two months after he announced, he would withdraw from the race, as he was running in only "a strong third position" in his home state of Connecticut.[25]

AT THE END OF April, Reagan officially opened his headquarters in Los Angeles, though he was still proclaiming that he had not yet decided on running. Then, on May 1, Ambassador George Bush officially jumped into the race. He had an impressively broad but somewhat shallow résumé and more personal resilience than a Timex watch. His campaign slogan, "A President We Won't Have to Train,"[26] was uninspiring, but it drew a contrast with the ever-shrinking Carter.

Bush's traditionalist positions on the issues—with the notable exceptions of a constitutional amendment to outlaw abortion, the Equal Rights Amendment (ERA), and the tax-cut bill sponsored by Jack Kemp in the House and William Roth in the Senate—might have won cheers from some of the conservatives who dominated the party. What's more, his culturally conservative upbringing, his service during World War II, and his experiences as a husband and father and as a businessman who had to deal with high taxes and excessive regulations aligned him with conservatives. But many conservatives just could not warm up to him, in part because he did not identify himself as one of them. As chairman of the Republican National Committee, Bush was asked if he was a conservative, a moderate, or a liberal and he dismissively said, "Labels are for cans."[27] Unlike Reagan,

Bush was not a big reader of conservative books or publications. He was more of an intuitive conservative, and often struck more moderate positions.

There also seemed to exist a cultural gap. Bush's Brooks Brothers suits, the tasseled loafers, the striped watchband, his good manners—all bespoke his privileged background, which included his education at the exclusive boys' boarding school Phillips Andover Academy and then Yale, where he was a member of Skull and Bones, a supersecret men's fraternity that only "old-money" sons could join. Some conservatives questioned Bush's "toughness," even though he had been a daring U.S. Navy pilot in the Pacific.

Bush's speech to the national media stressed his record of achievement rather than ideology. Carter's liberalism was an issue, yes, but this was not fertile ground for Bush to sow; this was where Reagan and others would take their stand.[28] Ideological passion was, well, kinda tacky with the Bush family. After Dave Keene had signed on with Bush, the candidate invited him to the family's summer home in Kennebunkport, Maine, to talk about the forthcoming campaign. There Keene asked Bush—rhetorically, he thought—"Why do you want to be president?" and was astonished to hear Bush reply, "Because I want to bring good people to government." Keene turned to Ambassador Bush, twenty years his elder, and said, "No, George, you want to be president because you want to save Western civilization."[29]

Almost everybody called Bush "Sir" or "Mr. Bush" or "Ambassador." Not so Keene, the son of a union organizer and saloon keeper. He despised elitism and went out of his way to disregard it, down to calling Bush by his first name. Bush of course never complained about it, but he didn't like it.[30]

Bob Dole was the next Republican to declare for president, in mid-May. Dole announced in his hometown of Russell, Kansas, and promised a positive campaign, prompting giggles from reporters who remembered him as the guy who once called opponents of the Vietnam War "left-leaning marshmallows."[31]

Dole, well regarded in Washington for his legislative skills, hoped that Reagan would not run or would falter so that the Kansas senator could pick up the conservative baton. Though he was at only 4 percent in new polls, Dole climbed to 15 percent when respondents were asked if they had a second choice.[32] He also assumed that if Ford did not run, Ford's support would go to him, not Bush, and that his friendship with Reagan staffers, including Lyn Nofziger, John Sears, Paul Russo, and Charlie Black, meant that they would come over to him if Reagan should stumble. It was, however, open to question whether Dole could overcome his image as a "combination of Attila the Hun, Sammy Glick and the sound of fingernails scratching down a blackboard," in the memorable words of the *Washington Star*.[33] Suffice it to say, there were a lot of "ifs" in the Dole campaign plan.

With Dole in the race and Weicker out, the 1980 GOP field remained at six candidates.

BY SUMMER, PRESIDENT CARTER was under fire from all sides. Some liberals tried to get Congressman Morris Udall of Arizona to run if Kennedy took a pass. When Carter caught wind of the fact that Udall was thinking about this, he called the congressman and specifically asked for his endorsement, but Udall refused. Others from the right side of the Democratic spectrum, such as Senator Pat Moynihan of New York, took soundings. Ted Kennedy was still undecided, even though polls continued to show him pounding everybody—including Reagan in Reagan's own state of California, 61–30 percent.[34]

A former Carter speechwriter, Jim Fallows, wrote an article for the *Atlantic Monthly* charging that the president personally approved who could and who could not use the White House tennis courts. Carter denied the micromanaging charge, but then told an astonished television interviewer that his secretary arranged tennis schedules "so that more than one person would not want to use the same tennis court simultaneously, unless they were on opposite sides of the net or engaged in a doubles contest."[35]

Carter one day lurched to the right, as when he proposed the deregulation of the railroad industry. Another day, he lurched to the left, as when he proposed massive new federal agencies such as the Departments of Energy and Education. His administration was spinning out of control.

Then it came to light that earlier in the spring, he had been fishing in a secluded pond near his home in Georgia when, startled, he was attacked in his boat by what became known as the "Killer Rabbit." The creature in question was not Bugs Bunny but a "swamp rabbit," large and unfriendly and, to judge by its menacing hiss and flashing teeth, probably rabid, making it potentially dangerous to Carter. But city folk simply didn't understand how a bunny rabbit could also be a vicious beast.[36]

White House press secretary Jody Powell had innocently told the story to Brooks Jackson, a reporter with the Associated Press, who wrote a small, light-hearted account of the incident. But then the *Washington Post*, the *New York Times*, and all three television networks picked up on it, putting a darker pall on the story. Everywhere Carter went, he was asked about the "Killer Rabbit." It was just one more embarrassing incident in a long line of embarrassing incidents.

To such embarrassments were added far more serious problems. Like Richard III, Carter was becoming "rudely stamped." It would be the political "winter" of his "discontent" yet would be a "glorious summer" for King Edward, the "sun" of

Massachusetts. Carter was a political cripple and was consumed with jealousy of the beloved Edward. Democratic men and women would adore Edward Kennedy, while "dogs bark" at poor Carter. President Carter had "no delight to pass away the time" and his supporters lamented the "deformed" quality of his administration.[37]

But it might have been Hamlet, not Richard III, on Carter's mind. Whether 'tis nobler to suffer the slings and arrows of outrageous fortune in the Oval Office—or, by taking leave of it, to end them?[38]

Carter's presidency had become a tragedy of Shakespearean proportions.

IN THE SUMMER OF 1979 the Soviets were making noises regarding the internal affairs of Afghanistan. The OPEC cartel had cut oil production and raised prices, a problem compounded by the fact that Carter had closed off exploration for oil and gas in much of Alaska, which by some estimates had 60 percent of domestic reserves. He had ordered oil companies to cut production of gasoline and instead produce home heating oil for the coming winter. Demand for gasoline now outstripped supply. Long gas lines snaked around blocks and through the suburbs in the late spring and summer of 1979. Bumper stickers appeared that read "Carter—Kiss My Gas."[39]

Fecklessly, Carter issued an executive order that nonresidential buildings in America, both government and private, could not set their thermostats lower than 78 degrees in the summer or higher than 65 degrees in the winter.[40] No one took Carter's order seriously.

RONALD REAGAN'S CAMPAIGN ALSO seemed to be paralyzed. In early June the *Los Angeles Times* reported that Reagan's support had "declined since the first of the year," as he was now favored by only 28 percent of GOP voters nationwide.[41] He was also lagging in fundraising. John Connally had raised about $2.2 million by mid-1979 and Phil Crane, mostly through direct mail, had raised $2.5 million, though he was heavily in debt to Richard Viguerie, his direct-mail sage. Reagan had raised only about $1.4 million.[42]

With John Sears still keeping Reagan on a tight leash, George Bush worked Iowa assiduously and in August unexpectedly won the Ames straw poll, which the *Des Moines Register* conducted at the annual fundraising dinner organized by the state GOP. Bush took almost 40 percent of the vote, with Reagan a distant second at 26 percent.[43] The Ames straw poll should have been a warning to Reagan and his flaccid operation, but the campaign made no changes in Iowa. Bush and his team could scarcely believe their good fortune.

Bush also signed up a veteran of the GOP wars in New Hampshire, former governor Hugh Gregg. Gregg had been Reagan's state chairman in 1976, but this was not the coup it might have seemed for Bush. The Gregg and Bush families were longtime friends, and in any case many Reaganites blamed Gregg for Reagan's losing New Hampshire by a whisker in 1976. Gregg had told his candidate to get out of the state the weekend before the primary, believing that Reagan's volunteers and town coordinators needed the time and space to get their voters out to the polls rather than hear the Gipper speak one more time. Reagan lost by about 1,300 votes out of 108,000 cast. Many thought that had he stayed to stump the state, he would have upset President Ford and perhaps won the nomination in 1976.[44]

Reagan, meanwhile, signed up Gerald P. "Jerry" Carmen as head of his New Hampshire operations. Carmen, who had been a GOP state chairman, was a shrewd and tough operator who had his critics. He had been flirting with Connally, but as soon as he joined the Reagan team, he signed up chairmen in nearly all of the Granite State's 236 towns, some of them hamlets that were nothing more than two roads crossing in the night. This operation in New Hampshire provided one of the few pieces of evidence that the Reagan campaign had not entirely stalled.

Around this time a seventh Republican presidential candidate, Congressman John B. Anderson of Illinois, emerged to replace Lowell Weicker as the GOP's "liberal" alternative. Anderson had begun his career as a conservative and a kooky one at that, as he introduced and reintroduced a bill in Congress that would specifically designate America to be a "Christian" nation.[45] But over the years, he had drifted to the left, and he became particularly miffed when social conservatives fielded a primary candidate against him in 1978. Although Anderson won, the challenger from the right gave him a scare—and a chip on his shoulder.

ON JULY 5, 1979, President Carter was scheduled to give a national address on the energy crisis, but his aides were divided over whether the president should give the address at all, let alone what he should say. Rosalynn Carter read the initial draft and didn't like it. Rumors leaked out of the White House that a shake-up of the cabinet was on the table. Just a day before the speech, Carter, who was at Camp David, abruptly and angrily canceled the address altogether when he hung up the phone on advisers Hamilton Jordan and Gerald Rafshoon and Vice President Walter Mondale.

The White House never fully explained why the speech had been canceled, and as the *Chicago Tribune* reported, this "inspired speculation that Carter was suffering from nervous exhaustion or a nervous breakdown."[46] The president was scheduled to return to the White House the following day, but he scrapped this plan too.

Carter officials told a *Washington Star* reporter that the administration was in "total disarray" and "chaos." "No one knows what the President is up to," one exasperated aide said.[47] Pat Caddell was called for a one-day meeting with Carter at Camp David, but it stretched into six days. All told, Carter remained at the secluded retreat for eleven days, summoning some 150 different people for meetings, including Democratic governors, a couple of GOP governors, Vice President Mondale, the Reverend Jesse Jackson, AFL-CIO leader Lane Kirkland, and Washington access-seller Clark Clifford. Most days, Carter was dressed casually—tennis shoes, no tie, slacks. Sometimes he would gather with his guests and sit on the floor, cross-legged. It was a group encounter session before the phrase came into common usage; Carter's aides called it a "Domestic Summit," trying to put the best face on things.[48]

At long last, Carter was ready to make a major television address. The July 15 speech was ostensibly to be about energy, but the real goal was the resurrection of the Carter presidency. The Georgian wanted to get back to the spirit of the 1976 campaign, when he had told the American people that they were good and that decency would cure all. In 1979, in the face of joblessness, long gas lines, high inflation, high interest rates, and high thermostats, Americans were scared and ornery. They wanted action.

The ironic truth is that Jimmy Carter never actually uttered the word "malaise" in his now notorious speech, but Caddell did in a memo to the president, and the word so perfectly fit Carter's tone and message that he was saddled with it anyway. It would bedevil him for the rest of his presidency—and his life. If the word "malaise" sounds suspiciously French, that is because it is. Dictionary.com has eight definitions for it, including "weakness," "discomfort," "mental uneasiness," and "lethargy."[49]

The president began the speech with a bit of a mea culpa, telling viewers that he had lost focus and admitting that he had become more worried about the "isolated world" of Washington than the larger welfare of the American people. Carter attempted to plumb the depths of the American psyche, dangerous ground for a president with a 25 percent approval rating. "It's clear that the true problems of our nation are much deeper—deeper than gasoline lines or energy shortages, deeper even than inflation or recession," he said. Carter told the American people they were suffering from "a crisis of confidence. It is a crisis that strikes at the very heart and soul and spirit of our national will. We can see this crisis in the growing doubt about the meaning of our own lives and the loss of a unity of purpose for our Nation. The erosion of our confidence in the future is threatening to destroy the social and the political fabric of America."[50]

No president had ever talked to the American people like this before: heavy, bordering on apocalyptic. David Broder of the *Washington Post* wrote the next day, "It will surely go down in history as one of the most extraordinary addresses a chief executive has ever given."[51] This was "Deacon Jimmy," the brooding, judgmental Baptist at his very worst.

In midstream of his speech, Carter changed abruptly and outlined a six-point program for energy independence and sacrifice. He promised action and new presidential initiatives; at no time did he prescribe free-market solutions to what ailed America, only more governmental measures. Carter closed the address by praising American resilience and resolve, and feebly urging his fellow Americans to "say something good about our country."[52]

Newspaper commentary the next day was for the most part guardedly supportive, and Carter's poll numbers actually went up. But some around the White House, including Vice President Mondale, thought the speech was a noble but wrongheaded effort. Mondale recalled warning Carter that "for an administration that got elected to be as good as the people, it's a bad idea now to say we need people as good as the government. And I said these are real problems out there, there's inflation, there's gas lines and that sort of thing, we ought to be working on that and not trying to psychoanalyze the emotional condition of the American people."[53] The vice president thought the speech would make Carter look like "an old scold and a grouch."[54] Mondale seriously contemplated resigning his office if Carter gave the address. He was that opposed to it.[55]

Reagan immediately denounced the speech, saying, "There really isn't any crisis in the country. There's just a crisis in the White House."[56] Armed with a scalpel, he added, "People who talk about an age of limits are really talking about their own limitations, not America's."[57]

By the summer of 1979, the president and the former California governor had virtually nothing in common. Reagan was an optimist and Carter a pessimist. Carter wanted to apologize to everybody and Reagan believed everybody should thank America. Reagan believed in the future while Carter feared the future. Reagan believed in conservatism while Carter believed in collectivism. Carter had come to Washington as a skeptic of government, but once he became president, his view on government changed dramatically. Reagan had started out as a New Deal Democrat who believed fervently in government, but had evolved over the years into a self-described "libertarian-conservative" who was deeply distrustful of centralized authority.

A STORM WAS BREWING in the Reagan camp. Lyn Nofziger quit the campaign in frustration. Nofziger had been a Reagan friend and aide since 1966, thirteen long years. He was one of the most respected operatives in the GOP and the conservative movement, in part because he said what was on his mind and didn't put up with any guff, especially from John Sears. Sears, Nofziger charged, was not only trying to moderate Reagan but also keeping the candidate from meeting with important people in conservative circles.

Nofziger was also miffed that Sears had made the odd decision to reassign him to fundraising. Nofziger had handled Reagan's press off and on since 1966, and he knew nothing about the niceties of polite political fundraising.[58] He had all the tact of a Mack truck; the last thing he should have been doing was dealing with anybody who didn't understand his off-color humor, his awful puns, or his rough-house rhetoric. The smoke-filled room, not the tearoom at some private club, was invented for Nofziger.

Reagan liked Nofziger, and tried to talk him out of leaving. "I don't want you to quit. We've been together too long," Reagan pleaded with Nofziger on a Saturday in late August. Reagan asked him to wait over the weekend, until he got back from the ranch.[59]

On Monday, Reagan held a meeting at his home in Pacific Palisades. Present were advisers Ed Meese, Sears, Charlie Black, Mike Deaver, and Jim Lake. The only two who spoke up in favor of Nofziger were Meese and Reagan himself. Nofziger was gone, which in Reagan's mind became one more strike against Sears.[60]

AS THE REAGAN CAMPAIGN struggled with infighting, the Gipper's fragile front-runner status was increasingly threatened. Over the summer, the *Washington Post* surveyed 1,310 delegates to the 1976 GOP convention and found that Reagan had the support of 43 percent. The *Post* wrote that Reagan was far and away ahead, which was true in one regard but overlooked the fact that Reagan had gotten nearly 50 percent of the delegates' votes four years earlier in Kansas City. Worse, of those who supported him in 1976, only 73 percent now favored him.[61] He had gone backwards.

Reagan's nomination was anything but a foregone conclusion. The field of potential Republicans wanting to take on Carter—and Reagan—was big and getting bigger. One who oddly declared for president but said he was also available to be vice president was Senator Larry Pressler of South Dakota. The thirty-seven-year-old first-term senator was a Rhodes scholar and a Vietnam War vet. He engendered little respect, though, not even from his own GOP state chairman,

Dan Parrish, who told the *Washington Post*, "My reaction in three words would be ha, ha, ha."[62] General Alexander Haig, who had served in the Nixon and Ford White House, was also making noises about running, but most saw him as simply a cat's-paw for his mentor, Henry Kissinger.

Gerald Ford liked to muse publicly about running, especially since Carter had fallen off so badly in the national polls. Ford and Reagan were statistically tied among Republicans, 30–29.[63] Though Ford often told the media that he was not a candidate for 1980, at other times he hinted at his interest, telling reporters, "You never say 'never.'"[64]

Ultimately, though, Ford was not about to go sloshing around New Hampshire or Iowa, grubbing for votes. Last time he'd done it, in 1976, he'd had the majesty of the office of the president to protect his honor, but if he were to do it again, he'd be treated like any other candidate, albeit one who had once accidentally occupied the office of the most powerful man in the world. No thanks. A draft, maybe. Or even better, a brokered convention in which the delegates, hopelessly deadlocked, would turn to the man from Michigan to whom they had turned once before. The convention would be held in Detroit, in his home state, and what better way to prove the old adage wrong? He could be a prophet in his own land.

With Ford staying out of the race and Reagan still reined in by Sears, the real showdown in the early days of the Republican campaign involved the two Texans, George Herbert Walker Bush and John Bowden Connally Jr. Anybody who knew anything about Texas politics knew that Bush and Connally loathed each other. Bush aide Richard Bond bluntly said it "was a hate-hate" relationship and that Connally thought Bush was a "bedwetting Trilateralist."[65] The Trilateral Commission, of which Bush was a former member, was a bogeyman to both the right wing and the left wing, believed to be bent on world domination by corporate interests. Think Nelson Rockefeller standing atop Lenin's Tomb.

It was the old Houston versus the new Houston—Connally's family went back generations in Texas, while Bush was a transplanted New Englander. But it went deeper than that. It was also "Old Cattle Money" versus "New Oil Money." It was the Alamo versus the *Mayflower*. Bush's friend Vic Gold said, "You knew who he regarded with a kind of disdain, and Connally was one of them." Connally, he said, was "high on" Bush's "shit list."[66] Bush considered the smooth, garrulous Connally "corrupt." The belief may have stemmed in part from the fact that in 1974 Connally had been charged with taking a $10,000 bribe over milk price fixing when he was treasury secretary. He was acquitted after hiring Washington superlawyer Edward Bennett Williams for $250,000. Williams battered the witness against Connally into submission. Connally had asked Bush to testify as a character witness in his behalf at the trial but Bush refused, and this solidified Connally's hatred of Bush.

While campaigning in 1979, Connally often said that he was "the only certified not-guilty candidate running in either party."[67] Audiences nervously laughed, but they were not convinced.

Connally regarded the blueblood Bush as "a little Lord Fauntleroy"[68] and derided him as "all hat and no cattle."[69] When a Bush aide once joshed him that he was afraid he'd find John Connally at his table at the Petroleum Club, Bush haughtily replied, "You don't really understand me, do you? The clubs I belong to wouldn't have John Connally as a member."[70]

The two candidates had only three things in common. They both had a remarkable politician's gift to remember everybody's name. They had both been on aircraft carriers in the Pacific for the Navy in World War II. And corporate America preferred either of them to the populist Reagan.

Connally's style of campaigning was dramatically different from Bush's. Connally couldn't care a whit for the living-room, retail aspects of politics, where Bush thrived. "If native Texan Connally is a little too big for this state [New Hampshire]," wrote Rowland Evans and Robert Novak in the *Washington Post*, "transplanted Texan Bush is the native New Englander who fits right in."[71] Connally was, as James Reston noted, "a superb public speaker,"[72] but he personified every non-Texan's cliché of the state: too big, too loud, and too pushy. The standard reporter's line about the 6'2", broad-shouldered, handsome Connally—nicknamed "Big John"—was that he "looks like a president,"[73] whatever that meant. Playing on his massive ego, the joke going around political circles was "Yeah, Connally might look like a president, but is the job big enough for him?" Every sentence he uttered seemed to begin with a personal pronoun.

Where Connally was "Big John," Bush had a kinder and gentler family nickname, "Poppy." His grandfather, George Herbert Walker, was "Big Pop," and his grandson was "Little Pop" and eventually "Poppy."[74] Bush hated it. Everybody in the family had a nickname, it seemed. His wife, Barbara Pierce Bush, was "Bar," his mother was "Gam," his brother Prescott was "Pressy," his daughter Dorothy was "Doro," and son Jeb was "Jebby." Even the family pooch was named "C. Fred."[75]

Others scoffed, but Bush believed in noblesse oblige. He believed his class had a duty to give back to society. It was as deeply ingrained in him as was his patriotism.

Bush could throw elbows, though. In a free-association interview, he described Reagan as "old," Connally as "slippery," and Bob Dole as "mean."[76] The self-aware Bush mirthfully described himself as "the elitist candidate." But he tried to distinguish himself from "those Brahmins," because he had not settled down in Connecticut, instead striking out for Texas to seek his own fortune and his own identity. He didn't go to Wall Street like so many of his school chums or indeed his own family.[77]

If Bush avoided labeling himself a conservative, Connally did not even grasp what conservatism meant. He had changed parties but not his views of the world. He believed government could solve most problems. A protégé of Lyndon Johnson, he defended the Great Society in one infamous meeting with conservatives in Washington. He also supported the ERA, abortion, and Carter's SALT II (the Strategic Arms Limitation Treaty) with the Soviet Union, which many Cold Warrior conservatives deplored. One disgusted conservative described Connally to columnists Rowland Evans and Robert Novak as "LBJ with charisma."[78]

Richard Viguerie, who had recently signed on with Connally after bolting from Phil Crane's campaign, tried to take him in hand and explain how populist conservatism worked. Connally would have none of it. He believed power flowed downward instead of upward. Connally was not building any sort of grassroots organization in Iowa or New Hampshire. It just wasn't the way you did politics in Texas, so why would it work anywhere else?

Connally and Bush even differed in their approaches to Ronald Reagan. While both recognized that their chances hinged on Reagan's faltering, Connally and his surrogates attacked the former California governor much more viciously. Connally took to slurring Reagan about his age by telling the national media that if someone was elected, he "ought to be able to serve."[79] Douglas Hallett, a Nixonian Republican from Reagan's California, wrote several columns for the *Wall Street Journal* eviscerating Reagan and thereby burnishing Connally's credentials. In one, Hallett wrote, "The Californian's increasingly lackluster rhetorical performance and aloofness from both new issues and the GOP's leadership have revived feelings that Mr. Reagan is too old and too indolent for the nation's top job. . . . Howard Phillips, chairman of the [Republican National] Conservative Caucus, puts it this way: 'Some (of us) suspect that Reagan is only a script reader, not a script writer. Nobody thinks that about John Connally.'"[80]

Privately, Bush did not think highly of Reagan, and the Bush camp knew that its candidate would have a shot at the nomination only if Reagan stumbled badly. But if Reagan did not mess up, Bush aides wanted to preserve a chance of getting their man on the ticket with him. In the early days, then, they proceeded more delicately than did the others, especially Connally, in public criticisms of Reagan. Not that they thought Reagan would actually win if he was the nominee, but getting Bush on the ticket would set him up nicely to be the nominee in 1984.

While Connally and Bush battled to position themselves as the best alternative to Reagan, another Republican long presumed to be running finally made his candidacy official: Senator Howard Baker of Tennessee. Baker was handsome, articulate, and exceedingly charming, and as Senate minority leader had proved himself an effective legislator. Most of official Washington thought Baker would be the best nominee against Carter—and indeed, Carter's White House feared Baker above all other candidates.[81] In his winning campaign in 1966 for the Senate seat once held by Estes Kefauver, Baker received an impressive 30 percent of the black vote in Tennessee.[82] Baker's foray into the race was not welcomed in the Bush camp, as he would be mining for the same moderately right-of-center voters that the tall Texan was.

Baker had been on Gerald Ford's short list for running mates in Kansas City three years earlier, but Ford chose Bob Dole when Reagan spoke up for the Kansan. Baker was ticked off, and vowed right then that he would be the master of his own fate next time. Another reason Baker may have been skipped over by Ford was his wife's struggle with alcoholism. Joy Baker was a very attractive woman, accomplished in her own right, and had apparently conquered her addiction by 1979.[83]

Baker showed that his campaign was serious when he signed up Ford's media man, Doug Bailey of the famous GOP consulting firm Bailey, Deardourff. Conservatives hadn't forgotten Baker's apostasy in supporting the Panama Canal treaties, but the Tennessee senator hoped that his strong opposition to Carter's SALT II would more than make up for this heresy.

Howard Baker also showed that he was targeting Ronald Reagan. Like all the other GOP candidates, Baker, fifty-four, made a special emphasis of his own age.[84] This pattern fit with the assessment of Lou Cannon, the political reporter who had covered Reagan for years. Cannon said there were two candidates in the Republican field: "Reagan and Stop Reagan."[85]

Problem was, it seemed too often that the most effective members of the "Stop Reagan" effort were Reagan's own blundering staffers.

BEFORE TED KENNEDY COULD jump into the presidential fray, he first needed to get his mother's permission to run.[86] Some rolled their eyes when they learned that Teddy wanted Rose Kennedy's consent, but they failed to remember that three of her four sons had died as young men—tragically and heroically. Ted was the only son she had left and she didn't want him prematurely cut down as well.

Senator Kennedy also had to ponder whether he wanted to endure renewed scrutiny over his fiasco at Chappaquiddick in 1969, when an attractive young woman, Mary Jo Kopechne, drowned under mysterious circumstances in a car that Kennedy drove off a small bridge late one summer evening. The unanswered questions about Chappaquiddick would haunt a Kennedy presidential campaign.

In addition, he needed to consider the scrutiny his wife, Joan, a sad alcoholic, would have to face. They had been living apart for several years and their uneasy marriage would be put under the microscope, as would his rumored dalliances with other women. She blamed her alcoholism on his philandering.[87]

Teddy also liked the sauce. A prominent Boston politician whose family had known the Kennedys for years was in Washington on business and had lunch with the senator. Prior to dining, Kennedy polished off a couple of highballs, then plowed through an exceptional amount of wine during their meal and afterward downed a couple of snifters of Courvoisier. Kennedy's guest, himself no stranger to drink, was nonetheless aghast at the senator's prodigious noontime thirst and asked Kennedy, "Do you do this every day?" Kennedy sheepishly replied, "Yeah, pretty much."[88]

The senator did have the Kennedy name, which conjured nostalgia for Camelot. But Ted was different from his brothers. JFK was smooth and reserved and RFK was intense and passionate, but Teddy was a bearish backslapper in the ward-heeler mode. He laughed easily and loudly, was given to silly pranks, and he always needed a haircut. Although forty-seven, the youngest Kennedy brother seemed pathologically boyish. If he entered the race, he would not be running just against Carter. He would also be running against ghosts: the memory of Jack and Bobby, who, especially after the dispiriting presidencies of LBJ, Richard Nixon, Gerald Ford, and Jimmy Carter, maintained a deep hold on the American imagination.

According to Walter Mondale, the memory of his brothers did not dissuade Kennedy from running for president. In fact, it may have compelled him to enter the race. "All this pressure was on Ted to fulfill the family tradition," Mondale recalled. "He really felt he was the holder of something precious in the Kennedy legacy."[89] Mondale always felt that Kennedy was forcing Carter's hand to give himself the reason to dive in to the race.

There was certainly little love lost between Carter and Kennedy. Real cultural and ideological difference separated the two men. Carter found Kennedy's undisciplined morals repugnant and Kennedy thought Carter sanctimonious. In addition, Carter, inside his party, was seen by doctrinaire liberals as a "mugwump"—someone who had broken faith with their party. Carter's preachy sermons about holding the line on spending and morality were not in keeping with the modern sensibilities of liberalism. They also disagreed about national health insurance, a pet Kennedy issue: Carter wanted it phased in slowly, while Kennedy demanded its immediate enactment. There was personal animosity as well: Congress had directed a gold medal struck commemorating the life of Robert F. Kennedy, but Carter refused to order it cast. The family of long memories would never forget this slight by Carter.

During the summer of 1979, Kennedy reportedly dropped twenty pounds (in part because he gave up ice cream), which was seen as another sign that he was moving toward a challenge of the president.[90] He was still trouncing Carter by more than 2–1 in the national polls.[91] The president of the United States was an underdog in his own party. This in and of itself was astonishing. In the twentieth century, this could only be said of William Howard Taft in 1912, when Teddy Roosevelt came out of retirement and beat Taft in nine GOP primaries. Yet because Taft, as the incumbent, controlled the levers of power at the national committee and the national convention, he, not Roosevelt, was nominated.

With the reforms of the Democratic Party that began after 1968, there would be no such "back-room deals"; primary voters in the various states would select the delegates almost entirely. This seemed to spell political death for Carter, whose national approval rating fell to 19 percent—even lower than Richard Nixon's the day before his resignation.[92]

The national media were ready to crown Kennedy. According to many stories, Kennedy would have the advantage not only against Carter but also, in a general election, over Ronald Reagan. Unlike Reagan, Kennedy would appeal to young voters and to the middle. The other Republican candidates encouraged this thinking, making the case that they matched up better against Kennedy than did Reagan.

According to the media, it didn't matter that the Massachusetts senator would be getting a late start on the campaign. He was well positioned to perform in the primaries, thanks to a "well-oiled Kennedy machine" that would be run by "old Kennedy hands." Jack Germond and Jules Witcover quoted "one old hand" saying, "You don't have that tooling up time with Kennedy."[93]

Another "old hand" was more realistic when he told the columnists, "A few years out of it is a long time. That clock rolls around pretty fast for campaigners."[94] The laws governing federal campaigns had changed greatly, too, and Joseph P. Kennedy was no longer around to write unlimited checks.

It also seemed that the Kennedy "machine" was not so well oiled. Michael McShane, a Mondale aide whose father had once worked for JFK, said, "I remember . . . talking to some of the Kennedy staffers that these guys would walk in 9:30, 10, they'd make a couple of phone calls, and then they'd go to lunch."[95]

In the early fall of 1979, after months of cagily telling the media that he "expected" that he would support Carter,[96] Ted Kennedy dropped the pretense.

Stephen E. Smith, Kennedy's brother-in-law, family confidant, and all-around utility infielder for the clan, announced the formation of a presidential exploratory committee to begin the organizational efforts. A date was announced, November 7, for the third Kennedy to formally declare his intentions to run for president of the United States. The headquarters was on 22nd Street NW in Washington, in what once was a Cadillac dealership.[97] In retrospect, it should have been an Edsel dealership.

The CBS television network announced that it would broadcast a one-hour documentary on Senator Kennedy. Called *CBS Reports: Teddy*, it would air on Sunday, November 4, at 10 P.M. eastern time. The executives at CBS rushed to get the show on the air before Kennedy officially announced his candidacy to prevent any "equal-time" claims from the others running for president.[98]

The Carter White House complained bitterly to CBS about the special, which had been in the works since the previous May, when it was becoming clear that Kennedy might indeed run for president. Carter aides believed that the show would be one giant wet kiss for Kennedy, especially since the host was Roger Mudd, an old friend of the Kennedy family.

Anyone who thought that CBS or Mudd would grovel before Teddy was sorely mistaken. The hourlong special was an unmitigated disaster for Kennedy. The interview began with Mudd asking Kennedy about the state of his marriage. The senator stammered: "It's—I would say that it's—it's—it's—I'm delighted that we're able to—to share the time and the relationship that we—that we do share." Several more questions dealt with his wife's alcoholism and Kennedy stumbled through these as well.[99]

Mudd later completely unnerved Kennedy with a simple yet devastating question: "Why do you want to be president?"

Kennedy, with a stunned look on his face, fumbled and bumbled and mumbled. "Well . . . I'm, . . . were I to make the announcement . . . and to run . . . the reasons that I would run is because I have great belief in this country . . . that it is . . . there's more natural resources than any nation of the world . . . there's the greatest educated population in the world . . . greatest technology of any country in the world . . . and the greatest political system in the world."[100] It went downhill from there.

Mudd was appalled that his old friend was so poorly prepared. He debated whether he should even bother to continue the interview.[101]

The rest of the special was almost as excruciating to watch. Mudd asked Kennedy whether he thought anyone would ever believe his version of the story about Chappaquiddick. Kennedy responded, "Oh, there's, the problem is, from that night, I, I found the conduct, the behavior almost beyond belief myself. I mean that's why it's been, but I think that's the way it was. Now I find that as I have stated that I have found the conduct that in, in that evening and in, in the, as a result of the accident of the, and the sense of loss, the sense of hope, and the, and the sense of tragedy, and the whole set of circumstances, that the behavior was inexplicable. So I find that those, those, types of questions as they apply to that, questions of my own soul, as well. But that happens to be the way it was."[102]

Kennedy, the vaunted public speaker, came across as babbling, dissembling, and unprepared. Chatter over his poor performance dominated Washington, the media, and Democratic circles for days, and shattered his legions of fans.

The Carter people could not believe their good luck. They were so delighted with how badly the special turned out that they copied the transcript and handed it out to anybody and everybody.

Kennedy moved on to Chicago and was promptly pelted with an egg.

One day after Kennedy's plunge into the campaign, Jerry Brown entered the race. He promised to "protect the earth, serve the people and explore the universe" and to "sense our unity in the spirit on this small speck of universal time."[103] "Governor Moonbeam" was at it again.

THE SAME DAY THAT Kennedy's disastrous interview with Mudd aired, events thousands of miles away would conspire to prevent Kennedy from winning the Democratic nomination and would reinvigorate, for a time, the fortunes of Jimmy Carter. On November 4, 1979, radical Islamic "students" charged the American embassy in Tehran, Iran, and took sixty-six Americans hostages.

The capture of the American hostages was ordered by the Ayatollah Khomeini, who had also commanded the overthrow of the shah back in February. As his country's leading cleric, Khomeini had more power than what passed for the new government in Iran, and he was whipping up anti-American sentiment. Each night, Americans watched rallies by terrorists whom the media kept referring to as "students." The daily frenzy would not be complete without the ritualistic burning of an American flag and chants of "Death to America." The American hostages were bound and blindfolded and paraded before the manic protesters so they could mock and threaten them, all for the benefit of the gaggle of Western reporters and cameras.

The hostage crisis allowed Carter to dominate the national stage. For months he had been dealing with reports about his sinking presidency, leaks about his dysfunctional White House, and rumors that his chief of staff, Hamilton Jordan, was using cocaine, but now he had an opportunity to display real leadership. Carter made it known to the ayatollah how much these Americans meant to him, which temporarily made him "look presidential."

Though Carter's performance over the course of the crisis could only be described as dithering—each and every day, new attempts to negotiate with the terrorists would spring forth—Kennedy went him one better. The senator inexplicably attacked the exiled shah, who was now battling cancer, and not the man who was holding the American hostages. Kennedy was widely denounced for "injecting politics" into the sensitive matter.

The only one who seemed to demonstrate a sophisticated understanding of American politics was the ayatollah, when he released the thirteen American women and blacks being held.

President Carter was soon getting the support of 70 percent of the American people for his handling of the crisis in Iran, because most believed he was doing all he could to secure the release of the hostages.[104] He now looked like the strong, decisive leader while Kennedy looked like the sad sack.

Such are the fortunes of war and politics.

4

THE FRONT-WALKER

"What am I supposed to do, skip rope through the neighborhood?"

Ronald Reagan's third drive for the White House was sputtering along as one old loyalist after another took a powder on the Gipper, mostly over the imperious management style of John Sears. Sears had become manager once again—over the protests of many—mainly because he had Mike Deaver's backing, which in turn meant that he had Nancy Reagan's backing. Now many Reaganites were being left out, ignored, or demoted as Sears and the campaign's national political director, Charlie Black, opted for "more important" state Republican operatives than the ones who had actually won primaries for Reagan in 1976.[1] In Texas, for example, Ernie Angelo, Ron Dear, and Ray Barnhart, who had beaten the GOP establishment in 1976, winning all one hundred delegates at a critical time for Reagan, had been demoted for the 1980 effort. All were crestfallen, especially the fiercely competitive Angelo.[2]

Sears had once wanted to be a psychiatrist. He was able to glean insights into people's pathologies, which gave him a distinct advantage in politics. The night before Richard Nixon resigned in August 1974, Sears bet some drinking buddies from the media that the "Trickster" would mention his mother in his pitiful remarks before departing the White House. Sears collected on his bet.[3]

Yet as well as Sears could read politicos, he had become insensate to the needs, desires, and wants of many Reaganites, including those in the grassroots. Sears had been forced out of the Nixon White House early on because Nixon's old friend, Attorney General John Mitchell, was fearful of the influence the young and moderate Republican would have over the Oval Office.[4] Now Sears was behaving just like Mitchell, forcing out the conservatives whom he feared had more influence over Reagan than he.

Years later, Sears compared the job of campaign manager to that of an orchestra conductor trying "to get everybody to sit in their chair and play their instrument."[5] The problem for the Reagan campaign was that not everybody was singing from the same sheet, and many did not even know which instrument Sears wanted them to play. Asked about the growing friction, Sears simply shrugged his shoulders, recalling, "There was a lot of pushing and shoving and that is normal."[6] Peter Hannaford, speaking for Reagan's Californians, dismissed Sears as "paranoid."[7] Another observer said that since 1976, "Sears had changed. Self-effacement had turned to arrogance, brilliance to egomania, self-mockery to aloofness and shyness to secretiveness."[8]

Reagan was dropping in the national polls among GOP primary voters. The candidate acted as if wrapped in gauze, because Sears would not allow him to campaign too often or too aggressively. Over cocktails, political journalists mocked Reagan's slow-motion effort, calling him the "front-walker" rather than the "front-runner," which also implied that Reagan was decrepit.[9]

The campaign's finances were a disaster, too. In September of 1979, it leaked out that Reagan's campaign was, incredibly, more than $500,000 in debt, even with former Democrat and now Reagan booster Frank Sinatra helping him raise money. The Reagan for President Committee was taking in around $300,000 per month but spending around $500,000 per month.[10] Sears's profligate ways had not changed since 1976. His splurging included renting a $1,700-per-hour private jet for Reagan. When asked about the indulgence he sniffed, "When you're a front-runner you must go in style."[11] A young aide, Doug Bandow, wondered why he and others in Reagan's entourage would stay in expensive hotels like the Waldorf in New York and not even "double up on rooms."[12]

Morale bottomed out. Internal strife was high among the survivors as they were engaged in a death struggle, battling for the soul of the campaign. Would Sears and his ally Deaver prevail along with a more "moderate" Reagan, or would the campaign get out of Reagan's way so he could follow his natural ideological instincts? The argument not only was insulting to Reagan, but demonstrated that even his own people often underestimated him. He had always known where he was going and how he would get there.

Sears's temporary alliance with Deaver was just that. Only several days before Reagan's announcement, Sears and Deaver got into a screaming match as Mrs. Reagan "sobbed in the background," according to Robert Scheer of the *Los Angeles Times*. Reagan and Paul Laxalt "joined in the shouting." Laxalt took Deaver's side and Reagan was yelling for a truce. But Sears got his way.[13]

The campaign had grown to more than 150 staffers, plus innumerable consultants, and Sears was hiring more. Many on the staff were new to Reagan. Lyn Nofziger, recently departed from the campaign, worried that Reagan was ignoring old friends and supporters, and that there was an ongoing effort to "repackage" Reagan.[14] Every conservative knew what that meant. Nofziger, Jim Lake complained, was "sowing seeds of discontent with the right-wingers."[15] Some of the new advance staff offended Reagan's old friends by keeping them at arm's length. They became known as "Reagan's SS."[16] With all the intrigue, much of it caused by himself, Sears quit. "Fuck it, I can't work here anymore."[17] The Reagans had to call him back from the ledge.

The Gipper regarded most of the strange new people around the campaign with bemusement and often simply nodded his head and then cocked it and smiled without saying a word. He would always listen to reason, but he was not about to alter his philosophy or ideology. Reagan was a master pragmatist when the need called for it, but he also had an utter belief in his abilities to lead people. Reagan was keeping his cool for the most part—and his sense of humor. He explained his reason for running to one reporter: "Well, there was an old saying in show business. If you don't sing and you don't dance, you'd better be able to do something else. . . . I don't sing and I don't dance."[18] He also had a standard one-liner about Jimmy Carter that drew laughs every time: "A man who tells you he enjoys a cold shower in the morning will lie about other things too."[19]

Publicly, Reagan continued to defend his beleaguered campaign manager, but he was deeply unhappy that old hands Nofziger and Marty Anderson were gone from the campaign and that money was being spent willy-nilly. At times, he was forced to apologize to old friends and supporters for Sears's decisions. Wooing moderate Republicans, Sears approached Governor Bill Milliken of Michigan, who had been a major Reagan basher in 1976; when Reagan's Michigan chairman, conservative state senator John Welborn, called Milliken a "skunk" to the media, Sears dismissed Welborn.[20] Reagan had to write a letter to a friend in Michigan apologizing for Sears's shabby treatment of his "good friend" Welborn and saying that Sears was "trying to moderate my views or make me less conservative."[21]

Reagan was becoming more and more uncommunicative with his campaign manager. Nofziger, years later, explained how he knew when Reagan did not like someone: Reagan would just clam up. The Gipper was far too polite to be overtly rude, but he would simply nod his head and smile and try to avoid direct engagement with the person. Peter Hannaford, another old Reagan hand, agreed that freezing people out was how Reagan dealt with people who got on his nerves. Increasingly in late 1979, this was how the Californian was acting with Sears.

When Reagan and Sears did talk, Reagan did most of the listening, often looking grim.

Archconservatives on occasion also got on Reagan's nerves. Some cited the fact that Reagan had not yet come out against Jimmy Carter's SALT II treaty as evidence that he was being "moderated," but Reagan was studying the document carefully. There would be no doubt that he would eventually oppose it if he deemed it a one-way street favoring the Soviets, but he wasn't going to be cowed into opposing something as important as an arms agreement if he hadn't reviewed it. In early October 1979, Reagan did indeed take a public position against the treaty, because it did not halt the spread of nuclear weapons. "SALT II is not a strategic arms limitation, it is strategic arms buildup," he said.[22]

Reagan's measured response did not satisfy some of the most avid Cold Warriors in the conservative movement, but he knew that if he was to become the fortieth president of the United States, he needed to lead more than the grassroots conservatives who had rallied to his side in 1976. He wasn't interested in leading another lost cause. He would campaign as what he was most comfortable being: a responsible conservative who knew the world he lived in.

ONE BRIGHT BIT OF news for the Gipper came when the California GOP decided to retain its winner-take-all primary. It was widely assumed that Reagan would swamp everybody in his adopted Golden State and take all 168 delegates bound for the national convention in Detroit. But California's primary was in June, months after Iowa and New Hampshire; the way things were looking to some in the Reagan camp, his campaign could be washed out to sea long before the June 3 primary. As of late September 1979, Phil Crane had campaigned in New Hampshire all or part of forty-five days, Bush had been there twenty-four days, Bob Dole twenty-one days, and John Anderson fifteen days. Reagan? He'd been to New Hampshire just once in two years, thanks to Sears's play-it-safe strategy.[23]

Reagan did make a rare trip to Indianapolis to address the National Federation of Republican Women (NFRW), a decidedly conservative organization with real grassroots strength. Its power and influence was such that all the announced or to-be-announced candidates had agreed to speak to the 2,500 women gathering in Indiana. When Reagan appeared, camera flashes went off continuously and some middle-aged women jumped up and down like teenyboppers, as many of the members were fans of Reagan from his movie days. "We all have sort of a love affair with Ronald Reagan," said one woman present.[24] Still, Reagan's reception was not as overwhelming as it had been in the past. James Dickenson of the *Washington Star* wrote that the women behaved as if Reagan had once been a "favorite boyfriend" but now they were "being wooed by all the good-looking guys in town."[25] Indeed, all the GOP candidates received warm welcomes from the gathering, including the newest suitor among them, General Alexander Haig. John Connally arrived via a two-block-long parade that included girls on rollerskates and a high school marching band.

Nancy Reagan was sometimes on the stump for "Ronnie," speaking and taking questions from audiences and reporters alike. In 1976, she had done some campaigning, but she would be more involved this time around, acting as Reagan's own "palace guard." She was on the lookout for people who were simply trying to use her husband; she knew all too well that this was Ronnie's last chance.

And she was becoming more and more concerned about Sears.

TOWARD THE END OF September, Reagan improved his financial situation by raking in more than $175,000 in one fell swoop at a dinner in New Jersey organized by Ray Donovan, owner of a construction company.[26] Donovan went on to become Reagan's beleaguered secretary of labor, but that would come later. For this one night, Donovan was a champ.

Reagan got an unexpected boost when his onetime aide Jeff Bell came back aboard the campaign. Bell, who had worked with Reagan from the early '70s right through the 1976 campaign, had been nursing a bruised ego since 1978, when Reagan refused to endorse him in his New Jersey Senate primary bid, which he won. Bell, in a fit of pique, refused Reagan's offer to come to New Jersey to campaign for him and asked Ford to do so instead.[27] Bell lost the general election, hooked up with a New York think tank, and became a charter member of the "supply-side mafia" of Jack Kemp, Art Laffer, Jude Wanniski, and Bob Novak. Now all was forgiven and Bell was back with Reagan. Bell would eventually take on a difficult and challenging part of the campaign, one that would help Reagan at a time when it looked as if all was lost.[28]

Although November 1 had tentatively been declared as the day of Reagan's formal announcement, the date was pushed back to November 13. The campaign had hoped to have a cash stockpile of around $4 million by the time of the declaration, but those plans were now inoperative. Just as bad, all three networks had turned down Reagan's request to purchase a half hour of broadcast time for the night of his announcement. It wasn't clear that the campaign could afford it anyway. The campaign had no recourse, as the networks had also turned down President Carter's similar request. The unwritten rule was to not sell any time to candidates before 1980.[29]

Although Reagan had lost the Iowa straw poll by a wide margin, amazingly he did not show when the Hawkeye State's GOP held its annual fundraising dinner in October. Every other candidate did. Sears told reporters, "The obligation of a frontrunner is to keep moving ahead. They can't hurt you as long as you're moving."[30]

Many observers thought Sears's strategy was ridiculous, and some saw it as dangerous. Reagan had deep roots and many friends in Iowa. In the 1930s, he'd become a local celebrity in Des Moines broadcasting on WHO radio and had returned many times to speak, including while he was on the "mashed potato" circuit. The Gipper had as much a claim on Iowa's Republicans as anybody—more than most—but he blew the chance to romance four thousand hard-core activists attending the box dinner.

George Bush won yet another Iowa straw poll, impressively, garnering almost 36 percent of the vote. Connally was a poor second at 15 percent. Bob Dole came in third, just behind Connally, though he had purchased hundreds of tickets for his "supporters" and should have gotten a far higher vote total. Reagan was a poor fourth, with 11 percent.[31] Bush's showing seemed extraordinary to everyone . . . except Sears and those in the Reagan high command. Bush was throwing a right hook and Reagan was about to lean into it.

Bush's young organizer in Iowa, Rich Bond, was exultant, gloating over Bush's win and Reagan's loss. Only twenty-nine, Bond was a brash, intense New Yorker and a huge fan of Bush's. In fact, Bond had started a scrapbook about Bush after meeting him seven years earlier. The young man was providing for his new wife, Valerie—a widow who had been married to Bond's closest friend—and for Valerie's four-year-old son. To save money, Bond lived in Ames, forty miles outside of Des Moines.[32]

Bond had been hired by Dave Keene. When Bush campaign manager Jim Baker had expressed cultural and ideological qualms about the liberal Republican from New York City, Keene said, "That's true . . . He also is so ambitious and hungry that he would kill his mother for the main chance and Iowa is the main chance."[33]

Bond assembled a political version of an Amway distributorship, with each person in the chain expected to recruit more people. He was a taskmaster, holding staff meetings at 8 A.M., even kicking Bush's son Marvin, the family cutup, out of the office, as he was a distraction to Bond's volunteers. "Marvin wanted to leave the office at 5:00, go to Vicky's Pour House, shoot pool and drink beer," Bond remembered. Jeb Bush was more helpful and was a hit with the College Republicans. All the Bush sons—Marvin, Jeb, and George W., the few times he came in for his father—slept on the couch at Bond's Ames apartment.[34]

George Bush was precisely following the plan executed by Carter four years earlier, but the Reagan team did not alter its approach one bit in Iowa. Sears consoled himself and the Reagans with some polling, which showed Reagan with handsome leads in Iowa and New Hampshire. In a Boston Globe poll, Reagan had 50 percent of the GOP primary vote in the Granite State.[35] What's to worry?

THE HAMLET-LIKE GERALD FORD made a seemingly firm decision not to seek the 1980 GOP nomination. He had barnstormed the country for two weeks in the fall of 1979 and then, in early October, met with five key supporters at his home in Rancho Mirage, California. Attending were Dean Burch, an old GOP hand; Bob Teeter, his pollster from 1976; John Marsh, a former White House aide; Stu Spencer, his chief strategist in 1976; and Dick Cheney, his former chief of staff and now a first-term congressman from Wyoming. Teeter's presence was odd, because he'd signed up with Bush's campaign months earlier. Teeter was from Michigan, like Ford, and was a moderate like Ford. This wasn't the first or the last time that Teeter would choose Ford over Bush, even while Bush was paying him. The group told Ford, in no uncertain terms, that if he wanted to be president, he would have to run in the primaries. Ford balked.[36]

Ford was still steadfastly opposed to a Reagan nomination and made it clear that he was available for a draft. He told his friends and supporters at the meeting and around the country to support anyone else, as long as it was not Reagan. George Bush and Howard Baker breathed a sigh of relief. Ford's retreat meant they would benefit from the release of those moderate voters waiting for the old Wolverine to jump in.[37]

Baker had carefully planned for an early win in the straw poll at the Maine state convention in Portland on the first weekend of November. He announced for president just two days before, in a mostly downbeat statement about America and the future. Baker had the support of his Senate colleague Bill Cohen of Maine.[38] Curiously, although Bush had spent most of the summers of his life just down the road in Kennebunkport, his campaign made little apparent effort in the Maine straw poll. He drove to the convention hall with only one lowly aide and his daughter, Doro, while Baker arrived with a plane full of national journalists, all ready to capture the moment when Baker won and solidified his position as the alternative to Reagan.[39]

Bush, though, gave a rousing speech that brought the crowd to its feet several times. Baker's speech did not go well. Bush, apparently not expecting to win, departed for Houston before the counting began. Baker waited anxiously for the voting. Alas for him, he lost narrowly, with 33 percent to Bush's 35 percent, and Bush grabbed the Sunday morning headlines across the country. The media had appointed Baker as the "thinking man's" alternative to Reagan, but they forgot to tell the Maine Republicans. A chagrined Baker appeared before the media and told them, "I have to move out of second."[40] He had, but in the wrong direction. Baker was dealt a severe blow, and would never be much of a factor again.

Reagan had not appeared in Portland for the event—as usual—and got a pathetic 7 percent of the vote.[41] Bush was on a roll, having won three straw polls in a row. The political establishment was beginning to take a closer look at Ambassador Bush.

REAGAN FINALLY PLUNGED INTO the campaign on November 13, 1979. Rather than launching his last quest for the GOP nomination from California or Dixon, Illinois, he made his announcement in New York City at a gala fundraising dinner at the New York Hilton. The campaign chose New York because it was still the media capital of the world, and because John Sears remained intent on wooing moderate northeastern Republicans. Sears invited some 250 neutral GOP political apparatchiks from the Northeast—state party heads, elected officials, and influential county chairmen.[42]

The morning of the announcement, Reagan went on NBC's *Today* show to be interviewed by Tom Brokaw. The only thing Brokaw seemed interested in talking to Reagan about was . . . his age.[43] By now, Reagan had become exasperated with the issue. He had joshed about his age for the past year or two, but he confided in private, "I've given all the light answers I can."[44] It didn't help that rival John Connally was taking an increasing number of shots at Reagan's age; columnist George F. Will wrote that "Connally's veiled references to Reagan's age . . . are nasty."[45] Connally's cutting remarks were making their way into political stories and columns, as political reporters like Tom Wicker of the *New York Times* frequently noted that Reagan's front-runner position was made tenuous "by the hazardous fact of Mr. Reagan's age—69 next year."[46] Frustrated, Reagan spluttered to reporters, "What am I supposed to do, skip rope through the neighborhood?"[47]

That night at the Hilton, Reagan's old friend Jimmy Stewart introduced him to the dinner crowd with a short biographical film. The staff referred to the film as "Tarzan Reagan" because Reagan had been depicted working at the ranch without his shirt on, young advance man Jim Hooley recalled.[48]

The packed hall of nearly two thousand included Bill Buckley and his wife, Pat, and many of the members of the Reagan Kitchen Cabinet. Ominously, Mike Deaver boycotted the event, a further sign of the internal deterioration of the campaign. In another indication of problems, only days before it had looked as if Reagan might announce before a half-filled ballroom; while some Reagan supporters paid $500 apiece to attend, campaign fundraisers had been forced to send out a last-minute telegram to those already attending, telling them that they could bring along a guest free.[49]

Reagan took the podium. Many of the 250 reporters covering the event probably anticipated that his remarks would be yet another variation on what they referred to as "The Speech," his milestone address for Barry Goldwater in 1964. Over the years, Reagan had endlessly polished the speech, all on four-by-six-inch index cards (not three-by-five, as the media often mistakenly said). Constantly updating the dozens upon dozens of index cards with new information from newspapers and letters, he would put the cards in a particular order for a particular group, varying things enough to keep the speech fresh. Always, though, Reagan's remarks advanced his philosophy of less government and more freedom.

The media thought they had heard it all before. But this speech was fresh, bracing. The address concerned itself with the national mood. He spoke movingly of a loss of confidence in government in America; unlike Carter, he blamed not the American people but rather the government itself. He said that he saw America as "a living, breathing presence, unimpressed by what others say is impossible, proud of its own success; generous, yes, and naïve; sometimes wrong, never mean, always impatient to provide a better life for its people in a framework of a basic fairness and freedom."[50]

Later in the speech he proclaimed, "The crisis we face is not the result of any failure of the American spirit; it is failure of our leaders to establish rational goals and give our people something to order their lives by. If I am elected, I shall regard my election as proof that the people of the United States have decided to set a new agenda and have recognized that the human spirit thrives best when goals are set and progress can be measured in their achievement."[51] Reporters hadn't heard that before from Reagan.

Reaching his peroration, Reagan did invoke a favorite phrase, saying that Americans had had a "rendezvous with destiny" ever since the moment in 1630 when John Winthrop told his followers, "We shall be a city upon a hill." Reagan concluded, "A troubled and afflicted mankind looks to us, pleading for us to keep our rendezvous with destiny; that we will uphold the principles of self-reliance, self-discipline, morality, and, above all, responsible liberty for every individual; that we will become that shining city on a hill."[52] Reagan's address had been pitched to the media as less strident than many of his previous speeches. John Sears and others wanted the national media to see that Reagan was a seasoned, thoughtful leader in a time of dwindling American morale.

The three networks stuck by their decision to withhold selling advertising time to any of the candidates. Reagan would have to settle for stringing together roughly eighty independent stations across the country, from which his campaign could purchase thirty minutes for his taped national address for the same night.[53] All told, these stations hit around 80 percent of the country. CBS had sold two five-minute slots to Reagan, one for the morning and one for the evening.

The Reagan speech was very good, with plenty of new content, and the candidate delivered it extremely well, even by his high standards. Yet reporters complained that they had a hard time getting their arms around it, charging that it lacked a central theme. Reagan just couldn't catch a break.

THE NEXT DAY, REAGAN struck out on a five-day, twelve-city tour, accompanied by a contingent of Secret Service agents newly assigned to his campaign.[54] Despite his intelligent delivery of good and substantive lines, there was great consternation and debate among some conservatives over the content and tone of the Reagan announcement. Had the moderates won the battle for the soul of Ronald Reagan? Had he lost his passion, his fire? What happened to bashing welfare queens and the Washington establishment?

Some of the disgruntled conservatives had in fact been off the Reagan bandwagon for several years now, convinced that he'd sold out or was too old. Or perhaps they just resented that they had too little influence.

At a press conference in Washington, Reagan announced that Congressman Jack Kemp would be the campaign's principal spokesman and the chairman of the "policy development committee."[55] Paul Laxalt had ably and tirelessly filled the role of spokesman in 1976, and had expected the role once again. But Sears saw Kemp as a means both to make inroads with northeastern Republicans and to lessen Laxalt's influence with Reagan. Laxalt, having put in thousands of hours for his friend in 1976, was deeply hurt by Sears's move.

Kemp's role as the campaign's "chief spokesman" unnerved those in Reagan's camp who knew the independent-minded Kemp could be difficult to control.[56] At the D.C. press conference, Kemp called the Gipper the "oldest and wisest of all the candidates who has embraced the youngest and freshest ideas."[57] The "oldest" comment did not sit well with Mrs. Reagan.

Word was leaking out that Kemp had been Sears's original choice to be campaign chairman until Laxalt caught wind of it. Laxalt went to Nancy Reagan to plead his case, but he didn't have to; Laxalt was a favorite of Mrs. Reagan's and the feeling was mutual. He was also popular with the political media, more so than Kemp, who some saw as arrogant. Others in the campaign, including younger Reaganites such as Jeff Bell and Roger Stone, the campaign's Northeast director, were already touting Kemp as the natural running mate for Reagan. Kemp had ruled out a primary challenge to liberal Republican senator Jacob Javits, and many saw a Reagan-Kemp ticket as the California–New York "dream ticket" for the GOP in 1980. Kemp's chief aide, Dave Smick, thought Sears was greasing the skids for Kemp not only to go on the ticket but also to become a presidential candidate in his own right eight years later.[58]

Reporters pressed Reagan on another issue: his refusal to do any joint appearances or debates with the other candidates, which was not sitting well with GOP voters. Reagan replied that he saw "no reason for a debate with other Republicans," and that such events would be "divisive."[59] The decision to bypass the debates came from Sears, of course, and was just more evidence that the candidate was overprotected. If Reagan had appeared at a few, there would have been no discussion about his missing debates. But Reagan ducked all of them in 1979, and this was fine as far as the other candidates were concerned. They could squawk about Reagan ducking the debates, plant innuendos about his age and mental prowess, and not have to compete with him for media attention at each GOP "cattle show." Sears scarily told reporters, "If we don't get licked early we don't get licked."[60] Problem was, what happened if Reagan did get "licked early"?

Although Ford, once again, dropped a hint that he might, just might, get into the race, citing "unforeseen circumstances," he would not elaborate on what those might be. Clearly, he wanted to stop Reagan, but by dangling himself out there he was freezing potential money and support for Baker and Bush. Many moderate GOP governors were aching to organize a late-starting Ford campaign, yet Ford held back. Reagan was holding on to his tenuous first-place position.[61]

Reagan's brief campaign for the GOP nomination in 1968 had begun badly and ended ignominiously. His campaign in 1976 had come out of the gate just as awkwardly, but finished magnificently though not victoriously. Now, once again, his drive for the GOP nomination was off to a blundering start, but the script had yet to be written for how this final grasp for the brass ring would end for Ronald Wilson Reagan.

5

THE UNDISCOVERED COUNTRYSIDE

"It's awfully hard to run a campaign in Iowa without the candidate here."

The Thanksgiving season greeted Ronald Reagan with more bad news. Despite Ted Kennedy's bumbling start, he was still overwhelmingly ahead of Reagan in the polls, 54–38 percent. Reagan was also losing to Carter, 48–42, according to Gallup.[1] The twelve-city tour that had followed the Californian's announcement had received generally good but not excellent reviews. Squabbling among the staff continued. Alarms were being sounded about his operation in Iowa, but they were going unheeded. A partial survey in October of two-thirds of Iowa's ninety-nine county GOP chairmen found that 34 percent favored George Bush and 24 percent were for Dutch Reagan.[2] Furthermore, the campaign was going deeper and deeper into debt.

Reagan came close to creating yet another controversy when it seemed he was advocating sending in U.S. troops to quell the uprising in Iran, but his biggest problem was that he was ignoring Iowa and interest in him was waning.

The age issue had grown to alarming proportions, but no one in the campaign seemed to know what to do. According to a Harris survey, 61 percent of voters, when told that Reagan would be seventy only two weeks after the 1981 inaugural, said that was too old. Polling showed it to be an even bigger issue among older voters.[3] Most oldsters felt that if they needed a nap or two a day and their bones creaked, then so too must Reagan's, and that meant he wouldn't be able to withstand the physical pressures of the presidency.

Yet Reagan had been in St. Petersburg, Florida, speaking to senior citizens, and as the *Washington Star* reported, "the contrast between his apparent vigor and that of those who sat on the benches . . . was striking."[4] Reagan had to deny that he took afternoon naps. For a man his age, his agility was impressive. He swung an ax, mounted and dismounted a horse like a teenager, pulled down trees. He'd played sports his whole life, though he had never learned to like tennis and found jogging faddish and unmanly.

After his straw poll wins, George Bush was the hot property, even though he was under 5 percent in most national polls. His speaking style had improved greatly and he had hit upon a theme that brought GOP crowds to their feet: "I am sick and tired of apologizing for the United States!"[5] The questions about his unusual résumé had faded somewhat; he did still need to talk about his work at the CIA, but in defending the institution he pleased Republicans. Bush's organization on the ground in Iowa was excellent, and he had assembled a Washington staff of talented, mostly moderate political operatives.

His senior advisers were masters at media schmoozing, led by campaign manager Jim Baker and political director Dave Keene. Both had heavy Washington experience and knew reporters needed to be kept happy and well fed with tidbits, quotes, and returned phone calls. Neither was a boozer, but they socialized with reporters over breakfast and lunch. Both were enthusiastic hunters and fishermen and would, when possible, use this inducement on like-minded journalists. They were two GOP operatives who did not routinely denounce the media, and thus were rewarded with good coverage. Bush's temperamental press secretary, Pete Teeley, could also network when the mood so moved him.

IN JUST A FEW years, the political "industry" had evolved. Power cannot be destroyed—only shifted—and the power in Washington had for a while been moving toward the media and away from the state party leaders; now it was also moving from elected GOP officials to the GOP operatives. In the old days, consultants and staff were seen but rarely heard. The "star" was always the candidate himself. FDR wanted staff "with a passion for anonymity." This began to change with Watergate. Political operatives and consultants were now becoming media stars.

A symbiotic relationship developed in Washington as the elected officials came and went, but the permanent classes of reporters and consultants stayed. This permanent class was what truly mattered in Washington. While consultants would publicly attack candidates they were working against, they would almost never attack one another, even across party lines. Bipartisan work on legislation, which many consultants also handled, was common, and it was not unusual to see prominent Democratic and Republican consultants dining cozily together at the Palm or the Monocle. The consultant you were opposing today could be your ally—even paymaster—tomorrow.

Lyndon Johnson, as perceptive a politician as ever lived, saw what was happening. He told David Halberstam, as related in *The Powers That Be*, "You guys. All you guys in the media. All of politics has changed because of you. You've broken all the machines and the ties between us . . . and the city machines. You've given us a new kind of people. . . . They're your creations, your puppets."[6]

While many consultants regarded candidates as little more than a means to gain exposure and make money, most levelheaded politicians understood this dynamic and were equally pragmatic. They routinely turned over staff. As the James Carville–based character in the novel *Primary Colors* told another political operative, "That's what these guys do. They love you, they stop lovin' you." Everybody used everybody, and as long as one understood this, one could prosper. It was symbiosis: the two organisms fed off each other.

In 1980, Iowa was smack dab in the middle of America in every measurable manner. Situated between the Mississippi and Missouri rivers, it was almost at the very middle of the continental United States. It had the twenty-sixth-largest population, with just under three million people; it was the twenty-fifth state in area; it had the twenty-first-largest median family income.[7]

Iowans were moderately conservative in their politics and their outlook. The state—nicknamed "Hawkeye" for an Indian scout from the classic James Fenimore Cooper novel *The Last of the Mohicans*—was generally Republican but not aggressively conservative. Iowa usually went Republican in presidential elections, but a streak of prairie populism often helped Democrats at the state and local levels. It was a common political dichotomy in the Midwest.

Agriculture dominated Iowa's economy: 12 percent of its citizens lived on farms and another 17 percent worked in farm-related manufacturing. Nationwide, the number of farmers had dwindled to about two million from almost seven million in the 1930s.[8] Iowa was a state of small towns; only seven cities exceeded fifty thousand people, and the largest city, Des Moines, had fewer than 200,000 people. Eighty percent of Iowa's residents had been born in the state, remarkable for a nation of transients.[9]

The image of Iowans depicted in *The Music Man* wasn't far from the truth.[10] (Favoring Reagan was "Mr. Music Man" himself, Meredith Willson, the famous musical writer and "Ioway" native. Willson thought the world of Reagan, even offering to lend his friend the music to "Seventy-Six Trombones" for his campaign.)[11] Toward the end of the 1970s the *Des Moines Register*, which dominated politics in the state, took a revealing survey of Iowa's citizens, asking them to rate thirty-three institutions in terms of trust. God came in first at 91 percent, as might be expected, but right behind was the Iowa State Police at 84 percent. Bringing up the rear were labor unions and farm organizations. More than 50 percent of Iowans said "I love you" to somebody at least once a day. A majority said they would rather live a hundred years in the past than a hundred years in the future. They went to the State Fair and when they did, by a margin of three to one, they preferred looking at the farm equipment and agriculture displays to going on rides on the midway. By the same margin they supported spanking in the schools, and while two-thirds believed in Heaven and thought they were headed in that direction, one-third said they knew someone who was going to Hell. The state ranked first in the nation in literacy, with 99.5 percent of everyone over the age of fifteen able to both read and write. The vast majority said their state was the best place to live and they had no desire to live anywhere else. A saying in Iowa, sometimes appearing on bumper stickers, proudly proclaimed, "Welcome to Iowa. Please set your clock back to the 1950s."

Political journalists from the East descended upon Iowa like a plague of Old Testament locusts. Some seven hundred reporters came to the state to cover its caucuses, the first major test of the 1980 campaign. Looking for colorful stories, they wrote romantically about Iowa's farmers as if they had just discovered a cure for cancer. The natives went along with bemusement, but were far more interested in the high school girls' basketball playoffs, which uniquely featured "six on six" rather than the "five on five" played everywhere else in the country. The media were shocked to learn that the bars in Iowa closed at 10 P.M.[12]

The locals made sport of the eastern city slickers behind their backs. A journalist for a big newspaper lamented the expanse of empty land in January. When Steve Roberts, the state Republican chairman, politely told her that that was where the grain grew in the summer, she replied, "But why don't you have something there in the winter?" Another reporter called and demanded to know where the pigs and corn were and could they take a taxi to film it?[13]

January 1980 was not a happy time for Iowa or Iowa's farmers. In addition to the national recession, acreage was falling in value for only the third time since the Great Depression, in some cases down by more than $500 per acre of land that had been fetching more than $4,000 per acre just a few years earlier. Just a year earlier, thousands of America's farmers driving hundreds of tractors had descended on Washington to protest government farm policies as part of the American Agriculture Movement. They jammed commuter roads into the capital and set up camp on the mall, where their farm equipment tore up the sod.

The protest took place during one of the worst winter storms in recent history, and in an effort to stay warm the farmers tore up benches and burned them in campfires. More recently, President Carter had imposed yet another hardship on Iowa's weary farmers when he implemented a grain embargo on sales to the Soviet Union.

The grain embargo was intended as punishment for the Soviets' invasion of Afghanistan. The Soviet Union had installed a puppet government in Kabul. In December 1979, after an uprising against the new government arose in the countryside, the Soviets used this pretext to send three battalions into Afghanistan, with more on the way. It was the first time since World War II that Soviet troops had gone into territory that was not a part of the Eastern bloc for the purposes of keeping a pro-Kremlin government from falling.

President Carter had warned Moscow not to invade Afghanistan, but the Soviets weren't listening. They had taken the measure of the man over three years and knew they could push him around. Within days, Soviet troop strength grew to more than fifty thousand men, and a full-scale invasion ensued. Carter seemed ill prepared to deal with the offensive other than to recall his ambassador to Moscow, Thomas Watson.

The Carter administration made clear that it would not link Soviet behavior, including the invasion of other countries, to its precious SALT II treaty. "We are not going to penalize the Soviets by cutting off our nose," said one White House official.[14] Carter called Leonid Brezhnev on the hotline, but was coldly rebuffed. Carter demanded that the Soviets reduce the size of their embassy staff in Washington, which everybody knew was stuffed with KGB agents.

Carter naïvely told his fellow Americans he was mystified that the Soviets would ever invade another country and further said his judgment of Moscow was undergoing a "dramatic change," as was his "opinion of what the Soviets' ultimate goals were." It was an extraordinary admission by the president of the United States.[15] Columnists Jack Germond and Jules Witcover compared Carter's statement to Michigan governor George Romney's comment in 1967 that American generals in the Vietnam War had "brainwashed" him, a remark that had torpedoed his presidential campaign.[16]

Ronald Reagan immediately issued a statement responding to Carter's naïveté, "congratulating the President on 'belatedly' making the discovery that the Russians are not to be trusted."[17] Afghan students in New Delhi protested the Soviet invasion of their homeland by taking over the Russian embassy and unfurled a banner that read, "We shall fight them here, we shall fight them there, we shall fight them anywhere."[18] It was *Dr. Seuss Meets the Mujahedeen*. Guerrilla operations formed very quickly. The Afghan people were not going to roll over and play dead for Moscow.

The Carter administration rounded up a handful of Western allies to boycott the 1980 Summer Olympics, due to be held in Moscow, which the Soviets were eagerly looking forward to as a public-relations bonanza. Alas for Carter, one by one, America's allies began to fall away as internal pressures and those of the International Olympic Committee forced them to weaken their resolve.

Inside the Reagan organization, power struggles continued between John Sears and anybody who had not already left the campaign in frustration. Sears had surrounded himself with his friends Charlie Black and Jim Lake, two dependable allies who had worked with him on the 1976 campaign. But things were different this time. In the 1976 quest, Citizens for Reagan was a gloriously haphazard operation where people worked long hours for little pay because they were on an ideological quest led by their hero, Ronald Reagan. An insurgent campaign against an incumbent president can't be picky about who wants to come to work for it, and Sears did not have full control of the 1976 operations. Most notably, Reagan's successful efforts in the North Carolina and Texas primaries were entirely locally run affairs, and won exclusively by grassroots "True Believers," not because of any substantial help from the national campaign.

Sears could be a lot choosier about staffing the 1980 campaign, since Reagan went into the race as the front-runner. But the campaign manager had changed. The chain-smoking, heavy-drinking Sears of 1976 was accessible and garrulous with the staff and volunteers, and especially with the Reagans. The Sears of 1980 was inward-looking, inaccessible, and paralyzed with concerns about turf. He was walling himself off, just as his mentor, Richard Nixon, had done.

Sears didn't want anything or anyone to screw up the 1980 campaign. His obsession led to infighting. Keene was the first to go, but this was easy for Sears, as old Reagan hand Mike Deaver agreed that he should go. Nofziger was next. Then Marty Anderson walked, furious that Sears had created a clandestine research operation in Washington when all campaign researchers were supposed to report to Anderson. These researchers were also being paid large amounts, with some getting as much as $10,000 for a single white paper at a time when the campaign was bleeding red ink. Anderson, ever the model of class and loyalty, did not speak out publicly against Reagan, saying only that he was scaling back his work to part-time. Nofziger also did not often comment publicly, but that did not stop him from raging privately against Sears to all who inquired. Rumors swirled around Washington and California that other departures were imminent, including Reagan's liaisons to the Jewish and black communities, John Erthein and Leo Taylor.

There were fewer and fewer old familiar faces around Reagan, and he grew more and more pensive. Sears was laying the groundwork for his own undoing by making unnecessary enemies. Though few Reaganites had wanted Sears back, no one was yet directly challenging his authority. Still, he was acting as if they were. In addition to Black and Lake, Sears brought in another old ally, Darrell Trent, who had battled with the 1976 Reagan campaign staff over expenses. The poor man was in an impossible position, courtesy of Sears. Trent's job was to hold the line on spending, but he couldn't stop the free-spending Sears; he could only stop the rest of the staff and vendors.

Now Deaver came into Sears's field of vision. In the power struggle of the previous August, when Nofziger fled, Deaver had sided with Sears, a clear indication of where Nancy Reagan stood in the choice between Nofziger and Sears. Mrs. Reagan liked the campaign manager and enjoyed talking politics with him over lunch. Sears was witty, erudite, cosmopolitan, and up on the latest gossip inside Washington. Nancy was less enamored with the cigar-chomping, plainspoken Nofziger.

But on the Sunday following Thanksgiving, Sears asked Reagan for an immediate meeting to discuss Deaver, who had taken over the finance director position for which Nofziger had been so ill-suited. Deaver had been invited to the meeting but, arriving a few minutes early, was surprised to walk into the Reagans' home and find Sears, Black, Lake, Mrs. Reagan, and Governor Reagan huddling together. Mrs. Reagan asked Deaver to wait in their bedroom, saying, "They are not quite through yet." After a few minutes of waiting, Deaver figured "what the hell" and left the bedroom. Walking back into the living room, he overheard Sears, Black, and Lake accusing him of bilking Reagan out of thousands of dollars. When they spotted Deaver, however, they would not look him in the eye.[19]

Like Nofziger, Deaver realized too late that he had been set up. He was no more a fundraiser than Nofziger was. Sears made it clear to Reagan that it was a "him or me" proposition; either Deaver had to go or Sears would, along with Lake and Black. Reagan was furious at the ultimatum, but Mrs. Reagan indicated her position when she said, "Honey, it looks as if you've got to make a choice." Recognizing that he'd lost the power struggle, Deaver said, "No, Governor, you don't have to because I'm leaving!" He bolted out with Reagan and Nancy following him, arguing for some other accommodation. Deaver declined. Reagan stomped back into the room, red-faced, furious. He hated blackmail and ultimatums.[20] Roaring at the three, he shouted, "You bastards! The biggest man here has just left the room!"[21]

Lake later said, "It was the blackest day of my life. I hated that day. I hated being there." He told Reagan he was siding with Sears for Reagan's own good.[22] Deaver's dramatic exit was marred a bit because his wife, Carolyn, had dropped him off and he had no way to get home. He sheepishly knocked on the door to borrow the Reagans' station wagon.[23]

The meeting with the others was over quickly and the Reagans showed little warmth toward the three as they departed. From then on, Sears was in Reagan's doghouse. Nancy Reagan later said, "I've never known Ronnie to carry a grudge, but after that day I think he resented John Sears."[24] Just a few more mistakes and Reagan would throw him to the wolves. Reagan's old friend and press aide Nancy Reynolds called the governor later to protest Deaver's departure and it was the first time that she remembered Reagan being ill-tempered with her.[25]

Deaver was crushed. He'd been with Reagan since 1967. He and Hannaford had traveled with Reagan for years, making him a pile of money with the radio commentaries, the syndicated columns, and the speakers' circuit.

Deaver was at his office the next morning when he bumped into Reagan, who'd had an office at Deaver & Hannaford since early 1975. Reagan was deeply bothered by the matter—he hated tension among the staff. He went into Deaver's office, shut the door, and said, "You know, if I knew yesterday what I know today, this would never have happened." Deaver replied, "You'd better be careful because I have been watching your planning and [you] have nobody now to watch your planning." Ominously, he said, "These guys, they do not believe what you believe."[26]

Reagan was truly between a rock and a hard place. For ten years, Sears's reputation had grown in the national media's estimation—often nurtured by Sears. To fire Sears now meant that Black and Lake would go, possibly along with many more staffers. The last thing Reagan needed at this point was more embarrassing news stories.

Deaver, as a small consolation, would become the Reagans' "personal representative" to the Kitchen Cabinet. But he was out of the campaign. The body count of old Reaganites strewn in Sears's wake was growing, but this one really stung Reagan. In many ways, Deaver was a surrogate son to him. More than anybody else, he had devoted his life to the needs of Ron and Nancy Reagan. Yes, the association had been financially advantageous for him, but he also had helped make the Reagans a great deal of money, while providing vital advice and counsel for many years. He'd earned a reputation as an SOB to some, but he also knew that every successful political leader needed such a person to do the nay-saying.

Deaver had once even saved Ronald Reagan's life. During the 1976 campaign, Reagan was on his campaign plane, playfully tossing peanuts into the air and catching them in his mouth. When one got caught in his throat, some thought the wildly gesticulating Reagan was having a heart attack, but Deaver knew better. He quickly seized Reagan from behind and performed the Heimlich maneuver, sending a fat wad of partially eaten peanuts shooting out of Reagan's mouth.[27]

Deaver's departure meant his partner, Peter Hannaford, another friendly face, also was gone from Reagan's orbit. Richard Wirthlin and Ed Meese were about the only familiar faces left around the campaign. Meese was at this point a seemingly nonthreatening issues adviser, while Wirthlin's polling operation was based in Salt Lake City, so Reagan saw him only sporadically—especially since Sears had told him not to do any polling in Iowa because "we've got it locked up."[28] Sears was trying to keep Meese in his place by making cutting remarks behind his back about his organizational skills.

Meese grew frustrated. Unbeknownst to Sears and company, he hopped aboard a red-eye flight from Los Angeles to Washington for a worried meeting with campaign chairman Paul Laxalt. Laxalt had his own ax to grind, as Sears had already tried to supplant him as chair of the campaign. Meese was steamed about how Sears had forced out Deaver and other old friends, and especially about how he treated Reagan; Lou Cannon wrote in *President Reagan: The Role of a Lifetime* that Sears "had little respect for Reagan's intelligence or work habits."[29] Sears had gone too far and had made too many adversaries. For the time being, he was in total control of the campaign, and the headquarters was being moved from Los Angeles to Washington, per his instruction. But Reaganites around the country were sticking pins in voodoo dolls bearing his name.

While Sears had driven out many of Reagan's old advisers, it was certainly not true that, according to a certain mythology that had grown up over the years, Reagan was a pawn of his campaign operatives. Reagan never cared much about the intricacies of a campaign operation. He did care passionately, though, about his freedom-based ideas and about America. If Reagan toned down his message it was because he knew what was at stake. He wasn't running for chairman of the conservative movement. He already had their votes. Reagan understood that millions of Democrats and independents were culturally conservative but that the GOP had repelled them with its country-club image and past corruption. He would direct his message to these people as well. After all, Reagan had grown up a New Deal Democrat.

The political season was roaring along like an eighteen-wheeler, picking up speed, and the best anyone could do was either hang on or get out of the way. Ending up as roadkill was always an option, but not a pleasant one. Howard Baker's campaign was looking more and more like it would be carrion, but he fought on. No one was more affable and kindly in the GOP field than Baker. But his duties as Senate minority leader had kept him from the retail campaigning in which George Bush had been able to engage; he wasn't a telegenic orator like John Connally; nor did he have the deep well of grassroots conservative support to call upon like Ronald Reagan. To jump-start his flagging effort, Baker fired his campaign manager, Don Sundquist, and replaced him with Wyatt Stewart, who had made his bones working for Richard Viguerie and later raising millions for the House Republicans.[30] Still, the media were beginning to write Baker off. It was very odd that of the four leading candidates—Reagan, Connally, Bush, and Baker—the last was the only one who had won an election over the previous ten years.

Bush, meanwhile, was on high octane. He was barnstorming all the important early primary states, and where his speeches and coffees a year earlier would draw a half dozen folks, he was now getting fifty and more at these events. The local media, which had been ignoring Bush, were now sending reporters out to cover him, a sure sign of progress. Even national reporters were beginning to go out on the road with him.

Bush was having a good time. He had outworked and outhustled the rest of the GOP field, having spent five weeks stumping in New Hampshire, nearly as much time in Florida, and more than three weeks in Iowa in 1978 and 1979. He was following the model of Jimmy Carter, who simply campaigned longer and harder than anyone else did in 1976. Adam Clymer of the *New York Times* got off one of the best lines of the 1980 campaign, writing of Bush, "There is no track record to suggest that the Republican Party is equally susceptible to guerrilla warfare, even if the Che Guevara of the movement is Yale, oil and banking and a former national party chairman."[31] George Will observed that Bush was "this year's happy warrior, the candidate having the most fun. This nation needs a demonstration that public affairs can be cheerful."[32] Bush was having an especially good time because his son Jeb was traveling often with him. The peripatetic elder Bush had frequently been away from his family over the years and it was in this race that he was able to spend so much personal time with his children, four of whom worked full-time on the campaign.[33]

Not all was perfect in Bushville. Bush was not in Reagan and Connally's class as a public speaker, and when this was pointed out, he bristled. Bush said, "To beat 'the bigger shots'" he would "outorganize 'em, outwork 'em, outspell-out-the-goals-of-the-country 'em."[34] In his now-familiar script, Bush talked to the media and crowds like a campaign manager instead of a leader, rattling off information about his fundraising, his name identification, his experience, his organization.

The Bush campaign experienced some low drama as well. A married major national political reporter was carrying on affairs simultaneously with two of Bush's female staffers, one in Iowa and the other in Washington. The reporter thought he had them at a safe distance, but when the two women crossed paths on the road and compared notes, they discovered to their surprise that they were sleeping with the same married man. The two ended up in a hair-pulling, screaming fight.[35]

While George Bush was doing well overall, Connally was becoming more and more frustrated that he couldn't catch Reagan. He began to attack the Gipper more directly. Connally told audiences that Reagan had cost Gerald Ford the election in 1976 by challenging him in the primaries. He whined that while he was criticized for switching parties, Reagan skated on the issue. He went back thirty years and attacked Reagan for campaigning for Helen Gahagan Douglas against Richard Nixon for the U.S. Senate in California in 1950, but as far as some conservatives were concerned, this was a point in Reagan's favor.[36]

Connally absurdly charged that Reagan had broken his own "Eleventh Commandment," which "Big John" interpreted to mean that one Republican did not criticize another. What Connally did not understand was that the Eleventh Commandment meant one Republican should not attack another Republican *personally*. On matters of policy, criticism and honest debate were welcomed and necessary. Indeed, it was the Ford campaign in 1976 that often attacked Reagan personally and not the other way around.

On one issue, however, Connally, had a point. He hit Reagan for ducking yet another debate, this time the upcoming *Des Moines Register and Tribune* free-for-all scheduled for January 5, 1980. The now galactically important Iowa caucuses would take place on January 21.[37] Puerto Rico entered the fray first with a primary on February 17, followed by the ever-vital New Hampshire primary on February 26. Those thirty-five days between Iowa and New Hampshire would prove to be the most important time in Ronald Reagan's political life.

FOUR YEARS EARLIER, RONALD Reagan had received 49 percent in an abbreviated Iowa GOP caucus and taken seventeen to Gerald Ford's nineteen Iowa delegate votes in Kansas City. The last reputable Iowa poll had been taken in August 1979 and that had Reagan at a stratospheric 48 percent, Howard Baker at 23 percent, and Bush dead last at 1 percent. All believed that Reagan would swamp the field here in 1980.[38]

Reagan, after all, was a local boy who made good. He had gotten his first big break after college as a sports announcer for WOC in Davenport, where he called a college football game that featured Michigan's standout center, Gerald Ford. Dutch Reagan moved to Des Moines in 1933 and spent more than four years on the 50,000-watt WHO station, becoming a minor celebrity in the community.

Plenty of people in Iowa knew and remembered Dutch Reagan. Now they were angry with their old friend. He'd snubbed them. Reagan's on-the-ground problems in Iowa went hand in hand with the fact that he was ignoring the state. "It's awful hard to run a campaign in Iowa without the candidate here," said the savvy Iowa GOP chairman, Steve Roberts.[39]

With only seven weeks to go before the caucuses, the Reagan for President Committee finally panicked and dispatched Peter McPherson and Kenny Klinge there to see what they could do to repair the situation.[40] McPherson had worked for Ford in 1976 in Jim Baker's impressive delegate operation. Klinge had worked for the Reagan campaign in 1976 and was a tough, unflinching conservative infighter. Four years earlier in Kansas City, when Reagan was meeting with his tearful staff, Clarke Reed of Mississippi had walked into the room, uninvited, and tried to make amends for betraying Reagan at the last minute and helping to swing the nomination to Ford by flipping his delegation's votes over to the president. Everybody, including Reagan, swung a cold shoulder toward Reed. Except Klinge. He swung his fists at Reed but was restrained by other staffers. Reed barely escaped.[41]

Despite the late start, Reagan's executive director in Iowa, Robert Collins, told reporters, "I'm looking for a majority of the caucus vote and I think I can get that."[42] Not only did he inflate Reagan's chances, but he also lowballed Bush's expected level of support. Collins was not on Bush's payroll, but you couldn't prove that as far as everybody else in the Reagan campaign was concerned.

Bush had signed up dozens of current and former state GOP officials, including former governor Bob Blue. The current governor, Bob Ray, though officially uncommitted, was thought to be clandestinely supporting Bush. Bush had also recruited some local GOP leaders, including Mary Louise Smith, former chair of the RNC.[43]

In December, Sears commissioned a poll in Iowa by the media-shy Arthur Finkelstein, and the results showed Reagan smashing all comers. The best course of action, Sears determined, was to take no action. He kept Reagan out of the line of fire in Iowa—or anywhere else, for that matter.[44]

Connally forged ahead, announcing with great fanfare that he was bypassing the matching funds the FEC offered presidential candidates if they complied with a mind-numbing set of rules. In 1980, those who abided by the convoluted system could raise and spend and accept in the form of matching funds only about $16.8

million in the primary season.[45] Connally's decision was motivated in part by the fact that he had been unable to implement his big-picture strategy of speaking to the American people directly in order to catch up to the name identification of Carter, Kennedy, and especially Reagan. "Big John" had wanted to buy national television time, but the networks had stuck to their plan of not selling anyone time before the arbitrary start date of January 1, 1980.

TED KENNEDY WAS ATTRACTING a land rush of media attention, and at any time on his plane there would be seventy or so reporters having a high time. "On the plane itself it is like the kids taking the bus to summer camp, laughs, much badinage between the press and a Kennedy staff that includes speechwriters, press agents and baggage smashers," wrote Jack Germond mirthfully.[46] Kennedy's personal wealth became known: it was around $20 million, and the entire Kennedy family estate was around $400 million. He was, by far, the richest candidate in the race.[47]

Yet Carter had halted the bloodletting of his campaign, while Kennedy was being bled white by a carping media and a newly skeptical public. A new national poll showed that Carter had moved into the lead over the prince of Massachusetts, 48–40 percent, among Democratic primary voters. It was the first time in two years that Carter had led Kennedy among Democrats.[48] It was an amazing 38 percent net change in the polls in just a little over one month.

This reversal occurred despite, or in part because of, the fact that Carter had abruptly announced that he would forestall any campaigning while he dealt with the hostage situation in Tehran. Carter was clearly being helped by the ongoing hostage crisis, though he had actually done very little since the Americans had been taken hostage. His aides recognized that by not campaigning formally, Carter was saving hundreds of thousands of dollars in campaign travel while staying above the fray of the media and the early contests.

Carter canceled a debate in Des Moines with Ted Kennedy and Jerry Brown, but in early December, he was forced to confront Kennedy at a Washington benefit for an academic chair at Boston College in the name of Tip O'Neill. Carter and Kennedy sat only a few feet from each other, but still managed never to make eye contact, and the room was thick with intrigue.[49]

Carter's point man, the wily Bob Strauss, could teach a fox a thing or two. He managed to convince the media that Carter was an underdog in Iowa because he would be doing no campaigning there while Kennedy was going hell-bent for leather. Further, he said, Carter could sustain a loss there and still go on. His sidekick Tim Kraft agreed and said, "Kennedy has done better than I thought he was going to do in getting organized in Iowa."[50] The media bought the Strauss ploy.

JOHN CONNALLY WAS BECOMING more and more frustrated over heavyweight contender Reagan. Reagan was still playing the rope-a-dope strategy devised by Muhammad Ali, when the ex-champ let champion George Foreman punch himself into exhaustion in Zaire in 1974. The madder Foreman became, the more Ali lay against the ropes, waiting for Foreman to exhaust himself. Ali regained the title in the eighth round, when he dropped Foreman like third-period French class.

Big John told reporters that Reagan should "come out of the closet" and debate, a slur on Reagan's manhood. He whined that Reagan had had years to run for president but the networks wouldn't allow Connally to buy broadcast time to try to match Reagan's advantage.[51]

Connally also said that Reagan's comments on Iran and the shah had been "more inflammatory" than Kennedy's. Reagan had proposed that America do the moral and courageous thing and grant the dying shah political asylum at a time when the Iranians were demanding his return.[52] While everyone—including Connally—was focused on knuckling under to the ayatollah and fretting about the hostages, Reagan was set on a display of strength and courage that would send a message to Iran and the rest of the world not to mess with America. "It's about time," he said, "that we stopped worrying about what people think about us and say we're going to be respected again. . . . Isn't it time that never again will a dictator invade an American embassy and take our people hostage?"[53]

Reporters clamored for a Reagan response to Connally's newest broadside. They asked whether Connally was trying to "buy" the election. Reagan deadpanned, "Why, you know, we never use expressions like that under the 11th commandment."[54] Reagan could be a pretty good counterpuncher when he needed to be.

Still, Reagan's campaign remained disorganized. With so many of his old friends now gone from the plane, he was surrounded by strangers or junior staffers who did not have the stature necessary to tell him when he was botching things, such as by ducking the Des Moines debate. Gerald Ford took a swipe at Reagan for not debating, saying that "those who do not participate will be the losers."[55]

ON ONLY HIS THIRD campaign swing since announcing his candidacy in early November, Reagan declared on December 14 that he would bypass the new Puerto Rico primary. The primary itself was not a big deal, but Reagan had proposed statehood for Puerto Rico in his November announcement and the Republicans there tended to be very conservative, so it should have been a chance for an early win. Reagan was forced to bow out now because his campaign had never gotten organized and didn't have the money to spend. His campaign was continuing to unravel. Reagan told befuddled reporters, "Well . . . the scheduling of my appearances . . . are up to the people in the field who have much more knowledge of the political situation than I do. It's my campaign, but there is no way I can be as familiar as they are with where are the spots that I'm needed most in my own behalf or where they can do without me."[56]

If Reagan's campaign was in trouble, Phil Crane's campaign was running on fumes. Crane had gone through new embarrassments involving his wife, Arlene. It seems the family dog bit a six-year-old boy and when the game warden showed up to take the dog away, she objected and was arrested.[57] Crane's campaign office in northern Virginia resembled a ghost town. His pollster, Arthur Finkelstein, had left months earlier and was now aboard the Reagan campaign, although his talents were not being exploited. Finkelstein had been a key figure in 1976, when he helped orchestrate Reagan's campaign-saving comeback in North Carolina and then his utter crushing of Ford in the Texas primary, winning all one hundred delegates at stake.

Reagan had had a pollster since 1966, Dick Wirthlin, and no pollster wants another around to question his methodology, tactics, or strategy. Rumors circulated that Finkelstein had been brought aboard by Sears just to keep him from working for any other candidate. Indeed, George Bush had made a run at Finkelstein but nothing had come of it. It was hard to imagine the scruffy Jewish kid from Brooklyn and the proper preppy from Connecticut sitting down together. The only thing they would have had in common was an obsession with baseball.

As for Connally, he finally acceded to his manager Eddie Mahe's pleas to get into Iowa and start meeting real voters. Since day one, Mahe had been undercut by Connally's yes men in Texas. To save money, twenty-five people were let go from Connally's campaign staff in Arlington, Virginia, nine days before Christmas. The money would be devoted to a last-minute retail effort in Iowa, in a desperate attempt to catch up to the others. Connally's finance director was a little-known banker from Phoenix, Charles H. Keating Jr., but he was promoted to head of the Arlington office. Mahe kept his title but was forced to go on the road both with and without Connally to see what he could do to patch together the very operation Connally had resisted for a year. Mahe was right, but Connally's pride would not allow him to admit he'd been wrong, so he undercut his manager's authority each day.[58]

Connally's campaign had flaws too numerous to mention. Most obvious was his certainty that Kennedy would be nominated by the Democrats; second worst had been his belief that all he had to do was give speeches on national television or before large audiences.[59] At some point, candidates must meet real people, if only to gain a better understanding that America does not look like the inside of a Houston country club.

Connally's strategy changed from day to day. The fifty-state strategy had been dumped. The late-starting retail effort in Iowa and New Hampshire was a joke. Everywhere Connally went in these two states, it was as if he found signs that read, "Bush was here first." Or "Reagan was here first." Or "Baker was here first." There was no room in the GOP inn for Big John except for possibly in South Carolina.

Connally's southern coordinator, Haley Barbour of Mississippi, said of the South Carolina primary, "This is the first crack we get at Reagan head-up, the first time these two go toe-to-toe with the others on the side."[60] The Connally campaign was convinced that if it could get into a "High Noon" showdown with Reagan, Connally would take Reagan out. South Carolina was shaping up as Big John's Alamo.

The FEC spending limit in the Gamecock State was around $423,000, but Connally, freed from those requirements because he had eschewed federal matching funds, would spend far more there. Governor Jim Edwards, who had been one of Reagan's strongest supporters in 1976 but had defected to Big John, would introduce Connally at rallies as "the most qualified man" in the race.[61] Connally had also gained the endorsement of another Reagan supporter from 1976, Senator Strom Thurmond. Internal politics had led Thurmond to flip to Connally. Reagan's new state chairman, the handsome young congressman Carroll Campbell, impoliticly let it be known that he wanted to run for Thurmond's seat in 1984, when the veteran senator was expected to retire. (As it happened, Thurmond did not leave the Senate until 2003, at the age of one hundred. Though Campbell, who did become governor, outlived Thurmond by two years, he died tragically of Alzheimer's in 2005 at the young age of sixty-five.)

Rather than lower expectations in the early states and especially in South Carolina, Connally's campaign staff openly bragged about the defections from Reagan to Connally. Ronald Rietdorf, Connally's in-state operative, said a "legion" of former Reagan fans were moving to Big John: "This kind of slippage is going on all over the state."[62] This would be the first GOP presidential primary ever held in South Carolina, so no one could be confident of anything, especially Reagan.

ON THE RARE OCCASION when he was on the stump, Reagan was getting an enthusiastic response from GOP crowds, but reporters were pressing him for the new proposals his campaign had promised. These had been delayed for weeks, another sign of disorganization in his operation. The plan all along had been to dominate the news and the other candidates with new concepts and ideas and to convince skeptical voters, especially in the East, that Reagan was not a "one-dimensional conservative." His overall schedule was still light, even at this late date. The plan was for Reagan to take a break over the Christmas and New Year's holiday from the little campaigning he was doing and start back up the second week in January.[63]

Bush, the only GOP contender whose campaign was not going off the rails, decided that he, too, might enter the South Carolina contest, despite a decision by Jim Baker and Dave Keene to stay out and let Reagan and Connally whale on each other while their resources bled.[64] Standing in the wings, waiting for the outcome, was Bush's best option, they believed. If Connally surprised Reagan, then Bush might emerge as the last man standing between Connally and a wounded Reagan and the nomination. If Reagan won, then Connally was through and Bush would again be the last man standing. He would get—if he did well in Iowa, New Hampshire, Vermont, and Massachusetts—what all the candidates had been maneuvering toward for two years: the opportunity to narrow the race to a choice between themselves and Reagan. Bush was a famously disciplined individual, but his loathing of Connally got the best of him and his better judgment.

Still, South Carolina was three months away. All eyes were on Iowa and New Hampshire—and on the hostages in Iran. Conservatives began to attack Carter, accusing him of hiding behind his "national unity" strategy.[65] Implicit in the Carter diagram was a not-so-subtle message that to criticize the president was to be unpatriotic and the not-so-subtle suggestion that any reckless comments could get the hostages killed.

Carter had publicly ruled out the use of force to retrieve his fellow Americans, taking yet another arrow out of America's quiver to use against the ayatollah. The only action taken was to send the unctuous, super-pacifist Ramsey Clark to Tehran, leading even the most dovish men around Carter to gag. Americans were told to write postcards to the hostages over the Christmas season.[66] In a public-relations "twofer," Carter asked Americans to dim their Christmas lights in a show of unity—while also saving on energy.

Christmas came a few days early for the candidates as the first matching funds were issued from the FEC to Carter and Howard Baker. Carter received a little over $1 million and Baker just shy of $800,000.[67] Reagan's and Bush's requests were still being processed. Connally had raised around $8 million and was bypassing the FEC.[68]

Almost forgotten in the field of GOP candidates was John Anderson, who was receiving scant attention from the voters and the media. He was convinced that he was the candidate of ideas, but so far his only ideas had been to slap a fifty-cents-per-gallon federal tax on gasoline and to cut Social Security taxes by 50 percent.[69]

He subscribed to most liberal nostrums: abortion on demand paid for by taxpayers, the ERA, and reductions in the Pentagon's budget. Anderson was reputed to be one of the best speakers in Congress, although he wasn't saying anything the voters hadn't heard before. But in this new era of conservative Republicanism, the media decided here was a truly new phenomenon: a "truth-telling Republican." Anderson eventually became the 1980 version of the "media's candidate," as Carter was for a time in 1976 and Gene McCarthy was in 1968.

RONALD REAGAN'S NEW HAMPSHIRE state GOP chairman, Jerry Carmen, was whipping his operation in the Granite State into shape even as Reagan's national campaign was a mess. Carmen wasn't going to let happen to Reagan what Hugh Gregg had allowed in 1976. He worked out of a decrepit Victorian mansion in Manchester, just down the street from the *Manchester Union-Leader*, his biggest ally.

Unfortunately, Reagan was avoiding New Hampshire. Carmen was confident that all was being done to ensure a Reagan victory, but he was missing a candidate in a state whose voters prided themselves on not picking their candidate until they had talked to all the hopefuls personally. The state GOP would send a meager twenty-two delegates to Detroit, but its first-in-the-nation status gave those delegates an outsized importance.

New Hampshire was not a simple state to categorize. It was fairly homogeneous in terms of race and religion but it operated under separate spheres of influence from Massachusetts, Vermont, and, to a lesser extent, Maine. The southern area up to Manchester was still dominated by a slowly deteriorating textile industry, which had moved north from Massachusetts because the business climate was more favorable. At the same time, imports were destroying the struggling shoe and garment manufacturers. The area adjoining Maine was wooded, and many paper mills operated there, processing cedar, pine, and birch. To the West was farmland, much of it devoted to dairy. Dartmouth College, inspiration for the movie *Animal House*, was also here.

The seacoast region included the naval ship and submarine operations in Kittery and Portsmouth. The farthest northern region, rural, bordered Quebec, and many American citizens in the area spoke French more than English. The state was also famous for its skiing and clear, cold lakes and fall foliage. It was from top to bottom one of the most picturesque states in the nation. Longtime residents could smell an outsider a mile away, and woe to any politician who mispronounced the name of Concord or the northern city of Berlin. The state capital was not pronounced like the grape, but as "Conk-ahd," as in a conk on the head. And it was "BURR-lyn," as in freezing cold, with the emphasis on the first syllable, unlike the German city.

Granite Staters had a proud heritage of self-reliance and respect for privacy. A strong libertarian streak flowed through the state. Reagan was their kind of politician. Trouble was, he wasn't spending much time there.

Reagan, when he was stumping, seemed to spend more time on planes and in limousines than in just plain old grip-and-grin campaigning, at which he was nonpareil. How to "handle" Reagan had been a subject of debate since 1966. Lyn Nofziger was one of the few who understood that Reagan, above all politicians of the era, had an uncanny ability to connect with voters. His charming candor, his self-deprecating humor, and his utter belief in the rightness of his ideas allowed him to motivate and connect with his fellow Americans in a manner that left his jealous opponents in awe.

Because his opponents could not compete with Reagan at this level, they rationalized that he was just a "performer," like some trained seal. Reagan had worked his whole life to perfect his presentation, from asking for voice lessons while on the radio in Des Moines in the 1930s to the tireless work he put in on his speeches. But it wasn't just how he said it; it was what he said that got people's attention.

THE NATIONAL ECONOMY WAS now in a full-blown recession. Inflation was galloping along as prices rose 1 percent in December alone. Inflation for 1979 was once again in double digits. Gas and oil prices were up, as were interest rates and housing costs. "Growth" was a feeble 1.5 percent annually, but this was negated by inflation.[70]

REAGAN WAS AHEAD IN all the polls among GOP voters, but none of the questions about his age, stamina, and conservatism had been answered. Could he take a licking and keep on ticking? George Bush was making headway, and the others, especially Connally and Baker, weren't about to leave the stage now, when the pressure or a gaffe or an ill-timed show of Reagan's age might destroy his candidacy. They were all banking on this, plus his inept campaign apparatus. Reagan's man Charlie Black laid it on the line when it came to Iowa: "I think we have to finish first to avoid getting hurt."[71]

6

THE ASTERISK ALSO RISES

"George has the momentum now."

George Bush had achieved the unimaginable. The "asterisk" of the Republican Party had come out of nowhere to bloody the front-runner, Ronald Reagan, in the Iowa caucuses. On a cold and blustery January 21, 1980, Bush defeated Reagan, 31.5 percent to 29.4 percent.[1]

The folks of Iowa had known Dutch Reagan for more than forty years. They had known George Bush for forty days. In the past year, however, Reagan had campaigned in their state for only forty hours.[2] It was a watershed moment for Bush. It appeared that his anti-Reagan tide might swamp the Gipper's last try for the GOP nod.

To his moderate supporters, St. George of Brooks Brothers had slain the conservative dragon. The fact that Bush wasn't really all that moderate, at least politically, didn't seem to matter. In politics, perception is everything. When Bush was in the Southwest, he emphasized his "roots" in the Texas oil industry and spoke with a drawl. When he was in New Hampshire, he reminded folks that he was born and raised in Connecticut, had a summer home in Kennebunkport, Maine, and was a blueblood product of Phillips Andover and Yale. In the South and Southwest, he conspicuously ate pork rinds. In the Northeast, he ate tuna fish with Tabasco. Bush was a chameleon. On his wrist was a preppy striped watchband; on his feet, depending on the region, cowboy boots or loafers. His audience saw what they most wanted to see. Reagan, on the other hand, was always . . . Reagan.

"If we blow it, we have no one to blame but ourselves," Paul Laxalt had told the media several months earlier.[3] Reagan had indeed blown it. Headlines across

America blared "Upset" or "Stunning" when describing Bush's big win over Reagan. In private, Laxalt berated Reagan, saying that he'd screwed up by "sitting on your ass." He also had some choice words about John Sears.[4]

Sears had told the media that Reagan would do very little meeting and greeting with Iowa's Republican voters: "It wouldn't do any good to have him going to coffees and shaking hands like the others. People will get the idea he's an ordinary man, like the rest of us."[5] Iowans, especially old friends, got the idea that Reagan didn't care about them anymore. John Maxwell, a native Iowan and GOP consultant who was working for Senator Roger Jepsen at the time, knew scores of people who remembered Reagan from the old days, when they "went out to have a beer with him after he got off work or . . . listened to him broadcast the Cubs games."[6]

Maxwell was more impressed with the Bush operation run by Rich Bond than with Reagan's. When Bush's phone operation called Maxwell, the woman on the other end of the line told him, after he said he supported Reagan, "I've always really liked Reagan, too, and I think of George Bush as being a younger Ronald Reagan." Tens of thousands of Iowans were being told this very thing by well-trained Bush callers. Several times Maxwell warned Reagan operatives Peter McPherson and Kenny Klinge about what was happening. The two took his concerns seriously enough to go to Iowa to try to salvage the Reagan campaign there.[7]

The inner circle of Sears, Jim Lake, and Charlie Black had agreed that Reagan could not be stopped. To a man, they were wrong. Revealingly, Black said of Iowa, "Hell, I didn't know it was gonna be a *primary*."[8]

Sears had violated his own maxim, "Politics is motion." Reagan hadn't been in motion for nearly a year, with the exception of his somewhat lackluster announcement tour. Sears wasn't letting Reagan say or do anything interesting. Truth be told, it was not all Sears's fault. It was Reagan's, too. He'd read the polls that showed him still out in front, and he had put himself on cruise control.

Outwardly, Sears projected an "it's all going according to plan" persona. His inner circle was panicking, though. According to Lake, the feeling was "We are up shit creek. What are we going to do?"[9] Many in Reagan's camp thought it was the end of the line for him.

Bush—for whom the word "competitive" never had to be explained—did not have time to sympathize with the Gipper. His campaign brochure boasted that "in contrast with" Reagan, Bush "has physical stamina."[10] In case anybody missed the less than subtle verbiage, Bush went to the YMCA in Concord, New Hampshire, and performed jumping jacks and push-ups for the benefit of the news media.

To be sure, the tall, lean Bush was an athletic man and an impressive physical specimen. He now flaunted those advantages and dared Reagan to take "the same [exercise] class next week."[11]

The two men had small use for each other and the campaigns detested each other. Bush "considered Reagan a lightweight," remembered David Keene, Bush's national political director who also had his own ax to grind against the Reagan campaign.[12]

There were just too many cultural, political, and ideological differences between the two combatants. *Time* journalist Larry Barrett later wrote, "Bush, like the patrician cousins he left behind in New England when he moved to Texas, regarded Reagan as a calcified yahoo, an ideologue unhealthy for the party and the country. When Bush's son George ran for Congress in west Texas in 1978, the conservatives already identified as part of the Reagan cadre savaged him as some kind of subversive. They did the same thing to the father in New England and the South during the 1980 primaries, using Bush's former membership on the Trilateral Commission as Exhibit A. Bush was justifiably bitter about it."[13]

Barrett elaborated on Bush's antipathy toward the Right: "One night . . . he told a few of us, 'I despise it. It's terrible the way I've been abused. You'd think the national press would have been more indignant over this sort of thing. It's—well, it's anti-intellectual, that's what it is. It's worse than the Birch stuff. And Reagan acquiesces—like he did when his people used it against my son George.'"[14] Bush was not one to let bygones be bygones. The Kennedys had little on the Bushes. The latter kept an unwritten "Enemies List" and checked it more than twice. Bush bitterly remembered years later how conservatives in his home state of Connecticut had attacked his father, Senator Prescott Bush.

He also resented having been passed over for the vice presidency three times in the space of three years—first by Richard Nixon in October 1973, after the resignation of Spiro Agnew; then by Gerald Ford in August 1974, when the new president opted for former New York governor Nelson Rockefeller; and most recently at the 1976 GOP convention, when Ford picked Bob Dole as more acceptable to the conservatives who dominated the convention. Reporter Jules Witcover, in his book about the 1976 campaign, wrote that Ford had passed over Bush because "everyone knowledgeable in Republican politics considered Bush incompetent to be president."[15] The rebuke stung Bush. He'd seen Lyndon Johnson, Richard Nixon, Gerald Ford, and Jimmy Carter at close range, and he believed they had nothing he didn't have.

Bush had been snubbed again in 1977, when Carter did not keep him on as CIA director, even after he had briefed the Georgian on covert intelligence and world affairs during the 1976 campaign and had heavily lobbied the incoming president to retain him as head spymaster. Bush loved the CIA; as director, he often signed his memos "Chief Spook." The brass ring had repeatedly been dangled in front of him and then jerked back. It was enough to drive any man bonkers. Bush's quest for the White House seemed at times to be more about score settling and putting a capstone on his résumé than it was about bringing great ideas to the presidency.

George Bush wasn't the only one who attacked Reagan in Iowa. The January 5 *Des Moines Register* debate took place before a live audience of 2,500 in the city's new Civic Center, was covered by more than 150 local and national reporters, and was broadcast live on PBS and tape-delayed for later broadcast on the CBS network. While Reagan was at his home in Pacific Palisades in sunny California, a thousand miles from the cold and mud of Iowa, the other six GOP aspirants pummeled the absentee Reagan throughout the course of the two-hour debate. Senator Dole said, "Ronald Reagan, wherever you are, I hope you're having fun."[16] Each candidate was asked individually where he differed with Reagan, and all did so with relish, especially John Connally. Fatuously, Connally said he had no idea where Reagan stood on the issues. He also said that they needed to do a few more debates to "smoke him out."[17] Charles Gibson, reporting for ABC, noted that "the only jabs were at Reagan."[18] All the candidates did well, save the one who didn't bother to show up. Everybody in Iowa now knew that Reagan had snubbed them.[19]

Dole and Bush were forced to sit next to each other in the setting, which did not make them happy, as they had nothing but contempt for each other. In character, during the debate, Dole needled Bush for losing a Senate race in Texas.

Fortunately, Dole was between Connally and Bush, which kept the two Texans from possibly coming to blows, as Bush and Connally detested each other even more than Bush and Dole did.

Before the debate, Bond, Bush's Iowa coordinator, had told the *Washington Post* that the debate "may hurt someone but I don't think it will help anyone very much."[20] Truer words were never spoken, and Reagan quickly found out how much he was hurt by not appearing. The *Los Angeles Times* took Reagan to task in an editorial, saying that "many should and will characterize his absence as a cowardly attempt to maintain a lead in the polls."[21] Reagan was steamed; he hated it when anyone challenged his manhood or his intelligence. Everybody was ripping into Reagan—David Yepsen at the *Des Moines Register*, Mike Glover at the Associated Press, all the local radio stations. "The media just went berserk," Bond recalled. "Nobody defended him."[22]

The day after the debate, while all the other candidates were squeezing as much campaigning into Iowa as possible, Reagan spent a single day in New Hampshire, whose primary was seven weeks off.

John Sears kept Reagan away from Iowa but arranged a three-day issues briefing for the candidate. The sessions, which started at 9 A.M. and usually finished by mid-afternoon, featured some thirty policy advisers, who briefed Reagan on all matters of national policy, from economics to trade to armaments. Participants included Art Laffer and Jack Kemp on economics, and Ken Khachigian, who had recently come aboard as a consultant to help Reagan with agricultural issues. Kemp aide Dave Smick kept getting peppered with notes from Congressman David Stockman, who was in the lobby, trying to horn in on the briefings.[23]

Smick was appalled at how little respect Sears and some of the others showed for Reagan behind his back. He did, however, remember Sears saying that Reagan's political instincts were "phenomenal . . . and that will carry him through."[24]

Reagan mostly listened during the briefings but sometimes asked questions. He came out of the meetings with stepped-up attacks on Carter. He began by urging the president to aid the "freedom fighters" in Afghanistan who were trying to dislodge the invading Soviet army.

On January 11, the Des Moines Register released a new poll showing that Reagan's support among GOP voters had plunged from 50 percent in December to 26 percent; Howard Baker went from 7 percent to 18 percent; Bush zoomed up from only 3 percent to 17 percent, just 9 points behind Reagan.[25] But Sears still saw Connally as Reagan's main competitor, and he remained unconcerned about Iowa. He rationalized that with such a big and diverse field, no one could get Reagan into a one-on-one contest early. "If we win Iowa, New Hampshire, Massachusetts . . . we'll have eliminated everybody and it will be a two-man race."[26]

Though he was mostly avoiding Iowa, Reagan did find time to go to New York to appear on Bill Buckley's TV debate program Firing Line.[27] He also sat down with the New York Times for a long interview. The questions ranged far and wide—from SALT II to energy to the federal government's Alaska land grab, which had prevented millions of acres from being explored for natural resources—and Reagan answered each with great detail and knowledge. He argued forcefully for returning authority and power to the states, demonstrating his refined understanding of federalism and conservatism. He was asked, "Do you favor a tax cut in 1980?" and with blue eyes twinkling, Reagan responded, "I favor tax cuts any time."[28]

Anybody who took the time to read the interview with Reagan would have discovered a cultured, thoughtful, and articulate conservative whose clarity of thinking had only been sharpened by his experiences and omnivorous reading.

Reagan's supporters griped that it was too bad this thinking man had not bothered to go to the Des Moines debate. Reagan's enemies were not about to give him the benefit of the doubt.

Bush, who had campaigned mainly by commercial travel for two years, traded up for a chartered Learjet that seated twenty and had a shower and, even more important, a bar. Leasing a private plane was a sure sign that a campaign was catching fire. His paid staff had grown to 215; most were in Alexandria, Virginia, across the Potomac from Washington, but 50 salaried staffers were toiling in Iowa. Each night, 300 volunteers and 60 paid locals worked the phones, calling Republicans in Iowa, exhorting them to support Ambassador Bush.[29] Jim Wooten of ABC reported that the hardworking Bush had "fifty-seven stops scheduled in the next week."[30]

On the other side of the aisle, Carter, like Reagan, had ducked the Des Moines debate, but it was to his benefit. Carter was smashing Kennedy, 57 percent to 25 percent, in surveys of Democrats in Iowa.[31] Kennedy shifted tactics, telling reporters that unless Carter got 50 percent in Iowa, it would be a "major setback." Reporters smirked behind their notepads at Teddy.

The less Carter campaigned, the more presidential he seemed and the more he went up in the polls. The less Reagan campaigned, the less courageous he seemed and the more he dropped. "Behaving almost as though he were an incumbent President," a reporter noted, "the former California governor visited Iowa rarely."[32] But Reagan was not an incumbent president. Voters, derided by some of the unblinking lizards who called themselves "campaign consultants," were a lot smarter than given credit for by these cold-blooded mercenaries. They clearly understood the important difference between holding the office and seeking the office. Carter was being rewarded for his "Rose Garden strategy" and Reagan was being punished for his.

Iowa's GOP voters were not mollified when Reagan made an abbreviated appearance in the state in mid-January. His Iowa tour did not go well. The media saw it as a panicky move, designed to stop his "severe erosion."[33] "One signal to emerge from all this," reported John Laurence with ABC News, "is that Reagan seems to be slipping not only in the polls but in his ability to concentrate as well. Even with his notes he has been having difficulty putting complicated new issues into understandable language."[34]

Reagan had also been to Florida and to South Carolina, to blunt the Connally effort there. One newspaper report said that he'd held "2,500 people spellbound" at an event in Florida.[35] Unfortunately, none of these folks would be voting in the Iowa caucuses.

HOWARD BAKER WAS UNDER no illusions about his chances. He knew his organization paled when compared with Bush's. He managed expectations, telling reporters, "Right now Reagan and Bush are ahead of me and Bush may be ahead of Reagan. . . . I wouldn't be surprised at all to see George make a serious challenge of Gov. Reagan."[36] Baker's campaign was faltering, but he was a disciplined man. In getting ready for the Senate Watergate hearings in 1973, Baker had lost twenty pounds in preparation through an unusual diet: "protein . . . and resuming smoking."[37]

Third place in the expectations game was getting crowded. Baker, Connally, and Dole all claimed they would come in third, while predicting Bush would come in first. Bush testily threw off the premature crown, and Reagan, showing weakness, openly said he'd do better in a primary than a caucus.[38]

The sharks of the national media smelled blood in the water. They began using words like "senility" and "staleness" when describing Reagan.[39] Reporters questioned Reagan's "stamina" and mockingly nicknamed his campaign plane the Ponce de Leon after the explorer who vainly searched for the fountain of youth. On the plane, Reagan would sometimes wander back to the press section to josh reporters that he was still awake or get on the intercom and announce a "four-hour disco party when we land."[40] But they were more interested in cutting up Reagan than cutting a rug.

Reagan was telling reporters he was "very cautiously optimistic" about the outcome in Iowa—this was a long way from the arrogance of his team just several weeks before.[41] It was a bad time.

Two days before January 21, the Reagan campaign hit upon the bright idea that Reagan should return to his old radio station, WHO, for an appearance. WHO was no mom-and-pop operation; it was a clear-channel, 50,000-watt station. Trouble was, Reagan called in from New York, which got things off on the wrong foot. He called in fifteen minutes late, which made things even worse. Reagan had expected a softball interview with the morning hostess, Susan Bray, but she hurled one beanball after another at the candidate. "Why haven't you campaigned more in Iowa? Why didn't you come to the Iowa Republican debate? Why are you acting as a recluse? Are you trying to conserve your strength?"[42]

If that weren't enough, one Iowan called in and said to Reagan, "You don't sound like a young man." For the fifteen minutes Reagan was missing, listeners were treated to commercials for George Bush ("We're going all the way," cried Bush in the spot) and Bob Dole. During Reagan's disastrous interview, an ad ran for a magazine with articles on restoring "potency to men whose sex lives are over" along with "ten ways to grow healthier as you grow older." The embarrassing show brought gales of laughter to the headquarters of other GOP candidates.[43]

Listening to the unmitigated failure, a Reagan aide shook his head and muttered the old conservative joke, "It's a Communist plot."[44]

There was a small bright spot in his January schedule when Reagan spoke to a group of high school students in New Hampshire. He received two standing ovations from the kids. Sixteen-year-old Tommy Duprey was not deterred by the fact that he couldn't vote, saying, "We're going to be 18 in two years and if he's president, we can re-elect him."[45]

IN A TESTAMENT TO the media's new regard for Bush, he was invited to appear on CBS's *Face the Nation* the day before the caucuses. Bush wisely refused to predict how Reagan would do in Iowa. He did tell the national audience, "But he's got to be stopped by me and he's got to be stopped before Illinois."[46] He was again talking more like a campaign manager than a presidential candidate. Bush missed his opportunity in the spotlight to talk about what he later derisively referred to as the "vision thing." Indeed, he lamented to a reporter that voters didn't know about "all these fantastic credentials" he had on his résumé.[47]

Bush's operatives were telling reporters half-jokingly that a blizzard on Monday was what they needed, in order to keep Reagan's soft support at home. Bush was frenetically campaigning; he attended fifty-four events in the month of January alone.[48] Connally decided to make a last-minute effort, spending more than $150,000 on television ads trying to catch up to Bush and Reagan.[49] Big John was now actually deigning to meet the little people of Iowa. Bob Dole spoke "midwestern" better than anyone else in the campaign, but dogs just didn't go for this dog food. More embarrassing for Connally, on the eve of the caucuses he was also hit with lawsuits charging that he had stiffed campaign vendors for hundreds of thousands of dollars.[50]

ON THE DEMOCRATIC SIDE, Ted Kennedy was jetting hither and yon, making a last-minute bid in Iowa. His wife, Joan, accompanied him. She got good reviews for her poise and a good laugh when she asked a group to vote "for the future of the country and for the future of Teddy." She gracefully defended her husband's behavior at Chappaquiddick.[51]

One of Kennedy's top lieutenants, Pat Lucey, the former governor of Wisconsin and until recently Carter's ambassador to Mexico, did his best to bring order to the stumbling campaign. Lucey was a Kennedy man through and through. He'd helped JFK in his crucial win in the Wisconsin primary in 1960 and had become close to the family. Still, he raised eyebrows when he abruptly left his diplomatic post in late 1979 to join Teddy's effort. Lucey's longtime political fixer, Paul Corbin, was small in stature but had often been at the center of big problems in American politics. Corbin had worked with Lucey in Wisconsin and caught Bobby Kennedy's attention, becoming the attorney general's political eyes and ears. Corbin now was naturally working on the campaign of RFK's younger brother.

Jerry Brown was campaigning in Iowa, but politicos considered his candidacy a punch line at this point. All the while Carter sat serenely above the fray, "acting presidential." The economy was in the toilet, the Soviets had overrun Afghanistan and were threatening the West in other arenas, Americans were being held hostage by a crazed religious fanatic in Iran, inflation was high, unemployment was high, gas prices were high, gold was at more than $500 per ounce, and American morale had bottomed out.[52] Carter had a nearly 60 percent approval rating. Go figure.[53]

BEGINNING AT 8 O'CLOCK on the windswept, wintry night of January 21, Iowa Republicans turned out in 2,531 precinct caucuses, which took place in churches, schools, bars, and living rooms, to begin the process of picking delegates to county conventions. Who in turn would pick delegates to go to congressional district conventions. Who in turn would pick delegates to go to the state convention. Who in turn would pick thirty-seven delegates to go to the national GOP convention. There was also a nonbinding straw poll, and it was on this that everybody's attention was focused.

Reagan had made radio commercials encouraging a big turnout. There was a big turnout—indeed a record turnout. Steve Roberts, the state GOP chairman, had thought that about 55,000 Republicans would show up. He was off by only 51,000. This rush of caucus voters ironically did Reagan in.[54]

The night of the caucuses, while Bush was squeezing the last bit of media coverage out of his foray into the Hawkeye State, Reagan was in Los Angeles, at home having dinner with friends and then watching a private screening of the new movie *Kramer vs. Kramer*.[55] The movie was about an ugly divorce and many saw it as a metaphor for the state of the Reagan-Sears marriage.

Sears called the Reagans that night to tell them the stunning news that Bush had won the caucuses. "They took it not well," he later said.[56] Reporter Lou Cannon said that the Reagans were "shattered" by the loss in Iowa.[57] Sears also called syndicated columnist Pat Buchanan and complained that Reagan had been using the same stump speech for the past year, even though the Gipper had barely been out in that time.[58]

Bush had not only upset Reagan but had left all the other Republican candidates in the dust. Howard Baker won the fight for third place with about 15 percent of the vote. Poor Bob Dole brought up the rear with a humiliating 1.5 percent.[59]

All three networks broadcast live coverage of the Iowa caucuses and Bush was seen all across the nation, with a slightly dazed look, in a room full of shrieking kids who looked as if they had just stepped out of a J. Press catalogue. One reporter said Bush "acted like a Yale undergraduate after the Elis had beaten Harvard."[60]

Sadly for Rich Bond, he could not celebrate the victory in which he'd invested a year of his life and for which he was most responsible. Jeb Bush recalled, "I was trying to find him to congratulate him and he was behind a screen in this . . . hotel reception room and he had just found out that his wife had a miscarriage that night." Bond told no one except his friend Jeb. Behind the stage, they embraced, Bond quietly weeping.[61]

Barbara Bush found out and the next morning was the first to call Bond and his wife, Valerie, at the hospital where she was recovering. Jim Baker later had the campaign pay for the Bonds to spend a week in St. Thomas.[62]

THE MORNING OF JANUARY 22, headlines across the country trumpeted Bush's "stunning" defeat of Reagan in Iowa. It was a genuine upset and people everywhere were bowled over that Reagan had lost. Tom Pettit of ABC said on national television the night of the caucuses, "We have just witnessed the political funeral of Ronald Reagan."[63]

Some Reaganites desperately claimed that Reagan really had not lost. They charged that because Bush's operatives controlled the GOP state party apparatus, they had simply stopped counting when Bush pulled ahead. A claimed computer malfunction made Reagan's supporters even more suspicious as the balloting resumed with a hand count. The "final" tally as announced by Steve Roberts, who if not a Bush supporter was certainly a cheerleader, was 33,530 for Bush and 31,348 for Reagan. When pressed, Roberts conceded that only 94 percent of the total vote had been counted. He claimed that the rest had never been phoned in or had been lost. He then halfheartedly said that maybe some would show up "in the mail."[64]

William Loeb of the *Manchester Union-Leader* said Bush's win in Iowa had "all the smell of a CIA covert operation."[65] If only the CIA were that competent. Marty Plissner, political director at CBS, thought the numbers that had been reported in for Bush from some precincts looked "funny."[66] Asked years later whether he knew anything about the missing Reagan votes in Iowa, Rich Bond simply rolled his eyes.[67]

Former Reagan aide Stu Spencer had been right when he told reporters that no one was going to beat Reagan for the nomination except Reagan himself.[68] Reagan had beaten himself in Iowa, and now it looked as if he may have lost his third and last chance to win the GOP nomination and the presidency.

Reagan and Sears tried to downplay the loss despite the fact that Reagan had spent more than $400,000 in Iowa.[69] Sears called the caucuses "essentially an organizational exercise," but that was an indictment of his own stewardship of the campaign.[70] Why didn't Reagan put together his own "organizational exercise"?

The day after the caucuses, Reagan bizarrely told reporters that losing in Iowa helped him because "I told you once before, I didn't like being a front-runner."[71] Reagan complained that his speech the Saturday before the voting, televised statewide, had been poorly promoted. He also told reporters there would be no change in strategy and no "heavying up" of his schedule in New Hampshire, a little less than five weeks away.

Sure enough, after only a minor campaign swing, Reagan returned home on Friday for some unnecessary "R and R." The wheels were coming off the Reagan for President campaign. Sears and his team had been overconfident for months, and now the Gipper was paying a heavy price. "The sons of bitches are dividing up the spoils and they haven't even won a primary yet," a GOP official had noted back in November about Reagan's team.[72]

Bush didn't waste a moment. He was winging his way to New Hampshire. Reagan forlornly said, "George has the momentum now."[73]

WHILE ONETIME REPUBLICAN FRONT-RUNNER Ronald Reagan was narrowly edged out in Iowa, onetime Democratic front-runner Ted Kennedy was routed. Jimmy Carter defeated him by 59–31 percent.[74] The embarrassing image of Carter the loser had been banished. Thirty days earlier, they'd been tied at 40 percent apiece in a Des Moines Register poll.[75] Kennedy's campaign was in complete disarray. It was the worst loss ever inflicted upon a member of America's political dynasty. Teddy and the Kennedy family were humiliated.

At a particularly bad time for Kennedy, both *Reader's Digest* and the *Washington Star* ran exhaustive stories that undermined two central theses of Kennedy's story about the night of the accident at Chappaquiddick. Kennedy had always contended that strong currents nearly swept him out to sea and it was this and his exhaustion at fighting the current which prevented him from saving Mary Jo Kopechne. But the *Star* reviewed tide and weather charts for that night and reported that in fact the tide was running in—slowly. The *Digest* reported that Kennedy was driving much faster than he'd previously stated.[76]

Kennedy and his staff attacked the two articles, but never said out-and-out that they were untrue. Joe Kopechne, Mary Jo's father, broke his eleven-year silence and took Teddy to task for lying.[77] Kennedy's campaign was forced to devote the first five minutes of a half-hour televised commercial to featuring him saying he did not cause the death of Mary Jo Kopechne.

Kennedy's campaign finances were in an even greater shambles than the rest of his campaign. In a short amount of time he had raised and frittered away $4 million, and he had less than $200,000 on hand as he limped into New Hampshire.[78] Campaign workers in the Granite State were notified that they could very well be going off the payroll. But no one was ready to give up on Teddy now, not after the seven-day-a-week, eighteen-hour-a-day investment they'd made. Nevertheless, already there were calls for Kennedy to get out, including by many of the union officials for whom he'd hauled water for years.

Kennedy had a bad habit of chewing his fingernails, and after all this he may have gnawed them down to the nub.

IN MID-JANUARY, LABOR LEADER George Meany passed away at age eighty-five. He'd been a fixture in the American labor movement for more than twenty-five years. Though a liberal Democrat, he was a vociferous anti-Communist and he had been an admirer of Reagan, in part because he saw Reagan's appeal with the American working man and woman. Meany went to great lengths to keep Communist unions from joining the AFL-CIO over the years, and in 1975 he had ordered union members to refuse to load American grain headed for Russia. Meany was deservedly mourned by hundreds of thousands of patriotic Americans.[79]

WINNING EARLY, THOUGH CERTAINLY preferable to losing early, brought with it its own problems for George Bush. The night of the Iowa win, Bush blurted out, "We'll do even better there," referring to New Hampshire.[80] At a subsequent press conference, he could not contain his glee and said confidently that if he won New Hampshire, "there'll be absolutely no stopping me."[81] The *Nashua Telegraph* upped the ante, running a wire story headlined "Bush Predicts N.H. Victory."[82] Jerry Carmen, Reagan's crafty director in the state, told the media that Bush "should get at least 50 percent in New Hampshire."[83]

The Bush campaign had wisely bought a great deal of television time in Boston, aimed at New Hampshire, with the notion that if Bush did well in Iowa, he had better follow it up with a strong performance in the next contest. But Bush eschewed the notion of getting too specific on issues. The tagline to the commercials was "George Bush—a president we won't have to train."[84] Once again, the focus was his résumé. He didn't have a story to motivate potential supporters, other than to say that he had "Big Mo," the silly, vaguely preppy slang Bush had used for his "Big Momentum" since Iowa.

Someone who did have a vital story to tell his fellow citizens was Ronald Reagan—if only he and his campaign would decide to tell it. Reagan's conservative ideology had become more refined and less dogmatic, more reflective and less reflexive. The "new" Reagan had not changed his basic ideology, only how he presented it. The focus became the positive aspects of his conservative philosophy. Rather than talking about balanced budgets, he spoke of limitless opportunities. He spoke of new horizons for the American people. His eye was on the dawn and not the dusk. Rather than dwelling on the past, he offered hope for the future. Rather than just denouncing collectivism, he expounded on the merits of freedom. Rather than being "anti-abortion," Reagan was "pro-life." To a degree, Reagan's message was a reaction to Carter's politics of scarcity, but it was also indicative of Reagan's own intellectual maturation.

The effervescent Bush was in motion, directly challenging Reagan. The Gipper was always at his best when challenged.

AFTER REAGAN'S DISASTROUS LOSS in Iowa, a young conservative activist received a call from Bob Heckman, founder of the Fund for a Conservative Majority (FCM). Heckman, who had worked for Citizens for Reagan in 1976, had started the political action committee three years earlier. He brought in John Gizzi, who would later become a longtime editor for *Human Events*, and another young conservative, Ralph Galliano, to help with the day-to-day activities. The three met with the young activist, who had knowledge of communications and New Hampshire politics, to discuss the faltering Reagan campaign.

It was quickly decided that Reagan desperately needed help. FCM had $750,000 on hand to assist Reagan. FCM hired the young conservative and he spent hours in a decrepit studio in the Georgetown section of Washington listening to tapes of Reagan's many speeches. Finally, thirty- and sixty-second radio spots were produced and he bought all the broadcast time available in New Hampshire, South Carolina, Alabama, Florida, Georgia, and Illinois.

Checks were sent along with reel tapes. In 1980, radio time was relatively cheap and in a state like New Hampshire, where television was expensive, it was the medium of choice. FCM bought time adjacent to news, weather, sports, and the farm reports. Flyers and newspapers ads were also prepared. The group spent tens of thousands of dollars in the Granite State alone. As an independent federal committee, FCM faced no limits on how much it spent on pro-Reagan activity.

There is no way to quantify its impact, but there can be little doubt that FCM's independent expenditure helped at the Gipper's most desperate hour, as Reagan was reeling after Iowa, with his campaign in disarray and heavily in debt.

With Reagan's astonishing loss in Iowa, his enemies and opponents came at him with all guns blazing, focusing of course on Reagan's age. In a CBS poll, half opposed a president who would turn seventy while in office.[85] A Carter official told reporters a joke that a farmer told him: "We wouldn't have these problems if Ronald Reagan were still alive."[86] A Carter factotum lamented to Lou Cannon that Carter campaign aides had thought they were going to face Reagan, but "now we are going to face Bush."[87]

Others piled on, telling the media that Reagan had slowed down, he'd gotten markedly older, and his voice wasn't as strong. Bush's New Hampshire director, Hugh Gregg, stuck a big needle in, saying the issue wasn't "age," it was "stamina."[88] A renewed debate ensued over whether Reagan took daily naps. Cannon said the age issue was starting to bother Reagan. "He got really down on himself for a while," the scribe said.[89]

Sears was insisting to anyone who would listen that Reagan could snap back in New Hampshire, but Reaganites asked the obvious question: Why did Sears put Reagan in the position where he would be forced to "snap back" in the first place?[90] In a postmortem, one Iowan complained that Reagan "doesn't seem to want to say anything. I remember when he could lift the roof right off this place. The old fire doesn't seem to be there now."[91]

Lyn Nofziger thought he knew the reason why. "They have him so intimidated, so convinced that he shouldn't speak out for what he believes that he's not Ronald Reagan."[92] Nofziger was right in part: Sears wasn't letting Reagan speak out. But he was wrong about something else: Ronald Reagan was never anything but Ronald Reagan.

Reagan had been here before. His 1976 campaign had begun tepidly and he lost the first five primaries. It was only after he tore up Sears's script and went after Gerald Ford on ideological grounds that he got back in the race and almost beat Ford for the nomination.

After Iowa, Reagan, the model of self-confidence, was filled with doubts. And anger, mostly at Sears. The campaign manager tried to tell Reagan he could not articulate his pro-life position. Patronizingly, Sears said, "That can be your private opinion, of course." Reagan stormed, "Damn it . . . I am running for president of the United States! You're not! Got it?"[93]

The capstone bad metaphor for Reagan post-Iowa was that "Bobo" went AWOL.

Who was Bobo?[94]

Bobo was a battery-powered, cymbal-clanking toy monkey that was a mascot of Reagan's Secret Service detail. Each time the Reagan entourage landed somewhere, Bobo was turned on to shriek, bang his cymbals, and celebrate. When he went missing, well, everyone went "bananas." The agents made T-shirts that read "Free Bobo."[95] They might have been better off if those T-shirts had read "Free Reagan."

After the Iowa caucuses the GOP county chairman in Marshall, Sheryl Readout, tartly summed up the situation: "Reagan was thumbing his nose at Iowa. Iowa has done the same thing to him."[96]

The question now was whether New Hampshire's Republicans would also thumb their noses at Reagan.

7

BUSH BEARS DOWN

"I just wish he wouldn't stand there and tell us he might drop dead."

"I wouldn't say he . . . was overrated, maybe I've been underrated," the new front-runner, George Bush, told reporters about his fading opponent as he raced across New Hampshire.[1] Bush was talking as if Ronald Reagan's campaign was over, and many in fact thought it was. One wag said that Reagan had been called the "front-runner" so many times over the past three years, some might have thought it was his real first name. No more. Ladbrokes, the giant London bookmaking house, installed Bush as the odds-on favorite to win the GOP nomination at 5–1. Reagan was behind even John Connally, who was installed at 6–1. The Gipper was going off at 7–1.[2]

Reagan was now running behind Bush by 16 percent in New Hampshire, according to Dick Wirthlin's polling, and his campaign staggered into the state— sans candidate.[3]

The day after the Iowa caucuses, Bush was in Keene, New Hampshire, with a large complement of national media in tow, while Reagan was still in California, at his home in Pacific Palisades. Reagan held an abbreviated press conference, where he was described as "crestfallen."[4] Bush had appeared on all three network morning shows before jumping into his sleek Learjet and heading for the first primary in the nation. He had already stumped more than fifty days in the Granite State over the past year, while Reagan had barely set foot there in more than two years. Ebulliently, Bush told a crowd, "There's no stopping me!"[5] Smug Bush staffers produced buttons proclaiming "FBBI": "For Bush Before Iowa."[6]

Reagan's campaign had no plans to get him into New Hampshire anytime soon, even with the primary just five weeks off. Almost everybody knew this was tomfoolery. Reagan's loss in Iowa "calls for a massive change in strategy," said Wyoming congressman Dick Cheney. "It makes New Hampshire critical. I don't think he can lose the first two and remain viable."[7]

Lyn Nofziger bluntly assessed the startling loss in Iowa. "He [Reagan] comes through to the voters as arrogant, rude to old friends. To get back [in the running] he's first got to eat a little humble pie."[8]

Reagan was doing anything but getting back in the running, as he defended his languid campaign style and restated his opposition to attending any "cattle shows" of GOP aspirants. On the days when Reagan was campaigning, often he didn't start until 11:30 in the morning. Mike Deaver talked hopefully of Reagan's supporters being shaken out of their complacency. Though both he and Nofziger had been thrown overboard, they were still rooting for the Gipper.

Yet this did not stop Nofziger from calling Dave Keene in the Bush camp the night of the Iowa caucuses and telling him, "Thank you for one of the most enjoyable evenings of my entire life."[9] Nofziger was mainlining schadenfreude, delighted at his enemy John Sears's growing discomfiture. For several days following the caucuses, Reagan had difficulty getting Sears on the phone, as he was holed up in a hotel room, brooding.

Howard Baker had come in a poor third in Iowa, and Bob Dole, John Anderson, and Phil Crane were being winnowed out. The race was quickly becoming a two-man contest. The scenario Reagan's opponents wanted—to emphasize Reagan's age, stop any thought of inevitability, and get him into a one-on-one contest—had come true for Bush. But Reagan and Sears could not even agree on this simple point. Sears was saying publicly it was a two-man race and Reagan was more wisely saying the other candidates were still "viable."[10]

Bush's campaign had exceeded even its greatest expectations. The goal of Bush advisers had been simply to come close to Reagan in Iowa, but they never imagined they would actually defeat him. In doing so, Bush accelerated the demise of all the others, save Connally, who was now basing his campaign on a last-ditch "stop Reagan" effort in the upcoming South Carolina primary. Reagan's campaign knew that sooner or later it would boil down to two men, but as George Will aptly put it, "Not even in their worst nightmares did they dream that it would begin the day after Iowa."[11] Giddily, Bush told a press conference that if he won the New Hampshire primary, Reagan's campaign would "unravel and unravel fast."[12]

Reagan's own supporters were mentioning his age, unprompted, in Wirthlin's polling. Some people frankly admitted to the media that the only reason they turned out at his speeches was that they were curious to see how he looked and handled himself. It didn't help that Reagan would turn sixty-nine on February 6.

The campaign, however, did not try to downplay the event, fearing that doing so would only make a bigger issue of Reagan's age. Instead, at the suggestion of a devoted Reagan aide, Lorelei Kinder, the campaign planned a very public celebration—a big fundraising party in Los Angeles with old friends Dean Martin and Frank Sinatra. Reagan quipped about birthdays, "They're OK—especially when you consider the alternative."[13] The campaign raised a much-needed $90,000 at the party.

But the campaign's problems were real—so real that Reagan convened an emergency meeting of his high command in Chicago. There, Nancy Reagan— once described as a "Metternich in Adolfo dresses"[14]—sternly pulled his advisers aside and demanded to know what had happened.[15] Before the strategy session, the plan had been for Reagan to visit New Hampshire for a half day the week following Iowa, and then to conduct an abbreviated four-day tour of other primary states before going back to Los Angeles. Incredibly, at this meeting the campaign altered nothing about the plan.

Later, at a press conference, Reagan had to fend off rumors that he was unhappy with Sears and Charlie Black. He took responsibility for the loss in Iowa, following Nofziger's long-distance advice. But Reagan specifically mentioned Ed Meese's name to the media as being in on the emergency strategy meeting. It was significant.

The long knives were out for Sears, less so for Black and press secretary Jim Lake. Sears had wagered that old Reagan hands could be forced out, that he could spend money incautiously, that he could keep Reagan under wraps for more than a year, and that he could hold Reagan's most fervent conservative supporters at arm's length and still win the nomination. His gamble was not paying off for the Gipper. The campaign had raised about $7 million but had little to show for it and little left to spend.[16] Reaganites "wanted the head of . . . John Sears," as the *Los Angeles Times* reported.[17] Nancy Reagan called Wirthlin to tell him she thought "Sears had to go," intimating that her husband's doubts were also growing.[18]

Lake suspected something was going down. Bob Novak asked him pointblank about a "breakup" and a "coup." Lake professed ignorance and chalked it up to the usual campaign intrigue, but he grew worried when his aide, Linda Gosden, ran into the mysterious attorney William Casey, a veteran of the Nixon administration, on an elevator accompanied by Dick Allen, Reagan's principal foreign-policy adviser.[19] Casey was also spotted going through the financial books at the L.A. offices.

Meese, Reagan's old counselor and friend from his Sacramento days who was now working on issues for the campaign, began to quietly flex his muscles. He was the only major Reaganite other than Dick Allen and Dick Wirthlin who hadn't yet been taken out by Sears. Meese went back many years with Mike Deaver, Peter Hannaford, Marty Anderson, and Nofziger. They all had special, personal relationships with Reagan as well. Deaver was in many ways a surrogate son to the Reagans. Anderson and Reagan played word games and often had deep philosophical discussions and exchanged books and articles. Hannaford was mannerly, understated, with a wry sense of humor that the Reagans enjoyed. He was also one of Reagan's favorite speechwriters. Blunt-talking, ribald, and disheveled, Nofziger was never much loved by Nancy Reagan, yet she knew how fond her husband was of Lyn and how effective he was as a political operative. He and Reagan told each other dirty jokes, and in private, Nofziger called Reagan "Ron," not "Governor" as everybody else did. Reagan, in turn, had a pet name for Franklyn Nofziger, calling him "Lynwood." Nofziger was a hero of World War II as a U.S. Army Ranger on Omaha Beach on June 6, 1944. Nazi shrapnel had carried away two fingers from his left hand. Reagan was always a sucker for war heroes.

Meese, a graduate of Yale with a law degree from Berkeley, had been in the middle of a successful career in law enforcement and gaining respect in California's conservative policy circles just as Reagan was gearing up for his first run for governor. Quiet and analytical, he knew Reagan's mind and Reagan's thinking better than anyone except Nancy Reagan and Paul Laxalt.

Increasingly distressed over both the dismissal of his friends and the faltering campaign, not to mention Reagan's sinking mood, Meese moved quietly behind the scenes. He told Reagan frankly that Sears had to be either reassigned or let go from the campaign. Otherwise, Reagan would never be president. Wirthlin and Senator Laxalt supported him in this. Tension already existed between Wirthlin and Sears, who said years later that the pollster "couldn't see a trend if it jumped on his head."[20] Laxalt had resented Sears ever since Sears had attempted to replace him with Jack Kemp as campaign chairman.

Meese met with the "Executive Committee," an expanded version of the Kitchen Cabinet that had supported and advised Reagan since the mid-1960s. Meese told the committee that if Sears remained in charge, Reagan was "doomed."[21]

When Mike Deaver was shunted aside in November, he had been given what was thought to be a meaningless job as the liaison between the campaign and the Executive Committee. But Reagan turned to his old friends for advice as the Sears controversy grew, and Deaver suddenly had supporters on the Executive Committee who thought it was time for Sears to go. A conspiracy was forming to take out Sears. Casey had a hush-hush dinner in Los Angeles with Meese and Deaver and told them about the campaign's bleak finances.[22]

Reagan's New Hampshire operation moved ahead without consulting Sears, as did independent groups all wanting to help the Gipper. Sears, the accused control freak, was losing control.

REAGAN STEPPED UP HIS rhetoric on the stump—though not his time. He said that Carter was "weak, deceitful, or a fool" for his tepid response to the Soviet invasion of Afghanistan. Then he went after Carter too hard, saying, "We are seeing the same kind of atmosphere as when Neville Chamberlain went tapping his cane on the cobblestones of Munich."[23] Later that day Reagan had to apologize to Carter for the harsh comparison to the flaccid British prime minister who had appeased the Nazis.

Once more Reagan was confronted with questions about his age. Reporters noted that he stumbled over several words in his "Neville Chamberlain" speech. He also became embroiled in a hypothetical discussion of whether he would step down as president if his health failed him. Reagan, ever polite in such settings, tried to deal with the asinine question, saying, "If that were ever a possibility, I'd be the first to recognize it, and the first to step down."[24]

Reagan did not stop taking a hard line. He denounced Carter's weakness in dealing with Iran, and called the president's proposal to restart Selective Service registration for young American men a "meaningless gesture" that would only "create a new bureaucracy."[25] Reagan opposed peacetime registration in a bow to his libertarian streak.[26] He returned to the Soviet question in a *60 Minutes* interview when he said that the Carter administration could have blockaded Cuba as a response to Soviet troops and fighter jets there. This comment, too, put him on the defensive; soon he was pleading to reporters, "I am not a warmonger."[27]

Reagan was stumbling on issues he'd owned for years—national defense and foreign policy. Foreign policy was Bush's strong suit. Fortunately for Reagan, the new front-runner was reluctant to get off his idiom of "Big Mo." Never big on ideas, Bush didn't get off the "Big Mo" in part because he didn't have anything to say, at least that he felt comfortable with.

Reagan had previously speculated that he, like Connally, might not take federal matching funds because he was philosophically opposed to taxpayer-financed elections. But in an awful show of weakness, he finally acceded to taking the first installment of $100,000 from the government because of the deplorable shape of his campaign's finances. In 1980, under FEC laws, a campaign could spend just under $17 million in the primaries, and the expenditure in each state was limited by a mind-numbingly complicated formula.[28] Reagan's campaign, under Sears, had squandered millions. Reagan told reporters that his campaign was having "cash-flow problems" and "there may have been a top echelon of executives in the campaign who have delayed taking [their salaries] because of cash flow." In fact, eight senior members of the campaign had gone off payroll in December and did not expect to begin being paid again until April. More went off the payroll in January. Lake said this was voluntary, but it was, in fact, essential. Staffers were told they would have to go without pay indefinitely.[29]

Reagan finally arrived in New Hampshire on January 28 and aimed more fiery rhetoric at Carter's foreign policy. Carter insisted that the Soviets withdraw from Afghanistan by February 20 or he would lead a world boycott of the Moscow Summer Olympics.

Carter was showing small signs of faltering. The media reported that Rosalynn Carter was becoming more involved in policy decisions in the White House, advocating drafting women, and it was later learned that she was sitting in on cabinet meetings. Ted Kennedy, however, was still not landing any punches. A Washington wag summed up how the world situation had helped the president: "Carter should deduct the Ayatollah as a campaign expense."[30]

REAGAN SWITCHED TACTICS FROM foreign policy to economics, giving speeches calling for the elimination of the federal inheritance tax, which sounded like a sop to the rich, and eliminating the minimum wage, which sounded like a sop to business.

As his campaign floundered, he decided abruptly that the GOP "cattle shows" were not such a bad thing and announced he would participate in one scheduled for South Carolina on February 28, just two days after the New Hampshire primary. But if Reagan lost again in New Hampshire, it would be a moot point. Bush accepted two invitations to debate in New Hampshire, but only if Reagan would agree to debate as well. Jim Baker, Bush's manager, said his goal was to "smoke Reagan out. We want to debate him. . . . We want him in New Hampshire."[31] Reagan was a wounded animal and the pack was on his trail.

Even though Reagan had accepted the invitation to debate in South Carolina, he waffled on any New Hampshire forum that might "divide" the Republican Party.[32] One was a League of Women Voters debate that had been scheduled for February 19 in Manchester, just seven days before the primary; all the candidates had accepted the invitation except Reagan.[33] The other debate under discussion was buried in most media reports; sponsored by the *Nashua Telegraph*, it would be for Bush and Reagan alone. The *Telegraph* had called a bluff by Jerry Carmen, Reagan's Granite State manager, who said that his man would debate Bush one-on-one. Carmen had made the challenge in order to buy time for Reagan and without asking anyone's approval.[34] But the disorganized national Reagan campaign did not respond to the *Telegraph*'s invitation. The paper's managing editor, John Stylianos, complained, "We couldn't get hold of Reagan. It's up to Reagan. Nothing has jelled."[35] For Reagan, the decision was call or fold.

Two competing power factions in the Reagan operation were at odds on the debate issue. On one side were Sears, Lake, and Black, who did not want to commit Reagan to any kind of debate in New Hampshire. Leading the other faction was Carmen, who thought that Sears and company had thoroughly botched Iowa and who knew that Reagan had a tendency to coast if he wasn't challenged. On his own, Carmen began telling the media that Reagan would debate all comers in New Hampshire. The tension would continue to mount in the short amount of time before the February 26 primary.

The whole matter of who wants to debate depends on where one stands in the polls. The conventional wisdom held that candidates or incumbents in the lead should not or would not debate, while those behind needed to change the subject and get the front-runner engaged. Bush's campaign had agreed to all debates before the stunning win in Iowa and before its own polling data showed Bush pulling out to a healthy lead in New Hampshire. Bush strategists began second-guessing their quick "yes" answers to all future joint appearances, which of course were what the other candidates wanted. Bush now wanted Reagan in a one-on-one showdown in the belief that he could finally show him to be a doddering old rigid fool. Sears wasn't so sure of either.

With the dynamics having also changed radically in the Democratic race since the late summer, Jimmy Carter flip-flopped his position on debating. When Carter was light-years behind Kennedy, he was eager to debate Teddy. Now that he was far ahead in the polls—54–36 in New Hampshire, according to a Gallup poll—Carter wanted no part of a debate.[36] Kennedy, having been run over and thrown into a ditch in Iowa, was cloyingly trying to get Carter to agree to a debate, but Carter brushed Kennedy off like some panhandler on the streets of Manchester.

Kennedy pulled off the road to reassess. Up until this point, there had been no rationale for a Kennedy bid except that he wasn't Carter; that might have sufficed but for the numerous foreign-policy crises that had exploded. In an effort to restart his campaign, Kennedy gave a barnburner speech at Georgetown University in which he chided Carter for his brand of liberalism and restated his own devotion to big-government liberalism.[37] If he was going to crash and burn, at least he wanted to go down knowing he'd said what was really on his mind.

Kennedy had finally outlined a theme for his flagging effort. Though his campaign remained a mess, deeply in debt, his speech immediately boosted his spirits and those of his few but fervent supporters.

One Irishman in the Democratic Party with the will to soldier on and stand by his principles was making a fight of it. No one knew whether the Irishman in the GOP was ready to do the same.

REAGAN WASTED MORE TIME playing defense. He lurched back toward foreign policy. His previous position on blockading Cuba, Reagan now said, was only "hypothetical." After he huddled with his foreign-policy adviser, Richard Allen, Reagan issued a statement in an attempt to clarify things. Reagan's statement said, "It's time to stop pretending that détente with the Soviet Union is still alive. . . . I say that Carter has the means at his disposal to stop" Soviet adventurism.[38] He told reporters that the blockade proposal was only one option and that he was not advocating using it—even though he thought Carter could have or should have used it. He also said he wasn't backing away from his earlier advocacy of using a blockade—even though he would not say whether he would use one if he was president.

Everybody was now thoroughly confused. Ironically, Reagan said, "We need to send the Soviet Union an unmistakable signal, one that they can understand."[39] Unfortunately, Reagan wasn't even sending his own supporters a message they could understand.

Yet another precious day trying to get back on the offense was lost. The defensive posture was especially frustrating to Reaganites given that Carter had told a group of reporters, absurdly, that the Soviets posed no military threat to the Caribbean—this despite the fact that the Soviets had been aiding Cuba for years and had begun funding the Communist government of Nicaragua. Carter had further said that he would not promise to use the U.S. military to defend the Caribbean if the Kremlin did have designs on it. Reagan called Carter's comments "incredible," but the story was lost in his own controversy.[40]

REAGAN GOT A LITTLE good news—the first in weeks—when he took six of twelve of the initial delegates selected in Arkansas, even though he had not campaigned there. Howard Baker took four Arkansas delegates. Bush surprisingly got only one delegate despite having committed serious resources to Arkansas. His aides had confidently predicted that their man would do well. It was their first real tactical mistake in an otherwise error-free campaign. Bush petulantly complained to UPI, "It's obvious to me that the Reagan and Baker people sided up against me."[41]

One delegate of the twelve remained uncommitted. This meant that John Connally had been skunked in Arkansas, even after he had spent thousands there to fete party officials. He went through yet another campaign shake-up, as man-

ager Eddie Mahe was kicked upstairs to handle "policy and strategy." If Connally
had listened to Mahe from the beginning, he might have been in better shape.

Reagan's campaign moved ahead, albeit in a desultory fashion. He made a
three-day swing that ended up in Minneapolis, but not once in that time did he
emerge from his cloistered compartment in the front of the plane to meet the
press. His flight out of Minnesota was delayed because of weather and Reagan
finally came out of seclusion, but only to stand off in the corner of the airport and
talk with some starry-eyed young staffers about Hollywood, being a lifeguard,
and growing up in the Midwest. As the "gentlemen of the press" headed for the
bar, Reagan instead reenacted a scene from an old movie to the delight of the
young Reaganites. "Mouth twisted into a grotesque half-grin, eyes out of focus, he
lurched forward, slurring his words as if drunk," one reporter recounted.[42]

A long piece in the Los Angeles Times was filled with wistful observations about
Reagan and his faltering effort—as if his campaign were all over. The feeling of
excitement in a presidential campaign, the Times reporter wrote, "does not last. . . .
At least, not on the Reagan campaign trail."[43] The Gipper's campaign was spiraling
down, as was his battered mood. In Florida, Reagan dejectedly told a crowd, "Way
down deep inside me . . . I believe one of my advantages is that I'm not running for
reelection . . . to hell whether there's a second term."[44] The room was filled with
embarrassed silence.

One saddened supporter at the event said, "I just wish he wouldn't stand
there and tell us he might drop dead."[45]

The bastards had finally gotten to Reagan.

Even he now seemed resigned to the prospects of his advancing years. He'd
publicly laughed the issue off, tossed off jokes, released medical reports, and
looked and acted to all like a man years younger. But his enemies wouldn't let it
go, chewing on Reagan's age like a mongrel dog on a soup bone. "Reagan dyes his
hair," "Reagan uses makeup," "Reagan had a facelift" (curious because his enemies
also went out of their way to point out his wrinkles), "Reagan is hard of hearing"—all the lies and mean-spirited venom, emanating from his own party, had
undermined the Gipper.

The corrupt bargain between some in the media and Republican Reagan-
haters had finally taken its toll. The whispering that had started two years earlier in
the highest echelons of the Republican Party—over lunches, drinks, golf, tennis,
and squash at their country clubs—was that the only way to stop Reagan was to
destroy Reagan. They could not destroy Reagan's ideas or character but they could
destroy Reagan the man. Bush aide Dave Keene, referring to the Gipper, brusquely
told Time magazine, "He is a great old dog, but he won't hunt this year."[46]

Reagan's enemies had tried the "he's too conservative" gambit but it hadn't taken hold. They had tried the "lightweight actor" bit but that hadn't worked either. In both cases, Reagan could not be typecast, because what people saw and heard from Reagan did not match the charges they heard from the GOP establishment. This was no "Bircher." This was not a "dangerous" man. Listening to those speeches and commentaries, and reading those columns, they recognized a man who quoted Alexander Hamilton, Cicero, Churchill, and Thomas Paine. This was no lightweight. This was a scholarly, thoughtful, and solicitous man.

But his age—ah, now there was the opening for the Washington insiders to obliterate Reagan once and for all.

Going after Reagan's age—especially since Sears had pulled Reagan back from any real campaigning over the past year—played right into their rumor-mongering game. "See, Reagan is back at the ranch, relaxing," they would say. "If Reagan were still alive . . . ," they'd say to sniggers and titters. "Reagan skipped all the debates because they were past his bedtime." "Reagan doesn't jog like Bush." "Reagan is lazy." The slurs and innuendos took hold, like a virus, in the media and in Republican circles throughout 1979 and into 1980.

The Reagan campaign's poor organization and failures to prepare the candidate properly fed the ugly talk. As the *L.A. Times* noted, Sears and other Reagan advisers had been accused of "deliberately shielding their candidate from close public scrutiny for fear, as one reporter put it, 'that he'll stick his foot in his mouth with some outrageous remark, probably about foreign policy, and scare people half to death.'"[47] But Sears wasn't being overprotective of Reagan now; having gone AWOL after Iowa, he was being underprotective. On a rare campaign appearance in New Hampshire, Reagan was stressing foreign policy and was embarrassed to be caught flatfooted when reporters asked him about an important development in the Iranian hostage crisis. No one in his campaign had bothered to tell him that the Canadian government had secreted six Americans out of Tehran.[48]

Sears, the venerable poker player, had had his pants taken off by the whist-playing Republicans and he didn't even know it. The campaign was out of money, out of morale, and out of steam because Reagan had been counseled to go against his own instincts by people who professed to know more about the American people and politics than he did. Reagan—who had crisscrossed the length and breadth of America for more than thirty years, who had spoken to millions and had met tens of thousands, who treated even the most common dirt farmer as if he were royalty—was listening to people whose view of America rarely extended beyond a barstool in Washington, D.C.

Reagan had suffered many indignities in his career—he had endured lies, gone though a divorce he didn't want, lost much of his movie career to World War II, lost his General Electric career to politics, lost the Republican presidential nomination in 1968 and 1976—but this was the worst it had ever been for him. The nomination had been within his grasp, and it was now slipping through his fingers. Washington insiders were proclaiming Reagan to be the William Jennings Bryan of the GOP, just another three-time loser. The country-clubbers of the GOP made fun of Reagan's movie career. Clinking wine glasses, they were toasting, "Bedtime for Bonzo and Reagan!"

David Prosperi, one of Reagan's young aides, suggested that at a campaign stop, a local band not play "I Left My Heart in San Francisco" but instead play the Bee Gees song "Stayin' Alive."[49] Black humor was running rampant in Reagan's waning operation.

All that was left was for Reagan to go through one more humiliating episode in New Hampshire, and then pack his bags and go back to his ranch in Santa Barbara.

Ronald Reagan was on the brink of political oblivion.

New Hampshire was an anomaly among New England states. Far more conservative, libertarian, quirky, and blue-collared than their neighbors, New Hampshirites generally had more affinity for the Reagan model than for the Bush model. But Bush had been ceaselessly campaigning in the state, sending notes, going hither and yon, while Reagan had been absent, it seemed, for years. The "asterisk" of American politics was on the verge of vanquishing the leader of American conservatism.

A new Boston Globe poll had Bush's lead in New Hampshire growing over Reagan, 45 to 36 percent.[50] Reagan had fallen well below the 49 percent he'd taken in 1976.[51] Dick Wirthlin's polling in New Hampshire had it even worse for Reagan. According to Carmen, Reagan had fallen 21 points behind Bush.[52] Bush's polling in August 1979 had shown Reagan with a commanding 53 percent of the primary field. That was all gone now.[53]

Bush moved in for the kill. At a town hall meeting in Lebanon, New Hampshire, a man in the audience asked, "Do you think 69 years old is too old to be president of the United States?" Bush cleverly answered, "Let the voters make that determination," and then dropped his anvil on Reagan, saying, "I am fit. I feel 35. I am 55."[54]

Reporters on the campaign plane got into a competition to see who could make the most vicious jokes at Reagan's expense.[55] One said Reagan's brain would be the most valuable for a transplant because it had never been used. When Reagan was tardy one morning, a network reporter got approving laughter by saying, "They're still rubbing life into his legs." Among themselves, they wondered which other campaign they would be assigned to cover once Reagan was driven out of the race.[56]

Reagan was sinking not only in New Hampshire but across the country. Just weeks earlier he had held a lead of 26 points over Bush among Republicans nationwide, but now an ABC News–Harris poll showed Reagan and Bush tied at 27 percent apiece.[57] Bush was handily ahead among moderate and liberal Republicans. Reagan led among conservative Republicans by only a 5–3 ratio.[58]

Worse for Reagan, Bush was ahead by 10 points in the East. Sears had obsessed about the East for Reagan since 1976, but it had come to naught.[59] And now the primaries in Vermont, Connecticut, and Massachusetts were looming soon after the New Hampshire vote. Each of these states was believed to be more hospitable to the moderate Bush, a former New Englander, than the conservative Reagan, a westerner. "With his shaggy good looks, Yale diploma and Ivy League wardrobe that give him the aura of an aging preppie," the *Nashua Telegraph* noted, "Bush feels at home in New England."[60]

Where Reagan was once confident of sweeping the southern GOP primaries, he was now talking guardedly about his chances there, saying, "I'm sure going to try."[61] Bush's pollster, Bob Teeter, ran the numbers in Florida and his man had vaulted to a 4-point lead there over Reagan, 35–31 percent, in the span of just a few days.[62] Among those Sunshine State Republicans who expressed a second choice, Bush was even stronger, while Reagan's support was soft. "This confirms Bush can increase his vote further in Florida," Teeter wrote. Potentially, Bush could defeat Reagan in Florida by a 2–1 margin, according to Teeter.[63]

It looked to everybody like it was all over but the shouting.

Reagan's campaign had collapsed.

8

DESCENT INTO THE MAELSTROM

"Reagan is a loser."

Ronald Reagan finally got angry.

Reagan was always at his best, most resolute, and toughest when he was angry. He hated losing. Losing Iowa, losing his national issues to the other candidates, and losing his old aides were more than he could stand. The lies and personal attacks by his political enemies only sharpened his anger. Hugh Gregg, Bush's New Hampshire coordinator, said, "I'll tell you, when Reagan gets tired, he's no good."[1]

The ridicule from some in the media was also contributing to Reagan's wrath. Political columnists Jack Germond and Jules Witcover described their poker buddy John Sears, the presumed puppet master, as "the man whose lips move when Ronald Reagan talks."[2]

Reagan furiously put his foot down. He impatiently told Sears that he would "campaign the way I like to campaign." That meant going to every corner of New Hampshire and not leaving the weekend before the vote, as he'd done in 1976.[3] It also meant speaking his mind and articulating his concerns to the American people, especially on the Soviet threat.

The Californian unveiled the "Reagan Doctrine," which was a complete refutation of the bipartisan Cold War containment and détente policies embraced by the intellectual classes of the previous four decades.[4] The Soviets were marching across the globe, with the acquiescence of much of the West. "Not so fast," said Reagan. His approach was, in essence, "What's ours is ours and what's yours is negotiable. Let's debate your ill-gotten territories." The elites hated it but the American people loved it. Reagan had found his voice.

Peter Hannaford said that Reagan's taking control of the campaign "was the beginning of the end for Sears."[5] Sears "was almost sulking . . . on the bus," remembered Ed Meese.[6] Poker-faced, Sears told the media, "It remains to be seen whether I'm great or a fool."[7] Reaganites already had an answer for Sears's self-query, but they were delighted that Reagan was finally taking control of his own destiny. Reagan wrote in confidence to one supporter, "I never thought the nomination was a sure thing [and] I don't think so now, but I'm going to fight like h—l."[8]

Only twenty-two delegates were at stake in New Hampshire, but much more was involved for Reagan. If he lost to George Bush in New Hampshire, his campaign would be over. Forever. There was no tomorrow. This was it for the Gipper.

Just a few days earlier, all the Reagan regional political directors had gathered together in secret to come to some consensus about the campaign. At this point, they were all temporarily off the payroll. There was no money to pay them. Together, they decided that the "handlers"—Sears chiefly—were getting in the way. Ernie Angelo, now running Texas, was deputized to go see Reagan and deliver their message. Angelo did in private, and though Reagan said little, the regional director could tell he was taking it in and was deeply troubled about his campaign.[9]

In late January Sears was summoned to Washington to face thirty of Reagan's congressional supporters, led by Congressman Tom Evans of Delaware. But Sears ducked the meeting at the last minute and instead sent Charlie Black. The furious Reaganites peeled Black's skin off and told him that the Reagan campaign manager should stop worrying about his own goddamn press and start worrying about Reagan's.[10] Black barely escaped.

Reagan and Sears were hardly speaking to each other now. When they did talk, Reagan complained, Sears "didn't look you in the eye, he looked you in the tie."

Late on a plane trip, Reagan was standing in the aisle, twirling his glasses at one o'clock in the morning while most of the press corps were sleeping off their evening booze session after filing their stories. Reagan joked aloud—to see whether anyone was paying attention—that maybe he needed a new campaign manager.[11] In fact, Reagan was not joking, but none of the slumbering and anesthetized journalists stirred.

NEW HAMPSHIRE WAS TYPICALLY cold, but the February chill was no match for the frosty relations between Jerry Carmen and John Sears. Carmen rarely spoke to the national office of Reagan for President anymore, except to tell them to stay out of his state or to schedule more days in New Hampshire for the Gipper to press the flesh. "From now on we are going to see the kind of campaign I have been wanting," he told the Associated Press.[12] Carmen, a chain smoker, was going through four packs a day of filterless Camels. The fingers on his right two fingers had been stained a sickly yellow.[13] He was locking horns almost daily with Reagan aide Helene Von Damm over money and the candidate's schedule. "He wanted all of Reagan's time," she lamented.[14] Carmen was also butting heads over all manner of things with Reagan's advance men, including the redoubtable Jim Hooley and Rick Ahearn. (The two burly Irishmen proved to be inventive as well as formidable. Off salary like the rest of the campaign, Hooley and Ahearn scavenged for food at receptions; after one poorly attended event, they gladly appropriated boxes of sad-looking roast beef sandwiches and lived off them for days.)[15]

Carmen sent word that Reagan must campaign much more than originally planned in New Hampshire or he would lose. Period. In the 1978 New Hampshire Senate campaign the conservative underdog, Gordon Humphrey, had shown the power of advertising on Boston television stations, which reached the populous regions of the southern half of the state, when he scored the biggest upset of the year over incumbent Democrat Tom McIntyre. But Reagan's campaign, nearly broke, had precious few dollars for the expensive Boston market. The cost to air a sixty-second prime-time commercial in Boston had gone up from $4,800 in 1976 to $7,400 in 1980.[16] If Reagan hoped to have any chance, he'd have to engage in the retail campaigning that traditionally had been the hallmark of the New Hampshire primary.

Television airtime wasn't the only major cost taxing the cash-strapped Reagan operation. Campaigns were getting more and more expensive, especially with double-digit inflation. The cost of brochures had doubled, as had the cost of a per-person interview by a pollster, from $8 to $16. A ninety-six-passenger Boeing jet, for a four-day charter, cost $37,500 in 1976, but by 1980, that same plane for the same amount of time cost more than $70,000. Consulting fees, natch, also went up. In 1976, Charlie Black was making $1,500 per month working for Reagan; in 1980, he was making $2,500.[17] However, if one calculated the untold hours staffers like Black put in, their take-home pay was less than that of a garbage collector. Sometimes these weary political operatives felt they were no different from trash men, cleaning up after their candidates.

Along with the growth in the consulting community, so too had the Secret Service grown in size, budget, and functions. In 1963, the "Service" had 389 agents and an annual budget of around $5.5 million. By 1980, there were 1,552 agents and a hefty budget of $157 million.[18] After the assassinations of President

Kennedy and Robert Kennedy, Congress greatly expanded the role of the Service to include protective details for, besides presidents and vice presidents, their spouses and children, former presidents—and viable presidential aspirants. This meant that Ted Kennedy was assigned a detail, as were Reagan, Phil Crane, John Connally, and George Bush; the Service deemed them viable candidates because of the amounts they had raised.

The Secret Service agents had to guard against becoming indifferent to someone who treated them badly, like Jimmy Carter. That was not a problem for Reagan's detail, who adored Reagan and looked forward to working with him. Sometimes, though, they were too obsessive in keeping supporters away from Reagan, and complaints were heard. Reagan had looked too imperial to Iowa Republicans; for that reason Bush had wisely refused the protective contingent before the Iowa caucuses.

Carter's code name was sometimes "Lock Master," sometimes "Deacon." Mrs. Carter's was sometimes "Lotus Petal," sometimes "Steel Magnolia." Kennedy's was "Sunburn." Bush's was "Sheepskin" and Mrs. Bush's was "Snowbank." The then hard-drinking "George Bush Jr.," as the Secret Service had him erroneously listed, was "Tumbler." Reagan's was "Rawhide" and Nancy's was "Rainbow."[19] The Reagans were so fond of their code names that they asked the Service to break precedent and keep them for the entire campaign, and later his presidency.[20]

Ted Kennedy's protective detail was the largest and most bureaucratic. He had three teams working to guard him, one that worked in advance of each stop, a second that traveled with him, and a third whose job it was to work with the local law-enforcement officials to block roads and traffic so Kennedy's motorcade could barrel through red lights and stop signs. It didn't win him a lot of votes, but these agents were doing their utmost to ensure that Kennedy was not lost on their watch. Because of the Service's zealousness, agents often ran roughshod over state and local law-enforcement officials. It was not unusual for fistfights to break out. Still, with thousands of nuts out there and more than four hundred people in the active files of the Service—people the agency believed were truly capable of killing a president or a candidate—diplomacy often took a backseat.[21]

Kennedy also traveled with a full-time doctor and nurse, skilled in trauma medicine . . . especially for gunshot wounds.[22]

Even as campaign costs were skyrocketing, new federal regulations imposed onerous spending limits on candidates. The sweeping reforms after the excesses of the 1972 Nixon campaign had resulted in the creation of the FEC. Reagan's campaign was bumping its head against the spending limit in New Hampshire, which was just under $300,000.[23] To stave off the FEC dogs, Reagan was staying at the

Sheraton–Rolling Hills Hotel Andover, just across the state line. Whenever possible, expenditures were being allocated against the Massachusett's FEC limits. Like many well-intentioned reforms, the post-Watergate campaign-finance laws spawned a host of unintended consequences that actually made regulation more difficult. Notably, the number of political action committees (PACs) had quadrupled since Nixon's day, because they provided a handy outlet to exceed proscribed limits.

HOWARD BAKER'S CAMPAIGN LIMPED into New Hampshire. Oddly, Iowa governor Robert Ray endorsed Baker *after* the caucuses, doing Baker absolutely no good in New Hampshire. Vermont governor Richard Snelling also endorsed Baker, but the support of this moderate-to-liberal Republican would prove of little help in New Hampshire.[24] Baker was now seen as a spoiler for Bush, since they were both competing for the same moderate votes.

Phil Crane was going after Reagan in New Hampshire, hoping, as one news report said, to feed "off Reagan's carcass."[25] But Crane had taken only 7 percent in Iowa, and was reduced to saying he'd be happy with a fourth-place finish in New Hampshire.

John Connally was not actively campaigning in New Hampshire and his drive for the White House had gone on life support. His "friends" in corporate America were turning to George Bush, as he looked to be a better bet against Reagan and Carter than Connally. *Dun's Review* surveyed 225 business executives and Bush was their overwhelming choice.[26] Connally was forced to borrow $500,000 because his campaign had spent lavishly, including, so far, more than $2.6 million just on the payroll. Over half the campaign staff of 140 was laid off and Big John replaced Eddie Mahe with Charles Keating. Connally may have won the 1980 prize for insensitivity when he referred to his former hardworking but now laid-off staff as "short-term volunteer help."[27]

Reagan's organization in New Hampshire was in good hands. Carmen's efforts had been hampered for the past year, as he rarely had a candidate on hand to tell his story to the voters. But now that Reagan had abandoned Sears's plan for limited campaigning in New Hampshire, Carmen would have the Gipper for sixteen full days.

Reagan hit the road hard in New Hampshire on February 5. He spoke at ten events that day, campaigning until almost midnight the day before his sixty-ninth birthday, or as he referred to it, the "thirtieth anniversary of my thirty-ninth birthday."[28] At nearly every stop, Reagan was serenaded with "Happy Birthday." Mrs. Reagan served him cake at each stop and Reagan, with his sweet tooth, ate with relish. The last cake of the day fortunately had only three candles on it for

Reagan to blow out. He joked that you know you are too old to be president "when your knees buckle and your belt won't."[29]

Despite the exhausting schedule, being back out on the stump revived Reagan. "His ready smile and good color made him seem all the more energetic and youthful in the crisp February air," remembered Peter Hannaford.[30] Reagan, Ed Meese later recalled, "campaigned in fire halls . . . in coffee shops, church basements, wherever they got a few people together."[31] Reagan, the old jock, was working out the kinks, finding his form again.

The hole Reagan had dug himself was deep, though. When *U.S. News & World Report* surveyed 475 members of the Republican National Committee and the state parties, it showed that they favored Bush over Reagan and thought the best nominee for the GOP would be a "philosophical moderate."[32] One Republican state chairman said that Reagan's intellect was "thinner than spit on a slate rock."[33] According to a Newsweek survey, in just ten days Bush's "favorable" rating among Republicans had jumped from 20 percent to an amazing 62 percent nationally.[34]

In New Hampshire, Bush was getting large crowds and was outspending his opponent.[35] Some of Bush's in-state supporters had an atrocious opinion of Reagan. The twenty-six-year-old mayor of Franklin, Stuart Trachy, said bluntly, "Reagan is a loser."[36] Bush was unfazed when asked about the Reagan campaign's claim that the Gipper "would take off the gloves when he got to New Hampshire and put Bush in his place." He replied, "Hooray! Reagan didn't even know I existed. Four or five weeks ago, I wasn't in the race as far as he was concerned."[37]

In a clear sign that Reagan was breaking from John Sears's reins, the Gipper admitted that he had made a mistake in refusing to debate in Iowa, and announced that he would attend all debates in New Hampshire. The old proverb was that "in poker, the losers yell 'deal,'" and the add-on in politics was, "in campaigns, they yell 'debate.'" Reagan was now yelling for a debate because he was losing the GOP nomination to the hard-charging Bush.[38]

Carmen, meanwhile, continued his efforts to arrange a one-on-one debate between Reagan and Bush—again without ever asking anybody at Reagan Central for permission.[39] "I am throwing the gauntlet down for the Bush people," the aggressive little businessman told the Associated Press. "If they will agree to a two-man debate, we will try to work out the details."[40] Suddenly Bush, who had wanted to get Reagan in a one-on-one debate, appeared to waffle. As the frontrunner he had more to lose in such an environment. Better to hide among the other candidates and sit on a lead.

Carmen was unrelenting. He told reporters in early February, "The one-on-one suggestion came from us and not the Bush campaign. We will meet George

Bush as soon as the details can be worked out and the times can be handled."⁴¹ The *Nashua Telegraph* was already busily arranging for the showdown between Governor Reagan and Ambassador Bush. The idea was for a ninety-minute debate, with forty-five minutes for questioning by reporters and forty-five minutes for questioning by a live audience.⁴²

Reagan swung hard at Bush. When someone asked about Bush's foreign-policy experience, Reagan replied, rapid-fire, "George Bush's experience in foreign policy was one brief term as ambassador to the U.N., special representative to mainland China and director of the CIA—which I don't think is exactly an education in foreign policy—in good foreign policy."⁴³

The voters began to learn more about the Reaganites' disenchantment with John Sears, who had long enjoyed favorable media coverage. Carmen, William Loeb, Senator Humphrey, and Paul Laxalt all went public against the beleaguered manager. In a *Manchester Union-Leader* editorial, Loeb acidly penned that Reagan had been "Searscumsized," and urged Reagan to fire the campaign manager: "The road to political victory is not the one being paved by Sears."⁴⁴ Laxalt said that Reagan was being "constrained, inhibited, packaged."⁴⁵ Humphrey was measured but firm, noting that Reagan had unaggressively stumped in Iowa and had paid dearly for turning all decisions over to Sears.

To make matters worse for Reagan, he had to contend once more with Gerald Ford. The former president made it known that he preferred Baker or Bush over Reagan, who Ford said was too conservative to win the presidency. Ford even made noises—yet again—about getting into the race. Reagan dared Ford, saying said he should "pack his long johns and come out on the campaign trail."⁴⁶

Bush was having his own problems, but of a different sort. Reagan was starting to get specific on the stump, and all of Bush's high command, from Jim Baker on down, knew that Bush had to do the same, in order to move from "George Who?" to "George What?" "The era of George Bush and the handshaking, cheerful politician is ended," Dave Keene told the *New York Times*. "The focus now . . . should be on George Bush and what he says."⁴⁷ Trouble was, somebody forgot to tell Bush.

Bush was being ridiculously cautious. A reporter innocently asked Bush, who often enjoyed a vodka martini at the end of the day, whether he favored a ban on the Russian vodka Stolichnaya. Bush acted as if "he had been thrown the world's hottest potato" as he wondered if it was bottled in the United States and how many people were employed.⁴⁸ When a journalist asked him whether he was a conservative, Bush gave a long and disjointed nonanswer when a simple "yes" would have served him better.

Bush also seemed a bit dazed on the hustings. His seemingly strong pronouncements of the past year melted away into mushy moderate Republicanism.
Perhaps from exhaustion, perhaps from the scrutiny, a "goofy side" came out.[49] He
kept telling everybody, "I'm up for the '80s." Indeed, it was his campaign slogan
for a time and was as vapid as "Big Mo."[50] "Up for the '80s" sounded to some like
a slogan for a new soda.

But Bush resisted the pressure of liberal Republicans to wage a "crusade
against Ronald Reagan and the Right." He refused not because he had any great
love for Reagan but because he was not sure it would work.[51]

It didn't help Bush that his press secretary, Pete Teeley, deprived the candidate of important opportunities to receive briefings from policy staffers. The
turf-conscious Teeley insisted that he, not any policy advisers, sit next to Bush on
the campaign plane. Even when a key adviser, Stef Halper, was summoned from
Washington to brief the candidate, Teeley wouldn't let him sit next to Bush. Teeley and Halper ended up in an obscenity-laced argument on a tarmac, which made
its way into a *Washington Post* story. Teeley "was a pain in the ass," Halper bluntly
said years later.[52] Halper was not alone in this opinion.

New Hampshire Republicans would eventually learn that Bush was plainly
and simply more moderate on almost everything than Reagan, with the possible
exception of homosexuality. Reagan took a distinctly libertarian approach, and
while Bush was tolerant, he also said the behavior was not "normal."[53] Neither
Reagan nor Bush—nor any candidate, for that matter—attended a forum held
by homosexuals in New Hampshire. Only a few candidates, including President
Carter, sent representatives to the forum. As a sign of the times, organizers asked
photographers not to take pictures of those in one section, as they were closeted
gays and feared "reprisals."[54]

Bush continued to highlight his jogging for the benefit of television cameras.
Each morning, in the frosty winter of New Hampshire, he was seen pounding
the pavement. Yet he was still saying little. The media were growing antsy, in
no small part because Teeley had not anticipated their increased demands on the
front-runner. Phones were often not available for reporters to call in their stories,
and the media were loaded onto an ancient prop plane, a Fairchild, which seated
only twenty and lumbered along at just a bit over 200 miles per hour . . . if there
was a good tailwind and the reporters got out and pushed.

Many in the media and Republican circles were taking a closer look at Bush,
and they weren't sure about what they were seeing. The résumé was good; he was
a war hero, and clearly a good husband and family man, but what did Bush really
stand for? New Hampshire's GOP voters wanted to know.

ON FEBRUARY 2, AS most attention was focusing on New Hampshire, ABC News revealed that the FBI had run a major sting operation, code-named "Abscam," in which agents posing as Arab businessmen dangled suitcases full of cash under the noses of congressmen and senators. The undercover agents invited government officials to a rented house in Washington where they offered the politicians money in exchange for their doing favors for a supposed Arab sheikh (who in fact had been made up). A secret camera captured virtually all of the targeted politicians—mostly Democrats—diving for the moolah without a moment's hesitation. Taking a bribe seemed the most natural thing in the world to them, even though it was of course against the law. One member of Congress and his aide got into a fight over the cash even before they left the room. In another case, a congressman was seen greedily stuffing the cash into the pockets of his suit.[55]

The only targeted politician who did not take the money was Senator Larry Pressler, Republican of South Dakota. Congressman John Murtha, Democrat of Pennsylvania, slipped the noose when he pulled back at the last instant and didn't take the proffered bribe, but he invited the would-be briber to stay in touch and suggested they could do business in the future.[56]

In the "Washington is a small town" category, the house that the FBI rented for its sting operation was owned by Lee Lescaze, a reporter for the *Washington Post*—though Lescaze didn't know who his tenants were until the story broke in his own paper.[57]

This would not be the last time that Abscam came up in the 1980 elections.

VOTERS WERE ONCE AGAIN scratching their heads over President Carter. First, the White House leaked that Carter prayed daily for the Ayatollah Khomeini.[58] Most Americans would have preferred that he bomb the ayatollah back into the Stone Age. Carter also let it be known that his administration would push for women to register for a military draft, though they would be in noncombat operations.

Reagan had always opposed a peacetime draft for America, and he definitely opposed the drafting of women into the military. "I wouldn't want to belong to a society that would put its women in trenches with men," he said in criticizing President Carter's plan.[59] Reagan instead stated his support for an increased military reserve and for greater benefits for American fighting men, many of whom were living hand to mouth, many on food stamps.

Favoring or perhaps following Reagan, the American people were demonstrating a significant rise in resolve. By large majorities—67 percent and 64 percent, respectively—they favored sending American troops to Europe to repel a Soviet invasion there and to the Middle East if the Kremlin sent forces into those countries. Moreover, 73 percent wanted a draft, 86 percent favored a grain embargo of the Soviets, and 66 percent supported boycotting the Moscow Summer Olympics.[60] Reagan had a novel idea on the Summer Olympics. Rather than subjecting them to political shenanigans by the host countries, his commonsense idea was, we should simply hold them every four years in Greece, where they had begun centuries before.

As Reagan tried to gain traction in New Hampshire with his more forceful campaigning, he encountered problems over the issues of taxes and federalism—the same matters over which he'd stumbled in New Hampshire four years earlier. New Hampshire famously had no state income tax and no state sales tax, and the *Concord Monitor* reported that Reagan in an exchange with a voter had called for the imposition of state income or sales taxes. It seemed Reagan had touched the third rail in the Granite State.

But Carmen immediately disputed the newspaper's account. Again without any help from the national HQ, the belligerent Carmen attacked the "liberal media" and issued statements jumping all over the story as it had appeared in the *Concord Monitor*. He was not going to let the issue become a millstone around Reagan's neck the way it had in 1976. William Loeb joined the effort, editorializing under the headline "Dirty, Dirty, Dirty!" that the charge against Reagan was a "14-Carat unadulterated pure lie."[61]

In fact, the *Concord Monitor* was essentially correct about what Reagan said. The candidate had told a New Hampshire voter about a hypothetical "broad-based" tax. The paper had a tape of the conversation. Carmen said he had a different tape of the conversation and promised to give the newspaper a copy of his transcription of the exchange as soon as he found the tape, which, he claimed, had been "misplaced."[62] Loeb, Carmen, and Reagan eventually pounded the story into the ground and moved on, but once again, precious time had been lost playing defense.

HOLLYWOOD'S BIG AND LITTLE celebrities hit the road for their favorite candidates. Cheryl Ladd of *Charlie's Angels* fame stumped for Carter, and Lauren Bacall campaigned for Kennedy. Reagan had an advantage here, since many old celebrities were old friends, including Ray Bolger, Pat Boone, Jimmy Stewart, Gloria Swanson, Jimmy Cagney, and Loretta Young.[63] Michael Landon was one of the younger Reagan supporters, as was rock star Alice Cooper.

Muhammad Ali supported Carter but Reagan counterpunched with Joe Louis. Others from Hollywood days who did not like either Reagan or his politics signed on with Kennedy, such as Gene Kelly, Warren Beatty, Bette Davis, and

Angie Dickinson. Carter, because of his southern roots, could count on country-and-western singers like Johnny Cash, Willie Nelson, and Tom T. Hall. Howard Baker of Tennessee had his share of these folks, including Johnny Russell, who had crooned "Rednecks, White Socks, and Blue Ribbon Beer."[64]

Reagan had Marty Robbins, Mel Tillis, and the great Merle Haggard. Jerry Brown had Linda Ronstadt, but his campaign was no good, no good, baby, no good.[65] Reagan's celebrity coordinator was the very young and very smooth Morgan Mason, the son of actor James Mason. Landon and Boone had already cut television spots for the Gipper. Boone had been a Reagan delegate four years earlier in Kansas City.[66]

Celebrities were becoming more and more involved in politics, especially their favorite causes. Robert Redford, on the day of the new Congress in January 1979, had visited his senator, Orrin Hatch, to talk about environmentalism. "Who may I ask is calling?" the nervous young receptionist said to one of the most famous men in the world and Redford deadpanned, "Paul Newman."

The celebs were also very high-maintenance. A young animated aide to Senator Humphrey, Eileen Doherty, was detailed to the New York office of the Reagan campaign to handle a very old and very demanding Gloria Swanson, who wanted Doherty to escort her to all events for Reagan. Swanson treated everybody like dirt, including Doherty for a time, but she later warmed up, regaling the young woman with sordid tales about her torrid affair with Joseph P. Kennedy.[67]

Reagan's celluloid career was years behind him . . . or so he thought. In Traverse City, Michigan, a tiny television station aired *Hellcats of the Navy*, a Reagan film memorable only because it was the first and only movie he and Nancy appeared in together. But the film did gain the attention of the Baker campaign, which filed a complaint with the Federal Communications Commission, charging that its airing violated "equal-time" provisions. The station, WGTU, agreed to give Baker an equal amount of time . . . in late March.[68]

On the road in New Hampshire, voters saw Reagan up close and they mostly liked what they both saw and heard. Fourteen-year-old Mary Ricci said, "I think he's kind of old for the job of president, but when you see him he looks like he can still do it." Another attendee, Peggy Weldon, gave voice to the other end of the age spectrum. "He looks great, doesn't he?" she said. She thought sixty-nine was a good age to be president: "You don't know anything about life 'til you hit fifty anyway."[69]

Just nine days before the New Hampshire primary, Reagan woke up early on a Sunday morning for fourteen hours of heavy-duty campaigning. Nearly ten inches of snow had fallen the previous day, but now the sky was blue and the air was crisp and clear. Bleary-eyed and hungover reporters crawled out of their warm beds to accompany Reagan. Reagan was crisp and clear himself. He shook hundreds of hands that day and at Wolfeboro told listeners how he refused to fill in that part of the government's census that asked how many bathrooms he had because it "was none of their business." He also joked that Nancy, who was with him, would not be attending cabinet meetings, a jab at Carter. Reagan was in fighting form.[70]

Bush's campaign was beginning to make tactical errors. In addition to not elaborating on what he stood for, he was also trumpeting the endorsements of moderate and liberal Republicans, such as Elliot Richardson and Henry Cabot Lodge, two scions of the Massachusetts liberal Republican establishment, and William Ruckelshaus, a prominent moderate Republican from the Midwest who became famous for being fired by Richard Nixon. Press secretary Teeley told reporters "we should be somewhere in the middle" between Reagan and John Anderson.[71] The Bush campaign completely misunderstood the dynamics of Republican politics in 1980. The GOP had swung wildly away from the progressive, pro-government Republicanism of its past. That fight had been won and it was the populist conservatives who ruled. The back door to the hunting club, not the front door to the country club, was now the main way into the Republican Party. Richardson, Lodge, and others were as out of place in the new GOP as George Wallace at an NAACP convention.

The cultural rivalries between the Bushies and the Reaganites led to a nasty, out-in-the-open fight in New Hampshire. Carmen picked the fight in an attempt to fire up the conservative base. He blasted the Bush effort for its "old school tie and inherited influence against the working middle-class Americans. . . . We're really running against the preppy . . . establishment."[72] Carmen and his Reaganites were convinced that the Bushies made fun of them behind their backs while meeting at "the club" for cocktails and cards. Loeb described Bush as a "clean-fingernail Republican" in his *Manchester Union-Leader*.[73]

Though Reagan was finally going all-out on the campaign trail and the Bush operation was now committing errors, the national media were convinced that Reagan's efforts would be "too little, too late," as ABC put it in one report.[74] After all, the New Hampshire vote was fast approaching and Bush remained well ahead. The Vermont, Connecticut, and Massachusetts primaries and the Maine caucuses were coming up as well, and Bush was poised to sweep all of them. And why not? He was born in one of the states and grew up in another, and his family owned a summer home in a third.

AS THE NEW HAMPSHIRE vote neared, Ted Kennedy's standing among Democrats was nosediving. Carter was now favored by a 3–1 margin nationally by his party.[75]

Kennedy was desperately trying to shake the Chappaquiddick can tied to his tail, telling voters to consider other "traumas" in his life as a way of taking the full measure of the man: "The loss of two brothers under very traumatic circumstances. A son who has experienced cancer and whose life I thought was going to be lost and a sister who was lost in a plane crash."[76] Kennedy was letting his morbid Irish show, which he very rarely did. Democratic voters were unmoved. The NRA was also unmoved, as it unveiled a campaign against Kennedy that was themed, "If Kennedy wins, you lose."[77]

On February 10 Kennedy got off the mat in Maine. Kinda. Though he didn't win, he beat expectations, losing by "only" 6 points to Carter, 45–39 percent.[78] Carter was still sticking to the White House, promising not to campaign until the hostages were released. The ploy was still working. Political cartoonist Jeff Mac-Nelly depicted two New England farmers walking from the barn to the house on a cold and snowy evening with one saying to the other, "Sure I voted for Carter. I'm for any politician who's smart enough to stay outta my sight."[79]

The Democrats' event in Maine was a one-day affair, but the Republican process was strung out over three months. Bush had started the ball rolling by winning the straw poll at the GOP state convention, which initiated the nightmarish and endless meetings by the dour Mainiacs.[80] They still had another month to go, but Bush was leading Reagan narrowly.

Bush showed continued strength when he came in a surprisingly close second in a Mississippi straw poll. Most had thought that Connally would come in first or second in the poll of more than a thousand Republicans at a GOP dinner. He had worked the state hard; Bush, not at all. But in fact Connally came in third, with 26 percent of the vote; Reagan won with 37 percent, and Bush finished in a strong second with 29 percent.[81] Iowa was continuing to pay dividends for Brahmin Bush.

The Winter Olympics in Lake Placid, New York, kicked off February 13. America was expected to be competitive in several sports, but certainly not hockey. The Soviets were heavily favored to win the gold again, as they had done every four years since 1964. The Americans hadn't been in a hockey medal round since 1960.

GEORGE BUSH GAVE A speech in Connecticut in which he promised "two guaranteed decades of peace" if he was elected president.[82] He was speaking of world peace, not political peace, because he and Reagan and the other candidates were about to explode into full-scale warfare.

The spark was the planned two-man debate sponsored by the *Nashua Telegraph*. All three parties—the *Telegraph*, Bush, and Reagan—had more or less agreed to the debate, and it was scheduled for February 23, just three days before the primary. The excluded candidates and their supporters were livid. Bob Dole and then Howard Baker announced that they would pursue legal challenges to the newspaper-sponsored debate as an illegal corporate contribution to the Bush and Reagan campaigns.[83] The government watchdog group Common Cause also protested the debate. Jon Breen, the paper's executive editor, pooh-poohed the complaints. He said that no one had seemed to care about the debate until Reagan and Bush both agreed to it, and that it would now be "logistically impossible" to include the others.[84]

The Gipper was aware of the stakes and now considered the one-on-one debate with Bush to be "necessary."[85] Reagan needed to draw distinctions between himself and Bush on several social and cultural issues, including gun control, abortion, welfare, and the Equal Rights Amendment. He also wanted to stress his commitment to across-the-board tax cuts and standing up to the Soviets.

But Reagan lost this much-needed opportunity when the FEC, responding quickly to Dole's complaint, ruled the *Nashua Telegraph* debate an illegal corporate contribution because it excluded "major candidates." The big showdown between Bush and Reagan was canceled.[86]

Though in motion, Reagan still sometimes stumbled. Always fond of a good laugh, he told an ethnic joke to several aides and then was asked by a reporter— off the record—to repeat it. Reagan did: "How do you tell the Polish one at a cockfight? He's the one with the duck. How do you tell the Italian? He's the one who bets on the duck. How do you tell when the Mafia is there? The duck wins." The reporters all laughed, but the joke earned the condemnation of several sanctimonious elements in the national media, including ABC, which incredibly aired the off-the-record gag.[87] Ed Meese quipped, "There goes Connecticut," an allusion to the state's heavy Italian population.[88]

The *New York Times* surprisingly defended Reagan in an editorial, saying the joke reflected his "geniality" and not "bigotry."[89] The whole thing became ridiculous when the president of Yale, Bart Giamatti, released a statement calling on Reagan to apologize to everybody, "including the ducks."[90] Reagan did a bit of tap dancing for the media, apologized, and promised to tell only Irish jokes in the future.

A RIVAL POWER CENTER inside the Reagan operation was coalescing, although Sears was slow to recognize the threat. Sears had all along relied on his two faithful allies, Charlie Black and Jim Lake. But Ed Meese, about the only old Reagan friend whom Sears had not forced out, did not like what Sears was doing to the campaign and was talking to the Reagans about it.

Sears, who had once considered becoming a "headshrinker," was good at read-ing people and their intentions. But here he was up against Meese, who gave the word "circumspect" new meaning. Though Sears didn't know it, he was also up against William Casey, who had ostensibly been called in to help Reagan prepare for the upcoming debates. Casey, the former Nixon administration staffer and one of the wise men of Wall Street, was an unlikely Reaganite, having supported Ford in 1976 as a New York Republican. But in fact he was part of a plan to replace Sears. Casey was tough to read, too; during World War II he had worked in covert operations for the OSS—the precursor to the CIA—and was experienced in psy-chological warfare and counterintelligence.

The undetected hand of Nancy Reagan was at work. Days before, she and Reagan were alone at the ranch, dismayed about the state of the campaign. Frus-trated, she picked up the phone and called their old friend Bill Clark, whom Rea-gan had appointed as chief justice to the California Supreme Court. Clark imme-diately drove to Rancho del Cielo and the three huddled in front of a fire with a plate of cold cuts. The Reagans asked their old friend if he would replace Sears and take over the campaign. Clark thought the world of Reagan but demurred, as several important cases were before his court.

Nancy had a yellow legal tablet and they began coming up with alternatives. One was Casey. No one remembers who actually came up with the name, but the Reagans asked Clark to call him and take his temperature. "I called him at his home on Long Island, got him out of bed," Clark later wrote. "And grumpy old Bill said, 'Let me think about it. I'll get back to you tomorrow.'" They spoke again the next day and Casey agreed, although not necessarily to take over the whole campaign.[91]

Casey's position was as yet undefined, and when a reporter in New Hamp-shire asked him about a more formal role in the Reagan campaign, he sent a shot across Sears's bow, saying, "I'm open on that."[92] Sears vowed to fight an insurrec-tion or rearguard action, though he was unsure what exactly was going on behind his back. Casey met privately in Worcester, Massachusetts, with Reagan, unbe-knownst to Sears. Reagan had also called Casey at his Florida retreat to discuss the top slot. Casey called Paul Laxalt to seek his advice. Laxalt told Casey that Reagan was affable and easy to work with, and that Nancy Reagan was a "smart, tough lady."[93] Publicly, Laxalt continued to criticize Sears's handling of the campaign. When a reporter asked about the charges that the Reagan campaign was error-prone, he drolly replied, "That's the understatement of the year."[94]

Around this time another old Reagan friend rematerialized. Peter Han-naford—Mike Deaver's business partner—returned early from an extended trip in Africa with his wife, Irene, after speaking with Ed Meese and Dick Allen about the state of their friend's campaign.

Casey spent several days in Los Angeles with Meese, and no one who knew about the covert meeting assumed they were talking about the upcoming Dodgers season. The Reaganites had finally decided to replace Sears with a triumvirate of Casey, Meese, and Dick Wirthlin. The only question now was how and when to ease Sears out. The Californians plotting against Sears feared that if they pushed too hard for executive control of the campaign and at the wrong time, Sears might resign in a fit of pique. This could set off a new round of anti-Reagan stories in the media, since Sears had better relations with the media than anyone else in the GOP. Reagan's campaign was just getting rebalanced after the disaster of Iowa, and an angry Sears could make life unbearable at precisely the wrong time for Reagan.

With less than three weeks to go before the crucial New Hampshire primary, Sears was in New York. He held a press conference to announce the filing of Reagan delegate slates for a primary that was almost three months off—and even then, he failed to file slates in two congressional districts, effectively ceding six delegates to Bush.[95] Rather than ministering to his wounded candidate in New Hampshire, Sears was holding unnecessary press conferences in the Big Apple. It was another strike against Reagan's manager.

As THE AMERICANS AND the Russians squared off in the world arena, everybody saw the Winter Olympics being held in the cold of Lake Placid as a metaphor for the Cold War. The Russians were scary, many believed they cheated, and they used intimidation tactics effectively in the sporting arena, just as they did in international politics.

The Soviets' predicted domination of the Winter Olympics got off to a rough start, though, when Eric Heiden of the United States upset the Russian in the 500-meter speed-skating competition. Also, the young American hockey team beat Norway handily, 5–1, after a surprising 7–3 win over Czechoslovakia. Most felt this represented the extent of their success. They were 2–0–1 but had yet to come up against the powerhouse Soviets.

IN THE FIRST WEEK of February, the newly active Reagan zipped through seven states in the South and the East. He gave a major foreign-policy speech in Macon, Georgia, in which he leveled Carter for the high number of members of the Trilateral Commission in his administration, including Zbigniew Brzezinski. Though he never mentioned Bush, he didn't need to. Everybody in the conservative move-

ment knew by now that Bush had been a member of the commission but had
resigned in preparation for pursuing the nomination.

William Loeb's *Manchester Union-Leader* beat Bush about the head and shoulders for this sin: "It is quite clear that this group of extremely powerful men is
out to control the world." Loeb also charged that Bush was using a Trilateral network of "banks, the media and oil companies" to steal the primary.[96] Loeb even
asserted that Bush's campaign was part of a CIA plot.[97] Mr. William Loeb, meet
Mr. Oliver Stone.

John Anderson was also a member of the commission, but he did not resign
and brushed off the conspiracists as "just old biddies." Bush finally was compelled
to put out a statement on the Trilateral Commission saying any charges of a conspiracy were "absurd."[98]

At each campaign stop Reagan was making proposals, making news, and
thrilling audiences with thunderous speeches. While in Georgia, Reagan spoke
forcefully to students at Columbus College: "No more Vietnams! No more aban-
donments of friends by the U.S. . . . We don't care if we're not liked! We're going
to be respected!" His young fraternity brothers of Tau Kappa Epsilon raised a banner that read, "RON-TKE-AND APPLE PIE." Two students performed a dance
routine and Reagan joined them in a bit of soft shoe. He was having fun again, he
wasn't soft-pedaling his conservatism, and he was back in motion.[99]

Also, in a nice redirection on his age and Bush's jogging for the media, Reagan told one individual who asked him about his years, "We don't elect presidents
to run foot races. We elect presidents to display experience and maturity."[100]

Charlie Black was comforted by the serendipitous early primary schedule.
New Hampshire was five weeks after Iowa. "If New Hampshire had been the
week after Iowa, we'd be in tough shape."[101] But Reagan's poll numbers still had
not recovered, and there were now only ten days left before the primary. Dick
Wirthlin conceded that for Reagan to win, he'd have to "come from behind."[102]
And Bush only added to his momentum when he won the Puerto Rico primary
on February 17.

Reagan finally got his television ads going. Initially, a Madison Avenue firm
that knew nothing about politics produced commercials of Reagan in a school-
room, talking to children about energy in front of a blackboard while holding a
piece of chalk.[103] The spots were ridiculous.

Black then called the old Reagan aide Jeff Bell and asked him to look at one
of the Madison Avenue commercials. "I told Charlie this was piece of shit," Bell
later recalled. Black concurred. The ads and the Madison Avenue empty suits
were sent packing, and Bell was brought on to produce new ads for the campaign

in New Hampshire. Bell also called in Elliott Curson, who had helped produce Bell's 1978 Senate campaign ads, to help on the Reagan spots. Bell and Curson went to Los Angeles to make the new spots. There they encountered two immediate problems. One was that Reagan had forgotten his contact lenses. "He was blind as a bat without them," Bell said. They had to make oversized cue cards that Reagan could see. The second was that Mrs. Reagan kept calling, telling Bell that "Ronnie" had to be home at 4 o'clock for a dinner party. Bell obediently followed Mrs. Reagan's urgent requests.

Despite the problems, Bell and Curson produced eleven commercials for $11,000 that were aired heavily in New Hampshire. Most touted Reagan's unvarnished support for tax cuts, and the effective ads helped bring the conservative base back to their hero.[104] The spots were in jest dubbed "The Good Shepherd" because Reagan, at the end of the ad, said, "We have to move ahead. But we can't leave anybody behind."[105]

Bush's commercials never got specific. According to Jim Baker, Bush canceled the long-planned issue ads in favor of continuing the "bio stuff."[106] Bobby Goodman, a man of indistinct ideology who had once written jingles for New York firms, was Bush's adman in 1980. The "bio spots" told the viewer that Bush had been a star baseball player at Yale and was a "legitimate American hero" because of his service in World War II. The five-minute commercial added that Bush offered "optimism and the promise of future accomplishment" but said nothing about what he would do as president. Goodman defended the spots, saying that "people vote for people they believe in as human beings."[107]

The increased media scrutiny was clearly taking its toll on Bush, as the other candidates had begun attacking him, following Reagan's lead. At one point he complained to the press about attacks from fellow Republicans, saying that their consultants were telling them to "go out there and go after George Bush."[108]

Cracks were beginning to appear in Fortress Bush. The New Hampshire primary was still more than a week away, and in politics a week is at least several eternities.

Anything could happen to front-runner George Herbert Walker Bush—Phillips Andover class of 1936, Yale class of 1948, hero pilot jock, and resident of Houston, Texas, and Kennebunkport, Maine.

And anything did happen.

9

FAST TIMES AT NASHUA HIGH

"I am paying for this microphone, Mr. Green!"

edical World News released health information on all the major candidates two weeks before the New Hampshire primary. The publication had solicited reports from each, and only Jerry Brown refused to comply. Jimmy Carter's was by far the briefest, with just a short statement from the White House physician, William Lukash, saying that the president was in excellent shape. Bob Dole may have once suffered from a "'silent' heart attack" based on his cardiogram, though his office strongly denied it. John Connally took medication for high blood pressure, Howard Baker recently had a CAT scan because of recurring headaches (which later went away), and both George Bush and Ted Kennedy had ulcers. Phil Crane's worst ailment was that his gums were receding.[1]

Ronald Reagan was in "remarkably good physical condition."[2] His blood pressure was 130/80; he had a pulse of eighty beats per minute; and he stood 6'1″ and weighed 194 pounds. The only minor notes were that he received occasional injections for his allergies and had a bit of arthritis in one thumb.[3] Lyn Nofziger always thought Reagan was one of those kids who were forced to change from a left-hander to a right-hander, which was not at all unusual at the time he began grade school. He wrote right-handed but chopped wood and fired a gun left-handed.[4] When the Gipper had been filmed smoking in his "Brass Bancroft" serials, he used his left hand.

Carter weighed but 155 pounds soaking wet; his blood pressure was 114/70 and he had an extraordinary pulse of only forty-two beats per minute. Unfortunately, it also came to light that he was afflicted with "chronic hemorrhoids."[5] This embarrassing tidbit became fodder for comics, notably in a cruelly funny *Saturday Night Live* sketch in which Dan Aykroyd, playing Carter, alluded to the president's indelicate affliction through a series of bad puns.

It was a new world in that Americans had previously known nothing of presidential health. Problems were routinely covered up—and some should have stayed that way, such as when LBJ vulgarly pulled down his pants to show the world a scar. Thomas Jefferson suffered from severe depression and migraines and sometimes rode off to be by himself for a good cry. Andrew Jackson had more maladies than could be listed, but to sum it up, though he stood six feet tall, he weighed less than 130 pounds. Abraham Lincoln had his bouts with melancholia. Woodrow Wilson, after a lifetime of sickness, was put out of action by a stroke. FDR not only had had polio that confined him to a wheelchair but also suffered from dangerously high blood pressure and possibly skin cancer. John F. Kennedy, despite his "vigah" and appearance, had Addison's disease and received regular cortisone shots for his searing back pain from an injury sustained when a Japanese destroyer sliced into his PT boat. More than one enemy in private conversation disparaged JFK as a "cripple." Richard Nixon's psyche and heavy drinking were dissected in a million articles, books, movies, and plays—once he left office.

But as the Associated Press noted in 1980, "The 'velvet barrier' between public service and private behavior has been virtually eliminated."[6]

ON THE NIGHT OF February 20, Manchester Central High School hosted the only scheduled debate that included all seven Republican candidates. The contenders, including Reagan, sat at a horseshoe-shaped table, facing moderator Howard K. Smith of ABC.

Reagan's goal that night was to highlight the dissimilarity between himself and Bush. He had spent time with his staff prepping for the debate by having Ed Meese and others throw questions at him while he honed his answers. The day before the debate Bush had sequestered himself in a remote cabin owned by Hugh Gregg and fielded question from Jim Baker, research director Stef Halper, and Pete Teeley. Reagan and Bush approached debates differently. Reagan looked at them as a chance to bring new people into his fold while Bush regarded debates warily, simply looking to survive them.

Bush was expecting the other candidates to gang up on him, but they mostly ganged up on Carter and the Soviets. Everybody was looking for a contretemps between Bush and Reagan, but in this they were disappointed. The only real confrontations came when Bob Dole repeatedly stuck it to Bush. Years earlier, in

1972, President Nixon had unceremoniously dumped Dole as RNC chairman, replacing him with the more suppliant Bush; Dole still hadn't gotten over it.

Reagan was only partially successful in his attempt to set himself apart from Bush. One account, in fact, described his debate performance as "lackluster."[7] But he did enough to counter the charges that he'd become too old to be president. The expectations going into the debate were so low that all he had to do was show up to prove he still had the vim and vigor. Writing of Reagan's performance in the *Washington Post*, Martin Schram acknowledged, "Tonight he showed that he could indeed debate the issues." Reagan responded "no more or less memorably than all the rest," wrote Schram, but that was all the candidate needed to do.[8]

Behind the scenes, Reagan's aides were attempting to revive the one-on-one confrontation with Bush that the FEC had squelched when it canceled the Nashua debate. The FEC finally ruled that a debate could go forward if it was funded by the two candidates, not the newspaper, and if it was not televised live, since showing the two candidates would trigger the FCC's equal-time provisions. Therefore, the debate would have to be covered as a news event by the networks' reporters and not broadcast in real time.[9]

To satisfy the FEC, the *Nashua Telegraph* suggested that the two campaigns split the $3,500 cost of the debate.[10] Bush's campaign balked. At this point, Bush's men really didn't want a debate with Reagan, hoping to nurse their lead home. "If they want to debate, let them pay for it," Hugh Gregg sniffed.[11] Jerry Carmen called Gregg's bluff and said that Reagan would foot the entire bill. Once again he did so without ever consulting anybody at the campaign.[12] Though it has been in dispute for years who really wanted to debate whom in Nashua, the Bush campaign confirmed that the push came from the Reagan camp, when Pete Teeley said, "We were challenged to a debate by Reagan and we felt if they wanted to debate then it is incumbent on them to pick up the tab."[13]

With the financial question settled, the debate was finally reset for Saturday, February 23, in the gymnasium of the Nashua High School.

TELEVISION ADS WERE NOW blanketing New Hampshire. Ted Kennedy hammered President Carter on the economy. Carter's spots emphasized that he was a family man. He was also running radio ads that had him reciting a portion of the Sermon on the Mount. As the *Miami Herald* reported, "The narrator says in the tones of a voice from Heaven: Vote for President Carter—peacemaker."[14]

On the Republican side, John Anderson's ads peddled "the Anderson difference." Bush continued with the bio spots, running commercials that emphasized his war record. Reagan played up his record of tax cuts as governor of California.[15]

The Republican race was quickly coming down to a two-man competition. Dole by now was simply going through the motions. His friends and family were telling him to get out and concentrate on being reelected to the Senate. Howard Baker was mired in third place. He was getting excellent press coverage, but did not have a sharp enough message for the GOP faithful. Not much of an elbow thrower either, he had no real story to tell except that he was a fresher face than Reagan and that he'd been elected more recently in Tennessee than Reagan had in California and Bush had in Texas—it wasn't rhetoric that would make the typical GOP voter's heart go pitter-patter.

Reagan got a boost when he learned he'd won the straw poll in Alaska, trouncing Bush 1,853 to 852.[16] The poll was nonbinding in the selection of delegates, but the Reagan campaign reacted as if it were news of the Second Coming. Reagan also took seven more at-large delegates selected in Arkansas. "Uncommitted" in the Razorback State came in a strong second with five delegates; Baker got four and Bush two. Connally finally won a delegate but his campaign was fading fast.[17] Nearly all his state offices around the country were closed with the exception of South Carolina and a smattering of others, in a last-ditch attempt to save cash.

With only six days to go before the New Hampshire primary, Bush was ahead of Reagan 37 percent to 33 percent in a University of New Hampshire survey.[18] Reagan's campaign coffers were nearly depleted. Reporters were now writing not only that a Bush victory was "conceivable" but that he could win "going away."[19] But Dick Wirthlin's tracking polls showed Reagan finally creeping up on Bush, whose numbers were ever so slowly trending downward.

THE CARTER ADMINISTRATION MADE it official: The United States would boycott the Moscow Olympics because of the invasion of Afghanistan. The administration made the announcement even though Secretary of State Cyrus Vance had failed to marshal a unified front among America's European allies. The ayatollah announced that the American hostages could not be released any sooner than April. At Lake Placid, the underdog American hockey team continued to surprise everyone by defeating the West Germans, 4–2, helping to guarantee a place in the medal round.

While so much was occurring on the international scene, word came down that an old and legendary "Grande Dame" of Washington, Alice Roosevelt Longworth, had died at the age of ninety-six. For more than eighty years, Alice, the eldest daughter of Theodore Roosevelt, had cut a wide swath through Washington society. When she was a young woman, her father, the president, had prohibited her from her smoking in the White House, so she went up on the roof to do so. In 1906 she married Congressman Nicholas Longworth of Ohio, who would become Speaker of the House. Neither she nor Longworth was a fanatic about being married and they were the subjects of extramarital rumors for years. When her husband was buried in Cincinnati in 1931 she was asked whether she would be buried alongside him. "That would be a fate worse than death itself," she replied.

Alice was beautiful and witty, and could be devastating in her humor. Though a lifetime Republican, in 1944 she described GOP nominee Thomas Dewey as looking like the "little man on a wedding cake." She also abhorred Joe McCarthy, a neighbor, and said her garbageman could call her by her first name but Senator McCarthy could not. She was banned from the Taft and Wilson White House after making jokes at their expense while attending parties in the Executive Mansion. In retaliation, she campaigned against Wilson's League of Nations and, through her charm, convinced enough senators to oppose it.

Described as "The Other Washington Monument," she was still entertaining guests over tea in her second-floor drawing room into her nineties. Alice had hosted prime ministers, kings, presidents, and other world leaders in her faded, five-story house.

Alice Roosevelt once said, archly, "If you can't say something good about someone, sit right here by me." When it was suggested to Theodore Roosevelt that he get his carefree daughter under control, he tartly replied, "I can be president of the United States or I can control Alice. I cannot possibly do both."[20]

NEW HAMPSHIRE WAS AN atypical state. First, there were few minorities. Second, more than 73 percent of the population was rural.[21] It also contained a disproportionate number of gun enthusiasts—or so the New York and Washington media crowd thought. There was no dominant television station inside the state and only one statewide newspaper, the *Union-Leader*, which was read by almost half the residents. Two hundred thousand new citizens had moved into New Hampshire over the previous decade, mostly from Massachusetts, attracted by the good schools, low taxes, and low crime rate. Still, they were Boston-centric. They read the *Globe* and watched Boston television, and the campaigns coughed up piles of dough for advertising to reach them in the southern portion of the state.[22] New Hampshire also had a disproportionate number of elected cranks, eccentrics, and oddballs.

Gun Owners of America sponsored a New Hampshire forum that all the GOP candidates attended. All the Republicans save John Anderson supported gun rights. Anderson, thinking of his friends in the national media, decided to challenge the crowd, half of whom were booing him and the other half yelling "bullshit!"[23] Bush was well received except when one questioner asked him whether he wanted "one-world" government, a reference to the Trilateral Commission. He sloughed it off and instead told the attendees of the time he tried to register his gun in Washington but was told by a government clerk that criminals did not register their guns, "just a bunch of suckers like you from Northwest Washington." Reagan received the warmest greeting when he told the gathering, "Thank you . . . my fellow members of the NRA."[24]

Jimmy Carter sent his son Jack to the forum. Surprisingly, Jerry Brown opposed gun registration based on his objection to more government involvement in private lives.[25]

THE EYES OF AMERICA were fixed on two usually snowy locations: New Hampshire and Lake Placid, New York. Speed skater Eric Heiden was the pride of America, winning five gold medals, the most ever won by an individual in singles competition events in the winter games.

But even Heiden was just a spectator at the greatest, most thrilling, and most shocking upset in the entire wide world of sports, when the U.S. hockey team, led by the great coach Herb Brooks, defeated the Soviets, 4–3. Sportscaster Al Michaels called the game for ABC and joyously cried out as the seconds ticked down, "Do you believe in miracles?" American exceptionalists yelled out in reply, "Yes!" The crowd in unison counted down the last ten seconds as if it were the final countdown for the Soviet empire.

Eight thousand, five hundred flag-waving Americans went bonkers in the Lake Placid arena. Across the nation, Americans wept, honked their automobile horns, danced in the streets, and clinked beer glasses toasting America's newest heroes, believing again in the miracle of America.

In the opinion of many, it was the greatest moment in all of sports. The Soviet hockey team had been undefeated in the Olympics since 1968, and had won the gold medal five of the past six Olympics. They were professional athletes, their average age in the thirties, and they had played together for more than six years; they'd been beaten by a bunch of American college kids whose average age was only twenty-two and who had been playing together for a mere six months.

The fact that the team was led by two alumni of Boston University—Mike Eruzione, who slammed home the winning goal in the final period, and Jim Craig in goal, who stopped a phenomenal thirty-nine shots—made the upset even more special for the people of Beantown and all of New England, including New Hampshire.

The Americans had to beat Finland the next night for the gold medal, 4–2, but the win over the Soviets was the first heartwarming, patriotic news for the battered American psyche in many years, possibly since the first moon landing in 1969. Many churches across the country let their parishioners leave early so they could be home to watch the gold medal contest. At the win over Finland, someone hung a sign, "Defectors Welcome," and listed a telephone number.[26]

Everybody in America saw the game for what it really was: a metaphor for the Cold War. The thuggish Soviets cheated while the clean-living Americans played by the rules. Yet in the end, right triumphed over might and truth was indeed stranger than fiction. Better, too.

Vice President Mondale was there for the gold medal victory over Finland. It was especially meaningful for him, as Coach Brooks and several of the players were from his native Minnesota.

The youthful American team gave their fellow citizens the same misty feeling they got when they looked at a Norman Rockwell painting. America, they believed, was a great country because America was a good country.

And no one believed this more than Ronald Wilson Reagan.

THE NIGHT OF THE win over the Soviets, Colin Clark, a twenty-year-old aide to Reagan and the son of Reagan friend William Clark, nervously approached the candidate with a handwritten message as the Gipper was giving a speech in Windham, New Hampshire. Mrs. Reagan, seated on the dais, looked at young Clark, wondering what the hell he was up to. But Reagan took the note, read it, smiled, and interrupted his speech to tell the audience, "Soviet Union 3, United States of America 4!" The hall went ballistic.[27] A man in the audience asked Reagan whether he too was going to win and Reagan replied, "You bet we are!"[28] Reagan was ready to rumble.

To the national media, though, it seemed that Reagan was bound to lose. Two new polls showed Reagan continuing to collapse nationally among Republicans. Where a month earlier Reagan had held a commanding lead of 40 points over Bush, a New York Times / CBS poll and a Time magazine survey showed his lead over Bush shrinking to 6 percent and 4 percent, respectively. In fact, Bush was leading among GOP voters most likely to vote in primaries. Even worse, Reagan had shot up to a 46 percent unfavorable rating, with only 38 percent of Republicans rating him positively.[29] Seeing such polls, Boston Globe columnist Robert Healy wrote, "Reagan does not look like he'll be on the presidential stage much longer."[30] Similarly, Germond and Witcover, never high on Reagan, said that "a rough consensus is taking shape . . . that George Bush may achieve a commanding position."[31]

But in fact, Reagan was gaining in New Hampshire, while Bush was losing votes to Baker and Anderson. One new poll, conducted by WNAC, had Bush ahead of Reagan by just 2 points, 34–32 percent.[32] The glow of Bush's big Iowa win was dimming. The *Union-Leader* produced a poll showing Reagan ahead by 5 percent, but the media discounted it, as the paper was in essence the house organ for the Reagan campaign.[33]

With his lead shrinking, Bush once again changed his mind on debating. Now it was he who wanted the debate restricted just to himself and Reagan. Giving any attention to the other candidates would simply drain away anti-Reagan votes. The Reagan camp knew what Bush needed—and that Bush and his team were becoming inflexible in their position that no other candidates could participate in the Nashua debate. By being so stubborn, Bush was about to set himself up as a patsy in a morality play by Reagan. Bush was assuming the role of the "Model Boy" Willie Mufferson, and Reagan was, of course, Tom Sawyer.

The other campaigns yet again vented their ire about being excluded from any debates. Howard Baker's press secretary, Tommy Griscom, angrily said, "Before this is over, the *Nashua Telegraph* is going to wish it never heard the word 'debate.'"[34] The candidates fired off telegrams to Reagan, citing "fairness." This weighed on the Gipper. Of the group, he was most fond of Dole and Baker, especially when they politely asked him to reconsider. He had nothing against Anderson, but Connally, Bush, and Crane were not high on his hit parade.

Just one day before the Nashua showdown, however, Jerry Carmen confirmed that the Reagan campaign still wanted a direct confrontation alone with Bush and not a multicandidate forum. "There are real differences . . . and we think people will be able to see those differences a lot better in a one-on-one debate than in a seven-way debate," he said.[35]

The *Nashua Telegraph*, Bush, Bush's men, Reagan, Carmen, Reagan's men—all had been boxed into the one-on-one debate format. All, that is, except for John Sears. He was looking outside the box. Sears had been keeping a low profile across the state line in Andover, Massachusetts, mostly dining and drinking in private with Jim Lake and Charlie Black or with national political reporters at the Wayfarer Hotel. He was in high dudgeon. ABC's Barbara Walters had already reported that if Reagan lost New Hampshire, Sears "may well be fired."[36] But before it was all over, he would give Ronald Reagan a final gift, one that would help open the front door to the White House for the Gipper.

And show to the world one last time the creative conceit of John Patrick Sears III, Esq.

The canny Irishman smelled an opportunity for Reagan to get the upper hand with a last-minute change to a multicandidate debate. His plan was to embarrass Bush into allowing Dole, Crane, Baker, and Anderson onto the stage, while making Reagan look magnanimous. Or perhaps the maneuver would create such chaos as to prevent Bush from winning the debate. Years later Charlie Black described Sears's strategy as "Let's put Bush under pressure." Black added, "We knew he would choke . . . in the debate."[37] Sears was blunter: "Our job was to show that Bush was not capable of being president."[38]

Sears reasoned that Reagan could have his cake and eat it, too. He could appear noble by relenting and inviting the other candidates at the last minute to participate while also dividing the anti-Reagan vote by giving them the spotlight to share with Bush. Sears also understood what no one else did: for one priceless moment, Reagan and the other candidates had a shared interest against Bush.

On Saturday, the morning of the debate, Jim Lake went to the Reagans' hotel suite to brief them on the new plan and to get their approval. Mrs. Reagan was in her slip, getting dressed, when Lake arrived. "What's up?" she said. Reagan was sitting on the bed talking on the phone, so she poked him in the shoulder and showed her husband the draft release Lake had written, announcing that Reagan was inviting all the candidates to attend. Reagan got off the phone, studied the release, and pronounced himself pleased with the change in plans.[39]

Bush gave his own preview of the debate when he said he would not "show my macho by pummeling Ronald Reagan" in Nashua. He further claimed that reporters were on a fool's errand if they looked for "bloodshed" or a "hemoglobin count" or expected him to go for the "jugular."[40] He "thanked" Reagan for underwriting the debate, implying that Reagan had only done so because he needed the confrontation more than Bush did. On this matter, Bush was right.

Around noon on the day of the debate, Sears got on the phone and tracked down all the other candidates. The only one who could not make it in time was Connally. He saw right through Sears's ploy to use him and the others as props, but he liked the idea of sticking it to Bush. Connally laughed and said, "Brilliant strategy, but I ain't coming. Fuck him over once for me."[41] Sears spoke to his old friend Dole, who in turn called John Anderson, his old friend, to discuss the new development. Paul Russo was working for Reagan but happened to be in the room with Dole and overheard him say to Anderson, "Yeah, I don't trust Sears either, but we still have to go!"[42]

At 2 P.M., Sears sprang his trap, publicly announcing that Reagan wanted to open up the debate to the other candidates. Lake issued the Reagan-approved press release, the first release the press secretary had ever written in his life.[43]

Bush took the bait. He immediately refused to include the others, saying that he'd been invited by the *Telegraph* to participate in a two-man debate and, in proper Yankee stiff-upper-lip mode, that he "played by the rules." A half hour earlier, Jim Lake had called the *Telegraph*'s Jon Breen to notify him that Governor Reagan, claiming enormous pressure from the other candidates, had decided to include them at the last minute. Breen became angrier when he found out that the other candidates had already been invited to his debate and he hadn't even been consulted. Sears was deliberately pushing both Breen and Bush into a corner, and they were pushing back, as Sears had hoped.

Breen tracked down Jim Baker, who told Breen that Bush would have "no objection" to the last-minute change, but also said, "We'll play by your rules." Breen and the paper were livid at Reagan for the last-minute switch. They decided that it was their debate and they would stick to their "rules"—the one-on-one format. In heated conversations later in the day in the halls of Nashua High School, Reagan's general counsel, Loren Smith, and deputy counsel, Stephen Thayer, were overheard arguing with angry representatives of the paper and Hugh Gregg's son, Judd Gregg. Smith and Thayer suggested that Breen and the paper's publisher, J. Herman Pouliot, meet with Reagan to discuss Reagan's position, but they refused. Several hours later, they reversed course and went looking for Reagan, but it was too late.[44]

Everybody was now on board with Sears's plan. Carmen told the Associated Press he believed in "confrontation politics."[45] Nobody for a moment thought he was kidding.

THAT EVENING, TENSIONS WERE high. About 2,400 people squeezed into the hot and stuffy gymnasium. There was a healthy mix of Reagan and Bush supporters, but in addition the crowd featured anti-abortion protesters, pro-abortion protesters, pro-ERA protesters, and representatives of the Clamshell Alliance, a scruffy, grassroots antinuclear group whose stated goal was to invade and "occupy" the construction site in nearby Seabrook, New Hampshire, where a nuclear plant was being built.[46] The gym was, as one GOP operative once said of another such event, "like the bar scene from Star Wars."[47]

The media turnout was huge, and the audience was thrilled to see national news anchors Walter Cronkite and John Chancellor milling about. Instamatic camera flashes from the audience went off constantly.

But tensions mounted as time passed and . . . nothing happened. The debate was scheduled to begin at 7:30, but at 8:15 there were still no candidates to be found. As spectators sat in the bleachers, with their coats across their laps, fanning themselves with programs, four media panelists from the *Chicago Tribune*, the *Washington Star*, the *Union-Leader*, and the AP sat and waited impatiently. What was the holdup?[48]

An advance man kept asking Reagan aide Russo how many chairs should he put on the stage, two or six? Russo could not give him an answer, replying, "I don't know."[49]

The two warring camps were assembled separately in classrooms. The other four candidates were in a music room at the back of the gymnasium. Some chubby staffers squeezed into the small high school desks. Campaign aides nervously smoked cigarettes and stubbed them out on the linoleum floors.

Neal Peden, Charlie Black's assistant, was sitting right behind Reagan as the candidate's bus approached the high school. "He [was sitting] very quietly . . . but you could see him come alive," Peden recalled. "He said, 'Here we go.' He was just up for it."[50] Some people standing outside the school in the cold applauded Reagan upon his arrival.

Reagan walked in and went directly to the back of the hall, where he spotted Sears. He sternly said, "I want to talk to George Bush." Reagan said the same to Paul Laxalt, but Laxalt suggested instead sending Senator Gordon Humphrey and Black to see Bush. It was agreed they would go as Reagan's emissaries, but Bush refused to see them. Instead, Jim Baker stepped out of Bush's holding room. "Hey, Senator, what do you want?" Baker said, not altogether warmly.[51]

Humphrey said, "I have a message for Mr. Bush that the one-on-one debate is not gonna happen," and that Bush had to let the others be included. Baker excused himself and stepped into the room to consult with Bush. A moment later he came back out and told the two the answer was still no.[52] Black pressed, but Baker, exercised, told him, "God damn it, you guys are not going to fuck this up! This is going to be a two-man debate and you are not going to do anything to change it!"[53]

When this was reported back to Reagan, who was now standing with the other four candidates, he stormed, "Dammit, this is unbelievable! I'm going to get you all in there!"[54] Breen later claimed that he tried to see Reagan to quell the situation or make some accommodation. Laxalt recalled Reagan being "P.O.'ed" and Bush acting like a "petulant child."[55]

Reagan adamantly wanted the debate opened. Bush adamantly refused. When Bush came out of his holding room and headed to the stage, Humphrey pleaded one last time to include the others in the name of "party unity." Bush spat back at Humphrey, whom he loathed, "No fucking way! I've worked all my life for this and I'm not giving it up. . . . I've done more for party unity than you'll ever know!"[56]

Sending Humphrey to appeal to Bush may have been a stroke of genius on Laxalt's part, since the plebeian brought out the worst in the patrician, and Humphrey reciprocated the feeling in spades. Originally from opposite sides of the tracks in Connecticut, Bush and Humphrey had a short history of contempt for each other.

Bush's position was now etched in granite: No other candidates.

Meese, Carmen, Laxalt, Loren Smith, Peter Hannaford, and others stood off in one corner, Sears, Black, and Lake in another. While battling Bush, they also found time to battle among themselves. Reagan, meanwhile, huddled with the other candidates backstage and decided to walk out of the whole mess, in unity with them. Nancy Reagan, Black, and Humphrey vociferously protested. Humphrey told Reagan he would lose the primary if he ran away and left Bush to have the stage to himself. Humphrey later told his aide Morton Blackwell that he was so intent on making his point, he discovered to his horror that he was poking Reagan in the chest.[57]

Mrs. Reagan suddenly said, "I know what you are going to do; you are all going to go in there together."[58] Reagan saw the wisdom in his wife's suggestion; he realized that if he walked out he would be seen as running away from a fight. He grimly shook hands with the four excluded participants and proceeded to the stage, escorted by Humphrey.

Standing in the wings, the candidates could hear the rowdy audience. Jim Lake could see that Reagan was livid. His face had become florid and his normally twinkly blue eyes had turned cobalt. Lake borrowed a piece of paper from NBC News anchor John Chancellor, who had sneaked backstage, and slipped Reagan a note telling him to keep his cool and that everyone was on his side. Reagan read it and winked at Lake but did not smile.[59]

Jim Roberts and his wife, Patti, also noticed Reagan's mood. Roberts, an executive with the American Conservative Union, had traveled to New Hampshire on his own dime to volunteer full-time helping Carmen, and he and his wife saw Reagan backstage. Patti Roberts, also a veteran of the conservative wars, including organizing the annual Conservative Political Action Conference (CPAC), turned to her husband and said, "He's going to be great tonight because he is just furious."[60]

Bush, accompanied by Breen, went onstage first to the subdued cheers of his supporters. Bush and his entourage swept right past Reagan in the back hall and neither man said a word to the other, although Teeley and Humphrey "had words," according to Carmen.[61] "And all of a sudden he [Reagan] sucks in his chest like this and says, 'Let's go.' And then he just moved to the door."[62]

Bush looked grim—stone-faced and unhappy. Reagan, glowering, climbed up on the stage a few moments later as his supporters repeatedly chanted, "We want Reagan!" He received more cheers than did Bush, but for once, the old performer did not notice. This was no act. Reagan was pissed off at Bush's and the newspaper's intransigence. As he brushed past Bush, he said nothing and barely shook his rival's hand.

The moderator, Breen, was lustily booed as he took his seat between the two combatants. Reagan and Bush did not look at each other. Reagan's microphone was already on because steps had been taken, according to Carmen, to make sure that the soundman, Bob Molloy, was under their control.[63] Reagan, standing, then motioned for the excluded candidates to come up to the stage, which they did happily.

Reagan, the old pro, tapped the microphone and then politely but firmly asked Breen if he could address the crowd. Breen rudely said, "No." Reagan spoke to them anyway. He began to tell the feisty throng that though the debate had initially been for just him and Bush, he now felt it was in the interest of fairness that all the candidates be included. He also said that the paper had rebuffed his plea to meet with the other candidates. Reagan then looked at Bush, but Bush just stared ahead, frozen, with his granny glasses on, refusing to meet Reagan's gaze. Breen interrupted Reagan . . . the crowd booed and hissed Breen again . . . and those who knew the Gipper said this was the angriest they'd ever seen him. His hands were shaking, he was so mad.[64]

Breen would not shut up and was rewarded with renewed boos as he talked over Reagan, who was still trying to explain why he thought the other candidates should be included. Reagan said testily to Breen, "I am the sponsor and I suppose I should have some right."[65] Breen ordered Reagan's microphone turned off, but the technician ignored him. Breen impatiently told Molloy a second time to turn off Reagan's microphone, and again he ignored Breen.

That was it. Reagan had had enough.

He turned to Breen with blood in his eye and thundered, "I am paying for this microphone, Mr. Green!"

The crowd went wild, hooting and yelling; the other four candidates forcefully applauded Reagan, and even the Bush supporters were cheering. The gymnasium was a madhouse. In case Breen missed Reagan's original meaning, the old lion roared again, "I am paying for this debate!"[66] Reagan called the editor "Green" instead of "Breen," but the newspaperman was lucky that Reagan didn't call him something far worse. Later, some thought Reagan was so mad he might throw his microphone at the man.

Several in the crowd inflamed the scene further when they shouted, "Get them chairs!" and "Let them speak!"[67] Reagan asked Breen one final time to include the others but was, astonishingly, rebuffed yet again. The scene was "total chaos," Molloy recalled.[68]

The confrontation energized Reagan. You could plead with Reagan, cajole Reagan, and reason with Reagan, but you could not push Reagan. He'd push right back.

Breen then talked down to Reagan, saying, "Are you through . . . ? Have you concluded your remarks?"[69] "Through all this, Bush sat woodenly at the debate table, staring straight ahead like a goody-two-shoes in the midst of a college cafeteria food fight," wrote one of Bush's longtime tormentors in the press, Jules Witcover.[70]

The "Nashua Four," as they quickly dubbed themselves—Dole, Baker, Crane, and Anderson—had come onstage to the cheers of the crowd, which was now a mob scene. They were photographed with Reagan, hovering over the scowling Bush. They all shook hands with Reagan, but not with Bush.

Reagan had completely outmaneuvered Bush. It didn't matter that after several unpleasantries hurled at Bush and pleasantries aimed at Reagan, the excluded candidates agreed to leave the stage—meaning that Bush got his two-man debate after all. According to Witcover, the incident in Nashua created the "perception" that "Bush had the backbone of a jellyfish."[71]

After this grand confrontation, the debate itself was anticlimactic. Reagan was on fire, though, as he showed his mastery of detail and great humor. When a questioner asked Reagan about raising the mandatory retirement age for Social Security, the Gipper joked, "Don't you think I have a conflict of interest on that issue?" Reagan's voice was strong and clear. When someone asked him about the toll the presidency takes on a man and how Carter had aged in the office, Reagan retorted, "It's the way you do the job. The way Carter does it, of course you would age." Reagan had the crowd eating out of his hand. When the issue of Vietnam arose, he parked it: "We should never let young men die in a war that their government is afraid to let them win."[72] The crowd responded with a one-minute round of applause. Breen petulantly threatened to stop the debate if they did not cease clapping.

Bush was asked by someone in the audience whether he thought Reagan was too old to be president, and he replied that he did not. Given a chance to reply, Reagan smiled and said, "I agree with George Bush."[73] The audience roared. That was the only nice word Reagan had for Bush this night. Reagan went after Bush for underestimating Soviet intentions while serving as head of the CIA. They also sharply disagreed over the size of a tax cut, Reagan favoring the bigger and Bush the smaller. Reagan got a standing ovation from the entire crowd when he sharply declared that the United States could never again abandon a "small country to Godless Communist tyranny."[74] Reagan tired a bit toward the end, but his people were completely energized.

Standing at the back of the hall, taking it all in, were Jim and Patti Roberts. Jim said later, "You had a feeling that history was being made there."[75]

FOLLOWING THE CONFLAGRATION, THE parking lot outside the school was littered with Bush campaign stickers and posters that Bush volunteers, called "Bush-whackers," had discarded.[76] After the debate, Teeley told Bush, "The bad news is that the media is playing up the confrontation. The good news is that they're ignoring the debate, and you lost that too."[77] Sears, proud of the riot of which he was the architect, stood off to the side and sardonically told a reporter, "We're just trying to be party unifiers."[78] For a politico like Sears with an appreciation for high drama, it didn't get any better than this. Hannaford said Sears was "smiling like the Cheshire cat."[79]

The Nashua Four retired to the school's Band Room, where they were met by a mob of media and joyously bashed Bush. Dole was the ringleader of the exiled four. Bush "wants to be king," Dole said. "I told him onstage there'll be another day."[80] Actually, he had leaned into Bush and loudly whispered, "I'll get you some-day, you fucking Nazi!"[81] Dole had also jammed a finger in Jim Baker's chest, promising retribution. Speaking to the media, he said that Bush "better find himself another Republican Party."[82] He even compared the hated Bush to the "Gestapo" and "Hitler's Germany."[83] Phil Crane made similarly dark references, intoning, "Shades of the beer-halls."[84] John Anderson joined in the Bush-bashing fun, saying, "He's awfully easily embarrassed for a man who aspires to sit in the Oval Office and deal with the leaders of the world."[85] Reporters had never seen the normally placid Howard Baker so mad. The four excluded candidates praised Reagan even though he hadn't asked for their participation until a few hours before the debate.

Nearly all the contenders had their own reasons for not liking Bush long before the Nashua debate. This night only exacerbated the bad blood. With Dole, the problem was cultural; Dole had grown up poor and resented people born of wealth. With Connally, it was Texas stuff. With Baker, it was because Bush had usurped his moderate position in the race. With Reagan, it was ideological, but had also become personal after all the age innuendos.

At midnight, Reagan was still so steamed that he called Howard Baker into his hotel room to vent about Bush.[86]

Though the event had not been televised live, the networks and local news ran footage, repeatedly, of a frozen Bush and the booming Reagan. New Hampshire had 482,415 voters, and most of them probably saw the film at least once.[87] Bill Loeb joyously editorialized that Bush looked "like the little boy who thinks his mother may have dropped him off at the wrong birthday party."[88]

Bush never knew what hit him. Shell-shocked, he kept muttering, "I kept my commitment. I kept my word."[89]

The next morning Senator Baker went on *Meet the Press* and called Bush "arrogant." Going further, Baker said, "If he is the front-runner in this race, he's wearing his crown without much grace."[90] Bush's New Hampshire chairman Hugh Gregg said Senator Baker was "lying through his teeth."[91]

Sears later expressed his surprise that Bush froze under pressure so easily. Embittered years later, he also said he thought the reason Reagan was so charged up was that to him it was a "movie scene."[92] The comment was ludicrous on its face.

While the Republican candidates had brought a surge of excitement to the New Hampshire primary, the Democratic race had far less drama. A final poll just before primary day showed Carter smashing Kennedy, 55 to 30 percent. Brown was stuck in single digits.[93] Kennedy's long-gone chartered 727, dubbed "Air Malaise," had cost thousands of dollars a day to operate. He would henceforth travel by commercial plane, or small, cheap charters—or by bus. Dozens of staffers were taken off the campaign's payroll.

The only thing Kennedy seemed to have left was a sense of humor. At a sparsely attended event, he turned to the press and joked, "Record crowds!" His campaign bus's theme song was "Take It Easy" by the Eagles. Kennedy had no choice.[94]

On the eve of the New Hampshire primary, Carter had more than $2 million cash in hand while Kennedy had less than $250,000.[95] Carter had been helped by contributions from avant-garde artist Andy Warhol and media baron Ted Turner, who thoughtfully sent $2,000 even though only $1,000 was allowable by law.[96]

The media would not let Chappaquiddick rest. Voters in New Hampshire did not often bring up the subject, but a young high school student asked Kennedy how he could be trusted in a "crisis when he didn't report for nine hours his automobile accident." The audience and media went dead. Kennedy paused in the embarrassing silence, then spoke in quiet tones about the many losses in his life. Afterward a reporter approached the student, Bruce Lary, for his response to Kennedy's answer. "I didn't think it was really an answer. I've been under a lot of stress, too. I've lost some family, too, but that doesn't make me qualified to be president."[97]

Out of the mouths of babes.

10

REAGAN ROMPS

"They finally got Rasputin, didn't they?"

There was a renewed bounce in Ronald Reagan's step after Nashua as he joyously hopscotched the Granite State in the final hours before the primary. Fresh in his mind was the lesson he had learned four years earlier, when he followed Hugh Gregg's advice to leave the state for the two days right before the primary and ended up losing by a razor-thin margin to Gerald Ford. "I'm not going to make that mistake this time," the Gipper vowed to an aide.[1]

Reagan was as firmly planted in the state as a stout maple tree. Over the final thirteen days, he spent ten of those in New Hampshire.[2] The *Washington Post*'s David Broder said it "was one of the most phenomenal pieces of personal campaigning I have ever seen."[3] Reporters on Reagan's bus, exhausted at the pace of a man twice their age, hung a sign that read, "Free the Reagan 44."[4]

Incredibly, George Bush did no personal campaigning in the state for the last seven days other than to appear at the two debates.[5] Gregg, now running Bush's campaign, was afraid to change plans in the wake of the Nashua debate debacle, fearing it would look as though they'd panicked.

Gregg was known for his temper but also a wry sense of humor. He once published a book titled *All I Learned About Politics*; all of the pages were blank. It was a joke, but the anecdote should have been a cautionary tale for Bush. Bush might also have taken note of the fact that Gregg had lost seven successive elections as either a candidate or a manager.

Instead, Bush took Gregg's advice—he left the state after the Nashua debate and went back to Houston for the Sunday and Monday before the primary. He was imprudently photographed jogging in shorts, in the warm Texas sun, while

Granite Staters were shoveling snow off their driveways and sidewalks, or shivering in their cold cars awaiting some heat.[6] The contrast was anything but helpful for Bush.

While Reagan tried to stay above the fray, joshing that the Nashua debate had been "kinda a fiasco," the other candidates didn't mind taking the low road against Bush.[7] Bob Dole, never at a loss, said that Bush "treated us like dirt under his feet."[8] From Chicago, John Connally piled on and said that Bush had displayed "pettiness and immaturity" in Nashua.

Gregg angrily told reporters, "It is obvious to me that this was a calculated strategy engineered by Ronald Reagan to embarrass George Bush." What was less obvious was why Bush's men let their candidate fall for the "calculated strategy." Reporters, smelling fresh ink, carried Gregg's charges to Reagan after he'd gone to church, and he did not disappoint: "Mr. Gregg must be feeling very desperate right at this moment because Mr. Gregg knows that this is a lie."[9]

Gregg had been snookered by Jerry Carmen to an extent, but also by his own stubbornness. The afternoon of the debate, Carmen went to Gregg and told him that Reagan was going to open the forum unless Bush put up half the money. Gregg told Carmen to go to hell. In doing so, Gregg gave the Reagan team the moral fig leaf it wanted to invite the four excluded candidates.

Years later, Carmen said that the Bush team had attempted a bluff of its own. The Bush people had hoped that Reagan would not go onstage if he couldn't bring the other four candidates into the debate, and that Bush would win the night and the bragging rights. "I think they thought we weren't coming in," said Carmen. If Reagan had backed off as he originally wanted, "it would have been a disaster," he added.[10]

The *Nashua Telegraph* attempted to draw some fire away from Bush by issuing a statement saying that even if Bush had agreed to allow the others to participate, the paper would have halted the event.[11] But Jon Breen had said just a day earlier that Bush's people had told him they would be comfortable with a change in the format.[12] Gregg also issued a terse, two-page, singled-spaced chronology of his version of events. Bush released a letter at a press conference in Houston explaining to the Nashua Four his version of events and apologizing to them. "Reagan . . . never had the courtesy to contact me. Frankly, I feel he used you to set me up."[13] The *Telegraph*, heavily invested on Bush's side, ran an unflattering photo of Reagan, and its account of the actual debate said that the two men had disagreed on little.[14] One had to wonder whether the reporter had covered a different debate.

Not even John Sears could have scripted that Bush would have frozen like a cigar-store Indian or that Reagan would respond so forthrightly. If Bush had been more nimble, he could have easily trumped Reagan by simply welcoming the other candidates. He would have earned points for his magnanimity. Bush's blunder was serendipitous for Reagan, who had up to this point been on a long streak of bad luck. It could not have come at a better time for the Gipper. Just that morning, Tom Wicker, in his *New York Times* column, confidently predicted that Bush would win the New Hampshire primary unless "Reagan mortally wounds him in their . . . debate tonight." What Wicker didn't foresee was that Bush might just mortally wound himself.[15]

Gregg whimpered that all the other candidates were ganging up on Bush. Bush himself said Monday morning on ABC's *Good Morning America*, "I'm worried about Reagan. I think he sandbagged me frankly."[16] John Anderson called Bush's charges the "petulant response of a spoiled child."[17] Of Bush's post-debate comments, Reagan said grimly, "I thought better of him." Red flags should have gone up in Bush's campaign at this statement by the Gipper.[18]

Bush was taking knocks from all sides. Conservative publications such as *Human Events* were leveling Bush. For months, Bill Loeb had been softening up Ambassador Bush in one long account after another in the *Union-Leader*. Lurid stories of power, access, and money used phrases like "Bush has been a loser," "Texas oil millionaire,"[19] and Loeb's favorite standby, "elitist preppy." Loeb also loved to torment Bush over the Trilateral Commission. In response, the Brahmin spluttered, "It just boggles my mind when I pick up newspapers and have allegations that I would belong to some conspiratorial organization. It simply isn't true."[20]

Bush's campaign wasn't paranoid. Everybody on Earth—or at least in New Hampshire—*was* out to get him, or so it seemed to his demoralized supporters. On Monday, Bush said from Houston, "I have been under constant attack in New Hampshire."[21] The Saturday before the primary, Loeb ran an editorial under the heading, "God Had Chosen Reagan to Lead Us."[22] Apparently even Heaven was now against Bush, at least according to Loeb.

On the day of the primary, Bush bought a front-page ad in Loeb's paper, trying to soften the hammering he'd been getting from the old yellow journalist. The *Union-Leader* was one of the few papers in America in which front-page ads could still be purchased. Bush attempted some levity: "Sure I have a sense of humor; Bill Loeb's editorials always give me a kick!" It was to no avail. That day three Loeb editorials were headlined "Only a Bush Leaguer," "George Bush Is a Liberal," and "George Can Return to China with Ron in the White House."[23] Five of the newspaper's front-page stories either assaulted Bush or praised Reagan. A flattering picture of Mrs. Reagan awarding a sled-dog championship also appeared on the front page.

JIMMY CARTER HAD NOT put one wet foot in New Hampshire, while Ted Kennedy was sloshing around the state, grubbing for votes. In the warmth of the White House, the president entertained the American Olympic gold medal hockey team.

Joan Kennedy had gained a great deal of confidence on the hustings. Since beating her alcoholism she looked radiant and exuded confidence, even as her husband's campaign was about to be buried under Avalanche Carter. Unfortunately, Mrs. Kennedy was constantly peppered with questions about their personal life and she kept repeating, "The state of our marriage is excellent."[24]

On Monday, February 25, the day before the vote, Reagan put in an eleven-hour day of campaigning and told supporters late that night, "I'm going to sleep well tonight."[25] He didn't take any chances, though, going out the next day and campaigning right down to the wire. He and Mrs. Reagan returned to their hotel late on Tuesday afternoon and Nancy wryly asked someone whether "they had a good remedy for a tummy ache" because she was headed to their room "to be nervous."[26]

After months of surviving on caffeine, nicotine, and adrenaline, Jerry Carmen likewise had frayed nerves. "The next 22-year-old snot that comes up to me is going to get his face pushed in," he stormed. He ordered a Reagan advance man out of his offices, threatening to call the police and the *Union-Leader* "to take the picture."[27] Carmen in calm moments was amiable. When riled, he swore like a longshoreman.

Most in the media thought the Reagans had good reason to be nervous and aggravated. Political observers felt that Bush still had the momentum and that the Nashua debate contretemps had come too late to help Reagan. Characteristic was the piece that E. J. Dionne of the *New York Times* wrote on primary day. Dionne praised Bush's ability to "transcend the factional fights that so roiled" the Republican Party in previous contests, and speculated that "the Reagan camp may be too late" in attempting to regain the offensive.[28]

Two of the few journalists who did see movement toward Reagan and away from Bush were Rowly Evans and Bob Novak in their syndicated column, published just one day before the primary. They had hired Carter's pollster, Pat Caddell, to do private polling for them. Caddell had gone into the town of Derry to sample GOP opinion. Bush was seen as just too "fuzzy" on the issues, while many liked Reagan and his positions. Of the sixty-two interviewed, fully thirty-nine planned on voting for the Gipper and only twelve for Bush.[29]

Some Bush aides fretted for the first time that the Nashua debate may have altered the dynamics of the race. Jim Baker second-guessed himself and said aloud that he wished Bush had met with the other candidates.

The first balloting on Tuesday, February 26, came in from Dixville Notch, whose two dozen cranky citizens voted—as was their peculiar custom every four years since 1960—beginning one minute after midnight. The tiny village was located high in the White Mountains of New Hampshire, only twenty miles from the Canadian border, and one had to question the sanity of these people going out in the subfreezing temperatures of midnight, deep into the February winter. For the other three years and 364 days, no one thought of Dixville Notch, but for one day—well, for a few hours on the morning of the New Hampshire primary—everybody following the results knew about Dixville Notch. Indeed, there were three times as many reporters on hand in the little town as there were people voting. Cameras whirred as the people went into the flag-covered voting booth in the Balsams Hotel.[30]

Reagan had lost to Ford in Dixville Notch four years earlier. When the ballots were counted this time around, Reagan initially won with six votes, followed by Bush with five votes, and Baker with four. Then a miscount was discovered and one vote was taken away from Reagan, so he and Bush tied in the metropolis of Dixville Notch.[31] When the reporters interrupted their late-night drinking in Manchester and Concord to learn of Bush's tie with Reagan there, it indicated to them that he hadn't been sufficiently damaged in Nashua and that the primary would be close, just as they had all written.

On the Democratic side, Carter won Dixville again, just as he had four years earlier, beating Kennedy in a landslide, three votes to two.[32]

ON THE DAY OF the New Hampshire primary, the ever-rumpled Carmen, who had slept only a few hours, said that the past week had been "the first good week we've had since Iowa," but that "Bush is widely regarded to be slightly ahead of Reagan." Indeed, yet another ballyhooed weekend poll had Bush up over Reagan by 6 points in the Granite State.[33]

Bush's people had to the end been pushing the envelope, suggesting to the media that when "the Ambassador" won New Hampshire, the other candidates, low on money, would collapse, including Reagan. More clear-thinking operatives not associated with any campaign said, "That's the kind of stuff, late at night, it's fun to drink and dream about."[34] Still, a new poll covering four southern states—South Carolina, Georgia, Florida and Alabama—had Bush leading Reagan, 42–36, and reporters drew the obvious conclusions.[35]

Some Reagan boosters, fearing a loss in New Hampshire, were already making their rearguard, "we'll come back in the South and the West" argument they'd made four years earlier. But that was the last war, and the critical mistake too many make in politics and warfare is to fight the previous war instead of the one in front of them.

Fortunately for the Reagan backers, Bush rushed out a radio commercial giving his side, yet again, of the Nashua story. The Reagan folks chuckled to themselves, as Bush was just keeping the story alive. They surmised that the contretemps must have hurt Bush worse than his people were letting on. Reaganites got a hold of the script for the commercial and distributed it far and wide. They were delighted to keep the story going.

Outside of Dixville Notch, the New Hampshire polls opened at 6 a.m. and would not close until 7 p.m. or 8 p.m., depending on the town. Though it was cold and windy, the skies were clear in most parts of the state. Turnout in the major cities started slowly, but picked up as the day went along.

New Hampshire had held its first primary in 1916, but it wasn't until 1952 that its presidential primary became the major proving ground for presidential candidates. Since then, no candidate had won the presidency without first winning New Hampshire's primary.[36]

While most towns still used paper ballots (aside from a few that were trying out a newfangled punch-style voting machine), a significant change had occurred since 1976. Previously, New Hampshire voters had picked the delegates associated with each candidate, but this time they voted for the candidates themselves.

The afternoon of the primary, the *Telegraph* ran a lead editorial praising not Reagan but John Sears for his "masterful stroke" at the debates. Calling him "skillful" and a "genius," the paper noted that Sears was "extremely fortunate in having an easily programmable candidate."[37] To little surprise, the *Telegraph* endorsed Bush over Reagan.[38]

The paper also reported that GOP pollsters said the race would be tight. This was the common refrain coming from the media. The previous day the *Washington Post* ran a story headlined "Bush, Reagan Even as New Hampshire Finish Line Nears."[39] Even as of Tuesday afternoon the Associated Press was releasing stories quoting experts saying that the Republican race was too close to call.

It was not even close.

Reagan romped in New Hampshire. It was a completely unexpected blowout, 50 to 23 percent. Turnout was huge among Republicans: more than 145,000 people.[40] In 1976, the turnout had been 111,000 for the GOP primary.

All were stunned at the margin of victory, including Reagan himself, his men, Bush, Bush's men, and the media. Dick Wirthlin's tracking polls had shown Reagan edging into a tie with Bush with less than a week to go and then going into a slight lead over the weekend, but even the esteemed pollster was taken aback at the Reagan landslide.[41] Dixville Notch had created an aura of suspense for the day, but late-deciding GOP voters—who made up about a third of those who went to the polls—went heavily for Reagan, by better than a 5–1 margin. Reagan won in almost every category, except among the affluent; Bush took those voters. Reagan won almost 2–1 among those making less than $10,000 per year.[42] He won among blue-collar voters, 51–20 percent, and among white-collar voters, 39–15. He won 2–1 in the rural areas and 3–1 in the towns.[43] Reagan even got a respectful number of self-identified moderate voters; most of the Ford vote from 1976, which Bush had hoped to claim, went heavily for the Gipper. Reagan of course won among voters who believed the GOP should pursue a conservative course. Overall Reagan took all ten counties in New Hampshire and eleven of thirteen cities. Loeb delivered for Reagan as he got a skyscraping 75 percent of the Manchester vote. The Gipper also took Concord, seat of the state's small liberal populace. And as a bonus, he took Nashua.[44] "Every single thing broke our way, everything," Carmen fondly remembered.[45]

"This is the first and it sure is the best!" an ebullient Reagan told the overflow crowd at the Holiday Inn in Manchester. Even in victory, Carmen was unrelenting with Bush: "I think George Bush is mortally wounded and not just in New Hampshire. . . . The silk stocking got a setback tonight." Hundreds had descended upon the overstuffed hotel. The *Washington Post* noted that the combined Lexington and Concord rooms were filled with "beer-drinking blue-collar supporters."[46] The victory rally was thick with smoke, heat, people, booze, polyester, and joy. The city's fire marshal had to close the hall, it was so crowded. Carmen had picked the too-small room without consulting with Reagan's advance men, Jim Hooley and Rick Ahearn, and they were fit to be tied. As a result, many of Reagan's supporters could not take part in the victory celebration.[47]

The Californian told his joyous supporters, "This is the way I want to continue campaigning, meeting the people of this country as I was able to meet you."[48] Reagan's supporters were even more jubilant than the Gipper himself. A truck driver, Ray Caron of Manchester, had driven Reagan voters to the polls all day. Caron said, "He's the only guy for us working people."[49]

Reagan couldn't resist taking a poke at Bush, saying that "the man who was supposed to be an alternative . . . is not really the alternative at all."[50] Nancy was beaming as Ronnie told the crowd, "I suppose you suspect that we're very happy! Well, we are!"[51]

Reagan got thirteen delegates in New Hampshire to Bush's five, Baker's two, and Anderson's two. In terms of overall delegates selected, Bush and Reagan were tied at twenty-two apiece, but the win had been so dramatic and the comeback so complete that Reagan was firmly reinstalled as the frontrunner.[52]

As Reagan departed the room around 10:30, he and Mrs. Reagan happened upon a young woman who went batty when she saw the former movie star. "Oh, what a wonderful face! I wish now I hadn't voted for Carter."[53]

Bush put the best face on his landslide loss, telling his supporters, "We've won two and lost one. That's .666. I used to hit about .240," a reference to his days playing baseball at Yale. His disheartened fans were not consoled. The chance to beat Reagan had been missed. Bush, standing in front of his supporters with wife Barbara, daughter Dorothy, and sons Neil and Marvin, conceded only forty-five minutes after the polls closed at 8 P.M.[54] He was asked whether the Nashua debacle had contributed to his loss, but he said little on the matter.

He returned to his room, slumped in a chair with a drink, and said of his landslide loss, "There's no excuse for it."[55] Bush called Reagan to congratulate him, saying, "You beat the hell out of us. . . . I'm not happy about it, but I'll see you in Massachusetts."[56]

Bob Dole was shut out of delegates in New Hampshire and harrumphed that his campaign was "not going anywhere."[57] The campaign had spent $219.58 at Sears Roebuck for a safe, but no one for a minute thought Bob Dole had a campaign plan worth stealing.[58] In short order, he dropped out of the upcoming debate in South Carolina and cut his already meager campaign staff to near nothing. He also speculated that President Ford, who had received a handful of write-in votes, would get into the race.

GOING INTO PRIMARY DAY, Ted Kennedy's team knew that the Massachusetts senator was in deep trouble. Kennedy's in-state director, an attractive blonde with the improbable name Dudley Dudley, had lamely joked that the "oil shortage is extending to the 'well-oiled Kennedy machine.'" The mood in Kennedy's headquarters was compared to "the end of a long death march." At the Kennedy "victory" party that night, the bandleader asked Mrs. Dudley if she had a request and she replied, "Camelot."

"Don't know it," he said.

She retorted, "That's the last thing I need to hear."[59]

Kennedy supporters were bracing for another loss, and they got it. President Carter knocked Kennedy down, 49–38 percent, not in his backyard but just down the street and in front of Teddy's friends, too.[60] Jerry Brown's campaign pulled up the rear, incredibly behind the even more eccentric Lyndon LaRouche.

Democrats began to call on Teddy to get out and fall in line behind the president, for the sake of party loyalty. But Kennedy understood all too well what his older brother Jack had meant when he said, "Sometimes party loyalty asks too much."[61] Teddy hated Carter. He declared, "Jimmy Carter ought not to be given a blank check. The last time we did that was to Richard Nixon."[62] In the Democratic Party, there was no lower blow than to compare someone to the odious Nixon.

Kennedy didn't care a whit. He'd found his voice on the road, and had actually been liberated by the prospect of almost certain defeat. The liberal lion was free to roar.

AFTER NEW HAMPSHIRE, IT became conventional wisdom to say that absent the Nashua debate, Reagan would have lost the primary. In fact, Reagan would have still won in New Hampshire but only narrowly—by less than 10 percent in all probability, which means the media would have portrayed the race far differently coming out of New Hampshire. Wirthlin's tracking polls had Reagan and Bush tied with five days to go—that is, even before the Nashua debate. Three days before that, Wirthlin's tabulations had Bush up by 9 percent over the Gipper.[63]

What the Nashua debate did do was to create doubts about Bush's ability to handle pervasive pressure. Such concerns had been an open secret in the GOP for years. In August 1974, when the tapes revealing that Richard Nixon had indeed orchestrated the cover-up of the Watergate break-in were released, Bush, then the party's chieftain, "broke out into assholes and shit himself to death," according to Dean Burch, one of last of the wise men of the GOP.[64]

Bush had made a dreadful mistake in not listening to James Baker, Dave Keene, and his press secretary and confidant, Vic Gold, who urged him to talk about issues rather than his "Big Mo." When asked why he was running for president, Bush had rattled off his résumé and then declared, "I look at it as the height of service."[65] For many Americans, Bush just didn't get it.

Also, in the last days of the campaign, the media began to turn against Bush and toward Reagan. Many reporters covering the campaign thought Bush had become arrogant. Reagan, whether up or down, always treated the gentlemen of the press like gentlemen. He rode the campaign bus together with the media "in New Hampshire day after day" and was always accessible, as Broder, grand old man of the *Washington Post*, recalled.[66]

ADDING TO THE HIGH drama of primary day was Reagan's startling, bloodless execution of John Sears, Charlie Black, and Jim Lake.

Sears and company had been in New Hampshire, but lying low. Carmen was running the entire show. Exactly one year earlier, Sears's friend Lake had told the

Washington Star that Sears "can talk anyone into anything . . . and not only con-vince you but get you to thinking it was your idea in the first place."[67] Now few in the Reagan camp were listening to Sears.

Congressman Mickey Edwards of Oklahoma, Congressman Bob Dornan of California, Senator Orrin Hatch of Utah, and Paul Laxalt stumped for Rea-gan in New Hampshire the day of the primary, and all had taken note of the poor condition of the campaign and had registered complaints with the Reagans. Edwards, Dornan, and Hatch talked among themselves about meeting in Wash-ington with Reagan to tell him he should fire Sears. Laxalt was more direct; when he bumped into Sears in the hotel lobby he bluntly told him, "If this was my campaign, you wouldn't be in it."[68] Sears had been on Laxalt's shit list for more than a year, but the Nevadan had become further inflamed when Sears "was briefing Ron and treating Ron like he was Charlie McCarthy," as Laxalt recollected years later. "Really, he was on a head trip, and it finally got to the point that he was insulting Ron in terms of his own capability and Nancy really got pissed off over that."[69]

Behind the scenes, efforts to either ease Sears out or limit his powers had accelerated over the previous several weeks. Mrs. Reagan was heading to Chicago and at the last minute asked Black and Lake—but not Sears—to accompany her. Seated in the first-class section, she told the two that "Ronnie has lost confidence in John." She then probed gently to see whether they would stay if Sears left. The two indicated that they thought Sears should continue to run the campaign and that if he went, they would be compelled to leave as well.[70]

A couple of days later, while on the campaign bus during a swing through Mas-sachusetts. Reagan asked Black to sit down with him. After telling a joke about an Irish gambler—one Black had heard a dozen times before—Reagan got down to business. "I'm really disappointed with the way John has been acting. . . . My friends are out of the campaign and I would like to bring them back in and he doesn't seem like he wants to do that." Black recalled Reagan pressing: "If anything did happen to John, would you stay?" Again, Black stood by Sears loyally: "I love you . . . no matter what, but I feel it's important to have John run the campaign."[71] That was it. If one went, then all three would have to go. Black now knew there was trouble in River City.

Reagan and his insurrectionists hit upon the idea of dismissing Sears—along with Lake and Black—the day of the primary, but before the results were in. They reasoned that if Reagan lost and then the three were fired, it would look like sour grapes and the campaign would be in even worse shambles. If Reagan won and then the trio was fired, Reagan would look ungrateful. On primary day itself, however, when no one yet knew the results, the news of the firings might be relegated to the back pages. It was a gamble.

Peter Hannaford had been out of the country, but when he returned, Ed Meese asked him to come to New Hampshire. Also part of the cabal was Laxalt, foreign-policy adviser Dick Allen, and Dick Wirthlin. All except Allen had been onetime supporters of Sears and all believed he had betrayed or burnt them. Reagan secretary Helene Von Damm heard rumors that Sears was now gunning for Allen as well.[72]

Sears knew straws were in the wind. Some time earlier, he had claimed to Nancy Reagan that he'd overheard Ed Meese in a men's room talking about how the campaign manager's departure was imminent.[73] Meese denied Sears's allegation and chalked it up to paranoia. At one point Sears directly confronted Bill Casey, when it was still unclear as to Casey's precise role in the campaign and when some felt it might be possible to keep Sears on, but without control of the checkbook. "Sears told Casey he could take any title he wanted," Hannaford later wrote. Casey was unable to determine whether Sears was bluffing or considering quitting.[74]

Five days before the voting began in New Hampshire, a gloomy dinner was held involving all the key players in this mini-drama—Sears, Black, Hannaford, Casey, Allen, Meese, Lake, and Reagan. The only one at the table in good spirits was the candidate himself. After Sears and company left, Hannaford urged Casey to formally join the campaign. That night the Reaganites hatched their plan for Sears's dismissal and presented it to the candidate for his approval.[75] A conference call took place the next day involving nearly all the conspirators and a new addition—Mike Deaver, who had his own giant ax to grind against Sears.

Just a couple of days earlier, a meeting between Reagan and Sears had not gone well. They had barely spoken in weeks, especially since Deaver had been thrown over the side. Now this meeting dragged on until two in the morning with nothing resolved. Sears and his allies started in on Meese, saying that he was a detriment to the campaign. Reagan dug in his heels. "Dammit, John, why do you always have to get your way? Why can't I get mine?"[76] Sears refused to back down and again went after Meese, throwing in Dick Allen for good measure.

Reagan finally exploded, became profane, and yelled at Sears, "Oh no, you're not going to get Ed, by God!"[77] Flushed and angry, Reagan jumped up and moved toward his campaign manager. Black thought Reagan was going to punch Sears, so he stepped in between the two and quickly escorted Sears from the room. Nancy Reagan pulled at her husband, saying, "Ronnie, Ronnie, come away."[78] But Reagan was still yelling at Sears, even as Nancy was tugging on him.

Reagan was so mad that Black feared they all might be fired right on the spot. Lake thought the Secret Service would break in because of all the shouting. Listening through the paper-thin wall in their hotel room and cheering Reagan on were two young campaign aides, Colin Clark and David Fischer.[79] Reagan later obliquely told Jim Dickenson of the *Washington Star* that he and Sears had "several meetings, you might even say confrontations."[80]

Meese described the contentious meeting as a "knock-down, drag-out thing." The problem, Meese said, was that "John always thought he was the smartest guy in the world . . . smarter than Ronald Reagan."[81]

Earlier, Sears had sought Stu Spencer's advice about the Californians around Reagan. Spencer, an on-and-off-and-on-and-off friend and adviser of the Reagans, told Sears that he'd better recruit an ally among the group. Sears had done so for a time with Deaver, but now he stood alone. Spencer warned Sears that "as things get tough . . . Reagan gets up in the morning, he likes to see a familiar face."[82] Meese was the one familiar face left. But he was more than that to Reagan. A constitutional lawyer and a thoughtful conservative, he never lost his cool and possessed an underappreciated sense of humor. Meese was Reagan's port in the storm of national politics. When asked to whom he would first turn in a crisis, Reagan once replied without hesitation, "Ed Meese."[83]

And Sears was now trying to get rid of Meese.

On the Sunday night before the New Hampshire voting, Reagan met one more time with Nancy, Meese, Allen, and Hannaford. Dick Wirthlin called with the happy news that his polling had shown Reagan opening a lead over Bush. But the order of business was the unhappy state of the campaign. Mrs. Reagan told her husband, "You know we just can't go on this way." Reagan replied, "Do we have to fire Jim and Charlie too?" Hannaford told Reagan yes, because the three of them had three times threatened to quit if they didn't get their way and it just didn't make sense to have people in the campaign more loyal to Sears than to Reagan. Reagan reluctantly agreed, telling Hannaford, "I understand."[84]

The day of the primary, Nancy Reagan, who was nursing a head cold, was deputized to ask Sears, Black, and Lake to meet with Ronnie in his suite at 2 P.M. The message came back that they were having lunch with several reporters, but that they could meet with Reagan at 2:30.[85]

As the three walked into what turned out to be their final meeting, Black suddenly knew it was over when he saw Mrs. Reagan sitting in a chair off in a corner of the room, instead of around the coffee table with the rest of them as she'd always done. She would not meet Black's gaze, or Sears's, or Lake's.

The three didn't know it, but Reagan had just that day received a letter from Paul Laxalt relaying conservatives' renewed complaints against Sears.

They sat down in the third-floor suite, the air thick with tension. Reagan was not smiling. He was holding a sheet of paper. Also present was the mysterious Casey, who said little. Reagan started by saying, "Well, fellas, I've been thinking about a change."[86] With that he handed the paper to Sears. It was a press release written by Hannaford announcing the "resignations" of the three. Hannaford had been so intent on secrecy that he kept his notes and the drafts of the release locked in his briefcase.[87]

Sears read it and then said softly, "I'm not surprised," but in fact he was. He handed it to Black. Instead of reading it, Black put the press release face down on the coffee table and said, "Wait a minute—before I read this, I quit."[88] The in-house coup was over in a matter of minutes. Lake and Black were devastated but they felt they owed Sears their loyalty. As they left the Reagans' suite, Charlie kissed Mrs. Reagan.[89] So did Lake, who also muttered bitterly, "Governor, Ed Meese manipulates you, he manipulates you."[90]

As Sears departed, Nancy Reagan asked, "Can we be friends?" He replied ominously, "That depends on you. If we have to defend ourselves then we will defend ourselves."[91]

THOSE INVOLVED IN THE plot to oust Sears had done the impossible in politics: they'd kept a secret. Reagan had agonized for a month over the problems, only talking with a trusted few.

Sears was truly stunned at his firing. He had thought he would be asked to stay as the campaign's chief strategist, with Casey taking over the day-to-day operations. But he had said only a few days earlier about the prospect of Casey's taking over, "You're talking about someone coming in as a co-equal, that's just not going to happen."[92] In fact, it had been reported that Sears had already threatened to quit if Casey joined the campaign.

Reagan, supposedly the passive instrument of John Sears, had concocted much of the scheme to fire his manager after talking with his son Mike several days earlier.[93] Reagan had been aware of how the media saw him and Sears and he didn't like it one bit. He wrote one supporter, "I've read all the eastern press . . . that Sears is pulling the strings and I'm the puppet."[94]

Sears, Lake, and Black went quickly to their rooms, packed, and left the state. Casey watched from a window as they walked across the parking lot to their car. John Sears had discovered too late that the fault was not in the star but in the underling.

Sears's and Lake's principal assistants quit in a show of loyalty. Black's assistant, Neal Peden, assumed she'd been fired and left with the others. She was delighted to learn later that she had not been fired after all and was asked to return to the campaign.

After the firings, Linda Gosden, Lake's aide, took it upon herself to confront Nancy Reagan in a hallway and scream several obscenities at her.[95] Peden, an attractive Mississippian and loyal Reaganite, said she was "horrified" when Gosden regaled the others over her confrontation with Mrs. Reagan.[96] Though her father had known Reagan in Hollywood, Gosden had a history of rubbing the Reagans the wrong way. Several days earlier, after spotting Bill Casey in an elevator, she pointedly asked Reagan about the matter just before the candidate was to give a speech. "It was not a good time to bring up the subject of staff tensions," Hannaford later wrote. "The conversation upset him, something that was noticed in his speech delivery by longtime Reagan-watchers among the news people covering the event."[97]

Meese was not in the room for the execution because he, like others in the conspiracy, was busy making phone calls around the country to Reaganites and reporters, "letting them know what was happening."[98] A list of VIPs was assembled for Reagan to call that afternoon. It included William F. Buckley, Laxalt, and Jack Kemp.[99] Talking points were compiled for the Reagan team as they hurriedly made their calls.[100]

Hannaford had aides deliver Reagan's bombshell to the flabbergasted national media at 3 P.M. in the form of a press release, just moments after the triple firing. Two hours later Hannaford held a press conference. He said the resignations were the result of a need for "a sharp reduction in expenses and a restructuring of our organization."[101] All were under strict orders not to cast aspersions on Sears, Lake, and Black. The three knew too much and were media favorites, and the campaign did not need to create any fresh problems for Reagan.

Lyn Nofziger bitingly said of Sears's firing, "They finally got Rasputin, didn't they?"[102] Appropriately, the foreign-policy adviser, Allen, called their successful coup a "Leninist plot."[103]

William J. Casey would immediately replace Sears as campaign chairman, but a triumvirate of Casey, Meese, and Wirthlin would in fact run the renewed campaign, coordinating with Laxalt. Hannaford would temporarily replace Lake until a full-time spokesman, Ed Gray, could be secured.

Years later, Meese reviewed Sears's undoing. "I think John was unable to move beyond the thinking of the Nixon campaign in 1968," in which "decisions were made in smoke-filled rooms. John . . . didn't communicate. He would do things without telling the Governor." Meese added, "He didn't like Lyn [Nofziger] being around, he didn't like Mike [Deaver] being around, he didn't want me around."[104]

Reagan had his own take on Sears in a conversation with Theodore White: "I don't fault his ability at political analysis, but he wanted to do everything. . . . Morale was at zero . . . There was . . . a feeling that I was just kind of a spokesman for John Sears."[105]

Casey had never run a national campaign. In fact, he had only performed minor tasks in the Eisenhower and Nixon campaigns. But he had been the head of the Securities and Exchange Commission (SEC) and held various other posts during the Nixon administration. Most important, he had Reagan's vote of confidence.[106]

The only apparent problem with Casey was that no one ever seemed to understand what he was saying. He quickly picked up—behind his back—the moniker "Mumbles."[107] Another benefit to selecting the balding and gray-haired Casey was that he looked much older than the Gipper, though in fact he was two years younger.

Not wasting time, other campaigns began to make overtures toward Sears, including, ironically, Dave Keene in the Bush operation. It had only been a year since Sears had hung Keene out to dry, prompting the young campaign aide to angrily leave Reagan for Bush. Politics does indeed make strange bedfellows.

WITH HIS REMARKABLE COMEBACK in New Hampshire, Ronald Reagan had staved off what had seemed his sure political death. At the same time, in one swift action, he had rid himself of the source of so many of the mistakes that had hampered his campaign: John Sears. He still had won fewer than two dozen delegates and had 976 to go before he'd have enough to claim the Republican nomination at the Detroit convention in July. Certainly a long road lay ahead, and many hurdles remained. But he was finally off and running.

Only two days before the New Hampshire primary, Reagan had told listeners, "This isn't a campaign anymore. It's is a crusade to save this nation."[108]

Millions of Americans seemed to agree.

11

UNDER NEW MANAGEMENT

*"You fellas are going to call me whatever you call me and
I have a hunch that you are going to settle on 'front-runner.'"*

The Columbia Broadcasting System, known as the "Tiffany Network" for its high standards of programming, made some news of its own in February 1980. The network announced with poignant fanfare that the grand old man of the *CBS Evening News*, Walter Cronkite, who had become permanent anchorman in 1962, would retire in 1981, to be replaced by longtime reporter Dan Rather.[1] A torch was passing for a generation that had grown up with "Uncle Walter." Cronkite had been voted time and again "the most trusted man in America." Cronkite was so revered that in 1972 the floundering Democratic nominee, George McGovern, had pleaded with him to become his vice-presidential running mate. Cronkite wisely demurred. After March of 1981, America would no longer hear Cronkite's signature sign-off, "And that's the way it is."

Cronkite, a seafaring aficionado with a summer home on Martha's Vineyard, cherished his sailboat, *On Assignment*, and on more than one afternoon he would depart CBS headquarters in New York, saying, "If anyone asks where I am, tell them I'm on assignment." For millions, Cronkite had been their captain, their calming presence, their voice of reason during the storms of the 1960s. Many remembered his hours upon hours of steady coverage of the assassination and funeral of President Kennedy; only once had he broken on air, slightly, when first announcing the death of his friend on the afternoon of November 22, 1963. Many others recalled his unprecedented step in the wake of the Tet Offensive in 1968: he editorialized on air against the Vietnam War. Lyndon Johnson remorsefully reflected that if he'd lost Cronkite, he'd "lost Middle America." Johnson shortly withdrew from the 1968 presidential campaign.[2]

In the morning, American kids' touchstone on CBS was Captain Kangaroo, played by the gray-haired and mustachioed Bob Keeshan, and in the evening, their parents' lodestone was Cronkite, who also had gray hair and a moustache. They served as reassuring father figures in an uncertain time

WITHIN A MATTER OF hours after its primary, New Hampshire's citizens were heaving sighs of relief as the quadrennial political stalkers left for home. Finally, no more volunteer door knockers, no more phone calls at all hours, no more junk mail. At the now abandoned Reagan headquarters in Manchester, coffeepots were still half-full and uneaten pastries were strewn about.

Calm had returned to the Granite State.

Except at the *Nashua Telegraph*, where they were still smarting over the debate disaster. Angry readers flooded the newspaper with letters, denouncing Jon Breen for being rude to Ronald Reagan. The paper published a series of post-debate editorials telling its side of the story. It revealed that Jerry Carmen and John Sears had conspired to install another moderator, George Roberts, Speaker of the State House, to replace Breen should the need arise. It was becoming clear how the cunning Reagan folks had set up poor George Bush in Nashua.

Never at a loss for a shiv, Carmen said that primary day in New Hampshire must have been "too cold for silk stockings."[3] The 6'3" Bush buttonholed the 5'6" Carmen and said he didn't like what Carmen was saying about him.[4] Nothing doing. It was impossible to intimidate Carmen and he poured it on Bush with even more glee.

GEORGE WILL HAD THE final say on the soon-to-be legendary Nashua debate. "Americans are getting angry and seeking authenticity, and Reagan gave them authentic anger. . . . When Reagan is aroused, he is the most effective campaigner in living memory."[5]

Reagan left New Hampshire on a high. Before he headed on to continue his newly resurgent campaign, he delivered a message to the media, who had been so surprised by his landslide victory. Smiling broadly, he told reporters, "You fellas are going to call me whatever you call me and I have a hunch that you are going to settle on 'front-runner.'"[6]

There was more good news for the Reagan team: the Secret Service's mascot had been found. "Bobo," the mechanical monkey that played Willie Nelson's hit song "On the Road Again," had been "lost" several weeks earlier, said campaign aide Cindy Tapscott. In fact, Reagan and two young aides, Colin Clark and Mark Hatfield Jr., had engaged in their own little prank: they had kidnapped Bobo. Clark sent the Secret Service a ransom note signed by the "Bobo Liberation Army." The agents couldn't find Bobo—because Reagan, in on the gag, had mirthfully hid the stuffed monkey in his suitcase.[7]

Reagan may have been laughing, but establishment Republicans were tearing their hair out over his rejuvenated campaign. They feared that Reagan, without Sears's moderating presence, would run wildly to the right and become a second Barry Goldwater, bringing a crashing defeat for the party in the fall. They thought George Bush and Howard Baker had blown it in New Hampshire and the only way to stop Reagan now was to get Gerald Ford into the race. Ford himself started making noises about coming in—again.

Bush and Baker saw things differently. Bush showcased his sense of humor in acknowledging the New Hampshire setback, saying that although he'd taken it "on the chin," in truth it seemed "I took it a little lower."[8] But he brushed himself off and Bush gamely challenged Reagan, saying, "I'm going out there and wear him down."[9] Clearly, Bush still thought that Reagan didn't have the stamina for the campaign trail and that it was all some kind of athletic competition rather than a contest of ideas and leadership.

Baker, for his part, believed that if Bush faltered even more, then he himself might emerge as the moderate alternative to Reagan.

Overlooked in all this discussion of Reagan's conservatism and the need for moderation was an extensive New York Times poll of voters nationwide, which found that 40 percent called themselves "conservative," while only 22 percent said they were "liberal."[10]

About the only certainty in the Republican race was that Bob Dole was near to dropping out. He'd collected roughly 0.4 percent of the vote in New Hampshire—around 600 votes—and as a result, was disqualified from receiving any more matching funds from the FEC under its convoluted qualifying plan.[11]

Within the Reagan campaign, great uncertainty remained over the matter of John Sears, Charlie Black, and Jim Lake. Though the three had so far gone quietly, they had many friends in the national media and could make things very unpleasant for Reagan. They also had allies in Republican circles, including twelve members of the Reagan campaign who had resigned in protest over their dismissal, such as Nick Ruwe, the scheduling director. More angry staffers were rumored to be on the verge of resigning in protest over the firings. Some worried that they'd be tagged as being loyal to Charlie Black and not Reagan and would be fired as a result.

The Reagan team hastily called a two-hour meeting at Washington's Dulles Airport to avert a new staff crisis. Present were Reagan, Mrs. Reagan, Bill Casey, Ed Meese, and the field staff—Roger Stone, Herb Harmon, Keith Bulen, Frank

Donatelli, Frank Whetstone, Andy Carter, Kenny Klinge, Rick Shelby, George Clark, Ernie Angelo, Don Devine, Lou Kitchin, Paul Manafort, Dale Duvall, Don Totten, and others. Lee Atwater and Lorelei Kinder did not attend, but they were also part of this crew. This was the crème de la crème of GOP organizers in 1980, and perhaps the most impressive group of political operatives ever assembled. They had come to Reagan because of conservatism and eschewed silly, puerile tactics. Dignity for their candidate and their campaign was important. Reagan utterly agreed.

But Black had recruited many of these operatives, and some directly confronted Reagan over the shake-up. Black was their friend and the meeting grew contentious. Mrs. Reagan sharply rebuked several who challenged Reagan over the firings.[12] Whetstone, one of those who challenged the candidate over the firing of Sears, Lake, and Black, had something else he wanted to get off his chest: "Ron, when are you going to get a hearing aid so you can hear people?"

Reagan, momentarily stunned by the attacks, pulled himself together and addressed the group with a little pep talk, but he "got a little bit pissed off a couple of times," Shelby recalled.[13]

Then Casey stood up and gave them unshirted hell about whether the meeting was necessary, warning them about future budget and personnel cuts, essentially playing bad cop to Reagan's good cop. This group had seen that ploy before and they weren't buying it. They wanted to know whether they still had jobs, and Reagan assured them they did, that he'd made a mistake in Iowa. Klinge recalled that Reagan said, "I want you all around. You guys have done, and gals, have done, [a great] job for me."[14] The meeting ended with the staff mostly satisfied; they had had their chance to blow off steam.

Lyn Nofziger was due to come back aboard the campaign in short order, but not before he wrote a long piece for the *Los Angeles Herald-Examiner* dumping all over poor John Sears. Nofziger then reprinted the article in the March newsletter of Citizens for the Republic, sending it out to tens of thousands.[15]

Nofziger was the Michael Corleone of the conservative movement. He didn't want to wipe out everybody—just his "enemies."

MANY IN THE MEDIA wrote derisively that the new team taking over for Reagan was inadequate to the task. One Sears-smitten reporter, Loye Miller, wrote that Meese, Casey, and Dick Wirthlin were "junior varsity" and that the campaign would "float dead in the water" for a time without Sears and company.[16]

The American voter in 1980 was becoming more aware of front-line political operatives. Political-operatives-as-celebrities were a new phenomenon in politics. It had taken off in 1976, starting with the media's love affair with Carter's aides and certified characters Hamilton Jordan and Jody Powell. The two made the cover of *Rolling Stone*. Behind the scenes were hundreds more, however, who toiled in anonymity for their candidates, including the personal assistants. Bush's was a pleasant young man, David Bates, who called himself a "gentleman's gentleman."[17] David Fischer did likewise for the Gipper. Their jobs were critical, as it was up to them to make sure their candidate was where he should be and when. To ensure that their clothing was cleaned and pressed. To get them a glass of water, hold their coats, write down names, or get them a bite to eat when needed. It wasn't glamorous, it wasn't highly paid, but it was important. In later campaigns, they would become known as "body men." They routinely put in eighteen-hour days and it wasn't unusual for the exhausted traveling staff to wake up not knowing what day it was or what city they were in.

These madcap campaigns were not for the faint of heart or connoisseurs of gourmet food. Staff subsisted on bad airplane food, greasy hamburgers, old coffee, and nicotine, and the evenings were fueled with too much alcohol. Most candidates avoided drinking on the road. Reagan had an occasional glass of wine; Bush, a martini; and Jimmy Carter, of course, was a near-teetotaler. Ted Kennedy, it appeared, was holding on to the wagon.

Reagan's favorite dessert was carrot cake, but he would devour any dessert put before him. Bush enjoyed granola and yogurt in the morning, while snacking on potato chips or popcorn on the campaign plane at other times. Jerry Brown nibbled on whole-wheat noodles and raw cauliflower. Bush ran each morning and Reagan worked out in his hotel room with an exercise wheel. Kennedy exercised infrequently because of his bad back, and he had to avoid ice cream and other rich foods, as he gained weight easily.

Food and drink in politics could be a delicate matter. George Wallace, stereotypically, filled his plane with MoonPies and Dr Peppers. John Kennedy and Bobby Kennedy more sensibly stocked their planes with cartons of Campbell's tomato soup. In 1968 Nelson Rockefeller thoughtfully provided oysters and a man to shuck them for the traveling press. In 1972 Sargent Shriver, stumping in New Hampshire, went into a blue-collar drinking establishment in Nashua with a throng of media. Shriver sidled up to the bar and ordered a round of beer for the house, earning cheers—until he asked for a snifter of Courvoisier for himself.

Later that year, George McGovern was campaigning in a Jewish section of New York, where he ordered a kosher hotdog and "a glass of milk."[18]

THE DAY AFTER THE big win in New Hampshire, Governor and Mrs. Reagan flew by commercial plane to Vermont, site of a primary in one week. Standing before the media, Reagan was asked about the departed aides. He refused to say they'd been fired. Indeed, he praised each, calling them "good men."[19] His campaign was doing all it could to avoid provoking Sears, Black, and Lake.

Reagan also took responsibility for Sears's profligate spending: "I went along with them too." But the fact was that his campaign's finances were in shambles. The FEC allowed candidates to spend approximately $17 million over the thirty-odd primaries, but Reagan's campaign had already spent more than $12 million. Bush, on the other hand, had spent only $6.3 million to date and had plenty in reserve. Reagan's campaign had been spending more than $500,000 a month just on salaries.[20]

Dealing with this financial crisis was Casey's first task. This unlikely Reaganite—a product of the East Coast moneyed elites, who were supporting candidates like Bush or Connally but not populists like Reagan—set about paring the campaign to a bare-bones operation in order to save the Gipper's chances for the nomination. Under Casey, the payroll was cut in half, from $500,000 per month down to $250,000. Fully half of the campaign staff of 275 was laid off.[21]

While Casey worked to get the operations in order, Reagan continued campaigning fiercely. He knocked the president hard on the hostage crisis, saying that Carter had "botched" it. He also said that by holding Americans, Iran was engaging in an "act of war."[22] Reagan hammered Ted Kennedy on Iran, too. Referring to Kennedy's proposal to set up an international tribunal to investigate Iran's complaints against Washington in exchange for release of the hostages, Reagan railed in his stump speech, "It's nice to be liked, but it's more important to be respected."[23]

With Reagan suddenly back in front, Bush's campaign eyed a new strategy. Stung by the criticisms that Bush had been too "vague" on the issues, his team debated whether he should make a major speech on foreign policy. The staff also wrestled with taking the gloves off on Reagan's age, but the idea of an advertising assault was set aside. It could backfire by making Bush look mean; it would certainly make Reagan and Mrs. Reagan more angry at Bush than they already were; and it would doom any chance whatsoever for Bush to go on the ticket with Reagan in Detroit if the governor won the nomination.

But Bush could not resist toying with the age issue. At a press conference in Florida, Bush denied that he was attacking Reagan for being sixty-nine years old but then said, "People are going to want a person who can be a president for eight years."[24]

The dynamics in Florida for Bush changed immediately following New Hampshire. Bush's office in Miami had been inundated with phone calls in the days leading up to New Hampshire. The day after, the phones went dead. "I think," admitted Bill Schuette, the Bush director in the state, "that this [New Hampshire] will slow that momentum." It was an understatement.[25]

Reagan's offices, which had been a lethargic operation, suddenly burst with new volunteers and contributors, according to his regional fieldman, Herb Harmon.[26] Reagan had been in trouble in Florida for months. One of the few state leaders for Reagan from 1976 who had survived the purges in preparation for 1980 was Tommy Thomas, a car dealer from Panama City. Thomas had the build and tact of a bull—without the etiquette. Thomas said whatever he was thinking. He had one piece of advice for Reagan, which he naturally gave in public: "Quit being such a nice guy."[27]

As Reagan's campaign began to take off, Bush's campaign struggled more and more. In Florida Bush was being dogged by newspaper ads, sponsored by the Florida Conservative Union and its chairman, Mike Thompson, detailing Bush's involvement with the Council on Foreign Relations, a right-wing bogeyman similar to the Trilateral Commission. Both—conservatives said—were bent on one-world government. The ads went after Bush and those members of his staff who had some sort of association with either organization.

As it happened, Bill Casey was also a member of the Council on Foreign Relations, but Reagan's new campaign manager was never attacked over this matter the way Bush was.

The pressures and frustrations seemed to be getting to Bush. At one Florida campaign appearance, pro-life demonstrators were heckling him. Bush walked over to their leader, a respected physician named Bart Heffernan, and whispered in his ear, "Go fuck yourself." Rather than doing that, Heffernan instead put Bush's anatomical observations in his newsletter and it got into the hands of the national media.[28]

Dave Keene prided himself on never lying to his friends in the media. He could spin with the best of them, so when reporters asked him whether Bush had really said this to Dr. Heffernan, Keene replied, "Now, does that sound like something George would say?" The ploy worked and the media moved on.[29]

TEDDY KENNEDY LIMPED INTO the South. He went to Alabama, where two dozen protesters heckled him at a speech at a steel mill in Birmingham. It was ugly. A handmade sign read, "How Can You Save the Country When You Couldn't Save Mary Jo?" Another steelworker yelled, "You're a murderer," and a medical student taunted Kennedy, "You cheated on a test!"—a reference to Kennedy's expulsion from Harvard.[30]

Kennedy did his best to ignore them and finished his speech, in which he promised to fight for gun-control legislation. Because of such statements, the

National Rifle Association had only accelerated its "If Kennedy Wins, You Lose" campaign as the primary season moved south.[31]

Although the president could claim only fifty-five delegates to Kennedy's thirty-six, Carter's team wondered how much more pounding Kennedy was willing to take. The national media had all but completely turned against Kennedy. They referred to his campaign as "The Bozo Zone," a send-up of *The Twilight Zone*. Reporters got on the public-address system of the plane to broadcast bogus news reports about the stumbles of the candidate and the comic story that Teddy's campaign had become.

Carter had walloped Kennedy in Iowa and New Hampshire, and now the White House aimed for a knockout. Carter didn't just want to beat Kennedy, he wanted to crush him, humiliate him. It would be Carter's revenge against the smarmy liberals from Georgetown who made fun of him and his clan. Carter wasn't just using the hostage crisis to maximum effect; the full force of his campaign and the government were brought to bear on poor, unsuspecting Teddy. Early on, Carter's team had worried that a bandwagon effect would take place, that terrified Democrats would quickly endorse Kennedy and run away from Carter's reelection campaign. So the president's operatives had organized assiduously for months in the early states, especially in lining up early endorsements. First they went after the big-city mayors, reminding them of the federal largesse given them over the past three years. The mayors, with their machines to consider, reluctantly signed up. Other sheepish Democratic politicians quickly fell in line behind the president, albeit with tails between their legs. Carter poured it on.

The president didn't need to worry about Jerry Brown by this point. Brown's campaign had devolved into a sad joke. Thousands of his petitions in New York were disqualified because two-thirds of the signers were not registered to vote. Brown's name was thrown off the ballot. His manager resigned, noting the difficulty of "working without salary."[32]

JOHN CONNALLY'S CAMPAIGN WAS a mess as well. He was now on his third campaign manager: his son, John Connally III. Connally's newest spokesman, Bill Rhatican, quipped, "I would say right now John Connally is his own campaign manager."[33] Despite the whipping administered to him so far, Big John said, "I could turn this country around in the first 24 hours if I was in office."[34] The words "humility" and "Connally" had never collided in the same sentence.

Connally decided to make South Carolina his last stand with Reagan. He had won the support of both Senator Strom Thurmond—who had played footsie with

Reagan in 1976 but had never come out for him—and Governor Jim Edwards, who had supported Reagan in 1976.

When Bush found out that Connally was making a big effort there to stop Reagan, he changed the agreed-upon strategy, which had been to stay out of the Gamecock State. Bush overruled the vigorous protestations of his campaign and paid the $1,500 filing fee. Jim Baker told reporters that Bush was going to South Carolina because Howard Baker was there, but the candidate was really going in because he hated Connally.

Bush had won the endorsement of Harry Dent of South Carolina, a former Nixon and Ford aide who made a big footprint in the GOP South. Dent despised Reagan and told Bush that he could win South Carolina, since he surmised that Reagan and Connally would divide the conservative vote. Dent immediately began to spread rumors that Connally's campaign was being run by blacks and homosexuals.

Connally replied by calling Dent "the original dirty tricks man."[35] Yet another of his temporary spokesmen, Jim McAvoy, told the media that Connally would not quit, even if he lost South Carolina, and that his goal was to hold Reagan to under 40 percent.[36] They were whistling past the kudzu.

BILL BROCK'S REPUBLICAN NATIONAL Committee was gearing up for the November elections. Brock had transformed the organization in just a few short years. The Republicans' house file list had grown to more than 650,000 names of proven givers—bigger, even, than it was after the 1964 Goldwater campaign—with an average return of $26 per name. The year before, the committee had spent $3.5 million on direct mail, which had impressively netted more than $9.5 million.[37] The RNC had fourteen trained regional political directors whose experience in running campaigns was put to use by sending them constantly on the road to give ideas, support, and advice to GOP candidates, managers, and committees.

Brock had instituted an impressive outreach program to minorities, women, labor, professionals, farmers, and other interest groups. He produced several widely read publications that not only boosted morale but also spread the Republican message. In addition, Brock was making plans to run a multimillion-dollar "institutional" campaign to further spread Republican cheer while taking it to the Democrats. His overall budget for 1980 was more than $20 million, up 200 percent in just four years.

Brock also rolled out one of the funniest and most effective commercials of the season. An actor who looked suspiciously like House Speaker Tip O'Neill was accompanied in a Lincoln Continental by a nervous young aide. "The Speaker" was depicted weaving down the highway, oblivious to his predicament as he ignored the aide's pleas to look at the gas gauge. Finally, as the car died on the side of the road, the comic faux O'Neill shrieked, "Hey, we're out of gas!" A voiceover intoned, "The Democrats are out of gas."[38]

The commercial (which later won a Clio Award for excellence in advertising) was a brilliant indictment of a Democratic Party that many believed hadn't had an original initiative in years, had poor energy policies, and was led in Congress by a man who was trapped in a New Deal past.

WITH THE DEPARTURE OF Sears from the Reagan campaign, all the old Reaganites began to come back into the fold. Lyn Nofziger, Marty Anderson, Mike Deaver, and others eventually returned to Reagan. The band was back together. A triumvirate of Meese, Casey, and Wirthlin was running the operation. The Californians, along with honorary new member Casey, were back. For the first time in a long time, Reagan was having fun again and there was joy in Mudville.

But Sears, Lake, and Black would not remain silent long. After their firing they had holed up in a Boston hotel to steer clear of reporters who were inundating them with interview requests, but they soon returned to Washington. Two days later they held a ninety-minute press conference at the National Press Club. The trio wanted to make it clear that they had not resigned. "I was fired," Black said, and the others concurred.[39]

The three avoided any personal criticism of the Gipper, but they portrayed the Reagan campaign as "an operation plagued with incompetence, internal rivalries and an indecisive candidate, unprepared on the issues and insulated from the problems on his staff."[40] Sears, of course, had been in charge of that operation. He and Black had hired much of the staff they now suggested was incompetent. And Reagan didn't look very indecisive when he participated in the scheme to fire them in New Hampshire.

Sears and Black both nervously smoked cigarettes as they sat during the press conference. Sears admitted that the financial mess was entirely of his doing, but he blamed Nofziger, Meese, and Deaver for sundry misdeeds. He also said Reagan had been poorly briefed, which is why he did not participate in the Iowa debates, a decision that Sears said was Reagan's decision, not his own.[41] This was true—in a way. Sears had recommended that Reagan not go and Reagan had acceded to the recommendation of the man in whose hands he'd put his career.

Bitterness sometimes crept into their comments. Black said, "If this [press conference] gets Gov. Reagan bad publicity, then I'm sorry. But we will not sit here and fail to tell you the truth."[42]

In character, Nofziger fired a salvo back from Los Angeles, saying that Sears was "paranoid, has been for a long time. He can't stand to have anybody disagree with him."[43]

The experience was terribly hard on the three men, as they had invested more than five years of their lives in Ronald Reagan, going back to 1975 as part of Citizens for Reagan. They had many friends there, and each had spent untold hours with Reagan on planes, in cars, in hotels, and over meals. It was clear that this was hardest on Black, the young conservative. For him, the campaign had been an ideological mission, much more so than for Lake and Sears. Reagan later told reporters that Black didn't have to resign.

When it came to Sears, Charlie Black put it best: "Reagan would never have become president had he not hired John in 1975 . . . and fired John in 1980."[44] There was wisdom in this observation. Sears was the only national GOP political operative in 1974 and 1975 who thought Reagan had what it took to be president. The other major GOP players—especially Easterners and moderates—thought Reagan was a certified yahoo, a shallow former B-movie actor who was the George Wallace of the Republican Party. To a person, by the time of Reagan's death in 2004, they would profess their love and devotion to Reagan and claim they were there from the beginning in 1974, which was a load of horse manure. The only one there was Sears, leading a small group of Californians, conservatives, and junior-varsity operators willing to take on the GOP establishment and Gerald Ford.

It was Sears who talked the Reagans into challenging the incumbent Ford. It was also Sears who came up with the idea of selecting Senator Dick Schweiker as Reagan's running mate before the 1976 convention, which kept Reagan's chances alive going into Kansas City. If Reagan hadn't run in 1976, he never would have run in 1980; he would have lived out his last years giving an occasional speech and spending his days at his ranch with Nancy and the horses.

Sears also understood better than almost anybody what was at stake in 1980: "I can tell you this particular election is more important than any I've seen before."[45]

The firings of Sears, Black, and Lake created bitterness on all sides. But over time, some of those wounds healed. Indeed, Black and Lake eventually became fixtures in the Reagan White House and on the 1984 campaign team.

Sears might have similarly worked his way back into Reagan's good graces. All he had had to do was pick up the phone and call and the forever-forgiving Reagan would have welcomed him warmly. Mrs. Reagan maybe less so, but she still would have been gracious. But according to Sears, after his firing in Manchester he never spoke with the Reagans again. On one or two occasions he saw Nancy at a Washington function, but they only waved from afar.[46]

Years later, Sears was philosophical about being dismissed. "I had already used my credibility and I was too controversial and they needed someone else. You go into politics . . . you're going to accumulate some shit. When you are in there too long, you should get out. It's a far nicer life when you are out."[47]

John P. Sears, campaign maestro extraordinaire—at only thirty-nine years of age—never again worked in national politics.

THE CAMPAIGN MOVED ON to the University of South Carolina, where four of the contenders met for a mostly civil ninety-minute debate moderated by Jim Lehrer of PBS.

Reagan was by now supremely confident at these "cattle shows" he had once derided. George Bush was forced to spend time on more mea culpas over Nashua. Senator Baker said he was no longer mad at Bush—which everybody knew was a fib. Connally lashed out at Bush, saying he must be a liberal, "because they are all for him." Bush replied weakly that "labels are not important."[48]

But Connally saved his hottest fire for Reagan, saying he had been running for president since 1964 and that he'd led the very liberal labor union the Screen Actors Guild. Reagan testily replied that he'd successfully fought off a Communist takeover of the union.[49] Big John had swung and missed.

The subject of the participation of African-Americans in the GOP came up. The other three candidates gave mostly stock answers about how many minorities were on their staff. Reagan said as much but then went much further than the other candidates did: "But what I think the Republican Party has to do today is recognize that the Democratic Party for years has humiliated and demeaned these people by saying the only way to approach them is by an offer of more government handouts. . . . We're coming to you because . . . we're Americans . . . with the same hopes and dreams. You want dignity . . . you want an opportunity to educate your children. We want you to have that and we believe the Republicans offer that more than the Democrats do."[50]

Reagan was also asked whether he supported counting illegal aliens from Mexico in the upcoming census. He replied that he was foursquare opposed, although he did express his opposition to a "nine-foot fence along the border," preferring instead an agreement between the two countries whereby citizens could cross the border legally, "with permits."[51]

Unlike the Nashua debate, the event at the University of South Carolina produced no dramatic confrontations. It certainly did nothing to allow George Bush to shift the momentum. Bush had to focus on Massachusetts and Vermont, which would hold their primaries on March 4, four days before the South Carolina vote.

These New England states were perceived as Bush's "firewalls"; they might halt Reagan's momentum after the Gipper's win in New Hampshire. Expectations remained high for Bush in the two states. Bush had the organizational jump on Reagan there. Besides, he had been born in Massachusetts and of course, there was Andover, and his list of supporters included some of the most prominent Boston Brahmins—Hatch, Lodge, Saltonstall. Recognizing these advantages, Reagan took only a cursory pass through the Bay State and made it clear that he expected Bush to win there. Polling seemed to confirm Reagan's point of view: a Boston Globe survey taken a month earlier had Bush up over Reagan by an incredible 61–16 margin.[52]

But after Reagan's big victory in neighboring New Hampshire, Massachusetts and Vermont had become "must-win" states for Bush. Bush's Bay State manager was the thirty-two-year-old Andy Card. Neither Card nor his assistant, Ron Kaufman, was anything like the Brahmins with whom they worked. Kaufman, who was Jewish, had grown up poor; his father once had a little shoe store where he made baseball cleats for Joe DiMaggio and Ted Williams. Kaufman was a self-described "underachiever"; he never went to college and had worked as a grocery clerk until he got involved in local politics and found out he was pretty good at it.[53] A tough kid, he'd once had the stuffing kicked out of him working on Election Day in South Boston. "Southie" was widely regarded as the roughest neighborhood in Beantown, intolerant of blacks, Jews, and Republicans, but Kaufman had made his bones and was ready for more action.[54]

Card had run into opposition from Jim Baker about hiring Kaufman as his deputy. Baker said, "Kaufman is wrapping lettuce for a living; he's not ready for politics." Card protested and finally Bush's manager relented.[55]

But now that the spotlight was on Massachusetts, Card showed his own inexperience. "Bush has to win here," he blurted out to reporters.[56] Yet in the wake of the New Hampshire landslide, Reagan's organizations in Massachusetts and Vermont showed new signs of life. Vermont allowed crossover voting, meaning that Reagan could hope to pick up votes from conservative Democrats there. John Anderson could also hurt Bush by attracting some Democrats in the Green Mountain State.

Anderson believed that his "Anderson Difference" era-of-limits message would go down well among the tweedy set of Vermont and the moderates of Massachusetts—the same voters Bush was counting on. Anderson had taken a beating in New Hampshire, winning only 10 percent of the vote, but the national media now got behind his flagging campaign. Some liberals, disappointed with Kennedy, were also kicking Anderson's tires.

The Reagan campaign recognized that the Bush campaign would be weakened further if he failed to live up to expectations in these states. Reagan's Massachusetts campaign director, the twenty-seven-year-old Robert Dawson, wisely kept the focus and expectations on the other candidates: "This is Bush's best state and it may be Anderson's best state."[57]

Facing unexpected challenges in Massachusetts and Vermont, the Bush team was forced to rearrange his schedule and spend even more time in those states. As a result, Bush could not devote as much attention to the tougher tests that would come later in the South and the Midwest.

The Bush campaign pushed a theme that was becoming prevalent in election reporting: that without Sears, Reagan would engage in some sort of ideological orgy and go too far to the right. Dave Keene, normally a shrewd operative, said he thought that Reagan would "move into an ideological corner" because his campaign could "fire up their base, but they can't expand their base."[58] He added that Reagan had let go "the 90 percent of the people who have talent." "If they think they . . . can win with the B team," Keene said, "then we're happy to play."[59]

Keene wasn't thinking right. He was going through a messy divorce and was in the unfamiliar Bush country club, working with moderates against all his friends in the Reagan campaign and the conservative movement. He was miserable and it showed. The crushing defeat in New Hampshire did not help his mood. Campaign secretaries fled his office in tears. He was so hard on one poor young woman that she quit in exasperation. The Bushes heard about the incident and indirectly let Keene know they were unhappy with his behavior. Jim Baker called Keene into his office ostensibly to deliver this message. Baker talked around the divorce and the Bushes' concerns. Keene, knowing how the Bushes felt about marriage, thought, "Uh oh, here we go," until Baker said, "Now, do you have a good lawyer?"[60]

THE GOP BASE OF support had changed over the past hundred years. In the years following the Civil War, the GOP's strength had been in the Northeast and the Midwest. States like Massachusetts, New Jersey, and Illinois were routinely Republican. The Democrats' stronghold was the South, fueled by anti-Republican rage over the Civil War, initiated by a Republican president, and Reconstruction, brought on by a vengeful Republican Congress. The New Deal and the rise of labor politics altered the course; onetime Republican states became Democratic. Jimmy Carter had won the presidency in 1976 by stitching together the old New Deal coalition of the South and the industrial Rust Belt.

But that was a last hurrah. The GOP's base had moved to the West and the South. Texas was moving into the GOP column and California, along with the rest of the West, was now reliably Republican, especially in presidential contests. It was significant that Reagan, Bush, Connally, and Howard Baker all hailed from the South or the West.

The new GOP embraced the western culture. These were states settled by men and women of courage and fortitude, by hardy individualists, conservative in their outlook and suspicious of government. The broad expanse of terrain imbued their culture and their character. Being at a great distance from the seat of their national government added to their "we don't need no stinkin' Washington" populist outlook. Notably, both Texas and California were once independent republics before they joined the Union.

The GOP was changing as America was changing. Texas and California together had more wealth than New York and New England combined.[61] Dallas, which had become a pariah city after 1963, had by the late 1970s been rejuvenated. It had even become the setting—and the name—of a hugely popular evening soap opera. American workers in the North, increasingly frustrated with the economy, government regulations, crime, education, and the weather, migrated in greater numbers to warmer climes than had those who had crossed the plains a hundred years earlier. The Democratic Northeast was losing population while the South and West gained voters.

The changing demographics were on the minds of all political types because the U.S. government was getting ready to launch the census. The Constitution required a nose count of Americans every ten years. At stake was the apportionment of congressional districts and thus presidential electoral ballots. Democrats worried that with the census counting illegal aliens, GOP states like California and Texas would pick up new congressional seats.

Like everything else bureaucrats and politicians got their hands on, the census had become grotesque and unwieldy. The short form had nineteen questions, eighteen of which conservatives thought were none of the government's business. The long form had a whopping forty-six questions. Bureaucrats arrogantly pointed out that the long form would take "just" forty-five minutes to complete. Even liberals worried about questions that could make people feel "uncomfortable." Indeed, the Census Bureau prepared a report revealing, "Many people believe that Americans are less willing now than in the past to cooperate freely with officialdom."[62] Big money, including the spread of federal pork, was at stake, and of course, many of the none-of-your-business questions were the result of lobbying by Madison Avenue. Marketers wanted taxpayers to pay for information they could use to cram new products down the American consumers' throats.

The nosiness of government was easy pickings for Reagan. He made bureaucrats look foolish when he told audiences that he refused to tell Uncle Sam how many toilets he had in his home.

George Bush, trying to recover from the loss in New Hampshire, went hard after Reagan. He wasn't about to roll over and play dead for anyone.

Bush told a group of reporters, "I can't see Reagan going much farther to the right, that's pretty hard to do." He also slammed Reagan on foreign affairs—a topic very much in the news and on the minds of government officials. Congress had approved a $75 million aid package for the "revolutionary junta" of the Sandinistas in Nicaragua, hoping to "curb the leftist tilt."[63] Meanwhile, the brutal fight in Afghanistan was raging, and it was dawning on the Soviets that their attempted takeover might take longer than expected. Bush attacked Reagan for his proposed blockade of Cuba to punish the Soviets for the Afghanistan invasion, calling it "almost an act of war"[64] and "irresponsible rhetoric."[65]

Bush also took it to Reagan on the economy. In Chicago he said that Reagan was making a "phony promise" to freeze or reduce federal spending. Bush said that his opponent needed to "get specific" about budget cuts and reduction in the size of the government, and accused Reagan of wanting to cut Social Security for retirees. "It's a cinch to go for the punch-line out there—the easy promise. But I'm going to avoid the simplistic."[66] Reagan was not about to let Bush's charges go without a response. He accused Bush of "bland generalities," adding, "I don't recall him ever being specific about anything."[67]

But if these guys thought national politics was tough, they hadn't seen nothin.' In Dade County, Florida, hundreds of people from all lifestyles were running for spots on the Democratic County Executive Committee. Each had a unique reason for running. "Michael Smyser is running against Seth Sklarey. He says Seth is ugly." Another candidate, Nancy Abrams, was said to be "easy to hate." Nancy and her ex-husband had carried some weight in Florida politics, but they went their separate ways in marriage and then again over Carter and Kennedy—Nancy stayed with Carter. *People* magazine did a story on their divorce.[68]

Of the whole local mess, the *Miami Herald* entertainingly wrote, "The rumors fly. So-and-so doesn't really live in her district. His endorsements are false. She never went to any party meetings. He's a homosexual. She's a power-hungry man-eater." The Republicans watched with bemusement from the sidelines. "We try to be polite, dear," Jane Warren, the Republican secretary, told the *Herald*. Of course, the local GOP had its own issues. In a recent Republican contest, Letitia Godoy found herself in a fight with her opponent over who would be listed first on the ballot. Her opponent was her own mother—Letitia Godoy.[69]

All of this Sturm und Drang was over offices that paid exactly nothing. There were some benefits to the job, though, by the account of one candid local official. "What do I do as a committeeman? Things like fixing traffic tickets and jury notices."[70]

Democracy in America was a beautiful thing.

12

FORD TEES OFF

"Maybe he's developed a slice."

In early March 1980, Lou Cannon wrote a remarkably candid piece about Ronald Reagan for the *Washington Post*'s "Commentary" section. "Reagan has been depicted in this newspaper and by this correspondent as being old, tired and hard of hearing," Cannon penned. "His capacity to be president has been questioned."[1]

But what was "remarkable," he added, was that Reagan had "chosen to grin and bear it. I have covered every campaign of Reagan's, seeing him on bad days and good. He can become angry or distraught or confused about what has been said about him. But I have never known Reagan to hide out on his ranch and refuse to answer questions. Nor has he treated those who reported critically about him with special disfavor. He has, on the contrary, been unfailingly courteous and responsive to his media critics, never whining about the treatment he has been given or suggesting that the liberties of the press should be curtailed.

"The word . . . to describe Reagan is 'manly.'"[2]

Now the "manly" Reagan was surging. George Bush's decision to redouble his efforts in Massachusetts and Vermont seemed not just prudent but critical by this point. A new Boston Globe poll released just four days before the primaries showed that Bush's once-massive lead in the Bay State had all but disappeared: Reagan and Bush were essentially tied, at 33 and 36 percent, respectively. John Anderson's strategy was paying off, as he scored an impressive 17 percent. Only Howard Baker fared poorly, polling at just 6 percent.[3] The race had gotten so tight that the candidates shuttled for a week between the two New England states by car and plane. Except for Reagan, that is: He adhered to the previous plan of spending only one day in Massachusetts. Most of his effort would go into a mailing to 270,000 of the state's Republicans.[4]

Bush was doing his best in Massachusetts to push Reagan into a right-wing corner and Anderson into a left-wing corner so he could seize the middle for himself. The primary, he said, would, "sort out the fringe candidates."[5]

The stunning breakdown in New Hampshire called for a radical change in Bush's message. Bush's adman, Bobby Goodman, huddled with Jim Baker, Dave Keene, and their candidate. They decided that they could not keep dancing around the age issue. The most effective way to attack Reagan's age, they concluded, was to create commercials featuring senior citizens speculating that Reagan couldn't have the necessary vitality anymore because they didn't have it anymore. "Onerous geriatric judgments" was how Evans and Novak put it.[6]

Bush began telling Republicans that "a vote for Anderson is a vote for Reagan."[7] Anderson didn't much like being called anybody's cat's-paw. He crisscrossed the state, and pledged to keep campaigning until he ran out of clean laundry. Anderson told voters, "There is something different about me," or, speaking in the third person, "There is something different about John Anderson." His speeches were liberally sprinkled with the words "I" and "my."[8]

Bush, more than gun-shy after the Nashua experience, ran away from a proposal to debate Howard Baker in Vermont, screaming "ambush." Baker wryly took stock of Bush's response and said, "George must have suffered more from New Hampshire than I thought."[9]

Adding to the Bush team's aggravation was the fact that the mudslinging was intensifying with John Connally in South Carolina. Connally had accused the Bush campaign of "dirty tricks,"[10] charging that a black supporter of Bush's was spreading "'walking-around' money" throughout the state. The charge was scurrilous, but Connally soon became embroiled in his own controversy. Bush backer Harry Dent—who loathed Connally almost as much as he despised Reagan—accused Connally of attempting to buy the black vote. Dent would not let the issue go, and the fight between the two campaigns turned ugly.[11] John Connally III, acting as his father's newest campaign manager, called Bush "reprehensible." A Bush spokesman fired back, using a polysyllabic obscenity, and called young Connally's charges "a lie."[12] Bush's aides fretted that their campaign was wasting time going after the wrong man, but Reagan couldn't have been happier. The more time the two Texans spent banging on each other, the less time they had to go after him. He could stay above the fray.

Connally was fighting hard in South Carolina, but he was not connecting with voters as one might have expected for a man who had plowed fields in Texas as a barefoot boy. At one stop in Greenville, *Newsweek* reported, he "declaimed on the virtues of revisited depreciation schedules as a means to promote capital formation." The crowd of working poor had no idea what he was talking about.[13]

President Carter was serenely riding the foreign-policy crises in Afghanistan and Iran—and using them to ride roughshod over Ted Kennedy. In polling in Illinois, whose primary was looming in mid-March, Carter was mauling Kennedy 64–17, according to the *Chicago Tribune*, while Bush was besting Reagan by an impressive 38–21 there.[14] Even in Kennedy's home state of Massachusetts, Carter was showing unexpected strength. A multitude of former Kennedy supporters had defected to the president, and Teddy was compelled to spend humiliating time campaigning there. Desperate to win, he was spotted at a factory gate in North Boston for the 6 A.M. shift change, shaking hands in the frigid cold.

Some of Carter's more seasoned operatives remembered the fickleness of the public. The president had gone from 70 percent approval in 1977 to 29 percent approval by late summer of 1979,[15] but had risen back to the 60s by December. He was due for another descent on the roller coaster. In fact, by late February 1980 his approval rating had already fallen to 52 percent.[16] Economic anxiety was hurting Carter—Americans expected prices to continue going up and the economy to continue downward—and Carter's stalled foreign-policy initiatives, including reinstituting a military draft, did not help him either. The only good news in America was that spring training opened on March 4.

Compounding the problem, Carter's team made its first serious mistake in several months. In early March, the United States astonishingly joined fourteen other countries at the United Nations in denouncing Israel over settlements in the West Bank. Many American Jews were already distressed with Carter over the Camp David Accords and his perceived kowtowing to Arab oil sheiks. The UN vote was the first time America had ever opposed Israel in the Security Council. Reagan said such a move by the United States was "preposterous."[17] Kennedy pounced on Carter, calling it an "appalling betrayal."[18]

Carter blamed the whole mess on miscommunication and said it was a mistake. The United States belatedly switched its vote, but the damage was done. It didn't help that the imbroglio emerged shortly before the forthcoming primaries in New York and Connecticut, two states with large numbers of influential Jewish Democratic liberal voters.

Gerald Ford finally came out from merely shadowboxing with Reagan and threw a big left hook at the Gipper. In an interview with his old friend Barbara

Walters of ABC he said there was a "50–50" chance that he would get into the contest. Ford denied to Walters that he would get in to "stop one candidate."[19] But soon, in an exclusive interview with Adam Clymer of the *New York Times*, Ford made his target clear: "Every place I go and everything I hear, there is the growing, growing sentiment that Governor Reagan cannot win the election."[20] He made the inevitable comparison to Barry Goldwater's crushing loss in 1964. When conservatives in the GOP responded with outrage, Ford backtracked, saying his comments had been taken out of context. "I said that there was a *perception* he was too conservative," Ford claimed, not too convincingly.

Reagan counterpunched, reminding reporters that he'd been twice elected governor of a state with a 2–1 Democratic registration edge—and that he'd beaten Ford in the 1976 southern primaries with the help of Democratic voters. Reagan challenged Ford's noncandidacy, saying he should "come out here. . . . There's plenty of room."[21]

Ford's posturing did nothing to help George Bush. Bush had already been accused of being a "stalking horse" for Ford, and if Ford got in the race, he would divide the anti-Reagan vote even more.[22] Ford supporters placed the former president's name on the ballot in relatively liberal Maryland. In Illinois, thirty-five former supporters of Howard Baker announced their intention to run as Ford delegates.[23] Bush's team now had something else to worry about. Bush said that he was not going to "roll over" for Ford, while Dave Keene said Ford was "mistaking affection for political support."[24]

Ford's narrow loss four years earlier to Carter ate at him more than he let on. He wanted another shot at Carter, and felt Reagan owed him that shot. Years later, journalist Tom DeFrank wrote that Ford "emphatically told me . . . that Reagan should have graciously stepped aside in 1980 so he could run against Jimmy Carter again and was monumentally irked when he didn't."[25]

While Ford was blasting Reagan, another former Republican standard bearer finally endorsed the Gipper for president. Barry Goldwater had supported Richard Nixon over Reagan in 1968 and Ford over Reagan in 1976. Reagan's famous speech in 1964 had raised hundreds of thousands of dollars for Goldwater, but it took sixteen long years for "Mr. Conservative" to return the favor.

Reagan had not yet consolidated the "New Right" behind his drive for the White House. More militant members had been withholding their support for various reasons while others had cast their lot with Phil Crane or Connally. The first to support Reagan was the Fund for a Conservative Majority, whose pro-Reagan independent expenditure effort had begun in New Hampshire and carried through all the primaries, including Illinois. The second to come on board was

Christian Voice, which launched an ambitious effort to contact five million Christian voters urging them to support Reagan and contribute to their organization. The funds were then used to put a half-hour interview with Reagan on independent television stations, including Christian stations in the South and Midwest, according to Gary Jarmin, head of the organization's Washington office. With Reagan speaking about his faith and moral stands, Christian Voice believed that this effort could mobilize millions of "moral" voters—born-again Protestants and conservative Catholics, Jews, and Mormons—in support of the Gipper.[26]

Another organization of the New Right, Americans for Conservative Action, blanketed South Carolina with anti-Bush flyers, charging him with being for gun control and federal funding of abortion. Bush was livid and was forced to defend himself yet again against spurious charges.[27]

The millions of dollars in independent support came none too soon for Reagan. Bill Casey had slashed campaign costs across the board. In South Carolina, for example, Casey canceled Reagan's charter plane, a Boeing 727, and instead rented a bus with "Reagan Express" signs taped on the side. The move saved tens of thousands of dollars, but it also created mayhem with the traveling press, some of whom were left high and dry, forced to hurriedly schedule commercial flights to cover Reagan's speeches. The decision to curtail the charters did not make for a happy press corps, but Reagan was in high spirits, out and about, meeting voters, listening to them, talking to them. He sat with a reporter from *The State*, Mike Clements, and mused about missing his ranch and the beautiful South Carolina countryside. After a grueling day, Reagan was still fresh as a daisy, while the staff and the reporters on the bus were dragging. Reagan explained, "You draw strength from the people."[28] Reporters were now noting how good Reagan looked, how ruddy and healthy and vibrant he seemed.

Riding on the bus with Reagan was the great former Yankee second baseman Bobby Richardson, but the biggest treat for Reagan came when he was introduced to a baby born just a month earlier on February 6, his birthday. The infant was named "Reagan."[29] The child would be the first of many to bear that honorific.

ON MARCH 4, GOP primary voters went to the polls in Vermont and Massachusetts. The day before the primaries, Bush was asked how he felt. The man who had been the front-runner just a week earlier replied, "Nervioso, muy nervioso."[30]

He was right to be nervous. His formerly massive lead in Massachusetts had practically vanished. Bush barely eked out the victory. He received 31 percent of the vote . . . but so did John Anderson; Bush edged Anderson by only 1,200 votes (124,316 to 123,080). And Reagan nearly matched them both; despite having done little campaigning there, he tallied 29 percent (115,125 votes). In Vermont, Bush came in a disappointing third with just 23 percent; Reagan came in first with 31 percent, while Anderson claimed 30 percent.[31]

The big winner of the day—though he won neither primary—was Anderson. After nearly stealing both primaries, he got the lion's share of laudatory media coverage, including an appearance on the *Today* show. Lots of independents and liberals had crossed over to vote for Anderson, which might have explained why he happily flashed the peace sign for photographers.

Moreover, a major constituency of Anderson's was young students, and New England was chock-full of them, especially Boston, where one in twelve inhabitants was enrolled in college. On primary night Anderson's young troops, students from Harvard, Tufts, Boston University, and dozens of other universities, gathered at his headquarters, drank beer, and screamed each time a network anchor gave out more favorable news about their man's progress. Anderson had attended Harvard Law, so he understood the culture of the campus. Bush referred to Anderson's showings as a "freak" occurrence,[32] and with that, when Anderson appeared on campuses, he addressed his young supporters as "my fellow Anderson freaks."[33]

Reagan was scored a survivor for having won two in the Northeast and been competitive in a third. But columnists pummeled poor Bush. He was only one delegate behind Reagan, 37–36,[34] but expectations had once again defeated him. He had been expected to score a major win in the Bay State instead of a narrow win and to place first or second in Vermont, not an unimpressive third. The *Miami Herald* called it a "minuscule boomlet" and Bush himself candidly said, "A landslide it wasn't."[35]

Moderates, growing more concerned about Reagan in Connecticut and other states around the country, began sending Ford telegrams of encouragement. It would be a major embarrassment for Bush to lose in the state where he had grown up.

LIKE THE GOP CANDIDATES, the Democrats split the Massachusetts and Vermont primaries. Ted Kennedy ended up winning his home state handily, taking 65 percent to Carter's 29 percent.[36] Predictably, the Carter White House pooh-poohed the results—Massachusetts, after all, was the Kennedy fiefdom—and Teddy caught no bounce out of it. Worse for Kennedy, Carter won neighboring Vermont convincingly.

The senator felt miserable with a bad cold. At this point, Kennedy was actually ahead of Carter in the delegate count, 113–89, but as the saying went, nobody paid this any never mind.[37] He was planning a last-ditch effort against Carter in Illinois and the New York and Connecticut primaries, all just over the horizon, but he got himself involved in a local dispute between the Chicago Firefighters Union and the city's mayor, Jane Byrne. Striking municipal workers in Chicago protested Kennedy—labor's best friend on Capitol Hill for years—and Carter, who had often been indifferent to the concerns of organized labor, was benefiting.

Nothing seemed to go right for Ted Kennedy.

AFTER HIS DISAPPOINTMENT IN New England, Bush pressed on to Florida. He took it to Reagan, reminding the GOP faithful that when they had nominated Goldwater in 1964, "the party self-destructed."[38]

Bush's campaign had produced some tough radio and newspaper ads going after Reagan, but then scrapped them at the last minute for fear of a backlash. The ads accused Reagan of "flip-flops" over the ERA and abortion. Then they made a harsh comparison between Carter and Reagan: "Can we afford the same mistake twice?" In a final blow, the ads said Reagan "has no real understanding of the dangers we face in the decade of the '80s. . . . He didn't even know who the president of France was"—a reference to an interview Reagan had done with Tom Brokaw of the *Today* show several months earlier.[39] Dave Keene had told reporters several days earlier that Bush's campaign would pursue a tougher line of attack on Reagan.

Although Bush was drawing big crowds throughout Florida, the volatility of the GOP contest fueled speculation that former president Ford might—or should—get into the race. Campaign maestro Stu Spencer made several probing calls around the country to Republicans, taking soundings as to how they felt about Ford jumping in. Since the calls were self-selected, naturally the vast majority were a go for Ford. Spencer was a laid-back GOP operative who had been active in grassroots politics until he ran Nelson Rockefeller's California primary campaign that ultimately lost to Goldwater in 1964. Reagan had picked Spencer and his partner, Bill Roberts, to run his winning gubernatorial campaigns in 1966 and 1970. But Spencer had been excluded from the early planning for Reagan's 1976 insurgent challenge, so he worked instead for his fellow moderate Ford. He complained privately that Reagan was too conservative to be president. He also groused that Ed Meese and others had cost him business in California, and this too prompted his desire to stop Reagan.

Ford went down to Florida to give a speech at Eckerd College in St. Petersburg—for which he was paid $50,000, as with all of his appearances. The three networks, the BBC, the *New York Times*, the *Washington Post*, and dozens of other outlets caught up with Ford at the small college to read the tea leaves.[40] The national media were on their guard. The past three years they had heard "Ford is running," "Ford isn't running," "Ford might run"; they referred to him behind his back as the "Hamlet of Rancho Mirage."[41]

Spencer coyly told the reporters, "I think you can look for a news story next week." An undergraduate who attended Ford's lecture on "National Character" was skeptical. "I've never heard anybody who can talk for an hour and not say anything," said Tim Storm.[42]

If Ford was going to take the plunge, he would have to decide quickly. Filing deadlines were looming in many states, fundraising was imperative, and there was the matter of staffing such an operation. Not to mention bank accounts, phones, stationery, office equipment, scheduling, babysitting the media, chartering a plane, food, coffee, liquor. It was akin to building a major corporation over a weekend.

Ford aides began drawing a campaign plan. In early March, a group led by Thomas C. Reed, Ford's former secretary of the air force, and Leonard Firestone, Ford's wealthy next-door neighbor in California, formally created the Draft Ford Committee. Reed, like Spencer, had once worked for Reagan. A young former Ford White House aide, Larry Speakes, was recruited as the committee's spokesman. Also working on the Ford campaign plan was none other than the Bush campaign's pollster, Bob Teeter.[43] People were gossiping about that one, but one source later said that Teeter had only done so with Jim Baker's approval.[44]

Everyone in Ford's inner circle was convinced that the former president was running. Ford had already met once in secret with John Sears, and he scheduled a second, more public meeting with Sears to discuss his campaign.[45] After the meeting, Sears and Ford held a press conference. Sears told the gathered media, "I believe Ford could be nominated. I don't think the timing is too late."[46] Sears was asked whether he thought Reagan was unelectable, but refused to answer.

More encouragement for Ford came from moderates in the GOP. Bob Dole, still not out of the race formally but out of the race in every measurable way, called Ford and urged him to jump in.[47] Any way Dole could, he would twist the knife into his old enemy Bush. Republican governors Robert Ray of Iowa, William Milliken of Michigan, and Richard Snelling of Vermont came out for Ford as well.[48]

Finally, Henry Kissinger came out publicly and called on Ford to jump into the GOP contest. Kissinger had met with Ford for more than two hours at Rancho Mirage and emerged saying Ford had a "duty" to run. Of all Ford's men, Kissinger may have been the most ideologically opposed to Reagan's election, as it would

mean a repudiation of détente. He'd said for months that the only candidate running whom he could not work with was Reagan.[49]

Kissinger told the press that Ford was the only Republican of stature in whom
foreign leaders had confidence. But he disavowed any knowledge of such earthly
matters; the master Machiavellian infighter and political operator told reporters
with a straight face, "I am not a politician."[50] Reporters giggled and smirked. It
was nearly as disingenuous as Ford telling reporters that he was not "scheming and
conniving" to get the nomination.[51] *Newsweek* reported that the former president
would reappoint Kissinger secretary of state if he once again occupied the Oval
Office.[52] Kissinger coveted a path back to power.

Ford went to New York City and met with a dozen prominent Republicans,
all Reagan critics, all of whom encouraged him to run, including Senator Jacob
Javits. They came away convinced that Ford would indeed make the race. Grassroots efforts to file slates of Ford delegates in New York, Connecticut, and Michigan were moving forward.[53]

ABC's *World News Tonight*, anchored by Max Robinson, opened dramatically
on March 7 with a report that "former President Ford, who four years ago went to
the political mat with Ronald Reagan and won, is apparently very close to getting
into this year's contest to try and head Reagan off once again."[54]

Evans and Novak reported that Ford had made the decision to get in once
and for all. He would become a formal candidate on March 20.[55] That was it.
The two columnists had the best sources in journalism, even though some critics
referred to them as "Errors and No Facts." Rowland Evans had spoken directly to
Ford, who had expressed his concerns that the primary season had not produced
a consensus candidate and said that he figured he could garner the entire Bush and
Anderson vote while cutting into Reagan's base.

Howard Baker by this point had finally dropped out of the race after repeated
weak performances, and two of his now unemployed aides, Doug Bailey and John
Deardourff, told reporters they were signing on to the Ford campaign. Lowell
Weicker endorsed the Ford candidacy, but most in the GOP viewed this as a
mixed blessing at best.[56]

In mid-March, Bob Mosbacher, a Bush confidant and fundraiser who nonetheless worshiped Ford, went into Dave Keene's office at Bush's headquarters.
Mosbacher shut the door and said to Bush's political director, "While we have
done a great job thus far, it is clear that only the president [Ford] is in a position to
stop Reagan and that we must therefore figure out how to get Bush to step aside
so that Ford can be convinced to enter the race." Keene was livid. As he recalled
years later, "I told Mosbacher the idea was absurd, and if he thought there was a

chance in hell that I'd participate in such a scheme or support Ford over Reagan, he was nuts." Keene, who had a temper like few men in politics, didn't stop there. His voice rising, he told Bush's fair-weather friend, "There are few times in life when one can say he made a real difference, but I could always look back on '76 and the fact that I'd played a role in ridding the nation and the GOP of Ford." Keene followed with a string of obscenities about Ford and Bush's betrayer sitting there in front of him. Mosbacher left Keene's office and they never spoke again.[57]

Keene later reflected, "The Bush campaign consisted of those who really thought Bush would make a good president and were supporting him for that reason; those who thought he'd make a stronger general election candidate than Reagan; and those who were simply using him because they hated and/or feared Reagan. Bush sometimes couldn't tell these folks apart."[58]

All the Republican candidates were forced to address the growing Ford rumors. Bush said Ford's entry would "complicate" things for him, but he kept telling people he didn't think Ford would get into the race. Anderson got off a good line when he said Ford should not "disturb his retirement."[59] Reagan kept his cool and showed off his wit. When reporters asked why Ford might be willing to give up the golf links for the campaign trail, Reagan quipped, "Maybe he's developed a slice." Reporters laughed.[60]

The next day, though, Reagan toughened up his message. "Frankly, I thought it was very thoughtless of him to say anything that could give comfort and aid to the enemy," referring to Ford's comments that Reagan could not win.[61]

Within a matter of hours, word leaked that it was official: Ford would get into the race the following week.[62]

Ford went through a charade with the media, proclaiming that he was playing no role in the draft-Ford campaign. In fact, behind the scenes, he was taking and making phone calls and lining up support for his imminent entry.

Reagan, however, was holding all the cards and he knew it. If Ford got in, it would doom Bush and Anderson, especially with the southern primaries coming up. They would divide the moderate GOP vote, leaving the conservatives for him. Asked whether he thought he could beat Ford, Reagan smiled and said, "Yep." When pressed as to whether Ford would tarnish his own image by joining the race, Reagan quipped, "It's a nice thing to think about."[63] Reagan was practically begging Ford to run.

RONALD REAGAN WAS IN Florida on the day of the South Carolina primary, but he still mangled both Bush and Connally in the Gamecock State. With help from his in-state organizer, an intense young man named Lee Atwater, Reagan took 54 percent of the GOP vote while Connally received 30 percent and Bush a paltry 15 percent. Reagan, helped by crossover Democrats, swept all six congressional districts and, with them, all twenty-five delegates.[64]

Democrats voting for Reagan did so at their peril. The state Democratic Party chairman, Donald Fowler, warned that they might not be allowed to vote in his party's caucuses the following week. Conservative Democrats in the state found Fowler repugnant. Turnout was five times as high as the record previously set in 1974. A furious Fowler threatened that he would force Democrats to sign a pledge of fidelity, but loyalty oaths had been out of fashion in the South since Reconstruction.[65]

If there had been a vote-buying scheme cooked up by either Bush or Connally, it had not produced. In one all-black precinct in Columbia, by 5 P.M. only two voters had shown up to vote in the GOP primary.[66]

Connally failed even in his modest goal of keeping Reagan under 40 percent. He'd spent $500,000 out of his own pocket in South Carolina, but it was for naught. Big John put what was left of his campaign on hold and went home to Texas to "reassess." He finally faced reality and referred to Reagan as "the champ."[67] Connally had been helped by one of the more creative media consultants, Roger Ailes, but even Ailes's powers could not stop the runaway train of Ronald Reagan. After thirteen months and millions spent, John Bowden Connally had nothing to show for his efforts save one lonely sixty-seven-year-old delegate from Arkansas, Ada Mills. She became known as the "$11 million delegate."[68] Toward the end of the road, Connally—who was all personal ambition—told a reporter, "I'm not consumed by personal ambition."[69]

Reporters mourned the demise of Connally. From his Stetson right down to his silver inlaid cowboy boots, he was always entertaining, always good copy, he always had a good joke, and he was a terrific public speaker.

Prior to his withdrawal, Connally called Reagan to inform him of his decision. Reagan listened but wisely did not ask for his endorsement; instinctively, he knew this would not have been the proper time. There was no report of Connally's calling Bush.

In the end, there was just too much of Connally for voters to swallow: too much Texan, too much wheeler-dealer, too much rumor and scandal and bravado. His campaign also spent foolishly, including furnishing and renting a lavish apartment in Virginia for his campaign treasurer. They had chartered expensive planes and expensive hotel rooms. His first manager, Eddie Mahe, was paid almost $9,000 a month. Of the $12 million Connally spent, about $10 million went to operations, staff, and consultants. Only about $2 million went into media.[70] But there was another reason why Connally never took off:

"What did us in?" lamented Connally's longtime aide Julian Read. "His name is Ronald Reagan. And he's been on the road and on television for years. He has a very solid, emotional constituency that we didn't penetrate. He just beat us."[71] Losing consultants never blame themselves and losing candidates never blame themselves.

George Bush's foolish diversion into South Carolina—a decision motivated by his contempt of Connally—hurt his campaign badly. The original plan had been to bypass the state and let Reagan and Connally beat the tar out of each other and deplete their resources. Bush could then take on either a weakened Reagan or a resurgent Connally. Bush had unwisely gambled time, money, and people in an attempt to achieve an impossible win. The two Texans made the classic mistake of getting into an ugly spraying match with each other; GOP voters, repulsed by the brawl, went with Reagan.

Reagan might have won South Carolina in any event, but the fight between Bush and Connally—with the Bush campaign producing seedy tape recordings of conversations between Connally's in-state and Washington staffers plotting a scheme to "buy" African-American votes in the state—pushed Reagan well over the 40 percent his campaign thought he'd get.[72] Reagan smilingly called himself "cautiously ecstatic."[73]

BEFORE THE SOUTH CAROLINA primary, Bush had been competitive with Reagan in Alabama, behind just 45–39 percent, according to a Darden poll.[74] He was shelling out several hundred thousand dollars, mailing the state heavily, and spending considerable time there. With Connally effectively out of the contest, Bush might have expected to reap some of the 10 percent support of his old antagonist. But when the ballots were counted on March 11, he was demolished in Alabama. Reagan, who had spent just a little over $30,000, took every county and received almost 69 percent of the GOP primary vote to Bush's 26 percent.[75]

In Georgia the same day, Reagan did even better, winning 73 percent to Bush's paltry 13 percent.[76] And in Florida, Reagan received more than 57 percent of the vote and Bush 30 percent.[77] On the day, Reagan took 105 delegates to only 9 for Bush.[78] It was especially embarrassing for Keene, who had billed himself in part as the Bush campaign's ace in the hole for the South.

Alabama and Georgia allowed crossover voting, and conservative Democrats helped add to Reagan's handsome victories in each. Florida had a closed primary and Reagan still won handily there, which should have been a wakeup call to those who said Reagan was not the favorite within the GOP. When Reagan won in crossover states, critics complained that Democrats should not be allowed to decide the nominee of the Republican Party. But in the same breath they said Reagan had no appeal beyond the conservatives in the GOP.

Reagan should have won Florida in 1976 and would have had he not unexpectedly lost New Hampshire to Ford and then stumbled on the Social Security issue in the Sunshine State. Reagan wasn't about to make the same mistake twice. This time he made it clear to the oldsters that the government-run pension plan would stay healthy if he was elected.

Reagan had also gone hard after the Cuban-American vote in Florida. He charged that Carter had "eliminated a clandestine radio station that was broadcasting messages of freedom to Cuba." He said "there was 'excessive surveillance' of anti-Castro refugees, and Cubans frequently were hauled up before grand juries." Reagan laid a wreath at a memorial for the Cubans who had died in the Bay of Pigs invasion.[79] Everywhere he went he was greeted with "Viva Reagan!" by the enthusiastic anti-Communists. He shucked his coat in the sweltering heat and told the crowd in Little Havana, "Our country still has an obligation." Someone yelled out, "We are ready again, anytime."[80] He then plunged into the gathering of thousands.

Bush limped back North after being bloodied in the southern primaries. But he was an extremely competitive man and turned away talk in his campaign to pack it in and call it a day. The good news was that Bush had beaten Reagan in Iowa, Maine, Puerto Rico, and Massachusetts; he still had money in the bank and more favorable terrain ahead in Illinois, New York, Connecticut, and Pennsylvania; he'd outlasted Bob Dole, Howard Baker, and John Connally; and he had become quite able on the stump, firing up crowds when he was moved to do so. The bad news was the specter of Gerald Ford getting in. In desperation, Bush suggested that Ford's age could be used against him, as it had been used against Reagan.[81]

Bush was distraught that he never had the chance for a two-man race with Reagan. Just when it appeared he might finally get his wish, John Anderson had appeared out of nowhere. Each vote Anderson was taking was coming right out of Bush's back pocket, it seemed to Bush's advisers. In the weeks up to and after Iowa, Bush had become the media darling. After the New England primaries, the white-haired, bespectacled Anderson stirred the passions of the national media. Reagan had the conservatives, Anderson had the media, and Bush was left holding air. Bush's press secretary, Pete Teeley, said Anderson was getting "the kind of influx of publicity, money, enthusiasm and support that we had after Iowa."[82]

Anderson had bypassed the southern GOP primaries, knowing his message would not go down well there. He was waiting for the chance to take on Reagan and a weakened Bush in the March 18 primary in Illinois, his home state. He also was making plans for Wisconsin's upcoming primary, counting on the state's progressive Republican tradition. Anderson was clearly courting liberals; he took out a full-page ad in the *New York Times* with an open appeal to its liberal readers for campaign contributions. The title of the ad was "Why Not the Best?" No one seemed to remember that this was the title of Carter's campaign book in 1976. The ad was plastered with kind comments from the Beautiful People, including writers Sally Quinn of Georgetown and Tom Wicker of Manhattan.[83] It also came to light that Anderson had signed a direct-mail fundraising letter for the National Abortion Rights Action League (NARAL), which planned to give the money to George McGovern, Morris Udall, and other pro-choice representatives.[84]

TED KENNEDY HAD BEEN wiped out in the southern primaries, as Jimmy Carter took 183 delegates on his home turf.[85] Carter humiliated Kennedy, winning 82 percent to 13 percent in Alabama, 88 percent to 9 percent in the president's native Georgia, and 61 percent to 22 percent in Florida.[86]

The outcomes weren't surprising. Kennedy not only had low expectations for Florida, he also had low funds. Carter could claim 390 contributors of $1,000 in Florida to Kennedy's 84. Even in Palm Beach, a second Kennedy home, he had only five $1,000 contributors—and one of those was his mother.[87]

Muhammad Ali worked the Sunshine State for Carter. "I'm here because I'm a brother. We got to pick the best of the whites and I say that is Carter."[88] On the eve of the Florida primary, the Carter administration announced that seniors would get a 13 percent cost-of-living Social Security increase.[89] Carter had mastered the spoils system.

A NEW ABC NEWS–HARRIS poll showed Ford to be favored over Reagan among Republicans, 36–32 percent. With independents thrown into the mix, Ford widened his lead over Reagan to 33–27 percent.[90]

Tom Reed of the Draft Ford Committee held a press conference in Washington and released the names of one hundred prominent moderate Republicans who supported Ford's entry into the race. Reed's scenario for Ford to win the nomination, however, stretched credulity. His plan was for a Ford surrogate to run in Ford's stead in Texas, since the filing deadline had closed there, and then beat Reagan in the Lone Star State. In addition, Ford would have to beat Reagan in California. Reagan had beaten—or more accurately, crushed—the incumbent Ford in both states in 1976.

Before sweeping the South, Reagan had wanted Ford to get in and divide the moderate vote. Now, with the momentum on his side, Reagan wanted Ford to stay out. Not because the former president might gain the nomination—there was little chance Ford could do this unless there was a brokered convention—but because a Ford entry into the race might marginalize Reagan. Nelson Rockefeller's late entry in 1964 had marginalized Barry Goldwater, preventing him from reaching out to middle-of-the-road voters in the general election.

Ford continued to draw extensive media attention. He leveled Jimmy Carter, saying, "My sole, single purpose . . . is to get President Carter out of the White House." Ford didn't stop there, telling a Republican audience, "The nation is in peril. Mr. Carter has forfeited his immunity at home. This country is in deep, deep trouble."[91]

Ford's attack was harsh, especially since he'd met with Carter that very morning and come out of it praising the president.[92] But that was Washington. Kiss 'em in private and bash 'em in public. A Carter man returned the Ford fire: "He's going to get chewed up alive if he comes in. He's a nice man, but let's face it, his were do-nothing years."[93]

In his *Washington Post* column, David Broder pointed out the practical impediments to a Ford candidacy. Ford would miss filing in twenty-one primaries that would choose 908 delegates out of 1,994. Also, Ford's charge that conservatives could not win a general election drove men and women on the right up the wall. They'd had it thrown in their faces ever since the days of Goldwater and Bob Taft, and if Ford got in and actually stopped Reagan, the party would be split so badly that it might never be repaired.[94]

Broder was one of the two or three best political reporters of the era. Soft-spoken, mannerly, but with a drive for the facts and boundless energy that few could match, he wrote long, thoughtful pieces that were considered "must-reads" in Washington. Even as Carter was sweeping away the Kennedy challenge and looking to stomp Reagan, Broder wrote a long piece in early 1980 about how Carter could be more vulnerable to Reagan than anyone realized.

POSTMORTEMS ON THE SOUTH were all good for Reagan, mostly good for Carter, and awful for both Kennedy and Bush. Carter was now ahead of Kennedy in the delegate count, 283–145. Reagan had opened up a delegate lead over Bush, 167–45.[95]

The presidential combatants descended upon Illinois, where new polls had Anderson surging into first place, Bush faltering, and Reagan moving into second place. It was the first midwestern primary and would also be a key battleground in the fall election.

All waited with bated breath for Ford's decision. Ford privately lamented that he was not getting the outpouring of support from around the country that he'd hoped for. He expressed a twinge of bitterness that few of the GOP officials he'd campaigned for had come out for his candidacy, especially key moderate governors Lamar Alexander of Tennessee, Dick Thornburgh of Pennsylvania, and John Dalton of Virginia.

In a meeting with reporters over breakfast, Ford was clearly having second thoughts. "Reagan has the strongest base of support I've seen in politics," he said.[96]

Two days later, Ford held a subdued press conference outside his home in California with wife Betty at his side and declared, once and for all, that he would not run in 1980. Her recent victory over addictions to alcohol and pills was a factor in his decision, but his supporters were crestfallen. Only twenty-four hours earlier, they had been happily preparing to relaunch the USS *Ford*. Now it was "final and certain" that he would not run.[97] Ford declined to endorse any candidate, but made it clear he intended on making it his business to defeat Carter in the fall. He choked up a bit during his remarks.

Ford came to his decision after one final meeting with his supporters who reviewed his bleak chances. Among those attending the two-hour meeting were Congressman Dick Cheney; Alan Greenspan, a former White House economic adviser; Doug Bailey, the former Baker media man; Tom Reed; and Stu Spencer.[98] Grassroots Republicans were sharply divided over Ford. A Gallup poll showed that while 49 percent said he should get in, 46 percent said he should not.[99] The most important poll, of his family, had his wife and three of his four children against his making the race.

Above all, the decision was about the numbers—the numbers on the calendar, the numbers of missing supporters, and the numbers of dollars he'd have to raise. If Ford believed he had a reasonable chance, he would have gotten in. He loved being president. But Reagan was piling up delegates and Ford would be competing with Bush and Anderson for the remaining moderate vote.

The Ford boomlet ended with a whimper. Larry Speakes, at the headquarters for the Draft Ford Committee, said, "About all we have is a phone bill to pay."[100] With that, Ford's thirteen-day campaign folded its tent.

Reagan was campaigning in his old stomping grounds in Rock Falls, Illinois, when reporters caught up with him to tell him the news about Ford. Reagan heaved a sigh of relief. So did Bush. So did Anderson. Reagan was speaking under a banner that read "Reagan Plays Well in Peoria," and indeed he did. A high school band played, a children's choir sang, and the crowd took part in a college-like cheer: "Give me an 'R,' give me an 'E,' give me an 'A' . . ." His old Eureka College football coach, Mac MacKenzie, introduced Reagan.[101]

The Gipper saw a former Eureka classmate and called out to her. Tressie Masocco Kazelka told the *Los Angeles Times*, "I'm surprised he even saw me out here!" She reminisced about Reagan at their alma mater, saying he'd been "president of everything," so it made sense that he was running for the White House.[102] The event was pure corn, which Reagan and most of his fellow Americans loved.

After the rally, a farmer tried to give Reagan a piglet as a gift but Reagan demurred, "gently tweaking its nose."[103] Instead, the farmer told Reagan he would give him the animal after he was elected, "so that the pig could graze on the White House lawn."[104]

Bush was exhausted. He'd lost weight, he had gone back to wearing the granny glasses his staff hated, and he looked haggard. His plane, Asterisk One, was long gone. He was so tired he did something unheard of. He took a day off.

"There is an air of desperation about the Bush campaign," the *Washington Post* noted. "A reporter joins the Bush traveling entourage and is promptly asked, 'You covering Illinois or writing a Bush obituary?'"[105]

And Reagan?

He was happily gallivanting across Illinois, routinely putting in fourteen-hour days. Bush had once believed he could run Reagan into the ground by simply out-hustling and outworking him, but in fact it was Reagan who had done precisely that to Bush. Reagan was concerned about losing Illinois to Anderson but he also had a "feeling," as he told reporters.[106]

Their ears perked up at this comment by Reagan. They had learned that no politician they'd covered since John Kennedy had as much a feeling for the American people as Ronald Reagan.

13

Now Anderson

"John, would you really find Teddy Kennedy preferable to me?"

T he four remaining GOP candidates—George Bush, John Anderson, Phil Crane, and Ronald Reagan—met in snowy Chicago for what turned out to be a fiery and freewheeling debate just days before the Illinois primary.

For months, Anderson had been largely ignored by the others, who regarded him as a bit of an oddball. Now he was the front-runner in his home state—according to newspaper polls—and as such was drawing extensive media attention. As a measure of his newfound celebrity status, he picked up a Secret Service contingent and was flush with cash, which included a transfusion from the FEC. Fittingly, his Secret Service code name was "Miracle."[1]

Crane, in contrast, had been denied FEC matching funds because of his poor primary performances. His campaign was broke, and he was simply not a factor by this point. He frankly told people he was only hanging around in case something befell Reagan.

That left Reagan, Bush, and Anderson as the real players in the ninety-minute Chicago barnburner. With no reporters and only a moderator, this was a freeflowing debate, especially as Bush and Anderson swung hard at each other. Bush, desperate to turn this back into a two-man race, aggressively tried to push Anderson out of the Republican mainstream and grab the middle for himself. Bush had been running television ads attacking Anderson for signing the direct-mail letter for NARAL, the pro-abortion group, and during the debate Anderson charged that Bush's commercials were filled with "half-truths," which was "worse than a lie."[2] Gesticulating, Bush pointed his finger at Anderson and hotly charged him with being disloyal to the party. Anderson angrily yelled at Bush not to point any fingers at him. Undeterred, Bush hammered Anderson's proposed fifty-cent-a-gallon tax on gasoline.[3]

Reagan, smiling, stayed above the fray. When he did get a chance to chime in, he referred back to the dramatic moment at Nashua. Addressing moderator Howard K. Smith, Reagan joked about having to wait to speak: "Thanks, Howard, I thought that not having bought the mike myself, I couldn't talk." The live audience laughed.[4]

The Californian was relentless. When Anderson tried to attack Reagan over his proposal to tell the Ayatollah Khomeini to release the American hostages by a "date certain" or else, Reagan responded forcefully that the Iranians needed to know that the United States meant business. When Anderson referred to liberal senators George McGovern and Frank Church as "good men," Reagan said, "You see, that's where we disagree. I don't think they're good men."[5] When discussing foreign policy, he blasted weak-willed U.S. politicians: "We seem to be only able to find human rights violations among allies. . . . We cozy up to and hug and kiss as he [Carter] did with Brezhnev—where no human rights exist at all. Let's thumb our nose at the Soviet Union."[6] When asked about a role for Henry Kissinger in a future Republican administration, Reagan mirthfully told the crowd he thought Kissinger had a bright future in academia.[7]

He also stated his objections to wage and price controls, asserting that they had never worked, even when the Roman emperor Diocletian 1,700 years earlier had threatened capital punishment to those who violated the law. Reagan said, "I'm the only one here old enough to remember it." The crowd roared again and the debate stopped as Smith waited for the laughter to subside.[8]

As the nationally televised conflagration wound down, Smith asked each of the four candidates whether they could support the others if they were the nominee. It gave Reagan the opportunity to issue one of his best lines of the year.

Anderson and Crane said flatly that they could not support each other. Crane told Anderson he was in the wrong party and Anderson tartly wondered when the GOP started administering saliva tests. Bush said he could support anybody on the stage. Reagan fudged on whether he could support Anderson because of the rumors that the Illinois congressman might run in the general election as an independent if he failed to gain the Republican nomination. Anderson denied that he would run as a third-party candidate, but he also indicated that he could not support Reagan if he was the nominee. Several weeks earlier, Anderson had said he would vote for either Carter or Kennedy over any of the other Republicans, including the Gipper.[9]

Reagan turned to his fellow Illinoisan and deadpanned, "John, would you really find Teddy Kennedy preferable to me?"[10]

Anderson, almost never at a loss for words, was struck dumb for a moment, but the nine hundred people attending the debate at the Drake Hotel roared with laughter. Anderson finally grumbled something unfunny during the hilarity of the moment, but Reagan added, "I'm still waiting for John to say!"[11]

Asked whether he had a "message for Gerald Ford," Reagan grinned and said, "Someone ought to point out if he's sitting in Palm Springs, it's snowing here!"[12]

When it was pointed out to Bush that both Anderson and Reagan had balked at supporting each other while he, Bush, had pledged to support whoever was the nominee, Bush picked sides and said of Reagan, "He's a good man."[13]

For the first time in the campaign, Anderson was on the defensive, mostly over the charges that he was a Democrat in Republican clothing. He was forced to hold a press conference with the state GOP chairman so he could say with certainty that, yes, Anderson really was a Republican. In fact, some liberals who had abandoned Carter but couldn't stomach Kennedy were helping Anderson around the country. Anderson's own place of worship, the Evangelical Free Church, passed a resolution denouncing his position on abortion, calling on "Brother Anderson" to mend his ways.[14]

Anderson stuck mainly to the campuses, where he was welcomed like a rock star by the kids. Sometimes they chanted, "You've got to believe!"[15] With his white hair and glasses, and propensity to lecture people, the fifty-eight-year-old Anderson walked and talked like a college professor. He quoted poets and philosophers, including Emerson. Anderson's message of a future of scarcity and his opposition to tax cuts and exploration for more oil was popular with the liberal elements of the academy. For them, Anderson was telling it the way it was. Except at Lewis and Clark College, where students wearing Reagan hats and buttons ambushed him.[16]

Reagan was anything but defensive, coming off his strong showing in the debate. The *Evans and Novak Political Report* said of the Gipper, "He has seemed like the Reagan of old, convincing a lot of skeptics. . . . His Illinois debate performance was superb; he was the clear winner—witty, quick, urbane."[17]

Reagan may have been doing well with Republican primary voters, but he still wasn't breaking through to the general population, according to a new poll in the *Chicago Sun-Times*. The survey showed that in a matchup against Carter, Reagan would get blown out in Illinois, 60–34. Bush was doing much better against Carter in Illinois, down only 42–36; Anderson was actually doing better than Carter in Illinois.[18] Losing Illinois in the general election would be no small blow; Illinois, with eleven million residents, was the fifth-largest state in the country.

The polls must have been maddening to Bush. Most believed he would do better as the GOP standard bearer in the general election, but he couldn't get past Citizen Reagan or separate himself from Anderson.

AS THE ILLINOIS PRIMARY was steaming along, the vilest mass murderer in the nation's history—John Wayne Gacy of Chicago—was convicted for the slaying of thirty-three young men and boys. Within a matter of hours, Gacy was sentenced to death, which at least thirty-three families thought was too good for this monster. Thirteen psychiatrists had testified at the trial. Four said Gacy was sane, four said Gacy was insane, and four had no opinion. The thirteenth couldn't make up his mind. Gacy was sentenced to twelve death penalties as well as twenty-one consecutive life terms. The jury deliberated for just over two hours, apparently unconcerned with Gacy's mental state.[19]

The macabre crimes and sensational trial had gripped Chicago for months, mostly pushing the presidential candidates off the Windy City's front pages. Gacy had been involved in local Democratic politics and had actually once shared a platform with Rosalynn Carter. In the photo of the two, Gacy was clearly wearing an "S" lapel pin, issued by the U.S. Secret Service. It was a huge embarrassment and black eye for the agency, which was supposed to do complete background checks on people who got that close to their protectees.[20]

Earlier in the year, George Bush had refused Secret Service protection when it was offered to him, but now he was forced to change his mind. On the morning of March 15, the Puerto Rican terrorist group FALN (Armed Forces of National Liberation) took over Bush's campaign offices in New York for several hours, binding and gagging ten staffers. On the same day the terrorists invaded President Carter's campaign headquarters. FALN had detonated more than one hundred bombs in the United States over the previous six years, killing five people. Fortunately, the hostage crisis in each city was eventually quelled by local and federal law enforcement.[21]

Bush's son Jeb had already had death threats made against him while stumping in Puerto Rico. Finally and reluctantly, Bush acceded to his family's and his staff's insistence that he get the Secret Service protection.[22]

But the campaign staffers, undeterred by the fact that their lives had been in grave danger, simply went back to work. They had a race to win.

NATIONAL JOURNALISTS GATHERED IN Washington for their annual Gridiron Dinner, at which they spoofed the high and mighty but rarely themselves. In one skit, Reagan was depicted as a forgetful Wizard of Oz.

The media had yet to add things up. Bush had lost by greater margins than expected in New Hampshire, South Carolina, Florida, Alabama, and Georgia. His win in Massachusetts was by a smaller margin than expected. Since Iowa, Bush had continually underperformed and Reagan had continually overperformed. Now, after leading handily in Illinois in late February, Bush had slipped to third place in the state; his numbers had fallen by 18 points in just two weeks, in the Chicago Tribune poll.[23] The accumulated bad news for Bush was blowing into Illinois, but he vowed to stay in the race and "keep plugging away."[24]

Many in the media had become mesmerized by "the politics of politics," which was about polls and money and consultants and gossipy conversations over drinks into the wee hours of the morning. The Bush campaign excelled at this, whereas Reagan's Ed Meese, Dick Wirthlin, and Bill Casey, all teetotalers, turned in as soon as the Gipper did. Lyn Nofziger and some lesser staffers enjoyed the late-night repartee with the national media, but Bush's Jim Baker, Dave Keene, Pete Teeley, and Bob Teeter outgunned them in this department.

Less and less attention was being devoted to message. Reporters' near-obsession with the mechanics of politics—the "horse race"—led an exasperated Bush to proclaim he would answer no more questions about his campaign's tactics, because he was being hit badly for avoiding any discussion of issues. Indeed, the Bush campaign produced one of the odder television spots of the season. In it, Bush was in an elevator with a young reporter to whom he curtly said, "I'm no longer going to talk about polls and strategy. I'll talk about issues, and that's all I'll talk about with you."[25]

Bush may have finally realized that issues were important, but his run of poor primary performances was hurting him even with members of the GOP establishment turned off by the conservative Reagan. The governor of Illinois, Jim Thompson, blew off Bush's request for an endorsement even though he'd been winking at Bush for the better part of a year. Thompson now told reporters that he'd seen Reagan's big wins and thought it would be better to stay out of the fight. Thompson called his confidants together and told them nothing could stop the Reagan express now and they'd better learn to live with that fact, despite their differences with the Gipper.

In Illinois, as in many other states, there was bad blood between the GOP establishment and the conservative rank and file. Thompson had invited Reagan to a private dinner at the Governor's Mansion, but at State Representative Don Totten's urging, Reagan turned down Thompson's invitation. In order to see the Gipper, Thompson sneaked into Reagan's suite on the ninth floor of the Drake Hotel just hours before the big debate.[26]

A curtain-raising story on Reagan ran on the front page of the *Chicago Tribune*. Although the article covered Reagan's prowess at public speaking, it featured a litany of quotes about Reagan's age. "Given the demands of the office, Reagan's age is a time bomb," said presidential scholar Fred Greenstein. Barry Goldwater was quoted warning Reagan to slow down: "I just hope he doesn't kill himself trying to prove that he is young."[27] Just several months before, Reagan had been widely admonished for inactivity; now he was being criticized for being too active.

But he was having too much fun. At one stop, a woman displayed a youthful photo of Reagan from his movie days. She sighed to Reagan, "You sent this to me!" Reagan looked at the photo and deadpanned, "I was never that young."[28] Two years earlier, Reagan had gone to Eureka College for a reunion, where he was seated next to a wheelchair-bound elderly man who knew all about Reagan. Reagan deliberately dropped some papers so he could get a close look at the man's name tag and was mortified to discover that it was his roommate from college.[29]

Reagan kept his eye on the ball in Illinois, telling voters that it was now about the all-important delegate count. At this point, he was ahead of Bush, 167–45. Illinois would hold a "blind" primary, meaning that candidates vying to be delegates to the Republican National Convention were listed on the ballot without any signal as to which candidate they supported. Accompanying that would be a nonbinding "beauty contest" vote for candidates. It was possible for a candidate to win the nonbinding Illinois primary and still lose delegates. To compete for the ninety-two delegates at stake on primary day (another ten delegates would be selected at the state convention), the candidates had to organize "mini-campaigns" around their chosen delegate nominees.[30] In order for primary voters to choose Reagan, they had to know who his delegate candidates were. The process put a premium on recruiting local celebrities whom friends and neighbors would recognize on the ballot.

Reagan drew big and enthusiastic crowds in downstate Illinois, his old stomping ground. The region was flat as a frying pan, with endless rows of soybean and corn, and was redneck conservative. The Chicago suburbs were moderate Republican territory.

Totten was running things for Reagan in Illinois, just as he'd done four years earlier. He was one of the few state operatives who were around in 1976 and hadn't been forced out or demoted by John Sears in the 1980 quest. Like Reagan's other men, Totten was a tough conservative whose hard work and loyalty were never in doubt. He was running an effective operation in Springfield, teeming with volunteers and an underpaid and overworked aide, Terry Campo, who was pressed into service one day as Reagan's spokesman because the woman assigned by the campaign had laryngitis. Campo didn't know a press release from a grape press but he struggled through, even as he was astonished at the unruly behavior of the horde of reporters, all barking questions at him.[31]

CARTER'S ROMP OVER KENNEDY continued without interruption. The same day that he trounced Kennedy in the Alabama, Georgia, and Florida primaries, he also won big in the Oklahoma, Delaware, and Hawaii caucuses. Only in Alaska's caucus did Kennedy defeat the president.[32] Carter also won the caucuses in Mississippi, South Carolina, and Wyoming, held four days later.[33] Kennedy's campaign was on the verge of being chloroformed, just in time for him to go back to Cape Cod and get ready for the coming spring sailing season.

The bad news never seemed to stop rolling downhill onto Kennedy. Long withheld evidence of the frantic phone calls he made in the hours after Chappaquiddick was released, and all the old questions arose anew about Kennedy's behavior that night in July 1969. Joan Kennedy stood by her man, even when reporters unchivalarously badgered her about Chappaquiddick. She also said bluntly, "I don't think much of President Carter."[34] The president's mother, "Mizz Lillian," had caused a bit of a stir earlier when she indelicately said of Kennedy, "I hope nothing happens to him."[35]

In desperation, Kennedy's campaign had detailed eighty staffers from the national office to Illinois, and a dozen or so members of his family worked the state as well.[36] Illinois would be the site of the first primary held on a neutral battlefield, neither Carter's South nor Teddy's New England. If Kennedy's campaign was to have any chance of rebounding, he would need to perform well in Illinois. Some Kennedyites were still in fighting spirit. Four women, including a Kennedy supporter, got into a fistfight at a Democratic precinct in Puerto Rico.[37]

From day one his plan had been to re-create the old liberal coalitions that his brothers had built. Illinois was large and diverse, and its biggest city, Chicago, was urban, ethnic, and heavily Catholic. The trouble was that the minorities whom his brothers had attracted thus far had been going for Carter. Meanwhile, the political machine of former Chicago mayor Richard Daley had for the most part collapsed after his death in 1976, so Kennedy could not count on its ability to deliver any votes, alive or dead.

A day before the Illinois primary, Kennedy marched in Chicago's St. Patrick's Day parade alongside the city's immensely unpopular mayor, Jane Byrne, who had endorsed him over Carter. Along the way, the boisterous crowd jeered and shouted obscenities at one of the most famous Irishmen in America. Kennedy flyers, in the shape of shamrocks, littered the wet sidewalks, making the puddles turn green. Joan Kennedy held close to her husband, a terrified look on her face.[38] Kennedy betrayed an assassination concern when some punks set off a string of firecrackers near him. "His hands shot to his head, his knees bent and the color drained from his face—but it all passed in a flash," one reporter wrote.[39]

Kennedy was able to secure a commitment from Barbra Streisand to do two fundraising concerts for his campaign, which he hoped would raise $1 million. Streisand had notorious stage fright and hadn't done a political concert since 1972, for George McGovern. Before he bowed out, John Connally had tried to recruit Wayne Newton, but the singer had already signed up with Reagan a year earlier. Newton did Reagan concerts and raised hundreds of thousands for the Gipper. Jimmy Buffett had signed on with Carter and Rockford's Cheap Trick with hometown boy John Anderson. If there was only one thing the various campaigns agreed upon, it was that celebrities were a pain to deal with. Their agents were even more insufferable. "I'm the no. 1 guy in the business," said music promoter and self-promoter Jerry Weintraub. "I can just pick up the phone and get anybody on the line . . . Kennedy . . . Bush . . . Mondale . . . the President, anybody."[40] The immodest Weintraub was a friend of the modest George Bush.

JESSE HELMS WAS A Reaganite's Reaganite, although the conservative North Carolina senator and his powerful political organization, the Congressional Club, had yet to publicly back Reagan, largely because they had been steamed at Reagan for keeping on John Sears as campaign manager. But Reagan would not have run at all in 1980 if it hadn't been for Helms and his top political aide, Tom Ellis; they had thrown their support behind Reagan at a crucial time in 1976. Reagan had been defeated in the first five primaries that year and was expected to lose to President Ford in North Carolina as well. Helms and Ellis furiously organized for Reagan in the Tar Heel State, with mailings, literature drops, phone calls, voter registration drives, and advertising. Combined with Reagan's last-gasp campaigning, this activity produced one of the greatest upsets in modern presidential political history. The victory revived the dying Reagan campaign and propelled him though the rest of the primaries and to the convention. Without the "Club," Reagan, as a political force, would have simply faded away after the 1976 North Carolina primary.

Now, with Sears dismissed, Helms's Congressional Club finally came off the sidelines and announced its support for Reagan. Reagan would benefit not only from the political and fundraising support of the powerful senator but also from Ellis's help. Ellis understood Reagan as did few other pros. One of his critical moves in 1976 was to put on all of North Carolina's television stations a half-hour address by Reagan. Even with the technical problems of the videotape, Tar Heel voters were drawn to the Reagan persona and message.[41]

In the early stages of the 1980 campaign, Reagan's advertising team had failed to appreciate this lesson. Before Jeff Bell rejoined the Reagan family, the campaign's television spots had been mostly a disaster. The old spots, produced by a Madison Avenue firm, had Reagan talking about inflation to schoolchildren, telling them it "could cost Joan and Billy here seventy-five thousand dollars to go to college."[42]

Bell and the new adman he had brought into the Reagan fold, Elliott Curson, worked on new television spots. The new commercials were simple and to-the-point. They opened with Reagan talking into the camera, saying, "This is a great country, but it's not being run like a great country," and ended with the slogan "Let's Make America Great Again."[43] The reaction among the elites was decidedly mixed; CBS analyst Jeff Greenfield was one of the few who recognized the power of the commercials, saying, "Reagan ran the least elaborate, least gimmicked-up, most issue-oriented ads of the entire campaign." Bush's ads, Greenfield said, were the most gimmicky.[44]

Bush had junked his earlier bio commercials in favor of talking-head ads in which he told voters, "Let's get down to cases." Carter, meanwhile, ran attack ads that left no doubt whom they were referring to, as the voiceover said, "You'll never find yourself wondering if he's telling you the truth." Kennedy's commercials were universally panned. One was a close-up of Teddy's hands, signing letters.[45] Another one contemplated but never produced was of him and his wife and children walking on the beach, which would have simply raised all the old questions about his marriage.

Curson was a big reason for the success of Reagan's ads. Curson, a long-haired and hip young conservative who lived in Philadelphia, was one of the young breed of new GOP ad makers who "got" Reagan. He eschewed trying to manage the Gipper or put him in a goofy setting, such as walking down the beach with his wife and dog, a coat slung over his shoulder—a style adopted in almost every other candidate's commercials in 1980. (The only candidates who did not do puerile "Man on the Beach" commercials were Reagan and Kennedy.) No balloons, jingles, or trite slogans for Curson. He put Reagan in front of a camera and just let the candidate talk. Curson defended the unslick commercials by saying, "We're trying to win an election, not an Academy Award."[46]

In short, Curson and Bell let Reagan be Reagan.

SHORTLY BEFORE THE ILLINOIS primary, Bob Dole at long last made it official and retired from the presidential field, saying he'd always been a long shot. The Kansan paid homage to Reagan in his remarks, a graceful move.

Since Dole had been a nonfactor in the race for so long, his departure did little to alter the dynamic in the Republican race. Anderson's unexpected success and now front-runner status in Illinois brought him a fundraising windfall and lots of media attention. But with that came increased scrutiny. As one of the last of a dying breed—a liberal Republican—he faced more and more questions about whether he would seek a third-party bid if he was not the GOP nominee. The sanctimonious Anderson, who on Capitol Hill had earned the nickname "St. John the Righteous,"[47] drew disparaging remarks from Republicans and Democrats alike. At one press conference Reagan poked fun at Anderson by saying that, unlike the Illinois congressman, "I have not endorsed Senator Kennedy."[48] Kennedy also had some fun at Anderson's expense. At one stop he noted Carter's absence and said that all the other Democrats were there, "including John Anderson."[49]

Although many in the media saw in Anderson's candidacy the chance for a new alignment in politics, merging the moderate Republican with the rural farm vote and the urban sophisticates, he could not avoid uncomfortable questions forever. Now the press began pressing him about his flip-flops. He'd once been a supporter of the Kemp-Roth tax cuts and nuclear power, but had switched in 1980.[50]

Anderson picked up another problem in the form of a new ad man, David Garth, a pushy, loud, and brilliant New Yorker with a flair for self-promotion. Any candidate had to understand that along with Garth's massive talent came an equally massive ego.

As Reagan had been aided in some primaries by crossover conservative Democrats, Anderson had been aided by crossover liberal Democrats. Since voters did not register by party in Illinois, anyone could vote in either the Democratic or the Republican primary. An under-the-radar fight was going on between Kennedy and Anderson for these prized voters, including college students and minorities. Anderson's presence in the race had hurt Bush and Kennedy. And both Reagan and Carter were benefiting as a result.

Bush tried to play his strong suit and restart his flagging campaign. He gave a major foreign-policy address in which he called for "economic warfare" to be used against Iran as a way to dislodge the hostages. Bush ripped into Carter, saying he'd demonstrated "an infinite capacity to be misled."[51]

Reagan stuck to his central message about tax cuts, government bureaucracy, and standing up to the ayatollah and the Soviets. In speech after speech, he thundered that "we're going to be so respected that never again will a dictator dare invade an American embassy and hold our people as hostages!"[52] Having lost badly to Ford in Illinois in 1976, he spent the entire week before the primary traipsing up and down and across the state. He was giving fewer prepared speeches and more off-the-cuff remarks, with plenty of time for questions and answers with voters.

Reagan kept his focus on Anderson in Illinois, hitting the congressman's liberal views and pointing up his disdain for his own party. Reagan told reporters, "A party isn't a fraternity; it isn't something you join because you like the school tie. . . . It is a gathering together of people who basically share the same political philosophy."[53] Anderson returned the volley, accusing Reagan of costing Ford the election four years earlier. "He could have elected Gerry Ford instead of sulking at home."[54] Reagan fired back by suggesting that Anderson was so out of touch with the GOP that he ought to consider leaving it.

The old Wizard of Oz knew what he was doing. As long as he engaged Anderson in a left-right squabble, he was depriving Bush of both media attention and liberal votes that might have gone to him but were going to Anderson because Reagan was attacking him.

Anderson had slipped a bit in his own internal polls, so he flew off for one final tour of the state. He charged that Reagan was embracing "Coolidge-era economics" and went hard after the Californian on foreign policy and national defense, saying that Reagan was unnecessarily saber rattling.[55]

Reagan was not backing away from issues of foreign affairs. In fact, that same day, speaking before the Council on Foreign Relations in Chicago, he gave what Dick Allen, his adviser on global and national defense matters, touted as a "major foreign-policy address." In the speech Reagan outlined his call for rebuilding the U.S. Navy and his support for an all-volunteer Army, provided that military salaries were raised enough to attract good people. He also called détente an "illusion" and tore into Carter's foreign policy, stating that it was marked with "vacillation, appeasement, and aimlessness" and that Carter was bringing shame to America. The audience warmly applauded Reagan.[56]

Reagan took questions from the crowd afterward. When asked about the Soviet Union, he said he would negotiate with the Soviets, but only from a position of strength. He called it his "grand strategy" based on three principles: that America was morally right and the Kremlin was morally wrong; that to have a strong military, America must have a strong economy; and that the way to peace was through strength.[57]

The media noted once again that Reagan was in fine form. He had worked hard on the speech with Allen, having met for three hours in Atlanta with seven experts, including Fred C. Iklé, former head of the Arms Control and Disarmament Agency. It was only the second time in the campaign that the text of a Reagan address was distributed to the media beforehand.[58]

Bush, however, was unmoved by the Reagan address. Challenging his opponent's lack of specifics, he said sourly, "Let's call it the Reagan secret plan for ending the Iranian hostage crisis," an allusion to Richard Nixon's secret plan in 1968 to end the Vietnam War.[59]

The day hadn't started well for Bush. In Chicago, several reporters had asked him when he was going to drop out of the race. Things didn't look good heading into the primary.

ON PRIMARY DAY, MARCH 18, John Anderson came crashing back to earth. Reagan won again, taking just under 50 percent, with Anderson at a disappointing 37 percent. Bush had collapsed to only 11 percent.[60] He had done worse than expected. He spent the day campaigning in Wisconsin, where he was heckled by a man who accused him of orchestrating murders while serving as head of the CIA.[61]

Anderson, voting in his home precinct in Rockford, told reporters that voting for himself made him feel "kind of funny."[62] Apparently, hundreds of thousands of GOP primary voters shared that view.

More than one million people voted in the Illinois GOP primary, up nearly half from 1976. Reagan was helped by the influx of conservative Democrats. He took 39 delegates and Anderson only 26. Bush got a paltry 2 delegates in Illinois. Reagan was now ahead in the delegate tabulation with 206 to Bush's 47 and Anderson's 39.[63] The only bad news of the day was that Reagan's Don Totten lost to an Anderson delegate. But across the rest of the state, Anderson had been swamped by Reagan's "rednecks," as Anderson derisively referred to Illinois conservatives.[64]

Reagan and his rednecks had a better feel for Illinois than did Anderson and the elites of the daily newspapers. The *Chicago Tribune* and the *Chicago Sun-Times* endorsed Anderson and the rest of the state's daily newspapers endorsed Bush. Not one daily newspaper in the state endorsed Reagan.[65]

The debate in Chicago had been crucial for Reagan. According to Dick Wirthlin, 52 percent of Republicans said Reagan had won the debate, 14 percent said Anderson, and only 3 percent said Bush. "Bush was the big loser," said Reagan's pollster. "People knew where [Reagan] stood on the issues. In the debate, however, they saw a different kind of man, a warm human being with a touch of humor. That's where Reagan picked up the extra votes that made this contest come out the way it did."[66]

Reagan had been born in Tampico, Illinois, growing up in various parts of the state; yet this primary and this campaign were not about where Reagan was from, but where he was going and where he wanted to take the country. He pledged to his supporters to keep going and not relax.

Anderson tried to say it was now a two-man race between him and Reagan—and since Reagan could not win in the fall against Carter, Anderson claimed he was the GOP's logical nominee. Losing his home state so badly, though, was a devastating blow. Jim Baker, while not happy with Bush's distant third, saw the silver lining in Anderson's not being able to win on his home court. Bush promised to make a last stand in upcoming Connecticut.

On the Democratic side, Carter routed Kennedy in Illinois, 65–30 percent.[67] Carter took 165 delegates to only 14 for Kennedy.[68] Mayor Byrne's endorsement had only hurt Kennedy's already faltering campaign. She was radioactive, and all of her endorsed local candidates lost that night as well. Kennedy had also been endorsed by Albert Shanker, head of the half-million-strong American Federation of Teachers.[69] Shanker's support was not the nuclear shot in the arm Kennedy had hoped for in Illinois. Kennedy had lost 2–1 among Irish and among Catholics.[70] He never had a prayer in Illinois.

Kennedy had now lost more than a dozen Democratic contests while winning almost zilch. Amazingly, he was performing so poorly in primaries while Carter was performing so poorly in the Oval Office. Despite unveiling plan after plan, President Carter had done nothing to get a hold on the dreadful economy. Interest rates had lurched up again, this time to 18.25 percent; mortgage rates were out of control.[71] Carter attacked the economy as half a budget-balancer and half-Keynesian. He proposed a ten-cent-per-gallon tax on gasoline, elimination of Saturday mail delivery, some cuts in the federal budget, and a mishmash of regulations, but also large increases in social spending and some largesse for the cities.

On foreign affairs, too, Carter was undermining his own strength. In a White House press conference, the president had told startled reporters and even more startled Kremlinologists that the United States would abide by SALT II, though the treaty had yet to be ratified by the Senate. A poll conducted by Lou Harris in mid-March showed that nearly half of all Americans thought Carter was "a failure" on the Iranian hostage crisis. His numbers had dropped precipitously in just a little over a month. A huge majority, 71 percent, said America had been made to look "weak and helpless" by the Ayatollah Khomeini.[72]

Yet although he tried, Kennedy couldn't capitalize on these mistakes. The Republicans were determined not to miss the same opportunity in the general election.

Reporters were beginning to write pieces speculating on Reagan's running mate, a sure sign that the press believed Bush and Anderson would soon throw in the towel. The usual suspects were being mentioned: Don Rumsfeld, Howard Baker, and Bill Brock, among others. Reagan's only stipulations at this point were that his running mate must be younger and agree with him philosophically.

And yet Reagan still hadn't captured the hearts of all Republicans. GOP voters had flirted with Bush, Ford, Connally, and Anderson and still had not set their hearts on Reagan. When queried by NBC whether anyone would emerge to stop his drive for the nomination, Reagan calmly replied, "They'll find someone."[73]

Like the tormented King Tantalus in Greek mythology, the more Reagan reached for the object of his desire, the more it eluded his grasp. In a New York Times poll, by a 52–27 margin, Republicans still favored Ford over Reagan as their standard bearer against Carter in the fall election.[74]

Reagan had miles of primaries to go—and, for his fellow Americans, promises to keep.

14

BUSH'S COUNTEROFFENSIVE

"Nobody said it would be easy. Nobody was right."

Fresh off his big win in Illinois, Ronald Reagan jetted to Brooklyn for a day of campaigning, but it didn't go according to plan. Hecklers chanting, "Reagan wants war!" greeted him. The Gipper shot back, "I'll tell you, you jokers. If I did want war, you're where I'd start it!"[1] Reagan had been in the Big Apple only a couple of hours and he was already starting to sound like a New Yorker.

He was welcomed more warmly later in Queens and Manhattan. Reagan had often been critical of New York City, but his initial strength in the Empire State could be found, perhaps surprisingly, in the city rather than upstate. The reason was that in New York City, the GOP "has tended to be more conservative as a counter to crime and decaying neighborhoods," in the words of the *New York Times*.[2]

Nancy Reagan got a taste of campaigning New York–style. State Senator John Calandra told her he would do everything he could to help her husband, "even if I'm invited to tea in a whorehouse."[3]

While campaigning in the city, Reagan praised Mayor Ed Koch, a Democrat, for his efforts to root out corruption, cut spending, and reduce crime. Koch in turn praised Reagan while complaining about the "Arabists" around the Carter administration. Carter's campaign chairman, the normally calm Texan Robert Strauss, referred to Carter's Jewish critics as "emotionally hysterical nuts."[4] Relations between Jewish Americans and the Carter White House were worsening. Vice President Walter Mondale spoke at an event in New York "attended by prominent Jews and was roundly booed virtually every time he mentioned Carter's name," the *Washington Post* reported.[5]

Anti-Carter sentiment offered an opening to Reagan, who expanded his message while stumping in New York state. As he talked about support for Israel and the plight of the inner cities, it was clear to reporters that he was already turning his attention to the fall contest. Reagan called for a partnership between government and private industry to help alleviate youth unemployment and said that any attempt to cut government "must not come at the expense of the poor and the disadvantaged."[6] He also called for increased funding for Radio Free Europe and the Voice of America as a way to undermine the Soviets—remarks pleasing to Americans of Eastern European descent, many of them traditional Democratic voters.[7]

In Syracuse, Reagan hammered Carter over his handling of the hostages in Iran. Up to this point, he'd pulled his punches on this issue. No more. "There must come a time, if we are to get them back, when we tell them [Iran] this is the end of the road," Reagan declared.[8] He had met in private with the mother of a hostage and came away disgusted when she told him President Carter would not meet with her.[9]

While Reagan turned an eye to Carter, the president's campaign began to plot its assault against Reagan. One column by James "Scotty" Reston of the *New York Times*, who frequently savaged Reagan, reviewed how the Carter White House feared all the Republican contenders except Reagan, who was "Carter's favorite opponent. . . . Seldom in the history of American politics has a party out of power shown so much generosity to a President in such deep difficulty."[10] Pat Caddell, Carter's pollster, was bragging that the president would not only hold on to his base in the fall but would also pick up a sizable number of Republican voters alienated by the "extremist" Reagan.

By this point most national political journalists were writing off George Bush's chances. Bush had staggered out of Illinois, stunned at the Reagan avalanche that had buried him. He'd flown to New York with no press in tow; they had been disinvited from his plane, as he didn't want to hash over the results of Illinois.

Many others who had dismissed Reagan were starting to recognize that his chances for the nomination looked good. A sure sign that the winds were shifting came when power junkie Henry Kissinger called Bill Casey and sanctimoniously told the campaign manager that he "would do nothing to hurt the governor." Casey, unmoved, queried why, then, had Kissinger stepped in front of the television cameras just a couple days earlier and urged Jerry Ford to get into the race? Kissinger answered sheepishly that he had done what he had to do.[11] Kissinger had flirted with John Connally the year before, when many thought Connally would be the Republican nominee. Now, with Reagan ascending, Kissinger deigned to say he could serve in a Reagan administration—as secretary of state, of course. As always, Kissinger's most important constituency was . . . himself.

Casey took control of the Reagan campaign. To be sure, he made missteps, such as telling ABC, NBC, and CBS after the fact that he'd canceled the campaign's charter plane, leaving three camera crews stranded in Atlanta.[12] Staffers joked behind his back about his forgetfulness, his wardrobe, his dandruff, and his dated knowledge of politics.

But the man had a set of brass ones. He brought sorely needed order and discipline to the Reagan campaign. He fired more than one hundred staffers, while others stayed without pay. Ed Meese said that Casey was "intelligent, exceptionally decisive, and easy to get along with."[13] But he was not always easy to understand. Reagan, Dick Allen, and Meese met Casey one day in the Midwest. After the meeting, in which Casey spoke in his trademark mumble, Reagan turned to Meese and said, "What the hell did he just say?"[14] Some thought the mumbling was an act to get people to pay attention. The media missed their old friend John Sears, but there was a new sheriff in town and they might as well get used to it.

NEW YORK AND CONNECTICUT would hold their primaries on the same day, March 25, a week after the Illinois contest. Up for grabs were a total of nearly 150 GOP delegates.

Bush was trying to pick up the pieces of his once-promising campaign, and Connecticut was a great place to start. The state was Bush country. He'd grown up there, and his father, Prescott, had once been a U.S. senator from Connecticut.

Newspapers used words like "shattering" and "crippling" to describe Bush's flagging effort.[15] After the devastating loss in Illinois, one aide at Bush headquarters had grumbled, "It's over. It's all over."[16] Others had wept. Days before the Illinois primary, Bush was already bracing for a loss; he wanly told one crowd, "Nobody said it would be easy. Nobody was right."[17]

But now Bush was back in his old stomping grounds, where he was warmly welcomed. He devoted six days of frenetic campaigning to the state, delivering speeches going after Carter and the scandals of the Democratic Party while touting his own tax-cut plan. He told reporters, "I'm not as far over on one side as Reagan is, and I'm certainly not as far over on the other side as John Anderson."[18] Bush was trying for a second introduction, this one centered on policy, not the "Big Mo." He went so far as to say, "I'm the new guy that's talking only about issues, not polls."[19] Bush realized too late that Jim Baker and other staffers had been right when they urged him to make that switch after Iowa.

Bush's chairman in Connecticut, Malcolm Baldridge, worked the state hard. He had an army of three thousand volunteers and coordinators in 150 towns and villages. Bush also had phone operations in six cities, attempting to call all 400,000 of Connecticut's Republicans.[20]

Reagan was under no illusions about his chances in Connecticut. The state had not held a primary four years earlier, but Reagan had been skunked at the Republican state convention that had been held instead. Now he was facing one of Connecticut's own. Reagan told reporters it was George Bush's "backyard."[21] Of course, he was inflating expectations for Bush. Reagan had some first-rate operatives in Connecticut, including state senator Nancy Johnson and former state Republican chairman Fred Biebel, and his campaign had assembled an impressive list of three hundred supporters that included many Italians and Roman Catholics, not to mention Andy Robustelli, the great former New York Giants football player.[22] At the very least the Reagan campaign hoped to take a few delegates in the state.

Reagan went to Connecticut, a shot across Bush's bow. He boarded the 7:11 A.M. commuter train in New Haven and rode along with the rest of the straphangers. It was a good media event for Reagan, especially because he took the train all the way into New York, where he was not at such a disadvantage compared with Bush. When he arrived at Grand Central Station just before 9 A.M, he was met by a small but enthusiastic crowd.[23] One rail user yelled out, "Win one for the Gipper!"[24] Reagan smiled and later went to the New York Stock Exchange, where he received a "tumultuous welcome on the trading floor," according to Peter Hannaford, who had accompanied him on the swing.[25]

Reagan was in better shape for New York's delegate-selection primary, at least as compared with 1976, thanks to longtime conservative operatives George Clark of Brooklyn and Roger Stone, Reagan's Northeast co-coordinator. Clark and Stone worked well together, despite the fact that Clark was as stable and low-key as Stone was colorful and controversial. Stone, though only twenty-nine, had seen a world of politics in his short life, including performing some junior-varsity dirty tricks for Nixon's Committee to Re-Elect the President ("CREEP") eight years earlier.

Like Illinois, New York then held a "blind" primary, in which delegates remained undeclared. Many of Bush's delegate slates had been disqualified in the Empire State, thanks to Clark and Stone's challenges, so Reagan delegates would run unopposed in five congressional districts. The Gipper and Bush would go head-to-head in another eighteen districts, while uncommitted slates were running in the remaining sixteen districts. Reagan was sure to add to his overall delegate lead, and his campaign hoped to take as many as 62 of New York's 123 delegates. The Reagan campaign passed out flyers and ran newspaper ads telling GOP primary voters who the Reagan delegates were. Also, a Reagan man of long standing, State Senator Fred Eckert of Rochester, declared himself no longer "uncommitted," though no one ever thought he was anything but.

Stone, like his counterparts in other states for Reagan, operated with an enhanced autonomy after the departure of Charlie Black and the arrival of Casey. Black knew politics as well as any man alive in 1980. Casey had far less experience and thus was forced to depend on the regional and state political directors assembled by Black. Not only were they skilled in organization and media, they were all dedicated conservatives who had come of age starting in 1964, with the rise of Barry Goldwater.

Reagan took his campaign to upstate New York. In Syracuse, reporters confronted him with a letter signed by a small coterie of Californians critical of his claims over cutting spending there while serving as governor. Reagan, quite out of character, wondered aloud about the "obscene phone calls" one of the signers had apparently been charged with, but the candidate, ashamed, quickly caught himself, saying it was a "dirty trick" to have brought up the matter.[26] Nancy Reynolds, an old friend, said that in all the years she had known him, she had "never heard him say a mean, unkind, vengeful word about anybody." She did say he would get mad, but it would pass in a moment.[27]

LIKE BUSH, TED KENNEDY was desperate to turn his campaign around in Connecticut and New York. Kennedy's ground forces in Connecticut had in fact organized very well for their beleaguered candidate. And despite Kennedy's awful performances thus far, the primary season was still young. It had been less than a month since New Hampshire and only a little over two months since Iowa. Two dozen primaries lay ahead over the next three months, culminating in no less than eight state primaries on June 3—including New Jersey, Ohio, West Virginia, Montana, and California—the "big enchilada," as Reagan was wont to refer to it.

But by now almost no one thought Kennedy would last until June. To the boys on the bus, the Kennedy operation was a running joke. It became the theater of the absurd when he attended a press conference with five black leaders from Harlem who spent forty minutes in a mutual admiration society while never once mentioning or endorsing Kennedy, which had been the purpose of the event. Kennedy's plane was then forced to wait on the ground in New York while Air

Force Two, with Vice President Mondale aboard, was given priority. Kennedy finally landed in a torrential rainstorm in Syracuse, where he was supposed to receive the endorsement of the local congressman, Jim Hanley. In front of the media, Hanley stammered and spluttered. When an exasperated reporter yelled out asking whether he was endorsing Kennedy, Hanley replied that he would have to keep that vital information "private." Everybody roared with laughter, including Kennedy, who put his arm around the befuddled congressman and said, "You can tell these guys, Jim, they won't tell anybody."[28]

During a harrowing leg of the trip, reporters broke out kazoos and played the theme to *The High and the Mighty*, a movie starring John Wayne about an airplane that almost crashed. Kennedy's sleek jet, Air Malaise,[29] had long since been grounded because of the cost, so his campaign had chartered a twin-engine old-timer from a regional airline, Air New England, nicknamed "Scare New England" by its terrified customers. The airline had a history of losing luggage—at five thousand feet, with suitcases landing in potato patches in Maine—and of losing propellers while in flight. The star-crossed airline would go out of business in 1981.

Kennedy moved on as best he could. He told reporters in Rochester that even if Carter got enough delegates for a first-ballot nomination, he still wouldn't drop out of the race. With polls putting him behind Carter in New York by a 2–1 margin, more and more prominent Democrats were urging Kennedy to call it a day.[30] John White, the respected chairman of the Democratic National Committee, admonished Kennedy and those liberals who said he should not get out, calling them the "masochist fringe of politics."[31]

The prolonged fight, White knew, was not going to be helpful to the party in the fall. Carter had pulled way out in front of Kennedy, with 615 committed delegates to Kennedy's 192.[32]

Kennedy was a young man selling old wares. The country was moving dramatically to the right. He'd been on the national scene for twenty years and was trapped in a time warp. He favored wage and price controls, though they had failed miserably under Nixon; he favored more government programs, though Americans now believed that government was the problem and not the solution and that Washington was mostly corrupt. He favored social activism and massive redistribution of wealth. When Chappaquiddick was added to the mix, it was just too much for too many Democrats.

He was undeterred. Teddy ran his staff ragged, turning in one sixteen-hour day after another. The only time he showed the wear and tear of the campaign was each evening, when a whirlpool machine was placed in his hotel room so Kennedy could treat his bad back.

Kennedy's campaign showed its first sign of life in weeks when a New York Times/CBS News poll indicated that he had actually gained on Carter nationally. Kennedy was still miles behind, of course, but Carter's national approval numbers, from Iran to the economy, continued to plummet. Carter's dive was the biggest one-month drop in the history of the poll. His approval rating had gone down 13 points from 53 in February, and 21 points since December, when he was at 61.[33]

The media were becoming fed up with Jimmy Carter and his arrogant White House. Michael McShane was a young advance man in Mondale's office. McShane remembered that many Fridays after work, White House employees would meet up for cocktails. He saw Carter staffers laughingly dig into their pockets and pull out thick wads of phone messages left on pink slips of paper, competing with one another to see who had returned the fewest calls that week.[34] Even worse, Carter's chief of staff, Hamilton Jordan, was facing a grand jury probe into alleged cocaine use at Studio 54.[35] (Jordan was later cleared.)

None of this was any help to Jerry Brown's quest. He was almost out of bio-fuel. Brown had never gotten beyond the caricature of himself as a California flake. As governor, Brown refused to live in the new executive mansion, built for the Reagans to replace the old Victorian firetrap in which Mrs. Reagan had refused to live. Brown instead threw his mattress down on the floor of a $275-a-month walk-up apartment near the state capitol building. The man who had once trained to be a Jesuit priest was spotted on occasion loitering around the California Zen Center in Marin County. At the Gridiron Dinner in Washington, reporters depicted him as a Hare Krishna wearing robes of saffron. He was clearly an intelligent man but wholly undisciplined and given to flights of rhetorical inanity. He pledged to keep going with his faltering campaign even if he had to hitchhike, which only fed the image of him as some freeloading, itinerant hippie.[36] His campaign hadn't gotten to that point of having to stick its thumb out, but it was close.

JOHN ANDERSON WAS A Harvard man, but he was nonetheless well received by the Yalies when he spoke there in search of votes for the upcoming Connecticut primary. One thousand kids jammed Battell Chapel and another thousand waited outside, whooping and cheering his call for austerity and environmentalism. He pounced on Reagan, saying, "He thinks in terms of a holy war against Communism."[37] Several days earlier, Anderson had mocked Reagan on a college campus in Wisconsin, charging, "You would think . . . that there is a sweeping red tide of Communism engulfing the globe and that he [Reagan] has been somehow destined to lead the charge against it."[38] Anderson, even in his sarcasm, was right.

Soviet Communism was on the march around the globe and Reagan did believe it was his destiny to defeat it.

Bush, a Yale boy who made good, was treated to a less-than-hoped-for welcome by the undergraduates there. They supported Anderson and accused Bush of misrepresenting Anderson's positions. Bush lost it: "For months, I let that character sit around and call me a Ronald Reagan in a J. Press suit. . . . I've got real differences with him! And I will support the nominee of the Republican convention, instead of sanctimoniously holding myself above the party!" Bush did get the kids laughing when he listed his rules for political survival. They included "Being a Yale graduate has certain political disadvantages" and "Never let your opponent pay for the microphone in a political debate."[39]

He had hoped to use this speech to jump-start his campaign. He also began to devote much of his time to pummeling Carter, and Republican audiences were receptive. His adman, Bobby Goodman, wanted to make commercials using Bush's recent primary defeats as analogous to having been shot down during World War II. The ads, fortunately, were never produced.[40] The growing power of media advisers was bipartisan. The year before, when President Carter was having his share of problems, his adman, Gerald Rafshoon, was given an office in the White House.

The media began to toy with the idea of Anderson's running as an independent in the fall election. Not only would this make for a great story, but some liked the idea of Anderson, the liberal, undermining Carter's bid for reelection. Stories exploring this possibility began to emerge in the major newspapers, and Anderson's campaign did little to dissuade the speculation.

Publicly, Anderson said he expected to be the GOP's nominee, but after Illinois, the odds had grown long for him. Deadlines were looming to get on the ballot in forty-five states (worth 486 electoral votes) as an independent for the fall campaign. Rich and powerful liberals such as Norman Lear and Paul Newman, whose company Anderson enjoyed, were turning his head. Both Reagan and Carter revolted them.[41]

Reaganites—after getting over their animosity toward the haughty Anderson—warmed to the idea of a third-party bid by Anderson. It would be a dagger aimed right at Carter, who needed the votes of liberals in New England and New York in the fall election.

Unctuously, Anderson denied that he would run as a third-party candidate, telling reporters, "I'm the only thing that stands between the Republican Party and defeat in November."[42] Vowing not to let the "Phil Cranes" push him out of the GOP, he took on Reagan: "I just cannot believe that the party will follow them and, lemming-like, rush to the sea and drown just so they can follow Ronald Reagan's banner as it sinks beneath the waves."[43]

PHIL CRANE FINALLY DROPPED out of the race—sort of. Though he released his four delegates to Reagan, Crane did not formally withdraw or endorse the front-runner, saying he wanted to hear from people around the country before finally deciding at the end of March . . . once and for all . . . maybe.[44]

There were now five candidates remaining in the race—Reagan, Bush, Anderson, Kennedy, and Carter. All five answered media questionnaires for the *New York Times*. Reagan was clearly the most distrustful of government, at any level. He cited rent control as the reason for New York's housing crisis. He cited gun control as what made New York so dangerous, whether day or night or "only half dark." He cited government social engineering as what had created the sad mess of the South Bronx.[45] In a sit-down interview with *Times* reporter David Rosenbaum, Reagan explained his view of government: "Government exists to protect us from each other. Where government has gone beyond its limit is in deciding to protect us from ourselves."[46]

The weekend before the Connecticut primary, a new poll out by the University of Connecticut had Reagan ahead, 43 percent to 30 percent for Bush and only 22 percent for Anderson.[47] Reagan hadn't been in the state since earlier in the week, while Bush was campaigning furiously there. Reagan's men drew comfort from the poll, though it was wildly different from newspaper polls.

Cautiously, they began to lay out a strategy for running in the general election against Carter. They surmised that Carter would attempt to brand Reagan as a "warmonger." Casey, Ed Meese, and Dick Wirthlin, less turf-conscious than most political operatives, discussed bringing in additional talent for the campaign. Discussions also began on a running mate for Reagan, with Howard Baker's name being floated. The Reagans liked Baker and had been guests at his home in Tennessee, but to Reagan's fire-breathing conservative supporters, Baker was the devil incarnate, mostly because of his support for the Panama Canal treaties. Other names mentioned included Congressman Jack Kemp and Senator Richard Lugar of Indiana.

TWO DAYS BEFORE THE primary, the *Hartford Courant* reviewed the remaining candidates in a long and thoughtful editorial. There were no gratuitous shots and the paper endorsed no one, but pleasing to the Reagan folks, the editorialists did not bash the Gipper as many others had done. He was praised for being specific on the issues and for his ability on the stump, and the paper went on to state that Reagan stood a better chance against Carter in the fall than was thought at the time. The paper actually gave local-boy-made-good Bush a bit of a going-over for not being specific enough, for not offering ideas, and for coming across as more conservative than he really was.[48]

The media had turned sour toward Bush. He simply didn't wear well with the ink-stained wretch crowd. A new, asinine theory was floated that Bush was not qualified to be president because he had not suffered sufficiently. Bush had had enough. When pushed, he testily asked the reporters whether they had ever had to watch a child die. They had not. "I did, for six months," Bush said irritably.[49] The Bushes had lost a little girl, Robin, to cancer in the 1950s. Of course, Bush was also a hero of World War II as the youngest flyer in the U.S. Navy, had built a successful business, and had risen in life mostly in spite of his upbringing and not because of it. The whole issue was absurd.

Although Connecticut and New York were looming, the candidates had to keep their eyes on Wisconsin, whose primary was scheduled for April 1. Anderson journeyed there, where he made his disdain for Reagan even more evident. He said he was going to "peel" Reagan's "fingers away from the nomination one by one." He called Reagan a "throwback" who was "simplistic, even primitive" in his views on foreign policy. Anderson then administered the coup de grace, calling Reagan's thinking "naïve and utterly misinformed."[50]

Early polling had Anderson scoring well in the Badger State, tied with Bush just behind Reagan.[51] Wisconsin, significantly, allowed for crossover voting. Reagan also made a trip into the state, and gave a barnburner of a speech in Waukesha to a thousand cheering Republicans. Congressman James Sensenbrenner endorsed Reagan on the spot and the crowd cheered wildly when he said he'd already cast his absentee ballot for Reagan.[52]

Reagan had been to Wisconsin dozens of times, including the night in 1976 of his stunning primary win over Gerald Ford in the North Carolina GOP primary. He was with Peter Hannaford and Marty Anderson that night to speak to Ducks Unlimited. When Hannaford asked Reagan if he wanted a speech prepared, the Gipper replied, "No, that's okay, I know what to say to a bunch of drunken hunters."[53] Reagan went out and told jokes that would have had the men laughing even if they'd been sober.

With nothing to lose, Kennedy went on the offense, hard. In speech after speech, he desperately thundered, "America means hope; America means opportunity; America means inspiration!" He ripped into Carter over the economy and foreign policy. The media had run out the string on Chappaquiddick and the trials of his campaign. All there was left to do was actually report on what Kennedy said. As the *Washington Post* observed, "Kennedy hasn't really recovered his political footing, but he has found his voice—and his themes."[54] Kennedy, after his incoherent start in the fall of 1979, had developed into a polished and effective speaker.

Bush was fighting off queries from reporters about when he would get out of the race. He pointed out that he had the money to keep going for a very long time. Bush still had coming $2.6 million in matching funds from the FEC. "Hell with 'em. We're going to win this nomination," he told a supportive crowd in Connecticut.[55]

Reagan spent the day before the Connecticut primary in Oklahoma, speaking at several rallies. He poked the Panamanian government for possible violations of the Canal treaties and told reporters that "millions of patriotic Democrats" would vote for him in the fall.[56] It was also announced that Reagan would stump in Texas the next day, accompanied by John Connally. Connally wasn't about to endorse Anderson or Bush, both of whom he detested. The next day, Connally urged all his supporters, including his lone delegate from Arkansas, Ada Mills, to swing their support to the Gipper.

Earlier in the day, Reagan had journeyed to Buffalo to put in a campaign appearance with Jack Kemp. Reagan was asked about the possibility of Kemp's going on the ticket with him, but demurred, saying only that he had "great admiration" for his young friend. Kemp was asked also but wisely ducked the question.[57]

THE DAY OF THE Connecticut primary was rainy, snowy, and otherwise miserable. But the sun shone on George Bush as he pulled out a surprise victory. Over the past week, some polls had put Reagan ahead, some had put Anderson ahead, but none had put Bush ahead. The unexpected win revived Bush and kept him in the race.

Once again, though, he was somewhat overshadowed. The real story of the day was Ted Kennedy's astonishing victories in the New York and Connecticut Democratic primaries. He trounced Carter 59–41 percent in New York and won Connecticut 47–41 percent. No one had seen Kennedy's upsets coming—not even the Kennedy campaign.[58] Before the results came in, speechwriter Bob Shrum had been drafting a withdrawal speech, and Kennedy himself apparently had been ready to call it day.[59] After the victories, old Kennedy hand Steve Smith was overheard in a Manhattan hallway saying to another old Kennedy hand, Eddie Martin, "What the f— happened?" to which Martin replied, "How the f— should I know?"[60]

Kennedy, grinning like the cat that just ate the canary, told the assembled press, "I love New York," quoting the Empire State's slogan in a national ad campaign. He did not overlook the Nutmeg State, adding, "And I love Connecticut too!"[61]

Kennedy had benefited greatly from the Jewish vote, which constituted 30 percent of Democrats in New York. Indeed, he won their votes by a 4–1 margin. For the first time, too, he won the Irish and the Catholic vote. New York had never been hospitable to Carter. He'd lost the primary badly in 1976, coming in a poor fourth.[62] He won it in the general over Gerald Ford, but by a margin far less than the percentage of registered Democrats.

At a press conference, State Department operative Hodding Carter unconvincingly dismissed Kennedy's twin victories as a meaningless "protest vote" against the president. The truth was that Carter had been deeply wounded, even if the president got nearly as many delegates as Kennedy that day, because of New York's proportional delegate selection. Carter's losses meant that he could not consolidate his party around his renomination before the convention. Of course, it would still be an uphill battle for Kennedy. He'd have to win three out of every five delegates up for grabs in the remaining primaries—a very tall order.

George Bush's victory on the Republican side in Connecticut—he took 39 percent to Reagan's 34 percent and Anderson's poor 22 percent—was overshadowed not just by Kennedy's wins but by his own loss in New York as well.[63] In New York, Reagan seized 73 of the 123 available delegates—more than expected—while Bush won only 6; the balance were uncommitted. Despite losing in Connecticut, Reagan took only one fewer delegate there than Bush did. Overall, Reagan now had 293 delegates to 68 for Bush and 46 for Anderson.[64]

Bush was nonetheless cheered by the results in Connecticut. The win would keep his campaign alive for another month. He had money in the bank, and the forthcoming Pennsylvania primary, where Anderson was not competing, would give Bush another crack at the Gipper, man-to-man. Bush would have around $1.5 million available for the next month, and even better, he had no debts. Reagan's campaign, in contrast, was still in debt, though treasurer Bay Buchanan had whittled the shortfall down from nearly $1.5 million to about $340,000.[65]

Reagan's campaign had made a major mistake in not contesting Connecticut harder. Had Reagan won, Bush would have been out and Reagan would have had months to consolidate the GOP. With Bush revived, Reagan had to continue working to win the nomination. The silver lining in all this was that Reagan, when tested, was a far better candidate than when he was coasting.

Bush headed right for Wisconsin to build on his renewed mini-momentum. He'd won the endorsement of the *Milwaukee Sentinel*, which called him "the best-equipped" of all the candidates.[66] Dave Keene bluntly assessed the chances for his candidate, saying that it was "improbable but not impossible."[67] Bush would have to come back very strongly in Pennsylvania, Michigan, Oregon, and other upcoming contests. Keene pointed out that if Bush's fortunes changed in these states, it could break loose some Reagan delegates in New York and Illinois, who were not compelled legally to vote for Reagan at the convention in Detroit. Kennedy's men believed the same, that Carter's delegate strength was soft.

AS A RESULT OF the March 25 primaries, the networks reported that both Kennedy and Bush had been "born again."[68] Brit Hume of ABC was more realistic, saying that Connecticut had given Bush's "campaign not so much a rebirth as a reprieve."[69]

Winning primaries had certainly been just the tonic Reagan's fundraising operation needed. New reports showed that he had taken in $4.3 million in February, besting Carter by almost $2 million. Bush had raised an impressive $2.8 million in February, but his fundraising tailed off badly in March.[70]

Politicos were now focused on the all-important Wisconsin primary. With its progressive tradition and allowance for crossover voting, no one was sure how it would play out. Kennedy was competing for liberals from both parties. So was Anderson. Reagan was competing for conservatives from both parties, struggling with Carter for the votes of conservative Democrats. Bush was counting on the newly resurgent Kennedy to pull liberal votes away from Anderson and drain his support in the state.

Ronald Reagan had not dispatched George Bush from the race but he was still turning his attention toward Jimmy Carter. His standard stump speech had become a bill of particulars against the president. He scored Carter, for example, on his statement several years earlier that America was "now free of that inordinate fear of Communism."[71] Reagan also offered solutions for what ailed America. He was honing his revolutionary economic message, complete with tax cuts for American taxpayers, cuts in federal spending and regulations, a reduction in inflation and interest rates—and prosperity for all.

Carter and Reagan were as different as night and day, and their respective approaches to economics were no exception. Reagan wanted the government out of the economy and Carter wanted it in. Reagan spoke of limitless horizons and Carter talked about limited futures. Carter said there was little a president could do to rescue the American economy. Reagan said take the yoke of government off the people and they will save the economy themselves. Carter wanted people to trust him. Reagan told Americans, "Don't trust me, trust yourself." Unfortunately for Carter, he was slowly becoming the Herbert Hoover of 1980 and Reagan was being cast as his political hero, FDR.

In 1932 the incumbent, Hoover, said that little could be done to stave off the Great Depression, while Roosevelt, the challenger, said that everything must be done to alleviate the plight of the American people. Under Reagan's emerging leadership, the GOP was becoming the party of hope. The role reversal of the candidates and the parties was astonishing.

Reagan was on the verge of making the GOP the party of the future.

15

REAGAN'S DEMOCRATS

"Reagan has the same image as these people have of themselves."

Ronald Reagan headed for Milwaukee's South Side, where he gave a rousing speech in Serb Hall. Speaking at this ethnic Mecca had been a rite of passage for Democratic presidential candidates over many years but verboten for nearly all Republicans. That is, until Reagan. The joint was packed to the gills, the cold beer was only fifty cents, and the crowd was rockin' with Ronnie.

This section of Milwaukee was 100 percent Democratic, 100 percent Catholic, yet Reagan wowed 'em that night. It was on the eve of the Wisconsin primary, and although the phrase "Reagan Democrat" had not yet been coined, everybody was coming to understand the Gipper's appeal with these flag-waving Americans. A young Democrat, Robert Ponasik, stood on a chair furiously waving a handmade sign that proclaimed, "Cross Over for Reagan."[1] Of the reaction to Reagan in Serb Hall, Lynn Sherr of ABC reported, "In judging from the way they showed up at a long-time Democratic meeting hall . . . a large number of blue-collar voters could go for Reagan."[2]

The white pages of the Milwaukee phone book were jammed with listings of people whose last names looked as if they'd gone through a Mixmaster. These were immigrants and first- and second-generation Serbs, Poles, Czechs, Russians, Ukrainians, Hungarians, and others who had escaped Stalin or Hitler and consequently were intensely anti-Communist and antisocialist. They were not the least bit interested in being dependent upon government. These Slavic-Americans were fiercely self-reliant and deeply patriotic. They loved America and many had already proven it in World War II, Korea, and Vietnam. Serb Hall was adorned with the names of ethnic Serbs who had fought and died for America.

There were no "fortunate sons" in these neighborhoods, and even if given the chance to avoid the military draft by joining the National Guard or gaining a college deferment, they would have scoffed. They had to go and fight or else their fathers would have knocked them through a wall.

These ethnics were Catholic and Eastern Orthodox, and as a matter of course intensely pro-life. They settled in the big and small cities of America: Youngstown and Cleveland, Ohio; Buffalo and Cortland, New York; and Milwaukee, where there was work and where the local political machines were reliably Democratic. The scions of the Republican Party didn't want these people with funny last names traipsing around their country clubs and private estates. Heavens to Betsy! These people drank cheap beer and ate kielbasa! Millions of Slavs who by their outlook if not their culture could or should have been Republicans were not, largely because the snobby Republicans didn't want them.

So they became Democrats, voting for Adlai Stevenson, LBJ, and in 1968, "Happy Warrior" Hubert Humphrey, whom they especially adored. In many of those Slavic Catholic homes, in a place of honor over the mantel were photos of their two heroes: John F. Kennedy and the pope. Many even supported George McGovern over the commie-bashing Richard Nixon in 1972.

In the 1960s and even earlier, the shrinking Republican Party in some northeastern and midwestern states had changed course and begun to open their primaries to Democrats and independents, hoping that doing so would make the practice of voting Republican more comfortable for the outsiders. Democrats responded in kind, allowing Republicans to vote in their primaries. In 1976, almost all the states Reagan won over Ford were with the help of Democrats crossing over to vote for him. No one really took notice of the phenomenon at the time, except some Ford supporters who complained vehemently that these people shouldn't be allowed in the front door of the GOP. A political party with only 18 percent support—falling apart at the seams—was complaining about people who wanted to come in to vote for Reagan.

Reagan spoke to these urban, ethnic Democrats in a way that no other politician had since JFK. He talked about community, responsibility, privacy, patriotism, the evils of Communism, and their children's future. Although Reagan was Protestant, his father had been Roman Catholic and he had inculcated in his young son a parish perspective. As an adult campaigner, the Gipper still preferred the pronouns "us" and "we" over "me" and "I," and these voters loved him for it. He made them feel good about themselves and, by extension, America. "Reagan has a personal following all his own," noted *Time* magazine.[3]

One member of that following was Muriel Coleman, who was organizing Wisconsin for Reagan. She'd been working in the Reagan scheduling office in Los

Angeles, but was detailed to her native Wisconsin. She was one of many young conservatives who had walked their own separate path to Reagan. In 1967, an old beau had been killed in South Vietnam. At his military burial, she vowed to make it her life's goal to fight Communism however she could. She found her means to do so in conservative organizations and in Reagan's 1976 and 1980 campaigns. Coleman adored Reagan. When her father died, she got a handwritten letter from her hero. Later in Madison, as they were going to the airport in the back of a car, Coleman gave Reagan a thank-you note and suggested he read it on the plane. Reagan replied, "Well, can't I read it now?" Taken aback, she told him of course. Reagan read it and then reached for her hand. Their eyes brimmed with tears as they both thought about fathers.[4]

Later in the year, Coleman became an elector to the Electoral College. In 1981, she saw Reagan at the White House and told him she'd had the pleasure of voting for him three times in 1980, without once breaking the law. Reagan laughed with delight.[5] Working with Coleman was Mike Grebe, a low-key but effective attorney in Milwaukee, and Joni Jackson, another longtime conservative activist in the Badger State. At one rally, the great ballplayer Sal Bando of the Brewers introduced Reagan.[6]

Restless Democrats in Wisconsin and elsewhere were ripe for Reagan's picking. By 1980 the fundamentals of America's economy and society had radically changed. Well-paying manufacturing jobs that allowed unskilled and semiskilled workers to enter the middle class had mostly dried up. Union membership was dwindling and the upheavals of the 1960s had left many traditional blue-collar Democrats alienated from society and from their party's intellectual elite. These reflexive Democrats in the heartland who had simply inherited their Democratic affiliation were tired of the party taking them for granted. Reagan, a product of the Great Depression himself, resonated with these voters on a profound, emotional level. In politics, timing is everything. A confluence of political and cultural factors ensured that, in this electoral season of discontent, Reagan's time had come.

The *Washington Post* assembled a focus group of voters in Albany, New York, to watch the television commercials of all the candidates. When the group viewed George Bush's commercials and heard the tagline, "A president we won't have to train," they broke out in laughter.[7] As for Reagan, the *Post* discovered an astonishing fact: the Gipper's commercials were more popular with Democrats than they were with Republicans. "Reagan's support among conservative, blue-collar Democrats has been one of the most underreported phenomena of the 1980 presidential race," the *Post* noted.[8] Reagan was pro–organized labor. He had proudly proclaimed in his autobiography, *Where's the Rest of Me?*, that he was a "rabid union man."[9]

Journalists were truly amazed at how lifetime urban Democrats were going bonkers for Reagan, and they began to speculate that Reagan was no Goldwater. He could not only keep his base of motivated Republicans, he could invade Jimmy Carter's base of traditional Democrats as well. Reagan's Milwaukee coordinator, Louis Collison, grasped the phenomenon immediately: "Reagan has the same image as these people have of themselves."[10]

Democrats at the grassroots were frustrated with the economy and the world situation. They believed that their party had become a tool of special interests. Reagan was "offering them a new home," as Jack Germond and Jules Witcover wrote.[11] This remarkable turn of events was noted in the White House. Carter's men recognized how well Reagan had done with Democratic crossover voters in Illinois, and suddenly they weren't so sure that they would knock the stuffing out of him. "To dismiss Ronald Reagan as a right-wing nut would be a very serious error—for us or anybody else," one Carter aide admitted.[12] At the end of March, Carter and Reagan were in a national dead heat, 45–44 percent, according to Gallup.[13] Reagan was getting a lot of Democrats, because there weren't that many Republicans around, certainly not almost half the country.

For three years, Jimmy Carter had been waiting to catch Br'er Reagan. It looked as if Carter the fox had indeed caught what he wanted: the Reagan rabbit. Only now, would he throw Reagan into the briar patch, just where Reagan wanted to be?

Before Carter could focus on halting Reagan's momentum, he needed to stop the newly resurgent Ted Kennedy. The president stepped up his efforts in Wisconsin. More than 350,000 Democrats received get-out-the-vote phone calls from the Carter campaign, and Carter's son Chip, his wife Rosalynn, and Vice President Walter Mondale all campaigned aggressively there.[14] Dozens of "vacationing" White House aides descended upon the state to stave off Kennedy, and new federal sewer construction grants were suddenly announced for Wisconsin.

Pat Caddell conceded that his polling showed the race closing there and Carter, in an interview for the *Milwaukee Journal*, savaged Kennedy just one day before the primary, accusing him of "cowardice and demagoguery."[15] Carter knew he was in trouble when Mondale reported back that while he was speaking at a high school in La Crosse, the kids laughed and mocked him when he mentioned the president by name.[16]

In the Milwaukee Journal poll, Kennedy had been behind Carter by a demoralizing margin of 61–11 percent—until New York and Connecticut, that is.[17]

Kennedy was forced to concede that he could not beat Carter in the upcoming Kansas primary, so he focused on Wisconsin and other states. He should have looked more closely at the Sunflower State. Farmers were increasingly angry with Carter, and defense cutbacks had resulted in unemployment in big airplane manufacturing plants in Wichita.

Kennedy had Pat Lucey on his side in Wisconsin. Lucey had been lieutenant governor in the 1960s and a popular governor in the 1970s. He was one of the most charming and gracious men in politics, with friends on both sides. Lucey had engineered John Kennedy's upset over Hubert Humphrey in Wisconsin in 1960, aided by his sidekick, the shadowy Paul Corbin. He hoped to do it again for Jack's youngest brother. The United Auto Workers had endorsed Carter, but that was it—none of the usual phone calls, organization, and graveyard voting that labor often did to help favored candidates.[18]

Kennedy decided to play the "Badger Game" in the Badger State. Originally, four days of campaigning had been planned, but it was then announced that this had been scaled back to one day. He was hoping to lower his expectations in Wisconsin, but he also realized that John Anderson might suck a lot of liberal Democrats into the GOP primary. Kennedy reasoned that if he performed poorly, he had an excuse, and if he beat expectations, then he would win the psychological day.

GEORGE BUSH HAD PULLED out a victory in Connecticut, but as the race moved to Wisconsin he slipped into an awkward mode of campaigning. His campaign instituted an "issue of the day," and Bush would talk only about that day's topic. When questioned about anything remotely related to campaign strategy, he refused to answer. Bush, offstage, was relaxed and could show a biting sense of humor with the media. Onstage, he too often tightened up.

He benefited, however, when Reagan's long-simmering "gaffe" issue finally boiled over onto the front page of the *Washington Post*, in a story written by Lou Cannon. In addition to stumbling over farm parity and several other issues, Reagan had fumbled answers about aid to New York City and the federal bailout of the Chrysler Corporation. "What emerges," Cannon wrote, "is the seeming paradox of a candidate who can out-debate rivals in candidate forums and outmaneuver contentious reporters in press conferences, yet still kindle questions about his intellectual capacities." The question Cannon posed was not whether Reagan was too conservative but "Does Ronald Reagan know what he's talking about?"[19]

Reagan knew all about farm parity; he just didn't want to say he was against it. He later admitted that he opposed parity because it subsidized inefficient farmers and kept them unfairly in the marketplace. But Reagan didn't want to turn potential voters away, especially conservative rural folks.

On other issues, though, Reagan had indeed fumbled. It was his campaign's fault and it was his fault: he wasn't prepared with the facts. The problem wasn't his command of issues; he had to read something only once and then he knew the issue cold. The "gaffe" problem was the result, rather, of his being too accessible to the media. On Reagan's chartered bus crisscrossing Wisconsin, reporters had pretty much unfettered access to the candidate, which inevitably led to "gotcha" questions.

Other chinks in the Reagan armor appeared. The *Wall Street Journal*, in an editorial, praised Reagan's apparent march to the nomination, but also expressed concern that he'd better learn more about his own campaign. After Reagan's appearance on ABC's news program *Issues and Answers*, some political reporters had been astonished that Reagan did not know the content of all his television ads. The *Journal* advised Reagan that he'd better bone up on the issues and read his briefing books—or else.[20]

Those briefing books, however, would not explain the philosophical debate inside the Reagan campaign over whether he should run in the general election as a populist reformer or a traditional Republican. Should he focus on government and government spending, or should he focus on massive tax cuts that would stimulate the economy while downplaying government spending cuts? Reagan tried to paper over the differences in his camp, but one thing was certain: he was four-square for the Kemp-Roth tax cuts.

The disagreement over tax cuts versus cutting government was a serious theoretical debate inside the GOP. The tax-cut gang—Kemp, Art Laffer, Jude Wanniski, and Jeff Bell—were not interested in the small-government arguments. People on the other side, like Bill Simon, Marty Anderson, and Alan Greenspan, felt that big government was the cause of many problems in the country and it had to be scaled back. They also believed that for the first time since the New Deal, Reagan's arguments for curtailing the size and scope of government were popular with the American people. Some on Reagan's team were hypersensitive about his looking like the candidate of moneyed GOP and big-business interests, which would undermine his appeal to blue-collar Democrats. The working poor and middle class wanted tax cuts, while the upper crust of the GOP wanted government reined in and tax cuts for businesses.

Anderson, Reagan's policy wonk, was struggling to produce an overdue white paper that would reconcile the two positions. But Reagan was not focused on the parlor-room niceties of economic theory. His interest was in restarting the American economy, which had slipped into its seventh official recession since the end of World War II. Inflation had risen sharply to 18 percent annually, even though Carter had hoped to hold it under 11 percent.[21] Interest rates, meanwhile, had rocketed to 19.75 percent.[22]

For Reagan, there was no debate to be had: in truth, he favored both cutting taxes and shrinking government. Endorsing both positions led to complaints from the media. How could he cut taxes, fund a military buildup, and still balance the federal budget? The Reagan campaign was desperate to find an answer. It feared stumbling into another political minefield over economics, as Reagan had in 1976 when he called for $90 billion in federal programs to be transferred back to the states without the apparent means of paying for them.[23] But Reagan told his staff, "Tell me what has to be done to restore economic health to this society—and let me worry about the politics of it."[24]

Reagan's tax-cutting commercials had been pulled after New Hampshire until the internal debate was settled. But his young regional field director, Frank Donatelli, insisted that the spots be aired in Wisconsin, believing that Democrats there would like the message, especially the link to John Kennedy's tax cuts.[25] The affable Donatelli had grown up in Pittsburgh, one of four boys, the son of Italian-Americans. Donatelli had worked for Reagan in 1976, had been courted by Bush and Phil Crane, but had chosen to stay with the Gipper for the 1980 effort. Mustachioed, he was also by reputation one of the nicest guys and one of the worst dressers in Washington, favoring god-awful polyester leisure suits. Like the rest of the field staff, he drove thousands of miles, was paid little, but always had a pocketful of dimes for pay phones to call his various coordinators across the Rust Belt.[26]

Besides targeting these new "Reagan Democrats," the Gipper's campaign also saw an opportunity with younger voters. Younger voters had for years tended to be more receptive to the happy-go-lucky Democrats than the staid and boring GOP. But inflation, unemployment, and high interest rates had led many demoralized young Americans to believe that the Democratic Party no longer was concerned about them and that the future was gone. They wanted the same chance at the American dream that their parents and grandparents had had. Eighteen-year-old college student Walter Hermann told the *Wall Street Journal*, "The Democrats haven't done a good job with the economy, especially not Carter."[27]

Reagan spoke in dozens of high school gymnasiums in the Badger State and the kids responded heartily. Though they were for the most part too young to vote, the imagery was great for the local television stations. Except in one, where a student sharply questioned Reagan and he replied, "I'd like to suggest some outside reading for you."[28]

At the end of March, Olympic hero Jesse Owens died at the age of sixty-six of lung cancer. Some Americans had urged the boycott of the 1936 Berlin Olympics, in protest of Adolf Hitler's Third Reich. Instead, the Americans sent a full complement of athletes, and Owens, a black man, beat the Nazis at their own games, winning four gold medals and doing so with grace. He later wryly noted that Hitler had not snubbed him at the Sports Palace in Berlin, but FDR did by never even sending a telegram of congratulations.[29]

The 1980 Olympics to be held in Moscow were no less controversial. Carter's boycott had faltered, and many American allies now were planning on sending delegations. Originally, Reagan had supported the boycott, but as time went on, he changed his mind and suggested that the athletes themselves vote on whether to go. Carter said he would enforce the boycott by not allowing visas to be issued to any of the Americans. He was dealing harshly with the athletes and this did not set well with their fellow countrymen, including Reagan, who said, "I find myself worrying about the young people who've worked so hard."[30]

President Carter fired a salvo at Reagan in a long interview with the *Washington Post*. While praising Reagan's skills as an orator, Carter dismissed his opponent's intellectual firepower, saying that Reagan could only "recite answers to the question concerning current events almost by rote" and that the Republican took "relatively simplistic approaches to issues."[31]

Walter Mondale also went after Reagan on the campaign trail, one time going too far with his humor. In a gag, he told a crowd of encountering an angry (mythical) Republican who was complaining about things in America and said, "You know, this would never happen if Ronald Reagan were alive." Later asked about the joke, Reagan said he thought it was "unkind,"[32] and the vice president got a call from an intermediary telling him that Nancy Reagan found the joke "very offensive." Years later Mondale recalled, "I said, 'Tell Nancy that it was a mistake and she'll never hear that joke again.'" Sure enough, Mondale, a gentleman, never told the joke after that.[33]

Mondale made a mistake in not recognizing what Reagan himself understood—that "the greatest humor is humor you use against yourself," as the Gipper told the *Los Angeles Times* in the early spring of 1980. Reagan demonstrated that self-deprecating humor repeatedly. Republican audiences loved it. "A few years ago—before anybody was trying to make anything of my age—I told the story of how I'd already lived ten years beyond my life expectancy when I was born, which was a source of irritation to a number of people."[34] Stumping in Kansas, Reagan bumped his head getting into a bus and, mindful of Gerald Ford's many pratfalls, said, "I know I can be president now."[35]

Jimmy Carter was notoriously unfunny, as was John Anderson. They were just too self-conscious. Jerry Brown may have been most incapable of seeing a good joke, even when it was literally under his nose. In New Hampshire, his campaign had provided chocolate-chip cookies and bean soup to a group of supporters. Brown got up to talk to them about fiscal discipline. Then he said there was no "free lunch" to a group that was enjoying that very thing. His supporters tittered, but Brown spluttered that somebody had to pay for it.[36]

Of course, a poor sense of humor may have been the least of Brown's problems. What was left of his long-shot campaign would collapse in Wisconsin. A statewide television broadcast, directed by Francis Ford Coppola of *Godfather* fame, was so weird and poorly produced—with bizarre lighting effects—that Brown was written off for good by most seasoned operatives. Coppola somehow projected an image of the Wisconsin statehouse onto Brown's forehead, prompting someone to say, "How can you vote for a candidate who shows you he has a hole in his head?"[37]

THE MONDAY BEFORE THE April 1 primaries, Reagan jetted off to Louisiana, where he was the featured speaker at a jambalaya fundraising dinner. In the question-and-answer period, someone, after nervously addressing Reagan as "Mr. President," asked about Gerald Ford going on the ticket with him. A chorus of boos descended upon the poor person. Responding, Reagan said he doubted that anyone who had once been president would be interested in going backwards one step. Reagan also told the crowd he would phase out the Departments of Energy and Education.[38]

On primary day, Reagan won both Wisconsin and Kansas. He took Kansas's closed primary handily, winning 63 percent of the vote to Anderson's 18 and Bush's 13.[39] Reagan had been helped by an unrestrained and unequivocal endorsement from native son Bob Dole, who said the weekend before the primary, "We're supposed to be a great nation. Well, I say it's about time to start to act like one! And Ronald Reagan can make that happen!"[40]

Reagan's victory in the hotly contested Wisconsin primary was much tighter. In fact, without the help of conservative Democrats, he would have lost. More than half of the votes cast in the GOP primary were by Democrats and independents, according to exit polls conducted by CBS and the New York Times.[41] Reagan ran strongly in the Democratic strongholds of Racine and Kenosha, along with the South Side of Milwaukee.[42]

Reagan took 40 percent to Bush's respectable 31 percent and Anderson's 28 percent.[43] But he did much better in delegates, because of Wisconsin's odd proportional delegate selection process, which awarded the slots by congressional district, with bonus delegates for winning the statewide contest. Reagan took home twenty-five delegates to only three for Bush.[44]

Bush had spent $500,000 in the state to Reagan's $200,000. Adding insult to injury, Reagan had campaigned in the state for only three days and had spent most of it making open appeals to Democrats and independents.

But Anderson had been the most damaged by the results in Wisconsin. He'd counted on the college kids and they had let him down, just as they often did their parents. Still, Anderson managed to claim six delegates, despite winning less of the popular vote than Bush did.

The day before the Wisconsin and Kansas primaries, Pat Caddell, the president's pollster, had Carter ahead in his polling in the Badger State, but he said, "I am not all that confident that those numbers will hold."[45] Ted Kennedy was surging after his surprise wins in New York and Connecticut, and Carter was showing more and more weakness. Though Carter's approval ratings had shot up after the Americans were taken hostage in Iran, it had now been five months and the president had taken little action to free them. Worse, Carter, trying to appear hawkish, had been badly embarrassed when the Iranians released to the media a private letter from the president to the Ayatollah Khomeini seeking to relax the tension between the two countries. The Carter White House vehemently denied that such a letter had been sent.[46]

The morning of the Wisconsin primary, with politicos thinking that Kennedy had an outside chance to win, President Carter engaged in what many later thought was an underhanded act. If nothing else, it was certainly cynical. Just forty minutes before the polls opened, Carter went on national television to announce a breakthrough—or as he said, a "positive development"—in the hostage negotiations.[47] In fact, there was no breakthrough—as the Iranians announced later in the day—but enough Wisconsin Democrats fell for the ploy that Carter won the state, 56–30 percent.[48] Carter also pummeled Kennedy in Kansas.[49]

No one knew whether Carter had been deceitful about the hostage situation, though many in Washington were becoming more cynical by the day. But the ploy worked. According to media polling, late-deciding Democrats broke heavily for Carter over Kennedy in Wisconsin.[50] Caddell blithely told reporters later that his man had been helped in Kansas and Wisconsin by the announcement.

President Carter had rolled back Kennedy's counteroffensive.

JOHN ANDERSON'S BID FOR the GOP nomination was fading and he, like Bush, was fulminating. Anderson lost any shred of gentility toward Reagan in Wisconsin. Frustrated, he lashed out, saying that Reagan "should go back to 'Death Valley Days' and simply imbibe some of those 20-mule team bromides."[51]

Bush's frustrations over his string of ill fortune sometimes came out nastily in public. Campaigning in New Orleans in anticipation of Louisiana's fast-approaching April 5 primary, Bush told a group that during the New England primaries, all the candidates had tried to show off their wares, telling citizens how deep their roots were in the region. "And Ronald Reagan told them he had dated Priscilla Alden," Bush said.[52] Alden had come over on the *Mayflower* in 1620, as every schoolchild knew.

It was one thing for Reagan to joke about his own age, but quite another for Bush to do so. The remark was noted and filed at Reagan Central.

Heavy rains had fallen across Louisiana, and though there was some flooding, the pumps that kept New Orleans dry were working. The Saturday primary in Louisiana was closed—no crossovers—but that didn't stop Reagan from washing over Bush, 74–19 percent.[53] Bush had set a modest goal of 30 percent for himself in Louisiana but failed to even achieve that. Reagan won twenty-nine of Louisiana's delegates, while two would go to Detroit uncommitted.[54]

After Louisiana, Reagan stood at 372 delegates to only 72 for Bush and 57 for Anderson.[55] Though Reagan was still more than 600 delegates short of a first-ballot nomination—a Republican needed 998 delegate votes—his juggernaut was rolling and most Republicans were falling in line behind him.

Carter swept past Kennedy in Louisiana, 56–22 percent,[56] but Kennedy's state coordinator, Judge Edmund Reggie, goofily called Teddy's performance "phenomenal."[57] Carter was ahead of Kennedy in delegates, 848–445. A Democrat needed 1,666 for the nomination.[58]

After the breakneck pace of the past two months, the campaigns now had a nearly three-week respite between primaries. The big Pennsylvania primary wouldn't come until April 22. Staff could go back home for a day or two to do laundry, pay overdue bills, check in at the office, and plan the next foray. Reagan took the time to beef up his press operation with the addition of Jim Brady to travel on the plane. Brady had been press secretary to John Connally and prior to William Roth, the easygoing senator from Delaware who was cosponsor with Jack Kemp on the big tax-cut bill (and who happened to sport the worst toupee in Washington).[59] Brady was affable and fun-loving and, like any good flack, enjoyed cocktails with reporters.

Reporters, too, needed this break in the campaign season. They'd been on the road constantly for months now, eating too much, boozing too much, sleeping too little, and not checking in with their spouses and kids enough. The three-week breather would also give them a chance to reflect on what the coming fall election might look like.

While reporters and politicos looked ahead to a Carter-Reagan showdown, Reagan refused to claim that the Republican contest was over. It was only "halftime," he said.[60] He remembered four years earlier, when he'd furiously come back in the second half against Ford and almost won. He was not going to do anything to jeopardize the outcome by taunting Bush now.

After all, Reagan had slipped at the end in Wisconsin. That gave Bush an opening, especially now that he had almost three weeks to focus on Pennsylvania's primary. On paper it looked good for Bush. First, Anderson had not qualified enough petitions, so he would not be on the ballot. Second, it was a closed primary. Third, Bush was the last man standing between Reagan and the nomination, which tightened the sphincter muscles of moderates; Bush put the heavy woo on them to come out once and for all for his nomination. At the top on this list was the moderate governor of Pennsylvania, the affable Richard Thornburgh.

But the terrain after Pennsylvania would be rocky for Bush. Many battles lay ahead in the twelve western "Reagan country" primaries. Reagan had taken 80 percent of these delegates four years earlier against Ford.[61] Moreover, the countryside of rural America was dotted with 1,300 Christian radio stations and forty independent Christian television stations, and most were already in Reagan's amen corner.[62]

Bush had one slim hope—namely, "that the frontrunner will make a major blunder and that their man will be the only one left to profit from the fallout," as Al Hunt wrote in the April 2 *Wall Street Journal*.[63]

LIKE REAGAN, JIMMY CARTER didn't have the luxury of overlooking his party's primaries. He had yet to dispose of Kennedy. True, the momentum Kennedy had gained in New York and Connecticut had dissipated in his losses in Kansas and Wisconsin, but the Massachusetts senator vowed over and over that he would stay in all the way to the convention in August. The fact that a sitting president was still slugging it out for the nomination of his own party so late in the game was a glaring sign of weakness.

And with every step he took, the president seemed only to weaken himself further. During a sit-down interview with Meg Greenfield of the *Washington Post*, Carter denied that three months earlier he'd said he was surprised, after the Soviet invasion of Afghanistan, to discover the USSR's "ultimate goals."[64] In fact, he had naïvely said on ABC that the Afghanistan invasion "made a more dramatic change in my opinion of what the Soviets' ultimate goals are than anything they've done in the previous time that I've been in office."[65] Those remarks to ABC were an astounding statement from the leader of the Free World; it was even more astounding that he would then try to deny what had been recorded on videotape and broadcast nationwide.

Carter's gambit of trying to "look presidential" in the face of international crisis had about run its course. Even the normally supportive *Washington Post* put its foot down over the hostage situation in Iran. Under a scorching editorial titled simply "Iran: Enough," the paper ripped Carter and an administration "that shrinks from asserting what even its enemies recognize as a legitimate interest in protecting its diplomats from a mob. . . . The United States has made concessions of the sort one might expect from a nation that had lost a war." The paper demanded a more forceful posture, à la Reagan. Reports were seeping out that the hostages were terribly demoralized and that some had attempted suicide, while others had been beaten, starved, and tortured.[66] Iranian diplomats functioned quite freely in and around their embassy in Washington, and the administration still hadn't decided whether to expel some of them. The daily crowds of anti-American protesters in Iran made crude signs for the Western media to record: "U.S. can not do anything."[67]

The Carter administration had fallen back to infighting and sniping at reporters for writing that the president was looking ineffectual against the ayatollah. Hawks in the administration complained about Carter's planned budget cuts in military spending, and spenders complained that Carter was being too chintzy. Jody Powell was harsh with reporters in the daily press briefing.

David Broder, dean of the Washington press corps, wrote a devastating column on the Carter White House. In caustic terms he did not often use, Broder catalogued, point by point, each time the White House had used its privileged position of power to create some sort of artificial positive news surrounding the hostages in order to help Carter win renomination. All incumbents use the powers of their office to help themselves politically, yet unmistakably clear in Broder's column was the motif that Carter was playing with people's hopes and the hostages' lives, cynically, in order to further his own political ambitions.[68]

After Broder's much-discussed piece, Carter would never again enjoy the benefit of the doubt from the national media, as he had since 1976.

Carter had pulled the "positive development" stunt one too many times for the American people. His approval numbers on the hostage crisis had fallen from 77 percent in December 1979 to 49 percent in March 1980. Caddell conceded that they'd used the issue to its maximum benefit and now it was working against Carter.[69] Carter soothed himself by meeting in the Rose Garden with a support

group, Intellectuals for Carter. The size of the group and the admission requirements were not disclosed.[70]

DURING THIS BRIEF DOWNTIME in the campaign, John Anderson's supporters
began to quietly organize for a third-party bid, which now appeared to be his only
option.

Anderson had good reason to consider the third-party route. A Gallup poll
in early April showed that in a hypothetical three-way race, Anderson would take
a very respectable 21 percent of the vote, with Carter winning 39 percent and
Reagan 34 percent. What was curious about the survey was that despite the rampant fear in the Carter camp that Anderson was a threat on the left, Anderson was
actually drawing equally from Reagan *and* Carter voters.[71]

But the third-party route was fraught with inequity. The FEC had been created in part by Republicans and Democrats to protect the two parties and punish
third parties that threatened them. Anderson would not qualify for the same federal funding—$29 million—that both parties' nominees would receive. At the
same time he would have to abide by the $1,000-per-individual limitation.[72] The
FEC hadn't even decided whether Anderson could go back and hit up again the
people who had given to him in the primaries. The injustice was indefensible and
perhaps unconstitutional, but Washington long ago had specialized in "political
parties first, principles and ethics last."

Just to get on the ballot in some of the states might cost Anderson $500,000,
and each state had its own requirements. For instance, North Carolina mandated
an astonishing 165,000 signatures to get on the ballot.[73] And there was not enough
practical time to form a legitimate third party that could raise money to pay for ballot access and then undertake all the work to overcome the significant obstacles.

For these and other reasons, third parties had achieved little in American
presidential politics. The most successful third-party candidate ever was Teddy
Roosevelt, running on the Bull Moose ticket in 1912. Roosevelt carried six states,
got 27 percent of the vote, and still lost. In 1968, George Wallace got less than
15 percent and carried but five states. It would take . . . well, it would take the
ego of a man like John Anderson to throw all to the wind and forge ahead with a
third-party presidential bid.

THE BREATHER ALSO ALLOWED time for the national media to focus on Nancy Reagan's influence over her husband and his campaign. Some had thought she was the
reason Reagan had moved to conservatism beginning in the late 1940s, but that was
nonsense, as Reagan had begun his journey while still married to Jane Wyman.

Nancy traveled often with her husband and rarely campaigned alone. The "Nancy gaze" had become something of a running joke in the media. "As she watches her husband give the speech she has heard countless times before, her look of rapt, wide-eyed adoration never falters," went one typical report.[74]

What they didn't know was that Reagan never would have come to the verge of the GOP nomination without her.

She was his confidante, his radar, his encourager. She would have, one friend said, made him the best shoe salesman in the world if he'd wanted to be a shoe salesman. Nancy, fifty-eight, was tough and tireless in pursuit of Ronnie's political career. She had had a direct hand in the ouster of John Sears several months earlier and was a powerful presence in Ronnie's campaign. Staff often ran ideas by her for her consideration and approval. On more than one occasion, Reagan had been the verge of a verbal slip, only to have his wife gently interject and push him onto safer ground.

Clearly, he was a happier candidate when she was with him on the road. On long flights, Nancy would put a pillow on his lap and take a nap. "They were crazy about each other," said Nancy Reynolds. "Her physical presence was a great balm to him."[75] Staffers knew it was best to stay on Mrs. Reagan's good side, but she could be playful. On the campaign plane during takeoff, she would get out of her seat and try to roll an orange down the aisle hoping to reach the back of the plane without hitting any reporters' feet.

When they were apart, Reagan wrote her notes and letters almost on a daily basis. Little drawings, too. One was a self-portrait showing him shedding tears over their separation. The caption read, "Look what happens when I'm without you. Your Roommate." He also wrote, "Maybe that job in Wash. wouldn't be so bad—you'd be right upstairs." He signed off as "Special Agent 33." Reagan considered it his lucky number, as it was his jersey number in college.[76]

By the last score of the twentieth century, all "first ladies" (the term may have been coined in 1863 by the British writer William Russell when describing Mary Todd Lincoln) were supposed to have pet causes.[77] "Causes" had started with Eleanor Roosevelt but had died down with Bess Truman and Mamie Eisenhower. Then Jackie Kennedy made the refurbishing of the White House her cause. That was it. Lady Bird Johnson's cause was "beautification," Pat Nixon's was literacy, and Betty Ford's was breast cancer. Rosalynn Carter went a step further than her predecessors, taking an active role in policymaking in her husband's administration to the point of sitting in on cabinet meetings. She also had a private lunch on Tuesdays with the president to discuss policy.[78]

But Nancy Reagan had no cause except the cause of her husband. When Reagan was asked what his wife's main interest would be in his White House if he was elected, he replied, "Me, first."[79] The elites and feminists were truly appalled that Mrs. Reagan didn't have a cause. Why, it was like saying that you preferred California wine to French wine. It was just simply not done, unacceptable, unsophisticated, and offensive to modern sensibilities.

Mrs. Carter made clear her differences with Nancy Reagan: "There was no way I could stay home and pour coffee and tea."[80] The divergence between the two men—and women—could not have been greater.

Reagan stepped in, ever the gentleman, to defend his wife. "I'm happy to say she would consider her first responsibility being Mrs. Reagan." He then pointed out that she had been involved in a foster grandparents program in California and had raised money for the families of Vietnam POWs.[81]

Reagan zinged President Carter on the subject: "I think Nancy would find things of that kind to do, but she wouldn't attend cabinet meetings."[82]

16

THE APPALACHIAN TRAIL

"Voodoo economics."

I t was in Pennsylvania where George Bush would make another assault on the formidable Mount Reagan. The state's difficult political terrain wasn't about to stop the stubborn Bush from trying to reach the summit and win the eighty-three GOP delegates at stake. Because John Anderson's campaign had not been able to land its candidate on Pennsylvania's Republican primary ballot, Bush was getting his long-hoped-for chance at a one-on-one against Ronald Reagan on neutral ground.

Bush wasn't ready to concede the race to Reagan. He was fighting tooth and nail to mount a comeback in Pennsylvania, devoting fourteen days to campaigning exclusively in the Keystone State. His campaign bought half-hour slots on local television stations to broadcast "Meet George Bush" extravaganzas in an attempt to flesh out what Bush stood for. He went after Reagan hard, claiming "jingoistic" comments by the Gipper over evacuating Cubans who wanted to flee Castro. Bush wanted to make clear how and where he differed with Reagan on the issues. "That was something I wasn't willing to do before," he said. "I made a mistake [by not doing it] months ago."[1]

Bush had won the support of the GOP state party chairman, old friend and fellow moderate Elsie Hillman, who, despite her breeding, had a tendency to say nasty things about Reagan to the media.[2] A young liberal Republican, Jim Coyne, a candidate for Congress, was part of a coterie of state politicians working hard to defeat Reagan.[3] Overall, however, Bush's support among elected officials in Pennsylvania was slim. The popular governor and lieutenant governor, Dick Thornburgh and William Scranton, though ideologically closer to Bush than Reagan, wisely decided to stay neutral, knowing how popular Reagan had grown in the state over the years.[4]

Pennsylvania was in many ways a microcosm of America. It was urban and rural, industrial and white-collar, sophisticated and simple, traditional and ethnic, nouveau riche and old-money. It had rivers and mountains, farmers and bond traders, colleges and cows, professional sports, halls of fame, skyscrapers, and grain silos. Like most of America, it was heavily Democratic yet attitudinally conservative.

The country was in a full-blown recession by now, but few states were as bad off as Pennsylvania. It was falling apart at the seams. The coal and steel industries, once the pride of the state, were mostly closed. Unemployment was rampant. The infrastructure was crumbling—roads and bridges were badly in need of repair. The cities were crime-ridden and filthy. The confluence of three rivers in Pittsburgh was a septic tank of grunge and waste. Years of neglect, corruption, and decay had taken their toll, and Pennsylvania's young citizens were fleeing for the Sun Belt, hoping to find opportunity. Farm prices in Pennsylvania were dropping even as grocery costs were going up. President Carter's secretary of agriculture, Bob Bergland, was scheduled to meet with the Pennsylvania Farm Association, which was composed of a number of Republicans. When he discovered this, Bergland refused to meet with the Republican farmers. This did not sit well with the rest of the farm community.[5]

Real wages had declined sharply across the country, and Carter's economists forecast high inflation through most of the 1980s. They seemed to have no consistent answer for the out-of-control price spiral. Americans' purchasing power had dropped an alarming 7.3 percent since April 1979. The New York Stock Exchange was down to 778, having plunged 14 percent in one month, one of the steepest declines in history.[6] Everything was either too expensive or in short supply or both. The national mood had sunk even further. An amazing 81 percent of Americans thought their country was in real trouble, the highest it had ever been in the history of the Yankelovich polling company.[7]

While Bush was devoting his energies to Pennsylvania, many observers had already counted him out. Names were being floated as candidates for Reagan's running mate. The media made much of the selection because of Reagan's age; conservatives considered the issue crucial as well, but for them it was a matter of ideology.

The name that reporters most frequently mentioned was their favorite, Howard Baker, with the rationale that he would help in the border states. The Reagans were fond of the well-respected Tennessean, but Paul Laxalt knew that with conservatives, the moderate Baker was a nonstarter, especially because he had supported the Panama Canal treaties.

Laxalt harbored his own ambitions for the number-two slot. He was Nancy Reagan's favorite, but he made little political sense as a running mate. Laxalt was from the West, like Reagan; Laxalt was as conservative as Reagan; and Nevada had only three electoral votes, which Reagan was sure to take anyway. Also, the libertine nature of the state, exemplified by its gambling and legalized prostitution, made "Reagan's Best Friend" a problematic choice at best. Rumors of Laxalt's ties to shady characters, including Howard Hughes, were unfounded, but they posed a potential political risk for Reagan nonetheless.

Conservative outsiders were pushing Jack Kemp, but Reagan insiders winced because they viewed the hyperkinetic and voluble forty-four-year-old as uncontrollable. Also, the idea of a ticket that featured a former movie star with a former football star offended some Reaganites' sensibilities. Even worse, nasty but baseless homosexual rumors had dogged Kemp from the time when he'd interned in Reagan's gubernatorial offices in Sacramento in the 1960s. These objections did not stop a group of starstruck New Right supporters from creating a draft committee to "Back Jack," with the winking support of Kemp's congressional office.[8]

Bill Simon was another possibility. He had governmental experience, was a Roman Catholic, and was a close friend of Bill Casey. Gerald Ford, however, was attempting to blackball Simon over offenses from four years earlier when Simon was in Ford's cabinet.[9]

Other names bandied about included Senator Richard Lugar of Indiana, RNC chairman Bill Brock, temperamental former Nixon and Ford aide Don Rumsfeld, and a handful of moderate senators and governors.

Some guessed that Reagan wouldn't pick anyone at all. Speculation swirled in Washington that he would throw the convention open to the delegates and let them decide who should be his VP, just as Adlai Stevenson had done at the Democratic convention in 1956.

A name rarely heard in the running-mate discussions was that of George Bush. He was low or nonexistent on most lists—especially those of Ron and Nancy Reagan. There was just too much lingering hostility and bad blood. That antagonism would only intensify in Pennsylvania.

THE MAYOR OF PHILADELPHIA, Bill Green, owed Ted Kennedy dozens of favors plus interest. Green ducked repeated entreaties to pay Teddy back before he finally came out and endorsed the senator. It was a significant if belated boost.[10] Kennedy also picked up the support of several important labor unions. He was in motion for the first time since winning New York and Connecticut and was undoubtedly helped by the fact that Carter had not been to Philadelphia once since winning the state in 1976. There was not much brotherly love for Brother Carter in April 1980.

John Anderson attempted a fool's errand of trying to mount a write-in effort in Pennsylvania. He seemed to be talking himself into the third-party effort, telling reporters that he would disappoint so many who had voted and contributed and who believed that "they thought John Anderson was different." The Harvard-educated pol told reporters he hadn't yet completed his "ratiocination," which sent them scurrying for their pocket dictionaries.[11]

It didn't seem to matter to Anderson that several years earlier, in a debate with former senator Gene McCarthy, he had criticized McCarthy for running as a third-party candidate in 1976 and had forcefully defended the "two-party system."[12]

Reagan, meanwhile, was coming under increasing scrutiny. The "gaffe issue" was growing. He claimed that Vietnam vets did not qualify under the GI Bill for benefits, a statement he later had to retract. Reagan took responsibility for his mistake, though two retired, high-ranking officers had in fact told him otherwise.[13] He joked "that having only been a captain himself he figured they were right."[14] But as reporters pushed, Reagan got testy, saying their preoccupation with his verbal mistakes was the result of "journalistic incest."[15]

Several days earlier, CBS had done an extensive report about a claim Reagan had made regarding the size of Alaska's proven oil reserves. Reagan did not back away on this question, charging, "They were doing exactly what they accused me of doing. . . . [They] went out and found some source that would give them a different answer and they then took that source as an absolute guarantee."[16] CBS also claimed that Reagan exaggerated the size of the 1963 Kennedy tax cuts and the extent to which the federal payroll had grown under Carter. Reagan, in turn, took a swipe at the network, saying that his figures were "not entirely [correct] but more correct than CBS."[17] The truth was, however, that the story nailed Reagan on several items, showing where he was just plain wrong.

Reagan and his men had gotten along well with many in the media, including ABC and NBC, but less so with CBS, which they believed had an institutional liberal bias against the Gipper. This particular story was assembled by a longtime Reagan basher, Bill Plante. His six-minute piece ended with him speculating on Reagan's intelligence: "Does it really matter? To some, it's a sign that Reagan isn't smart enough for the job he seeks."[18]

The strain of the campaign trail got to all the candidates, and Reagan was not immune. Some were bothered more than others. Carter easily showed displeasure with reporters and his staff. Bush was almost unfailingly polite, as was Kennedy. Reagan for the most part had a superb temperament, but even he had his moments. On a bus during the Connecticut primary, Reagan wanted to read a newspaper before meeting with some reporters. Why? "I want to see what the bastards are saying so I can protect myself. You can sure tell when you're in hostile territory."[19]

The *Los Angeles Times* published an extensive account in which Reagan's claims as governor were challenged. Reagan had often done battle with the *Times*, but this piece was symptomatic of the growing scrutiny Reagan faced as the front-runner. A Reagan aide patronizingly explained away one gaffe: "He read that in *Reader's Digest*. He reads everything he can get his hands on and he remembers this stuff. Unfortunately nobody has been checking it out for him."[20]

Ed Meese saw the growing problem and told reporters that he would ensure that Reagan's team would review everything "with a fine-tooth comb" before showing it to the governor.[21] The gaffe difficulty wended its way up the food chain to Paul Laxalt. Laxalt was no spin doctor. He said simply, "I think it's a problem. It's going to have to be met and it's going to have to be met factually."[22]

Reagan was asked at one press conference why he was making so many mistakes on the road. Rather than blaming his staff, Reagan said he was doing his own research and not checking his facts thoroughly the way he should have been.

Newsweek published its own detailed story compiling Reagan's string of misstatements. When the magazine asked Congressman Guy Vander Jagt, head of the GOP's House campaign committee, whether he thought Reagan was "shallow," he coldly replied, "It depends on how you define 'shallow.'"[23]

The gaffe issue became an out-of-control brushfire. Long reports in the *New York Times*, *Washington Post*, *Time*, and other media outlets detailed Reagan's problem with misstatements. Reagan was right when he spoke about "incest" among the media: one story tended to generate another story in which the first story was cited. This had happened to Reagan the year before with the age issue, and now he was going through it again with questions about his intelligence. Some of the "catches" by the media, such as how many employees worked just on government compliance forms at General Motors, were legitimate errors by Reagan. He said the number was 23,000. In fact, 24,000 worked on government-mandated programs at the automaker, but only 5,000 actually filled out reports for Washington. Other errors were niggling. Reagan sometimes mentioned that the third chief justice of the United States, John Marshall, was not a lawyer. Reporters jumped on him for this. Actually, Marshall had not gone to law school but had "read for the law."[24]

In April, the remaining candidates of both parties appeared in close succession before the annual convention of the American Society of Newspaper Editors in Washington. Reagan, in his speech before the newspaper editors, seemed uneasy and tentative. He read from a prepared text instead of from his usual note cards. His campaign was test-driving some new themes: that "blue-collar workers, ethnics, registered Democrats and independents with conservative values" would be part of his new majority coalition. They would be brought together because of shared values: "the family, neighborhood, work, peace-through-strength and freedom-through-vigilance."[25]

The *Los Angeles Times* noted that Reagan's speech "was received in utter silence" by the editors.[26] Before taking questions from the hostile crowd, Reagan nervously joked, "Do I get a cigarette and a blindfold?"[27] One editor in attendance, Edwin Guthman of the *Philadelphia Inquirer*, expressed his disdain for Reagan, saying that the governor "is living in a world that is as remote from the realities and challenges of the 1980s as any 1930s Hollywood happy ending could be."[28]

Americans, though, did not agree with the mandarins of the press. About 60 percent of his countrymen now thought Carter had been too weak in dealing with the ayatollah and that his handling of the Soviets had been too soft, according to a survey commissioned by *Time* magazine. Carter's image as a strong leader was in full retreat and Bush's had evaporated. The only candidate whom the American people regarded as a strong leader was Reagan.[29]

Bush still could not figure out that Reagan's appeal wasn't just about delivering a good speech. In his own remarks before the newspaper editors, Bush said, "The process has put a lot of emphasis on theater, on charisma. What I must do is recognize that I will not be able to outdo my principal opponent on the 30-second clip. Nor can I outperform him on the applause meter. . . . He's just better than I am at that."[30]

Reagan and his followers, however, found vindication for what they were doing. For the first time in the campaign, Reagan actually moved ahead of Carter in the national polls, 44 percent to 43 percent.[31] True, it was within the margin of error, but they took the poll as a sign that his conservative message was getting through to his fellow citizens. The gaffe issue was so much eyewash as far as Middle America was concerned.

Religious conservatives were becoming fully engaged in the 1980 campaign, mostly supporting Reagan, despite the fact that he was a divorced man who had once supported the ERA and that as governor he had signed one of the most liberal abortion laws in the country. Reagan flipped on the ERA, and shortly after signing the abortion bill he said he'd been sold a bill of goods and expressed lifelong regret over signing it.[32]

Religion had been a part of the American political scene since the days of the Revolution, but never had political participation been organized from the pulpit in this fashion, with the possible exception of the activist clergy of the 1960s who protested against the Vietnam War and in favor of civil rights. But the right-wing evangelical tide now swelling in America was dwarfing anything the Berrigan brothers and their cohorts had done during the heady days of the counterculture.

Most religious leaders had eschewed direct activism ("Render unto Caesar . . ."). Politics was of this world, while they were concerned with the next world. Carter, Communism, and the culture changed their outlook. Carter had run as a born-again Christian in 1976, making much of his faith, and evangelicals had responded enthusiastically, giving him 60 percent of their vote over Ford and Ford's outspoken wife, Betty, who supported the ERA and abortion and had scandalously condoned a hypothetical affair by her daughter. But evangelical leaders and voters quickly became disaffected with Carter and the Democratic Party, which was more and more being dominated by sideshow politics and special-interest groups. They also were motivated by the profound changes wrought during the 1960s and 1970s. Sex, drugs, and rock 'n' roll didn't sit too well with these people. Finally, they were terrified by the march of atheistic Communism around the world, and by President Carter's inability (or disinclination) to halt it.

The "Silent Majority," as Nixon had once called them, would be silent no longer. Evangelicals formed their own political organizations, including the Moral Majority, the Religious Roundtable, and the National Christian Action Network, and were marshaling their resources to stand up to the cultural forces they feared were tearing society apart—and to do battle with the president.

Bush acknowledged the rise of religion in speeches across Pennsylvania. In Doylestown, he told Christian voters, "The proper role of government in the 1980s should and must be to encourage the institution of home and community on which our society is based and to preserve our religious diversity." It was a significant break from the past for the reticent Episcopalian. By his culture and his faith, Bush was taught not to talk about religion in public. Now he went even further, contrasting the religious tolerance in America with the intolerance he had witnessed as U.S. envoy to China.[33]

THE PENNSYLVANIA GOP PRIMARY was part "beauty contest" and part delegate selection, but one had no bearing upon the other. It was possible to lose the beauty contest and still win the majority of delegates. Pennsylvania's primary rules made it possible for GOP voters to pick their neighbor who was running as a delegate for one candidate while also pulling the lever for another candidate. Delegate candidates would not be identified as to whom they were affiliated with, the same as in Illinois, so the Reagan and Bush operations would have to conduct guerrilla activities to alert the local Republicans.

Not so on the Democratic side, where apportionment of delegates would be directly tied to the popular vote.[34] Carter was in a tailspin, and even though logic dictated that Kennedy could not catch him, logic was suspended. Kennedy continued to batter the president day in and day out, predicting a worse economy than under Hoover.[35] Oddly, Kennedy was now earning the hosannas of devoted liberals who had watched him get pasted in one primary after another. As he soldiered on, a certain nobility attached to him. The media and the elites had turned on Carter and now they cheered the valiant Kennedy. He must have felt like a modern-day Caesar. First the media hordes loved him, then they killed him, and now they mourned him.

Kennedy was so devoted to his cause that he had attempted to get Congressman Morris Udall of Arizona, a liberal of great self-deprecating wit who had run a fairly strong campaign for the Democratic nomination in 1976, to run in his stead, but the legal hurdles were too great, so Teddy vainly fought on.[36] He must have been bitterly disappointed that so many friends he'd helped over the years had cut and run on him, but he never complained, at least publicly. His aides and family were less circumspect. When he became reflective, he twisted a lock of hair behind his left ear, a habit eerily reminiscent of his brothers. He contemplatively told a reporter, "Everyone . . . is three individuals. What you think you are. What you are. And what others think you are."[37]

REAGAN'S POLLSTER, DICK WIRTHLIN, was not only a quiet and gentle Mormon; he was also one of the most perceptive students of American culture and politics. In mid-April, he did a remarkable thing. He took a poll in which he did not ask the American people what they thought about Reagan or Bush or Kennedy or Carter; he asked Americans what they thought of themselves. The results were starkly revealing. Those at the highest end of the scale of "well-developed confidence in self" were Reagan's strongest supporters. Another pro-Reagan group consisted of those who could be labeled "self-assertive." These people typically took responsibility for their actions and tended to be pro-life and pro–gun ownership. According to Wirthlin, these Reagan supporters skewed heavily Catholic, ethnic, blue-collar, and Democratic. Another group in Reagan's camp was the "optimistic." These were Americans who believed in the future and that they had control over their own destinies.[38]

The pollster found, in short, that Reagan was appealing to a new values system that was not part of the old formulaic Republican message. By narrowing his message, Reagan was broadening his base. Wirthlin said, "The statements that Reagan makes about what the nation can do to recover its freedoms and its greatness help reduce the uncertainty of the future. . . . The assumption that we're making is that [these voters] will vote for a political change."[39]

On the stump, Reagan was often just winging it, without using his speech cards. As the long primary season wore on his voice sometimes weakened, especially at the onset of making remarks. But as the crowd warmed to him, he seemed to gather strength from them and his voice would mostly boom again.[40] Eleanor Roosevelt once observed that John Kennedy had the same quality as her husband, that they gathered inner strength from their audiences.[41] Reagan was in the same mold.

"Americans aren't losing their confidence, they're losing their shirts," Reagan said to supportive crowds.[42] But to seasoned Reagan watchers, he was getting ragged and sloppy. He didn't have the time now to work on the details of his speeches the way he had before, and there wasn't enough staff help. It was the price one paid for being a front-runner with little money.

Even as elites in the media, government, and the academy were scrutinizing Reagan's every move, they were coming to terms with the possibility that he could be elected president of the United States. Many were manifestly scared. Even the moderately conservative British magazine *The Economist* had a cover that announced, "It's time to think the unthinkable," referring to a possible Reagan win.[43] This from a publication that had supported, albeit with doubts, the election of Margaret Thatcher a year earlier in Great Britain.[44]

During a campaign stop in North Carolina, whose primary would be held two weeks after Pennsylvania's, Reagan was introduced by the Tar Heel State's own Jesse Helms. Senator Helms spoke of a "coalition of shared values" and referred to a movement that was as much about spiritual matters as it was about ideology. He said, "It may well be that God is giving us one more chance to save America."[45] The elites snickered, but millions not only knew what Helms meant, they agreed with him.

A COMIC-DRAMA WAS PLAYING out in the Bush campaign. Months earlier, while assembling the campaign's operation, both Jim Baker and Dave Keene had resisted traveling with Bush. It wasn't personal, but both could take candidates only in small doses. So they recruited a stalwart conservative, writer Vic Gold, to travel full-time with the candidate. Gold suffered no fools and was a rough operator, but he was a superb, erudite attorney and one of the best wits and writers in Washington. He also had a temper like few men in politics.[46]

Gold had come out of southern politics in the 1950s. He worked as deputy press secretary for Barry Goldwater in 1964 and later was press secretary for Vice President Spiro Agnew in the Nixon White House. Gold had left, quitting many times in a fit of pique, before Agnew resigned. He was already a legend before he swore off politics to concentrate on his writing career. The specter of out-of-control journalists and dumb Republicans playing into their hands disgusted him. He became a feature essayist for a number of publications, including *National Review*, *The American Spectator*, and the *Washingtonian*, and a regular commentator on ABC's *Good Morning America* opposite longtime liberal and scion of Hollywood royalty Frank Mankiewicz. Gold's dinner friends included Frank Sinatra and baseball great Stan Musial. In 1979, Gold was a contented man, far from the political free-fire zone.

He was far more conservative than Bush and had known Reagan for years, but thought, like most, that Reagan was too old to run. The nascent Bush operation wasn't happy with the speeches being written by David Gergen and others, so Gold was introduced to Bush. He met with Bush over drinks at the Alibi Club in Washington, and during a later trip to Houston they bonded by jogging together. He was introduced to Jim Baker and was talked into traveling with Bush as a speechwriter—but Gold would be more than that. He was Bush's peer, and the adult confidant that every candidate needs to talk frankly and confidentially to and with. Gold assumed that Bush's effort would be respectable but would come up short. He hadn't counted on the failings of the Reagan campaign in the early going or the tenacity of Bush.[47]

Bush hung in there like a terrier and Gold with him. But by the eve of the Pennsylvania primary, Gold had suffered one insult too many and furiously quit the campaign. The final straw had come when Bush aide Jennifer Fitzgerald showed one of Gold's speeches to Gergen and Gergen made a few minor edits. When Gold found out, he hit the ceiling.[48]

As soon as Bush was without Gold, he began to make glaring mistakes on the road and was taking the wrong advice. By this time, with Reagan strongly in the lead, Jim Baker was looking to make a soft landing of the Bush campaign. Baker's notion was to get Bush out of the race gracefully, not offend Reagan and Nancy any more than the campaign already had, and angle to get his candidate the second slot leading up to Detroit. That meant that Bush could no longer insult Reagan on the campaign trail.

Gold acutely understood this, but Pete Teeley, Bush's liberal press secretary and Reagan skeptic, did not. For months, Bush had been bedeviled by the political advantage Reagan had gained with his proposal for massive tax cuts. Bush was an old-fashioned balance-the-budget Republican. Bush's advisers convinced him to propose his own modest tax-cut plan, which he reluctantly did, even though it was focused more on cuts for business than for individuals.

It was in Pennsylvania, at the prodding of Teeley and Bush researcher Stef Halper, where Bush unveiled a line that, while sounding good at the time, would become a source of enormous tension between him and Reagan for a long time.[49] He called Reagan's 30 percent tax-cut plan "voodoo economics."[50] "I went off the campaign trail for a while and voodoo economics comes up and Teeley writes the goddamn speech," Gold later recalled.[51]

It was a good line. Too good. The media immediately picked up on it. As soon as Baker and Keene heard about it, they knew Bush's chances for going on the ticket were headed into the toilet. If Bush was making fun of Reagan's plan, he might as well be making fun of Reagan. And while Reagan could laugh at himself, Nancy flipped out when anybody made fun of her Ronnie.

Bush dropped the voodoo-economics bomb during a speech before students at Carnegie Mellon University. In it he accused Reagan of "phony promises" and "economic madness."[52] Bush wanted to know where the corresponding cuts in spending would come from to pay for huge tax cuts. He did not believe in the supply-side theory that the tax cuts would generate more revenues for the federal treasury than they would cost. Bush previously had danced around the policy differences between the two men, but this speech went full-bore against the Gipper. Bush was as dismissive of Reagan's ideas as he was of someone not using the correct fork at dinner.

Baker and Keene knew they needed to get Gold back out on the road with Bush, if only to protect the candidate from himself. They delicately suggested to Ambassador Bush that he call Gold at his home and ask him to come back. Bush balked. He didn't understand why he had to apologize. Finally he acceded. Bush called Baker and Keene at the campaign office, not knowing that he was on a speakerphone. "So how did it go?" Keene asked. Bush snapped back, "Well, I did what you asked me to do." Keene replied, "Yeah, so everything's fine?" "He told me to go fuck myself and hung up." As Keene and Baker rolled on the floor laughing, Keene choked out, "Well, it usually works!"[53] Baker and Keene did not immediately respond to Bush's lamenting. They were still too busy laughing hysterically.

Reagan's Pennsylvania coordinator, Frank Donatelli, was a native of the state and knew the political landscape. Equally adept was another key member of the Reagan operation in Pennsylvania, the widely respected Drew Lewis, whom John Sears had recruited. Lewis was one of the most influential GOP leaders in the state, and when working for Ford in 1976 he had held the line against any defections engineered by Reagan's running mate, Pennsylvania senator Richard Schweiker. Lewis and Schweiker had been boyhood friends, but 1976 caused a temporary rift in their friendship. Schweiker's aides called Lewis a "Judas" for supporting Ford.[54]

Lewis earned the undying respect of many in the GOP because he was a terrific fundraiser and because he was a man of his word, loyal to a fault.[55] Lewis even won the support of the tough-minded Billy Meehan, the old boss of the Philadelphia GOP, who delivered his thirteen delegates after Reagan agreed to appear at a fundraiser for him.[56]

Lewis once told Al Hunt of the *Wall Street Journal* that "most of my business and political friends had little nice to say about Reagan; the only people I enjoyed talking to about Reagan were the gas station attendant and the guy at the parking garage."[57]

Reaganites dominated the heavily Republican counties of Bucks, Montgomery, Delaware, and Chester, while Bush's support would come from the blue-blooded "Main Line" of Philadelphia's western suburbs. Two of Lewis's notable conservative recruits were Faith Whittlesey and Congressman Bud Schuster.[58] On the other hand, John Eisenhower, son of the former president, was vehemently opposed to Reagan.[59]

Bush's newest strategy was to declare he was going to tell the truth, Harry Truman–style. He repeatedly said, "I'm going to resist the popular appeal." He claimed that Reagan was proposing ideas that sounded good but would not work.[60] Bush was often angry on the stump and it showed, as he frequently balled up his fist for effect. His attempts at humor rarely came off well.

Washington insiders familiar with Bush said that for all his obvious talents, the man was just tone-deaf when it came to politics. The reputation had deepened when, in the black depths of Watergate, Bush, as head of the national Republican Party, did not speak out against President Nixon and his cronies. The party was falling apart, and yet Bush chose to be loyal to Nixon instead of the GOP. Many in the media and the Republican Party became deeply disappointed over Bush's timidity. At the very time when he should have shown caution and gone easier on Reagan, he did just the opposite and endangered the slim chance he had to go on the ticket with Reagan in Detroit.

It was time for Vic Gold to get back on the plane. Gold called Keene at 2 o'clock one morning and barked, "Where is he? It's time to save the son of a bitch from himself."[61] His pride salved, the high-maintenance Gold did eventually return to the road with the low-maintenance Bush.

Gold's return to the Bush entourage was evident immediately. Bush adopted a softer approach and David Broder of the *Washington Post* took note: "Only in the past month . . . has Bush begun to recover. He has finally begun to distinguish his own 'reasonable' conservatism from Reagan's more free-swinging variety. Republicans have begun to notice that Bush is making sense and scoring points in his criticisms of President Carter's foreign and domestic policies."[62]

Reagan addressed 1,200 rabid fans in Philadelphia. The Gipper was introduced by Governor Thornburgh, who was booed by the crowd for not doing more for their city, and because he was taking a neutral stance in his state's presidential primary (though he did call Bush's campaign "hopeless"). Reagan walloped Carter, charging him with costing the city 2,000 defense-related jobs at the recently closed Frankford Arsenal because of cuts in Pentagon spending. Reagan said America's military might should be so great that "no nation on this earth will dare to lift a hand against us."[63]

Earlier in the day, Reagan had plunged into an excited, mostly Democratic crowd at the South Philadelphia Italian Market, accompanied by Senator Dick Schweiker and an overcaffeinated supporter, Paul Giordano, owner of a locally well-known grocery store. Giordano took note of the makeup of the crowd and told a reporter that Carter might do well there because the president was "a babbling idiot."[64] A street band played the theme to *Rocky* . . . again . . . though Mr. and Mrs. Balboa were not spotted.

TED KENNEDY RETURNED TO Pennsylvania in mid-April and got some unexpected good news. Arizona Democrats had held their state convention, and he'd surprisingly won there over Carter.[65] He was hoping the trend would move northeast to a state where his brother the president had been greeted like a god. The other reason for the spring in Kennedy's step was that a poll taken by the Carter-Mondale campaign leaked and had Kennedy ahead of the president in Pennsylvania, 43–40 percent.[66]

Kennedy was running tough television ads against Carter. One showed the president at bat in a softball game. A pitch slowly went by Carter and the bat never came off his shoulder. The heavy metaphors were impossible to miss about Carter's manhood, as he missed the "softball" pitch, a fat strike over the plate. Kennedy had another ad featuring Carroll O'Connor, television's "Archie Bunker," telling audiences, "Jimmy's Depression is going to be worse than Herbert's," a reference to Hoover and to a line from the *All in the Family* theme song. Carter responded with peel-your-skin-off ads eviscerating Kennedy over character and family.[67]

IN THE JUST COMPLETED North Dakota convention, Reagan took twelve of the seventeen delegates chosen. Bush took only one. The other four were technically "uncommitted," but if you scratched any of them, underneath you found yet another hard-core Reaganite.[68]

In Arkansas, John Connally's "$11 million delegate," Ada Mills, did not follow Big John's lead to endorse Reagan. Instead, she chose Bush.[69] In better news for Reagan, he took all seventeen delegates in the Nevada state convention.[70] Even more promising, Reagan hit the sweet spot in New Jersey, as a preliminary report said he would win sixty of sixty-six delegates there in June. Four years earlier, Reagan had taken only a few of the state GOP's sixty-seven delegates.[71]

Ray Donovan, a contractor with a superb political reputation, was running things in the Garden State for the Gipper. Donovan had raised $650,000 for Reagan, more than had been raised in any other state except Reagan's California. He was being assisted by an original Reaganite, Thomas Bruinooge from Bergen County, who had been one of the few courageous New Jersey delegates to support Reagan over Ford in 1976.[72] Reagan was also getting the reluctant support of much of the state GOP, which had snubbed him four years earlier. New Jersey politicians knew when they were licked.

Speaking at his alma mater in Ann Arbor, Gerald Ford was asked whether he would consider going on the ticket with Reagan. He shot it down, saying the notion was "totally impractical."[73]

Just three days before the Pennsylvania primary, John Anderson dropped any remaining pretense and announced that he would run for president as an independent.[74] Absolutely no one was surprised.

WITH THE PENNSYLVANIA PRIMARY now just days away, Bush complained about the polls, which showed him losing the state to Reagan: "I don't believe all these damned polls. They've been wrong, wrong, wrong."[75] For the Sunday before the April 22 primary, Bush had bought a full-page ad in the *Philadelphia Inquirer*, taking on not Ronald Reagan but Jimmy Carter. The tagline, "He's the one man Jimmy Carter hopes he'll never have to run against," was clunky, but it did the trick.[76] For the first time since the Iowa caucuses, George Bush was giving a clear reason why Republicans should choose him to lead the GOP in 1980.

Bush was back on message, spending a boatload of money and all his time in the state. Reagan's support was dropping; Pennsylvania Republicans thought he was snubbing them, because he had spent only a couple of days campaigning there. The Reagan campaign was repeating the mistake of Iowa.

Panicked, Reagan returned to Pennsylvania for a final two-day swing.[77] Team Reagan now feared that Bush might just win the state. Bush picked up some additional momentum on the eve of Pennsylvania by seizing seventeen of Maine's twenty-one delegates in its final selection round.[78]

The Sunday before the primary, Senator Howard Baker startled everyone when he swung his support to Reagan. Baker got out of a sickbed and abruptly appeared in Pennsylvania, where he warmly endorsed and then embraced a very pleased Gipper. Baker minced no words about Bush, the animosity still evident: "Reagan would make a much better GOP nominee and a better president."[79] Jim Dickenson of the *Washington Star* had the best take on the Baker endorsement: "An increasingly confident and assertive Reagan put Baker on display much as ancient Roman generals paraded defeated chieftains who then swore fealty to the conqueror."[80]

Before appearing with Reagan, Baker had called Bush to inform him of his decision. Bush was not happy. But he sloughed off the Baker endorsement by citing the support he had won from Penn State football coach Joe Paterno, a godlike figure in the state: "One Joe Paterno is worth five Howard Bakers."[81]

Bush and Reagan raced through a frenetic schedule in the final days. Bush was well received at Villanova University, where he took it to Carter.[82] Reagan went to a horse auction in Lancaster, put on a funny straw hat, and helped auction off a baby donkey. He had fun, telling the prospective bidders, "All these months that's what I'm trying to do is get rid of a jackass." Several people gasped at the harsh reference to Carter, but Reagan recovered when he quipped, "I have to pretend it's an elephant with a short trunk." Later in the day, children from a nearby Christian school, dressed in red, white, and blue, held up a sign, "God Bless America and Ronald Reagan." The state was thick with candidates and surrogates. In Wilkes-Barre, Reagan had his remarks drowned out by the approach of Air Force Two carrying Vice President Mondale.[83]

The vice president was in rare form. Though he was booed at a labor speech in Pittsburgh, he joked, "There are always more Democrats than Republicans, and for a good reason: we're sexier and it's inevitable we have more kids. That's why Republicans are so sour all the time, things aren't good at home."[84]

WHEN THE POLLS CLOSED in Pennsylvania on the night of April 22, the Keystone State shocked the political world with a pair of upsets. Ted Kennedy stunned

Carter and won the state narrowly, despite having been outspent $750,000 to $300,000.[85]

George Herbert Walker Bush emerged with a stunning victory of his own. He had come from 30 points behind to defeat Reagan.[86] Bush closed fast and his win was wide and deep. He won with 53 percent of the GOP vote to Reagan's 46 percent, beating his opponent by almost 100,000 votes.[87] Drew Lewis had run a shoestring Reagan operation as well as he could, but in the end he could not overcome being outspent $1 million to somewhere around $100,000.[88]

Having lost the beauty contest, Reagan consoled himself with the fact that he had taken fifty of the eighty-three delegates at stake.[89] Reagan was now at approximately 460 delegates.[90] Bush's win had clearly slowed the Gipper's momentum, though. Bush's forces called attention to the fact that most of Reagan's delegates were "pledged" but not "mandated" to vote for him.[91] Dick Schweiker knew the Reagan team had blown a big opportunity. "The pressure from all party sources [for Bush to withdraw from the race] would be overwhelming" if Reagan won, he said.[92] Reagan kissed off Bush's victory, calling it "meaningless."[93] He predicted flat out that he would win the nomination. But at this point, who knew? Reagan had let Bush get off the mat.

On May 3, Reagan and Bush would come to death grips in the dusty streets, country roads, bumpkin byways, and city-slick high-rises of Texas.

17

West of Eden

"Nothing can stop Reagan from getting the nomination
unless he gets hit by a bus."

Ronald Reagan wasted no time. He headed to George Bush's hometown for a League of Women Voters debate with his last remaining opponent. All the others had fallen by the wayside. Only the resilient Bush was still in the race. There in Houston, the two weary contestants eyed each other, circled each other, and sized each other up. Bush promised to "hammer at the differences" between the two.[1]

The one-hour session, moderated again by Howard K. Smith, was contentious. The candidates fell into sharp disagreement over Reagan's tax-cut proposal, with Bush arguing for balancing the federal budget instead, and charging that the radical plan offered by Reagan would "emasculate government."[2] When Reagan accused his opponent of wanting to continue the status quo, Bush sharply retorted, "That's not what I'm proposing!"[3] Bush shook his finger at the Californian, and Reagan looked anything but pleased.

They also clashed over a blockade of Cuba as a means of pushing back against the Soviets over the invasion of Afghanistan, with Reagan favoring the action and Bush opposing it. An edgy exchange took place over illegal immigration: Bush supported allowing the children of illegal aliens into public schools, while Reagan favored requiring work permits and mandating that illegal aliens pay taxes.[4]

The next day the *Dallas Morning News* boomed a headline: "Chance of Reagan-Bush Ticket Slim." Toward the end of their debate, Reagan had said that whoever his running mate was would have to agree with him on his tax-cut plan.[5]

The debate was a victory for Bush. They'd had three confrontations up until then, in Manchester, Nashua, and Chicago, and Reagan had gotten the best of

Bush in each instance. In the Houston debate, Reagan coasted and it showed, while Bush was sharp, unrelenting.

Meanwhile, a super-secret "worst-case scenario" report in Reagan's campaign projected that by early June, at the conclusion of the primaries, he could have just 951 delegates, which would leave him short of the nomination by 47 votes.[6] He'd lost by a handful in 1976 and it was possible he could do so again. Bush's men, led by James Baker, were whispering sweetly in the ears of GOP delegates that they'd be throwing away their votes on Reagan. Why not go with someone younger, like Bush, someone who could beat Carter? Reagan was prone to verbal mistakes and no telling when his age might catch up with him, Bush's men argued.

Baker knew that of the delegates headed to Detroit, 49 percent were only morally but not legally bound to vote for the candidate to whom they were pledged. They'd have to be convinced of the error of the Reagan ways, that Reagan's ideas were so much carrion on the side of the road, and that he wouldn't be able to win states in the Northeast if he were the nominee—a case the Bush campaign could press harder now that Reagan had fallen short in places like Pennsylvania and Connecticut.[7] For obvious reasons, a political operative went on background when he told the *Los Angeles Times*, "Both Teddy and George are like vultures, circling, waiting for their opponents to die."[8]

Jimmy Carter had the same problem with Ted Kennedy as Reagan had with Bush: neither could put the other man away. Reagan was battling unfounded complacency, in both himself and his campaign. His money problems continued, too. In the month of March, Bush had outraised him by better than 2–1, $5.3 million to $2.5 million. The campaign was still in debt, and Reagan was perilously close to his primary-season financial limits with some twenty contests to go. As a result, he had nothing to spend on television advertising in Texas, while Bush had a massive advertising budget ready. [9] Bush's ads attempted to exploit Reagan's gaffe problem with the tagline "Vote for the man who has the deepest knowledge and understanding of the facts."[10] It was a less-than-subtle swipe at the Gipper's supposed lack of mental acuity. Added to all that, Reaganites grew concerned that conservative Democrats in Texas so loathed Teddy Kennedy they would be tempted to vote in that primary for Carter instead of crossing over for Reagan. A key source of Reagan's strength would then be neutralized.

With his newfound impetus, Bush was hoping to win his adopted Lone Star State and then move to more favorable territory in the Michigan, Maryland, and Ohio contests. His chances to do just that improved when he received the endorsements of many Texas newspapers.[11] Still, the shrewd Jim Baker lowballed his man's chances in Texas, saying Bush would be pleased to get one-third of its eighty delegates.[12] Not without reason, perhaps: an early poll by the *Austin American-Statesman* had Reagan blowing Bush away in Texas, 75–21 percent.[13] Fred Biebel, a vice chairman of the Reagan campaign, said overconfidently, "Nothing can stop Reagan from getting the nomination unless he gets hit by a bus."[14] Everybody thought Reagan would win Texas comfortably. The newspaper poll was the last public poll taken before the primary, still two weeks away.

Ernie Angelo was running Texans for Reagan. Angelo, along with several others, had engineered Reagan's huge win over Gerald Ford in 1976, taking all one hundred of the state's delegates. Aiding Angelo was Rick Shelby, a pleasant, soft-spoken, and respected Oklahoman who had also worked on the '76 Reagan campaign. Shelby handled a giant swath of the country for the Reagan operation, from North Dakota all the way south, but he later said that he spent "an inordinate amount" of his time focused on Texas, "probably . . . 75 percent."[15]

Shelby needed to devote as much time as he could to Texas, since Angelo's whole budget was only around $200,000.[16] The Reagan headquarters in Virginia bought into the notion that it could scrimp in Texas, especially since Reagan had taken 66 percent to Ford's 34 percent there four years earlier.[17] Reagan had a following in Texas but Bush had one as well. The national Reagan office failed to appreciate the severe split in the Texas GOP between the Reagan folks and the Bush brigades. The divide was exacerbated when Reagan had campaigned against young George W. Bush in his 1978 congressional primary. "The Bushes took it personally," said one insider. "The senior Bush has always been credited with a long memory about things like that."[18]

THE DIRE SITUATION IN Iran took center stage. A joint U.S. military rescue operation called "Desert One" failed ignominiously in the sands outside of Tehran. For several weeks, rumors had flown around Washington that President Carter was preparing to take military action to free the hostages, since all attempts at diplomacy had failed miserably.

The mission was a disaster from the beginning. The filters on the helicopters were not sufficient to strain out the fine Iranian sand and the engines consequently overheated. One of the rescue helicopters slammed into a parked C-130 plane and together they exploded in a fireball. Eight young American soldiers died in the desert. Carter belatedly canceled what was left of the operation. Photos of the ravaged landscape, which included charred American bodies and incinerated aircraft, flashed across the world. If it were possible, American morale sank even lower.[19] The hostages found out later and their morale was crushed too, according to Bruce Langdon, the chargé d'affaires.[20]

The response from the Carter White House was initially confusing and garbled. Clearly, they did not know how to handle the crisis. Carter was personally devastated. He addressed the country, obviously shaken by the disaster. In a bizarre understatement, he said the action had been performed "without complete success."[21]

Tens of thousands of frenetic "students" descended on the American embassy in Tehran. Some thought the mob might tear the American hostages apart there and then. Khomeini batted Carter and America around to the world press, which in turn attacked Carter for the feeble military attempt. Families of the hostages took to the airwaves, denouncing Carter and pleading with the ayatollah to spare their loved ones' lives. The Iranians separated the hostages to deter another attempt to rescue all of them in one fell swoop.[22]

Despite the catastrophe, Carter was not, in the short term, wounded politically. In fact, he shot up 10 percent in his approval ratings, and 70 percent of Americans supported the action even though it had been a disaster.[23]

The Iranians eventually turned over the remains of the American military personnel to the International Red Cross for transference to loved ones, but only after displaying their charred remains in the compound of the U.S. embassy in Tehran. Jody Powell condemned this "moral depravity."[24] The wounded but surviving members of the rescue attempt went to Texas, and the president went to visit them at their bedsides. As he left, he met the five children of one of the injured servicemen and paternally told them, "Behave yourself while your father is in the hospital."[25]

Carter then held a prime-time press conference where he turned in a well-received and heartfelt performance, though he privately feared that a reporter might ask him "why he should not resign." Secretary of State Cyrus Vance, the leading dove in the administration, sent a handwritten letter of resignation, partly in protest over the rescue mission but also because he'd lost a power struggle with National Security Agency head Zbigniew Brzezinski. Privately, Brzezinski was underwhelmed with most of Carter's minions; they in turn referred to him behind his back as "Dr. Strangelove."[26]

Kennedy and Bush supported Carter, John Anderson blasted him, and Reagan, after spending a few hours studying the situation, supported the action yet called it "long overdue."[27] Reagan hurled words like "delayed," "vacillated," and "grave peril" at Carter. He also addressed the global ramifications, becoming the first politician to speak to the issue beyond just the lives of fifty-three Americans. He called attention to the weakness of the Carter administration in its dealings with the ayatollah—and what this meant for the security of all Americans.[28] Reagan's condemnation was fueled by the fact that military advisers had told him that the force used was far too small for a decisive action and that Carter should have sent in as many as thirty-five helicopters and four hundred troops.[29]

The failure in the Iranian desert underscored one of Reagan's main campaign themes: the need for upgraded military strength. It turned out that the helicopters deployed in the mission were ancient and shoddy—this at a time when Carter was again trying to cut the military budget. When the U.S. Navy asked the White House for replacements for the aircraft lost in Desert One, it was rebuffed.[30] *U.S. News & World Report* said of the failed rescue operation that Reagan was the "big political winner."[31]

The big political loser may have been John Anderson; *Time* and *Newsweek* had planned cover stories anticipating his third-party run, but he was booted off by the huge Desert One story.

The boost of support Carter had received soon sank in the quicksand of public opinion. House Speaker Tip O'Neill told President Carter over breakfast, "You seem snakebit." Carter, always awkward in the face of O'Neill's Irish bluntness, sat in stony silence.[32]

REAGAN MADE A QUICK swing through Tennessee, where he picked up the endorsement of Governor Lamar Alexander.[33] While in Tennessee, Reagan was expected to say nice things about Howard Baker and nothing bad about the Tennessee Valley Authority (TVA).

Four years earlier, he had been scorched on the eve of the Tennessee primary for suggesting that he would "look at" selling the multibillion-dollar federal project. To Reagan, the New Deal–era electrification venture was a boondoggle, but to thousands of locals, it was an icon of "good government" activism that had raised them up from wretched poverty. In a surprise, he ended up losing the Tennessee and Kentucky primaries to Gerald Ford by hair-thin margins, and most felt the furor over his remarks was the reason. In 1980, Reagan—once burnt, twice smart—addressed the issue right off the bat, telling a small crowd that he "had no intention of selling" the TVA. "I thought we might as well get that settled," he said with a grin.[34]

Still, the Tennessee tour didn't go smoothly. First, the always punctual Reagan was a half hour late for a rally of three hundred fans who awaited his arrival; to make matters worse, he then ducked into a one-hour meeting with campaign advisers. It was bad advance work all the way around. The campaign event took place at the Stage Door Lounge, which was too small, meaning that influential Republicans had to be turned away. The local media were also kept at arm's length, and Reagan got poor press reports as a result.[35] Clearly, the frenetic pace of the campaign was taxing his campaign staff.

AT A PRESS CONFERENCE at the National Press Club in Washington, Anderson formally announced his third-party pursuit of the presidency and said that it would be called the National Unity Campaign for John Anderson. During the press conference he blasted Reagan, calling him a "dangerous" man.[36] He released his fifty-six GOP delegates and returned to the FEC $307,000 in unspent matching funds.[37]

The Reagan and Carter camps were alarmed, as both saw Anderson with the potential to take voters away from them in the fall. But those in Bush's camp were thrilled. For months, they had groused that Anderson had been taking moderate GOP voters from Bush even though Anderson never had a realistic chance of winning the nomination. For the last round of primaries, Bush would finally have Reagan all to himself.

Nonetheless, Anderson had done a huge favor for future political strategists and consultants: he had identified the swing vote in American politics. In his corner stood middle-of-the-road, nonaligned, antiestablishment voters who swung back and forth between the two major parties. Disaffected visionaries on white steeds regularly ride into American political lore in search of an alternative to the two-party status quo. Whether the standard bearer was Teddy Roosevelt, George Wallace, or John Anderson (or, one day, Ross Perot), the quest always proved quixotic. But the aftereffects of a third-party challenge lingered, because one of the major parties ultimately absorbed and co-opted the message of the outsider.

Despite the formidable odds against his third-party candidacy—or perhaps because of them—Anderson took on a renewed faddish appeal. Liberals, especially in Hollywood and the media, took up his cause—including multimillionaire Stewart Mott, crown prince of hopeless liberal causes. Mott, an unreconstructed liberal, was quirky but had a heart of gold. The political cartoon strip *Doonesbury* started touting Anderson, and he landed a guest appearance on *Saturday Night Live*.[38] Rumors made the rounds, fed by an interview with Morton Kondracke of *The New Republic*, that CBS anchor Walter Cronkite might agree to become Anderson's running mate.[39]

ALTHOUGH KENNEDY HAD WON Pennsylvania over Carter, he still faced very long odds. On Saturday, April 26, he tied Carter in the Michigan caucuses, and neither candidate was helped. Kennedy needed more than a draw, but it was enough to keep him in the race, and by keeping Teddy in the race, it prolonged the fight for Carter. This could only spell trouble for the president, whose approval rating had plummeted again after the momentary spike resulting from the aborted Iranian rescue attempt. The miserable economy had quickly sent it back down. By the end of the month a New York Times/CBS poll put his approval rating at 21 percent.[40]

Carter's men looked to sharpen their attacks on Kennedy. They were disturbed by the fact that the Pennsylvania primary had marked the first time middle-class conservative Democrats had swung their support to the challenger. By this point, Carter had 1,109 delegates to 639 for Kennedy.[41]

Over the last weekend in April, Reagan took more GOP delegates in state meetings in Minnesota and Missouri. He now stood at 429 delegates to 96 for Bush. Reagan was still less than halfway to the 998 needed for a first-ballot nomination.[42]

ON THE STUMP IN Texas, Leon Jaworski, the famous Watergate prosecutor, Houston native, and supporter of George Bush, tore into Reagan. "Is it to be Ronald Reagan, extremist, whose over-the-counter simplistic remedies and shopworn platitudes . . . or is it George Bush, moderate, sensible and sound in his views and objectives?" Bush "rolled his eyes heavenward" while listening to Jaworski's over-the-top rhetoric, although he was also clearly enjoying it.[43]

Jaworski also ripped John Connally for endorsing Reagan. It was all complicated by the enigmatic customs of Houston society and politics, as socialite Joanne Herring knew all too well. The striking blonde said it was about money, one-upmanship, the right parties, the right clubs, and the right church. If your great-granddaddy hadn't fought at the Alamo, you were a newcomer. Bush, despite living there for more than thirty years, was made to feel like a greenhorn by the folks around Connally. Bush was oil, and for many in Houston, that was new money. It was laugh-aloud ironic, because he'd come from the oldest money in America, New England society. But to Herring and her high-society friends, it was a matter of the highest import. Herring was friends with both Connally and Bush, but she was supporting Reagan. He was the toughest anti-Communist, and killing commies in Afghanistan had become her pet charity.[44]

An outsider in the state, Reagan did his best to win over Texans. At Baylor University in Waco, Reagan offered the school's mascot, a live bear, a soft drink. The bear happily accepted the gift and Reagan quipped, "I'll tell you one thing, I'm not going to take it away from him."[45] A member of the drill team kissed Reagan, leaving a large set of red lip prints on his cheek.

He was less welcomed at the LBJ Library in Austin, where a small group of student protesters chanted, "Reagan go home!" They also carried signs that said, "LBJ is rolling in his grave." Some got downright nasty when they displayed a Reagan campaign poster covered with Nazi swastikas.[46] The irony of students sticking up for Johnson because Reagan was speaking at his presidential library was lost on no one. Twelve years earlier, tens of thousands of student protesters had camped out at the White House and chanted morning, noon, and night, "Hey, hey, LBJ, how many kids did you kill today?" Johnson cursed a blue streak about the anti–Vietnam War protesters, but their relentless harassment led in part to his abrupt departure from the political scene.

Despite the handful of youthful protesters at the Johnson Library, Reagan confidently campaigned among young Americans at high schools and college campuses, where he was often greeted warmly. Just the week before, he'd been on the campus of St. Mary's, a Catholic women's college affiliated with Notre Dame. Reagan was welcomed wildly by the students and he told them of coming to Notre Dame years before when he was filming the part of George Gipp for the movie *Knute Rockne, All American*. The kids rewarded Reagan with a blue and gold jersey inscribed "Gipper" and the number 80.[47]

On April 24, he paid a courtesy call on Governor Bill Clements, who, while blowing Reagan a big wet kiss, officially stayed neutral in deference to his fellow Texan Bush.[48] As Reagan walked through the state capitol, a group of older women saw the Gipper and, well, they swooned, sighing and cooing. One exclaimed, "He is still so cute."[49]

The Bush campaign, recognizing the financial advantages it had over Reagan, was planning on spending at least $600,000 on television advertising in Texas.[50] The campaign was so pleased with the "Ask George Bush" half-hour TV productions done in Pennsylvania that it also aired them in Texas.[51] Nervous local television operators rifled their inventories of films to weed out old Reagan movies and keep them off the air, for fear of triggering the FCC's equal-time provisions.

Bush, exhausted, gave a poor performance in Dallas by mangling his speech in front of a crowd that had begun by being supportive but became quiet and uncomfortable as he struggled to finish. Later in the day, an empathetic supporter asked Bush where he was off to next. The exhausted Bush replied, "Oh gosh, I don't know. Just on and on and on."[52]

Though Reagan didn't have much money to spend, he was being aided—indirectly—by an outspoken Texan, Eddie Chiles, who put his enormous wallet where his mouth was. Chiles was the head of the Western Company, which supplied equipment to oil companies. Chiles ran ads throughout the South that opened with an announcer saying, "What are you mad about today, Eddie?" Chiles would then expound on some aspect of government or the culture, making a conservative case against each. In the background was patriotic music. He also distributed tens of thousands of bright red bumper stickers that shouted, "I'm mad as hell too, Eddie!"[53] Chiles never mentioned Reagan in his ads but he didn't have to. Everybody knew who and what he was talking about. Some local stations, fearing FCC complaints, refused to run his spots.

Texas was a hothouse for conservative activism. Reaganites such as Tom Pauken had been aggressively organizing and running for office.[54] Joanne Herring, the beautiful Houston socialite and popular local television hostess, was a staunch anti-Communist who was egging Democratic congressman Charlie Wilson to join her one-woman crusade against the Soviets' invasion of Afghanistan. The Hunt brothers of Dallas—William Herbert Hunt and Nelson Bunker Hunt—funded many conservative and patriotic organizations, as did T. Boone Pickens, Harold Simmons, Dick Collins, and others. Most of these superrich Texans, unknown to the country at large, were superstars in GOP and conservative circles. Most shunned the limelight, but Chiles bathed in it. Always fascinated with playthings, he bought the hapless Texas Rangers baseball team in 1980 for $4 million. Nine years later, he sold the team to a group of investors headed by a ne'er-do-well oil-man, George W. Bush. Young "George W." was sometimes mistakenly referred to as "Junior," an appellation he detested.

As in previous primaries, Ambassador Bush was dogged by right-wing literature that accused him, because of his former membership in the Trilateral Commission, of being part of a conspiracy to bring "one-world" government to America. It clearly got under his skin, and he was forced to denounce the unsigned pamphlets yet again. He went to Dallas and appeared on a local talk show hosted by Charlie Rose. The set featured an all-female audience that, together with Rose, hurled questions at Bush, who did well in the setting. After a year of this, Bush had become an old hand at working a live audience. Yet, once again, he was asked about the Trilateral Commission, and once again, he was forced to deny being part of a conspiracy.[55]

In Fort Worth, Bush said that Reagan had "absolutely none" when it came to foreign- policy experience.[56] He then threw gasoline on the fire by suggesting that Reagan's campaign was responsible for the malevolent brochures. Return-ing Bush's fire, Reagan denied knowing anything about the brochures, but he let loose on his opponent when he said, "The only person I've seen raise the Trilateral issue is George Bush and maybe he should tell us why he resigned?"[57] The battle escalated when Bush pointed out that Reagan campaign manager Bill Casey and longtime adviser Caspar Weinberger were also members of the commission. Rea-gan said that Weinberger never thought it was a conspiracy and asked again why Bush had resigned.[58]

Bush did not back down from his accusations that Reagan's campaign was behind the brochures. In fact, Ernie Angelo had previously sent a memo out to his Reagan team across the state telling them to stop distributing this material if, indeed, they were.[59] Angelo got in a lick when he said of Bush, "George isn't given to taking criticism too well."[60]

Reagan said he wished Bush "would accept my word that we don't know anything about this Trilateral issue."[61] Bush wouldn't let it go, calling the material "vicious." Yet when he appeared on the Houston television station KTRK immediately after Reagan had told the station that Bush's claims were a "desperation gambit," Bush—informed that Reagan was on camera elsewhere—suddenly backed down. Now he said the pamphlets were "not a big deal, frankly." Bush's backpedaling came "to the surprise and disgust of the Reagans," as Lou Cannon later reported. Nancy Reagan asked pointedly, "If it's no big deal, then why does he keep raising it?" Later, Reagan told aides, in confidence, that Bush "just melts under pressure." Ominously, he said this in response to a suggestion about Bush going on the ticket with him. He also dismissed Bush as lacking "spunk."[62]

Bush was getting more pressure from the groups calling for him to drop out of the campaign. He was getting agitated. He also told reporters how proud he was of one of his sons for almost getting in a fistfight with someone who had questioned their father's patriotism. Bush did not say which of his four sons was involved in the dustup. He became angry in front of a crowd in Austin, saying he did not "need any lectures" about getting out of the race. "Hell with 'em. We're in this thing to win."[63]

Reagan was equally angry, but at Bush, for mischaracterizing his beloved Kemp-Roth plan. Bush was telling crowds it would cost $90 billion in the first year alone. "I am not out here in left field all alone with some cockamamie proposal," the Gipper stormed to the press.[64] This episode in the Bush-Reagan range war only confirmed that relations between the two men were a dead letter.

Despite all this, Jim Baker and the Bush troops did a good job keeping expectations low. All the media bought the line that Bush would be happy with 40 percent of the popular vote and just twelve delegates. Some of Reagan's undisciplined zealots, on the other hand, were predicting that Reagan would get seventy-five out of eighty delegates and 60 percent of the GOP vote.[65]

ALTHOUGH TED KENNEDY NEEDED big wins if he was to have any chance of ripping the Democratic nomination from Carter, he made only a cursory pass through Texas. Meanwhile, Mrs. Carter and other surrogates worked the state for the president. That legwork paid off for Carter, who stomped Kennedy on primary day in Texas, 56–22 percent.[66] It was, however, only an underpublicized "beauty contest," with no delegates chosen. Ominously for Carter, 19 percent of Texas Democrats pulled the level for "uncommitted."[67]

The Bush-Reagan contest in the Lone Star State was surprisingly close. Bush won an impressive 47 percent of the vote to Reagan's unimpressive 51 percent.[68] None of the early polling had predicted such results, nor had the state's GOP county chairmen, 70 percent of whom were supporting Reagan.[69]

Bush's team had played the expectations game perfectly. Even though he lost, he got a media boost from the unexpectedly tight contest. He would live to fight another day. After the results were counted, Bush said that his narrow loss wasn't "much of a downer," because no one had expected him to perform well in Texas.[70] He lamented that if he'd had another week in the state, he might have won. Given his rise in the polls, he may have been right.

But it was Reagan who had won. He offered his take on why Bush had lost Texas despite having lived there for thirty-one years: "Maybe it's because the people of Texas are aware that he has also run as the native of three other states."[71] For Bush, such swipes were not nearly as big a problem as the fact that, because of the manner in which Texas's delegates were apportioned, Reagan had taken the lion's share of them, with sixty-two to only eighteen for the Houstonian.[72]

This was the second primary in a row in which Bush had performed well in the popular vote but not received anywhere near a proportional share of the delegates. Reagan must have understood Bush's frustration, having experienced it in 1976. Reagan had arrived at the Kansas City convention actually having won more of the popular vote in the contested primaries than did Ford, but because of bossism, mistakes by his campaign, and the vicissitudes of politics in New York, Pennsylvania, New Jersey, and Ohio, he got nowhere near his proportional share of delegates.

If Reagan empathized with Bush's position in 1980, he did not show it. After Texas he told reporters that Bush "has no mathematical excuse for continuing."[73] Ford had taken a similar approach in 1976, telling Reagan to get out. Back then, Ford had overplayed his hand, and now Reagan was doing the same with Bush. In each case, the calls to drop out of the race created a more fearsome, more resolute challenger. Bush tartly replied to Reagan's comments, "I'm going to stay in this race all the way . . . because I believe the country deserves a choice."[74] It was a statement eerily reminiscent of what Reagan had said four years earlier to Lyn Nofziger when the Gipper was being badgered to get out.

Reagan increased the pressure on Bush when he picked up another eighty-five delegates in weekend conventions in Missouri, Oklahoma, Arizona, Minnesota, and Guam.[75] Moving on to North Carolina, Reagan was welcomed like a son of the Confederacy. Everywhere he went, adoring fans mobbed him. He met with Billy Graham, and aides said with a straight face that the meeting had nothing to do with politics. Reagan also spoke before 15,000 devoted Amway distributors in Charlotte. Kenny Klinge, one of Reagan's more talented fieldmen, said of the Amway rally that he'd never seen a crowd so frenzied, nor had he ever seen so many bouffant hairdos.[76] North Carolina had a special place in Reagan's heart. It was where his dead-in-the-water campaign came back to life in 1976, as he stunned Ford after losing the first five contests.

Bush looked at the remaining primary schedule and claimed a new strategy to win the GOP nomination that would include beating Reagan in his home state of California. Everybody in politics knew that Bush's chances of beating Reagan in the Golden State were almost as good as Reagan's chances of being asked to join Yale's Skull and Bones society, which counted Bush among its members. Polls had Reagan ahead of Bush 7–1 in California.[77] Still, Bush stubbornly announced that he would raise $1 million to campaign there.[78]

Bush certainly had the will and the resources to fight on, but the schedule ahead was anything but favorable. He had been able to outspend Reagan massively in recent primaries and was preventing Reagan from beginning the long process of consolidating the Republican Party. Not surprisingly, then, the Reagan campaign seemed finally, if reluctantly, willing to call off the dogs and let Bush get out gracefully. Angelo told reporters that Bush was "an articulate spokesman for the Republican philosophy" and predicted that Bush would drop out and endorse Reagan.[79] Reagan was asked whether he thought the results in Texas might convince Bush to finally drop out and he said, gently, "It would ease my travel."[80]

Reagan was well on his way toward the nomination, but the road before him would not be easy. Jimmy Carter likewise was on his way, but the cost of his journey had been high. As the primaries wore on, he was weakening politically. Though Kennedy's plan for a breakthrough against him was not coming to fruition, the president needed to start consolidating his party and making the case against the Republicans and especially Ronald Reagan. Vice President Walter Mondale was ready to be typecast as the heavy in this drama. "I'm confident this party will unite very quickly, particularly against Ronald Reagan," Mondale said. "The country just isn't ready yet for an actor who in his first movie lost the girl to Gabby Hayes."[81]

Carter could not rely on his surrogates forever, though. And now he made a pivotal announcement. For months, he'd been under self-imposed house arrest, saying that he would not actively campaign in the presidential race (though for

months he'd been burning up the phone lines calling supporters) "until the status of the hostages had changed."[82] His staff had badgered him to abandon the
"Rose Garden strategy," and Carter, because of his isolation in the White House,
had been smirkingly referred to in Washington's drinking establishments as "the
fifty-fourth hostage."[83] (Later the number of American hostages in Iran would
be reduced by one, from fifty-three to fifty-two, after one hostage, Richard
Queen, fell grievously ill and the ayatollah released him to the International Red
Cross.)[84]

Now the president abruptly announced that the crisis was "manageable," and
Mrs. Carter said that in the wake of the failed rescue attempt the hostages' status
had indeed "changed."[85] Carter would join the presidential race in earnest—never
mind that the hostages seemed in greater danger than ever as a result of the Desert
One fiasco. When told of Carter's decision, Reagan crisply said, "If he feels freed,
I wonder if he thinks now that the hostages have now been somehow freed."[86]

Deacon Carter was finally coming down from the mountain. The office had
aged him visibly, as it did most presidents, but he was not about to relinquish the
position to anybody. Carter had fought tenaciously for the job in 1976 and he was
a tenacious man still.

Three other tough-minded men—Kennedy, Bush, and Reagan—were not
about to give up either.

18

WINNING IS GOOD

"Well, I've got the delegates."

The oft-cited rap against George Bush was that he was a political journeyman who had held many jobs with little to show for it. He had a golden résumé but no gravitas. Something else he did not have was any Republican mayor in Indiana on the eve of its big primary, which came just three days after Texas. Every single one of the fifty-three city executives endorsed Ronald Reagan for president. Even Indianapolis mayor William Hudnut, who had previously supported Bush, jumped ship to Ronald Reagan.[1] Dejected, Bush withdrew from the Indiana contest.

Texas had only briefly reinvigorated his campaign. On May 6 there would be primaries not only in Indiana but in Tennessee, North Carolina, and the District of Columbia as well. Reagan had a hammerlock on all but the nation's capital, where he was not on the ballot. With Reagan poised to grab most of the 146 delegates at stake, Bush said somberly the day before the primaries, "I'm not looking forward to tomorrow."[2] But he vowed to keep fighting until June 3, when eight GOP primaries would take place.

Jim Baker spelled out Bush's Hail Mary effort: It would require Bush to split the Ohio and New Jersey primaries with Reagan, win California, and raid state delegations that were only pledged and not mandated to vote for Reagan. It was a tall order, especially the California notion, but it was not harebrained. California was a winner-take-all primary. Months earlier Bush supporters had strongly objected to this setup as giving Reagan an advantage and had tried to have the rules changed. Now they saw that it could help Bush. He had the money to contest the Golden State and Reagan's budget was exhausted.

It was political trench warfare. Reagan aide Keith Bulen spoke for many about the months-long political process when he said, "I'm tired, the campaign's tired. It's a ridiculous sort of thing."[3] Bulen was a tough, chain-smoking operative who had a core of devoted political allies, despite his reputation for angry outbursts. In Bulen's native Indiana, Reagan's team was working tirelessly—and trying to set limits on the press. Reagan's advance schedule in the state directed staff that when the candidate was in a church while on the road, reporters must be told "to remain outside unless they wish to worship."[4]

Republican National Committee high priest Bill Brock was reluctant to declare the race over. Reagan aides, especially Lyn Nofziger and Jerry Carmen, had been openly dismissive and suspicious of the moderate Brock. They began to eye hungrily Brock's well-financed fiefdom at 310 First Street in Southeast Washington, where almost three hundred staffers were laboring for the party. They were whispering in Reagan's ear that Brock was no friend and that the establishment Republicans thought Reagan and his followers were déclassé. "They wondered who this interloper was from the West," Ed Meese later said. "He was not the Establishment guy."[5] Brock's ace in the hole was Senator Howard Baker, his friend and go-between with the Reagans.

While looking over his shoulder at his conservative critics, Brock burrowed into the planning of the national convention. The first announcement was that former president Ford would open the quadrennial gathering on Monday, July 14. Congressman Guy Vander Jagt, also of Michigan, would give the keynote address the following night. The idea of having Ford and Vander Jagt speak had come not from Brock but from Reagan's men, who pragmatically wanted to show a unified GOP face to the world.

But the Reaganites made the new order clear to all, telling reporters that they were "calling the shots" and that if Brock wanted to keep his job, he'd better dance to the Reagan tune. They let Brock make the Ford announcement only as a "matter of courtesy."[6] Former president Richard Nixon, by everyone's agreement, would not be invited to speak to the party that he'd once lorded over.

When a reporter asked Brock whether he would stay on if Reagan was the nominee, he guardedly said, "I think the Governor would prefer to speak for himself."[7] Brock got some good news when a survey he'd commissioned found that Republican Party identification had grown to 30 percent, up from the 24 percent where it had been stagnating. Meanwhile, Democratic Party identification had dropped, from 46 percent to 40 percent.[8] It was the first inkling of a Reagan-spearheaded realignment.

In even better news, Brock's RNC was light-years ahead of the Democratic National Committee in fundraising. The RNC had already raised $9 million of an expected $19 million while the DNC, despite the advantages of incumbency, had raised only $1.5 million with a staff of just fifty.[9]

Reagan went to Indiana for a whirlwind of campaigning. Pennsylvania and Texas had thrown a scare into him. It was not beyond possibility that Bush could rebound, especially given his huge money advantage. Reagan couldn't coast or stumble again.

Thousands of energized Hoosiers met Reagan across Indiana. On the stump, he said it might be possible for the GOP to gain control of the U.S. Senate for the first time since the early 1950s.[10] He also loved to tell a corny joke that always got a big laugh. He would relate to audiences about how he and Nancy were campaigning in the Midwest when they met up with an old man who didn't recognize the Reagans. Reagan gave a hint: "We're from California." No response. "We're in the movies." No response. "My initials are RR." Eyes brightening, the old man yelled, "Ma, come quick. Roy Rogers and Dale Evans are running for president."[11]

While in Indiana, Reagan went to see an old friend, Colonel H. N. Park. They had been pals years before in Des Moines. Park remembered Reagan in those days as someone "who made things happen." Reagan, he said, was "handsome, well-mannered . . . yet could party with the best of them on a Saturday night." As young men, they often gathered at the Moonlight, a gin mill outside of town.[12]

Dick Wirthlin was already writing a 176-page plan for the fall campaign. He identified several "Conditions of Victory" needed for Reagan. These included expanding his appeal to draw the support of "moderates, Independents, soft Republicans and soft Democrats." He advocated holding back on campaign spending until the final twenty days before the November election. Reagan's pollster also urged the campaign to search for ways in which to "neutralize Carter's 'October Surprise,'" which Reagan's men believed would be the dramatic release of the hostages in Iran.[13]

Reagan's campaign temporarily dealt with the gaffe issue by eliminating any statistics he might cite in a speech unless and until they were verified and reverified. By now, many in the media were lying in wait, just hoping to catch Reagan making a mistake on the stump. So was Bush.

Another solution under discussion was to bring Stu Spencer back into the Reagan fold. Spencer, since 1966, had had an "off again, on again" relationship with the Reagans. He'd run Reagan's successful campaign in 1966 for governor and was involved in the successful 1970 reelection. Around that time, he'd lost some political business and blamed Ed Meese and others around Reagan for dropping dimes on him. The relationship bottomed out after that. In 1976, Spencer signed up with Gerald Ford, telling people, "It's one thing to elect that right winger governor, it's another to elect him as president."[14]

Late in the spring of 1976, in the heat of the campaign, Reagan had been asked a hypothetical question about quelling the situation in Rhodesia, which was going through a bloody civil war as it transitioned from white minority rule to black majority rule. Reagan postulated some sort of international peacekeeping force, including American troops to prevent more bloodshed, nothing more. Spencer wrote radio and television scripts for Ford making an analogy to Vietnam. The tagline was, "Remember, Governor Reagan couldn't start a war. President Reagan could." Reagan was beyond furious, first at Spencer and then at Ford because he defended the commercial and made sport of Reagan's anger. The "warmonger" issue backfired on Ford in the California primary, because the charge just didn't jibe with the voters' actual experiences of Reagan as governor. But it contributed to the deterioration of an already bad relationship between the two men.[15]

Four years later, the rift between Reagan and Spencer had somewhat healed. Mrs. Reagan, to her credit, knew that her husband, despite all the past dustups, respected Spencer and that Reagan needed someone on the plane to hold his hand and eliminate or at least minimize the misstatements. Spencer also had front-line experience in presidential campaigns and knew that general elections were fought differently from primary contests. At Nancy's direction, Mike Deaver and Wirthlin quietly approached Spencer about the Prodigal Son coming home. Spencer laid out some conditions, and when these were met, he later joined the campaign.[16]

At an early meeting, Karen Spencer joined her father for a drink with Bill Casey. Spencer already had a reputation for having terrible taste in clothes, but even his daughter was appalled when he showed up wearing "white socks, yellow pants, a blue shirt, and a red tie." If that weren't bad enough, he was also wearing golf shoes—with the cleats still in them. She remembered that neither she nor her father could understand one word Casey said: "He just sat and mumbled into his tie."[17]

At one point—before Spencer came back aboard—he and Deaver had run into each other in the lobby of a New York hotel. There had been bad blood between the two for a number of years, but they decided to get a drink and hash things out. Many drinks later—Spencer was counting swizzle sticks—they patched things up and renewed their old friendship. But Spencer also warned Deaver, "If you ever fuck with me again you are going to rue the day you were born."[18]

The Reagan campaign was looking ahead to the Republican convention. There would be headaches from dealing with strident conservatives who wanted to tear the GOP platform apart and include all manner of proposals, such as "repealing the Panama Canal treaties, breaking diplomatic ties with the Soviet Union, or pulling out of the United Nations," according to the *Wall Street Journal*. Fights were anticipated over abortion and the Equal Rights Amendment.[19] Reagan's men agonized that their conservative supporters might want to hold show trials and symbolic beheadings of moderate and liberal Republicans to avenge past offenses.

The city of Detroit was preparing for the convention as well. City fathers saw the opportunity to showcase Detroit, so to forestall anything like the riots between leftist protesters and cops in Chicago at the 1968 Democratic National Convention, Detroit officials designated several protest sites far from where the Republicans were to meet. Protesters had to make reservations to use the sites. To hold a spontaneous protest, applicants were asked to write a certified letter of request to the city council and specify the time, the number of protesters, and what they were protesting. So far, only the Citizens Reacting Against a Sick Society and the Irish National Caucus had made spontaneous-protest reservations.[20]

UNLIKE RNC CHAIR BILL Brock, the chairman of the Democratic National Committee showed no reluctance in calling a winner. John C. White proclaimed the fight between President Carter and Ted Kennedy "resolved." Though respected on both sides of the aisle and in the media, White had been handpicked by Carter, and Kennedy aides called for his resignation.[21]

Still, Carter's advisers were already looking ahead to the fall campaign, just like Reagan's team. Carter maintained a huge advantage over Reagan on the "war and peace" issue, even among Republicans, who by better than 2–1 thought Carter more likely than Reagan to keep the country at peace.[22] Carterites felt this would be the issue the campaign would ultimately turn on, as voters would forgive Carter for the bad economy as long as he could keep the world from blowing up.

What worried Carter's strategists was the recent phenomenal growth of the Sun Belt across the South, from Carter's beloved Georgia to Reagan's adopted California. Lower taxes, a lower cost of living, open space, plentiful sunshine, less government interference, and other inducements brought jobs and prosperity to this conservative and increasingly Republican region. During the economic upheavals of the 1970s, the Sun Belt suffered less, at least in terms of unemployment, than did the Rust Belt and other regions. For the first time in American history, according to the Census Bureau, more Americans lived in the South and the West than in the rest of the country.[23] Texas had passed Pennsylvania in the 1970s to become the third most populous state in the Union.[24]

In 1976 Carter had only narrowly won several states in his native South against Gerald Ford. It was an inherently conservative region where Reagan had far greater appeal than Ford ever did. Reagan was counting on sweeping the West, knowing that Carter was unlikely to make a dent there, with the possible exceptions of Oregon and Washington, two western states that represented an unpredictable blend of frontier conservatism and liberal urbanism. Reagan could pin Carter down, forcing him to defend his Democratic stronghold of the Northeast, the upper Midwest, and some states in the South. Reagan's initial campaign plan called for picking off a couple of states in the South while grabbing the swing state of Ohio, which Carter had won narrowly four years earlier. The goal was 302 electoral votes, just 32 more than needed to win the presidency.[25]

Even New York was now in Reagan's crosshairs. Reagan had strong appeal with ethnic voters, and the state, though Carter had also carried it narrowly in 1976, always held the Georgian at arm's length. The state GOP was falling in line behind Reagan. Even the Republican machine boss of Nassau County, Joe Margiotta, opened his arms to a candidate for whom he had previously no use; Reagan ended up raising untold dollars for the county organization. The Gipper was being ably assisted in New York by one of the most streetwise of operators, Mike Long, a leader in the conservative party, who by day owned a liquor store in Queens and had the dubious honor of once being shot by a would-be robber.[26]

Reagan would run in the Empire State on the Republican line along with the Conservative line and the Right-to-Life line.[27] Carter might appear only on the Democratic line, as the Liberal Party was playing footsie with John Anderson.[28]

REAGAN MATCHED UP WELL with Carter in one important regard that was difficult to measure but too obvious to overlook: happiness. As the new decade of the 1980s got under way, people in the South and Southwest seemed—on the surface, anyway—to be friendlier, more garrulous, and more confident. All one had to do was drive across the Mason-Dixon Line and go into a coffee shop. In the North, if you asked for a second cup of joe, you might get a resentful stare instead. In the South and West, you'd get a bottomless cup, and with a smile, too. Reagan's optimistic outlook was clearly appealing to these folks. Their attitude seemed to match the limitless horizon of the skies in the West. In contrast, "Carter has almost no positive-issue profile in the West that makes Westerners comfortable with him," said Earl deBerge, a Phoenix-based pollster.[29]

Reagan sat down for an unusually introspective interview with Howell Raines of the *New York Times*. Raines found a man who loved the crowds and loved the stage, but who, paradoxically, was deeply committed to his own private world, a world that no one entered except for Nancy. Reagan illustrated for the journalist how zealously he guarded his privacy. As a boy, his brother had once asked their father how much money he made. Jack Reagan turned on his two young sons: "That's a question you don't ever ask anyone. That's a private question that belongs to the individual."[30] It was a revealing peek into Reagan's personal and political philosophy. His refined conservative worldview included a deep respect for individual rights and privacy.

Reagan also chortled to the reporter that his heavy campaigning had tuckered everybody else out, but he was still raring to go. In another burst of Socratic insight ("Know thyself"), he said, "Maybe one of the reasons that the fellows in the back of the plane are astonished that I'm not in a state of collapse . . . with the schedule we keep, is maybe there is something that is stimulating to me about having that contact."[31]

BIG LABOR HAD NEVER been a big fan of Jimmy Carter's. Labor leaders from the North regarded Carter as an odd duck and they'd had a long love affair with Ted Kennedy. Yet Carter was the incumbent and had done labor a few favors. As it appeared more and more likely that Carter would be renominated, labor leaders faced an uncomfortable situation. Their cultural animosity toward the president ran strong. One of the more aggressive and liberal union heads, Jerry Wurf of AFSCME, a Kennedy acolyte, was asked whether he would support Carter if and when Kennedy faltered. He replied, "I'll jump off of that bridge if I get there."[32]

Many others, however, were prepared to hold their nose and get behind the president. "The true enemy of labor is Reagan, not Carter," spluttered one top leader in the AFL-CIO, "and we are almost certainly going to be backing Carter in the fall after the primaries are over. We can't go all-out for Kennedy without hurting Carter."[33] It didn't matter that Reagan, unlike Carter (or Kennedy or Anderson), was a union man. Reagan still paid his annual dues to the Screen Actors Guild. As six-time president of the union, he'd skillfully led it through many negotiations with the feared heads of the studios.

The opposition of labor was a real concern for Reagan. Unions could and did spend millions of unaccounted dollars outside the strictures set down by the FEC. Labor was specifically exempt from any campaign laws passed by Congress, accountable to no one.

Big Labor had a long list of grievances against Reagan. He opposed the minimum wage as well as Davis-Bacon, which mandated that the government pay the prevailing wage in any area in which it awarded contracts.[34] Davis-Bacon was one way for labor to undermine right-to-work states—many of them in the Sun

Belt—which prevented compulsory union membership, also opposed by Reagan. Reagan favored applying antitrust laws to labor as a means of undermining collective bargaining. As far as Reagan was concerned, if the government could break up American businesses that had too much control over an aspect of the marketplace, then why couldn't that same logic apply to labor unions?

To GEORGE BUSH'S AIDES, May 6 became known as "Black Tuesday."[35] On that day, Reagan wiped out Bush in Tennessee, North Carolina, and Indiana. In Tennessee and Indiana, Reagan took an amazing 74 percent of the vote, and in North Carolina, 67 percent. Only in the District of Columbia, where Reagan was not on the ballot, did Bush win.[36]

After his big day, Reagan stood at nearly 800 delegates. Still, Bush would not quit. He talked about spending $1 million in California against Reagan.[37] Bush sequestered himself with Jim Baker and others to discuss his next move.

President Carter also romped on May 6, winning all three states easily. Jody Powell, Carter's White House press secretary, told the assembled media that the results of May 6 meant that only one of two men would be in the White House in January 1981: Reagan or Carter.[38]

Carter's men were plotting their summer offensive against Reagan. "You won't hear any more of that malaise malarkey," one said. They had but one option against Reagan and that was to send surrogates out to tear the hide off the Gipper. "We've got to crack the veneer of the Reagan appeal," another said. Their goal was to show that Reagan was an "untried lightweight." Another goal was to discredit Anderson as some sort of nut. Carterites hoped to use Anderson's earlier attempt to declare America a "Christian" nation to scare Jewish voters back into the fold.[39]

The wise old man of the Democratic Party, Robert Strauss, renewed his call for Kennedy to bow out.[40] He sent a memo to Democratic Party leaders, urging them to call on Teddy to do that as well.[41] Kennedy reacted as Reagan had in 1976 when Gerald Ford tried the same ham-handed tactic: he dug in. No one was going to tell him to exit the race. Bush aides, meanwhile, claimed that the Reagan campaign had tried to get former president Ford to call Bush and tell him to get out of the race, but Ford aides denied it. Indeed, Ford the next day said Bush should stay in the race.[42]

Bush also claimed he was not interested in being Reagan's running mate, a pro forma position for any aspirant while still in the heat of battle. On the other hand, Reagan wasn't offering it. "No one in the Reagan camp can be found who expects Bush to be Reagan's running mate," wrote Lou Cannon in the *Washing-*

ton Post. Adding gasoline to the fire, Cannon noted, "Reagan and his aides are concerned about how a running mate would fare in debates with Vice President Mondale, a respected adversary." No one missed the skillfully planted suggestion to the respected journalist about Bush's suspect debating skills.[43]

Anderson was starting to search for a running mate, but he was embarrassed when Congressman Mo Udall of Arizona, who had already endorsed Kennedy, rebuffed him.[44] Udall was engaged in a tough contest for reelection, and though no one knew it at the time, he was also engaged in a fight with Parkinson's disease.[45]

CARTER'S DRIVE FOR RENOMINATION was not helped when the governor of New York, Hugh Carey, abruptly called for an "open convention" and asked that both sides release their delegates to be reshuffled in a new deal. Carey ominously said that the Democratic Party was in trouble, real trouble, and cited the reasons why: "The interest rates, the discharge of auto workers, the near collapse of the economy on the housing side, unemployment raging upwards, skyrocketing inflation unchecked, a lack of consistency and total uncertainty in foreign policy for starters."[46]

Carter's aides immediately shot down the Carey proposal, but curiously, so did Kennedy's men. Some thought Carey was angling for the nomination for himself as a compromise choice. Others speculated that he would support Anderson's insurgent effort.[47]

A day later, Carey renewed his call, attacking the "flacks, managers and self-styled political pundits" who had attacked him. He then asked, rhetorically, "If conventions were entirely predictable, why hold them?"[48] Why indeed?

Carter's men fussed that the prolonged fight would spoil their eventual nomination. Even as Kennedy faltered, those opposed to Carter questioned whether he should be the Democratic standard bearer. "Dump Carter" movements were rumored around the country. Few were enthralled with Kennedy as the alternative, and several names popped up, including that of Senator Daniel Patrick Moynihan of New York, a moderate intellectual who challenged liberal orthodoxy without wanting to upend it. Moynihan's neoliberal views about reforming the welfare state and the importance of buttressing the family unit would one day prove farsighted. But in 1980, he was little known outside of New York.

Carter wasn't helped when David Broder of the *Washington Post* speculated that the president might be forced to withdraw from the contest to deal with the hostage situation.[49] Rowly Evans and Bob Novak took it one step further and suggested that Vice President Mondale was emerging as a "consensus choice . . . to replace Jimmy Carter."[50] An editorial in the *Des Moines Register* bluntly said that

Carter should "get out" because it was impossible for him to "campaign and lead the nation at the same time."[51]

Anti-Carter sentiment helped Ted Kennedy in Colorado's caucus. For the Rocky Mountain Democrats, supporting Kennedy had little to do with pro-Camelot enthusiasm; it was merely a process of elimination. One Kennedy man explained his loyalty to Teddy by dismissing Carter as "the most incompetent President since Millard Fillmore."[52]

LIKE CARTER'S MEN, REAGAN's campaign just wanted to get past the nomination fight. The Gipper was now steaming toward an apparently inevitable nomination. The Republicans in Colorado did not even bother to total up the local votes after holding their precinct caucuses on May 5, as all knew Reagan would get the thirty-one delegates chosen at the state convention in early June.[53] On May 10, Reagan took sixteen of Wyoming's nineteen delegates and skunked Bush in the first round in Virginia, taking all six initial delegates selected.[54]

But George Bush pushed on. Trying desperately to rally his dwindling troops, he went to New Jersey to campaign before the big June 3 primary. Reagan shook his head at his opponent's stubbornness in the face of all odds. Secretly, Reagan must have identified with this trait in Bush.

With the odds of his nomination looking stronger than ever, one might have expected that Reagan would follow the maxim of Richard Nixon about running to the right in the primaries but then running to the middle in the general election. Reagan did no such thing and stuck to his conservative, anti-Washington message.

"I think the biggest single cause [of the breakdown in the family] has been the bureaucratic role of government and the insistence by government that it knows more about raising children than parents do," he said. And this: "I would like to take government back from being—or attempting to be—parent, teacher and clergyman and make government what it is intended to be in the first place and that is the servant of the people."[55]

On May 13, Reagan won the Maryland primary by a surprisingly comfortable margin over Bush of 48–41 percent.[56] The state was one of those on Bush's "needed" list if he was to mount his desperate comeback, so the loss was a severe blow. Don Devine, a cerebral conservative who could have easily passed for a longshoreman, was running Reagan's operation in the state. Devine cannily filed four times as many Reagan delegates as necessary, hoping to roadblock Bush. He did.

Reagan had zipped through the first three weeks of May, winning one primary after another, piling up delegates, moving inexorably closer to the magic number of 998. A new ABC–Louis Harris poll had him in front of Carter, 39–33 percent, with Anderson at 23 percent.[57] Most observers believed that like other third-party candidates, Anderson would fade over time and that most of his support would go to the president.

The media noted for the first time in the campaign that Reagan was getting the support of the front-runners of American politics: corporate America. Their first love had been John Connally, their second Bush. Reagan, suspicious of the concentration of power, governmental or corporate, simply wasn't high on the executives' hit parade, despite his many years as a pitchman for General Electric. Sheepishly, William Agee of the Bendix Corporation said at a lavish fundraiser for the Gipper, "His message has not changed. We have."[58]

The mountain had come to Mohammed.

RONALD REAGAN'S LONG QUEST to be nominated for president of the United States was nearly over. It had been a long and winding road. Only eighteen years earlier, Reagan had been a registered Democrat. He had once campaigned for liberal Helen Gahagan Douglas and against Richard Nixon for the Senate in California in 1950 and before that for Harry Truman in 1948. In his salad days in Hollywood, Reagan had been a self-proclaimed "bleeding-heart liberal" and a rip-roaring supporter of FDR and the New Deal.

He now was on the verge of becoming the leader of the Republican Party and maybe—just maybe—leader of the Free World.

19

Six Men Out

*"Maybe someplace along the line later today I'll go home
by myself and let out a loud yell."*

T he political classes in the spring of 1980 were all over the lot as they considered the prospect of a "President Ronald Reagan." Many feared him, a few welcomed him, some reevaluated their previous opinions of him, and others did not know what to make of him. European journalists were positively apoplectic. Across the continent, newspapers editorials bewailed the nominees of the American parties. A Frenchman lamented to America, "You lack a man!"[1] The rest of the French media simply referred to the Gipper as "le Cowboy."[2]

Back in the United States, story after story analyzed the Gipper's appeal to union households, corporate boardrooms, rural Baptist farmers, ethnic and Catholic factory workers—and, most mystifying of all, young voters. Youthful voters had been the province of the Democratic Party since the New Deal, and in 1980, it was assumed that John Anderson's "difference" would make him the candidate of the campuses. Yet a poll of students at Ohio State showed Reagan virtually tied with Jimmy Carter, with 35.3 percent to the president's 36.6 percent, and well ahead of John Anderson, who drew 14.6 percent.[3]

Reagan, the oldest candidate, knew what was on the minds of young Americans: they had been robbed of their future and they didn't like it one bit. The economy lost almost 900,000 jobs in May alone, and it was reported that between eight and nine million people were out of work for this period.[4] What prospects did a well-scrubbed college grad, résumé in hand, have in a job market that couldn't provide work for his or her own parents? What chances did a young graduate of vocational school have for honest work as a skilled craftsman, when his old man had been laid off at his factory job months earlier?

For the first time in polling history, parents did not believe the future would be better for their children. Reagan told them he wanted to be president so their children would "know the freedom that you and I knew when we were their age, and which has greatly disappeared in recent years."[5]

Carter's campaign, looking ahead to the general election, said that it would welcome a debate with Reagan, as the president believed he would pound Reagan in verbal combat. On the other hand, Carter said there was no way he would debate Anderson. His press secretary, Jody Powell, said the idea was a "fantasy."[6] Carter's men worried that in a close election, Anderson would siphon off liberal votes from the president, costing them reelection. They began rolling out the phrase "A vote for Anderson is a vote for Reagan" as a way to scare errant liberal sheep back into the Carter flock.[7] The president's campaign had already generated a blizzard of paper to keep close track of Anderson's ballot-access progress across all fifty states.[8]

The problem for Carter was that Reagan had already said he would be happy to debate Anderson in the fall. "Sure, that's alright with me," the governor good-naturedly said. "I'd like to hear him explain some of his positions."[9] Reagan's casual announcement put Carter on the spot, making the president look weak for refusing to debate Anderson.

Reagan's canny comments kept the three-way-debate issue alive for weeks. The national media pounded Carter over ducking Anderson. Polls showed that a majority of Americans supported a three-way debate. It didn't matter that, given the substantial obstacles to any third-party candidate's viability at the federal, state, and local levels, Anderson was marginalized to the point of being an entertaining sideshow. Reagan's pressure, the media fixation on the debate issue, and public sympathy for including Anderson ensured that Carter faced yet another embarrassment.

Of course, the Carter campaign caused many embarrassments of its own. The campaign staff decided to "deemphasize" the Iranian hostage crisis, as if it could somehow make more than fifty Americans just disappear.[10]

ON MAY 13, THE same day that Reagan won the Maryland primary, he also took the prize in Nebraska.[11] He now needed just a handful more delegates to go over the magic mark of 998, and on May 20 he would have a shot at Michigan's 82 delegates and Oregon's 29. He was confident about both states, even though he had lost them to Ford in 1976.[12] George Bush knew the situation was bleak, telling reporters that the numbers were "discouraging."[13]

Rumors, hushed conversations, smoke signals, and veiled signs went back and forth between Gerald Ford and Reagan at the staff level. Bryce Harlow, who had served every Republican president since Eisenhower, wrote to Ford advocating a Dream Ticket.[14] The letter was leaked to reporters, who took the notion seriously because Harlow was one of the wise old men of the GOP. Reagan's men now signaled via *Newsweek*'s Periscope section that Reagan was indeed interested in the revolutionary idea of running with the former president.[15] Likewise, a Reagan man told the *Baltimore Sun* that the idea "warrants close examination and serious consideration."[16] Paul Laxalt did little to shoot down the idea, saying it had "a lot of support . . . but it is a long shot."[17] No one knew for sure how far the Ford talk would go or how serious it was, or whether Reagan was simply flattering his old adversary in hopes of enticing him to lend his aggressive support in the fall. If the Ford discussions were real, the Reagan and Ford people would need to address the obvious problem that both men were residents of the same state. The Twelfth Amendment to the Constitution prohibited a member of the Electoral College from casting both his votes for candidates from his own state, and California was too rich in electoral votes to trifle with.[18] Ford would need to change his residence back to his native Michigan.

Though struggling to survive, Bush, like Reagan, had utterly devoted young people working for him, most now without pay. Some, such as Ron Kaufman, traveled to Michigan on their own dime. "As hokey as it sounds, I think working for Bush is the best thing I can do for the country," Kaufman said, and no one doubted his sincerity.[19]

Bill Peterson, a thoughtful journalist for the *Washington Post*, summed up what working in a national campaign meant in 1980. No outsider would ever really understand it. Peterson did: "You have to remember the kind of people who go to work in political campaigns. They are young, ambitious, fascinated with the process. People with few enough attachments that they can afford to gamble. The Bush campaign was a big gamble for all of them from the beginning."[20]

Peterson's prose applied to all the campaigns and nearly all the workers in them. They were patriots, devoted to their candidates, believers in the rightness of their cause. They worked long hours for little or no pay. For most, it was not about money, power, or glory; they believed the man they worked for had the answers and was the leader America needed in the dark days of 1980. There was not one campaign in 1980 where devoted staffers did not, at some point, go without pay, and many were never reimbursed for lost wages.

They were so emotionally invested in their candidate, their cause, and one another, that the thought of giving up and walking away was abhorrent. When they were paid, they worked for what UPI described as "coolie wages."[21]

On the Reagan campaign, one of the impressive young staffers was the conservative writer Anthony Dolan. Dolan had won a Pulitzer Prize for exposing local corruption in Connecticut, and he wrote occasionally for *National Review*.[22] He was also a certified character. In an earlier incarnation, he composed and sang right-wing folk songs in Greenwich Village coffeehouses. Dolan got his opportunity with the Reagan campaign when one top aide, with the unlikely name of Anderson Carter, resigned after feuding with some on the campaign staff and went back to his New Mexico ranch.[23] As longtime Reaganite Carter was walking out the door, in walked Dolan, becoming an aide to campaign chief Bill Casey.

Another young operative in 1980 was Charlie Black, who reemerged after his dismissal from the Reagan campaign by busily organizing a political action committee for Congressman Jack Kemp.[24] No one doubted for a moment that the real purpose of the group was to boost Kemp for the ticket with Reagan.

Former American Conservative Union executive Jim Roberts and direct-mail strategist Bruce Eberle were busily organizing their own draft-Kemp organization called Republicans for Victory in 1980. Kemp aide Dave Smick did not discourage the effort for his boss, but he told them to be careful.[25] Others championing Kemp as the vanguard of the Reagan future were Congressmen Trent Lott of Mississippi, David Stockman of Michigan, and Newt Gingrich of Georgia, along with neoconservative writer Irving Kristol.[26] While one of Kemp's colleagues told the *New York Times*—on background of course—that he was a "light-weight," in fact Kemp was exploding with ideas, mostly economic. From enterprise zones to incentives for individuals, schools, and small businesses, he loved the arcane world of economics. Woe to the young staffer who asked Kemp a question about some obscure economist; while the aide might receive an excellent lecture, it could go on for hours.[27]

Kemp himself was intrigued with the idea of joining the ticket, but said nothing publicly.[28]

ON THE DAY OF the primaries in Oregon and Michigan, Reagan stood at 939 delegates, according to the generous media accounts at UPI.[29] The wins he expected in the two primaries would put him over the top at last.

Reagan, however, clearly needed to take a break from his arduous schedule. Speaking at the University of Oregon, he was hissed and booed by some students, and his temper got the better of him. To one heckler who was especially boorish, Reagan bellowed, "You don't want to hear the truth! That's why you're stupid!" Reagan was trying to give a speech on how the Carter administration's tight credit policies were choking off small businesses, but instead it looked as if he might put his own fingers around the throat of the student. He cooled down . . . mostly. "I said 'stupid.' I shouldn't have said that. It was very impolite. He was just rude."[30]

The next day, Reagan got an even more unwelcomed retort from the people of Michigan: he was completely routed in the state's Republican primary. Bush won Michigan big, 57 percent to Reagan's 32 percent. Nobody saw it coming. The media hadn't bothered to do any polling, since they assumed that Reagan would win, and neither campaign had had the money to poll the state. The turnout in Michigan was paltry, only 13 percent, but it didn't matter. Bush had won big; it was his biggest win yet, in fact. Although Reagan won Oregon, most media organizations—and even his own campaign—showed him still short of the delegates needed for the nomination.[31]

It was Bush's night, or at least he and his team thought it should have been. Bush had won Michigan on sheer grit. Reagan had seventeen primary wins to Bush's six, but the results in Michigan opened up questions anew about the Gipper's ability to carry big northern states in the fall. For a moment, Bush was exultant, his campaign reinflated.

Yet at precisely the moment that Bush seemed to have again jump-started his campaign, ABC and CBS called the nomination for Reagan. ABC was the first to call it, at 11:30 P.M. eastern time, at the top of *Nightline*: "ABC News projects that Ronald Reagan has now gained enough delegates to clinch the Republican nomination for president." CBS followed minutes later.[32] Reagan appeared on both networks, where he was congratulated by reporters. Bush's men were galled when they later found out that the networks had told Reagan the day of the primaries, when votes were still being counted, that they would declare him the nominee of the Republican Party.[33]

Frustrated and furious, Bush told reporters he "shouldn't be written off."[34] Jim Baker was as angry as Bush at the networks for prematurely calling the race. The normally calm Texan said raising money for the upcoming California contest in this environment would be "goddamn tough."[35]

Reagan said he wasn't going to argue with ABC and CBS, although he stopped short of actually claiming victory. He issued a statement saying, "The future looks very good," but conceding that "we don't have the number needed for nomination." Reagan was secluded at his ranch, but later went down the mountain to meet with reporters gathered in Santa Barbara.[36]

Members of his staff spoke on background to Lou Cannon of the *Washington Post* and were far less gracious than Reagan was. "Within the Reagan camp, there are those who care less for Republican rival Bush than they do for Jimmy Carter, or maybe even the Ayatollah Khomeini," Cannon wrote. "These Reaganites see Bush as a party wrecker whose persistence in a long-lost cause diminishes the chance for Republican Party unity in November. They would like to criticize their opponent in these terms."[37] No one need guess who these erupting Reaganites were. Lyn Nofziger and several others detested Bush. Reagan, though, was keeping his own counsel on Bush's departure from the race.

Reagan's own ultracautious count showed him at 910 delegates.[38] There was also the matter of technically uncommitted but in fact pro-Reagan delegates already selected. And in one week, on May 27, the primaries in Kentucky, Nevada, Arkansas, and Idaho would take place. No one thought for a moment that Reagan would not do well in each. Then one week after that, hundreds of delegates would be selected in not only California, Ohio, and New Jersey but also Montana, New Mexico, and South Dakota. Reagan had an 8–1 polling lead over Bush in his home state and strong delegate slates in the Buckeye State and the Garden State.[39]

Even with Bush running out of time, money, and primaries, Ford publicly encouraged him to hang in there. Clearly, the Reagan staff's proffered olive branch of a Ford VP slot was not having the desired effect. By this point, it was the political equivalent of drawing to an inside straight for Bush.

The Reagan operation leaked to reporters that if Bush got out now, Reagan just might consider him for the ticket. Few, if any, in the media or either camp believed that was based in reality. Bush obviously didn't believe it, because he pushed on to New Jersey for a day of campaigning.

Jim Baker and Dave Keene met on Capitol Hill to review the bleak situation with a couple of dozen Bush supporters, but the group of congressmen came out of the meeting declaring that Bush should get out and endorse Reagan for the sake of the party. The leader of Bush's supporters on Capitol Hill was Barber Conable, the venerable congressman from western New York. When reporters confronted Bush with his erstwhile supporters' statement, he was "visibly shaken," according to the *Washington Post*.[40]

Bush conceded to reporters that he did not believe he would have sufficient resources to contest California unless he went into debt for $250,000. His campaign, however, said money was budgeted and available for Ohio and New Jersey.[41] A Potemkin Village–like office had been opened in San Francisco for Bush, manned by son Jeb Bush and Rich Bond, and then was just as quickly closed.[42] Bond was sent back to Washington to wait for the final decision. He had organized Bush's big win in Iowa, and there was a poignant symmetry to his being in on the first victory for Bush and now the possible last defeat.[43]

Ambassador Bush was sequestered in a reeking Holiday Inn located in a swamp just off the New Jersey Turnpike. The mangy hotel didn't even have a bar, just a corner where one could get a lukewarm beer.[44] Bush was out of touch with his campaign team in Virginia. With his nerves frayed, he went on a local radio show, where a caller harassed him and told Bush he ought to get out of the race. Bush lost it. "I don't need a lecture from you on that," he shot back.[45] He also spoke in private with former president Ford, who was in New Jersey. Ford, the old Navy man, encouraged Bush, another old Navy man, once again not to give up the ship.[46]

Incredibly, at the same time, Ford was talking to Reagan by phone, promising to campaign hard for him—if he was the nominee, and if Reagan made some concessions, including granting Ford veto power over the Gipper's running mate. Reagan went along with Ford's demands for the time being and told reporters that the former president would be part of his planning team.[47]

Reagan still refused to say anything one way or the other about Bush's getting out except that "there is the smell of roses in the air."[48] He acknowledged that it was time for him to carefully consider a running mate, but he said that as long as Bush kept fighting, then he was going to keep on fighting.

Of course, the question was not whether Reagan would go over 998 delegates, but when. Bush's dying campaign was now speaking in contradictory voices. One day, Baker was saying one thing, Keene something else, and Bush yet another thing. It was clear that it was the end of the line for Bush, but he was unwilling to withdraw formally. He'd invested two years of his life in the race and the final primaries were only two weeks away. Keene, too, was in favor of pressing on. By winning Ohio and New Jersey, Keene reasoned, Bush would increase his leveraging power at the convention and establish "a strong base for whatever he wanted to do in the future."[49]

Reporters rolled their eyes at Bush for refusing to withdraw. "There are dangers in any campaign," wrote Judy Bachrach in the *Washington Star*, "one of the most subtle and nefarious being that when a guy is losing, and losing big, and accepting defeat with a modicum of grace and class (a talent Bush has only recently acquired), you start to like him. There is, after all, a fine line between pity and affection."[50]

Bush had read his political obituary before. He'd come back from New Hampshire to win in Massachusetts. He'd come back from Illinois to win in Pennsylvania. He'd almost won in Texas. He'd come back from Indiana to win in Michigan. He wanted to fight on. First, though, he would head home to Houston and reevaluate his situation. Bush canceled the rest of his schedule in New Jersey for the weekend of May 23 and hopped on a private jet back to Texas.

Unbeknownst to Bush, once he was in the air his press aide Susan Morrison told reporters on the ground, "We're putting the campaign on hold."[51] And Jim Baker issued a statement—without Bush's approval—announcing that Bush was suspending his campaign. Bush learned of Baker's action only when he landed in Houston. Suffice it to say, he was not happy.[52]

THE ALLEY FIGHT OVER Bill Brock's stewardship of the Republican National Committee spilled out into the streets. Brock and Reagan had met in early May, and Brock told people after the meeting that he had Reagan's blessings to stay on as party chairman through the fall election. Paul Laxalt challenged Brock's version, telling reporters that Reagan may have wanted Brock to continue only "through the convention," at which point he might exercise his option as the nominee to pick his own man to run things at 310 First Street, SE.[53] Laxalt hinted that Lyn Nofziger might go over to the RNC as Reagan's in-house man, which sent chills up the spines of the staffers, who knew of Nofziger's low opinion of them.[54]

Reagan's men were anxious to dump others in the RNC also. Brock's key deputy, Ben Cotten, was a ringleader of the Reagan critics inside the RNC and was still feuding with Reagan's campaign, even on the eve of his nomination. Not normally interested in lower-level personnel matters, Reaganites took a special interest in seeing Cotten thrown out on his ear.[55] The cochair of the RNC, Mary Dent Crisp, was likewise on double secret probation because of her accumulated four years of gossip and harsh criticism of Reagan. Rumors were going around that she was about to endorse Anderson but she denied them, telling the *Washington Post,* "I'm not a flake." Many thought otherwise.[56]

Brock had revolutionized the committee, creating a house file of 650,000 names whose average contribution was $26, thus lessening the dependence on fat cats. He developed a program to help local candidates, building a farm team for the future. His projected budget of $31 million for 1980 was twice that of four years earlier. The party's slogan was "Vote Republican—For a Change."[57]

Meanwhile, as *Newsweek* reported, Jerry Carmen from the Reagan headquarters was prowling the building on a daily basis, "frightening the help with asides about the high volume of 'deadwood' he has been finding."[58] Nancy Reagan had already made her displeasure with Brock known when someone alerted her to an RNC publication that extensively covered a speech by Gerald Ford but devoted not a drop of ink to her husband.[59]

Things were no better between Reagan and Bush in the spring of 1980 than they'd been six months earlier. Reagan's inner circle was newly angry with Bush for a joke he was telling at Reagan's expense: "What's black, flat, and glows in the dark? Iran after Reagan bombs it." They were also convinced that Bush did not want to be Reagan's running mate and that Bush was playing for the 1984 nomination because he assumed Reagan would lose in the fall to Carter.[60]

TANNED, RESTED, AND REVIVED after a couple of days at his ranch, Reagan hit the road again, campaigning in California, Missouri, New Jersey, and Ohio. Missouri was a telling inclusion. Unlike the other states, it was not hosting an upcoming primary; in fact, its GOP caucus had already passed. Rather, Missouri would be an important state in the general election.

Bush hadn't formally withdrawn from the race, but when he canceled his schedule and flew home to Texas, Reagan for the first time seemed to be claiming victory. Even then, it was a modest claim. "I guess I have to accept that I should start looking ahead to beyond the convention," Reagan cautiously said to reporters.[61] The long primary battle between Bush and Reagan seemed to be finally ending, but with a whimper and not a bang.

Reagan threw out an enticing offer to Bush. If he quit, Reagan would help him eliminate whatever campaign debt he might have left. Jim Baker called Vic Gold and asked him to go to Houston and convince Bush that it was fruitless to continue. "Vic," Baker pleaded, "he won't listen to me. You have got to go." Gold reluctantly boarded a plane for Houston.[62]

Bush was still telling crowds that his instinct was to "fight, fight, fight."[63] But Baker had been telling reporters for a few days that Bush was finally getting out—again without first telling the candidate or getting his approval. Baker was leading Bush to his own execution.

At first Bush didn't want to listen to Gold's pleas, either. He couldn't drop out, the candidate said; people in California and New Jersey had been working for two years for him. So Gold laid it out for Bush: "George, if you carry this to the convention, you will end up like Nelson Rockefeller. . . . The party will hate you, so when are you going to concede?" At that, Bush finally gave in. Gold said, "Okay, I will write the goddamned statement."[64]

Bush met with his family and his closest campaign advisers, reviewing the delegate count and the budget. Of his family, his son Jeb took the news the hardest; he urged his father to stage an "Alamo-style" last stand against Reagan.[65] But there would be no more last stands for George Bush. On May 26, he at last ended his presidential sojourn.[66]

Bush was forced to offer up tribute to Emperor Reagan to gain any favor in his court, and he made a good stab at it by announcing that he would release his delegates at the convention and call on them to vote for Reagan. He also sent a telegram to Governor Reagan praising his "superb campaign."[67]

Bush had waged a spirited effort and he might have beaten Reagan after his stunning upset in the Iowa caucuses if just a few things had gone his way. Politics is about timing and judgment as much as anything else, and if Bush had displayed better judgment after his win, he and not Reagan might have been on his way to Detroit as the nominee. Yet Bush had refused to move off the "Big Mo" message. He never did anything with the spotlight once it had been put on his candidacy. Ultimately, there was no "there there" except for a résumé, "Big Mo," and a bland version of Republicanism.

His timing had been off in the Nashua debate; in his comeback wins in Massachusetts, Connecticut, and Pennsylvania; in his near-win in Texas; and of course in his big win in Michigan. Each time, Bush had been trumped by events favoring Reagan, especially the vote-robbing candidacy of John Anderson.

Bush was proud that he was a literalist and not a lyricist. He wasn't very interested in highfalutin ideas. In his concession speech, he told a weeping crowd in Houston, "I see the world not as I wish it were, but as it is."[68] Bobby Kennedy and Ronald Reagan would have argued with that. RFK had famously quoted George Bernard Shaw, "I dream things that never were and ask, 'Why not?'"[69] Reagan had once paraphrased the journalistic muckraker and socialist Lincoln Steffens, giving one of Steffens's famous lines about the Soviet Union an ironic twist, saying, "I have seen the conservative future . . . and it works."[70]

Bush was never comfortable with inspirational, straight-from-the-heart rhetoric, seeing it as a sign of weakness. His discomfort with emotion was a product of his Episcopalian upbringing. Brahmins like Bush just didn't like to wear their feelings on their Brooks Brothers sleeves; it was considered gauche to betray too much passion. Bush may have portrayed himself as a twang-voiced Texan to the voters, but make no mistake, his genuine personality had been forged on the privileged playing fields of Andover and Yale.

Even in the concession speech, Bush didn't want to back down. He'd "never quit a fight," he said.[71] He did take the measure of the man who had just beaten him, saying, "Losing to Reagan isn't that bad." Even so, he didn't blame himself for the loss; he blamed ABC and CBS. When they'd called the race for Reagan, he complained, his money flow dried up.[72] Like most politicians, Bush overlooked his own failings.

Bush, with wife Barbara at his side, told reporters, "I made a point."[73] What that point was, he failed to explain.

During the press conference, he faced the inevitable question about whether he would consider being Reagan's running mate. Bush snapped at the reporter who posed the question, saying once again that he was obdurately uninterested.[74]

As much as Bush had resisted conceding, a huge burden seemed to lift from his shoulders as soon as he made the announcement. After the press conference, he invited reporters to his home for cocktails. There he was the picture of relaxation, lounging barefoot in yellow slacks as he chatted with journalists.[75] When some reporters noticed the Yale alumni magazine resting on the coffee table, Bush said, "That's the first time we've been able to put that out for months." Then he held up a copy of *National Review* and said, "I guess we can put this away now."[76]

Bush ostensibly was kidding around, but people often reveal a lot about themselves when they're supposedly being facetious. Now that his campaign was over, Bush's social mask had slipped a bit, and his little "joking" revealed how he really felt about the conservatives in his party.[77]

Bush had garnered around 270 delegates, had raised and spent $15 million,[78] had made a lot of friends, had written thousands of thank-you notes, and had earned the respect of many in the media and the ire of a few others. And yet, after his two-year political jog across the country, no one knew any more about where George Bush stood on the issues than they had before he started out on his quest. All they knew was that he hinted he was more physically up to the presidency than Reagan, had no family problems like Ted Kennedy, and would bring "excellent, good people" to government.[79] In the end, it just wasn't enough for GOP voters. "Poppy" Bush remained a cipher in a rep tie.

Lyn Nofziger, the unparalleled quipster in Reagan World, said that Bush's "Big Mo" had slowed to "slo mo" and finally "no mo."[80]

Ronald Reagan, finally, was the last man standing in the Republican field. Ever gracious, he called Bush to thank his former opponent for his promised support. Even at this point, Reagan did not make a bold statement of victory. "I don't think it's quite sunk in yet," he told reporters when asked about having locked up the nomination. "Maybe someplace along the line later today I'll go home by myself and let out a loud yell."[81]

Reagan recognized that he did not have time to celebrate; he had to get on with the business of taking on the incumbent president. "It isn't the end of the road," he said. "It's a beginning. There's another long road ahead."[82]

20

Coming of Age

"My message has not been for Republican ears alone."

The day after George Bush withdrew from the contest, the Kentucky primary took place, and Ronald Reagan, as if to put an exclamation point on his now inevitable nomination, won there by an incredible 11–1 margin, tallying more than 78,000 votes to less than 7,000 for his now-departed opponent. Reagan stomped out the dying embers of Bush's campaign in the Nevada and Idaho primaries as well, getting 83 percent in each.[1]

As Bush left the field, John Anderson took a parting shot, saying that Bush reminded him of "a Hardy boy trying to be Winston Churchill."[2] Being forced to exit the race was particularly painful to Bush because numbers showed that on the national level he was competitive. A new Time-Yankelovich poll showed that he had closed the national gap among Republicans to just eight points, 48 percent for Reagan to Bush's 40 percent. Three months earlier, Reagan had been leading 49–17.[3] Also, in a head-to-head with Jimmy Carter, Bush was now just as competitive as Reagan. Bush had peaked too early in Iowa and then too late in Michigan—he'd never peaked at the right time.[4]

The poll did provide some good news for Bush: it showed that by a wide margin, he was the preferred running mate for Reagan.

Having sewn up the nomination, Reagan was spreading his gospel in California, speaking to four thousand at the Western Desert Gospel Singers picnic. He told the pro-family group, "I think this country is hungry today for a spiritual revival." Elaborating, he said, "You know, there are people in our land today who want to take 'In God We Trust' off our money. I've never known a time when it needed to be there more."[5]

Mary McGrory of the *Washington Star* noted how well winning suited the Gipper. "Reagan looked wonderful," she wrote of the presumptive nominee. "His dark blue eyes were sparkling and his cheeks had the rosy glow of conquest."[6] Yet the man who had such an ear for politics and theater had missed an important cue. For sixteen long years, thousands of his supporters had wished and dreamed and worked for this moment of triumph; after coming so close in 1976, and his failed effort in 1968, he had overcome his doubters—not least within his own party—to claim the Republican nomination at last. When it happened, Reagan and his campaign neglected the opportunity to make it magical. They also missed a chance to begin the process of healing the party.

Instead, the campaign focused on more mundane matters. Reagan's national headquarters had been in Los Angeles, but after months of internal skirmishes on this question, the Reagan team finally decided to move headquarters to northern Virginia. The decision reflected the fact that so much of America's power structure was built around the nation's capital: the money, the political media, the party establishment, and the government. Carter had made a critical mistake in 1976 by not moving his headquarters from Atlanta to Washington after winning the nomination, earning the ire of the D.C. establishment and ensuring that he remained mired in parochial thinking.

A search was under way for a place in rural Virginia for the Reagans to hang their hat. Whatever was selected, it had to be large enough for Reagan to go horseback riding. Eventually the Reagans rented a secluded estate in the hunt country, about an hour from downtown Washington, that had once belonged to John F. Kennedy. Jackie Kennedy had found and decorated the estate, known as Wexford, as a getaway for JFK. After his assassination, she never again visited Wexford.

The Reagan campaign also started looking at potential running mates. Dick Wirthlin began a national poll testing the names of eighteen prospective vice-presidential candidates. The poll took about one hour per sample; the unlucky Republican who was called had better have a pot of coffee nearby. Wirthlin would not reveal the names of the candidates to the media, but Reagan did mention two women he thought qualified, Senator Nancy Landon Kassebaum of Kansas and former ambassador Anne Armstrong of Texas.[7] Kassebaum, however, quickly said she felt unqualified for the position and ruled herself out.[8]

The group touting Jack Kemp as Reagan's running mate—Republicans for Victory in '80—cleverly conducted a survey of 4,096 delegates and alternates to the 1976 convention. Kemp came in impressively with 28.3 percent. Closely behind were Howard Baker at 27 percent and George Bush at 19.6 percent. Gerald Ford was at 1.4 percent.[9]

The Gipper was flying high, even if his campaign plane didn't always get off the ground. Attempting a takeoff from Lindbergh Field in San Diego, his private Learjet had accelerated to top speed when the hydraulics blew, three-quarters of the way down the runway. Steering and brakes wouldn't work, but the pilot averted a disaster by aborting at the last moment. Reagan, never a good flyer to begin with, nonetheless got into another plane. He was probably just as glad to get out of San Diego, where, the Associated Press noted, he "suffered from a fat lip and taunts from a group of angry hecklers."[10] The AP story did not elaborate on how Reagan got the fat lip.

Before leaving the city, Reagan spoke to a crowd of supporters, who pushed the protesters to the back as one shouted, "I want Teddy." Reagan didn't waste a second telling the friendly crowd in front of him, "There's a fella back there who wants Teddy—he's sick!"[11]

Something else moving was the sick economy, and it was going down, down, down. The government released the Index of Leading Economic Indicators at the end of May and they had dropped a mind-boggling 4.8 percent, the worst dive in thirty-two years.[12] Economists predicted it would get even worse, if that were possible. The White House's response was that the president was "concerned."[13] The administration did the best it could to point out that interest rates and inflation had momentarily slowed, but to the consumer, soothing words meant little.[14] Inflation was now running at 18 percent per annum. Gas, which had cost 58 cents per gallon a couple of years earlier, was now running at $1.20 per gallon. Banks were offering certificates of deposit for over 11 percent interest.[15] Saving was no option, as one lost money, somewhat gradually. Spending was the only other option, but with things so expensive, consumers were forced to hold onto increasingly worthless dollars.[16] Americans were caught in an inflationary spiral.

Several days later, the government announced that unemployment had climbed to 7.8 percent. More than eight million people could not find a job.[17]

TED KENNEDY WAS PROVING even more stubborn than George Bush. President Carter rolled over him in Kentucky, Nevada, Idaho, and Arkansas, but still Kennedy wouldn't withdraw from the Democratic contest. Only technically in the game, he continued to angle for delegates and a rule challenge at the Democratic convention in August.

The whole exercise reminded many in the media of Reagan's last gasp in 1976. In fact, Reagan had won far more primaries and state conventions against the incumbent Gerald Ford than Kennedy had against the incumbent Carter in

1980. As quixotic as Reagan's challenge to Ford may have seemed at the time, Kennedy's was even more so.

Carter offered an olive branch to Kennedy and invited him to work together on the Democratic platform with "concessions in every direction."[18] Kennedy brushed aside the Carter offer and talked up the Anderson candidacy just to torment Carter.[19] Several of Kennedy's men advised him to get out gracefully, but he was having none of it.[20] There had never been any love lost between the two candidates or their families, and now Kennedy just hated Carter.

To almost everyone but Kennedy, it was clear that Jimmy Carter and Ronald Reagan were headed for a titanic showdown. Despite being governors simultaneously, the two adversaries had never met personally, according to President Carter.[21] Still, it was apparent that they already didn't like each other. Carter met with a group of editors and cast aspersions on Reagan's work during meetings of the nation's governors. He said Reagan would "come into a meeting . . . without doing the long, tedious work . . . would call a press conference and because of his fame, would attract a great deal of press attention and then he would be gone." When asked about Carter's comments, Reagan responded, "I remember a young newcomer coming aboard as governor of Georgia. For the life of me, I can't remember anything he ever did."[22] It would go downhill from there.

Carter and Reagan crossed paths in Ohio at the end of May. The president was in the Buckeye State in hopes of securing the last delegates he needed for his party's nomination. It was his first overtly political trip since vowing to stay in the White House until the hostages were released. Ohio would also be a key battleground state in the general election, as polling had Reagan and Carter tied in the mid-30s.[23]

Campaigning in Columbus, Reagan and Carter found themselves within spitting distance of each other. Reagan remarked that he and Carter were "about two blocks apart physically. I think spiritually and mentally and philosophically, we're a million miles apart."[24] In front of the statehouse he told the crowd, "I understand that there are two candidates in town today. [Sounds of laughter and applause] As a matter of fact somebody said that they were having a little trouble telling which motorcade was ours and which was the other one. Well, you could tell his—it turns left at every corner! [Sounds of laughter]"[25]

Legendary Ohio State football coach Woody Hayes was on the dais for Reagan. But not everybody was glad to see the Gipper. Several protesters were dressed as clowns and holding signs that said, "Bozos for Reagan" and "Robots for Ray-Gun."[26]

Before leaving Ohio, Reagan met with a group of editors and acidly said that when he'd heard Carter's State of the Union address in January, "I didn't know what country he was talking about."[27]

The Democrats began to crank up the anti-Reagan rhetoric. First out of the block was Pat Brown, with whom Reagan had wiped the floor in California's 1966 gubernatorial race, denying Brown reelection by almost a million votes. Brown, fourteen years later, still hadn't gotten over the humiliation. After having a White House lunch with Carter, presumably to give him tips on how not to lose to Reagan, Brown said a Reagan presidency would be "tragic" for America. Brown called Reagan "a very poor governor," stating that he "hurt" people and that his policies were "cold-blooded."[28]

Carter got in on the act when he described the Republican in apocalyptic phrases, accusing Reagan repeatedly of "simplistic beliefs" and "demagoguery" to a group of Democratic state party bigwigs. He also implied that Reagan was a warmonger.[29]

It was not all harmony in the GOP, but Carter was a great organizing principle. Inside Reagan's new coalition were neocons and paleocons, libertarians and theocrats, fusionists and federalists, family groups and foreign-policy groups, pro-lifers and proletarians. The neoconservatives, old anti-Communist "Humphrey Democrats," were, as the *Washington Post* noted at the time, "uncomfortable with traditional Republicans, who favor trade with the Soviet Union and are mildly hostile to labor unions." The neocons had their differences with the New Right as well. "Those people are different," lamented one neocon. "They believe Communism comes to power beginning with OSHA [the Occupational Safety and Health Administration]. They believe the Soviet Union is one giant OSHA with nuclear weapons."[30] OSHA was the conservatives' poster child for waste, fraud, and abuse in the federal government. The New Right had less influence with Reagan than the traditional conservatives—as he kept some conservative social activists at arm's length. But he did owe a great deal to many in the New Right, such as Richard Viguerie, Paul Weyrich, and Phyllis Schlafly, as they had done much to prepare the GOP and the conservative movement for the coming revolution.

A "conservative enlightenment" was in full flower. At the core, more or less, was a philosophy based on, as Reagan had said in 1964, "maximum freedom consistent with law and order." Most of the players from all the seemingly dissociated groups agreed with this. They believed that with the exception of national defense, the problems that afflicted Americas were best handled by the states and localities, and then only after the individual and the free market could not address such issues. Across the board, they were strident anti-Communists who thought that only a strong national defense would roll back Soviet hegemony. Combined, they were a muscular new phenomenon in American politics. Pro-family conservatives attempted to take over a White House Conference on Families, and when they failed to prevent passage of pro-choice and pro-ERA planks, they stormed out en masse for the benefit of the media. Saul Alinsky would have been proud of the street theater protests of the guerrilla conservatives.

When the exemplar of Soviet accommodation, Henry Kissinger, sat down to break bread—at Kissinger's request—with Reagan's top national security adviser, Richard Allen, the avatar of "peace through strength," all knew which side had won. Allen had once worked for Kissinger in the Nixon administration, and Kissinger had fired the brash young man. Now Allen, on Reagan's behalf, was not interested in lording it over his vanquished foe. Much. Rather, he was extending an olive branch. Allen told the *Washington Post* that he and Kissinger "see the world approximately the same way."[31] Jaws dropped all around Washington as establishmentarians read Allen's comments in the *Post* that morning.

Allen's move, and other Reaganite efforts to reach out to the Republican establishment, demonstrated a new level of sophistication not exhibited by either Barry Goldwater or Richard Nixon. Upon his nomination in 1964, Goldwater stuck a thumb in the eye of the moderate elements of the GOP by picking as his running mate Congressman Bill Miller of New York, another conservative who enjoyed tormenting liberals—and liberal Republicans—even more than Goldwater did.

The supposedly "new" Nixon came to Washington in January 1969, president of a badly broken country, and proceeded to engage in antics that earned him not the coveted respect of the liberal establishment but only the ire and eventual contempt of the conservatives who had once cautiously supported him. In the end he was alone, sinking in the muck of corruption of his own doing. There was no one left to offer him any support. He'd simply made too many enemies on both the Left and the Right.

Reagan wasn't about to make the mistakes of Goldwater or Nixon.[32] Besides, it wasn't in his character or temperament to make enemies he didn't need. Over the years, he'd learned to become a pretty good politician and had always been a savvy negotiator. He was a good poker player in that he never cleaned out his opponents. He let them keep a little and was satisfied with a 70 percent victory, knowing he'd get another shot at their wallet—or legislation—later.

Even at this late date, some doubted that Reagan was engaged in his campaign and philosophy, but as if to prove otherwise, he walked into a meeting where a half dozen of his economic advisers were huddling in San Francisco and said with a smile, "This must be what's known as the battle for my mind."[33]

Across the aisle, the Democrats' dismay was spreading like a virus throughout their party, even as George Wallace had announced he'd voted for Carter in the primaries.[34] President Carter was drawing withering criticism even from the mainstream press corps. David Broder of the *Washington Post* wrote a column in early June comparing Carter and Nixon.[35] Although Broder was skeptical of Reagan, he was downright scornful of Carter. Pat Oliphant, the acerbic cartoonist for the *Washington Star*, depicted Carter as literally a stuffed dummy in a mock debate with John Anderson.[36] Reagan had kept that issue alive by once again telling reporters that John Anderson should be included in the presidential debates. Carter continued to oppose any debate that included Anderson, saying that the independent candidate was irrelevant. That was a difficult argument to make at a time when, according to a poll by Louis Harris, Anderson was pulling 29 percent compared with Carter's 31 percent and Reagan's 35 percent.[37]

It didn't help Democrats that the Abscam indictments started trickling in. Congressman John Murtha, who hadn't taken the money during the FBI's sting operation but who but indicated on the videotape that he was interested in doing business in the future with the "Arabs," now turned stool pigeons against two fellow Democrats, John Murphy of New York and Frank Thompson of New Jersey.[38]

Worse, disdain for liberalism, big government, and public-sector solutions had settled across the land. The Democratic Party seemed tired and worn out. The New Deal and Great Society were being held up to ridicule. Liberalism became a dirty word. People, especially young Americans, wanted to make a buck, laugh, and have fun for once. Carter was the dour Baptist minister. Reagan was the happy and indulgent grandfather, giving the kids the keys to his car over the disapproval of the parents—in this case, government.

THERE WERE ONLY ELEVEN weeks until the GOP's hoped-for love-in in the Motor City and there was plenty of work to go around for everybody. Debts had to be retired, platform work begun, a running mate found, the campaign reorganized and retooled, affairs at the Republican National Committee settled, the convention planned and scripted, and everything kept generally in motion. The greatest threat to Reagan was complacency. As ever, in the background, continued the burble of political talk about a "Reagan-Ford" ticket. It showed up in political columns and barroom talk and no one seemed to find any objection to it. Momentum for the Dream Ticket slowly gathered through June of 1980.

As an example of the Republicans' newfound self-confidence, the mayor of New York accepted the invitation to address the GOP platform hearings. It was the first time anyone remembered a prominent Democrat going willingly into the lion's den. This Daniel, though, was quite a lion himself—for Ed Koch often took on bruising fights, and even Carter, when he thought it right.[39]

With George Bush out of the race, the last remaining liberal Republicans began to issue sheepish statements of support for Reagan. RNC chairman Bill Brock grudgingly jumped on the Reagan bandwagon, saying that the Gipper would "beat Jimmy Carter like a drum."[40] Even Gerald Ford finally endorsed Reagan . . . kinda. "I have always supported the Republican nominee and will do so in 1980." Ford also ruled himself out as the Gipper's running mate.[41]

Conservatives began a pressure campaign to keep Reagan from choosing Howard Baker for veep. The conservative weekly *Human Events* lashed Baker heavily in an editorial. This was not insignificant, as *Human Events* was Reagan's favorite conservative publication, much to the dismay of some around him. Reagan said, "Not a week goes by during my campaign that I don't . . . read [it] from cover to cover." The publication had only sixty thousand subscribers but exerted influence out of proportion to its size. Co-owned by Tom Winter and Allan Ryskind, two rough-and-tumble conservatives, *Human Events* feared no one, not even Reagan. Earlier in the year it had blasted Reagan for opposing the grain boycott of the Soviets. Now the intense Ryskind said his publication might not support Reagan if Baker was selected as running mate.[42]

The Right's anger over Baker's support for the Panama Canal treaties was well known, but conservatives were also angry with Baker for supporting the ERA and the creation of the Departments of Energy and Education, and for being questionable on homosexual rights and on abortion. Most conservatives were just as vehemently opposed to Bush, but New Right leader Richard Viguerie surprisingly told the *Wall Street Journal*, "I don't have as much a problem with Bush" as did the other conservative ringleaders.[43] Viguerie's comments must have been music to the ears of another Houstonian, James Baker, who was attempting to lay the groundwork for Bush to go on the ticket with Reagan, despite Bush's public utterances.

Baker planted the notion with the media that Reagan needed to do well in the big industrial states and his man Bush had done just that in the primaries, and that Reagan needed someone with Washington experience and with foreign-policy experience. Oh yes, and Bush wasn't interested in the job. Wink, wink.

Turning to Carter and the fall campaign, Reagan's men focused renewed attention on staffing. They wanted to beef up operations both in the headquarters and on the plane. An old Reagan aide, Ed Gray, had been serving as the press officer on the plane with Reagan since the firing of Jim Lake several months earlier. Gray, however, didn't get along with the national media, and many reporters didn't respect him. In early June, Lyn Nofziger returned to the fold, replacing Gray.[44]

Staffing moves prompted a burst of second-guessing—one of Washington's favorite indoor sports. Bill Casey made two personnel decisions, hiring respected conservative activist Morton Blackwell as the campaign's youth coordinator and Peter Dailey of Los Angeles to handle Reagan's advertising. The hue and cry from Washington's establishment Republicans could be heard from the Capitol to the Lincoln Memorial, as they had their own candidates for these positions.[45] Blackwell immediately tried to get the necessary funding—$75,000—for a youth operation but was being stymied at every turn. A flurry of memos went back and forth in the campaign, equivalent to a small forest of trees and maybe as much paper as it would have cost Blackwell's program before he finally got his funding.[46]

Several days later, Casey announced that the well-regarded GOP operative Bill Timmons would serve as Reagan's convention director, and that Mike Deaver and Marty Anderson would return to the campaign, reprising their old roles. Timmons had worked for Nixon and Ford, but he moved easily between the GOP establishment and the conservatives, both sides impressed with his honest counsel.[47] All the Californians and most of the old Reaganites were finally back with Reagan now.

Always in the background was Reagan's original Kitchen Cabinet, the wealthy California businessmen he'd first met in 1964. Henry Salvatori, Holmes Tuttle, Justin Dart, William Wilson, and Alfred Bloomingdale were confidants and frequent dinner partners of Reagan's.[48] They would exert a strong opinion on actions made and people hired by the campaign. And in a small townhouse in Old Town Alexandria, a group led by Ed Meese and assisted by Helene Von Damm was working quietly to assemble a government if Reagan won.[49]

HAVING COME TO REAGAN'S rescue in the primaries with a massive independent expenditure, the Fund for a Conservative Majority reloaded its guns and announced a $3–10 million effort for Reagan in the general election under the heading Citizens for Reagan in '80.[50] By the time of the convention, a half dozen more such efforts would be launched. They were all perfectly legal as a result of the landmark ruling by the Supreme Court in *Buckley v. Valeo*, which allowed for groups to pool resources and participate in elections.

Yet another group, Americans for Change, led by Clare Boothe Luce and Republican senator Harrison Schmitt of New Mexico, announced that it would raise and spend $20 million to get Reagan elected. Pulling this operation together was an eclectic and brash young conservative, Brad O'Leary.[51] Also gearing up were Jesse Helms's organization, Americans for Reagan, and the Ronald Reagan Victory Fund, which the National Conservative Political Action Committee was assembling.

These political action committees (PACs) had to file quarterly returns with the FEC including background information on every individual who contributed over $200. They could not take more than $1,000 from any individual, could not take corporate money, and to maintain an independent status, could not "coordinate" activities with the candidate they were supporting, which made for tricky maneuvering in the small and very social world of Washington politics. Conservatives had many friends in the Reagan campaign; in order to not run afoul of the law, they had to be careful who they talked to and about what, in the summer and fall of 1980. Intrapolitical dating also became thorny, as pillow talk was considered the province of the FEC.

ON JUNE 3, REAGAN swept the eight remaining primaries without breaking a sweat, taking almost all of the 418 delegates available. Bush was out, but the Reaganites still wanted to party, so the campaign rented a room at the Ambassador Hotel in Los Angeles, the same room Bobby Kennedy had been assassinated in twelve years earlier. Reagan told the gathered, "My message has not been for Republican ears alone. I am deeply grateful for the large number of Democrats and independents who have supported my candidacy."[52]

On the Democratic side, matters were more complicated. Having failed to persuade Kennedy to drop out of the race, Carter proceeded to lose five of the eight primaries that night. The president was doing little to strengthen his case, either against Kennedy or to the American voters. But he had backed into the Democratic nomination; he had secured enough delegates to give him a comfortable cushion, 1,965 to 1,214 for Kennedy, according to the *Washington Star.* Carter's forces held a celebration in Washington, but so did Kennedy's.[53]

Carter continued his "peace offensive" and invited Kennedy to visit him at the White House. The two Democrats met alone in the Oval Office for more than an hour, but Kennedy remained adamant. He was not getting out. When the meeting ended in the late afternoon, more than two hundred reporters were waiting for Kennedy on the White House lawn. It was a media circus, and Kennedy was clearly having fun. He told the reporters, "I finally saw the Rose Garden—through the window."[54]

Relations were just as bad between the candidates' wives. Joan Kennedy sniped, "Rosalynn Carter doesn't have a master's," referring to her own advanced degree in comparison to Mrs. Carter, who had attended junior college.[55] Wisely, Mrs. Carter didn't take the bait.

Reagan was engaged in his own peace offensive. He headed for Rancho Mirage to see none other than Gerald Ford. After meeting privately in Ford's home for an hour and a half, the two stepped outside to chat with the press, on the thirteenth hole. They spoke so kindly of each other, so warmly that reporters ribbed each other, knowing these two old antagonists were snowing them.[56]

JIMMY CARTER WAS PLANNING to make foreign policy an issue against Reagan in the fall campaign. Even though the Soviets were still in Afghanistan and Americans were still in captivity in Tehran, Carter wanted to remind the American voter that on the "keeping America out of war" issue, it was he and not Reagan whom the American people could trust.[57]

After Reagan secured the nomination, his team contemplated sending him on a trip to Western Europe as a way to keep him in the news and burnish his foreign-policy credentials. But nothing came of the idea. He was coasting again, always dangerous for Reagan. His momentum since clinching the nomination had slowed, and the age and gaffe issues started creeping into stories again.

Blue-collar voters who had supported Carter in 1976 were ready to abandon the president, and the erudite Anderson was not their cup of tea, but they worried whether Reagan was up to the task. "He's articulate, smooth, handsome, but just too old," a female union worker lamented.[58]

AFTER LONG AND GRUELING fights among many competitors, the parties' candidates for the presidency—along with a rare independent competitor—were finally in place. Ronald Reagan, Jimmy Carter, and John Anderson would now slug it out through the summer and into the fall.

At this point the financial assets of Reagan, Carter, and Anderson were released. Anderson, after a lifetime in the public sector, was worth around $350,000. Carter, the thrifty and successful farmer, was worth just over $1.3 million. Reagan, for all the criticism about his being for the rich, was worth just a bit more than Carter, with $1.5 million in assets.[59]

Both the Democrats and the Republicans had staged thirty-four primaries in 1980; Carter had won twenty-four primaries to Kennedy's ten, while Reagan had won twenty-eight to Bush's six.[60]

At first blush and from the safe perch of history, Reagan's nomination seemed as if it was a cakewalk. But in fact, it had been the toughest and most grueling street fight of Reagan's career—a fight he had nearly lost because of his own inattentiveness to his campaign, because he underestimated Bush, because of the infighting and incompetence of some of his staff, and because the Republican establishment and elements of the media were in league to destroy him.

Reagan, having faltered badly, had been compelled to fight with all his might to get back in the game. He had gritted his way back into the race, but he did so with his customary aplomb.

He only made it look easy.

21

THE ROAD TO DETROIT

"Dr. Jimmy Carter is fixing to carve up Mr. Reagan and show the voters he hasn't got what it takes to be President."

The gaffe and age issues collided into one big mess in mid-June 1980, when Ronald Reagan announced to the media that if elected president and later found to be senile, he would resign.[1]

The Gipper had been given a better-than-clean bill of health by six physicians. He proclaimed that he "never felt better." According to the actuarial tables, he could expect to live to almost eighty-one years of age.[2] Reagan was simply trying to reassure Americans that he understood what was at stake. Among the bloodhounds of the national media, however, the statement resurrected all the long-festering concerns about Reagan's age and mental acuity. Pack journalists were always sniffing around for an issue to sensationalize; Reagan's age filled the bill yet again.

Jimmy Carter could only watch and smile as his opponent committed another faux pas. Carter's campaign had yet to develop any positive reasons why he should be reelected, but it was fine-tuning its line of attack on Reagan. The president's men were bent on sowing panic among the electorate by suggesting that Reagan suffered from incipient senility, and Reagan's remarks—together with the media's tabloid fixation on the issue—only aided their cause.

Joining in Carter's anti-Reagan efforts was the Chinese Communist government. Beijing blasted Reagan for daring to suggest that America pursue a "two-China policy"—that is, recognizing both the pro-Western government on Taiwan and the Communist government on the mainland.[3] Reagan had been on record for the past year and a half opposing the Joint Communiqué issued by the Carter administration and China renouncing American diplomatic relations with Taiwan.

Attacks by Communist leaders may have helped Reagan with voters, but the foreign-policy establishment was in high dudgeon, convinced that Reagan simply didn't understand. Establishmentarians thought that his notions of morality and righteous indignation over Communist aggression were out of touch with the modern world. Sophisticated people didn't think in such black-and-white terms. The "striped-pants set" at the State Department didn't approve of Reagan, whom they viewed as a simpleton and a cowboy. Strobe Talbott of *Time* magazine (who would later become a key Clinton administration adviser on Russian affairs) reflected the prevailing attitudes about Reagan within the foreign-policy establishment. Talbott called Reagan's anticommunism "visceral, unequivocal and global," a "Manichaean view of a struggle between the forces of light and the forces of darkness [that] is . . . old-fashioned and yet also very much back in fashion."[4]

But Reagan did not back off his anti-Soviet views. He sat down for a two-hour meeting with the editors of the *Washington Post* and elaborated that his plan for a military buildup would put undue strain on the Soviet economy and "force the Soviets to the arms control bargaining table." Nor did he back down when questioned about an apparent conflict of interest within his campaign: it had been disclosed that two of his close aides, Mike Deaver and Peter Hannaford, had a long-standing lobbying contract with Taiwan. Coming to Deaver and Hannaford's defense, Reagan told the *Post*, "Hell, I was the one who was selling them on Taiwan."[5]

THE DEAVER-HANNAFORD FLAP WASN'T the only public-relations headache for the Reagan campaign. Eyebrows were raised when it was revealed that Frank Sinatra had listed Reagan as a character reference in an application to buy a casino in Las Vegas.[6] Sinatra had long been rumored to have close ties to organized crime, and newspaper stories and photos started to appear about the shady characters— "wise guys" with pinkie rings and surnames that ended in vowels—who were good buddies of the "Chairman of the Board."

Reagan advisers surely would have preferred to avoid another round of bad press, but in fact Sinatra and Reagan had a lot in common. They were roughly the same age and they had both been New Deal–worshipping, Democratic Party liberals in their youth. Walter Winchell and other newspaper columnists had smeared Sinatra in the 1940s as a Communist. Sinatra had been particularly close to the Kennedys, pulling many strings to help get his friend and party-mate Jack elected in 1960. But after the election, Bobby Kennedy's callous and ungrateful treatment of Sinatra, as well as the advent of the rock 'n' roll counterculture, soured Sinatra on anything that smacked of liberalism. The Kennedys had broken his heart; the

Beatles and their ilk had threatened his career. Sinatra rejected those on the Left who had rejected him, and he embraced the Republicans.

Despite the Reagan campaign's continuing hiccups, Jimmy "The Greek" Snyder, the famous Vegas oddsmaker, was laying odds on the Gipper to win in November and to choose George Bush as his running mate.[7] The folks who published the *New Webster Encyclopedic Dictionary* seemed to agree. Their new edition listed Reagan as the fortieth president, despite the fact that the encyclopedia was released in the summer of 1980, when the election was still months away.[8]

REAGAN GRUDGINGLY DECIDED TO keep Bill Brock as chairman of the Republican National Committee. Stories had been leaking out yet again that Brock's days were numbered. Jerry Carmen had written a scathing report about Brock's stewardship of the committee, and Carmen had a powerful ally in Paul Laxalt, who wanted Brock ousted. Brock, however, whipped up a public-relations campaign to fight off the insurgency, persuading elected officials and friends to contact Reagan to plead for clemency. They included Jack Kemp, Bill Timmons, and Howard Baker.[9] The gambit worked.

Reagan did not, however, give Brock carte blanche. He installed another aide—Drew Lewis, from his Pennsylvania operation—as his eyes and ears at the RNC to ensure that the committee worked in good faith for his election and to "ride herd" on Brock, according to Ed Meese.[10] Moreover, two other irritants to the Reaganites, RNC cochair Mary Dent Crisp and top aide Ben Cotten, were severely marginalized, though not fired as the conservatives wanted.

Brock had already written the loquacious Crisp a memo warning that she "should adopt the lowest profile possible." She had become an embarrassment: she had claimed her offices at the RNC were bugged, but when police investigated they discovered that the wires in question were part of the building's Muzak system. Frustrated, Brock now ordered Crisp not to talk to the press, and two events in her honor scheduled for the convention were canceled. Rumors still ran that the Reagan-loathing Crisp was on the verge of endorsing John Anderson.[11]

Brock was bloodied and slightly bowed, but the fact that he was still at the RNC came down as a big loss for Carmen, Laxalt, and Lyn Nofziger, who had been gunning for Brock since the Panama Canal fight. Reagan's close confidant Ed Meese had also supported Brock's ouster, but had been less public about it than the other three.

The Democrats were coping with their own internecine fighting. Jimmy Carter's aides referred to Ted Kennedy as a "fat, spoiled, rich kid." Teddy's staff returned the kindness, calling Carter "that redneck Southern Baptist."[12]

Carter was struggling to get support. In Miami, he was booed lustily, obscene gestures were made in his direction, and bottles were thrown at his motorcade—including his own limousine—by out-of-work blacks. One sign read, "Hail to the Chief Racist."[13] In Washington, his proposal for a new oil import fee was pilloried by members of his own party. At an event on the South Lawn, Carter asked his fellow Democrats for a round of applause supporting the proposal but "the silence was so resounding the English boxwood could be heard growing," in the words of the New York Times.[14]

Though Carter labeled Reagan's economic proposals as "facile" and "ideological nonsense," he hinted at minor tax cuts and budget cuts to stimulate the economy, a plan that sounded suspiciously like a pale version of "Reaganomics."[15] This time the president was undercut by a member of his own cabinet. Commerce Secretary Philip M. Klutznick said that he "saw no possibility" for tax cuts in 1980.[16] Federal taxes were scheduled for another rise in January 1981, up billions.

Reagan's men, especially his new ad team, led by Peter Dailey, were only now starting work on their own anti-Carter themes. After four years, there was an embarrassment of riches for the Republicans to mine against the incumbent, but the Gipper's campaign was drifting. Dailey, though talented, was getting little direction from Bill Casey.

Reagan had won the nomination, and now no one seemed to know what to do to gear up for the summer and fall campaigns. The first tier of advisers—Meese, Casey, and Dick Wirthlin—was talented, but the only media schmoozer on the team was Nofziger, who was irreverent to the point of sometimes making jokes at his candidate's expense. With no national political director in place, regional directors went without guidance and the campaign was downright listless. The candidate was being poorly briefed or not at all. The Reagan campaign was making embarrassing mistakes, too. The Gipper had been invited to address the annual meeting of the NAACP, but Reagan's scheduling office and the RNC dropped the ball and left the invitation unanswered for weeks.[17] By the time the mishap was discovered, there was nothing to do except to politely decline. Carter, Kennedy, and Anderson all spoke before the influential group. The Reagan campaign scrambled to accept the invitation of another African-American organization, the Urban League.[18]

Reagan was in New York for important editorial board meetings with the New York Times, but the aides there were vacillating. Reagan was angry, telling them he didn't want any "yes men" around him and "that if they did not level with him, he would take drastic physical retaliation against them."[19]

Efforts to bring in a top political director were also ineffectual. Bill Timmons had been brought aboard to direct the convention, but was unavailable to help with anything else. Charlie Black, who had been fired four months earlier, was offering his services to come back, but no one was returning his phone calls. John Sears's onetime protégé David Keene, Bush's former political director, had made too many enemies in the Reagan camp to be seriously considered. He had been "blackballed" by a few Reagan advisers, reported the *Wall Street Journal*.[20] And Mrs. Reagan had never been fond of him. Years later, at a Washington dinner, when told she would be seated between Keene and conservative polemicist Pat Buchanan, Mrs. Reagan rolled her eyes heavenward and said sarcastically, "Oh great!"

The Reagan team eventually wised up and let it be known that Timmons, once his duties were done at the convention, would become the campaign's de facto political director.[21] The national media liked the soft-spoken Tennessean. He was seen as conservative, but not someone likely to grab you by the lapels. The media backed down on the issue of Reagan's campaign staff—for a time.

JOHN ANDERSON'S INDEPENDENT QUEST was qualifying for the ballot in more and more states, so the Democratic National Committee set up a $225,000 fund to stop Anderson from succeeding any further.[22] DNC chairman John C. White, normally unflappable, charged that Anderson and Reagan had hatched a "plot" to stick it to Carter.[23] Nothing could have been further from the truth; Anderson thought Reagan was not up to the challenge, while Reagan returned Anderson's malice, telling a group of editors that the only Anderson "difference" was "an ego trip."[24]

The real question was who would be hurt more by Anderson's continued presence, Reagan or Carter? Anderson did not shy away from attacking Reagan. In a speech before the New York Stock Exchange, Anderson made several nasty references to Reagan's age. "I wasn't old enough, maybe he was, to remember what things were like in 1923 and 1924, but it isn't appropriate for the problems we have to face in 1980." Some of the brokers booed Anderson.[25]

But much of Anderson's impact would hinge on how Reagan campaigned. If Reagan ran a typical Republican race, then Anderson, the Republican, would take votes away from him. If, however, Reagan ran a conservative race, then Anderson, the liberal, would take votes away from Carter.

The independent posed a threat to Carter in another way: The dour Anderson was working the same "woe-is-us" patch of earth that Carter had been hoeing for the previous four years. In the words of *Newsweek*, Anderson specialized in "brooding, son-of-malaise sermons everywhere about the decline of American optimism and the need for discipline and sacrifice."[26]

In addition to worrying about Anderson, the Carter campaign still had to deal with Kennedy. Although the Democratic nomination was now out of his reach, Kennedy refused to go away. He went so far as to hint that he might not campaign for the president's reelection. Carter was losing much of his essential constituency in the South, with blue-collar workers, Catholics, and evangelicals, but it remained to be seen whether the Republicans could get out of their own way and take advantage of his problems. Carter's men understood this. "Carter may not be able to win this election, but Reagan sure can lose it," one said. Their plan was simple: to "scare the hell out of them with Ronald Reagan."[27]

Most polls over the spring of 1980 had the race close, swinging back and forth between Carter and Reagan. In the states, it was just as close. Carter was ahead in sixteen states and the District of Columbia with 154 electoral votes, and Reagan was ahead in twenty-two states with 160 votes. Twelve states with 224 electoral votes were too close to call.[28]

With the stakes so high and with Carter's campaign struggling, the president's chief of staff, Hamilton Jordan, took a leave of absence from the White House and assumed command of the reelection committee. Jordan knew what Carter needed to do. He needed to slice and dice Reagan before the Gipper could get going in earnest with his own national campaign. As the *Wall Street Journal* noted at the time in an editorial, "Dr. Jimmy Carter is fixing to carve up Mr. Reagan and show the voters he hasn't got what it takes to be President."[29]

As JORDAN BEGAN TO make his battle preparations, the Republicans held the first of a series of "unity dinners." The $500-per-plate dinner in Beverly Hills featured Reagan alongside his six former challengers. The event was designed to pay off the fallen challengers' campaign debts. Not surprisingly, then, love was in the air. George Bush called Reagan an "honorable, honest, decent man." Bob Dole, the stand-up comic of the GOP, said his own campaign was "such a secret that nobody noticed it." Reagan spoke last and said of his former rivals, "You have seen six examples of real class, real dignity, real sportsmanship."[30]

The event raised $550,000, but as it turned out, little would go to retire campaign debts after all. A bait-and-switch was employed. The money would pay for a national television broadcast in which donations would be solicited. If money came in from this, only then would it go toward the various candidates' debts.[31] The extravaganza was broadcast on CBS the following Saturday at 10:30 P.M. eastern time.

Reagan had the backing of most of his family members as well as former opponents. Son Michael and daughter Maureen enthusiastically participated in their father's campaign. Mike had even played a role in the dismissal of John Sears. When his father called him in frustration from New Hampshire, Michael had advised Reagan to fire Sears.[32] Maureen, meanwhile, was an active campaigner, giving well-received stump speeches. She was a natural politician, some said even more so than her father.

The other two children, son Ron and daughter Patti Davis, were not involved to any great extent, pursuing their own lives and interests. Ron had dropped out of Yale and in 1980 was trying out for the Joffrey Ballet. The campaign was worried about the image of a ballet-dancing son of a rugged movie hero but decided to leave well enough alone. Reagan was asked about his son and, like any protective father, replied that he was "all man." Patti was a struggling actress. She took her mother's maiden name for the stage and grew up a typical California flower child, pursuing fads, partying with rock stars, and generally irritating her parents. She loathed her father's conservatism.

Reagan did get a boost from Republicans in Congress. Working in harmony with the Reagan campaign, the GOP members introduced an immediate across-the-board 10 percent tax cut, a down payment on the 30 percent being proposed by their presumptive nominee.[33] The ploy forced Carter and the Democrats to go on record opposing Reagan's proposal. On permanent offense, the Republicans kept attaching tax-cut legislation to bill after bill, compelling the Democrats to oppose them over and over.

Carter's men were looking for inspiration and they turned to Harry Truman, just as Gerald Ford had four years earlier. A new book had been released on Truman, and circulated in Democratic circles was a 1948 memo about Truman's campaign written by the longtime Washington insider Clark Clifford.[34]

Democrats needed all the help they could get, because in a new poll released at the end of June, Reagan for the first time had broken into a healthy lead over Carter. The New York Times/CBS survey had Reagan out in front, 47–37, and even with Anderson in the mix, Reagan still led with 41 percent to 30 percent for Carter and 18 percent for the independent candidate. Reagan also got high ratings on leadership and—defying the pundits—the voters said that Reagan was as smart as Carter. College graduates supported Reagan over Carter by a larger margin, 48–35, than non–college graduates, 47–37.[35] A poll by Newsweek showed a similar strengthening of Reagan's position with the American people.[36]

Nothing monumental had occurred in the past several weeks to turn the tide. Reagan had, of course, won the nomination, but he had made few speeches during that time. Simply, Carter was floundering, and the voters were tiring of the president. They were willing to look at Reagan's solutions, no matter how radical they might seem.

REAGAN'S SELECTION TEAM HAD narrowed the number of prospective running mates down to eight. All were asked for, and submitted, extensive medical, personal, and financial documents. They included Howard Baker, George Bush, Jack Kemp, Don Rumsfeld, Richard Lugar, Paul Laxalt, and one surprise, Congressman Guy Vander Jagt of Michigan.[37] Vander Jagt was of indistinct ideology but had done a yeoman's job retooling the National Republican Congressional Committee. He was not only charming but also one of the best orators in politics. He never used a prepared text or teleprompter. Instead, he memorized his speeches, some of them extensive.

Conservatives heaved a sigh of relief that Gerald Ford was not on the list. Yet they worried because the list indicated that the Reagan campaign was searching for someone more "moderate" than Reagan, despite his oft-repeated comments that his running mate would have to be of the same ideological stock. Conservatives complained about Howard Baker the most. Baker didn't help his cause when he went on CBS's *Face the Nation* and said what the country needed in a president was "not necessarily the most cerebral, the most intellectual person." Implying that Reagan lacked a first-rate intellect was not a way to win over the Reagan campaign, Nancy Reagan, or conservatives.[38] For good measure, Baker and poor George Bush got the virtual kiss of death from the liberal Republican senator Jacob Javits, who said he supported either as Reagan's running mate.[39]

AT THE BEGINNING OF July, a new report on the TV networks' political coverage confirmed what everybody knew: CBS, NBC, and ABC were slobbering all over John Anderson. The Media Analysis Project, generated by George Washington University, said that "Anderson is an articulate, liberal spokesman and . . . the press also regards itself as articulate and liberal." One interesting finding was that Carter was getting even worse coverage than Reagan. But it was not as if the Republican was receiving good media, just less bad than Carter. Stories about Reagan on the networks ran 6–1 unfavorable to favorable.[40]

To bypass the networks, Reagan's campaign began buying broadcast time on national radio networks. Reagan had been comfortable in front of the microphone for almost fifty years, going back to his days on WHO in Des Moines. In his addresses, he urged the American people to avoid the "trust me" government of Carter, because it bestowed too much on one man, which was contrary to the republican form of government created by the Founding Fathers. Explaining his view of "not only the power but the limits of the presidency," Reagan made clear his sophisticated understanding of the American federalist system.[41]

On the campaign trail, Reagan reinforced the message about federalism and his desire to scale back federal power. In the 1970s the so-called Sagebrush Rebellion had erupted in the American West, where the federal government controlled huge swaths of land—an incredible 544 million acres in twelve states—that were off-limits to any form of use or access. Groups had organized to fight for a return of the lands to the states. The "rebellion" had been going on for years, but Reagan took the opportunity to endorse their position. "Count me in as a rebel," he told a cheering crowd of ranchers, miners, and oilmen in Salt Lake City.[42]

Reagan wasn't the only one on the attack. President Carter went into Reaganland, traveling to Los Angeles to speak to the annual gathering of the National Education Association. Eight thousand (mostly women) teachers chanted Carter's name over and over. Carter ripped Reagan's tax-cut proposal, labeling it a "free lunch," which was mildly amusing since that is what Republicans had charged the Democrats with for years.[43] He also warned the crowd about Reagan's supposed extremism, saying that if elected, the Republican would choose conservative judges. Finally, he defended his administration's actions against the Soviets over their invasion of Afghanistan as "effective" but "peaceful in nature."[44]

Carter then got nasty in a speech that had been billed as "nonpolitical." He said, "We cannot allow nostalgia built on an incorrect memory to blind us to what life is like when government did nothing to protect minorities, the working people, or the poor."[45]

It was a foreshadowing of the coming fight.

Work was proceeding apace in Detroit on the convention. Political conventions had changed greatly over the years and not altogether for the better. As television dominated the gatherings more and more, the political consultants took control and squeezed tension, emotion, and drama out of the quadrennial gatherings, reducing them to infomercials and the delegates to a one-dimensional caricature of their former selves.

Once, delegates had been the muscle of the party. In 1952 Senator Robert A. Taft of Ohio, "Mr. Republican" himself, arrived at the Philadelphia convention with 530 delegates, well ahead of Dwight D. Eisenhower and just 74 short of a first-ballot nomination. Delegates maneuvering for Ike's eleventh-hour bid, along with a typical underhanded assist from Senator Richard Nixon, helped rob Taft of the nomination.

That same year, when the Democrats gathered, Governor Adlai Stevenson of Illinois had next to nothing in delegate strength, only 41, while Senator Estes Kefauver of Tennessee had 248, Senator Richard Russell of Georgia had 121, and Governor Averell Harriman of New York, 108.[46] Yet it was Stevenson who left Chicago as his party's nominee.

The delegates had also been responsible for writing their parties' platforms. For years the conventions had been preceded by "Platform Week," in which delegates gathered in committees and subcommittees to work out their party's position on a host of issues, ranging from social policy to economics, national defense, and foreign policy. Delegates in their committees would hear testimony from elected officials, philosophers, economists, labor leaders, and foreign-policy experts. After endless debate and discussion, these delegates—housewives, small businessmen, religious leaders, retired military, a cross section of America—wrote impressive documents setting a philosophical and ideological direction for their political party, all without the interference of self-inflating political consultants. Over the years issues from nullification to slavery to prohibition to suffrage to war and peace were endlessly debated and discussed. What a party stood for at these affairs was just as important as the man it nominated. Notably, the media covered these weeklong events just as enthusiastically as the nomination week itself.

Those days were quickly passing into history, but the platform remained a crucial document for the political parties. And for the GOP in 1980—a party at a crossroads—the debate over the platform would be especially important. Reagan's point man at the 1980 platform hearings was Marty Anderson, his longtime policy adviser. As well as anyone, Anderson knew the political, cultural, and governing philosophy of Ronald Reagan.

THE REAGAN CAMPAIGN'S POLLS on a running mate found that only Gerald Ford helped Reagan in the general election, and it was by a minuscule 2 percent. All the other prospective choices were a drag on his campaign.[47] Reagan understood that the best choice was to avoid "buying yourself a negative."[48] Richard Nixon had confessed to a friend at Miami Beach in 1968 that he wished he could run alone. He wasn't the only one on either side of the aisle who felt this way. Kennedy reportedly expressed similar sentiments about Lyndon Johnson.

Other than presiding over the Senate, the second man had no required duties. The Founders thought so little of the office that they didn't even come up with a residence, like the White House, for the vice president. Most stayed in boardinghouses or hotels when they were in Washington, waiting to be told the president had died so they, too, could become a part of history. An official VP residence had emerged only when Gerald Ford took pity on Nelson Rockefeller and gave him the official residence of the chief of naval operations, a Queen Anne–style estate in northwest Washington. Rocky, in character, refused to stay there, but Number One Observatory Circle thereafter became the home for the number-two guys.

Sometimes the choice of a running mate spilled over into the bizarre and even tragic. In 1972 Democratic nominee Senator George McGovern took Senator Tom Eagleton of Missouri as his running mate. McGovern said he was "1,000 percent" behind his choice when it was revealed that Eagleton had been institutionalized in a mental hospital and had even undergone electroshock therapy. McGovern then went south on Eagleton and engaged in a bizarre search for a running mate, enduring the sorry spectacle of almost everybody turning him down until party man Sargent Shriver, a Kennedy in-law, gamely went on with McGovern—and later down in flames with him.

Reagan didn't want a similar embarrassment, so Bill Casey hired a private investigator to check out the men remaining on Reagan's list—peeping through keyholes, dumpster diving, talking to enemies, making sure there was nothing that would embarrass Reagan. At some point, Reagan's men would speak to each person on the list, and if a VP candidate passed muster, he could meet with Reagan himself. Anyway, that was the plan.

Bush's stock began to rise. Indeed, a plurality of Republican delegates in a survey conducted by the *Washington Post* showed a strong preference for the Houstonian. Bush was well out in front with 34 percent and Kemp a disappointing second at 21 percent.[49] Similarly, a survey of the fifty Republican state chairmen showed that Bush was the most popular choice.[50]

The problem was, Reagan—and especially Mrs. Reagan—just could not warm up to Bush. The *Washington Star* reported that Reagan had "private reservations" about his rival, who had "choked up" in their debate in Nashua months earlier. Reagan reportedly told an aide, "If he couldn't stand up under that much pressure, how could he be president?"[51]

ONE OF THE MOST significant stories of the campaign was first reported by Rowland Evans and Robert Novak in early July. The columnists wrote about a meeting of two hundred Protestant evangelicals and fundamentalists who had passionately supported the born-again Jimmy Carter in 1976 but after four years had soured on him. One Georgia pastor in attendance at the Atlanta meeting clearly had a sense of humor; he said, "The problem is to get any of them to confess they voted for Carter last time. But believe me, they did."[52]

The meeting had been organized by New Right leader Paul Weyrich, whose specialty was grassroots pulpit politics. The leaders in attendance felt betrayed by Carter and were eager to support Reagan, who was on their side on abortion, prayer in school, and private Christian education.[53]

Grafting this new coalition onto the GOP would not be easy, as the old elements of the party viewed the interlopers with suspicion. Reagan's campaign faced a stiff challenge in trying to keep these various coalitions together. Much of the hard work would have to be done at the convention, and especially in the debate over the party's platform. Reagan had already gotten an idea of how difficult this work would be when he tried to find a compromise on the ERA, only to anger both sides.

It was clear that the some in the New Right would not give up the platform without a fight. Senator Jesse Helms and his men had been stewing over being left out of key campaign decisions, including those involving staff. In 1976 Helms had offered substitute planks to the Republican platform at the Kansas City convention, and he was threatening to do the same in Detroit.[54] He went public only days before the platform hearings, charging that convention managers were playing "hardball" because his request to testify in Detroit had gone unanswered. It had already been confirmed that Henry Kissinger and other moderates would appear before the platform committee. Angry over Reagan's choice of Alan Greenspan, another Fordite, as principal adviser on the budget, Helms railed, "The Ford people are taking over the Reagan campaign. And now it looks like they're taking over the platform as well."[55]

The summer of 1980 was shaping up as a scorcher. In early July the temperature in some parts of the country lingered above 100 degrees for days on end.

It remained to be seen how hot it would get politically in Detroit for Ronald Reagan.

22

SUMMER IN THE CITY

*"Republicans have been running around on Democratic turf.
I don't blame them. We left a vacuum."*

L ong before the oppressive, sticky, and sweltering summer of 1980, Detroit
had descended into a pit of urban rot. Things had started out just fine in
1701, when French officer Antoine de la Mothe Cadillac founded a settle-
ment there with permission from the French Crown. The city grew prosperous
through water and overland trade, and its healthy commercial development fos-
tered a vibrant city culture. Detroit became known as "the Paris of the West" for
its architecture and wide, tree-lined avenues. Industrial production boomed after
Henry Ford and the rest of the automobile industry settled in Detroit; by the
1920s word was out that Ford was paying extraordinarily high wages on his state-
of-the-art assembly lines. During World War II, Detroit's huge industrial plant
was turned into a massive arsenal for democracy, churning out tanks, airplane
engines, troop transports, and other war matériel.

But in the ensuing decades the city had become a burnt-out shell of its former
self. Though millions of poor blacks from the agrarian South had migrated north
in search of less racism and more economic opportunities, they found to their
dismay that in Detroit and in so many other northern cities the conditions were
far from ideal. (Dr. Martin Luther King Jr. once said that Chicago was the most
racist city in America.) Detroit, like other American cities, erupted in race riots
in the 1960s. That only accelerated the massive "white flight" to the suburbs that
hollowed out Detroit.

It wasn't just white residents who left. Motown Records, founded in Detroit
in 1959 by Berry Gordy Jr., was one of the best-recognized labels in the country and the most prominent record company owned by an African-American.

Motown had discovered and promoted one great musical act after another—Smokey Robinson and the Miracles, Marvin Gaye, Diana Ross and the Supremes, Gladys Knight and the Pips, the Jackson Five, and dozens of others. But in 1972, the Motown label fled Detroit and headed for Los Angeles.

Now the once-confident metropolis was continually plagued with municipal strikes and was often without dependable police or fire protection, not to mention satisfactory trash removal. Frequent teacher walkouts and interrupted bus service only added to the city's woes. Unemployment in 1980 hovered just under a heartrending 20 percent, a level not seen since the Great Depression.[1] When Hollywood film directors needed a convincing backdrop for science-fiction movies about futuristic "dystopias," they would often choose the grim city streets of Detroit—without changing a thing.

Detroit's proud professional sports teams, the Lions, the Tigers, the Pistons, and the Red Wings—often derided as the "Dead Wings"—had become struggling, losing franchises. The two-dollar-per-seat bleachers at Tiger Stadium became a no-man's-land as inebriated fans took to throwing cherry bombs and other assorted items at players on the field. The bleachers were closed.[2] The fortunes of all four teams had spiraled downward right along with those of their host city.

Eyebrows had been raised, then, when Republican chieftain Bill Brock announced his plans a year and a half earlier to hold the GOP's quadrennial confab in the Motor City. Conservatives like Senator Paul Laxalt furiously fought Brock over the decision. Laxalt wanted the convention in Dallas, capital of the New West. The committee members voted and it came up a tie, with one woman, a Reaganite, who nonetheless had promised Brock that she'd vote for Detroit, missing. Brock sent aides to find her and finally discovered her in the ladies' room, standing on the toilet seat in a stall, hiding. When she was finally cajoled out, she reluctantly voted for Detroit, just as she'd promised Brock.[3] A blue-collar city, largely ethnic, unionized, and in a heavily Catholic state—this was just what Brock wanted to counter the white-bread, Protestant, Buick-driving, country-club image of the GOP.

Detroit was struggling to right itself, just as the GOP was in the latter part of the twentieth century. Detroit mayor Coleman Young, famous for his all too frank comments, was a shrewd executive who saw the convention as a way to showcase his city in the hopes of attracting new businesses and investments. It would be the city's first chance to gain positive coverage since the race riots of 1967. Mayor Young was an urban liberal Democrat who normally had little use for the country-club Republicans, but he and Brock worked well together and the city rolled out the red carpet for the Republicans. City fathers chose the welcoming slogan of "Detroit Loves a Good Party" to greet the thousands of Republicans who would stream into town.[4] The center of the festivities would be the Renaissance Center, a new, gleaming high-rise that had cost hundreds of millions of dollars and now towered over the burnt-out slums of the rest of the city.

Brock had invested plenty of resources reaching out to black America, even though in 1980 only 2.8 percent of the GOP's delegates were black, down from the 3.4 percent of four years earlier.[5] In 1976 Jimmy Carter had received almost 90 percent of the black vote,[6] so Republicans had nowhere to go but up with this relatively small but politically important voting bloc. The image of the party as one of privilege and access had to be jettisoned in favor of inclusion and opportunity for all. The theme of the 1980 Republican Convention, "Together . . . A New Beginning,"[7] summed up perfectly Young's goal for his city, Brock's goal for his party, and Ronald Reagan's message to America.

Of Brock's choice of Detroit the head of the United Auto Workers, Douglas Fraser, observed, "Republicans have been running around on Democratic turf. I don't blame them. We left a vacuum."[8] The Democrats had certainly left a vacuum in Detroit. Despite being the party of the workingman, they had never held their national convention in the U.S. capital of the workingman. Now the Republicans were stepping in—and hoping to appeal to those same working people. The autoworkers had supported the Democratic Party for years, but some labor management and a great deal of the rank and file had become increasingly dismayed with its economic policies. Fraser made clear his disdain for Carter when he noted the "correlation" between the rise in unemployment and the rise in Reagan's support.[9] The American workingman was also hard-core anti-Communist and didn't like to see the president knuckling under to the Russians. Reagan, a union man and tough guy when it came to the Kremlin, was more to the liking of the working class.

Brock's bold choice of Detroit came with more than a little risk. As thousands of fussy Republicans and thousands more indifferent journalists prepared to descend on the city for the GOP jamboree, a new strike by trash collectors meant that refuse was piling high and stinking deep. Mayor Coleman was working furiously to settle the strike and get his city's streets cleared of the piles of garbage before the convention got under way.[10] Another strike had sidelined the *Detroit Free Press*. The paper had invested hundreds of thousands of dollars to cover the first national convention in the city's history, but the editors' and reporters' hands were tied, as the Newspaper Guild ordered them to abide by the Teamsters' strike.[11]

Some Republicans were skeptical of Brock's choice of Detroit and reportedly brought Mace with them. One woman from the South was walking along the Detroit waterfront when a boat passed with several black people on board. She turned to a friend and said, "I didn't know blacks had boats."[12] The poor woman, guilty of cultural clumsiness, was overheard by a reporter for the *Washington Star*.

CARTER, TAKING SOME VERY bad advice, made a political swing through Detroit on the eve of the Republican convention. He succeeded only in embarrassing himself, as news reports used the unemployment plight of the city as a metaphor for his presidency. The visit came across as a cheap political stunt. A Reagan spokesman, James Brady, zapped Carter, saying, "It was like Sherman visiting Atlanta. He was returning to visit the scene of his crime."[13]

Weighing down Carter politically was that fact that more than fifty Americans were still being held hostage in Tehran. The ayatollah had still released only one American, who was very sick. The others continued to languish with no hope in sight.[14]

MARTY ANDERSON WAS LOOKING after Reagan's interests as the GOP gathered in Detroit to write the document spelling out the party's philosophy. Anderson was a slight, bookish type with an undergraduate degree from Dartmouth and a Ph.D. from MIT. He certainly had the rumpled, slightly disheveled look of an academic, complete with papers under one arm and a briefcase in the other hand. Anderson was a passionate conservative who got along well with the other Reagan insiders. And with his charming, unassuming manner along with his heavy campaign experience, he could reason with Republicans and conservatives outside the Reagan inner circle. He was the perfect choice to calm the stormy waters of the Republican platform fights.

The platform battle royal kicked off over the pro–Equal Rights Amendment plank, which had been in the party's platform since 1940. In the subcommittee, it easily went down to defeat, 11–4.[15] Watered-down language making vague promises about equality for women was substituted, which pleased neither side. Still, it was a small victory for conservative grassroots activist Phyllis Schlafly and her legions of women supporters, who had wanted a strongly worded denunciation of the amendment.

A plank supporting a Human Life Amendment to the U.S. Constitution was easily adopted, though a majority of GOP delegates to the convention opposed the measure, according to a partial survey by the *Washington Post*.[16] The platform committee also approved language opposing federal funding for abortion. Pro-choice and pro-ERA supporters made noises about bringing their positions to the full convention for its consideration, but they could not muster the twenty-seven signatories among the full platform committee members needed to file a minority report.

RNC cochair Mary Dent Crisp was photographed dissolving in tears as her beloved ERA was cut from the platform. Crisp had not been removed from her post, but she was not running for reelection the following week, as she knew she would have been in for a crushing defeat. The convention scene only heightened speculation that she would bolt the party and endorse John Anderson.[17]

For the past four years, Reagan had gotten one report after another on Crisp's nasty comments about him, to the point that even his good manners were tested. "Mary Crisp should look to herself and find out how loyal she's been to the Republican Party for quite some time," he said tartly.[18]

The controversial Crisp left Detroit several days before the beginning of the convention to the catcalls of her conservative enemies. The Reagan forces moved quickly to nominate a successor to Crisp: Betty Heitman, chair of the National Federation of Republican Women. Heitman, from Louisiana, was a conservative, a Reagan fan, and a team player who was popular at Republican headquarters.[19]

Crisp's departure wasn't enough to mollify some conservatives. Senator Jesse Helms and his followers were unhappy with the "compromise" on women's rights and wanted punitive language on the Panama Canal, Taiwan, and other foreign-policy matters in the platform. One plank offered by the Helms forces called for the resurrection of the House Committee on Un-American Activities, the controversial commie-hunting group of the 1950s.[20] Helms, unwittingly, was serving Reagan's purposes. In taking such hard-line stances, he was moderating Reagan's image with the media.

Other subcommittees adopted language supporting Reagan's tax cuts and billions for a defense buildup, as well as military superiority over the Soviets. Conservatives and Reaganites rammed through one initiative after another.

Ted Kennedy was having far less luck on the Democratic side. His proposed planks to allow the delegates already pledged to President Carter to be freed essentially to revote at the Democratic convention were going down in flames, one by one.[21] Carter's men had a hammerlock on the platform process.

THE FINAL DRAFT OF the 1980 Republican platform was approved on Thursday, July 10. It might as well have been lifted from Reagan's commentaries and speeches over the previous four years. The platform dealt with pro-life judges, the decontrol of oil and natural gas, more domestic exploration, repealing the national 55-mile-per-hour speed limit, busing, gun control, new defense systems, and increased pay and incentives for the American GI and military reserves.[22] It called for rejection of SALT II and for "military superiority" over the Soviets. It was the most conservative and most specific platform in the history of the party.[23]

The 1980 Republican Party platform was clear and unequivocal: "Mr. Carter must go! For what he has done to the dollar, for what he has done to the life savings of millions of Americans, for what he has done to retirees seeking a secure old age, for what he has done to young families aspiring to a home, an education for their children and a rising living standard, Mr. Carter must not have another four years in office." When the final draft was offered to the committee for passage, Representative Ed Bethune of Arkansas offered a floor amendment to add the exclamation point at the end of the first sentence. The motion was carried unanimously, to the cheers of the members of the platform committee.[24] The final sentence of the preamble presented to the full committee read, "Let us now together make America great again, let us now together make a new beginning." Mrs. Patric Dorsey, a delegate from North Carolina, proposed that the sentence begin, "With God's help," and this amendment, too, was accepted.[25]

The final GOP document, a tough denunciation of all things Carter, all things Communist, and nearly all things liberal, would have been even harsher had not Marty Anderson and other Reagan men been on watch to prevent the hard-liners from inserting even stronger verbiage. Jack Kemp had been one of those deputized by the Reagan forces to mollify Helms and his team so as to keep the platform from lurching too far to the right. Kemp had helped dial back the more assertive members of the platform committee, so much so that he joked that he looked "like a Communist."[26]

EVEN WHILE CONSERVATIVES WERE fighting over the Republican platform, they had stayed focused on the issue of Reagan's running mate. Richard Viguerie's *Conservative Digest* devoted most of one issue to making the case against Howard Baker. The magazine's cover ruthlessly portrayed Senator Baker wearing a yellow dunce cap.[27] *Human Events*, no slacker in the ideological wars, was still running its own jihad against Baker. The newspaper was championing Kemp as Reagan's running mate.[28]

Human Events was not alone in backing Kemp. Many conservatives and most of the GOP's delegates wanted the former quarterback on the ticket. The independent group Republicans for Victory, organized by Jim Roberts and Bruce Eberle, had already raised $70,000 for its draft-Kemp effort, which included distributing bumper stickers, posters, and free copies of Kemp's book.[29] The group even opened up a storefront in Detroit to tout the young congressman for the ticket. Kemp worried that the grassroots effort might actually backfire and hurt his chances. He must have been surprised, then, when Bob Dole, a longtime skeptic of supply-side economics, spoke up in favor of Reagan's selecting Kemp for the ticket.[30]

Reagan liked Kemp a lot, and intellectually he was most comfortable with the New York congressman. Maybe it was their unusual backgrounds: as a former movie actor and pro football player, respectively, each man had to deal with those who doubted his intellectual capacity. Perhaps as a way to compensate for being thought of as a lightweight, both Reagan and Kemp read everything under the sun, especially on economics and political science. After the platform committee passed the huge tax-cut plan, Kemp proudly proclaimed, "This is a radical plan for us. Republicans can no longer be called conservatives. We are radical and I am proud of it."[31] Only a few, including the Gipper, understood the significance of what Kemp was saying.

Although Kemp was rumored to be a Reagan favorite, an insider told the *Washington Post* that the former quarterback was "too immature" for the ticket. George Bush, meanwhile, did not appeal to the Gipper himself—according to the insider, Reagan didn't think the Texan was "presidential"—but he was drawing the eye of many other Republicans.[32] Surprisingly, a handful of southern state Republican chairmen came out for Bush as the best choice for Reagan. Bush also got support from an even more unexpected quarter. The American Conservative Union held hearings in Washington to review the merits of potential running mates. Afterward, the attendees were surveyed, and Bush tied conservative favorite Bill Simon at 25 percent, one point ahead of Jack Kemp. It boded well for Bush that he had made so much headway with some in the Old Right and the New Right.[33]

Other candidates were in the mix. More and more attention was centering on the respected Richard Lugar of Indiana, a moderate-to-conservative senator who offended no one but whose public-speaking style put people to sleep. The joke running around in Reagan circles was "Most people think Lugar is a pistol, not a senator."[34] Lugar was also laboring with a millstone hung around his neck some years earlier, when he was mayor of Indianapolis: Nixon's henchmen had let it be known that Lugar was Nixon's "favorite mayor."[35] Lugar was still trying to recover.

On the eve of the convention, a leak to the *Los Angeles Times* said that Reagan had suddenly ruled out his old friend Paul Laxalt for the second slot.[36] It appeared that Reagan, despite his and his wife's affection and high regard for Laxalt, recognized that choosing the Nevadan would bring little if any political benefit to the ticket and could actually hurt in the general election because of his state's legal-ized gambling and prostitution.

Even with Laxalt out of the running, a number of prospects were still under consideration. One thing Reagan steadfastly refused to do was to have the pro-spective candidates trudge up the long road to his ranch in Santa Barbara for an embarrassing dog-and-pony show the way Carter had put everybody on his short list through an awkward display in Plains, Georgia, four years earlier. One of Reagan's goals was to maintain dignity for all.

Reagan insiders fretted over the seemingly slim pickings for the number-two slot. One told the *Washington Star*, "Is that all there is? There's got to be something better out there."[37]

Reagan himself betrayed doubts over at least some of the candidates. Stu Spencer saw this firsthand. It was just before the convention that Spencer came back aboard the Reagan campaign. Spencer noted that after all the old fights and animosities, the Reagans simply picked up the friendship where it had left off five years earlier. Reagan, though, was anything but pleasant when Spencer raised George Bush's name. "He just looked at me like I hit him in the stomach," Spencer later recalled. "He spent fifteen minutes jumping on George Bush."[38]

Spencer made a case for picking Bush, given the conservative nature of the plat-form, Bush's second-place finishes, and his impressive foreign-policy credentials.

Reagan only replied, "Hmmm, interesting, interesting."[39]

ON SUNDAY, JULY 13, Reagan, Nancy, his key staff, and several journalists flew into Los Angeles before his passage to Detroit the next day. As the plane nosed its way through the clouds, Reagan sat down to chat with the traveling reporters. One tried to bait him, asking whether he still believed, as he had charged years earlier, that a "progressive" income tax was the vile contrivance of Karl Marx. Reagan didn't bat an eye: "Well, it was. He was the first one who thought of it."[40]

Some of the newer members of the Reagan team were at cross-purposes with their boss. They kept telling reporters that Reagan was really "compassionate" and "kinder and gentler," but Reagan kept talking about Godless Communism and face-less bureaucrats. Confronted with the conflict, Reagan's new adman Peter Dailey suggested that it was simply a matter of trying to "change the speeches." Even at this late date, some of those around Reagan still thought he was an empty suit.[41] These underlings did not understand him.

Reagan's campaign staffing problems continued. Bill Casey had an organiza-tional chart in his office that showed the lines of communications flowing from staff through himself to Reagan, but everybody knew it was nonsense. Dick Allen, Marty Anderson, Lyn Nofziger, Dick Wirthlin, Mike Deaver, Peter Hannaford, and a couple of the others inside the bubble had direct access to Reagan. When they wanted to talk to him about something, they just stopped by his hotel suite or office, called him at home, or wandered up to the front of the plane. Some had this relationship with Reagan going back years and they weren't about to put up with some damned organizational chart.

THE REPUBLICAN CONVENTION OPENED in Detroit on Monday, July 14. The three networks estimated that more than forty million Americans would tune in, even though everybody knew what the outcome would be—or at least thought they knew the outcome. A GOP functionary, Ken Reitz, told reporters, "The whole idea is to make the event into a TV production instead of a convention."[42]

With the media swarming Detroit and so many millions tuning in on television, Mayor Coleman Young and city officials did all they could to put lipstick on their pig. The city's garbage and bus strikes were settled just before the convention opened. The remaining trash was picked up, potted plants lined the streets and interstates, graffiti were painted over, hoboes were given the bum's rush, potholes were filled in, and the marquees of X-rated movie theaters were covered over. Since hotel space was so limited in the Renaissance Center, many delegates and reporters found themselves in third-rate hotels in other parts of the city or in the suburbs—or even in another country, probably a first for an American political convention. Numerous attendees stayed across the river in the Canadian city, Windsor.

One thing Mayor Young and his officials couldn't control was the weather. The week of the GOP convention was hot and humid, and the afternoons were punctuated several times by violent thunderstorms. Still, Detroit did its best to entertain the visitors. The city allowed bars and restaurants to stay open until 4 A.M. to accommodate the GOP night owls. A madam thoughtfully offered to make her prostitutes available to the male conventioneers and even offered to throw in a "free sample" for the head of Detroit's finest. Another gentleman said he would use his divining rod to help the city find water, since he predicted that all the thirsty Republicans would cause the municipality to run out.[43] City officials declined both charitable offers.

None of these sideshows could distract Reagan from his mission. His acceptance speech would be the most important moment in his political life. He had a small lead over Carter, but at the same point four years earlier, Carter had enjoyed a much greater advantage over Ford and yet had almost lost on Election Day. The media were full of advice for Reagan. Lou Cannon offered this: "Reagan must demonstrate on . . . his acceptance speech Thursday, that he can reach beyond his standard rhetorical banquet fare and speak to the needs and aspirations of the nation." Cannon observed that Reagan "remains a vaguely out-of-date and somewhat stereotyped political figure in key sections of the northeast and Midwest."[44]

David Broder recognized that something bigger might be at stake than just another election. Broder wrote, "Ronald Reagan began his political life as a 21-year-old follower of Democrat Franklin Delano Roosevelt. Now there are sober people who think Reagan, at age 69, might become the FDR of a born-again Republican Party."[45]

Peter Hannaford, a Reagan favorite, was hard at work on drafting the acceptance address, but as with everything else the Gipper said in speeches, commentaries, or his columns, the final work would be pure Reagan. And Reagan knew what he had to do.

FOR THE FIRST TIME in years, the GOP was earning praise in the media. Many had grown weary of the holier-than-thou Carter and his tired, run-down Democratic Party, but they were equally impressed that the Grand Old Party had become a Brand New Party with a coherent philosophy, confidence, and the will to win. The stench of Watergate had been vented. Most of the old, creaky alliances of convenience were gone. Regional differences still existed, but far less so than in years past.

Behaviorally and attitudinally, the party was in many ways one big extended family. There were fights, to be sure, but blood loyalty kept the fights in the family. Liberals in an increasingly conservative party were not gone, but those left knew to keep their mouths shut or mouth the party line if they wanted to take part in the spoils of victory.

Consequently, Reagan arrived in Detroit without the burden of having to make the type of deals many of his predecessors had been forced to make. In 1952 Eisenhower had to pick Richard Nixon to placate the anti-Communist elements in the party. In 1960 Vice President Nixon humiliated himself by detouring from the GOP convention to pay homage—and make concessions—to Governor Nelson Rockefeller of New York, the prince of the East Coast establishment. The agreement between the two became known infamously as the "Compact of Fifth Avenue," but Barry Goldwater acidly referred to it as the "Munich of the Republican Party."[46] Goldwater himself failed to make any deals in San Francisco four years later, and thus liberal Republicans ran for the hills. In 1968 Nixon made many deals but broke all of them, and with them the hearts of Republicans. In

1976 Ford chose Bob Dole as his running mate to try to appease the conservatives who had nearly given the nomination to Reagan.

Reagan was freed of the petty, sail-trimming politics that had bedeviled the GOP men who went before him. He was assuming command of a party that had mostly grown to adore him. He was a politician, like the others, but he was also about to take the helm of a new GOP, unbattered, unbowed, unencumbered by political deal-making. One delegate from Arkansas hand-lettered a sign for her convention boater that simply and pointedly read, "This Time."[47]

In a sense, Reagan benefited from his party's lackluster recent history. Whereas the Democrats were struggling to live up to the legacy of Franklin Roosevelt, John Kennedy, Bobby Kennedy, and other leading lights, the Republicans of recent years had only the demon-haunted Nixon, the kind but accidental Ford, and the hands-off Eisenhower. These GOP leaders were not giants; they seemed to hold on to power only to deny it to the Democrats, not because they sought to do anything bold or great.

Ronald Reagan, in contrast, had a bold agenda, a plan for his presidency and for his country. Before he could achieve that plan, he needed to inspire his own party—the conservatives and the moderates, the social conservatives and the sociable conservatives. In Detroit, he would bring them all together for a big prayerful hootenanny.

Or so he hoped.

23

AT CENTER STAGE

"There are always brush fires in politics."

Gerald Ford appeared on ABC's *Issues and Answers* the Sunday before the proceedings began in Detroit and was forced once again to knock down the rumors that he would be Ronald Reagan's choice for the ticket. He was as Shermanesque as possible, saying, "Under no circumstances would I be the candidate for the vice presidency." Ford then praised George Bush to the heavens, calling him "very attractive, very dedicated, experienced."[1] Ford's denial was a page-one story in newspapers across the country.

Ford had ruled himself out, Howard Baker was being ruled out by conservatives, and Reagan was truly stymied. The redoubtable Tommy Thomas, Reagan's state leader in Florida, was adamant that Reagan not take Bush, who he believed was "part of a liberal Republican 'conspiracy' to take control of the government."[2] Even the most optimistic of Bush's men were dubious that he'd be picked.

Reagan seemed to be publicly talking himself out of choosing Bush. He told the *Los Angeles Times*, "I think there's something cynical in choosing someone of a different political view than your own with the idea in mind of getting votes. I think your choice should be based on who do you feel could be a President if he had to be."[3] Reagan was still miffed at Bush over "voodoo economics" and other offenses, as well as Bush's poor performance at the Nashua debate.

He had shown just how miffed, days before the Detroit convention in a private meeting with field staff. Most members of the staff were for Jack Kemp as running mate, but when asked his opinion, Don Devine, the campaign's political director for Maryland, voiced his opinion that Reagan should choose Bush. Devine told the candidate, "I gotta lot of problems with Bush myself, ideologically, but I think we need to do that . . ." Before Devine could finish, Reagan stormed, "I'll never choose that man; he lied about my record!" The meeting ended abruptly as Reagan stormed out. Devine was "scared shitless," he remembered in an interview. According to Devine, Frank Donatelli, another field director, later told him privately, "Thank God you did it, because I was going to say the same thing and you got yelled at!"[4]

In choosing a running mate, Reagan needed someone who was qualified and was comfortable with his conservatism but who could also reach out to the dwindling moderates in the party and unify the convention while earning the respect of the national media. And given Reagan's age, he needed someone who could step into the role of president. Eight VPs in American history had been required to assume the presidency. Reagan was mindful of what the first vice president, John Adams, had said. "I am Vice President. In this I am nothing. But I may be everything."[5]

Reagan wanted to be certain that there were no embarrassments or hiccups of the sort that vice-presidential nominees had created in the past. Four years earlier, Bob Dole had embarrassed Ford by talking about "Democrat Wars" and generally ignoring the demands of the national campaign office.[6] Typically, Dole would get on his plane, throw away the schedule, point in a given direction, and tell the pilot to go that way.

Too often, there had been a slapstick quality to the selection of the second man for the ticket. The very first political convention, 1832, was not even for the purpose of selecting a president; it was for dumping a vice president. President Andrew Jackson couldn't wait to get rid of John C. Calhoun and replace him with Martin Van Buren.

In 1900 Teddy Roosevelt was put on the ticket with William McKinley mainly because he had become such a pain to the New York GOP party bosses that they hoped he would never be heard from again. To their dismay, McKinley was assassinated in 1901 and they heard far too much for far too long from the old Rough Rider. The office had opened in the first place only when McKinley's first vice president, Garret Augustus Hobart—who was a threat to no one except an open bar and a free buffet—literally partied himself to death. As one writer recounted, Hobart "went to six dinner parties and a dozen receptions a week. He died in office, some say the first politician to be killed by the Washington social scene."[7]

In 1960, in an eleventh-hour deal in Los Angeles, John F. Kennedy offered the vice presidency as a conciliatory gesture to his main opponent, Lyndon Johnson. JFK needed Johnson's support in the general election but assumed that the proud Texan would turn him down. To his and his brother Bobby's consternation,

LBJ said yes—and then tearfully refused to step aside when the Kennedy camp tried to get him to do so.

In 1964 Barry Goldwater selected little-known conservative congressman William Miller from upstate New York because he "bugged" Lyndon Johnson.

A famous Hubert Humphrey campaign ad in 1968 targeted Richard Nixon's running mate, the little-known Spiro Agnew. The commercial's soundtrack featured nothing but a man's nonstop, derisive laughter at the prospect of Agnew as VP. Later Agnew set a new standard for embarrassment, as far as the Washington establishment was concerned.

And, of course, in 1972 George McGovern went through a comedy of errors because his campaign failed to look carefully into running mate Tom Eagleton's history of severe mental health problems.

Reagan was intent on avoiding such pitfalls. A press conference was scheduled for 11 A.M. on Thursday morning to make the announcement. He wanted this thing to go smooth as silk.

Right.

REAGAN OFTEN JOKED THAT in his Hollywood days, he made some pretty bad movies, which "didn't have to be made well, they had to be made by Thursday." This time he would have plenty of time to prepare for an audience of thousands in Detroit and millions across America. This performance, though, would be live. There would be no directors yelling "cut." He had to get it right on the first take. The media understood the importance of his acceptance speech. "Most of the national television audience," the New York Times observed, "has never heard him give [a] speech."[8]

To espouse his statecraft, Reagan would first need great stagecraft. Detroit's Joe Louis Arena would help give him that. The visuals looked terrific, with the speaker's platform high above the convention floor. The platform, a deep blue half circle, boasted the convention's slogan in huge letters across the front: "Together . . . A New Beginning." Splayed under the motto was a sea of red and white carnations. On either side of the stage were two huge American flags, the thirteen-star flag on the left and the fifty-star flag on the right. The lighting and the camera work, though maybe not up to Hollywood standards, would be sufficient for Reagan's purposes.

The rest was up to the Gipper. The old trouper had always known when to manfully leave the stage, but he also took pride in knowing how to gracefully make an entrance.

CONSERVATIVES COULD SCARCELY BELIEVE it. At last, their man, Reagan, was about to become the GOP nominee. Some bitterly remembered how their first hero—Senator Robert Taft of Ohio—had, in their view, been robbed of the nomination in 1952. Forces supporting Dwight Eisenhower challenged the seating credentials of some southern delegates supporting Taft, who were then replaced with delegates for Ike. Conservative boos rained down on Eisenhower's forces, especially New York governor Tom Dewey. In 1956 conservatives may even have cheered Democrat Frank G. Clement, governor of Tennessee, who blasted Republicans for choosing as their standard bearer a general "who didn't know up till that time whether he was a Democrat or a Republican" instead of "their logical leader from Ohio."[9]

True Believers were never completely enamored of Richard Nixon and would have been even less so had they known that he'd maneuvered behind the scenes to cut the legs out from under Taft in Chicago. They went along in 1960, although a number of conservatives quietly voted for Kennedy because he came off as far more anti-Communist, especially when it came to Castro's Cuba and the supposed "missile gap" with the Soviets. (The old soldier Eisenhower was annoyed with Kennedy, knowing that in reality there was no missile gap.)

Barry Goldwater was the Right's real first love. When conservatives temporarily seized control of the party at the Cow Palace in San Francisco in 1964, they ironically joined in with Eisenhower as he attacked the media; the conservative delegates turned and shook their fists and shrieked at the press section in the hall.

In 1968 Nixon convinced much of the conservative movement, including the exuberantly polysyllabic Bill Buckley, that he'd learned his lesson, that he was one of them and would govern as a conservative. Within a matter of weeks of his inaugural, Nixon was careening off on a binge of liberal policies that eventually included wage and price controls, détente, and overtures to Communist China. Conservatives grumbled and, in 1972, fielded a sacrificial lamb, Congressman John Ashbrook, in the primaries. Nixon waxed the conservative.

Nineteen seventy-six was a magnificent, memorable, messy, and thrilling roller coaster ride for the conservatives. Gerald Ford had never been one of theirs, going back to his days in the House of Representatives. When conservatives met in Washington, certain members of Congress had to be present to make the meeting meaningful—Goldwater, Senator Everett Dirksen, Ashbrook, others—but no one ever thought that Ford's presence was necessary. So when he became president in August 1974, the conservatives had nothing invested in Ford, because he had nothing invested in them. They were free to criticize his administration, which they did with relish. That led to the extraordinary insurgent campaign of Ronald Reagan in 1976.

The campaign, Citizens for Reagan, was a splendidly haphazard and rollicking movable feast, one day brilliant, another day bungling, but with few exceptions, the staffers were devoted to one another and venerated their man Reagan. Friendships developed that lasted a lifetime among the overworked and underpaid campaign crew. So on the last night of the 1976 convention in Kansas City, when Reagan gave his memorable, bittersweet, touching, and heartrending comments, upstaging Ford, there wasn't a dry eye among his followers. "I felt torn apart, just tragic," said Cynthia Bunnell, a 1980 Reagan delegate from California, about the 1976 convention.[10]

But the losing quest had left a legacy upon which to build a movement and rebuild a party. Conservatives flocked to Reagan's banner in 1980. One young woman, Michele Davis, was offered other jobs in other campaigns for far more money, but she decided, "I want to follow this guy. He's got that special something that makes me feel like we've actually got a chance. Let's go!"[11] Now this hardy and growing band of conservatives felt utterly and completely vindicated. After Goldwater's loss in 1964, the mantra among conservatives was: twenty-seven million people could not all be wrong. Sixteen years later, these conservatives stood atop the GOP. "The ideas that were frighteningly radical when Barry Goldwater espoused them in 1964 are what is called moderate conservatism today," wrote Jack Germond. "The notion that the government can be an effective agent for citizens has been challenged across the ideological spectrum."[12]

The conservatives had taken over the Republican Party in a bloodless coup, and the country was becoming more conservative as government was failing at almost every level. Sometimes it was hard to believe. Sometimes they had to pinch themselves. It seemed as if they'd always been in the minority, as if they had always been derided. They had heard all the shopworn jokes about meeting in phone booths, or been reminded of the smug proclamations of Lionel Trilling, a sanctimonious liberal who years earlier had sniffed in his book *The Liberal Imagination* that conservatism was irrelevant, just a rash of "irritable mental gestures."[13] Trilling died in 1975, coincidentally as liberalism's decline and conservatism's ascendancy were accelerating.

The contributions of Buckley and *National Review* could not be underestimated in the growth of conservatism. From the 1950s right up to the impending nomination of Reagan, Buckley, his message, and his magazine had been a beacon of brilliant light slicing through a fog of ignorance and incoherency. Buckley was every conservative's hero. He made conservatives feel intelligent, and beat back the dyspeptic prattling of liberals such as Trilling. Every man admired his breezy style, his writings, his wit, his urbane and laid-back manner, and his many interests. Women admired him as well and he was in many ways the movement's first sex symbol. Buckley certainly made it "cool" to be a conservative. He was a true Renaissance man, a swashbuckler who sailed the Atlantic. He admonished his young son, Chris, that "industry is the enemy of melancholy."

This new movement also contained a healthy dose of elements of the Christian Right. "The white, right, born-again faithful, once safe in the fold of Jimmy Carter, or abstaining from the deviltry of politics altogether, are flocking to the Republican mother church this year where they feel they have a friend in Ronald Reagan," the *Washington Post* rightly noted.[14] Jerry Falwell's Moral Majority had taken over or exerted considerable influence in a number of state Republican parties. Reaganites now held sway over nearly every element of the GOP.

The remaining moderates and liberals in the Republican Party were reduced to sitting around the Salamandre Bar in Detroit, literally crying into their beer. Their drinking establishment, one reporter wrote, "is dimly lit, which puts it in marked contrast to the moderate Republican national committeeman who, at 1:15 A.M., is well lit."[15] The tables had turned for the moderates in the party, and they were decidedly unhappy.

Someone else who was miffed over being left behind was Reagan's former campaign manager, John Sears. He wrote a scathing piece for the *Washington Post* essentially dismissing Reagan as a lightweight who was a creation of his staff. The candidate "simply looks to someone to tell him what to do," Sears claimed.[16]

THE FIRST DAY OF the convention began only two minutes behind schedule. Bill Brock used an oversized gavel to bang the hall to attention. After the call to order, Pat Boone led the delegates in the Pledge of Allegiance. (The next night, Tuesday, a U.S. Marine veteran of the Vietnam War named James Webb would lead the delegates in the Pledge.) Glen Campbell and Tanya Tucker sang "The Star-Spangled Banner." Brock got down to party business—the roll of states, the election of temporary convention officers, and the adoption of rules.[17]

Later in the morning, Senator Richard Lugar spoke. Delegates were still arriving, checking into their hotels and meandering over to Joe Louis Arena for the pro forma session. Being handed such a lousy speaking slot, well out of the glare of prime-time coverage, was a sure sign that Lugar was off the list of potential running mates. Bob Dole was on the floor and quipped to a reporter, "Poor Lugar. [He's] up there speaking and really wondering if his phone is ringing right now."[18]

Two others cited as VP possibilities, Don Rumsfeld and Bill Simon, scored prime-time speeches that night. But like Lugar, both had dropped down considerably on the veep list kept by the "Great Mentioner"—a.k.a. the national media.

The entertainment the Republicans rolled out was better than the Lawrence Welk fare of previous conventions, although they could have used a George Jones or Johnny Cash in Detroit. It featured Donnie and Marie Osmond, Vikki Carr, Dorothy Hamill, Richard Petty, Ginger Rogers, Jimmy Stewart, Michael Landon, Wayne Newton, and several others.[19] The television critic at the *New York Times* couldn't resist a shot: "There is no need to switch channels in search of an old movie."[20]

On Monday afternoon, "Commitment '80" was announced: a massive door-knocking operation that would involve as many as half a million grassroots Republicans in the fall. The goal was to take maximum advantage of the thousands upon thousands of the Gipper's fans. The plan was enormously ambitious, with video-tape pitches from Reagan and his running mate as well as from Brock, simultaneous meetings in three hundred locations coordinated by satellite downlinks, phone conference call-ins, and direct mail. It was back to the future for the GOP, which for too long had eschewed the shoe-leather politics that was so vital in campaigns. Brock had appointed a drawling and effective Virginian, Dennis Whitfield, to supervise the massive affair.[21]

Two independent groups held press conferences in Detroit that day to announce specific plans for independent expenditure campaigns in support of Reagan in the fall election. Terry Dolan, head of the National Conservative Political Action Committee (NCPAC), previewed ten commercials for the media, some praising Reagan but most blasting Carter. Dolan, as always, made grandiose announcements and then left the details to underlings.[22] The fundraising for the NCPAC's campaign fell on the shoulders of a young conservative, L. Brent Bozell III.[23]

Bozell, a chain smoker with a thatch of red hair and matching red beard, was the son of one of the seminal writers and thinkers in the early days of the conservative movement. The elder Bozell had ghostwritten *The Conscience of a Conservative* for Barry Goldwater. Young Brent's mother was the sister of Bill and Jim Buckley, which meant he grew up reading not *Spiderman* and *Batman* but *National Review* and the *Pink Sheet on the Left*, and being bounced on the knee of some of the most important political leaders of the Right, including "Uncle Bill."

Despite that pedigree, young Bozell was modest and down-to-earth, never lording his kinship over others. He was also a hell-raiser who would have been more comfortable organizing a party at Delta House than hanging with some of the more stuffy elements of the conservative movement. He was one of ten children and their mother, Patricia, did not so much raise them as simply take attendance. She was herself one of best writers and editors in politics.[24]

That the conservative movement was already deep into a second generation of activists and leaders was a testament to its durability and staying power. Conservatives weren't going anywhere.

GOVERNOR REAGAN AND NANCY arrived at the Detroit Plaza Hotel at 3:30 on Monday afternoon. The pair looked great. Deeply suntanned, Reagan was wearing blue pants and a creamy colored tropical sports jacket, while Mrs. Reagan was positively radiant in a Chanel suit. They were greeted by banners that read "Viva Reagan" and "Enough of Carter,"[25] as a throng of enthusiastic supporters standing on balconies and stairways cheered, "Rea-gan! Rea-gan!" He quipped, "Are you sure there's a room left for me?"[26] The crowd roared in the affirmative. He then told the crowd that he'd had a dream in which "Carter came to me and asked why I wanted his job. I told him I didn't want his job. I want to be president!"[27]

Reagan was having fun, but he turned serious when he told the Republicans, "All of us know why we're here—the need for a crusade in this country today . . . a crusade to make America great again."[28]

A day at a convention would not be complete without trouble and squawking interest groups, and this day was no exception. Reagan's men had to beat back an attempt by "bitter-ender" conservatives to get Henry Kissinger thrown off the program for the next night. On cue, four thousand protesters organized by the National Organization for Women (NOW) took to the streets for the Equal Rights Amendment (ERA), and the national media were there to dutifully record the event. Reagan also had to meet with black Republicans and female Republicans to hold their hands—with women over the ERA and with blacks over the lack of high-profile African-Americans on the campaign staff.[29] He was philosophical about the flare-ups, though. "There are always brush fires in politics," he muttered.[30]

That evening, Reagan attended a small reception and offered the group his definitions of liberalism and conservatism: "A conservative is a fellow that if he sees someone drowning, will throw him a rope that's too short and tell him that it would be good for his character to swim for it. A liberal will throw him a rope that's long enough, but when he gets hold of it he'll drop his end and go away to look for someone else to help."[31]

Reagan's four children were meeting up in Detroit. As with all conventions on both sides of the aisles, the national media devoted long personal stories to the candidate, and his wife and children. Charitably, Reagan's children in 1980 were "finding themselves," to use a popular phrase of the era. The two older children, Michael and Maureen, were in their thirties, both already divorced and both college dropouts. Michael was officially in boat sales and periodically raced speed-boats. Maureen had tried a career in acting but it hadn't come to much, but both were enthusiastically helping their father. They were the products of Reagan's first marriage to actress Jane Wyman, though Michael had been adopted. After the divorce, both stayed close to their mother and tried to stay close to their father, but he was in the process of a second marriage, to Nancy, and now had two more children, Patti and Ron—whom his father called "Skipper," which young Ron hated. Michael and Maureen were far more interested in their father's politics and political career than the younger two, whose politics skewed left.

No one can ever really know the inner workings of a family, and the Reagan family was no different. What was clear was that the two elder and the two younger Reagan children were mostly indifferent to each other.

For the sake of family unity, not to mention party unity, the four Reagan children met up in Detroit to root for their father. None of the four, however, flew out on the chartered plane with their parents. All took commercial flights instead.[32]

MONDAY'S HIGHLIGHT WAS THE prime-time speech by former president Ford. He and Reagan were never terribly fond of each other, but Ford detested Carter, and at the end of the day he was a party man, ready to support even the man he believed had cost him the election four years earlier. Ford, who had once been at best a mediocre public speaker, had become pretty good on the stump since leaving the White House. The confidence of becoming a beloved elder statesman surely helped, but when it came to Carter and the Democrats, he needed little motivation. Ford ripped into Carter. The Georgian had "sold America short," he said. He went on, "You've heard all Carter's alibis. . . . We must lower our expectations. We must be realistic. We must prudently retreat. Baloney!"[33] Ford concluded by telling the Republicans something they hadn't heard in a while: "Let's start talking like winners and being winners."[34]

Joe Louis Arena went wild. Delegates were hanging from the balconies, whooping and cheering for their now adored "Jerry."

Earlier in the day, Ford had met with Reagan, and once again the subject of his going on the ticket had come up. In their meeting, Ford specifically questioned the qualifications of Lugar, Kemp, and Bill Simon. So Reagan and some of his men perked up that night when Ford told the thousands of devoted Republicans, "I am not ready to quit yet," and that when the GOP fields "the team for Governor Reagan, count me in." Maybe Ford had changed his mind after all about being on the ticket.[35]

Reagan and Ford met in private again on Tuesday. During the hour-long meeting on the sixty-ninth floor of the Detroit Plaza, they spoke once more about the vice-presidential slot. Ford was dubious, but this time he did not reject the idea out of hand. Rumors began to build in Detroit that the Dream Ticket was possible.[36]

Bush, knowing his tenuous position with the Reagans, wisely decided to do nothing to look as if he was campaigning to be vice president. He would stay above the fray, let the others go through their machinations. Strict orders went out to his supporters: no one was to organize for Bush.

TUESDAY'S PROCEEDINGS BEGAN PROMPTLY at 5 P.M., but the convention quickly fell behind schedule.

The party's 40,000-word platform was adopted with little discussion. It was the longest platform in GOP history, but it passed with far less drama than the one in Kansas City four years earlier.[37] Kansas City had been a bloodbath, with fights over détente, the Panama Canal, and Henry Kissinger. This time, the only hiccup occurred when the delegation from Hawaii moved for a suspension of the rules so a debate could be held over the ERA's removal. But the Hawaiians failed to get another delegation to second their motion, and that was that.[38] Marty Anderson and the rest of the Reaganites were thrilled.

Tuesday's speaking schedule was laden with Republican heavyweights. Speakers included Jack Kemp; Senator John Warner of Virginia, considered a talented up-and-comer, and the subject of much media attention because of his marriage to actress Elizabeth Taylor; John Connally, who was always good for a stem-winder; Barry Goldwater, who still made the hearts of conservatives go atwitter; and, sandwiched in among all these conservatives, lonesome Henry Kissinger.

In addition to all that, Guy Vander Jagt was scheduled to deliver the convention's keynote address. Vander Jagt had been the 1953 national debate champ in college, and with his dulcet voice he could transfix a room. Most good politicians could give short extemporaneous remarks, but Vander Jagt was from the old school, the really old school: he delivered even his longest speeches from memory.

Vander Jagt prepared for this speech diligently, in no small part because he believed he was auditioning to be Reagan's running mate. He was never seriously considered.[39]

There was nothing fundamentally wrong with Vander Jagt's going on the ticket with Reagan. He was conservative enough, was an excellent campaigner, and had IOUs built up from here to Kingdom Come. True, he was rumored to have a wandering eye, but many men in politics had as much said about them. His big problem, it seemed, was that he had received bad advice from his staff about becoming Reagan's running mate. He seemed to want it too badly. Just weeks before the convention, Vander Jagt shucked the steel-rimmed glasses he'd worn for years and switched to contact lenses. He also produced a slim self-published book that did not go over well with some of the Reaganites.

MRS. REAGAN MADE HER first appearance before the convention Tuesday evening, looking lovely in a white dress. The delegates warmly welcomed her. The rumors all over the convention were that she was stridently opposed to Bush's joining "Ronnie" on the ticket.[40] As always, Bob Novak and Rowly Evans had the inside dope. "[Reagan] and Nancy Reagan have made clear to their aides that they simply do not think Bush is up to the presidency," they wrote. "That judgment, highly colored by Bush's performance in New Hampshire, seems an ineradicable mind set."[40] Deep down, the Reagans insistently wanted Laxalt as the Gipper's veep—especially Mrs. Reagan. Just as insistently, they were being told no by Reagan's men.

THE CONVENTION CROWD WAS energized when Goldwater was introduced by his son, Barry Jr., a congressman from California whose jawline was even more pronounced than his father's. "In our hearts, we knew he was right," the son told the delighted crowd, playing on the campaign's slogan in 1964. Junior elaborated: "A prophet in his own time? You're damn right!"[42]

The seventy-one-year-old senator, who was locked in a tight race for reelection in Arizona, took to the stage. Barry did not disappoint. He jokingly asked the crowd whether he could accept their nomination and they cheered. At one point, Goldwater departed from his prepared text to tell the sweaty delegates that the arena was "the hottest damn place I've been all year."[43] Some things never changed.

Goldwater admonished the conservatives at the convention to do "less carping" and refrain from "thousands of interpretations of morality and conservatism."[44] It was vintage Goldwater. Twenty years earlier he told conservatives they needed to "grow up."

But the carping and fighting that Goldwater warned against would never die completely. The New York delegates asked for a way to memorialize Nelson Rockefeller, who had died a year earlier, but they were rebuffed by convention officials. Conservatives had waited for years to dance on Rocky's grave and now—finally—they were.[45]

Following Goldwater on the dais was another Arizonan, House Minority Leader John Rhodes, who had been installed as permanent chairman of the convention. Rhodes gave an uncharacteristically thunderous speech that accused Carter of playing politics with the American hostages in Iran.[46]

Jack Kemp spoke afterward, as the proceedings continued to fall behind. He was greeted with a sea of printed signs that read "Reagan-Kemp" and a giant banner that proclaimed "Jack Kemp—the GOP's No. 1 Draft Choice."[47] Kemp was proud of his football career, but even he sometimes got sick of the gridiron analogies.

Spot surveys of the Virginia, Washington State, Oklahoma, and Arizona delegations showed support for Kemp as the running mate. Meanwhile, Bush was getting support from some key delegations, including, surprisingly, the conservative delegations of Alabama and Idaho. NBC had surveyed 77 percent of the conventioneers and Bush was preferred with 47 percent to Kemp's 35 percent.[48] Reagan had doubts about the youthful Kemp. "Reagan himself has never been convinced that he had the weight of experience or ability to be a president," reported Jack Germond.[49]

Lugar had fallen badly off the pace, especially after his bland speech on Monday. One Reagan aide quipped, "The best thing that happened to Lugar was that Reagan was flying to Detroit at the time and didn't see it." Caspar Weinberger was asked his opinion of Don Rumsfeld's going on the ticket with Reagan and minced no words, saying, "He's a pretty abrasive fellow and he's no admirer" of Reagan's.[50] George Romney, the former governor of Michigan, weighed in with his own blunt opinion: "Reagan's got two problems. He's an amateur with no experience in Washington. And he's ultraconservative. Ford would answer both questions. It would sweep the convention. If he doesn't take Ford, he better take Bush or he'll be in trouble."[51] Just as emphatically, however, Jesse Helms and other conservatives were still vowing publicly to stop Bush from going on the ticket. The vice-presidential issue was spinning out of control.

With Jack Kemp attracting so much attention in Detroit, some of his enemies began recycling nasty rumors about him that had sprung up in 1967. That year the native Californian Kemp, then the quarterback for the Buffalo Bills, had interned in the offices of Governor Reagan in Sacramento. Columnist Drew Pearson, who was always on the hunt for misinformation, exposed a homosexual "ring" (two men on Reagan's staff). An unnamed "athlete" was also mentioned in the scurrilous column. The two men were fired from the governor's staff and faded into obscurity. Kemp went back to his job as quarterback of the Bills.[52] Not long thereafter Bill Buckley founded the National Committee to Horsewhip Drew Pearson. Pearson was the bane of every conservative's existence.

The issue faded until late 1978, when columnist Bob Novak discovered top Carter aides, including DNC chairman John White, spreading the ancient rumors about Kemp. White told Novak that he'd heard about it from another reporter, who in turn said he'd been told by a high White House aide. Novak queried Lyn

Nofziger, who had handled the investigation into the scandal in 1967. Nofziger told the columnist that Kemp was not involved, and that in his opinion Kemp was not gay. Novak even went to San Francisco to track down one of the men fired years earlier and asked him point-blank whether Kemp had been involved. The man replied in no uncertain terms that Kemp was not involved. Novak wrote a column detailing the smear campaign against Kemp in December 1978, and the issue faded again until Detroit.[53]

Anybody who knew Kemp knew the whole thing was nonsense. Kemp liked women and women liked Kemp. Nevertheless, as Reagan approached decision hour on his running mate, the rumors were back in circulation.

WHEN HENRY KISSINGER SPOKE near midnight, the word had already been spread throughout the hall to please not boo him and embarrass the party, the convention, or Reagan. Some of Jesse Helms's supporters had threatened an anti-Kissinger demonstration on the floor of the convention, but cooler heads prevailed. One Helmsite astonishingly told the *Washington Post* that "this is 'a unity convention.'"[54] Then hell froze over.

Kissinger was not lustily cheered, but he was surprisingly well received by the red-meat conservatives. He called Reagan the "trustee of all our hopes" and later self-deprecatingly joked at his ability to unite people, as liberals and conservatives alike had booed him.[55]

The convention was now running two hours behind. Try as he might to get Vander Jagt on in prime time, John Rhodes was unable to do so. The idea had been suggested to get Kissinger to go last, but no one had the energy to take on Kissinger and his ego.[56]

The hour was extremely late, and there were still parties to get to, a lot of drinking to be done, gossip to exchange. The delegates had been listening to speeches and introductions for more than seven hours, and they were on tilt. Even these fanatical Republicans and conservatives could take only so much speechifying. Those delegates still on the floor were restless. One put a sign on her chair, "Wake me at 9:30."[57]

And yet there were still other speakers to go. A former Reagan basher, Richard "Rosey" Rosenbaum of New York, was in Detroit to support the nominee. No GOP cavalcade of the era was complete without the towering, bald old Rockefeller retainer. His rendition of "Ronnie Reagan!" in his high-pitched voice made people double over with laughter. Rosenbaum, a liberal Republican through and through, had been a hate figure to Reaganites four years earlier, but this time around he had signed on with Reagan. And he wasn't anything if he wasn't effective. A wizard at organization and fundraising, he had helped the naïve Reaganites navigate through the moderate backwaters of New York Republican politics. Rosey had done such a good job that he was asked to give one of the seconding speeches for Reagan.[58]

There was even a surprise last-minute addition to the already-heavy speaking schedule. The 121 black Republican delegates had come up with the brainstorm of inviting the president of the NAACP, Benjamin Hooks, whose annual conference Reagan had missed several weeks earlier. Now was a chance for some real fence mending. Though the black delegates had to threaten a symbolic walkout to make their point, when their idea got through to the Gipper, he embraced it immediately.[59]

Hooks was given twenty minutes to speak. He was received politely if not wildly, and the delegates even interrupted him several times with a smattering of applause. Hooks—given the fact that Reagan had skipped his conference—could have justifiably leveled Reagan, but he decided to take the high road. When asked by reporters whether Reagan had written off the black vote, Hooks dismissed the idea: "I don't believe he has written off any vote."[60]

Prime time had ended hours before. So convention planners were forced to move Vander Jagt's keynote address—again. The Michigan congressman had already been bumped from Monday night, the traditional slot for the keynote address. Now he would be pushed back to Wednesday.[61] While the GOP was showing more unity than it had in years, the convention was not turning out to be the smooth operation that the Reagan campaign had imagined. And the woes would quickly intensify.

More worrisome for Reagan than the schedule changes was the incessant prattling about a Dream Ticket, with Gerald Ford starring as Reagan's sidekick. In the movies, Reagan had often been the classic sidekick who critics said never got the girl—although the Gipper sometimes complained that this characterization wasn't true: he almost *always* got the girl. Now some, including Reagan, thought that he ought to try to get the former president.

Yet what would start out in Detroit as a "dream" would end up very quickly as a nightmare for Dutch Reagan. Reagan was about to be reminded of the old saw "Be careful what you wish for."

24

Motown Madness

"We heard from Senator Schweiker that Senator Laxalt told someone else who then told Senator Schweiker that it would be Gerald Ford."

After the 1924 Democratic convention, which notoriously went to 103 ballots over sixteen days before choosing John W. Davis of West Virginia, satirist H. L. Mencken had had enough and wrote, "There is something about a national convention that makes it as fascinating as a revival or a hanging. It is vulgar, it is ugly, it is stupid, it is tedious, it's hard upon both the higher cerebral centers and the *gluteus maximus*, and yet it is somehow charming. One sits through long sessions wishing heartily that all the delegates were dead and in hell—and then suddenly there comes a show so gaudy and hilarious, so melodramatic and obscene, so unimaginably exhilarating and preposterous that one lives a gorgeous year in an hour."[1]

On Wednesday, July 16, 1980, the Republican National Convention put Mencken's disparagement of conventions to shame, though no one would be sitting on his keister this day. You couldn't gossip sitting down.

The grand old man of the *Wall Street Journal*, the wonderfully named Vermont Connecticut Royster, reflected the widespread sentiment that the GOP convention had so far been a dull affair. There were no fights like in the old days over rules or platforms or "over the vice-presidential choice," he wrote. But Royster, a perceptive political observer who had won two Pulitzer Prizes, noted toward the end of his column that it was possible Reagan "could shoot himself in the foot with his vice-presidential nominee."[2]

As the sun rose over Detroit's boarded-up slums and shuttered factories on July 16, the buzz was growing about the Dream Ticket of Ronald Reagan and Gerald

Ford. The gossip had been stoked by a Bill Plante report on CBS several nights earlier. Plante ran through the list of prospective running mates and concluded, "Everyone does agree . . . around here, that the Dream Ticket would have been Ronald Reagan and Gerald Ford. And that rumor surfaced again today."[3] A pretty young Reagan aide, Michele Davis, wrote in her diary, "We are all abuzz about the Ford rumors. . . . I think it's nuts." As it turned out, she was way ahead of the gray heads at the convention. (She also had strong opinions about the "fatcats" she had to babysit there, calling them "obnoxious, boorish assholes.")[4]

The Reagan team let it leak that morning that Howard Baker could help Reagan more by staying in the Senate. Loosely translated, it meant Baker had been officially dumped from consideration. Actually, Baker had appeared on *Face the Nation* several weeks earlier and disavowed any interest in the job. Within the Reagan campaign, Senator Baker already had his opponents, notably including Paul Laxalt; it was rumored that the two senators did not get along. After the *Face the Nation* appearance, Reagan called his old friend Baker to tell him he was taking him at his word, and Baker assured Reagan that if he was asked, he'd join the ticket, but otherwise, he wasn't interested. Baker had begun to gently close the door and Reagan helped him do so. Word never leaked out—astonishing in politics—until the convention.[5]

Throwing Baker over the side was a tactical mistake by the Reagan forces. With Howard Baker out, conservatives such as Jesse Helms could concentrate their fire on George Bush. Even Helms now said—amazingly—he could "live with a Reagan-Ford ticket."[6] Helms went even further, saying he preferred that pairing to a "Reagan-Helms" ticket.[7]

That was it. Reagan's men got the ideological cover they needed to seriously negotiate with Ford. Reagan was seeking "a good reason to pick somebody else," not Bush, according to the *Washington Star*, and that somebody else was starting to look like it could be Ford.[8] Among Reagan's men, there had been no consensus candidate save maybe Jack Kemp, and this vacuum also sucked people in toward Ford.

According to Dick Wirthlin, the idea of asking Ford was never meant to be a serious proposal. Wirthlin and Bob Teeter cooked it up, he said years later, as a sign of good faith on Reagan's part. Wirthlin and Teeter expected Ford to graciously turn down the offer, and that would be it.[9] Among Reaganites, the consensus was definitely against Bush. As Jim Baker saw it, it was "ABB—Anybody But Bush."[10] Reagan's men were narrowing down the list quickly, and it seemed there were no good alternatives to Ford.

When the name of the arrogant and manifestly ambitious Don Rumsfeld came up in one meeting of Reaganites, Lyn Nofziger bitingly said, "Rummy would be fine, but you realize we'll have to hire a food taster for Reagan!"[11] Rumsfeld was winnowed along with Dick Lugar and Bill Simon.

Laxalt's name kept coming up, because the Reagans wouldn't let the idea go. But even Laxalt was leaning toward the Dream Ticket, telling Mary McGrory of the *Washington Star*, "I've been nursing this along for months."[12] On Reagan's confidential schedule was an 8 P.M. meeting in his suite Tuesday evening denoted simply as "PRIVATE."[13]

Time was running out for Guy Vander Jagt. He still hadn't given his keynote speech, and as the morning progressed, the networks were breaking into regular programming to speculate about the Dream Ticket.

Almost everybody who was awake and not too hungover in Detroit was talking about Reagan-Ford now. A mass self-hypnosis—or mass hysteria, depending on your point of view—began to take hold among the Republicans, so caught up were they in the romance of Reagan and Ford bringing the party together and putting Carter away in the fall.

Around 9:30 the night before, a half dozen prominent Republicans had joined Reagan for yet another private meeting in his suite on the sixty-ninth floor of the Detroit Plaza Hotel. The small group included Reagan's 1976 running mate and friend, Senator Dick Schweiker of Pennsylvania. The conversation turned toward Ford. The "how wonderful it would be" chatter piqued Reagan's interest.[14]

Reagan and Ford met later that night, and Reagan made a gracious pitch to Ford to join the ticket. Ford was briefly touched by Reagan's sincerity. The icy relations between the two men seemed to be thawing.[15] Ford raised the objection that the Twelfth Amendment might cost such a ticket California's electoral votes because both men lived there. He was dubious that he could simply change his residency back to Michigan, but one report had it that Reagan was willing to make the race with Ford even if it voided the Golden State's forty-five electoral votes.[16]

After a boat reception on the Detroit River later that evening, Ford met with a small group of aides to discuss the merits of Reagan's offer. Henry Kissinger, the doctor of hidden agendas, as much as said that for the sake of the country, Ford had to accept. The conversation in Ford's suite did not end until 3 A.M. Ford had to get up in several hours for a live appearance on the *Today* show.[17]

After his television appearance, Ford reluctantly sent his advisers off to negotiate on his behalf. One confidant said that though Ford was still unconvinced, "he was willing to let us talk to the Reagan people to see if we could give some meaning to the definition" of Reagan's offer. They met that morning with Reagan's negotiators—Ed Meese, Dick Wirthlin, and Bill Casey—and were pleased to find that the two sides "very much agreed on the broad conceptual framework. There were no significant differences at all."[18]

The devil, as they would soon learn, was in the details. Reagan's men and Ford's men met again later that afternoon to try to hammer out an agreement about power sharing. Casey and Kissinger did most of the talking. "They discussed which cabinet appointments President Ford would control and what authority he would have," recalled Casey's secretary, Barbara Hayward. "The more power Mr. Kissinger expected for Ford, the more annoyed I could see Mr. Casey getting."[19]

Wirthlin was with Reagan for much of the day and later remembered, "There was an assurance and calmness about Reagan that I think added a very sustaining influence to what we were trying to do, tactically, even in spite of the Ford thing."[20]

When Wirthlin's family came by the suite to see the governor, Reagan took them into one of the adjoining bedrooms. He seemed as if he had something he wanted to share with somebody.

Wirthlin asked Reagan how he felt, and the governor replied, "Let me tell you, I feel like the man who was walking along the beach and offered a prayer that he might be sustained. And as he walked along the beach, there were really two [sets of] footsteps, his own and that of the Heavenly Father. And as he turned around and looked at where he'd come, he saw just one at a time when he was under terrific stress. And he said, 'Why did you leave me when I needed you so much?' And the answer was, 'I didn't leave you; I was carrying you.'"[21]

AT 8 O'CLOCK WEDNESDAY morning, Bill Brock convened a meeting in his suite with some of the "wise men" of the party—Bryce Harlow, Howard Baker, Kissinger, Senator John Tower, Alan Greenspan, several governors, and other luminaries. The purpose of the meeting was to orchestrate a full-scale lobbying campaign for the Dream Ticket. One of the wisest men, Congressman John Rhodes, was the skunk at the party when he pronounced the idea "cockamamie" and stormed out. At 9 A.M., he had a meeting with Reagan, who asked Rhodes who should be on the ticket. Rhodes unhesitatingly told him Bush.[22]

By noon on Wednesday, almost all other leaders of the Republican Party were openly advocating the Ford plan, thinking it was brilliant. Brock and Howard Baker met with Ford and urged him to accept Reagan's offer. Then Dole, Governor Jim Thompson, and several others weighed in, telling Ford he needed to go on the ticket. Bob Teeter, even though he was supposedly working for the Bush campaign, urged his former client Ford to do it as well. Congressman Silvio Conte of Massachusetts was dubious. "Ford is not going to give up his gosh-darned golf game," he said.[23]

That morning, a Reagan aide told Al Hunt and Jim Perry of the *Wall Street Journal* that the deal was "90 percent done." The story picked up additional momentum when Ford began sending public signals in chats with reporters and politicos that he might, just might, be interested.[24]

Betty Ford told Barbara Walters of ABC that the idea was fine with her.[25] Ford's extended entourage and sycophants were starting to spread the word that it was nearly a "done deal," though they had never been given real knowledge or direct authority to do so.

Reagan was spotted around 2 P.M. heading for a luncheon, accompanied by his protective detail. When Reagan saw two reporters he knew, he walked over to greet them. Naturally, they asked the governor whether the rumors about Ford as his running mate were true, and he replied, "Oh sure. That would be the best."[26]

As the day progressed, a new rumor, that Reagan and Ford would make a joint appearance that night before the delegates, swept the Motor City.[27] Two of the few in Detroit who thought the ticket was crazy were Stu Spencer and Dick Cheney, good friends from working together on the 1976 Ford campaign. Both were asked to help in the negotiations, but they made themselves scarce, instead going fishing for the afternoon on the Detroit River.[28]

Like Spencer and Cheney, Bill Timmons, one of the keener heads in the GOP, believed the idea was nuts. He was already running everything in Detroit, but he decided he'd better stay close to the situation to see whether he could lend some sanity and keep Kissinger, who was angling for the State Department and God knows what else, from grabbing too much power. Timmons only had a convention to run, a thousand staffers to supervise, eight thousand reporters who all needed babysitting, and more than four thousand delegates and hundreds of high-maintenance politicians to look after. The last thing he needed on his plate was some wacko idea about a co-presidency. He also got pressed into service because, as he later joked, "I was the only one who could type."[29] Paul Russo, the Reagan's campaign's remarkably patient congressional liaison, described Timmons as a "godsend" to the campaign.[30]

TIME WAS OF THE essence for the Dream Ticket, which only added insanity to the already hectic convention schedule. As Reagan aide Neal Peden recalled, conventions are always "a blur of faces. People just go 'vroom' around you day and night."[31] Now the Reagan and Ford camps worked furiously to come up with a proposal that would be acceptable to both sides.[32] Ford's men—Greenspan; Kissinger; John Marsh, a former Ford White House aide; and Bob Barrett, Ford's former military aide, who was in way over his head—aggressively pursued the deal.

Reagan's men were more passive. Casey "was insisting it didn't make a difference" who Reagan chose, although at other times he was pushing for Ford. Meese "was prepared to do anything Mr. Reagan wanted."[33]

Peter Hannaford was pulled into the mess, too, even though he was hard at work on Reagan's acceptance speech for the next night. Peter Rusthoven, whose writings in the *American Spectator* Hannaford had taken note of, had been asked to join the convention writing team to help contribute to the crafting of the speech. Rusthoven was also editing the daily newsletter of the convention.[34] The ultracautious Hannaford drafted a statement for Reagan, half announcing, half imploring that Ford should go on the ticket with him.[35]

It was unclear whether the swirling rumors were pushing the deal or whether it was the other way around. All anybody talked about at the convention was the Dream Ticket. Reporters chased down gossip from delegates and Reagan and Ford staffers, who in turn passed what they heard from reporters along to other staffers and reporters, which started the whole process over again. It was a gigantic Rashomon effect, where one person might convey only partially correct information to another, who in turn would pass along just a fraction of what he'd really heard but would fill in the details with more speculation. The phrase "Well, I heard . . ." echoed throughout the convention.

All the GOP's careful convention preparations were thrown out the window. From the standpoint of convention planners, the day was an utter disaster. Reagan's private schedule said he would call at 9:45 P.M. "1. VP nominee. 2. Former President Ford. 3. Other VP nominee candidates."[36] Then Reagan was to proceed to the hotel of his running mate. That plan had gone all to hell.

IN THE NOT-SO-SECRET MEETINGS high atop the Detroit Plaza Hotel, variously on the sixty-eighth, sixty-ninth, and seventieth floors, the Ford high command happily and the Reagan high command now less so began to slice up the White House, the cabinet, and apparently the Constitution.

The proposal as it evolved over just a few short hours called for Ford to act as a super-empowered chief of staff and Reagan as a benign chairman of the board. All information for Reagan would flow through Ford, and Reagan's White House staff would have to go through Ford first. The proposal also gave Ford veto power over Reagan's cabinet choices, The proposal gave Ford the authority over the budget, the Domestic Council, the National Security Council, the Pentagon, and the State Department—where Ford insisted that Kissinger be reinstalled. There would also be a "mutual veto" scheme.[37] Left untouched at this point was the White House gardener, but who knew?

The deal in the works essentially emasculated Reagan and would have made him seem what he wasn't but what his critics charged he was: an empty suit who just sat there while Ford and his cronies really ran the government. A joke was already making the rounds that Reagan would be "acting president" from nine to five and Ford would be president before nine, after five, and on weekends. Jim Baker could only watch the insanity from the sidelines. He mirthfully wondered how Ford would be addressed. Would it be "Mr. President–Vice President" or "Mr. Vice President–President"?[38]

As the day wore on, Reagan's men experienced more and more doubts. They began to believe that they were being snookered by Kissinger and Company, and wondered whether Ford really knew what his team was pushing for. Timmons had already typed up several iterations of what later became known as the "Treaty of Detroit," although at the time the documents were referred to benignly as "talking points."[39]

The first several drafts were quite specific regarding the proposed new duties and power for a Ford vice presidency, but Reagan's men then produced their own, newer scheme, which was far vaguer and spoke only in generalities about the parameters of the agreement. Ford's negotiators pushed for more talks, hoping to wear down their counterparts, and a kind of shuttle diplomacy took place between the various floors of the Detroit Plaza Hotel.

What had started out as a show of good manners to some and a bad joke to others had evolved into a serious offer by Reagan to Ford. But neither of them knew that their staffs were running amok, especially the Ford staff.

Ford was physically tired and impatient with the whole nonsense. He pleaded with his staff, "I've done the whole sled run. . . . I'll campaign for the ticket in the fall. But don't ask me to do this." Yet he also said that if he was going to do this, it would not be as a regular vice president.[40] Ford was giving conflicting signs even to his own team; they decided to interpret only the ones they agreed with, and kept negotiating hard.

Some of Ford's aides wondered why he kept sending mixed signals. The answer was that Ford was a competitive SOB. Ever since losing to Jimmy Carter in 1976, he had seethed over his defeat. He felt he'd done much to heal the country and the economy, which had been staging a comeback of sorts in 1976, but he'd never gotten a clean shot at his own term of office.

On one hand, Ford really liked being an ex-president. As one of two living former Republican presidents—the other in hiding and reviled—Ford was now beloved, and he enjoyed the creature comforts that came with the high honor. On the other hand, he'd always wanted another crack at Carter. To run in the primaries would have meant stepping off his pedestal, so he hoped his nascent draft committee would develop momentum. He was surprised and disappointed when it didn't, and had a hard time letting go of his dream when it became clear that his old nemesis Reagan was on his way to the nomination.[41]

When Reagan first presented his idea, Ford understandably demurred.[42] He'd been second banana once before and did not want to go through that thankless hell again, having neither authority nor responsibility. According to his former chief of staff Dick Cheney, Ford "hated . . . those nine months he was vice president under Nixon."[43] It made Ford gag to think of once more having to defend someone else's policies, as he'd been forced to do as Nixon sank in the quagmire of Watergate.

But as the "co-presidency" power pot became sweeter and sweeter, Ford listened more and more. Marty Schram of the *Washington Post* nailed it: "The portrait of the former president moving toward his onetime foe . . . as revealed in interviews with a number of the principals involved, is a picture of a man wrestling the conflicting forces of pride, responsibility and ambition . . . a man keeping a hectic schedule with little sleep . . . who allows himself to be nudged and finally budged by advisers whose motives ranged from patriotic duty to party loyalty to personal career gains."[44]

GEORGE BUSH STARTED OUT Wednesday morning thinly hoping that he'd get the phone call asking him to go on the ticket.[45] He didn't know then that informal conversations had already begun between Ford's men and Reagan's men. Bush had read the stories of the past several months about the Reagans' concerns about him, yet many running mates in the past hadn't gotten along. Just ask anybody in the Kennedy family what JFK really thought of Lyndon Johnson. Politics, Bush knew, was about compromise and finding common ground. That's how you won elections.

Yet as the morning wore on and talk of the Dream Ticket drifted up to Bush's suite on the nineteenth floor of the Pontchartrain Hotel, Bush grew testy. He became convinced that Reagan and Ford would run together, which didn't help his mood as he prepared for his speech that evening. It seemed as if all forces were arrayed against Bush: the Reagans, the conservatives, the politicians, the media—and now apparently Ford, who had previously touted Ambassador Bush in two meetings with Reagan.

Jim Baker's aide Margaret Tutwiler was so distraught by the Ford buzz that she called her wealthy father from a pay phone outside the convention hall, asking him to send a plane ticket for her. She'd been the second person hired by Bush for his presidential run, and after more than two years, she was exhausted.[46]

HAND-PAINTED SIGNS BEGAN APPEARING on the floor of Joe Louis Arena proclaiming "Ron and Jerry." Just as quickly, a manufactured sign declaring "Reagan-Bush" disappeared. Reagan and Ford met again around 5:30 P.M. with no conclusive results, but all reported that it had gone well between the two men.[47] By this point, Ford was under unrelenting pressure from his fellow Republicans to join the ticket. Bob Dole saw Ford after the former president's afternoon meeting with Reagan and told everybody "the deal was on."[48]

Dick Allen passed Ford and his Secret Service escort in the hall as he made his way to Reagan's suite. He walked into a quiet room, where Casey, Hannaford, Meese, and Wirthlin were sitting on a large "U-shaped couch, hushed," Allen later remembered. Allen had stopped by to see whether Reagan needed anything before heading over to the convention hall. Reagan said, "No, but thanks," and then asked Allen, "What do you think of the Ford deal?" Allen, startled, said, "What deal?" Reagan responded, "Ford wants Kissinger as secretary of state and [Alan] Greenspan at Treasury." Spluttering, Allen said, "That is the craziest deal I have ever heard of."[49]

Lyn Nofziger stopped by just before 6 P.M. and Reagan matter-of-factly told him about the Ford proposal. Forty minutes later, Kissinger came by for a private chat with Meese.[50]

At 7 P.M., an old friend and adviser of Reagan's dropped by his suite and was surprised to find Reagan dining alone, quietly looking out the picture window at the view of the Detroit River. Reagan told his friend: It's Ford.[51]

Allen believed that the only logical choice for Reagan was Bush. He reached out to Stefan Halper, a second-tier Bush aide who had been handling foreign policy and research. Halper, like the other Bush folks, was becoming convinced that the Dream Ticket was a reality, but Allen told him that if it wasn't, his man had to be prepared to tell Reagan he supported the entire platform, including dropping his opposition to the tax cuts and the pro-life plank. Halper took it under advisement.[52]

JUST AFTER THE EVENING's procedures got under way, Ford dithered once again, this time leaning toward the Dream Ticket in front of millions of Americans. He did a television interview on CBS with Walter Cronkite at 7:15 P.M. and said, "If I go to Washington, and I'm not saying that I'm accepting, I have to go there with the belief that I would play a meaningful role, across the board."[53] He added, "I have to have responsible assurances."[54] Ford was negotiating with Reagan on national television, with Cronkite in essence brokering the deal by specifically asking about a co-presidency.

News of Cronkite's interview with the former president caused a wave of jubilation throughout the hall. As far as the delegates were concerned, the Dream Ticket was now a fact. "A palpable euphoria swept through Joe Louis Arena, television speeding it along like a hot wind pushing a hungry fire," wrote Peter Boyer of the Associated Press.[55] All that was needed now was for Reagan to accede to Ford's demands and the delegates could get on with the coronation.

In Reagan's suite, the feeling could be described as less than euphoric. Everyone was genuinely astonished that Ford did not balk when Cronkite mentioned a co-presidency. Allen said that Reagan was "appalled."[56] Wirthlin concurred, saying that Reagan exclaimed, "Did you hear what he just said?"[57] Reagan himself later confided that the Cronkite interview forced him to wonder what the hell he'd gotten himself into. "Wait a minute," he recalled thinking, "this is really two presidents he's talking about."[58]

George Bush's team was just as shocked by the Cronkite interview. When Ford said that pride would not stop him and Mrs. Ford from going back to Washington as an "executive vice president" or "deputy president,"[59] Bush aide Vic Gold blew up at the television. "Pride!" Gold screamed. "What the fuck does he know about pride, that horse's ass!"[60]

Ford later conducted a similar interview with Barbara Walters of ABC and upped the ante. "I was a vice president and I had problems," he told Walters.[61] To get Ford to agree to the last-minute interview, Walters, practically crying, had repeatedly begged and pleaded with the former president.[62]

Network reporters were out of control. It was a media riot, and "the relentless speculation and pursuit of the rumors by network 'floor reporters' seemed to create a life of their own," as the *New York Times* observed at the time.[63]

Lynn Sherr of ABC—one of those "floor reporters"—took to the airwaves to announce excitedly, "We heard from Senator Schweiker that Senator Laxalt told someone else who then told Senator Schweiker that it would be Gerald Ford!"[64] Sherr was not alone in such schoolyard journalism that night. Besides Tom Brokaw of NBC, about the only network journalist who was keeping his wits about him was Frank Reynolds of ABC. On air, he speculated that the deal could be "ephemeral."[65] Then again, Reynolds knew Reagan better than anyone else in the electronic media did; though he was a liberal, the Reagans adored him and he returned the affection. Reynolds knew, or should have known, Reagan would never go along with a deal that would undercut his own authority or majesty. For Reagan, it was never just about the art of the deal—any deal—but the deal itself.

AFTER FORD'S INTERVIEWS, REPORTS began leaking out that Reagan's staff was angrily fighting among themselves, frustrated with the corner they had apparently painted themselves into.[66] Some conservatives were frustrated also, including Reagan's longtime friend and supporter Tom Winter, co-owner and co-publisher, along with Allan Ryskind, of *Human Events*. Reagan had been a faithful subscriber for years, corresponded with the two men, had dinner with them—and in turn the publication was devoted to Reagan. On the other hand, they reviled Ford. When Winter heard about the Dream Ticket he went off and got so sullenly drunk that he was later found by his friends slumped in a chair, babbling incoherently.[67]

Jimmy Lyons, another old Reagan friend, stopped by Reagan's suite to throw in his two cents that he thought the Ford idea was "insane." Lyons could talk to Reagan like that.[68] First, he was a Texan, and second, his bank, River Oaks, had made an unsecured $100,000 loan to Reagan's campaign at a critical point in 1976.[69]

Shortly after the Cronkite bombshell, Reagan and Allen were alone in the suite. Allen pressed Reagan to think about Bush, but Reagan balked, citing abortion and "voodoo" economics. Allen pressed him, asking whether the governor would reconsider Bush if he pledged to support the entire platform. Reagan saw an out: "Well, if you put it that way, I would agree to reconsider." Stef Halper, having handled his side of the agreement, later called Allen to tell him Bush would agree to support the platform if picked by Reagan.[70]

THE CONVENTION'S SCHEDULED AFFAIRS were almost an afterthought amid all the Dream Ticket excitement. The roll call of state delegations confirming their selections for the party's nominee would only officially pronounce what everyone already knew: that Reagan would be the GOP's standard bearer. The drama involving Reagan's running mate was much more exciting.

There were only three principal convention speakers on the list that night: Bush, Brock, and Guy Vander Jagt, who would finally get to give his keynote speech. Vander Jagt asked and had been assured by the Reagan camp that no final decision would be made on the vice presidency until he spoke.

Bush's self-deprecating if somewhat brief remarks that night were a good, solid effort—better than the "gentleman's C" he had often earned at Yale—and he was warmly received by the delegates. "If anyone wants to know why Ronald Reagan is a winner, you can refer him to me," Bush said. "I'm an expert on the subject. He's a winner because he's our leader, because he has traveled this country and understands its people. His message is clear. His message is understood."[71]

With nothing to lose now that Ford apparently was getting the VP spot, Bush was publicly relaxed, calm, and effective.[72] Privately, he seethed. While Bush waited underneath the stage to give his remarks, a convention aide said, "I'm sorry, Mr. Bush, really sorry. I was pulling for you." Bush curtly replied, "Sorry about what?" "You mean you haven't heard? It's all over. Reagan's picked Ford as his running mate."[73] Bush snapped, "Well thanks a lot!"[74]

After his speech, as Bush headed to his car to take him back to his hotel, Stef Halper tried to tell Bush that it was not over, that he'd been in back-channel conversations with Dick Allen. Halper had never seen Bush rage like this. "Don't you get it? It's over!" Bush slammed the car door in Halper's face, leaving him standing there sheepishly on the curb.[75] ABC's Jim Wooten caught the private George Bush and reported that the Houstonian was "shaken . . . bitter."[76]

Reagan, on the other hand, was becoming more and more pensive. Just before 8 P.M., the presumptive nominee was munching his preferred snack of jelly beans and watching Dole on ABC saying, "Ford and Reagan can work it out." Reagan replied to the television, "No, Bob. I cannot give him what he wants."[77] Yet he did not halt the negotiations. Reagan was invested in his own proposal and wasn't about to quit now, since he was, as Mike Deaver once said, "the most competitive son of a bitch who ever lived."[78]

FINALLY AT THE CONVENTION podium, Vander Jagt did not disappoint. In a thirty-five-minute address, he wowed the delegates, prompting David Brinkley of NBC to comment, "Well I've got to say he turned them on."[79] But some media observers viewed his speech as pompous and overwrought, in the manner of William Jennings Bryan. One hard-bitten reporter turned to another and called it a "goddamn snake-oil speech."[80]

Whatever the case, the speech came too late to make a difference for Vander Jagt's cause. Reagan and his men would not pick him for the number-two slot—though exactly who they would pick remained very much in doubt.

ED MEESE WENT BY Reagan's suite at around 8:30 P.M. to happily inform his man that Ford had backed off on previous demands to take over the National Security Council. Then, just a few minutes before 9 o'clock, Reagan withdrew to his bedroom to call Ford. When he reemerged, the presumptive nominee announced that Kissinger had taken himself out of contention for the State Department, but no one bought that for a second.[81]

In the background on one of Reagan's three television sets, Frank Reynolds could be heard betraying his own good judgment, telling viewers, "We now have reports that a deal has been made between Governor Reagan and former president Ford and that it has been accepted and agreed to, and that former president Ford will be Governor Reagan's choice to be the number-two man on the ticket to run for vice president. That is historic. It is unique. It is unprecedented, and we don't know it for sure, but there are reports confirming what our correspondent Jim Wooten told us some time ago, that the deal was under way."[82]

Sam Donaldson, also of ABC, announced at 9:30 that Ford and Reagan would make an appearance in Joe Louis Arena before the night was over. At twenty minutes to ten, Garrick Utley of NBC interviewed former senator Robert Griffin of Michigan, a Ford intimate, who said, "It looks good." Utley said, "This is practically a confirmation." Practically.[83]

At ten minutes after ten, Walter Cronkite solemnly told his viewers, "CBS has learned there is a definite plan [that] the nominee of this party, Ronald Reagan, [will choose] the former president of the United States, Gerald Ford . . . as a vice-presidential running mate . . . an unparalleled, unprecedented situation in American politics. They are going to come to this convention tonight to appear together on this platform to announce that Ford will run with him."[84] That was that. If "Uncle Walter" said it was so, you could bank on it.

Yet all Cronkite had to go on was what his correspondents were telling him. And they were going on what the correspondents for the other networks were reporting, fanned by GOP operatives who had no idea what was really going on. Reporter Dan Rather broke in breathlessly at 9:10 P.M. to tell the anchor, "Walter, the number of sources on the floor who say a deal has been cut is increasing."[85] Earlier, Cronkite had presciently said to Ford, "Well, we're going to jump to conclusions all over the place tonight."[86]

Ted Koppel of ABC seemed about the only sane person now on the tube, as he mused, "I hope we're all not feeding off each other. . . . The delegates feeding off the television reports and the television reporters feeding off the delegates."[87]

JUST A FEW MINUTES after 10 o'clock, Reagan's name was placed in nomination—for the third time in twelve years. The delegates went bonkers, cheering, applauding, using the same air horns that had filled Kemper Arena four years earlier, prompting the New York Times to compare their noise to the "ululations of Arab women."[88]

Paul Laxalt fired up the crowd, asking, "Who is this man who will not make any more weak, ill-advised decisions like the Panama Canal giveaway? Who is this man who will stand by our allies and not indulge in any more 'Taiwan sellout'?" Each time Laxalt asked another question, the delegates would scream in unison, "Reagan!" Laxalt concluded his remarks to warm applause and the hall got down to the actual voting.[89]

Alabama went first and served up a plate of 27 deep-fried delegates for Reagan. Then the Alaska delegation, recently taken over by the Moral Majority, delivered its 12 votes for the Gipper. California, with its controversial winner-take-all primary, gave all 168 of its votes to its favorite son. Reagan's daughter Maureen made the announcement on national television to the cheers of Joe Louis Arena. Boos were heard when John Anderson received votes from the Illinois and Massachusetts delegates, but the boos were loudest when the band played the Ohio State fight song just as Michigan was getting ready to announce its vote tally.[90]

As the delegates continued their roll call, the Reagan and Ford negotiators frantically held two more meetings high atop the Renaissance Center, one at 9 P.M. and another at 10 P.M.[91] The Ford men kept excusing themselves to go meet with the former president, leading Reagan's negotiators to believe that their counterparts were negotiating power for themselves. The Reaganites whispered that Ford's men were trying to talk Ford even at this late hour into committing completely to their plan. In fact, Ford was telling his aides, "Go back and get more."[92]

Bill Simon stopped by the Reagan suite and told the Californian in no uncertain terms that the whole Ford thing was nuts. Simon, though he had been Ford's treasury secretary, made it clear to Reagan that he didn't trust the man.[93] Reagan respected Simon and listened to him.

Reagan's men were dismayed. It was now sinking in that they were inadvertently working on "a return of the Ford White House." They mostly respected their counterparts and believed the ticket would be good for the country, but they also had a nagging suspicion about hidden agendas. Although Kissinger claimed that Meese, Wirthlin, and Casey had asked him to use his influence with Ford to get him to go for it,[94] Meese was already having second thoughts. Meese told Reagan, "You know, I don't think this is going anyplace." Reagan replied, "I don't think it's going to come to any fruition either."[95] Cheney, meanwhile, was astonished at the concessions Casey was making in Reagan's name.[96]

Reagan's doubts were gnawing at him. He called Stu Spencer and asked, "You still feel the same way about Bush?" Spencer assured him that nothing had changed his opinion that Bush was Reagan's best choice.[97]

Bill Casey had been invested in the Ford idea ever since he had visited the former president several weeks earlier and come away believing that Ford wanted to go on the ticket. Now he needed to buy time for the negotiators, so he sent word down to the convention floor to "keep the 'spontaneous' demonstration marking the end of the roll call and Reagan's nomination going as long as possible," as the *Washington Post* reported.[98]

Reagan and Ford talked once again by phone but nothing was resolved. In the 10 o'clock meeting, the Ford people, sensing that they'd tried to grab too much in earlier negotiations, backed off on some of their demands. Meese, at 10:45, briefed Reagan on the new framework: Ford still wanted veto power over Reagan's cabinet selections, and he would also name the head of Office of Management and Budget and the head of the National Security Agency.[99]

Over at Joe Louis Arena, Reagan's nomination was imminent. David Broder and Lou Cannon filed a story with the headline "Ford Reportedly Accepts No. 2 Spot on GOP Ticket." The headline reflected the doubts of the two scribes. Cannon once again was proving his perspicacity as a political reporter. All week he had been telling anyone who would listen that it would be Bush, not Ford.[100]

The Reagan-Ford deal was unraveling, but nobody in the hall knew it. Former Michigan governor George Romney was a Bush delegate, but this did not stop him from spreading the word on the floor that Ford would be on the ticket with Reagan. Romney had gone so far as to tell Bush face-to-face that morning that he was dumping him for Ford.[101] Bob Dole had been led to believe it was all set. But as the evening went on, he later said, "I got nervous because it was taking too long. Something happened. Maybe we left the wrong people in charge."[102]

RONALD WILSON REAGAN WAS finally nominated for president at 11:13 P.M., when the Montana delegates put him over the top.[103] A prolonged demonstration of almost forty minutes took place. The band played "California, Here I Come," and 12,000 red, white, and blue balloons fell. Delegates joyously popped them.[104] For sixteen years, since Reagan's speech for Goldwater, conservatives had waited for this moment. Their man, their leader, had finally won the Republican Party's nomination for president of the United States.

Reagan received 1,939 delegate votes; John Anderson 37; George Bush, 13; and Anne Armstrong, former U.S. ambassador to the Court of St. James, 1. Four delegates abstained.[105]

Photographers were invited into Reagan's suite to memorialize the occasion and the nominee looked serene. His family members—Nancy, daughter Patti, sons Mike and Ron, and daughter-in-law Colleen—were smiling brightly. Casey, Wirthlin, and Meese, on the other hand, had no time to savor the nomination they'd worked so hard for. They were up in Ford's suite desperately trying to salvage the Dream Ticket, but it was falling apart.

Allen informed Hannaford, Nofziger, and Marty Anderson of his unauthorized initiative to Bush via Stef Halper and the good news that Bush would support the platform. Hannaford, with Mike Deaver also present, told the group that it might be best to start arguing for another option for Reagan.[106]

Ford, on the advice of his men, had told Reagan when the Gipper called earlier that he wanted to sleep on the whole matter, but Reagan dug in his heels. He told Ford in no uncertain terms that he needed to have Ford's answer that night. Deaver said Reagan was "not happy."[107] Reagan's men later realized that the Ford team wanted to wait another twelve hours so the Dream Ticket would become an unmistakable fact with the world, making it impossible for Reagan to back out without losing face.

Just before 11:30 P.M., Meese, Casey, and Wirthlin reported back to the governor that negotiations were not going well.[108] Deaver warned Hannaford and Nofziger that the convention "is about to go up in smoke, out of control . . . if we don't give them a decision." Nofziger proposed that they go upstairs and tell the negotiators. They bounded up the stairs to find Kissinger, Greenspan, and Barrett in the room.[109] Deaver told them that it was decision time and added, "The governor wants us to see President Ford."[110] After a brief silence, Barrett excused himself to go into Ford's room. He soon came out and said, "He's going downstairs, and I think the answer is 'No.'"[111]

Around 11:30, Ford, with Barrett in tow, arrived at Reagan's suite. Reagan and Ford closed the door and went into the dining room by themselves. Five minutes later they emerged and shook hands, and Ford departed after they bade each other goodnight.

"I have to say the answer is 'No,'" Reagan told his men. Ford had told Reagan that his "gut reaction" was that it "just wouldn't work."[112] Maybe Reagan was acting. No one will ever really know. He had outmaneuvered the fearsome Hollywood moguls as head of the Screen Actors Guild, and it was possible he'd just forced a former president's hand, leading Ford to pull out of the co-presidency concept. Hannaford said years later that it was typical Reagan to let all the "elements play out."[113] In any event, Reagan had just dodged a bullet. He was relieved.

The Candidate said, "Well, what do we do now?"[114]

After a prolonged silence, Peter Hannaford said, "Governor, maybe it's time to call George Bush."[115]

Seeing no objection from his most trusted advisers, Reagan reluctantly said, "Well, let's get Bush on the phone."[116]

BUSH HAD BEEN IN the downstairs bar of the hotel with two of his sons, George and Jeb, having a quiet beer. When they got back to the suite, Jeb grabbed his friend David Bates and said, "Let's go drink some scotch," and they went to another room to be alone.[117] Bush stayed in the suite with Jim Baker, Vic Gold, and some family and other close aides. Drinking a Heineken, he awaited a courtesy call from a Reagan aide to formally tell him that Ford was going to join the ticket, as if he didn't already know that.

The phone rang, but it wasn't from Reagan. It was the Secret Service, telling Bush that they had taken up a position two floors down. They wanted to know whether Bush needed anything. "Need anything? What the hell's that supposed to mean?"[118] To this day, no one can account for the speedy actions of the Secret Service, although it is plausible that agents assigned to Reagan heard about the movement toward Bush and took action, detailing agents to the soon-to-be running mate even before Reagan had called Bush.

At 11:37, shortly after the mystifying Secret Service call, Bush's phone rang again.[119] This time it was Mr. Reagan calling.

Jim Baker answered, handed the phone to Bush, and then just as quickly cleared the room of nearly everybody except Barbara Bush, their son Marvin, and Dean Burch, the former head of the party. Reagan brightly said, "Hello, George, this is Ron Reagan. George, I would like to go over there and tell them that I am recommending you for vice president. Could I ask you one thing—do I have your permission to make an announcement that you support the platform across the board?"[120] Reagan asked specifically about the pro-life plank. Bush, flabbergasted, readily agreed to support the conservative document "across the board" per his testy but productive conversation with Halper.[121] "I'd be honored, Governor."[122] And that was that.

Someone knocked on the door of Jeb's room and told him that his father wanted to see him. Jeb, halfway into his cups, went and saw his parents "not looking very happy." He asked whether Reagan had made a courtesy call and the elder Bush languidly said, "Yes." After a pause, the father added, "Yeah, he asked me to be his running mate." Jeb almost fainted. Ambassador Bush pulled the same gag on Vic Gold, but rather than fainting, Gold jumped five feet in the air.[123]

A few minutes later a television set in the Bush suite showed a network reporter shouting, "Not Ford! It's Bush!"[124] The suite quickly filled with a crush of friends and well-wishers. Bush was absolutely stunned by Reagan's call. Before the phone rang he'd been sitting in his suite, nursing bruised feelings toward Reagan and Ford. Vic Gold had been so angry at Ford for touting Bush, telling everyone he didn't want the vice presidency—and then apparently taking the post—that Bush aides felt compelled to gently escort Gold away from the few reporters who were attending what they thought was Bush's political deathwatch.

Now reporters descended on the suite for the celebration. Bush didn't even have time to put on a suit and tie, so he met with the media wearing a red Polo shirt. He frankly told them how shocked he was: "Out of a clear blue sky . . . Governor Reagan called me up and asked if I would be willing to run with him on this ticket. He was most gracious in the invitation and I, of course, was very, very pleased to be invited to do this. . . . I was surprised."[125]

Just as shocked were the media outlets that had breathlessly reported the Dream Ticket story most of the day as if it were a done deal. As Reagan was calling Bush, a network anchor told his audience that "it would be an electrifying moment" when Reagan and Ford appeared together on stage that night.[126] The Associated Press and *United Press International* had already moved several stories about the Reagan-Ford tandem, and the *Chicago Sun-Times* and the *Wall Street Journal* had even printed early editions announcing the news of the Dream Ticket.[127]

REAGAN HAD FINALLY MADE his choice, but he still faced the real danger of a runaway convention. Deaver "had just been down to the convention and he came in and said, 'Boy, this place is so tense down there it is about to explode,'" recalled Hannaford.[128] The situation would become even more disastrous if the delegates retired for the evening thinking that the choice was Ford only to wake up the next morning and find out it was Bush.

It was a taboo in politics for a candidate to appear before he'd actually accepted the nomination. But the normally superstitious Reagan listened to Deaver and recognized that he needed to get the convention under control. If he waited to the make the Bush announcement until the press conference scheduled for the 11 o'clock the next morning, there would be mass confusion—and mass disappointment. Worse, the media would become fixated on picking apart what had happened in the Ford negotiations. The Gipper knew he needed to change the subject quickly, and get people to focus on Bush, not Ford. Consequently, he broke with precedent and went to Joe Louis Arena.[129]

The networks informed their viewers of the Bush selection before Reagan got the chance to tell his own convention. NBC went first, less than fifteen minutes after Reagan had called Bush. Chris Wallace, the thirty-two-year-old son of television legend Mike Wallace, was covering his first convention, but he got the biggest scoop of the night. Sporting the standard-issue headphones, he was on the floor with the Illinois delegation, which included Reagan's Midwest political director, Frank Donatelli. Reagan operatives had just passed Donatelli the stunning news, but the campaign had given no directives about what to tell the media. Donatelli wasn't sure, but figured what the heck, so he told Wallace, who at 11:55 P.M. went live with the dramatic news bulletin that Reagan was headed to Joe Louis Arena to announce his surprise choice of Bush.[130]

CBS went with the story maybe thirty seconds later.[131] When a stunned Cronkite was told on air by Lesley Stahl that it would be Bush—and not Ford—the newscaster "buried his head in his hands."[132] Stahl went with the story only because yet another Reagan official was screaming it in her ear.

NBC came in dead last in the announcement. Sanctimoniously, John Chancellor told his audience, "You have just seen an example of politics out of hand in an electronic age," as if his network had had nothing to do with the "out of hand" quality of the day.[133]

By now, all the networks, having been a part of the problem, upbraided Reagan for allowing the situation to get out of control. Hal Bruno of ABC said the fiasco "doesn't show very good judgment" on Reagan's part. David Brinkley complained that the networks had been used as "something of an intercom" by the Ford and Reagan camps and their supporters.[134] Only Tom Brokaw at NBC had given the story a wide berth, having been warned by Stu Spencer that it was all nonsense.[135]

Reagan, accompanied by Nancy to help soften the blow, addressed the hall around 12:15 A.M.[136] The place exploded when the Gipper arrived. Everybody was cheering but nobody seemed to know what for: Reagan-Ford, Reagan-Bush, or Reagan-Ford-Kemp, which would have made a pretty good touch-football team.

The hall became hushed as Reagan mounted the podium. Many of the delegates were surprised that Ford was not there with the Gipper, as had been previously billed. Reagan told the audience that he'd come down there to straighten out "the rumors and the gossip."[137] He informed the astonished conventioneers that he and Ford "have gone over this and over this and over this, and he and I have come to the conclusion, and he believes deeply, that he can be of more value as the former president, campaigning his heart out, as he has promised to do, and not as a member of the ticket."[138]

The Dream Ticket was dead.

Reagan took four minutes to get to the other subject he wanted to discuss, and he did not seem completely comfortable with the idea yet. He announced the Bush selection "with a taut smile on his face," as Hedrick Smith reported in the *New York Times*. Reagan called Bush "a man we all know and a man who was a candidate, a man who has great experience in government, and a man who told me that he can enthusiastically support the platform across the board."[139]

The hall rang with cheers for Bush, or perhaps because the long night of drama, which had frayed everyone's nerves, was coming to a close.

Reagan's quick announcement of the Bush selection had succeeded in keeping a bad situation from getting worse: reporters were forced to deal with the new story rather than just pick apart what was now an old story.

As for what had scuttled the Reagan-Ford negotiations, both camps stayed tight-lipped. The line coming out of Team Reagan was "The governor finally decided the price they wanted was too high."[140] Maybe.

The official line from Team Ford was that the former president had never wanted to do it in the first place and had finally said, "Goddamn it all, it's not going to work. I knew it wouldn't work." Maybe.[141]

WITH HIS DRAMATIC POST-MIDNIGHT announcement of his running mate, Reagan had stanched the wound he and his team had inflicted by getting caught up in the high-profile Dream Ticket negotiations. Had he not moved so quickly, the bloodletting would have been much worse.

But that didn't mean Reagan had defused all criticism.

Ed Rollins, a GOP consultant from California and a Nofzinger protégé, was in the command-post trailer when the phone call came down saying that Bush was the pick. "Fuck," Rollins grumbled. Then he was told he needed to break the bad news to Paul Laxalt. Not wanting to deal with an angry Laxalt, Rollins turned to Frank Fahrenkopf, Laxalt's friend from Nevada, and told him, "It is going to be Bush. And they want *you* to tell Laxalt."[142]

But before Fahrenkopf could reach his friend, Laxalt spotted Bill Timmons on the phone writing down names: "Baker, Kemp, Vander Jagt . . ." Realizing that Timmons was on the line with Reagan, Laxalt tried to speak to his old friend, but Timmons was saying to Governor Reagan, "You can't call them yet. You've got to call Bush." Laxalt suddenly understood that Reagan had chosen Bush; Timmons was writing down the names of the men Reagan had passed over, who would need to be notified of the nominee's decision. Jack Germond and Jules Witcover reported that Laxalt "turned white" and grabbed the phone from Timmons, but found Ed Meese now on the line. Laxalt pleaded, "Ron, Ron. I've got to talk to Ron." Meese replied, "He can't talk to you, he's on the phone to Bush." Laxalt implored Meese to delay the announcement until the next day, but to no avail; Reagan had already left for Joe Louis Arena.[143]

Laxalt was "pissed off" when he found out about the Bush selection, as he acknowledged years later. "And then I was pissed off at Judy Woodruff, too, who was pestering the hell out of me."[144] It wasn't just that the conservative Laxalt had deep reservations about the Brahmin Bush; Reagan's old friend and adviser was especially angry that he hadn't been consulted on the choice after the Ford deal had fallen through.

When a reporter asked Laxalt about his feelings on Reagan-Bush, he gamely replied, "I think it's a winnable ticket."[145] Then he stormed out of the convention.

Laxalt wasn't alone in doubting Reagan's decision. One of Reagan's closest confidants—someone who had been with his campaign for six years—grumbled on background to a top political reporter, "This is the sorriest day in a decade for Republicans."[146]

Reagan had to figure out how to turn this lemon into lemonade.

25

FAMILY, WORK, NEIGHBORHOOD,
PEACE, AND FREEDOM

*"With a deep awareness of the responsibility conferred by your trust,
I accept your nomination for the presidency of the United States."*

The Jazz Age American novelist F. Scott Fitzgerald famously wrote, "There are no second acts in American lives."[1] He wrote those gloomy words in the immediate aftermath of World War I, when an entire generation of artists—a "Lost Generation"—looked with revulsion at the devastation wrought by the great powers. The "War to End All Wars" had snuffed out seventy-two million lives; it introduced the world to mechanized death, trench warfare, and gas attacks. The horrific carnage of that conflict ushered in an age of existential uncertainty and, in the view of Fitzgerald and his disillusioned and drunken peers, of mindless materialism.

Fitzgerald may have been right in his time, but his poignantly tragic aphorism didn't apply to Ronald Reagan—certainly not in Detroit. The Republican Party's convention in 1980, for Reagan, represented his third presidential act, after he had tried and failed to gain the GOP's nomination in 1968 and 1976. Considering his many successes, failures, and varied careers, along with his divorce and second marriage, Reagan had had many debuts, both triumphant and otherwise. Much like the protagonist Jay Gatsby in Fitzgerald's novel *The Great Gatsby*, Reagan had chosen through sheer force of will to rise above his difficult roots and, in the classless and upwardly mobile landscape of the New World, invent himself, though without Jay's corrupt past or fallen future.

In this sense, Ronald Reagan was quintessentially American.

The question in the 1980 election was whether America itself would begin a new act, or whether the same troubling scene was unceasing. Rarely had two presidential candidates been so diametrically opposed on virtually every public-policy issue. Jimmy Carter and Ronald Reagan disagreed on everything from the size and scope of government, to U.S.–Soviet relations, to military spending, to the conduct of foreign policy, to abortion, tax cuts, and the free market. "Make no mistake about it: the election of 1980 is one of those critical events that will shape this country's future for many years to come," wrote leading conservative theoretician Irving Kristol as the Detroit convention was reaching it climax. He elaborated, "The Republican Party too is on its way to changing its character, and the nomination of Mr. Reagan . . . will ratify the permanence of this change."[2]

BEFORE REAGAN WOULD FACE Carter in the fall, he had to first convince his doubting supporters of the choice of Ambassador Bush as the stand-in running mate, and clean up the mess left over from the day before over the whole co-presidency nonsense.

On Thursday morning, just hours after the drama of the announcement, the Bushes headed to the Reagan suite in the Detroit Plaza Hotel for a private breakfast.[3] It was the first time Reagan and Bush had been together since their contentious debate in Houston several months earlier. They hit it off fine, but when network cameras were invited in to record the meeting, Reagan did not yet look altogether comfortable with his last-minute choice. Mrs. Reagan seemed even less comfortable with the Bushes. The fact that both she and Barbara Bush had attended Smith College did little to break the ice between the two women.

Some conservatives in Detroit shared Nancy Reagan's doubts about George Bush. The Texas delegation was in near revolt. But Reagan's state director, Ernie Angelo, told the delegates they would be "nuts" if they cut and ran on Reagan on the very first decision he made as the party's nominee. "I don't want one negative vote on the floor," Angelo warned. The room went silent, and that night the entire delegation voted for Bush.[4]

Weeks before the convention, a number of New Rightists, such as Richard Viguerie, had given signs that while Bush would not be the conservatives' ideal choice, he was acceptable. That was then. Now that the choice was official, many were openly displeased. Almost all the leading members of the New Right endorsed a plan to try to draft Jesse Helms as the vice-presidential nominee. On Thursday, seventeen conservatives met with Senator Helms, who called Bush "unpalatable" and "unacceptably liberal."[5] Other conservatives wanted to stage a walkout at the convention. Helms buttonholed a young convention page, Quin Hillyer, to go find Tom Ellis, his chief political aide, to discuss the draft or a walkout.[6]

Terry Dolan, head of NCPAC, fired a salvo at Bush: "For 30 years the Republicans have tried to convince people they aren't a party of country clubs and prep schools. I find it ironic that the party is now nominating an absolute stereotype of that image."[7] Dolan, from the wrong side of Connecticut, would make himself a *bête noire* to Bush.

One group pleased with the messy selection of Bush was the Carter White House. The notion of a Reagan-Ford tandem had terrified Carter's people, even though it would have been the oldest ticket in American history. The Democrats were relieved that Ford was out of the picture, though one aide to Carter got it right when he told the *New York Times* that a Reagan-Ford ticket "would have been a disaster. It would have all fallen apart within two days because of turf battles, ideological upheavals, even fights between Nancy Reagan and Betty Ford."

Regardless of the merits of a Reagan-Ford pairing, Democrats were excited by what had happened in Detroit, especially because the no-deal/deal/no-deal spectacle had played out on national television. They believed that Reagan had badly flubbed his first test as presidential nominee.[8] The Democratic National Committee produced talking points bashing Reagan for almost choosing Ford— points that were almost precisely the same as those that some Republicans had made the night before in opposing the ticket, including doubts about the constitutionality of a "shared-power arrangement with Ford."[9]

Lyn Nofziger, during a morning briefing on Thursday, tried to turn aside doubts raised by the events of the day before. He said with nearly a straight face that George Bush was the only one Reagan had asked to be his running mate and that the campaign was "a very well-run operation."[10]

Many in the press, perhaps defensive about their own appalling performance the day before, pronounced that Reagan had blundered. Jack Germond and Jules Witcover of the *Washington Star* started right in: "Ronald Reagan has managed to achieve the worst of both political worlds by his off-again, on-again handling of his decision on a vice-presidential nominee." They lambasted Bush as a "wallflower" and Ford for "his own penchant for seizing the limelight."[11] James Dickenson, also of the *Washington Star*, turned in the most creatively descriptive prose about the events of Wednesday, calling it "a fiasco that made [Reagan] and almost everyone else prominent enough to get on television look like people who should be wearing caps and bells and hitting each other with inflated pig bladders rather than posing as saviors of the Republic."[12]

John Sears offered his own take on how his old boss Reagan would be affected by all the confusion over his VP process: "He's shot himself in the foot."[13]

In the wake of the Ford affair, questions were being raised about Bill Casey's capacity to run the fall campaign. Casey had been an instigator behind the co-presidency idea. Rumors of friction between Bill Timmons and Casey were already

AT LONG LAST: Ronald Reagan finally accepted the Republican Party's nomination for president on his third try—twelve long years after his first failed attempt.

A NEW BEGINNING: Reagan's 1980 campaign was not simply a turning point in his own political career; it marked a bold new path for the Republican Party and the rise of a new generation of conservatism.

"I AM PAYING FOR THIS MICROPHONE!": Reagan rescued his collapsing campaign with an extraordinary performance at the Republicans' Nashua debate. Looking on are moderator Jon Breen (seated, center), front-runner George Bush (seated at right), and the other GOP candidates, John Anderson, Howard Baker, Bob Dole, and Phil Crane.

BIG JOHN: Many Republicans thought former Texas governor John Connally was the man to beat in 1980. But his campaign strategy was flawed from the start.

THE ANDERSON DIFFERENCE: John Anderson (left) washed out in the GOP field but ran in the general election as an independent. Running mate Pat Lucey, a Democrat, despised Carter.

"Morale was at zero": Reagan fired controversial campaign manager John Sears and top aides Charlie Black and Jim Lake the day of his triumph in New Hampshire. A few days later the ousted operatives held this press conference to fire back at the Reagan campaign.

Under new management: The new Reagan regime, led by William J. Casey (right) and long-time Reagan adviser Ed Meese (left), helped turn around a campaign that under Sears had been riddled with problems.

Reagan's closest friend: Senator Paul Laxalt of Nevada was national chairman of the 1980 campaign, but he stormed out of the Republican convention before Reagan accepted the nomination.

THE "DREAM TICKET" DIES: Only after the exhausting negotiations to get Gerald Ford onto the ticket collapsed at the eleventh hour did Reagan—reluctantly—call George Bush to be his running mate. Surrounding Reagan are (left to right) Mike Deaver, Peter Hannaford, Dick Wirthlin, Drew Lewis, Dick Allen, and Bill Casey.

RUNNING MATES: Given all the hopes invested in a "co-presidency" with Ford—not to mention Reagan's own coolness toward George Bush—the Reagan-Bush ticket got off to a rocky start, but the pairing quickly proved to be a plus for the Republicans.

THE CONSERVATIVE CRUSADE BEGINS: The convention delegates cheered wildly for their new nominee and his clan—from left, son Ron, daughter Patti, wife Nancy, Reagan, grandson Cameron, son Mike, daughter-in-law Colleen, and daughter Maureen.

THE NEW GOP: Reagan, the conservative, was leading the new Republican Party into the future; moderates like Bush and Gerald Ford were along for the ride.

CARTER ATTACKS: President Jimmy Carter viciously attacked Reagan throughout the campaign and even intimated that the Republican was a racist. *Washington Star* reporter Lisa Myers called out the president on this nasty insinuation, in an exchange that reportedly left Carter "shaken."

"THE DREAM SHALL NEVER DIE": Ted Kennedy challenged President Carter for the Democratic nomination, and the fight went all the way to the convention. There, Kennedy stole the show by giving the best speech of his life.

THE VP: Walter Mondale, bored with his job as vice president, relished going on the campaign trail and playing the attack dog. But he sensed better than many other Democrats that Carter was in trouble against Reagan.

THE DEBATE: Reagan scored a small psychological advantage before his debate with Carter by crossing the stage to offer his best wishes to the president. Reagan's debate performance closed the sale with the American voter.

ELECTION DAY: Reagan's long quest for the White House came down to one day. After he and Mrs. Reagan cast their ballots, he was asked who he voted for. "Nancy," he replied.

LANDSLIDE: The election thought to be "too close to call" ended up a massive victory for Ronald Reagan. Carter called to concede the election when it was still only 5:35 P.M. on the West Coast.

RENDEZVOUS WITH REAGAN: Ronald Reagan and the author enjoy a laugh together, 1985.

NOFZIGER: The author with Lyn Nofziger, one of Reagan's closest aides going back to California days.

CHENEY: Dick Cheney, shown here being interviewed by the author, served as President Gerald Ford's chief of staff but was a Reaganite by 1980. The congressman who led the investigation into the theft of Carter's debate briefing books was puzzled by something Cheney told him.

making the rounds, and it was an open secret that Casey was disdainful of Bush, thinking him "too liberal and his character too soft."[14]

Reagan knew he needed to rewrite this script. On Thursday morning, he and Bush, together with their wives, held a press conference. The first six questions, not surprisingly, were about the failed "Treaty of Detroit." Reagan spoke warmly about Ambassador Bush, saying that he wasn't his second choice but only that the Ford opportunity was "so unique." Bush, for his part, was touchy about the nonsense of the day before: "What difference does it make? It's irrelevant. I'm here."[15]

The Reagan campaign was sufficiently worried about the reaction to the Bush selection that it sent out emissaries to plead with various delegations to support the ticket. Helms sequestered himself in his suite with Congressman Bob Bauman of Maryland, head of the American Conservative Union, and Phyllis Schlafly, longtime conservative leader and organizer. Bauman made his displeasure with moderate Republicans such as Bush well known, saying, "They are elitists. They are out of touch with the supermarket counters. Their view of Communism is that it is a market to be sold to, not a system that may destroy their children's freedom."[16] Helms then appeared on ABC and seemed to stick to his guns, saying, "We are still holding the option of . . . having my name placed in nomination tonight."[17]

But in the end, Helms countenanced no official effort on his behalf or an organized walkout over Bush. Helms was given a prime-time speech at the last minute as a reward for calling off his troops. In it, he announced to the delegates that he would not permit the VP draft to go forward, because Bush had pledged to support the entire platform. One more disaster was averted. While a small cadre of hard-liners continued to deliberate offering Helms's name for the vice-presidential nomination, to do so would require negotiating a thicket of rules, which included getting a certain number of state delegations to support such a floor action. In the end, conservatives pulled back their threats and reluctantly supported the ticket. Frankly, Helms didn't have enough time or the troops to mount any real insurrection. He could, however, have embarrassed Reagan, which Helms never would have done. He'd been a close friend for too long, a conservative soldier in arms with the Gipper.[18]

Far more Republicans openly endorsed the Reagan-Bush pairing. Even Jack Kemp, who had been subjected to all that malicious old gossip and then passed over for the number-two spot, pronounced the ticket to his liking. He pointedly said that Bush was an asset to Reagan.[19] If Kemp was bitter about being passed over or the generally rude treatment he had received from some of the Reaganites, he didn't betray it. Reagan aide Paul Russo said years later that much of the fanning of the womanizing and gay rumors against Kemp had been by Ford operatives.[20]

Kemp was a team player, but his assessment also happened to be accurate. Bush was the best choice for Reagan, as Jim Baker had asserted all along.[21] He'd come in second for the nomination, had deep roots in the party, was more moderate than Reagan, had more foreign-policy experience than Reagan, and in the primaries had won several big industrial states, including Pennsylvania and Michigan. With the possible exception of Kemp himself—who was, of course, far less experienced—Bush was the best choice to unify the convention.

In fact, the last-minute pick of Bush was already proving beneficial to Reagan. A new Gallup survey, taken the weekend before and testing hypothetical running mates for Reagan, showed that the addition of Bush increased the Republicans' advantage over the Democrats. Running alone against Carter, Reagan was ahead 38–32, but the ticket of Reagan-Bush versus Carter-Mondale was leading 43–34.[22] Another poll, by the Associated Press and NBC, showed Bush helping Reagan more than Gerald Ford did.[23] Though the margin was small, the irony was deep: much of what had spurred the frenzied momentum behind the Dream Ticket was an early poll by Dick Wirthlin that showed Ford helping Reagan more than anyone else.

Better still for the Republicans, the Reagan-Bush team was unifying the GOP, and was competitive or leading in all regions of the country and even tied with Carter in his beloved South. And according to polling done for the Republican National Committee, majorities of Americans thought the Republicans were better at holding the line on government spending, better on tax cuts, better on standing up to the Communists, and better on reining in inflation. Adding insult to injury, a majority of Americans thought it would be better if the Republicans controlled Congress. Four years earlier, who'da thunk it? Sampling conducted by CBS and the *New York Times* in April 1980 confirmed that respondents "by wide margins" supported "cutting taxes, balancing the budget."[24]

Even some in the mainstream media recognized that the Bush choice could be a boon for Republicans. The lead editorial in the *New York Times* reviewed the madness of July 16 in Detroit and, while questioning Reagan's pursuit of Ford, still praised the Republican candidate for acting "decisively" at the last and asking the convention to nominate Bush. Bush also came in for praise from the paper: "He is a serious, able and likeable man. Ronald Reagan's second choice is not second-rate."[25]

Meanwhile, some of Bush's consultants tried to spin the media, saying that for the past two years Bush had in fact always been running for vice president, not president. The story—made up out of whole cloth—got the attention of some reporters; it appeared in at least one major national publication.

For all the drama surrounding the vice-presidential pick, Bush himself had a levelheaded assessment of the job of veep. He'd seen the daily reality of several vice presidents up close and knew the talk about expanding the duties of the office was so much hooey. The day before he was chosen by Reagan, he told a reporter, "Everyone says they are going to reinvent the wheel, that their Vice President is going to be in on developing North-South strategy and other great projects. But it never happens. Two years later, you wake up and find he's still going to funerals."[26] Still, Bush hoped for more than casting tie-breaking votes in the Senate and wondering about the health of the president. Certainly more than Richard Johnson, Martin Van Buren's second banana, who one summer had so little to do that he went home and managed an inn. Woodrow Wilson's vice president, Thomas Marshall, couldn't get a private audience with Wilson for a year and a half.

THE LONG, AGONIZING DECISION over a running mate, along with the introduction of Bush to the media, was finally behind the Reagan campaign. Still, Reagan and Bush had plenty of work ahead of them. Both had speeches to give that night.

For Bush, there was almost no time to prepare for such an important address. While the running mates did their meet-and-greet in the Reagan suite that morning, Vic Gold was sequestered in his room, furiously writing Bush's acceptance speech. He'd already written Bush's speech to the convention the night before, and now he and the other Bush aides were pulling a double shift, without any shop steward to complain to.

With Gold's help, Bush pulled off the important task that had been handed him. In a five-minute speech accepting the nomination for vice president, Bush both signaled to conservatives that he was on board with Reagan and the muscular platform and reached out to voters outside the party. First he proclaimed, "I enthusiastically support our platform. It's up to each and every one of us to help carry Ronald Reagan's message of a strong, free America the length and the breadth of this land." That message was unmistakable, as was his next one, in which he called on "disillusioned Democrats and disappointed independents" to join Reagan's cause.[27]

Unlike Bush, Reagan had had plenty of time to prepare for his acceptance speech, but his challenge was far greater than that of his new running mate. Indeed, the speech he gave that night would be the most important of his life up to that point. He was not simply accepting the nomination of the Republican Party and trying to unify his own party; he also needed to speak directly to the American people. A recent AP–NBC poll showed that Americans, by a slim margin of

44–42, thought Carter would win the fall election.[28] With the news media blasting Reagan for the chaos of the day before and questioning his decision-making abilities, the credibility issue was all the more pressing. Reagan had his work cut out for him. He would have to put on a stellar performance to ensure that Ford and the co-presidency fiasco didn't overshadow his convention.

Recognizing the importance of the moment, Peter Hannaford had worked on the speech with Reagan for six long weeks.[29] It would run for approximately forty-five minutes.

THAT NIGHT, CONVENTION PLANNERS thought it would be a good idea to put the Reagan and Bush families into one room together so they could get to know one another. Jeb Bush recalled that the older Reagan children, Mike and Maureen, could not have been nicer, "completely gregarious, nice, easy to deal with." The same could not be said for "the two other children, who were quite unhappy," sitting "off in the corner." "I walked over and tried to introduce myself," Bush said, "and they were basically rude."[30]

Jeb's father got a warmer reception from the delegates. That night, George Bush's name was placed in nomination for vice president of the United States. The "Reagan-Ford" handmade signs from the night before had disappeared and Joe Louis Arena was now filled with professionally printed "Reagan-Bush" signs in red, white, and blue. Since no other names were placed in nomination, the delegates got down to business quickly. Bush won 1,832 votes, with only 162 diehard conservatives voting against him.[31]

Four years earlier, when Gerald Ford accepted the GOP nomination in Kansas City, a cloud of blue smoke choked Kemper Arena from cigarettes, pipes, and cigars. Now only an occasional puff of smoke could be seen in Joe Louis Arena. The air had cleared for the Republicans in more ways than one. In 1976, in the wake of Watergate, there were few real heroes left in the Republican Party to join Ford at the dais on the night of his nomination. This time a galaxy of GOP stars was out for Reagan. President Ford and Mrs. Ford were seated in the hall in a place of honor. All the contenders for the Republican nomination were in Joe Louis Arena as well. They had been allowed to address the convention—all except for Phil Crane, that is. The snubbing of Crane was punishment for past offenses against Reagan.

One VIP sadly not in evidence for Reagan's acceptance speech was Paul Laxalt, who had been as responsible for this moment as anyone. He was still angry that he hadn't been consulted on the choice of Bush and felt the whole mess of the previous day could have been avoided.

Laxalt had a legitimate beef. Since 1975, he'd been Reagan's campaign chief. Laxalt traveled endlessly for his friend, whom he'd known since 1966, when both were running for governors of their respective states. Laxalt had pushed for Reagan, argued for Reagan, defended Reagan, and campaigned for Reagan. The night that his friend who owed him so much was nominated, Laxalt went out to dinner. The next morning, he skipped the all-important Republican Party meetings and flew back to Washington.[32]

Laxalt was far too polite to go public with his frustrations. When queried as to why he went to dinner rather than attend Reagan's acceptance speech, he said he just got sick of "eating a hot dog every night" for a meal. No one in the press corps was buying that.[33] Yet another rumor made the rounds that Laxalt had quit the campaign. As if Republicans hadn't already overdosed on unsubstantiated rumors.

Once George Bush's nomination was made official, the convention watched a biographical movie about Reagan, produced by Peter Dailey.[34] As it ended, the Reagans suddenly materialized on the podium, and the hall went berserk. If the old performer was nervous, he didn't show it. The band struck up Reagan's signature song, "California, Here I Come," and the faithful roared their approval.

As the Reagans appeared on the dais, the crowd began a prolonged, frenzied demonstration, with thousands of delegates waving signs and Americans flags, flashing Instamatics, blowing banned air horns, screaming, stomping, and yelling. A giant banner at the back of the hall proclaimed "Reagan Country" and was accompanied by what would become an iconic photo of Reagan, with the signature slightly lopsided smile, wearing a white cowboy hat, and looking every inch the rugged cowboy.

The California and Texas delegations reprised their back-and-forth chant of Kansas City. The California Reaganites would raise their white cowboy hats and yell, "*Viva!*" to which the Lone Star Reaganauts would raise their blue cowboy hats and reply, "*Olé!*" Indeed, it seemed as if the entire arena was filled with cowboy hats, even though some of the city slicker delegates' only brush with a ranch was their salad dressing.

Pretty soon, the entire arena joined in the fun. Reagan could only watch and laugh, sharing the amusement with thousands of people, many of whom had waited a goodly portion of their life for this scene. Chuckling over the prolonged demonstration, the Gipper quipped, "We're using up prime time!"[35]

Nancy Reagan was seated to "Ronnie's" left, looking lovely in a soft peach-colored dress, eyes fixed on her husband with adoration. Next to her was Maureen. The rest of Reagan's family, along with George Bush and his extended family, sat on stage as well.

When Reagan finally got the raucous delegates to settle down, he joked, "The first thrill tonight was to find myself for the first time in a long time in a movie on prime time!"[36] The crowd roared with laughter.

Reagan had addressed the 1964 Republican convention as a private citizen; the 1968 gathering as a governor and erstwhile presidential candidate; the 1972 coronation of Richard Nixon as a governor again; and the 1976 convention as a failed presidential candidate and private citizen once again.

The term "citizen" had great meaning to the Gipper, a student of the American Revolution and the federalism created by the Founding Fathers. Reagan knew that these men believed the citizen to be of more importance in their American experiment than all the elected officials combined. These men were "Citizen Franklin" and "Citizen Adams" on July 4, 1776, and September 17, 1787. Thus Reagan called his 1976 quest "Citizens for Reagan"; his political committee was "Citizens for the Republic"; and he always referred to himself as a "citizen-politician" because he truly believed in the concept. Now, in Detroit, Reagan opened his speech by appealing to "my fellow citizens."[37]

Reagan looked every inch the leader and prospective president. He wore a dark blue suit, a spread-collar white shirt, a maroon pin-dot tie in his usual Windsor style, and, of course, a folded white handkerchief in the left breast pocket of his suit jacket. In his left lapel was a tiny American flag. His hair wafted a bit, as a small fan blew air at him in the overly hot convention hall.

Reagan had a fan club started in the 1940s by Mrs. Zelda Multz of Brooklyn. She'd kept the club going for almost forty years. Now the Gipper was poised to swell the ranks of that club. First, though, Reagan, ever mannerly, thanked the host city and the state of Michigan for "the warm hospitality we've enjoyed." Reagan was growing comfortable with the choice of George Bush and went out of his way to twice refer to Bush. He thanked the delegates "for your wholehearted response to my recommendation in regard to George Bush as the candidate for vice president."[38]

He swung into his speech, beginning, "With a deep awareness of the responsibility conferred by your trust, I accept your nomination for the presidency of the United States." This set off a new round of celebration by the delegates. Reagan moved ahead and made an appeal not just to Republicans but also to Democrats and independents to join a "community of shared values."[39]

This address, so obviously crucial for Reagan, would not be another variation of "The Speech," his bread and butter of the past sixteen years. He only sparingly inserted the phrases and sentiments he had used so many times. His rhetoric was soaring, melodic. Even people who worked for Reagan and had heard him speak a hundred times were truly amazed at what a moving, lofty speech this was.

During the address Reagan invoked the names of three presidents, only two of them with praise: Abraham Lincoln and his personal favorite, Franklin Roosevelt. The third, Jimmy Carter, he eviscerated for his "mediocre leadership."[40] His approach to FDR was unusual, but true to his conservative philosophy and fitting for his Republican audience: he cited Roosevelt in 1932 criticizing the excessive spending by the federal government under Herbert Hoover.

Though the Republicans could get behind calls to curb the size of government, they didn't know what to make of Reagan's warm words about a politician they had grown up despising, and the applause was light to say the least. It was true that Reagan had no intention of dismantling Roosevelt's New Deal. He had abandoned his opposition to Social Security back in the late 1960s. He also remembered that his out-of-work father had gotten a job in the New Deal, in the depths of the Great Depression, and he saw the New Deal not so much as socialism but as a form of government insurance that would help the free market operate. It was the Great Society that Reagan wanted to dismantle, as he later wrote in his diaries.[41]

Reagan moved to the heart of his address and declared, "Never before in our history have Americans been called upon to face three grave threats to our very existence, any one of which could destroy us. We face a disintegrating economy, a weakened defense, and an energy policy based on the sharing of scarcity." He did not hesitate to hold President Carter and the Democratic Congress accountable, saying that they had a "direct political, personal, and moral responsibility" for "this unprecedented calamity which has befallen us." Reagan continued:

> They say that the United States has had its day in the sun, that our nation has passed its zenith. They expect you to tell your children that the American people no longer have the will to cope with their problems, that the future will be one of sacrifice and few opportunities.
>
> My fellow citizens, I utterly reject that view.
>
> The American people, the most generous on earth, who created the highest standard of living, are not going to accept the notion that we can only make a better world for others by moving backward ourselves. And those who believe we can have no business leading this nation.[42]

Reagan was even more pointed in his indictment of President Carter's administration. "Back in 1976," he reminded his listeners, "Mr. Carter said, 'Trust me.' And a lot of people did. And now, many of those people are out of work. Many have seen their savings eaten away by inflation. Many others on fixed incomes, especially the elderly, have watched helplessly as the cruel tax of inflation wasted away their purchasing power. And, today, a great many who trusted Mr. Carter wonder if we can survive the Carter policies of national defense."[43]

As Reagan built his case against Carter, the crowd joined in. Reagan asked, "Can anyone look at the record of this administration and say, 'Well done'?"[44] The partisan audience roared, "NO!"

"Can anyone compare the state of our economy when the Carter administration took office with where we are today and say, 'Keep up the good work'?" Reagan issued what only could be called a sarcastic wink to the crowd.[45]

They cried out, "NO!" to his refrain.

"Can anyone look at our reduced standing in the world today and say, 'Let's have four more years of this'?"[46]

"NO!"

Reagan drew energy and strength from the delegates, and only minutes into the speech he had found his stride. "I will not accept," he thundered, "the excuse that the federal government has grown so big and powerful that it is beyond the control of any president, any administration or Congress. We are going to put an end to the notion that the American taxpayer exists to fund the federal government. The federal government exists to serve the American people. On January 20, we are going to reestablish that truth."[47]

He stated his view of the role of governments and the role of people, doing the Founders proud. "My view of government places trust not in one person or one party, but in those values that transcend persons and parties. The trust is where it belongs—in the people. The responsibility to live up to that trust is where it belongs—in their elected leaders. That kind of relationship, between the people and their elected leaders, is a special kind of compact."[48]

Reagan's speech was infused with words and phrases such as "unify," "future," "dedication," "commitment," "clarity of vision," "forward momentum," and "courage"—all new idioms to a GOP once obsessed about the past and had been forced onto the defensive over Herbert Hoover, isolationism, anticommunism, traditional values, and the corruption of Richard Nixon and his betrayal of conservatism. Reagan also used the phrase "a new beginning," as well as "new consensus" and "the time is now," several times.[49]

Reagan proposed to take positive action, announcing specific freezes in federal hiring and cuts in federal spending if elected. He also made his case for the Kemp-Roth across-the-board tax cuts:

Work and family are at the center of our lives, the foundation of our dignity as a free people. When we deprive people of what they have earned, or take away their jobs, we destroy their dignity and undermine their families. We can't support families unless there are jobs; and we can't have jobs unless the people have both money to invest and the faith to invest it. . . .

The American people are carrying the heaviest peacetime tax burden in our nation's history—and it will grow even heavier, under present law, next January. We are taxing ourselves into economic exhaustion and stagnation, crushing our ability and incentive to save, invest and produce. This must stop. . . .

I've long advocated a 30 percent reduction in income tax rates over a period of three years. This phased tax reduction would begin with a 10 percent "down payment" tax cut in 1981, which the Republicans in Congress and I have already proposed. A phased reduction of tax rates would go a long way toward easing the heavy burden on the American people. [50]

Reagan did not stop there, proposing new and additional tax cuts for businesses as a means to jump-start the torpid American economy. Some of his heartiest applause came at his tax-cut proposals.

The GOP's nominee also made a direct challenge to minorities to join his cause. "We have to move ahead, but we're not going to leave anyone behind. . . . That may be the Democratic leadership's message to the minorities, but it won't be our message. . . . It's time to put America back to work, to make our cities and towns resound with the confident voices of men and women of all races, nationalities and faiths bringing home to their families a paycheck they can cash for honest money." [51]

During long applause, the networks' "pool" camera (to save costs, the three networks shared the same camera and broadcast content) cut away to show viewers what the hall looked like and who was there. Frank Sinatra and his wife, Barbara, were in a VIP section. George Bush, wearing the same granny glasses his aides had begged him to get rid of, was wreathed in smiles. So was Barbara Bush and the rest of their family, with the exception of their eldest son, George, who looked bored and not terribly happy. Mostly, though, television viewers saw in Joe Louis Arena people pretty much like themselves.

Reagan turned to foreign policy, his staple issue for many years, especially his opposition to Soviet Communism. In a clear, forceful tone, Reagan said, "When we move from domestic affairs and cast our eyes abroad, we see an equally sorry chapter in the record of the present administration." He catalogued Carter's abdication of responsibility: "A Soviet combat brigade trains in Cuba, just 90 miles from our shores. A Soviet army of invasion occupies Afghanistan, further threatening our vital interests in the Middle East. America's defense strength is at its lowest ebb in a generation, while the Soviet Union is vastly outspending us in both strategic and conventional arms. Our European allies, looking nervously at the growing menace from the East, turn to us for leadership and fail to find it."[52]

Reagan then took on the sensitive issue of the American hostages long held in Iran. "And incredibly . . . more than fifty of our fellow Americans have been held captive for over eight months by a dictatorial foreign power that holds us up to ridicule before the world."[53]

He turned the snarky comments made about his movie career around on Carter, charging the president with living "in the world of make-believe. . . . But you and I live in a real world, where disasters are overtaking our nation without any real response from Washington. This is make-believe, self-deceit and, above all, transparent hypocrisy. For example, Mr. Carter says he supports the volunteer army, but he lets military pay and benefits slip so low that many of our enlisted personnel are actually eligible for food stamps." Reagan elaborated on the poor condition and morale of the U.S. military and then swung yet again at Carter. "There may be a sailor at the helm of the ship of state, but the ship has no rudder."[54] The crowd laughed and Reagan smiled.

The candidate was not finished with Carter, serving up his most powerful bill of particulars against the administration. "Who does not feel a growing sense of unease as our allies . . . reluctantly conclude that America is unwilling or unable to fulfill its obligations as leader of the free world? Who does not feel rising alarm when the question . . . is no longer 'Should we do something?' but 'Do we have the capacity to do anything?' The administration which has brought us to this state is seeking your endorsement for four more years of weakness, indecision, mediocrity, and incompetence. No American should vote until he or she has asked, 'Is the United States stronger and more respected now than it was three-and-a-half years ago? Is the world today a safer place in which to live?'"[55]

The delegates responded in unison, "NO!"

Waiting for the applause to die down, Reagan spotted a group of supporters from the Young Americans for Freedom in the crowd, furiously waving signs, and the Gipper gave them a warm wink.[56] He was the national chairman of their advisory board. These kids adored Reagan, and he always seemed to find time to attend their conferences and answer their requests.

"It is," he went on, "the responsibility of the president of the United States, in working for peace, to ensure that the safety of our people cannot successfully be threatened by a hostile foreign power. As president, fulfilling that responsibility will be my number one priority."[57] Nothing less than the outcome of the Cold War was at stake in this election, many believed, and Reagan picked up the mantle of the anti-Communist John F. Kennedy, who said in 1961, "For only when our arms are sufficient beyond doubt can we be certain beyond doubt that they will never be employed."[58] In 1980 Reagan said:

> Four times in my lifetime America has gone to war, bleeding the lives of its young men into the sands of island beachheads, the fields of Europe and the jungles and rice paddies of Asia. We know only too well that war comes not when the forces of freedom are strong, it is when they are weak that tyrants are tempted. . . .
>
> But let our friends and those who may wish us ill take note: the United States has an obligation to its citizens and to the people of the world never to let those who would destroy freedom dictate the future course of life on this planet. I would regard my election as proof that we have renewed our resolve to preserve world peace and freedom. That this nation will once again be strong enough to do that.[59]

Nearing the close of his remarks, Reagan became misty, reflective. "This evening marks the last step, save one, of a campaign that has taken Nancy and me from one end of this great nation to the other, over many months and thousands and thousands of miles." He then gave testament to the person-to-person campaigning on which he thrived. "There are those who question the way we choose a president, who say that our process imposes difficult and exhausting burdens on those who seek the office." Softly, with his blue eyes flashing, he said, "I have not found it so."[60]

Then Reagan spoke of America and the American people with a poignancy that few politicians could match:

> It is impossible to capture in words the splendor of this vast continent which God has granted as our portion of His creation. There are no words to express the extraordinary strength and character of this breed of people we call Americans.
>
> Everywhere we've met thousands of Democrats, Independents and Republicans from all economic conditions, walks of life bound together in that community of shared values of family, work, neighborhood, peace and freedom. They are concerned, yes, they're not frightened. They're disturbed, but not dismayed. They are the kind of men and women Tom Paine

had in mind when he wrote, during the darkest days of the American Revolution, "We have it in our power to begin the world over again."

Nearly 150 years after Tom Paine wrote those words, an American president told the generation of the Great Depression that it had a "rendezvous with destiny." I believe this generation of Americans today also has a rendezvous with destiny.[61]

Hannaford knew the speech cold from having worked on it so long with Reagan, but even the favored wordsmith wept when he heard Reagan deliver it.[62]

Joe Louis Arena was still, the delegates rapt with attention. Helene Von Damm, Reagan's utterly devoted secretary for so many years, was crying tears of joy. She could scarcely believe that this moment had finally come[63] As few other American leaders have, Reagan made Americans weepingly happy and proud. Men and women were snuffling, crying unabashedly, not only in Detroit but across the country, in saloons and firehouses, on farms and in fishing villages, in American Legion halls and college dormitories. Reagan spoke to all of them, reaching into their homes, their minds, and their hearts. Concluding, the Gipper said:

> The time is now, my fellow Americans, to recapture our destiny, to take it into our own hands. And to do this it will take many of us, working together. I ask you tonight, all over this land, to volunteer your help in this cause so that we can carry our message throughout the land . . .
>
> Can we doubt that only a Divine Providence placed this land, this island of freedom, here as a refuge for all those people in the world who yearn to breathe free? Jews and Christians enduring persecution behind the Iron Curtain; the boat people of Southeast Asia, Cuba and of Haiti; the victims of drought and famine in Africa, the freedom fighters in Afghanistan, and our own countrymen held in savage captivity.

Reagan's voice began to crack slightly as he revealed the depth of his feelings about America.

"I'll confess that I've been a little afraid to suggest what I'm going to suggest. I'm more afraid not to. Can we begin our crusade joined together in a moment of silent prayer?"[64] He bowed his head and more than twenty thousand people fell silent. Except the low hum of the air conditioning, nary a sound was heard. As he lifted his head, Reagan's eyes misted over and he struggled to keep his composure. He gained it and ended simply, elegantly, and fervently.

"God bless America."[65]

26

Horse Latitudes

"We are not that dumb."

In the early days of sailing between Europe and the New World, sea captains who navigated too close to a subtropical stretch of still weather along either side of the equator would find themselves becalmed, as the winds became insufficient to propel their ships forward. Adrift for weeks on end, they would find their water supply running perilously low. To husband what little water was left for the crew and save their thirsty animals from further suffering, the captains would order the horses thrown overboard. These waters into which they were tossed became known to seafaring men as the "horse latitudes."

Ronald Reagan didn't know it, but beginning shortly after the Republican convention, his campaign would drift into its own horse latitudes. Given his love of horses and George Bush's love of the sea, perhaps between the two men they should have forecast this spell that threatened to overcome their campaign in the scorching summer of 1980.

THE DETROIT CONVENTION ENDED well enough. Joe Louis Arena went bonkers with cheering the last night of the convention when George Bush joined Reagan in a victory clasp. Then their wives, Barbara and Nancy, joined them. When former president Ford appeared, the applause and cheers continued unabated. T-shirts on the floor read, "Why not an actor—we've had a clown for 4 years."

The highlight of the night, of course, was Reagan's speech. Reaction was almost universally positive from the American media, political observers, and the party the Gipper now led. According to a young researcher, Mitchell Shirley, Reagan was interrupted eighty-nine times in forty-six minutes by the delirious

Republicans. Just as important, this speech and this conservative leader were giving rise to a second generation of optimistic conservative leadership in politics and the culture. Names that meant nothing in 1980 were just foot soldiers in Reagan's revolution, including twenty-somethings (and even some teens) such as John Fund, Mark Levin, Grover Norquist, Mark Tapscott, Steve Moore, Frank Luntz, Tony Fabrizio, Kirby Wilbur, Jack Abramoff, Alex Castellanos, Diana Banister, Laura Ingraham, John McLaughlin, and Mike Pence. They were among thousands of young Americans touched and moved by Reagan and his message. Soon, many of these young upstarts would become the resurgent conservative establishment.

Plenty of Americans, of all ages, were called to join the "crusade" Reagan spoke of in his acceptance speech. People such as Diana Evans, a fifty-two-year-old housewife from Oregon. Before 1964 she had barely given any thought to Reagan, but then she saw Reagan's speech for Goldwater. That was it. She became a Reaganite and volunteered on his 1968 campaign. She rose through the ranks through hard work to become a Reagan delegate in 1976 and again in 1980. As a reward for her years of thankless effort, Diana was asked to give a short speech in Detroit seconding her hero, Ronald Reagan. According to *Time* magazine, she was "superb." She cried tears of joy as she watched Reagan up on the stage giving his acceptance speech.[1]

The Gipper's speech succeeded because Reagan knew that campaigns and conventions and all the minutiae they entailed were not about the candidate or the party or the media. Ultimately, politics was about what a politician was going to do for the voters and where he wanted to lead them. Reagan told the American people he trusted them to trust themselves—which meant, in turn, they could trust him.

Wall Street was pleased by the speech. Traders went on a buying spree and sent the stock market up nearly 9 points to a three-year high of 923. Brokers openly told the media that Reagan's talk of massive tax cuts coupled with giant increases in defense spending helped push the market up.[2]

The media widely commended Reagan's speech. The network anchors, to a person, were impressed. Speaking for all, John Chancellor of NBC said of the address, "Well, Ronald Reagan has done it again." The lead editorial in the *New York Times* the Sunday after the convention was headlined "Franklin Delano Reagan." Quite a statement coming from a pillar of the liberal eastern elite. The paper called Reagan's handling of the convention and his speech "audacious, even brilliant," noting that "if Ronald Reagan casts himself as the latter-day equivalent of Franklin Roosevelt, guess which part Jimmy Carter is meant to play." The *Times* even praised Reagan's attempt to coax Ford onto the ticket, saying it "demonstrated a clear Reagan willingness to reach out. So did the ultimate choice of

George Bush." Tongue-in-cheek, the paper added, "So did the effort to kidnap Franklin Roosevelt."[3]

The same Sunday, the *Washington Post*'s lead editorial said that Reagan had unleashed an "intellectual revolution in American politics" and that "there could be no better political news than that one of the country's major parties in fact had something new to say."[4] *Time* magazine's cover story was an illustration of a GOP elephant as a convention delegate tearing off his shirt and tie, Superman-style, to reveal the familiar red "S" and blue superhero outfit. "Feeling Super in Detroit" shouted the headline. An accompanying story said, "The great strength of the speech was Reagan's relaxed but forceful delivery."[5] The publication called Reagan's speech "very likely the best" of his career.[6]

One of the most talented political cartoonists of the era, Jeff MacNelly, whose cartoons tended to favor the Republicans (unlike those of virtually all of his brethren), humorously drew a horde of hungry GOP elephants breaking into a barn labeled "The Carter Record" to find it full of peanuts, plenty for them to munch on.[7]

Even the very liberal Meg Greenfield of the *Washington Post* said that "Reagan's lack of guile is one of the things that he has going for him" and that he'd run "what seems to have been an unusually aboveboard, uncrooked and uncompromised campaign."[8]

Only overseas was Reagan routinely panned. Britain's *Daily Mail* eviscerated the Republicans, while the *Times* of London called the convention a "debacle." The Egyptian media predictably blasted Reagan and the "Zionist forces surrounding him."[9]

Everyone else, it seemed, was suddenly reevaluating his opinion of the Gipper. Corporate America, long skeptical of Reagan's populism, was taking a closer look and consoling itself with the notion that Reagan's record in Sacramento wasn't nearly as conservative as his rhetoric. The venerable Veterans of Foreign Wars, representing millions of former American GIs, broke with their tradition of sixty-six years of neutrality and went to battle stations for Reagan. There were approximately thirty million vets in the country in 1980.

Remarkably, the Reverend Jesse Jackson hinted just days after the GOP convention ended that he could "support Republican efforts to take over the White House this year."[10] Black Americans had voted overwhelmingly Democratic for decades, but Reagan aides reached out to Jackson for a meeting, and not without reason. As part of Operation PUSH (People United to Save Humanity), Jackson went into inner cities to exhort young black children to hit the books, get good grades, and pull themselves up by their bootstraps. At the time, too, Jackson was pro-life. In the 1960s and 1970s, African-Americans consistently polled more pro-life and more conservative on cultural issues than whites. Even if Reagan could not make major inroads with the black community, open relations would at least comfort moderate Republican and independent voters.

The eventual meeting with Jackson was a washout, though. Reagan flew to Chicago and met in private with the Reverend Jackson. All seemed to go well—that is, until Jackson walked Reagan to his car. Spotting the television cameras, Jackson embarrassed Reagan by asking him in front of the media if he would renounce the endorsement of the Ku Klux Klan, which Reagan did not seek, did not want, and found detestable. Reagan told Jackson he was unaware of the odious endorsement and denounced the organization.[11]

Reagan's progress with African-Americans was slow, but with Hispanics, especially the heavily anti-Communist Cuban, Nicaraguan, and Salvadorian communities in America, who had fled Communism, he had hero status. It wasn't unusual for Reagan, when he campaigned in front of Hispanic audiences, to see signs such as "Only Reagan can halt Communism."[12]

Despite all the good signs, Reagan had only a mere twelve hours after his acceptance speech in Detroit before he hit another bump in the road. On Friday morning, July 18, he met in private with his field staff, most of whom had wanted Jack Kemp on the ticket and felt little compunction about saying so to Reagan. When Roger Stone, the campaign's regional political director in New York and Connecticut, pointedly asked why Reagan hadn't picked Kemp, the nominee shrugged his shoulders and made an oblique reference to the rumors.[13] Later, Lyn Nofziger told reporter Bob Novak that Kemp had been passed over because of "that homosexual thing. The governor finally said, 'We just can't do this to Jack.'" Reagan wanted to spare Kemp and his family from the vicious and untrue rumors that surely would have come up had he chosen the tax-cutting acolyte.[14]

Reagan's meeting with his field staff ended uncomfortably. Kenny Klinge, another member of the field staff, remembered Bill Timmons saying at the time, "I'm going to get fired because I'm going to have to say something to the governor about this. I mean, we can't have him making these kinds of comments."[15] Ed Meese concurred.

Reagan's comments seemed even less politic in light of claims made by many sources that what ultimately kept Kemp from real contention was not any rumor but that he was "uncontrollable." What ultimately put George Bush on the ticket was that he was controllable, according to Kemp aide Dave Smick.[16]

The same day that Reagan met with his field staff, the Republican National Committee met in Detroit for its annual election of officers. RNC chairman Bill

Brock was basking in the glow of a well-fashioned convention, for having the vision to choose Detroit over many objections, for turning the party around over the past three and a half years, and for raising millions for the GOP. As much as anybody, Brock had helped to bring his party back from the dead. Since the disastrous 1974 elections, the GOP under Brock's leadership had regained 358 state legislative seats, a net of six governorships, and a handful of congressional seats.[17]

For all this, Brock was rewarded with an embarrassing, temporary reelection that would allow him to serve as chairman only until after the election, at which time a permanent replacement could very well be chosen. Brock still had two members of Reagan's campaign team looking over his shoulder at the RNC, Jerry Carmen and Drew Lewis. Conservatives were delighted to see their old adversary Brock continue to lose face.[18]

ON THE FRIDAY AFTER the convention, the Reagans jetted off to Houston to join the Bushes. After a private lunch at the Bush home in the wealthy enclave of Memorial, the running mates appeared at a public rally at a shopping center. Both Reagan and Bush wore white cowboy hats. The appearance was indoors, and good thing, too, because the temperature outside was 103 degrees. Apparently, not everybody had gotten comfortable with the Reagan-Bush ticket. Former ambassador Anne Armstrong mistakenly introduced the "Reagan-Ford ticket" to gasps, but quickly corrected herself.[19]

After the Houston appearance, Reagan headed west to his ranch in Santa Barbara and Bush headed north to his family's oceanside estate in Maine. They both needed some rest. The previous week—indeed, the previous three years—had been a roller coaster ride. They needed time to reflect on recent events, the swirl of history and fate that had brought together two vastly different men—two men who, up until just a few hours before, really didn't know each other, had little use for each other, and often didn't like each other.

Bill Timmons, having successfully run the convention, moved over to become the political director for Reagan-Bush. He was already in combat mode, as he gleefully expressed to the media. "We will charge the Carter administration is dumb, dangerous and deceitful," Timmons told the *Wall Street Journal*.[20]

President Carter was not letting Republican attacks go unanswered. Upon Reagan's nomination at the GOP convention, Carter called his opponent and sent him a congratulatory telegram.[21] But just as quickly he began bashing the Republicans and challenging Reagan to a series of debates. He reminded an audience of Democrats at a fundraiser in Florida that Republicans "brought us the disgrace of

Watergate."[22] Carter's record as president was open to question, but as a politician in the hunt, he was relentless.

Ted Kennedy, still hanging on for the Democratic convention, also attacked Reagan and the GOP. He compared Reagan's tax-cut proposal to Laetrile, a substance long touted as an anticancer agent that clinical trials and other investigations had shown to be useless—and dangerous to boot. In other words, Kennedy was calling Reagan a snake-oil salesman. His analysis of the Democrats' situation displayed a bit more concern than did Carter's, however. Kennedy said, "We have only four more months to convince the voters that America is not Hollywood, the Republicans are not the party of the future, and Ronald Wilson Reagan is not Franklin Delano Roosevelt."[23]

Reagan and Bush met back up in Los Angeles toward the end of July with some staff to review their strategy for the summer and fall effort. But before battling with the Democrats, the two former combatants had to referee the battles between their respective staffs. Lyn Nofziger, now firmly ensconced as the campaign's spokesman and chief punster, said of merging the two campaigns, "It's a hell of a mesh, I'll tell you." The Los Angeles meeting took place in the Tokyo Room of a Travelodge across the street from Reagan's original campaign headquarters. Nofziger said the room "would be a good place to orient people."[24]

Some members of the Reagan staff were attempting to dictate personnel policy to the grafted-on Bush team—or what was left of it. Nofziger was gunning for Pete Teeley, Bush's press secretary, whom he didn't like and whose liberal politics he despised. Nofziger tried to supplant him with Jim Brady, who had come aboard after his candidate, John Connally, had nosedived. Nor did Jim Baker want Teeley back. But other Bush aides intervened and Teeley ended up staying on with Bush.[25]

Baker didn't want David Keene back either. Keene was long gone from the Bush operations, having earned the enmity of Mrs. Bush over his personal life and of Ambassador Bush for being a profligate leaker and for verbally abusing the campaign staff, according to sources. Keene had reportedly tried to rejoin the Bush campaign in Detroit after learning that Bush had been chosen for the Republican ticket.[26] Mike Deaver, Keene's "*bête noire* within the Reagan camp" (as the *Washington Star* reported), was keeping him out of the Gipper's operation as well.[27] Keene was regarded as having one of the best minds in Republican politics, but he'd dealt himself out of the high-stakes game of 1980.

The group assembled in Los Angeles included fifteen or so Reaganites, among them Ed Meese, Marty Anderson, Nofziger, and Peter Dailey, who had worked with the legendary Roger Ailes producing ads for Richard Nixon in 1972. The

meeting was light on Bush aides. Bush attended the meetings only with the beleaguered Teeley and Dean Burch, a gray eminence of the GOP who hadn't played
a significant role in Bush's campaign. The rest of Bush's staff was three thousand miles away back in Washington, dry-docked. An aide on the Reagan plane,
Michele Davis, dropped by the campaign headquarters in Arlington, Virginia,
which the Reagan team had taken over in a sublease from John Connally's long-
expired campaign. Davis later confided in her diary, "Not too many happy faces
around there."[28] She also noted that between the Reaganites and the Bushies there
existed "a real 'we' 'they' attitude."[29]

Dick Wirthlin briefed the L.A. group on the fall campaign strategy. He had
written a two-hundred-page plan titled the "Great American Team" that detailed
the regions of the country he believed were ripe for Reagan, many of which had
been only sporadically available to the Republicans before. One key step of Wirthlin's plan had already been taken: he had urged picking a moderate running mate
at the convention in order to unify the party.[30]

Wirthlin was encouraged that Reagan-Bush could take all the states Gerald Ford had carried in 1976 with the possible exception of Michigan and would
be very competitive in Carter's South as well as heavily Catholic states, including New York, Ohio, and Pennsylvania, all of which Carter had carried in 1976.
Wirthlin's larger strategy called for making the case against Carter in the Northeast, from New York across the Rust Belt to Illinois. That meant going after the
blue-collar vote and shelving Reagan's past attacks on labor unions. "There will be
no union baiting in this campaign," said one campaign official. Wirthlin harbored
no illusions that Reagan would get the 54 percent of the labor vote that Richard
Nixon had in 1972 when the AFL-CIO sat on its hands. That was especially so
because the AFL-CIO had issued an all-points bulletin to affiliated unions to turn
up the heat on Reagan, and was expected to spend as much as $10 million in
the campaign. Still, Wirthlin was confident that Reagan, the first major-party
presidential candidate to hold an active union card, would get more than the 36
percent of the labor vote that Ford had four years earlier.[31]

Wirthlin thought Connecticut could be in play because of George Bush's roots
there. No one in the campaign, however, thought Massachusetts, which George
McGovern had carried singularly in 1972 and which Carter had won handily in
1976, was anything close to being up for grabs.[32] Columnists Bob Novak and
his partner Rowly Evans discerned something else though in the Bay State. They
commissioned Carter's pollster, Pat Caddell, to focus on precinct 7-1 in Waltham,
a blue-collar Catholic suburb of Boston. What they found was astonishing. Carter
had carried the precinct in a landslide in 1976, but now, among the 79 registered

voters, Reagan was getting 37, John Anderson 22, and Carter just 12, with the rest undecided. By large margins, the voters of 7-1 favored the Reagan tax cuts, cuts in the federal government, and a military buildup. The columnists concluded that precinct 7-1 portended not just "another swing by supposedly volatile voters, but a basic revolution in American political attitudes."[33]

Such attitudes were crucial to Wirthlin's plan to fight hard in Carter's South. The Reaganites understood that the South, though behaviorally Democratic, was nonetheless attitudinally conservative. Reagan had already proven in the primaries of 1976 and 1980 his crossover appeal in such states as Texas and South Carolina. The Reagan campaign therefore had high hopes for Texas, which Carter had carried by the skin of his teeth over Ford. Wirthlin assumed that with Reagan, hugely popular in the Lone Star State, and Bush, who had adopted Texas as his home, plus John Connally's help, they might win it.

Wirthlin had put together an impressive political plan. The problem for the Reagan-Bush team was that it had done little to assemble an operational campaign to marry up with the plan. Fissures soon began to appear between Reagan's "Californians" and the "Easterners," and each side leaked to the media against the other. Skeptically, Nofziger said of the Bush staff, "It's a matter of bringing them into the Reagan campaign."[34] One GOP consultant, more sarcastically said, "We'll have to get along for only about three months."[35] Whether they could was open to question.

As a start down the road of internal reconciliation, the campaign hastily arranged a press conference in Washington to announce that Paul Laxalt and Anne Armstrong would be cochairs of the general-election campaign. It had taken a bit of cajoling to get Laxalt back after he'd left the convention ticked off, but the Nevadan wasn't going to miss this one last roundup with his old friend. Laxalt was one of the most easy-going and most forgiving men in politics. At the press conference he spoke up for Bush and said that conservatives upset over the choice of running mate would come back into the family. The Reagan team also took the opportunity to announce that Jim Baker had become a senior adviser to the campaign; the former Bush manager would assume a full-time if undefined position.[36]

A new poll by the Associated Press–NBC had Reagan opening up an eye-popping 55–24 percent lead over President Carter. John Anderson had dropped to 15 percent.[37] In a Lou Harris poll, Reagan was leading by a whopping 61–33 percent. No one thought the margin would hold, but Reagan clearly got a better convention bounce than anyone had expected. More sober Reaganites remembered the gigantic lead Ted Kennedy had held over Carter just a year earlier, and, even more relevant, Carter's huge 62–27 lead over President Ford four years earlier, following his convention.[38] They knew that in politics, what went up must come down.

The truth was that the thought of going up against Carter's tough campaign operatives terrified the Reagan-Bush team. "We look at the Carter operation and we worry a lot," fretted one campaign staffer. "On this stuff, they're big-leaguers. We're still babes in the woods."[39] This fear was real, even though Carter's approval rating had bottomed out at 22 percent yet again, just where he'd been in his "malaise" slump of one year earlier.[40] Carter was a tough hombre, at least as a campaigner, and had all the power of incumbency at his disposal. Polling also showed the antiabortion plank in the GOP platform to be a drag with some voters. No matter what the early sampling said, this fight wouldn't be some walk in the park for Reagan—especially because Carter had yet to get his own convention bounce.

Problems began to mount for the Reagan campaign. Bush was continually asked why he was the second pick for the second slot. Ten days had passed since the convention and the stories still hadn't died down about the "co-presidency." The *Wall Street Journal* ran the distracting headline "Reagan, Bush Start on Fall Campaign, Haunted by 'Dream Ticket' Nightmare."[41] A headline in the *Los Angeles Times* blared, "Nettled by Rumors . . . ," and the story reviewed the discord inside the merged Reagan and Bush operations.[42] Still under fire, the Reagan campaign announced that it would produce its own account of what really happened with Ford and release it to the media, then abruptly changed field and said it would not release such a report.[43]

A new story surfaced in the media, bizarrely claiming that Reagan "had encouraged Bolivian military officials in what turned out to be a successful overthrow of the Bolivian government a week ago." Lyn Nofziger had to go out and knock it down, saying, "We are not that dumb."[44] Another rumor claimed that Ford had been offered both the vice presidency *and* defense secretary.

These stories had no sooner cooled down when the media turned their attention to a fresh controversy: Would Reagan release his income-tax statements, and if so, when?

Yet another media frenzy resulted when Reagan went to get . . . a haircut. "Did he or didn't he?" had been a running question for years—did he dye his hair, that is. Now under constant press scrutiny, Reagan was trailed by reporters when he stopped in at Drucker's barbershop, where he had been going for forty years.[45] On at least one occasion reporters actually took the cuttings from the floor of the barbershop to have them tested. The samples came back proving that Reagan was telling the truth and did not dye his hair, but that didn't stop reporters from continuing to speculate on why Reagan had so few gray hairs. Actually, he only shampooed with Head & Shoulders and then used a little dab of Brylcreem along with copious amounts of water. Before this campaign was over, however, Reagan would accumulate a few more grays, as would Bush.

A story buried in the *New York Times* in late July casually mentioned an invitation Reagan had received to attend the Neshoba County Fair in Mississippi in early August, just one day after a planned speech to the National Urban League meeting in New York. The Urban League speech was part of an effort by the Reagan campaign to make amends for skipping the annual meeting of the NAACP. The paper ominously described the region of Mississippi where Neshoba was as "a setting that was once a favorite stumping ground for segregationist politicians."[46]

Dick Wirthlin tried to talk Reagan out of going to Neshoba. Alone in Reagan's bedroom, the pollster made his case that he thought it was a mistake. He must have pushed the issue too hard, because, as he later remembered, Reagan "got so mad at me, he threw his speech papers at me and scattered them all over the bedroom." When Reagan calmed down, he said, "Dick, I've already given a commitment on it. I'm not going to disappoint these people."[47]

NATIONAL DEMOCRATS BECAME MORE vocal with their concerns about nominating either Carter or Kennedy. A small group of Democrats, convinced that neither could beat Reagan, had met quietly in Philadelphia to create the Committee for an Open Convention. Its purpose was to investigate the possibility of the party's turning to either Secretary of State Edmund Muskie, formerly a senator from Maine and Hubert Humphrey's running mate in 1968, or Senator Henry "Scoop" Jackson of Washington, two of the most respected men in the Democratic Party.[48] Forty members of Congress lent their names to a move to find an alternative candidate. Vice President Mondale had already had his tires kicked, but he was a loyalist and said "no way."[49]

Some saw the move as a ploy by Kennedy forces. Kennedy was hundreds of delegates behind Carter in the count, yet an odd sort of hopefulness took hold in his campaign and in the media that, somehow, he might still win the nomination. Kennedy's plan rested on a slim reed: that a sufficient number of delegates would vote to suspend Rule F(3)c. According to the rule, delegates were required to cast their first roll-call votes for the candidate to whom they were pledged. The open-convention scheme necessitated a suspension of that rule so that those committed to Carter could reverse field, presumably on the basis that Carter had so badly faltered in the last primaries. In short, Kennedy wanted a new deal of the delegate cards. It was not likely to happen. Already a majority of Democratic state chairmen had called on Teddy to give up the ghost. But the rumors of a "Dump Carter" movement grew.

THE SHAH OF IRAN passed away in late July. He'd been suffering from cancer for months. Carter refused to send any representative from Washington to the funeral and said nothing publicly. His administration's only acknowledgment of the shah's passing came in a statement released by the State Department—which went out only after both Carter and his national security adviser, Zbigniew Brzezinski, reviewed the draft personally. Reagan, in contrast, called the shah a "loyal and valued friend" and said that his death "reminds us of the value of remaining true to our friends."[50]

THE REAGAN CAMPAIGN AND the Carter team had the same essential strategy for November: to make the election about their opponent. Dick Wirthlin recognized this when he said that the Reaganites' task was to make the election a referendum on Carter's presidency, and that it would be "problematical" if they allowed Reagan to become the issue.[51]

To underscore Reagan's supposedly controversial economic agenda, the Carter campaign for a time referred to the "Reagan-Kemp-Roth" tax bill. Democrats confidently predicted that Reagan would be running away from the plan by the fall.

Going on the attack against Reagan, the Carter administration rolled out some big guns. Brzezinski broke conventions as a diplomat and negotiator by going right at Reagan on the war-and-peace issue, attempting to exploit the Republican's image of having an itchy trigger finger. Brzezinski attacked the GOP platform and Reagan's call for military superiority over the Kremlin, saying that containment combined with diplomacy would keep the Russian bear from prowling outside his territory.[52] Secretary of State Muskie broke the tradition into a thousand pieces by saying that Reagan could kick off a new arms race; however, Soviet officials were at the same time, attempting to get a private meeting with Reagan's aides just "in case" he won.[53]

Carter then trotted out Secretary of Defense Harold Brown, who called Reagan "simplistic," "unrealistic," and "dangerous."[54] The Carter administration was going to use every resource at its command.

Although the Democrats were attempting to portray the Republican candidate as an extremist, Reagan showed no signs of moving to the middle now that he had secured the GOP nomination. During an extensive interview with *U.S. News & World Report* he detailed the government agencies he would cut or eliminate, including the Departments of Energy and Education, and he insisted on pushing tax cuts and big increases in defense spending.[55] He said he planned on delegating authority to people who understood his framework of governance, a point Lyn Nofziger reiterated when he harked back to California and said, "cabinet officers were Reagan's men in the departments; they were not the departments' men in the Reagan cabinet."[56] Reagan did show his pragmatic side in the interview, saying he'd learned in Sacramento that "if I found . . . that I could not get 100 percent of what I asked for, I took 80 percent."[57]

John Anderson had faded somewhat into the background over the summer. Though he had managed to qualify for the ballot in all fifty states, money had slowed to his campaign and the media attention had tailed off. As a result, Anderson was stuck in the polls somewhere between 15 and 25 percent.[58] Reagan's pick of Bush had assuaged some moderate Republicans and persuaded them to stick with the party rather than bolt for Anderson.

Anderson still hadn't selected a running mate. It appeared his best opportunity for choosing a vice-presidential partner would come after the Democrats held their convention in August, when—assuming Kennedy lost to Carter—some hard-core Kennedyites who couldn't stomach Carter might be willing to support the independent ticket.

Anderson and Kennedy got together on Capitol Hill for no reason other than to give the media something to cover. It was a pure photo op as the two met briefly with no agenda and then addressed the media and had nothing to say. It was dutifully covered by all the major media, including the networks. All the while Kennedy had a slightly dazed look on his face. The only "news" to come out of it was that Anderson "might reassess" his independent bid if Carter was not renominated.[59]

As renegade Democrats continued calling for an open convention, Kennedy worked the phones hard, leaning on wavering delegates. His argument was a difficult one to make. As the champion of "reform," Kennedy had been on the side of letting the primaries rather than the political bosses select the delegates. Now he was arguing for a return to the legendary "smoke-filled rooms."[60] In politics, where you stood was often defined by where you sat.

Carter got support from an unusual quarter: Reagan. He wasn't being cynical about it, either. Reagan said, "When you free the delegates, you disenfranchise the voters who elected them."[61] It was the best argument in support of Carter's renomination.

Reagan's campaign courted new controversy when it finally released the nominee's tax returns for 1979, which showed his income at $515,878. Between federal and state taxes, more than half—$262,936—went to government. Most of Reagan's income had come from his speeches, radio commentaries, and newspaper columns.[62]

To the media, the bigger news was that he had donated just a little over $4,000 of his six-figure income to charity—as compared with the $15,000 Carter had donated. Moreover, he had checked "No" on a voluntary one-dollar contribution to the "presidential election campaign fund"—a fund that had just given him, as the Republican nominee, $29.4 million to finance the balance of his campaign. The media also howled because Reagan took an operating loss of more than $9,000 on Rancho del Cielo even though it was only technically a working ranch, and because he had charged his daughter Maureen $481 interest on a loan he'd made to her.[63]

An old allegation surfaced against Reagan, one that Ford's campaign had investigated in 1975, over a real estate deal Reagan had made with Twentieth-Century Fox when he became governor. In the 1950s, Reagan had bought a tract of 290 acres adjacent on three sides to land owned by Fox Realty, a division of the film company. Reagan bought it for just $65,000 and sold it to Fox Realty in 1966 for more than $1.9 *million*.[64] The documents had been leaked to the Ford campaign by Reagan's Democratic enemies in California, and in 1980 they were leaked to the media. The truth of the matter was that real estate prices had gone through the roof in the Golden State for years and it wasn't unusual to realize such profits—or for movie studios to be sloppy with money.

Reagan suffered still another embarrassment when the Right to Life Party withdrew its endorsement. The national pro-life group called the choice of Bush "unacceptable" and took Reagan off its voter line. This move jeopardized Dick Wirthlin's strategy for taking New York in November. His ambitious plan was contingent on Reagan's running on the Republican, Conservative, and Right to Life lines to scoop every vote possible in the state, and on Anderson's getting the Liberal Party line to deny Carter those votes.[65]

With Reagan still not out on the stump, the media began to intensely scrutinize his big proposals: a massive tax cut, a giant increase in defense spending, and a balanced budget. Alan Greenspan was asked how these seemingly conflicting goals could be reconciled; he said, "There are any number of answers on how to resolve these goals," although he didn't give any specific examples.[66]

It had been more than two weeks since the end of the convention and yet Reagan seemed stuck in neutral. Even the reliably pro-Reagan conservative weekly *Human Events* was taking the Gipper to task over the Ford mess, over his stalled campaign, over the poor treatment afforded Jack Kemp, and over the choice of Bush.

About the only bright sign came when Fidel Castro of Cuba said, "The fate of humanity would be at stake if Ronald Reagan won the presidential election."[67] There was no truth to the rumor that Ed Meese sent a bouquet of flowers to the Communist dictator to thank him for attacking Reagan.

Jimmy Carter suffered an embarrassment of his own, over the simmering problem of his brother Billy's six-figure contract with the renegade terrorist nation of Libya. Probes had been announced by Congress as well as by the Justice Department. The president finally as much as said that he had, in fact, been in contact with his brother on the matter—something he had previously denied. Because Muslims put a "great importance on family ties," Carter said, he felt that asking his brother to bring a Libyan diplomat to the White House for a quiet meeting might help spring the hostages in Iran.[68] The whole exercise was asinine.

Carter was attempting to follow the advice of George Bernard Shaw, who said, "If you cannot get rid of the family skeleton, you may as well make it dance."[69] The mess was particularly devastating for a politician who had come into office sanctimoniously proclaiming, "I will never tell a lie."[70] Carter's greatest asset, his supposedly unassailable integrity, was besmirched.

Carter at least could take some solace from the fact that the Soviets had blown their chance for the public-relations bonanza they had hoped for with the Moscow Olympics. Dozens of other countries had joined the American boycott, and the Summer Games ended quietly in early August.

Reagan finally hit the road to fulfill his commitment to speak in Neshoba County, Mississippi. Wirthlin and other aides had wanted him to skip the trip there because it was a tinderbox of racial hatred. Three civil-rights organizers had been murdered there in 1964 and the Ku Klux Klan still operated in the area. Yet the media gave Reagan's Mississippi trip short shrift—for the time being, anyway. Unfortunately, this would not be the last Reagan heard about Neshoba.

After Neshoba, the Republican nominee moved on to New York City to speak to the National Urban League (even though the Urban League appearance had originally been scheduled first). He met with the organization's president, Vernon Jordan, who was in a hospital recovering from a gunshot wound.[71] The two immediately hit it off and found they had many friends in common. Surprisingly, Reagan was received nearly as well when he gave his speech before the Urban League. Refusing to pander, he rejected public housing and called for "urban homesteading" where residents could buy their dwellings from the government for a nominal fee.[72] He opposed affirmative action and told the audience so, even though several black leaders had urged him to change his stance. He opposed set-aside programs, the minimum wage, and federal intervention in local schools. The solution to the plight of the black family, he said, was not to argue over a "shrinking economic pie" but to produce "a bigger pie so that everyone will have a chance to be better off."[73]

Reagan pointed to his record of black advancement while governor of California: over eight years, the percentage of African-Americans hired in the state government increased 23 percent.[74] He asked the attendees not to look at him as a "caricatured conservative."[75]

Reagan received his biggest round of applause when he said, "We must adopt the goal of making black Americans more economically independent, through means of black enterprise and lasting, meaningful jobs in the private sector. We must assure that four years from now public sector jobs can't be dangled like carrots; that welfare can't be used as a lever to pry loose urban votes; that black Americans have captured more of their destiny."[76]

He was interrupted fifteen times with applause and was cheered "politely at the end," according to the Washington Star.[77] A black columnist, Earl Caldwell with the New York Daily News, was "stunned" at the warm reception Reagan received.[78]

While in New York City, Reagan also visited the burned-out slums of the South Bronx, which Carter had famously toured in 1977, vowing to improve the lot of its poor. Nothing had been done in three years since, and the Reagan campaign saw the opportunity to capitalize on the issue. Aides envisioned a photo op with Reagan standing before the decay of boarded-up buildings and offering hope to the out-of-work and desperate people.

It did not quite work out that way.

On a sweltering day, around a hundred African-Americans, whites, and Hispanics greeted Reagan with boos and catcalls. He said, "This is an example of how the federal government can fail," but he was drowned out by the crowd, which chanted, "1–2–3–Boo-oo-ooo!" Reagan tried again, his frustration and anger rising, shouting, "You will listen to me!" The catcalls grew even louder. "Down with Reagan!" they chanted. A Chicano woman kept badgering him, asking repeatedly, "What are you going to do for us?"

Reagan tried to reason with the hecklers, asking them to look at his record of job growth in California. They shouted back, "We don't need them in California, we need them here!" He got even madder and shouted, "Stop talking and listen!" Some in the crowd tried to listen but the rest were not buying it, chanting, "Go home! Go home! Go home!"

Finally, Reagan exploded, "I can't do a damn thing for you unless I am elected!"[79]

Defeated, he retreated to his twelve-car motorcade and the safety of his air-conditioned limo, where Mrs. Reagan had wisely stayed. But asked whether he planned any more urban tours, Reagan surprisingly said yes. Despite his rough treatment in the South Bronx, he wasn't shutting the door to the dispossessed. In 1968, when asked why he and Richard Nixon weren't campaigning in urban America, Spiro Agnew declared with characteristic artlessness, "If you've seen one city slum, you've seen them all." Reagan was far less harsh. He truly felt bad about the plight of the poor, perhaps because the memories of his own deprivations during the Depression were deeply etched in his psyche. "There we were, driving away, and you think of them back there in all that ugliness and they have no place to go," he recalled with genuine compassion. "All that is before them is to sit and look at what we just saw."[80]

27

The Democrats

"This election is a stark choice between . . . two futures."

Everybody, it seemed, was in a bad mood by August 1980. Millions of fans of the evening soap opera *Dallas* were angered by the strike of the Screen Actors Guild and the American Federation of Television and Radio Artists. In the spring the hit program's season had ended on a cliffhanger when an angry, unknown assailant shot the odious oilman J. R. Ewing. The series was supposed to resume in September, but if the strike was not settled soon, no one would find out the answer to "Who shot J. R.?"—the catchphrase on everybody's lips in the summer of 1980.

The irate actors in Hollywood weren't the only ones striking. Angry garbagemen in Boston went on strike, as did hotel workers in San Francisco. American productivity had declined for six quarters in a row, according to the Labor Department.[1] Consumer spending was down dramatically, output was down, and a July report from the White House predicted that the recession would deepen even more than previously thought.[2] Even the most optimistic economists called for only an anemic recovery in late 1981.

Millions of Americans were out of work and could not find employment. The unemployment rate had jumped fully 2 percentage points since February.[3] Americans were angry and scared. An out-of-work steelworker in Homestead, Pennsylvania, crossly said, "All we got is unemployment. . . . The lines are getting longer. Men with families and no work. We're getting butchered." An angry young man in Miami lamented that though Cubans could get work and Haitians were willing to work for little, there were no jobs available for him. "Foreigners got it made over here, especially if they speak Spanish." Among black Americans, it was not a recession—it was a depression. Joblessness among African-Americans had climbed to over 14 percent. Among all teenagers, unemployment hovered just under 20 percent, but among black teenagers, it was an appalling 36 percent.[4]

It didn't help anyone's spirits that the drought and heat wave that had afflicted the nation for weeks still had not abated. Dallas and Fort Worth went thirty-three days in a row in which the temperature topped 100 degrees. By late July the death toll nationwide had exceeded 1,200 Americans. Otherwise healthy men and women were dying from heart attacks and heat stroke. Crops had shriveled, lakes and streams had dried up, livestock were dying, chickens had stopped laying eggs, and there was still no end in sight. The governor of Oklahoma, George Nigh, organized a state-sponsored day of prayer for rain. In St. Louis, baseball's Cardinals drenched their feet in cold water—without removing socks or shoes— as the temperature on the artificial turf spiked to 146 degrees.[5]

In Washington, pro-Khomeini Iranians showed up at the White House to protest angrily whatever it was they were protesting. In response, a group of Americans spontaneously took up battle positions and began their own counter-protest, yelling obscenities and insults at the Iranians. President Carter had issued a ban on Iranian protests at the White House, but somebody forgot about it and gave the "Khomeiniacs" a permit.[6]

Naturally, the Summer of Anger spilled into domestic politics. Americans were angry at Jimmy Carter for his handling of the economy, unemployment, the hostage crisis—practically everything. Fully 86 percent criticized his management of the economy, according to an ABC–Harris poll. If that were not bad enough, two-thirds of Democrats attacked his stewardship of their party.[7]

Democrats were angry that the best they had to put up was either the incompetent Carter or the badly flawed Ted Kennedy. Democratic officeholders were angry that if Carter was renominated, he might drag the whole lot down to defeat. A Carter operative counted his blessings and said, "If it had been anybody else but Ted Kennedy, Carter would be long gone."[8] Still, Carter's men couldn't rest too easy: the "Dump Carter" rumors kept cropping up.

Kentucky's first lady, former Miss America Phyllis George Brown, was angry with Carter because she thought her husband, Governor John Y. Brown, should have been asked to give the keynote speech at the upcoming Democratic convention.[9] Carter's brother, Billy, was furious that people were interfering in his business deals with Libya, and that his brother's campaign had told him his help was not needed. President Carter was angry that Congress was not letting him testify soon enough to deny that he had done anything to help his brother.

Republicans and independents were angry, too—Republicans, because Reagan was dawdling; independents, because John Anderson was not making his case more effectively. In Denver, Anderson suffered the indignity of being hit with eggs thrown by angry Communist protesters.[10]

Carter's campaign was angry at the Anderson candidacy. "We are caught in the middle," one Carter aide whined in a memo. On the other hand, "Ronald Reagan's candidacy poses a more complex problem. Reagan's style, rhetoric and conservative philosophy are attractive to many disaffected Democrats."[11] Reagan was cutting into Carter's base, and the Democrats were not happy about it. Carter himself was angry about the relentless criticisms coming from his opponents. He lashed out at Ronald Reagan, calling the Republican "irresponsible." Reagan sharply responded, "I'll admit to that, if he'll admit that he's responsible."[12]

The newspapers and magazines were filled with annoyed letters, firing back and forth over Reagan, Carter—whatever was steaming them. Nancy Reagan sent in her own hot dispatch to *Time*, blasting the magazine for an unfair and inaccurate portrayal. "Just to keep the record straight: I do not buy $5,000 dresses [July 7]; I do not have an extensive jewelry collection, or paintings, or antiques; and I do not have a hairdresser and interior decorator in tow. I get my hair done once a week, and I'm at a loss as to what an interior decorator would do. Perhaps rearrange the furniture in all the Holiday Inns I've been staying in."[13]

It was also the silly season, or maybe the brutal August heat was just making everybody swoon. Ron Dellums, a black congressman from California, declared his candidacy for the presidency, and the president of the New York City Council, Carol Bellamy, also announced her intention to seek the Democratic Party's nomination. Farmers were looking to nominate one of their own as well.[14]

Ronald Reagan may not have been angry, but he had reason to be frustrated about backbiting and negative press coverage. The media were kicking over the dead embers of his decision to go to Mississippi. The Reagan-Bush campaign began to leak to reporters that it had been a mistake to go to the Neshoba Fair, that the symbolism and history were just too burdensome, especially for a conservative trying to fight off false charges of racism. The media leveled Reagan for using the phrase "states' rights" while at the fair, because some saw it as a code phrase for racism.

Reagan strongly begged to differ. Ever the Jeffersonian Republican, he had used the phrase "states' rights" for years, North and South, East and West. To Reagan, the Tenth Amendment, limiting the power of the national government, was just as important as the nine previous amendments to the Constitution. He said, "I believe in states' rights; I believe in people doing as much as they can at the private level." He wanted to "restore to states and local governments the power that properly belongs to them."[15] Yet to Reagan's critics, all that mattered was that he had once opposed the 1964 Civil Rights Act and the 1965 Voting Rights Act. The fact that he later recanted, saying his opposition had been a mistake, seemed irrelevant. The Neshoba appearance would haunt Reagan.

Kenny Klinge, running part of the South for Reagan, had successfully argued for the Mississippi appearance as part of an effort to go after Carter right in his own backyard. Klinge was already in hot water with Mrs. Reagan for insisting that they leave the ranch early to go to Mississippi. At the end of Reagan's remarks in Neshoba, he was unexpectedly given a rocking chair, and Klinge along with advance man Lanny Wiles cringed, sensitive to the age issue. But Reagan didn't miss a beat. He sat in the rocker and pulled Nancy down onto his lap. The crowd, as well as the media, ate it up.[16] What could have been a disaster turned into a charming photo of the two, which appeared in newspapers throughout the South.

As the Reagans walked through the muddy field back to the bus, Mrs. Reagan spotted Klinge and said, "You're a pretty lucky boy, you know that?" Klinge sheepishly replied, "Yes, ma'am." She stayed mad at Klinge for several weeks, and it became a running comedy for the staff to hide Kenny before she could spot him and demand he be fired.[17]

The Reagan campaign's fumbles led more and more reporters to openly criticize the operation. "More than most campaigns, the Reagan effort has been hampered by logistical problems," wrote Lou Cannon of the *Washington Post*. "Schedules are slow to be prepared and changed frequently." An ongoing gag on his plane among reporters was that Reagan "would have to manage the country much better than he does his campaign schedule."[18]

DESPITE ALL THE PROBLEMS Jimmy Carter had experienced, he was not always angry. In fact, there was, at least briefly, a light spring in the president's step— what *Newsweek* described as a "preternatural serenity."[19] New polling came out showing that he had drawn much closer to Reagan. In only about three weeks since the Republican convention, Reagan's lead had already been cut in half, from nearly 30 points over Carter to 14.[20] Reagan's men had expected that his numbers would come back to earth, but he was sinking more quickly than anticipated. Reagan's campaign was stumbling. Even better for Carter, the president had received good reviews for his nationally televised press conference in which he handled rough questions about his ne'er-do-well brother; Carter got a bit of sympathy for manfully dealing with Billy's bumbling.

Carter remained confident that he could portray Reagan as another Goldwater. Hamilton Jordan, his erstwhile White House chief of staff who was now running the reelection campaign, recognized that Reagan was a tougher cookie than was widely assumed. Later, in his memoirs, Jordan recounted that he alone among the Carterites sized up Reagan properly.[21] He planned accordingly for the fall assault on the Gipper, and would earn every bit of the $161,000 per annum he was paying himself.[22]

Jordan knew he had history on his side. The American people did not like to fire their presidents. Indeed, at this point Carter should have been marching to his own coronation, as most incumbent presidents did. On a number of issues, the American people were on Carter's side, not Reagan's. From the pro-life amendment in the GOP platform to federal controls on the price of oil to the 55-mile-per-hour speed limit, Americans took Carter's side. They had also become ambivalent about Reagan's economic proposals. Yet here Carter was, still dealing with Ted Kennedy. The delegate math clearly didn't work for the challenger, but Kennedy wouldn't bow out gracefully. He went on *Face the Nation* the Sunday before the convention and airily said, "I think the vote itself will be decided by fifty votes one way or the other."[23]

President Carter did harbor some anger, though at Camelot's prince. He was resolutely rejecting all suggestions of magnanimous gestures to heal the breach between himself and Kennedy. He wanted to crush Kennedy in the delegate vote for all the world to see. The enmity went back a long way. When Kennedy had criticized Carter in 1976, the then-candidate responded to an aide by saying, "I don't have to kiss Teddy's ass" to win. Two years before that, when both Kennedy and then-governor Carter were invited to speak at the University of Georgia, Carter had offered Kennedy the use of his state airplane, only to renege at the last minute. Kennedy had to scramble to find a car and almost missed his speech. Kennedy would not have been faulted for thinking that Carter intentionally sabotaged him so that when Carter spoke at the same event, he would get better reviews than Kennedy, especially since Carter delivered possibly the best speech of his career until then.[24] The man from Plains who had once spoken so unabashedly of his "love" for the American people was sometimes revealed to have a vindictive streak.

In this case, Carter clearly had the upper hand on Kennedy. The president had a comfortable cushion of 316 delegates beyond what he needed for the nomination, giving him an iron grip on the upcoming convention. Supporters of an "open convention" were still pushing for a suspension of Rule F(3)c, which would be voted on during the first day of the convention, Monday, August 11. In fact, several dozen protesters gathered outside the convention site, New York's Madison Square Garden, to chant, "One, two, three, F-C-3!"—until, that is, the organizer corrected them: "No, no, guys—it's F-3-C!"[25] But Carter's team was taking special precautions to prevent defectors from voting for the rule suspension: setting up 128 whips—dressed in green—on the floor to keep delegates in line. The Carterites held a dress rehearsal to test their communications equipment, quell imaginary delegates, and hold a mock roll-call vote.[26] Moreover, Vice President Walter Mondale and cabinet officials were working individual delegations in preparation for the showdown vote on Monday.[27] Kennedy had no such plan or organization.

As THE DEMOCRATS BEGAN gathering in New York City for their quadrennial convention, they had problems on their hands. The fact that their sitting president was still battling a Democratic challenger at what was supposed to be a show of party unity was symptomatic of the deeper problems plaguing their party. Some columnists were writing openly about the death of the Democratic Party. Judy Bachrach, a columnist for the *Washington Star* whose prose could make grown men cry, wrote, "About the only thing that makes the Democratic Party bearable is its passion for suicide."[28]

All the weeklies and big newspapers were running in-depth articles on Carter, attempting to probe the depths of his psyche and evaluate his presidency. It was revealed that West German chancellor Helmut Schmidt cried bitterly because "Carter did not grasp his true responsibility as leader of the U.S." The head of Singapore, Prime Minister Lee Kuan Yew, told Hugh Sidey of *Time* that Carter's worldview was "a sorry admission of the limits of America's power."[29] Even members of Carter's own party were quoted speaking critically of the president. In more than three years in office, Carter had never ventured forth to establish a personal power base in the environs of Washington. He was a captive of the White House and his own Georgian culture. He had no friends on Capitol Hill and he resisted socializing with members of Congress. A former aide to Lyndon Johnson lamented, "Carter is alone in this city."[30] LBJ had loved the courting and give-and-take of politics. Carter hated it. Instead of behaving as a politician, Carter comported himself with the self-righteous rectitude of a Baptist minister. Many in his own party despised him for it.

New York had hosted the Democratic National Convention four years earlier, too. Back then, the city went all-out to welcome the Democrats. Streets were cleaned, bums were given the rush and outsourced to other locales, grumpy cabbies turned their frowns upside down, and the weather was remarkably pleasant for the visiting Democrats. But now New Yorkers, suffering through the hot and sticky summer, barely concealed their contemptuous yawns and made only a minimal effort to greet the party and the president who had showered so much largesse on their city. If the Moscow Olympics had a competition for peevishness, New Yorkers would have been gold medalists.

The city would surprisingly be short on the glitterati parties Manhattan was known for, simply because the Carter folks did not engender these affairs. The Georgians asked themselves why anybody would live on an island that did not have good fishing. Besides, it was August, and anybody who was anybody was in the Hamptons or The Vineyard. At one of the few hoity-toity parties held, a man kissed Phyllis George's hand and consequently was kicked in the rear by Carter's mother. "You shouldn't kiss a married lady," Mizz Lillian said sternly. Pat Caddell was seen escorting Christie Hefner, daughter of *Playboy* magnate Hugh Hefner, but protested, "We're just good friends."[31]

The Democrats also faced a problem of a logistical nature: Madison Square Garden was too small. Fifty-six hundred party officials, including delegates and alternates, had credentials; when divided into the square footage of the floor of the Garden, that left about two square feet per person, according to the *Washington Post*.[32] When the media, security, volunteers, and hangers-on were thrown into the mix, it was shaping up to be one giant can of sweaty sardines. And smoking was allowed on the floor.

All of the White House staff, along with Carter, Vice President Mondale, cabinet officials, and members of Congress, would be on hand in New York. The current joke was, "Who's running the government this week?"[33] Special interests abounded on the floor. Feminists (wearing the white dresses of the suffragettes), labor, Hispanics, and gays "seemed to glory in their diversity," as Haynes Johnson of the *Washington Post* put it.[34] Columnist Mark Shields, a former Democratic consultant who found writing less time-consuming and more profitable, lamented that his party had become dominated by hyphenated Democrats.[35]

Another small controversy broke out before Carter went to New York. The head of the Moral Majority, Jerry Falwell, had attended an off-the-record session with Carter and other religious leaders. Falwell queried Carter about having "known practicing homosexuals on your senior staff here in the White House." According to a transcript of a tape Falwell surreptitiously made during the meeting, Carter replied, "Well, I am president of all the American people, and I believe I should represent everyone." To which Falwell replied, "Why don't you have some murderers and bank robbers and so forth to represent?"[36] The White House transcript of the meeting differed vastly from the one released by Falwell, and no one knew who was telling the truth. Regardless, Falwell had provided more grist for the mill among grassroots Christians.

CARTER WENT TO CAMP David to prepare for his acceptance speech. He would not arrive in New York until Wednesday, the day of the vote, as befitting the incumbent. Kennedy, however, arrived in the Big Apple the Sunday before the convention, there to hustle for last-minute votes. To mark his arrival at the Waldorf-Astoria Hotel, Kennedy's staff selected "Fanfare for the Common Man," by Aaron Copland, but with so many limousines, security vehicles, and buses in front of the luxury hotel, the scene looked nothing like what a "common man" was used to.[37]

Kennedy was doing his best to project confidence on the eve of the convention. He called Ronald Reagan to say that if he became the Democratic nominee, he wanted to debate both Reagan and Anderson, unlike Carter, who had already signaled his opposition to any three-way debates. Team Reagan thought it was a hoax, so they asked Kennedy for his private number. Calling back, they found that, indeed, it was Kennedy calling Reagan.[38]

In truth, Senator Kennedy had no hope of winning the nomination. The Associated Press released a survey of Carter's delegates and found that 87.5 percent intended on sticking with him over the rules-suspension fight, and that 95.5 percent would vote for his renomination.[39] In other words, even if the rules were suspended to allow delegates to freely vote their preferences, their preference was still to renominate Carter. It was a myth that Carter's delegates were remorseful about supporting their man over Kennedy. They were just depressed about the general election. Carter was also the preference of Democrats nationwide, 49–38 over Kennedy, according to the newest New York Times/CBS poll. They had previously been tied at 43 percent apiece.[40]

At the very least, Kennedy and his platform manager, an attractive young activist named Susan Estrich, were intent on making a defense of liberalism through a couple of planks in the platform. Carter and his campaign were delighted to throw Kennedy that consolation prize. What must not have thrilled the president were the attacks that Kennedy continued making on Carter. In reality, all Kennedy could do in New York was damage Carter's chances for November. At this, he did not disappoint. He told a crowd, "We cannot afford to nominate a Democratic candidate who will be quoting Herbert Hoover in the fall."[41] In Democratic circles, comparing someone to Hoover was akin to calling him a child molester.

The rules vote Kennedy had long been jockeying for finally arrived on Monday night. Several of the big states supporting Kennedy passed in the first go-round, and for a moment Carter's men thought Kennedy had something up his sleeve. But like everything else in Kennedy's operation, these states were just disorganized. They were having trouble counting their delegates. Kennedy wandered across the hall to get something to eat.

The result of the vote was never really in doubt. Carter won by 1,936.4 to 1,390.6 (don't ask), finally ending the talk of an open convention. Even in Kennedy's home state of Massachusetts, thirty delegates—more than a quarter of his state's delegation—voted against him, something that never would have happened to Jack or Bobby Kennedy. Conversely, in Carter's Georgia, the president received sixty-two votes while Kennedy got only one.[42]

Kennedy watched the balloting from his suite with his wife, Joan; his sister-in-law Ethel; his sisters Jean Smith and Pat Lawford; and several campaign retainers, including Bob Shrum. His children—Teddy Jr., Kara, and Patrick—were also there. Even after this definitive setback, some wanted him to stay active as a candidate for the balloting Wednesday night. Kennedy made a surprise statement to the media and, in typical Kennedy style, used self-deprecating humor: "I am deeply gratified by the support I received on the rules fight tonight—but not quite as gratified as President Carter."[43]

Kennedy briefly considered hanging on until Wednesday, but then abruptly decided to pull the plug on what was left of his campaign. His sisters went through books of quotations to find something appropriate for his remarks but were unable to come up with anything. Teddy no longer wanted to rage against the dying light.

Compounding the frustration and disappointment of the moment was an unexpected reminder of the family's tragic past. Kennedy's sisters, upon their arrival, had accidentally walked into the wrong suite, where a television set was on, airing a special on ABC about the Secret Service. Suddenly the horribly familiar footage from so long ago in Dallas appeared. Eunice Shriver was observed "burying her face in her hands." Pat Lawford sadly "shook her head."[44] The assassinations of his two brothers also hung over Teddy, and on the trail, with the slam of a door or when photographers' flashbulbs went off, he "winced noticeably."[45]

Some wounds would never heal for the Kennedy family. Two thousand miles away in Dallas, the medical examiner tastelessly announced that he would exhume Lee Harvey Oswald's remains to determine whether it was indeed the body of JFK's assailant. A British writer had a book out claiming that the body was actually that of a Secret Service agent.[46] It was just another conspiracist the family had to put up with.

JUST BEFORE 10 P.M. Ted Kennedy called Carter to congratulate him on winning their party's nomination. A final indignity came when he couldn't even get Carter on the phone. Kennedy aide Richard Burke placed the call to the White House, and a surly operator told Burke that Carter was "too busy" to talk to Kennedy. Burke finally got to the operator's supervisor, who transferred the call to Camp David.[47]

A little over an hour later, Kennedy gathered his weary and weeping troops together. The announcement was anticlimactic. "I'm a realist," he told them. "My name will not be placed in nomination."[48]

When he met one last time with his staff, some chanted, "Eighty-four! Eighty-four!" but that was a long way off.[49] The supposedly well-oiled Kennedy machine was finally scrapped and the old Kennedy hands would have another four years to get older. Kennedy's 1980 quest was over.

He had spent $15 million over nine months and, according to accounts, traveled in the neighborhood of 300,000 miles in the air.[50] He had gotten up early, gone to bed late, eaten on the run, been pelted with eggs, been booed by crowds—only to suffer the humiliation of losing to Jimmy Carter.

Yet Ted Kennedy also gained something. He had lived in the shadows of his brothers his whole life. With this quixotic campaign, he had gained his own distinctiveness, given testament to his liberal beliefs, and though he would never again seek the presidency, he made himself a political and legislative force to be reckoned with. In primary loss after primary loss, he never whimpered, never complained, and exhibited that "grace under pressure" of which his brother John had often spoken. Teddy, before this campaign, had run only in Massachusetts for his brother's old Senate seat. Unlike his brothers, he had not been seen as a serious individual. The odor of playboy privilege clung to him, especially after Chappaquiddick. Everything had been handed to him on a silver platter. Against Carter, however, he had fought tirelessly and until the very end. Though he started out fumbling, he became a crusader who could fire up any crowd.

Teddy's campaign had been fruitless—or worse, as it laid bare the divisions inside the Democratic Party. But this campaign had been everything for Edward Moore Kennedy. Though he lost the nomination, he gained his own self.

CARTER HAD "WHIPPED" KENNEDY's "ass," just as he had vowed almost a year earlier, and yet Carter's supporters, with few exceptions, were not exultant, just downright rude.

Roughing up a Kennedy was a touchy matter, as the family had dominated the Democratic Party and much of American politics for years. Personal animosity remained between the two men. Hamilton Jordan conceded as much on the *Today* show, saying, "Both [Carter] and Senator Kennedy realize that some of the real differences between them cannot be lightly glossed over."[51] Jordan coldly told Adam Clymer of the *New York Times*, "He doesn't matter so much himself, but his people do."[52] Kennedy took note of the final insult and, as of midweek, still had not formally endorsed Carter for reelection.

Carter now had to pull together his badly fractured party if he hoped to defeat Reagan and fend off the challenge from the left in the form of John Anderson. It would be a monumental task. Carter's emphasis was on "unity," but Kennedy and his 1,200 delegates had something else in mind.

Carter was due in Wednesday morning. Oddly, he would land not at John F. Kennedy International Airport, as chief executives normally did, but instead at Newark Airport in New Jersey.[53] No one knew whether Carter was sending one more signal to Ted Kennedy.

KENNEDY HAD FINALLY DROPPED out of the contest, but he got his opportunity to address the convention. On Tuesday night Madison Square Garden turned into a poignant tribute to the last son of Camelot. The floor of the convention was a sea of supporters waving blue and white "Kennedy '80" signs that included his handsome profile. The noise Kennedy's supporters made was off the scale. The band played an old family favorite, "McNamara's Band."[54]

The crowd roared as Kennedy went to the podium at 8 P.M., on time for once. When the din finally died down, the senator opened with a joke: "Things didn't work out the way I wanted them to, but I still love New York."[55] He spoke wistfully of his campaign, saying, "We have learned that it is important to take issues seriously, but never to take ourselves too seriously."

Kennedy then tore into Ronald Reagan and predicted a "march toward a Democratic victory in 1980." He offered to "congratulate President Carter," but still did not actually endorse Carter for reelection. No one missed the nonendorsement.

Seeing that Reagan was trying to cast himself and his party as the agents of the future, Kennedy said, "We must not permit the Republicans to seize and run on the slogans of prosperity. Progress is our heritage, not theirs. What is right for us as Democrats is also the right way for Democrats to win."[56] Kennedy was interrupted numerous times with chants of "We want Ted! We want Ted! We want Ted!"[57]

He took a populist line, noting that government officials from the president to congressmen to the bureaucrats all had free health insurance, and if they did, why shouldn't the rest of America? He quoted FDR in making the case against Reagan: "Can the Old Guard pass itself off as the New Deal? I think not. We have all seen many marvelous stunts in the circus—but no performing elephant could turn a handspring without falling flat on its back."

Kennedy thundered that Reagan "has no right to quote Franklin Delano Roosevelt!" This set off a thirty-minute demonstration, despite the efforts of House

Speaker Tip O'Neill, serving as convention chairman, to bring the hall under control. Kennedy's address was an indictment of Reagan and the Republicans and a cry for the Democratic Party to return to its liberal roots. The words "justice" and "compassion" were thick through his remarks.

Nearing the end, Kennedy spoke reflectively of his campaign, his party, and his brothers. In true Kennedy fashion, he waxed literary, quoting Tennyson: "I am a part of all that I have met: Tho' much is taken, much abides. . . . That which we are, we are. . . . One equal temper of heroic hearts . . . strong in will. To strive, to seek, to find, and not to yield." Thousands of Democrats were reduced to tears.

Kennedy closed with the sort of eloquence his frustrated supporters—and indeed the country—had expected of him from the beginning of his campaign: "For me, a few hours ago, this campaign came to an end, for all those whose cares have been our concern, the work goes on, the cause endures, the hope still lives, and the dream shall never die."[58] With a boyish, almost puckish grin that evoked the eternal youth of his martyred brothers, he waved to the crowd and walked off.

Twenty thousand Democrats exploded.

After another thirty minutes of adoring clamor, they were still chanting, "We want Ted!" O'Neill could not get control of the hall and finally surrendered to reality, signaling the band to play "Happy Days Are Here Again" and "For He's a Jolly Good Fellow."[59] Kennedy had left the podium with his family, but then reappeared halfway into the spontaneous demonstration, to the heightened frenzy of the delegates.

The address had been worked on and polished by Bob Shrum and Carey Parker, Kennedy's two principal speechwriters. Ironically, Shrum had quit the Carter campaign in 1976. Ted Sorensen, JFK's old wordsmith, had added his two cents to the draft. Kennedy, meanwhile, had practiced using a teleprompter.[60] It all added up to the finest speech of his life. The performance renewed speculation that he should or would run again in four years.

Such is often the case with losing politicians. Unsophisticated commentators say in such circumstances—as they did in Kennedy's case—"If only he'd spoken like that in the primaries, the results might have been different." What these observers failed to understand is that it is precisely because the circumstances are different that losing candidates speak differently. The reason is simple: they have nothing more to lose.

THOUGH TED KENNEDY'S LONG struggle had ended, one of his key aides and close friends, former Wisconsin governor Pat Lucey, was still thinking about what he could do to hasten Carter's defeat in November. He was being encouraged to do something to undermine Carter by his old friend Paul Corbin, political operator extraordinaire and one of the truly great characters of American politics.

The day before, Lucey had resigned as a member of the Badger State's delegation in protest over the defeat of the rules suspension. Dismayed that Kennedy had lost, Lucey said ominously that he would "reserve the right" to support someone other than Carter.[61]

It so happened that John Anderson was in New York at the time. He was there for a press conference to announce that Mary Dent Crisp, who had been forced out of the Republican National Committee for her anti-Reagan stances, would become chair of his independent campaign. Sure enough, Lucey was spotted paying what he thought was a covert visit to Anderson's hotel, where the two met in private. When Governor Lucey emerged, he praised the independent candidate, saying that he and Kennedy had "very similar positions. I am not at this moment prepared to endorse either Mr. Anderson or Mr. Carter."[62] Lucey and Corbin were up to something.

ON WEDNESDAY EVENING, CARTER was renominated, winning 2,129 delegate votes to 1,146.5 for Kennedy and 53.5 for a smattering of other aspirants. Texas put Carter over the top. With that, Kennedy's political ally and close friend Thomas P. O'Neill III, the lieutenant governor of Massachusetts and the son of the House speaker, moved that the convention unanimously renominate Carter, at Kennedy's urging, and the delegates did so—although some protested, shouting, "No!"[63] Kennedy sent a statement to the hall, and O'Neill, the father, read it to the delegates: "It is imperative that we defeat Ronald Reagan in 1980. I urge all Democrats to join in that effort."[64] Kennedy also sent word that he would appear on the dais with the president Thursday evening, signaling his awaited endorsement.

The hall mostly cheered Carter's renomination. The rebel yells of several joyous southern delegates reverberated around the Garden. Jody Powell, Carter's loyal and effective press secretary, choked up over his boss's renomination, which many had thought impossible less than a year earlier.[65] The convention again sang "Happy Days Are Here Again," but were they?

A behind-the-scenes kabuki dance had gone on all day long between the Carter team and the Kennedy men over the platform and Kennedy's statement, and the president and Senator Kennedy spoke by phone to try to hash things out. In another sign of weakness, Carter had to send the platform committee a long letter outlining his positions on various issues and where he disagreed with Kennedy. Rumors of a walkout by disappointed liberals and feminists also had to be quashed.[66]

Many Democrats were less than enthusiastic about the party's presidential ticket. "It's just not there this year," said Bill Clinton, the thirty-three-year-old governor of Arkansas. "You can only do that one time—elect the first southern president."[67] Clinton had given one of the best speeches of the week, contrasting the Democrats' past with America's future, but it was largely overlooked.[68]

ON THURSDAY, AUGUST 14, the night Carter accepted the nomination, the Kennedy blue signs gave way to the president's green placards. Before Carter spoke, Vice President Mondale addressed the crowd. A favorite of the delegates, Mondale had been renominated with ease (although one delegate cast a ballot for George Orwell).[69] Now he gave a highly partisan speech that energized the convention. In refrain after refrain he said, "Most Americans believe," after which he would cite a federal program. The crowd then answered, "But not Ronald Reagan!" Mondale tore into Reagan's tax-cut proposal, saying that the only way it could be funded would be to wreck every social program, including Social Security, Medicare, Medicaid, aid to veterans, aid to children, aid to cities, and aid to the states. He also went after Reagan for wanting to use the U.S. military to quell crises around the world.[70]

After Mondale's spirited speech and especially the Kennedy stem-winder of two nights earlier, President Carter had tough acts to follow. Like Mondale, Carter aimed his fire at Reagan. Unlike Mondale, he distinctly underwhelmed the delegates with his speech.

The president entered Madison Square Garden to "Hail to the Chief," the very song he had banned in 1977.[71] Before Carter laid into Reagan, he honored the Democratic Party's long tradition. But when he tried to pay tribute to a fallen hero of the party, Hubert Humphrey, the name came out "Hubert Horatio Hornblower . . . err . . . Humphrey!"[72] The crowd tittered. It was not an auspicious beginning.

Carter quickly shifted his focus to accusing Reagan of having an itchy trigger finger: "The life of every human being on earth can depend on the experience and judgment and vigilance of the person in the Oval Office. The president's power for building and his power for destruction are awesome. And the power's greatest exactly where the stakes are highest—in matters of war and peace."[73] Of course, with the American hostages still being held captive in Tehran, Carter himself was plagued by rumors that he was planning a full-scale invasion of Iran.

"This election," the president intoned, "is a stark choice between two men, two parties, two sharply different pictures of what America is and what the world is. But it's more than that—it's a choice between two futures."[74] He envisioned a future of "security and justice and peace," but the other possible future, he said, would be one of "despair," "surrender," and "risk." His voice rising, Carter said that Reagan would "launch an all-out nuclear arms race" and initiate "an attack on everything that we've done in the achievement of social justice and decency in the last fifty years."[75]

Here, the president was signaling the rough treatment that he and his Georgians had in store for Reagan in the fall campaign.[76] Carter suffered under few illusions about Americans' attitudes toward his presidency, so with little to trumpet over the past four years, he would need to turn all his guns on Reagan, in an attempt to destroy the Republican's legitimacy as a candidate. "The question in the fall," admitted a Carter aide, "is who is the bigger turkey? I think people will decide that Reagan is."[77]

By this point in the speech, sweat was pouring off the president's face, and the front of his shirt was noticeably damp. Not much of what he was saying was sticking, though. Indeed, toward the end of the speech, bored delegates could be seen yawning and fidgeting. One problem was that the address—crafted primarily by Hendrik "Rick" Hertzberg, who with Pat Caddell had fashioned Carter's now-orphaned "malaise" speech—reflected the input of a number of different Carter advisers. It ended up touching the bases of all the Democratic constituencies—labor, minorities, women, Jews, farmers, teachers, and others—and a laundry list of typical activist initiatives.

Things did not get better for Carter after he concluded his bland and uninspiring fifty-one-minute speech. Embarrassingly, a scheduled balloon drop failed, robbing the Democrats of the celebration they had planned for the national television viewership. Tom Brokaw of NBC tried to query a visibly upset Hamilton Jordan on the floor, asking whether the failed balloon drop was a metaphor for the Carter campaign.

In an attempt to show unity, the Democrats trotted out an array of famous and not-so-famous Democrats—cabinet officials, governors, members of Congress, White House staff. Mondale joined him on the stage, then their families, and then a goofy display of Democratic power brokers appeared as Bob Strauss, chairman of the Carter campaign, screamed out their names as the Democratic power brokers joined Carter on stage. It looked like a badly organized high school assembly in which everybody was included so as not to offend anyone.

When Zbigniew Brzezinski was announced, the somnolent delegates booed lustily. Some delegates booed Carter himself, while the rest of the crowd offered tepid applause. Then, like the cavalry coming over the hill, Ted Kennedy appeared on stage. The delegates perked up and the noise in the hall grew appreciably louder and warmer. They began chanting, "We want Ted!" as they had two nights before. Kennedy, with a small smile pasted on his face rather than his usual broad grin, waved to the audience and moved from one side of the dais to the other, always away from Carter. Carter kept following Kennedy, like a little kid, trying to engage Kennedy in the traditional victory clasp, but Kennedy would have none of it. It was embarrassing and Carter was furious.[78]

The bitterness between the two men only deepened. Carter complained that Kennedy was not on the stage immediately at the conclusion of the speech, while Kennedy claimed that he'd done exactly what the president's men wanted, so as to not show Carter up. Kennedy then walked off the stage, when decorum demanded that the president leave first.

A Carter aide said ruefully, "He wanted to put that last wound into us."[79] In an interview with the former president years later, it was clear that the old animosities still existed.[80]

The night of Ted Kennedy's speech, a family retainer, Paul Corbin, was standing on the floor of the convention with his friend Bill Schulz of Reader's Digest, watching Kennedy concede the nomination to Carter. Corbin hated Carter. He turned on his heel to leave, and as he was storming out, Schulz called after him, asking what his plans were now that Kennedy was out of the race.

Corbin, a Kennedy Democrat, labor organizer, former Communist agitator, and political troublemaker par excellence, yelled back, "I'm going to go work for Reagan!"[81]

28

CORBIN

"I can argue it both ways."

It would be too easy to call Paul Corbin "Runyonesque." A better question might be which one of the two inspired the other.

Damon Runyon, the cocksure novelist, had a taste in his writings for the slangy-type phrase, and Corbin certainly "cracked wise." Since they both lived in New York City in the 1930s, no one will ever know whether they knew each other, but one thing is for sure: they would have liked each other.

Runyon, the chronicler of the New York netherworld, drank heavily, smoked, and cheated on his wife. Corbin did all of these things, too, but was particular about his brand of cigarettes, smoking only blue-and-white Pall Malls. Runyon once quoted Ecclesiastes, with a twist: "The race is not always to the swift, nor the battle to the strong, but that's the way to bet."[1] Corbin would have fixed the race or the fight so there would be no risk involved, at least for him. He then would have figured out how to get his enemies to bet the other way, to increase his payout.

Corbin, in later years, resembled the actor Barry Fitzgerald in *The Quiet Man*, gray-headed, lines deeply etched in his face. With his fedora, gangster-like black suits, gravelly voice, whispered late-night phone calls, nefarious deals, and bizarre collection of friends, he intrigued some. Most people who knew him, though, used obscenities in describing the diminutive, shadowy character. When he walked into a restaurant, he would greet the waiter by shouting, "Fellow worker!" and then ask how poor the working conditions and the pay were: "How do the bosses treat you around here? They treat you like shit, don't they?"[2] He had a variety of mistresses throughout his life and even in his late seventies he was supporting a woman in Nashville who referred to herself as "The Wanton Woman."[3]

An FBI file was opened on Corbin in 1940[4]—only four years after he entered the country illegally from his native Canada[5]—and entries were still being made twenty-eight years later.[6] The initial report said he was 5'6" and weighed 145 pounds, with black hair and blue eyes. The bureau assigned him a number, 2417609.[7] For nearly three decades the FBI filled Corbin's ever-growing file with hundreds of documents, news clips, photos, arrest records, and informants' reports. He was under almost constant FBI surveillance through the 1940s and '50s and into the early '60s.

By the time of his death in early January 1990, Corbin had accumulated an FBI file of nearly two thousand documents. Yet when a Freedom of Information Act request was filed seventeen years later, the FBI held back several hundred pages, the oblique reason cited being "national security." The documents that were released, if reluctantly, were heavily redacted.

The papers released by the bureau revealed the life not of an apparent national-security risk but of a crook and a rogue—sometimes charming, mostly not. His was a lifetime spent in labor, left-wing, and Democratic politics, but also in business and personal dealings with Republicans and conservatives. A common thread through the files was that Corbin liked to cheat, especially the system and his enemies, but also friends.

Corbin cheated even when he didn't have to, as when he played poker with his friends, just to see if he could get away with it. Democratic operative and later columnist Mark Shields, one of the most genial men in Washington, declined an invitation to a friendly weekly poker game that Corbin played in because he refused to sit at the same table, still detesting Corbin over some ancient disagreement. When Shields was told Corbin had died, he retorted, "Yeah? Prove it!"[8] Corbin was a man of utterly no convictions except self-interest and loyalty to a small circle of associates—and he grifted even them once in a while.

In the late 1980s, Corbin, who for years had been very close to Robert Kennedy's family, convinced two of his conservative friends to contribute to the debt retirement of Kathleen Kennedy Townsend, RFK's eldest daughter. She'd lost a race for Congress, so Corbin took his conservative friends to Hickory Hill, long-time residence of Robert and Ethel Kennedy. There, at the reception, he ushered them around as if he'd just delivered tribute. Corbin's out-of-place right-wing friends gamely went along, chatting with Ethel, the kids, and the dozens of liberals who had gathered. Their one stipulation was that Corbin tell no one that they had contributed money to a Kennedy. One month later, in Chuck Conconi's gossip column in *Washingtonian* magazine, an embarrassing item appeared detailing how two conservatives had given money to Kathleen.

They smelled a rat and burned a phone line to Corbin. He responded with that rough little laugh of his and as much as admitted that he'd called Conconi. As much as cheating people, he loved upsetting them, especially the high and mighty of Washington. Whenever he saw Ted Kennedy, he was forever embarrassing him, doing such things as telling him to get his suit pressed.[9]

As a result—and for hundreds of other reasons—Corbin made enemies as easily as eating breakfast. He was loved by a handful that understood him and hated by hundreds more who understood him. At his sparsely attended funeral in January 1990, his longtime friend and pallbearer Bill Schulz quipped, "There wasn't a wet eye in the house."[10]

Kennedy Townsend said simply, "He was a rascal. He created trouble. He upset people. . . . He didn't respect people." As she was preparing for her wedding, Corbin went to her future husband to give him conjugal advice. "Make her come to you" was Corbin's gravelly counsel to Kathleen's beau.[11]

In 1989 Corbin had known for several months he was dying of cancer. Despite their rocky relationship, Teddy Kennedy had arranged for Corbin to get preferential treatment at the National Institutes of Health. A young friend of Corbin's would often drive him there, and sometimes Corbin would get in the car and with black humor say, "Well, it's Boot Hill for me!" Other times, he wanted his friend's assurance that God loved and forgave all.[12] Yet when an old friend, Ray Thomasson, went to see him in late 1989, Thomasson grew weepy and tried to hug the frail old man. "What the hell are you trying to do, kill me?" was Corbin's grumpy response.[13] Joseph Sweat, another friend, asked Corbin how he was feeling. "Goddamn it, how the hell do you think I'm doing, you son of a bitch? I'm dying!"[14]

On his last Christmas, Kathleen's mother, Ethel Kennedy, and several of her children went to his home to sing Christmas carols for the failing man. He hadn't completely lost his humor. "I really must be going," he joked, making allusions to hearing crooning heavenly angels.[15] When Corbin died, the Kennedy clan turned out in force for his wake and funeral. For years, the children of Robert and Ethel Kennedy called Corbin "Uncle Paul."

Kennedyite John Seigenthaler, one of the most ethical and moral men in American politics, delivered a touching eulogy for one of the most unethical and immoral men ever to work in American politics.

Much of Corbin's life had been spent one step ahead of the law, grand juries, the FBI, and union thugs wanting to beat him up. Even into his late sixties, he was still evading investigating committees, including a congressional committee formed in 1983 to try to solve a crime. Someone in 1980 had stolen top-secret debate-briefing books from deep inside the Carter White House and had clandestinely given them to the Reagan-Bush campaign. Three years later, when the theft became known, the city of Washington was in an uproar over the scandal, which became known as "Debategate." Congressman Donald J. Albosta, Michigan Democrat, headed the congressional investigation, and the FBI and everybody in the national media were trying to find out who'd stolen the Carter briefing books.

Albosta's committee interrogated hundreds of witnesses, and the FBI interviewed as many suspects, including a Carter White House aide, Bob Dunn, who had known Corbin for years. John Seigenthaler said Dunn had "worked his way into Paul's life."[16] Dunn was also a protégé of Ted Kennedy ally Pat Lucey, who would become John Anderson's running mate in 1980. Pat's daughter, Laurie, worked in the Carter White House as well. Both Luceys were close friends of Corbin's.

Albosta's investigation produced a report totaling nearly 2,500 pages, yet the congressmen on the panel never solved the crime—even as the answer was right under their noses.[17] In an interview years later, Stu Spencer explained, "[Bill] Casey had some guy that got the book for him, and he gave it to [Jim] Baker."[18] Baker confirmed this, saying that Casey "gave it to me. He said, 'Here is something that you might give to your debate prep team,' and I thumbed through it . . . sent it down to [David] Gergen or somebody."[19]

It was Paul Corbin, a Democrat late of the 1980 Ted Kennedy campaign, who—with a little help from some friends—stole the Carter briefing books and gave them to Ronald Reagan's campaign.[20]

HIS NAME AT BIRTH was not Corbin but Kobrinsky. His parents, Nathan and Anna Kobrinsky, were Jewish émigrés from Russia.[21]

Born in Winnipeg, Canada, Corbin was a troublemaker from an early age. His sister recalled how Corbin at age five kicked their grandmother in the shins.[22] Years later, after Corbin came to New York, FBI documents indicated a "possible cancellation of CORBIN's naturalization due to his subversive activities."[23] U.S. immigration officials apparently deported him to Canada on several occasions in the 1930s because of his illegal status, but Corbin just sneaked back into the United States.[24]

In mid-November 1940 he registered with the Selective Service, though he did not bother to become an American citizen until 1943. In 1943 Corbin also joined the Marines and served as a cook in the Pacific.[25] He later claimed to some friends in Tennessee that while in the Pacific, he had shot and killed a Japanese soldier trying to steal food.[26] He also claimed that he'd led a platoon.[27] Previously he had told the FBI "that he had been a major in the Canadian Army." In typical FBI understatement, the bureau observed that he seemed to be a "prevaricator."[28] Indeed, with Corbin it was sometimes difficult to know where the cock-and-bull ended and the truth began.

In 1939 Corbin abandoned his first wife and young daughter in Brooklyn and headed for Minnesota and Wisconsin.[29] His first wife, Seena, happened to be his first cousin. He did not again lay eyes on his only child, Darlene, until she was fourteen, and then only for ten minutes.[30] Corbin freely admitted to the FBI under questioning that he sent money to his wife only "from time to time," but he lied about his previous arrests—and later he even claimed that his wife had abandoned *him*.[31]

On the day of his divorce from Seena in 1944, Corbin married Gertrude McGowan, whom he had met during the war. Gertrude apparently lied on her marriage license: she claimed that she'd never been married, although an FBI investigation uncovered that she had once been listed as "Gertrude Cox" and "previously married to Harvey Cox, whom she divorced for non-support in 1938."[32]

Years later, Corbin's only daughter alternately sympathized with and criticized her father. On the one hand, she said she "didn't respect him as a human being." On the other hand, she admitted that she understood why he had abandoned her mother: Seena was "crazy as a loon."[33] Darlene was an elderly woman at the time she was interviewed, but it was clear she had to be Paul Corbin's daughter: in conversation she had absolutely no compunction against hurling obscenities.

Out in the Midwest, Corbin ran afoul of various law-enforcement agencies. Purporting to represent a number of unions, he threatened businesses with strikes unless they bought ads in union publications. The publications were fraudulent, and Corbin pocketed the ad money. The FBI file noted another scam, one that led to his arrest in September 1940: Corbin, "an excellent dice-man, had 'taken the house' at a local saloon, which unfortunately was owned by a deputy sheriff." The FBI report called Corbin and his associates "amateur hoodlums." After spending three days in custody he was let off upon paying costs and pleading not guilty.[34] Only a month later, Corbin was arrested for "obtaining money under false pretenses" and was freed again after pleading not guilty.[35] According to FBI records he was taken into custody twice more in 1941, including another arrest for obtaining money under false pretenses. Apparently none of the charges stuck, since he was found not guilty by the municipal judge in Wisconsin.[36] Corbin was fingerprinted at least four times, including when he was registered as an alien in late December 1940.[37]

Over the years Corbin drifted in and out of labor politics, working for both the AFL and the CIO,[38] and was beaten up more than once by labor goons.[39] At various times he worked for the Longshoremen's and Warehousemen's Union and the Furniture Workers. He was listed in FBI documents as a "union organizer" for United Public Workers, but then abruptly showed up in Baton Rouge at the headquarters of the Marine Corps League, attempting to "take over and step up the operations of that office." He succeeded and was, for a time, the national chief of staff for the league.[40]

Allegations surfaced repeatedly that Corbin had Communist connections. A confidential informant in his FBI file stated that he was "a member of the Rockford [Illinois] branch of the Communist Party and active in the infiltration of labor unions."[41] Other FBI entries noted that Corbin "was a subscriber to the *Daily Worker*," the publication of the Communist Party USA,[42] and "was in frequent contact with Communist Party officials in Milwaukee, Wisconsin, during 1946."[43] An informant told the FBI in 1946 that Corbin was a card-carrying member of the "Communist Party, (registration card number 62908) made out in the name of PAUL CORBIN." Informants confirmed Corbin's membership in 1947 and 1948.[44]

In 1950, however, another informer told the FBI that "in his opinion, CORBIN may be a Socialist but he [redacted] did not think CORBIN was a Communist."[45] Eventually Corbin himself told the G-men that he had "never been a member of the Communist Party and that he did not agree with the Communists."[46]

Despite the conflicting reports, Corbin's old friend Adam Walinsky had no doubt about Corbin's allegiances. "He was a real Commie," Walinsky said matter-of-factly in an interview decades later. "He got thrown out of the United Auto Workers by Walter Reuther."[47] A passionate liberal who served as a top aide to RFK in the 1960s, Walinsky was respected on both sides of the aisle for his integrity and acumen.

In this case, the FBI files confirm his assessment: the bureau secured copies of Corbin's Communist Party membership card.[48]

Remarkably, at the very time when Corbin was under constant FBI surveillance and being investigated by the House Committee on Un-American Activities for suspected Communist ties, he was doing brisk though surreptitious business with the biggest anti-Communist headline seeker in America: Senator Joe McCarthy of Wisconsin.

McCarthy was barnstorming the Midwest in the early 1950s, gaining steam in his hunt for suspected Communists in the U.S. government. Typically, he would go into a small town and give fiery speeches in legion halls, Grange halls, Masonic halls, or just on the front steps of the county courthouse. The towns were often sleepy affairs, thought "Reds" were everywhere, and wanted to be there when their hero, McCarthy, eviscerated the "fifth column" inside the U.S. government.

Before McCarthy arrived in said town, Corbin would have been there with a truck filled with American flags to sell to the locals—big American flags, little American flags, American flags with gold trim. No one wanted to go see "Tail Gunner Joe" without an American flag to wave. Corbin cleaned up.

He didn't think it was necessary to tell the suckers that he and McCarthy were in business together; Corbin and the senator split the profits from the sale of the flags.[49]

A constituent whose name was redacted by the FBI wrote Senator McCarthy a letter in May 1951, expressing his concerns about Corbin's suspected Communist ties: "He entered the U.S. through Canada in the middle Thirties. This, as you know, was the route traveled by many Communists during that period. I have learned that he has had several clashes with the law in some cities along the Lake front."[50]

McCarthy referred the letter to the FBI, but then within a matter of hours had it withdrawn. An agent recording McCarthy's abrupt change of heart noted that the senator said "that Corbin was alright and that he did not want the name check, and that he would rather not have any record made that he had requested it." The FBI had presumably briefed the senator on its intelligence showing that Corbin "had been a Communist Party member since 1939."[51] The bureau had had Corbin under active surveillance for years by this point, and at least several memos went directly to FBI director J. Edgar Hoover, meaning that the bureau considered Corbin potentially dangerous to national security.[52] Hoover himself had generated memos concerning Corbin.[53] Despite all that, McCarthy made his sudden about-face. When asked years later whether Corbin may have threatened or blackmailed McCarthy, Adam Walinsky simply looked at the ceiling and smiled.[54]

Corbin got out of business with Joe McCarthy when the Red-hunter's reputation began to suffer. "The bottom dropped out of the flag market," Corbin later obliquely joked in a Wisconsin newspaper.[55]

In 1954 Corbin was ordered out of Rochester, Minnesota, for running his advertising scam, suspected of hustling dozens of businesses for thousands of dollars. Corbin's operation was exposed when one of his targets was bowling with a union official, who casually told his companion that there were "no advertising cards at the new Union Hall." The FBI report on this one operation of Corbin's was sixty pages long. Yet, once again, Corbin escaped prosecution.[56]

IT IS UNCLEAR PRECISELY when Paul Corbin and Bobby Kennedy met, though it seems likely that they crossed paths in the early 1950s as a result of their mutual association with Joe McCarthy. RFK worked for McCarthy's Senate Subcommittee on Investigations, probing Communism in the government. The Kennedy family—especially patriarch Joe Kennedy—applauded McCarthy's work. Ambassador Kennedy contributed to McCarthy's Senate campaign. McCarthy dated Kennedy's daughters and attended the wedding of his Senate colleague John Kennedy to Jacqueline Bouvier.

Corbin's relationship with RFK began to flourish in 1960, when they both worked on Jack Kennedy's presidential campaign. Bobby served as his brother's very young but very tough and very capable campaign manager, while Corbin signed up early to help Kennedy out in the Wisconsin primary. At a time when anti-Catholic sentiment ran high in the state, Corbin reported to the FBI that an anonymous caller had asked him, "How much is the pope paying you?" and that another caller had instructed Corbin's wife to tell her "no good husband that the KKK is riding tonight."[57] Later, Corbin inflamed voters in Wisconsin's heavily Catholic districts by distributing anti-Catholic literature that was supposedly being passed out in Protestant precincts. JFK's opponent, Senator Hubert Humphrey, was blamed for the flyers. As far as anybody knew, however, Corbin may have printed up the anti-Catholic flyers himself—and may have invented the anonymous phone calls.[58] There was a reason that Kennedy campaign aide Helen Keyes said, "If you have a job and you want to get it done, and you don't care *how* it's done, send Paul Corbin out to do it."[59]

While in Wisconsin, Corbin invited his daughter, Darlene, out to visit him at the campaign. He had finally begun to cultivate a relationship with her. He took her to an event with JFK. Kennedy, not knowing she was Corbin's daughter, made a pass at her. "He was flirting with me," she recalled, "but I wasn't flattered after I heard that he slept with everybody."[60] When Corbin later attempted to introduce his daughter to Senator Kennedy, the candidate blushed.

The Kennedy campaign moved on to West Virginia, and Corbin was put in charge of "Protestant precincts." Loosely translated, that seems to have meant that he spread cash around the streets for JFK. A later FBI report said that Corbin, while "under the influence of intoxicating liquor" at a party, "stated that he had swung the election in West Virginia for President-elect KENNEDY by passing out $10 bills."[61]

According to Walinsky, Corbin got the money from Park Agency, the Kennedy family's business office at 200 Park Avenue in New York.[62]

Walinsky, an attorney, was once a deputized "bagman" for the family. In 1968, exhausted after days on the road for RFK, Walinsky needed a day off with his family in New York. Someone with the campaign asked him to stop by the Kennedy offices to pick up a Gladstone bag. Walinsky did and later peeked inside, only to see it was filled with cash—"at least a couple of hundred thousand." The Kennedy family political machine, Walinsky stressed, ran on "trust." "Nobody was writing cover your ass memos." When the Kennedy family passed out cash to trusted aides, no one was asked for receipts. Secrets were kept, and if you kept your mouth shut and did your job, the family took care of you and yours.[63]

Robert Kennedy was finding that Corbin was one of those men he could trust. Corbin worked hard to impress RFK—so much so, according to at least one FBI informant, that in front of Kennedy he took credit for other people's work.[64] Eventually he became a "Bobby Kennedy guy." John Seigenthaler, one of Corbin's few friends, said years later, "He was very unscrupulous, but he was a good political organizer."[65]

Corbin had also become a close friend and adviser to Pat Lucey, Wisconsin's up-and-coming Democratic Party chairman. Lucey would eventually become lieutenant governor and then governor of the state, after a tour of duty in the Kennedy administration, where RFK placed him in charge of all patronage for his home state. It was Lucey who had brought Corbin into the Kennedy campaign in Wisconsin. The two men developed a friendship that lasted a lifetime. Corbin also took Lucey's daughter, Laurie, under his wing. When she was married, Corbin gave her a gift with a note that read, "To Laurie Lucey on the occasion of your first marriage."[66]

IN THE 1960 GENERAL election, Corbin worked on the Kennedy campaign out of the Hotel Syracuse in upstate New York. No one was impervious to Corbin's taunts. When Pat Moynihan arrived at the headquarters, he walked in dressed as if he'd just arrived from a British boarding school. Corbin took Moynihan's measure and proclaimed, "Well, if it isn't Mr. Chips!"[67]

Corbin rubbed the local Democrats the wrong way and some tried to have him removed, calling Bobby Kennedy in Washington to complain. RFK "dumped it on me," remembered Seigenthaler, who was working in the national campaign headquarters. The New Yorkers came to Washington to tell Seigenthaler that Corbin's work for Kennedy was upsetting the entire Democratic slate in New York. Corbin had recently walked into the local Democratic Party headquarters and announced, "On the day after the election, the only people who are going to get jobs in the federal government are working at Citizens for Kennedy." Seigenthaler could only hold their hands and tell them, "I will do all I can to muzzle him." But he told them in no uncertain terms that RFK was "not going to move him. He thinks he's doing one hell of a job."[68]

On the night of the 1960 election, Corbin was one of the privileged few to be invited to the Kennedy compound in Hyannisport.[69]

After JFK won in 1960, Paul Corbin wanted a job in the new administration. RFK was happy to help out, but one Friday afternoon, the new attorney general called in Seigenthaler, whom he had brought aboard as his principal assistant. Seigenthaler recalled that the outgoing attorney general, William Rogers, left RFK a fountain pen to sign judicial appointments with and "a bottle of aspirin for all the headaches the judicial appointments would give him."[70]

On Kennedy's desk was an oversized binder—Corbin's FBI file, complete with an updated background check. Even before Kennedy had become attorney general, he'd asked the FBI to undertake a full field check on Corbin. RFK told Seigenthaler, "I am not going to look at this, but I want you to look at it over the weekend. All Paul wants is a little desk out of the way—Stew Udall will take Corbin at Interior—so he can bill for a federal pension. He can work eight years in Jack's administration."[71] Corbin had told friends that his plan was to work in Washington for sixteen years—eight for President John Kennedy and eight for President Robert Kennedy.

An FBI teletype had gone out to nine field offices, including those in Milwaukee and Minneapolis. They were ordered to comb their files for any and all material on Corbin and to conduct field interviews. The report was to be "personally delivered to Mr. Robert Kennedy." The request was given top priority and marked "expedited" by the director himself, J. Edgar Hoover.[72]

When the FBI interviewed Corbin, he of course denied any Communist affiliations and completely whitewashed his background. The agent conducting the interview described Corbin's narrative as "vague."[73] Within days, teletypes clacked with reports from the FBI's field offices, loaded with information on Corbin, virtually all of it shocking.

From the Omaha office came rumors of domestic problems between Corbin and his wife. One source, whose name was redacted, "considers Corbin emotionally unstable, untrustworthy and unreliable." The memo also went into detail about Corbin's contributions to and membership in the Communist Party USA.[74]

The Springfield, Illinois, office said that Corbin was "impetuous, inclined to be belligerent."[75] The report from the Baton Rouge office was no better. Another field office interviewed a source from the 1940s who remembered Corbin as a "playboy" and someone "out for a good time and a fast buck. Corbin appeared to be frequently under the influence of liquor." This last report further noted that

Corbin had been a high official of the United Public Workers Union, which was expelled from the CIO for its Communist leanings.[76]

Someone in Rockford, Illinois, vouched for Corbin's character, but virtually everybody else questioned every aspect of his character. Of the dozens of people the FBI's Chicago office interviewed, nearly all condemned Corbin in harsh terms, some questioning his patriotism.[77] A second reference was made to family problems with his wife. Women mentioned his "suggestive statements and actions,"[78] and one claimed that he'd attempted to sexually assault her and had backed off only after she hit him.[79] It was revealed that he'd briefly been in the employ of Congressman Gerald Flynn of Wisconsin, who had asked for Corbin's resignation when he discovered the operative's nefarious activities.[80] Corbin claimed that he had resigned because of a "misunderstanding."[81]

A detailed report filed from the Milwaukee office stated that an informant called Corbin a "tap man," meaning someone whose job it was to raise funds for union activities, but "Corbin had the reputation of keeping a large portion of such collected funds for himself." The individual said the thought of Corbin working in the government made "his skin crawl." Others remembered hearing Corbin make favorable comments about Joseph Stalin.[82] He also had been denied membership in the Janesville Country Club.[83]

A theme was emerging in the FBI field reports, as nearly all were shot through with terms like "controversial," "troublemaker," "untrustworthy," and "crude"; one report said that Corbin "played one Democratic group against the other." When people were asked about Gertrude Corbin, however, it seemed she was universally liked.[84]

Gertrude herself was interviewed by the FBI, and though the document redacted her name, the last sentence said that she "stated, of course, that she would not hesitate to recommend PAUL CORBIN for a position of trust in the government."[85]

A telling report from the FBI office in Racine, Wisconsin, based on an interview with Congressman Flynn, might have explained RFK's attraction to Corbin: "He was much hated by his fellow members of the Rock County Democratic organization . . . but as a campaigner, he was an extremely hard worker and when he tackled a job he always put it over. It was just this same ability that appealed to the JOHN F. KENNEDY campaigners." This report credited Corbin with doing much to win upstate New York for JFK in 1960, something no one thought possible in this Republican stronghold. The report concluded, "As a tireless perfectionist in whatever job he is engaged in, he is of unquestioned value and to that end, despite his reputation, may lie his greatest attraction."[86]

For Seigenthaler, however, those talents weren't enough to overcome the obvious red flags. When he met with Kennedy, he informed the attorney general that under no circumstances could Corbin be given a job in the Kennedy administration: "You can't hire him! You can't hire him!" RFK responded, "I don't want you to tell me what's in [the FBI file], but why?"[87] Kennedy pleaded that all Corbin wanted was a salary, a desk, and a phone at the Department of the Interior.

Seigenthaler made it clear to RFK that the worst thing that could be done would be to give Corbin a job in the government, especially with access to a phone. "It won't be too long before he's . . . an embarrassment to the administration," Seigenthaler said.[88]

At RFK's direction, Corbin was instead quietly put on retainer with the Democratic National Committee. According to Walinsky, his role there was straightforward: to act as the eyes and ears of the Kennedy White House and especially of Bobby Kennedy. "Corbin's function was to be snooping around," Walinsky remembered. "His job was to find out who was stealing anything before the FBI and the newspapers found out so that person could be quietly gotten rid of."[89]

CORBIN ALMOST GOT HIMSELF thrown out of the DNC by JFK personally. One day Kenneth O'Donnell, the president's scheduler, was having lunch at a Washington hotel when he spotted Corbin sitting by the pool, having a drink and sunning himself. When O'Donnell—who never liked Corbin—got back to the White House, he told President Kennedy, "I want you to know that Paul Corbin is helping you get reelected in '64 by sunning himself by the pool."[90] According to Seigenthaler, Ben Bradlee of *Newsweek*, a close friend of JFK's, called Corbin at the hotel wanting to know why he wasn't at the DNC working for Kennedy's reelection. Corbin must have suspected that President Kennedy was listening on an extension, as he began to jerk Bradlee's chain. "I'm out here, Ben, by the pool, with a broad in one hand and a drink in the other," he said. He added, "Look, if Jack doesn't straighten up we're going to have to pull him out of there and run Bobby in '64."[91]

JFK called his brother and demanded that Corbin be fired. RFK stormed to Seigenthaler, "Why can't he just work over there and keep his mouth shut?"[92] The attorney general told Seigenthaler to call DNC chairman John Bailey and have Corbin fired. Seigenthaler talked Robert Kennedy out of it and then told Corbin to make himself scarce for a couple of days. Corbin's little joke had backfired and it nearly cost him his job. Bradlee wrote an embarrassing squib about the incident for the Periscope section of *Newsweek*. Corbin had to go to Hickory Hill and grovel to RFK as per Seigenthaler's counsel. It worked: Seigenthaler recalled that their breakfast was "like old home week."[93] Later, Corbin was invited to Madison

Square Garden to witness Marilyn Monroe seductively sing "Happy Birthday, Mr. President" to JFK.[94]

John F. Kennedy was often indifferent to or not sure about Corbin, and Corbin's relationship with Teddy Kennedy was complicated. Most of the "Irish Mafia" around President Kennedy despised Paul.[95] Only Dave Powers liked Corbin. But Corbin had a strong rapport with other Kennedys. He intimated that the head of the Kennedy clan, Ambassador Kennedy, took a shine to him. And why not? They were cut from the same cloth.

Most important, RFK, Ethel Kennedy, and their brood loved Paul and Paul's wife, Gertrude. When Bobby became the attorney general, he was issued two keys to the private elevator at the Justice Department, which went directly to his office on the top floor. Kennedy kept one and gave the other to Corbin. While others scraped and bowed to RFK, calling him "Mr. Attorney General" and later "Senator," Corbin simply and always called him "Bob."[96] (RFK hated being called "Bobby.")

This relationship with RFK made Corbin practically bulletproof in the Democratic Party and in Washington. Few understood Bobby's close friendship with Corbin, however. Old Kennedy hand Joe Dolan called Corbin "the dark side of Bobby Kennedy." Columnist Rowly Evans, a social friend of the Kennedy family, once said to RFK, "You ought to drop Paul Corbin. He's really hurting you." Kennedy barked back, "Listen, Rowly, when I want your advice, I'll ask for it!"[97] Evans did not know what RFK's daughter Kathleen Kennedy Townsend knew: "My father appreciated somebody who would find out what's going on in the government or in politics and would be forthright about telling him so that he could have eyes and ears in places that he wouldn't normally have them."[98] Columnist Drew Pearson characterized Corbin's role more bluntly: he was "Bobby's backstage henchman."[99]

For the next few years, Corbin lurked in the shadows, handling political matters for RFK, gathering political intelligence, and looking out for Kennedy family interests. Corbin successfully ratted out a number of corrupt government officials and they were gently eased out before becoming an embarrassment. As Walinsky said, "It takes a thief . . ."[100]

Gertrude Corbin served as Ethel Kennedy's private secretary for a time. In 1961, Corbin and his wife became Catholics and Bobby and Ethel Kennedy became their godparents.[101] Corbin's sister said Paul had been born Jewish but later become an atheist.[102] Indeed, the Catholic conversion was probably a matter of political convenience for Corbin. According to Walinsky, who knew both Corbin and Kennedy well, it may have been RFK's idea that Corbin become a Catholic, as a way of appeasing Congressman Francis Walter. A devout Catholic, Walter happened to be chairman of the House Committee on Un-American Activities, which, like the FBI, remained very interested in Paul Corbin.[103]

THE FBI CONTINUED TO monitor Corbin and asked the House Committee on Un-American Activities for any information it had on Corbin.[104] Congressman Mel Laird, a Republican from Wisconsin, confidently predicted that Corbin would be dismissed from the Democratic National Committee.[105] The FBI, in an attempt to embarrass the Kennedy administration, did an "information dump" with the *Milwaukee Journal* in August 1961. The paper published a long story covering Corbin's Communist ties and his numerous scams, under a large headline, "Many Are Wondering: What of Corbin's Part?"[106] In September the *Journal* headlined a piece "Reds Backed Corbin at Divorce Trial," reporting that two Chicago Communists, Kenneth Born and Ishmael P. Flory, had been character witnesses at his divorce trial in the 1940s.[107]

DNC chairman John Bailey was forced to publicly defend Corbin, dismissing the mountains of evidence and saying simply that Corbin was a "controversial figure." Laird inserted in the *Congressional Record* the unbelievable rumor about Corbin's both being a Communist *and* having business affiliations with the late Joe McCarthy.[108] Corbin denied having embraced either Communism *or* Joe McCarthy. Another Wisconsin representative, Democrat Clement Zablocki, sent a letter to Bobby Kennedy asking that Corbin's FBI file be released, but Seigenthaler rebuffed Zablocki.[109] One FBI report written around this time observed that Corbin "has been continuously defended by the Attorney General in these criticisms,"[110] while another complained that "the Attorney General . . . seems to have gone completely overboard in trying to defend Corbin. He has suppressed any and all references to our report detailing Corbin's Communist activity."[111]

On July 2, 1962, Corbin testified before the House Committee on Un-American Activities. Predictably, he denied ever having been a member of the Communist Party.[112] For the benefit of the congressmen, he went through a play-act with his flamboyant attorney, John Jay Hooker. Turning to his lawyer, Corbin said in an indignant stage whisper, "I do not care what you say, Hooker! I am not going to lie to this august group!"[113]

In a 1962 deposition a Marine who served with Corbin in the South Pacific said that while Corbin was "a radical . . . I consider him an opportunist and it is my opinion that he would affiliate himself with any group if he thought it would be profitable to him financially."[114] Corbin had once growled to a young Republican friend, "I can argue it both ways."[115]

J. Edgar Hoover, who hated the Kennedys, saw Corbin as a way to embarrass his nemeses. A later document confirmed their ongoing war, as it noted that the

FBI director was furious "over the personal attack which Senator Kennedy made on Mr. Hoover."[116] Dozens of Corbin-related memos were flying around the FBI by December 1962. One report cited Corbin's "perjurious statements during testimony before HCUA."[117]

But then, that same month, the FBI's intense interest in Corbin ended abruptly. An almost completely redacted memo said, "No further action will be taken by this office."[118]

It is unclear what caused this sudden turnabout. The FBI had dug up a lot of incriminating information on Corbin. The bureau had clearly been stymied—and would remain so for nearly two years.

IN JUNE 1963, CORBIN was part of a group of Democrats in Washington who formed the "New Frontier Club" as an organizing tool for JFK's reelection campaign.[119] Five months later, President Kennedy was dead and Robert Kennedy was devastated, a lost soul. Several weeks after JFK's assassination, Corbin showed once more the special relationship he had with Bobby Kennedy. Those were understandably black days for RFK, but several weeks after the shooting Corbin concluded that Bobby had moped around long enough. According to Walinsky, Corbin yelled at the mourning attorney general, telling him to pull himself together. "Corbin went to him at one point and said, 'You've just got to get off your fucking ass, Bob, and stop this bullshit sitting around crying and get up off your ass and . . . run for the U.S. Senate.' Nobody in the whole world said that to Robert Kennedy . . . except for Paul."[120]

A short time after November 22, a bereaved RFK went through the Oval Office and gave Corbin many personal effects of the late President Kennedy's, including a cut-glass water pitcher that Lyndon Johnson and the Kennedy cabinet had given to JFK on his birthday in 1961.

A FEW MONTHS LATER, Corbin found himself—and his friendship with Bobby Kennedy—under renewed scrutiny. In early 1964 the new president, Lyndon Johnson, caught wind of the fact that Corbin was orchestrating a "Draft Kennedy for Vice President" write-in effort in the New Hampshire primary. LBJ was no fan of the Kennedys, and the last thing he wanted was a restoration, even a partial one, of Camelot. Johnson had already stopped referring to the New Frontier and begun using his own catchphrase, the Great Society.

Johnson called John Bailey at the DNC to ask what he knew about Corbin.[121] Corbin was the subject of at least nine presidential phone calls between February 10 and March 12, 1964, as LBJ reached out to Bailey, O'Donnell (who had stayed

on in the Johnson White House), Ben Bradlee, Jack Valenti, Bill Moyers, and
Larry O'Brien.[122]

On March 10, LBJ won the New Hampshire Democratic primary with ease.
But RFK received nearly as many votes as a write-in candidate for vice president as
Johnson did for the top spot on the ticket—an astounding 25,861 write-in votes
versus the 29,635 votes that LBJ received.[123]

Corbin hadn't even traveled to New Hampshire, but by working the phones
he had scored this victory for Bobby Kennedy, which was an embarrassment to
President Johnson. John Seigenthaler's worries about Corbin and access to a telephone had been prescient.

Suddenly the FBI set its sights on Corbin again. In April 1964 agent N. P.
Callahan sent J. Edgar Hoover an internal memo complaining that someone was
protecting Corbin from Justice Department prosecution and FBI investigation.
Agent Callahan was clearly frustrated by Corbin's prevarications. He wrote,
"How familiar is the Attorney General [Robert Kennedy] with these unresolved
contradictions and has the Department of Justice exhausted all possibilities of
resolving them? At this point, I do not profess to know.—Especially, in view
of the reported new political activities of Mr. Corbin, I am totally unwilling to
regard the subject as closed."[124]

President Johnson angrily had Corbin thrown off the DNC payroll in August
1964 (though it was reported that he had "resigned"). When LBJ told Kennedy he
was getting rid of Corbin, the attorney general said, "President Kennedy wouldn't
approve of that." Johnson tersely replied, "But Bobby, I'm president now."[125]

The Kennedy family—they of the long loyalties and even longer memories—
put Corbin on the payroll of the Merchandise Mart in Chicago, an enormous
wholesale-goods business that Joe Kennedy had purchased in 1945. Corbin was
still on the Merchandise Mart payroll at the time of his death in 1990.[126] A news
report in 1964 said that Corbin had also been placed on the payroll of the Joseph
P. Kennedy Jr. Foundation.[127] The family was taking care of its own.

In September, a month after President Johnson forced Corbin out of the
DNC, RFK resigned as attorney general in order to run for a U.S. Senate seat
in New York. Naturally, Corbin was involved in the campaign. He ran around
upstate New York making "his usual underhanded deals," joked Walinsky.[128] Eventually, though, Corbin stepped on so many toes that he was banned from the
Empire State and had to operate out of New Jersey, according to Kathleen Kennedy Townsend.[129]

The troublesome Corbin was mostly sidelined in the 1968 presidential campaign by old Kennedy hands Kenny O'Donnell and Larry O'Brien, who were

nominally in charge of the freewheeling operation. They prohibited Corbin from traveling, but made the mistake of giving him a phone and a desk at the headquarters in Washington. Corbin spent his days "trashing them," said Walinsky. He once compared Corbin to RFK's dog, Brummus, a large Newfoundland, which RFK once told him "did not have a single redeeming social characteristic." At Kennedy lawn parties, recalled Walinsky, "Brummus literally just walked up to some woman, lifted his leg, and drenched her. Paul was like a human version of Brummus."[130]

When RFK was assassinated in June 1968, Corbin was shattered. His friend, his political protector, the center of his universe, was gone. He had loved Robert Kennedy and RFK had loved Corbin.[131]

But his friend's death did not exactly soften Corbin.

Corbin was on the funeral train carrying RFK's remains from the service in New York to Washington for burial. On the train, a bereaved Kennedy man who had often knocked heads with Corbin sidled up to his old adversary and offered an olive branch. Crying uncontrollably, Joe Dolan, who had been RFK's top aide on Capitol Hill, said to Corbin, "Let's let bygones be bygones."

Corbin squinted at the weeping Dolan and growled, "Bob never trusted you."[132]

AFTER THE FUNERAL, SEIGENTHALER saw the rough time Corbin was having and advised him to leave Washington and politics. Seigenthaler, who had become editor of the *Nashville Tennessean*, urged Corbin to move to Nashville to better deal with his grief. In Nashville, Seigenthaler tried to put Corbin into several business deals, including a publishing venture, but Corbin had trouble with the other partners. In his first meeting with the others, Corbin promised to "only skim 10 percent off the top." The partners laughed, thinking Corbin was kidding.[133]

Corbin then got involved with the Country Music Wax Museum and delighted all by taking the boots off such wax figurines as Johnny Cash and wearing them around town. He became an immediate hit with the locals and cultivated a young activist, Bob Dunn, a student at Vanderbilt. He later helped Dunn get a job on the staff of his friend Governor Pat Lucey.[134]

Slowly recovering from his anguish, Corbin looked to get back into politics. In the 1970s he made a run at doing business with Tennessee governor Ray Blanton but was rebuffed.[135] Blanton's tenure was marked by charges of corruption. He was accused of selling pardons, in particular to a double murderer whose father was a political supporter. Once he left office, Blanton was pursued by the FBI for illegally selling liquor licenses.[136] He was convicted and sentenced to federal prison, although the conviction was later overturned on a technicality.[137]

Corbin was also an early organizer in a string of Minnie Pearl fast-food restaurants, but only made more enemies, including former Republican congressman
Robin Beard, who lost his shirt in Corbin's scheme when it went belly-up. In another
caper, Corbin became close to Lafayette C. "Fate"Thomas, a sheriff in the Volunteer
State who went to federal prison for, among other crimes, having prisoners work on
his summer home.[138] Thomas and Corbin had once traveled to Moscow together and
Thomas said that "Corbin almost got him thrown into a Russian prison."[139]

A Corbin crony claimed that Corbin helped out with Lamar Alexander's
gubernatorial campaign by spreading disinformation about Alexander's Democratic opponent, Jake Butcher.[140] Corbin himself later bragged to some poker
friends that he had the goods on Democrat Al Gore. Joseph Sweat, one of Corbin's
associates in Tennessee, remembered that Corbin accused Gore, then a young
congressman, of renting rooms in a motel in Cookeville to watch pornography.
"That goddamn Gore, he is up there in a motel . . . watching those dirty movies!"
Corbin exclaimed. Asked how he knew, Corbin replied, "The desk clerk, I paid
him a little bit and he gave me the receipt."[141]

In the late 1970s Corbin went back to Washington. But he was held at arm's
length by the Carterites, because they didn't know him or, even worse, because
they *did* know of him, at least his reputation of being a Kennedy man. Naturally he
supported Ted Kennedy's presidential bid in 1980. The senator himself, however,
was dubious about Corbin, despite his long history with the family. Corbin had
no formal role in the 1980 Kennedy campaign except to "stir up trouble," according to Walinsky. Walinsky did not take a role but left no doubt as to his loyalties.
When asked about supporting Carter, he simply replied, "Fuck him."[142]

Some others in the Kennedy family, including Kennedy brother-in-law Steve
Smith, who was running the campaign, were happy to have Corbin's help. Corbin
hated Carter and his people. According to Seigenthaler, Corbin once got a hold of
a phone bank and "screw[ed] up the Carter campaign headquarters telephones."[143]
Corbin claimed that his prank took out all the Carter campaign's phones in New
York City.

JUST BEFORE TEDDY KENNEDY officially jumped into the campaign in the fall of 1979,
President Carter's ambassador to Mexico, Pat Lucey, abruptly quit his post and took
a position in the Kennedy campaign. When he resigned, Lucey bluntly told reporters about his loyalty to the Kennedy family and his intentions to help Teddy.[144] It
struck at least a few in Washington as odd that Lucey's loyalty to Carter was so tenuous. He had been given a plum diplomatic assignment and enjoyed a close friendship
with Vice President Walter Mondale. Years later Mondale said of Lucey's resigna-

tion, "We were pissed at that."[145] On the other hand, the Carter White House had been leaking stories dumping on Lucey's work since the previous summer. Lucey was steamed. The Carter team was good at making unnecessary enemies.

Lucey's daughter, Laurie, had been working in the Carter White House at the time as a confidential assistant to Landon Butler, deputy to Chief of Staff Hamilton Jordan.[146] But just days before her father quit his post in Mexico, she resigned from her White House job.[147]

Around the same time that Laurie Lucey was leaving the White House, Bob Dunn was coming in. Dunn went to work for Carter's head of scheduling, Phil Wise. Dunn was Pat Lucey's longtime aide, having worked for the governor in Wisconsin and then having accompanied Lucey to Mexico when he was appointed ambassador.[148] And Dunn was Corbin's friend. Their friendship went back to 1971, according to Dunn.[149]

"Dunn's new job has attracted some attention since Lucey joined the campaign for Sen. Kennedy," *National Journal* reported at the time.[150] But it should have done more than attracted "some attention"; Corbin's close relationships with Dunn, Laurie Lucey, and Pat Lucey should have set off alarm bells in the Carter White House. The Carter team took no action.

In 1980 Corbin should have been enjoying retirement and grandchildren, like most other men his age. Not Corbin. He hated kids. Instead, he was still plotting shadowy deals, still scheming against his enemies. In fact, the old man orchestrated the biggest heist of his life: stealing—and delivering to the Reagan campaign—President Carter's secret debate briefing books.

IT WAS AT THE 1980 Democratic convention in New York, as Ted Kennedy gave the best speech of his life, that Corbin yelled to his friend Bill Schulz, "I'm going to go work for Reagan!"

Schulz's friendship with Corbin was odd, but that was the way Washington often worked. Schulz, a friendly bear of a man, had been a founding member of Young Americans for Freedom, had worked for syndicated conservative columnist Fulton Lewis, and by 1980 was the Washington editor of *Reader's Digest*, often derided by liberals because of its conservative content. (Reagan was one of its most ardent readers.)

Way back in 1961, material on Corbin's Communist affiliations had been leaked to Schulz. He called Corbin at the Democratic National Committee and said, "Mr. Corbin, I am an assistant to Fulton Lewis, the columnist and radio commentator. I wanted to get your reaction to a report that I have. . . . Individuals have identified you in closed-door testimony before the House Committee on Un-American

Activities as a one-time member of the Communist Party USA." Corbin growled back, "Mr. Schulz, you can kiss my fucking ass!" Then he hung up.[151]

Sixteen years later, in 1977, they were reintroduced at a poker game at GOP operative Dave Keene's home in Alexandria, Virginia. Keene said, "You might not know Paul Corbin." Corbin replied cryptically, "I know Mr. Schulz. We had a conversation once."[152] Keene's father, a labor organizer in Wisconsin, had also had a run-in with Corbin, like everybody else, it seemed. "Didn't my father once have you beaten up and thrown into a ditch?" Keene asked the grizzled little man. Corbin replied, "Yeah, but the son of a bitch is dead!"[153]

Just after the Democratic convention in 1980, syndicated columnist Charles Bartlett, a fixture on the Washington social scene, introduced Corbin to Bill Casey. Bartlett was great company, up on all the latest gossip, and knew everybody in Washington. He had famously introduced John Kennedy to Jacqueline Bouvier at a dinner party in 1951.[154] Bartlett called Casey and told him Corbin could help Reagan.[155]

In August, Corbin contacted Casey and proposed to assist Reagan, ostensibly with organized labor. Casey agreed, putting Corbin on retainer to the Reagan campaign. Thus the former Communist organizer Paul Corbin (and former business partner of Joe McCarthy) began to work for the ardently anti-Communist Ronald Reagan.

Corbin was not the only old RFK retainer who wanted to help Reagan defeat Carter. Adam Walinsky wrote a six-page memo to Casey on how Reagan could score points in a debate with the president.[156] Walinsky later met with Casey to discuss the campaign.

A later news report said that Jim Baker had a hand in bringing Corbin into the Reagan campaign.[157] But the fact was that Baker never liked Corbin. Keene had introduced the two in 1979 after a lunch in which Corbin and Bartlett gave Keene "advice" for his candidate, George Bush. "In Kennedy's case, we just put a girl on the plane," the two men told Keene. "That gives us a much better candidate. And we think you need to do this with Bush." Keene told them, "I made a deal with Jim Baker that he's in charge of the campaign and I'm in charge of the political organization. And it seems to me that this would fall within his domain rather than mine." So Keene, who liked a good joke, called Baker and suggested he meet with Corbin and Bartlett. Baker agreed to the meeting, and shortly after the two men departed, he yelled at Keene, "You son of a bitch, you could have at least told me!"[158] Keene was proud of his little prank.

According to Keene as well as Adam Walinsky, it was also Corbin's idea to convince Pat Lucey, once Ted Kennedy was out of the race, to go on the ticket with John Anderson so as to bleed more liberal votes away from Carter.[159] Lucey didn't need much convincing, as he loved Kennedy and despised Carter and his aides.[160] This approach fit the two-step plan that Corbin was formulating: The first step was to defeat Carter to exact revenge. The second was to mount a second campaign by Ted Kennedy in 1984 as a way to restore Camelot.

Corbin's work for the Reagan campaign was, of course, crucial to ensuring that the first step of the plan was achieved. Corbin first visited the Reagan-Bush headquarters in Arlington on September 29, meeting with Jim Baker and then with Bill Casey. He would make at least three more visits, signing in on October 11, October 25, and November 3.[161]

On October 25, Corbin signed in at 9:35 A.M., gave his destination as "Casey," and picked up a check for $1,500. It was just three days before the big debate between Reagan and Carter.[162]

On November 3, the day before the election, Corbin picked up a second and final check from the Reagan campaign, this time in the amount of $1,360.[163] He also spent nearly two hours meeting with Casey. The report that the campaign filed with the Federal Election Commission said that Corbin received this check for "professional services and telephone" (with $160 of the final $1,360 covering reimbursement of phone expenses).

Corbin's invoices claimed that he produced research reports on Florida for the Reagan campaign. He did go to the state, but no evidence of his doing any work there for the Gipper surfaced. No one at the campaign recalled ever seeing a report from him. The idea that Corbin would put anything in writing was absurd. He certainly wasn't breaking a sweat for Reagan while in Florida. In the back of his rental car were several boxes filled with Reagan-Bush campaign materials, but he asked a friend to throw them in the trash as a favor.[164]

PRESIDENT CARTER'S DEBATE BRIEFING books had been assembled and copied in the White House starting the night of October 23 and finishing around 11 o'clock the next morning. A White House aide, James Rowland, stood at a copying machine to prepare the briefing books for Carter and his debate-prep team.[165] There were actually three books: one on domestic policy, one on foreign policy, and a third for Vice President Mondale's perusal.[166]

Jerry Rafshoon, in charge of President Carter's media, recalled seeing Corbin around the Carter White House late in the 1980 campaign and thought it odd that this Kennedy man and Carter hater would be there.[167] He had no idea at the time that Corbin was covertly working for Reagan.

Copies of the Carter briefing books arrived at the Reagan campaign's headquarters not long after the White House had put them together. Reagan adviser

David Gergen later recalled a package arriving at the Reagan-Bush campaign on a rainy Saturday, "probably October 25."[168] October 25 was indeed a rainy Saturday in Washington.[169] It was also the same day that Corbin met with Bill Casey at Reagan campaign headquarters.

Within a short period of time, everybody in the Reagan-Bush campaign knew about the purloined Carter briefing books. Jim Baker knew about them. Stef Halper, the Bush research aide who by the fall was working for Ed Meese, knew about them.[170] So apparently did the campaign's national political director, Bill Timmons.[171] So did Gergen, a former Bush aide (although he first denied and then later admitted to Congress that he knew of the books).[172] So did Congressman David Stockman of Michigan, who in Reagan's practice debates stood in for John Anderson and then Carter.[173] So did Francis Hodsoll, who was coordinating papers for the debate prep with Reagan.[174] Wayne Valis, a staffer at the American Enterprise Institute who was volunteering at the Reagan campaign, later recalled that pretty much everybody knew about the material through the grapevine.[175]

Nevertheless, the story of the pinched Carter briefing books did not go public during the 1980 campaign. On the day of the debate, October 28, David Stockman did make reference in a speech to the "pilfered" briefing books.[176] Later, after Reagan's victory, a "collector of campaign memorabilia" searching for souvenirs found Carter campaign memos among the Reagan campaign's trash.[177] But it would be another three years before the stolen-briefing-books story made national news, when Laurence Barrett of *Time* reported on the episode in a mostly harsh book about Reagan, *Gambling with History*. In a small item tucked inside the book, Barrett said that someone in the Reagan camp had "filched" Carter's briefing material, and insinuated that Jim Baker had an ethical problem because he had "looked the other way."[178]

Right after publication of Barrett's book, former Carter press secretary Jody Powell wrote a column flaying the national media for showing so little interest in the story. Within days, Washington was engulfed in a "Debategate" inferno. A congressional committee was duly appointed to investigate the theft in the late spring of 1983.[179]

The congressional investigation headed by Don Albosta took ten months and cost $500,000.[180] A number of figures came under suspicion but were never charged. The FBI accused Wayne Valis under questioning of sleeping with women in the Carter White House in order to get sensitive documents, to which Valis responded, "Gentlemen, when I sleep with women, it's not to get papers. Why do you sleep with women?"[181] Reagan's national security adviser, Richard Allen, told the Albosta committee that after the 1980 election Jerry Jennings, a staffer at Carter's National Security Council, was "seen associating" with Tony Dolan, an aide to Ed Meese at the Reagan campaign who was also close to Bill Casey.[182] Jim Rowland, the White House aide who had photocopied the briefing books, came under suspicion because he had once worked for "the very conservative *Human Events*" and had been overheard criticizing the Carter administration, although the committee later cleared him.[183]

Of course, the committee could not fail to take note of Paul Corbin. With attention focused on the old Kennedy operator, the media began staking out Corbin's home. To avoid the press he would jump the back fence and walk into his neighbor's basement, and he would then put on a disguise and be sneaked out in a car. Corbin knew what it was to be stalked by federal investigators, as he'd once secreted accused GOP dirty trickster Roger Stone during the Watergate investigation.[184] At the height of the investigation, Phil Gailey of the *New York Times* tracked down Corbin in Aruba, and Corbin denied knowing anything about the Carter briefing books. He did confirm that he had spoken with Casey about the matter, however. Casey ducked Gailey's repeated calls. The story revealed that Reagan White House counsel Fred Fielding had given the FBI a list of "secretaries and low-level employees who had worked in the Nixon and Ford Administrations and were held over by the Carter White House."[185]

Corbin submitted a sworn statement to the Albosta committee, and in his interviews with the committee and with the FBI he was again full of denials.[186] Frustrated, Congressman Albosta acknowledged his committee's inability to pin Corbin down, saying, "He denies everything . . . doesn't even know his own name. This leads people to suspect he had some effort and involvement."[187]

Furthering suspicion was the fact that, as phone logs revealed, Corbin had called Bill Timmons at the Reagan campaign "on several occasions."[188] The Albosta committee reported that Corbin was informing Timmons of Carter's travel in advance, and noted that a memo by Reagan aide Jerry Carmen to a field staffer "proceeded to discuss President Carter's scheduled stops for two dates a week-and-a-half away."[189]

The Albosta committee concluded that the Carter debate briefing books were most probably taken from either the National Security Council offices or the White House Situation Room, both in the West Wing and both with tightly controlled access.[190] Albosta himself said in an interview years later that he thought the briefing books had been lifted from the office of National Security Adviser Zbigniew Brzezinski. "The papers were left on his desk," Albosta recalled, "and this one night they . . . disappeared, and they became gone."[191]

The Albosta committee's final report, in 1983, stated the committee's belief that there existed "organized efforts to obtain from the Carter administration, and from the Carter-Mondale campaign, information and materials that were not publicly available."[192] The investigators could not come to more precise conclusions, in part because the Carter White House—featuring many holdovers from the Ford and Nixon administrations who didn't like the Carter gang—leaked like a sieve. According to the final report, the investigation found that thirteen Reagan staffers had either received or were aware of Carter material that had come into the possession of the Reagan campaign.[193] With so many possible culprits, Corbin escaped the noose. The investigators were forced to admit their failure, saying that the committee "was unable to state how Corbin may have obtained those materials himself."[194]

Years later Congressman Albosta said he felt that he'd been hoodwinked, especially by David Stockman, though he did not elaborate.[195] He was also frustrated that when his committee interviewed Bill Casey, they couldn't understand a word he said. The only thing that was clear was that Casey denied giving Jim Baker the Carter briefing books, as Baker had claimed in the media and to the Albosta committee.[196]

These counterclaims led to squabbling within the Reagan administration. Casey, by then the CIA director, challenged Baker, Reagan's White House chief of staff, to take polygraphs. Baker fretted that Casey, from his OSS and CIA experience, would know how to "game the polygraph" tests and hang him out to dry.[197] Casey confirmed Baker's fear when he told his friend Bill Safire, "I know how to handle those things."[198] For days, the two Reagan aides engaged in public finger pointing. Paul Corbin's name was lost amid this high-profile spat.

At the height of the Albosta investigation, Baker received a call from Congressman Dick Cheney. Cheney told Baker that a member of his staff, Tim Wyngaard, confided that Corbin had privately acknowledged orchestrating the theft of the Carter briefing books and giving them to Casey.[199] Corbin and Wyngaard, a former reporter, had known each other a long time, going back to Wisconsin politics. Wyngaard, the executive director of the House Republican Policy Committee, confirmed to Albosta committee investigators and to the New York Times that Corbin had claimed credit for lifting the briefing books.[200]

Regardless, Corbin, the old master, once again had left no fingerprints—in this case, literally. Although the FBI found both Jim Baker's and David Gergen's fingerprints on the Carter briefing books, they found none of Corbin's, or of Casey's for that matter.[201]

Corbin was too smart to make that dumb mistake. After all, how many Washington political operators had a downtown office with an unlisted phone number? Jim Baker despised Corbin but there was also grudging respect. He once told the old man, "I got to say this about you Kennedy guys. You really know how to keep your mouths shut."[202]

ON JUNE 5, 1981—THIRTEEN years to the day after RFK was shot in L.A.'s Ambassador Hotel—President Ronald Reagan awarded to the Kennedy family the Congressional Gold Medal commemorating the life of Robert Francis Kennedy. This was the very same medal that Jimmy Carter had refused to present, causing deep resentment among Kennedyites.

Just before noon, the entire Kennedy clan, along with close friends and supporters of RFK, returned to the White House for the bittersweet and long-delayed Rose Garden ceremony.

Camelot rematerialized for one brief shining moment.

The day was magnificent. Blue skies, temperature in the mid-eighties, puffs of clouds, with a light offshore breeze and low humidity.[203] Kennedy sailing weather.

President Reagan greeted all in his customary gracious style. "President Reagan was very kind to our family," remembered RFK's eldest daughter, Kathleen.[204] Reagan told the small gathering, "Those of us who had our philosophical disagreements with him always appreciated his wit and his personal grace."[205] He then turned to Ethel Kennedy and said, "So Mrs. Kennedy, this medal has been waiting patiently to be presented."[206] Everybody knew to what and to whom Reagan was referring.

Speaking for the family, Ted Kennedy was equally genial, drawing a connection between his own brother's shooting and Reagan's, offering thanks to God that Reagan had survived. He then thanked Reagan and reminisced about his beloved brother, including RFK's famous internationally television debate with Reagan in 1967. "My brother Bob said that Ronald Reagan was the toughest debater he ever faced—and obviously, he was right."[207] Everybody knew to what and to whom Kennedy was referring.

But as gracious as Reagan was, and as much as the Reagans and the Kennedys were united in their aversion to Jimmy Carter, this lovely and overdue event did not just happen. Somebody had had to cut the deal and keep the pressure on Reagan chief of staff Jim Baker to make sure that the Kennedy family finally got the Congressional Gold Medal for their adored RFK. Someone who was irascible, unrelenting, who would call and push and agitate and irritate and cajole and threaten until he got what he wanted for his old friend Bob Kennedy.

Standing in the background of the Rose Garden, quietly taking it all in, was a wizened, tough, hard-bitten old political operator, perhaps the greatest, most controversial, and most unethical of them all—Paul Corbin.

29

GENERAL QUARTERS

"The way things are going now, we are going to lose."

Ronald Reagan emerged from seclusion atop the Santa Ynez Mountains, 2,400 feet above sea level. During the week of the Democratic convention, Reagan had been happily alone with Nancy at Rancho del Cielo, only once taking time to meet with a group of supporters. The supporters, whom the Reagans had met in Mississippi at the Neshoba County Fair several weeks earlier, had been invited to the ranch—a rare treat—to present a horse-drawn wagon built by Amish artisans. Several reporters were on hand, and the presentation was cut short when they violated the ground rules of the event by asking Reagan about politics.[1]

Reagan's celebrity neighbors in Santa Barbara, such as Sylvester Stallone and John Travolta, worried that if Reagan won, their quiet town might be overrun with reporters and tourists, but in truth they had little to fear. Reagan's ranch was nearly thirty miles outside of town, and nobody in his right mind would drive the seven-mile-long road up through the mountains to 333 Refugio Road—a harrowing trip along sheer cliffs without guardrails—unless he really had to. The road was closed frequently due to floods, and only a few months earlier, a pregnant woman, had to be carried out on horseback.[2] Reagan loved the seclusion.

Now, however, he had to come down from the mountain. The Democrats had their official nominee at last, and this election was shaping up as the most polarizing of the twentieth century. Several days earlier, Reagan had issued a statement saying that although Ted Kennedy's speech had been the indisputable highlight of the Democratic convention, it had changed nothing: "The issue is still the Carter record."[3]

A casual examination of the two parties' platforms made the contrast between the Republicans and the Democrats clear. The GOP platform fretted about government interference, while the Democratic platform embraced it by saying that jobs were the "government's most important product."[4] The Republicans stressed a strong national defense as a means of dealing with the Soviets, while the Democrats stressed arms control and diplomatic relations. From education to welfare to tax cuts to preferential treatment for minorities and women, the parties and their nominees agreed on virtually nothing.

The Democratic Party's organizing principle had evolved over time into the concept of "justice." The new organizing principle of the GOP—as espoused by Reagan—was "freedom." Of course, one man's idea of justice can often conflict with another person's belief in freedom.

As the years went by, it would become more and more difficult for the two parties to find common ground.

FRESH OFF HIS LACKLUSTER acceptance speech, Jimmy Carter received some good news in late August: support for John Anderson was slacking and more of the Democratic core base was coming home, including Jewish voters. A prominent Jewish attorney, Justin Feldman, recalled that in 1948, "Jews all said they were going to vote for Henry Wallace until they walked into the [voting] booth."[5] Feldman's point was that although Democrats may have been unenthused about Harry Truman at the time, they still returned to the New Deal coalition and voted for him, rather than voting for the third-party candidate, Wallace—and a substantial turnout for the left-wing Wallace might have thrown the election to Republican Tom Dewey. Likewise, labor was coming home for Carter, despite its highly public grousing about the incumbent. As a bonus, the national television audience for Carter's convention topped 115 million viewers over the four days, beating the Republican convention in Detroit by a healthy 15 million Americans.[6]

The Carter campaign's goal was to use the Rose Garden to its maximum advantage. The president would campaign only two days a week until two weeks before the election, when he would go on the road right up to Election Day, November 4. Meanwhile, Walter Mondale and surrogates would take it to Reagan.[7] Even Mondale's wife, Joan, would be deployed. A pleasant and soft-spoken lady, Mrs. Mondale was an "amateur potter" and the plan was to use her in the "arts and crafts" community.[8]

Carter's plan for reelection was reasonable—on paper, anyway. He would hold on to what he'd won in 1976: the South, big Democratic states like New York and Pennsylvania, and Mondale's home state of Minnesota. The only western state he needed was Hawaii. Those states put him at 279 electoral votes, nine more than needed. A cushion was sought from Oregon, Wisconsin, Ohio, and Washington.[9] Carter was also making a serious play for Reagan's California, which, given its huge Democratic registration advantage, made sense. That left Reagan only the rest of the West and such reliably Republican states as New Hampshire, Maine, and Vermont.

The Carterites were quite organized, even if they walked close to the ethical line. Government employees were practically ordered to raise money for the reelection campaign. They were told what amounts they had to raise, and deadlines were set for dozens of government workers. A memo went out from Tim Finchem saying, "Each team will include 10 or more political appointees and/or government employees each of whom will be asked to solicit and collect a minimum of $5,000 from non-government employees." The organizing meetings took place in Hamilton Jordan's campaign office. Mid-level government employees did not say no to the president of the United States.[10]

But the Carter campaign was not a seamless operation. There were internal disputes over tactics, strategy, and turf. If the Carterites were good at anything, it was writing memos. Memo after memo went out laying out various opinions and positions. Pat Caddell alone was a threat to American forestry, notorious for excruciatingly long memos. Carter's team heard complaints from some state leaders centering on the president's adman, Gerald Rafshoon.[11] They were barking up the wrong tree in going after Rafshoon, who was close to Carter and a member in good standing of the Georgia Mafia.

Rafshoon began testing several anti-Reagan themes under the headings "He's not acting" and "Empty Oval Office." Carter's researchers were hard at work poring over every utterance Reagan ever made, going back to his days in Hollywood. They went through thousands of columns, radio commentaries, and speeches, trying to find ammunition to use against Reagan. Rafshoon was also exploring pro-Carter themes, but he and the rest of the Carter campaign team believed there was so much "low-hanging fruit" to use against Reagan that going negative was the way to go.[12]

The emerging strategy would be "a broad-scale offensive designed to force Reagan out of the meticulously packaged, cue-card campaign he would like to run," wrote Lisa Myers of the *Washington Star*. The goal of the Carter campaign, said Myers, was to convince voters of the "'danger' of electing an aging actor whose concepts of diplomacy allegedly are lifted from his old scripts in shoot-em-up westerns."[13]

The Carterites' opinion of Reagan was so low that they thought Carter would mop the floor with him in a one-on-one debate. "The Carter operatives have always been convinced that the president would obliterate Reagan in a debate format," wrote columnists Jack Germond and Jules Witcover.[14] Tim Smith, chief counsel to the campaign, wrote in a memo, "We are for more debates, not fewer; beginning earlier, rather than later."[15]

What Carter's advisers meant was that they wanted as many debates as possible *with Reagan only*. The League of Women Voters had set a threshold of 15 percent in the polls for John Anderson to be included in presidential debates, but Carter objected to setting the bar that low.[16] Carter butted heads with the league,[17] but Reagan, who just wanted to debate somebody, anybody, stayed out of the dustup. The White House's heavy-handedness toward Anderson benefited Reagan. Anderson abhorred Reagan's ideology but had nothing against him personally at this point, as he did Carter. This resentment was a big factor in who Anderson eventually selected for his running mate.

THE GOP NOMINEE HEADED for Chicago to accept the endorsement of the Veterans of Foreign Wars—the first time the organization had ever backed a presidential candidate. In his speech, Reagan lambasted Carter, accusing him of allowing America's defense posture to weaken. Reagan pledged a program of "peace through strength" and said that as president, while building up the nation's armaments, he would continue negotiations with the Soviets. To illustrate his philosophy, he told the five thousand veterans, "The great American humorist Will Rogers some years ago had an answer for those who believed that strength invited war. He said, 'I've never seen anyone insult Jack Dempsey.'"[18]

Reagan spoke of the American efforts to stave off the fall of South Vietnam as a "noble cause," saying, "It is time we recognized that ours was, in truth, a noble cause. A small country, newly free from colonial rule, sought our help in establishing self-rule and the means of self-defense against a totalitarian neighbor bent on conquest." Reagan brought the crowd to its feet when he thundered, "Let us tell those who fought in that war that we will never again ask young men to fight and possibly die in a war our government is afraid to let them win." Of Carter's treatment of veterans, he used words such as "regrettable and insensitive," "unconscionable," and "betrayal."[19]

The national media received Reagan's VFW remarks poorly. Like his trip to the Neshoba County Fair in Mississippi, his calling the Vietnam War a "noble cause" would come back to haunt the Californian.

Before that media frenzy erupted, Reagan had to confront another problem: by late August, his once-commanding lead was gone.

Gallup's new national poll had it 39 percent for Reagan and 38 percent for

President Carter, with John Anderson at 14 percent. And when the survey only pitted Carter against Reagan, Carter was comfortably ahead, 46 percent to Reagan's 40 percent.[20]

The Harris poll had it better for the Gipper, with Reagan at 42 percent, Carter at 36, and Anderson at 17. In the NBC–Associated Press poll, Reagan was also ahead, 39 percent to Carter's 32 percent and Anderson's 13 percent.[21] But regardless of which poll you picked, one thing was clear: Carter was surging. The Gipper's confident team had thought the president might get a smaller-than-usual bump from his convention because of the lingering fight with Ted Kennedy. Now it was evident that Carter was actually extending his post-convention bounce. Reagan was in trouble, despite the spin of his campaign aides.

The Republican candidate pushed on to Boston to address the annual convention of the American Legion. The four thousand attendees rabidly received him, but once again the media complained that the speech was short on substance. He did, however, blast Carter on the deterioration of the military, the absence of replacement parts for equipment, and the low military morale while voicing support for the GI Bill of Rights.[22]

NOW THAT THE DEMOCRATIC convention was over and Ted Kennedy was finally out of the race officially, John Anderson had more options for running mates. Among the names bandied about were Hugh Carey, the governor of New York, and Kevin White, the mayor of Boston.[23] Anderson had also talked with Congresswoman Shirley Chisholm, who in 1972 had mounted the first serious attempt by an African-American to win a presidential nomination.[24]

But Paul Corbin was secretly engineering a deal with Pat Lucey, who had resigned as Carter's ambassador to Mexico in the fall of 1979 to join the Kennedy campaign. Discussions had been going on for more than a month, and Anderson and Lucey now met in seclusion. Anderson needed a running mate who was respected by the media and the political establishment, and the former Wisconsin governor filled the bill. Lucey was also a New Deal liberal and would appeal to voters on the Left.

Lucey told everybody he was leaving the decision to his wife, Jean, who, like her husband, adored the Kennedy family and despised Carter. It was easy to see where this was going. Jean Lucey told reporters, "Anderson is certainly the best of the lot."[25]

THE REAGAN TEAM ANNOUNCED that the official kickoff of its fall campaign would be at Liberty State Park in New Jersey on Labor Day. The candidate would give a major speech with the Statue of Liberty and Ellis Island as a backdrop.[26] Reagan would then return to Detroit. Democrats often kicked off their campaigns there, but this time the Republican candidate was competing for the workingman's vote.[27] George Bush was to begin with a rally at the airport in Portland, Maine, and then stump in New Jersey.[28]

Carter announced that the launch of his fall campaign would be at a picnic in Tuscumbia, Alabama.[29] Four years earlier, Carter had begun in Warm Springs, Georgia, where FDR had often vacationed.

REAGAN'S "NOBLE CAUSE" COMMENT was beginning to generate manufactured indignation among the elites. In 1980 the Vietnam War was a taboo subject, at least any defense of it. The dominant culture subscribed to the argument that America had lost Southeast Asia because America was corrupt, the Pentagon was evil and incompetent, and there was moral equivalency between the North Vietnamese and the South Vietnamese—the killing fields of the puppet Cambodian regime set up by Hanoi notwithstanding. Reagan would not keep quiet, though. He said the North Vietnamese could not beat America in the field, so they beat America in its living rooms, with a propaganda campaign designed to weaken American resolve.

The phrase "noble cause" pushed buttons. Whether to use it at all had been hotly debated inside the Reagan campaign. It had been taken out of the original draft, but Reagan put it back in.[30] It came out of the second draft. Reagan put it back in. It came out a third time. Reagan put it back in.

Liberal columnists such as Mary McGrory of the *Washington Star* denounced Reagan for making the remark. Even Rowly Evans and Bob Novak pronounced the comment "inexplicable."[31] A disloyal member of Reagan's campaign told Evans and Novak that he was "appalled" by the "noble cause" statement. Another aide, clearly more loyal, told the columnists that Reagan had a need "to tell it like he feels."[32] A split was developing in the campaign between men like Richard Allen and Ed Meese, who had been with Reagan for years and were more conservative, and more moderate latecomers like David Gergen. The hardliners had won out over the toughness of Reagan's speeches, even as the moderates attempted to reduce on-the-fly press conferences and to take Reagan out of the loop on his own speeches.

In the "noble cause" speech Reagan had also said that the Carter administration was turning a blind eye to Soviet hegemony. The White House response to developments in Poland illustrated his point. Workers across that Eastern Bloc nation, led by an unassuming, pipe-smoking electrician named Lech Walesa, had gone on strike for the right to create their own labor unions and to protest the abysmal conditions in their country, where simple consumer goods that Westerners took for granted—light bulbs, toiletries, stationery—were either luxury items or unattainable. Poland's Communist government called out the riot squad, sending thousands of troops and policemen into the street to quell the protesters. Despite the Communists' heavy-handed response, the Carter administration refused to support the striking workers. Secretary of State Ed Muskie called for "restraint."[33] Such was the Carter administration's fear of antagonizing the Kremlin.

THE MEDIA DETONATED ANOTHER bomb over Reagan's comments about "upgrading" relations with Taiwan without reducing recognition of China. The Communist regime that controlled the Chinese mainland was outraged by Reagan's desire to return to the "two-China" policy that existed before Carter canceled relations with the island country. Reagan had been to Taiwan in 1978, accompanied by Peter Hannaford and Dick Allen along with their wives. Like all anticommunists, he had deep feelings of support for the beleaguered Taiwan Chinese, often referring to their country by its official name, the Republic of China.

The Reagan campaign had sent Bush—a former envoy to China—off to Asia. The goal was to showcase Bush's foreign-policy expertise, but even before he left the matter of China and Taiwan had become a subject of dispute. At the send-off event for Bush, the media pressed the campaign over whether Reagan would reject Carter's policy and reinstitute recognition of Taiwan. The campaign unsuccessfully tried to assure the media that the policy would not be reversed.[34]

Now the Chinese used the opportunity of their old friend Bush's visit to attack Reagan in the state-controlled media. Bush had a two-hour meeting in private with Communist Chinese leader Deng Xiaoping and emerged "looking chastened," according to *Newsweek*. He was also reported to be in a state of "testiness."[35]

When Bush was asked about Reagan's comments concerning improving U.S.–Taiwan diplomacy, "He put his hand to his forehead and groaned," the *Washington Post* reported.[36] Reporters kept pressing Bush on the matter, but the running mate refused to elaborate on his outward display.

REAGAN PRESSED ON TO Dallas, where he gave a barnburner of a speech to thousands of religious leaders, who four years earlier had overwhelmingly supported the born-again Carter. Reagan made a profound statement that later became emblematic of his political skills: "I know you can't endorse me, but I endorse you."[37] The event was organized by the televangelist Reverend Jerry Falwell and his Moral Majority. Anderson and Carter also had been invited to speak but had turned Falwell down. Billed as the Roundtable National Affairs Briefing, the conference was officially nonpartisan, yet these pastors and laymen were gearing up to mobilize their congregations for the fall election.

The audience and Reagan had far more in common than not, especially when Reagan said the theory of evolution was just that, a theory, and that the "Biblical story of creation should be taught as well."[38] Reagan then knocked it out of the park, concluding, "The First Amendment was written not to protect the people and their laws from religious values but to protect those values from government tyranny."[39]

But the event was not stress-free for Reagan. Because of poor advance work by his campaign, he was stuck on the stage with a fire-and-brimstone pastor who said America should be governed by the Bible and not the Constitution.[40] The entire national media took note of Reagan's discomfort.

The year before, Falwell had said that a liberal could not be a good Christian. When reporters caught up with Reagan, he went out of his way to disagree with Falwell, saying that it was possible "for a true Christian to support the Equal Rights Amendment" and "homosexual rights."[41]

Reagan represented a paradox: although culturally conservative by nature, he also had been steeped in Hollywood's more tolerant, cosmopolitan way of life. Throughout his life and especially as an actor the gregarious Reagan socialized with all types. He never disavowed his days in Hollywood Babylon and always reminisced fondly of his old movie pals.

When it came to his personal dealings with individuals, Reagan was nothing like the man his enemies tried to portray. He was nonjudgmental with a generosity of spirit. Consequently, Reagan's relationship with the Religious Right would always remain a complicated one, a *pas de deux*. He periodically—and convincingly—threw them rhetorical red meat and they, in turn, threw him their votes. Whether Reagan—or anyone—could tangibly deliver what they actually wanted was, given the realities of modern American society, another matter.

THE CARTER BATTLE PLAN was taking shape. They would paint Reagan as a warmonger, a dangerous, trigger-happy nuclear cowboy unfit to hold high office. Rafshoon was preparing a hit commercial on Reagan named "Places he would attack." Carter wasn't going to bother convincing voters that he was up to the task but rather would convince them that Reagan was not. Pat Caddell bluntly summarized his mission: to separate the voters who thought "Reagan is going to be worse" from those who felt "Reagan can't be any worse."[42] A Carter campaign memo clearly spelled out this agenda: "Our goal must be to establish the shadow of doubt about Reagan's ability to handle the Presidency. His age, lack of foreign-policy experience, and simplistic economic philosophy are exploitable."[43]

As most vice presidents do, Walter Mondale had become bored with his job. He was known to sometimes take a nap in his office or knock off early and go home. So getting back on the stump and making the partisan case against Reagan suited him just fine. Talking tough with reporters, Mondale said, "The other thing is that I believe when Reagan starts to fall, he'll fall like a crowbar." He was asked, "Just how does a crowbar fall?" Mondale deadpanned, "Awfully fast."[44]

The Reagan campaign continued to worry—deeply—that the White House was planning to spring an October surprise. Reagan strategists lay awake at night visualizing Carter going on national television to announce that the hostages had been released from Iran and were flying to Andrews Air Force Base, where Carter would greet them. Then there would be a ceremony on the South Lawn of the White House and a procession up to Capitol Hill. Carter would get such a boost from the grateful American voters that he would bound right over Reagan and into a second term.

AMBASSADOR BUSH RETURNED TO bad reviews from his trip to Asia. Indeed, many media outlets pronounced the trip a failure.[45] Bush was in a difficult position, in part because of Reagan's comments about "upgrading" an American presence on Taiwan as part of a "two China" policy.[46] Even former president Ford criticized Reagan's position on China, saying that Carter had done the right thing in cancel-ing relations with Taiwan. But Ford did say he thought the controversy would not affect the outcome of the election.[47] Lyn Nofziger agreed, telling reporters, "This campaign is not going to be won or lost on China."[48]

Rather than backing away from the controversy, Reagan showed that he would not knuckle under to the Chinese. In Los Angeles, with Bush standing at his side, he read a two-thousand-word statement in which he said, "As president I will not accept the interference of any foreign power in the process of protecting American interests." Reagan conceded that he might have "misstated" what he really meant about recognizing both countries, and he now made clear, once and for all, that if elected he would maintain full relations with the People's Republic of China but would also embark on reinstituting official recognition of Taiwan.[49]

The media tried repeatedly to get both men off stride. Reagan's jaw clenched and he raised his voice several times. Bush strongly rejected the reports that his trip had been unsuccessful and said clearly that the Chinese understood Reagan's position.[50] The two men then swung into an attack on Carter, accusing him of creating the mess in the first place with the abrogation of the mutual-defense treaty with Taiwan that had been supported and endorsed by every president since Truman.

The *New York Times* turned to John Sears, Reagan's former manager, for his analysis of the imbroglio. Vengefully, he remarked, "You can find yourself explaining every day why you're not an idiot. He's got some work left to do."[51]

The Reagan-Bush press conference was important, though, as it got Reagan off the defensive. He realized the situation was a test of his command abilities and he had but three choices: to continue to stew in his own juices, to back off and essentially endorse the Carter position, or to enunciate his policies, firmly. Reagan chose the third option, and after his show of strength and decisiveness, the matter began to fade. Even the oft-critical columnists Germond and Witcover said, "Reagan's defense of his friends in Taiwan could be considered an act of political principle, conviction above pragmatism."[52]

At another press confab, three thousand miles away in Washington, Governor Pat Lucey announced at the National Press Club that he would go on the ticket with Anderson. Lucey took a jab or two at Reagan, as would be expected, but he saved his strongest punches for Carter. He referred to "the human wreckage Jimmy Carter's presidency has left in its wake. Jimmy Carter has not seen this. He has been hiding in the Rose Garden trying to escape debates." Lucey said he would campaign among labor unions, attack Carter, and make the case for Anderson.[53]

It was now clear that Anderson and Lucey would run as unreconstructed liberals, the left of Carter. Paul Corbin's plan was coming together. With Carter battling Anderson for liberal votes, Reagan, with conservatives in his hip pocket, could move toward the middle.

In yet a third press conference, Ted Kennedy emerged from a one-hour meeting at the White House with Carter. The Carter White House had tried since the end of the convention to get a meeting with Kennedy to put on a show of unity. Teddy finally agreed, having nothing to gain at this point by being seen as a poor loser. He did his best to talk up Carter, but the skeptical White House press corps wasn't buying it.[54]

WITH THE REAGAN CAMPAIGN still happy to include Anderson in three-way debates, Carter tried to get ahead of the story by accepting an invitation from the National Press Club—which his White House had generated—to debate Reagan one-on-one. Carter also accepted the offer of *Ladies' Home Journal* to debate Reagan, again without Anderson.[55] Jim Baker, representing Reagan in preliminary negotiations on debates, defended Anderson's right to debate because he was a viable candidate. The Carter debate proposal would not work because it excluded the ladies of the League of Women Voters, "Gentleman Jim" added with a straight face.[56]

Reagan headed for Ohio, where he spoke to the Teamsters. Labor unions traditionally did not endorse Republicans, but the Teamsters had supported Nixon over George McGovern in 1972 as part of the deal to release Jimmy Hoffa early from prison, so there was an outside chance they would support Reagan as well.[57]

Reagan attended a private lunch with Teamster officials including William Presser, who had been convicted of bilking employees; his son Jackie Presser, who was under constant investigation over his handling of the pension fund; and Roy Williams, who only the day before had "taken the Fifth" before the Senate Investigations Committee.[58] Press reports did not indicate whether the union officials' parole officers accompanied them. Reagan aides could only shrug their shoulders about the Teamsters' choices of luncheon guests and the poor advance work.

Reagan's speech before the Teamsters rank and file was warmly received, however. He charged that Carter had created a "depression" and that American families were "suffering more than at any time since the Great Depression of the thirties."[59] Reagan was knocked for using the term "depression," but the head of his Economic Advisory Group, Alan Greenspan, came to his defense, saying, "The facts are that the economy is in terrible shape and what you choose to call it is a terribly secondary question."[60]

Carter responded to Reagan's rhetoric about the awful economy by proposing his own tax cuts for businesses and individuals, as well as a new bureaucracy to deal with the recession. Carter made clear that while the government must defend the American people when it came to the economy, Washington was not the generator of jobs—the marketplace was. Washington's job was to be the referee and help business and labor, he said. It wasn't quite Adam Smith, especially since he also called for $4 billion in stimulus spending, but it was to the right of liberals such as Kennedy.[61] The president was sometimes more moderate on economic issues than many others in his own party. In fact, his tax-cut pitch was in direct violation of the Democratic platform.[62]

Still, Reagan blasted Carter's economic proposal. Because Carter's tax-cut plan was linked to an increase in Social Security taxes, the Reagan campaign slammed it as "the pickpocket theory." The Reaganites produced a report showing that for a worker making $15,000 a year, Carter's tax cut was almost entirely wiped out by the Social Security tax increase. Over the course of a year the worker would end up netting *two dollars*. Reagan warned that the president's proposal would have "only delayed the day of reckoning in Social Security."[63]

The Carter proposal was small-bore—a little here, a little there, a distillation of Carter's minimalist approach to problems. The plan was not easily understood, as Reagan's was. It was not bold, and it did not go over well.

Carter then proposed a 9 percent pay hike for all federal employees, higher than what Congress was considering.[64] Reagan watched Carter's speech on television and dismissed the proposal out of hand, commenting, "[He] seems to be saying more government will solve the problems government itself has caused."[65]

ANDERSON'S CAMPAIGN STRUGGLED TO get on track. He was in debt, despite having created an impressive mailing list, and he had not received any federal funds, as had Reagan and Carter.[66] The White House was pressuring the Federal Election Commission not to release any funds to Anderson. This became just another reason for Anderson to despise Carter.

Garry Trudeau's popular political cartoon strip, "Doonesbury," had taken lighthearted jabs at the kids running the Anderson campaign, and it obviously bothered the candidate. Anderson defensively said his operation was not a "Doonesbury campaign." To show how serious he was, he handed his campaign over to New York political consultant David Garth—a feared and reviled figure. Garth was so despised that when Anderson announced that he was taking over, three top aides promptly resigned and several volunteers broke into tears.[67]

Reagan also worried about the quality of his campaign operation. "To get his faltering presidential campaign back on track," as Jack Germond reported, Reagan called an emergency all-hands-on-deck meeting at his rental home, Wexford, in the Virginia countryside.[68] Attending the meeting were Bill Casey, Ed Meese, Lyn Nofziger, Dick Wirthlin, Bill Timmons, Mike Deaver, Drew Lewis, Jim Baker, and Dean Burch. (Stu Spencer hadn't been invited to the meeting and Nancy Reagan was furious when she found out.)[69] Reagan wanted to know why he was not being properly briefed on the trail, why he couldn't shake bad media coverage, and why the campaign plane was coordinating so poorly with the national office in Virginia.[70] Also, leaks had become a big problem again, for the first time since John Sears had been fired. Indeed, all the major media reported on this supposedly top-secret, hush-hush meeting.[71]

The gathering ended inconclusively, with no major changes instituted, though shortly thereafter, Meese and Spencer asked Ken Khachigian, a Nixon vet, to come aboard the plane to help with speechwriting. Khachigian, short, swarthy, and affable, agreed, met the plane in Los Angeles, and then didn't get off for five weeks, writing nearly all of Reagan's day-to-day speeches. Doug Bandow worked on research, assisting the speechwriters as they huddled in a little corner of the plane. Khachigian had to come up with new content every day in order to keep the press satisfied.[72]

Reagan and his aides certainly weren't satisfied with what had happened to their lead. A new poll released by the Roper organization confirmed the earlier numbers: Reagan was at 38 percent, Carter at 37, and Anderson at 17.[73] Morale was low at the Reagan campaign, and the Republican's top advisers were "clearly apprehensive about the general election outlook," as the *Washington Star* reported. One Reaganite was even more blunt, saying, "The way things are going now, we are going to lose."[74]

Once again, Reagan had been coasting. The campaign had made too many mistakes since Detroit and had squandered his lead. Reagan had wasted August, to the delight of the Carter campaign.

IN PREPARATION FOR THE Labor Day campaign kickoff, President Carter retreated to Camp David. He wanted to rest and, more importantly, to work on his speeches. Carter's chief speechwriters—Rick Hertzberg and Chris Matthews—were generally regarded as good writers. The problem was that Carter could not stop tinkering and then inviting everybody else to tinker with his speeches, which they were more than happy to do. Tribute for White House staffers is often measured in small, even petty ways. Nothing gets attention in a Washington saloon after work more quickly than for a staffer to say, "Well, as I told the president today," or "That draft speech was a piece of shit until I cleaned it up." Such were the rewards for the unctuous factotums who sniffed power in Washington.

The Carterites may have been mediocre at governing, but at politics they excelled. Once Labor Day rolled around, they would be able to focus on what they did best. As one of Carter's men said of the upcoming campaign kickoff, "Starting Monday, the blow torch is on."[75]

30

SLOUCHING TOWARDS NOVEMBER

*"Doubts about him are growing, his lead is shrinking,
and more and more people are wondering whether he's up for the job.
If this impression hardens, he'll be out of the race."*

Only sixty-five days remained until the election. From here on, the staffs of both campaigns were required to focus all their attention on the task at hand. Staffers were expected to work 24/7, and most ailments to be handled by taking two aspirin. Going to the emergency room or staying home sick were options of last resort. You had better know, as pro athletes did, the difference between pain and injury. What couldn't be fixed with something out of the campaign's medicine cabinet—or coffee, alcohol, or tobacco—would have to wait until after the election.

Arriving at the campaign office late, say after 7 A.M., or leaving early, say before 10 P.M., was not only frowned upon, it could get you fired. There were people who would give their eyeteeth to work on a presidential campaign for little money. Both campaigns had filing cabinets bulging with résumés of eager, passionate, young supplicants willing to be treated like dirt as long as they got a start in politics.

If you were on the road, tardiness meant the plane or motorcade would simply leave you behind. You'd have to catch up on your own, then sheepishly explain how you had screwed up. Toward the end of the campaign, clean underwear became an option for young men. Some simply and repeatedly turned theirs inside out. It was all splendidly ludicrous.

In Michigan, the Republican nominee in the seventeenth congressional district, Alfred L. Patterson, was released from a psychiatric hospital in order to campaign in the fall election.[1] His condition only proved what everybody in politics already knew: you had to be crazy to be in this business.

As JIMMY CARTER KICKED off his fall campaign, Speaker of the House Tip O'Neill was telling fellow Democrats that a "smell of victory" was in the air.[2] After all, Carter was on the verge of surging into the lead over Ronald Reagan, and his single-mindedness, especially in electoral politics, was legendary. But some of Carter's aides felt that the president performed better as an underdog and worried that the focus might now shift from Reagan's mistakes to Carter's ineffectiveness. In the parlance of the era, they did not want to "peak too soon."

Carter began his fall drive at a Labor Day picnic in Tuscumbia, Alabama. The *Los Angeles Times* reported that Tuscumbia was the "national headquarters of the Knights of the Ku Klux Klan."[3] Twenty thousand people attended the event despite the ninety-plus-degree heat. Perspiring heavily, the president said, "It's good to be home!" and got a generous round of applause from the sweltering crowd. He joked, "I just want to say how great it is to be with folks who don't talk with an accent."

On the dais with Carter was former Alabama governor George Wallace, permanently confined to a wheelchair after being shot while competing for the Democratic nomination in 1972. Carter wheeled Wallace forward and hugged him; then the president's daughter, Amy, kissed the old segregationist on the cheek.[4] Wallace was the only Democratic politician so singled out by President Carter, though many others were present.

Carter also singled out the Ku Klux Klan. Sixty Klansmen had marched to the park where Carter was speaking. Clad in heavy white robes and hoods (anyone who added unnecessary clothing in the heat and humidity of the day had to be nuts), the Klansmen came in time to hear the president attack them. "As a southerner," Carter declared, "it makes me feel angry when I see them use the Confederate battle flag."[5]

Carter told the crowd, "We southerners believe in the nobility of courage on the battlefield. And because we understand the costs of war, we also believe in the nobility of peace."[6]

In the entire speech Carter never mentioned Ronald Reagan's name. This was not an augury of things to come: soon he would begin bashing his opponent with glee.

The president jetted back to Washington on a smaller-than-normal Air Force One in order to save the campaign some cash, as the trip to Alabama was overtly political. Back at the White House, he entertained a thousand labor leaders and their families on the South Lawn, wooing them with barbecue and whiskey.[7] Carter was eager to patch up his relationship with Big Labor, especially since Reagan was making a play for the blue-collar vote.

The real action of Labor Day involved a firestorm of words between Reagan and Carter. Appearing at the Michigan State Fair in Detroit, Reagan departed from his prepared remarks to tell the crowd that Carter was "opening his campaign down in the city that gave birth to and is the parent body of the Ku Klux Klan."[8] Reagan was mistaken: though the city had been made the national headquarters of one of the vile organization's largest factions, the Knights of the Ku Klux Klan, the birthplace of the Klan was actually fifty miles away in Pulaski, Tennessee.[9]

Carter, when told of Reagan's erroneous comments, said, "Anybody who resorts to slurs and innuendo against a whole region of the country based on a false statement and a false premise isn't doing the South or our nation a good service." He said the Gipper's comments were "uncalled for" and added that "as an American and a southerner, I resent it."[10]

Reagan knew immediately that he had made a giant mistake. As soon as he was alone with his staff after his Detroit speech, he said, "I blew it."[11] A worried Ed Meese confirmed Reagan's instincts when he called the traveling party to warn about the criticism the comments had already sparked. The candidate issued an apology of sorts, one that clumsily tried to make the controversy about Carter: "I am greatly disturbed about efforts to make the Ku Klux Klan an issue in this campaign. I also regret that certain remarks I made . . . are being misinterpreted to mean something that was never intended."[12] But it was too late.

On the plane after the Michigan event, Lyn Nofziger had gotten into a rancorous shouting match with reporters over the accuracy of Reagan's comments. Several days later, campaign manager Bill Casey yanked Nofziger's stripes, turning communications over to Bob Gray, a Washington P.R. executive.[13] Some friends worried that Nofziger was drinking too much of his favorite Bombay gin, but within a short time, he pulled himself together.

Over the previous weeks, Carterites had frequently made allegations of racism against Reagan. Andrew Young, Carter's controversial former ambassador to the United Nations, was one of those who went after Reagan for appearing at the Neshoba County Fair. Young penned a scathing op-ed that as much as said Reagan was a racist for using so-called code words such as "states' rights." He wrote, "One must ask: Is Reagan saying that he intends to do everything he can to turn the clock back to the Mississippi justice of 1964?"[14] Patricia Harris, Carter's secretary of Health and Human Services, had repeatedly assaulted Reagan because the Klan had endorsed him—an endorsement Reagan had repudiated. Secretary Harris said, "When I hear Reagan's name, I see the spectre of white sheets."[15]

Reagan had put up with smears much of his adult life, but the racist charge stung more than anything else. He found the Ku Klux Klan repugnant, beyond contempt, and became furious when anyone tried to suggest that he was a racist. But now the attacks from some black leaders intensified. Congressman Parren Mitchell of Maryland said that Reagan was "a clear and present danger to black America." Aaron Henry of the Democratic National Committee charged, "When you say Reagan to the black community, you might as well say Hitler in terms of the turn-off you get."[16]

Seven Democratic southern governors sent Reagan a telegram demanding an apology. Pat Caddell chortled to Hamilton Jordan, "If Reagan keeps putting his foot in his mouth for another week or so, we can close down campaign headquarters."[17]

Carter didn't let up for a moment. Here was the blowtorch his aides had promised. Carter practically ran to every microphone to blast Reagan over the Klan comment. Evans and Novak, who had observed Carter for years and knew him for the political street fighter he was, wrote in their column that "the president engages in hyperbole when attacking his opponent that has been his political trademark."[18] Reagan was furious with Carter, as the Republican made clear when he phoned both the mayor of Tuscumbia and the governor of Alabama to express his regrets over the incident. Reagan later called on the president to disavow the ruthless comments made by Secretary Harris and Andrew Young, but Carter merely took it under advisement.[19]

Desperate political need was driving Carter to go after Reagan so intently. The South had comprised 40 percent of Carter's electoral votes four years earlier, and in order to defeat Reagan he needed to hold on to what was his.[20] Secretly, Hamilton Jordan had already put Texas, Florida, Louisiana, Tennessee, Mississippi, and Alabama, all states that Carter carried in 1976, in the "marginal/ minus" column.[21] Carter saw Reagan's Klan comment and his campaign's subsequent mishandling of the situation as an opportunity to revile the Republican as a carpetbagger below the Mason-Dixon Line. Because Reagan had spoken out about states' rights and because many liberals harbored doubts about conservatives' position on race, Carter was able to get traction with his attacks.

The president turned up the pressure on Reagan the day after Labor Day in a town hall meeting at Truman High School in Independence, Missouri.[22] Carter's "give 'em hell" rhetoric was hotter than anything Truman had ever said and even hotter than the day before.[23] After refraining from mentioning Reagan in his Alabama speech, the president now made frequent stinging references to his GOP opponent.

Carter charged Reagan with wanting to start a "massive nuclear arms race." He implied that Reagan's position on increasing national defense was "one of the most serious threats to the safety and the security and the peace of our nation and of the world that is being dramatized in this 1980 election."[24] Carter elaborated: "I believe in peace. I believe in arms control. I believe in controlling nuclear weapons. I believe in the rights of working people of this country. I believe in looking forward and not backward. I don't believe the nation ought to be divided one region from another. In all these respects, Governor Reagan is different from me."[25]

THE KLAN CONTROVERSY WAS doubly problematic for Reagan because it obscured what should have been a powerful kickoff to his fall campaign.

The setting that the campaign had chosen for the Labor Day launch provided a striking visual. With the Statue of Liberty in the background and the wind tousling his hair, Reagan looked virile and in command. The day was hot and humid, and Reagan shucked his tie and jacket, undid the top two buttons of his shirt, and rolled up his sleeves, but not before giving his cufflinks to an unknown man in the crowd who had complimented them.[26] Mrs. Reagan was presented with flowers "by children in ethnic dress," according to Colin Clark's advance schedule.[27]

This event was about more than good stage management. Reagan's speech was a biting commentary on the failures of the Carter presidency. While Carter did not mention Reagan in Tuscumbia, the Gipper had no compunction against tearing into Carter. On this Labor Day he scored the president for having "betrayed" the working men and women of America. Gesturing to the statue behind him, he said, "The Lady standing there in the harbor has never betrayed us once." Then, referring to the criticism he had provoked by using the term "depression," Reagan proclaimed: "Let it show on the record that when the American people cried out for economic help, Jimmy Carter took refuge behind a dictionary. Well, if it's a definition he wants, I'll give him one. A recession is when your neighbor loses his job. A depression is when you lose yours. Recovery is when Jimmy Carter loses his!"[28] The crowd went wild.

At the conclusion, Reagan led the crowd—which featured many ethnics who waved the flags of multiple nations—in singing "God Bless America." Then he embraced Stanislaw Walesa, the father of Polish labor leader Lech Walesa, to the cheers of the audience.[29]

One of the few problems Reagan encountered was heckling from a handful of protesters. But Lou Cannon, in his coverage for the *Washington Post*, had a different spin on the event. Cannon had been covering Reagan for the better part of fifteen years, and though there was a mutual fondness, the reporter was now bristling over the increasingly limited press access the campaign had imposed.

In his piece, he pettily pointed out that while Reagan referred to the "great lady looking on," in fact the crowd was viewing the back side of the statue.[30] Cannon also wondered—oddly—how it was that Reagan could make an open appeal for ethnic voters when his two lead advancemen were Irish Americans.[31] That would be Rick Ahearn and Jim Hooley, both of whom had the map of Ireland all over their faces. Burly, effective, tough, well respected, these two Irishmen loved the Irishman they were working for and handled all of his important trips over the years (including his last, in June 2004).

Reagan went to Detroit after the Liberty State Park event. The ill-considered remark about Carter and the Klan was the obvious lowlight of the Detroit visit but not the only difficulty he encountered in the Motor City. Reagan seemed to suggest that he would favor some sort of restrictions on the importation of Japanese cars until Detroit got back on its feet, though he had previously said that the automakers' problems were the result of excessive government regulations. When he toured the Chrysler plant the workers gave him a lukewarm reception, some booing and some cheering. While there he indicated that he had come around on the loan guarantee for Chrysler, of which he had previously been dubious.[32]

Blue-collar voters were not the only traditionally Democratic bloc that Reagan was targeting. He was also attempting to take advantage of Carter's problems with American Jewish voters. Reagan traveled to New York to address B'nai Brith. Speaking to an audience of 1,500 under the theme "A Covenant with Tomorrow," Reagan leveled Carter over the administration's refusal to veto a resolution which criticized Israel for enunciating that Jerusalem was the capital of the Jewish state.[33] He also assailed Carter for refusing to call the Palestine Liberation Organization a terrorist organization. "They are terrorists and they should be identified as such," Reagan said bluntly.[34] Al Spiegel, head of the coalition of Jewish Americans supporting his candidacy, introduced Reagan. He told the audience that "long before he was a candidate for public office," Reagan had tendered his resignation from the Lakeside Country Club in Los Angeles because of its policy against Jewish members.[35]

Carter also spoke before the organization, but comments like "cracker" and "I doubt that Carter knew any Jews in Plains, Georgia," were overheard. One attendee resignedly said, "I guess I'll vote for Reagan. I'm not a flaming liberal anymore."[36]

CARTER'S CAMPAIGN FILED A complaint with the Federal Communications Commission to prohibit independent conservative groups from running television ads in an attempt to aid Reagan. The groups and their commercials were legal, but the complaint and the attendant publicity, the Carterites knew, would have the effect of intimidating local station owners. The "equal-time" argument was used, but that law did not apply to independent groups, only to federal candidates.[37] The Carter team had already filed a complaint with the Federal Election Commission charging collusion between the official Reagan-Bush campaign and the independent groups.[38]

The FEC didn't weigh in on that complaint, but it did, by a vote of 5–1, decide to give John Anderson's campaign federal funds, just as it had already released funds for Carter and Reagan. This was a boon for Anderson, who needed an infusion of money. The bad news was that he would not actually receive the federal funding until *after* the election, based on a complicated formula involving percentages and vote totals.[39] Nevertheless, simply knowing that some money was guaranteed by the FEC meant that he now could get bank loans.

INCUMBENCY HAS ITS PRIVILEGES. In Philadelphia, Carter announced that the USS *Saratoga* would be dry-docked for refitting, this saving 9,000 shipyard jobs and adding as many as 2,600 more. He picked up the endorsement of the feared American Federation of State, County, and Municipal Employees union, one million strong.[40]

Reagan also pushed onto Philadelphia. There he gave a speech to a senior-citizens group, organizing under the awkwardly alliterative "Super Senior Sunday."[41] Carter accused Reagan—falsely—of wanting to make the federal retirement system "voluntary," a code word to the oldsters that Reagan wanted to throw them out into the snow. Reagan, he said, "would destroy the system."[42] In fact, Reagan had mused publicly years before about a system whereby individuals, if they demonstrated they had already made plans to fund their own retirement, might be "excused" from participating in the poorly managed program. Though Reagan told the seniors organization that he pledged to "defend the integrity of the Social Security system," he received only a halfhearted response.[43]

A better campaign event was held outside the Philadelphia Museum of Art. Reagan spoke from the steps that Sylvester Stallone had made famous by running up them in the Oscar-winning film *Rocky*. After his remarks, Reagan, dressed in a brown plaid suit, danced a few steps with Nancy to "In the Mood" performed by the Glenn Miller Orchestra, making for a nice photo-op.[44]

Carter didn't let up on Reagan. He told an audience in Philadelphia that "the poor and minorities" would be hurt under a Reagan presidency. He also claimed that advances in civil rights "came to a screeching halt" when Richard Nixon was elected, implying the same fate if Reagan won. For good measure, he hit Reagan on Social Security, saying once again that he might "destroy the system."[45]

Carter attacked Reagan so vehemently that even some of his out-of the-loop aides worried that it was too much. These advisers believed that while the American people may have thought the Georgian was not up to the job of the presidency, they at least thought he was a decent and honorable man. Now the president's men worried that Carter was squandering this reservoir of good will. But when this concern was pointed out to the president, he responded "with an ambivalent shrug," *Newsweek* reported.[46]

In fact, Carter was following to the letter the campaign script written by his maven, Pat Caddell.[47]

REAGAN RECEIVED HIS FIRST good coverage in weeks when he finally got off the defensive. During a campaign stop in Jacksonville, Florida, he went after the Carter administration, accusing it of deliberately leaking information about the new "Stealth" plane in development. The GOP nominee accused Secretary of Defense Harold Brown of a breach of security, saying that it was "unacceptable and intolerable for [Brown] to play politics with America's national security."[48] Reagan pinned Carter with giving the Soviets the jump on developing anti-stealth technology because of the leak of the classified information.

Pentagon civilian officials began to bicker publicly with the military brass over the Stealth Bomber leak. At the White House, Jody Powell called Reagan's accusation "false" and "unforgivable," saying it "goes far beyond the acceptable bounds of political partisanship." Powell also claimed that no damage had been done to U.S. national security since the Soviets had known about the Stealth technology for years.[49] Yet a handful of former military brass, including retired admiral Thomas H. Moorer, former chairman of the Joint Chiefs of Staff, and Admiral Elmo R. Zumwalt, former chief of naval operations, blew Carter out of the water over the leak.[50]

Watching the president flail around over the Stealth issue, Reagan joshed to an audience about Carter's famous "I'll never lie to you" statement of 1976. "After hearing that line about twenty times," Reagan said, "I was reminded of Ralph Waldo Emerson's line: the louder he talked of his honor, the faster we counted our spoons."[51]

Reagan was finally making some headway. But then, on the morning of September 5, a rumor swept Wall Street that he had suffered a heart attack. When traders began minor sell-offs, nervous investors called offices across the country to find out why the market was declining. As they were told of the rumor, the selling off of stocks became much more intense. Not until almost the time of the closing bell was an alert sent out by the Dow Jones News Service that Reagan was hale and hearty. By then, the market had dropped 22 points.[52]

Some thought the rumor had been planted deliberately as a way for investors to make money by going short. Reagan denounced the scheme as "sleazy." Later, he kidded reporters, "Well, if any of you want to make some money in the market, just let me know."[53]

Still more bad press came Reagan's way when Angela Fox Dunn, the daughter of his drama coach at Warner Brothers, alleged that astrologers guided the Reagans' lives. Reagan was forced to write a letter defending himself to a group of Nobel laureates who had complained about the astrology charge via the Federation of American Scientists. "Let me assure you that while Nancy and I enjoy glancing at the daily astrology charts in our morning paper (when we are home, which isn't too often these days), we do not plan our daily activities or our lives around them," the Aquarius whimsically wrote. He was happy to report, though, that astrologer Jeane Dixon supported his candidacy.[54]

CARTER WAS PUSHING HARD for early-and-often debates with Reagan, believing that his opponent would make more mistakes and that the contrast with the president would convince voters Reagan was just not presidential timber. "The more debates there are, the greater the chance Reagan will screw up," chortled one confident Carter staffer.[55]

There remained the sticking point of whether John Anderson would be included. The League of Women Voters was holding to its 15 percent threshold for Anderson, and Reagan had already agreed to abide by whatever the league wanted.[56] Carter, of course, didn't want Anderson making his presidency the issue or taking attention away from any verbal miscues by Reagan. He also was miffed at the ladies of the league because they hadn't chosen a site in the Deep South for one of the four debates being considered.[57]

Reagan and Carter disagreed over debate format as well. Reagan wanted a freewheeling affair, with the opportunity to show off his style and passion. Carter wanted the nondebate debate format, with reporters and a moderator, who would focus on more technical and quantitative aspects of the office, which Carter's men believed would favor their man, the engineer. One Carter man would live to rue what he told *Newsweek* about Reagan in such a debate setting: "He gives the best 30-second answers in America. The question is what's beyond the 30 seconds if he gets extended."[58]

IN NEW ORLEANS, REAGAN spoke to a group of supporters aboard a riverboat. He told the crowd, "I know it's tough when you have got a brother who has been a national disgrace for three and one half years. But so far Billy has not complained!"[59] Reagan had been given a gift from the campaign gods when it was revealed that First Brother Billy Carter apparently had a second secret deal in the works with the terrorist nation of Libya, and it seemed the Justice Department was not on the ball in pursuing the issue. Billy claimed the $220,000 the Libyans had given him was a "gift."[60] Over in the Reagan camp, Bill Casey called for the resignation of Attorney General Benjamin Civiletti over contradictory statements involving the president's brother.[61]

Reagan needed such a gift, since his decline in the national polls was now showing in state-by-state polls. Florida, where Reagan once had a massive lead, was neck and neck. Carter was slightly ahead in New York, Illinois, and Minnesota. In California, where Reagan once led Carter 51–20 percent, he'd fallen to 39 percent and Carter had climbed to 29 percent. Connecticut was tight. Carter was slightly ahead in Alabama and only slightly behind in Mississippi, two states Reagan was aiming to pick up.[62]

For Carter, the bad news in the polls was that Anderson was definitely costing him. In many states where Carter was behind, Anderson's votes, when added, would have vaulted Carter into the lead. The "Anderson Difference" was taking on a whole new meaning for the Carterites.

As a result, it was a blow to Carter when Anderson won the support of New York's Liberal Party. The Liberal Party had broken with the Labor Party in New York in the 1940s when the Laborites had refused to ban Communists from joining. At one time, Liberals had been a real power in the state, often providing the margin of victory for statewide candidates. They were now a sleepy party dominated by aging Manhattanites. In New York, the bigger the party, the higher on the ballot the party was listed. The Liberals had been reduced to Row E.[63] Still, it was not a vote of confidence for the sitting Democratic president that he could not win the Liberal Party's nomination.

Running on the Liberal line was a plus for Anderson but was a sad lot for an ailing old lion of the Senate, Jacob Javits, who had been defeated in the Republican primary by Alfonse D'Amato. Javits was one of the last of New York's "Tom Dewey Republicans," his old friend Nelson Rockefeller having died the year before. D'Amato had run a vicious campaign against the old man, with commercials whose tagline was: "And now, at age seventy-six and in failing health, he wants six more years."[64]

Speaking on background—perhaps knowing how vengeful D'Amato could be—someone who knew the young politician said frankly, "He is . . . the toughest, meanest, nastiest guy you'd ever want to meet." Javits, in contrast, was beloved by his staff and took care of them, even in retirement or sickness. He loaned them money and then somehow forgot to collect.

The final sad irony was that in running on the Liberal line, Javits was aiding D'Amato by taking away votes in the general election from Elizabeth Holtzman, the Democratic nominee.

THE LEAGUE OF WOMEN Voters was moving toward its deadline in the hope that all three candidates would debate. Reagan wanted in unconditionally. Anderson wanted in unconditionally. Carter wanted in, conditionally. His position was "no" on Anderson or it would be "no" for Carter.

Jim Baker, Reagan's cool Texan, and Bob Strauss, Carter's calm Texan, were going eyeball to eyeball with each other. Strauss was waiting to see whether Baker would really allow Reagan to go into a debate with Anderson and without the president of the United States. When the deadline came and Anderson was over the necessary 15 percent in the polls, Baker said he certainly would allow that. Strauss blinked first and said no, Carter would not debate under these terms.

Reagan could not resist tweaking Carter, telling reporters, "I can't for the life of me understand why Mr. Carter is so afraid."[65]

The president complained that Anderson should not be included because he was "primarily a creation of the press." Then Carter did what no southern gentleman should ever do: he attacked Anderson's wife, saying, "He doesn't have a party. He and his wife handpicked his vice-presidential nominee."[66] That was it. Any lingering doubts about the animosity Anderson and Pat Lucey had for Carter were gone.

GERALD RAFSHOON WAS GEARING up his productions for the fall, as was his Republican counterpart, the equally talented Peter Dailey. Rafshoon was producing spots depicting Carter in the Oval Office, wearing a white sweater, the weight of the world on his shoulders. The spots made it clear that the burdens of the office were awesome and only a few men could stand up to the pressure. "The responsibility never ends," intoned the voiceover, accompanied by violins. "Even at the end of a long working day there is usually another cable."[67]

Dailey knew what few others knew: the best and indeed only way to sell Reagan was to let Reagan be Reagan. Most of the Dailey spots, whether the five-minute or thirty-second ads, were of Reagan looking into the camera, in a library setting, speaking his mind.

Dailey finished each spot with the new slogan for the campaign: "The Time Is Now for Reagan—Reagan for president." The voiceover was done by Reagan's old buddy Robert Stack, famed for his role as Eliot Ness on the television series *The Untouchables*. Sometimes a choir would sing the tagline. It was hokey but it worked.[68]

While the ad creators were trying to sell their candidates to the American people, campaign surrogates played hardball. Walter Mondale hit the road to hit Reagan. Mondale loved politics, the give and take, the speechifying, and was relishing his role as attack dog. And clearly he had better joke writers than Carter. He joshed about Reagan's prior statements on evolution and the Bible, saying that the Republican had picked up "a hot potato last dropped by William Jennings Bryan fifty-five years ago."[69]

Someone who knew about hardball politics—hell, he practically invented the game—was Richard Nixon. The former president sat down for a series of taped interviews with famed political author Teddy White for the *Today* show. Nixon was unimpressed with Reagan's staff, saying they weren't covering for him enough. "The candidate makes a boo-boo—you go out and take the heat yourself, and that's what the Reagan staff had better learn." He was more impressed with Carter's staff, which he called "ruthless." "They're a tough bunch . . . these Georgia boys. They may play softball down in Plains, but they play hardball in the country."[70]

The former president said that Carter was "very tough," "very shrewd."[71] Nixon had never liked Reagan much, once telling his own ruthless White House staff that his fellow Californian was odd. This from a man who ran the air conditioning at the same time as logs crackled in the fireplace in the White House residence.

Academics also began weighing in on the candidates. James David Barber, a professor and expert on presidential temperament at Duke University, worried that if elected Reagan would be a weak president. "The character-rooted danger of the Reagan type in the presidency is that he will cave into pressure. Mr. Reagan hates a scrap, especially close up."[72]

REAGAN WENT TO CHICAGO to make a major economic speech to quell a growing controversy about his tax plan.[73] For months, a battle had been waged against his tax-cut proposal. Anderson had come up with a good sound bite: when asked how Reagan could cut taxes, maintain social spending, and build up the military, Anderson said, "It's very simple. You do it with mirrors."[74] Reagan's Chicago address, unofficially among the staff, became known as the "mirrors speech."

Addressing the three hundred attendees of the International Business Council, Reagan answered the establishment's questions about his program by explaining that going after the billions in waste, fraud, and abuse would not do the trick alone. Fixing the terrible economy and the crumbling military were, he said, bigger priorities than balancing the budget, though his plan did call for a balanced budget by the fifth year.[75] When asked how long it would take for his plan to take effect, Reagan said, "It took Mr. Carter three and a half years of hard work to get us into this economic mess. It will take time to get us out."[76]

In the speech, Reagan said that revenue from a restarted economy would not by itself pay down the deficit and so some already scheduled tax increases would have to go forward as well. He also abandoned his earlier support for elimination of taxes on interest and inheritance.[77]

But the Chicago address did not end the controversy over his economic plan. It only angered the business community and supply-siders. The National Federation of Independent Businesses and the National Association of Manufacturers blasted Reagan for proposing more tax cuts for individuals than for businesses.[78] Meanwhile, doctrinaire supply-siders found Reagan's speech appalling. These purists screamed that establishmentarian economists from the Nixon and Ford administrations, including Alan Greenspan, had watered down Reagan's original bold proposals. And it was true that the Reagan campaign had shunted aside Jude Wanniski and Art Laffer, architects of the original economic proposal. Even a Reagan favorite, Jack Kemp, was not being sought out for his economic advice. One new Reagan insider opposed to the supply-side philosophy said, "None of us wanted to have to sell that notion in a political campaign, because none of us really believes it."[79]

Reagan seemed to be doing better with working people. When Mondale, a union champion, went to Columbus, Ohio, to tour a Western Electric plant, he was unexpectedly greeted with signs that read, "Happy Retirement, Walter Mondale, Jan. 21, 1981," and "I used to be a Democrat." Reporters talked to the workers and several said they thought Reagan would carry a majority of the seven thousand employees there.[80]

Reagan embarked on a blue-collar tour that took him to Cleveland, Buffalo, and Erie, Pennsylvania. In Cleveland at Public Square, Reagan pummeled Carter over the administration's energy policies, saying they had discouraged domestic production for nearly four years. Carter had to deny the charge, which gave Reagan a new opening. In Erie, the Gipper told the sign-waving, button-sporting crowd, "My analysis of our energy situation evidently touched a nerve in the administration, because Mr. Carter responded immediately and personally."[81] He added that Carter had engaged in "half-truths." Anyone who thought Reagan was not competitive or did not keep score knew nothing about the man.

That morning, Reagan had breakfast in Buffalo with Thomas Gleason, president of the International Longshoremen, making a bid for the union's endorsement. At a planned rally, however, only around fifty longshoremen showed up, including a small group of protesters.[82] More dockyard workers might have shown up for Reagan if there was work to be had, but a boat had not pulled into to be unloaded in almost two years, such was the sorry state of the shipping industry.

CARTER HIT A BUMP in the road when it was disclosed that his nominal campaign manager, Timothy Kraft, was under investigation for possible cocaine use. Given that Hamilton Jordan had faced similar charges previously, this was the last thing Carter needed. Kraft took a leave of absence from the campaign and Jordan shortly reprised his 1976 role, having been cleared of the drug allegations.[83]

Kraft was an old Carter hand, though he was not a Georgian. After the 1976 campaign, a retreat was organized outside of Washington for the staff. Jordan led the meeting and introduced each, most with a wicked comment. When he came to Kraft, he pointed out that the tradition of the campaign had been for the staff to sleep in the homes of supporters to show a feel for the people. "I want to introduce a guy who's slept with more supporters than anyone in the campaign. In fact, instead of sending Tim his salary each month, we send him a dose of penicillin." Kraft reportedly was not happy with Jordan's comments, but did not back down. In front of a crowd that included Jordan's wife, Nancy, he said, "Well thank you, Ham. And I'd like to say you've been an inspiration to us all."[84]

REAGAN WAS STILL GETTING pummeled in the news media about his campaign's poor decisions, his gaffes, and the way that his advisers were sequestering the candidate to prevent further adlibs. Words like "problem," "damage,"[85] "ill-prepared,"[86] and "disarray"[87] peppered the news stories analyzing the problems of the Reagan campaign. Reporters quoted officious GOP operatives, most not affiliated with the campaign, offering their unwelcome advice to Reagan, Bill Casey, Meese, and others. A Republican from California showed up in Washington and when reporter Bob Shogan of the *Los Angeles Times* asked why, he replied, "I'm here to see old-foot-in-the-mouth."[88] The major newspapers rolled out stories recounting past misstatements by Reagan—or past misunderstandings, depending on one's point of view.

The Carter team was thrilled, since the media were doing exactly what the president wanted: making Reagan the issue. Pat Caddell said, "Doubts about [Reagan] are growing, his lead is shrinking, and more and more people are wondering whether he's up to the job. If this impression hardens, he'll be out of the race."[89]

In mid-September the *Washington Post* released a new poll that showed the two combatants tied at 37 percent apiece. Carter scored well ahead of Reagan on getting the hostages out of Iraq, but Reagan bested Carter on the ability to "get things done." In two crucial areas Reagan was losing. By a 48—40 percent margin, voters sided with Carter, wanting military parity with, instead of superiority over the Soviets. They also now sided with Carter on the issue of the conservative's tax cuts, opposing them by a margin of 51—39 percent.[90]

Reagan had not even come close to closing the sale with the American voter.

31

The Torrents of Autumn

*"The past few days have revealed a man capable of far more petty vitupera-
tion than most Americans thought possible even in a dank political season."*

As the presidential race tightened, the war of words between Jimmy Carter
and Ronald Reagan only escalated. Reagan said Carter had replaced the
Declaration of Independence with a "Declaration of Indifference" over
the broken American dream, and blasted the Carter record as a "litany of despair,
of broken promises, and sacred trust abandoned and forgotten."[1] Carter returned
fire, accusing Reagan and the Republicans of behaving in a "distorted and irresponsible fashion."[2] Both candidates knew the stakes: political experts rated the
race a tossup in seventeen states that accounted for a pivotal 236 electoral votes.[3]

With tensions boiling over, debate negotiations between the Carter and Reagan campaigns broke down. No future meetings were contemplated between
Robert Strauss and Jim Baker. In the eyes of the media, Round One of the debate
over the debates had gone to Reagan and his corner man, Baker, as Carter had
come off looking petty for not allowing John Anderson to participate. This was
quite an achievement for Baker and the Reagan campaign, since Strauss was without peer as a media schmoozer.

George Bush attacked Carter for not agreeing to debate his two opponents.
When journalists asked Bush about his own experience debating Reagan in their
Nashua Telegraph confrontation months earlier, the VP nominee was ready. "I
learned the hard way. Jimmy Carter will learn too."[4] The Houstonian's mission
was clear: Take it to Carter, don't screw up, and focus on the local media, not the
national media.

Cynicism was rampant across the land. Many voters had tuned out all three
candidates, complaining about the same old, same old. A lot of them were telling

pollsters they had no plans to vote. It was the most fluid election anyone could remember in a long time.

MANY, BUT NOT ALL, of the kinks had been worked out on Reagan's plane and back at his Virginia headquarters. The speechwriting was being vetted better, the schedule made more sense, the candidate was doing only a couple of big speeches a day, usually on the same theme, and the media for the most part were being held (unhappily) at bay. Reagan had just completed a successful tour of the industrial Midwest, meeting tens of thousands along the way while providing good visuals for the cameras. With the media off his back temporarily, Reagan went back to using the four-by-six cards that he preferred but that his advisers had stopped him from using to try to curtail gaffes.

As part of the effort to smooth out operations, the campaign had taken control of the press shop at the campaign HQ away from Lyn Nofziger. Nofziger did retain the title of press secretary, but now his role was limited to the plane.[5] The hand of Jim Baker, who was quietly asserting himself more and more, was suspected in some quarters. The two men never had much use for each other and would shortly come to loathe each other.

Reagan's plane was officially named LeaderShip '80 by the staff and unofficially the Ponce de Leon by the traveling press. Life on the stretched-out Boeing 727 was for the most part riotous, if also tiring and haphazard. In addition to Mrs. Reagan's trick of bowling an orange down the aisle, takeoff was often marked by enterprising reporters and staffers putting food trays in the aisle and attempting to "surf" their way down the plane.[6] Things were even more rollicking on the second, "chase" plane that the Reagan operation leased as the campaign moved into overdrive. This one was nicknamed, not too inaccurately, *The Zoo Plane*. The campaign referred to the tarmac press conferences as "feeding the animals."[7]

One might think that traveling with the president of the United States would be more prestigious and luxurious, but the Carter team had turned Air Force One into a model of penny-pinching. The law stipulated that when a president was traveling for even partially political purposes, his campaign had to reimburse the federal treasury in full. It was not unusual for the Carter campaign to bill the traveling media at twice or even three times the cost of flying first class on commercial airlines. The campaign even billed senators and representatives for the privilege of flying with the president. Most campaign staffers were banned from the plane, as their seats could be turned into profit centers for the Carter campaign.

Walter Mondale's plane was an even less desirable spot. For fiercely competitive reporters, and especially for the network correspondents, it was all about covering the presidential candidate, not the understudy. Mondale made so little news that the media dubbed his plane Morpheus 2.[8]

While Reagan was marginally ahead of Carter in several regions of the country, he was again well behind the president in most of the South. To try to make inroads there, the campaign sent Reagan and Bush on a trip to Texas. Reagan always liked the Lone Star State, and more importantly, Texas loved Reagan. Reagan's field staffers liked Texas, too. Whenever one staffer would stop by the state headquarters of Democrats for Reagan, a former funeral home, he and a comely young assistant would quietly retire to the basement, where they would avail themselves of a left-behind coffin for an afternoon assignation.[9]

Carter headed to Texas as well, needing to carry the state as he had in 1976. In Houston he spoke before enthusiastic Democrats, hitting Reagan for being "muzzled" by his staff.[10] The president seemed to believe that the only way to get his second term would be to increase the attacks on Reagan. That was certainly what Pat Caddell was advising campaign surrogates: pound Reagan. Any hope Carter had of riding a revived job market into a second term had been dashed by the latest economic reports. The second quarter, in which the economy had perked up a bit, had proven to be an anomaly; the newest projections for the third quarter had the economy in negative growth, as it had been for much of 1980 and all of 1979. Two million Americans had lost their jobs in the previous twelve months. Economists everywhere were gloomy.[11]

The prospects looked little better on the foreign-policy front. Secretary of State Edmund Muskie told the American people it was doubtful that Tehran would release the hostages before the election.[12] Carter said something more hopeful while in Texas, but he quickly scaled back his Pollyannaish view when reporters complained about the contradiction. The first anniversary of the taking of the hostages would fall on November 4—Election Day. Privately, the president fretted that this would hurt his chances unless the hostages were released beforehand.[13]

Muskie wore a yellow pin to signify support for the captives. Yellow ribbons had adorned America's trees, buildings, and cars for the past year. The ribbon campaign was taken from a Tony Orlando song about a released convict. Some Americans didn't like the implication, the color long being associated with cowardice. Americans no longer wanted to be cowards on the world stage.

The GOP was eager to highlight party unity, and in mid-September Reagan and Bush joined Republican members of Congress and 150 aspirants to House and Senate seats for a major rally on the steps of the U.S. Capitol. Reagan spoke, proposing a "solemn covenant with the American people." Reagan and the GOP congressional leadership announced five goals, among them tax cuts, budget cuts, and increased defense spending. All the attendees signed a document pledging their fealty. Congressman Guy Vander Jagt jibed that the Democrats were "running away from their nominee" while "we are proud of our nominee."[14] The event concluded with Reagan and Bush clasping hands over their heads as the harmonically challenged Republicans sang "God Bless America" whether the audience wanted them to or not.[15]

The rally almost did not come off. A freshman congressman from Georgia, Newt Gingrich, had fought with some in the campaign to make the event substantive rather than just a big photo-op. He'd been working with Bill Brock on the ceremony but threatened to have it canceled unless Team Reagan supported at least the semblance of a framework for Republican governance. "Young man, I assumed you wanted my attention," Bill Casey condescended to Gingrich in a phone call. "This is going to be horseshit," Gingrich shot back. He pushed the five-point plan, arguing that it "is just a perfect example of . . . where is Reagan." After a short discussion, the Reagan campaign endorsed the Gingrich model.[16]

Though Gingrich was only a freshman, he spoke frankly about the GOP's problems: "We have a party here that's not very used to winning. It's not even used to fighting very well."[17]

ACCORDING TO A GALLUP poll, Carter was getting the lion's share of the evangelical vote, 52 percent to only 31 percent for Reagan.[18] A Los Angeles Times poll, however, showed it much closer, 40 percent for Reagan and 39 percent for Carter.[19] The Religious Right was assiduously organizing for Reagan. Carter's relationship with the evangelical community had soured badly since his 1976 election eve broadcast with Reverend Pat Robertson.[20] He received no help from his controversial secretary of Health and Human Services, Patricia Harris, who compared the "Christian Right" in America with the "mullahs" running Iran. She said she was scared that America might one day have its own "ayatollah," but that instead of "a beard . . . he will have a television program."[21]

The Reagan campaign hired from the Moral Majority a man named Robert Billings to act as a liaison. Reagan was also making inroads with the Catholic community. There were those, though, who worried about the explosive mixture of God and state. A Reagan staffer, a self-described conservative, told *U.S. News & World Report*, "This marriage of religion and politics is the most dangerous thing, the creepiest thing I've ever seen."[22]

CARTER ACHIEVED THE DESIRED result from his weeks of pounding Reagan. A New York Times–CBS poll showed Carter moving again ahead of Reagan. This survey put the race at 38 percent for Carter, 35 percent for Reagan, and 14 percent for Anderson. According to the poll, Carter was winning the South and East handily, he and Reagan were tied in the Midwest, and in the West, Reagan's lead was down to 5 percentage points. Carter led for the first time in the seven largest electoral states, 39–34 percent. He led among African-Americans, 77 percent to 6 percent, and was almost splitting the white vote, 38 for Reagan and 34 for Carter. The president was even getting a healthy percentage of the conservative vote, 31 percent to Reagan's 46 percent. Conversely, Carter was getting 48 percent of the liberal vote and Reagan only 23 percent. Carter was also winning every age category; only among voters under thirty was Reagan competitive with his Democratic opponent. Since the previous Times poll, in August, Carter had gained in every category, every region.[23]

When word leaked out that the Republicans would not release details of a poll taken by Bush's former numbers man, Bob Teeter, the gossip fed media suspicions that Reagan was faltering. Carter's men were growing in confidence daily, believing that only Anderson stood between them and a big win in November. Their internal polling had shown movement away from Reagan toward "undecided" or to Anderson, so they needed to wheedle these voters to keep moving to Carter.

Carter kept taunting Reagan. In Texas he said, "You probably noticed that the campaign staff of my Republican opponent have put him under wraps."[24] In Georgia he tried out a new campaign theme: charging Reagan with being a racist.

President Carter went to Atlanta to speak at the Ebenezer Baptist Church, home of Dr. Martin Luther King Sr. "You've seen in this campaign," Carter said, "the stirrings of hate and the rebirth of code words like 'states rights' in a speech in Mississippi, in a campaign reference to the Ku Klux Klan relating to the South. This is a message that creates a cloud on the political horizon. Hatred has no place in this country."[25]

Carter's newest barb at Reagan started the race debate anew. It also galled his opponent.

Reagan was slow to anger, and for the most part he had kept his temper in check during the campaign. But when he did get mad, watch out. Lyn Nofziger said there was the real Reagan fury and the bogus Reagan anger. When Reagan tossed his eyeglasses on a table, that was just for effect, such as when someone interrupted him while he was working on a speech. When he broke a pencil or threw something across the room, you knew that was the real anger.[26] Once, in 1973, he threw his keys into Mike Deaver's chest, furious over Spiro Agnew's resignation.[27] Reagan got especially angry when he was called a racist.

The mistake many of Reagan's foes made was in going too far in attacking him. When Reagan got angry, he became more focused and he improved as a campaigner. In 1966 Governor Pat Brown ran a mean-spirited ad that made Reagan furious, and the Gipper went out and mowed over Brown, winning by nearly a million votes. In 1976, as his campaign was faltering in the late stages, Reagan got angry after Ford's campaign ran an appalling commercial implying that Reagan was a warmonger; the ad spurred Reagan to push through to the convention, despite all odds. And during the 1980 primaries, Reagan had gotten angry at George Bush over the attacks on his tax-cut plan and the hints that he was too old.

Now many felt Jimmy Carter had gone overboard. A headline in the *Washington Post* screamed, "President Says Reagan Has Injected Hatred and Racism into Campaign."[28] Every other newspaper in America picked up the president's charge.

Carter had ignored a warning from Pat Brown. In a letter to the president that was released for publication, Brown advised, "First and above all, don't underestimate Mr. Reagan personally. He's not a clown or a buffoon. . . . He is a very astute—even superb politician. Second, you've got to take his views seriously."[29]

Disgusted over Carter's comments, Reagan held his first impromptu press conference in weeks. Taking a break from campaigning in 106-degree heat among the Mexican-American community in Texas, Reagan went right at Carter's remaining strength—his perceived decency. "It's harmful and it's shameful because whether we're on the opposite sides or not, we ought to be trying to pull the country together, not tear it apart," he said, with just the right touch of moral indignation.[30] Reagan then fired at Carter: "I just don't know how much further he'll go to try and divert attention from the fact that he could say all these things to a nationwide audience . . . if he just wanted to debate."[31]

Bush jumped in and sharply attacked Carter for "ugly little insinuations" against Reagan, calling them a "new low."[32] Gerald Ford also came to Reagan's defense with a contemptuous condemnation of Carter: "Mr. Carter does not just owe Governor Reagan and the Republican Party an apology. . . . Mr. Carter owes the American people an apology. His intemperate . . . misleading statements demean the office of the presidency itself."[33]

Ford's well of good will was deeper than Carter's and the former president's comments especially stung.

Jody Powell was sent out to deny that Carter had called Reagan a racist. Notably, many prominent Democrats did not defend the president. Lieutenant Governor Mario Cuomo of New York said of Carter's charges against Reagan, "It's not nice. It's not sporting."[34]

The Georgians knew Carter had a self-inflicted wound that badly needed tending. Gerald Rafshoon fretted privately to Hamilton Jordan, "It's that old Carter hyperbole. He just can't help himself sometimes."[35]

On September 17 Carter held a press conference to try to quell the growing controversy. The president had held only seven press conferences in all of 1980, "hardly a record of openness and accountability," Reagan acidly stated.[36] Now Carter leveraged the live network television coverage to give an opening statement that was a five-minute recitation of his administration's accomplishments. When he turned to his comments about Reagan, he refused to apologize and denied that he had called Reagan a "racist in any degree." He then attacked Reagan yet again for bringing up "code words."[37]

But Carter was nailed by an unexpected source: Lisa Myers of the *Washington Star*, whose writings some Reaganites thought too harsh on their man and too easy on Carter. Myers pointed out to President Carter that "it was your own cabinet secretary, Patricia Harris, who first interjected the KKK into the presidential race."[38] Following Myers's lead, other reporters bore in and asked Carter whether he was being too "mean" in attempting to "savage" Reagan.[39] Carter's White House aides glared at the nervous but determined young "Brenda Upstart." She did not back down and pressed Carter even harder about bringing race into the election. It was an important turning point, sparked by Myers.

Carter spluttered, "I am not blaming Governor Reagan. That's exactly the point. The press seems to be obsessed with this issue."[40] The *Los Angeles Times* reported that Carter was "shaken" by the exchange.[41] The event did not go at all as Carter's aides had planned.

The gentlemen and gentle ladies of the press may have been more left-of-center than Reagan, but they had a refined sense of fair play, and after four years of covering Carter, some had had it with the Georgian's sanctimonious behavior. While Carter now wanted the whole incident to go away, Myers noted that the White House had made "no similar complaints . . . when the media was hammering away at Reagan during the initial days . . . after the Republican incorrectly stated that Carter launched his re-election drive in the Alabama city which gave birth to the Klan. Then, Carter and his lieutenants labored to keep the issue alive."[42]

Reagan filed an "equal-time" request with all three networks to respond to Carter's statements, but they turned him down, saying the president's press conference was a legitimate news event. Nonetheless, CBS went on record as stating that it had been badly used by Carter.[43]

Then the Carter campaign really got down and dirty. It ran ads in black-owned newspapers charging that Reagan wanted to defeat Carter because of the president's record on appointing African-Americans. The ad read, "Jimmy Carter named 37 black judges, cracked down on job bias, and created 1 million jobs. That's why the Republicans are out to beat him."[44] But Carter had overplayed his hand. He had done precisely what he did not want to do: he made Reagan a victim.

Republicans screamed bloody murder, and many in the press, still steaming over being used in the White House press conference, thought Carter had gone too far again. The Carter campaign withdrew the ads. Gerald Rafshoon released a statement that sheepishly read, "We will not run this ad again. We believe that the facts support the statements in the ad. However, because of the publicity about the ad, we feel that it's lost its effectiveness, and we won't run it again."[45] The Carterites knew what they were doing. Pat Caddell years later made clear that there was a purpose to the ongoing hammering of their opponent: "It was part of the risk strategy, anything to drive up that variable that [Reagan]'s too risky to be president."[46] They didn't mind taking on water, as long as they could drown Reagan in the process.

The *Washington Post* editorialized that Carter was "running mean" and said he had a "miserable record of personally savaging political opponents."[47] The *Washington Star* referred to Carter's campaign against Reagan as a "squalid exercise."[48] Jack Germond and Jules Witcover, normally critical of Reagan, upbraided Carter over his tactics. They noted that Carter had used the same devices in the 1976 primaries and that no one, in Reagan's years in politics, had ever seriously suggested he was a racist.[49] Even the reliably liberal columnist James "Scotty" Reston said that Carter's supporters were "deeply disappointed by the mean and cunning antics of his campaign." Reston concluded that Carter "is extremely confident, angry and vindictive, and thinks that concentrating on the weaknesses of his opponents is the way to win."[50]

The wise and urbane Hugh Sidey of *Time* said of Carter, "The past few days have revealed a man capable of far more petty vituperation than most Americans thought possible even in a dank political season. The wrath that escapes Carter's lips about racism and hatred when he prays and poses as the epitome of Christian charity leads even his supporters to protest his meanness."[51]

Though the Carter campaign had pulled the appalling newspaper ads, it went ahead with a television ad that asked, "When you come right down to it, what kind of person should occupy the Oval Office? Should it be someone who, like Ronald Reagan, has a fractured view of America, who speaks disdainfully about millions of us as he attacks the minimum wage and calls unemployment insurance a 'prepaid vacation'? Or should another kind of man sit here, an experienced man who knows how to be responsive to all Americans, all 240 million of us? Figure it out for yourself."[52]

Paul Laxalt had seen and heard enough. The ultra-cool Nevadan stormed that Carter had "slandered and vilified a decent and honorable man—but, more than that, he brought dishonor on the high office of the presidency."[53] Laxalt had the goods on Carter. He said that in 1964, while Carter was in the Georgia state senate, the future president had voted "for legislation which for all intents and purposes circumvented the Civil Rights Act" by "preventing school desegregation" while prohibiting any county in Georgia from "enacting open accommodation and fair employment laws."[54] Carter, in 1964, was a Jim Crow man. He hadn't changed by 1970, when his campaign distributed brochures with photos of his opponent, Carl Sanders, with African-American members of the Atlanta Hawks basketball team. Laxalt said of Carter's style, "This is his record. This is how he plays—hard ball, below the belt."[55]

Indeed, both Hubert Humphrey and Ted Kennedy had complained bitterly about Carter's style of campaigning in the past.

After months of negotiations, the League of Women Voters was finally ready to host the first presidential debate, but between Reagan and Anderson, and sans Carter. The GOP nominee had been truly astonished when Mike Deaver told him some time earlier that Carter would not participate. "What? I don't believe it," he said to Deaver. He then ordered his aide to make some phone calls and reconfirm the information. Reagan's "sense of fair play was totally offended," as one a senior aide told Newsweek.[56] Of Carter's refusal to debate, Reagan said bitingly, "He couldn't win a debate if it were held in the Rose Garden before an audience of Administration officials with the questions being asked by Jody Powell."[57]

Baltimore was the location for the debate between Reagan and Anderson, which was held on Sunday night, September 21. The city was delighted to host the event. It had fallen on hard times after the Second World War, and only in the 1970s, with urban homesteading and the revitalization of its Inner Harbor, did Charm City begin to sparkle again. Mayor Donald Schaefer, one of most creative and effective city executives in the country, had engineered the renaissance. Schaefer, a Democrat, had also worked some magic on behalf of President Carter. The League of Women Voters had promised the Reagan campaign that the debate stage would feature an empty chair to represent the missing president, which Jim Baker had negotiated for.[58] Carter was furious about the planned chair stunt, and Schaefer at the last minute convinced the league to nix it.[59]

The debate was held in the Baltimore Convention Center. The arena seated 2,600 people, but after the campaigns, the media, and the league took their tickets, a princely one hundred seats were available for the general public.[60]

The moderator of the debate was Bill Moyers, whom the Associated Press identified only as a "news producer and reporter for public television" but not as the highly partisan former press aide to Lyndon Johnson. The panel of questioners featured several journalists, including the popular economic writer Jane Bryant Quinn of *Newsweek*. Both NBC and CBS broadcast the debate, but ABC took a pass.[61]

As soon as the Baltimore debate kicked off, it was clear that the real target of the two combatants was the absent President Carter. Anderson set the tone early when he said, "Governor Reagan is not responsible for what has happened over the last four years, nor am I. The man who should be here tonight to respond to those charges chose not to attend."[62] Reagan, relaxed and in control, referred to the deficient Carter as "the man who isn't here tonight." Later he said, "It's a shame now that there are only two of us here debating, because the two that are here are in more agreement than disagreement."[63] Reagan was exaggerating, as he and Anderson agreed on little. They disagreed, albeit gently, over tax cuts; Reagan pointed out that a year and a half earlier Anderson had supported the original plan offered by Jack Kemp. They disagreed over defense spending and whether conservation was the only way to fight the energy crisis. They disagreed on abortion and a gas tax.

Some had expected this debate to be a sideshow since Carter wasn't there. But Reagan and Anderson benefited from the event. Some fifty million people watched the debate on NBC and CBS, millions more than watched the movie (*Midnight Express*) offered by ABC.[64] Both debaters won plaudits from the media and viewers. Anderson even scored an endorsement from the influential liberal magazine *The New Republic*, which in sixty-six years had endorsed only Democrats for president.[65] Reagan's performance, meanwhile, lifted the morale of the campaign and of the candidate. He hit a couple out of the park and committed no errors. The Gipper had been guided in part by a memo authored by Dick Wirthlin advising him to have a good time, show that he was "capable of enjoying a laugh," and keep his answers short and tight.[66]

Reagan had been the candidate most clearly helped by agreeing to show up in Baltimore. Voters who saw the debate preferred Reagan of the three candidates.

Carter and his men had miscalculated. In arguing for not participating, they got hung up on the internal minutiae of politics—"inside baseball" stuff. Their arguments were lost on the American people, who wanted concrete solutions to their plight. Anderson and Reagan offered those in their reasoned and reasonable debate. Carter, who gave up the chance to offer any such solutions by ducking the debate, bore the brunt of criticism.

Carter needed to change the subject back to questions about Reagan. The next day in Illinois and then in California, the president said the 1980 election would determine "whether we will have war or peace."[67] Carter thought he had found his opening with the "Tolstoy" issue.

Reagan privately seethed when informed of Carter's newest assault. He publicly labeled it "beneath decency."[68] Stumping in the panhandle of Florida, thick with retired military, Reagan said, "History will record that under Jimmy Carter, our military personnel had first-class equipment taken out of their hands—and food stamps put in them."[69]

Carter went right back at Reagan's throat, criticizing him for too often suggesting the use of power to confront enemies of America and the West. Calling Reagan's aggressiveness "disturbing," Carter said that "to call for the use of military forces in a very dangerous situation has been a repeated habit of his."[70] Jody Powell handed out reams of clips going back to 1968 highlighting instances in which Reagan suggested military interventions by the United States.[71] In an interview with Los Angeles station KNBC, Carter said, "I don't know what he would do if he were in the Oval Office, but if you judge by his past highly rhetorical calls for the use of American military forces in these altercations, it is disturbing. What he would do in the Oval Office I hope will never be observed by the American people."[72] On the "warmonger" issue, unlike the others rolled out, Carter was not going to back down.

Reagan had indeed called for military action at least ten times in twelve years, including as a means to rescue the Americans held captive by North Korea aboard the USS *Pueblo* in the late 1960s, as a way to keep the peace in Rhodesia in 1976 as it transitioned from a minority white government to a majority black government, and as a response to the Soviet invasion of Afghanistan. In 1975, when Ecuador took American fishing boats, Reagan had suggested a naval escort to prevent it from happening again.[73]

It was all Reagan could do not to leap for the bait and respond too aggressively. To win, Reagan must come across to the American public as a man of reason and depth and not given to angry outbursts. Carter was doing his best to goad the Gipper and attempt to show that he was unfit for the Oval Office. To tear too aggressively into Carter would have been exactly what Carter wanted Reagan to do.

When told that Carter refused to apologize for his most recent remarks, Reagan shook his head and said, "That doesn't surprise me. That's in character."[74]

Later, he calmly pointed to the war that had just erupted between Iran and Iraq to call attention to Carter's weak-willed foreign policy. Iraq only days earlier had invaded Iran. Reagan believed, had President Carter supported the shah of Iran, this newest war between Iran and Iraq might never have happened, and Americans would not have been taken hostage, as the Ayatollah Khomeini would not have come to power. "What is happening in Iraq and Iran," Reagan said, "is the consequence of policies this administration has followed during the last three-and-a-half years—a vacillating foreign policy and a weakened defense capability are largely to blame."[75]

It was not the response that Carter's men expected. Rather than crying foul for days on end, putting himself on the defensive, Reagan in measured tones redirected the voters' attention to Carter's military and foreign-policy weaknesses. The response was a testament to Reagan's new discipline and how much his campaign operations had improved in a few short weeks. Reagan said, "I'm not going to bother every day trying to answer those things. The issue of this campaign is his record and I'm just going to keep talking about it."[76]

Carter's warmonger insinuations, coming hard on the heels of his racism allegations, drew even more condemnation from journalists. Germond and Witcover called Carter's latest remark "a rabbit punch in its way even lower than his earlier suggestion of racism on Reagan's part."[77] Another reliably liberal columnist, Mary McGrory, castigated Carter, acerbically penning, "It isn't exactly hit-and-run, because Carter sticks around the scene of the accident long enough to say he didn't mean it."[78]

Carter's comments on foreign affairs also provided an opening for Reagan. Every time Reagan, Anderson, or their surrogates talked about the hostages, Carter and his aides "sternly lectured them on the risk of upsetting secret but delicate diplomacy," in the words of Adam Clymer of the *New York Times*. But then the president made the odd comment that the war between Iran and Iraq might "induce [the Iranians] to release the hostages." Here was Carter engaging in the same sort of unfounded speculation for which he had attacked his opponents.[79] The president's comments freed Reagan. When asked what he would have done differently from Carter, Reagan replied, "Everything."[80]

Of course, while Carter was admonishing his opponents not to politicize the plight of the hostages, Hamilton Jordan and other members of the staff were plotting to do precisely that. Carter said he worried about being seen as "using [the hostages'] return improperly." Jordan said, "What I would like to do, Mr. President, is use their return improperly and not be blamed for it." Carter laughed.[81]

REAGAN'S SWING THROUGH THE South took him not only to Florida but to Tennessee and Louisiana as well. Polls still put Reagan behind in Carter's "Solid South," and his campaign needed to press its opportunity in this culturally conservative region

In Florida, Reagan spoke to Cuban-Americans, fervent anti-Communists and just as fervent Reaganites. He praised most Cubans, except those "hardened criminals" Fidel Castro had cleaned out of his prisons and dumped on the United States.[82] Most were quarantined in Florida, but Carter had moved some to Arkansas, where they became the headache of Governor Bill Clinton, who was running for reelection. Carter made a calculated move: since Arkansas was his second-best state after Georgia in 1976, he thought he could take a hit in the state and still win it. Clinton, however, was furious with Carter.

In Tennessee, Reagan once again had to assure voters that he had no intention of dismantling their beloved Tennessee Valley Authority. Then, just as he had promised, he kept talking about the Carter record, hitting it hard. "By every way we have of measuring failure, his policies have failed."[83]

Reagan's move through the South was his best yet, as media polling confirmed. The Gipper was having fun on the stump for the first time in days. He drew energy from the audiences; the warmer they were, the better he was in addressing them. In Missouri, Reagan was caught on film autographing the arm cast of a beaming little boy.[84] He told audiences—above the Mason-Dixon Line—"Jimmy Carter is the South's revenge for Sherman's march through Georgia."[85]

Morale in the Reagan campaign was rising.

THE DECISION FOR REAGAN to debate Anderson had been, in retrospect, more critical than anyone knew at the time. Since Detroit, Reagan had been reduced to a one-dimensional figure by his own mistakes and the Carter battering. Coming out of the debate, he began to climb back into contention. Carter had slipped and Anderson, despite what the media thought of his performance, had gone backwards. Was it possible that the "Anderson Difference" was just warmed-over liberalism? Most reporters and sages settled in with the idea that the election would be very close, as in 1960, 1968, and 1976.

Carter's men—as well as Reagan's—thought that sooner or later there would be a debate between the two antagonists. Indeed, Carter was preparing for such an eventuality even at the time of the Anderson–Reagan debate. As *Newsweek* reported, the president was "studying a thick, black, 200-page notebook entitled 'Reagan Information' and divided into chapters detailing Reagan's past and present stands on critical issues."[86] Everybody seemed to know about the

Carter debate book, contents of which became the worst-kept secret in Washington.

Now the League of Women Voters abruptly altered plans and offered to sponsor a two-man debate between Reagan and Carter, to be followed by a three-way debate. Carter accepted the invitation for a one-on-one debate. Anderson naturally objected to the new offering. Reagan, too, rejected the offer.[87] He would not go back on his word by excluding Anderson.

Besides, the new setup meant that Reagan would have to debate three times and the other two men only twice. With his campaign nearly righted and Reagan hitting his stride on the road, Reagan's team saw no need for any more debates, though it meant he might lose the high-road argument.

Bizarrely, the league called on the public to whip up a grassroots campaign to pressure Reagan and Anderson to accept the new parameters.[88]

A Mondale–Bush debate had also been kicked around. In fact, shortly after accepting the GOP's vice-presidential nomination, George Bush had been in Kennebunkport relaxing when he received—and accepted in principle—an invitation from Vice President Mondale to debate.[89] Later, when more formal discussions began, Bush said no to the idea of debating, and now, that confrontation was off the table. In interviews years later, Bush recalled, incorrectly, that no debate had been planned at all, while Mondale recalled accurately that one had been in the works.[90] The Reagan team must have breathed a sigh of relief when the VP debate idea was shelved. Bush had a shaky debate record, and Mondale was such a pro that he had whipped Bob Dole in 1976. (In 1984 Mondale would become the only person to defeat Ronald Reagan in open debate.)

Reagan picked up the endorsement of an old liberal antagonist from California, Republican congressman Pete McCloskey. He'd been a burr under Reagan's saddle for years, having opposed every campaign of the Gipper's. Reagan once jokingly said that McCloskey's district ought to be moved to the San Andreas Fault.[91] In one of the weirder media events of the campaign, aides pushed McCloskey's ancient Volkswagen Bug onto the tarmac where Reagan's plane awaited. In front of the Gipper, McCloskey put a Reagan bumper sticker on his jalopy and then saluted the sticker, Marine-style.[92]

Another old rival, Jerry Ford, was campaigning aggressively for Reagan—though some Reagan aides thought it more than coincidence that the former president seemed to stump near every championship golf course in America. Ford zapped Carter over the "misery index." Carter had employed the cockamamie phrase in 1976 to refer to the combination of unemployment and inflation. Back then the index had stood at around 15 percent. Unfortunately for Carter and even more so for the average American, by 1980 it had rocketed up to over 21 percent.[93]

The Carter team had taken a calculated risk in making the warmonger charge against Reagan, and the president had endured his share of criticism for making the allegation. Still, Carter's campaign remained convinced that Reagan was vulnerable on issues of war and peace. Confirming their strategy, a new poll by NBC News and the Associated Press showed that 41 percent of Americans thought Carter would do the best job at keeping the country out of war; only 16 percent said Reagan. The same poll revealed that voters believed Reagan would do a better job on the economy.[94] Carter's men needed to keep attention on the issues which benefited them, and Team Reagan likewise.

Unfortunately for the Reagan campaign, the media were still picking up on the divisions between the Ford/Bush insiders and Reagan's Californian outsiders. Stories in the *New York Times* and the *Los Angeles Times* quoted campaign officials citing chapter and verse against the conservatives while making the former Ford and Bush operatives look smooth and debonair. The biggest target was Lyn Nofziger, who was taken to task for his demeanor, his rumpled clothing, and his inability to kiss the media's asses. Nofziger, as always, had the last word, even in the story: "I see certain people here who were for Ford, certain who were for George Bush and other people I don't like. This is the way I feel: I'll love you until November 4, and then, I'll be out to get you."[95] Not for a moment did anyone doubt Nofziger, who had been a contributor to Richard Nixon's notorious "Enemies List." It was for this and a million other reasons that Nofziger was simultaneously beloved and feared.

Fortunately for the candidate, such distractions were more than offset by his strong performance in Baltimore and his recent successful stumping. Polls showed that Reagan's fortunes had rebounded somewhat. The *New York Times*, which before the debate had had him down to Carter, 40–36, now had him up, 40–35, and a new NBC–Associated Press poll showed that he had regained the lead over Carter by a wider margin, 42–33.[96]

Still, Reagan's team felt the need to step things up. Specifically, longtime Reagan aides such as Jeff Bell worried that the campaign needed to do more than simply convince Americans that Carter needed to get kicked out of office. If Reagan won, he would need a mandate to do things. Gauzy, nonspecific ads were finally scrapped near the end of September in favor of more issue-oriented messages offering bold solutions to the ailments of America.

Conservatives did not want another empty win, as in 1972. They wanted this election to stand for something.

32

Mission from God

*"Americans might be separated, black from white, Jew from Christian,
North from South, rural from urban."*

Although Ronald Reagan had moved slightly ahead of Jimmy Carter in the national polls in late September, his lead was within the margin of error. And while a new Associated Press survey showed Reagan ahead in states with 236 electoral votes, 34 short of the 270 needed, his campaign described his lead in many of these states as "shaky."[1] Gerald Ford, the Reaganites reminded themselves, had topped out at 240 electoral votes four years earlier. More telling was the *Washington Post*'s in-depth polling in seven battleground states, which showed Carter ahead in New York, Reagan ahead in California, and the race dead even in the other five states, including Texas, Michigan, and New Jersey.[2]

Some voters were slowly migrating away from either John Anderson or Carter, because they were coming to believe that one was unelectable and the other was unacceptable. But just as Jeff Bell and other conservatives feared, these voters weren't embracing Reagan because of his ideas, at least not yet; they were simply dubious about the other two candidates and were now in the undecided column.[3]

Even Reagan's alma mater, Eureka College in downstate Illinois, seemed ambivalent about him. Reagan was clearly Eureka's most famous alumnus, and if he became president it would rain attention and much-needed endowments onto the sleepy, perpetually cash-strapped school. Still, there were no outward signs of support for Reagan at Eureka. The tiny school did not even bother to display the rare items and documents he had donated over the years. The material instead was stored in the basement of one of the institution's six red brick buildings.

In the 1940s Reagan and his then-wife, Jane Wyman, had approached the school about funding a performing arts center named after the two of them. The school excitedly said yes and Reagan wrote out a sizable check. But in the intervening time, Reagan and Wyman entered into divorce proceedings (at her insistence) and thus Wyman's check never arrived at the school. The plans for the center were quietly shelved by the school's administration.[4]

Reagan's hometown was less circumspect than his alma mater. Dixon's city fathers, having bought the old Reagan homestead, took out ads in the *New York Times* and other major newspapers touting their new book, *Reagan's Dixon*. "Before you vote," the ad urged, "this should be must reading for you."[5]

There was little more than a month to go before Election Day, and voters were still trying to figure out who Ronald Reagan was.

Reporters would have liked to supply their own answers, but the Reagan campaign continued to curtail media access to the candidate. Many of the hard and often boiled gentlemen of the press sat at the back of the plane, sucking on adult beverages and cigarettes, with little to do except sulk and complain to each other and the staff.

Carter's campaign remained intent on defining Reagan for voters. Not only was the president going hard after the Republican in speeches, but the campaign had also rolled out attack ads "designed to stir questions about Ronald Reagan's ability, at the age of 69, to handle the job," as the *New York Times* reported.[6] One "man on the street" ad featured an American saying, "Reagan scares me," and another commercial pointed out that while governor, Reagan acted as if California had its own foreign policy.[7]

Pat Caddell, the president's pollster, saw nothing to dissuade Carter from savaging Reagan. Citing polls showing that Anderson was falling, Caddell believed that the independent would soon be below 10 percent and that Anderson's wandering sheep would eventually rejoin Carter's flock.[8]

But Caddell's Republican counterpart, Dick Wirthlin, had detected signs in his surveys that Carter's harsh attacks were no longer working. The president, he believed, was playing with fire by continuing to go after Reagan so viciously. Even some White House aides leaked to the press their concerns that the president had "gone overboard" and had "overstated" his arguments against the GOP nominee.[9]

In a column on Carter's attack apparatus, Tom Wicker of the *New York Times* concluded: "He may win re-election by exaggerations, distortions and innuendo designed to 'reinforce' public fear of Mr. Reagan, as well as by clever exploitation of a short public memory for his own promises and pretensions. But next year, when the bands have been stilled and the lights dimmed, what Adlai Stevenson called 'the stark problem of governing' will remain. And Jimmy Carter, in a second term so won, may find himself less admired, less trusted, therefore even less able to lead and achieve than he was in his first. Think of that."[10]

Carter was not thinking about the long-term implications of this election. In a confidential memo written months earlier, one of his campaign aides, Karl Struble, had bluntly assessed the situation. "The electorate is more volatile and less committed to a presidential candidate . . . since World War II," Struble incisively wrote. "Every 30–40 years, the United States has experienced a realigning election (1828, 1860, 1896, 1932). . . . The last realigning election occurred in 1932. Similar unstable economic conditions and the inability of the dominant party to cast off obsolete ideology, made the 'New Deal Coalition' possible. Historically, we are overdue for another realigning election."

Struble continued: "There is mounting evidence that blue collar workers, urban white ethnics and Southern Democrats are slowly disintegrating as cornerstones of a Democratic majority. . . . Reagan . . . could become the lightning rod which realigns our political parties."[11]

THE REAGAN CAMPAIGN'S PUBLIC position at this point was that there would be no new debates. Jody Powell accused Reagan of "duplicity" for refusing to debate without Anderson.[12] In truth, there was no clear consensus inside Reagan Central on whether the Gipper should debate again. Indeed, a dispute had broken out among Reagan's inner circle on the subject.

On one side of the divide were the pro-debate "hawks," including Ed Meese and Bill Casey, who argued for a one-on-one debate with Carter and abandoning the campaign's position that Anderson needed to be included. On the other side were the anti-debate "doves," such as Bill Timmons, Lyn Nofziger, and Dick Wirthlin, who felt that a debate gaffe would halt the momentum Reagan had recently been building. One dove anonymously told the New York Times, "Debates are tough. You're rolling the dice every time you go out."[13]

Before the internal debate over debates was over, individuals would shift sides more than once. Three people had yet to really be heard from: Nancy Reagan, Jim Baker, and the Gipper himself.

Another debate was playing out on Capitol Hill. Republican senators wanted to get the first installment of the Reagan tax cut up for a vote, to show voters that Carter and the Democrats were on the wrong side of the issue. Senator Bob Dole was Reagan's chief spear-carrier, and if anyone knew how to take a minority of recalcitrant GOP senators and beat the Democrats, or at least put them on the defensive, it was Dole, the legislative magician. Dole could not muster enough support and the measure failed, along party lines, 54–38, but the Republicans had made their point: the GOP was foursquare for personal income tax cuts and the Democrats were on record opposing them.[14]

CARTER HAD NOT BACKED off on his attacks, and now even John Anderson criticized the president for the warmonger swipes at Reagan. Carter, Anderson said, had made "an unfair, highly political, and undocumented charge" against Reagan and was using "scare tactics" to suggest "that the election in November is a choice between peace and war."[15] The president was being "demagogic," according to Anderson.[16]

The Reagan campaign believed, before most of the president's team did, that Carter's harsh rhetoric was beginning to backfire, that voters wanted something more uplifting, more inspiring, than two men slugging it out in the gutter. Nofziger, always with his finger on the pulse of the people, said, "Clearly there is no great demand for this kind of campaign anymore."[17] With that, the Reagan-Bush campaign made a critically important strategic decision: it resolved to take the high road.

Reagan's message changed dramatically on the road. In Florida he spotted a sign that read "Blacks for Reagan." Smiling broadly, Reagan departed from his speech and said, "God bless you, and God bless those who brought that sign and, by golly, it shows that you can't fool all of the people all of the time."[18]

This change in sentiment eventually infused the entire campaign. Whereas Carter had continually attacked Reagan the man, Reagan's campaign would mostly stick to questioning Carter's record as president. In a major address to the World Affairs Council, George Bush characterized Carter's foreign policy as one of "bluff, bluster and backdown" and accused the president of weakening American influence. Bush reminded his audience of Carter's surprise a year earlier when the Soviets invaded Afghanistan. "Ronald Reagan would take office next January with a full understanding of the expansionist nature and geopolitical intentions of the leaders of the Soviet Union."[19] Loosely translated, this meant that if elected, Reagan was going to ride roughshod over the Russians.

REAGAN WAS STILL WELL behind in North Carolina and several other southern states, and Carter was fighting hard to hold on to what had been his. But it now looked as if the walls of Carter's once "Solid South" might tumble down. New polls showed Reagan creeping into small leads in Texas, Louisiana, Mississippi, and Florida. He was also leading in Virginia.[20]

The votes in the South, according to political observer Michael Barone, broke down into three categories: blacks, "country club whites," and the swing vote of

culturally conservative, rural, blue-collar Democrats. Grit by grit, a slow, trickling stream of southern Democrats was moving toward Reagan or undecided,
dismayed with their cultural brother, Carter. Jimmy Buffett was surprised to hear
boos from a young crowd in Georgia when Carter's name was mentioned at a
fundraising concert for the incumbent.[21]

A new category had also emerged in the South beginning in 1976: that of the
politically active Evangelical church. Reagan continued to court this fast-growing
constituency. He journeyed to Lynchburg, Virginia, to address thousands of supportive evangelicals at the National Religious Broadcasters Association Convention, telling them that if elected, he would push for voluntary prayers in public
schools. Reagan sidestepped a controversy when asked whether he agreed with a
recent statement by the Reverend Jerry Falwell that God heard the prayers only
of Christians. "No," he replied. "Since both the Christian and Judaic religions
are based on the same God, the God of Moses, I'm quite sure those prayers are
heard."[22]

Reagan was also making some inroads up north. Nancy Reagan, on a rare
solo mission, held a high-profile event in New Jersey with a number of current
and former Democratic officeholders, including sheriffs, town mayors, and ward
leaders, who endorsed her husband.[23] When Reagan arrived for his own tour in
New Jersey, he reminded the heavily Catholic state of his support for tax credits
for parochial schools. A heckler yelled out that it was not constitutional and Reagan, not missing a beat, fired back, "Yes it is! Separation of church and state does
not mean we have to separate ourselves from our religion." A few other hecklers
joined in and Reagan joshed to the overwhelmingly supportive crowd, "I wish
they'd shut up!"[24]

When Ray Donovan, the developer who was the head of the Reagan campaign
in New Jersey, and Roger Stone, the campaign's regional political director, were
not butting heads, they were organizing a very effective operation in the state.

In New York City, of all places, Reagan inveighed against government. The
Environmental Protection Agency (EPA) under Carter had halted the construction of the badly needed replacement for the West Side Highway; the crowd of
hardhats and unionists, who supported the $1 billion project, loudly cheered Rea-
gan. Lou Cannon noted that Reagan was striking a New Deal theme when he told
the workers, "I happen to think that the best social program is a job."[25] The union
workers gave Reagan a hardhat, an item that would come in handy given all that
Carter was throwing at him.

The Republican candidate moved on to Pennsylvania and discovered to his
delight that he'd moved ahead of Carter there, 40–33 percent, according to a Gal-

lup poll. Reagan told a crowd in Wilkes-Barre, "Mr. Carter does not represent the same values as such great Democrats as John F. Kennedy or Harry Truman."[26]

As certain pockets in the East were moving toward Reagan, the western states were beginning to fall in line behind the Gipper, with only Hawaii looking dubious. The West, from the election of Dwight Eisenhower up to 1976—excepting LBJ's landslide in 1964—had been reliably Republican in presidential elections. And of course, the West was Reagan Country. Carter's forays into this region were not bearing fruit.

By early October, Carter was stymied. His recovery in the polls had stalled after the Reagan-Anderson debate, and now reporters were beginning to ask him about the "meanness" issue. When Reagan criticized the SALT II treaty with the Soviets, saying that "the one card that's been missing in the negotiations has been the possibility of an arms race," Carter surprisingly did not respond. While the president's advisers may have finally been considering a new approach, they still had Walter Mondale to go on the attack. "This underscores what I think is a reckless, irresponsible and dangerous attitude by the Republican nominee," the vice president said of Reagan's comments.[27]

Carter didn't hold his tongue long, however. Speaking at a black-tie Democratic Party fundraiser, he threw a below-the-beltway punch, stating that if Reagan was elected, he would bring about "the alienation of black from white, Christian from Jew, rich from poor, and North from South."[28] The *Washington Post* had become so inured to Deacon Carter's "mission from God" inflammatory rhetoric that the story ran on page two and the appalling language was buried at the end of the article.

The Carter campaign tried to enlist other attack dogs. Pat Caddell called Bob Shrum, Ted Kennedy's speechwriter, to ask him to have Teddy attack Reagan as "anti-Catholic." Shrum replied, "Well, I'll ask him, but he isn't going to do it. Not in a million years."[29] Shrum knew his man. Teddy rejected the request out of hand.

Carter got a bit of good news on the economy for the first time in a long time. The unemployment rate dipped from 7.6 percent to 7.5 percent, and inflation had actually gone down for the first time in more than four years, dropping 0.2 percent for the month of September.[30] If Carter could convince enough voters that the economy was on the way back and that Reagan was not the way to go, he still had time to eke out a win, as in 1976.

To help along the process, the Carter administration was spreading federal aid around as if it were manure. Millions for a gasohol plant in Michigan, tens of millions in largesse for Chicago, all announced by Carter or cabinet officials on the stump.[31] There was little Reagan could do except cry foul, just as he'd done in 1976 when Ford was rolling out the federal pork in primary after primary.

AT THE BEGINNING OF October, Washington's attention temporarily shifted from the presidential race to a pair of Capitol Hill scandals. First, Michael Myers, Democrat of Pennsylvania, became the first congressman to be expelled from the House of Representatives in nearly 120 years. Myers was one of the politicians whose hand had been caught in the Abscam cookie jar. He had already been convicted in court, despite his imaginative defense that the video of him stuffing money into his pockets was in actuality of another man; if it was him, Myers claimed, he was only "play acting."[32] He would ultimately be sent to federal prison.

The day after the House voted to expel Myers, Congressman Robert Bauman of Maryland, a fiery young conservative and chairman of the American Conservative Union, was charged with soliciting sex from a sixteen-year-old male prostitute.[33] Bauman, who had a wife and four children, admitted to "homosexual tendencies" and blamed those "tendencies" on alcoholism.[34] He checked into rehabilitation and conservatives checked Bauman off their lists.

REAGAN'S OPPONENTS STEPPED UP their attacks. A heckler in New Jersey called him a "pig."[35] The National Organization for Women (NOW) said he was "medieval." At their convention in Texas, NOW members broke out into a chant: "ERA, here to stay! Ronald Reagan, no way!" The women's group adopted a resolution to picket Reagan and Bush, though it did not go so far as to endorse Carter's candidacy.[36]

Carter was back in the role of the underdog—a role his campaign always said he preferred. The president's supporters redoubled their attacks on Reagan. Mondale said Reagan's position on the SALT treaty "threatens civilization."[37] Edmund Muskie, the secretary of state, said that if Reagan was elected, the country would be in a perpetual state of war.[38] Even Mrs. Carter, in her own way, knocked Reagan. She told crowds she was "proud" that her husband was the "president of peace," and as the New York Times reported, her message was "a mixture of not-so-subtle digs at Ronald Reagan's conservatism, age and competence."[39]

Carter's union supporters began to plan their own attacks on Reagan— largely because they had almost nothing positive to say about the president. In the battleground state of Pennsylvania, labor officials held a crisis meeting in Harrisburg. Jim Mahoney of the AFL-CIO's political committee said frankly, "Let's face it—Carter is a tough job to sell. . . . We have to do a hatchet job on Reagan." Another said, "I can't tell Joe Worker that Jimmy Carter is great. He knows he is worse off today than he was four years ago. . . . What I have to do is make Reagan a devil."[40] Carter gave his presidency a better grade than did his union supporters. The president went on *60 Minutes* and said, "Under the circumstances, I think about a B. The actual results, maybe a C."[41]

Carter himself continued to tear into Reagan. Appearing before thousands in downtown Chicago, he labeled Reagan's rhetoric on national defense "jingoistic" and "macho" and said that his opponent wanted to "push everybody around."[42] That night at a party fundraiser, Carter restated the sinister theme he had unveiled a few days earlier: "You'll determine whether or not America will be unified, or if I lose this election, whether Americans might be separated, black from white, Jew from Christian, North from South, rural from urban—whether this nation will be guided from a sense of long-range commitment to peace, sound judgment and broad consultation."[43] Again Anderson condemned Carter for using "feverish, anything-goes tactics."[44]

Since the end of September, Reagan had been mostly circumspect about Carter's attacks, talking about what he wanted to talk about and not allowing himself to be diverted. Indeed, he'd joked with audiences that his secret agenda was to cancel Social Security and start World War III. Yet when reporters confronted him with the newest broadside from Carter, Reagan became visibly irritated. His response was mostly measured nonetheless: "I'm saddened that anyone . . . could intimate such a thing. . . . Certainly he's reaching a point of hysteria that's hard to understand."[45]

Carter was the subject of another round of editorials blasting him for his ruthless speechifying against Reagan. The president's high command convened an emergency meeting and determined that a change in tactics was required. The Carterites finally had to face facts: the president's relentless assault on Reagan had blown up on Carter. Not only had Carter been unsuccessful in provoking Reagan, but he had also tarnished his image as a decent man and instead developed a reputation for nastiness. The president's men acknowledged as much, saying that the strategy "ends up backfiring. . . . What we're doing isn't working."[46] Even Bob Strauss was critical of Carter, saying he "used a poor choice of words sometimes. . . . He gets into personal confrontation."[47] Carter had no choice but to tamp down his rhetoric. Reagan campaign aide Michele Davis went out drinking one evening with a group of reporters covering the campaign and was astonished to hear them. She wrote in her diary, "They sure do talk shit about the Carters. Funny."[48]

The president went on ABC for an interview with Barbara Walters, a rite of passage for public officials wanting to express public contrition. Yet it may have been the oddest nonapology in American political history: "I think it's true that when Mr. Reagan says that I'm desperate or hysterical or vindictive that he shares part of the blame that I have assumed."[49] Carter explained away some of his over-heated rhetoric by saying, "It's not a deliberate thing. Some of the issues are just burning with fervor in my mind and in my heart, and I have to sometimes speak extemporaneously and I have gotten carried away on a couple of occasions."[50] The president did tell Walters that he wanted to get his campaign "back on the track" and that he should not have implied that Reagan was a warmonger.[51] Going forward, he said, he would tone down his attacks on Reagan and instead give a series of long, issues-oriented speeches.

When told about Carter's "apology," the Gipper replied, "Well, I think that would be nice if he did . . . if he's decided to straighten up and fly right."[52]

Despite Carter's promise to clean up his act, Anderson was unmoved. He told liberals in New York that the president was "incompetent," that he had "no clear and compelling vision of our nation's future," and that Carter was simply an "opportunist" who craved power.[53]

Carter's quasi mea culpa seemed too little and certainly came too late. He was still forced to address the issue on the campaign trail. During a swing through the South he acknowledged before a large crowd that he'd been "overly enthusiastic" in his comments about Reagan. During a town hall meeting with 4,400 people at Nashville's Grand Ole Opry, Carter was taken aback when a high-school student came full bore at him, asking, "Sir, why is it that if you are the right man for the job, that you and your staff have to lower yourself to the extent of slinging mud and making slanderous statements [against] your rival, Ronald Reagan?" The hall exploded in applause at the young man's brazenness.[54]

In his postpresidential memoir, Carter did not express much regret at having directed "a harsh phrase" at Reagan. The media, he wrote, had misinterpreted his attacks on Reagan as being "personal." What really bothered Carter was that the "political damage" from the attacks "was afflicting me as much as it was him."[55]

REAGAN HAD BEGUN INCHING toward the middle. First he had softened his position on the bailout of Chrysler and on federal aid to New York City, causing conservatives to squawk. Now, during yet another tour of Ohio, a battleground state, his campaign distributed hundreds of thousands of flyers in which he reversed his earlier stance on subjecting unions to antitrust laws.[56]

Unexpectedly, Reagan also called on the government to speed up the purchase of cars from Detroit as a means of helping the ailing industry. The Carter White House was livid, believing that Republican moles had found out that Carter was going to take just this action. Reagan had stolen the president's thunder.[57]

Moderates in the campaign even tried to convince Reagan to give up on his tax-cut plan and to drop his support for eliminating the Departments of Education and Energy, but on these and other issues, his position was unshakable.

The campaign's sudden moderation reflected how close the race was in vital swing states. Reagan had picked up his share of protesters and picketers on the campaign trail, in part because his operation continued to have problems with the local advance work. The protests became an outsized problem for the Reagan campaign because the media often highlighted boos or heckling. During his latest Ohio tour, for example, hecklers came out to a poorly advanced event in Steuben-ville, and the *New York Times* duly noted their presence in its news report.[58] The focus on the protesters detracted from Reagan's message. In this case the candidate was calling for a close examination of the Clean Air Act, which he claimed had closed many factories in the Buckeye State.[59] Ohio, where unemployment had approached 9 percent, was the rustiest of all the Rust Belt; from Akron to Zuck, factories were boarded up.[60] Reagan knew that Ohio was crucial for him. Carter had carried the state by only a handful of votes in 1976, and in the twentieth century, no Republican had won the presidency without carrying Ohio.

The Reagan campaign enlisted Bush to make the case in battleground states. Once relegated to the backwaters, Bush was now put in a series of television broadcasts modeled on his effective "Ask George Bush" formats from the primaries, only these were billed as "Ask Reagan/Bush." The shows were broadcast all over the northeast and Midwest along with Texas. Stu Spencer told reporter Lisa Myers, whom the *Washington Star* had promoted to the Reagan plane, that Bush would be especially helpful in American suburbs.[61]

Bush's prominent role in the campaign was a surprising break from GOP precedent. Ford had tried to muzzle his running mate, Bob Dole, and Nixon had put a leash on his rabid dog, Spiro Agnew. Nixon himself was ground under Eisenhower's heel for eight years. Bush, however, benefited because Reagan was growing more comfortable with him and because some of Bush's staff had emerged in key positions in the campaign, especially Jim Baker.

Another Reagan effort to reach beyond conservative voters—his courting of traditionally Democratic groups—was paying off. A month earlier, the National Maritime Union had strongly denounced Reagan in its newsletter. But Reagan attended a meeting of the union in St. Louis, and by voice vote the seamen changed course, endorsing the GOP nominee for president.[62] Reagan himself seemed stunned at the development.

Almost as surprising, and much more significant, was the endorsement of the 2.3–million–member International Brotherhood of Teamsters.[63] Reagan had been warmly received by the Teamsters back in August, but the endorsement was nonetheless unexpected.

Odd as the Teamsters' endorsement of Reagan seemed at the time, nothing nefarious—at least on the surface—was involved, according to Myron Mintz, a veteran of the Nixon White House and a tax attorney for the controversial union and its then president, Frank "Frankie" Fitzsimmons, a protégé of Jimmy Hoffa's. The union was angry with the Carter administration and Ted Kennedy for supporting deregulation of the trucking industry. The Teamsters had flirted with endorsing John Connally in the primaries, but Fitzsimmons's rival, Jackie Presser, later held a rally for Reagan in Ohio over the summer of 1980. Anxious not to be cut off from Reagan inside his own union, Fitzsimmons agreed to endorse Reagan; he did so at the urging of Mintz during a game of gin rummy with Mintz.[64] Fitzsimmons, a lifelong Republican, wasn't that difficult to persuade. Presser needed to do more work with the board. He said: "You Italians, listen up! More than anyone else in this room, you should be supporting Reagan! Reagan has agreed to lay off of us! The Justice Department will not be on our backs for once!"[65] He also told them that Reagan would not pursue trucking deregulation as aggressively as Carter had. They immediately voted to support Reagan.

Mintz, who grew up on the rough-and-tumble streets of Philadelphia, was well suited to be a union lawyer, a world in which allegations of mob ties were routine. He'd once gotten into a fistfight with government officials who had come to his office with a search warrant for union documents. A lifelong Jew, Mintz changed his religion to Baptist during his divorce proceedings with his first wife so he could get their children on Christian holidays. When the court awarded their unoccupied house to his former wife, he went there one Friday afternoon, put a garden hose in the basement window, turned on the water, and left.[66]

The welcomed union endorsements were mostly lost in a miniflap over Reagan's assertion that the EPA was too aggressive in pursuit of a clean environment. Reagan had gone off script, and he and his campaign ended up stuck in a debate with Carter's EPA and the media over what constituted air pollution and how it was created. The controversy reminded people of an earlier comment he had made to the effect that "trees cause more pollution than automobiles," a statement for which he had been roundly denounced.[67] Worse, Reagan tried to suggest that the spill of more than 200,000 gallons of oil off of Santa Barbara was no big deal. From an environmental standpoint he was right, for as Lou Cannon wrote in *Governor Reagan*, the "long-term biological effects of the spill were negligible." But the political impact of the spill was "enormous," as Cannon said; it gave force to the environmental movement and led to a ban on drilling in federal waters.[68]

Michele Davis confided in her diary, "Old RR came out with some real off-the-wall bloopers on the environment today."[69] Reagan opened himself up to attacks with such remarks. One environmental activist said Reagan had "a Neanderthal understanding" of the problems of the environment and the media whipsawed him over his comments.[70] Reagan was tired and he needed to get off the road to recharge his batteries.

Adding to Reagan's embarrassment was a case of bad timing. On the heels of his assertion that air pollution was coming under control in America, two press planes following his campaign aircraft into Los Angeles had to be diverted because of poor visibility due to smog. Later, at a rally with Roy Rogers, he was met by environmental activists who heckled him, one carrying a sign that read, "Stop Pollution; Choke Reagan."[71]

CARTER'S NEWEST PROMISE TO elevate the tone of his campaign lasted exactly twenty-four hours. On a swing through Florida, he said Reagan would not be "a good man to trust with the affairs of this nation in the future." Jody Powell was sent to the back of the plane to clean up Carter's mess. Reagan that day had said the hallmark of the Carter presidency was "a string of broken promises and trusts that have been betrayed." Powell made the equivalency argument: "If one is a harsh personal attack, the other damn sure is."[72]

Reagan might have been expected to receive sympathetic coverage in the wake of Carter's newest assault, but then he accused the president of plotting an "October Surprise," the first time the candidate had used this phrase in public. Reagan simply let it be known that "presidents can make things happen." Carter hotly denied that his administration was cooking up an October Surprise, but the Reagan campaign had injected the issue into the national debate, attempting to tap into voters' cynicism about Carter.[73]

Reagan went off message when he charged that Carter engaged in "fits of childish pique" and that he was the "greatest deceiver ever to occupy the White House." Reagan added, "We trusted him and now as president he's broken probably more promises than any president in United States history."[74] Reagan was off his game, which was precisely what Pat Caddell had hoped to achieve with his attack strategy.[75] Up to this point, though, Reagan had mostly avoided such attacks and spoken directly to the voters. "Keep in mind," he said, "this dream is not so much for those who are already well-off as it is for . . . the great majority of Americans who are less fortunate—for the poor, for minority Americans and for the elderly."[76]

Traveling through the Sunshine State, Reagan told elderly voters that he favored repealing a law which prohibited them from making outside income without reducing Social Security benefits. The limitations, dating back to the Depression, did not apply to government officials, known at the time as "double dippers." Reagan told a crowd at Al Lopez Field in Tampa that he would work to preserve the oft-maligned retirement system.[77] From Florida he headed back to California for a much-needed weekend of rest.

When he was on message, evident in Reagan's speeches and at his rallies, was a renewed appeal to American patriotism that had been out of fashion for years. The elites had made patriotic Americans a caricature, from Johnny Carson's dim-witted "Floyd R. Turbo" to comedian George Carlin's rants against traditional American values and the culture; and the counterculture had made anybody who wore an American flag lapel pin out to be some sort of Bozo. Many sports facilities simply stopped playing the national anthem. In a country where it was once impossible for a man in uniform to walk into a bar and not have someone buy him a beer, by the 1970s servicemen were sometimes spat upon. But Reagan spoke unabashedly about loving his country and old-fashioned values, and also about his hope for the future. One wag said it best about Reagan: he was nostalgic for the future.

The sophisticates who could rarely find anything good to say about America continued their derision of Reagan and patriotism. But it was they who had become a joke, not those who agreed with Reagan. Patriotism had become hip again, at least for the middle and lower classes.

Of all the unwritten stories of the 1980 campaign, one of the most significant was that the fever of anti-Americanism had run its course and Dr. Reagan was chiefly responsible for breaking it.

33

STALLED

"If the guy can't debate Jimmy Carter for one hour,
maybe we're all making a mistake."

By mid-October the Reagan momentum had faltered once again, and the Democrats had the wind at their backs. In Texas, which Reagan should have put away long before, polling showed the race tied.[1] Ernie Angelo, who was running Reagan's operations in the state, worried that with a large Hispanic turnout, Texas might go for Jimmy Carter again. He was working to get a healthy share of that vote for Reagan, but a pro-Carter Hispanic leader retorted, "If we wanted an actor, we would vote for Ricardo Montalban."[2] Two former Democratic governors were supporting Reagan, Preston Smith and Allan Shivers[3], but if anyone knew how to deliver the state to Reagan, it was the tall, lanky, soft-spoken, and well-regarded Angelo. He was up against a Carter import, Bob Beckel, a large, hard-drinking, garrulous gun-for-hire.

George Bush headed for Virginia, another state that should have been tucked away months earlier. Also in play was Michigan, where labor unions were working hard for Carter—motivated in part by the administration's $1.3 million grant to create counseling centers for unemployed autoworkers.[4] Although Gerald Ford had carried his Wolverine State in 1976, the moderates who dominated the state GOP were decidedly unenthusiastic about Reagan.

The only major industrial state in the Northeast where Reagan was holding a lead was New Jersey, and soon even that state would move into the toss-up category. Connecticut was still up for grabs, despite the campaign's attempt at a merger between Bush's blue bloods and Reagan's blue collars. Reagan punster-in-residence Lyn Nofziger called it the "blue woo."[5]

Illinois, land of Reagan's birth, which Ford had carried in 1976, fell back into the undecided column. A Chicago Sun-Times poll as of the third week of October had Carter ahead, 43.9 to 41.5 percent.[6] Carter's surge had come primarily from suburban voters, who were moving away from John Anderson and had lingering doubts about Reagan. The state was a bellwether, as it had gone for the winner in seven out of the eight previous presidential contests.

Ohio's status also slipped back into the toss-up category, despite a statewide unemployment rate of around 9 percent and the Reagan campaign's considerable expenditure of resources in the Buckeye State.[7] The newest polling had Reagan at 36 percent and Carter at 34 percent in the state. Amazingly, among the self-described conservatives in Ohio, Reagan was getting only 54 percent of the vote and Carter was taking a respectful 25 percent. The Democratic chairman of Cuyahoga County, Timothy Hagan, summed it up: "With all his problems, Carter should be blown out of the water by now, but he obviously isn't, so he's still in the game."[8] Republican governor Jim Rhodes, a slightly unsavory character, was campaigning hard for Reagan. Typically, he would slam his wallet on a lectern and tell the crowd, "That's the issue—who puts something in there rather than who takes it out."[9]

In Florida, a newspaper poll had it 42 percent for Reagan and 40 percent for Carter, but Jewish voters there were overwhelmingly for the president, 61–14 percent. Carter was hitting Reagan hard in the state on Social Security and Medicare.[10] And Reagan had protracted problems in Alabama because of his comments several weeks earlier about the Klan.[11]

All told, a dozen battleground states were considered toss-ups by mid-October, and both campaigns were working overtime to determine where to deploy their limited financial and manpower resources in the final weeks.

In many states, Carter had two aces in the hole. The first was that organized labor controlled most of the levers of power, from the election boards to the public schools to the state legislatures. Second, most states had Democratic governors and many of these had their own effective political machines they were only too willing to loan to Carter.

Ted Kennedy had made some campaign appearances with the president, but with his standoffishness he telegraphed that he was holding his nose in supporting Carter—a point Kennedy speechwriter Bob Shrum confirmed in an interview years later.[12] Now Kennedy reluctantly agreed to do commercials for the president, with the proviso that Carter's media man, Gerald Rafshoon, not be anywhere near him. Kennedy held a grudge against Rafshoon over what he believed were heavy-handed ads in the primaries. Teddy's former media adviser David Sawyer bluntly said, "They were mean," and speculated that the residual bad feelings had hurt Carter among traditional Democratic voters because the ads "were so intensely personal, raising inferences about Chappaquiddick."[13]

But Carter needed Kennedy's help, and he knew it. As Carter later remembered, "I was never reconciled to the more liberal wing of [the] Democratic Party as long as I was in office." He fretted over the Catholic vote going to Reagan and the liberal vote going for John Anderson, and so he was working hard to hold on to these traditional Democratic voters.[14]

Mondale, Carter, and Bush were all available to talk with the media, but not Reagan and the complaints became more insistent. Reporters began to wonder amongst themselves why Reagan seemed to be ducking a one-on-one debate with Carter, since John Anderson had faltered and because Reagan initially had said he would welcome such a confrontation with Carter. Reagan began receiving renewed tough critiques from the nation's columnists. David Broder of the *Washington Post* said that some of the Reagan campaign's tactics were downright "preposterous" but that Carter was too much of a stiff to take advantage; many other politicians had successfully stopped their opponents by making fun of them.[15]

Reagan was trying to stay on offense. He charged the Carter administration with "doctoring" the new economic figures, but the charge did not stick.[16] He was still bedeviled over his comments that air pollution in America was essentially under control and that the massive oil spill in Santa Barbara in 1969 wasn't a big issue.

The GOP nominee was mostly sticking to his script, talking again and again about "family, work, neighborhood, peace, and freedom." His staff referred to it as the "FWNPF" speech and the media had their own impolite way of describing it. Reagan was not saying anything new.

Although Carter's attacks on Reagan had come at a serious price for the president, they did at least slow the Republican down. The assaults had, for example, limited Reagan's ability to call for military action to free the hostages, as this would play into Carter's hands and renew suspicions that Reagan was "trigger happy."

Pat Caddell saw "softness" in Reagan's support, including in his adopted home state of California.[17] A good deal of the softness, according to Caddell, was with women voters, who were more supportive of Carter. Reagan was touchy about the subject and suggested that his support among women might be higher absent Carter's "warmongering" attacks. Caddell said, "All elections involve a certain amount of seeding. Carter has succeeded in seeding certain doubts about Reagan."[18]

As was the case four years earlier, Carter was once again relying upon a small coterie of fellow or honorary Georgians. Hamilton Jordan was at the headquarters full-time, delighted to be away from the stuffiness of the White House. Jordan found governance to be a bore. His office at the campaign reflected his irreverence: the only item adorning the walls was a poster that read "Luciano Pavarotti for President."[19] Each morning, Jordan convened an 8 o'clock strategy meeting. Most nights, the Carterites retired to the Class Reunion bar around the corner from the White House for further talks, cigarettes, and booze. The smelly dive was a favorite haunt of the Carter gang and political reporters. In the rear, next to the men's room, was a door to the alley, where a dumpster was often covered with rats.

John Anderson's candidacy appeared to be waning, but not fast enough for Carter's nerves. Four years earlier, Eugene McCarthy's quixotic candidacy had, Carter believed, cost him a handful of states as liberals threw in their lot with the erudite Minnesotan.

Only in the rural West was Carter unable to make much of a dent. One large reason why the president had not cracked the region was his hostility toward federal water projects there, essentially sacred cows in this perpetually parched land. Farmers, ranchers, and developers prized these projects. Spurred on by the "Sagebrush Rebellion" that had grown up in opposition to the federal government's control of so much western land, the region had become increasingly anti-Washington on issues ranging from water to taxes to gun ownership to the fifty-five-mile-per-hour speed limit, which Westerners saw as hugely impractical in a land where one might have to drive for hours just to go grocery shopping.

About the only other good news for Reagan at this time was that he appeared to be making inroads with Catholic voters nationally. Catholics had supported Carter 54–44 over Ford in 1976.[20] Chipping away at Carter's lead with Catholics could help Reagan in battleground states.

A final piece of promising news for the Republicans went underreported: the results of a national survey of the rank-and-file of the labor movement taken by the AFL-CIO. Surprisingly, 72 percent of members opposed any cuts in defense spending, 65 percent favored a balanced-budget amendment, 60 percent remained opposed to the Panama Canal treaties, more than 50 percent opposed new gun-control laws, and 44 percent stood in opposition to abortion.[21] No wonder the leadership at the AFL-CIO tried to keep a lid on the results.

On the whole, though, the election indicators were growing poor for Reagan and the GOP. The Republican National Committee was so fearful of a Reagan collapse that it began telling its candidates to run from Reagan and localize their efforts.[22] Where once the GOP had been favored to take control of Congress, the Democrats had regained the lead, 51–42 percent, according to a Gallup poll released in mid-October.[23] A Republican sweep appeared to be slipping away.

As PART OF THE evolving tone of his campaign, President Carter began a series of twenty-minute radio broadcasts, the first detailing his new economic plan, which he said would lead to an "economic renaissance." Without mentioning Reagan by name, Carter excoriated those who pined for "earlier times." Carter then headed for New York, New Jersey, Connecticut, Pennsylvania, Missouri, Illinois, and, curiously, Massachusetts, which everyone assumed would be a lead-pipe cinch for the Democrats.[24] Carter's closing argument would have to be directed at undecided voters and wavering liberals who had flirted with Anderson over the summer and fall but were succumbing to the argument that a "vote for Anderson is a vote for Reagan," as Carter's campaign had charged.

To make his case, Carter needed to rekindle a message of hope and opportunity, a message he'd thrown away over the past several years, repeatedly telling the American people of a world of scarcity and sacrifice. Reagan had happily picked up the message of hope. Carter would also have to continue to shift the focus from the current state of the economy to questions about Reagan and nuclear war.

In addition, the Democrats wanted to remind voters of Reagan's flip-flops, and this Vice President Mondale did with relish, hoping to prod disgruntled Democrats back into the fold. Reagan indeed had changed his positions on federal aid to New York City, the grain embargo of the Soviets, the federal loan guarantee for Chrysler, and the sale of the Tennessee Valley Authority, and Mondale wasn't about to let anyone forget it.

Mondale was from the old school, the Harry Truman school. As a young man, he been on the train with Truman in 1948 when the thirty-third president was "giving 'em hell" and Mondale always remembered three lessons from the old machine pol: "Tell the voters what you have done and where you are going and, above all, have some fun along the way."[25]

THE ELECTION WAS NOW less than three weeks away. Tempers rose and patience was practically nonexistent. Subtlety was in short supply. Andrew Young, Carter's former UN ambassador, opened his mouth again—always a dangerous proposition. In Ohio, he said that Reagan's support for "states' rights . . . looks like a code word to me that it's going to be all right to kill niggers when he's president." The White House immediately repudiated Young's horrendous comments, and Ed Meese, who was almost always a study in dispassion, stepped out of character and called Young's comments "low and vicious demagoguery . . . part of the continuing Carter hatchet attack."[26]

Reagan, in an effort to close the sale in his home state, went back to California for a hoped-for favorable tour, complete with good visuals for the networks.

The stop at Claremont College was anything but favorable, as hundreds of chanting students from a half-dozen colleges ambushed him as he attempted to speak. The wittiest sign was attached to a tree, and it said, "Chop me down before I kill again," a reference to Reagan's earlier statement about trees and pollution.[27] Chanting "We Want Bonzo!" "Smog!" and "ERA!" some protesters waved coat hangers signifying their support for legal abortions and tried to drown out Reagan's speech by singing "America the Beautiful," prompting Reagan to gibe, "They can't even sing."[28] Reagan smiled and watched the protesters until they began yelling "Heil Reagan!" and making the Nazi salute in his direction. Reagan's visage became grim and he said, "Those who would deny the right to speak to others who don't share their particular views were raising their hands in a salute that was more familiar in my younger days. . . . Well, you know I take a little pride, if you'll forgive me, that if it wasn't for our generation they'd be saying 'Heil' somebody today."[29]

Reagan was treated far better at an event in Orange County that included skydivers and fireworks. He shouted to the thousands assembled, "Are you better off than you were in 1976?" and "Do we really need more spending programs?" The crowds shouted back, "No! No!"[30] But more and more hecklers were showing up at every Reagan appearance.

Carter had his own trouble with hecklers. In New York, he pledged continued support for Israel in the Jewish Community Center in Queens, but a handful yelled "Liar!" back at him.[31] Carter would need the support of Jewish Americans if he were to carry New York again. Reagan, in California at Temple Ner Tamid in Van Nuys, attacked Carter for failing to denounce the bombing of a synagogue in Paris and other apparently coordinated attacks on Jews in France. Wearing a white yarmulke, Reagan was well received.[32]

The ERA protesters appearing at every rally were getting under Reagan's skin. He became defensive over the issue of women's rights. In an attempt to address the matter and regain his waning momentum, Reagan announced at a rare press conference—his first in a month—that if elected, he would fill one of the first openings on the Supreme Court with a woman.[33]

The move did nothing to help his faltering effort. Indeed, it only invited conservatives to criticize him and liberals to doubt him. A spokeswoman for the National Women's Political Caucus said, "It won't do him much good." She said he could help himself only by changing his position on abortion and the ERA.[34] The press saw the announcement of a woman on the Supreme Court as gimmicky and pandering. Reporters who had not had the opportunity to cross-examine Reagan for a month peppered him with questions, such as whether a female appointee would be pro-life. He dodged the question. Photos of the event showed an unhappy candidate.

Carter hit Reagan from the right, saying it was inappropriate to hold a slot on the court "for a particular kind of American."[35]

Paul Conrad, the political cartoonist for the *Los Angeles Times*, had been another ruthless burr to Reagan for years. On this matter, he depicted Reagan as a sleazy lounge lizard trying to pick up an equally sleazy girl in a disco. "Haven't we met before? Do you come here often? Can I buy you a drink? How about a seat on the U.S. Supreme Court?" The cartoon was widely reprinted.[36]

Conrad was but one of hundreds of political cartoonists in America, many being very good even as they were overtly liberal in their perspective. The *Washington Post*'s Herbert Block was considered the dean of the fraternity along with Bill Mauldin of the *St. Louis Post-Dispatch*, who was beloved by World War II vets for his depiction of two dogfaces, "Willie and Joe." The funnier, up-and-coming cartoonists included Mike Peters of the *Dayton Daily News*, Pat Oliphant of the *Washington Star*, and the favorite of conservatives, the irrepressible Jeff MacNelly of the *Richmond Times-Dispatch*. Since all were syndicated in hundreds of newspapers, millions saw their handiwork. MacNelly, a college dropout, had already won two Pulitzers despite his rightward tilt. Like most cartoonists, MacNelly had started out drawing Carter as normal-sized. As the president diminished in the polls, however, the cartoon versions of Carter shrank as well, and in most depictions, he was comically small, always looking up at people and events. Herblock, Oliphant, and MacNelly were not in high favor in the Carter White House for their depictions of the president.

Reagan, like Carter, had evolved coming out of the inkwell. For years, most cartoonists had emphasized the wrinkles under the Gipper's jaw line, but as he began winning—and maybe fearful of a backlash with seniors—cartoonists began making Reagan appear younger, emphasizing his pompadour instead. Cartoonists fretted that Reagan was hard to characterize because, complained Paul Szep of the *Boston Globe*, "he is still a very good-looking man."[37]

NOW ON THE DEFENSIVE, Reagan jetted off for a couple of days of campaigning in South Dakota and Idaho—two more states that he should have locked up already. Meanwhile Carter took wing on Air Force One through New York, Missouri, and Illinois. In the Land of Lincoln, he spoke to sooty-faced coal miners and told them how their coal would one day replace oil from the Middle East.[38]

In many of his appearances, Carter held town hall meetings with American citizens. He excelled in these forums, asking for the questioners' first names and then using the names and answering their questions with great flourish and detail. Sometimes too much. At Hofstra University on Long Island, a thirteen-year-old girl stood up to ask Carter a question and when he was finished, he said, "Thank you, sweetheart. I love you." Later, a young man said to the president, "I voted for you and it's the biggest mistake I ever made."[39]

Carter continued to have difficulty with New York City's mayor, the colorful Ed Koch, who often complained about the president's stance toward Israel. At one point, Koch had refused to appear on the same dais with Carter in the Big Apple. To tweak Carter, Koch invited Reagan to Gracie Mansion for a meeting and then held a widely covered photo op.[40] Reagan was only too happy to take advantage of Koch's gesture, but the Carter campaign made sure New Yorkers didn't forget what Reagan had once said about federal aid to their city. Carter was running billboard ads quoting Reagan as having said, "I have included in my morning and evening prayers every day the prayer that the federal government not bail out New York."[41]

"RONALD REAGAN'S PRESIDENTIAL CAMPAIGN may be running out of steam." So wrote two of the *Wall Street Journal*'s top political reporters, Al Hunt and James Perry, in a lead story published on October 16. The story detailed gloomy assessments of the Reagan campaign, including those offered by Democrat Peter Hart and Republican Bob Teeter. Confidence in the Carter campaign was "surging," according to the journalists.[42]

Polling confirmed that Reagan's campaign had ground to a halt. Bob Strauss crowed to journalists that Pat Caddell's surveys showed Carter "pulling ahead, or at least even, in all of the key industrial states."[43] More telling, an ABC News poll released a few days later showed that Reagan had slid backwards in the Electoral College tally, and that the growing mass of toss-up states now accounted for 182 electoral votes.[44] Then a New York Times–CBS poll revealed that Carter had pulled out to a nine-point lead over Reagan in the state of New York, 38–29 percent. Anderson was at 10 percent and 23 percent were undecided.[45]

Anderson concluded that he was nearing the end of the road. Though his bank account was heavily in the red, reporters noted a devil-may-care attitude in the candidate aboard his plane, *Rocinante*, named for Don Quixote's horse. He was telling jokes on the stump, mostly at Carter's expense, referring to Reagan as "Ronnie," and generally having a good time. He confided to a reporter, "I'm loosening up. It's almost over."[46] After months, Anderson was finally relaxing.

Reagan was anything but relaxed. Desperate to turn things around, he flew to Flint, Michigan, where he was greeted warmly by 1,200 out-of-work autoworkers. The city's unemployment rate was over 20 percent and the state's jobless rate was over 12 percent. Reagan hit Carter hard on importation of foreign automobiles, as the U.S. government levied certain taxes on American-made cars—in the range of $200 to over $500 per vehicle—but not on Japanese-manufactured cars sold in America. Reagan issued one of his better lines: "You remember when they promised us two cars in every garage? We've got them now—both Japanese and out of gas."[47]

While in Michigan, Reagan received unexpected endorsements from two legendary civil-rights leaders, Ralph Abernathy and Hosea Williams. Both men were important lieutenants of Dr. Martin Luther King Jr. and both were high officials in the Southern Christian Leadership Conference (SCLC). Abernathy spoke to the congregation of the St. John's Christian Methodist and Episcopal Church in Birmingham, outside of Detroit. Referring to Carter, he said, "We don't need this doctor anymore, because we as the patients are getting sicker. We need to change doctors." Reagan was deeply touched by the decision of Abernathy and Williams: "I just didn't realize such a thing could happen. I was overwhelmed." Black leaders including Coretta Scott King, widow of the slain civil-rights icon, roundly denounced the two men.[48] African Americans, who had provided the margin of victory for Carter in seven states in 1976, were expected to heavily support the Democrat again.

Stepping up the pressure, Carter yet again called on Reagan to meet him in a one-on-one debate. Just as in the Reagan camp, a hotly argued debate had been going on among Carter's men over a debate. Pat Caddell, in particular, argued vociferously against any debates now. The pollster knew that undecided voters had broken for the incumbent in the closing days of every presidential election since World War II, with the exception "the big landslides in '64 and '72, which were locked in very early." More important, Carter was surging and Reagan was faltering. A debate at this point was an unnecessary wild card, with Carter in danger of losing more than he would gain. "I kept saying no, no, no," Caddell later remembered. But Bob Strauss and Hamilton Jordan were "unwilling to shut the door" on the debate negotiations after the Reagan-Anderson debate, Caddell said.

There was another, even more important factor: the president himself wanted to debate. Carter was contemptuous of Reagan and wanted the chance to make mince meat of his conservative opponent. Caddell later said, "I don't think the president . . . felt Ronald Reagan was well informed. I think that's a nice way to put it."[49]

Caddell was overruled by Carter and the hierarchy.

The Reagan campaign was unsurprisingly uncoordinated in its response to Carter's challenge. Bill Casey agreed in principle that the voters would find a debate between the two men useful, and Ed Meese said such a meeting was "highly possible," but Reagan told ABC News that he was still opposed to excluding Anderson.[50] Inside the campaign, the hawks and doves were going at it over whether to debate. Speaking for the doves, Stu Spencer said, "We don't need a debate."[51] Others were dubious. One Reagan aide said on background, "If the guy can't debate Jimmy Carter for one hour, maybe we're all making a mistake."[52] The Democrats, meanwhile, pressed the advantage. Strauss told reporters, "Carter does not need the debate. Reagan needs the debate."[53]

The editorialists who had praised Reagan only a short time earlier for bravely wanting to include Anderson in the fall debates now hotly denounced him for "ducking" a two-man confrontation, especially since the wind was going out of Anderson's sails.

Surprisingly, however, these editorial pages were supporting Reagan by a healthy margin over Carter. *Editor & Publisher* magazine surveyed hundreds of newspapers and as of the third week of October, 221 newspapers had endorsed the Gipper while only 59 supported Carter. The survey did not take into account the size or circulation of the publications or that 303 papers had yet to announce their decision, but it did defy the notion that the editorial pages were overwhelmingly liberal or biased against Reagan.[54]

Reagan got some more welcomed news when he received the endorsements of the National Association of Police Organizations, the largest police union in the country, and of the New York Patrolmen's Benevolent Association.[55] Beat cops had always liked Reagan.

But even with those small advances, Reagan wasn't slowing Carter down. The president got still another boost in the form of new government reports showing that the dead economy might slowly be coming to life. In September, production increased 1 percent, the first increase since May 1979, and personal income likewise moved up nearly 1 percent.[56] Detroit and the housing industry, too, were slowly getting off the mat. Inflation, interest rates, and unemployment remained terribly high, but Carter welcomed any good economic news.

IT REMAINED UNCLEAR WHETHER Reagan and Carter would ever participate in a one-on-one debate, but they engaged in a showdown of sorts at the annual Alfred E. Smith Memorial Foundation dinner in New York City. The white-tie charity event had become practically a command performance for presidential candidates, who were expected to entertain the dinner guests with irreverent and self-deprecating humor. The foundation had been created back in the 1940s to honor the memory of Al Smith, the New York governor who in 1928 became both the first Catholic and the first Irish American to win the presidential nomination of a major party. The Democrat was pummeled by Republican Herbert Hoover, but in that election Smith began to pull together the seemingly disparate groups of ethnic voters, city workers, blacks, rural folks, Roman Catholics, and southerners who, beginning with Franklin Roosevelt, would become the foundations of the modern Democratic Party. Carter had skillfully rebuilt this coalition in 1976, and now he needed to do so again.

But Carter stumbled badly as he addressed the crowd at the Al Smith event. The president did not help himself by blowing off the dinner and only arriving afterward to make his comments. Reagan, as was his custom, was there for the entire event, meeting people and taking the temperature of his audience before speaking. Carter goofed again when he told several jokes at Reagan's expense; at best they fell flat and at worst were booed—and this by an overwhelmingly Democratic crowd. Nancy Reagan fixed an icy cold gaze on Carter. The president's speech went downhill from there, as he then lectured the audience about religious tolerance in America. "I've studied the Bible all my life. But nowhere in the Bible, Old or New Testament, are there instructions on how to balance the budget or how to choose between the B1 bomber and the air-launched cruise missile."[57] The audience groaned loudly at Carter's sanctimonious remarks.

Reagan clearly understood the mood of the event much better than his opponent did. His speech was lighter, his jokes self-deprecating. Reagan led off with a yarn about a recent phone conversation he had supposedly had with Carter. In Reagan's tale, Carter said with amazement (here Reagan put on a mock southern accent), "Ronnie, how come you look younger every time I see a picture of you riding a horse?" To which Reagan said he responded, "It's easy, Jimmy. I just keep riding older horses."[58] Reagan played off the age issue again when he quipped that there was no truth to the "rumor that I was present at the original Al Smith dinner."[59] Then Reagan took note of Al Smith's first career: "What a president he would have made! He started out as an actor."[60] The audience roared.

Reagan turned serious for a moment when he brought up the issue of the hostages in Iran. Rising above all the rumors that the hostages would be freed before the election—including his own previous reference to a possible "October Surprise"—he said, "No one in America will rejoice more than I when America's long wait for a resolution of this crisis is over." He concluded by making moving remarks about Al Smith, "a man of peace, good will and profound faith." Reagan told of how Smith did not descend into bitterness the night he suffered his crushing defeat to Hoover, but instead said, in reference to his wife, "This is Katie's birthday, let's go upstairs and cut the cake." Reagan added, "That's what I call real class." The Gipper was rewarded with a standing ovation.[61]

Reagan had clearly won this round with Carter. Now his campaign faced a decision on a bigger fight—the one-on-one debate.

The Reagan camp was still divided on this issue. Stu Spencer and Bill Timmons remembered Gerald Ford's disastrous performance in his second debate with Carter in 1976 and didn't want to see a repeat of it. But even some of the doves recognized that Carter was scoring political points by repeatedly challenging Reagan on this subject. Carter continued to rise in the polls and Reagan continued to decline. Finally, the night Reagan addressed the Al Smith dinner, Spencer convened an emergency meeting of the campaign's high command to decide the issue once and for all. The Reaganites commandeered a suite on the top floor of the Waldorf Astoria to hash things out.

After a couple of hours spent arguing in the deep of night, the high command reached a virtually unanimous decision: Reagan would have to debate Carter to stop the hemorrhaging of his campaign. The following morning, over a 6 A.M. breakfast, Reagan met with his men, who told him of their view that the confrontation was now necessary. The strongest advocate was the newest member of the team, Jim Baker.[62] Baker's show of confidence in his candidate meant a lot to Mrs. Reagan.

But Spencer could tell that the Gipper was way ahead of them. A couple of days earlier, during his campaign swing through South Dakota, Reagan had told Nofziger, "Lynwood, I think we're going to have to debate."[63]

Reagan announced on the tarmac at LaGuardia Airport that he would now debate Carter, dropping his stance that Anderson had to be included. In his statement, Reagan said that given the independent's sagging support in the polls, the League of Women Voters was justified in excluding him.[64] Anderson squawked, but there was little else he could do.

The League of Women Voters immediately issued revised invitations to a forum at the Cleveland Convention Center, tentatively scheduled for October 28, only one week before the election. A hurried meeting was arranged for representatives of both camps to haggle over the details. Jim Baker didn't try to spin things, saying bluntly that Reagan was debating only because he had fallen in the polls. The truth was that a lack of enthusiasm for Jimmy Carter was not enough of a reason to vote for Reagan. Reagan had yet to convince the American people that he would be an acceptable alternative to Carter.

The ferocious campaign between Ronald Reagan and Jimmy Carter in many ways had come down to an all-or-nothing proposition for both men. A Reaganite complained that it would be like "rolling the dice in one big crapshoot that could blow it all."[65] With only a week to go after the debate, the loser would have little time to repair the damage. In all likelihood, the winner would be the next president of the United States.

Once the debate was on the schedule, both campaigns' advertising went negative. The Carter campaign ran five-minute spots featuring the president saying that Reagan wanted to engage in a "shootout at the O.K. Corral" with the Soviets. Reagan's commercials stuck to the economy. The ads showed him standing in a field, looking into the camera, saying, "Everywhere I travel in America I hear this phrase over and over again. 'Where is it going to end?' Record inflation has robbed the purchasing power of your dollar. . . . I'm prepared to do something about it."[66]

Reagan also used television to try to refute Carter's attacks. The campaign purchased a half-hour on CBS for $150,000 for Reagan to talk about foreign policy in an attempt to reassure nervous voters, especially women. The theme of the address was "Strategy of Peace in the '80s."[67] Reagan used the word "peace" so often in the speech that some writers referred to Reagan's "peace offensive." The GOP nominee made his case that peace would come from strength, and that nothing would force the Soviets to the negotiating table quicker than a militarily strong America. He called for junking SALT II and starting over with SALT III: "The way to avoid an arms race is not to simply let the Soviets race ahead. We need to remove their incentive to race ahead by making it clear to them that we can and will compete if need be." Reagan cited Senator John Glenn of Ohio, a Democrat who also opposed SALT II.[68]

Carter didn't let up, charging that Reagan's position on nuclear armament could lead to war because he sought superiority over the Soviets. The president claimed in a live radio broadcast from the Oval Office that Reagan was pushing America toward the "nuclear precipice," and called Reagan "extraordinarily naïve."[69] Carter announced that he would once again seek Senate ratification of SALT II, even though the Democratic-controlled body had put the treaty on ice after the Soviets invaded Afghanistan.

More and more columns appeared speculating that Reagan was about to blow the election. In state after state, it was too close to call. Confidentially (but lacking in confidence), one of Reagan's key aides told a reporter, "I think Reagan is slipping everywhere . . . If he doesn't do something dramatic, he's going to lose it by attrition."[70]

Most of the Carterites were almost giddy. They had gotten the debate they wanted with Reagan and the president was on offense. Despite some lingering concerns about several states in the South, they felt, to a person, that the president's home region would not give up on one of its own. One Carter aide confidently told *Newsweek*, "The pieces are in place for us to win."[71]

To shore up his backyard, Carter headed to Texas, Florida, and Louisiana. On the stump, his touch was noticeably lighter, less abrasive than it had been. Ted Kennedy had finally fallen into line, working crowds in New Jersey and other states, exhorting them to send Carter back to the White House. Kennedy had come around for two good reasons. One, his own political future: his aides were already plotting a 1984 campaign. Second, money: half of the money he raised on the trail for Carter would go toward the $1.7 million debt his own campaign had rung up. At one joint event, the two men finally clasped hands over their heads in the very pose that Carter had coveted at their convention.[72]

JACK GERMOND AND JULES Witcover, the perceptive political duo for the *Washington Star*, paid a visit to the youthful governor of Arkansas, Bill Clinton, for his assessment of how the campaign was shaping up. Though Carter was well ahead of Reagan in Arkansas, young Clinton, who was already a Jedi Master when it came to politics, distanced himself from the president and said that Reagan "comes across here as a guy who has a coherent vision."[73] Clinton was running for reelection and had his own headaches, including the thousands of Cuban criminals Carter had dumped on his state after Castro had dumped them on Carter.

NO ARMS NEGOTIATIONS INVOLVING heads of state were as deliberative as the talks setting the ground rules for the first and only debate between Jimmy Carter and Ronald Reagan. The campaigns spent two days fighting over the finest points of format and presentation. From the reporters who would serve on the panel, to camera angles, to tickets for the live debate, to who would walk on stage first, nothing was too petty to squabble over.

Jim Baker urged the same format as in 1976, but Bob Strauss wanted fewer reporters on the panel and time for the candidates to cross-examine each other. Baker shot down cross-examination by the contestants.[74]

Carter's team wanted the presidential seal on the front of his podium. "Yeah, right," was Baker's reply. No seal.

The Reagan men wanted the podiums as close together as possible to accentuate the difference in height between the 6'1" Reagan and the 5'9" Carter. Nothing doing, said Strauss. They would be as far apart as possible without actually going off the stage.

Carter's men pressed for a two-hour debate. The thinking was that over a long confrontation the older Reagan might tire in front of millions of Americans. Baker suggested one hour. The two sides compromised on ninety minutes.[75]

There would be no opening statements, but there would be closing statements. A coin toss backstage would decide who got to choose who would take the first question and who would make his closing comments first.

Symbolically, Reagan would stand to the audience's right, Carter to the left.

Sandwiches were brought in to slake the hunger of the debate negotiators. At one point, reporters in the hallway heard Strauss through a partially opened door yell, "I don't think you've heard anything I've said since we came in here!"[76]

A Bush-Mondale debate was junked, as the Reaganites secretly wanted. Baker said with a straight face that Bush was one of only two surrogates on the road for Reagan and he was needed out there. Mondale's chief of staff, Dick Moe, stormed out halfway through the second day of the session when it became clear that Bush would not be allowed to debate.[77]

At one point, Strauss excused himself to call Jody Powell at the White House for a clarification. He joked to Baker, "You know, I'm pretty close to Carter. I can go in the bedroom with Carter and ask him anything in the world, but Jody can go into the bathroom."[78] Four years of fighting and drinking on the East Coast's "Cannery Row" had taken their toll on Powell, though he was still a young man of thirty-seven. He had permanent dark circles under his eyes and was a chain smoker. Burning the candle at both ends was beginning to wear him down. The tough town had also rubbed the wedded Georgian the wrong way, as when he awoke one morning to see in black and white in the *Washington Post* an unsourced allegation that he was engaged in an extramarital affair.[79] By all other reports, Powell was a happily married man.

Baker, a.k.a. "The Waco Kid," ran a successful bluff, audaciously suggesting that the debate should be held the night before the election, pitching it in the guise of good government. In between the two days of negotiations, Baker went on ABC's *Good Morning America* to float the notion.[80] The Carterites countered instead with October 28 . . . which was exactly the date Baker and the Reaganites wanted in the first place. Holding a debate the night before the election would have left the Reagan campaign absolutely no time to fix things if Reagan, as some in his camp feared—and the Carter camp hoped—made a gaffe in the live, nationally televised debate. October 28 also appealed to the Reaganites because it allowed their candidate more than a week to get ready for the debate.

Carter, of course, was born ready. Yet he faced a problem. For weeks he had been daring Reagan to debate. His men had gone further, letting it be known that they were champing at the bit for a debate and that they were utterly convinced that the president would trounce Reagan in a one-on-one setting. Now the debate was a go, and they had managed to inflate expectations sky high.

REAGAN PRESSED ON. HE went to Illinois, yet again, accompanied by Nancy and two hundred reporters and staffers who filled seven buses. In Springfield he laid a wreath at Lincoln's tomb and then, in the fashion of the state, rubbed the nose on the statue of Abe for good luck. The night before, he'd gone back to Eureka for a boisterous homecoming rally in the Reagan Gymnasium. The last time he'd been there, his alma mater was unmoved. This time, however, they welcomed the football team's old right guard. He attended the homecoming football game the next day against Concordia. At the rally, Reagan's old coach, Ralph McKinzie, eighty-six, presented the Gipper with a jersey that read "Reagan 80" on the back. Ominously, Concordia clobbered Eureka, 33–13.[81]

BOTH REAGAN AND CARTER were playing it safe until their showdown at the Mistake by the Lake. Heading into their one and only debate, Carter had made it pretty well known what he thought of Reagan, which was not much. "Word went around that Carter expected to swamp Reagan," recalled Reagan speechwriter Peter Hannaford.[82]

The Gipper, on the other hand, had been more circumspect. Only years later would it become clear what Reagan really thought of the thirty-ninth president. When asked in an interview whether Reagan was intimidated by being on the same stage as Carter, Stu Spencer replied that, no, Reagan wasn't intimidated because he didn't see Carter so much as the president of the United States and Leader of the Free World.

Reagan simply saw Carter as a "little shit."[83]

34

ON DECK

*"Since we can't do anything about the hostages anyway,
we might as well go on doing what we can do."*

James Addison Baker III had not taken his grandfather's advice to stay out of politics. He might have listened to the old man had he not lost his young wife, Mary, to cancer in 1970. A widower at the age of thirty-nine, Baker was alone, trying to raise four sons. He was shattered, tried alcohol for solace, but was fortunate to find out that, unlike other men in his family, he had no stomach for booze. The former U.S. Marine did, however, have more than enough intestinal fortitude for the political game. The tall and cool Texan may have missed his calling by a hundred years, though. Unflappable, Baker would have been the best poker player west of the Pecos had he lived in those times.

In addition to building the family law practice in Houston, he turned to politics, at the suggestion of his tennis partner, George H. W. Bush, as an outlet for the pain and emptiness in his life. Baker soon made the Harris County GOP into a potent operation. His appetite whetted, he eventually went to Washington to work in the Commerce Department during the Ford administration. But he wanted more, and fate lent Baker a hand.

In 1976 a heavy-drinking crony of Gerald Ford's, Jack Stiles from Michigan, died in an accident one night, wrapping his car around a tree. Stiles was slated to be Ford's delegate hunter but the job fell to Baker, who—probably more than any other man—kept Ronald Reagan from winning the 1976 nomination with his yeoman's efforts. Baker orchestrated the campaign to woo some 150 uncommitted delegates while also keeping wavering delegates in the Ford camp by holding their hands and listening to their gripes and demands. Only a man with the patience of Job—someone like Jim Baker—could have handled the job so well.

In gratitude, Ford promoted Baker to run the fall campaign. Though the president did not win reelection, Baker got high marks from many for bringing Ford from thirty points down in the polls to losing by less than two. There was some grumbling because Baker had left $1 million in the Ford coffers unspent when it could have helped in close states. Baker later said that because of the Ford committee's accounting glitches, he hadn't known that money was still available.[1] After 1976, Baker liked to joke that he was the only Republican in recent memory to have run an incumbent's campaign and not run afoul of the law, unlike Ike's Sherman Adams and Nixon's John Mitchell.

After Ford's loss, Baker headed back to Texas and ran for attorney general in 1978, losing. His campaign manager was Frank Donatelli. Years later, Baker, by then a national power broker, liked to josh people, "I owe everything I have become to Frank Donatelli, because if he had been a decent campaign manager, I would have been stuck down in Austin!"[2] Baker was only ribbing Donatelli, who in fact had done a good job under difficult circumstances.

Ronald Reagan came in to campaign for Baker and Baker received a generous contribution from the National Conservative Political Action Committee, but to no avail. Immediately after losing, Baker was approached by his old friend Bush about pitching in on his longshot presidential quest. (In the process he managed to irk his old boss Ford, who even at the Republican convention in 1980 was still miffed that Baker and Bush had not kept their powder dry until he made his decision whether or not to run.)[3] Though Bush failed to wrest the nomination from Reagan, his shocking win in Iowa, his other primary wins, and the fact that his campaign lasted well beyond what it should have, were chalked up to Baker's skills and Bush's tenacity.

Baker had come to the Reagan operation almost by accident. At the convention he was certain that Reagan was going to take Ford as his running mate. Headed to the airport on his way out of Detroit, Baker bumped into Stu Spencer, who urged him to delay his plans and stick around. Spencer advised the campaign to grab Baker, though he was 0-for-2 at the national level.[4]

The first entreaty Baker received from the Reagan campaign came from Lyn Nofziger, a man with whom he would later become bitter enemies. Baker demurred, but when he was approached a second time, this time with Bill Casey offering an elevated title, he jumped at the chance. Conservatives around Reagan grumbled about the moderate Baker, whom they saw as an interloper. Nonetheless, he brought with him the reputation of a man who got things done. Most importantly, Nancy Reagan liked him. That was that.

Bill Casey handed Baker the entire debate portfolio. He would be responsible for negotiating the arrangements and preparing the candidate. With just over a week to go before the Carter-Reagan debate, the campaign set aside a full three days out of Reagan's schedule for Baker and his team to get the Gipper ready.

Casey also handed Baker a large envelope and told him he might find something interesting in it. He did not tell Baker where he'd gotten it.[5] Baker opened the package and inside were three large bound books. He flipped through the pages and then sent them along to David Gergen, who had come over from the Bush operation as well, handling research. The bound tomes were briefing books that had been compiled for Jimmy Carter's own debate prep.[6]

Around this time, the shadowy and unsavory Paul Corbin would show up occasionally at the Republican nominee's headquarters in Virginia. Sometimes Corbin would sign in to see Baker, other times to see Casey. Several of the meetings lasted well over an hour.[7]

CARTER'S CAMPAIGN WAS GOING for broke. Every staff member brought in by Carter was given a second job of delivering his reelection. Many members of the administration received the very same talking points that went to Carter himself, and they were tasked with campaigning for the president across the country—working the press more than the public.[8] Cabinet officials alone reportedly spent one hundred days crisscrossing America. Only Attorney General Benjamin Civiletti, mired in the Billy Carter scandal, was not campaigning.

Government officials spread out across the heartland, awarding federal contracts high and low—three million dollars for retraining displaced workers in Toledo; money for industrial parks and urban projects, most in battleground states. All of the money was handed out with the cautionary note that if Reagan were elected, the goodies would run out. President Carter himself directed the release of $238 million in previously frozen highway-building funds for Texas—where polls had the presidential race dead even—even though the state had yet to comply with the minority-hiring strings that came along with the federal money.[9] Walter Mondale got in on the fun in New Jersey when he announced a $6 million aid package to build a water pipeline for the state.[10] Carter also halted the purchase of military equipment by Saudi Arabia, which Israel had opposed. The *Washington Star* described it as a "policy change." Indeed, earlier Carter had personally overruled his own national security adviser and defense secretary to allow the sale of refueling equipment for F-15 jets to the Saudis.[11]

The Republican opposition called the Carterites' politicization of the bureaucracy "unprecedented," and others leveled charges of misuse of federal funds.[12] Carter's people simply shrugged their shoulders at such charges, knowing that after the election any corruption accusations would be swept under the rug, regardless of who won.

The business of Washington had ground to a halt. Congress was in recess, campaigning for reelection, the cabinet was on the road for Carter, and the mice of the bureaucracy were playing—coming in later, taking long lunches, and leaving early. The halls of Congress were hushed, empty of members, staff, and lobbyists. Barstools and lunch tables went begging. Washington hostesses stopped holding parties until the matter was settled in November. No sense in insulting the eventual winners by casting canapés before swinish losers.

Carter held an Oval Office press conference in which he said that Reagan "did not understand." Reagan, on the trail in Kentucky that day, threw some hot rhetoric back in Carter's face. Standing on the flatbed of a blue truck provided by the Teamsters, Reagan said it was true, he didn't understand—he didn't understand why America was losing the Cold War, why people went without jobs, why inflation was raging out of control, or "why fifty-two Americans have been held hostage for almost a year now!"[13] A man yelled out in response, "Because Carter's incompetent!"[14] Reagan was on fire and the crowd went wild.

Reagan now grabbed the hostage issue by the throat and told audiences the long captivity was "a humiliation and disgrace" to the country.[15] He walloped Carter, saying, "I believe that this administration's foreign policy helped create the entire situation that made their kidnap possible."[16]

By now the bad blood between the candidates was palpable. There was no doubt that Carter would return fire in this war of words. The president charged Reagan with breaking a campaign pledge not to make a "political football" out of the hostages. Carter also implied that Reagan was endangering the lives of the hostages.[17]

Reagan, angry from the months of attacks from the Carter campaign—the racist charges, the slurs on his intelligence—shot right back. "I don't think I've broken that pledge," Reagan acidly told reporters in Kansas City. "I would think that breaking such a pledge might be if I waited until 7:15 on Election Day and then brought the subject up, as he did in the Wisconsin primary."[18] Carter's cheap bit of political theater from back in the spring—going on national television to announce a breakthrough in the negotiations when apparently there was nothing of the sort, at a time when Ted Kennedy was closing the gap—was coming back to haunt him.

Carter continued his counterattack on the hostage issue. In Texas he chided Reagan for having a "secret plan" to secure the release of the hostages. The president drew a comparison to Richard Nixon's statements in 1968 that he had such a plan to end the Vietnam War. "Republicans have a habit of spreading a lot of horse manure around right before an election," Carter railed, "and lately, it's getting pretty deep all over this country." The partisan crowd in Waco ate it up, though Reagan had never suggested that he had a "secret plan," only "some ideas" (not specified) on how to win their release.[19]

Carter's campaign was convinced that Reagan had made a major mistake in bringing up the hostages, that it was a sign of weakness and that Reagan's faltering campaign was getting desperate. In the end, the president's men felt, the issue would favor Carter and not Reagan. Or so they hoped.

But Reagan was getting political cover from John Anderson. The independent candidate weighed in on the hostage issue, saying that the president had failed to see it coming.[20] The stakes had gotten personal for Anderson, too. Even as his political hopes dwindled, he made sure to blast his political enemy, Carter.

The campaign was now downright ugly. Carter, in Florida, told an audience, "When you're sitting across the negotiating table with President Brezhnev . . . you can't rely on three-by-five cards, and you can't read a TelePrompTer." Carter implied that unlike Reagan, he was able to "think on his feet."[21] In Texas, the Republican governor, William Clements, called Carter a "goddamned liar," and former senator Ralph Yarborough retorted that Clements was a "guttersnipe." Democrats said Clements's outburst was just more evidence that Reagan was slipping in the Lone Star State. Mondale, in the state, said Reagan was "an enemy of Mexican-Americans and blacks."[22]

A television station in New Orleans received a death threat aimed at Carter. The threat was on the Secret Service agents' minds when some lights loudly went out during the president's rally in the Big Easy.[23] They moved quickly, but it turned out to be only a blown fuse.

Reagan also received his fair share of death threats, which the Secret Service and the FBI had to track down and monitor. One threat came from the "American Indian Party," which asked Senator S. I. Hayakawa to help "even to the point of killing" Reagan.[24] Another warned Reagan not to go to Oregon: "If Reagan comes here he may get his head blowen [sic] off."[25]

THE IVY LEAGUE HAD weighed in on the election without anybody asking it to do so. In a poll of 2,500 undergraduates attending Harvard, Cornell, Penn, Brown, and Princeton, 41 percent were for Anderson, 29 percent for Carter, and fewer than 15 pvercent for Reagan. Modestly, 45 percent of those students surveyed thought they were smarter than any of the three men running; at Harvard, unsurprisingly, that figure shot to over 50 percent.[26] Not to be outdone, the supercilious

Harvard Crimson endorsed the socialist candidacy of Barry Commoner, running on the "Citizens Party" ticket.[27]

A poll that people actually cared about came from the *New York Times* and CBS News with just ten days to go until the election. The poll confirmed Carter's lead over Reagan, 39 percent to 38 percent. Anderson was at 9 percent. To be sure, those numbers made the race a virtual tie, but the trends of all the national polling favored the president. Carter now had the advantage after he and Reagan had traded places four times in the past several months in the New York Times poll. He was ahead in the South and the Midwest, essentially tied in the East; and appeared to be coming on strong in the West, down only 40–34 percent. Independents were moving toward Carter, when only a few months earlier they had strongly favored Reagan.[28] All that seemed left for Carter was to polish off Reagan in their debate.

Jimmy Carter was on the verge of one of the biggest comebacks in American political history. He had proven himself to be one of the toughest (and, some thought, meanest) political operators around. Like his predecessors Truman and Nixon, he was obsessed with politics, down to the minutiae of polling and cross-tabs and precinct voting histories. Truman and Nixon had few interests outside of politics, and Carter, just a bit more. Truman liked to drink and play cards. Nixon used to be a very good poker player, before he quit. Carter, a severe Baptist, did not play cards, but he did enjoy political gambling. Now, on a winning streak, he was ready to put all of his chips into the middle for the biggest pot in the world: the presidency of the United States.

MRS. REAGAN, WHO NORMALLY did not get into the public hurly-burly of campaigning, had finally had enough. In a campaign commercial, she went right after Jimmy Carter, saying, "I deeply, deeply resent Mr. Carter's attempt to paint my husband as someone he is not." She also called Carter "vicious."[29]

If Reagan could be irresistible on some matters, Nancy could be downright immovable, especially when it came to people she believed were hurting "Ronnie's" career. As of October 1980, it had become apparent that she'd had a much bigger—if subtle—role in the dismissal of John Sears, Jim Lake, and Charlie Black on the day of the New Hampshire primary months earlier. Michele Davis, an attractive blonde aide, was told almost as soon as she went on the Reagan plane that as far as Mrs. Reagan was concerned, good looks were no substitute for good works.[30]

Now, as the maelstrom of the closing days of the campaign swirled around them, Nancy proved once again to be Reagan's port in the storm. If possible, the tumult of the final days drew the Reagans closer together. They turned to each other even more for comfort. She really was his best friend and confidante. For his part, he had to be something very special for Nancy Reagan. After all, years before, as an aspiring actress, she had once dated Clark Gable.

THE REAGAN CAMPAIGN WAS desperate to reverse Carter's momentum. Dick Wirthlin, Reagan's placid pollster, disputed the new poll by the *New York Times*, but the media—who love a horse race—weren't listening.[31] Several of the bigger newspapers concluded in-depth studies of the nine "big ticket" states with the bulk of the Electoral College votes, and they all came to the conclusion that the race was too close to call.

Wirthlin, though, was right: hidden in the polling data were a couple pieces of good news for Reagan. First, 18 percent of Democrats were prepared to cross over and vote for Reagan.[32] Second, Jewish voters were holding back on Carter; in 1976 the Georgian had received 64 percent of their vote, but in the new polling he could not top 40 percent. Though Jewish Americans constituted less than 3 percent of the vote, they were a hugely influential voting bloc, especially in New York and Florida, two states that had gone for Carter in 1976 but that Reagan was fighting hard for in 1980.[33]

Reagan was picking up support from figures across the political spectrum. Filling his plane were GOP establishmentarians including Senator Howard Baker, former ambassador to Great Britain Anne Armstrong, and two former secretaries of state, William Rogers and Henry Kissinger.

Reagan welcomed the endorsement of former Minnesota senator Gene McCarthy, whose surprisingly strong showing as an antiwar Democrat in the 1968 New Hampshire primary had prompted President Lyndon Johnson not to seek reelection. The former garden-variety liberal had evolved into a libertarian, especially on free-speech matters. On such issues he and Reagan were in complete agreement. Besides, McCarthy loathed Carter and had little use for his old Senate colleague Walter Mondale.[34] McCarthy once dismissed Mondale as having "the soul of a vice president."[35] In endorsing Reagan, McCarthy said he hadn't been enthusiastic about a presidential candidate since Adlai Stevenson. When an incredulous reported asked, "Including yourself?" without missing a beat McCarthy replied, "Probably least enthusiastic about myself!" The reporters laughed uproariously.[36]

In Mississippi, Reagan received endorsements from two men who had been on opposites sides of the civil rights issue. One was Democrat John Bell Williams, the former segregationist governor of Mississippi. Williams told a crowd that

Carter was "a man who put aside [Thomas] Jefferson and picked up Karl Marx." The other was Charles Evers, the well-known black leader in Mississippi whose brother, civil-rights leader Medgar Evers, had been killed by a sniper in 1963.[37] Reagan's tough but able southern field director, Kenny Klinge, was handling the balancing act in the South of reaching out to blacks without antagonizing whites.

Reagan also picked up the endorsement of Republican Edward Brooke of Massachusetts, the first African-American to be popularly elected to the U.S. Senate. The former senator said that the Gipper's election would "herald a bright day . . . for many minorities who believe that this man is very sensitive to their problems."[38]

Not surprisingly, Reagan did not win the endorsement of the *New York Times*. The Gray Lady hadn't endorsed a Republican since the war hero Eisenhower in 1952. Still, the paper's selection of Carter was reluctant at best. The paper praised Reagan's compassion, saying that he was "clear, self-confident, optimistic." But the *Times* argued that Reagan was guilty of "appealing simplicity," that "his political values are idyllic." "Too often," the paper concluded, "Ronald Reagan's clarity and robustness sound more like bluster, bravado and refusal to recognize that America is no longer, if it ever was, king of the world."[39] The *Times*'s halfhearted endorsement of Carter only reflected the fact the paper was ideologically closer to the president than to the Californian.

The Gipper even managed to get the backing of another union. This endorsement would, in retrospect, seem ironic: it came from the Professional Air Traffic Controllers Organization (PATCO).[40]

AT 901 SOUTH HIGHLAND Street in Arlington, Virginia, the headquarters of the Reagan-Bush campaign, Bill Casey was utterly convinced—as were many staffers—that Carter was doing his utmost to get the hostages released before the election. Casey had recruited hundreds of retired military and CIA agents to monitor the news and global rumors about the hostages and any development in Iran. Every morning at 6 o'clock he convened a meeting with Wirthlin and the campaign's research director, Reserve Admiral Robert Garrick, to review the day's news on the hostages.[41]

Asked by a reporter what the Reagan campaign would do if the hostages were released before the election, an aide replied somberly, "Punt. If he [Carter] gets the bodies out, that's the ballgame." Yet not all Reaganites were so fearful of an October Surprise. Some simply recognized that the matter was out of their hands and not worth obsessing over. One aide said, "Since we can't do anything about the hostages anyway, we might as well go on doing what we can do."[42] Others within the Reagan camp were less resigned. They believed that there was a down-side for the Carter campaign in all the talk about the hostages' release. Rumors had been flying for weeks that a deal was imminent—the latest buzz held that the hostages would be repatriated the day of the debate—so expectations had been raised yet again. If the fifty-two Americans did not come home soon, Carter would have to face an even more demoralized electorate.

The Reagan campaign had done a good job raising the issue, playing on peo-ple's cynicism about Carter's perceived manipulation of the crisis. Casey sent Rea-gan a memo arguing that release of the hostages at this point would be seen as a "political trick . . . and the American people would wonder why Carter hadn't done it sooner."[43]

In any case, Washington was awash in hostage and political rumors.

BOTH THE DEMOCRATS AND the Republicans were targeting toss-up states. Since Texas was still a dead heat, Ted Kennedy went to San Antonio to fire up enthusi-astic Hispanic voters—an important bloc for Carter, since they now represented nearly 15 percent of the electorate in Texas. To rally the crowd, Kennedy invoked the memory of his long-dead brother. "The thousand days are like an evening gone, but they are not forgotten." Teddy made his wistful remarks at John F. Ken-nedy High School.[44]

Reagan was campaigning through the South at the same time, pushing on to Florida after stumping in Mississippi. Even with the hostages going on one year in Tehran, the economy was his bread-and-butter issue. Making his case against Carter in Florida, he charged that inflation had destroyed the fixed earnings of retirees.[45]

The latest economic news reinforced Reagan's message. As if in anticipation of Carter's reelection, the stock market, which had been staging a comeback since the GOP convention, pulled back sharply, falling more than 15 points to close at 939.[46] Then, on the last Friday of October, the Bureau of Labor Statistics released the final inflation report before the election. Inflation for September, the last month measured, was one full percent, making the annualized rate 12.7 percent.[47] This marked the third year in a row of double-digit inflation. Everything was up again: food, gasoline, clothing. Reagan ripped Carter over the new inflation report, and Carter weakly replied to a town-hall audience in New Jersey that the bad inflation report was just one more reason why Reagan's huge tax cuts were to be avoided. Implementing Reagan's tax cuts would be "just like pouring gasoline on a fire," the president said, reminding his audience that George Bush had once called them "voodoo economics."[48]

Reagan shot back that by reminding voters that back in 1976, when the "misery index" (the combination of unemployment and inflation) stood at 12, Carter had said that Gerald Ford was unqualified to be elected. The misery index in October of 1980 was over 20. "By his own words, he has no right to seek reelection," Reagan declared.[49]

Carter headed to his home court, the White House, where he addressed two hundred black ministers, calling on them to help with a big turnout. The Reverend Joseph Lowery, head of the Southern Christian Leadership Conference, endorsed Carter and said "the forces of insensitivity to human suffering, of racism, of militarism, of violence, of negativism are gravitating in and toward" Reagan.[50] The networks later broadcast the successful event.

Frustrated, Reagan said, "I think it is apparent that his whole campaign effort has been one of personal attacks, trying to make the issue of this campaign me, rather than his record of failure."[51]

SINCE ANDERSON WAS EXCLUDED from the debate to be broadcast live on all three networks, Ted Turner, who took a backseat to no one when it came to promotion, announced that Anderson would participate—in a fashion. The independent would appear on Turner's tiny cable system, CNN, to answer the same questions posed to Reagan and Carter, complete with rebuttal, all through the magic of taping and splicing.[52]

In a converted garage at Wexford, Jim Baker assembled his team of debate briefers and mock questioners, which included columnists George Will and Pat Buchanan and foreign-policy adviser Jeane Kirkpatrick. Playing the role of Carter, because he'd done such a good job mimicking Anderson, was a young congressman from Michigan, David Stockman.[53] Stockman, just thirty-three years old, was considered a wunderkind, a real up-and-comer in GOP politics. All foresaw a bright future for the young man.

JUST FOUR DAYS BEFORE the debate, Reagan took to the airwaves in a nationally televised address on ABC. Unlike the peace-through-strength speech of a week earlier, these remarks contained nothing even slightly apologetic or explanatory. Reagan focused on the terrible conditions of the economy. He opened by quoting Thomas Wolfe, who once wrote about the "mighty music" of America; that music, Reagan said, had been replaced by the silence of the Carter malaise. "In many places the mighty music has been all but silenced. Where once there was the great, confident roar of American progress and growth and optimism, there is now the eerie, ghostly silence of economic stagnation, unemployment, inflation, and despair." The "silence" of the shuttered factory, the "silence" of the neighbor-hood, the "silence" of the desolate farm now cast a pall over the nation.[54]

Reagan recounted a story in which a young woman asked Carter how it was that government could not fix inflation and unemployment. The president replied, "You know, people tend to dwell on temporary inconveniences and the transient problems that our nation faces." Reagan was aghast at Carter's insensitivity. He reviewed the evidence: Housing starts were down 30 percent in four years, and a thirty-year mortgage on a $47,000 house had gone from $306 per month to $556 per month—an 81 percent rise in just four years. The ruin of Carter's economy was "on a scale so vast in dimensions, so broad, with effects so devastating, that it is virtually without parallel in American history."[55]

Reagan closed his address in the most human terms possible. He told of a fifth-grade girl in Fort Wayne, Indiana, Andrea Baden, who wanted a pair of roller skates. So she saved her allowance and went to the store, only to find that the price had gone up. She waited and saved some more and went again to the store, only to find that the roller skates had gone up in price once more. So she patiently saved some more but then found to her dismay that the price had gone up yet again. Plaintively, she said, "It's just not fair." Reagan replied, "Well that's right, Andrea: What Mr. Carter has done to this country's economy just isn't fair. It just isn't right."[56]

He closed by saying, "I would like very much to do something about that lack of fairness to hard-working Americans and, Andrea, to thrifty Americans like you. I need your help, your support. But first of all, I need your commitment, your hope, and your belief in this great nation's ability to begin again. I think the time has come for fair play for Americans. If you agree, together we can have a new beginning, for ourselves and for our children."[57]

The campaign had plunked down $150,000 for this speech, but if it had been ten times that amount, it still would have been a bargain.[58] A Reagan aide said, "We're going to beat [Carter] over the head with the incompetence thing from now until the election."[59] In the days leading up to the debate, Reagan settled on this theme and audiences reacted favorably.

Peter Dailey's ads focused on the competence question. The Reagan cam-paign was running hard-hitting spots focused on Carter's record. Dailey had capi-talized on an oversight by Gerald Rafshoon: the Democratic adman had neglected to copyright the commercials he had produced for Carter in 1976, meaning that they were on the open market for anybody to use—or abuse. Reagan's campaign and conservative independent groups employed the four-year-old ads to mock Carter for his broken promises.[60]

Reagan wanted the competence issues front and center, and on the eve of the big debate he got an assist in this area from an unlikely source: Libya's dictator, Muammar al-Gaddafi. Gaddafi ordered his French-made Mirage fighter jets and Soviet MIG-23s and 25s to harass U.S. Navy jets in the Mediterranean. The unstable dictator then sent letters to Carter—and to Reagan in the form of a full-page ad in major newspapers—telling them to stay out of the affairs of the region. Under Carter, the American fighters were under standing orders not to engage the Libyans in aerial combat, even as the Libyan fighters locked their missiles on the American planes.[61]

American fecklessness was on display for all the world to see.

For Reagan, the incident was just more evidence of Carter's "demonstrated inability to govern our nation."[62]

CARTER DIDN'T RESPOND TO Reagan's ABC speech. There wasn't much he could say to spin the economic news. Instead, he hit Reagan for changing his position on the grain embargo of the Soviets over their invasion of Afghanistan. Reagan had initially supported it, but when farmers pointed out that they alone were bearing the burden, he called for a general boycott of trade with the Russians or the blockade of Cuba.[63] Carter didn't address his own shift on the matter, as the United States had recently begun selling grain to the Soviets once again. Alas, the Russians reported yet another crop failure, this one owing to too much rain.[64] In the past, it had been not enough rain. In the Soviets' collectivist world, things were never "just right."

Agriculture Secretary Bob Bergland, complying with the White House's directive to all cabinet secretaries, did his part to help the president's campaign. Carter's remarks were rebroadcast on rural radio stations.[65]

Now the president needed to hunker down and get ready for the big debate. He jetted from Ohio to Camp David for a day of preparation. Sam Popkin, a college professor, had been recruited to stand in for Reagan in their mock debates. Several of their sessions were contentious, and Carter stormed out more than once, so angry was he with Popkin's rhetorical hits.[66]

At one point in the debate prep, the president made a reference to asking his daughter, Amy, for advice. Jody Powell said that the comment "had not come across, did not quite work."[67] Carter's aides advised him not to make any policy references to his thirteen-year-old daughter.

The president's plan for the debate was to go right at Reagan, hitting him on several issues of which he had changed his mind. Carter also wanted to show off his own command of data. But the Reaganites questioned the president's unwavering confidence in his ability to take on Reagan. A few days earlier Ed Meese had pointed out to the *Wall Street Journal* that Carter would have a harder time making assaults on Reagan with the Republican standing right there on the stage.

"We've found," Meese said, "that when more people see Ronald Reagan, they like what they see."[68]

35

CLEVELAND

"Are you better off than you were four years ago?"

Kennedy family confidant and historian Arthur Schlesinger bumped into his old friend Bill Casey in Washington just as autumn was deepening and there was a snap in the air. They had first met in the Second World War when Casey was stationed in London working for the OSS. The two men had little in common, politically, but they were both members in good standing of the Washington–New York political establishment.

Casey introduced the Kennedyite to Reagan's top aides Ed Meese and Dick Wirthlin. Since Schlesinger loathed Jimmy Carter, they knew he was a temporary ally. They confided the bad news revealed by Wirthlin's polling: under Carter's relentless attacks, Reagan had "lost 12 points on capacity to keep the peace" but Carter had only "lost 3 points on decency"—"a pretty good trade-off from Carter's viewpoint."[1] As Carter's mother, "Mizz Lillian," once said, her son was "a beautiful cat with sharp claws."[2]

The latest polls showed that the race was as tight as ever. Most national surveys had Carter ahead of Reagan or the race statistically tied with the momentum on Carter's side. An ABC poll released just before the debate did show that Reagan had moved into a small lead over the president, 45–42 percent.[3] It had Reagan leading in twenty-four states with 217 electoral votes and Carter ahead in fourteen states with 146 electoral votes.[4] But Republicans could not rest easy with that assessment, since a new poll by *Time* had Carter ahead, 42–41 percent. In *Time*'s breakdown of seven Rust Belt states, Carter had broken out to a seven-point edge over Reagan. Even more important, 62 percent of Americans had confidence in Carter's ability to handle foreign affairs. Moreover, support for Carter's economic programs had improved markedly, with 69 percent of Americans expressing confidence in them.[5]

The Midwest was, as *U.S. News & World Report* called it, a "slugfest."[6] While a St. Louis Post-Dispatch poll had Reagan at 36 and Carter at 32 in Missouri,[7] a St. Louis Globe-Democrat poll had it just the opposite, with the president at 35 and Reagan at 28 percent.[8]

"Tense" was the oft-used—overused—phrase in both camps. Even the placid Meese was observed snapping at reporters. Press aide Jim Brady ran down the aisles of the campaign plane as it flew over a forest fire in Louisiana, joking to reporters, "Killer trees! Killer trees!" It was a mirthful reference to Reagan's earlier claim about trees and air pollution, but he was temporarily banished from the aircraft.[9] Speechwriter Ken Khachigian also joined in the fun, but he was not caught and punished like Brady.[10]

Many had lost what they needed most in these last few hours: a sense of humor.

Gerald Ford had temporarily set aside his animosity for Reagan to rally support for the GOP candidate. Ford and Reagan—especially Ford—still had little use for each other.[11] But Ford was a competitive and partisan Republican, happy to do his part to hammer Carter. On CBS's Sunday morning show, *Face the Nation*, he returned to the rumors that Carter might orchestrate the release of the hostages for his own political gain. "There is no doubt in my mind," Ford said, "that President Carter will do whatever he can in political terms to ensure his reelection."[12]

Henry Kissinger, Howard Baker, and Dick Allen all echoed Ford's charges. Allen was an intellectual, urbane and sophisticated, yet underneath the surface lurked someone who could take care of himself in a bar fight. In the 1950s he had competed against Paul Hornung for the quarterback position at Notre Dame—though, as Allen himself would good-naturedly acknowledge years later, it wasn't much of a competition: he ended up tutoring the Heisman Trophy winner in Spanish for $2.50 an hour.[13]

The Carter campaign was once again forced to deny the charges of a secret deal to free the hostages. Walter Mondale was trotted out to issue a denial, while Jody Powell labeled Ford's charge as "trash." Ford did not back off, however. The next day, he cranked it up another ten notches when he asked, "Why didn't Carter show the same initiative over the past fifty-one weeks" as he was with the election looming?[14]

Panicked that Anderson would drain off enough voters to deliver the election to Reagan, liberal groups in the last days rallied to Carter's cause. The Americans for Democratic Action, one of the oldest liberal organizations around, gathered together the best and the brightest to endorse Carter. Clarence Mitchell of the NAACP and Gloria Steinem, utility feminist, held a press conference in which he repeatedly called Reagan a "racist" and she said she was "fearful" for women and minorities if Reagan won. She also said that Reagan was the candidate of the John Birch Society.[15]

Actually, the Birch Society opposed Reagan's election, saying he was a "lackey" of "Communist conspirators."[16] All the nuts were now coming out, from the Left and the Right.

His days on the road were winding down, and for the most part, Reagan had had a ball. Several weeks earlier in Philadelphia, he'd been taught a new greeting backstage so he went out to the Polish audience and said, "Dziekuje and dzien dobry." The crowd ate it up. Reagan then rattled off the names of Phillies slugger Greg Luzinski and Eagles quarterback Ron Jaworski and the audience exploded again. He also mentioned Pope John Paul II and eviscerated the Democrats, charging that they no longer represented the values of Polish-Americans.[17] That was it as far as they were concerned; Reagan was now an honorary Pole.

Reagan won the endorsement of Oscar-winning actor George C. Scott, though it was doubtful his endorsement would carry much weight among his liberal colleagues in Hollywood.[18] More big-city newspapers weighed in with their endorsements. The *Philadelphia Inquirer* supported Carter's reelection "with grave misgivings,"[19] and the *Chicago Tribune* threw its qualified support behind Governor Reagan, saying, "There is good reason to worry" about him.[20] Carter won the support of the *Youngstown Vindicator* and Reagan nailed the *Indianapolis Star.*[21]

Wexford was the perfect site for Reagan's debate practice sessions. The driveway alone was two miles long, making the secluded estate safe from prying reporters' eyes.

In a garage made to look like a debate set, Reagan went up against David Stockman as Carter. Stockman had been the final recipient of the purloined Carter briefing books and absorbed them to channel Carter. The books, having been given to Bill Casey by Paul Corbin, went first to Baker and then to David Gergen and finally to Stockman. George Will, helping prepare Reagan, looked at the Carter material for all of thirty seconds, dismissing it as meaningless.[22]

Will had a critical point. The books were simply a recitation of Reagan's comments, positions, columns, and radio commentaries. It was all a part of the public record, and Reagan had been hit on all this by his political opponents and reporters for years.

Baker was on hand, pencil behind one ear, cursing and telling ribald jokes. The candidate often dressed in cowboy boots and western shirts for these sessions. At any one time up to twenty people were hanging around, until Meese and Baker called the drill to order and a small group got down to work with Governor Reagan. Jeane Kirkpatrick, Marty Anderson, Howard Baker, and others would pepper him with questions while "Carter" went after him, hammer and tong. Reagan lost his temper more than once. A young aide to Ed Meese, Marc Rotterman, was at Wexford and during a break Reagan sidled up to him and said, "They are taking me to the woodshed out there."[23] The candidate later said, "After Stockman, both Anderson and Carter were easy."[24]

At one point Reagan was withering under Stockman's assault and stormed in frustration, "Damn it, here you go again!" The briefers laughed, startling Reagan. He told them he was going to tuck the phrase away and "may save it for the debate."[25]

One of Meese's aides, Tony Dolan, had written a long, thoughtful memo that had influenced the debate prep. Reagan should not try "to outpoint the other guy," Dolan wrote; rather, the candidate should "speak directly to the American people."[26]

The Sunday before the debate, Reagan canceled a previously scheduled taped interview with *Good Morning America* to spend more time getting ready for the debate. He also took time to watch video of the Carter-Ford debates of 1976.

Gerald Ford visited Reagan at Wexford for some last-minute tips on facing Carter. Ford was fully engaged now, lashing the president for "demagoguery."[27] Reagan, he warned, "has to anticipate some show of typical Carter meanness . . . vindictiveness."[28] Ford would know.

The president was in fighting trim, having spent time with his trusted advisers Powell, Hamilton Jordan, Gerald Rafshoon, Pat Caddell, and Stuart Eizenstat at Camp David, boning up for the debate.[29] Carter was poring over the massive briefing books covering Reagan's record over the years on all matters, foreign and domestic.

As Reagan had been active in public discussion since the late 1940s, it was a prodigious amount of material. The domestic book alone totaled several hundred pages.[30] Three sets of books had been prepared—though one set had disappeared from the White House.

No one seemed to want to claim credit for selecting Cleveland as the site for the debate, though it was generally agreed that the idea had come from the League of

Women Voters. Of all the decrepit, falling-down cities in the Rust Belt, Cleveland may have been the saddest. Its river was so polluted that it had once caught on fire. Looming over the city was "Terminal Tower," and no one doubted it for a moment.

Yet the media were thrilled to descend on the struggling city. This was the showdown that had been argued and negotiated over for weeks—months, even— and now it was finally here. Some 1,500 reporters and media support-types arrived in the city for the debate. In gratitude, the town took them to its bosom and treated them like royalty, giving them chauffeur-driven cars and limousines, baskets of fruit, receptions with shrimp and oysters, and—as always—copious adult beverages.

The ninety-minute debate was to be broadcast live on NBC, ABC, CBS, and PBS, and many national, regional, and local radio stations. It would be beamed overseas to twenty-six countries via four Intelsat satellites.[31] People around the country organized debate parties to watch and cheer their favorite candidate. It was the first televised presidential debate that would feature a live studio audience.

That morning's *Washington Post* had a big story trumpeting "Carter Goes Into Debate With Lead in New Poll." The breathless story by Martin Schram detailed, "Their clash comes on the heels of a Gallup Poll report yesterday that voters have swung sharply toward Carter in the last two weeks—a six-point shift that now gives the president a three-point lead over his Republican challenger."[32]

Nonetheless, Reagan was "serene" the day of the debate, according to Jim Baker. Sitting backstage just moments before being introduced, Reagan asked Baker if he could have the holding room to himself for a moment. "I want to have a word with the man upstairs."[33]

Carter's horoscope the morning of the debate said, "Confront adversaries."[34] But the president received a less auspicious sign when he arrived at the Cleveland Convention Center's Music Hall, site of the debate. He was startled to see Reagan T-shirts on the workers backstage. The men were members of the Teamsters union, which had endorsed Reagan; they hoped to throw Carter off his game with this bit of psychological warfare.[35]

Meanwhile, a memo authored by Reagan top aide Paul Manafort went out to the entire field staff, urging them to organize "surrogates and leadership persons for favorable debate reaction statements." Ominously, Manafort warned, "This is an important exercise."[36]

CBS OPENED ITS PRE-DEBATE show with Walter Cronkite telling millions of viewers, "It's not inconceivable that the election could turn on what happens in the next ninety minutes."[37]

As the hour of the debate finally arrived, Carter appeared stage right, wearing a dark blue suit, white shirt, nondescript tie, and a collar bar, which had recently come back into vogue. He caught wife Rosalynn's eye and smiled, then went back to writing notes (neither candidate was allowed to bring any prepared text). Reagan, still in the wings, was also in a dark blue suit, white shirt, and nondescript tie, but no collar bar, though he did have his always present folded white handkerchief in the left breast pocket of his suit jacket.

Somehow, Henry Kissinger had finagled his way into the wings with the Reagan team. He stood where he made sure the audience in the hall could see him.

Reagan looked robust, suntanned, his pompadour held in place with a bit of water and a little dab of Brylcreem. Only the veins on his hands betrayed his age. Reagan had had a light dinner and one glass of wine, "a little color for his cheeks," Mike Deaver said.[38] He was ready.

Carter's hair had been blow-dried and was neatly in place. He was wearing makeup to give his sallow skin a bit of color and to hide some liver spots. Though he was only fifty-six, his four years in the Oval Office had aged him ten years, rounding his shoulders. The famous toothy grin of 1976 had given way to a somber, burdened man. The stress of the job had clearly taken its toll on the president. Mondale worried that "Carter looked pale and drawn and sort of tense."[39] Nevertheless, the Carterites were confident. "Carter seemed intellectually poised to devastate Reagan," said Peter Bourne.[40] They didn't seem concerned that Carter hadn't debated anybody since 1976 while Reagan had already debated six times in the past year—winning all except for a debate with Bush in Texas when there was little on the line.[41]

While waiting for the cue from the television producer, Reagan bounded up the stairs, stage left, and strode across the stage to proffer his hand to the president. Carter, who was looking down at his lectern, jotting down notes, was momentarily taken aback when his opponent was suddenly standing there, right hand extended. Carter smiled and accepted Reagan's hand but said nothing, and Reagan walked back to his side of the stage. It was not televised, but Reagan had scored a small psychological advantage with his sporting gesture. Photographers captured the moment.

THE "TALE OF THE Tape" stood as follows.

Carter—once known as "Jimmy Who?"—was the defending champion with a lifetime record of 126 wins and 46 losses. His wins included the presidency of the Future Farmers and Future Homemakers of America Camp Development Committee, the Georgia Crop Improvement Association, the Lions International, the Georgia state senate, the Georgia governorship, the Democratic presidential primaries of 1976 and 1980, and the U.S. presidency of 1976. The champ weighed in at 155 pounds, and stood 5'9". The "Bantam Rooster" of the South had a deceptively good left uppercut but preferred body blows while sticking and moving, sticking and moving. Political pugilism was in his blood, though the word on the street was that he tended overestimate his own skills. He'd won the title four years earlier when his opponent, Gerald Ford, made a critical mistake in the late rounds.

The challenger—Ron "The Gipper" Reagan out of the West—stood 6'1" and weighed 194 pounds. The East Coast writers knew less about him. His overall record was 86 wins and 31 losses, with his victories including his high-school and Eureka College class presidencies, the presidency of the Screen Actors Guild, the California gubernatorial primaries and general elections, and the Republican presidential primaries of 1976 and 1980. The book on Reagan was that he coasted in the early rounds while taking the measure of his opponent. He sometimes used a "rope-a-dope" strategy, slipping punches and letting his opponents thump themselves weary, although he was often accused of tiring in the late rounds himself.

When aroused, Reagan had a lightning-fast right cross. Though some thought he was not a terrific puncher, most agreed that he was a great counterpuncher. He was also more nimble on his feet than many scribes gave him credit for.

Most observers expected the defending champ to wear down his challenger. But it was precisely one year earlier that Jimmy Carter had confided to Hamilton Jordan that he thought he'd be running against Reagan and that "it would be a mistake to underestimate him."[42] Carter was about to learn how right he had been.

THE PROCEEDINGS OPENED WITH a statement by a very nervous Ruth Hinerfeld, president of the League of Women Voters. Hinerfeld in turn introduced Howard K. Smith, who would serve as the debate's moderator, just as he had in the GOP debates during the primaries. Smith coolly explained the ground rules and introduced the panelists: William Hilliard of the *Portland Oregonian*, Harry Ellis of the *Christian Science Monitor*, Marvin Stone of *U.S. News &World Report*, and Barbara Walters of ABC. An unusual seating arrangement kept Smith and Walters away from each other; when they once shared coanchoring duties at ABC, they had spent most of their off-camera time bickering over who got more "face time" on camera.

A coin toss backstage had determined who would receive the first question. Carter had won the toss, and in a bit of a surprise he chose to have Reagan field the first question and then go last with his closing remarks. As to why the president made these choices, Jody Powell joshed, "Good manners."[43]

So it was Reagan who fielded the first question, from Marvin Stone, on the use of military power. The Carterites smiled. A Tolstoy question. "War and peace" was the issue the president had been clubbing Reagan with for weeks.

Sure enough, Reagan seemed a bit nervous, tentative in his response. He did, however, hit Carter hard at a couple of points. Asked to explain the specific differences between his approach to the use of military power and that of the president, Reagan said, "I don't know what the differences might be, because I don't know what Mr. Carter's policies are." He outlined his position on how a strong military would not invite aggression, and condemned the Carter administration for continually letting "events get out of hand" until the point that the United States was faced "with a crisis." Stone followed up, asking how Reagan could increase the military budget, cut taxes, and balance the budget all at the same time. Reagan's answer was a bit meandering and disjointed.[44]

When it was Carter's turn to rebut Reagan, he, too, was nervous and halting. But he touched all the right bases on peace, building up the military, and the treaty he'd negotiated between Israel and Egypt. He quoted H. L. Mencken—patron saint of cynical journalists—and made a passing reference to "simple" solutions. No one needed to guess to whom he was alluding. Stone, in his follow-up, tried to pin the president down on how and when he might use military power. Carter calmly replied that he had worked for "security" in the Middle East and that he'd deployed two carrier task forces to the region. He restated that the military budget had gone up on his watch after going down during the Nixon and Ford administrations.[45]

Reagan, given the chance to respond, went after Carter on this matter, making the point that military spending had declined as America was pulling out of Vietnam and that the Democrats in Congress refused to go along with any increases in the Pentagon's budget. This time, his answer was tight. He rattled off a series of military programs Carter had canceled, saying that the president had cut "sixty ships out of the Navy . . . , stopped the B-1, delayed the cruise missile, stopped . . . the Minuteman missiles, stopped the Tridents." It was a strong swipe at Carter, but the president recovered when he accused his Republican opponent of "habitually" supporting "the injection of military forces into troubled areas" whereas he and previous presidents had exercised caution. Carter also got a dig in on the use of nuclear weapons. The president won the exchange on points when he said his military buildup would mean that defense forces would never be used and soldiers would not die in combat.[46] Reagan scowled at Carter; he must have wondered whether the Democrat had stolen one of his old speeches.

Carter took the first question from Harry Ellis, this one regarding inflation and what, in the future, he would do for workers. The president faltered as he blamed the oil-producing countries for the high inflation while seeming to suggest that the problem had started before he was elected. He was tap-dancing on the issue. Ellis followed up and gave Carter another chance to spell out what he'd do in a second term, but the president did no better, focusing on the "sacrifice" he had "demanded" from the American people. Carter came across as patronizing. He said oil imports had dropped 33 percent, which was true, but around the bars and living rooms of America, voters knew why demand had dropped: because the bottom had fallen out of the economy.[47] At the time, a barrel of American-produced oil was selling for $6.50 per barrel, but the fear was that it could rise as high as $36 if price controls were lifted.[48]

Carter again talked about "sacrifice," "conservation," and a government jobs program for young Americans along with tax credits for businesses. Now he was coming off like a scold. He wasn't really addressing the problem in a way that would resonate with the voters; the American people did not believe inflation was their fault. Carter took a shot at the "Reagan-Kemp-Roth proposal," calling it "irresponsible" and reminding the audience that George Bush had once called it "voodoo economics."[49] Reagan, upon hearing this, caught his running mate's eye in the audience and smiled, giving him a friendly wink.[50] He shifted his feet, as if he couldn't wait to respond to Carter's comments.

Ellis turned to Reagan and the Gipper was primed. He utterly rejected what he characterized as Carter's suggestion "that inflation somehow came upon us like a plague and therefore it's uncontrollable and no one can do anything about it," calling the idea "entirely spurious" and "dangerous." Contrary to Carter's argument, Reagan calmly pointed out, inflation in Ford's last term was at a tolerable 4.8 percent, but by 1980 it was at an annual rate of 12.7 percent, not the 7 percent that the president had argued. Reagan agreed that some new jobs had been created under Carter, "but that can't hide the fact that there are eight million men and women out of work in America today and two million of those lost their jobs in just the last few months." He blasted Carter for saying that to get inflation under control, America would have to accept more joblessness and less productivity.[51]

Reagan laid into the root cause of inflation: out-of-control government spending. He said Carter had blamed a host of other actors for inflation, including OPEC and the Federal Reserve; Carter, Reagan said, "has blamed the lack of productivity on the American people; he has then accused the people of living too well, and that we must share in scarcity, we must sacrifice and get used to doing with less." That would not do for Reagan: "We don't have inflation because the people are living too well. We have inflation because the *government* is living too well."[52]

Recognizing that his time was running short, Reagan summarized his position succinctly: "Yes, you can lick inflation by increasing productivity and by decreasing the cost of government."[53]

It was a turning point, though few in the hall knew it. Reagan was making the case to the American people that they were not to blame, as it seemed Carter and official Washington had suggested for four years. Inflation could be beaten. Reagan had settled in, had shaken off the early jitters, and was talking to the American people—more than 100 million of whom were watching, with millions more listening on their radios.[54]

At his next chance to speak, Carter chided Reagan again on the "Reagan-Kemp-Roth" plan, calling it "highly inflationary." Carter said Reagan's suggestion to eliminate the minimum wage was "a heartless kind of approach to the working families . . . which is typical of many Republican leaders."[55]

The GOP nominee homed in on the savaging of his tax-cut plan. "I'd like to ask the president: Why is it inflationary to let the people keep more of their money and spend it the way they'd like, and it isn't inflationary to let him take that money and spend it the way he wants?"[56] Bingo. Reagan's so-called simplicity must have grated on Carter, but his common sense struck a chord with the American worker.

When William Hilliard asked a question about the plight of the cities, Reagan had a proposal courtesy of Jack Kemp. Reagan proposed "development zones" to provide tax incentives and reduced regulations in distressed urban areas as a means of attracting business and investment to the municipalities. He painted a picture for the audience of his recent unpleasant experience in the Bronx: "You have to see it to believe it. It looks like a bombed-out city—great gaunt skeletons of buildings, windows smashed out, painted on one of them 'Unkept Promises,' on another 'Despair.'" Reagan reminded his audience that Carter had gone there in 1977 promising everything, delivering nothing.[57] Though Reagan handled Hilliard's follow-up question awkwardly, he had skillfully reminded Americans of the failed Carter record, of four years of broken promises.

Carter, in his rebuttal, offered the usual liberal bromides of more government spending. Speaking like a technocrat, he threw out statistics and big figures that surely sounded like fingernails across a blackboard to the people watching at home. At his conclusion, he accused Reagan of being insensitive to racism.[58] It was clear that Reagan's calm demeanor was starting to annoy Carter.

Carter spoke of America as if it was no longer a melting pot but instead something akin to a patchwork quilt, where immigrants could preserve "their ethnic commitments" and "their relationships with their relatives in foreign countries."

Carter was in full pander mode now, as he spoke about the exclusion of minorities from "the affairs of government" and how he had appointed blacks, women, and Hispanics to government jobs. Patronizingly, he said, "To involve them in administration of government and a feeling that they belong to the societal structure . . . is a very important commitment."[59]

Reagan should have knocked it out of the park in his response, but instead he answered disjointedly about unemployment among blacks and the minimum wage. He only touched on government programs as "dead-end" jobs. He had given Carter an opening, which the president took advantage of when he again accused Reagan of "insensitivity" to the plight of poor people. "This, to me, is a very important difference between him and me," Carter said.[60]

Now it was Barbara Walters's turn. She did not ask the president what kind of tree he was. Rather, she bore in on the issue of the hostages, which had been the eight-hundred-pound gorilla in the room for the past forty-five minutes. She pointed out that Israel had a zero-tolerance policy on hostages: Israeli hostages were treated the same as soldiers, and the government would not negotiate with terrorists for the lives of either. Carter, of course, had spent a year negotiating with terrorists for the lives of more than fifty Americans in Tehran. He ducked the question and talked obliquely about how terrorism was "one of the blights on this world." He meandered and took another shot at Reagan, accusing him of supporting the spread of nuclear weapons.[61]

Walters was unsatisfied with Carter's answer and got more specific, asking whether offering military spare parts wasn't "reward[ing] terrorism." He answered weakly again, using only a few seconds of his allotted time.[62] Clearly, he wanted to move on.

Walters repeated her original question to Reagan, and the challenger jumped all over it—nailing Carter in the process: "Barbara, you've asked that question twice. I think you ought to have at least one answer to it." Reagan, though, was in a predicament. As much as he wanted to slam Carter's policy toward the ayatollah, the situation in Tehran was ticklish. "Your question is difficult to answer because [of] the situation right now," he said cautiously. As he acknowledged in his response, he didn't want to say anything overtly aggressive that might inadvertently delay the return of the hostages or cause them harm.[63]

So he pursued a safe course, defending himself over Carter's false accusation that Reagan had a "secret plan" to secure their release and then calling for a "complete investigation as to . . . why they [the hostages] have been there so long. . . . And I would suggest that Congress should hold such an investigation. In the meantime, I'm going to continue praying that they'll come home."[64]

Walters asked Reagan a follow-up on overthrowing or supporting govern-ments that did not conform to the principles of the United States. Reagan was dubious about interfering in the internal affairs of sovereign nations, as a new government installed by the United States might be more noxious than the old one. Carter, when he was offered rebuttal time, said petulantly, "I didn't hear any comment from Governor Reagan about what he would do to stop or to reduce terrorism in the future."[65]

At the debate's halfway mark, two things were clear. The first was that Rea-gan was the master of subtlety while Carter had all the subtlety of a blunderbuss. The second was that Reagan was getting under Carter's skin. Carter glared at Reagan periodically.

In the second half of the debate, the format changed: there would be no fol-low-up questions from the panelists, but the candidates themselves could take two cracks at rebutting, offering a follow-up question, or just making a comment.

Stone asked Reagan about arms control and his suggestion to "scrap" SALT II. Reagan handled the question with aplomb. He pointed out that while both Carter and Mondale blamed him for blocking their cherished treaty, it was the Senate Armed Services Committee, controlled by the Democrats, which had "voted ten to zero, with seven abstentions, against the SALT II treaty and declared that it was not in the national security interests of the United States." Reagan once again got in a subtle dig at Carter when he reminded the president that when he had pushed the Soviets for actual reductions in nuclear arms, the response from the Kremlin was "nyet."[66] A murmur of laughter was heard in the hall.

The same question went to Carter and he moved in on Reagan like Sugar Ray Leonard. "There is a disturbing pattern in the attitude of Governor Reagan" on the issue of arms control, Carter curtly said. "He has never supported any of those arms control agreements. . . . And now he wants to throw into the wastebasket a treaty to control nuclear weapons." Carter closed in. "When a man who hopes to be president says, 'Take this treaty, discard it' . . . that is a very dangerous and disturbing thing."[67]

When it came time for Reagan's rebuttal, he threw it back in Carter's face. "If I have been critical of some of the previous agreements, it's because we've been out-negotiated for quite a long time. And they [the Soviets] have managed, in spite of all of our attempts at arms limitation, to go forward with the biggest military buildup in the history of man." Carter had noted that the SALT treaty had been negotiated "by myself and my two Republican predecessors," but Reagan dismissed this comment as misleading, pointing out that Gerald Ford "is emphati-cally against this SALT treaty." Reagan buttressed his case by telling the audience that it was two Democratic senators, Henry Jackson of Washington and Fritz Hollings of South Carolina, who were carrying the fight against the treaty on the floor of the U.S. Senate. Finally, Reagan rejected claims that he supported "throwing away" the treaty: "I am not talking of scrapping. I am talking of taking the treaty back and going back into negotiations" with the Kremlin to press for real arms reductions.[68]

Carter was finding to his dismay that Reagan was not an empty suit who was lost without his four-by-six cards. He seemed to be frustrated that Reagan had parried so many of his punches. "Governor Reagan is making some very misleading and disturbing statements," he said. Carter scored Reagan for wanting nuclear superiority over the Russians, even though recent polling showed that a strong majority of the American people wanted superiority, not the parity that Carter was advocating. He closed his rebuttal by saying that Reagan's "attitude is extremely dangerous and belligerent in its tone, although it's said with a quiet voice."[69]

Reagan began his rebuttal by saying, "I know the president is supposed to be replying to me, but sometimes I have a hard time in connecting what he's saying with what I have said or what my positions are."[70] Then he calmly restated his position on reopening negotiations with the Soviets.

Carter had the last word on this question. One that would haunt him for the rest of his life.

"I think to close out this discussion it would be better to put into perspective what we're talking about. I had a discussion with my daughter, Amy, the other day before I came here to ask her what the most important issue was. She said she thought nuclear weaponry and the control of nuclear arms."[71]

The crowd tittered with derisive laughter, and Carter's aides buried their faces in their hands. Carter looked up into the audience as he heard their reaction. Americans around the country laughed aloud. Reagan knew well enough to leave things alone when your opponent was screwing up. No one bothered to pay attention to the rest of Carter's answer.

The questioning moved on to energy, exploration, conservation. Little interesting was said by either man except that Carter kept pawing at Reagan. "Governor Reagan says that this is not a good achievement." "Governor Reagan's approach to our energy policy . . . is to repeal or to change . . ." "The air pollution standard laws . . . were passed over the objections of Governor Reagan, and this is a very well-known fact."[72] Reagan brushed off the charges.

The topic moved to Social Security. This issue was supposedly another hot potato for Reagan, but he fielded it cleanly. Indeed, he displayed complete command of the subject, conducting a national tutorial on the troubled and bankrupt retirement system as he explained how a program "trillions of dollars out of balance" must be "put on a sound actuarial basis." He even managed to turn the topic around and hit Carter for the "biggest single tax increase in our nation's history."[73]

Carter jabbed Reagan on his previous musings about making Social Security voluntary, but patiently, as if leading a slow student through a lesson. Carter grinned, pleased with himself. Reagan replied, "Mr. President, the voluntary thing that I suggested many years ago was that [with] a young man, orphaned and raised by an aunt who died, his aunt was ineligible for Social Security insurance because she was not his mother. And I suggested that if this is an insurance program, certainly the person who's paying in should be able to name his own beneficiaries. That's the closest I've ever come to anything voluntary with Social Security."[74] Reagan looked directly at the president as he spoke. Carter returned Reagan's gaze for a time, but then turned his head to look out at the panel of questioners.

Carter was on the defensive over Social Security, pledging not to change the system or the relationship between Social Security and Medicare. Then he attacked Reagan again—one time too many as it turned out. "Governor Reagan, as a matter of fact, began his political career campaigning around this nation against Medicare." Carter added a few perfunctory comments about national health insurance and then finished by saying, "Governor Reagan again, typically, is against such a proposal."[75]

Howard K. Smith turned to Reagan and said, "Governor?"

Reagan had had enough. Emitting a low chuckle, he turned to his right, smiled his famous crooked smile, looked at Carter, and delivered his immortal line:

"There you go again."[76]

The audience forgot the earlier admonition to be silent, and laughter rolled across the Music Hall. The Gipper had just thrown his famous thundering counterpunch.

Reagan then detailed how he had favored another plan, offered by the American Medical Association, based more on the marketplace than on the incompetence of government bureaucrats, but nobody was really listening to the rest of Reagan's reply, as heads huddled together and people whispered about the debate. Carter, smiling, hesitated in his response and went back to the safety of vilifying the Republican Party as being heartless, unlike the Democratic Party, whose historical commitments "to the working families of this nation have been extremely important to the growth in their stature and in a better quality of life for them."

He peevishly criticized Reagan for quoting Democratic presidents, as if Reagan had taken his ball away on the playground. In his next response, Reagan replied to this complaint by saying, "I was a Democrat. I said many foolish things back in those days."[77] The audience couldn't help themselves and laughed again.

Barbara Walters asked Carter about leadership and why he thought Reagan should not be president. It was one of the few times during the debate when Carter smiled. The president deadpanned, "Barbara, reluctant as I am to say anything critical about Governor Reagan, I'll try to answer your question."[78] Ripples of laughter came from the audience at Carter's uncharacteristic wit.

Other than that, throughout the evening, he'd been stern, trying to convey a seriousness of purpose. He quickly reverted to that mode, swinging into yet another attack on Reagan, saying that his opponent posed a danger in that he represented, on some key issues, "a radical departure . . . from the heritage of Eisenhower and others" in the Republican Party. Carter also snuck in a cutting remark about how Reagan had "been running for president, I think, since 1968." In concluding, he returned to the warmonger theme, attacking Reagan once again for "careless" and "belligerent" attitudes.[79]

Walters turned to Reagan and asked why he should be president and why his opponent should not. She noted that Reagan "may be equally reluctant to speak ill of your opponent." Reagan replied, "Well, Barbara, I believe that there is a fundamental difference. And I think it has been evident in most of the answers that Mr. Carter's given tonight that he seeks the solution to anything as another opportunity for a federal government program." Reagan swung into his federalism view of government, saying that Washington "has usurped powers and autonomy and authority that belongs back at the state and local level. It has imposed on the individual freedoms of the people, and that there are more of these things that could be solved by the people themselves if they were given a chance or by the levels of government that were closer to them."[80]

Somewhere, Thomas Jefferson was smiling.

Reagan finished his response strongly, stating his belief that "millions of Democrats . . . are going to vote with us this time around. Because they too want that promise kept. It was a promise for less government and less taxes and more freedom for the people."[81]

Carter flailed desperately in his rebuttal. "I mention the radical departure of Governor Reagan from the principles or ideals or historical perspective of his own party." He went after what the Democrats thought was Reagan's weakness, his opposition to the Equal Rights Amendment. Carter made a good case for the amendment and the GOP's historic support of the idea. Reagan answered, not well, but adequately, discussing his support for full rights for women while governor of California.[82]

With time running out, both men meandered further. Carter went through a litany of items such as deregulation of trucking and airlines, as if he was mentally checking off a list of things to throw out there in defense of his four years in office. Reagan oddly went back to the Equal Right Amendment, as if he wasn't satisfied with his first answer, and then did his own checklist, as he reminded the viewing audience that he'd been a union president and still carried a union card.[83]

That was the end of the questioning. The time had come for the candidates' closing statements.

It was now 11 p.m. on the East Coast, and each candidate would have three minutes to give his summation. Carter went first. He opened with praise for the League of Women Voters and the city of Cleveland, as befitting any good guest. The president made clear to the American people his belief in the "stark differences" between himself and his California opponent. He spoke of peace and fairness, of the loneliness of the presidency and how he'd fought to keep America out of conflicts with other nations. He did not speak of the economy, jobs, or inflation.[84]

The verdict of the American people was at hand and Carter made his best case. "The American people now are facing, next Tuesday, a lonely decision," he said. "Those listening to my voice will have to make a judgment about the future of this country, and I think they ought to remember that one vote can make a lot of difference." For a moment, Carter had regained some of his old form and almost had the people again, but then he reverted to the lecturing schoolmarm, talking about how one vote per precinct put JFK in office in 1960 and how the lack thereof kept Hubert Humphrey out of office in 1968.[85]

He concluded by speaking of human rights and American leadership in that world: "To stay strong, to stay at peace, to raise high the banner of human rights, to set an example for the rest of the world, to let our deep beliefs and commitments be felt by others in all other nations, is my plan for the future."[86]

In another era, another time, another economy, it might have sufficed, but this was 1980 and the American people couldn't save the world until and unless somebody saved their own country.

At this point Americans had suffered through seventeen long, horrible years. They had lost a golden champion, cut down by an assassin's bullet in Dallas. They had lost a war, the first in the nation's history. They'd lost another president, because of his corruption and contempt for the Constitution. They were losing a so-called Cold War to an Evil Empire. They were losing their jobs, they were losing their homes, and they were losing the value of a hard-earned buck. The country had lost the respect of its former allies and earned only the scorn of enemies. Years of bad news piled atop more bad news had battered the "can-do" American psyche into the ground.

RONALD WILSON REAGAN HAD traveled the length of breadth of America for more than forty years, seeing the best—and the worst—of his country and his fellow countrymen. After all these years, after listening—really listening to tens of thousands of his fellow citizens, especially over the past four years—he knew their hearts, he believed in their goodness, he felt their pain, and he desperately wanted to do something about their plight.

He hadn't only spoken with and listened to Americans. Other politicians sloughed off their mail to factotums to answer. Not Reagan. He read his mail. Not all of it, to be sure, but enough to gain an understanding and perspective that eluded other politicians. Reagan called himself a "citizen politician" and he really believed it.[87]

In those letters, Reagan read of joy and sorrow, of gain and loss, of hopes and dreams, of life and death. And to each, Reagan answered—not with a dashed-off note, but often with long handwritten letters, tender letters offering advice, offering counsel, articulating his philosophy, giving solace.

He also read through a file of news clips prepared for him each morning by his staff. The file contained the news of the day, coverage of Carter, himself, world events, and the like, but what he was most interested in were the other stories, often from small-town newspapers, about the American people. About blue ribbons awarded at livestock shows, about boys winning Eagle Scout, about the charity of Girl Scouts, about unselfish and heroic deeds performed by what he called the "quiet, everyday heroes of American life."[88] Reagan believed America was a great country because America was a good country.

Through all this Reagan gained an insight and honed a political philosophy that was based upon the most fundamental creed of the founders: That power should reside with the many people and not the few elites. That power should flow upward and not downward. That elected officials were truly "public servants" who had a solemn compact with those who put them into power. And that the first obligation of the national government was to secure the peace and freedom for those who allowed them to govern.

He understood the quintessential American because he *was* the quintessential American. He'd never forgotten where he'd come from.

Ronald Reagan, age sixty-nine, now stood before the American people, exactly in the place he wanted to be and in the moment he wanted to possess. Now was his chance to make the case he'd always wanted to make since that time long ago when he was a dreamy boy whose ambition was to one day save others.

As the camera ever so slowly moved in for a close-up, Reagan began his remarks by thanking the "ladies" of the league and expressing his regret that John Anderson couldn't have been on the stage that night. He moved quickly into his closing argument to the American people:

Next Tuesday is Election Day. Next Tuesday all of you will go to the polls, you'll stand there in the polling place and make a decision. I think when you make that decision it might be well if you would ask yourself:

Are you better off than you were four years ago?

Is it easier for you to go and buy things in the stores than it was four years ago? Is there more or less unemployment in the country than there was four years ago? Is America as respected throughout the world as it was? Do you feel that our security is as safe? That we're as strong as we were four years ago?

And if you answer all of those questions yes, why then I think your choice is very obvious as to who you'll vote for.

If you don't agree, if you don't think that this course that we've been on for the last four years is what you would like to see us follow for the next four, then I could suggest another choice that you have.

This country doesn't have to be in the shape that it is in. We do not have to go on sharing in scarcity, with the country getting worse off, with unemployment growing.

We talk about the unemployment lines. If all the unemployed today were in a single line, allowing two feet for each one of them, that line would reach from New York City to Los Angeles, California.

All of this can be cured. And all of it can be solved. . . . I know that the economic program that I have proposed for this nation in the next few years can resolve many of the problems that trouble us today. . . .

I would like to have a crusade today. And I would like to lead that crusade with your help. And it would be one to take government off the backs of the great people of this country and turn you loose again to do those things that I know you can do so well, because you did them and made this country great.

Thank you.[89]

36

MELTDOWN

"Ask Amy, She Knows."

At the conclusion of the debate, as at the beginning, Ronald Reagan walked across the stage and met President Carter at his podium. The president was bending over, picking up a piece of paper or perhaps trying to undo his microphone wire. When he saw Reagan he stood up, clasped Reagan's right hand with both of his, and smiled genuinely, as if he had just discovered newfound respect for his adversary.

The Reagan and Carter families and friends gathered on the stage, smiling and mingling. The contenders were hugged and kissed by their wives. Nancy Reagan was the first one on stage to greet her husband. Mrs. Reagan had been opposed to the debate, worried about what Carter might do to "Ronnie." It was one of the few times that Reagan did not seek her counsel.[1] Now Mrs. Reagan was beaming. Reagan, too, seemed pleased with how things went. He told friends of the encounter, "I've examined myself and I can't find any wounds."[2] The next day he would say he hadn't been nervous about being on the same stage as the president, quipping, "No, I've been on the same stage with John Wayne."[3]

President Carter and First Lady Rosalynn Carter left the hall. They forced smiles, but in his diary the night of the debate, Carter memorialized his contempt for Reagan: "Reagan was, 'Aw, shucks, this and that. I'm a grandfather, and . . . I love peace,' etc. He has his memorized lines, and he pushes a button and they come out."[4] Carter's media man, Gerald Rafshoon, had written a memo back in July saying that the cornerstone of the campaign should be, "Carter Is Smarter Than Reagan"; the president would not let the idea go.[5] But at least Carter was not as cocksure as he had been before the debate, which he walked into completely confident in his ability to obliterate Reagan. The morning after, when asked whether he had won the debate, Carter surprisingly said, "It's hard to say."[6] Years later, Carter maintained that the debate was "a standoff," because "my folks thought I won . . . his folks thought he won."[7]

Carter's mission had been to "make Reagan the issue," and unfortunately for the president, he succeeded beyond his wildest expectations. More than 105 million people had watched the debate, according to *Newsweek*, making it by far the most viewed debate in American history.[8] Those millions of viewers had learned that the Californian was not a mad bomber, he was not an empty suit, he was not a mean man who would throw old people out into snow banks, he was not a bigot or stupid. They discovered a man far different from the one portrayed by the Carter campaign; Rafshoon's July memo, typical of the way the president's men dismissed their opponent, contemptuously referred to Reagan as "too old, not smart, too simplistic, doesn't read, naieve [*sic*], inexperienced, right-wing."[9] Instead, viewers saw a man of humility but self-confidence, a conservative who believed that compassion came from the home, the church, and the community and that it could not—and more importantly should not—be imposed by governmental fiat.

Carter had been right when he said that there were "stark differences" between the two candidates.[10]

But many of the elites—a.k.a. the "Beautiful People"—were not sure how to respond. It couldn't be possible that Ronald Reagan—*that actor*—had beaten President Carter, could it? Nawww.

Therefore, like the townspeople in the tale of *The Emperor's New Clothes*, they scurried to the safety of their elitist friends to say that President Carter had won the debate because other members of the elites said Carter won the debate. "All the people throughout the city had already heard of the wonderful cloth and its magic and all were anxious to learn how wise or how stupid their friends and neighbors might be."[11]

In their postdebate analysis, CBS correspondents Dan Rather, Lesley Stahl, and Bill Plante all chatted up Carter's performance. In the minority were Walter Cronkite and Bruce Morton, who were mildly impressed with Reagan, but only because he had not screwed up. Jack Germond and Jules Witcover agreed and wrote backhandedly that Reagan hadn't done "anything stupid."[12] The next morning on the *Today* show, anchor Tom Brokaw dwelt favorably on Carter's handling of the SALT II issue.[13]

The *Washington Post* gave additional comfort to the elites the morning after as David Broder wrote in a story headlined "Carter on Points, but No KO" that Carter had kept Reagan on the defensive throughout. "In a confrontation where most of the time was spent on Carter's preferred issues—and not the economic record of the last four years, on which Reagan would have preferred to focus—the incumbent repeatedly managed to work in a partisan appeal to his fellow Democrats."[14]

The TV critic for the *Post*, Tom Shales, wrote, "As TV personality, Carter looked . . . basically unflappable. Reagan let himself be backed into corners by Carter punches to the face and body."[15]

In the *Washington Star*, the august Mary McGrory wrote, "Ronald Reagan showed the superficiality and insensitivity to such matters as the nuclear threat and race relations that makes people nervous about putting him in the Oval Office."[16]

Fred Barnes, a reporter for the *Baltimore Sun*, watched the debate and, like his peers in journalism, thought Carter had won. After the debate Barnes headed to Philadelphia to cover a campaign story, and while listening to Larry King's radio show during the drive he was astonished to find all the callers saying that Reagan had won.[17]

The callers' response was no fluke. The *New York Times* had assembled a focus group made up of a cross-section of voters from the greater New York area, including many who before the debate had planned to vote for Carter or had been undecided. Not now. One pre-debate undecided voter, a woman from Connecticut, said Carter was "offensive and belligerent." She was among those now leaning toward Reagan. Even some of those who said they planned on voting for Carter praised Reagan's performance and panned Carter's. A Rutgers professor from Brooklyn said of Reagan, "I had to hand it to him. He is very reassuring. He comes across so graceful. Without substance, though." She complained bitterly about Carter's "self-righteousness, his hyperbole." What's more, the group exploded in guffaws over Carter's assertion that he'd discuss nuclear policy with his daughter, Amy.[18]

Still, there was an utter and complete chasm between the paper's coverage of the debate and the reporting on its little focus group.

Even more telling was the Associated Press poll taken immediately after the debate. The survey showed that fully 46 percent of the respondents thought Reagan had done a better job while only 34 percent said Carter had performed better.[19]

The poll was conducted too late in the evening for the East Coast papers to report on it. When mainstream media figures did learn of the late-night survey, they generally dismissed it, claiming that the poll had been tilted toward "Reagan Country" in the West.

Conservative columnist R. Emmett Tyrrell saw it differently, saying that it was the distinction between the "Wise and the Wisenheimers."[20] Tyrrell had a point. There was a huge disconnect between the insulated elites and the rest of the country. The difference was as stark as that between a delightfully amusing little Chardonnay and a frosty bottle of Carling Black Label beer. A union man with the roofers said after the debate, "If Reagan was a Democrat, he'd been in the White House in January."[21] For millions of Democrats, Reagan spoke their language, even if he didn't mangle his verb usage.

One of the few Beautiful People who did understand what had transpired in Cleveland was Sam Donaldson of ABC News. After leaving the hall, he spotted Jody Powell and Hamilton Jordan backslapping each other and congratulating themselves on Carter's "win." Donaldson knew otherwise and yelled out, "Your man blew it!"[22]

Ted Kennedy was another exception among the elites. He watched the debate with a group of high-powered Democrats at the Century Plaza Hotel in Los Angeles. At the conclusion, remembered Bob Shrum, "they're all cheering and they're saying Carter won." When Shrum got into the limousine with Kennedy to head to the airport, Kennedy told Shrum, "He just got killed."[23] Kennedy wasn't referring to Reagan.

Warren Mitofsky, the much-esteemed head of survey research for CBS, said on the night of the debate that instant public commentary after such debates meant little. What was more meaningful, he argued, was what people thought several days after, when they had time to digest things, talk to friends and family, and formulate an opinion.[24]

Dick Wirthlin had been running daily tracking polls for weeks now. Wirthlin's overnight tracking after the debate had Carter blip up by three points in a head-to-head matchup. But a few days after the debate, the Republican pollster's internal numbers on the "who won the debate?" heavily favored Reagan: 41 percent thought the Republican had won, while only 26 percent thought Carter had, with the balance saying either "undecided" or "neither."[25]

Wirthlin's internal numbers were supported by an ABC call-in poll done the night of the debate. Although mired in controversy (as we'll see later), the callers overwhelmingly supported Reagan by a 67 to 33 percent margin.

Two days after the showdown, CBS News released a nationwide poll that only confirmed what Middle America already knew: Ronald Reagan had won the debate—by a margin of 44 percent to 36 percent, Americans thought Reagan had outperformed the president.[26]

NEW ENDORSEMENTS ROLLED IN for Reagan. For the first time in its history, the National Rifle Association fired a twenty-one-gun salute and warmly endorsed the Gipper. In addition, *TV Guide*, with a circulation of 18.9 million, endorsed

Reagan—the first endorsement ever by the popular magazine. The publisher was Walter Annenberg, who had once been Richard Nixon's ambassador to the Court of St. James.[27]

The *Washington Post* issued its judgment the Friday before the election, coming in for Carter, but only reluctantly. The long piece actually had more praise for Reagan than Carter. The *Post* conveyed its lack of enthusiasm when it sourly noted, "A just God will hear the prayers of *all* those who wish this campaign soon to be over."[28]

The *Post* was like many of the big-city newspapers in endorsing Carter over Reagan. It was not representative of newspapers overall, however. In fact, *Editor and Publisher* magazine found that 443 daily newspapers with a combined circulation of 17.6 million had endorsed the Gipper, while the president had received the support of 126 editorial pages with only 7.8 million readers.[29] When the *New York Post* endorsed Reagan, Carter petulantly called the publisher, Rupert Murdoch, to chew him out. He complained that "the Australian-born Murdoch is not even a U.S. citizen."[30]

THE DAY AFTER THE debate Carter went to Pittsburgh to begin the frenetic last days of campaigning. One newspaper called this closing segment of the campaign a "six-day political death march."[31] After spending so many months employing the Rose Garden strategy, Carter was now campaigning all-out. He was covering as much ground as possible, putting in long days until Americans voted on Tuesday, November 4. Pennsylvania, New York, New Jersey, Florida, Mississippi, Missouri, Texas, Tennessee, and California were just some of the pivotal states he would hit in the scant few days remaining.

The last-minute swing through Reagan's California was a shot across the Republican's bow, but Reaganites dismissed the president's incursion to reporters. Dick Richards, Reagan's political director for the West, considered Carter's planned trip to California no less than a fool's errand.[32] But the Reagan campaign sweated enough to buy an additional $25,000 worth of TV time in Los Angeles to run the weekend before the election.[33]

The mood on Carter's plane was jovial. The president voiced confidence on the trail. In Missouri, he reminded the audience that JFK had once said that in twenty years Republicans would praise Harry Truman, then added, "I predict that twenty years from now Republican candidates might even be saying nice things about Jimmy Carter's second term."[34] After being met by tens of thousands of union members in New York City's Garment District, Carter wrote in his diary, "A lot of electricity. Excitement." Clearly, he thought he was going to win.[35]

There were, however, reasons for apprehension. The fact that he had to devote so much time to southern states was itself a problem. Carter had taken all of the South in 1976, and now his administration was serving up millions in federal pork to the region. It was a worrisome that Florida, Mississippi, Texas, and Tennessee weren't safely in his column.

The "big four" industrial states bordering the Great Lakes—Ohio, Michigan, Pennsylvania, and Illinois, for a total of ninety-nine electoral votes—were all too close to call.[36] But Don Totten, Reagan's Midwest political director, knew the region like his own mother's face and was confident about his on-the-ground squad.[37] Meanwhile, Carter himself acknowledged that he was trailing in New Jersey.

A new national survey said that 48 percent of adult blacks either were not registered to vote or were not planning on voting.[38] This was further bad news for Carter, who needed the black vote badly. In several states, including Ohio and Mississippi, black voters had provided the critical margin for him four years earlier.

An embarrassing story came out that Carter's campaign was running ads in urban areas falsely charging John Anderson with having opposed the Civil Rights Act of 1964 and the Voting Rights Act of 1965 when in fact he had voted for both. Trying to keep blacks from switching to Anderson, the Carter campaign ho-humly took credit for the ads without apologizing for the lie.[39]

Adding to Carter's worries were continued rumors about the Iranian hostages. The latest rumor the administration had to fight off held that the president was about to fly to a military base in Wiesbaden to greet the released hostages. Evans and Novak breathlessly reported that a deal had been worked out two weeks before the election, "sealed in a handshake" between White House counsel Lloyd Cutler and Iranian negotiators. Cutler hotly denied the column.[40]

There was no such deal. In fact, as Walter Mondale remembered years later, "Khomeini was playing us like a cat and a mouse . . . dangling hope and then crushing it."[41]

ALTHOUGH MULTIPLE INDICATORS SHOWED that at least a plurality of Americans thought Reagan had bested Carter during the debate, a minor controversy arose relating to a poll run by ABC's popular news program *Nightline*.[42] In the days before the debate ABC had heavily promoted a survey in which people could phone in to vote on who they thought won the showdown. Once the debate ended, ABC revealed two phone numbers that viewers could call: one to register a vote for Reagan and another to vote for Carter. Each call cost fifty cents.[43]

AT&T was inundated with phone calls—an astonishing 725,000 in about an hour and a half, from just before the end of the debate at 11 P.M. eastern time until

12:30 A.M. The results of the phone-in poll were announced on *Nightline*: 483,815 votes for Reagan and 243,563 for Carter—a smashing 67 percent to 33 percent victory for the Republican.[44]

The survey provided great fodder for *Nightline*, as millions watched, anxious to learn the final results. Host Ted Koppel periodically announced that Reagan was maintaining his 2–1 edge in the voting, and he and guest commentator George Will discussed the meaning of the results. The next day the results were widely reported in newspapers and on radio; the *Washington Star* actually put the results on the front page.[45]

There was only one problem: the so-called poll was utterly worthless. In pollster-talk, it was representative only of the universe of those who participated; in other words, it did not represent the entire electorate. Plus, it did not discount multiple calls. Technical difficulties were reported as well. Cities that had crowded phone exchanges had more trouble with jammed lines than did rural areas, and the system would not accept calls from hotels or pay phones.[46] In Atlanta, Carter supporters were appalled to find that when their calls did go through, a tape-recorded message said that they had just voted for *Reagan*.

Nor did the ABC survey account for the fact that Republicans could call the Carter phone-in line and stay on the line, preventing Carter's supporters from legitimately casting a ballot for the Democrat. Or vice versa. As it happened, some twelve thousand Carter backers complained that they had tried repeatedly to call in and vote for their man but could not do so because the lines were jammed.[47]

A Carter aide bitterly objected that the phone-in poll could allow someone to "stack the deck."[48] He was right. Bill Timmons, Reagan's national political director, revealed years later that the Reagan campaign had been tipped off to the Reagan call-in phone number by a source at ABC several days before the debate. The campaign distributed the number among grassroots Republicans, who in turn passed it along to family, friends, and neighbors, all urged to call in and vote for the Gipper.[49]

Other media outlets, including the *New York Times*, viciously attacked the poll, even as they were declaring Carter the winner of the debate. "On content and meaning, Mr. Carter won," the *Times* editorialized.[50] The president of ABC News, Roone Arledge, was so incensed he wrote a letter ripping into the paper.[51] Faced with the uproar, Ted Koppel went so far as to host a half-hour show to defend the poll.

Despite—or perhaps because of—the controversy, ABC was pleased with the effects of the poll. Interest in the results had boosted the network's ratings during the debate, and in such big markets as New York and Chicago, ABC easily bested NBC and CBS.[52]

What was not discussed on *Nightline*, and what was not known to viewers at the time, was that George Will, who warmly praised Reagan's performance in his role as a guest commentator for ABC, had participated in Reagan's debate preparation. Will's lack of disclosure was the second controversy that grew out of *Nightline*'s coverage of the Carter-Reagan debate. This kerfuffle, however, would not emerge for another few years; Will's small role in the debate prep became known in the summer of 1983, as Congress was investigating the matter of the pilfered Carter briefing books. The revelation sparked a series of denunciations from other members of the media.[53] But the "controversy" was silly, frankly. Will was a well-known conservative who in his political commentary made his support for Reagan abundantly clear. In any case, columnists had play-acted being consultants for years, dispensing advice in print and over cocktails.

Two DAYS AFTER THE debate, the federal deficit for the year was announced at a staggering $59 billion—the second biggest on record (after the 1976 deficit of $66.4 billion). Normally, the Treasury Department would have made such an announcement the previous Friday. When pressed as to why the delay had occurred, a Treasury official shrugged his shoulders and said, "I can't think of a single reason."[54] But had the announcement been made on the usual schedule, it surely would have pushed the economy to the forefront of the debate agenda—and would have put President Carter on the defensive. Not surprisingly, tongues were wagging about the delay of the announcement. Though suppression of such government information could bring criminal charges, no formal accusations were leveled.

Then, of course, there was the ongoing saga of the Billy Carter investigation. Had the White House been obstructing the Justice Department's inquiry? The Reagan campaign weighed in. Jim Baker issued a statement saying that a subpoena might be necessary to force President Carter to cooperate, while Reagan told a local Pittsburgh television station that the president "does seem to be dragging his feet."[55]

It didn't help Carter that the Abscam scandal continued to cast a pall over his party. All but one of the Abscam targets were Democrats, and the story was still alive. In fact, one Democrat caught taking a bribe from FBI agents, Senator Harrison Williams of New Jersey, was indicted day just six days before the election.[56] Williams wasn't up for reelection, but others implicated, including Congressman John Jenrette of North Carolina, were fighting for their political lives.[57]

So was Jimmy Carter.

REAGAN'S SCHEDULE WAS JUST as hectic as Carter's, but the Gipper was having a good time. He took wing to Texas after the debate for an appearance with his old friend Roy Rogers. Rogers was a good sport and sang a few lines from "Happy Trails" at the behest of the traveling press corps. Reagan pointed out how Carter liked to mention other Democratic presidents, then added, "You know there's one Democrat president he doesn't talk about and that's Jimmy Carter." In Fort Worth, when Reagan asked rhetorically whether someone else had been in charge at the White House the way Carter was talking, the audience spontaneously yelled out, "Amy!" Reagan lost it. Laughing, he replied, "Maybe."[58]

He had fun telling crowds in the final days that Carter reminded him "of someone who can name the fifty parts of an automobile—he just can't drive it or fix it."[59] Mrs. Reagan was also having fun, telling women to "let the dust accumulate" at home and get out and campaign for "Ronnie."[60]

Reagan went to Dallas and as he walked onto the stage, the band struck up "Happy Days Are Here Again," which had been the Democratic Party's unofficial official song since 1932. It was the final insult of the campaign. Check that. It was the next to last. The last was when someone in the crowd yelled out, "Give 'em hell, Ronnie!" The phrase had oft been associated with Harry Truman's upset campaign of 1948.[61]

Joining Reagan on stage were Dallas Cowboys quarterback Roger Staubach and head coach Tom Landry. The men, as far as Texans were concerned, could have been the thirteenth and fourteenth disciples. The Cowboys cheerleaders were on hand too. A giant American flag adorned the background and red, white, and blue streamers and balloons dropped. A sign among the boisterous audience read, "Amy for Secretary of Defense."[62]

It was not all festivity. On a local Dallas television show, Reagan betrayed how angry he was about the personal attacks by Carter: "Criticizing each other belongs in a campaign . . . but I think Carter has lowered himself to a personal type of attack against me. And it's an attack based on falsehoods and distortions." He elaborated, "He doesn't know me enough to charge me with being a racist. He doesn't know me enough to suggest that I am trigger-happy and would cause a war and so forth, such things as saying if I were President I would separate Christians from Jews, blacks from whites and so forth. This is a personal type of campaign that's unworthy of the office he holds. I can hardly have a warm feeling in my heart for someone who's been attacking me on a personal basis for many months now in the campaign."[63]

Like Carter, Reagan had to deal with controversy in the final hours. A mini-crisis came up when allegations arose in the *Wall Street Journal* about the business dealings of his national security adviser, Richard Allen. Some of the charges went back to Allen's days in the Nixon administration, including a suggestion that Allen had used inside information to assist some clients, including the shady Robert Vesco.[64] Reagan said Meese would look into the allegations. Allen took a leave of absence from the campaign until the matter was cleared up, but both Meese and Nofziger publicly stood by their old friend.[65]

As newspaper stories appeared about Allen's problems, reports began popping up about a possible role for Henry Kissinger in a Reagan administration. The two sets of stories closely tracked with one another, but only a cynic would suggest that enemies of Allen had coordinated the whole thing. It was widely known that Kissinger and Allen despised each other and had for years. The two badmouthed each other constantly. Observing the mortal enemies in the same room, a campaign staffer said, "It was like a scene from a Fellini movie."[66] Conservatives gagged on the idea of Kissinger being let even in the back door of a Reagan administration instead of their friend Allen.

Reagan made one more pass at New Jersey and picked up the endorsement of the Democratic mayor of Lodi, a heavily blue-collar town in Bergen County. He stopped by Barrett's, a local gin mill popular with Democrats. Reagan, who almost never swore in public, slipped and said of Carter, "I'll be damned if we'll let him get reelected!"[67] He told the mostly Democratic crowd, "I know what it's like to pull the Republican lever for the first time, because I used to be a Democrat myself, and I can tell you it only hurts for a minute and then it feels just great."[68]

With just a few days to go, the Reagan plane, LeaderShip '80, had become a moveable feast of wine and song. Drinks were being consumed at all hours. The chase plane was even more of a rollicking good time. Lyn Nofziger, who sometimes preferred to travel on this plane, could always count on a bottle of Bombay gin waiting for him.

Reagan was on high octane, but his staff was running on fumes. At one point, an exhausted Michele Davis fainted in the aisle of the plane. Like most of the other campaign aides, she had been burning the candle at both ends, working all day, drinking all night, dating on the run. She was surprised to wake up and find a compassionate conservative, Ronald Reagan, hovering over her, trying to revive her.[69] Davis wrote in her diary that people were "getting kind of punchy."[70]

Meals were served endlessly to the press—steaming platters of macaroni and cheese, pots of beans and sausage, giant frankfurters. Upon every takeoff, Mrs. Reagan would go through the press section handing out chocolates. Not everybody wanted the chocolates and some reporters complained of the poundage they had gained since being assigned to the Reagan campaign. But they knew it was best to accept the proffered candy, even if it meant depositing it in the pouch in front of them.

Some women in the press corps just didn't like Mrs. Reagan for whatever reason—she was old-fashioned, they didn't like her clothes, she didn't have a cause, whatever. Judy Bachrach of the *Washington Star* wrote a vicious column about her for handing out chocolates![71] After the column, Mrs. Reagan jokingly wore a sign around her neck as she handed out the candy. It read, "Take One! Or Else!"

Bachrach might have been more open-minded had she known how little the Carter White House thought of the press corps. One Carter campaign memo went so far as to refer to the reporters as a "flock of sheep."[72]

THE CHEER AND OPTIMISM that had dominated the Carter campaign immediately after the debate was gone, finito. By the weekend, his aides were quietly conceding that Reagan had "profited the most" from the debate. One Carterite said that Reagan "came across as appearing much more credible . . . as we're all now discovering."[73] Pat Caddell grudgingly accepted that maybe Reagan had gotten a "slight advantage."[74] Caddell was relentlessly spinning, but privately, he buried his head in his hands and lamented, "I just wish we hadn't debated."[75]

The momentum had shifted abruptly. Dick Wirthlin's internal polling suggested that Reagan had overtaken Carter in the race, and Reaganites were feeding these tidbits to reporters. The media's own polls showed motion toward Reagan also. In addition, the press could see on the ground the ever-swelling throngs for the Gipper, and the morale of the campaign staff and the candidate himself as he effortlessly worked a crowd.

Carter's fall offensive was faltering. In Mississippi just three days before the election, Carter bluntly told the crowd that his reelection was "very much in doubt." One aide, in an understatement, said that there was "a pause in the momentum" for Carter.[76] While Carter was getting great receptions from black audiences, the whites who came to hear him speak now were underwhelming, listless. Mondale, who had as good a feel for the game of politics as anyone, later remembered, "It was after that debate you could feel it drifting away. . . . You can see it in their faces. . . . You can see it in the way they applaud. . . . You can tell when they're kind of dispirited."[77]

The president staggered into Florida. Reagan, in contrast, was rolling now. He told crowds, "He did not give us a government as good as the people, as he said he would! He only gave us a government as good as Jimmy Carter! And that isn't good enough!"[78] Audiences ate it up. Signs materialized proclaiming, "Ask Amy, She Knows," including one that adorned the door to the head on Reagan's plane.[79]

In Wisconsin, before a large, friendly labor crowd, Reagan just could not resist. Speaking of Carter, he mirthfully said, "I know he touched our hearts, all of us, the other night. I remember when Patti and Ron were little tiny kids and we used to talk about nuclear power."[80] When he openly wondered who had "been in charge for the last three-and-one-half years," the crowd began chanting, "Amy! Amy!" "That could be," Reagan drolly replied.[81]

On the Reagan plane's PA system the campaign broadcast, for the benefit of reporters, Carter's much-mocked comments on discussing nuclear proliferation with his daughter, as well as his remarks about how he and Rosalynn read the Bible to each other in Spanish.[82] The Carter team employed the same device aboard Air Force One, broadcasting an old speech of Reagan's from 1961 in which the Republican warned that Medicare was a step toward "socialized medicine."[83]

But Carter just couldn't escape the ridicule. "Ask Amy" had taken on a life of its own. On the Sunday before the election, during the CBS broadcast of the Cowboys-Cardinals football game, quarterback-turned-commentator Roger Staubach was asked how Dallas could stop the potent St. Louis offense. "I talked to my daughter, Amy, this morning about it," he replied, "and she said the number-one problem was the bomb." Staubach, a Reagan supporter, did have a daughter named Amy, though she was just four years old.[84]

Carter was stumbling at the worst possible time, but the Reagan campaign wasn't content to wait and see how things would play out. Bill Timmons was organizing a massive get-out-the-vote effort, the biggest in the history of American politics, using possibly 500,000 motivated Republicans. Phone calls were being made, doors knocked on, rides to the polls arranged. Television and radio advertising was broadcast playing up Reagan's record as governor. Even Betty Ford had signed a letter to more than a million GOP women in targeted states.[85] In Texas, Gary Hoitsma with the Reagan campaign in Austin proudly told reporters that the campaign had fifty phone banks there and had already called one million voters.[86] Bob Beckel, Carter's point man in the state, paddling along on denial, said, "We're moving and Reagan's stalled."[87]

However, respected columnist and former Democratic consultant Mark Shields flatly predicted that Reagan would win the election on Tuesday, possibly by a big margin.[88] Tom Shales, who had ripped Reagan's debate performance, three days later did a 180-degree turn and wrote a long piece defending Reagan while tearing into the three networks, their anchors, and reporters for gross unfairness in their coverage of Reagan over the past year.[89]

Reagan streaked to Michigan on Sunday morning for one more joint appearance with his new best friend, Gerald Ford. Ford, the former center, and Reagan, the former right tackle, went high and low on Carter. Reagan praised Ford's time in office and Ford said Carter had "screwed up" the country. Ford also tried to chide Carter for accidentally referring to "Grand Rapids" as "Cedar Rapids." Ford told the audience that, in his opinion, Grand Rapids was "the most wonderful community in all the forty-eight states—er, fifty states."[90] One Reagan aide, remembering Ford long history of malapropisms, shook his head and said, "He who lives by the sword, dies by the sword."[91]

Some protesters heckled the Gipper, chanting, "Bonzo! Bonzo! Bonzo!" Reagan, grinning, won the discussion when he told them and the supportive audience, "Well, they better watch out! Bonzo grew up to be King Kong!"[92] Pleased with himself, Reagan said to an aide, "Eh—that got 'em."[93]

So much had changed in a short time. By this point Reagan had even developed a solid partnership with his running mate—a partnership that would eventually bloom into a genuine friendship. George Bush was out on the road taking the fight to the incumbent, proving himself to be tougher than Reagan had once thought. And Reagan had shown himself to be deeper, more reflective than Bush had expected. The running mates now spoke on the phone two or three times a week—at Reagan's insistence.[94]

Things were suddenly looking very good for Ronald Reagan. Superstitious, he almost never said "when we win," but rather "if we win." He always reminded aides of "President Dewey."[95]

Others were more bullish. Perhaps peering into the future, a fortune cookie company in New York began marketing cookies under the heading "Reagan Says"; each cookie had a saying or parable by the Gipper.[96]

IF THERE WAS A scent of victory in the air for Reagan, there was a smell of death around Carter's term of office. The rats were beginning to jump ship. Lane Kirkland, the head of the AFL-CIO, had been supporting Carter's reelection, but secretly opened back-channel communications to Ed Meese. The chancellor of West Germany, Helmut Schmidt, was quietly reaching out to Reagan, suggesting a mid-November meeting.[97] Caddell conceded that, for the first time in a long time, his polling had Reagan in the lead.[98]

Other rats were leaking their names for a role in a possible Reagan administration. World-class self-promoters such as Al Haig were being "mentioned" for State. Others, more modest and class acts, like Dick Schweiker and Drew Lewis, were finding their names showing up for possible roles in the cabinet without any impetus from them. For the Departments of Energy and Education, no names made the list of the "Great Mentioner," as Reagan saw them as worthless and wanted them dismantled. Some other interesting names were being floated, including Thomas Sowell, an African-American at the vanguard of conservative intellectuals, for Labor and the young Michigan congressman David Stockman, who had so effectively portrayed Carter in the mock debate with Reagan, for a White House staff position.[99]

THE WEEKEND BEFORE THE election, most political writers were still saying the election was too close to call. The media generally stuck to predictions of only modest GOP gains in the House of ten to fifteen seats and three to six in the Senate. As for the presidential race, a huge block of undecided voters remained, making the whole situation just too fluid to gauge. Many political watchers felt that, in the end, voters would settle for the Carter they knew rather than the Reagan they did not. That's what Jody Powell told himself, saying that when "people really start to think about Ronald Reagan in the White House," they would opt for Carter.[100]

But something was going on out there. GOP phone banks were showing an enormous upswing in Reagan support since the debate. Morale among the workers and party people was sky-high. Everybody was working twenty-hour days and loving every second of it. Some Reagan teams had so many volunteers on their hands that there wasn't enough work to go around. Michele Davis penned in her campaign journal, "I know we are going to win . . . everyone is so UP. Even Stu Spencer is smiling outright."[101]

For the Democrats, it was just the opposite. Low morale and low volunteer activity plagued them across the nation. Carteritis had set in. Democratic candidates were desperately running away from the president, hoping not to be caught in his undertow. "A lot of us could lose, and Carter isn't worth it," one confided to writer Elizabeth Drew.[102]

Reagan could feel the difference from the crowds. He'd always drawn his strength and sustenance from people, and he had hit his stride at just the right time, exhorting crowds who were, in turn, exhorting him. The ground was cracking underneath Carter and the Democrats as Reagan's crowds continued to swell. Lou Cannon reported that Reagan's supporters "now press in on the candidate in what sometimes seems an almost atavistic urge to touch their leader."[103]

The primitives were massing, the elites nervous.

And the political Richter scale was beginning to gyrate.

37

ENTRANCE, STAGE LEFT

*"I am not frightened by what lies ahead. And I don't believe
the American people are frightened by what lies ahead."*

In the lead-up to Election Day—Tuesday, November 4—the weather across the country was unusually warm for so late in the year. States in the South were still hitting highs in the mid-seventies and northern cities such as Boston were downright balmy, with daytime temperatures in the high fifties.

But ominously, rain was pouring down when President Carter returned to the White House before lunchtime on Election Day. He had just come back from voting at his old high school in Plains, Georgia. There had also been a steady rain in Seattle the night before at Carter's last stop. For Carter, it seemed like it was raining all over the world.

In the past week, he had gone to twenty-six cities in fifteen states, logging more than fifteen thousand air miles.[1] His face was "puffy and lined from the relentless pace he had set," in the words of the *New York Times*, and his right hand was "red and bruised from endless hand-shaking," covered in nicks from the rings and fingernails of people clasping.[2]

At 8 A.M. in Plains, he spoke to old friends and neighbors—people who used to call him "Jimmy." Carter's voice quavered as he tried to find the words to defend his first term of office. He said ruefully, "I am ready to abide by your judgment," like a man on trial who was not hopeful for a favorable verdict from the jury.[3] Carter struggled, choking up as he bit his lip. His remarks were "tinged with foreboding," Sam Donaldson reported.[4] Mrs. Carter stood beside him, looking stoic but sad.

Later that morning, five hundred administration employees—not knowing whether they would be employed for much longer—waited in the rain for President and Mrs. Carter on the South Lawn. After landing in *Marine One*, the president addressed the crowd. He spoke in past tenses—not "We will" but rather "We have."[5] It was not very reassuring.

Carter somberly reminded his audience to vote and then walked into the White House with the first lady. Observers could not tell whether that was rain or tears streaking down their faces.

RONALD REAGAN, BACK AT his home at 1669 San Onofre Drive in Pacific Palisades, cast his ballot several hours after Jimmy Carter. A voting precinct had been set up at a neighbor's house, so he and Mrs. Reagan made a short and leisurely trip down the street to vote just after 10 A.M. pacific time.[6] Robert and Sally Gulick had made their home available for seventeen years as a polling place to their neighbors. Lawrence Welk, Sylvester Stallone, and Vin Scully had all voted at their house.[7]

Reagan was dressed in a god-awful red-and-white-checked blowsy shirt and brown pants. Mrs. Reagan looked terrific, as always. Friends and well-wishers lined the street and the Reagans stopped frequently to shake hands, chat, and hug. Mrs. Reagan told a friend, "I'll be glad when the day is over."[8] They voted by paper ballot and Reagan was spotted wearing his reading glasses in the open voting booth, something he rarely allowed the public to see. Television cameras and reporters were everywhere, and autograph hounds badgered the Reagans. He was besieged with questions but said lightheartedly, "I can't answer till I get on my mark," like the old pro he was. On the ground were two taped Xs, one marked "R. R." and the other "N. R." Someone had scribbled on Reagan's mark "O. & W.," a joking reference to a phrase coined by Jack Kemp the year before, when he called Reagan the "oldest and the wisest" of the GOP candidates. Nancy Reagan hated the expression.

Reagan was asked whom he voted for and he quipped, "Nancy."[9] When asked whom she voted for, he wisecracked, "Oh, Nancy voted for some has-been actor."[10]

As Reagan got into his limousine, reporters clamored to know whether he thought he was going to win.[11] "You know me," he replied. "I'm too superstitious to answer anything like that." Mrs. Reagan said softly that they were "cautiously optimistic," prompting Reagan to tell the throng, "Yes, I'm cautiously optimistic."[12]

Whatever the outcome, he was making plans to head to his ranch to recharge his batteries. In the last two weeks of the campaign, he'd stumped in fifteen states and was exhausted.

THE 1980 CAMPAIGN HAD begun more than two years earlier, when Congressman Phil Crane launched his long-shot bid for the GOP nomination in the late summer of 1978. For some, the quest for the White House had started even earlier—much earlier. Ronald Reagan had begun officially in 1968 at the GOP convention in Miami Beach and unofficially as a kid in Dixon, Illinois. Jimmy Carter had been bent on securing a second term ever since he audaciously ran for president in 1976 as a former one-term governor of a backwater state—a victory as extraordinary and unexpected as any since the election of former one-term congressman Abraham Lincoln in 1860.

After two years of electioneering by nearly a dozen men, after some thirty-five primaries and more than $255 million spent by all the contenders and pretenders, the national debate had come down to this one day, November 4. An estimated eighty-five million people would go to the polls, voting not only for their chief executive but also for 34 senators, 435 members of the House, and roughly 6,000 state legislative seats, not to mention local offices and various referenda.[13]

Holding Election Day in early November was a holdover from America's agrarian past. Back in 1792 Congress had specified only that presidential electors be appointed "within thirty-four days preceding the first Wednesday in December, in every fourth year." This was to give the members of the Electoral College time to meet and count their ballots and thus proclaim a new president-elect. It wasn't until 1845 that Congress had officially designated "Election Day" across the country as the "Tuesday next after the first Monday in the month of November." Early November was the most convenient time because it fell after farmers had pulled in their harvest, meaning they could afford to take the time to travel to vote, but before the snows of winter had arrived, which would make travel from remote farms much more difficult. Election Day was set for a Tuesday because traveling to vote could take a day or more, and activity on a Sunday, the Lord's Day, was verboten for many Christians.[14]

On the eve of the 1980 election some columnists and academics worried that with John Anderson on the ballot, neither Reagan nor Carter would get a majority of the popular vote or a majority of the Electoral College vote. Failing to get a majority of the popular vote was not, in fact, all that unusual: it had happened fourteen times up to that point, the most recent instance coming in 1968. It was far less common for no presidential candidate to receive a majority of the Electoral College vote: this had happened only twice before, in 1800 and 1824. In each case, per the system set up by the Founding Fathers, the House of Representatives handled the matter—messily, maybe, but handled it nonetheless. Similarly, only twice—in 1876 and 1888—had a presidential candidate secured the required votes in the Electoral College but failed to win the popular vote.

If such a case were to occur in 1980, the electoral map indicated that Carter might be the one to benefit: the census was ten years old, and as a result tradition-ally Democratic-leaning states such as Pennsylvania and New York retained their Electoral College muscle even though they had lost thousands upon thousands of voters in the past decade.

It was a thin reed for Carterites to clutch.

While in Chicago on the Sunday before the election, President Carter awak-ened at 4 A.M. to a phone call from Deputy Secretary of State Warren Christopher informing him that the Iranian parliament had announced its terms for the release of the American hostages. Carter was exhausted from campaigning nonstop since the debate, but wearily, he put on the suit he'd worn earlier and left his suite on the twenty-ninth floor of the Hyatt Regency near O'Hare Airport and flew back to Washington, canceling that day of campaigning. Some reporters, rousted from their slumber, fumbled for their passports, assuming that the phone call meant they were off to Germany with the president to greet the returning hostages.[15]

The U.S. government had made a last-minute offer to end the trade boycott of Iran and release frozen Iranian assets in the United States if the hostages were released. Now Carter met for several hours in the White House Cabinet Room with members of his administration to thrash out the latest proposal from the Ira-nians. Later in the day, he made a three-minute televised address to the country about the Iranian offer, describing it as a "positive basis."[16]

Still, the hostages were in Iran with no end of their humiliation in sight. As one reporter noted, "Carter's strategists have been hoping that the president would reap an 11th-hour benefit from the apparent prospect that the hostages will soon be freed."[17] But any presumed political advantage from the release of the hostages had drained away by this point. According to news polls, Americans by a 4–1 margin opposed the release of the hostages if it meant renewing relations with the Iranians, and more than half the country now believed that Carter would "give up too much" in order to secure their freedom.[18]

Many Americans couldn't decide whether they had been played as fools by Carter or if he'd been played for a fool by the ayatollah. The fact that Carter's tele-vised remarks broke into the live broadcast of NFL football games probably did not help his cause.[19] Nor did the fact that Election Day would mark the first anni-versary of the taking of the American hostages—something Carter noted bitterly years later, especially because all the networks trumpeted the anniversary.[20]

The Iranians were not looking forward to the American elections. They had contempt for Carter, regarding him as "weak," according to Bruce Langdon, the American chief of mission in Iran, who was the top-ranking hostage. At the same time, however, they hated and feared Reagan. Said Langdon, they were concerned about Reagan's "tough bombast . . . what that might mean in the long run."[21]

IN THE LAST DAYS of the campaign, Reagan was a study in both adrenaline and cool. On his plane, he kidded with photographers, even as one mistakenly referred to him as "President Reagan" while asking him to sign some photographs. Reagan replied, "You know, after you've canceled Social Security and started the war, what else is there for you to do?"[22]

As his 727 took off, Reagan stood in the passageway—temporarily substituting for Mrs. Reagan—to attempt to roll a small pumpkin down the aisle rather than the usual orange. When the plane's public address system played "On the Road Again" by Willie Nelson and a less well-known number called "Ronald Reagan for President," the candidate was back up, clapping his hands and performing a "hoedown," as one reporter observed. On another takeoff, Reagan attempted to roll the pumpkin down the aisle again, but this time a reporter had given him an incentive: there, in the middle of the aisle, was a rubber mask of Jimmy Carter. Reagan threw a ten-strike, hitting the mask squarely in the kisser.[23]

Reporters noted the difference between Reagan's LeaderShip '80 and Carter's Air Force One at campaign's end. The Reagan plane resembled a flying Delta House, with laughing, practical jokes, whistles blowing, booze freely flowing. Reagan easily mingled with the media and the staff. Reporters jokingly serenaded the Reagans with "Happy Trails." Air Force One, by contrast, was a dirge, and Carter kept to himself in the front section of the plane. He was closely monitoring the latest news from Tehran, via Ed Muskie at the State Department.

On Sunday, Reagan made his way to Cincinnati with Gerald Ford, George Bush, and Bob Hope in tow. Hope made a joke about Reagan appointing acerbic comedian Don Rickles as America's ambassador to Iran and fifteen thousand people laughed uproariously.[24]

Although the running mates had grown to like and respect each other, all was not sweetness and light between their respective camps. The Bushies privately complained that Reagan had run a "bumbling campaign"; one unnamed Bush adviser told *Time* that "if Bush had been the nominee, he would have been leading in the polls by 20 points."[25]

Monday was a whirlwind of campaign activity, as Reagan moved from Peoria, Illinois, to Oregon before going to San Diego. At the last stop Reagan noted to a big, friendly crowd outside a shopping mall that he'd finished his 1966 campaign for governor in San Diego as well. A solitary heckler would not be quiet, yelling repeatedly. Reagan finally said, "Aww, shut up!" The crowd went wild. The dutiful son said that his mother had told him he should never use that word but he figured one time wouldn't do any permanent damage.[26]

Reagan's plane then headed home to Los Angeles, but because of fog, Leader-Ship '80 was forced to land at Burbank instead. On the plane, he rolled the orange one more time down the aisle, and reporters good-naturedly chanted, "Drop the bomb!" Reagan was in high spirits as he told the airborne crowd, "I've just decided that the whole thing has been so much fun, to hell with the election, we're going to keep on campaigning."[27]

Carter made a mad dash to Ohio, Illinois, Oregon, and Washington State before flying home to Georgia late Monday evening so that he and the first lady could vote Tuesday morning. In Seattle, Carter implored Democrats to "come home." Plaintively and repeatedly, he said, "I need you, I need you." His voice was croaky, after one more long day of exhorting wavering Democrats not to "waste your vote."[28]

On the plane back, he had little time to rest, as he was getting updates from officials about the hostages as well as the state of his campaign. Neither situation was going well for Carter.

John Anderson, lance still firmly in his grip and a windmill in his vision, ended his campaign in Minnesota, naturally on a college campus.[29] Toward the end, he had discovered the simple joys of being out and about with his fellow Americans. He knew he wasn't going to win, his supporters knew it, but it did not matter. Anderson—now "Stardust" to his Secret Service contingent—wanted to speak his mind and make his point, and he got that chance.[30] The interior of his plane was a menagerie of oddball banners, bumper stickers, and posters. His staff had taken up the habit of blowing duck and moose calls as the plane took off. Reporters organized a "kazoo band," and when Anderson walked down the aisle of the plane, they mirthfully played "Hail to the Chief." Aides tried to steal a large potted plant from the Milwaukee airport to decorate their plane, but were foiled by local officials.[31] No one outside of politics would ever understand how joyously puerile a losing campaign at the end could be.

The Reagan campaign used the night before the election to broadcast across the nation a half-hour speech by the candidate. Reagan had taped it earlier in a Virginia studio. It was one of his best speeches, though it never got the recognition it deserved.

Reagan, looking into a camera, gave his testament to America, describing it as mankind's "last best hope." Carter was mentioned just twice, and only in passing. The Republican spoke of the impending election and of his hopes for the safe and imminent return of the fifty-two imprisoned Americans.

Reagan turned to two of his favorite subjects: the future and young Americans. "A child born this year will begin his or her adult life in what will be the twenty-first century. What kind of country, what kind of legacy will we leave to these young men and women who will live out America's third century as a nation?"

He reviewed the stakes, describing Americans' unhappiness about the "worsening economic problems, about the constant crisis atmosphere in our foreign policy, about our diminishing prestige around the globe, about the weakness in our economy and national security that jeopardizes world peace, about our lack of strong, straight-forward leadership." Reagan addressed the threat of the national government to the citizenry: "And many Americans today, just as they did two hundred years ago, feel burdened, stifled and sometimes even oppressed by government that has grown too large, too bureaucratic, too wasteful, too unresponsive, too uncaring about people and their problems. Americans, who have always known that excessive bureaucracy is the enemy of excellence and compassion, want a change in public life—a change that makes government work *for* people."

Reagan then moved to hope. "I believe we can embark on a new age of reform in this country and an era of national renewal. An era that will reorder the relationship between citizen and government, . . . that will revitalize the values of family, work, and neighborhood and that will restore our private and independent social institutions." He didn't stop there—no sail-trimming for the old Jeffersonian. Reagan championed the "individual" over the "state" and said that private "institutions, not government, are the real sources of our economic and social progress as a people." Reagan stated once again his desire to cut taxes and curb the growth of government, calling it and the accompanying "waste and fraud" a "national scandal." He referred to America as a "federation of sovereign states."

Reagan spoke of his view of the presidency as a "bully pulpit" and not a managerial concern. "No person who understands the American presidency can possibly hope to make every decision or tend to every detail in the national government." Reagan did not mention that Carter kept the schedule for the White House tennis courts, but everybody knew what he was referring to.

The GOP nominee cited some of the reforms he would seek if elected: reining in the bureaucracy, saving Social Security, going after corruption in government and organized crime, including the horrendous drug traffic.

Reagan came to the meaning of the election of 1980. "That's why I want to talk with you—not about campaign issues, but about America, about us, you and me. Not so long ago, we emerged from a world war. Turning homeward at last, we built a grand prosperity and hoped—from our own success and plenty—to help others less fortunate. Our peace was a tense and bitter one, but in those days the center seemed to hold. Then came the hard years: riots and assassinations, domestic strife over the Vietnam War and in the last four years, drift and disaster in Washington. It all seems a long way from a time when politics was a national passion and sometimes even fun. . . .

"That is really the question before us tonight: for the first time in our memory many Americans are asking: does history still have a place for America, for her people, for her great ideals? There are some who answer 'no': that our energy is spent, our days of greatness at an end, that a great national malaise is upon us. They say we must cut our expectations, conserve and withdraw, that we must tell our children . . . not to dream as we once dreamed."

Reagan's eyes glistened, his voice became husky, as he told of his old friend John Wayne. The Duke, said Reagan, was "more than a symbol of the Hollywood dream industry; to millions he was a symbol of our country itself. And when he died, the headlines seemed to convey all the doubt about America, all the nostalgia for a seemingly lost past. 'The *Last* American Hero,' said one headline. 'Mr. America Dies,' said another. Well, I knew John Wayne well, and no one would have been angrier at being called the '*last* American hero.'"

Reagan spoke of the heroes of Vietnam, the prisoners of war whom he and Mrs. Reagan had welcomed to America and entertained in their home. The Reagans had heard their tales of torture, of "tapping code on the wall that divided their solitary confinement cells. One night . . . I asked Nancy, 'Where did we find such men?' The answer came to me as quickly as I had asked the question. We found them where we've always found them. In our shops, on our farms, on our city streets, in our villages and towns. They are just the product of the freest society the world has ever known."

Reagan turned to spiritual matters. "Since her beginning America has held fast to this hope of divine providence, this vision of 'man *with* God.' It is true that world peace is jeopardized by those who view man not as a noble being, but as an accident of nature, without soul, and important only to the extent he can serve an all powerful state. But it is our spiritual commitment—more than all the military might in the world—that will win our struggle for peace. . . . It is humility before God that is ultimately the source of America's strength as a nation."

After telling his story about the Puritans and their "city upon a hill," Reagan moved toward his conclusion, talking about the past year on the campaign, meeting and talking with so many of his fellow Americans. "I find no national malaise,

I find nothing wrong with the American people. Oh, they are frustrated, even angry at what has been done to this blessed land. But more than anything they are sturdy and robust as they have always been." Reagan then offered not an empty promise but a wish, a hope, and a pledge to "stand by" the oppressed of the world, the tortured, the enslaved, the victims of persecution. He challenged Americans, quoting Dr. Joseph Warren, who had been killed at the battle of Bunker Hill and who said to his fellow patriots before the clash, "Act worthy of yourselves."

In closing, the Gipper reminded Americans of the past four years, the dire economy, and America's diminished standing across the globe. He quoted Lincoln's admonition etched at his memorial: "Let us bind up the nation's wounds." And then, as always, Reagan returned to the young men and women of his country.

"At this very moment, some young American, coming up along the Virginia or Maryland shores of the Potomac, is seeing for the first time the lights that glow on the great halls of our government and the monuments to the memory of our great men. Let us resolve tonight that young Americans will always see those Potomac lights; that they will always find there a city of hope in a country that is free. And let us resolve they will say of our day and our generation that we did keep faith with our God, that we did act 'worthy of ourselves,' that we did protect and pass on lovingly that shining city on a hill."[32]

THE ELECTION-EVE SPEECH COST $400,000 to broadcast on all three networks.[33] It was worth every penny.

Reagan's hard-bitten press aide, Jim Brady, shed tears when he saw the speech. Lisa Myers wrote in the *Washington Star*, "It was a speech of hope, designed to soothe and stir rather than incite." It was, she said, "presidential in tone."[34] Howell Raines of the *New York Times* was also impressed, calling it "evocative."[35] *Time* magazine called it "superbly moving."[36]

The remarkable address, which Reagan did on the second take, had been drafted by one of Reagan's favorite speechwriters, Ken Khachigian. Word had already leaked out that if Reagan won, Khachigian was favored for the top speech-writing post in the White House. Khachigian had been traveling on the plane with Reagan throughout the fall, banging out speech after speech on his IBM Selectric II. Stu Spencer, who had seconded Ed Meese's decision to bring Khachigian aboard, years later said, "He was the best speechwriter I ever saw."[37]

Khachigian and Reagan's other favorite speechwriter, Peter Hannaford, were so successful at least in part because they understood Reagan and listened to him. Before they touched a keystroke, they would sit with Reagan and take notes, getting direction on content. They would then draft the speech and give it to Reagan, who would edit it—adding, deleting, moving paragraphs around.[38]

IN ACCORDANCE WITH TRADITION, Election Day voting began in Dixville Notch, New Hampshire, just after midnight. Reagan crushed Carter in this tiny New England village, 17–3.[39] He had finally won Dixville Notch, after losing there to Ford in the 1976 primary and tying with Bush in the 1980 primary.[40]

Democratic leaders knew their base was demoralized, while the Republicans were energized. In St. Louis County, Missouri, GOP chairwoman Pat Keyes called Kenny Klinge and said, "I've got a problem." Klinge expected her to say no one had shown up to work the twenty-five phones. Instead, she said, "I've got five hundred people, what am I supposed to do?" A platoon system was hastily arranged.[41]

The pollsters were working the phones, checking key precincts in early states, trying to determine a trend, if any. Dick Wirthlin was detecting unusual strength for Reagan among Catholic and blue-collar voters in the Northeast.

Bill Casey and others were also working the phones, calling their CIA and military contacts around the world, trying to find out about any unusual troop movements or unexplained activity by American military planes. Casey, even on Election Day, was worried that Carter might pull the hostages out of a hat.

ABOUT TWO HOURS AFTER the old cranks of Dixville Notch voted, Jody Powell took a phone call on Air Force One as the big plane was on approach to the Seattle airport. It was from the White House. On the other end of the line were Hamilton Jordan and Pat Caddell. The connection was bad, but Powell could hear well enough to know the news was bad. "We need to talk to the president," his friend Jordan said. "The bottom has fallen out. It's all over."[42]

As soon as the plane landed, Powell called back on a land line and pressed for more information. Caddell told him that on Saturday his polling had had the race statistically tied, with Carter at 41 and Reagan at 40 percent. On Sunday night, his polling had had Reagan going up by 5 percent over Carter. And by Monday night, Reagan had opened up 7 to 10 percent lead over the president.[43]

The young press secretary, grasping at straws, asked whether the poll was an aberration. Caddell told him that a trend had begun over the weekend and was only accelerating. A landslide was coming their way and there was nothing they could do to get out of its path. Dejectedly, Powell hung up. He then watched as the president spoke to a hangar full of enthusiastic Democrats. Though Carter's voice was nearly gone, he gave a good performance, even as he choked up a bit. Powell remorsefully thought that it was the best rally of the year.[44]

He decided not to tell the president yet; he would wait until they were alone on the Boeing 707 and headed back to Georgia. Problem was, he couldn't get Carter alone. Around 11:30 P.M. pacific time, as the plane took off, Powell went to the galley, fixed himself a stiff drink, and waited.[45] Carter had come out of his two-room private compartment to chew the fat with the staff in their section of the plane and have a rare double martini. The president was "joshing around . . . that sort of thing," Powell recalled. "I thought, 'This is such a nice one that I cannot break into this and take him back up there and tell him he's got a call, because I know what he is going to hear.'"[46]

Carter decided to invite reporters into his private quarters for a chat. Finally, as the plane was halfway across the country and the reporters had been dismissed, Powell went to the forward section of the plane and told Carter about his phone call with Jordan and Caddell. It was now almost 4 A.M.

"What did they find?" Carter asked.

"They said it looks bad," Powell told him. "It's probably all over."[47]

Carter was first shocked and then disheartened. "So finally," Powell remembered, "one of the stewards came . . . and said, 'Mr. Caddell and Mr. Jordan are on the phone and they said they need to talk to the president.'" Caddell's latest numbers showed an utter and complete collapse for the Georgian, across the board, with nearly all groups and in nearly all regions. He was losing whites overwhelmingly, he was losing the Catholic vote, and Reagan was extremely competitive with union voters. Carter was being wiped out in the suburbs and in the rural areas. Reagan was scoring impressively with Hispanics and Jewish voters. Carter's beloved South had also apparently found a new hero in Reagan. Carter was running far behind in every category from four years earlier, even among the evangelicals he'd carried so handsomely in 1976.

"Are you sure about this?" Carter asked.

"Yes. There is just no way."

With little else to say, both men apologized to the president. Carter hung up. Powell, weeping, said, "I'm really sorry, Mr. President. . . . We could have done a better job."[48] Carter called Rosalynn at their home in Plains and told her, "We are going to lose."

The president, alone in the darkened Air Force One, gently wept.[49]

SOMETIME LATER, POWELL ASSEMBLED White House staffers and told them what he'd told the president. In the dim plane racing over the slumbering countryside, they learned that the election was "hopeless."

All cried but promised Powell that they would not tell anybody else. Understandably, Powell described the rest of his day as "miserable." He did tell his wife, Nan, and daughter, Emily, that the president was going to lose. His twelve-year-old daughter burst into tears. "No! That cannot be! That cannot be!"

Powell ruefully remembered all the insults piled on the Carter gang by the Washington establishment. "They were all cheerleaders for Camelot." He also remembered the false story in the *Washington Post* accusing him of having an affair. His family saw the awful story and Powell furiously demanded a retraction, which the paper published. He said the Style Section of the *Post* was "totally out of control" in those days and that his wife never forgave the paper.[50]

THE MORNING OF THE election, George Bush met with his campaign team in Houston and spoke to them affectionately about the trail, the travails, and now, a possible triumph. Earlier, a thick fog had enveloped Houston as he and Mrs. Bush went to their polling place. Later that day, friends, campaign workers, and reporters milled about the Bush home in Houston. The Bushes were born blood donors, always kind to strangers, even those they did not depend on. Their door, it seemed, was always open to friends. In the evening, the entire Bush clan gathered in a hotel suite. George and Barbara Bush sat on the floor watching the returns on three television sets as their four sons joyously roughhoused with one another. Bush several times had to gently admonish them, "Respectful, respectful."[51] A photographer was attempting—vainly—to get the Bush boys to knock off the horseplay and stand still for the historic photograph.

Vice President Mondale voted that morning in the Afton, Minnesota, town hall, accompanied by his wife, Joan, and their children.[52] Mondale, of all the candidates, may have pulled the toughest duty. It was up to him, the old New Dealer, to convince wavering Democrats, distrustful of Carter, to come back to the fold. He loved campaigning but had been on a whirlwind tour for months and was exhausted. And he knew. Carter had called him earlier to tell him they were going to be wiped out.[53]

Carter spent the afternoon in the Oval Office and the family residence of the White House. He knew the end was coming but believed it was not a reflection on him. He blamed Walter Cronkite for trumpeting Election Day as the anniversary of the hostage taking and for heightening the American people's frustration.[54] He blamed the personal problems of his staff, including Bert Lance and Hamilton Jordan. He blamed the increases in the cost of oil from the Arab countries, the fight over the Panama Canal treaties, and the appointment of "so many minority members" to federal posts.[55] Only later, in a moment of private candor, did he say, "I lost it myself."[56]

After Carter spoke to the staff on the South Lawn, the bad news raced through the White House complex. By late afternoon, almost everybody knew the election was going to go badly. Carter went for a jog alone in the rain, lost in thought. He asked Powell to arrange a meeting in the Oval Office at half past five with Jordan, Robert Strauss, Stuart Eizenstat, and Jack Watson, who had replaced Jordan as chief of staff. The depressing discussion was about what he should say to the Democrats gathered at the Sheraton Washington Hotel and when he should call Governor Reagan. All agreed that he should not concede until the polls had closed on the West Coast.[57]

Carter called a cabinet meeting for 7 P.M. He did not attend, but he sent Jordan and Watson to tell the members of his cabinet that he was going to lose. No one was to criticize or attack Reagan. Just a few hours earlier, Carter had called Reagan a "right-wing Republican."[58]

As darkness enveloped Washington, Carter was biding his time in the twenty-five-room private residence at the White House, his family somberly gathered around watching television. Understatedly, Caddell said, "No one was feeling very good."[59]

REAGAN, AFTER VOTING, GOT a quick haircut at Drucker's Barber Shop in Beverly Hills. The trim set him back $7.50. While there, he also got a $1 shoeshine and a $7 manicure. Later, over a lunch of tuna salad, iced tea, and iced milk, Ed Meese and Mike Deaver joined Reagan to discuss the transition of power in the government. The Gipper, superstitiously, knocked on wood and was hesitant to talk about such matters unless and until he actually won.[60] Ken Khachigian had drafted a victory speech, but the ultra-cautious Reagan refused to look at it.[61]

Reagan was operating under the assumption that the election would be a close one. Wirthlin had advised him that their last national sampling had Reagan ahead by six points, but Reagan knew it was now all about turnout.[62] Wirthlin called Reagan just after noon to tell him about the early numbers. Reagan responded by crossing his fingers and knocking on wood at the same time. He and Nancy tried to busy themselves by taking and placing phone calls.

Carter knew he was going to lose and Reagan believed he might win, but neither man was prepared for the political earthquake that was rumbling its way across the country, precinct by precinct, county by county, and state by state.

THE THREE MAJOR TV networks—ABC, CBS, and NBC—went live with their news at 6:30 P.M. eastern time and then swung right into their open-ended election coverage beginning at 7 P.M. In a sign of things to come, two small cable stations were also broadcasting election-related content that evening. Ted Turner's CNN was offering its first coverage of a presidential campaign. Meanwhile, a tiny cable station called the Cable Satellite Public Affairs Network, which had a miniscule budget of $100,000 for the night, planned to broadcast old speeches by the candidates and raw footage from campaign events, interspersed with call-in shows. The concept was the brainchild of a formerly obscure staffer in the Ford White House, Brian Lamb. The phrase "low-key" was invented for Lamb, the president of C-SPAN, who rarely showed any emotion whatsoever. Lamb had assembled a network of 850 cable systems that reached six million houses.[63]

But it was definitely the major networks that ruled the roost. And they promised "wall-to-wall" Election Night coverage. For the hypercompetitive political junkies at the networks' news divisions, this was their Super Bowl. As the *New York Times* observed, "To television news officials, the contest between Jimmy Carter and Ronald Reagan almost pales beside the fierce competition among the three major commercial networks over which will name the national and statewide winners."[64] Nobody wanted to screw up, as CBS had in 1976, prematurely calling Ohio for Ford, only to have to withdraw the call and award it later to Carter. But this was war, as far as they were concerned, and the intense pressure to be first would lead to more wrong calls on this night that would have to be reversed.

The networks' election coverage was lavishly produced. Each network had full-fledged political units including political directors, pollsters, consultants, and aides skilled in analyzing key precincts in the states, especially those thought to be close. The "nets" had computers, calculators, runners, makeup artists, phone lines everywhere, cute little jingles, state-of-the-art graphics, and cars with drivers at the ready to fetch a guest at a moment's notice. Correspondents had been dispatched to all the important locations. These included the hotel in Washington where the Republicans were gathering, the Hilton; the Reagan hotel in Los Angeles, the Century Plaza; the Democrats' hotel in Washington, the Sheraton; the White House; the Reagans' home in Pacific Palisades; even John Anderson's command station (Anderson's inevitable concession speech being an unlucky draw for network reporters). The networks also had reporters stationed with several key Senate candidates around the country. A handful of longtime liberal senators had been under assault from independent conservative and Christian organizations, and all wanted to see if they would be able to withstand the withering challenge from the Right.

The anchors were in New York and Washington. For ABC, Frank Reynolds and Ted Koppel were in the pilot and co-pilot seats. ABC had a small army of other commentators, including Max Robinson, Barbara Walters, Peter Jennings, and Robert MacNeil, along with columnists George Will and Tom Wicker and correspondents Catherine Mackin, Lynn Sherr, Steve Bell, and Brit Hume. Barry Serafin was with the Reagan entourage in LA and the irrepressible Sam Donaldson was with Carter at the White House.

Venerable Walter Cronkite was manning the desk for CBS along with his designated replacement, Dan Rather, whom Cronkite treated like an errand boy. This would be "Uncle Walter's" last election. It was also his sixty-fourth birthday. Correspondent Bill Plante was with Reagan and Phil Jones with Carter, while Lesley Stahl was on hand as well. For commentary CBS had Bill Moyers, who had worked for Lyndon Johnson, and Jeff Greenfield, who had worked for Bobby Kennedy, along with conservative columnist James J. Kilpatrick, whose famous "Point-Counterpoint" exchange on *60 Minutes* with liberal Shana Alexander had been uproariously parodied on *Saturday Night Live*.

Over at NBC, John Chancellor was holding down the fort, aided by David Brinkley and Tom Brokaw. It was an open secret that Chancellor and Brinkley detested each other. Brinkley was under doctor's orders not to push it too hard, as he had just gone through gallbladder surgery.[65] The greatest of all the presidential campaign biographers, Teddy White, was on hand to lend his substantial presence for NBC. Jessica Savitch was covering the congressional race, and Heidi Schulman and Chris Wallace were in Los Angeles with the Reagan campaign.

None of the networks had any political consultants in the wings to pontificate. All three used their own correspondents or print journalists and elected officials.

The networks' political directors—the bookish Hal Bruno at ABC, the quietly charming Marty Plissner at CBS, and NBC's Gordon Manning, who kept a lower profile—had been relentlessly preparing for this one big night. They had been running the numbers for days now, looking at all possible election scenarios. They also had the private phone numbers for all the high-ranking officials of the Reagan and Carter campaigns. Throughout the day they had been gathering tidbits, rumors, and anecdotes from around the country. ABC had interviewed voters in three hundred key precincts. CBS, together with the *New York Times*, interviewed 15,000 voters that day. NBC conducted an astounding 28,500 exit interviews with voters.[66]

For sheer glitz and exceptional content, ABC led the way. This was the era of the legendary Roone Arledge, whose creative stewardship had turned ABC into a broadcasting juggernaut. The network's round, two-tiered set looked like the bridge of the starship *Enterprise*, filled with analysts; giant, brightly lit maps; television and computer monitors; and colorful graphics. NBC was not far behind in the department, featuring a massive, twenty-four-by-fourteen-foot Plexiglas map that was being operated by a squad of electricians in charge of 7,324 tiny lightbulbs.[67]

All three networks employed colored maps, taking advantage of the fact that by 1980 most Americans had color television sets. States on the ABC board that might go for Reagan would be lit in a bright red while those that might go for Carter would be lit a bright blue. For NBC and CBS, it was just the opposite: Reagan states would be blue; Carter states, red. But Democrats complained about being so closely identified with red, the color of Communism. Within a few years, all three networks would make the GOP the "Red State" party.

The elaborate studios were hives of activity. For every person in front of the lens, there were hundreds working in support of him or her, behind the camera. Tables groaned under the weight of shrimp, sandwiches, fruit, and other delectables for staff and guests. Wine and beer was even available, though it was discouraged for those going on camera. Despite the amenities, the atmosphere wasn't entirely comfortable. To counter all the equipment and the klieg lights, the studios had been super-cooled. Woe to those who sat still too long; their feet got cold.

The huge armies covering the election were gearing up for a long night.

It wasn't to be.

THE END CAME QUICKLY, but not mercifully, for Jimmy Carter. At 6:30 P.M. eastern time, ABC's Frank Reynolds announced that Reagan had already carried the state of Indiana and that a thirty-three-year-old GOP congressman, J. Danforth Quayle, had defeated three-term incumbent Democratic senator Birch Bayh. The polls were still open in parts of Indiana. Over at NBC, John Chancellor came on at 7 P.M. and predicted, "Ronald Reagan will win a very substantial victory tonight—that's our projection."[68]

At the top of the hour, Reynolds called Ohio for Reagan. The ABC newsman hadn't even had a chance to tell viewers that Reagan had also taken Virginia and Kentucky. Carter had won West Virginia and, as expected, Georgia and the District of Columbia. The polls were still open in some of these states. Florida fell quickly for Reagan—the first breach of Carter's "Solid South." At seven minutes after seven, Reynolds called New Hampshire for Reagan.

Barbara Walters, widely known to have a nuclear-powered Rolodex, came on at 7:12 P.M. to report on a startling phone conversation she'd just had with Caddell. "He did say that last night he told President Carter he was going to lose." She said she had pressed Caddell, asking if there was any chance, and he replied, "Look up at the board and you can see it spelled out."[69]

Oklahoma and its eight electoral votes quickly fell into the Reagan column, and minutes later Tennessee went for the Gipper, as did New Jersey. States were falling as if autumn leaves. Maine, North Carolina, and Wisconsin went for Reagan too, adding to his electoral vote total.

When the national ABC broadcast came back on at 8 P.M., Reynolds said that Carter had carried Massachusetts and that in North Carolina, incumbent Democrat senator Robert Morgan had staved off the challenge of Professor John East. ABC later had to reverse both calls. East won a huge upset in North Carolina and Reagan, astonishingly, won Massachusetts by a razor-thin margin. Reagan was aided heavily in the Bay State by the 23 percent Anderson took there.[70]

When NBC came back on at 8 P.M., David Brinkley and John Chancellor called in rapid- fire succession Mississippi, Florida, Alabama, and, a few minutes later, Michigan, Ohio, Illinois, New Jersey, and Pennsylvania for Reagan. In the Keystone State, Reagan had taken 25 percent of the Democratic vote.[71]

By 8 o'clock NBC had 295 electoral votes in the Reagan column—twenty five more than was needed to clinch the election. A few minutes later, Reagan took Texas. A rout was on and the on-air reporters were speculating that Carter's surrender was imminent.

IN THE PRIVATE RESIDENCE of the White House, Carter bitterly wanted to give his concession speech and be done with the whole thing. Jody Powell was in his office in the White House complex when Carter called him at 8 P.M., demanding that he go to the hotel and concede. "It's ridiculous," Carter stormed to his press secretary. "Let's go and get it over with quickly." Powell talked Carter out of it, urging him to "wait a little longer."[72]

Fifteen minutes later, at 8:15 eastern time, NBC gave up the charade and called the election. Not just one state, but the entire national election. Only 5 percent of votes had actually been counted. Chancellor, unsmiling, intoned, "Ronald Wilson Reagan, former sports announcer, a film actor, a governor of California, is our projected winner."[73]

AN HOUR AFTER THE president's testy exchange with Powell, the phone rang in the Reagan home in Pacific Palisades. Phone numbers had been exchanged by the two campaigns for this perfunctory but all-important call. Reagan was taking a long shower. Nancy Reagan said he liked to take long showers because he could do some thinking in private, then write down his thoughts later.[74] He'd already taken a phone call from John Anderson. Henry Kissinger had also called to offer his best wishes.

Mrs. Reagan was luxuriating in a hot bath in her own home after months of strange hotels. In the background, she heard John Chancellor "saying Ronnie had won the election," she later remembered. "I banged on the shower door, and Ronnie came out. We stood before the set wrapped in our towels and listened. 'I don't think this is the way it is supposed to happen.'"[75]

It was 8:35 on the East Coast and only 5:35 in the afternoon in California when the phone rang in their bedroom. Mrs. Reagan answered it. It was the White House calling. Reagan, clad in only a towel, took the phone. A White House operator said, "Governor Reagan? Please stand by for the president."

A moment later, Carter was on the line, conceding the election to Reagan and congratulating him on a "fine victory."[76]

THE PRESIDENTIAL MOTORCADE WENT directly to the Sheraton just after Carter's historic phone call to Reagan. The demoralized Democrats were sullenly gathered in the same hotel that the losing Ford forces had used in 1976. Many were crying, and just as many were plain old-fashioned face-down-in the-gutter drunk. Carter walked in amidst a swarm of people in the hotel lobby, but there were no magnetometers, no pat-downs, no searches of women's purses, no invasions of personal privacy, no thuggish police-state tactics, and only a small retinue of Secret Service agents.

As Carter entered, the band was incoherently playing "Let a Winner Lead the Way" and then swung into the party's old standby, "Happy Days Are Here Again."[77] The crowd—which was witnessing in real time the loss of the presidency, the loss of control of the Senate, the loss of nearly three dozen congressional seats, and the rise of hundreds of newly elected Republicans in the state legislatures—bleakly sang along.

Carter mounted the stage, accompanied by Mrs. Carter and their children, including Amy, who had received so much unwanted attention over the past week. The band struck up "Hail to the Chief" as he was shaking hands. It was odd and bittersweet. The room was filled almost to capacity, because a convention of defense contractors meeting in the same hotel had flooded into the room when they heard that the president was coming.

On the stage and in the hall were Democrats great and small. Ed Muskie was there, as were the Reverend Jesse Jackson and many White House and cabinet officials, including a hollow-eyed Powell, Zbigniew Brzezinski, Hamilton Jordan, and Pat Caddell, curiously smiling broadly. When he shook Jordan's hand, Carter could be heard saying, "It's okay" to his beleaguered manager.[78]

Carter was introduced by Bob Strauss. Forcing a wan smile, Carter said, "I promised you four years ago that I would never lie to you—so I can't stand here tonight and say it doesn't hurt."[79] Mrs. Carter looked stricken, her face swollen from crying. People later found out the depth of the animosity she felt toward Reagan, with Rosalynn Carter saying that she was "bitter enough for the both of us."[80] The president looked down for a moment, his eyes misting.

Carter told the audience that he had called "Governor Reagan" to congratulate him and that he promised a smooth transition. Carter had also sent Reagan a gracious telegram, which read: "It's now apparent that the American people have chosen you as the next president. I congratulate you and pledge to you our fullest support and cooperation in bringing about an orderly transition of government. . . . My best wishes are with you and your family . . . Jimmy Carter."[81] There was a prolonged cheer, as if the Democrats were applauding not only Carter's generous telegram but also the magnificence of the peaceful transfer of power that was unique to their country.

Carter spoke eloquently about his love of America and the American people and about how blessed he'd been to do all that he'd done and see all he'd seen. Someone in the audience cried out, "We love you, Jimmy!" and applause broke out, as Carter struggled to hold it together.[82] He ended by quoting an old Yiddish proverb: "God gives burdens, also shoulders."[83] Carter's voice trailed off and, fighting back tears, he told the audience that he had not lost his love for either America or his countrymen.

Departing, Carter worked the crowd, shaking hands, as the band played "Everything's Coming up Roses."[84]

TIP O'NEILL WAS ONLY a few blocks away at the U.S. Capitol. Carter had invited the Speaker of the House to attend his concession, but O'Neill refused, enraged that Carter was doing so while the polls were still open on the West Coast. Several days earlier O'Neill had learned from pollster Lou Harris that the house was about to drop on his House, but now Carter was making it that much harder for Democrats down the ticket.[85]

Indeed, out West, word spread like wildfire that Carter had conceded. It was only 5:50 and many people were standing in line to vote. When they heard about the concession, demoralized Democrats fell out of line and headed home, believing that there was no point to voting now. Some Democrats who lost narrowly on the West Coast would blame Carter and would never forgive him. Nor would O'Neill, who never had any use for Carter or his band of Georgians.[86]

Carter's concession speech was the earliest one since 1904, when Teddy Roosevelt slaughtered the Democratic Party's sacrificial lamb, Alton B. Parker.[87]

ANDERSON, WHO HAD NO chance in hell of winning, conceded also—one hour *after* the president of the United States did. The good news for Anderson was that he had scored more than the 5 percent of the national vote needed to guarantee him federal matching monies; those funds could go toward paying off his campaign debts. There was also some idle chatter about starting a permanent third party. Bitter toward Carter right to the end, his wife, Keke, fixed his tie and remarked, "Smile. Carter is not elected."[88]

THE REAGANS BEGAN THEIR evening with an early dinner at the Bel Air home of Earle Jorgensen and his wife, Marion, along with other members of the Kitchen Cabinet and their wives, including the Bloomingdales, the Salavatoris, and the Tuttles. In all, about fifty people attended. Marion Jorgensen served veal stew and coconut cake, just as she had for Reagan on the election nights of 1966 and 1970. By now, all knew about the phone call from Carter and the early call by NBC. The mood was festive, even as dragoons of additional Secret Service agents arrived to protect the new president-elect. Though Mrs. Reagan was described as "abubble," her husband, the next president of the United States and future leader of the Free World, was low-key, amiable, "oddly untouched," and "aw-shucks cool."[89]

Afterwards, the Reagans journeyed by motorcade to the Century Plaza Hotel and immediately went to a suite on the nineteenth floor, where Reagan placed and took phone calls for an hour and a half. He spoke to Bill Brock, the party chairman he'd butted heads with off and on over the past four years. Gerald Ford tried to reach Reagan, but missed him several times. The Gipper spoke with Governor Jim Rhodes of Ohio as well as his dear friend Paul Laxalt, who was handily winning reelection as senator from Nevada. Reagan also spoke with his new vice president–elect.

At dinner Reagan had seemed cool and relaxed, but at times in the suite he seemed slightly subdued, quiet, as possibly he was considering the awesome duties awaiting him. Though many Reaganites had believed Reagan would win, no one—not even Reagan himself—was prepared for the awesome nature of the moment.

In Honolulu, Jane Wyman, who so many years earlier had sought a divorce from Reagan because of his growing passion for politics, broke her long silence and told United Press International that she thought his win was "marvelous" and that she "of course" had voted for her former husband. "My children have worked long and hard for that campaign."[90]

Reagan overheard a report on one of the TV networks that Anderson's percentage meant he would get matching funds from the Federal Election Commission and thus could pay off his debts. "Oh good," Reagan said.[91]

Bill Casey, in Los Angeles with Governor Reagan, was interviewed by CBS, and in language clear as a bell he spoke about the campaign, the polling, and the transition of power. Rumors were already floating that either Jim Baker or Ed Meese would head up the transition team.

Doug Bandow, a young researcher on Reagan's chartered plane, had had a front-row seat for history for nearly a year. Now he was numb, not from exhaustion but from "pure exhilaration." He described the evening as "shared warmth. It is one night you forget all of the disputes . . . all of the arguments."[92]

Mrs. Reagan hugged her husband's aide—and her confidant—Mike Deaver. Dick Allen had reappeared, once again wearing a staff badge. Charlton Heston was there as well. By phone, Reagan spoke to the Republicans gathered in Washington and to their cheers called the night "one of the greatest Republican victories of all time."[93]

Oregon, Washington State, California (which was never in doubt, despite Carter's heavy expenditure of time and money), Nevada, Idaho, Iowa, Montana—all tumbled before the Reagan juggernaut. Minnesota went for Carter, sparing Mondale that embarrassment. Mississippi had finally gone for Reagan. ABC's Frank Reynolds noted, "It was Mississippi that refused to go for Ronald Reagan four years ago at the Republican national convention . . . [and] spelled the death knell of his hopes for the nomination."[94]

Reagan took a phone call from Ted Kennedy, who offered his good wishes, which Reagan found especially touching. The extended Kennedy family had voted that morning—and nearly all had voted for Ronald Reagan, Maria Shriver told Stu Spencer.[95] The family of long memories had not forgotten that Carter had beaten their Teddy, denying them the restoration of Camelot. Nor would they ever forgive Carter for what they saw as a ferocious and sometimes unfair campaign against their beloved brother, uncle, son, father, and brother-in-law. The Kennedy women, being Catholic, were pro-life, and that made it easier to vote for the pro-life Reagan. Kathleen Kennedy Townsend, Bobby Kennedy's eldest daughter, did vote for Carter, but even she expressed her disdain for the Georgian. Kathleen took her three-year-old daughter, Meaghan, into the voting booth and let her pull the lever so she could always say she never pulled the lever for Carter.[96] Jackie Onassis, President Kennedy's widow, couldn't pull the lever for Carter, either; she voted for Anderson.[97] Ted Kennedy's limo driver told a stunned GOP operative that he'd voted for Reagan and "I think a lot of people around here did."[98]

Carter had a long memory himself, and he never forgave Teddy for taking him on in the Democratic primaries. It was clear in an interview with President Carter more than a quarter century later that none of the hostility had diminished.[99]

MURIEL COLEMAN HAD BEEN working in Chicago helping Don Totten run the Reagan campaign in the Midwest. After months of fourteen-hour days, she was exhausted. The night of the election, a young volunteer was driving her to the election party in Milwaukee when she dozed off for what seemed only a moment. When she stirred, she asked, "How are we doing?"

"We won," he replied.

"You mean New Hampshire or some other states?"

"No, we won the whole thing."[100]

As SANDER VANOCUR OF ABC reported live from the Sheraton around 11 P.M. in Washington, there was no sign of the Democrats who had been gathered there earlier in the evening. All that could be seen behind Vanocur was an empty stage, an empty room, and several workers stacking chairs and sweeping up the floor. Over at the graceful brick townhouse of Averell and Pamela Harriman on N Street in Georgetown, the cream of the liberal Democratic establishment was curdling. Joe Califano, Clark Clifford, Robert McNamara, Henry and Muffie Brandon—one by one, they got into their limousines to leave what a reporter described as a "wake." As always, the Beautiful People were worried about their "standing in a new town."[101]

Liberals had reason to be depressed. When the final election results were tallied, they were stunning, especially in the Electoral College. Reagan won nearly 44 million votes and 51 percent to Carter's 35.5 million votes and 41 percent. Reagan took forty-four states and 489 electoral votes to Carter's six states and paltry 49 electoral votes.[102] Even Herbert Hoover, crushed in 1932 by FDR, took ten more electoral votes than Carter did. Carter carried the same number of states as Barry Goldwater had in his landslide loss to LBJ in 1964.

Anderson took around 7 percent of the vote and flunked out of the Electoral College.[103] Though he got the lowest percentage of the three candidates, he gave the longest speech of the night.

Many commentators were using the word "mandate" in speaking of Reagan's win. The electoral-vote landslide was the third-biggest in history, behind Nixon's 1972 performance of 97 percent and FDR's mind-boggling 1936 "squeaker" of 98 percent.

Reagan won 51 percent of the Catholic vote and 62 percent of the evangelical and Protestant vote. He won a plurality of the Jewish vote with 39 percent and held Carter to only 66 percent of registered Democrats. He won the vast majority of Americans who did not believe they were better off than they had been four years earlier. Young Americans, once considered the domain of the Democrats, split their vote, giving Reagan and Carter 43 percent apiece.[104]

For all the talk during the campaign about the "Anderson Difference," it turned out that John Anderson had little effect on the election's outcome. Only in Massachusetts and possibly New York did Anderson's margin make a difference. Despite what Carter wanted to believe, in the end even many of Carter's aides recognized what the election amounted to: "a personal rejection of Jimmy Carter."[105]

In the process of dominating the election, Reagan had made Jimmy Carter the first president in forty-eight years—and the first Democrat in ninety-two years—to lose his bid for reelection. Carter was only the seventh incumbent president to lose a general election.

Reagan also had long coattails. He brought along enough GOP senators to take control of that body for the first time since 1954. In all, twelve Democratic senators were felled, left and moderate, including Frank Church of Idaho, John Culver of Iowa, Warren Magnuson of Washington, Gaylord Nelson of Wisconsin, George McGovern of South Dakota, and John Durkin of New Hampshire. Reagan swept thirty-three Republicans into the House; these GOP representatives would for a time band with the Boll Weevil Democrats, who would later become known as "Reagan Democrats."[106] The Democrats' cushion in the House, which had stood at a comfortable 149 seats in 1977, had been cut to only 49.[107]

Another Democrat who lost was the young first-term governor of Arkansas, Bill Clinton, in a shocking defeat at the hands of the unknown Frank White, a banking executive.[108] Arkansas had been Carter's second-best state after Georgia in 1976, but it fell narrowly into Reagan's lap this night.

OVER AT THE CENTURY Plaza Hotel in Los Angeles, Reagan had ditched the red-and-white-checked shirt and put on a dark suit with white shirt, striped tie, and his ever-present white, pocket handkerchief. Only now did he agree to look at the remarks Ken Khachigian had drafted. The two went into a room alone for a moment to review the statement.[109]

Just before 8 P.M. pacific time, the crowd in the jam-packed hall on the first floor began to chant, "We want Reagan! We want Reagan!" A few minutes later, the president-elect arrived, stage left. He and Mrs. Reagan went up before the throng. Reagan, who bent over to shake hands with some fans in front, was grinning from ear to ear, his cheeks flushed with joy.

The Reagan offspring were introduced. Maureen exuberantly threw her arms around her father and stepmother. Michael, wife Colleen, and their baby, Cameron, were introduced next, and Mike and his father kissed each other on the cheek. Ron and Patti came on together. The body language and space between the

Reagan children was unmistakable. Maureen, Mike, and Colleen gathered on one side while Ron and Patti stood on the other side, holding hands. All except Patti embraced their parents. Reagan reached out toward his younger son with his left hand and "Skipper," with a look of hero worship on his face, reached back for his father with his right hand, affectionately.

Also on stage were Reagan's older brother, Neil, and his wife Bess, along with members of the extended family, including Maureen's husband, Dennis Revell.

Finally it was time for Reagan to speak. He started slowly but firmly. "There's never been a more humbling moment in my life," he began. Pausing, the history of the moment sinking in, he told the thousands in the hotel and millions watching, "I consider the trust that you have placed in me sacred, and I give you my sacred oath that I will do my utmost to justify your faith."

Reagan spoke warmly of the call from President Carter and the outgoing president's pledge to ensure a smooth transition. Out of the blue, some unknown aides came on stage carrying a tremendous cake in the shape of the continental United States. Nervously, they tipped it so everybody could see it and the massive confection started to slide off, nearly coming down on Mrs. Reagan. For a moment, her smile faded, but Reagan moved to catch the cake and help tilt it back. Reagan's smile had also left his face; he had just been warming up when the staffers interrupted him. The aides with their cake departed the stage quickly.

The president-elect went back to his remarks, thanking the staff, the volunteers across America to whom he owed "an immeasurable debt of thanks," and then George and Barbara Bush. "We're going to have true partnership and a true friendship," he said of the vice president–elect. That elicited another cheer. He thanked his family, then thanked Nancy and said adoringly, "She's going to have a new title in a couple of months." The crowd cheered lustily. He pointed out that it looked at though the GOP would "control one house of the Congress for the first time in a quarter of a century," and the audience shouted approval again. Someone in the crowd held up a hot-off-the-presses *Los Angeles Times* that proclaimed, in big letters above the fold, "Reagan Landslide!"

Reagan reminded the audience of what Abraham Lincoln had told a group of reporters the day after his election: "Well, boys, your troubles are over now; mine have just begun."

Nearing the end of his brief remarks, Reagan summed up his view: "I am not frightened by what lies ahead. And I don't believe the American people are frightened by what lies ahead."[110] *Time* later said the president-elect had given his remarks with "the same mixed tone of humility and boyish glee that so obviously had charmed American voters during the campaign."[111]

To leave no doubt about his priorities, Reagan added firmly, "Together, we're going to do what has to be done. We're going to put America back to work again!"

He paused for a moment. His speech was short and lacking some of the soaring rhetoric usually associated with the Gipper. The end had come so swiftly for Carter—and the beginning so quickly for Reagan—that he had little time to review or work on his remarks, but Reagan did not doubt that he was ready for the colossal mission handed him by the American people. "I aim to try and tap that great American spirit that opened up this completely undeveloped continent from coast to coast and made it a great nation, survived several wars, survived a great depression, and we'll survive the problems that we face right now."

A reverent mood came over Reagan. "When I accepted your nomination for president, I hesitatingly . . . asked for your prayers at that moment. I won't ask them for this in particular moment, but I will just say, I would be very happy to have them in the days ahead." His voice caught for a moment.

"All I can say to all of you is thank you." Then, revealingly, his thoughts drifted back to Tampico and Dixon, the two little towns in Illinois where he'd grown up. The old broadcaster had arranged to have his message aired on a small radio station in downstate Illinois to reach the folks there. He wanted to tell them that he was still thinking about them. "So to all of them," he said, "thank you, too, back there in the hometown."[112]

There—sixty years earlier—a wistful boy had dreamed of being a hero, of saving people, of saving his country one day when it needed him most. The little boy's dream had come true. He would get his chance to save America.

RONALD WILSON REAGAN, THE president-elect of the United States, departed the Century Plaza's stage to step shortly onto a much bigger stage—in fact, the biggest stage of his life. He'd been on stages big and small his whole life—high-school stages, soundstages, convention stages—but this was something different, bigger, more vast, indeed all-encompassing.

Ronald Reagan would finally get a chance to ply his trade.

On a world stage.

Epilogue

DESTINY

"Now that damned cowboy is in the White House!"

S o exclaimed the Karl Rove of his era, Mark Hanna, when his man President
William McKinley succumbed to an assassin's bullet and the irrepressible
Theodore Roosevelt became president.[1] The reaction to Ronald Reagan's
election, another cowboy, was much the same among the country-club moderates
who still made up a portion of the Republican Party of 1980 and still loathed Reagan. They could not forgive a man who had said, in a 1977 speech before a group
of conservatives, "The New Republican Party I envision will not be, and cannot
be, one limited to the country club–big business image."[2]

Reagan and the elites had little use for each other. Helene Von Damm, Reagan's longtime secretary in Sacramento, recalled an item from *National Review*: "It
seems no one likes him . . . except the voters."[3]

It took a man from another country, Aleksandr Solzhenitsyn, to express
the prideful sorrow Americans felt days after Reagan died on June 5, 2004. "In
July 1975, I concluded my remarks in the Reception Room of the U.S. Senate
with these words: 'Very soon, all too soon, your government will need not just
extraordinary men—but men with greatness. Find them in your souls. Find them
in your hearts. Find them within the breadth and depth of your homeland.' Five
years later, I was overjoyed when just such a man came to the White House. May
the soft earth be a cushion in his present rest."[4]

Solzhenitsyn had been a Soviet dissident, had been imprisoned for ten years,
beaten and starved by the Communists, but refused to bend or break. His "crime"
was that he had criticized Joseph Stalin in a private letter. In prison, he kept writing. His words in *The Gulag Archipelago* and *One Day in the Life of Ivan Denisovich*

spoke the truth to millions about the terrors of the Soviet regime. At Henry Kissinger's urging, President Ford refused to meet with the famed Nobel Prize–winning author who had been banished from the Soviet Union, fearing the wrath of the Kremlin.[5] Two and only two senators had the courage to officially greet Solzhenitsyn: Jesse Helms of North Carolina and Joe Biden of Delaware. Former California governor Reagan greeted him unofficially. Reagan also wrote a column excoriating Ford and Kissinger, and this latest knuckling under to the Soviets may have been the last straw in making him decide to challenge Ford in the 1976 primaries.[6] Had Ford told the Soviets where to get off and met with the famed author, Reagan might not have run for president in 1976. Had Reagan not run and lost then, he never would have run in 1980.

But after he won, he too continued to write and speak out and take actions against the Soviet Union, telling audience after audience that the USSR would be consigned to "the ash heap of history" and that it was "the focus of evil in the modern world." Reagan called Communism "another sad, bizarre chapter in human history whose last pages even now are being written."[7] Another imprisoned dissident, Natan Sharansky, gives Reagan the credit for the fall of the Berlin Wall and the victory of the West over Soviet Communism. Sharansky recalled being imprisoned with "a Christian named Volodya. We called our [Bible reading] sessions Reaganite readings."[8] Of Reagan's impact, former Estonian prime minister Mart Laar said simply, "Without this man, I would be somewhere in Siberia in chains."[9]

Reagan abhorred Communism. He told the annual gathering of the 1977 CPAC, "When a conservative says that totalitarian Communism is an absolute enemy of human freedom, he is not theorizing—he is reporting the ugly reality captured so unforgettably in the writings of Aleksandr Solzhenitsyn."[10] After Reagan was reelected in 1984, the diplomatic tags on the cars used by the Soviet Embassy in Washington were changed to begin with the initials "FC." Nobody needed to guess what it stood for.[11]

The Communist nations didn't much like Reagan either. "Probably no American policymaker at any time during the Cold War inspired quite as much fear and loathing in Moscow as Ronald Reagan," according to a definitive book on the Cold War, *The Sword and the Shield*. The Communists began tracking Reagan years before he was elected president. The East German secret police, the Stasi, maintained an ever bulging dossier on Reagan, while Soviet agents, beginning in the mid-1970s, were under orders to find "compromising material" on him. After 1976 the Soviets worked covertly in America to undermine his political career and to plant anti-Reagan stories in the world press, courtesy of "Service A" and the "Centre," two Soviet-funded propaganda operations.[12]

And of course, history has recorded how Reagan put the neck of Soviet Communism under his cowboy heel and crushed the life out of it, freeing millions, winning the Cold War. Some academics and historians try to make the case that Reagan "ended" the Cold War with Mikhail Gorbachev's cooperation. Nonsense. From 1917 up until 1991, no Soviet dictator ever willingly gave up power. From 1917 up until 1980, the Soviets gained territory against every American president—until Reagan, working with Margaret Thatcher and Pope John Paul II, turned the tide toward freedom.

There was no doubt in 1980 about the Soviets' intentions. The Carter years were "frightening," Newt Gingrich recalled. "I think that the real risk was the Soviet Union winning the Cold War. They were in Nicaragua, they were in El Salvador, they were in Cuba, they were in Mozambique, they were in Afghanistan, they were paying . . . partisans in Germany and Great Britain. . . . There is no reasonable way that they would not have attempted under a Carter II to expand their capacity very significantly." Gingrich, the history professor, rated Carter as "the second most destructive president after James Buchanan."[13]

The stakes, in short, were sky high in the 1980 election. Conservative writer and commentator George F. Will said, "For the first time in my life, I regarded an election as a national emergency."[14]

Another influential conservative writer, R. Emmett Tyrrell Jr., founder of *The American Spectator*, summed up the stark choice American voters faced in the fall of 1980. Carter, he said, had an "antipodal view of mankind. Reagan is the optimist. Carter is the pessimist. Reagan sees us as capable. Carter sees us as inept and wobbling for Skid Row were it not for government's watchful eye."[15]

Tyrrell and Will were among the conservative columnists who began to flourish in the mid- to late 1970s. The political fires of the '60s had forged these commentators and now they were shaping political thought in America. In an era before cable television, the Internet, talk radio, and the explosion of conservative think tanks, their writings and pronouncements and thus their influence could not be underestimated. Both Will and Tyrrell had Reagan into their homes for dinner parties. Tyrrell, who enjoyed suits from London's Savile Row, expensive wine, and good cigars, was known for the sumptuous dinners he hosted.

History has recorded, too, how Reagan restored American morale, its "can-do" spirit, patriotism, and the notion of American exceptionalism. Reagan also revived the American economy after the devastating Carter Recession through revolutionary tax cuts and tight monetary policies, which drastically lowered the terrible inflation, interest rates, and unemployment. The economic growth that began in 1982 continued unbroken for a remarkable ninety-two months, during which time nearly thirty-five million new jobs were created.[16] And in fact, the soaring growth carried on almost unabated until the last months of the George W. Bush administration in 2008—an unprecedented twenty-six-year run of growth, which was due to some of Reagan's economic policies being carried forward, especially by Gingrich and Bill Clinton.

As long as these things are recorded, the word "morale" will always be associated with Reagan while the word "malaise" will always be associated with Jimmy Carter. Yet Reagan did more, much more, than accomplish these three big goals. He changed American politics for a lifetime.

"Once he was the most underestimated man in American politics—a washed-up movie star, it was said, who was too old, too simple and too far right to be President," wrote Peter Goldman of *Newsweek* several days after the election of 1980.[17] How did Reagan manage to overcome all those perceptions not only to win the GOP nomination but also to defeat an incumbent president and a third-party candidate? Dick Wirthlin, Reagan's one and only pollster from 1966 until 1984, had understood early on what Reagan needed to do to win: he needed to achieve realignment. Wirthlin's detailed campaign plan presented at the end of June 1980 laid out how to do just that. It wasn't enough to get the Republican vote, Wirthlin wrote, because, as his surveys revealed, the country was 51 percent Democrat, 30 percent Republican, and 19 percent independent.[18] Reagan needed to scramble the old New Deal coalition and create a new ideological and cultural coalition. He needed "Reagan Democrats" to win (though the term would not be coined until after the election).[19]

Sure enough, that's what Reagan pulled off. George Church of *Time* summed up the remarkable realignment that occurred on November 4, 1980: "Landslide. Yes, landslide—stunning, startling, astounding, beyond the wildest dreams and nightmares of the contending camps, beyond the furthest ken of the armies of pollsters, pundits and political professionals. After all the thousands of miles, the millions of words and dollars, the campaign that in newspapers across the land on the very morning of Election Day was still headlined TOO CLOSE TO CALL turned out to be a landslide. The American voter had struck again. Reagan's triumph dismembered the old Democratic coalition. Jews, labor-union members, ethnic whites, big-city voters—all gave Reagan far more votes than they usually cast for a Republican. The disaster left the Democratic Party, which has held the presidency for 32 of the 48 years since 1932, badly in need of a new vision and a new agenda."[20]

Reagan became, in the opinion of renowned historian John Patrick Diggins, one of America's greatest presidents, alongside Washington, Lincoln, and Franklin Roosevelt. Similarly, the great historian James MacGregor Burns in 1999 said that he would rank Reagan in the "great" or "near-great" category, alongside FDR.[21] A good case can be made that Reagan was actually a better president than FDR. Both were confronted with "guns and butter" issues, yet FDR never solved his economic calamity in eight years; only when America went to war did the Great Depression end. Reagan solved the Carter Recession in two years, and his work from 1981 to 1989 caused the collapse of the Soviet threat in 1991, and with it the triumph of freedom over Communism.

Tributes poured in from Congress when Reagan died, but one of the most gracious and eloquent came from Ted Kennedy. The old liberal spoke of Reagan's conservatism, his love of country, and his convictions, with no bitterness or rancor, but with a genuine affection for the man. Kennedy gave Reagan all the credit as "the president who won the Cold War," and added, "His deepest convictions were matters of heart and mind and spirit—and on them, he was no actor at all."[22]

It spoke very well of Reagan also that his first wife, Jane Wyman, admitted she had voted for him gladly in 1980 and 1984, and that when he died, she broke her silence of more than fifty years to say, "America has lost a great president and a great, kind and gentle *man*."[23]

Indeed, Reagan was one of the most incredibly relaxed men in politics. As reporters watched him doing remote TV interviews one sweltering day in a Los Angeles studio in 1980, he suddenly realized that the reporters couldn't hear the broadcasters, only him. Between interviews, a mischievous smile crossed Reagan's face and he began calling an imaginary baseball game, but with a political twist: "And now, Teddy Kennedy is coming to the plate. Kennedy has hit for five out of eight in the primaries today. Kennedy looks loose." The people in the studio laughed.[24] During his mock debate with David Stockman in 1980 to prepare for the real debate with John Anderson, Stockman was pummeling Reagan over the environment when Reagan retorted, "Well, John, sounds like I better get a gas mask!"[25]

Still, Reagan, like all men, was flawed. He had a temper, although it mellowed in later years. Once as governor, speaking to a political ally who had betrayed him, he pointed to a baseball bat on display in his office and said, "I should have shoved it up your ass and broken it off!"[26] Actor Arthur Kennedy, an old friend, said the Gipper's anger "flares like magnesium powder and disappears in a cloud of smoke."[27]

Such foibles do not by any means diminish Reagan's significance or, indeed, greatness. His old friend Lyn Nofziger explained it better than anybody: "Our problem is we are trying to make a saint out of a man who certainly wasn't perfect. But he was a unique president. He believed in three things: God, the American people and himself. And that's kind of unique."[28]

PHIL ALEXANDER, A YOUNG aide on the 1976 and 1980 campaigns, was at Belmont race track in New York the day Reagan died, June 5, 2004. Reagan's death was announced over the public address system and the crowd of unruly thousands was asked to observe one minute of silence in remembrance of the Gipper.

Alexander was astonished when the tough and cynical New Yorkers did just that.[29]

Alexander wasn't the only young American to be drawn to Reagan. In the 1980 election he received a plurality of voters under the age of thirty, and in 1984 he received more than 60 percent of the under-thirty vote. When he left office in January 1989, Reagan's overall approval rating was 68 percent, making him the most popular president at the end of his term since the Second World War, more popular even than the beloved Ike. Among African Americans he drew 40 percent support, amazing for a post–New Deal Republican. But most incredible was his approval rating among voters under thirty—a stunning 85 percent.[30]

In 1976 an eleven-year-old Minnesota boy, John McConnell, heard that his hero, Ronald Reagan, was coming to St. Paul. He badgered his mother into allowing his twenty-year-old brother to drive him 250 miles to see Reagan, and giving them twenty dollars to cover the cost of gas and a meal. Young McConnell was so nervous when he met Reagan that he dropped his camera, but he shook Reagan's hand and got a treasured autograph. McConnell went on to become a vice-presidential and presidential speechwriter for Dan Quayle, Dick Cheney, and George W. Bush.[31]

Longtime conservative leader Grover Norquist, who was a youthful Reagan aide in Massachusetts in 1980, explained why Reagan held such appeal for young Americans: "What Reagan sells is liberty and freedom and optimism. And if you're seventy-five, what good is that? A limitless future in front of America makes more sense to a thirty-year-old than a sixty-year-old."[32]

Newt Gingrich went even further. Reagan, he said, "was actually something quite different for the young." Young people admire revolutionaries, and in 1980 Reagan brought a revolution, with a replacement not merely of the "people who were in power" but also of "the principles by which power is exercised." Reagan, Gingrich said, always challenged the status quo; the president "almost never got trapped in the destructive choices of the modern elite, but would simply keep reframing the question." Gingrich was in his thirties in 1980, in just his first term in Congress, when he heard Reagan speak before the NAACP. The Gipper's clear and insightful remarks changed the young politician's life.[33]

William F. Buckley Jr., interviewed before he passed away in 2008, said he saw Reagan's appeal with the young as evidence that they viewed him as "anti-establishment."[34] Ron Robinson, president of Young America's Foundation, observed that some of Reagan's important speeches challenging the status quo were given before college audiences—for example, at Notre Dame in 1981, when he said, "The West won't contain Communism; it will transcend Communism;" and at Moscow State University in 1988, when he told Soviet students of his hope that freedom "will blossom forth at least in the rich fertile soil of your people and culture."[35] In each case, Reagan issued a challenge to his young listeners, but he also provided hope for a future of freedom and opportunity.

Reagan retained his appeal to young Americans to the end. Karen Spencer, daughter of longtime Reagan aide Stu Spencer, once watched as Reagan's helicopter landed on a softball field in Mission Viejo, California, before he was to give a speech. The field adjoined a grade school. Reagan had been out of office for years, but "the kids were just standing by the windows. And they burst out the door, about 200, 250 of them, and they just mobbed him, mobbed President Reagan. The Secret Service went nuts. He just smiled. He loved it. That was the last time I ever saw him."[36]

AS OF FEBRUARY 2009, 11,800 books have been written about Reagan, second only to Christ, according to *Newsmax*, and well ahead of JFK and Lincoln.[37]

Within the GOP, and indeed across the political spectrum, Reagan is now revered, even beloved. But it wasn't always so. Within the party establishment, Reagan was never much loved, even after his election. After the 1982 elections, in which the GOP suffered reversals, a Republican National Committee functionary taped a piece of paper to her door announcing the signup for the 1984 Bush for President campaign. Today, most party apparatchiks who were around in the late 1970s and early 1980s will plead how much they always loved Reagan. But Ed Blakely, who ran the media division for the National Republican Congressional Committee all those years and at the time was no fan of Reagan's himself, had a simple response when asked about such claims: "Bullshit." Reagan was not liked and was barely tolerated in the various national GOP committees, according to Blakely.[38] As Dick Cheney recalled in an interview, however, "By the end . . . we were all Reaganites."[39]

If Republicans entertained doubts about Reagan, the feelings were far more intense among liberals. A *Washington Post* critic aptly observed that for many on the left in the 1980s, "hating Ronald Reagan was as elemental as hating August without air conditioning."[40]

The notion that Reagan was universally loved while in office is just one of many myths that have surrounded him. One widely accepted in political circles in the late 1970s was that Reagan was lazy. This myth was best dispelled by an aide who said, "He isn't lazy. He just doesn't like to hang around the office."[41]

The laziness idea has largely faded, but other myths, large and small, still abound.

One of the more popular is that Reagan changed the inaugural ceremony from the East front to the West front of the U.S. Capitol. In fact, that decision had been made months earlier by the congressional committee with the oversight for one simple reason: to save money. Carter's inaugural stand in 1977 cost $825,000, but because the West front could accommodate so many more without costly temporary construction, Reagan's inaugural stand in 1981 cost only $463,000. The East front of the Capitol had been used by every president starting with Andrew Jackson in 1829.[42]

Another myth is that Reagan and Tip O'Neill were great friends. O'Neill in his autobiography revealed his low opinion of Reagan, saying it was "sinful" that he'd become president and that Reagan was the worst president O'Neill had ever known.[43] To the House Speaker's everlasting credit, however, when Reagan was shot, O'Neill quietly slipped into the president's hospital room at George Washington University, got on his knees, held Reagan's hand, and they prayed, reciting the Twenty-third Psalm. O'Neill then kissed Reagan. According to White House aide Max Friedersdorf, the Democrat wept at Reagan's bedside.[44]

It has also become common to conclude that Reagan made the final decision to reject the "co-presidency" in Detroit with Gerald Ford. In fact, both President and Mrs. Reagan wrote in their autobiographies that Ford took himself out of contention.[45] (Nancy Reagan also acknowledged her opposition to Ford.) Of course, we will never know what Reagan and Ford said to each other in private that night they secreted away to try to hash it out one more time. Reagan had clearly grown uncomfortable with any power-sharing arrangement, and it may be that Reagan—the *über*-negotiator—simply let Ford talk himself out of the idea. That would have allowed Ford to save face while keeping the former president on Reagan's side for the fight ahead against Jimmy Carter. Ford later told NBC that "it might have turned out differently" if they hadn't run up against the deadline Reagan had set.[46]

Those looking to attack the Reagan legacy often seize on a myth about spending and the size of government. According to this line of argument, despite his rhetoric about reducing government, Reagan did nothing to tame spending or unnecessary programs and a result sent federal deficits soaring. In fact, setting aside the very necessary defense buildup after Richard Nixon, Gerald Ford, and Jimmy Carter had allowed the military to fall into ruination, discretionary federal spending under Reagan *fell* 13.5 percent. Government spending as a percentage of gross domestic product also fell under Reagan. Moreover, the number of subsidy programs in the federal budget was cut back after Reagan entered office, dropping from 1,123 in 1980 to 1,013 in 1985. (Such subsidies took their greatest leap under George W. Bush, from 1,425 in 2000 to 1,804 in 2008.)[47] Reagan also used the veto pen more than any president since Eisenhower.[48]

A particularly persistent and pernicious myth holds that Reagan's appearance at the Neshoba County Fair in Mississippi in the summer of 1980 was part of some nefarious plot to woo white racist voters. Liberal commentator Paul Krugman seized on this point with a nasty insinuation: "[Reagan] began his 1980 campaign with a speech on states' rights at the county fair near Philadelphia, Mississippi, the town where three civil rights workers were murdered in 1964. Everyone got the message."[49] But even longtime Democratic operative Bob Shrum acknowledges that Reagan didn't know the symbolism of the location.[50] In truth, Reagan didn't have a racist bone in his body, and it pained him terribly when people falsely charged him with racism.

Yet another myth is that Reagan was somehow "unknowable." I did not know the man well, but after working on his campaigns; after immersing myself in his writings, speeches, columns, diaries; after conversations with countless who knew him; and after reading hundreds of books and articles and monographs about him, I feel I at least understand him.

Reagan often said that he genuinely liked people and maybe that's why they liked him. He was garrulous, chatty, could be very thoughtful, but when people disturbed him or got on his nerves, especially strangers, he'd simply clam up. With friends, close aides, and associates, he might let on some anger, break a pencil, but he would also verbally express himself. With two people, he never clammed up. Peter Hannaford and Ken Khachigian were clearly his and Mrs. Reagan's two favorite speechwriters. For all of his big speeches, from his acceptance speech in Detroit to his breathtaking remarks on the eve of the 1980 election to his inaugural address, he always turned to Peter and Ken.[51]

The people who didn't know Reagan would draw the wrong conclusion that he had some sort of mysterious zone of privacy. While he clearly relished his solitude with Nancy, especially alone at the ranch, his life was not a mystery. They had their private corners like all happily married couples and he could easily make himself happy alone, reading, writing, working at the ranch.

Many who felt they couldn't know Reagan probably never really understood him. That category may include his own vice president. George Bush, in 1989, told the Gridiron Club in Washington, "Let's face it. If I was funnier than Ronald Reagan, I would have won in 1980."[52] The same went for Reagan's erstwhile campaign manager, John Sears, who slammed Reagan for simply looking to others "to tell him what to do."[53]

The unknowable Reagan seems to be a myth created by people who weren't paying attention.

Despite his landslide victory, not everyone was happy about the election of Ronald Reagan in 1980. At Berkeley, two thousand students and professors took to the streets, rioting for three days. The violent protests, which resulted in scores of arrests, were sponsored by Students for Peace.[54]

Edward Heath, the former British Conservative prime minister, said on the BBC that while he was pleased Reagan had been elected, "it would be disastrous if Reagan really let people believe that there were simple ways to solve the problems of terrorism or oil prices."[55]

Radical chic conductor Leonard Bernstein said Reagan's election would unleash the forces of fascism in America.[56] Columnist Judy Bachrach of the *Washington Star* had come up with a term of derision to describe Reagan: the "Great Communicator." She never knew that one day he and his supporters would embrace it.[57]

The Soviets weren't happy about Reagan's victory either. Several days after the election, on the anniversary of "Revolution Day," a giant parade was held in Moscow, complete with tanks, "goose-stepping troops," and "missile carriers that roared across cobblestoned Red Square," as UPI reported. Defense Minister Dmitry Ustinov said the Soviets "would never accept second place to the Americans."[58]

Even some of Reagan's conservative supporters seemed unhappy after Election Day. Campaign aide Michele Davis, who had traveled for several months and hundreds of thousands of air miles with the Gipper and the staff, went into a funk when it all ended. "Everything is different," she confided in her diary. "There are different Secret Service agents, advance men that I've never seen before and guys in dark suits in every nook and cranny. And my traveling buddy the Gipper is far away from us all. Sigh." She later did what any sane campaign worker would do at the end of a glorious campaign. She took a bottle of Courvoisier to the headquarters and, with some friends, got drunk.[59]

Within days of the election, Reagan was being zinged in the pages of the conservative newsweekly *Human Events* under the headline "Mixed Reviews for

Reagan Transition Team." A five-member team of "coordinators" had been created to begin the process of staffing the new government. It was headed by Bill
Timmons, Reagan's 1980 political director, whom conservatives held in suspicion
for his longtime association with moderate Howard Baker. Of the members of
the group, only Loren Smith, Reagan's 1976 and 1980 general counsel, was considered a "movement conservative." The paper also ran a sidebar item in which it
quaintly noted that "many talented conservatives from around the country have in
the past shown little interest in relocating in Washington. We hope, however, that
the November 4 election may have changed their thinking." *Human Events* solicited résumés from conservatives and promised to send them along to the Reagan
transition team.[60]

But out west—in the heart of Reagan Country—billboards materialized
overnight after the 1980 election proclaiming, "Welcome to the Reagan Revolution."[61]

Fearing Reagan, while also contemptuous of Carter, the Ayatollah released the
hostages—only after the fortieth president replaced the thirty-ninth president.

The stock market was also pleased with the Reagan tide. The day after the
election was the second busiest day of trading in the market's history, and stocks
soared.[62] And while scholars since the death of JFK had lamented that the job of
president was "too big for one man," all that talk stopped abruptly after the election of Reagan.

Solzhenitsyn's three young sons, Ignat, Yermolai, and Stephan, were among
those pleased by Reagan's victory—though they paid a price for it. By this point
they had settled in Vermont with their parents after their father had been exiled
from the Soviet Union. On the day after the 1980 election, their teacher was
mourning the election of Reagan, referring to the "dark night of fascism descended
under the B-movie actor." When the teacher asked his students whether any disagreed with him, the three Solzhenitsyn boys raised their hands. Outraged, he
sent the children out into the cold November morning without their coats, under
an American flag that had been lowered to half mast. The boys saw the bright side;
the hour they spent shivering "was a relief from sitting in the auditorium listening
to the party line."[63]

Then, of course, there were Reagan's legions of devoted followers across the
country. He had plenty of fan clubs, and not just from his movie days. Muriel
Coleman, a devoted conservative and Reagan staffer, told of the hundreds of "R.
Clubs" that dotted the Midwest. For an annual fee of $50 or $100, you became a
member and got a little pin. Muriel said many people were buried wearing their
"R. Club" pins.[64]

During the campaign, Jeb Bush discovered Reagan's extraordinary appeal to Americans—and found out what it was like to play second banana to the Gipper. In North Dakota, eight thousand people filled a hall, rabid for Reagan. When young Bush went on the stage to make a pitch for his father, there remained only about "two hundred people in the room."[65]

TO BE SURE, REAGAN had a different view of the GOP from the country clubbers. He often said that the GOP was "not the party of big business and the country club set, but the party of Main Street, the small town, the shopkeeper, the farmer, the cop on the beat, the guy who sends his kids to Sunday school, pays his taxes, and never asks anything from government except to be left alone."[66]

What kind of conservative was Reagan then? He flirted with liberalism in his youth, but after seeing the government take up to 90 percent of his income in the 1940s, and the efforts of thuggish Communism provocateurs in Hollywood, Reagan began his historic move to the right. Yet during the hearings of the House Committee on Un-American Activities, while some, like his friend and fellow actor Robert Taylor, called for the expulsion of Communists from America, Reagan said, no, that would be contrary to the principles and spirit of America.[67] We were strong enough to tolerate all political points of view, as long as they were peaceful. At that stage, he was pretty much a garden-variety man of the right, more anti-liberal than pro-conservative. As he grew older, his political philosophy matured, became refined. Thoughtful. Reagan realized that nothing was more sacred than the privacy and dignity of individuals.

Maybe the best place to start is with a policy statement he issued in April 1980, in the heat of the primary battle, on "homosexual rights." "While I do not advocate the so-called gay lifestyle, all citizens have equal rights before the law," he said. "I believe the government should not interfere with the private lives of Americans, nor should there be any place in our society for intolerance and discrimination. So long as a person's private life is private and does not interfere with his or her job performance, it should have no bearing on private-sector or government hiring."[68] At the same time he believed that "gay ordinances" were wrong that compelled an employer to hire someone simply because he or she was gay.

Reagan was not a libertarian who denied political realities. He was also pragmatic, telling a group of conservatives that he did not view the GOP as a party "based on a principle of exclusion. After all, you do not get to be a majority party by searching for groups you *won't* associate or work with. Conservatism is not a narrow ideology nor is it the exclusive property of conservative activists."[69]

In addition, Reagan was a constitutionalist who honored the federalist system set up the Founders. In his first inaugural address, which he wrote largely himself, Reagan said, "From time to time we have been tempted to believe that society has become too complex to be managed by self-rule, that government by an elite group is superior to government for, by and of the people. But if no one among us is capable of governing himself, then who among us has the capacity to govern someone else?"[70]

In a letter to this author, historian John Patrick Diggins told of how in he reviewed a collection of writings by American conservative Russell Kirk and discovered that in six hundred pages, Ronald Reagan's name was never mentioned. It then dawned on Diggins that Kirk's inspiration was Edmund Burke and Reagan's was Thomas Paine.[71] Burke and Paine, contemporaries, reviled each other. Where Burke believed in the divine rights of kings, Paine despised royalty, or any concentration of power, and celebrated the citizenry. Paine, like Reagan, believed in challenging the status quo, not defending it. Paine, like Reagan, believed that power should flow upwards and not downwards. Reagan articulated his views when he said, "I've always thought of myself as a citizen politician, speaking up for the ideas and values and common sense of everyday Americans."[72] Paine also happened to be fond of the phrase "common sense."

Some on the right were less than thrilled with Reagan's high regard for Paine. A notable example is Reagan's friend George Will. Will criticized Reagan for being "inexplicably" and "painfully" fond of quoting Paine's line "We have it in our power to begin the world over again," which the columnist dismissed as a "preposterous cry" and "the most unconservative statement that ever issued from human lips."[73]

The question of how to define Reagan's conservatism is crucial at a time when politicians routinely attempt to claim the Reagan mantle. The regular appeals to Reagan's legacy are easy to understand, given that Reagan has become adored, his name gracing thousands of buildings, roads, medical centers, and schools. His statue, incredibly, stands in former Communist countries where his name was once jeered and assassination plots were hatched against him.[74]

The fortieth president's name was invoked many times, in all manner of things, by the forty-third president, George W. Bush, in justifying the inconsistency of "compassionate conservatism." While the 2000 election offered a clear choice between a right-of-center candidate, Bush, and a left-of-center candidate, Vice President Al Gore, libertarians and some conservatives were not altogether pleased with Bush's election. Three years later, Ed Crane, head of the respected Cato Institute, penned this: "The philosophical collapse of the GOP came with the 2000 campaign of George W. Bush, who ran without calling for a single spending cut, much less the elimination of programs, agencies or departments. Worse, neoconservatives moved to fill the philosophical vacuum created by the supply-siders."[75]

Today, the Republican Party is back in the wilderness. A key reason is that the GOP of the early twenty-first century has largely discarded Reaganism. In his farewell address to the nation on January 11, 1989, Reagan summed up his philosophy: "'We the People' tell the government what to do, it doesn't tell us. 'We the People' are the driver—the government is the car. And we decide where it should go, and by what route, and how fast. Almost all the world's constitutions are documents in which governments tell the people what their privileges are. Our Constitution is a document in which 'We the People' tell the government what it is allowed to do. 'We the People' are free. This belief has been the underlying basis for everything I tried to do these past eight years."[76]

Freedom was the Republican Party's organizing philosophy from 1856—when the first GOP nominee, the great explorer and military leader John C. Frémont, ran with the campaign slogan "Free Speech, Free Press, Free Soil, Free Men, Frémont"—extending through Lincoln, Teddy Roosevelt, and Reagan. But now that organizing principle has been abandoned, replaced by "security." Security—like "justice," the organizing principle of the Left—requires a large, centralized government. Reagan's freedom needed only a Bill of Rights and a Constitution, intelligent courts, and a restrained police force.

The GOP has also been besmirched by corrupt politicians, lobbyists, and "Republican strategists" who had neither the discipline, the courage, the conviction, nor the understanding to extend and enlarge the Reagan Revolution. The siren song of command and corporate largesse, mixed with easy entrée to sleazy politicians, combined to create the downfall of Republicanism.

Author Tom Wolfe once observed, "At a Washington party, it is not enough that the guests feel drunk; they must feel drunk and important."[77] The Republican gatecrashers came; got drunk on power, easy money, and easier access; felt important; and destroyed the home of Abe, Teddy, Ike, Barry, and Ronnie.

In 2003 George W. Bush's handpicked chairman of the Republican National Committee, Ed Gillespie, attended an editorial meeting of the *Manchester Union-Leader*. Afterward, the paper wrote that Gillespie "said in no uncertain terms that the days of Reaganesque Republican railings against the expansion of the federal government are over. . . . Today the Republican Party stands for giving the American people whatever the latest polls say they want. . . . The people want expanded entitlement programs and a federal government that attends to their every desire, no matter how frivolous? Then that's what the Republican Party wants, too."[78]

Was Gillespie right? Is it all over? Reagan populism as a force inside the Republican Party has since been replaced by a belief that America needs two big-government parties. Whether the GOP ever returns to its pro-freedom, smaller-government roots is open to question.

The week of the Reagan funeral, time seemed to stop in America. Margaret Thatcher, ailing, was not intending to make the trip, but at the last, she summoned the strength to see her old friend and fellow warrior off one more time. In the guest book she wrote, "To Ronnie: Well done, thy good and faithful servant."[79]

As his body lay in state in the U.S. Capitol Rotunda, more than a hundred thousand people waited patiently in a line that snaked from the Capitol all the way back to the Air and Space Museum. The Rotunda was open for a number of days, twenty-four hours per day. People traveled hundreds and even thousands of miles just to pay their respects. As his casket was moved to the Capitol—led by a rider-less horse with Reagan's own scuffed but polished riding boots turned backwards, in the fashion of fallen military leaders—tens of thousands lined the streets, just as they did when he was moved to the National Cathedral and then to Andrews Air Force Base for his final trip home to his beloved California. And then, as the funeral procession made its way from Los Angeles up the highway to Simi Valley, an amazing thing happened.

All along the route, people stopped and got out of their cars to pay their respects.[80]

Old Reagan aide Jim Stockdale said, "I don't think the Washington press corps had any concept of how Americans felt about Ronald Reagan until that funeral."[81] Stockdale had been with the Gipper going all the way back to Reagan's wilderness days. Like everybody, it seems, he has stories about Reagan's kindnesses, such as the day his thirteen-year-old son, Marty, was sent to get Reagan some lunch. Stockdale heard a crash. Marty had dropped the lunch, but there was Reagan on the floor, helping the boy pick it up.[82]

For this author, the most memorable moment came at the end of the services at the National Cathedral as the casket was being taken to the hearse waiting outside; suddenly a ray of sunlight broke through the gray, overcast, drizzly day—and shone on Reagan's casket.

That day, June 9, 2004, the Washington transit agency, the Metro, experienced its busiest day ever, as 850,636 hardy Americans used the rail system.[83] The programs from the Reagan funeral at the National Cathedral showed up quickly on eBay, fetching as much as $250 each. The hand cards passed out in the Rotunda were going for $46, and the programs from the final service in Simi Valley were getting $455.[84]

In the U.S. Navy, sailors forcefully compete with each other to serve on the USS *Reagan*, so revered is the ship and her namesake.[85] Reagan's library is, by far, the most popular of all the presidential libraries, surpassing even JFK's in annual attendance, despite the fact that the Reagan Library is somewhat off the beaten path compared to most others. Reagan's presidential alumni association remains the largest of all, and seems to grow each year, even though his presidency ended twenty years ago.[86] The postage stamp bearing Reagan's image remains one of the most popular ever issued by the U.S. Post Office. When it was released in January 2005, it sold out instantly. When the Richard Nixon stamp was unveiled, no one wanted it, and the Postal Service ended up destroying hundreds of thousands of stamps bearing the visage of "Tricky Dick."[87]

The outpouring for Reagan was not universal. At the time of his death, a Broadway play entitled *Assassins* featured an actor portraying John Hinckley—who almost shot Reagan to death in early 1981—firing away repeatedly at a cardboard cutout of the Gipper.[88] This tasteless "art" recalled the liberal radio announcer who, when Reagan was shot, bewailed the fact that Hinckley hadn't used a more powerful weapon like a .45. Many left-wing activists hadn't softened their views since the days when they had excoriated him for all manner of things, from wanting to start World War III to hating the homeless.

When news of Reagan's death reached a march sponsored by the radical protest organization ANSWER, "the crowd whooped and cheered," *National Review* reported.[89] One commentator, Adrian Wooldridge of *The Economist*, said upon Reagan's death that he represented "wild-eyed lunacy."[90] CBS, always Reagan's worst critic among the three networks, produced a docudrama called *The Reagans*. The made-for-TV movie was supposed to be historical, but the producers consulted not one person who knew the couple. Reagan biographer Lou Cannon was appalled at all the mistakes in the smear job, and the outrage from millions of Americans was such that the movie was pulled from network programming at the last minute and offered only on a flimsy CBS-owned pay-cable channel.[91]

ONE MONTH BEFORE THE 1980 election, Scotty Reston, fabled liberal columnist for the *New York Times*, wrote that Reagan "hates races, even the tiresome race for the Presidency. He may not have a sense of history but he has a sense of humor and knows he cannot reform the world."[92]

With the exception of the remark about Reagan's wittiness, untruer words were never penned.

Reagan had a clear sense of history, and even more important, he had a sense of duty and destiny that propelled him. The Reagans' old friend Nancy Reynolds said, "He always thought he had a purpose. . . . He believed in destiny."[93] Candidate Reagan, both modest and superstitious, was reluctant to say too much about coveting the presidency. But quietly, he believed it was his calling to occupy the Oval Office, and therefore to save America and change the world. On rare occasions he let this quiet confidence slip to reporters. Once on the 1980 campaign trail, he mused that it's not enough for a candidate simply to *want* to be president. "There is," he said, "more of a feeling that maybe you *should* be."[94]

Contrast that with Jimmy Carter, whose makeup was astutely captured by the liberal writer John Stacks: "Once in office, Carter failed to respond to the different demands on him as president. He failed to project the sense of sureness, of direction, of certainty that is required of any president. The irony was that as a campaigner, Carter often seemed to me an arrogant man decked out to seem humble. As a president, he seemed a humble man pretending to power and decisiveness. Too full of self-doubt to be a certain leader, he was at the same time too proud to admit his real shortcomings."[95]

Bill Buckley made the same point simply and elegantly, saying that Carter was "lost in power." But Reagan, Buckley said, had a sureness both about himself and about America. The Gipper "believed in . . . the basic premises of American society," and he was also a leader "who would face the Soviet threat with ingenuity and adamancy and determination."

Of Reagan's own rendezvous with destiny, his old friend Buckley said that "his extensive use of language occasionally suggested that he thought that he and divine destiny were loosely synchronized."[96]

It would seem so.

Author's Note

Surprisingly, few books have been exclusively devoted to the monumental struggle in 1980 between Jimmy Carter and Ronald Reagan for the presidency of the United States, certainly one of the most important campaigns in American history. Jack Germond and Jules Witcover wrote a short book immediately after the election, *Blue Smoke and Mirrors*, which was fairly derisive toward Reagan. John Stacks of *Time* wrote a quickie entitled *Watershed* that came out in 1981 that was also somewhat disdainful of Reagan. Elizabeth Drew wrote *Portrait of an Election*, but it was mostly from Carter's vantage point. And Andrew Bush wrote a fine textbook entitled *Reagan's Victory*.

Portions of other books have looked at the 1980 election. The great Lou Cannon covered the campaign along with other parts of Reagan's life and presidency in his book *Reagan*. Peter Hannaford also devoted several chapters to the 1980 campaign in his book *The Reagans*, as did Steven Hayward in *The Age of Reagan*. Teddy White broke ground with his masterful *The Making of the President* books starting in 1960 and continuing until 1972. He did not write a book focused on 1976 or 1980, though he did produce the highly enjoyable *America in Search of Itself*, which touched on the 1980 campaign. Both President Carter and President Reagan devoted several pages in their autobiographies to 1980.

Nearly as important, there has never been a book comprehensively detailing Reagan's wilderness years. These years of 1977 to 1979 were extremely important to Reagan, as he honed his message and ideology while mulling whether to make one last run when he would be sixty-nine years old.

My daughter Taylor's high school textbook *The American Pageant*, published in 2002 by Houghton Mifflin, devotes a large chapter to Reagan, more than twenty pages. But it illustrates the need for clarity in this important story. Titled "The Resurgence of Conservatism," the chapter attempts to document the rise of the fortieth president and the conservative movement he sometimes led. A portion of the work is acceptable, but most areas are shot through with bias and errors. For example, the text says that Reagan was guided by "neoconservatives," which is nonsense, and states that Reagan's campaign slogan in 1980 was "It's morning again in America." That was the slogan in the 1984 campaign. The slogan for 1980 was "The time is now." Far worse, the work claims that Reagan "renew[ed] the Cold War" and gives Mikhail Gorbachev the lion's share of the credit for "bringing an end to the Cold War." This is simply ridiculous, as all now know. What's more, the work associates Reagan with greed, Iran-Contra, deficits, and the declining economy in the early 1990s, though Reagan had been out of office for four years. Snarky references are made to Reagan's previous careers and his intellect. The chapter is clearly written by liberals bending over backwards trying to prove they don't despise Reagan. Unfortunately, they don't succeed.

For all these reasons, other works of history are necessary in order to present the facts of the rise of conservatism as led by Reagan beginning in the latter half of the 1970s. I hope some will say this book was necessary.

JUST DAYS BEFORE THE 1980 election, supermodel Cheryl Tiegs came through the nation's capital on a media tour. Washingtonians for the most part simply shrugged their shoulders at the passing through of Miss Tiegs. Nothing got the city's denizens as hot and bothered as politics and campaigns—not even a leggy 5'10" blonde.

No wonder someone once said that Washington was too small to be a state and too large to be an insane asylum.

At that point, of course, the political hacks were still relishing the prospect of a "too close to call" election. So in the days after the vote, they were trying to make sense of what happened. Six days after the election, the "Godfather of the New Right," Richard Viguerie, was invited to the elite private breakfast of Washington journalists hosted by Godfrey Sperling of the *Christian Science Monitor*. Sperling and the other scribes, still shell-shocked over the Reagan earthquake, asked Viguerie how it had come off without the elites' knowing. Viguerie, known for cutting to the chase, bluntly said, "With all due respect . . . I can't tell you how many press conferences we called where you guys didn't show up, how many press releases we put out that you didn't cover and print. And there probably never was a revolutionary moment that was so open and so ignored by the Establishment."

The establishment would need to catch up to history.

POLITICS, AS MR. DOOLEY said, "ain't beanbag." And good campaigns are, as GOP consultant Eddie Mahe once quipped, "Garbage moving in the right direction." Politics is messy, and even the best campaigns don't hold up well under close scrutiny. They can't, not with so many egos involved, hidden agendas, flawed human beings, mistakes, mismanagement, broken promises, incompetence, alcohol, lust, unforeseen external events, money woes, *ad nauseam*. Like all campaigns, the Reagan campaign of 1980 was, to quote Don Devine, Reagan's political director for Maryland and later a member of his cabinet, a "mess." At the top there was the mismanagement of John Sears and later the inexperience of Bill Casey. "It was the regional directors . . . they kept this thing moving," Devine explained. "And they would bullshit—including me—they would bullshit the local people and tell them that they had the approval for things they didn't have the approval for."

Campaigns are sloppy as well. Some have asserted that the local operations of both Reagan and Carter didn't always do everything by the FEC book; that is, local money was allegedly used to augment activities, outside the scope of the federal government. Meanwhile, the organizational charts for the Reagan campaign were hastily drawn affairs, with names scratched out, lines going everywhere, and not always a clear line of authority. The youth directors at the campaign, Steve Antosh and Morton Blackwell, flooded campaign offices with their memos complaining about not being able to get any funds or support for their efforts. Eventually, $75,000 was scrounged up for the Youth for Reagan program and the RNC kicked in another $75,000. But then they immediately got caught in a legal sticky wicket when Loren Smith, the campaign's attorney, advised them that they had to sever any ties to independent groups such as Young Americans for Freedom and the Fund for a Conservative Majority.

For a time, the Reagan campaign couldn't even agree on an official poster. Lorelei Kinder, who was running California, took it upon herself to design a poster with low-quality artwork and a photo of Reagan with a crinkly smile wearing a white cowboy hat and a blue denim shirt, which was snapped by Michael A. W. Evans in 1976. The poster was titled "America. Reagan Country." Most people in the campaign disliked it, including Mrs. Reagan. Three decades later, the photo is iconic, and the poster is still a popularly selling item in the Reagan Library. The Gipper was so impressed with Evans's work that Reagan asked him to become his personal photographer. Evans passed away in 2005.

Campaigns bring out all sorts of people. Two enterprising songwriters penned the music and lyrics to "Hello Ronnie, Good-Bye Jimmy" and submitted it to Ed Meese. The song was not adopted; nor were two other unsolicited songs, "We Need a Change in Washington" and "Let Ron Do It."

The technology associated with campaigns of the twenty-first century was simply not available in 1980. A "high-speed" copying machine spat out replicas at a blazing ten seconds per. Phone calls were made from an office, hotel, or pay phone. There were no cell phones, no Internet, no Twitter, no e-mail, no fax machine (except for a smelly and rudimentary Quip machine). Computers were used to process numbers, but speeches, statements, and press releases were produced on typewriters, the better ones having correcting ribbon. Either that or use white paint from a small bottle to obliterate typographical errors.

Many of the campaign daily schedules listed a "twenty-four-hour call assignment." Usually it was Cindy Tapscott from the scheduling office; her office and home phone numbers were given for anyone to call, night or day, to complain or ask questions about Reagan's itinerary.

Mark Tapscott, Cindy's brother, was a young, newly hired press secretary to Senator Gordon Humphrey in the summer of 1980. Lyn Nofziger needed an assistant at the Reagan operation. He walked into Humphrey's office and, without consulting the senator, hired Tapscott on the spot. Tapscott immediately left for his new job with Reagan. When Humphrey found out, he was not pleased. Nofziger never worried about niceties.

In the fall of 1980, Bill Casey thought he was running the campaign from Virginia while Stu Spencer and the boys on the plane with Reagan thought they were running things. Roger Stone, running New York and Connecticut, and many others in the field had a generally poor impression of Casey. Behind Casey's back, they called him "Bill Spacey" and "Mumbles." (Apparently Jim Baker used to do a dead-on impression of Casey.) Stone later quipped to Kenny Klinge that no one needed to worry about CIA chief Casey giving away state secrets to the Russians because they would never "understand a fucking word he was saying."

Years later, Casey was briefing the Reagan cabinet and, according to Jim Baker, sounded as if he had "marbles in his mouth." Reagan turned to his then–chief of staff, Howard Baker, and said, "Howard, I have never been able to understand Bill Casey." The chief of staff replied, "Mr. President, that is the scariest thing I have ever heard."

Still, Casey brought order to the chaotic mess left behind by his predecessor, John Sears. And later, as Reagan's head of the CIA, he too embraced Reagan's vision of the rolling back of Communism in the Western Hemisphere and the eventual destruction of Soviet Communism.

Casey even to this day is underappreciated as a courageous Cold Warrior.

ALMOST THIRTY YEARS LATER, some wounds are still not healed and some will never be.

Many conservatives never liked or trusted RNC head Bill Brock, and he reciprocated the sentiment. Rich Bond, hero of George Bush's astonishing win in Iowa, ended up estranged from Bush's eldest son, George W., even as Bond had in many ways become the unofficial fifth Bush son. According to Bond, there was also "bad blood" between Jim Baker and Karl Rove stemming from 1980. Baker and Lyn Nofziger ended up despising each other, with Nofziger late in his life saying bluntly, "I don't think he's an honorable man. And you can quote me."

John Sears and Senator Paul Laxalt never recovered from their falling out. In 2007, twenty-eight years after Sears had tried to supplant Laxalt as chairman of the campaign, the former senator asked me to lunch and I suggested that Sears join us, thinking the wounds had healed. Laxalt replied, "Oh, Craig, there's just been too much water over the dam."

Gerald Ford never really got over his animosity toward Reagan. Neither did Carter.

Meanwhile, Gordon Humphrey has become a recluse in New Hampshire, dodging old friends. John Sears became a lightning rod for criticism, with people to this day either worshipping him or worshipping the quicksand he walks on.

Still, Sears was one of the few in 1980 who saw the Reagan crusade as epochal, a "game changer" in the parlance of the modern era. Almost everybody else simply saw it as just another presidential campaign, to battle over and to do battle with each other.

Old Reagan hand Jeff Bell summed it up in the *Weekly Standard*: "Many of us on Team Reagan often found ourselves at each other's throats."

Some of that happened in the Bush camp, too. Dave Keene and George Bush had a tempestuous relationship, to say the least. Keene told me he was convinced that Bush thought he was an "asshole." Bush may have had some reason to think that. During the campaign, Bush complained to Keene that he was always criticizing him. Keene replied that he "did not know my job description included kissing your ass; I thought there were a lot of people around that would do that for free."

WAS THE 1980 ELECTION settled on ideology or was it simply a rejection of Carter? The evidence is overwhelming that the election was by and large a rejection of big-government liberalism. As Tom Brokaw told me in an interview, "It was the end of the New Deal." The young TV reporter had covered Reagan for KNBC in Los Angeles, and when he moved up to the network, he warned the easterners not to underestimate Reagan. They scoffed. Americans had come to see that after forty-plus years of looking to Washington, their government was no longer capable of solving their problems. It was now time for a new approach. Reagan's approach.

Don Devine made the critical point that up until the last days of the campaign, voters were "mainly anti-Carter and not pro-Reagan." It wasn't until after the debate one week before the election that people began to move into the pro-Reagan column. His debate performance, while unconvincing to the elites, closed the sale with the American voter. As occurred throughout Reagan's political life, his fortunes improved when he took control of his own "rendezvous with destiny." The old master Walter Mondale knew the night of the debate that the Democrats were in trouble. "I don't think Reagan ever talked about limits," Mondale told me. "Carter came in and he's talking about scarcity, he's talking about sacrifice."

President Carter, of the choice offered the American people, said to me succinctly, "What was at stake for the whole country was just a difference in basic philosophy."

He was right.

How CLOSE WAS REAGAN to losing the nomination to George Bush after Iowa? According to Dick Wirthlin's polling in New Hampshire, in April 1979 Reagan stood at 55 percent and Bush at 4 percent. After the Iowa caucuses, Reagan plummeted to 35 percent while Bush surged to 41 percent, a massive shift.

Fate and luck helped save Reagan. Nowadays, only one week separates Iowa's caucuses and the Granite State primary. Had that schedule been in place in 1980 Reagan would have lost New Hampshire and with it the nomination. But in 1980 there were five weeks between the caucuses and the New Hampshire vote. Those five precious weeks gave the Gipper time to recover and the voters and the media more time to look closer at Ambassador Bush.

Reagan, though, certainly had the energy to win the nomination. In 1980, Nancy Reagan told the *Washington Star*, "I can assure you . . . Ronnie's a young man mentally *and* physically." This would have come as news to her childhood friend Mike Wallace, who told a young Californian Reaganite, Pat Nolan, that Reagan was "too old" to run again. Wallace told Nolan this in 1968.

WHAT IS FASCINATING IS how many people will tell you today how much they supported Ronald Reagan in 1980 or that they worked for him. Much of it is poppycock. One low-level numbers cruncher in Bush's campaign insisted to me that he actually ran the Bush campaign and then moved over to run the Reagan campaign after Detroit. Another person who clearly worked for John Connally in the primaries swore that he was always with Reagan. The party committees, including the Republican National Committee and the National Republican Congressional Committee, were essentially incubators of anti-Reagan sentiment all through the late 1970s, but now most who worked there will tell you they supported Reagan from the get-go. I will not embarrass them by naming names, but their revisionist claims are simply not true.

Ernie Angelo, a loyal Texas Reaganite, was repulsed by the GOP operatives who "made fun" of the conservatives and Reagan. "Principle or philosophy had nothing to do with it for them; it was winning."

THE FIRST ANSWER IS yes, Paul Corbin delivered the stolen Carter briefing books to the Reagan campaign in the fall of 1980. There is little doubt of his involvement. George Will was delighted to learn this from me, as Jimmy Carter for years has falsely blamed him for giving them to the Reagan campaign. Nobody but Carter would ever cast Will as a second-story man. Carter has made some other odd assertions over the years, including that Will had asked Carter for forgiveness, which, if anyone knows the taciturn columnist, is claptrap. In his own inimitable fashion, Will called the former president a "recidivist fibber" in a 2005 column.

A number of sources confirmed various aspects of Corbin's role in the caper, including Dick Cheney, John Seigenthaler, Bill Schulz, and others. Corbin, at various times, admitted directly or at least hinted that he'd stolen the briefing books. Vice President Cheney recalled that his former aide the late Tim Wyngaard had said that Corbin had told him of passing the briefing books to Bill Casey; Wyngaard himself told this to the congressional investigating committee headed by Democratic congressman Don Albosta. Casey gave up Corbin's name to the Albosta committee in early July 1983, but said that Corbin had given him only "some material," not the actual briefing books. Corbin denied having given Casey the books, natch.

Jim Baker told the Albosta committee in 1983 that Bill Casey had "indicated to me" that Corbin "might have been a source" for the books. When I interviewed Baker, he said Dick Cheney had told him that Corbin had taken the briefing books, and we joked about the statute of limitations.

Plus, I knew Paul Corbin. Paul Corbin was a friend of mine. For years, we played together in a weekly poker game, and while he never came right out and told us that he'd stolen the debate books, none of us doubted for a moment that he did it and did it willingly, happy to stick it to Carter. Diogenes' lamp would have never shone on Corbin.

Corbin did deny in a sworn statement to the Albosta committee that he'd given the briefing books to the Reagan campaign. But lying to federal officials was old-hat for Corbin. As *Time* magazine politely said, his "reputation for veracity is uneven."

How Corbin got the briefing books out of a sensitive area of the Carter White House is less clear.

In 1983, when the story of the stolen books broke out, the Reagan White House reviewed the guest logs for the Carter White House for the fall of 1980. They did not show a "Paul Corbin" signing in, but security in those days was extremely lax.

Laurie Lucey has been the subject of quiet rumors of involvement for years because of her friendship with Corbin and because she worked in the Carter White House. When I interviewed her in 2008, Lucey repeatedly and emphatically denied playing a role in the briefing-books escapade. She actually left the Carter White House in the fall of 1979, almost a year before the debate books were stolen, and it seems improbable that she would have been able to get back inside the White House complex, given the bad blood between her father, Pat Lucey, and Jimmy Carter.

However, John Seigenthaler told me that he felt Laurie Lucey might have been some sort of "go-between," saying, "There is no other way." The courtly, elderly man also believed that Carter aide Bob Dunn had a role. Seigenthaler is not alone in thinking this. Dunn knew Corbin. He was also a protégé of Pat Lucey. Indeed, he had worked for Lucey in Mexico and in Madison, Wisconsin. But surprisingly, Dunn went to work in the Carter White House just as Lucey was resigning as ambassador to Mexico to join Ted Kennedy's campaign in the fall of 1979.

The FBI tracked Dunn down in San Francisco in 1983, but according to Dunn, the agent never even asked him about his relationship of long standing with Corbin. Dunn expressed amusement to the *Washington Post* that the FBI agent knew so little about the case.

When I finally interviewed Dunn after trying repeatedly over three years to speak with him, he denied any role in the heist.

In the exhaustive search for the full story, I attempted to interview Wilma Hall, a secretary in the Carter White House and later the Reagan White House. She refused to talk. Her daughter later worked as an aide to Colonel Oliver North, author of the Iran-Contra scandal. Name of her daughter? Fawn Hall.

The receptionist at the Reagan campaign, Justine Marks, told investigators in 1983 that she recalled a "young, clean-cut man" delivering to the headquarters a package of materials that resembled the Carter briefing books. She said that she did not remember much about the incident or the person. When asked by the FBI to undergo hypnosis to jog her memory, she demurred. She did, however, recall stopping the stranger, who, she claimed, "had material related to the briefing material for Carter."

Marks worked on, and controlled access to, the fourth floor of the Reagan campaign headquarters. Both Bill Casey's and Jim Baker's offices were located on that floor. It is of course possible that Corbin simply employed someone to deliver the package for him. But records also show that Corbin was meeting with Casey on October 25, the day the books showed up.

When I interviewed Don Albosta many years after his committee's investigation wrapped up, he was still frustrated by what had gone down. The investigation had proved inconclusive. Albosta said that he found both the Carter men and the Reagan men less than forthcoming. He was especially frustrated with Bill Casey, whom he could not understand, and Jim Baker, whom he knew and did understand. He also told me he thought it was odd that Congressman Dick Cheney came to his office to tell him he had nothing to do with the caper when Albosta hadn't even suspected the Wyoming congressman.

The final report produced by Albosta's committee (officially titled *Unauthorized Transfers of Nonpublic Information during the 1980 Presidential Election*) roughed Casey up while giving Baker the benefit of the doubt. Casey issued a statement in which he said, "The campaign management never contemplated, directed or authorized seeking any inside information from the Carter camp." True enough, except the statement never said anything about *accepting* anything stolen from the president's campaign.

Corbin became closer to Bill Casey after Reagan appointed Casey as head of the CIA. Corbin used to tell his daughter, Darlene, that he was going to Nicaragua to help the Contras, and he also used to josh his poker pals about his long absences, saying that he was "running guns" in Central America. With Corbin, anything was possible.

One thing is for sure: Corbin was sui generis, even in a time when American politics was filled with colorful characters who rarely ended up in the newspapers and never on television. There were times when anonymity was necessary in this game. Tom Brokaw neatly summed up the differences between that era and the modern era: "In those days, you couldn't get anybody to talk; now you can't get anybody to shut up!" The era of the political operative as colorful and mysterious has passed and it should be lamented. Men like Corbin and Lyn Nofziger would despise the current consultant-as-celebrity culture of Washington, and the modern, TV-obsessed political operators would have been eaten alive by Nofziger, Corbin, and others of their era.

The second answer is no, the outcome of the election was not affected by the briefing books. President Carter, to this day, is still deeply upset about his purloined briefing books and it was evident in our interview. "I don't think there's any doubt that it made some difference," he complained.

But the briefing books were little more than a compendium of Reagan quotes, comments, speeches, columns, and radio commentaries spanning his public life. Reagan knew what he'd said during all that time, because he had deviated little from his fundamental philosophy over the previous twenty to thirty years. He himself acknowledged that he'd pretty much been saying the same thing; it was just that by 1980, more people were agreeing with the Gipper.

But if the briefing books were filled with pedestrian public-record material, the fact of the matter is that all sorts of other White House documents did show up in the Reagan files, just as Reagan material showed up in the Carter campaign files (and can now be found in archives in the Carter Presidential Library). In September 1980 Reagan-Bush staffer Stefan Halper passed along an internal Carter/Mondale memo advising President Carter on how to deal with various issues Reagan was advocating. *Newsweek* reported that another internal Carter document arrived on Reagan aide Bob Gray's desk with a note saying, "Bob—Report from a White House mole." The Carter White House leaked like a sieve.

And no, no evidence or even the tiniest shred of accusation has ever emerged that Reagan knew about the briefing books coming into his campaign's possession. Everybody knew that if he had been told, his reaction would have been to send them back with an apology to President Carter.

Pat Caddell years later asserted in our conversation his belief that Bill Casey set up a covert operation using former CIA operatives to steal documents out of the Carter White House. Caddell may be right, but no evidence has been forthcoming of such a conspiracy involving so many people.

Likewise, there has never been any evidence that the Reagan campaign sent George Bush to Paris in October 1980 to orchestrate a reverse "October Surprise" by meeting secretly with the Iranians to ensure that the hostages would not be released before the election. As with the stolen briefing books, some Carter supporters have pointed to this alleged secret mission to explain why Carter lost the election. But there is plenty of suspicion that Carter manipulated the hostage crisis for his own political gain, as written by the renowned David Broder of the *Washington Post* then, and by others since.

Carter was also deeply bitter over Ted Kennedy's primary challenge and the fact that liberals went with John Anderson in the fall rather than sticking with him. "I was never reconciled to the more liberal wing of [the] Democratic Party as long as I was in office," he told me. "And there is no doubt that the Kennedy supporters in the left wing of the Democratic Party, the liberal wing, supported John Anderson over me in campaigning."

President Carter did not lose the 1980 election because of the stolen briefing books. He lost because the economy was a catastrophe, because the world situation was worsening, because he could not get the American hostages out of Iran, and because the citizenry was downright scared, ready to listen to Reagan's message, which he delivered at the Cleveland debate. If President Carter is bitter over the election (and by all accounts he is), it could be because he did not listen to Caddell, who opposed any debates and instead devised a campaign plan to destroy Reagan and force voters, reluctantly, into reelecting Carter. A Carter aide said at the time, "The whole thrust of our media this Fall will be to paint Ronald Reagan as dangerous and stupid."

After the election, it leaked out that Rosalynn Carter had opposed the debate, which is interesting, as so too did Mrs. Reagan. It also leaked out that Carter's men had warned him against invoking his daughter, Amy, in the context of a serious policy debate on nuclear armaments. Almost to a man, Carter's aides believe he lost the election because he lost the debate. Pat Caddell said in our interview, Carter was ahead in national polling before the debate, and although he was behind in the electoral vote count, Reagan was nowhere near the needed 270. Even as Reagan won an electoral-vote and popular-vote landslide, many, many states went only very narrowly for the Gipper, Caddell bitterly remembered.

One of the best postelection lines to come out of the 1980 campaign was from Tim Kraft of the Carter campaign, who quipped to Jerry Rafshoon that they should have taken the $30 million spent on the campaign and instead put it into buying two more helicopters for the ill-fated rescue attempt of the hostages in Iran. And who is to say that Kraft's whimsical notion might not have changed the outcome? Had the hostages been rescued, it may have boosted American morale enough that a majority of voters might have forgiven Carter for the terrible economy and given him his second term. We'll never know.

One thing is certain, though: Carter's fall campaign repulsed many Americans, and not just conservatives. The president was eviscerated by liberal columnists and editorialists for the meanness of his campaign. Recall Hugh Sidey's denunciation of Carter in the pages of *Time* magazine in late September 1980: "The past few days have revealed a man capable of far more petty vituperation than most Americans thought possible even in a dank political season. The wrath that escapes Carter's lips about racism and hatred when he prays and poses as the epitome of Christian charity leads even his supports to protest his meanness." Sidey was one of those writers everybody read and took to heart, and was among the most gentle of men. For this urbane and regarded man to pen a column so contemptuous of Carter was stunning. And he was not alone. In turn, the *Washington Post* and even the liberal Scotty Reston of the *New York Times* took Carter to task for his vicious campaign.

AFTER THE PUBLICATION OF my book on Reagan's 1976 insurgent attempt to steal the GOP nomination away from Gerald Ford, *Reagan's Revolution*, I was surprised but obviously also delighted to receive favorable reviews from across the political spectrum. But the issue came up a few times then and now as to whether I am a "Reagan worshipper," as one person put it. No, I am not a "Reagan worshipper." While I am in awe of the man's many and varied accomplishments, I am also in awe and respectful of JFK. In any case, looked at factually and critically, Reagan certainly looms as one of the half dozen most influential men of the twentieth century. And history is being good to him.

I worked for Reagan's 1980 election and reelection in 1984, running and supervising large independent expenditure (IE) campaigns. In 1980, after Reagan lost Iowa and was reeling, I was approached by Bob Heckman, John Gizzi, and Ralph Galliano of the Fund for a Conservative Majority (FCM) and asked whether I was interested in running an IE in support of Reagan. At twenty-three years of age, I jumped at the chance, even though, according to the election laws of the time, I could not work for the official campaign thereafter. I'd met Reagan on a campaign in New Hampshire in 1978, and though he didn't know me from Adam's off ox, he afforded me kindness and sincerity.

Heckman et al. gave me free rein and a check for $750,000. Remembering what my old friend Lyn Nofziger said about people messing around with Reagan's presentation, I decided simply to buy as much radio time as humanly possible beginning in New Hampshire and "just let Reagan talk," as Nofziger said. In a decrepit old studio in Georgetown, for hours at a time, I listened to Reagan's speeches, picked out the best passages, and produced thirty- and sixty-second commercials. With no Internet then, reel-to-reel tapes—complete with the federally mandated disclaimer identifying FCM as the sponsor—were boxed and mailed to hundreds of radio stations in New Hampshire, South Carolina, Florida, Alabama, and Illinois.

In those days, $750,000 went a long, long way on radio. FCM's commercials pretty much ran wall-to-wall in every market in New Hampshire for weeks before the primary. No other group on the Left or Right was conducting a significant independent campaign, and I like to think that Bob, John, Ralph—and

I—deserve a small amount of credit for coming to Reagan's aid when he needed it the most, when his campaign was collapsing, out of money, and beset by internal discord after the stunning loss to George Bush in Iowa.

After Reagan went to Washington, I worked at the Republican National Committee at the behest of Nofziger for the 1982 cycle and later went to the National Conservative Political Action Committee, helping to manage a $14 million IE in support of Reagan's reelection. And during those eight years, it seemed as if I was always at the White House, pitching in on a variety of issues, attending speeches, seeing friends, drinking beer and smoking cigars on Frank Donatelli and Frank Lavin's balcony in the Old Executive Office Building on Friday afternoons.

Still, to write a work of history, a writer must present the facts and let readers draw their own conclusions. The facts I present show Reagan at his best and his worst. I tried to follow the maxim of Jeane Kirkpatrick, who in 1979 told Wayne Valis, "I want to be a good scholar; to unearth the truth, and follow the truth no matter where it leads; and to expose falsehood and lies. That is the definition of a good scholar."

The story is favorable to Reagan because the facts are favorable to Reagan.

The facts are less favorable to Carter. He was, all objectively agree, an unsuccessful president. He came to the presidency with the best of intentions: human rights around the world, reorganizing government, cleaning up Washington, reducing the nuclear threat. But he was simply overwhelmed by the office—"lost in power," as Bill Buckley succinctly told me. Still, I believe that Carter deserves more credit than history has given him in undermining the Soviets. He was the first president to call attention to the human-rights abuses behind the Iron Curtain, and he increased the funding for Radio Free Europe and secreted thousands of copies of *The Gulag Archipelago* behind enemy lines.

Some will argue that in addition to being a bad president, Carter was also a bad man. Others dispute that. My own opinion is that Carter was a good man who had bad days, as opposed to a bad man who had good days. On one particular bad day in 1979, when confronted with the petition of the deposed shah of Iran to enter the United States for cancer treatment, Carter replied, "Fuck the shah."

Carter experienced his share of difficult days after he lost to Reagan. He suffered the humiliation of being the first incumbent Democrat ejected by the voters in almost a century and then, to make matters worse, of having the Iranians wait until minutes after he left office to release the hostages. Worn out after four years in Washington and a brutal campaign, he had planned to spend time alone in a Georgia cabin near a favored fishing stream. But when Carter arrived home in Plains, he discovered to his horror that his carefully constructed finances were a shambles and that he was near bankruptcy. He had to set to work trying to paying the bills.

And so it goes, as Billy Joel wrote in 1983.

Funny how things go. My father was a self-taught historian and a good writer, and loved politics. He died in 1977, but the farther in time I get away from him, the more it seems I am becoming like him. He was certainly more prescient than many in 1965, when he told my brother, my sister, and me after listening to a Reagan speech that the former actor should be president.

This book for me has been a frustrating but wonderful labor of love.

I wouldn't have had it any other way. The search for facts and telling the story combined research, reading, writing, meeting people—some of the things that make living enjoyable.

I plan on writing other books on Ronald Reagan, including one on the 1984 campaign, but I am also planning on writing other works on American political and cultural history. I discovered in my last book that recording history is the imperfect search for perfection. Records go missing, memories fade, people prevaricate, and reporters file mistaken stories.

But excepting God's love, there is no perfection in this life.

Notes

Prologue: A New Beginning

1. Norman C. Miller, "The Republican Revival," *Wall Street Journal*, July 16, 1980, 24.

2. Theodore H. White, "The Small-Town Boys Who Seek to Govern," *Washington Star*, September 29, 1980, A3.

3. "Beyond Packaging," *Wall Street Journal*, July 16, 1980, 24.

4. Jessica Savitch, in discussion with the author, October 1980.

5. Tom Marganthau, Gloria Borger, and James Doyle, "Republican of the Future?" *Newsweek*, July 28, 1980, 33.

6. Tom Wicker, "The Politics of Taxes," *New York Times*, July 25, 1980, A25.

7. "Campaign '80: A Spirited GOP Gears Up for Its Big Show," *U.S. News & World Report*, July 14, 1980, 27.

8. John F. Kennedy Presidential Library and Museum Historical Resources, "Inaugural Address of President John F. Kennedy," John F. Kennedy Presidential Library and Museum, http://www.jfklibrary.org/Historical+Resources/Archives/Reference+Desk/Speeches/JFK/003POF03Inaugural01201961.htm.

9. David Lucey, in discussion with the author.

10. Robert Scheer, "Collapse of Reagan-Ford Deal Blamed on Kissinger," *Los Angeles Times*, July 20, 1980, A22.

11. Don Oberdorfer, "Kissinger Said to Have Courted Both Sides in '68," *Washington Post*, June 2, 1983, A1; Terence Smith, "Kissinger Role in '68 Race Stirs Conflicting Views," *New York Times*, June 13, 1983, B6.

12. "Washington Whispers," *U.S. News & World Report*, May 8, 1978, 16.

13. Michael Barone, "Big Stick Politics," *U.S. News & World Report* (Special Issue), July 17, 2002.

14. Franklin Delano Roosevelt Presidential Library and Museum Audio Clips, "Rendezvous with Destiny," Franklin Delano Roosevelt Presidential Library and Museum, http://www.fdrlibrary.marist.edu/audio.html; Thomas V. DiBacco, "Nothing Conventional about Democrats' History," *Washington Times*, August 13, 2000, C6.

15. Robert G. Kaiser, "Smooth Operator," *Washington Post*, February 22, 2004, T3.

16. Victor Gold, in discussion with the author, April 16, 2007.

17. Lou Cannon, "Man from Main Street, Middle America," *Washington Post*, April 25, 1980, A1.

18. Howell Raines, "From Film Star to Candidate: Ronald Wilson Reagan," *New York Times*, July 17, 1980, A1.

19. *A Time for Choosing: The Speeches of Ronald Reagan, 1961–1982* (Chicago: Regnery Gateway, 1983) 57.

20. James C. Roberts, ed., *A City Upon A Hill: Speeches by Ronald Reagan Before the Conservative Political Action Conference, 1974–1988* (Washington, DC: The American Studies Center, 1989), 13–21.

21. Cannon, "Man from Main Street."

22. "Living Over the Store," *Newsweek*, February 16, 1981, 21.

23. Arnold Koch, "The Lifeguard," *Melrose Mirror*, December 3, 1999.

24. *A Time for Choosing*, 219.

25. "'The Time Is Now . . . to Recapture Our Destiny,'" *Washington Post*, July 18, 1980, A10.

26. "Reagan's Announcement of Running Mate, and Comments by Bush," *New York Times*, July 18, 1980, A12.

27. "Text of Reagan's Speech Accepting the Republicans' Nomination," *New York Times*, July 18, 1980, A8.

28. Ibid.

29. Ibid.

30. Ibid.

31. Jon Meacham, Andrew Murr, Eleanor Clift, Tamara Lipper, Karen Breslau, and Jennifer Ordonez, "American Dreamer," *Newsweek*, June 14, 2004, 22.

32. Koch, "The Lifeguard."

Chapter 1: Exit, Stage Right

1. Frank van der Linden, *The Real Reagan: What He Believes, What He Has Accomplished, What We Can Expect from Him* (New York: William Morrow, 1981), 143–44.

2. Lyn Nofziger, *Nofziger* (Washington, DC: Regnery Gateway, 1992), 206.

3. Lou Cannon, "Reagan: A Healing Hand on the GOP," *Washington Post*, August 21, 1976, A1.

4. Peter Hannaford, *The Reagans: A Political Portrait* (New York: Coward-McCann, 1983), 137.

5. Nancy Reagan with William Novak, *My Turn: The Memoirs of Nancy Reagan* (New York: Random House, 1989), 201.

6. Tom Mathews, Gerald C. Lubenow, and William J. Cook, "Into the Sunset," *Newsweek*, August 30, 1976, 45.

7. Reagan with Novak, *My Turn*, 197.

8. Richard Cheney, in discussion with the author, June 9, 2004.

9. Nofziger, *Nofziger*, 199.

10. Ronald Reagan, *Reagan: A Life in Letters*, ed. Kiron K. Skinner, Annelise Anderson, and Martin Anderson (New York: Free Press, 2003), 219.

11. Peter Hannaford, in discussion with the author, March 24, 2006.

12. Mike Deaver, in discussion with the author, October 18, 2006.

13. Ibid.; John Carmody, TV Column, *Washington Post*, July 21, 1983, D8.

14. Lou Cannon, *Governor Reagan: His Rise to Power* (New York: PublicAffairs, 2003), 433.

15. Peter Hannaford, in discussion with the author, June 30, 2009.

16. John Sears, in discussion with the author, March 18, 2004.

17. United Press International, "Reagan to Appear on TV Tomorrow to Assist GOP," *New York Times*, September 18, 1976, 10.

18. Christopher Lydon, "Reagan Ads for G.O.P. Set for Television, *New York Times*, October 11, 1976, 18.

19. Hannaford, *The Reagans*, 137.

20. Associated Press, "Reagan Bars Aiding Ford in 3 Key States," *New York Times*, October 28, 1976, 47.

21. Christopher Lydon, "Reagan Is Too Busy to Aid Ford in 5 States," *New York Times*, September 20, 1976, 22.

22. Lou Cannon, in discussion with the author, December 5, 2006.

23. Ibid.

24. Michael Reagan, in discussion with the author, July 2, 2004.

25. Lydon, "Reagan Is Too Busy."

26. *National Review*, October 15, 1976, 1098.

27. Jimmy Carter, in discussion with the author, July 11, 2006.

28. United Press International, "Reagan Will Not Bar Another Try in 1980," *New York Times*, November 3, 1976, 17.

29. Reagan, *Reagan: A Life in Letters*, 224.

30. United Press International, "Goldwater Bars G.O.P. Fund Role," *New York Times*, January 6, 1977, 18.

31. Warren Weaver Jr., "Top Republicans Unable to Agree on Filing Two Major Party Posts," *New York Times*, January 7, 1977, 10; Warren Weaver Jr., "Brock Takes Lead for G.O.P. Chairman," *New York Times*, January 14, 1977, 8.

32. Lou Cannon, "Disunity, Nixon Debacle Plague, GOP," *Washington Post*, August 15, 1976, A1.

33. Jack Bass, "Southern Republicans: Their Plight Is Getting Worse," *Washington Post*, July 12, 1977, A4.

34. Ronald Reagan, "Ronald Reagan Speaks Out," *Citizens for the Republic Newsletter*, February 1, 1977.

35. Cindy Tapscott Canevaro, in discussion with the author, November 3, 2006.

36. James Stockdale, in discussion with the author, February 15, 2007.

37. Fred Ryan, in discussion with the author.

38. Walter R. Mears, Associated Press, June 13, 1977.

39. Ronald Reagan, *Reagan, In His Own Hand: The Writings of Ronald Reagan That Reveal His Revolutionary Vision for America*, ed. Kiron K. Skinner, Annelise Anderson, and Martin Anderson (New York: Free Press, 2001), xvi.

40. Hedrick Smith, "Carter So Far: Mix of Symbol and Substance," *New York Times*, March 6, 1977, 144; Jimmy Carter, *Keeping Faith*, 27.

41. Douglas E. Kneeland, "Carter's Style as President Has Drawn Mixed Reviews," *New York Times*, February 13, 1977, 26.

42. Jimmy Carter, *Keeping Faith: Memoirs of a President* (New York: Bantam Books, 1982), 27.

43. Dennis Franey, "GOP's Old Pros Take Stock of Jimmy Carter," *Wall Street Journal*, June 27, 1977, 10.

44. *A Time for Choosing: The Speeches of Ronald Reagan, 1961–1982* (Chicago: Regnery Gateway, 1983) 183.

45. Ibid., 184.

46. Ibid., 185.

47. Ibid., 189.

48. Ibid., 200–201.

49. Ibid., 185.

50. Lou Cannon, "Reagan Criticizes Carter for Proposing Defense Budget Cuts," *Washington Post*, February 6, 1977, 20.

51. David Broder, in discussion with the author.

52. Howard Phillips, in discussion with the author.

53. Lou Cannon, "Tapping the Little Guy," *Washington Post*, March 6, 1977, A1.

54. Ronald Reagan, *Reagan's Path to Victory: The Shaping of Ronald Reagan's Vision: Selected Writings*, ed. Kiron K. Skinner, Annelise Anderson, and Martin Anderson (New York: Free Press, 2004), 132.

55. Associated Press, June 27, 1977; Walter R. Mears, Associated Press, June 13, 1977.

56. Don McLeod, Associated Press, June 10, 1977; Joseph B. Treaster, "Reagan Is Critical of Carter on Rights," *New York Times*, June 10, 1977, 5.

57. *Washington Star*, "Much Ado about Panama," May 2, 1976.

58. Eric Pace, "Reagan Declares Canal Treaties Should Be Rejected by the Senate," *New York Times*, August 26, 1977, A1.

59. Reagan, *Reagan, In His Own Hand*, 201.

60. United Press International, "Ford Gives Support to New Agreement on Panama Canal," *New York Times*, August 17, 1977, A1.

61. "Panama; A Doomed Treaty?" *U.S. News & World Report*, September 19, 1977, 18.

62. Tom Raum, Associated Press, September 8, 1977.

63. Walter R. Mears, Associated Press, November 4, 1977.

64. Charles Black, in discussion with the author, January 16, 2007.

65. Associated Press, December 20, 1977.

66. Ibid.

67. United Press International, "Reagan Protests Party Fund Drive," *New York Times*, December 21, 1977, A14.

68. Ibid.

69. Albert R. Hunt, "Reagan: 'A Man, a Plan, a Canal . . . ,'" *Wall Street Journal*, August 26, 1977, 8.

70. Rowland Evans and Robert Novak, "Reagan in '80?" *Washington Post*, January 16, 1978, A21.

71. James R. Dickenson, "Reagan's Man Sears Is Ready to Roll," *Washington Star*, February 26, 1979, D1.

CHAPTER 2: RETURN OF THE REPUBLICANS

1. Terence Smith, "Carter, in TV Talk, Asks Canal Backing," *New York Times*, February 2, 1978, A1.
2. Ibid.
3. Donald M. Rothberg, Associated Press, February 8, 1978.
4. Robert G. Kaiser, "Senate Votes First Canal Treaty, 68–32," *Washington Post*, March 17, 1978, A1.
5. Donald M. Rothberg, Associated Press, April 18, 1978.
6. Associated Press, April 18, 1978.
7. Associated Press, May 24, 1978.
8. Albert R. Hunt, "Carter and the '78 Elections," *Wall Street Journal*, December 27, 1977, 8.
9. "Generals of a Rebellion by California Taxpayers: Howard Arnold Jarvis and Paul Gann," *New York Times*, June 8, 1978, A25.
10. Wallace Turner, "Brown, in Shift, Now Sees Opportunities in Tax Cut," *New York Times*, June 8, 1978, A25.
11. Doug Willis, Associated Press, June 7, 1978.
12. "Generals of a Rebellion by California Taxpayers."
13. Susanna McBee, "Prop 13 Spawns Tax-Curb Votes on 16 State Ballots," *Washington Post*, November 1, 1978, A4.
14. Rowland Evans and Robert Novak, "A New Tax-Cut Theology for the GOP," *Washington Post*, June 8, 1978, A23.
15. Arthur Laffer, in discussion with the author, January 18, 2007.
16. Ibid.
17. Ann Crittenden, "The Economic Wind's Blowing Toward the Right—for Now, *New York Times*, July 16, 1978, F1.
18. Jeb Bush, in discussion with the author, August 22, 2006.
19. *U.S. News & World Report*, June 13, 1977, 16.
20. "Tax-Cut Plan Gives GOP a New Issue and a New Face," *Wall Street Journal*, September 19, 1978, 1.
21. Bill Peterson, "Rep. Crane Informs Reagan of Plans for '80 Presidential Bid," *Washington Post*, July 27, 1978, A3.
22. Richard Pyle, Associated Press, July 28, 1978.
23. Adam Clymer, "Rep. Crane Weighs Race for President," *New York Times*, July 20, 1978, A17.
24. John W. Mastheck, Thomas J. Foley, and Jack McWethy, "'80 Sweepstakes: At Starting Gate," *U.S. News & World Report*, June 4, 1979, 28.
25. Michael K. Deaver with Mickey Herskowitz, *Behind the Scenes: In Which the Author Talks About Ronald and Nancy Reagan . . . and Himself* (New York: William Morrow, 1987), 75.
26. Frank Donatelli, in discussion with the author, July 26, 2006.
27. PostScript, *Washington Post*, August 28, 1978, A3.
28. Ronald Reagan, *Reagan: A Life in Letters*, ed. Kiron K. Skinner, Annelise Anderson, and Martin Anderson (New York: Free Press, 2003), 116.
29. Peter Hannaford, *The Reagans: A Political Portrait* (New York: Coward-McCann, 1983), 175.
30. John Milne, "'New Right' Exclusion Cost Sears," *Miami Herald*, March 2, 1980, 23A.
31. Lou Cannon, "Reagan Described as Ready to Campaign Hard and Early for the Presidency," *Washington Post*, August 13, 1978, A3.
32. Ibid.
33. Walter R. Mears, Associated Press, October 16, 1978.
34. George Gallup, "Kennedy Gains as Top 1980 Choice," *Washington Post*, August 13, 1978, A15.
35. Associated Press, October 6, 1978.
36. Victor F. Zonana, "California Is Roiled by a New Initiative, Over Homosexuals," *Wall Street Journal*, October 10, 1978, 1.
37. Ed Meese, in discussion with the author.
38. Lyn Nofziger, in discussion with the author.
39. "After Elections—Challenges for Carter and Congress," *U.S. News & World Report*, November 20, 1978, 20.
40. "Looking Ahead to 1980 Elections," *U.S. News & World Report*, April 16, 1979, 37.

41. Nancy Reagan with William Novak, *My Turn: The Memoirs of Nancy Reagan* (New York: Random House, 1989), 189.

42. Deaver with Herskowitz, *Behind the Scenes*, 85.

43. "Going Far by Going Slow," *Time*, January 21, 1980, 32.

44. Jack W. Germond and Jules Witcover, "Retooling Ronald Reagan," *Washington Star*, August 15, 1979, A11

45. Jeffrey Bell, in discussion with the author.

46. Germond and Witcover, "Retooling Ronald Reagan."

47. Hannaford, *The Reagans*, 177–81.

48. James Reston, "When Old Men Dream," *New York Times*, January 26, 1979, A25.

49. Jack W. Germond and Jules Witcover, "Connally Hits N.H. First Time Pouring Out Political Confidence," *Washington Star*, March 22, 1979, A4.

50. David Keene, in discussion with the author.

51. Ibid.

52. David Keene, in discussion with the author, October 10, 2006.

53. Ibid.

54. David Keene, in discussion with the author, March 17, 2006.

55. "Dole Files with Election Panel," *New York Times*, February 22, 1979, A20.

56. Douglas E. Kneeland, "Republican Hopefuls Tread the Carter Path to Iowa," *New York Times*, March 4, 1979, E4.

57. Bill Peterson, "Reagan for President Committee Is Formed, but He Hasn't Announced Candidacy—Yet," *Washington Post*, March 8, 1979, A2.

58. Hannaford, *The Reagans*, 201.

59. Peterson, "Reagan for President Committee Is Formed."

60. Jeffrey Bell, in discussion with the author.

61. Reagan with Novak, *My Turn*, 205.

62. Memorandum from Peter Hannaford to Governor Reagan, "Your Access to the News Media," October 26, 1979, Peter Hannaford Collections, Hoover Institution, Stanford, CA.

CHAPTER 3: LE MALAISE

1. Eugene Kennedy Franklin, "The Looming '80s," *New York Times Magazine*, December 2, 1979, 17.

2. *Time*, "Now, the Self-Centered Generation," September 23, 1974, 85.

3. Ibid.

4. Ibid.

5. Chris Connell, Associated Press, October 23, 1979.

6. Columbia University Augustine Club, "Text of Address by Alexander Solzhenitsyn at Harvard Class Day Afternoon Exercises, A World Split Apart, June 8, 1978," Columbia University, http://www.columbia.edu/cu/augustine/arch/solzhenitsyn/harvard1978.html.

7. Lee Lescaze, "Solzhenitsyn Says West Is Failing as Model for World," *Washington Post*, June 9, 1978, A1.

8. Ibid.

9. Ibid.

10. Ibid.

11. George Will, "Solzhenitsyn's Critics," *Washington Post*, June 18, 1978, B7.

12. Reuters, "New Year's Day Brings New York a Homicide Record," *Washington Post*, January 3, 1980, A14.

13. Jack W. Germond and Jules Witcover, "Pollster's Cleveland Poll Offers Unkindest Cut of All for Carter," *Washington Star*, May 20, 1979, A4.

14. Steven V. Roberts, "Carter, at Midterm, Is Still 'Outsider' to Many in Congress," *New York Times*, March 7, 1979, A18.

15. Lee M. Cohn, "0.7 Pct. Rise in GNP Just Above Recession Level," *Washington Star*, April 19, 1979, A16.

16. Michael Getler, "OPEC Increases Oil Price by 9%, Allows Surcharge," *Washington Post*, March 28, 1979, A1.

17. Rowland Evans and Robert Novak, "Shameful Treatment of the Shah," *Washington Post*, April 27, 1979, A23.

18. United Press International, "Kennedy Leading Carter by 2 to 1 in Poll of New Hampshire Voters," *New York Times*, April 12, 1979, A20.

19. Donald M. Rothberg, Associated Press, June 13, 1979.

20. Kati Marton, *Hidden Power: Presidential Marriages That Shaped Our Recent History* (New York: Pantheon Books, 2001), 236–38.

21. James R. Dickenson, "Crane's Fledgling Presidential Campaign Beset by Full Share of Woes," *Washington Star*, May 13, 1979, A4.

22. Peter Goldman and Tony Fuller, "The Early Bird," *Newsweek*, March 19, 1979, 37.

23. Ronald Reagan, *The Reagan Diaries*, ed. Douglas Brinkley (New York: HarperCollins, 2007), 227.

24. Diane Henry, "Weicker Joins Race for the Presidency," *New York Times*, March 13, 1979, A1.

25. Ibid.

26. John W. Mashek, "Preview '80; Bush's Theme: Time for Insider in White House," *U.S. News & World Report*, October 22, 1979, 65.

27. Dale Russakoff, "Cheerleader Style Further Blurs Bush Image," *Washington Post*, November 3, 1984, A1.

28. Bill Curry, "Bush Declares Presidential Candidacy," *Washington Post*, May 2, 1979, A3.

29. David Keene, in discussion with the author, March 17, 2006.

30. David Keene, in discussion with the author.

31. Adam Clymer, "Senator Dole Joins G.O.P. Race for '80 Presidential Elections," *New York Times*, May 15, 1979, A1.

32. James R. Dickenson, "Dole Formally Joins Six Others in GOP Race," *Washington Star*, May 14, 1979, A1.

33. James R. Dickenson, "Dole Seeks to Portray Self as GOP Pussycat in Presidential Campaign," *Washington Star*, May 15, 1979, A3.

34. Associated Press, June 1, 1979.

35. Edward Walsh and Martin Schram, "Carter, Kennedy Clash Sharply on 'Windfall' Oil Tax," *Washington Post*, May 1, 1979, A1.

36. Steven F. Hayward, *The Real Jimmy Carter: How Our Worst Ex-President Undermines American Foreign Policy, Coddles Dictators, and Created the Party of Clinton and Kerry* (Washington, DC: Regnery, 2004), 155.

37. William Shakespeare, *The Tragedy of King Richard III*, ed. John Jowett (Oxford: Oxford University Press, 2000), 147–49.

38. Vermont Royster, "Thinking Things Over," *Wall Street Journal*, February 22, 1978, 22.

39. Peter Goldman, James Doyle, Thomas M. DeFrank, Eleanor Clift, and Susan Agrest, "The Politics of Gas," *Newsweek*, July 9, 1979, 29.

40. Frank Cormier, Associated Press, July 11, 1979.

41. *Los Angeles Times*, "Reagan, Ford in Near Tie in Gallup Poll," June 3, 1979, A2.

42. Fred Barbash, "Reagan Raises $1.4 Million in Campaign Funds," *Washington Post*, July 26, 1979, A8.

43. Douglas E. Kneeland, "Bush Is Buoyed by Iowa Straw Poll," *New York Times*, May 24, 1979, B12.

44. Lou Cannon, "Bush Is Crushed by Wide Margin," *Washington Post*, February 27, 1980, A1; R. W. Apple Jr., "Long Fight Likely," *New York Times*, February 26, 1976, 1.

45. James Gerstenzang, Associated Press, May 16, 1980.

46. Harry Kelly, "Nation's Morale Torments Carter" *Chicago Tribune*, July 15, 1979, A12.

47. Roberta Hornig, "Aides in 'Disarray' as Deadline Looms on Energy Policy," *Washington Star*, July 6, 1979, A1.

48. Peter Goldman, Thomas M. DeFrank, Eleanor Clift, and Rich Thomas, "Carter's Secret Summit," *Newsweek*, July 16, 1979, 19.

49. Dictionary.com, "Malaise," http://dictionary.reference.com/browse/malaise.

50. "Transcript of President's Address to Country on Energy Problems," *New York Times*, July 16, 1979, A10.

51. David S. Broder, "After 30 Months, Self-Criticism, Sense of Purpose," *Washington Post*, July 16, 1979, A1.

52. "Transcript of President's Address," *New York Times*.

53. Walter Mondale, in discussion with the author, February 28, 2007.

54. Mark O. Hatfield, with the Senate Historical Office, *Vice Presidents of the United States, 1789–1993* (Wash-

ington: U.S. Government Printing Office, 1997), 517–25, http://www.senate.gov/artandhistory/history/common/generic/VP_Walter_Mondale.htm.

55. Walter Mondale, in discussion with the author, February 28, 2007.

56. Adam Clymer, "Reagan: The 1980 Model," *New York Times Magazine*, July 29, 1979, SM6.

57. Hayward, *The Real Jimmy Carter*, 141.

58. Edwin Meese, in discussion with the author, May 6, 2006.

59. Lyn Nofziger, *Nofziger* (Washington, DC: Regnery Gateway, 1992), 236.

60. Ibid.

61. Barry Sussman, "Early Poll Shows Reagan Far in Lead," *Washington Post*, June 23, 1979, A1.

62. Bill Peterson, "'Long Shot' Pressler Enters GOP List," *Washington Post*, September 26, 1979, A6.

63. Jack W. Germond and Jules Witcover, "Admits His 'Interest' as Carter Slips," *Washington Star*, August 5, 1979, A1.

64. Adam Clymer, "Ford Weighs a Low-Key Drive for G.O.P. Nomination," *New York Times*, October 1, 1979, A12.

65. Richard Bond, in discussion with the author, October 4, 2006.

66. Victor Gold, in discussion with the author, April 5, 2007.

67. John F. Stacks, *Watershed: The Campaign for the Presidency, 1980* (New York: Times Books, 1981), 55.

68. Victor Gold, in discussion with the author, April 5, 2007.

69. Tom Wicker, "A Balance for Bush," *New York Times*, July 29, 1988, A27.

70. David Keene, in discussion with the author, March 17, 2006.

71. Rowland Evans and Robert Novak, "George Bush, Jogging," *Washington Post*, August 8, 1979, A17.

72. James Reston, "When Old Men Dream," *New York Times*, January 26, 1979, A25.

73. Michael Graczyk, "Texas Gov. John Connally Dead at 76," Associated Press, June 16, 1993; James Reston, "When Old Men Dream," *New York Times*, January 26, 1979, A25.

74. Paul Hendrickson, "The Long Journey of George Bush," *Washington Post*, January 13, 1980, F1; Aaron Latham, "How History Would Vote," *Washington Post*, October 23, 1988, C1.

75. James M. Perry, "To George Bush, Seeking Presidency Seems Almost a Duty," *Wall Street Journal*, July 6, 1979, 1.

76. Ibid.

77. Maurice Carroll, "Bush Emphasizes His 'Fantastic Credentials' in Race," *New York Times*, January 5, 1980, 10.

78. Rowland Evans and Robert Novak, "Connally's Populist Push," *Washington Post*, August 13, 1979, A21.

79. United Press International, "Chappaquiddick Warning," *Washington Post*, October 13, 1979, A5.

80. Douglas Hallett, "John Connally's Slick Image," *Wall Street Journal*, May 17, 1979, 26.

81. James Gerstenzang, Associated Press, August 20, 1979; Bill Brock, in discussion with the author, October 15, 2006.

82. John W. Mashek, "Preview '80; Howard Baker Takes Aim at Carter's Southern Turf," *U.S. News & World Report*, July 30, 1979, 49.

83. Myra MacPherson, "Talmadge Is Back on the Hill and the Tributes Flow," *Washington Post*, March 2, 1979, E1.

84. Peter Goldman, Gerald C. Lubenow, Tony Fuller, and James Doyle, "A Royal Progress," *Newsweek*, November 26, 1979, 50.

85. George F. Will, "Characteristically Connally," *Washington Post*, October 18, 1979, A19.

86. Mike Feinsilber, "Today's Topic: Mother, May I?" Associated Press, September 14, 1979.

87. Adam Clymer, *Edward M. Kennedy: A Biography* (New York: Perennial, 1999), 226, 243–44, 252.

88. Confidential interview with the author, 1991.

89. Walter Mondale, in discussion with the author, February 28, 2007.

90. Associated Press, November 2, 1979.

91. Ann Blackman, Associated Press, September 7, 1979.

92. Associated Press, "Carter's Job Rating at 19%, The Lowest Since the 1950s," *Washington Post*, September 14, 1979, A2.

93. Jack W. Germond and Jules Witcover, "Team of 3 Paves Way for Kennedy Campaign," *Washington Star*, October 11, 1979, A3.

94. Ibid.

95. Michael McShane, in discussion with the author.

96. Martin Schram, "Kennedy's Intensified Rhetoric Fuels '80 Speculation," *Washington Post*, June 11, 1979, A1.

97. T. R. Reid, "Kennedy to Declare Nov. 7 in Boston," *Washington Post*, October 30, 1979, A1.

98. Les Brown, "'Teddy' on CBS Sunday," *New York Times*, November 1, 1979, C19.

99. Roland Perry, *Hidden Power: The Programming of the President* (New York: Beaufort Books, 1984), 74.

100. Clymer, *Edward M. Kennedy*, 286–87.

101. Roland Perry, *Hidden Power*, 77.

102. Clymer, *Edward M. Kennedy*, 286.

103. James R. Dickenson and Duncan Spencer, "Gov. Brown Launches His Run for Presidency," *Washington Star*, November 8, 1979, A1.

104. Associated Press, "Public Would Back Retaliation, Poll Shows," *Washington Star*, November 30, 1979, A1.

Chapter 4: The Front-Walker

1. Charles R. Black, in discussion with the author, March 20, 2006.

2. Ibid.; Ernie Angelo, in discussion with the author, November 13, 2006.

3. Albert R. Hunt, "Reagan Strategist Surveys Scene—and Picks a Winner," *Wall Street Journal*, August 30, 1979, 18.

4. "Sears: Reagan's High-Roller," *Time*, August 16, 1976.

5. John Sears, in discussion with the author, July 26, 2006.

6. Ibid.

7. Peter Hannaford, in discussion with the author, March 24, 2006.

8. Joseph E. Persico, *Casey: From the OSS to the CIA* (New York: Viking, 1990), 176.

9. Robert Lindsey, "Reagan Campaign Said to Be in Debt as Donations Lag," *New York Times*, September 6, 1979, B11.

10. Al Martinez, "Presidential Campaigns: Money Plus Manpower," *Los Angeles Times*, November 1, 1979, I1.

11. Doug Bandow, in discussion with the author, October 10, 2006.

12. Robert Scheer, "'California Cronies' Have Reagan's Ear," *Los Angeles Times*, June 26, 1980, A9.

13. Richard Bergholz, "Former Aide Says Reagan Staff Is Too Big, Arrogant," *Los Angeles Times*, October 27, 1979.

14. Jim Lake, in discussion with the author, September 19, 2006.

15. Martinez, "Presidential Campaigns."

16. Jim Lake, in discussion with the author, September 19, 2006.

17. Martinez, "Presidential Campaigns."

18. Ibid.

19. Adam Clymer, "Kennedy Candidacy a Big Topic at Michigan Republican's Parley," *New York Times*, September 24, 1979, A17.

20. Ronald Reagan, *Reagan: A Life in Letters*, ed. Kiron K. Skinner, Annelise Anderson, and Martin Anderson (New York: Free Press, 2003), 232–33.

21. Robert Lindsey, "Reagan Urges Senate to Reject Arms Pact, but His Tone Is Softer," *New York Times*, September 16, 1979, 39.

22. "Reagan, Already the Front Runner, Formally Enters GOP Race Tuesday," *Washington Star*, November 11, 1979, A4.

23. Hedrick Smith, "Candidates Running for Visibility in New Hampshire," *New York Times*, September 17, 1979, A22.

24. "Republicans Take Turns Criticizing Kennedy as Haig Hints He Will Run," *New York Times*, September 30, 1979, 18.

25. James R. Dickenson, "Reagan Is Favorite at GOP Women's Meeting," *Washington Star*, September 30, 1979, A1.

26. "Reagan's Jersey Backers Help Campaign at Dinner," *New York Times*, October 1, 1979, B2.

27. Jeff Bell, in discussion with the author.

28. Terence Smith, "Aides Say Carter Will Enter Race On Dec. 4 and Make a 4-Day Tour," *New York Times*, October 5, 1979, A21.

29. James Dickenson, "Reagan, Already the Front Runner, Formally Enters GOP Race Tuesday," *Washington Star*, November 11, 1979, A4.

30. Douglas E. Kneeland, "Bush Easily Wins Iowa Straw Vote for Republican Presidential Choice," *New York Times*, October 16, 1979, B10.

31. David Keene, in discussion with the author, March 17, 2006.

32. Richard Bond in discussion with the author, October 4, 2006.

33. Ibid.

34. Thom Mathews and Gerald C. Lubenow, "The Leading Man," *Newsweek*, October 1, 1979, 20.

35. Adam Clymer, "Ford Rules Out Active Candidacy; Calls on Supporters to Back Others," *New York Times*, October 20, 1979, 28.

36. Clymer, "Ford Rules Out Active Candidacy."

37. George F. Will, "Connally's Recklessness Makes Reagan Look Better for GOP," *Los Angeles Times*, October 22, 1979, C7.

38. Martin Schram, "Maine Vote Gave All the GOP Strategists a Surprise," *Washington Post*, November 5, 1979, A2.

39. Richard L. Lyons, "Bush's Victory Surprises Baker in Maine Voting," *Washington Post*, November 4, 1979, A1.

40. Schram, "Maine Vote Gave All the GOP Strategists a Surprise."

41. Adam Clymer, "Poll Finds Reagan Keeping Lead; More Democrats Back Kennedy," *New York Times*, November 6, 1979, A1.

42. Frank Lynn, "Reagan Plans New York Announcement of Candidacy," *New York Times*, October 18, 1979, A17.

43. Lou Cannon, "Reagan Announces, Urges Strength at Home, Abroad," *Washington Post*, November 14, 1979, A1.

44. Tom Mathews and Gerald C. Lubenow, "The Leading Man," *Newsweek*, October 1, 1979, 20.

45. Will, "Connally's Recklessness Makes Reagan Look Better for GOP."

46. Tom Wicker, "Up & Down in N.H.," *New York Times*, October 30, 1979, A19.

47. Dickenson, "Reagan, Already the Front Runner."

48. Jim Hooley, in discussion with the author.

49. Helene Von Damm, *At Reagan's Side* (New York: Doubleday, 1989), 106–9.

50. Ronald Reagan Presidential Library Foundation Speeches, "Intent to Run for President; Official Announcement, November 13, 1979," Ronald Reagan Presidential Library Foundation, http://www.reaganlibrary.com/reagan/speeches/speech.asp?spid=4.

51. Ibid.

52. Ibid.

53. Robert Lindsey, "Reagan, Entering Presidency Race, Calls for North American 'Accord,'" *New York Times*, November 14, 1979, A1.

54. Tom Raum, Associated Press, November 14, 1979.

55. James R. Dickenson, "Reagan Won't Debate Party Rivals," *Washington Star*, November 14, 1979, A1.

56. Tom Raum, Associated Press, November 14, 1979.

57. Lou Cannon, "Reagan Refuses to Debate His GOP Opponents," *Washington Post*, November 15, 1979, A3.

58. David Smick, in discussion with the author, October 18, 2006.

59. Robert Lindsey, "Reagan Bars Debate with Rivals for Fear of Dividing the G.O.P.," *New York Times*, November 15, 1979, B16.

60. Adam Clymer, "Both Reagan and Rivals Are Depending on Early Victories," *New York Times*, October 8, 1979, A14.

61. Bill Curry, "GOP Governors in No Hurry to Endorse," *Washington Post*, November 20, 1979, A5.

CHAPTER 5: THE UNDISCOVERED COUNTRYSIDE

1. Adam Clymer, "Reagan Wins a Poll of G.O.P. in Florida," *New York Times*, November 18, 1979, 1.

2. Bill Peterson, "Republican Hopefuls Grasp at Straws in Iowa Wind," *Washington Post*, October 15, 1979, A5.

3. Jack W. Germond and Jules Witcover, "Concern for Reagan's Age Strongest Among Elderly," *Washington Star*, December 26, 1979, A1.

4. Ibid.

5. Associated Press, January 6, 1980.

6. David Halberstam, *The Powers That Be* (Chicago: University of Illinois Press, 2000), 6.

7. Adam Clymer, "The Pulse Remains Steady Across Iowa Heartland," *New York Times*, January 20, 1980, E2.

8. William Serrin, "Down on the Farm, Changing Times Are Driving Many People to Find Work in Town," *New York Times*, August 12, 1979, 20.

9. Clymer, "The Pulse Remains Steady Across Iowa Heartland."

10. Ibid.

11. Tom Buckley, "'Music Man's' Music Man at 78," *New York Times*, June 5, 1980, C17.

12. "Where Are the Pigs and Corn?" *Time*, February 4, 1980.

13. Ibid.

14. "Carter Denounces Russia's Intervention in Afghanistan," *Washington Star*, December 29, 197, A5.

15. George F. Will, "Games People Shouldn't Play," *Washington Post*, January 6, 1980, B7.

16. Jack W. Germond and Jules Witcover, "Carter Sets a Political Time Bomb for Himself," *Washington Star*, January 4, 1980, A3.

17. Ibid.

18. Robert H. Reid, "Afghans Continue Fierce Fighting," *Washington Post*, January 3, 1980, A1.

19. Mike Deaver, in discussion with the author, October 18, 2006.

20. Nancy Reagan with William Novak, *My Turn: The Memoirs of Nancy Reagan* (New York: Random House, 1989), 205.

21. Mike Deaver, in discussion with the author, October 18, 2006.

22. Jim Lake, in discussion with the author, September 19, 2006.

23. Mike Deaver, in discussion with the author, October 18, 2006.

24. Reagan with Novak, *My Turn*, 205.

25. Lou Cannon, *Reagan* (New York: G. P. Putnam's Sons, 1982), 239.

26. Mike Deaver, in discussion with the author, October 18, 2006.

27. Reagan with Novak, *My Turn*, 183.

28. Dick Wirthlin, in discussion with the author, November 8, 2006.

29. Lou Cannon, *President Reagan: The Role of a Lifetime* (New York: Public Affairs, 1999, 2000), 46.

30. Bill Peterson, "Shaken by Election Loss, Baker Switches Managers," *Washington Post*, November 17, 1979, A3.

31. Adam Clymer, "Optimistic Bush 'Fired Up,' Feels Drive 'Is Moving,'" *New York Times*, November 23, 1979, A24.

32. George F. Will, "The Joy of Politics," *Newsweek*, November 26, 1979, 128.

33. Jeb Bush, in discussion with the author, August 22, 2006; *Washington Star*, "George Bush: Urbane, Unflappable, Unknown," October 28, 1979.

34. Maurice Carroll, "Bush, in Illinois, Pleased by Rapid Rise in Attention," *New York Times*, November 30, 1979, A23.

35. Confidential interview with the author.

36. Douglas E. Kneeland, "Connally, Stumping Middle West, Intensifies His Attacks on Reagan," *New York Times*, December 1, 1979, 39.

37. Ibid.

38. Hedrick Smith, "Optimism Is Fading for Reagan in Iowa," *New York Times*, December 10, 1979, D10.

39. Ibid.

40. Adam Clymer, "Reagan's Fortunes in Iowa Caucuses Appear to Hang on Strength of Local Organizations," *New York Times*, January 13, 1980, 20; Rowland Evans and Robert Novak, "Reagan: Once Invincible, Now Invisible," *Washington Post*, January 14, 1980, A23.

41. Lyn Nofziger, *Nofziger* (Washington, DC: Regnery Gateway, 1992), 205; Kenny Klinge, in discussion with the author, July 12, 2006.

42. Smith, "Optimism Is Fading for Reagan."

43. Susan Drake, "Bush's Iowa Bandwagon," *Newsweek*, September 3, 1979, 15; Richard Bond, in discussion with the author, October 4, 2006.

44. Memorandum by Arthur Finkelstein, Kenneth Klinge Archives Collection.

45. "The Strings on John Connally," *New York Times*, December 13, 1979, A30.

46. Jack W. Germond, "Is Kennedy Flying . . .", *Washington Star*, December 2, 1979, A4.

47. Philip Taubman, "With a Fortune Over $20 Million, Kennedy Is Wealthiest in '80 Race," *New York Times*, December 30, 1979, 1.

48. Hedrick Smith, "Poll Finds Carter Leads Kennedy in a Reversal Among Democrats," *New York Times*, December 12, 1979, A1.

49. Jeremiah O'Leary, "Carter, Kennedy Exchange Light Quips at Dinner for House Speaker O'Neill," *Washington Star*, December 10, 1979.

50. Jack W. Germond, "Carter Needn't Win Early Test, Aide Says," *Washington Star*, December 17, 1979, A3.

51. Hedrick Smith, "Reagan Challenged to Join Iowa Forum," *New York Times*, December 13, 1979, A20.

52. Ibid.

53. Robert Lindsey, "Reagan Suggesting Few New Programs," *New York Times*, December 16, 1979, 38.

54. Robert Lindsey, "Reagan Is Undecided on Taking U.S. Funds In Primary Campaign," *New York Times*, December 13, 1979, A20.

55. Adam Clymer, "Ford and His Old Advisers Meet to Talk Current Issues," *New York Times*, December 15, 1979, 12.

56. Robert Lindsey, "Reagan Decides at the 11th Hour to Forgo Puerto Rico's Primary," *New York Times*, December 15, 1979, 13.

57. Ronald D. White, "Rep. Crane's Wife Acquitted of Pet Law Charges," *Washington Post*, December 19, 1979, B1.

58. Douglas E. Kneeland, "Connally Is Dropping His TV Drive for Primary Contests with Reagan," *New York Times*, December 16, 1979, 36; Tom Morganthau, Tony Fuller, and James Doyle, "Connally Dials Back," *Newsweek*, December 17, 1979, 49.

59. Douglas E. Kneeland, "Connally's Campaign Tactics," *New York Times*, January 15, 1980, D14.

60. Hedrick Smith, "GOP Race Focuses on South Carolina," *New York Times*, December 17, 1979, A21.

61. Ibid.

62. Ibid.

63. Lindsey, "Reagan Suggesting Few New Programs."

64. David Keene, in discussion with the author, March 17, 2006; Smith, "GOP Race Focuses on South Carolina."

65. Tom Mathews, Eleanor Clift, Fred Coleman, Thomas M. DeFrank, and William E. Schmidt, "The Chill of a New Cold War," *Newsweek*, January 14, 1980, 24.

66. "Held Hostage in Iran—60 Americans," *New York Times*, November 11, 1979, E1; "State Dept. Issues Plea on the Hostages' Mail," *New York Times*, December 14, 1979, A16.

67. United Press International, "U.S. Funds Allocated for Carter and Baker," *New York Times*, December 21, 1979, A21.

68. Caroline Rand Herron and Daniel Lewis, "Connally Passes Up Matching Funds for a Free Rein," *New York Times*, December 16, 1979, E4.

69. Dan Balz, "Anderson Climbs Uphill Toting Heavyweight Issues," *Washington Post*, November 17, 1979, A2.

70. "Analysts See U.S. Economy Growing Again," *Globe and Mail* (Toronto), December 22, 1979.

71. Robert Shogan, "Candidates as Thick as Corn as Caucuses Near," *Los Angeles Times*, December 4, 1979, B1.

CHAPTER 6: THE ASTERISK ALSO RISES

1. Judy Daubenmier, "Bush Margin Drops as Tally Ends," Associated Press, January 24, 1980.

2. James Wooten, "George Bush's Organization and His Own 'Peddler' Style of," *World News Tonight*, ABC News Transcripts, January 22, 1980.

3. Bill Peterson, "Many See Threat Greatest to Reagan," *Washington Post*, September 23, 1979, A1.

4. Lou Cannon, *Reagan* (New York: G. P. Putnam's Sons, 1982), 249.

5. Bill Peterson and Margot Hornblower, "Reagan Returns to WHO . . . What Hit Him?" *Washington Post*, January 19, 1980, A1.

6. John Maxwell, in discussion with the author, July 20, 2006.

7. Ibid.

8. James A. Baker III and Steve Fiffer, *Work Hard, Study . . . and Keep Out of Politics!* (New York: G. P. Putnam's Sons, 2006), 87.

9. Jim Lake, in discussion with the author, September 19, 2006.

10. Maurice Carroll, "Bush Campaign Is Flying, but Has It Really Taken Off?" *New York Times*, January 6, 1980, E4.

11. Andrew Schneider, "George Bush Exercises His Campaign Style," Associated Press, January 10, 1980.

12. David Keene, in discussion with the author, May 12, 2009.

13. Laurence I. Barrett, *Gambling with History: Ronald Reagan in the White House* (New York: Penguin Books, 1983), 376–77.

14. Ibid, 377.

15. Jules Witcover, *Marathon: The Pursuit of the Presidency, 1972–1976* (New York: Viking Press, 1977), 504.

16. Richard Bergholz, "GOP Candidates Differ on Iran, Grain; Chide Reagan," *Los Angeles Times*, January 6, 1980, 1.

17. Ibid.

18. Charles Gibson, *World News Tonight Sunday*, ABC News Transcripts, January 6, 1980.

19. Jack W. Germond, "GOP's Iowa Debate Fails to Draw Blood," *Washington Star*, January 6, 1980, A1; James R. Dickenson, "The Absent Reagan Looms Large at Des Moines Republican Debate," *Washington Star*, January 6, 1980, A5.

20. Bill Peterson, "Though Main Tent Folded, the Show Must Go On," *Washington Post*, January 5, 1980, A2.

21. William Endicott, "Reagan Steps Up Criticism of Carter," *Los Angeles Times*, January 9, 1980, B14.

22. Richard Bond, in discussion with the author, October 4, 2006.

23. David Smick, in discussion with the author, October 18, 2006.

24. Ibid.

25. "Reagan Popularity Drops In Iowa; Carter Tops Kennedy," Associated Press, January 11, 1980.

26. James R. Dickenson, "Early Political Tests to Be Different This Year," *Washington Star*, January 6, 1980, A3.

27. William F. Buckley Jr., *On the Firing Line: The Public Life of Our Public Figures* (New York: Random House, 1989), 178.

28. "Talking Politics: Ronald Reagan," *New York Times*, January 2, 1980, A1.

29. Carroll, "Bush Campaign Is Flying."

30. Wooten, *World News Tonight Sunday*, ABC News Transcripts, January 6, 1980.

31. United Press International, "President Leads Kennedy in Iowa Poll; Reagan Slips," *Los Angeles Times*, January 11, 1980, A1.

32. Robert Shogan, "Carter Leads Kennedy 57% to 25% in Iowa Poll; Reagan Slips" *Los Angeles Times*, January 12, 1980, A6; "And Now It Begins—Sort Of," *Time*, January 21, 1980.

33. Tom Jarriel, *World News Tonight*, ABC News Transcripts, January 11, 1980.

34. John Laurence, *World News Tonight*, ABC News Transcripts, January 11, 1980.

35. William Endicott, "Reagan's Strategy: Say What They Like to Hear," *Los Angeles Times*, January 11, 1980, B6

36. Shogan, "Carter Leads Kennedy 57% to 25%."

37. Albert R. Hunt, "Howard Baker Steers Center-Stream Tack in the GOP Regatta," *Wall Street Journal*, October 23, 1979, 1.

38. Walter R. Mears, Associated Press, January 21, 1980.

39. Colman McCarthy, "Reagan: Not His Age, His Staleness," *Washington Post*, January 20, 1980, E5.

40. William Endicott, "Reagan Facing Up to His Age by Flaunting It," *Los Angeles Times*, January 18, 1980, A9.

41. "Campaign Notes," *Washington Post*, January 18, 1980, A3.

42. Peterson and Hornblower, "Reagan Returns to WHO . . . What Hit Him?"

43. Ibid.

44. Ibid.

45. William F. Endicott, "Reagan Says Iran May Be Next Soviet Target," *Los Angeles Times*, January 17, 1980, B19.

46. Margot Hornblower, "Iowa Politicians Say Bush May Extend Reagan," *Washington Post*, January 21, 1980, A4.

47. Maurice Carroll, "Bush Emphasizes His 'Fantastic Credentials' in Race," *New York Times*, January 5, 1980, 10.

48. James R. Dickenson, "Size of Iowa Turnout," *Washington Star*, January 20, 1980, A3.

49. Jack W. Germond, "The Changing Face of Iowa Caucuses," *Washington Star*, January 18, 1980, A1.

50. Robert Meyers, "Firm Claims Sen. Dole Owes for Campaign Job," *Washington Post*, January 18, 1980, C13.

51. David Wood, "A Relaxed Kennedy Makes Last Iowa Swing," *Washington Star*, January 19, 1980, A3.

52. Associated Press, "Gold Price Tops $510 in European Markets," *Washington Star*, December 27, 1979, A1; Molly Sinclair and Jane Seaberry, "Panicky Investors Push Gold to Record $575.50," *Washington Post*, January 3, 1980, A1.

53. "Carter Slips in Poll on Handling of Iran," *Washington Post*, January 11, 1980, A8.

54. "Iowa Precinct Caucuses at a Glance," *New York Times*, January 21, 1980, A14; United Press International, "Final Figures in Iowa Show Bush Received 36.5% of Caucus Votes," *New York Times*, January 24, 1980, B9.

55. Richard Bergholz, "Reagan Shrugs Off Loss to Bush in Iowa Caucuses," *Los Angeles Times*, January 23, 1980, 23.

56. John Sears, in discussion with the author, July 26, 2006.

57. Lou Cannon, in discussion with the author, June 6, 2006.

58. John Sears, in discussion with the author, July 26, 2006.

59. United Press International, "Final Figures in Iowa Show Bush Received 36.5% of Caucus Votes," *New York Times*, January 24, 1980, B9.

60. John F. Stacks, *Watershed: The Campaign for the Presidency, 1980* (New York: Times Books, 1981), 107.

61. Jeb Bush, in discussion with the author, August 22, 2006.

62. Richard Bond, in discussion with the author, October 4, 2006.

63. Lou Cannon, in discussion with the author, June 6, 2006.

64. Judy Daubenmier, "Bush Margin Drops as Tally Ends," Associated Press, January 24, 1980.

65. "In New Hampshire, They're Off!," *Time*, February 25, 1980.

66. Martin Plissner, in discussion with the author.

67. Richard Bond, in discussion with the author.

68. "Can Reagan Be Stopped?" *U.S. News & World Report*, December 3, 1979, 41.

69. "Candidates Spending a Total of $2.8 Million in Iowa Caucuses, 10 Times the '76 Level," *New York Times*, January 21, 1980, A13.

70. Peter Goldman, Frank Maier, Richard Manning, James Doyle, John Walcott, and Gerald C. Lubenow, "Iowa: Two for the Seesaw," *Newsweek*, January 21, 1980, 38.

71. John Laurence, *World News Tonight*, ABC News Transcripts, January 22, 1980.

72. Peter Goldman, Gerald C. Lubenow, Tony Fuller, and James Doyle, "A Royal Progress?" *Newsweek*, November 26, 1979, 50.

73. Bergholz, "Reagan Shrugs at Loss in Iowa," *Los Angeles Times*, January 23, 1980, B1.

74. Donald M. Rothberg, Associated Press, January 22, 1980.

75. Donald M. Rothberg, "After Wide Swings in the Opinion Polls, Iowans Caucus," Associated Press, January 21, 1980.

76. Walter R. Mears, Associated Press, January 18, 1980.

77. "Dead Woman's Father Reportedly Not Surprised at Kennedy Report," Associated Press, January 24, 1980; Mears, Associated Press, January 18, 1980.

78. T. R. Reid, William Greider, Maralee Schwartz, Basil Talbott, and Fay Joyce, "Funds Depleted, Kennedy Juggles Campaign Plans," *Washington Post*, January 25, 1980, A1.

79. Lance Gay, "Meany Buried in Maryland After Service Attended by Carter, About 1,100 Others," *Washington Star*, January 16, 1980, A6; Martin Weil and Warren Brown, "Labor Leader George Meany Dies of Cardiac Arrest at 85," *Washington Post*, January 11, 1980, A1; Associated Press, January 11, 1980.

80. Associated Press, "Reagan Ambushed in Iowa; Carter Whips Kennedy, 2–1," *Concord* (NH) *Monitor*, January 22, 1980, 1.

81. George Esper, "Buoyed by Iowa Victory, Bush Campaigns in New Hampshire," Associated Press, January 23, 1980.

82. Tim Ahern, Associated Press, "Bush Predicts N.H. Victory," *Nashua* (NH) *Telegraph*, January 24, 1980.

83. Paul Carrier and David Olinger, "Gallen, Others Say Iowa Vote Will Change Strategies Here," *Concord* (NH) *Monitor*, January 22, 1980, 1.

84. Robert G. Kaiser, Lou Cannon, and Maralee Schwartz, "The John, Jerry, Howard, George, Teddy and Jimmy Show," *Washington Post*, February 10, 1980, A4.

85. "Reagan," *Concord* (NH) *Monitor*, January 22, 1980, 1.

86. Ibid.

87. Lou Cannon, in discussion with the author, June 6, 2006.

88. "Reagan," *Concord* (NH) *Monitor*, 1.

89. Lou Cannon, in discussion with the author, June 6, 2006.

90. Goldman, Maier, Manning, Doyle, Walcott, and Lubenow, "Iowa: Two for the Seesaw."

91. Lou Cannon, "After First Blush, Reagan Losing Bloom . . . ," *Washington Post*, January 25, 1980, A3.

92. Ibid.

93. Richard Allen, in discussion with the author, June 14, 2006.

94. Cindy Tapscott Canevaro, in discussion with the author.

95. Cathleen McGuigan, "Newsmakers," *Newsweek*, January 21, 1980, 59.

96. "Surprise Harvest in Iowa," *Time*, February 4, 1980.

CHAPTER 7: BUSH BEARS DOWN

1. Richard Bergholz, "Reagan Shrugs at Loss in Iowa," *Los Angeles Times*, January 23, 1980, B1.

2. Associated Press, January 22, 1980.

3. Richard Wirthlin, in discussion with the author, November 8, 2006.

4. Robert Lindsey, "Reagan Meets to Review Strategy," *New York Times*, January 24, 1980, B9.

5. Douglas E. Kneeland, "Bush, in New Hampshire, Buoyed by Iowa Victory," *New York Times*, January 23, 1980, A16.

6. Stefan Halper, in discussion with the author, March 20, 2007.

7. "On the Hill: New Respect for Bush, Doubt on Reagan," *Washington Star*, January 22, 1980, A1.

8. Bergholz, "Reagan Shrugs at Loss in Iowa."

9. David Keene, in discussion with the author, March 17, 2006.

10. Walter R. Mears, Associated Press, January 22, 1980; Linda Deutsch, "Reagan Hints Changing Stance on GOP Debates," Associated Press, January 22, 1980.

11. George F. Will, "Iowa Isn't Heaven, but It's a Step Up," *Los Angeles Times*, January 25, 1980, C5.

12. "Reagan Likes Birthday, Considering Alternative," *Los Angeles Times*, February 4, 1980, A14.

13. Robert Lindsey, "As Reagan Goes, So Goes John P. Sears 3d," *New York Times*, January 27, 1980, E4.

14. Joseph E. Persico, *Casey: From the OSS to the CIA* (New York: Viking, 1990), 177.

15. Charles R. Black, in discussion with the author, March 20, 2006.

16. Merrill Hartson, Associated Press, February 5, 1980.

17. Bella Stumbo, "On the Campaign Trail with Reagan," *Los Angeles Times*, February 4, 1980, B1.

18. Richard Wirthlin, in discussion with the author, November 8, 2006.

19. Jim Lake, in discussion with the author, September 19, 2006.

20. John Sears, in discussion with the author, July 26, 2006.

21. Persico, *Casey*, 177.

22. Ibid., 178.

23. Richard Bergholz, "Reagan Says Carter Is to Blame for Afghanistan," *Los Angeles Times*, January 25, 1980, B23.

24. Adam Clymer, "Reagan Suggests Blockade of Cuba on Soviets' Move into Afghanistan," *New York Times*, January 28, 1980, B5.

25. Bernard Weinraub, "Reagan Blames Carter 'Failure' for Soviet Move," *New York Times*, January 25, 1980, A12.

26. Marjorie Hunter, "Wife Hints Carter Backs Female Draft," *New York Times*, January 26, 1980, 9.

27. Clymer, "Reagan Suggests Blockade of Cuba."

28. Richard Bergholz, "Reagan Decides to Take Federal Matching Funds," *Los Angeles Times*, January 29, 1980, B9.

29. Richard Bergholz, "Reagan Modifies His Stand on Cuban Blockade—Says It Was Only Hypothetical," *Los Angeles Times*, January 31, 1980, A15.

30. Steven V. Roberts, "Ted Kennedy: Haunted by the Past," *New York Times*, February 3, 1980.

31. Bill Stall, "Reagan Agrees to Carolina Debates," *Los Angeles Times*, January 31, 1980, 6.

32. Margaret Nelson, "Republicans Revive Debate Over Debate," *Nashua* (NH) *Telegraph*, January 29, 1980, 3.

33. Associated Press, "Reagan Is Heating Up Campaign," *Nashua* (NH) *Telegraph*, January 31, 1980.

34. "Reagan-Bush Debate Sought by Telegraph," *Nashua* (NH) *Telegraph*, January 30, 1980, 1.

35. Stall, "Reagan Agrees to Carolina Debate."

36. Richard Reeves, "The President Loses Reagan," *Washington Star*, January 29, 1980, A11.

37. "Transcript of Kennedy's Speech at Georgetown University on Campaign Issues," *New York Times*, January 29, 1980, A12.

38. Bergholz, "Reagan Modifies His Stand."

39. Ibid.

40. Donald M. Rothberg, Associated Press, January 31, 1980.

41. United Press International, "Reagan Wins 6 Arkansas Votes, Baker Captures 4," *Los Angeles Times*, February 3, 1980, A15.

42. Stumbo, "On the Campaign Trail with Reagan."

43. Ibid.

44. Ibid.

45. Ibid.

46. "A Patrician Entry for the GOP," *Time*, May 14, 1979.

47. Stumbo, "On the Campaign Trail with Reagan."

48. Dennis Farney, "Reagan Is Stressing a Tough U.S. Stance in Foreign Affairs in Bid to Gain Ground," *Wall Street Journal*, January 31, 1980, 8.

49. Stumbo, "On the Campaign Trail with Reagan."

50. "Bush, Reagan in 'Dead Heat' Race in New Hampshire," Associated Press, February 2, 1980.

51. Hugh A. Mulligan, "New Hampshire Primary," Associated Press, February 6, 1980.

52. Gerald Carmen, in discussion with the author.

53. Memorandum by Market Opinion Research, "New England Primary Study Analysis," August, 1979, Robert Teeter Papers, #9646, Box 1, George H. W. Bush Presidential Library, College Station, TX.

54. Donald M. Rothberg, "Bush Back in New Hampshire—Again," Associated Press, February 13, 1980.

55. Stumbo, "On the Campaign Trail with Reagan."

56. Robert Scheer, "Reagan: Long in Spotlight, Still Enigmatic," *Los Angeles Times*, June 25, 1980, B1.

57. Associated Press, "Reagan, Bush Tied for Vote, Poll Finds," *Los Angeles Times*, January 24, 1980, B28.

58. United Press International, "Bush and Reagan Tied With 27% in Republican-Independent Poll," *New York Times*, January 25, 1980, D14.

59. Ibid.

60. George Esper, Associated Press, "Suddenly, It's No Longer 'George Who?'" *Nashua* (NH) *Telegraph*, January 28, 4.

61. Donald M. Rothberg, "Reagan Faces Crucial Challenges in South," Associated Press, February 2, 1980.

62. Memorandum by Market Opinion Research, "Summary of Republican Presidential Primary Polls: Post Iowa," January–February, 1980, Robert Teeter Papers, Box 1, Bush Primary States, Wave I, Data-Analysis, George H. W. Bush Presidential Library, College Station, TX.

63. Memorandum by Market Opinion Research, "Florida: Executive Summary," January–February, 1980,

Robert Teeter Papers, Box 1, Bush Primary States, Wave I, Data-Analysis, George H. W. Bush Presidential Library, College Station, TX.

CHAPTER 8: DESCENT INTO THE MAELSTROM

1. Francis X. Clines, "In Praise or in Criticism, Bush at Center of Debate," *New York Times*, February 14, 1980, A22.

2. Jack W. Germond and Jules Witcover, "Sears' Risk Is Almost as High as Reagan's," *Washington Star*, January 30, 1980.

3. Peter Hannaford, in discussion with the author, June 25, 2009.

4. Donald M. Rothberg, "Reagan Spells Out Soviet Policy," Associated Press, February 1, 1980.

5. Peter Hannaford, in discussion with the author, June 25, 2009.

6. Edwin Meese, in discussion with the author, May 6, 2006.

7. "Chilly New England for Kennedy, Reagan?" *U.S. News & World Report*, February 11, 1980, 6.

8. Ronald Reagan, *Reagan: A Life in Letters*, ed. Kiron K. Skinner, Annelise Anderson, and Martin Anderson (New York: Free Press, 2003), 240.

9. Ernie Angelo, in discussion with the author, November 13, 2006.

10. Germond and Witcover, "Sears' Risk Is Almost as High as Reagan's."

11. Haynes Johnson, "Reagan Finds Himself Racing Clock," *Washington Post*, February 4, 1980, A1.

12. Margaret Nelson, Associated Press, "The Republicans," *Nashua* (NH) *Telegraph*, February 4, 1980, 1.

13. Gerald Carmen, in discussion with the author.

14. Helene Von Damm, in discussion with the author, May 17, 2006.

15. Jim Hooley and Rick Ahearn, in discussion with the author, February 4, 2009.

16. Adam Clymer, "Inflation and a Limit on Contributions Strain Presidential Hopefuls' Budgets," *New York Times*, February 4, 1980, A14.

17. Ibid.

18. Robert Blair Kaiser, "Presidential Candidates Disagree on Value of Secret Service Watch," *New York Times*, February 10, 1980, 1.

19. "Who?" *Wisconsin State Journal*, July 26, 2007, F5; Myra MacPherson, "Joan's Journey," *Washington Post*, December 14, 1979, B1.

20. "Washington Whispers," *U.S. News & World Report*, February 23, 1981, 16.

21. Kaiser, "Presidential Candidates Disagree."

22. Stewart M. Powell, "Can Kennedy Get Back Up Off the Floor?" *U.S. News & World Report*, February 4, 1980, 36.

23. Clay F. Richards, United Press International, "Latest New Hampshire Polls Give Leads to Carter, Bush," *State* (SC), February 20, 1980, 11B.

24. David S. Broder, "Iowa, Vt. Governors Supporting Baker," *Washington Post*, February 7, 1980, A3.

25. Jack W. Germond and Jules Witcover, "Other GOP Conservatives Now Taking Aim at Reagan," *Washington Star*, January 27, 1980.

26. "Surprise Harvest in Iowa," *Time*, February 4, 1980.

27. Adam Clymer, "Connally Is Scrambling to Keep Troubled Presidential Bid Afloat," *New York Times*, February 7, 1980, 18.

28. Walter Mears, "Reagan Makes a Date for a Debate," Associated Press, February 5, 1980.

29. Richard Bergholz, "Reagan Mercifully Hears the Last Happy Birthday," *Los Angeles Times*, February 7, 1980, B18.

30. Peter Hannaford, *The Reagans: A Political Portrait* (New York: Coward-McCann, 1983), 228.

31. Edwin Meese, in discussion with the author, May 6, 2006.

32. "It's Reagan vs. Bush: A Survey of Republican Leaders," *U.S. News & World Report*, January 28, 1980, 57.

33. Richard Reeves, "The President Loses Reagan," *Washington Star*, January 29, 1980, A11.

34. "Newsweek Poll: A Big Boost for Bush," *Newsweek*, February 4, 1980, 33.

35. Jane Anderson, Associated Press, "Candidates Big Spenders in N.E.," *Nashua* (NH) *Telegraph*, February 6, 1980, 3.

36. Francis X. Clines, "In Praise or in Criticism, Bush at Center of Debate," *New York Times*, February 14, 1980, A22.

37. Andrew Schneider, Associated Press, "Bush Revels In New-Found Attention," *Nashua* (NH) *Telegraph*, February 5, 1980, 3.
38. Linda Deutsch, "Reagan Hints Changing Stance on GOP Debates," Associated Press, January 22, 1980.
39. Gerald Carmen, in discussion with the author.
40. Associated Press, "Reagan Is Key in Efforts to Set Up Debates," *Concord* (NH) *Monitor*, January 30, 1980, 4.
41. Andrew M. Nibley, United Press International, "Reagan Agrees to N.H. Debate," *Nashua* (NH) *Telegraph*, February 6, 1980.
42. "Reagan, Bush Forum Feb. 23," *Nashua* (NH) *Telegraph*, February 12, 1980, 1; Associated Press, "Reagan and Bush Agree to Forum," *Concord* (NH) *Monitor*, February 13, 1980.
43. Richard Bergholz, "Reagan to Join Six in N.H. TV Debate," *Los Angeles Times*, February 6, 1980, B14.
44. Dennis A. Williams, Martin Kasindorf, and Tony Fuller, "Boys in the Back Room," *Newsweek*, February 4, 1980, 37.
45. William Endicott, "Reagan Aide Fends Off Critics," *Los Angeles Times*, February 10, 1980, A13.
46. "What's News," *Wall Street Journal*, February 1, 1980, 1.
47. Adam Clymer, "Candidates Shifting Tactics," *New York Times*, January 23, 1980, A1.
48. Bill Peterson, "The Old Intimacy of Winner Bush Has Disappeared," *Washington Post*, February 1, 1980, A3.
49. Robert D. Novak, *The Prince of Darkness: 50 Years Reporting in Washington* (New York: Crown Forum, 2007), 348.
50. Lou Cannon, Bill Curry, Margot Hornblower, Robert G. Kaiser, George Lardner Jr., Lee Lescaze, Kathy Sawyer, and Maralee Schwartz, "George Bush: Hot Property in Presidential Politics," *Washington Post*, January 27, 1980, A1.
51. David Keene, in discussion with the author, March 17, 2006.
52. Stefan Halper, in discussion with the author, March 20, 2007.
53. Allan J. Mayer, Stryker McGuire, Jerry Buckley, Ronald Henkoff, Gloria Borger, Richard Manning, and Martin Kasindorf, "Bush Breaks Out of the Pack," *Newsweek*, February 4, 1980, 30.
54. Associated Press, "N.H. Gays Want Say in Primary," *Nashua* (NH) *Telegraph*, February 4, 1980, 9.
55. Charles R. Babcock, Spencer Rich, Timothy S. Robinson, Chip Brown, and Tom Sherwood, "FBI 'Sting' Snares Several in Congress," *Washington Post*, February 3, 1980, A1.
56. Martin Schram, Tom Sherwood, and Chip Brown, "Sen. Pressler: He Spurned the 'Arabs,'" *Washington Post*, February 4, 1980, A1; Charles R. Babcock, George Lardner Jr., Thomas O'Toole, and Warren Brown, "Ethics Aide, GOP Urge 'Sting' Probe," *Washington Post*, February 4, 1980, A1.
57. Associated Press, February 4, 1980.
58. "Carter Prays Daily for the Ayatollah," *Washington Star*, February 6, 1980, A6.
59. George Esper, "Reagan Calls for Strengthening Reserves, Opposes Drafting Women," Associated Press, February 9, 1980.
60. E. J. Dionne Jr., "Surveys Find Crises Stir Militant Mood," *New York Times*, February 5, 1980, B14.
61. David Olinger, "Reagan's Tax Remarks Verified by Recording," *Concord* (NH) *Monitor*, February 8, 1980, 1; Richard Bergholz, "Reagan Tries to Clarify Tax Remark," *Los Angeles Times*, February 10, 1980, A13.
62. Olinger, "Reagan's Tax Remarks Verified by Recording."
63. David Larsen, "The Stars Come Out in Election Year," *Los Angeles Times*, February 11, 1980, B20.
64. Ibid.
65. Ibid.
66. Maxine Cheshire, "Sinatra Due at Detroit Doings," *Los Angeles Times*, July 11, 1980, F6; Larsen, "The Stars Come Out in Election Year."
67. Eileen Doherty, in discussion with the author, April 11, 2007.
68. United Press International, "1948 Reagan Movie Gains Baker TV Time," *Los Angeles Times*, February 13, 1980, B19.
69. Francis X. Clines, "Reagan Turns 69 with Vigorous Burst of New Hampshire Politicking," *New York Times*, February 6, 1980, 20.
70. James J. Kilpatrick, "Reagan Proves He's Far From Bush-ed," *Newark* (NJ) *Star-Ledger*, February 22, 1980.

71. Douglas E. Kneeland, "Bush Clinging Fast to Center of Party," *New York Times*, February 7, 1980, 19.

72. Hedrick Smith, "In New Hampshire: G.O.P. Family Feud," *New York Times*, February 7, 1980, 18.

73. Albert R. Hunt, "Subtlety Isn't One of Mr. Loeb's Strengths," *Wall Street Journal*, February 12, 1980, 24.

74. James Wooten, *World News Tonight*, ABC News Transcripts, February 18, 1980.

75. United Press International, "Poll: Kennedy Losing Ground," *Boston Globe*, February 20, 1980, 13.

76. United Press International, "Kennedy: Consider Other Traumas in Life as Well," *State* (SC), February 20, 1980, 11B.

77. Clay F. Richards, United Press International, "Latest New Hampshire Polls Give Leads to Carter, Bush," *State* (SC), February 20, 1980, 11B.

78. Walter R. Mears, "Carter Won't Consider Changing His No-Campaign Policy," Associated Press, February 11, 1980.

79. Jeff MacNelly, *Burlington* (VT) *Free Press*, February 20, 1980.

80. Jerry Harkavy, "Kennedy Needs Decisive Victory in Maine Caucuses," Associated Press, January 27, 1980.

81. Associated Press, "Bush in 'Surprise' Showing," *New York Times*, February 14, 1980, A22.

82. "Bush: 'Guaranteed' Peace," *Concord* (NH) *Monitor*, February 12, 1980.

83. United Press International, "Dole Wants to Join Nashua Debate," *Nashua* (NH) *Telegraph*, February 14, 1980; Associated Press, "Dole, Baker Seeking to Halt Telegraph-Planned Debate, *Nashua* (NH) *Telegraph*, February 16, 1980.

84. Tom Oppel, "Common Cause Protests 2-Man Debate," *Nashua* (NH) *Telegraph*, February 14, 1980.

85. Walter R. Mears, Associated Press, February 6, 1980.

86. Walter R. Mears, Associated Press, "Bush Wins 1st Issue; Reagan Funds Forum," *Nashua* (NH) *Telegraph*, February 14, 1980, 10.

87. John Laurence, *World News Tonight Sunday*, ABC News Transcripts, February 17, 1980.

88. Wayne King, "Reagan, After Apology, Explains His Recounting of an Ethnic Joke," *New York Times*, February 19, 1980, A14.

89. Editorial, "Jokes, and Echoes, in New Hampshire," *New York Times*, February 20, 1980, A24.

90. "Yale Head Hits Reagan," *Boston Globe*, February 21, 1980, 12.

91. Paul Kengor and Patricia Clark Doerner, *The Judge: William P. Clark, Ronald Reagan's Top Hand* (San Francisco: Ignatius Press, 2007), 102–3.

92. "Lawyer May Fill Top Reagan Post," *Los Angeles Times*, February 19, 1980, 1.

93. Joseph E. Persico, *Casey: From the OSS to the CIA* (New York: Viking, 1990), 178–79.

94. "Lawyer May Fill Top Reagan Post," *Los Angeles Times*, February 19, 1980, 1.

95. Maurice Carroll, "State G.O.P. Girds for 3-Way Presidential Primary," *New York Times*, February 8, 1980, A12.

96. James M. Perry, "Conspiracy Theorists Point Darkly to Bush as a 'Trilateralist,'" *Wall Street Journal*, February 26, 1980, 1.

97. Hunt, "Subtlety Isn't One of Mr. Loeb's Strengths."

98. Perry, "Conspiracy Theorists Point Darkly to Bush as a 'Trilateralist.'"

99. "Reagan Races a Little Faster," *Time*, February 11, 1980.

100. Ibid.

101. James R. Dickenson, "Reagan Taking Pains to Fight Bush's Resume," *Washington Star*, February 15, 1980, A3.

102. Tom Morganthau, Tony Fuller, Stryker McGuire, Gloria Borger, and Gerald C. Lubenow, "GOP Shakedown Cruise," *Newsweek*, February 25, 1980, 32.

103. Jeff Bell, in discussion with the author; Bill Roeder, "Reagan Toughens His Ad Campaign," *Newsweek*, February 11, 1980, 25.

104. Jeff Bell, in discussion with the author.

105. Novak, *The Prince of Darkness*, 349.

106. James Baker, in discussion with the author; Victor Gold, in discussion with the author.

107. Tom Morganthau and James Doyle, "The Prime-Time Players," *Newsweek*, January 28, 1980, 34.

108. Donald M. Rothberg, "Bush Criticized by GOP Opponents," Associated Press, February 14, 1980.

Chapter 9: Fast Times at Nashua High

1. Kevin McKean, "Magazine Reports on Health of Presidential Candidates," Associated Press, February 12, 1980.

2. Ibid.

3. "The Candidates: Just How Healthy?" *U.S. News &World Report*, February 25, 1980, 8.

4. Lynn Nofziger, *Nofziger* (Washington, DC: Regnery Gateway, 1992), 222.

5. "The Candidates: Just How Healthy?"

6. Dom Bonafede, "Covering the Presidential Elections—Despite the Cost, the Press Is Ready," *National Journal*, February 2, 1980, 192.

7. "Cautious Confrontation," *Time*, March 3, 1980.

8. Martin Schram, "Bush Survives Debate Unscathed," *Washington Post*, February 21, 1980, A2.

9. Adolphe V. Bernotas, "Reagan Campaign Agrees to Pay to Debate George Bush," Associated Press, February 22, 1980.

10. Lou Cannon, "Reagan Forces to Pay Costs of Debate with Bush," *Washington Post*, February 22, 1980, A2.

11. Adam Clymer, "Reagan to Finance His Debate Tomorrow with Bush," *New York Times*, February 22, 1980, A14.

12. Peter Hannaford, in discussion with the author.

13. Benjamin Taylor, "Twists and Turns on Debate in N.H.," *Boston Globe*, February 22, 1980, 11.

14. Saul Friedman and Remer Tyson, "Big Fanfare, Small Delegation in N.H.," *Miami Herald*, February 26, 1980, 1A.

15. Scott Mackay, "Presidential Hopefuls Begin Final Media Blitz," *Burlington* (VT) *Free Press*, February 24, 1980, 1A.

16. United Press International, "Reagan Landslide Winner in Alaskan Precinct Straw Poll," *Los Angeles Times*, February 23, 1980, A22; Merrill Hartson, Associated Press, February 22, 1980.

17. United Press International, "Reagan Clings to Lead as Arkansas Picks Delegation," *Los Angeles Times*, February 17, 1980, A11; Bill Simmons, "Reagan and Baker Major Victors in Arkansas Contest," Associated Press, February 17, 1980.

18. Lou Cannon, "Risk Higher in N.H. for Bush Campaign," *Washington Post*, February 20, 1980, A4.

19. David Nyhan, "What to Check in N.H.," *Boston Globe*, February 20, 1980, 15.

20. Melvin Maddocks, "Politics and the Taste of Pickles," *Christian Science Monitor*, March 3, 1980, 23; James Prichard, "The Life and Times of Alice Roosevelt Longworth," Associated Press, October 22, 2007.

21. Richard Bergholz, "Carter Holds Lead as N.H. Vote Nears," *Los Angeles Times*, February 25, 1980, 1.

22. Bernard Weinraub, "Ads Underscore Boston Media's Role in Campaign," *New York Times*, February 23, 1980, 8.

23. Martin Schram, "The Guns of the N.H. Skirmishing," *Washington Post*, February 20, 1980, A1.

24. Francis X. Clines, "New Hampshire Gun-Control Forum Brings Out Presidential Vote Hunters," *New York Times*, February 20, 1980, A19.

25. Ibid.

26. Associated Press, "Hockey Win Stirs Flag-Waving Rush," *Miami Herald*, February 25, 1980, 1.

27. Colin Clark, in discussion with the author, September 22, 2006.

28. Walter R. Mears, Associated Press, February 24, 1980.

29. Mary Thornton, "Carter Gaining in Poll; Reagan Lead Narrows," *Washington Star*, February 19, 1980, A1.

30. Robert Healy, "The Bush Wagon Rolls On," *Boston Globe*, February 22, 1980, 15.

31. Jack W. Germond and Jules Witcover, "King of the Hill?" *Boston Globe*, February 22, 1980, 15.

32. "Carter Ahead in Poll," *Boston Globe*, February 21, 1980, 12.

33. Clay F. Richards, United Press International, "GOP Rivals Blast Bush," *State* (SC), February 25, 1980, 2A.

34. Benjamin Taylor, "Twists and Turns on Debate in N.H.," *Boston Globe*, February 22, 1980, 1.

35. Ibid.

36. Barbara Walters, *World News Tonight*, ABC News Transcripts, February 22, 1980.

37. Charles R. Black, in discussion with the author, March 20, 2006.

38. John Sears, in discussion with the author, July 26, 2006.

39. Jim Lake, in discussion with the author, September 19, 2006.

40. Harry F. Rosenthal, "Bush Won't Attack Reagan," Associated Press, February 23, 1980.

41. Charles R. Black, in discussion with the author, March 20, 2006; Jim Lake, in discussion with the author, September 19, 2006.

42. Paul Russo, in discussion with the author, September 8, 2006.

43. Jim Lake, in discussion with the author, September 19, 2006.

44. Editorial, "A Bizarre Chain of Events," Nashua (NH) Telegraph, February 28, 1980.

45. Andrew Schneider, "Two GOP Candidates Differ on Importance of Debate," Associated Press, February 15, 1980.

46. Mickey Baca and Cynthia Jones, "Forum Reaction Varies Widely," Nashua (NH) Telegraph, February 25, 1980.

47. Peter Secchia, in discussion with the author.

48. "2,300 Hear Reagan-Bush Forum Tonight," Nashua (NH) Telegraph, February 23, 1980, 1; United Press International, "Reagan-Bush Debate Sparks Anger," State (SC), February 24, 1980, 2A.

49. Paul Russo, in discussion with the author, September 8, 2006.

50. Neal Peden, in discussion with the author, July 6, 2006.

51. Charles R. Black, in discussion with the author, March 20, 2006.

52. Ibid.

53. Jim Lake, in discussion with the author, September 19, 2006.

54. Charles R. Black, in discussion with the author, March 20, 2006.

55. Paul Laxalt, in discussion with the author, July 31, 2006.

56. Jim Lake, in discussion with the author, September 19, 2006.

57. Morton Blackwell, in discussion with the author, February 28, 2007.

58. Peter Hannaford, in discussion with the author, March 24, 2006.

59. Jim Lake, in discussion with the author, September 19, 2006.

60. Jim Roberts, in discussion with the author, July 2006.

61. Gerald Carmen, in discussion with the author, July 25, 2006.

62. Ibid.

63. Jim Lake, in discussion with the author, September 19, 2006; Gerald Carmen, in discussion with the author.

64. Peter Hannaford, in discussion with the author.

65. Germond and Witcover, "GOP Rivals Gang Up."

66. Walter R. Mears, "Bush and Reagan Poised to Square Off in Debate," Associated Press, February 23, 1980.

67. Francis X. Clines, "A Reporter's Notebook: Grand Old Pandemonium," New York Times, February 25, 1980, A18.

68. Jack Kenny, "Campaign Tales Are Told by the Man Who Provides Sound, Video to Candidates," N.H. Business Review, January 28–February 10, 2000. http://www.molloysoundandvideo.com/articles.html.

69. Associated Press, February 25, 1980.

70. Jules Witcover, Crapshoot: Rolling the Dice on the Vice Presidency (New York: Crown Publishers, 1992), 306.

71. Ibid., 307.

72. Robert Shogan, "Reagan Effort to Expand Debate Leads to Dispute," Los Angeles Times, February 24, 1980, 1.

73. David Nyhan and Robert Healy, "Nashua Debate Turns into a Fight to Speak," Boston Globe, February 24, 1980, 1.

74. Hedrick Smith, "Excluded from G.O.P. Debate, Four Attack Bush," New York Times, February 24, 1980, 1.

75. Jim Roberts, in discussion with the author, July 2006.

76. Ronald Reagan, An American Life: The Autobiography (New York: Simon & Schuster, 1990), 213.

77. Lou Cannon, Reagan (New York: G. P. Putnam's Sons, 1982), 253.

78. Don Campbell, "Bush and Reagan Debate Ends Up a Party Battle," Burlington (VT) Free Press, February 24, 1980, 1.

79. Peter Hannaford, *The Reagans: A Political Portrait* (New York: Coward-McCann, 1983), 238.

80. Shogan, "Reagan Effort to Expand Debate."

81. David Keene, in discussion with the author, March 17, 2006.

82. Mears, "Bush and Reagan Poised to Square Off."

83. David Nyhan, "'Just Politics' or a 'Lockout,'" *Boston Globe*, February 25, 1980, 1; Rochelle Share, "Shadow Outshines Nashua Debate," *Concord* (NH) *Monitor*, February 25, 1980, 1.

84. Jack W. Germond and Jules Witcover, "GOP Rivals Gang Up on Bush as Debate Turns into a Brawl," *Washington Star*, February 24, 1980, A1.

85. James R. Dickenson, "Fallout Over Debate Could Decide GOP's Primary Contest," *Washington Star*, February 26, 1980, A1.

86. Robert Healy, "Nashua Debate and a New Unity," *Boston Globe*, February 25, 1980, 6.

87. Richard Bergholz, "Carter Holds Lead as N.H. Vote Nears," *Los Angeles Times*, February 25, 1980, 1.

88. William Loeb, "*Only a Bush Leaguer*" *Manchester* (NH) *Union-Leader*, February 25, 1980, 1.

89. Mears, "Bush and Reagan Poised to Square Off."

90. Richard Bergholz, "Reagan and Bush Battle for Lead in N.H. Primary," *Los Angeles Times*, February 26, 1980, 2A.

91. Clay F. Richards, United Press International, "GOP Rivals Blast Bush," *State* (SC), February 25, 1980, 2A.

92. John Sears, in discussion with the author, July 26, 2006.

93. Walter R. Mears, "New Hampshire Tests Kennedy, GOP Challengers in First Primary," Associated Press, February 26, 1980.

94. David Espo, Associated Press, "On the Road with Ted," *Nashua* (NH) *Telegraph*, February 25, 1980, 11.

95. Warren Weaver Jr., "Carter Far Ahead of Kennedy on Campaign Funds," *New York Times*, February 22, 1980, A14.

96. Patrick Riordan, "Lions Fatten President's War Chest," *Miami Herald*, February 25, 1980, 1A.

97. Thomas Oliphant, "New Hampshire: The Image and the Reality," *Boston Globe*, February 26, 2.

CHAPTER 10: REAGAN ROMPS

1. Lou Cannon, Martin Schram, Myra McPherson, Judy Nicol, Art Harris, and David S. Broder, "Bush Is Crushed by Wide Margin," *Washington Post*, February 27, 1980, A1.

2. *U.S. News & World Report*, February 25, 1980, 23.

3. David S. Broder, in discussion with the author, June 23, 2006.

4. Lou Cannon, *Reagan* (New York: G. P. Putnam's Sons, 1982), 249.

5. Cannon et al., "Bush Is Crushed by Wide Margin."

6. David S. Broder, "Dramatic Reversal of Fortune in New Hampshire," *Washington Post*, February 28, 1980, A1.

7. Associated Press, "Debate Fiasco: Who's to Blame?" *Miami Herald*, February 25, 1980, 25A.

8. Remer Tyson and Saul Friedman, "Republican Campaign Turns Nasty," *Miami Herald*, February 25, 1980, 25A.

9. Richard Bergholz, "N.H. Voting in Presidential Primary Today," *Los Angeles Times*, February 26, 1980, A10.

10. Gerald Carmen, in discussion with the author, July 25, 2006.

11. Tyson and Friedman, "Republican Campaign Turns Nasty."

12. Associated Press, "Debate Fiasco."

13. Bruce Nichols, United Press International, "Bush Labels Debate Furor Ploy," *Nashua* (NH) *Telegraph*, February 26, 1980, 1.

14. Tom Oppel, "Reagan and Bush Stands Similar," *Nashua* (NH) *Telegraph*, February 25, 1980.

15. Tom Wicker, "A Trail of Peanut Hulls," *New York Times*, February 24, 1980, E19.

16. Remer Tyson and David Hoffman, "Bush Fears Debate Flap Backlash," *Miami Herald*, February 26, 1980, 11A.

17. Walter R. Mears, "Poll Says Carter Over Kennedy; Bush, Reagan in Squeaker," Associated Press, February 25, 1980.

18. United Press International, "Reagan 'Sandbagged Me,' Bush Says of Debate," *Miami Herald*, February 26, 1980, 8A.

19. Warren Pease, "George Bush: Often a Candidate, Rarely Chosen," *Manchester* (NH) *Union-Leader*, January 15, 1980, 1.

20. James Wooten, *World News Tonight*, ABC News Transcripts, February 24, 1980.

21. Walter R. Mears, "New Hampshire Tests Kennedy, GOP Challengers in First Primary," Associated Press, February 26, 1980.

22. Walter R. Mears, "Poll Says Carter Over Kennedy; Bush, Reagan in Squeaker," Associated Press, February 25, 1980.

23. "Read All About It . . . ," *Miami Herald*, February 26, 1980, 11A.

24. Tom Oppel, "Joan Kennedy Ventures into Primary," *Nashua* (NH) *Telegraph*, February 20, 1980, 3.

25. Bergholz, "N.H. Voting in Presidential Primary Today."

26. Donald M. Rothberg, Associated Press, February 26, 1980.

27. David Nyhan, "Reagan's Mr. Inside in N.H.," *Boston Globe*, February 28, 1980, 1.

28. E. J. Dionne Jr., "Bush Viewed as Above Faction Fights," *New York Times*, February 26, 1980, B11.

29. Rowland Evans and Robert Novak, "Reagan's Solid Base," *Washington Post*, February 25, 1980, A23.

30. Jerry Harkavy, Associated Press, "Dixville Notch: Bush, Reagan Tie," *Nashua* (NH) *Telegraph*, February 26, 1980, 1.

31. Associated Press, "Turnout Mixed in New Hampshire Vote," *Washington Star*, February 26, 1980, 1.

32. Ibid.

33. James R. Dickenson, "Vote to Show Whether Reagan Can Regain His Frontrunner Status," *Washington Star*, February 24, 1980.

34. Jack W. Germond and Jules Witcover, "Insiders Think Bush Soon Can Lock Up Lead," *Washington Star*, February 21, 1980, A1.

35. Stephen Doig, "Poll: Bush Leading Reagan in South," *Miami Herald*, February 25, 1980, 23A.

36. Francis X. Clines, "New Hampshire Hears the Final Vows," *New York Times*, February 26, 1980, A1.

37. Editorial, "Mr. Sears' Masterful Stroke," *Nashua* (NH) *Telegraph*, February 26, 1980, 5.

38. Associated Press, February 27, 1980.

39. Lou Cannon, "Bush, Reagan Even as New Hampshire Finish Line Nears," *Washington Post*, February 25, 1980, A2.

40. Chris Black, "Voter Turnout Sets a Record," *Boston Globe*, February 27, 1980, 1

41. Broder, "Dramatic Reversal of Fortune."

42. Bill Boyarsky, "Carter, Reagan the Victors," *Los Angeles Times*, February 27, 1980, 1.

43. Cannon et al., "Bush Is Crushed by Wide Margin."

44. Remer Tyson, "Month After Iowa, Bush is N.H. Loser," *Miami Herald*, February 27, 1980, 1A.

45. Gerald Carmen, in discussion with the author, July 25, 2006.

46. Cannon et al., "Bush Is Crushed by Wide Margin"; Myra MacPherson, "Reagan, Gaining Steam, Changes Horses," *Washington Post*, February 27, 1980, A1.

47. Jim Hooley and Rick Ahearn, in discussion with the author, February 4, 2009.

48. Associated Press, "Reagan Switches Top Aide," *State* (SC), February 27, 1980, 1.

49. MacPherson, "Reagan, Gaining Steam."

50. Adam Clymer, "Reagan Easily Defeats Bush and Baker in New Hampshire; Carter Victor Over Kennedy," *New York Times*, February 27, 1980, A1.

51. Associated Press, "Reagan Switches Top Aide."

52. "Delegate Tally," *Miami Herald*, February 27, 1980, 8A.

53. MacPherson, "Reagan, Gaining Steam."

54. Tyson, "Month After Iowa."

55. D'Vera Cohn, United Press International, "Bush: 'There's No Excuse for It,'" *Nashua* (NH) *Telegraph*, February 27, 1980, 10.

56. Clymer, "Reagan Easily Defeats Bush."

57. Associated Press, "Reagan Switches Top Aide."

58. Donald M. Rothberg, "Presidential Campaigning Getting More Expensive," Associated Press, February 9, 1980.

59. Associated Press, February 27, 1980.

60. Saul Friedman, "Victory for President Another Blow to Ted," *Miami Herald*, February 27, 1980, A1.

61. Michael Putzel, "Former Democrats Welcomed by President," Associated Press, June 10, 1985.

62. "In New Hampshire, They're Off!" *Time*, February 25, 1980.

63. Broder, "Dramatic Reversal of Fortune."

64. Bob Woodward and Carl Bernstein, *The Final Days* (New York: Simon & Schuster, 1976), 369.

65. Harry F. Rosenthal, Associated Press, February 27, 1980.

66. David S. Broder, in discussion with the author, June 23, 2006.

67. James R. Dickenson, "Reagan's Man Sears Is Ready to Roll," *Washington Star*, February 26, 1979, D1.

68. Peter Goldman, Gerald C. Lubenow, Stryker McGuire, James Doyle, Phyllis Malamud, and Martin Kasindorf, "Reagan Is Back in the Saddle," *Newsweek*, March 10, 1980, 26.

69. Paul Laxalt, in discussion with the author, July 31, 2006.

70. Charles R. Black, in discussion with the author, March 20, 2006.

71. Ibid.

72. Helene Von Damm, *At Reagan's Side* (New York: Doubleday, 1989), 117.

73. John Sears, in discussion with the author, July 26, 2006.

74. Peter Hannaford, *The Reagans: A Political Portrait* (New York: Coward-McCann, 1983), 232.

75. Ibid., 233–35.

76. Charles R. Black, in discussion with the author, March 20, 2006.

77. Charles R. Black, in discussion with the author.

78. Jim Lake, in discussion with the author, September 19, 2006.

79. Ibid.; Colin Clark, in discussion with the author, September 22, 2006.

80. James R. Dickenson, "Reagan Fires Campaign Manager Sears," *Washington Star*, February 27, 1980.

81. Edwin Meese, in discussion with the author, May 6, 2006.

82. Stuart Spencer, in discussion with the author, September 28, 2006.

83. Lou Cannon, "Reagan Moves to Cut Costs by Reorganizing," *Washington Post*, February 28, 1980, A7.

84. Peter Hannaford, in discussion with the author, March 24, 2006.

85. Dickenson, "Reagan Fires Campaign Manager."

86. Charles R. Black, in discussion with the author.

87. Memorandum by Peter Hannaford, February 26, 1980, Peter Hannaford Papers, Box 5, Reagan for President Committee, Hoover Institution Archives, Stanford, CA.

88. Goldman, et al., "Reagan Is Back in the Saddle."

89. Robert Shogan, "Sears Ousted as Top Reagan Campaign Aide," *Los Angeles Times*, February 27, 1980, A6.

90. Lou Cannon, *Governor Reagan: His Rise to Power* (New York: PublicAffairs, 2003), 463.

91. John Sears, in discussion with the author, July 26, 2006.

92. Shogan, "Sears Ousted."

93. Michael Reagan, in discussion with the author, July 2, 2004.

94. Ronald Reagan, *Reagan: A Life in Letters*, ed. Kiron K. Skinner, Annelise Anderson, and Martin Anderson (New York: Free Press, 2003), 240.

95. Charles R. Black, in discussion with the author.

96. Neal Peden, in discussion with the author, July 6, 2006.

97. Hannaford, *The Reagans*, 231.

98. Edwin Meese, in discussion with the author, May 6, 2006.

99. Memorandum, unsigned, "Call List," February 26, 1980, Peter Hannaford Papers, Box 5, Reagan for President Committee, Hoover Institution Archives, Stanford, CA.

100. Memorandum, unsigned, "Telephone Talking Points," February 1980, Peter Hannaford Papers, Box 5, Reagan for President Committee, Hoover Institution Archives, Stanford, CA.

101. Donald M. Rothberg, "Reagan Replaces Campaign Chief as He Reclaims Frontrunner Role," Associated Press, February 26, 1980.

102. "'He Was the Cruiser,'" *Time*, March 10, 1980.

103. Richard Allen, in discussion with the author, June 14, 2006.

104. Edwin Meese, in discussion with the author, May 6, 2006.

105. Theodore H. White, *America in Search of Itself: The Making of the President, 1956–1980* (New York: Harper & Row, 1982), 251.

106. Walter R. Mears, Associated Press, February 26, 1980.

107. James Baker, in discussion with the author, September 6, 2006; confidential interview with the author.

108. "Campaigns Finish in High Gear," *Concord* (NH) *Monitor*, February 25, 1980, 1.

Chapter 11: Under New Management

1. Les Brown, "Dan Rather to Succeed Cronkite," *New York Times*, February 15, 1980, C30.

2. Harry F. Waters, "A Man Who Cares," *Newsweek*, March 9, 1981, 57.

3. David Nyhan, "Reagan's Mr. Inside in N.H.," *Boston Globe*, February 28, 1980, 1.

4. Gerald Carmen, in discussion with the author; Nyhan, "Reagan's Mr. Inside."

5. George F. Will, "30 Seconds Over Nashua," *Washington Post*, March 2, 1980, C7.

6. Tom Pettit, *NBC Nightly News*, NBC News Archives, February 27, 1980, http://www.icue.com/portal/site/iCue/flatview/?cuecard=5175.

7. Paul Kengor and Patricia Clark Doerner, *The Judge: William P. Clark, Ronald Reagan's Top Hand* (San Francisco: Ignatius Press, 2007), 104; Colin Clark, in discussion with the author, September 22, 2006; Ken Khachigian, in discussion with the author, May 2007.

8. Mary Elson, "I'll Criticize Reagan, Bush Tells Club Here," *Chicago Tribune*, March 1, 1980, 5.

9. Richard Bergholz, "N.H. Winners, Losers Plotting Next Moves; Candidates Planning Their Next Moves," *Los Angeles Times*, February 28, 1980, A9.

10. E. J. Dionne, "New Hampshire Poll Backs View of Volatile Mood Among Voters," *New York Times*, March 2, 1980, 1.

11. Don McLeod, Associated Press, "Some Losing Candidates Face Loss of Funds," *Nashua* (NH) *Telegraph*, February 28, 1980, 1; "Primary Picture," *Miami Herald*, February 27, 1980, 1.

12. Edwin Meese, in discussion with the author, May 6, 2006; Kenny Klinge, in discussion with the author, July 12, 2006.

13. Rick Shelby, in discussion with the author, September 12, 2006.

14. Kenny Klinge, in discussion with the author, July 12, 2006.

15. Lyn Nofziger, "Sears Saga—Rise and Fall of 'Political Genius,'" *Citizens for the Republic Newsletter*, March 21, 1980, 1.

16. Loye Miller Jr., Newhouse News Service, "Primary Victors Still Face Tough Road," *Newark* (NJ) *Star-Ledger*, February 28, 1980, 1.

17. Fred Ferretti, "Political Valets Provide Clean Shirts and Sympathetic Ears," *New York Times*, February 25, 1980, B5.

18. B. Drummond Ayres Jr., R. W. Apple Jr., Douglas E. Kneeland, and Wayne King, "The Feeding of the Candidates," *New York Times*, February 27, 1980, C1; Linda Carol Cherken, "Candidates Are as Different as Favorite Foods," *Miami Herald*, February 28, 1980, 11E.

19. James R. Dickenson, "This Time Reagan Leaves N.H. as Victor, but Burdened with Spending Problems," *Washington Star*, February 28, 1980, A3.

20. David Hoffman, "Republicans' Big Spender Nearing His Limit with 34 Primaries to Go," *Miami Herald*, February 28, 1980, 28A.

21. Lou Cannon, "Reagan Moves to Cut Costs by Reorganizing," *Washington Post*, February 28, 1980, A7.

22. Scott Mackay, "Carter Botched Hostage Crisis, Reagan Charges," *Burlington* (VT) *Free Press*, February 28, 1980, 1A.

23. "In New Hampshire, They're Off!" *Time*, February 25, 1980.

24. Mike Feinsilber, "Bush Tackles Vagueness," Associated Press, March 6, 1980.

25. Tom Fiedler, "Campaigns in Florida Feeling N.H. Ripples," *Miami Herald*, February 28, 1980, 28A.

26. Ibid.

27. Howell Raines, "Republicans Girding for Florida Battle," *New York Times*, February 24, 1980, 16.

28. Lawrence Martin, "U.S. Publisher Who Beached Muskie Is Out to Fell Bush," *Globe and Mail* (Toronto), February 22, 1980.

29. David Keene, in discussion with the author.

30. Willard F. Rose, "Kennedy: Hecklers Greet Him in South, Saying, 'You Killed That Girl,'" *Miami Herald*, February 28, 1980, 29A.

31. Art Harris, "Anxious N.H. Candidates Assail Taciturn Yankees' Ears," *Washington Post*, February 21, 1980, A3.

32. "Brown Chief Is Quitting Campaign," *Miami Herald*, March 2, 1980, 21A.

33. "Campaign Notes," *Washington Post*, February 29, 1980, A3.

34. Peter Goldman and Tony Fuller, "Big John: Whistling Dixie," *Newsweek*, March 3, 1980, 30.

35. David S. Broder and Bill Peterson, "Despite Barbs, GOP Debate Produces Little Disagreement," *Washington Post*, February 29, 1980, A6.

36. Thomas C. Cothran, Associated Press, "Some Say GOP Primary May Be Pivotal," *State* (SC), February 25, 1980.

37. David Wald, "GOP Mails Ford Fund Pitch Amid Heavy Betting He'll Declare," *Newark* (NJ) *Star-Ledger*, March 7, 1980, 7.

38. Tom Raum, "The Selling of the GOP," Associated Press, January 29, 1980.

39. Hedrick Smith, "Ousted Reagan Aide Shuns Baker's Bid," *New York Times*, February 29, 1980, B5.

40. Margot Hornblower, "Sears Details 'Disorder' in Reagan Camp," *Washington Post*, February 29, 1980, A1.

41. Ibid.

42. Tom Raum, "Former Reagan Aides Say They Were Fired," Associated Press, February 28, 1980.

43. Paul Houston and Carol Blue, "Reagan Fired Them, 3 Top Aides Say," *Los Angeles Times*, February 29, 1980, B25.

44. Charles R. Black, in discussion with the author.

45. Hornblower, "Sears Details 'Disorder.'"

46. John Sears, in discussion with the author, July 26, 2006.

47. Ibid.

48. Richard Bergholz, "GOP Candidates Swap Barbs in Debate in South," *Los Angeles Times*, February 29, 1980, B1.

49. Ibid.

50. Associated Press, February 29, 1980.

51. Ibid.

52. Associated Press, "Newspaper Polls Show Kennedy and Bush Leading in Massachusetts," February 11, 1980.

53. Jack W. Germond and Jules Witcover, "Reagan Closing Up on Bush in Massachusetts," *Washington Star*, February 29, 1980; Ron Kaufman, in discussion with the author, August 25, 2006.

54. Ron Kaufman, in discussion with the author, August 25, 2006.

55. Ibid.

56. Bernard Weinraub, "Kennedy and Bush Face Key Tests Tuesday in Massachusetts Primaries," *New York Times*, February 29, 1980, B5.

57. Ibid.

58. Adam Clymer, "Triumph by Reagan Stirs Fears of Shift to the Right," *New York Times*, February 28, 1980, A19.

59. Loye Miller Jr., Newhouse News Service, "Primary Victors Still Face Tough Road," *Newark* (NJ) *Star-Ledger*, February 28, 1980, 1.

60. David Keene, in discussion with the author.

61. William K. Stevens, "Texas and California Are Forging a New Axis of Power for the '80s," *New York Times*, February 29, 1980, A1.

62. Arlen J. Large, "Complex Arithmetic: As Census Nears, Issues of Compliance, Aliens, and Adjusting for Undercount Bedevil Bureau," *Wall Street Journal*, February 27, 1980, 48.

63. United Press International, "House OKs Aid to Nicaragua," *Boston Globe*, February 28, 1980, 6.

64. Ellen Hume, "Bush Assails Reagan Views on A-Waste," *Los Angeles Times*, March 2, 1980, A26.

65. Jules Witcover, "Reagan Challenges Ford to Enter Primary Race," *Washington Star*, March 3, 1980, A1.

66. David S. Broder, "Bush Aims to Fling More Zings at Reagan," *Washington Post*, March 1, 1980, A2.

67. Bill Peterson and David S. Broder, "Reagan Criticizes Bush for 'Bland Generalities,'" *Washington Post*, March 2 1980, A2.

68. Sara Rimer, "Politicians Snarl Over Lowliest Job," *Miami Herald*, March 2, 1980, 1A.

69. Ibid.

70. Ibid.

CHAPTER 12: FORD TEES OFF

1. Lou Cannon, "Kennedy and Reagan: Grinning and Bearing a Lot," *Washington Post*, March 2, 1980, A4.

2. Ibid.

3. United Press International, "Massachusetts Poll Has Bush, Reagan Dead Even," *State* (SC), March 2, 1980, 12A.

4. F. Richard Ciccone, "Forget Moral Victories, Massachusetts Counts," *Chicago Tribune*, March 2, 1980, 12.

5. David S. Broder, "Kennedy, Bush Campaigns on Line in Massachusetts," *Washington Post*, March 3, 1980, A1.

6. Rowland Evans and Robert Novak, "A Get-Tough George Bush?" *Washington Post*, March 3, 1980, A23.

7. Lou Cannon, "Anderson Battles 2-Man GOP Race Idea," *Washington Post*, February 14, 1980, A2.

8. Elizabeth Rathbun, "John Anderson: 'There Is Something Different About Me,'" *Miami Herald*, March 4, 1980, 12A.

9. United Press International, "Massachusetts Poll Has Bush, Reagan Dead Even," *State* (SC), March 2, 1980, 12A.

10. James M. Perry, "Connally Woos Voters in South Carolina, His Last Stand, with Help of Thurmond," *Wall Street Journal*, March 3, 1980, 8.

11. Bill Peterson, "Reagan Keeps Clean While Bush, Connally Sling Mud in S.C. Race," *Washington Post*, March 5, 1980, A9.

12. United Press International, "Texans' Camps Slugging It Out," *Miami Herald*, March 5, 1980, 10A.

13. Tony Fuller, "Connally's Bitter End," *Newsweek*, March 24, 1980, 37.

14. F. Richard Ciccone, "Kennedy Trailing Badly Here," *Chicago Tribune*, March 2, 1980, 1.

15. Roper Center for Public Opinion Research, "Job Performance Ratings for President Carter," University of Connecticut, http://webapps.ropercenter.uconn.edu/CFIDE/roper/presidential/webroot/presidential_rating_detail.cfm?allRate=True&presidentName=Carter.

16. "Carter's Popularity Still Falling as Economy Gets More Attention," *Miami Herald*, March 6, 1980, 24A.

17. United Press International, "Reagan Calls U.N. Shift 'Preposterous Situation,'" *New York Times*, March 9, 1980, 34.

18. Aaron Epstein, "Ted: Was U.N. Blunder 'Calculated'?" *Miami Herald*, March 11, 1980, 13A.

19. Barbara Walters, *World News Tonight*, ABC News Transcripts, March 5, 1980.

20. Adam Clymer, "Ford Declares Reagan Can't Win; Invites G.O.P. to Ask Him to Run," *New York Times*, March 2, 1980, 1.

21. Jules Witcover, "Reagan Challenges Ford to Enter Primary Races," *Washington Star*, March 3, 1980, A1.

22. Tom Wicker, "The Ford Shadow," *New York Times*, March 7, 1980, A27; Peter Goldman, James Doyle, Thomas M. DeFrank, Gloria Borger, Stryker McGuire, Martin Kasindorf, and Tony Fuller, "Ford vs. Reagan Again?" *Newsweek*, March 17, 1980, 33.

23. "Ford Is Put on Ballot in Maryland," *New York Times*, March 4, 1980, B9; Adam Clymer, "35 Delegate Candidates in Illinois Switch From Baker Drive to Ford," *New York Times*, March 10, 1980, B10.

24. "Bush Says No One Will 'Roll Over,'" *New York Times*, March 3, 1980, D9; Hedrick Smith, "Baker Out of Race; Pressures Increase for Entry by Ford," *New York Times*, March 6, 1980, A1.

25. Thomas M. DeFrank, *Write It When I'm Gone: Remarkable Off-the-Record Conversations with Gerald R. Ford* (New York: G. P. Putnam's Sons, 2007), 110.

26. Russell Chandler, "'Christian Voice' Political Action Group Plans Massive Drive on Reagan's Behalf," *Los Angeles Times*, March 6, 1980, 10.

27. Herb Frazier, "Bush Says Position Distorted," *State* (SC), March 8, 1980, 1A.

28. Mike Clements, "Reagan's 'Express' Tours S.C.," *State* (SC), March 7, 1980, 1A.

29. Mike Clements, "Confident Reagan Expects Victories Across South," *State* (SC), March 8, 1980, 1A.

30. John Herbers, "Record Massachusetts Vote Is Seen Today in First Large-State Primary," *New York Times*, March 4, 1980, A1.

31. Associated Press, "Baker Quits; Ford Says Even Chance He Will Start," March 5, 1980.

32. Mike Feinsilber, "Bush Happy with New England Vote," Associated Press, March 5, 1980.

33. Dan Balz, T. R. Reid, and Joseph A. O'Brien, "John B. Anderson: 12 Years on the Road to Discovery," *Washington Post*, March 6, 1980, A3.

34. "Delegate Tally," *Miami Herald*, March 6, 1980, 16A.

35. Tom Fiedler and William J. Mitchell, "Bush Aims at Reagan in Florida After Tiny Massachusetts Victory," *Miami Herald*, March 6, 1980, A21.

36. "Baker Quits; Ford Says Even Chance He Will Start," Associated Press, March 5, 1980.

37. "Delegate Tally," *Miami Herald*, March 6, 1980.

38. Tom Fiedler, "Bush Will Step Up Attacks on Reagan," *Miami Herald*, March 7, 1980, 18A.

39. Tom Fiedler, "Bush Pulls His Punches at Reagan," *Miami Herald*, March 8, 1980, 16A.

40. Sara Rimer, "Ford Plays Cool at College: No, Not Yet—but Maybe," *Miami Herald*, March 7, 1980, 17A.

41. Dennis A. Williams, Thomas M. DeFrank, and Martin Kasindorf, "The GOP's Hamlet," *Newsweek*, March 10, 1980, 28.

42. Rimer, "Ford Plays Cool at College."

43. Adam Clymer, "Ford Supporters Organize Group to Spur a Draft," *New York Times*, March 7, 1980, A1; Adam Clymer, "2 Major Issues Raised in Ford's Potential Candidacy," *New York Times*, March 8, 1980, 9.

44. David Keene, in discussion with the author, November 18, 2007.

45. David S. Broder, Bill Peterson, Martin Schram, Lou Cannon, Dan Balz, and Maralee Schwartz, "GOP Game: Will Ford Deal Himself In?" *Washington Post*, March 6, 1980, A4.

46. Clymer, "2 Major Issues Raised."

47. Bob Fick, "Dole Pulls Out of South Carolina Primary," Associated Press, February 27, 1980.

48. Clymer, "2 Major Issues Raised."

49. "Kissinger Urges Ford to Join the Presidential Race," *New York Times*, March 9, 1980, 34.

50. "Kissinger Urges Ford to Enter Race," *Miami Herald*, March 9, 1980, 20A.

51. Williams, DeFrank, and Kasindorf, "The GOP's Hamlet."

52. Bill Roeder, "Jerry Ford Would Reappoint Kissinger," *Newsweek*, March 10, 1980, 23; Associated Press, "Ford Opens Door to Candidacy," *Burlington* (VT) *Free Press*, March 3, 1980, 1A.

53. Adam Clymer, "Ford Supporters Organize Group to Spur a Draft," *New York Times*, March 7, 1980, A1.

54. Max Robinson, *World News Tonight*, ABC News Transcripts, March 7, 1980.

55. Associated Press, "Ford Is Moving to a Candidacy as Groundswell Grows," *Newark* (NJ) *Star-Ledger*, March 7, 1980, 1.

56. Martin Schram and David S. Broder, "Prospective Candidacy Muted," *Washington Post*, March 14, 1980, A1; Robert M. Andrews, "Ford Claims Broad Support to Enter GOP Race," Associated Press, March 6, 1980; Jack W. Germond and Jules Witcover, "Ford's Advisers Test Waters for Expected Entry," *Washington Star*, March 11, 1980.

57. David Keene, in discussion with the author, October 4, 2007.

58. Ibid.

59. Associated Press, "Ford Is Moving to a Candidacy."

60. "Reagan Returns Barb for Ford's Putdown," *Newark* (NJ) *Star-Ledger*, March 3, 1980.

61. "Kennedy, Bush Take Last Swipes at Carter Before Today's Vote," *Miami Herald*, March 4, 1980, 12A.

62. Tom Fiedler, "Ford to Run Again, Ex-Aide Reed Says," *Miami Herald*, March 8, 1980, 16A.

63. David Hoffman, "Optimistic Reagan Keeps Watchful Eye on Ford," *Miami Herald*, March 11, 1980, 14A.

64. Hedrick Smith, "Reagan Victorious in South Carolina by Decisive Margin," *New York Times*, March 9, 1980, 1.

65. Smith, "Reagan Victorious."

66. Bill Peterson, Jack Bass, Lou Cannon, and Martin Schram, "Reagan Crushes Connally, Bush in S.C.," *Washington Post*, March 9, 1980, A1.

67. Ellen Hume, "Connally Goes Home to 'Reassess' Campaign," *Los Angeles Times*, March 9, 1980, A18.

68. Bill Peterson and Tom Curtis, "The Best Roadshow in Politics Ends," *Washington Post*, March 10, 1980, A1.

69. Linda Kuntz Logan, United Press International, "Connally Describes Himself," *State* (SC), March 5, 1980, B1.

70. Patrick Riordan, "Connally's Big Purse Spent on 'Junk Food,'" *Miami Herald*, March 11, 1980, 15A.

71. Bill Peterson and Tom Curtis, "The Best Roadshow in Politics Ends," *Washington Post*, March 10, 1980, A1.

72. Bill Peterson, "Reagan Keeps Clean While Bush, Connally Sling Mud in S.C. Race," *Washington Post*, March 5, 1980, A9.

73. Associated Press, "Reagan Routs Foes in S.C. Vote," *Montgomery* (AL) *Advertiser*, March 9, 1980, 1A.

74. Frank Blanchard, "Reagan, Bush Said Close; Carter Leading Demos," *Montgomery* (AL) *Advertiser*, March 4, 1980, 1.

75. Peggy Roberson, "Candidates Pour Funds into Alabama Primary," *Montgomery* (AL) *Advertiser*, March 10, 1980, 1; Associated Press, "Alabama and Georgia Both Go to Carter and Reagan," *New York Times*, March 12, 1980, A17.

76. Associated Press, "Alabama and Georgia."

77. Howell Raines, "Clear-Cut Triumphs," *New York Times*, March 12, 1980, A1.

78. Walter R. Mears, Associated Press, March 11, 1980.

79. Lou Cannon and Martin Schram, "Reagan: Administration Harasses Cuban Exiles," *Washington Post*, March 10, 1980, A5.

80. David Hoffman, "Castro Foes Chant Out: Viva Reagan," *Miami Herald*, March 10, 1980, 16A.

81. "Bush Tells Ford to Stay Out of Race, Raises Issue of Age," *Miami Herald*, March 10, 1980, 16A.

82. Fiedler and Mitchell, "Bush Aims at Reagan in Florida."

83. Advertisements, *New York Times*, March 9, 1980, E22.

84. David S. Broder and Bill Peterson, "Rivals Take Turns Ripping Anderson's Loyalty to GOP," *Washington Post*, March 14, 1980, A6.

85. David S. Broder, "President Captures Lead in Delegates," *Washington Post*, March 12, 1980, A1.

86. Associated Press, "Alabama and Georgia"; Howell Raines, "Clear-Cut Triumphs," *New York Times*, March 12, 1980, A1.

87. Patrick Riordan, "Florida's Big Money Flowing to Carter," *Miami Herald*, March 8, 1980, 1A.

88. Susan Sachs, "Stumping for Himself, Carter," *Miami Herald*, March 9, 1980, B1.

89. Associated Press, "Benefits Won't Suffer From Budget-Cutting, HEW Chief Predicts," *Miami Herald*, March 9, 1980, 23A.

90. Louis Harris, "Republican, Independent Voters Pick Ford in Poll," *Washington Post*, March 10, 1980, A6.

91. Don McLeod, "Ford Attacks Carter Policies, Says He'll Decide Next Week," Associated Press, March 12, 1980.

92. Howard Benedict, "GOP Candidate Debate Tonight; Ford Still Considering Race," Associated Press, March 13, 1980.

93. "Reagan's Bandwagon Rolls," *Time*, March 24, 1980.

94. David S. Broder, "The Ford Fantasy," *Washington Post*, March 5, 1980, A23.

95. "Delegate Tally," *Miami Herald*, March 13, 1980, 16A.

96. Martin Schram and David S. Broder, "Prospective Candidacy Muted," *Washington Post*, March 14, 1980, A1.

97. Martin Schram, "Ford Says He Won't Be a Candidate," *Washington Post*, March 16, 1980, A1.

98. Ibid.

99. "Idea of Ford Candidacy Gets Grassroots Support," *Miami Herald*, March 10, 1980, 4A.

100. Schram, "Ford Says He Won't Be a Candidate."

101. William Endicott, "Reagan Pleased That Ford Won't Run," *Los Angeles Times*, March 16, 1980, A23.

102. Ibid.

103. Ibid.

104. Bill Peterson and Lou Cannon, "Illinois: Bush Weary, Reagan Hopeful, Anderson Ecstatic," *Washington Post*, March 16, 1980, A4.

105. Ibid.

106. Ibid.

CHAPTER 13: NOW ANDERSON

1. NNDB, "Secret Service Codename Lists," http://www.nndb.com/lists/050/000140627/.

2. David S. Broder and Bill Peterson, "Rivals Take Turns Ripping Anderson's Loyalty to GOP," *Washington Post*, March 14, 1980, A6.

3. Ibid.

4. Brit Hume, *World News Tonight*, ABC News Transcripts, March 14, 1980.

5. Jules Witcover, "Rivals Gang Up on Anderson in GOP Debate," *Washington Star*, March 14, 1980, A1.

6. David Hoffman, William Mitchell, and Remer Tyson, "Anderson's GOP Foes Join Forces, Attack His Loyalty to Party," *Miami Herald*, March 14, 1980, 31A.

7. Witcover, "Rivals Gang Up on Anderson."

8. Adam Clymer, "Campaign Report," *New York Times*, March 17, 1980, A14.

9. James Yuenger, "Anderson's Goal: Show GOP Loyalty," *Chicago Tribune*, March 15, 1980, 8; Merrill Hartson, "Anderson Says He's Tired of Having His GOP Loyalty Questioned," Associated Press, March 14, 1980; Witcover, "Rivals Gang Up on Anderson."

10. Broder and Peterson, "Rivals Take Turns Ripping Anderson's Loyalty."

11. Witcover, "Rivals Gang Up on Anderson."

12. Hume, *World News Tonight*, ABC News Transcripts.

13. Witcover, "Rivals Gang Up on Anderson."

14. "Anderson's Church Raps His Position on Abortion," *Chicago Tribune*, March 13, 1980, 12.

15. "Now It's the Anderson Phenomenon," *U.S. News & World Report*, March 17, 1980, 25.

16. James Yuenger, "Anderson Gets Look of Big Leaguer," *Chicago Tribune*, March 12, 1980, 10.

17. Rowland Evans and Robert Novak, "GOP," *Evans-Novak Political Report*, March 19, 1980.

18. Bill Peterson and Lou Cannon, "Illinois: Bush Weary, Reagan Hopeful, Anderson Ecstatic," *Washington Post*, March 16, 1980, A4.

19. Jane Fritsch, "Gacy Found Guilty," *Chicago Tribune*, March 13, 1980, 1.

20. "Gacy Clearance Probe Set," *Chicago Tribune*, January 22, 1979, 3.

21. Kathy Sawyer and Edward Walsh, "Terrorists Invade Offices of Carter, Bush Campaigns," *Washington Post*, March 16, 1980, A6.

22. Ibid.

23. Mitchell Locin, "Bush 'to Keep Plugging' Despite Losses in South," *Chicago Tribune*, March 12, 1980, 10.

24. F. Richard Ciccone, "Poll Puts Anderson on Top in State," *Chicago Tribune*, March 12, 1980, 1.

25. James R. Dickenson, "Reagan, Master of GOP Heartland, Shows He Still Can Play in Peoria," *Washington Star*, March 16, 1980.

26. Rowland Evans and Robert Novak, "Learning to Live with Reagan," *Washington Post*, March 17, 1980, A23.

27. Steve Neal, "Scripts Have Changed, but Reagan Remains a Star," *Chicago Tribune*, March 7, 1980, 1.

28. Gerald C. Lubenow, "Reagan: Secret of Success," *Newsweek*, April 7, 1980, 26.

29. Michael Reagan with Joe Hyams, *Michael Reagan: On the Outside Looking In* (New York: Zebra Books, 1988), 169.

30. David S. Broder, Lou Cannon, Myra MacPherson, Bill Peterson, and Kathy Sawyer, "Anderson Beaten Despite Crossover," *Washington Post*, March 19, 1980, A1.

31. Terry Campo, in discussion with the author, February 7, 2007.

32. "Carter and Reagan Duplicating Primary Showings in Caucuses," Associated Press, March 12, 1980; Associated Press, March 12, 1980.

33. "Carter, Buoyed by 3 Caucus Wins, Aims for Puerto Rico Victory," Associated Press, March 16, 1980.

34. United Press International, "Chappaquiddick Proved Kennedy's 'Guts,' Wife Says," *Washington Post*, March 17, 1980, A3.

35. Patricia Avery, "Running for President Is a Family Affair," *U.S. News & World Report*, March 10, 1980, 19.

36. "Illinois—Where Survival Is at Stake," *U.S. News & World Report*, March 17, 1980, 26.

37. United Press International, "Fists, Curses Fly as Incidents of Violence Mar Primary Elections," *San Juan* (PR) *Star*, March 17, 1980.

38. Edward Walsh, "Inhospitable Day a Gloomy Omen for Sen. Kennedy," *Washington Post*, March 18, 1980, A1.

39. Robert J. Rosenthal, "He Is a Man of Myth—and Mystique," *Philadelphia Inquirer*, April 16, 1980, 10A.

40. Mike Qualls, Mary Murphy, and Mitchell Fink, "The Politics of Holly-Tics: Campaigners Woo the Stars," *Chicago Tribune*, March 8, 1980, 13; "A Holly-Tics 'Who's for Whom,'" *Chicago Tribune*, March 8, 1980, 14.

41. William M. Welch, "Helms to Launch TV Campaign for Reagan," Associated Press, March 8, 1980; James R. Dickenson, "Republicans Start Battle for No. 2 Spot on Ticket," *Washington Star*, March 19, 1980, A1.

42. Jeff Greenfield, *The Real Campaign: How the Media Missed the Story of the 1980 Campaign* (New York: Summit Books, 1982), 141.

43. Ibid.

44. Ibid., 138.

45. Raymond Coffey, "Selling the Candidates," *Chicago Tribune*, March 16, 1980, A1.

46. Ibid.

47. Bill Peterson, "Saint's Halo Slips; Anderson Turns Expedient, Lusts for Bloodbath Among Democrats," *Washington Post*, August 9, 1980, A2.

48. Dickenson, "Reagan, Master of GOP Heartland."

49. Tom Wicker, "Kennedy vs. Anderson," *New York Times*, March 14, 1980, A27.

50. Albert R. Hunt, "Anderson Draws Fire from Both Parties as He Becomes Focus of Illinois Primary," *Wall Street Journal*, March 17, 1980, 6.

51. Adam Clymer, "Use 'Economic Warfare' on Iran, Bush Demands," *New York Times*, March 15, 1980, 8.

52. Anthony Lewis, "The Reagan Prospect," *New York Times*, March 20, 1980, A27.

53. Steven V. Roberts, "Anderson Drive Appears to Be Slowing at Home," *New York Times*, March 17, 1980, A14.

54. Leslie Bennetts, "Anderson Condemns Stances of Bush and Reagan," *New York Times*, March 22, 1980, 7.

55. James Yuenger, "Anderson Disputes Polls but Staff Admits He's Behind," *Chicago Tribune*, March 18, 1980, 12.

56. Steven V. Roberts, "Reagan, in Chicago Speed, Urges Big Increases in Military Spending," *New York Times*, March 18, 1980, B8.

57. Ibid.

58. Lou Cannon, "Reagan Is Conciliatory in Foreign Policy Statement," *Washington Post*, March 18, 1980, A4.

59. Ibid.

60. Lou Cannon and David S. Broder, "Despite His Rivals, He Looks to Carter," *Washington Post*, March 20, 1980, A1.

61. Mike Shanahan, Associated Press, March 18, 1980.

62. Associated Press, "Anderson Finds Voting for Himself as President 'Kind of Funny,'" March 18, 1980.

63. Cannon and Broder, "Despite His Rivals, He Looks to Carter"; Mike Robinson, "Anderson Woos Independents in Illinois Primary," Associated Press, March 18, 1980.

64. William Safire, "Third Party A-Comin'?" *New York Times*, March 20, 1980, A27.

65. Associated Press, March 17, 1980.

66. Cannon and Broder, "Despite His Rivals, He Looks to Carter."

67. Adam Clymer, "A Blow to Kennedy," *New York Times*, March 19, 1980 A1.

68. Adam Clymer, "Carter Gets 165 Delegates to Kennedy's 14 in Illinois," *New York Times*, March 20, 1980, B10.

69. David Espo, "Kennedy Sees Narrow Loss in Puerto Rico as 'Encouraging,'" Associated Press, March 16, 1980.

70. Walter R. Mears, Associated Press, March 19, 1980.

71. James L. Rowe Jr., "Banks Raise Prime to 18¼%," *Washington Post*, March 14, 1980, E1.

72. Louis Harris, "Carter Rated as 'Failure' on Hostages," *Washington Post*, March 17, 1980, A18.

73. Donald M. Rothberg, "Reagan Beginning to Act Like He's the GOP Nominee," Associated Press, March 19, 1980.

74. Hedrick Smith, "Carter's On-Job Rating Falls in Poll Because of Foreign Policy Concerns," *New York Times*, March 18, 1980, A1.

Chapter 14: Bush's Counteroffensive

1. Lou Cannon and David S. Broder, "Despite His Rivals, He Looks to Carter," *Washington Post*, March 20, 1980, A1.

2. Frank Lynn, "In New York, Leadership Is Diffuse and the Delegates Are Up for Grabs," *New York Times*, March 21, 1980, A16.

3. Dennis Farney, "Reagan's Time?" *Wall Street Journal*, July 15, 1980, 1.

4. Rowland Evans and Robert Novak, "Carter's Big Apple Blues," *Washington Post*, March 24, 1980, A23.

5. Martin Schram, "Kennedy Upsets Carter in N.Y., Conn.," *Washington Post*, March 26, 1980, A1.

6. Cannon and Broder, "Despite His Rivals, He Looks to Carter."

7. Allan J. Mayer and Martin Kasindorf, "Reagan on the Key Issues," *Newsweek*, March 31, 1980, 26.

8. Douglas E. Kneeland, "Reagan Sees Need for President to Draw the Line with Iran on Hostages," *New York Times*, March 25, 1980, B10.

9. James Gerstenzang, "Reagan Urges Tougher U.S. Stand in Iranian Hostage Crisis," Associated Press, March 27, 1980.

10. James Reston, "Carter's Secret Weapon," *New York Times*, March 21, 1980, A27.

11. William Safire, "Third Party A-Comin'?" *New York Times*, March 20, 1980, A27.

12. Lou Cannon, "Reagan's New Campaign Chief: So Far, So Good," *Washington Post*, March 18, 1980, A4.

13. Ibid.

14. Edwin Meese, in discussion with the author; Richard Allen, in discussion with the author.

15. Edward Walsh, "Kennedy Defeat a Crippling Blow," *Washington Post*, March 19, 1980, A1; David S. Broder, Lou Cannon, Myra MacPherson, Bill Peterson, and Kathy Sawyer, "Anderson Beaten Despite Crossover," *Washington Post*, March 19, 1980, A1.

16. Peter Goldman, James Doyle, Eleanor Clift, Thomas M. DeFrank, Gerald C. Lubenow, Stryker McGuire, Richard Manning, and John Walcott, "National Affairs," *Newsweek*, March 31, 1980, 22.

17. Douglas E. Kneeland, "Bush and Aides Seek Ways to Steady a Faltering Drive," *New York Times*, March 21, 1980, A17.

18. "Bush Labels President's Policy Toward Iran 'a Farce,'" *New York Times*, March 21, 1980, A17.

19. George Esper, "Bush Hopes U.S. Helps See That Shah Gets Medical Treatment," Associated Press, March 23, 1980.

20. David S. Barrett, "Large GOP Enrollment Believed Aid to Anderson," *Hartford* (CT) *Courant*, March 21, 1980, 1.

21. Richard L. Madden, "Bush Opens Drive in Connecticut After His Poor Showing in Illinois," *New York Times*, March 20, 1980, A1.

22. Mark Shields, "Reagan May Get His Chance," *Washington Post*, March 21, 1980, A19.

23. Donald M. Rothberg, "Reagan Trades Taunts, Vows No Letup," Associated Press, March 19, 1980.

24. Matthew L. Wald, "Reagan Tour of City Draws Cheers, Some Boos and Forecast of Victory," *New York Times*, March 20, 1980, B13.

25. Peter Hannaford, in discussion with the author.

26. James Gerstenzang, "Reagan Tours Upstate New York; Aides Predict Victory," Associated Press, March 24, 1980.

27. Nancy Reynolds, in discussion with the author, October 3, 2006.

28. T. R. Reid, "Kennedy: Laughing on a Day When All Else Seems to Fail," *Washington Post*, March 22, 1980, A4.

29. T. R. Reid, "Trucking Plan Wins Kennedy Unlikely Fans," *Washington Post*, December 4, 1979, A3.

30. Reid, "Kennedy: Laughing on a Day When All Else Seems to Fail."

31. Warren Weaver Jr., "An Independent Anderson Seen as 'Problem' for Carter," *New York Times*, March 20, 1980, B11.

32. Hedrick Smith, "President and Regan Now Appear Likely Contenders in Fall Elections," *New York Times*, March 20, 1980, A1.

33. Hedrick Smith, "Carter's On-Job Rating Falls in Poll Because of Foreign Policy Concern," *New York Times*, March 18, 1980, A1.

34. Michael McShane, in discussion with the author.

35. Robert Pear, "Grand Jury Convened in Inquiry on Jordan," *New York Times*, March 2, 1980, 1.

36. David Harris, "Whatever Happened to Jerry Brown?" *New York Times Magazine*, March 9, 1980, 9.

37. David S Barrett, "Primary Frenzy Eases as State Voting Nears," *Hartford* (CT) *Courant*, March 23, 1980, 1A.

38. Mike Shanahan, "Anderson Says He Will Wrest GOP Nomination from Reagan," Associated Press, March 20, 1980.

39. David S. Broder and Martin Schram, "Bush, Vowing to Continue, Flays Rivals," *Washington Post*, March 25, 1980, A4.

40. Dave Goldberg, Associated Press, March 22, 1980.

41. Myra MacPherson, "'WOW!' Said John Anderson After the Tuesday Count, but Can His Dark Horse Go the Distance?" *Washington Post*, March 6, 1980, D1.

42. Hedrick Smith, "President and Reagan Now Appear Likely Contenders in Fall Elections," *New York Times*, March 20, 1980, A1.

43. Kathy Sawyer and Margot Hornblower, "Anderson, Chastened but Determined, Looks to Wisconsin," *Washington Post*, March 20, 1980, A8.

44. Associated Press, "Crane Urges Supporters to Back Reagan's Drive," *New York Times*, March 21, 1980, A17.

45. "The Candidates on Issues of Interest to New York and Connecticut," *New York Times*, March 23, 1980, 30.

46. David E. Rosenbaum, "On the Issues: Ronald Reagan," *New York Times*, March 22, 1980, 8.

47. "Reagan, President Ahead in Poll; Many Undecided," *Hartford* (CT) *Courant*, March 23, 1980, 1.

48. "The Presidential Primary," *Hartford* (CT) *Courant*, March 23, 1980, 34.

49. George F. Will, "The GOP's Own Class Struggle," *Newsweek*, March 17, 1980, 108.

50. Donald Pfarrer, "Reagan's Ideas Worry Anderson," *Milwaukee Journal*, March 20, 1980, 16.

51. Joel McNally, "Running or Not, Ford Leads Here as GOP Choice," *Milwaukee Journal*, March 23, 1980, 1.

52. Daniel P. Hanley Jr., "Reagan Stumps for Votes," *Milwaukee Journal*, March 23, 1980, 1.

53. Peter Hannaford, in discussion with the author.

54. David S. Broder, "Leader of the Opposition," *Washington Post*, March 26, 1980, A19.

55. Bill Peterson and Robert G. Kaiser, "The Eagle's Nose Dive," *Washington Post*, March 22, 1980, A1.

56. Douglas Shuit, "Reagan Says He Is in Tune with the People," *Los Angeles Times*, March 25, 1980, B15.

57. James Gerstenzang, "Reagan Wins Connally Support," Associated Press, March 25, 1980.

58. Frank Lynn, "Wide Margin in City," *New York Times*, March 26, 1980, A1.

59. Robert Shrum, in discussion with the author, March 19, 2008; Robert Shrum, *No Excuses: Concessions of a Serial Campaigner* (New York: Simon & Schuster, 2007), 103; David Espo, "Kennedy Says He'll Go On," Associated Press, March 24, 1980.

60. Peter Goldman, John Walcott, Jacob Young, James Doyle, Eleanor Clift, Thomas M. DeFrank, and Susan Agrest, "Carter Is in Trouble Again," *Newsweek*, April 7, 1980, 22.

61. Robert Shogan, "Kennedy Upsets Carter in N.Y.," *Los Angeles Times*, March 26, 1980, B1.

62. William Schneider, "Carter's New York Woes: Good News for Kennedy—and for Reagan," *Los Angeles Times*, March 30, 1980, D1.

63. Maurice Carroll, "Republican Buoyed," *New York Times*, March 26, 1980, A1.

64. Linda Charlton, "Campaign Report," *New York Times*, March 27, 1980, B6.

65. Warren Weaver Jr., "Reports on Expense Show Bush in Lead," *New York Times*, March 27, 1980, B7.

66. Steven V. Roberts, "Anderson Pins Hopes on Belief Anything Can Happen," *New York Times*, March 29, 1980, 8.

67. David S. Broder, Edward Walsh, Lou Cannon, T. R. Reid, and Maralee Schwartz, "Mathematics Working Against Kennedy and Bush," *Washington Post*, March 27, 1980, A1.

68. Max Robinson, *World News Tonight*, ABC News Transcripts, March 26, 1980.

69. Brit Hume, *World News Tonight*, ABC News Transcripts, March 26, 1980.

70. George Strait, *World News Tonight*, ABC News Transcripts, March 21, 1980.

71. James Gerstenzang, Associated Press, May 22, 1977.

CHAPTER 15: REAGAN'S DEMOCRATS

1. Steven V. Roberts, "Crossovers Are Forsaking Tradition in Wisconsin," *New York Times*, March 30, 1980, 18.

2. Lynn Sherr, *World News Tonight*, ABC News Transcripts, March 30, 1980.

3. "But Can Reagan Be Elected?" *Time*, March 31, 1980.

4. Muriel Coleman, in discussion with the author, May 2, 2007.

5. Ibid.

6. Memorandum, unsigned, "Governor Reagan Detailed Schedule for Trip to Milwaukee Area," October 31, 1980, Colin Clark Archives Collection.

7. Robert G. Kaiser, "TV Veteran Reagan Gets Good Reviews on Ad Performance," *Washington Post*, March 25, 1980, A3.

8. Bill Peterson, "Restive Crossover Vote in Wisconsin May Benefit Reagan," *Washington Post*, March 31, 1980, A3.

9. Ronald Reagan with Richard G. Hubler, *Where's the Rest of Me?: The Ronald Reagan Story* (New York: Duell, Sloan, and Pearce, 1965), 133.

10. Peterson, "Restive Crossover Vote."

11. Jack W. Germond and Jules Witcover, "Reagan, Too, Goes Courting for Crossovers," *Washington Star*, March 31, 1980.

12. "But Can Reagan Be Elected?"

13. "Kennedy Vows to Stay in Race, Reagan Shrugs Off Rivals for Veep," Associated Press, March 23, 1980.

14. William Endicott, "Wisconsin Voting Uncertain at Best," *Los Angeles Times*, March 31, 1980, B1.

15. T. R. Reid, "President Lashes Out at Kennedy as Wisconsin Primary Approaches," *Washington Post*, March 31, 1980, A3.

16. Rowland Evans and Robert Novak, "On to Wisconsin," *Washington Post*, March 31, 1980, A23.

17. Jules Witcover, "Kennedy 'Rejuvenation' Faces Wisconsin Test," *Washington Star*, March 30, 1980, A3.

18. David S. Broder, "Mondale Rallies Carter Supporters in Wisconsin Blitz," *Washington Post*, March 29, 1980, A3.

19. Lou Cannon, "The Reagan Paradox," *Washington Post*, March 31, 1980, A1.

20. "Reagan Takes New York," *Wall Street Journal*, March 27, 1980, 26.

21. Eileen Alt Powell, "Economists Predict Higher Inflation and Recession," Associated Press, April 1, 1980.

22. "Chase Manhattan Lifts Prime Rate to 19¾ Percent," *Washington Star*, April 1, 1980, A1.

23. Albert R. Hunt, "Which Conservatism, Traditional or Populist, Will Reagan Stress?" *Wall Street Journal*, March 27, 1980, 1.

24. Allan J. Mayer and Martin Kasindorf, "Reagan on the Key Issues," *Newsweek*, March 31, 1980, 26.

25. Rowland Evans and Robert Novak, "Reagan, JFK and Taxes," *Washington Post*, April 7, 1980, A25.

26. Frank Donatelli, in discussion with the author, July 26, 2006.

27. Paul Ingrassia, "Inflation's Rigors Mold Politics of One Group of Voters Aged 18 to 26," *Wall Street Journal*, March 31, 1980, 1.

28. James Gerstenzang, "Reagan Goes to the Head of the Class," Associated Press, March 26, 1980.

29. Frank Litsky, "Jesse Owens Dies of Cancer at 66; Hero of the 1936 Berlin Olympics," *New York Times*, April 1, 1980, 1.

30. "Reagan Would Let Athletes Vote on Boycott of Moscow Olympics," *New York Times*, April 1, 1980, B10.

31. Meg Greenfield, "Jimmy Carter Talking About Himself . . . His Record . . . His Campaign," *Washington Post*, March 29, 1980, A13.

32. Marlene Cimons, "For Politicians, Humor Is a Serious Business," *Los Angeles Times*, March 22, 1980, A1.

33. Walter Mondale, in discussion with the author, February 28, 2007.

34. Cimons, "For Politicians, Humor Is a Serious Business."

35. Associated Press, "Reagan Pokes Fun at Former President," *Kansas City Times*, March 24, 1980, A4.

36. Cimons, "For Politicians, Humor Is a Serious Business."

37. Adam Clymer, "Kennedy Cheered on Eve of Primary in Wisconsin; Difference Cited by Reagan Two Appearances Canceled," *New York Times*, April 1, 1980, B11.

38. Iris Kelso and Ed Anderson, "Reagan Is Seeking Big Win in Louisiana," *Times-Picayune* (LA), April 1, 1980, 1.

39. Associated Press, "Reagan Wins Overwhelmingly in Kansas Primary; Carter Beats Kennedy," *New York Times*, April 2, 1980, A18.

40. David Chartrand, "Dole's Support Goes to Reagan," *Kansas City Times*, March 31, 1980, B1.

41. Hedrick Smith, *New York Times*, "Wisconsin Voters Defy Political Forecasters, Go with Leaders," *Kansas City Times*, April 2, 1980, A6.

42. James R. Dickenson, "Carter, Reagan Favored Today in Wis. Primary," *Washington Star*, April 1, 1980, A3.

43. Adam Clymer, "Carter, Reagan Take Wisconsin; Brown Pulls Out," *New York Times*, April 2, 1980, A1.

44. Walter R. Mears, Associated Press, "Brown Drops Out After Wisconsin," *Kansas City Times*, April 2, 1980, A1.

45. E. J. Dionne Jr., "Iran and Wisconsin Primary," *New York Times*, April 3, 1980, 36.

46. Charles Mohr, "Iran Reports Conciliatory Message from Carter, but U.S. Issues Denial," *New York Times*, March 30, 1980, 1.

47. Associated Press, "Iran Timing Aided Carter, Caddell Says," *Washington Star*, April 3, 1980, A3.

48. Clymer, "Carter, Reagan Take Wisconsin."

49. Associated Press, "Reagan Wins Overwhelmingly in Kansas Primary."

50. Walter R. Mears, "Carter Half-Way to Nomination; Reagan Marches Upward," Associated Press, April 2, 1980.

51. Bill Peterson, "Anderson Damaged by Twin Defeats," *Washington Post*, April 2, 1980, A1.

52. Iris Kelso, "Bush Talk Light Rap at Reagan," *Times-Picayune* (LA), April 4, 1980, 7.

53. Associated Press, "Carter and Reagan Enjoy Victories Won in Louisiana Primary Contest," *New York Times*, April 7, 1980, D9.

54. Ed Anderson, "Carter, Reagan Sweep Louisiana Primaries," *Times-Picayune* (LA), April 6, 1980, 1.

55. Ed Anderson, "La. Campaign Workers Bemoan Low Turnout," *Times-Picayune* (LA), April 7, 1980, 14.

56. Associated Press, "Carter and Reagan Enjoy Victories Won in Louisiana Primary Contest," *New York Times*, April 7, 1980, D9.

57. Anderson, "La. Campaign Workers Bemoan Low Turnout."

58. David Broder, "Kennedy Falters; Brown Withdraws," *Washington Post*, April 2, 1980, A1.

59. Howell Raines, "Reagan's Campaign Style Is Creating a Varied Coalition of 'Shared Values,'" *New York Times*, April 12, 1980, 10.

60. Peterson, "Anderson Damaged by Twin Defeats."

61. Albert R. Hunt, "Carter and Reagan Win Races in Kansas and Wisconsin to Solidify Lead Positions," *Wall Street Journal*, April 2, 1980, 2.

62. Francis X. Clines, "Visit with an Election-Year Lobbyist," *New York Times*, March 31, 1980, D10.

63. Hunt, "Carter and Reagan Win Races in Kansas and Wisconsin."

64. Greenfield, "Jimmy Carter Talking About Himself."

65. Stephen J. Lynton, "President Rebukes Brezhnev, Assails 'False' Response," *Washington Post*, January 1, 1980, A1.

66. Editorial, "Iran: Enough," *Washington Post*, April 6, 1980, E6.

67. Jonathan C. Randal, "Bani-Sadr, Clergy in Power Struggle," *Washington Post*, April 4, 1980, A1.

68. David S. Broder, "Jimmy Carter's 'Good News' Strategy," *Washington Post*, April 6, 1980, E7.

69. Terence Smith, "Iran's Shadow on Primary," *New York Times*, April 2, 1980, A1.

70. Anthony Lewis, "With Flexible Firmness," *New York Times*, April 3, 1980, 23.

71. Linda Charlton, "Campaign Report," *New York Times*, April 2, 1980, A18.

72. Tom Wicker, "Looking to the Future," *New York Times*, April 6, 1980, E17.

73. Warren Weaver Jr., "Message for John Anderson: Independents Fare Not Well," *New York Times*, April 13, 1980, E4.

74. Leslie Bennetts, "Strong Wives Keeping Pace with Front-Runners," *New York Times*, April 5, 1980, 1.

75. Nancy Reynolds, in discussion with the author, October 3, 2006.

76. Nancy Reagan, *I Love You, Ronnie: The Letters of Ronald Reagan to Nancy Reagan* (New York: Random House, 2000), 132–33.

77. William Safire, "Women and Power," *New York Times*, May 19, 1980, A21.

78. Ibid.

79. Melinda Beck, Gerald C. Lubenow, and Martin Kasindorf, "The Woman Behind Reagan," *Newsweek*, April 28, 1980, 33.

80. Leslie Bennetts, "Strong Wives Keeping Pace with Front-Runners," *New York Times*, April 5, 1980, 1.

81. Mary Thornton, "Carter Is 5 Months Late on Iran, Reagan Says," *Washington Star*, April 9, 1980, A3.

82. Ibid.

Chapter 16: The Appalachian Trail

1. Rick Nichols, "Bush Takes the Road of the Moderate," *Philadelphia Inquirer*, April 12, 1980.

2. Paul Taylor, "How Pa. Stacks Up: Carter-Kennedy Race Close," *Philadelphia Inquirer*, April 14, 1980, 1A.

3. Maida Odom, "Bush Pursues Ethnic Vote," *Philadelphia Inquirer*, April 14, 1980, 3A.

4. Nichols, "Bush Takes the Road of the Moderate."

5. Lee Egerstrom, "All a Mistake," *Philadelphia Inquirer*, April 16, 1980, 4A.

6. "A Time of Wild Gyrations," *Time*, April 7, 1980.

7. "And Reagan Catches Carter," *Time*, April 14, 1980.

8. David Smick, in discussion with the author, October 18, 2006; Bruce Eberle, in discussion with the author, March 4, 2007; Jim Roberts, in discussion with the author, July 2006; Randal C. Teague, in discussion with the author, August 22, 2006.

9. Allan J. Mayer, Gerald C. Lubenow, and James Doyle, "Search for a Running Mate," *Newsweek*, March 31, 1980, 26.

10. Paul Taylor and Robert R. Frump, "Green Gives Backing to Kennedy," *Philadelphia Inquirer*, April 16, 1980, 1A.

11. David M. Alpern, Richard Manning, Tony Fuller, and Howard Fineman, "A Third Party for Anderson," *Newsweek*, April 7, 1980, 25.

12. Bill Peterson and Lou Cannon, "For Anderson, the (Grand Old) Party's Over," *Washington Post*, April 25, 1980, A1.

13. "Reagan Rejects Charge by Carter on Criticism," *Washington Star*, April 11, 1980, A3.

14. Max Robinson, *World News Tonight*, ABC News Transcripts, April 10, 1980.

15. Lou Cannon, "Reagan Turns Testy on Misstatements," *Washington Post*, April 11, 1980, A3.

16. Terence Hunt, "Reagan's Changes Tune on Veteran Charge," Associated Press, April 10, 1980.

17. Cannon, "Reagan Turns Testy."

18. Jeff Greenfield, *The Real Campaign: How the Media Missed the Story of the 1980 Campaign* (New York: Summit Books, 1982), 89.

19. Gerald C. Lubenow, "Reagan: Secret of Success," *Newsweek*, April 7, 1980, 26.

20. Bill Stall and William Endicott, "Record Doesn't Always Support Reagan's Claims," *Los Angeles Times*, April 12, 1980, A1.

21. Howell Raines, "Reagan Attacks Press Analyses Calling His Speeches Inaccurate," *New York Times*, April 11, 1980, D14.

22. Steven Rattner, "Ronald Reagan's Economic Policy," *New York Times*, April 13, 1980, F1.

23. Peter Goldman, James Doyle, and Martin Kasindorf, "How's That Again, Ronnie?" *Newsweek*, April 21, 1980, 47.

24. Douglas E. Kneeland, "Challenges to Statements Putting Reagan on the Defensive," *New York Times*, April 13, 1980, 16.

25. Edwin Guthman, "Compared to the Facts, Reagan's Story Falls Apart," *Philadelphia Inquirer*, April 13, 1980, 9L.

26. Richard Bergholz, "Reagan, Editors Face Each Other; It's a Standoff," *Los Angeles Times*, April 9, 1980, C17.

27. Lou Cannon, "Reagan Preaches 'New Economics' Gospel," *Washington Post*, April 9, 1980, A3.

28. Guthman, "Compared to the Facts, Reagan's Story Falls Apart."

29. "And Reagan Catches Carter," *Time*, April 14, 1980.

30. *Washington Star*, April 8, 1980.

31. "And Reagan Catches Carter."

32. Robert Scheer, "Reagan Views Issues at Home, Abroad," *Los Angeles Times*, March 6, 1980, B1.

33. Maida Odom, "Bush Pursues Ethnic Vote," *Philadelphia Inquirer*, April 14, 1980, 3A.

34. Thomas Ferric Jr., "Presidential Race Narrows in Pennsylvania," *Philadelphia Inquirer*, April 15, 1980, 3A.

35. Merrill Hartson, "Kennedy Rips Carter on Inflation; Reagan Wins Dole Support," Associated Press, March 30, 1980.

36. Curtis B. Gans, "A Force, Not a Candidate," *Washington Post*, April 8, 1980, A19.

37. Robert J. Rosenthal, "He Is a Man of Myth—and Mystique," *Philadelphia Inquirer*, April 16, 1980, 10A.

38. Lou Cannon, "Assertive, Optimistic Support Reagan, Pollster Says," *Washington Post*, April 9, 1980, A3.

39. Ibid.

40. "On the Road: Long Hours but High Praise from His Fans," *U.S. News &World Report*, April 7, 1980, 24.

41. Arthur M. Schlesinger Jr., *Journals: 1952–2000* (New York: Penguin Press, 2007), 92.

42. Howell Raines, "Reagan Says His Drive Is Backed by New Coalition of Middle Class," *New York Times*, April 9, 1980, A24.

43. "President Reagan?" *Economist*, March 29, 1980, 17.

44. "Only One Prime Minister," *Economist*, April 28, 1979, 13.

45. Howell Raines, "Reagan's Campaign Style Is Creating a Varied Coalition of 'Shared Values,'" *New York Times*, April 12, 1980, 10.

46. Victor Gold, in discussion with the author, March 27, 2006.

47. Ibid.

48. Victor Gold, in discussion with the author, December 19, 2007.

49. Stefan Halper, in discussion with the author, March 20, 2007.

50. Robert Shogan, "Bush Accuses Reagan of 'Economic Madness,'" *Los Angeles Times*, April 11, 1980, B20.

51. Victor Gold, in discussion with the author, March 27, 2006.

52. Shogan, "Bush Accuses Reagan of 'Economic Madness.'"

53. David Keene, in discussion with the author, March 17, 2006.

54. Paul Taylor, "A Pol's Pol Strokes and Cheerleads for Reagan," *Philadelphia Inquirer*, April 20, 1980, 21A.

55. Ibid.

56. Jack Germond and Jules Witcover, "A Poll on Reagan vs. Carter," *Philadelphia Inquirer*, April 20, 1980, 11L.

57. Albert R. Hunt, "Bush Hoping for Upset in, Pennsylvania, but Reagan Is Favorite in Primary Test," *Wall Street Journal*, April 21, 1980, 12.

58. Paul Taylor, "How Pa. Stacks Up: Carter-Kennedy Race Close," *Philadelphia Inquirer*, April 14, 1980, 1A.

59. Germond and Witcover, "A Poll on Reagan vs. Carter."

60. Rick Nichols, "He Wants to Be Powerful—and Nice, Too," *Philadelphia Inquirer*, April 14, 1980, 1B.

61. David Keene, in discussion with the author, March 17, 2006.

62. David Broder, "Bush on the Comeback Trail?" *Philadelphia Inquirer*, April 16, 1980, 13A.

63. Charles B. Fancher Jr., "Thornburgh Booed; Reagan Cheered," *Philadelphia Inquirer*, April 17, 1980, 6A.

64. Ibid.

65. Robert R. Frump, "Kennedy Back Here, Buoyed," *Philadelphia Inquirer*, April 14, 1980, 3A.

66. Taylor, "How Pa. Stacks Up."

67. David Zucchino, "Candidates Fine-Tune Penna. Ad Campaign," *Philadelphia Inquirer*, April 18, 1980, 1A.

68. Robert R. Frump, Ray Holton, and Bruce Keidan, "Bush, Reagan Get Some Help from Their Friends Outside Pa.," *Philadelphia Inquirer*, April 18, 1980, 8A.

69. "A Costly Vote Goes to Bush," *Philadelphia Inquirer*, April 18, 1980, 1D.

70. Lee Linder, Associated Press, April 21, 1980.

71. Dale Mezzacappa, "State GOP Takes a Right Turn to Reagan," *Philadelphia Inquirer*, April 20, 1980, 1B; Terence Hunt, "Reagan Wins Endorsement of Howard Baker, Ohio Governor Rhodes," Associated Press, April 20, 1980.

72. Mezzacappa, "State GOP Takes a Right Turn to Reagan."

73. Associated Press, "Ford Rejects Running on Ticket with Reagan," *Washington Star*, April 17, 1980, A4.

74. Donald Kimelman, "Anderson to Begin His Run as Independent Next Week," *Philadelphia Inquirer*, April 19, 1980, 1A.

75. Ibid.

76. Advertisements, *Philadelphia Inquirer*, April 20, 1980, 9L.

77. Terence Hunt, "Reagan Wins Endorsement of Howard Baker, Ohio Governor Rhodes," Associated Press, April 20, 1980.

78. Walter R. Mears, Associated Press, April 21, 1980.

79. Bill Peterson, "Baker Urges Unity, Endorses Reagan," *Washington Post*, April 21, 1980, A1.

80. James R. Dickenson, "Baker Endorses Reagan in Move Keyed to Primary," *Washington Star*, April 21, 1980, A1.

81. "Bush Scores Apparent Upset of Reagan in Pennsylvania; Democratic Race Tight," *Wall Street Journal*, April 23, 1980, 6.

82. Paul Taylor, Ray Holton, Charles B. Fancher Jr., Donald Kimelman, and Joyce Gemperlein, "Penna.'s Jury of 5.1 Million Is Out on Fate of Politicians," *Philadelphia Inquirer*, April 22, 1980, 1A.

83. William Endicott, "Reagan, Donkey Bring Down House," *Los Angeles Times*, April 22, 1980, B14.

84. Walter Mondale, *World News Tonight*, ABC News Transcripts, April 15, 1980.

85. Judy Wiessler, "Pennsylvania Primaries May Be Last Chance for Kennedy, Bush," *Houston Chronicle*, April 20, 1980, 24.

86. David S. Broder, "Reagan Builds Delegate Total," *Washington Post*, April 23, 1980, A1.

87. Edward Walsh, "David S. Broder, and T. R. Reid, Kennedy Gains Slim Pa. Victory," *Washington Post*, April 24, 1980, A1.

88. Judy Wiessler, "Pennsylvania Primaries May Be Last Chance for Kennedy, Bush," *Houston Chronicle*, April 20, 1980, 24.

89. David S. Broder, "Reagan Builds Delegate Total," *Washington Post*, April 23, 1980, A1.

90. Remer Tyson and Rick Nichols, "GOP Race Is by No Means Finished," *Philadelphia Inquirer*, April 24, 1980, 7A.

91. Paul Taylor and Mary Walton, "Reagan Trailing Across the State," *Philadelphia Inquirer*, April 23, 1980, 1A.

92. Tom Masland, "Reagan Troops Temper Sadness with Hope for the Delegate Vote," *Philadelphia Inquirer*, April 23, 1980, 5A.

93. "Kennedy Edges Out Carter, Bush Beats Reagan by 54% to 45% in Pennsylvania," *Wall Street Journal*, April 24, 1980, 7.

Chapter 17: West of Eden

1. David Hoffman, "Bush-Reagan 'Debate' Is a Carter Grilling," *Philadelphia Inquirer*, April 24, 1980, 8A.

2. Ibid.

3. Howell Raines, "Reagan and Bush Debate in Texas but Disagree on Few Major Points," *New York Times*, April 24, 1980, A25.

4. Norman Baxter and Cragg Hines, "Bush, Reagan Find Lots of Commons Ground in Forum," *Houston Chronicle*, April 24, 1980, 1.

5. Carolyn Barta, "Chance of Reagan-Bush Ticket Slim," *Dallas Morning News*, April 24, 1980, 14A.

6. Richard Bergholz, "Carter, Reagan Winning What Counts: Delegates," *Los Angeles Times*, April 24, 1980, B1.

7. Douglas E. Kneeland, "Bush, Buoyed by Pennsylvania, Emphasizes His Determination," *New York Times*, April 24, 1980, A24.

8. Bergholz, "Carter, Reagan Winning What Counts."

9. "Reagan Raises $2.5 Million, Nears Ceiling," *Washington Star*, April 25, 1980, A5.

10. Adam Clymer, "It's Bush vs. Reagan, Reagan vs. Complacency in Texas," *New York Times*, May 2, 1980, B6.

11. "Carter, Bush Deserve Votes," *Austin* (TX) *American-Statesman*, April 21, 1980, A8; "Primary Elections Endorsements," *Austin* (TX) *American-Statesman*, May 3, 1980, A10.

12. Donald M. Rothberg, "Bush Campaign Rejuvenated by Victory in Pennsylvania," Associated Press, April 23, 1980.

13. "Reagan Far Ahead in Texas GOP Poll," *Austin* (TX) *American-Statesman*, April 28, 1980, B2.

14. "Carter, Reagan Victors in State Party Sessions," *Washington Star*, April 21, 1980, A3.

15. Rick Shelby, in discussion with the author, September 12, 2006.

16. Norman Baxter, "Reagan's Texas," *Houston Chronicle*, April 25, 1980.

17. James P. Sterba, "Democratic Vote Propels Reagan to Texas Sweep," *New York Times*, May 3, 1976, 1.

18. Confidential interview with the author.

19. "Planes Collide; Carter Calls Off U.S. Mission," *Philadelphia Inquirer*, April 25, 1980, 1A; Associated Press, April 26, 1980; Lise Stone, "Sikorsky Officials Won't Discuss Helicopter's Failure," Associated Press, April 29, 1980.

20. Bruce Langdon, in discussion with the author.

21. Peter Goldman, Eleanor Clift, Thomas M. DeFrank, Fred Coleman, and John J. Lindsay, "Another Rescue Mission," *Newsweek*, May 12, 1980, 26.

22. Bruce Langdon, in discussion with the author.

23. Associated Press, "Poll Backs Action Taken in Iran," *Washington Star*, April 26, 1980, A7; Jack W. Germond, "Political Damage to Carter Is Immediate and Obvious," *Washington Star*, April 26, 1980, A3.

24. William Branigin, "Pledge to Return Corpses in Doubt," *Washington Post*, April 28, 1980, A1.

25. Alan Ehrenhalt and Phil Gailey, "Carter Met Raid Team Secretly; Sets Press Conference for 9 P.M.," *Washington Star*, April 29, 1980, A1.

26. Goldman et al., "Another Rescue Mission."

27. Lou Cannon, "Reagan: Action to Rescue Hostages 'Long Overdue,'" *Washington Post*, May 1, 1980, A3.

28. Doulas E. Kneeland, "Reagan Says Carter Acted Too Late with Iran Mission," *New York Times*, May 1, 1980, B10.

29. Richard Burt, "Many Questions, Few Answers on Iran Mission," *New York Times*, May 11, 1980, E3.

30. George F. Will, "Just What You'd Expect from This Administration," *Washington Post*, May 1, 1980, A19.

31. *U.S. News & World Report*, May 5, 1980, 13.

32. Goldman et al., "Another Rescue Mission."

33. Larry Daughtrey, "Mondale, Bush, Reagan Poised for State Push," *Nashville Tennessean*, April 28, 1980, 1.

34. Larry Daughtrey, "Reagan Mum on Baker, Backs TVA," *Nashville Tennessean*, May 2, 1980, 1.

35. Robert Sherborne, "Reagan Disdain Offends Backers," *Nashville Tennessean*, May 2, 1980, 6.

36. Ronald J. Ostrow, "GOP's Anderson to Run for President as an Independent," *Los Angeles Times*, April 25, 1980, B1.

37. David M. Alpern, Tony Fuller, Richard Manning, James Doyle, Susan Agrest, and Martin Kasindorf, "Campaign '80: The Third Man," *Newsweek*, May 5, 1980, 46.

38. Ibid.

39. United Press International, "Cronkite Won't Enter Politics," *News and Observer* (NC), April 30, 5.

40. Steven V. Roberts, "As Prices Rise, Carter's Rating in Poll Declines," *New York Times*, April 28, 1980, D10.

41. Donald M. Rothberg, "Kennedy Bolstered by Twin Victories in Industrial States," Associated Press, April 27, 1980.

42. Ibid.

43. Cragg Hines, "Bush Admits He's an Underdog, Vows to 'Fight My Heart Out,'" *Houston Chronicle*, April 29, 1980, 8.

44. Joanne Herring, in discussion with the author.

45. Norman Baxter and Cragg Hines, "Bush, Reagan Find Lots of Commons Ground in Forum," *Houston Chronicle*, April 24, 1980, 1.

46. Dave McNeely, "Reagan's Call for Strong America Pleases Supporters," *Austin* (TX) *American-Statesman*, April 25, 1980, A1.

47. Lou Cannon, "Reagan Discounts Bush, Says Nomination Near," *Washington Post*, April 23, 1980, A12.

48. Norman Baxter, "Clements Visits with Reagan, but Stays Neutral," *Houston Chronicle*, April 25, 12.

49. Jim Baker, "He Still Draws 'Em," *Austin* (TX) *American-Statesman*, April 25, 1980, A14.

50. Dan Balz, "Reagan Is Winner in Texas Race," *Washington Post*, May 4, 1980, A1.

51. Larry Jolidon, "Bush Is Biggest Buyer," *Austin* (TX) *American-Statesman*, April 25, 1980, B9.

52. Dick Stanley, "Bush Magnetic, but Less Effective before GOP Faithful," *Austin* (TX) *American-Statesman*, April 30, 1980, B7.

53. Dennis A. Williams, Henry W. Hubbard, Jeff B. Copeland, Stryker McGuire, and Jerry Buckley, "Congress: GOP Fall Offensive," *Newsweek*, April 21, 1980, 42.

54. Ibid.

55. Dick Stanley and Dave McNeely, "GOP Foes Bypassing Unity Vow," *Austin* (TX) *American-Statesman*, May 2, 1980, B10; Dick Stanley, "Bush Chides Carter for Selecting 'Soft-Liner' Muskie," *Austin* (TX) *American-Statesman*, May 1, 1980, B9.

56. Stanley and McNeely, "GOP Foes Bypassing Unity Vow."

57. Lou Cannon, *Governor Reagan: His Rise to Power* (New York: PublicAffairs, 2003), 472.

58. Stanley and McNeely, "GOP Foes Bypassing Unity Vow."

59. Ernie Angelo, in discussion with the author.

60. Adam Clymer, "It's Bush vs. Reagan, Reagan vs. Complacency in Texas," *New York Times*, May 2, 1980, B6.

61. Associated Press, "Reagan, in Texas, Assails Bush Campaign Statements," *New York Times*, May 3, 1980, 9.

62. Lou Cannon, *Reagan* (New York: G. P. Putnam's Sons, 1982), 263.

63. Dan Balz and Lou Cannon, "GOP Shootout in Texas: Survival or Quick Kill?" *Washington Post*, May 2, 1980, A3.

64. Associated Press, "Reagan Shows Impatience with Bush," *Indianapolis Star*, May 3, 1980, 7.

65. Balz and Cannon, "GOP Shootout in Texas: Survival or Quick Kill?"

66. Adam Clymer, "Reagan Heads for Narrow Victory Over Bush in Texas Primary Vote; Carter Wins the Balloting While Kennedy Hopes for Share in Caucuses," *New York Times*, May 4, 1980, 1.

67. Walter R. Mears, "Bush, Kennedy Taunts May Soon Be Moot," Associated Press, May 5, 1980.

68. David McNeely and Andrew Mollison, "Mix-Up Gives Bush 3 Delegates," *Austin* (TX) *American-Statesman*, May 6, 1980, A1.

69. "GOP Officials in Texas Back Reagan in Survey," *Houston Chronicle*, May 1, 1980, 12.

70. Walter R. Mears, Associated Press, "Reagan Has Razor-Thin Texas Lead," *News and Observer* (NC), May 4, 1980, 1.

71. Norman Baxter, "Texans Rebuff Kennedy, but Keep Bush GOP Hopes Alive," *Houston Chronicle*, May 4, 1980, 10.

72. McNeely and Mollison, "Mix-Up Gives Bush 3 Delegates."

73. Dave McNeely, "Bush Buoyed by Texas Showing," *Austin* (TX) *American-Statesman*, May 5, 1980, A1.

74. Walter R. Mears, Associated Press, "Reagan Has Razor-Thin Texas Lead," *News and Observer* (NC), May 4, 1980, 1.

75. McNeely, "Bush Buoyed by Texas Showing."

76. Kenny Klinge, in discussion with the author, July 12, 2006.

77. Lou Cannon, "Reagan Aides Fear Bush May Reopen Old Wounds," *Washington Post*, May 3, 1980, A4.

78. McNeely and Mollison, "Mix-Up Gives Bush 3 Delegates."

79. Sam Kinch Jr., "Clements Follows Cue, Endorses Reagan," *Dallas Morning News*, May 6, 1980, 14A.

80. "Reagan Arrives Here for 2-Day Campaign," *Indianapolis Star*, May 4, 1980, A1.

81. Ernest B. Furgurson, "Mondale's Mission," *Baltimore Sun*, May 4, 1980, K5.

82. "President Plans to Resume Campaigning Although Situation in Iran Is Unresolved," *Wall Street Journal*, May 1, 1980, 10.

83. Caroline Rand Herron, Michael Wright, and Daniel Lewis, "The Nation," *New York Times*, May 4, 1980, E4; Goldman et al., "Another Rescue Mission."

84. Angus Deming, Elaine Sciolino, and Christopher Ma, "A Hostage Returns," *Newsweek*, July 28, 1980, 45.

85. "President Plans to Resume Campaigning."

86. Herron, Wright, and Lewis, "The Nation."

CHAPTER 18: WINNING IS GOOD

1. "Mayors Endorse Reagan," *Indianapolis Star*, May 3, 1980, 7.

2. Hedrick Smith, "Carter and Reagan Expected to Widen Delegate Leads in Today's 4 Primaries," *New York Times*, May 6, 1980, D18.

3. "Mayors Endorse Reagan."

4. Memorandum, unsigned, May 3, 1980, Colin Clark Archives Collection.

5. Edwin Meese, in discussion with the author, May 6, 2006.

6. Eleanor Randolph, "Reagan Quietly Planning July Convention Roles," *Los Angeles Times*, May 9, 1980, B24.

7. Associated Press, "Ford Gets Republican Convention Role in Unity Bid," *New York Times*, May 9, 1980, A23.

8. Associated Press, "Brock Says Survey Shows Gain in Republican Voters," *New York Times*, May 10, 1980, 9.

9. Hedrick Smith, "Reagan and Carter Gearing Up and Winding Down," *New York Times*, May 19, 1980, B12.

10. Edward Wills Jr., "Reagan Sees Senate in GOP Hands Soon," *Indianapolis Star*, May 5, 1980, 1.

11. "Campaign Notebook," *Detroit News*, May 15, 1980, 18A.

12. Susan Headden, "Reagan a Go-Getter as Young Man, Recalls Park," *Indianapolis Star*, May 5, 1980, 25.

13. Richard Wirthlin, "Reagan for President Campaign Plan," June 29, 1980, Richard Wirthlin Archives Collection.

14. Craig Shirley, *Reagan's Revolution: The Untold Story of the Campaign That Started It All* (Nashville, TN: Nelson Current, 2005), 84.

15. Ibid., 236, 239.

16. Stuart Spencer, in discussion with the author, September 28, 2006.

17. Karen Spencer, in discussion with the author, December 20, 2006.

18. Stuart Spencer, in discussion with the author, September 28, 2006.

19. Albert R. Hunt, "Eyes of Reagan Are upon Texas but Gaze Is Turning More Frequently to Autumn," *Wall Street Journal*, May 2, 1980, 12.

20. Susan Ritchie, "Detroit—1980 GOP," *Detroit News*, May 13, 1980, 4A.

21. Adam Clymer, "Chief of Democrats Declares Race Over," *New York Times*, May 3, 1980, 10.

22. "Gallup Finds Public Backs Carter Over Reagan on Avoiding a War," *New York Times*, May 4, 1980, 24.

23. Howell Raines, "Newcomers to South and West Reinforcing Reagan's Strength," *New York Times*, May 3, 1980, 1.

24. "Texas Primary: The State," *New York Times*, May 3, 1980, 9.

25. Wirthlin, "Reagan for President Campaign Plan."

26. Mike Long, in discussion with the author, April 19, 2007.

27. William Safire, "Reagan in New York," *New York Times*, May 8, 1980, A35.

28. Ibid.

29. Raines, "Newcomers to South and West."

30. Howell Raines, "Reporter's Notebook: Reagan's Style," *New York Times*, May 4, 1980, 24.

31. Ibid.

32. Harry Bernstein, "Labor's Fear of Reagan Bars Support of Kennedy," *Los Angeles Times*, May 2, 1980, B1.

33. Ibid.

34. Ibid.

35. James M. Perry, "Carter, Reagan Take 3 State Primaries; Kennedy, Bush Win District of Columbia," *Wall Street Journal*, May 7, 1980, 6.

36. "Voting Results in 4 Primaries," *New York Times*, May 7, 1980, 7.

37. Perry, "Carter, Reagan Take 3 State Primaries."

38. Associated Press, "Carter Victories Virtually Eliminate Kennedy as Challenger, Powell Says," *Indianapolis Star*, May 7, 1980, 8.

39. Timothy D. Schellhardt, "Carter's Post–Rose Garden Strategy," *Wall Street Journal*, May 8, 1980, 26.

40. Terence Smith, "Confident Carter Aides Shifting Focus to General Election," *New York Times*, May 7, 1980, B9.

41. What's News, *Wall Street Journal*, May 8, 1980, 1.

42. Hedrick Smith, "Carter and Reagan Expected to Widen Delegate Leads in Today's 4 Primaries," *New York Times*, May 6, 1980, D18.

43. Lou Cannon, David S. Broder, and Maralee Schwartz, "Reagan Campaign Looks to Running Mate," *Washington Post*, May 13, 1980, A4.

44. United Press International, "Udall Reportedly Bars No. 2 Spot with Anderson," *New York Times*, May 9, 1980, A22.

45. Associated Press, "Udall Discloses He Suffers from Parkinson's Disease," *New York Times*, October 18, 1980, 8.

46. Richard J. Meislin, "Carey, Saying Nation Is 'In Trouble,' Calls for Open Convention," *New York Times*, May 6, 1980, A1.

47. Ibid.

48. Maurice Carroll, "Carey Renews Call to Democrats for 'Open' National Convention," *New York Times*, May 9, 1980, A22.

49. David S. Broder, "Carter's Cabinet Power," *Washington Post*, May 4, 1980, C7.

50. Rowland Evans and Robert Novak, "The Mondale Alternative," *Washington Post*, May 2, 1980, A17.

51. Adam Clymer, "Disquiet Among Democrats," *New York Times*, May 8, 1980, B11.

52. Adam Clymer, "Democrats Divided in Colorado Voting," *New York Times*, May 7, 1980, B8.

53. Ibid.

54. Associated Press, "Wyoming and Virginia Give Support to Reagan," *New York Times*, May 11, 1980, 21.

55. William Endicott, "Reagan Selling a Return to the 'Good Old Days,'" *Los Angeles Times*, May 6, 1980, B1.

56. Jackson Diehl and Felicity Barringer, "Voters Express Disenchantment," *Washington Post*, May 14, 1980, A1.

57. Associated Press, "New Poll Finds Reagan Leading," *Washington Post*, May 15, 1980, A4.

58. Bill Peterson, "Reagan Is Finally Picking Up Support in the Boardrooms," *Washington Post*, May 16, 1980, A2.

CHAPTER 19: SIX MEN OUT

1. R. W. Apple Jr., "Europe Looks Askance at Choice for U.S. President," *New York Times*, June 6, 1980, A13.

2. William Safire, "Ronnie Le Cowboy," *New York Times*, June 16, 1980, A23.

3. David S. Broder, "Columbus Cool to Campaigners Carter, Reagan," *Washington Post*, May 30, 1980, A1.

4. Jonathan Fuerbringer, "Jobless Rate Climbs to 7.8 Pct. Sets 3½-Year Record, but Inflation Off," *Washington Star*, June 6, 1980, A1.

5. Steven R. Weisman, "Carter and Reagan 'Debate' in Ohio, Six Blocks Apart," *New York Times*, May 30, 1980, A1.

6. Terence Smith, "President Won't Debate Anderson; Independent Hopes Called Fantasy," *New York Times*, May 28, 1980, B5.

7. "A Look Ahead from the Nation's Capital," *U.S. News & World Report*, May 12, 1980, 13.

8. Memorandum by Martin D. Franks, "Anderson," May 13, 1980, Jimmy Carter Presidential Library, Atlanta, GA.

9. Tom Wicker, "An American Style," *New York Times*, May 25, 1980, E19.

10. "A Look Ahead from the Nation's Capital," *U.S. News & World Report*, May 12, 1980, 13.

11. Associated Press, "The Vote Tally," *New York Times*, May 14, 1980, A18.

12. Lou Cannon, "Reagan, Ignoring Bush, Assails Carter's Policies," *Washington Post*, May 20, 1980, A8.

13. William Endicott, "Reagan, Carter Win 2 Primaries," *Los Angeles Times*, May 14, 1980, B1.

14. "Top GOP Adviser Urges a Reagan-Ford Ticket," *Baltimore Sun*, May 15, 1980, A7.

15. Bill Roeder, "Reagan and Ford Play Games," *Newsweek*, May 12, 1980, 25.

16. "Top GOP Adviser Urges a Reagan-Ford Ticket."

17. Associated Press, "Report of Ford Candidacy with Reagan Held Unlikely," *New York Times*, May 16, 1980, B5.

18. "Top GOP Adviser Urges a Reagan-Ford Ticket."

19. Bill Peterson, "Bush Campaigners Insist He Can Win, Despite the Odds," *Washington Post*, May 19, 1980, A3.

20. Ibid.

21. United Press International, "Working on the Campaign Trail: It's Frustrating but Addictive," *Providence* (RI) *Journal*, May 25, 1980, A11.

22. "Pulitzer-Winning Reporter Joining Reagan Campaign," *New York Times*, May 22, 1980, B8.

23. Adam Clymer, "Bush Wins Michigan; Reagan and Carter Are Oregon Victors," *New York Times*, May 21, 1980, A1.

24. Kathy Sawyer and David S. Broder, "Jack Kemp: Galileo of GOP Economics," *Washington Post*, May 20, 1980, A3.

25. Jim Roberts, in discussion with the author, July 2006; Bruce Eberle, in discussion with the author, March 4, 2007; David Smick, in discussion with the author, October 18, 2006.

26. Sawyer and Broder, "Jack Kemp."

27. Judith Miller, "Reagan's Quarterback," *New York Times*, June 8, 1980, F1.

28. Jack Kemp, in discussion with the author.

29. Lou Cannon, "Reagan, Ignoring Bush, Assails Carter's Policies," *Washington Post*, May 20, 1980, A8.

30. Ibid.

31. Associated Press, "Primary Results," *New York Times*, May 21, 1980, A26.

32. T. R. Reid, "Delegate Noses Are Hard to Count, the Media Find," *Washington Post*, May 22, 1980, A3.

33. Richard Bergholz, "Reagan Says He Might Back Higher Tax Cuts," *Los Angeles Times*, May 20, 1980, B18.

34. Bill Peterson, David S. Broder, and Lou Cannon, "Bush Scores Upset in Michigan Primary," *Washington Post*, May 21, 1980, A1.

35. David Broder and Maralee Schwartz, "Despite Michigan Win, Bush 'Reassessing' Prospects," *Washington Post*, May 22, 1980, A1.

36. Lou Cannon, "Optimist Reagan Will Speak No Evil of His Dogged GOP Rival," *Washington Post*, May 21, 1980, A3.

37. Ibid.

38. Broder and Schwartz, "Despite Michigan Win, Bush 'Reassessing' Prospects."

39. Richard Bergholz, "Reagan Confident About Delegate Count," *Los Angeles Times*, May 22, 1980, B22.

40. Bill Peterson and David S. Broder, "Bush All but Abandons California Race, Plans Think Session," *Washington Post*, May 23, 1980, A3.

41. Ibid.

42. Richard Bond, in discussion with the author, October 4, 2006.

43. Associated Press, "Bush Quits Calif. Race; Campaign in Doubt," *Providence* (RI) *Journal*, May 23, 1980, A1.

44. Susan Morrison, in discussion with the author.

45. Bill Peterson, "Bush Does Not Want to Quit," *Washington Post*, May 24, 1980, A1.

46. Associated Press, "Bush Quits Calif. Race; Campaign in Doubt," *Providence* (RI) *Journal*, May 23, 1980, A1; Susan Morrison, in discussion with the author.

47. Jack W. Germond and Jules Witcover, "Will Ford Pick Reagan's GOP Running Mate," *Washington Star*, May 25, 1980, A3.

48. Jules Witcover, "Bush Is 'Reassessing' Race Despite Victory in Mich.; But His Aides Deny Reagan Over Top," *Washington Star*, May 21, 1980, A1.

49. James M. Perry, "Bush's Camp, Hurt by Tepid Response to Michigan Victory, Weighs Giving Up," *Wall Street Journal*, May 22, 1980, 5.

50. Judy Bachrach, *Washington Star*, May 20, 1980.

51. Associated Press, "Bush Campaign Fizzles; Calif. Operations Closed," *Sioux Falls* (SD) *Argus Leader*, May 23, 1980, 1A.

52. James Baker, in discussion with the author, September 6, 2006; Victor Gold, in discussion with the author, March 27, 2006.

53. Associated Press, "Reagan Plans Intense Primary Season Windup," *Washington Star*, May 24, 1980.

54. Adam Clymer, "Reagan, Confident of Victory, Faces GOP Problems," *New York Times*, May 22, 1980, A1.

55. Bill Roeder, "Shaking Up the GOP Committee," *Newsweek*, May 19, 1980, 27.

56. Bill Peterson, "Democrats Working to Block Anderson," *Washington Post*, June 5, 1980, A1.

57. Peter Goldman and James Doyle, "The GOP Renaissance Man," *Newsweek*, May 26, 1980, 34.

58. Ibid.

59. Bob Colacello, *Ronnie and Nancy: Their Path to the White House, 1911 to 1980* (New York: Warner Books, 2004), 486–87.

60. Jack W. Germond and Jules Witcover, "Will Ford Pick Reagan's GOP Running Mate?" *Washington Star*, May 25, 1980, A3.

61. United Press International, "Reagan Says He Has Won Republican Nomination," *New York Times*, May 24, 1980, 9.

62. Victor Gold, in discussion with the author, March 27, 2006.

63. Lawrence L. Knutson, "Bush Appeals for Democratic Support in Michigan Primary," Associated Press, May 19, 1980.

64. Victor Gold, in discussion with the author, March 27, 2006.

65. George Bush with Victor Gold, *Looking Forward: An Autobiography* (New York: Doubleday, 1987), 213.

66. Douglas E. Kneeland, "Bush Says He'll Quit Active Campaigning, Ending 2-Year Quest," *New York Times*, May 27, 1980, A1.

67. Ann Devroy, Garnett News Service, "Bush Quits, Supports Reagan," *Idaho Statesman*, May 27, 1980, 1A.

68. Kneeland, "Bush Says He'll Quit Active Campaigning."

69. Evan Thomas, "RFK's Last Campaign," *Newsweek*, June 8, 1998, 46.

70. Walter R. Mears, Associated Press, January 15, 1977.

71. Bill Peterson, *Washington Post*, "Bush Quits GOP Candidacy, Pledges Support to Reagan," *Courier-Journal* (KY), May 26, 1980, A1.

72. Bill Peterson, "Bush Ends 2-Year Quest, Concedes '80 Republican Nomination to Reagan," *Washington Post*, May 27, 1980, A1.

73. Ibid.

74. Ibid.

75. Kneeland, "Bush Says He'll Quit Active Campaigning."

76. Douglas E. Kneeland, "Bush, with Time to Relax Again, Ponders Political Future," *New York Times*, May 28, 1980, B5.

77. Ibid.

78. United Press International, "Bush Bows Out, to Back Reagan," *Atlanta Journal Constitution*, May 26, 1980, 1A.

79. "George Bush's Distance Race," *New York Times*, May 27, 1980, A26.

80. Lyn Nofziger, *Nofziger* (Washington, DC: Regnery Gateway, 1992), 239.

81. Kneeland, "Bush Says He'll Quit Active Campaigning."

82. Martin Smith, "Reagan on VP Pick: 'Moderate Like Me,'" *Sacramento Bee*, June 4, 1980.

Chapter 20: Coming of Age

1. James R. Dickenson, "Carter, Reagan Win Primaries in Landslides," *Washington Star*, May 28, 1980, A1.

2. Dennis Farney, "Ability to Stand Alone Is Anderson's Strength and His Weakness," *Wall Street Journal*, May 29, 1980, 1.

3. Mary Thornton, "Gloomy Voters Lack Confidence in Candidates, New Poll Shows," *Washington Star*, May 26, 1980, A1.

4. Ellen Hume, "Bush Ends His 2-Year Quest for Presidency," *Los Angeles Times*, May 27, 1980, B1.

5. Andrew J. Glass, "Reagan: Nation Today Wants a Spiritual Revival," *Atlanta Journal Constitution*, May 27, 1980.

6. Mary McGrory, "The Lesson Reagan Hasn't Learned," *Providence* (RI) *Journal*, May 28, 1980.

7. Associated Press, "Reagan Cites 2 Women for Second Spot," *Providence* (RI) *Journal*, May 29, 1980, A2.

8. William Endicott, "Reagan to Poll Party on Choice of Running Mate," *Los Angeles Times*, May 28, 1980, B1.

9. United Press International, "Vice-Presidential Poll Puts Kemp and Baker in the Lead," *New York Times*, June 6, 1980, A17.

10. Associated Press, "For Reagan, San Diego Trip Had Ups, Downs," *Sacramento Bee*, May 25, 1980, A32.

11. Lou Cannon, "Reagan Vows Better U.S.-Business Ties," *Washington Post*, June 3, 1980, A5.

12. Herbert Denton, "Carter Sees Sharp Drop in Economy," *Washington Post*, June 1, 1980, A1.

13. "Index Points to Economy in Nosedive," *Atlanta Journal Constitution*, May 31, 1980, 1A.

14. David S. Broder and Myra MacPherson, "Reagan Says U.S. 'Can't Afford' Four More Years of Carter," *Washington Post*, May 30, 1980, A2.

15. William Glasgall, "Money Supply Drops $2.9 Billion," Associated Press, May 9, 1980.

16. Owen Ullmann, "Inflation Eases Significantly in April," Associated Press, May 23, 1980.

17. Eileen Alt Powell, "Unemployment Rate Rockets 7.8 Percent in May," Associated Press, June 6, 1980.

18. Adam Clymer, "President Praises Kennedy and Says Fight Helped Party," New York Times, June 1, 1980, 1.

19. Adam Clymer, "Kennedy Bars Talk Offered by Carter on Party Platform," New York Times, June 2, 1980, A1; Donald M. Rothberg, "Kennedy Refuses to Say Whether He'd Support Carter This Fall," Associated Press, June 1, 1980.

20. Hedrick Smith, "Carter and Kennedy to Meet Today to Cope with Democratic Breach," New York Times, June 5, 1980, A1.

21. Jimmy Carter, in discussion with the author, July 11, 2006.

22. Broder and MacPherson, "Reagan Says U.S. 'Can't Afford' Four More Years of Carter."

23. David S. Broder, "Columbus Cool to Campaigners Carter, Reagan," Washington Post, May 30, 1980, A1.

24. Donald M. Rothberg, Associated Press, May 29, 1980.

25. Ken Kashiwahara, World News Tonight Sunday, ABC News Transcripts, May 29, 1980.

26. Thomas K. Diemer, "4 Blocks, Mental Miles Divide the Candidates," Plain Dealer (OH), May 30, 1980, 8A.

27. Associated Press, "Reagan Ridicules Carter Over Progress as President," New York Times, May 31, 1980, 8.

28. Leo Rennert, "Pat Brown on Reagan . . . 'Bad Governor, Good Actor,'" Sacramento Bee, May 29, 1980, A1.

29. Phil Gailey, "Carter Blasts Reagan for 'Quick Fixes,'" Washington Star, June 7, 1980 A1.

30. Nicholas Lemann, "The Republicans: A Government Waits in Wings," Washington Post, May 27, 1980, A1.

31. Ibid.

32. Ibid.

33. James R Dickenson, "Reagan Backs Big Cuts for Biggest Taxpayers," Washington Star, June 1, 1980.

34. Kendal Weaver, "Presidential Campaign Is Conducted Without a Familiar Face," Associated Press, May 31, 1980.

35. David Broder, "Carter on Brink of Rigging Election," Sioux Falls (SD) Argus Leader, June 1, 1980, 2D.

36. Sioux Falls (SD) Argus Leader, June 4, 1980, 2C.

37. Editorial, "Let's Have a Three-Way Political Debate," Providence (RI) Journal, May 31, 1980.

38. Charles R. Babcock, "Abscam Net Spreads," Washington Post, June 19, 1980, A1.

39. Ronald Smothers, "Koch Plans to Appear Before Panel Drafting Republicans' Platform," New York Times, June 1, 1980, 1.

40. "Bush Withdraws Candidacy, Throws Support to Reagan," Sacramento Bee, May 27, 1980, A1.

41. Associated Press, "Ford Endorses Reagan, Saying He Has Nomination," New York Times, May 28, 1980, B5.

42. James M. Perry, "Conservatives Mobilize to Block Reagan from Choosing Baker as Running Mate," Wall Street Journal, May 30, 1980, 6.

43. Ibid.

44. James R. Dickenson, "Reagan Begins Beefing Up Campaign Staff," Washington Star, June 5, 1980, A3.

45. Adam Clymer, "Doubts About Reagan Staff," New York Times, May 30, 1980, B6.

46. Memorandum from Steve M. Antosh and Morton C. Blackwell to William J. Casey, "Starting the Fall Youth Effort," August 6, 1980, Box 311, Ronald Reagan Presidential Library, Simi Valley, CA.

47. Dickenson, "Reagan Begins Beefing Up Campaign Staff."

48. Robert Lindsey, "Reagan's Inner Circle of Self-Made Men," New York Times, May 31, 1980, 9.

49. Helene Von Damm, in discussion with the author, May 17, 2006.

50. Jack W. Germond, "2 GOP Groups Using Loophole to Aid Reagan," Washington Star, June 1, 1980, A1.

51. Bill Peterson, "Funds Loophole Exploited," Washington Post, June 6, 1980, A1.

52. Jules Witcover, "Reagan Runs Score Up in 9 Landslides," Washington Star, June 4, 1980, A1.

53. Jack W. Germond and Jules Witcover, "Delegate Race Goes to Carter but Kennedy to Stay Until Convention," Washington Star, June 4, 1980, A1.

54. Terence Smith, "Kennedy Meets with the President and Declares He Is Still Candidate," New York Times, June 6, 1980, A1.

55. Ann Blackman, "Joan Kennedy Surprises the Skeptics and Survives the Campaign," Associated Press, June 2, 1980.

56. Lou Cannon, "Ford Meets Reagan, and They Denounce Incumbent President," *Washington Post*, June 6, 1980, A3.

57. "Gallup Finds Public Backs Carter Over Reagan on Avoiding a War," *New York Times*, May 4, 1980, 24.

58. Timothy D. Schellhardt, "Midwest Mood," *Wall Street Journal*, June 2, 1980, 1.

59. "A Look at Finances of Front-Running Candidates," *U.S. News & World Report*, June 2, 1980, 56.

60. Associated Press, "Vote Totals for Presidential Primaries," *Los Angeles Times*, June 8, 1980, A14.

CHAPTER 21: THE ROAD TO DETROIT

1. Lawrence K. Altman, "Reagan Vows to Resign If Doctor in White House Finds Him Unfit," *New York Times*, June 11, 1980, A1.

2. Ibid.

3. "China Hits Reagan's 'Two-China' Plan," Associated Press, June 14, 1980.

4. "Reagan Confronts the World," *Time*, June 9, 1980.

5. Lou Cannon, "Arms Boost Seen as Strain on Soviets," *Washington Post*, June 19, 1980, A3.

6. United Press International, "Sinatra Names Reagan in Casino License Request," *Los Angeles Times*, June 17, 1980, A1.

7. "Campaign Notes," *Washington Post*, June 16, 1980, A7.

8. United Press International, "Dictionary Outdoes Polls, Names Reagan as President," *New York Times*, June 25, 1980, A20.

9. Hedrick Smith, "Move to Oust Brock Poses Test of Reagan's Leadership," *New York Times*, June 13, 1980, A14.

10. Edwin Meese, in discussion with the author, May 6, 2006.

11. Maurice Carroll, "Eclipse of Republican Co-Chairman Is Explained by Harsh Brock Memo," *New York Times*, June 19, 1980, A17.

12. John W. Mashek, "Will Democrats' Split Cost Them Election?" *U.S. News & World Report*, June 30, 1980, 26.

13. Phil Gailey, "Carter Pelted After Pledging to Aid Miami," *Washington Star*, June 10, 1980, A4.

14. Steven R. Weisman, "The President and Congress Are Certain to Clash Again," *New York Times*, June 15, 1980, E4.

15. Brooks Jackson and Richard J. Levine, "Carter Considers Proposing Tax Cuts, More Spending Later This Year If Slump and Joblessness Don't Abate," *Wall Street Journal*, June 11, 1980, 3.

16. Associated Press, "Klutznick Rejects 1980 Tax Cut," *New York Times*, June 16, 1980, D1.

17. Sheila Rule, "Reagan Turns Down Invitation to Address NAACP," *New York Times*, July 1, 1980, B6.

18. Hedrick Smith, "Urban League to Hear Rival," *New York Times*, July 4, 1980, A1.

19. Howell Raines, "A Reporter's Notebook: Reagan Holds Running-Mate Auditions," *New York Times*, June 22, 1980, 30.

20. Albert R. Hunt, "Many in GOP Charge Reagan Campaign Is Falling into Disarray, Losing Support," *Wall Street Journal*, June 12, 1980, 6.

21. Lou Cannon, "Reagan Staff: Hesitant, Faction-Ridden," *Washington Post*, June 22, 1980, A4.

22. Mike Shanahan, "Debates Now Likely to Include Anderson," Associated Press, June 11, 1980.

23. David Wood, "Democratic Chairman Says Reagan Camp Aids Anderson Drive," *Washington Star*, June 10, 1980, A5.

24. James R. Dickenson, "Reagan Says Anderson Running on 'Ego Trip,'" *Washington Star*, June 23, 1980, A3.

25. Eleanor Randolph, "Anderson Calls Reagan Tax Plan Old-Fashioned," *Los Angeles Times*, June 24, 1980, 10.

26. Peter Goldman, Tony Fuller, Richard Manning, James Doyle, Henry W. Hubbard, Gloria Borger, and Howard Fineman, "John Anderson: The Wild Card," *Newsweek*, June 9, 1980, 28.

27. Albert R. Hunt, "As Carter Falls Further in Polls, He Now Lacks Any Solid Political Base," *Wall Street Journal*, July 1, 1980, 1.

28. "Now for the Real Campaign," *U.S. News & World Report*, June 16, 1980, 22.

29. Norman C. Miller, "Perspective on Politics; The Rest of Reagan?" *Wall Street Journal*, June 26, 1980, 26.

30. Robert Lindsey, "Six Losing Candidates Vow Fealty to Reagan at GOP Unity Fete," *New York Times*, June 15, 1980, 1.

31. Ibid.

32. Michael Reagan, in discussion with the author, July 2, 2004.

33. Jack W. Germond, "Reagan, GOP Hill Leaders Seek Tax Cuts," *Washington Star*, June 25, 1980, A1.

34. James R. Dickenson, "Carter Men Reading Up on Truman," *Washington Star*, June 22, 1980, C1.

35. Adam Clymer, "Approval of Carter's Foreign Policy Drops in Poll to Pre-Hostage Level," *New York Times*, June 25, 1980, A1.

36. David M. Alpern, "Carter Is the Underdog," *Newsweek*, June 23, 1980, 24.

37. Jack W. Germond, "Reagan Thins Choice for Veep to 8 Names," *Washington Star*, June 30, 1980.

38. United Press International, "Reagan Is a Winner, If Not an Intellectual, Baker Says," *New York Times*, June 30, 1980, B13.

39. Maurice Carroll, "Javits Says He'll Spend $1 Million in Battle to Win GOP's Primary," *New York Times*, July 1, 1980, B6.

40. Bernard Weinraub, "Study Finds Networks 'Infatuated' with Anderson," *New York Times*, July 1, 1980, B6.

41. Associated Press, "Reagan Explains Idea of Presidency's Limits," *New York Times*, July 3, 1980, A15.

42. Howell Raines, "States' Rights Move in West Influencing Reagan's Drive," *New York Times*, July 5, 1980, 7.

43. Steven R. Weisman, "Warm Greeting for President," *New York Times*, July 4, 1980, A1.

44. Herbert Denton and Lou Cannon, "Reagan Would Turn Judiciary to Right, Carter Tells Blacks," *Washington Post*, July 5, 1980, A1.

45. Eleanor Randolph, "Carter in L.A., Hits Reagan Tax Plan as 'Free Lunch,'" *Los Angeles Times*, July 4, 1980, A1.

46. Associated Press, "Line-Up of the Delegates for Presidential Contest," *New York Times*, July 17, 1952, 7.

47. George Will, "If Only Reagan Could Run Alone," *Washington Post*, July 3, 1980, A15.

48. Richard Bergholz, "Reagan Looks for No. 2 Methodically," *Los Angeles Times*, July 4, 1980, A1.

49. Barry Sussman, "Bush Top Choice of Delegates to Run with Reagan," *Washington Post*, July 5, 1980, A1.

50. Associated Press, "Bleak Poll for Democrats," *Washington Post*, July 4, 1980, A4.

51. Jack W. Germond and Jules Witcover, *Washington Star*, July 1, 1980, A3.

52. Rowland Evans and Robert Novak, "Belted in the Bible Belt," *Washington Post*, July 4, 1980, A15.

53. Ibid.

54. Lou Cannon and Bill Peterson, "Reagan at Odds with Conservatives on ERA Platform Plank," *Washington Post*, July 4, 1980, A3.

55. "Reagan Appoints Greenspan as Chief Adviser on Budget," *Washington Post*, July 6, 1980, A4; David S. Broder, "Helms Accuses GOP Platform Panel of 'Hardball' Tactics," *Washington Post*, July 6, 1980, A3.

CHAPTER 22: SUMMER IN THE CITY

1. Allan J. Mayer and James C. Jones, "A Renaissance in Trouble," *Newsweek*, July 21, 1980, 54.

2. Mitchell Ross, "'Detroiters Are Simply Awaiting This Chance to Applaud Themselves,'" *New York Times*, July 8, 1980, A17.

3. Bill Brock, in discussion with the author, October 15, 2006.

4. Iver Peterson, "Ribs and Beer and Much More Are Features of a 'Good Party,'" *New York Times*, July 14, 1980, A11.

5. Richard Bergholz, "Script All Set for Reagan to Steal Scene at Detroit," *Los Angeles Times*, July 13, 1980, A1.

6. Betty Anne Williams, "Black Delegates Meet with Carter," Associated Press, August 15, 1980.

7. Kathy Sawyer, "It'll Be Gee Whiz and Show Biz," *Washington Post*, July 14, 1980, A1.

8. Bill Peterson, "Job-Conscious GOP Watches an Incumbent Woo the Jobless," *Washington Post*, July 9, 1980, A3.

9. Bill Peterson, "Auto Union Chief Fraser Sees Reagan Tide Rising," *Washington Post*, July 12, 1980, A7.

10. Mike Feinsilber, "Republican Convention a Glittering Sign of Detroit Renaissance," Associated Press, July 13, 1980.

11. Keith Richburg, "Detroit News to Print Its Strikebound Rival," *Washington Post*, July 14, 1980, A15.

12. Phil Gailey, "Detroit GOP Are Hoping for Better Images," *Washington Star*, July 13, 1980, A4.

13. Peterson, "Job-Conscious GOP."

14. Angus Deming, Elaine Sciolino, and Christopher Ma, "A Hostage Returns," *Newsweek*, July 28, 1980, 45.

15. Robert G. Kaiser, "Conservatives Prying ERA from GOP Draft Platform," *Washington Post*, July 9, 1980, A1.

16. Bill Peterson, "GOP Moderates March in Protest of ERA Stance," *Washington Post*, July 15, 1980, A1.

17. Bill Peterson, "In Her Farewell, Mary Crisp Blasts GOP 'Sickness,'" *Washington Post*, July 10, 1980, A1.

18. Ibid.

19. Adam Clymer, "GOP Retains Brock as Chief," *New York Times*, July 19, 1980, A4.

20. Phil Galey, "Made-for-Reagan Platform Is 'Radical' on Economics," *Washington Star*, July 11, 1980, A1.

21. David S. Broder, "Democratic Camps Spar Over Delegates," *Washington Post*, July 2, 1980, A4.

22. Tom Raum, "Highlights of GOP Platform as Approved by Resolutions Panel," Associated Press, July 10, 1980.

23. Gregory Nokes, "GOP Platform Most Conservative in 16 Years," Associated Press, July 16, 1980.

24. Warren Weaver Jr., "GOP Policy Panel, in Platform, Says 'Carter Must Go!'" *New York Times*, July 11, 1980, A1.

25. Warren Weaver Jr., "Platform Drafters Prove Pragmatic," *New York Times*, July 12, 1980, 6.

26. Phil Gailey, "GOP Rightist Tamed by Ex-Pro Quarterback," *Washington Star*, July 12, 1980, A3.

27. Martin Schram, "Reagan Would Rather Go It Alone, but Choose He Must," *Washington Post*, July 10, 1980, A3.

28. Albert R. Hunt, "As Ronald Reagan's Star Rises, So Does That of the Conservative Newspaper Human Events," *Wall Street Journal*, July 9, 1980, 44.

29. Francis X. Clines, "Roads to the Vice Presidency," *New York Times*, July 8, 1980, B6.

30. Martin Tolchin, "Kemp's Friends Push Him as Vice-Presidential Choice," *New York Times*, July 12, 1980, 6.

31. Phil Galey, "Made-for-Reagan Platform Is 'Radical' on Economics," *Washington Star*, July 11, 1980, A1.

32. Schram, "Reagan Would Rather Go It Alone."

33. Joseph F. Sullivan, "Will Reagan Tap Simon?" *New York Times*, July 13, 1980, nj13.

34. Lou Cannon and Katharine MacDonald, "Reagan Rules Out Laxalt of Nevada as Running Mate," *Washington Post*, July 12, 1980, A1.

35. Judy Bachrach, "Richard Lugar Might Just Be Too Honest," *Washington Star*, July 11, 1980.

36. Cannon and MacDonald, "Reagan Rules Out Laxalt."

37. James R. Dickenson, "Reagan's List for Ticket Is Still Open," *Washington Star*, July 10, 1980, A3.

38. Stuart Spencer, in discussion with the author, September 28, 2006.

39. Ibid.

40. Howell Raines, "Reagan Words Often Conflict with Strategy," *New York Times*, July 13, 1980, 1.

41. Ibid.

42. Adam Clymer, "Republicans Are Buoyed by Survey on Party's Image," *New York Times*, July 7, 1980, A1.

43. Phil Gailey, "Detroit, GOP Are Hoping for Better Images," *Washington Star*, July 13, 1980, A1.

44. Lou Cannon with David S. Broder and Maralee Schwartz, "Ahead: Prime Time for Reagan Campaign," *Washington Post*, July 13, 1980, A1.

45. David S. Broder with Maralee Schwartz and Lou Cannon, "Republicans Dream of Watershed Year," *Washington Post*, July 13, 1980, A1.

46. Mike Feinsilber, "Here's How the Republicans Have Done It, from Ike to Bush," Associated Press, August 16, 1992.

47. Mary McGrory, "Clamor on ERA Fails to Wake Sleeping Party," *Washington Star*, July 15, 1980, A4.

Chapter 23: At Center Stage

1. Adam Clymer, "A State of Some Confusion," *New York Times*, July 14, 1980, A14.

2. Jack Nelson, "Decisions by Reagan May Affect Campaign," *Los Angeles Times*, July 14, 1980, B1 .

3. Ibid.

4. Don Devine, in discussion with the author, September 14, 2006.

5. "Choosing a Vice President," *New York Times*, December 12, 1963, 38.

6. Francis X. Clines, "No. 2 Spot on Ticket: Party's Last Surprise," *New York Times*, July 14, 1980, A10.

7. Ibid.

8. "TV Convention-Watching Should Give Few Thrills," *New York Times*, July 14, 1980, A10.

9. "Text of the Keynote Address by Governor Clement at the Democratic Convention," *New York Times*, August 14, 1956.

10. Haynes Johnson, "The Reagan Faithful Savor Their Moment of Vindication," *Washington Post*, July 15, 1980, A1.

11. Michele Davis, "My Recollections of Detroit; 1980 Diary," July 17, 1980, Michele Davis Archives Collection.

12. Jack W. Germond, "Gift for Talk, TV Era Put Reagan Up Front," *Washington Star*, July 14, 1980, A1.

13. Lionel Trilling, *The Liberal Imagination: Essays on Literature and Society* (New York: Viking Press, 1950), xv.

14. Kathy Sawyer and Robert G. Kaiser, "Evangelicals Flock to GOP Standard Feeling They Have Friend in Reagan," *Washington Post*, July 16, 1980, A15.

15. Martin Schram, "The Moderates: Disappointed, but Ready to Give Reagan and Platform a Chance," *Washington Post*, July 15, 1980, A11.

16. John Sears, "Reagan: How He Decides," *Washington Post*, July 16, 1980, A19.

17. Republican National Committee, "Order of Business '80; 32nd Republican National Convention," July 14, 1980, Ashbrook Center for Public Affairs.

18. Francis X. Clines, "Convention Journal: Conservatives Are Mellow at the Top," *New York Times*, July 15, 1980, B8.

19. "Schedule of Events," *New York Times*, July 14, 1980, A10.

20. "TV Convention-Watching Should Give Few Thrills," *New York Times*, July 14, 1980, A10.

21. Adam Clymer, "Aides to Reagan Plan a Door-to-Door Effort by Mass of Volunteers," *New York Times*, July 15, 1980, A1.

22. Don McLeod, "Two Groups Announce Independent Fund-Raising Drives for Reagan," Associated Press, July 14, 1980.

23. Brent Bozell, in discussion with the author, January 4, 2007.

24. Ibid.

25. Hedrick Smith, "Reagan Is Promising a Crusade to Make Nation 'Great Again,'" *New York Times*, July 15, 1980, A1.

26. Clines, "Convention Journal: Conservatives Are Mellow at the Top."

27. Kathy Sawyer, "Reagan Welcomed as a Hero," *Washington Post*, July 15, 1980, A12.

28. Richard Bergholz, "Reagan Promises to Lead GOP 'Crusade,'" *Los Angeles Times*, July 15, 1980, B1; Smith, "Reagan Is Promising a Crusade."

29. "The GOP Gets Its Act Together," *Time*, July 28, 1980.

30. Howell Raines, "Reagan Voices Optimism on Unity for Convention," *New York Times*, July 15, 1980, B6.

31. "Quotation of the Day," *New York Times*, July 15, 1980, B1.

32. Leslie Bennetts, "The Reagan Family: Husband and Wife Inseparable, 4 Children Go Own Way," *New York Times*, July 15, 1980, B6.

33. Smith, "Reagan Is Promising a Crusade."

34. Bergholz, "Reagan Promises to Lead GOP 'Crusade.'"

35. "Text of the Address by Former President Ford Before Republicans' Convention," *New York Times*, July 15, 1980, B7.

36. Donald M. Rothberg, "Reagan Awaits the Crown; The Convention Awaits His VP Choice," Associated Press, July 16, 1980; Lou Cannon, Martin Schram, David S. Broder, Felicity Barringer, and Kathy Sawyer, "Ex-President Sees a Tough Campaign," *Washington Post*, July 16, 1980, A1.

37. Adam Clymer, "The Conservatives' Message," *New York Times*, July 16, 1980, A1.

38. "Moderate Republicans Fail to Open Platform for ERA Debate," Associated Press, July 15, 1980.

39. Nancy Sinnott, in discussion with the author, March 29, 2007.

40. Cannon et al., "Ex-President Sees a Tough Campaign."

41. Rowland Evans and Robert Novak, "The Trouble with Bush," *Washington Post*, July 16, 1980, A19.

42. Francis X. Clines, "Convention Journal: Goldwater Briefly Relives the Glory of '64," *New York Times*, July 16, 1980, A18.

43. Ibid.

44. David S. Broder, Glenn Frankel, Bill Peterson, David Maraniss, Keith Richburg, Kathy Sawyer, and Martin Schram, "Carter Is Flayed from the Podium," *Washington Post*, July 16, 1980, A14.

45. Clines, "Convention Journal: Goldwater Briefly Relives the Glory of '64."

46. Broder et. al., "Carter Is Flayed from the Podium."

47. Hedrick Smith, "Reagan Woos Ford as Top Republicans Denounce President," *New York Times*, July 16, 1980, A1.

48. Lou Cannon, David S. Broder, Bill Peterson, Martin Schram, David A. Maraniss, Peter Osnos, and William Greider, "Some States Back Kemp," *Washington Post*, July 15, 1980, A1.

49. Jack W. Germond, "GOP Field Narrows on VP Choice," *Washington Star*, July 16, 1980, A1.

50. Cannon et al., "Some States Back Kemp."

51. Germond, "GOP Field Narrows on VP Choice."

52. Robert D. Novak, *The Prince of Darkness: 50 Years Reporting in Washington* (New York: Crown Forum, 2007), 354.

53. Ibid., 354–55.

54. "A Nervous Kissinger to Address GOP Tonight," *Washington Post*, July 15, 1980, A10.

55. Steven Rattner, "Kissinger, Addressing Convention, Calls Carter's Policies 'Incoherent,'" *New York Times*, July 16, 1980, A15.

56. James Wooten, *World News Tonight*, ABC News Transcripts, July 16, 1980.

57. Germond, "GOP Field Narrows on VP Choice."

58. Frank Lynn, "Former Top Aide to Rockefeller Turns to Reagan," *New York Times*, July 16, 1980, A18.

59. Joyce Purnick, "Hooks Urges GOP to Pursue Equality," *New York Times*, July 16, 1980, A17.

60. Ibid.

61. Smith, "Reagan Woos Ford."

CHAPTER 24: MOTOWN MADNESS

1. H. L. Mencken, *On Politics: A Carnival of Buncombe*, ed. Malcolm Moos (New York: Vintage Books, 1960) 83.

2. Vermont Royster, "Peace, Harmony and Problems," *Wall Street Journal*, July 14, 1980, 14.

3. Jeff Greenfield, *The Real Campaign: How the Media Missed the Story of the 1980 Campaign* (New York: Summit Books, 1982), 161.

4. Michele Davis, "My Recollections of Detroit; 1980 Diary," July 14–16, 1980, Michele Davis Archives Collection.

5. James R. Dickenson, "Reagan Agrees Baker's Best Role Lies in Senate," *Washington Star*, July 16, 1980, A1.

6. Albert R. Hunt and James M. Perry, "Reagan Picks Bush to Be Running Mate as Ford Deal Fizzles," *Wall Street Journal*, July 17, 1980, 1.

7. Mary McGrory, "A Brief Paradise for the GOP, Then Reality," *Washington Star*, July 17. 1980, A4.

8. Jack W. Germond, "GOP Field Narrows on VP Choice," *Washington Star*, July 16, 1980, A1.

9. Dick Wirthlin, in discussion with the author, November 8, 2006.

10. James A. Baker III and Steve Fiffer, *Work Hard, Study . . . and Keep Out of Politics!* (New York: G. P. Putnam's Sons, 2006), 98.

11. Lyn Nofziger, in discussion with the author, 2004.

12. McGrory, "A Brief Paradise for the GOP."

13. Memorandum, unsigned, "Ronald Reagan Detailed Schedule," July 14, 1980, Colin Clark Archives Collection.

14. Lawrence Martin, "How Ford's Demands Scuttled the Republican Dream Ticket," *Globe and Mail* (Toronto), July 18, 1980.

15. Thomas M. DeFrank, *Write It When I'm Gone: Remarkable Off-the-Record Conversations with Gerald R. Ford* (New York: G. P. Putnam's Sons, 2007), 115.

16. "Top GOP Adviser Urges a Reagan-Ford Ticket," *Baltimore Sun*, May 15, 1980, A7.

17. Haynes Johnson, David S. Broder, Lou Cannon, Bill Peterson, Martin Schram, and Felicity Barringer, "The Cement Just Wouldn't Set on GOP's Ideal Alliance," *Washington Post*, July 18, 1980, A1.

18. Ibid.

19. Joseph E. Persico, *Casey: From the OSS to the CIA* (New York: Viking, 1990), 188.

20. Dick Wirthlin, in discussion with the author, November 8, 2006.

21. Ibid.

22. John J. Rhodes, "The 1980 Republican National Convention," Arizona State University Libraries, http://www.asu.edu/lib/archives/rhodes/essay8.htm.

23. McGrory, "A Brief Paradise for the GOP."

24. Hunt and Perry, "Reagan Picks Bush to Be Running Mate."

25. Ibid.

26. Jules Witcover and James R. Dickenson, "A Dream Ticket Dissolves Over Ford Reluctance," *Washington Star*, July 17, 1980, A1.

27. David M. Alpern, Martin Kasindorf, Thomas M. DeFrank, Henry W. Hubbard, John J. Lindsay, Gloria Borger, and Deborah Witherspoon, "How the Ford Deal Collapsed," *Newsweek*, July 28, 1980, 20.

28. Richard Cheney, in discussion with the author, March 19, 2007; Stuart Spencer, in discussion with the author, September 28, 2006.

29. Bill Timmons, in discussion with the author, September 6, 2006.

30. Paul Russo, in discussion with the author, September 8, 2006.

31. Neal Peden, in discussion with the author, July 6, 2006.

32. Johnson et al., "The Cement Just Wouldn't Set."

33. Albert R. Hunt and James M. Perry, "Reagan Plan Is to Make Carter the Issue, Stress Large Industrial States," *Wall Street Journal*, July 14, 1980, 1.

34. Doug Willis, "Reagan Acceptance Speech Six Weeks in Making," Associated Press, July 17, 1980.

35. Peter Hannaford, "Mon. Reception Remarks," July 17, 1980, Peter Hannaford Papers, Hoover Institution Archives, Stanford, CA.

36. Memorandum, unsigned, "Ronald Reagan Detailed Schedule," July 14, 1980, Colin Clark Archives Collection.

37. Howell Raines, "Ford Advisers Reportedly Asked Wide Concessions from Reagan," *New York Times*, July 18, 1980, A1.

38. Baker and Fiffer, *Work Hard, Study . . . and Keep Out of Politics!*, 100.

39. Alpern et al., "How the Ford Deal Collapsed."

40. Martin Schram, "Ford, Roused by Last Hurrah, Clung for a While to the Torch," *Washington Post*, July 18, 1980, A9.

41. Ibid.

42. DeFrank, *Write It When I'm Gone*, 115.

43. Richard Cheney, in discussion with the author, March 19, 2007.

44. Schram, "Ford, Roused by Last Hurrah."

45. Victor Gold, in discussion with the author.

46. Margaret Tutwiler, in discussion with the author, December 1, 2006.

47. Johnson et al., "The Cement Just Wouldn't Set"; Witcover and Dickenson, "A Dream Ticket Dissolves."

48. Lawrence Martin, "How Ford's Demands Scuttled the Republican Dream Ticket," *Globe and Mail* (Toronto), July 18, 1980.

49. Richard V. Allen, "The Accidental Vice President," *New York Times Magazine*, July 30, 2000, 36.

50. Ibid.

51. Johnson et al., "The Cement Just Wouldn't Set."

52. Allen, "The Accidental Vice President."

53. Adam Clymer, "Reagan Says Bush Backs Platform; Ford Was Offered Major Authority," *New York Times*, July 17, 1980, A1.

54. James Gerstenzang, "Reagan Dumps Ford, Picks Bush for Veep," Associated Press, July 17, 1980.

55. Peter J. Boyer, Associated Press, July 17, 1980.

56. Allen, "The Accidental Vice President."

57. Dick Wirthlin, in discussion with the author, November 8, 2006.

58. Ronald Reagan, *An American Life: The Autobiography* (New York: Simon & Schuster, 1990), 215.

59. Schram, "Ford, Roused by Last Hurrah."

60. Ibid.; Victor Gold, in discussion with the author, March 27, 2006.

61. Richard L. Strout, "The Summing Up: What Historians Will Remember About This GOP Convention," *Christian Science Monitor*, July 18, 1980, 4.

62. Greenfield, *The Real Campaign*, 164.

63. Clyde Haberman, "Convention Replay: When TV Runs Hot, Politics Boils Over," *New York Times*, July 20, 1980, E2.

64. Ibid.

65. Ibid.

66. Robert Shogan, "High Tempers, Secret Meetings Mark Process," *Los Angeles Times*, July 17, 1980, B1.

67. Jim Roberts, in discussion with the author, July 2006.

68. Ernie Angelo, in discussion with the author, November 13, 2006.

69. Jim Lake, in discussion with the author, January 16, 2004.

70. Allen, "The Accidental Vice President."

71. Hedrick Smith, "Reagan Wins Nomination and Chooses Bush as Running Mate After Talks with Ford Fail," *New York Times*, July 17, 1980, A1.

72. Stefan Halper, in discussion with the author.

73. George Bush with Victor Gold, *Looking Forward: An Autobiography* (New York: Doubleday, 1987), 11.

74. Stefan Halper, in discussion with the author.

75. Ibid.

76. Greenfield, *The Real Campaign*, 166.

77. Allen, "The Accidental Vice President."

78. Mike Deaver, in discussion with the author.

79. Haberman, "Convention Replay."

80. Lyle Denniston, "Bush's Speech Gave Convention Its Heart," *Washington Star*, July 17, 1980, A3.

81. Allen, "The Accidental Vice President."

82. Greenfield, *The Real Campaign*, 166.

83. Ibid., 166–67.

84. A. O. Sulzberger Jr., "Officials of 3 Networks Defend Coverage of Night of Speculation," *New York Times*, July 18, 1980, A12.

85. Haberman, "Convention Replay."

86. Greenfield, *The Real Campaign*, 164.

87. Ibid., 167.

88. R. W. Apple Jr., "Ford Takes Nomination on First Ballot; Reveals Vice-Presidential Choice Today," *New York Times*, August 19, 1976.

89. Smith, "Reagan Wins Nomination."

90. Lou Cannon, "A Triumph for the Man, and the Party," *Washington Post*, July 17, 1980, A1.

91. Alpern et al., "How the Ford Deal Collapsed."

92. Martin, "How Ford's Demands Scuttled the Republican Dream Ticket."

93. Allen, "The Accidental Vice President."

94. Johnson et al., "The Cement Just Wouldn't Set."

95. Edwin Meese, in discussion with the author, May 6, 2006.

96. Richard Cheney, in discussion with the author, March 19, 2007.

97. Stuart Spencer, in discussion with the author, September 29, 2006.

98. Johnson et al., "The Cement Just Wouldn't Set."

99. Allen, "The Accidental Vice President."

100. Lou Cannon, in discussion with the author.

101. McGrory, "A Brief Paradise for the GOP."

102. Martin, "How Ford's Demands Scuttled the Republican Dream Ticket."

103. Allen, "The Accidental Vice President."

104. Denniston, "Bush's Speech Gave Convention Its Heart."

105. Walter R. Mears, Associated Press, July 17, 1980.

106. Allen, "The Accidental Vice President."

107. Mike Deaver, in discussion with the author, October 18, 2006.

108. Allen, "The Accidental Vice President."

109. Peter Hannaford, in discussion with the author, March 24, 2006; Peter Hannaford, *The Reagans: A Political Portrait* (New York: Coward-McCann, 1983), 276–77.

110. Mike Deaver, in discussion with the author.

111. Hannaford, *The Reagans*, 277.

112. Peter Hannaford, in discussion with the author, March 4, 2008.

113. Peter Hannaford, in discussion with the author.

114. Allen, "The Accidental Vice President."

115. Peter Hannaford, in discussion with the author, March 24, 2006.

116. Allen, "The Accidental Vice President."

117. Jeb Bush, in discussion with the author, August 22, 2006.

118. Bush with Gold, *Looking Forward*, 14.

119. James M. Perry and Albert R. Hunt, "The Reagan-Ford Deal Was Built Bit by Bit and Then Fell Apart," *Wall Street Journal*, July 18, 1980, 1.

120. Allen, "The Accidental Vice President."

121. Stefan Halper, in discussion with the author.

122. Bush with Gold, *Looking Forward*, 15.

123. Jeb Bush, in discussion with the author, August 22, 2006.

124. Bush with Gold, *Looking Forward*, 15.

125. "Reagan's Announcement of Running Mate, and Comments by Bush," *New York Times*, July 18, 1980, A12.

126. John J. O'Connor, "TV: Covering the Big Story That Never Became Reality," *New York Times*, July 18, 1980, A12.

127. Betty Anne Williams, "The Reagan-Ford-Bush Ticket Caused Some Red Faces," Associated Press, July 18, 1980; O'Connor, "TV: Covering the Big Story That Never Became Reality."

128. Peter Hannaford, in discussion with the author, March 24, 2006.

129. Mike Deaver, in discussion with the author.

130. Tom Shales, "Camera Madness," *Washington Post*, July 18, 1980, C1.

131. Frank Donatelli, in discussion with the author.

132. Haberman, "Convention Replay."

133. Peter J. Boyer, Associated Press, July 17, 1980.

134. Haberman, "Convention Replay."

135. Stuart Spencer, in discussion with the author, September 28, 2006.

136. McGrory, "A Brief Paradise for the GOP."

137. Lou Cannon, David S. Broder, Martin Schram, Felicity Barringer, and Keith Richburg, "Efforts to Forge 'Dream Ticket' with Ford Fail," *Washington Post*, July 17, 1980, A1.

138. Smith, "Reagan Wins Nomination."

139. Ibid.

140. Johnson et al., "The Cement Just Wouldn't Set."

141. Ibid.

142. Bill McInturff, in discussion with the author.

143. Jack W. Germond and Jules Witcover, "Reagan Handling of VP Choice Creates Serious Rift with Laxalt," *Washington Star*, July 19. 1980, A1.

144. Paul Laxalt, in discussion with the author, July 31, 2006.

145. Clymer, "Reagan Says Bush Backs Platform."

146. James R. Dickenson, "Ford Episode Displays Reagan in a No-Win Situation," *Washington Star*, July 17, 1980, A3.

Chapter 25: Family, Work, Neighborhood, Peace, and Freedom

1. "Second Acts in American Lives," *Time*, March 8, 1968.

2. Irving Kristol, "The New Republican Party," *Wall Street Journal*, July 17, 1980, 20.

3. Lawrence L. Knutson, Associated Press, July 17, 1980.

4. Ernie Angelo, in discussion with the author, November 13, 2006.

5. Martin Tolchin, "Conservatives First Recoil, Then Line Up Behind Bush," *New York Times*, July 18, 1980, A9.

6. Quin Hillyer, in discussion with the author, May 5, 2006.

7. Albert R. Hunt and James M. Perry, "Reagan, Bush Strive to Repair the Image of a 'Dream Ticket,'" *Wall Street Journal*, July 18, 1980, 2.

8. B. Drummond Ayres Jr., "Democrats Get a Laugh and Lift at Vice-Presidential Puzzlement," *New York Times*, July 18, 1980, A9.

9. Memorandum, unsigned, "Talking Points," 1980, Box 54, Jimmy Carter Presidential Library, Atlanta, GA.

10. Elizabeth Drew, *Portrait of an Election: The 1980 Presidential Campaign* (New York: Simon & Schuster, 1981), 215.

11. Jack W. Germond and Jules Witcover, "Running Mate Snag Gets GOP Off to Shaky Start," *Washington Star*, July 17, 1980, A1.

12. James R. Dickenson, "Ford Episode Displays Reagan in a No-Win Situation," *Washington Star*, July 17, 1980, A3.

13. "A Special Weekly Report from the Wall Street Journal's Capital Bureau," *Wall Street Journal*, July 18, 1980, 1.

14. Joseph E. Persico, *Casey: From the OSS to the CIA* (New York: Viking, 1990), 188.

15. Associated Press, "Reagan-Bush News Conference and the Bush Acceptance Speech," *New York Times*, July 18, 1980, A12.

16. "Reagan Takes Command," *Time*, July 21, 1980.

17. Sam Donaldson, *World News Tonight Sunday*, ABC News Transcripts, July 17, 1980.

18. Quin Hillyer, in discussion with the author, May 5, 2006.

19. "Why Bush Wound Up on the Ticket," *U.S. News &World Report*, July 28, 1980, 21.

20. Paul Russo, in discussion with the author, September 8, 2006.

21. James Baker, in discussion with the author, September 6, 2006.

22. E. J. Dionne Jr., "Survey Reports Reagan's Slate Leads Carter's," *New York Times*, July 18, 1980, A9.

23. Hedrick Smith, "Laxalt Calls Bush Strongest Running Mate; 'A Difference of Opinion,'" *New York Times*, July 23, 1980, A14.

24. Memorandum, unsigned, "Carter vs. Reagan," April 1980, Carter–Mondale Book, Jimmy Carter Presidential Library, Atlanta, GA.

25. Editorial, "Mr. Reagan's Second Choice," *New York Times*, July 18, 1980, A24.

26. "The GOP Gets Its Act Together," *Time*, July 28, 1980.

27. "Reagan-Bush News Conference and the Bush Acceptance Speech," *New York Times*, July 18, 1980, A12.

28. Dionne, "Survey Reports Reagan's Slate Leads Carter's."

29. Peter Hannaford, in discussion with the author, March 24, 2006.

30. Jeb Bush, in discussion with the author, August 22, 2006.

31. Hedrick Smith, "Prudence Is Stressed," *New York Times*, July 18, 1980, A1.

32. Adam Clymer, "Reagan Hails Republicans' Unity; Carter's Aides Defend Jobs Policy," *New York Times*, July 19, 1980, 1.

33. Jack W. Germond and Jules Witcover, "Reagan Handling of VP Choice Creates Serious Rift with Laxalt," *Washington Star*, July 19. 1980, A1.

34. Lynn Sherr, *World News Tonight Sunday*, ABC News Transcripts, July 13, 1980.

35. "Text of Reagan's Speech Accepting the Republicans' Nomination," *New York Times*, July 18, 1980, A8.

36. Ibid.

37. Ibid.

38. Ibid.

39. Ibid.

40. Ibid.

41. Ronald Reagan, *The Reagan Diaries*, ed. Douglas Brinkley (New York: HarperCollins, 2007), 65.

42. "Text of Reagan's Speech Accepting the Republicans' Nomination."

43. Ibid.

44. Ibid.
45. Ibid.
46. Ibid.
47. Ibid.
48. Ibid.
49. Ibid.
50. Ibid.
51. Ibid.
52. Ibid.
53. Ibid.
54. Ibid.
55. Ibid.
56. Glenn Frankel, "Reagan's Triumph Parallels YAF's Resurgence," *Washington Post*, July 21, 1980, A2.
57. "Text of Reagan's Speech Accepting the Republicans' Nomination."
58. John F. Kennedy Presidential Library and Museum Historical Resources, "Inaugural Address of President John F. Kennedy," John F. Kennedy Presidential Library and Museum, http://www.jfklibrary.org/Historical+Resources/Archives/Reference+Desk/Speeches/JFK/003POF03Inaugura101201961.htm.
59. "Text of Reagan's Speech Accepting the Republicans' Nomination."
60. Ibid.
61. Ibid.
62. Peter Hannaford, in discussion with the author, March 24, 2006.
63. Helene Von Damm, *At Reagan's Side* (New York: Doubleday, 1989), 124.
64. "Text of Reagan's Speech Accepting the Republicans' Nomination."
65. Ibid.

Chapter 26: Horse Latitudes

1. "The Long March," *Time*, July 28, 1980.
2. H. J. Maidenberg, "Stocks Post Sharp Rise; Dow at 923," *New York Times*, July 19, 1980, 23.
3. Editorial, "Franklin Delano Reagan," *New York Times*, July 20, 1980, E20.
4. Editorial, "The GOP's Man Who," *Washington Post*, July 20, 1980, E6.
5. "The GOP Gets Its Act Together," *Time*, July 28, 1980.
6. "How to Leave Them Cheering," *Time*, July 28, 1980.
7. Jeff MacNelly, *Time*, July 28, 1980, 13.
8. Meg Greenfield, "Taking Reagan Seriously," *Washington Post*, July 23, 1980, A21.
9. R. W. Apple Jr., "Republican Ticket Sparks Some Foreign Animosity," *New York Times*, July 19, 1980, 6.
10. Warren Brown, "Could Back GOP, Jesse Jackson Hints," *Washington Post*, July 21, 1980, A1.
11. Doug Willis, "Reagan Gets Mixed Reception from Blacks," Associated Press, August 6, 1980.
12. Steven Strasser, Larry Rohter, and Tessa Namuth, "Latin America; Back to Square One with Reagan?" *Newsweek*, August 18, 1980, 50.
13. Kenny Klinge, in discussion with the author, June 27, 2006.
14. Robert D. Novak, *The Prince of Darkness: 50 Years Reporting in Washington* (New York: Crown Forum, 2007), 354.
15. Kenny Klinge, in discussion with the author, June 27, 2006.
16. David Smick, in discussion with the author, October 18, 2006.
17. Hedrick Smith, "GOP Hopes Go Beyond 1980 and Beyond the White House," *New York Times*, July 20, 1980, E1.
18. Alice J. Porter, "On the Campaign Trail," *National Journal*, July 5, 1980, 1114.
19. Lou Cannon, "GOP Team Opens Campaign in Houston," *Washington Post*, July 20, 1980, A4.
20. James M. Perry and Albert R. Hunt, "Reagan Plan Is to Make Carter the Issue, Stress Large Industrial States," *Wall Street Journal*, July 14, 1980, 1.
21. Jimmy Carter to Ronald Reagan, telegram, July 1980, White House Files, Carter Presidential Library, Atlanta, GA.
22. Steven R. Weisman, "Carter Terms GOP 'Afraid of Future,'" *New York Times*, July 18, 1980, A1.

23. Frank Reynolds, *World News Tonight*, ABC News Transcripts, July 18, 1980.

24. Douglas E. Kneeland, "Reagan and Bush Meet for Briefings," *New York Times*, July 25, 1980, A8.

25. Confidential interview with the author.

26. Ibid.

27. Jack W. Germond and Jules Witcover, "Smiles Masking Friction Among Reagan Aides," *Washington Star*, July 20, 1980, A3.

28. Michele Davis, "1980 Diary," August 11, 1980, Michele Davis Archives Collection.

29. Michele Davis, "1980 Diary," August 27, 1980, Michele Davis Archives Collection.

30. Perry and Hunt, "Reagan Plan Is to Make Carter the Issue."

31. Sara Fritz, "Unions' Drive to Stop Reagan's Inroads," *U.S. News &World Report*, July 21, 1980, 75.

32. Douglas E. Kneeland, "Reagan to Focus on Northeast, Midwest and Texas," *New York Times*, July 26, 1980, 7.

33. Rowland Evans and Robert Novak, "Stronghold Lost," *Washington Post*, August 4, 1980, A17.

34. Peter Goldman, Eleanor Clift, John Walcott, Gloria Borger, and Howard Fineman, "The Mutinous Democrats," *Newsweek*, August 4, 1980, 21.

35. "A Tamer for the Reagan Lions," *Newsweek*, July 14, 1980, 26.

36. "Armstrong, Baker Join Reagan Unit," *Washington Post*, July 23, 1980, A3.

37. Hedrick Smith, "Laxalt Calls Bush Strongest Running Mate," *New York Times*, July 23, 1980, A14.

38. T. R. Reid, "Reagan Far Ahead of Carter in Poll Just After Convention," *Washington Post*, July 24, 1980, A2.

39. Perry and Hunt, "Reagan Plan Is to Make Carter the Issue."

40. Jules Witcover, "Carter's Rating Sets All-Time Low in Poll as Public Sifts Libya Fallout," *Washington Star*, July 30, 1980, A1.

41. Albert R. Hunt, "Reagan, Bush Start on Fall Campaign, Haunted by 'Dream Ticket' Nightmare," *Wall Street Journal*, July 21, 1980, 18.

42. William Endicott, "Nettled by Rumors, Reagan's Aides Plan 'Definitive Report' on Talks with Ford," *Los Angeles Times*, July 24, 1980, B21.

43. Ken Kashiwahara, *World News Tonight*, ABC News Transcripts, July 25, 1980.

44. Lynn Sherr, *World News Tonight*, ABC News Transcripts, July 25, 1980.

45. Kneeland, "Reagan and Bush Meet for Briefings."

46. Ibid.

47. Dick Wirthlin, in discussion with the author, November 8, 2006.

48. Jules Witcover, "Drive Launched to Make Sen. Jackson the Nominee," *Washington Star*, July 28, 1980, A1.

49. Hedrick Smith, "Carter's Odds at Convention," *New York Times*, July 29, 1980, A1.

50. A. O. Sulzberger Jr., "U.S. Quietly Acknowledges Death of Shah," *New York Times*, July 28, 1980, A11.

51. Associated Press, "Reagan Was Willing to Join Ford Ticket in '76," *Los Angeles Times*, July 27, 1980, A11.

52. Michael Getler, "Administration Willing to Confront Reagan on Arms Limits," *Washington Post*, July 23, 1980, A2.

53. "Washington Whispers," *U.S. News &World Report*, July 21, 1980, 12.

54. Richard Halloran, "Defense Secretary Criticizes GOP on a 'Simplistic' Military Platform," *New York Times*, July 29, 1980, A13.

55. John W. Mashek, "What Kind of President," *U.S. News &World Report*, July 21, 1980, 16.

56. "People to Watch If GOP Wins the White House," *U.S. News &World Report*, July 21, 1980, 19.

57. Mashek, "What Kind of President."

58. Albert R. Hunt, "Anderson Race Is Helped by Carter Woes, Hurt by Reagan's Overture to Moderates," *Wall Street Journal*, July 29, 1980, 8.

59. David Espo, "Kennedy Exuding Confidence on Open Convention," Associated Press, August 1, 1980.

60. John W. Mashek, "Can Carter Hang On?" *U.S. News &World Report*, August 11, 1980, 16.

61. William Endicott, "Reagan Says He Doubts Carter Will Be Dumped," *Los Angeles Times*, July 30, 1980, B16.

62. "Ronald Reagan's Taxes," *Newsweek*, August 11, 1980, 31.

63. Associated Press, "Reagan Paid $262,936 in U.S., State Income Taxes," *Los Angeles Times*, July 31, 1980, A1.

64. Jim Drinkhall, "Film Company Paid the Candidate a Steep Price for Some Steep Land to Make Him a Millionaire," *Wall Street Journal*, August 1, 1980, 30.

65. Maurice Carroll, "Right to Life Leaders Say Choice of Bush Bars Backing of Reagan," *New York Times*, July 30, 1980, B6.

66. David Wood, "Reagan Advisers Deny Slump Is Easing; Insist Kemp-Roth Tax Cut Is a Remedy," *Washington Star*, August 2, 1980.

67. Reuters, "Castro Issues a Warning About Reagan Candidacy," *New York Times*, July 28, 1980, A16.

68. Allan Frank and Lyle Denniston, "Use of Brother on Hostages Is Defended," *Washington Star*, August 5, 1980, A1.

69. Daniel Dervin, *Bernard Shaw: A Psychological Study* (Lewisburg, PA: Bucknell University Press, 1975), 114.

70. "What's Behind the Carter Magic?" *Economist*, April 17, 1976, 31.

71. Lou Cannon, "Reagan Campaigning from County Fair to Urban League," *Washington Post*, August 4, 1980, A3.

72. Doug Willis, "Reagan Outlines Plans for Cities Before Civil Rights Convention," Associated Press, August 5, 1980.

73. David Wood, "Reagan Tells Blacks GOP Best for Them," *Washington Star*, August 5, 1980, A4.

74. Lou Cannon, "Reagan Makes Appeal for Black Votes," *Washington Post*, August 6, 1980, A1.

75. Gordon Crovitz, "The Urban League Meets Reagan," *Wall Street Journal*, August 8, 1980, 12.

76. Ibid.

77. Ibid.; Wood, "Reagan Tells Blacks GOP Best for Them."

78. Crovitz, "The Urban League Meets Reagan."

79. David Wood, "Reagan Finds South Bronx Has a Feel for Politicians," *Washington Star*, August 6, 1980, A1; William Endicott, "Reagan Tells Urban League His Plans to Revivify Cities," *Los Angeles Times*, August 6, 1980, A1; United Press International, "Reagan Booed in Bronx Slum," *Los Angeles Times*, August 5, 1980, A1.

80. Tom Wicker, "A Time to Reach Out," *New York Times*, August 8, 1980, A29.

Chapter 27: The Democrats

1. United Press International, "U.S. Productivity Drops for Sixth Quarter in Row," *Washington Star*, July 28, 1980, A1.

2. Harry Anderson, Rich Thomas, and Pamela Lynn Abraham, "Carter's Sea of Red Ink," *Newsweek*, July 28, 1980, 55.

3. Jonathan Fuerbringer, "Unemployment Levels Off at 7.8 Percent," *Washington Star*, August 1, 1980, A1.

4. Christopher Byron, "The Idle Army of Unemployed," *Time*, August 11, 1980.

5. "The Misery Spreads," *U.S. News & World Report*, August 4, 1980, 14.

6. Jube Shiver Jr. and Bob Gettlin, "New Protests Launched by Pro-Khomeini Iranians; N.Y. Detainees Back to Join D.C. March," *Washington Star*, August 7, 1980, A1.

7. Walter Isaacson, Ed Magnuson, and Christopher Ogden, "Carter Battles a Revolt," *Time*, August 11, 1980.

8. Jack W. Germond, "Carter Seen Lucky Foe Was Kennedy," *Washington Star*, August 11, 1980, A1.

9. G. B. Trudeau, "They Shouldn't Put It All in Writing," *Washington Star*, August 12, 1980, A3.

10. Associated Press, "Agitators Hit Anderson with Egg, Say They're Communist Workers," *Washington Star*, August 6, 1980, A4.

11. Memorandum from Karl Struble to Tim Kraft, "General Election Observations," May 12, 1980, Carter/Mondale Presidential Committee, Jimmy Carter Presidential Library, Atlanta, GA.

12. Lou Cannon, "Reagan Campaigning from County Fair to Urban League," *Washington Post*, August 4, 1980, A3.

13. "Less Is More," *Time*, August 11, 1980.

14. Jules Witcover, "Ron Dellums Declares Self a Candidate," *Washington Star*, August 11, 1980, A1.

15. Douglas E. Kneeland, "Reagan Campaigns at Mississippi Fair," *New York Times*, August 4, 1980, A11.

16. Kenny Klinge, in discussion with the author, June 27, 2006.

17. Ibid.

18. Cannon, "Reagan Campaigning."

19. Peter Goldman, Eleanor Clift, Thomas M. DeFrank, Henry W. Hubbard, Gloria Borger, John Walcott, and Fred Coleman, "The Drive to Dump Carter," *Newsweek*, August 11, 1980, 18.

20. Barry Sussman, "New Polls Show Closer '80 Race," *Washington Post*, August 10, 1980, A1.

21. Hamilton Jordan, *Crisis: The Last Year of the Carter Presidency* (New York: G. P. Putnam's Sons, 1982), 302–4.

22. Memorandum, unsigned, "1976 Democratic Presidential Campaign Summary Of Expenditures by Function; AIGN Expenditures," Carter/Mondale Book, Financial Sector, Jimmy Carter Presidential Library, Atlanta, GA.

23. James M. Perry and Albert R. Hunt, "Carter Seems in Command Despite Drive by Kennedy Forces as Convention Opens," *Wall Street Journal*, August 11, 1980, 2.

24. Martin Schram, "Candidates: Intractable and Proud," *Washington Post*, August 10, 1980, A1.

25. "Delegates Hard at Work Before the Call to Order," *New York Times*, August 12, 1980, B12.

26. "Madison Square Garden of Briars," *Time*, August 25, 1980.

27. Terence Smith, "Carter Confident as Aides Meet with His Delegates," *New York Times*, August 11, 1980, B7.

28. Judy Bachrach, "A Split Party Again Is Flirting with Suicide," *Washington Star*, August 12, 1980, A5.

29. Hugh Sidey, "Assessing a Presidency," *Time*, August 18, 1980.

30. Ibid.

31. Claudia Wallis and Melissa Ludtke Lincoln, "People," *Time*, August 25, 1980.

32. Bill Peterson and Edward Walsh, "The Convention Floor: A Wall-to-Wall Crush," *Washington Post*, August 11, 1980, A9.

33. Ibid.

34. Haynes Johnson and Barry Sussman, "Party Paradox," *Washington Post*, August 11, 1980, A1.

35. Mark Shields, "Wanted: Democrats Plain," *Washington Post*, August 22, 1980, A15.

36. Dudley Clendinen, "White House Says Minister Misquoted Carter Remarks," *New York Times*, August 8, 1980, A16.

37. T. R. Reid and Martin Schram, "Upbeat but Facing Loss, Kennedy Arrives in N.Y.," *Washington Post*, August 9, 1980, A1.

38. Bill Peterson and T. R. Reid, "Anderson May Quit If Party Dumps Carter," *Washington Post*, August 1, 1980, A1.

39. Hedrick Smith, "Strauss Predicting Some Carter Losses on Party Platform," *New York Times*, August 9, 1980, 1.

40. Adam Clymer, "Poll Finds Carter Gaining in Party After News Conference on Brother," *New York Times*, August 10, 1980, 1.

41. B. Drummond Ayres Jr., "Kennedy, in New York, Sees 'Real Chance,'" *New York Times*, August 9, 1980, 7.

42. Associated Press, "Roll Call on Rule," *Washington Star*, August 12, 1980, A5.

43. T. R. Reid, "Facing Up to Defeat," *Washington Post*, August 12, 1980, A1.

44. Judy Bachrach, "Tenderness Has Bitter Flavor in Kennedy Circle," *Washington Star*, August 13, 1980, A5.

45. B. Drummond Ayres Jr., "Kennedy Race Ends, but Cause Continues," *New York Times*, August 13, 1980, B1.

46. Associated Press, "Oswald's Body to Be Exhumed," *Washington Star*, August 14, 1980, A1.

47. David M. Alpern, John Walcott, Thomas M. DeFrank, Eleanor Clift, Henry W. Hubbard, Stryker McGuire, and John J. Lindsay, "A Veneer of Unity," *Newsweek*, August 25, 1980, 24.

48. Reid, "Facing Up to Defeat."

49. "Madison Square Garden of Briars."

50. Reid, "Facing Up to Defeat."

51. Jack W. Germond, "Challenger Quits After Rules Loss," *Washington Star*, August 12, 1980, A1.

52. Adam Clymer, "A Graceful Withdrawal," *New York Times*, August 12, 1980, A1.

53. David S. Broder, Edward Walsh, Karlyn Barker, Lou Cannon, Herbert Denton, Helen Dewar, Stan Hinden, T. R. Reid, and Maralee Schwartz, "Kennedy Ends Fight for Nomination," *Washington Post*, August 12, 1980, A1.

54. Edward Walsh, Robert G. Kaiser, David S. Broder, Lou Cannon, Kathy Sawyer, and Martin Schram, "Kennedy Rips Reagan, Electrifies Convention," *Washington Post*, August 13, 1980, A1.

55. Hedrick Smith, "A Bid to 'Keep Faith,'" *New York Times*, August 13, 1980, A1.

56. "Text of Kennedy's Address to Democratic National Convention," *Washington Star*, August 13, 1980, A7.

57. Walsh, et al., "Kennedy Rips Reagan."

58. "Text of Kennedy's Address."

59. "Madison Square Garden of Briars."

60. Alpern et al., "A Veneer of Unity."

61. Walsh et al., "Kennedy Rips Reagan."

62. United Press International, "Mary Crisp Gets High Post in Anderson's Campaign," *Washington Star*, August 14, 1980, A5.

63. David S. Broder and Edward Walsh, "An Uphill Race Against Reagan," *Washington Post*, August 14, 1980, A1.

64. Hedrick Smith, "Carter Wins Nomination for a Second Term; Gets Kennedy Pledge of 'Support and Work,'" *New York Times*, August 14, 1980, A1.

65. Broder and Walsh, "An Uphill Race Against Reagan."

66. Robert G. Kaiser, Martin Schram, Lou Cannon, Helen Dewar, Herbert Denton, Bill Peterson, T. R. Reid, Kathy Sawyer, and Chris Colford, "A Formal Peace Over Platform," *Washington Post*, August 14, 1980, A1.

67. Howell Raines, "Among Southern Delegates, Enthusiasm Is Hard to Find," *New York Times*, August 14, 1980, B2.

68. Elizabeth Drew, *Portrait of an Election: The 1980 Presidential Campaign* (New York: Simon & Schuster, 1981), 256.

69. Edward Walsh, Robert G. Kaiser, Helen Dewar, Martin Schram, Bill Peterson, Lou Cannon, David S. Broder, Kathy Sawyer, T. R. Reid, Eugene Robinson, Jackson Diehl, and Karlyn Barker, "Carter Asks Kennedy to Join Reagan Fight," *Washington Post*, August 15, 1980, A1.

70. Maureen Santini, "Mondale Says Reagan 'Out of Step with America,'" Associated Press, August 14, 1980; Jeremiah O'Leary, "Gusto Marks Mondale's Acceptance," *Washington Star*, August 15, 1980.

71. Haynes Johnson, "Running Then as a Farmer, Running Now as a President," *Washington Post*, August 15, 1980, A10.

72. Edwin Warner, Christopher Ogden, and Joanna McGeary, "Drawing the Battle Lines," *Time*, August 25, 1980, http://www.time.com/time/magazine/article/0,9171,948979,00.html.

73. David S. Broder, "Carter Strategy Aims to Plant Doubts About Reagan Abilities," *Washington Post*, August 16, 1980, A10.

74. "Transcript of Carter's Speech Accepting His Renomination at Party Convention," *New York Times*, August 15, 1980, B2.

75. "Carter: Running Tough," *Time*, August 25, 1980.

76. Warner et al., "Drawing the Battle Lines."

77. Broder, "Carter Strategy Aims to Plant Doubts."

78. Jimmy Carter, in discussion with the author, July 11, 2006.

79. "Madison Square Garden of Briars."

80. Jimmy Carter, in discussion with the author, July 11, 2006.

81. Bill Schulz, in discussion with the author, January 23, 2007.

CHAPTER 28: CORBIN

1. Cheryl Lavin, *Chicago Tribune*, November 5, 1995, 12C.

2. Adam Walinsky, in discussion with the author, June 10, 2005.

3. Paul Corbin, in discussion with the author.

4. Federal Bureau of Investigation, Report, "Paul Corbin wa. Paul Kobrinsky," file no. 100–10181, February 13, 1952, Milwaukee, WI.

5. Memorandum from A. H. Belmont to D. M. Ladd, "Paul Corbin wa. Paul Kobrinsky; Name Check Request—Senator Joseph R. McCarthy," United States Government, June 2, 1951.

6. Memorandum from Director FBI to the Attorney General, United States Government, January 9, 1968.

7. Federal Bureau of Investigation, Report, "Paul Corbin wa. Paul Kobrinsky," file no. 100–8584, June 27, 1944, Chicago, IL.

8. Mark Shields, in discussion with the author.

9. John Seigenthaler, in discussion with the author, November 15, 2007; Kathleen Kennedy Townsend, in discussion with the author, December 18, 2007.

10. Bill Schulz, in discussion with the author.

11. Kathleen Kennedy Townsend, in discussion with the author, December 18, 2007.

12. Paul Corbin, in discussion with the author.

13. Ray Thomasson, in discussion with the author, February 12, 2007.

14. Joseph Sweat, in discussion with the author, February 12, 2007.

15. Ray Thomasson, in discussion with the author, February 12, 2007.

16. John Seigenthaler, in discussion with the author, March 25, 2008.

17. House Committee on Post Office and Civil Service, Subcommittee on Human Resources, *Unauthorized Transfers of Nonpublic Information During the 1980 Presidential Election*, 98th Cong., 2d sess., 1984, Committee Print 98–12; Mike Feinsilber, Associated Press, May 24, 1984. Hereinafter cited as House Committee report.

18. Stuart Spencer, in discussion with the author, September 28, 2006.

19. James Baker, in discussion with the author, September 6, 2006

20. David Keene, in discussion with the author, October 10, 2006; Richard Cheney, in discussion with the author, March 19, 2007.

21. Federal Bureau of Investigation, Report, file no. 161–107, January 13, 1961, Washington, DC.

22. Frida Shankman, in discussion with the author, 2007.

23. Memorandum from SAC, Milwaukee to Director FBI, "Paul Corbin; G. M. Corbin," United States Government, April 12, 1954.

24. Lewis E. Glenn, Federal Bureau of Investigation, Report, file no. 161–14, January 16, 1961, Waterloo, IA.

25. "Many Are Wondering: What of Corbin's Past?" *Milwaukee Journal*, August 24, 1961.

26. Joseph Sweat, in discussion with the author, February 12, 2007.

27. "Many Are Wondering."

28. Federal Bureau of Investigation, Report, "Paul Corbin wa. Paul Kobrinsky," file no. 100–5813, August 3, 1944, Saint Paul, MN.

29. Federal Bureau of Investigation, Report, "Paul, Aka.," file no. 161–84, January 17, 1961, Chicago, IL.

30. Darlene Corbin, in discussion with the author, December 11, 2007.

31. Federal Bureau of Investigation, Report, "Paul Corbin wa. Paul Kobrinsky," file no. 100–8584, June 27, 1944, Chicago, IL; Jack E. Ison, "Paul Corbin," *ASC Newsletter*, September 30, 1961, 2; Federal Bureau of Investigation, Report, file no. 161–166.

32. Ison, "Paul Corbin"; Federal Bureau of Investigation, Report, file no. 161–166.

33. Darlene Corbin, in discussion with the author, December 11, 2007.

34. Gordon B. Playman, Federal Bureau of Investigation, Report, "Paul Corbin," file no. 161–15, January 20, 1961, Chicago, IL.

35. Memorandum from SAC Milwaukee to SAC Minneapolis, "Paul Corbin," file no. 161–17, United States Government, January 16, 1961.

36. Federal Bureau of Investigation, Report, "Paul Corbin wa. Paul Kobrinsky," file no. 100–8584, June 27, 1944, Chicago, IL.

37. Federal Bureau of Investigation, Report, "Paul Corbin wa. Paul Kobrinsky," file no. 100–10181, February 13, 1952, Milwaukee, WI.

38. Federal Bureau of Investigation, Report, "Paul Corbin wa. Paul Kobrinsky," file no. 100–8584, June 27, 1944, Chicago, IL.

39. Adam Walinsky, in discussion with the author, June 10, 2005.

40. Federal Bureau of Investigation, Report, "Paul Corbin wa. Paul Kobrinsky," file no. 100–10181, February 13, 1952, Milwaukee, WI.

41. Ibid.

42. Federal Bureau of Investigation, Report, "Paul Corbin wa. Paul Kobrinsky," file no. 100–8584, February 7, 1950, Chicago, IL.

43. Federal Bureau of Investigation, Report, "Paul Corbin, with alias Paul Kobrinsky," file no. 100–10181, February 28, 1950, Milwaukee, WI.

44. Federal Bureau of Investigation, Report, "Paul Corbin wa. Paul Kobrinsky," file no. 100–10181, February 13, 1952, Milwaukee, WI.

45. Ibid.

46. Federal Bureau of Investigation, Report, "Paul Corbin," file no. 161–17, January 17, 1961, Milwaukee, WI.

47. Adam Walinsky, in discussion with the author, June 10, 2005.

48. Memorandum, unsigned, "Paul Corbin Special Inquiry," United States Government, December 12, 1966.

49. Bill Schulz, in discussion with the author, January 23, 2007; Paul Corbin, in discussion with the author; David Keene, in discussion with the author.

50. Letter to Joseph McCarthy, May 22, 1951.

51. Memorandum from A. H. Belmont to D. M. Ladd, "Paul Corbin wa. Paul Kobrinsky; Name Check Request—Senator Joseph R. McCarthy," United States Government, June 2, 1951.

52. Memorandum from Hoover to Communications Section and SAC Milwaukee, Federal Bureau of Investigation, April 20, 1954.

53. Memorandum from Hoover to SAC Milwaukee, Federal Bureau of Investigation, April 28, 1954.

54. Adam Walinsky, in discussion with the author.

55. Milles McMillin, "Curious Lack of Publicity about Paul Corbin," *Capital Times* (WI), January 2, 1961.

56. Richard N. Pranke, Federal Bureau of Investigation, Report, "Paul Corbin; G. M. Corbin," file no. 33–101, April 5, 1954, Minneapolis, MN.

57. Memorandum from SAC, Milwaukee to Director FBI, "Paul Corbin; SM–C: SGE; Security Matter—Communist," file no. 100–10181, Federal Bureau of Investigation, April 9, 1959.

58. Adam Walinsky, in discussion with the author, June 10, 2005.

59. Jeff Shesol, *Mutual Contempt: Lyndon Johnson, Robert Kennedy, and the Feud That Defined a Decade* (New York: Norton, 1997), 183.

60. Darlene Corbin, in discussion with the author, December 11, 2007.

61. Federal Bureau of Investigation, Report, "Paul Corbin, aka Paul Kobrinsky," file no. 161–17, January 15, 1961, Madison, WI.

62. Adam Walinsky, in discussion with the author, June 10, 2005.

63. Ibid.

64. Federal Bureau of Investigation, Report, "Paul Corbin, aka Paul Kobrinsky," file no. 161–17, January 17, 1961, Milwaukee, WI.

65. John Seigenthaler, in discussion with the author, November 15, 2007.

66. David Lucey, in discussion with the author, December 8, 2006.

67. Paul Corbin, in discussion with the author.

68. John Seigenthaler, in discussion with the author, November 15, 2007.

69. Milles McMillin, "Curious Lack of Publicity about Paul Corbin," *Capital Times* (WI), January 2, 1961.

70. John Seigenthaler, in discussion with the author, November 15, 2007.

71. Ibid.

72. Memorandum to Mr. Rosen, "Paul Corbin Special Inquiry," United States Government, January 12, 1961.

73. Federal Bureau of Investigation, Report, "Paul Corbin, aka. Paul Kobrinsky spi," file no. 161–107, January 13, 1961, Washington, DC.

74. Federal Bureau of Investigation, Report, "Paul Corbin, spi," file no. 161–14, January 14, 1961, Omaha, NE.

75. Federal Bureau of Investigation, Report, "Paul Corbin, spi," file no. 161–19, January 14, 1961, Springfield, IL.

76. Federal Bureau of Investigation, Report, "Paul Corbin, Special Inquiry," file no. 161–17, January 17, 1961, Milwaukee, WI.

77. Federal Bureau of Investigation, Report, "Paul, Aka.," file no. 161–84, January 17, 1961, Chicago, IL.

78. Federal Bureau of Investigation, Report, "Paul Corbin, Special Inquiry," file no. 161–17, January 17, 1961, Milwaukee, WI.

79. Federal Bureau of Investigation, Report, "Paul Corbin," file no. 161–17, January 15, 1961, Madison, WI.

80. Federal Bureau of Investigation, Report, "Paul Corbin, Special Inquiry," file no. 161–17, January 17, 1961, Milwaukee, WI.

81. "Many Are Wondering."

82. Federal Bureau of Investigation, Report, "Paul Corbin, Special Inquiry," file no. 161–17, January 17, 1961, Milwaukee, WI.

83. Federal Bureau of Investigation, Report, "Paul Corbin, Special Inquiry," file no. 161–17, January 16, 1961, Janesville, WI.

84. Ibid.

85. Ibid.

86. Ibid.

87. John Seigenthaler, in discussion with the author, November 15, 2007.

88. Ibid.

89. Adam Walinsky, in discussion with the author, June 10, 2005.

90. John Seigenthaler, in discussion with the author, November 15, 2007.

91. Ibid.

92. Ibid.

93. Ibid.

94. Darlene Corbin, in discussion with the author, December 11, 2007.

95. Kathleen Kennedy Townsend, in discussion with the author, December 18, 2007.

96. Adam Walinsky, in discussion with the author, June 10, 2005.

97. Shesol, *Mutual Contempt*, 183.

98. Kathleen Kennedy Townsend, in discussion with the author, December 18, 2007.

99. Drew Pearson, "R. Kennedy Refused Bow to LBJ," *Washington Post*, July 6, 1965, B11.

100. Adam Walinsky, in discussion with the author, June 10, 2005.

101. Ibid.

102. Frida Shankman, in discussion with the author, 2007.

103. Adam Walinsky, in discussion with the author, June 10, 2005.

104. Memorandum from C. D. DeLoach to Mr. Mohr, "Paul Corbin; House Committee on Un-American Activities," Federal Bureau of Investigation, July 27, 1962.

105. United Press International, "Inquiry Is Planned on Democratic Aide," *New York Times*, September 1, 1961, 18.

106. "Many Are Wondering."

107. Edward S. Kerstein, "Reds Backed Corbin at Divorce Trial," *Milwaukee Journal*, September 14, 1961.

108. Associated Press, "Bailey Clears Corbin of Red-Link Charges," *Washington Post*, September 9, 1961, A6.

109. "Corbin Data Kept Secret," *Milwaukee Journal*, January 26, 1961.

110. Memorandum from M. A. Jones to Mr. DeLoach, "Paul Corbin," United States Government, February 16, 1962.

111. Memorandum from C. A. Evans to Mr. Belmont, "RE: Paul Corbin," Federal Bureau of Investigation, February 1, 1962.

112. Memorandum from C. A. Evans to Mr. Belmont, "Paul Corbin," United States Government, July 3, 1962.

113. Ray Thomasson, in discussion with the author, February 12, 2007.

114. Federal Bureau of Investigation, Report, "Paul Corbin," file no. 161–84, December 21, 1962, Rockford, IL.

115. Paul Corbin, in discussion with the author.

116. Memorandum from SAC, WFO, to Director FBI, "Paul Corbin SPI," file no. 161–107, Federal Bureau of Investigation, December 19, 1966.

117. Memorandum from SAC, Omaha, to Director FBI, "Paul Corbin Aka, SPI Dash Perjury," file no. 161–14, Federal Bureau of Investigation, December 13, 1962.

118. Memorandum, unsigned, Federal Bureau of Investigation.

119. Judith Martin, "New Frontiersmen Stake Out a Homestead," *Washington Post*, June 9, 1963, F8.

120. Adam Walinsky, in discussion with the author, June 10, 2005.

121. Lyndon B. Johnson to John Bailey, telephone conversation, tape: WH6402.14, February 11, 1964, Lyndon Baines Johnson Presidential Library, Austin, TX.

122. Ibid.; Lyndon B. Johnson to Ken O'Donnell, telephone conversation, tape: WH6402.14, February 11, 1964, Lyndon Baines Johnson Presidential Library, Austin, TX; Lyndon B. Johnson to Ben Bradlee and Jack Valenti, telephone conversation, tape: WH6403.04, March 7, 1964, Lyndon Baines Johnson Presidential Library, Austin, TX; Lyndon B. Johnson to Bill Moyers, telephone conversation, tape: WH6403.07, March 9, 1964, Lyndon Baines Johnson Presidential Library, Austin, TX; Lyndon B. Johnson to Larry O'Brien, telephone conversation, tape: WH6403.09, March 11, 1964, Lyndon Baines Johnson Presidential Library, Austin, TX.

123. Anthony Lewis, "Kennedy Denies a Johnson Feud," *New York Times*, March 13, 1964, 1.

124. Memorandum from N. P. Callahan to the Director, "The Congressional Record," United States Government, April 6, 1964.

125. "The Choice of Humphrey, Step by Step," *New York Times*, August 27, 1964, 1.

126. Paul Corbin, in discussion with the author.

127. Joseph A. Loftus, "'Draft Kennedy' Unit Files in Wisconsin," *New York Times*, March 11, 1964, 1.

128. Adam Walinsky, in discussion with the author, June 10, 2005.

129. Kathleen Kennedy Townsend, in discussion with the author, December 18, 2007.

130. Adam Walinsky, in discussion with the author, June 10, 2005.

131. Kathleen Kennedy Townsend, in discussion with the author, December 18, 2007.

132. Adam Walinsky, in discussion with the author, June 10, 2005.

133. John Seigenthaler, in discussion with the author, March 25, 2008.

134. Ibid.

135. Ray Thomasson, in discussion with the author, February 12, 2007; Joseph Sweat, in discussion with the author, February 12, 2007.

136. "Ray Blanton: A Synonym for Controversy," United Press International, June 9, 1981.

137. Sue Allison, "Blanton Takes Political Spotlight," United Press International, July 30, 1988.

138. Ray Thomasson, in discussion with the author, February 12, 2007; Joseph Sweat, in discussion with the author, February 12, 2007; Kirk Loggins, "Legendary Sheriff Fate Thomas Dies," *Tennessean*, July 26, 2000, 1A.

139. Joseph Sweat, in discussion with the author, February 12, 2007.

140. Ray Thomasson, in discussion with the author, February 12, 2007.

141. Joseph Sweat, in discussion with the author, February 12, 2007.

142. Adam Walinsky, in discussion with the author, June 10, 2005.

143. John Seigenthaler, in discussion with the author, November 15, 2007.

144. Bill Peterson and Basil Talbott Jr., "Carter Scores in Iowa Straw Ballot, but Kennedy Parries in Cook County," *Washington Post*, November 6, 1979, A6; David S. Broder, "It Was a Family Picnic, Touched by Eloquence and Poignancy," *Washington Post*, October 21, 1979, A4.

145. Walter Mondale, in discussion with the author, February 28, 2007.

146. Jimmy Carter Presidential Library, Atlanta, GA, "Oral Histories at the Jimmy Carter Library," http://www.jimmycarterlibrary.org/library/oralhist.phtml; Dom Bonafede, "At the White House, You Can't Tell the Players without a Scorecard," *National Journal*, October 6, 1979, 1641.

147. Bonafede, "At the White House"; Broder, "It Was a Family Picnic."

148. Bonafede, "At the White House"; Alice J. Porter, "All the President's Men and Women," *National Journal*, November 17, 1979, 195; Associated Press, November 11, 1979; Robert Dunn, in discussion with the author, June 23, 2009.

149. "The FBI Didn't Even Ring Once," *Washington Post*, March 18, 1984, C4.

150. Porter, "All the President's Men and Women."

151. Bill Schulz, in discussion with the author, January 23, 2007.

152. Ibid.

153. David Keene, in discussion with the author; Adam Walinsky, in discussion with the author, June 10, 2005.

154. Charles Bartlett, in discussion with the author, November 4, 2007.

155. "Casey Affidavit," *Washington Post*, May 24, 1984, A16.

156. Gregory Gordon, "Casey Submits to House Interview," United Press International, November 9, 1983.

157. Mary McGrory, "Where's the Liar?" *Washington Post*, May 27, 1984, C1.

158. David Keene, in discussion with the author, June 10, 2005.

159. David Keene, in discussion with the author, October 10, 2006; Adam Walinsky, in discussion with the author, June 10, 2005.

160. Patrick Lucey, in discussion with the author, December 5, 2006.

161. House Committee report, 114.

162. Ibid., 114; Gregory Gordon, "Consultant Visited Casey's Office Three Days Before Debate," United Press International, January 8, 1984.

163. Howard Kurtz, "Timing of Visit Poses Questions in Debate Case," *Washington Post*, January 9, 1984, A5.

164. House Committee report, 114–15.

165. Gregory Gordon, "The Briefing Papers Mystery: Leaked? Stolen? Investigations Spawn Contradictions, Unanswered Questions," United Press International, July 24, 1983.

166. House Committee report, 101–2.

167. Gerald Rafshoon, in discussion with the author, March 20, 2008.

168. Joseph E. Persico, *Casey: From the OSS to the CIA* (New York: Viking, 1990), 331.

169. Weather Underground, Daily History for the District of Columbia, October 25, 1980, http://www.wunderground.com/history/airport/KDCA/1980/10/25/DailyHistory.html?req_city=Washington&req_state=DC&req_statename=District+of+Columbia.

170. Stefan Halper, in discussion with the author, March 20, 2007.

171. House Committee report, 114.

172. Ibid., 7, 104.

173. Ibid., 109–110.

174. Ibid., 105.

175. Wayne Valis, in discussion with the author, March 27, 2008.

176. House Committee report, 5–6.

177. Martin Schram, "'Preposterous': Carter Aide Says Debate-Book Rumor Dismissed," *Washington Post*, July 10, 1983, A1.

178. Laurence I. Barrett, *Gambling with History: Ronald Reagan in the White House* (New York: Penguin Books, 1984), 382.

179. House Committee report, 6–7.

180. David M. Alpern, Elaine Shannon, and Gloria Borger, "The Issue That Won't Die," *Newsweek*, June 4, 1984, 24.

181. Wayne Valis, in discussion with the author, March 27, 2008.

182. House Committee report, 91–92.

183. Ibid., 98.

184. Adam Walinsky, in discussion with the author, June 10, 2005.

185. Phil Gailey, "Casey Made Call on Carter Papers," *New York Times*, July 4, 1983, 8.

186. House Committee report, 113, 123; Mike Feinsilber, Associated Press, May 24, 1984.

187. Martin Tolchin, "Inquiry on Carter Data Said to Focus on 2 Men," *New York Times*, December 7, 1983, A15.

188. House Committee report, 114.

189. Ibid., 74.

190. Ibid., 95.

191. Don Albosta, in discussion with the author, January 5, 2007.

192. House Committee report, 3.

193. Ibid., 100.

194. Ibid., 124.

195. Don Albosta, in discussion with the author, January 5, 2007.

196. House Committee report, 111–12.

197. James Baker, in discussion with the author, September 6, 2006.

198. Persico, *Casey*, 329.

199. Richard Cheney, in discussion with the author, March 19, 2007; Persico, *Casey*, 327, 329.

200. Tolchin, "Inquiry on Carter Data."

201. House Committee report, 2073.

202. Adam Walinsky, in discussion with the author, June 10, 2005.

203. "The Weather," *Washington Post*, June 5, 1981, B2.

204. Kathleen Kennedy Townsend, in discussion with the author, December 18, 2007.

205. Elisabeth Bumiller, "RFK and the Spirit of a Generation," *Washington Post*, June 6, 1981, C1.

206. B. Drummond Ayres Jr., "Reagan Joins a Kennedy Remembrance," *New York Times*, June 6, 1981, 1.

207. "Newsmakers," *Newsweek*, June 15, 1981, 57.

CHAPTER 29: GENERAL QUARTERS

1. Douglas E. Kneeland, "Reagan Resting Up at Ranch on Coast," *New York Times*, August 14, 1980, A21.

2. Alison Muscatine, "Reagan's Neighbors Shun Life in Fishbowl," *Washington Star*, August 16, 1980, A3.

3. Alison Muscatine, "Reagan Critical of the Oratory at Convention," *Washington Star*, August 15, 1980.

4. United Press International, "Parties' Platforms: The Contrasts on Issues," *New York Times*, August 18, 1980, A14.

5. Robert G. Kaiser, "The Jewish Voter: Giving Up on Carter," *Washington Post*, August 17, 1980, A6.

6. Associated Press, "115 Million Saw Convention, NBC Estimates," *Washington Star*, August 16, 1980, A3.

7. John W. Mashek, "Carter's Second Chance," *U.S. News & World Report*, August 25, 1980, 16.

8. "Carter Family: 'Old Pros' on Campaign Trail," *U.S. News & World Report*, August 25, 1980, 58.

9. "How Carter Plans to Win; Needed: 270 Electoral Votes," *U.S. News & World Report*, August 25, 1980, 18; Memorandum from Karl Struble to Tim Kraft, "General Election Observations," May 12, 1980, Carter/Mondale Presidential Committee, Jimmy Carter Presidential Library, Atlanta, GA.

10. Memorandum from Tim Finchem to Hamilton Jordan, Jack Watson, and Landon Butler, "Political Appointees Fundraising Program—Talking Points," September 26, 1980, Carter/Mondale Re-Election Committee, Box 142, Jimmy Carter Presidential Library, Atlanta, GA.

11. Lisa Myers, "Carter Camp Shows Signs of Strategy Split," *Washington Star*, August 16, 1980, A1.

12. James M. Perry, "Carter Plans to Win by Depicting Reagan as Shallow, Dangerous," *Wall Street Journal*, August 14, 1980, 1.

13. Myers, "Carter Camp Shows Signs of Strategy Split."

14. Jack W. Germond and Jules Witcover, "Carter Is Stuck on Defensive as Clock Ticks," *Washington Star*, August 8, 1980, A3.

15. Memorandum from Tim Smith to Hamilton Jordan and Bob Strauss, "Preliminary Debate Discussions," August 21, 1980, Carter/Mondale Presidential Committee, Box 55, Jimmy Carter Presidential Library, Atlanta, GA.

16. Terence Hunt, "Reagan Proposes Only Two Campaign Debates," Associated Press, August 25, 1980.

17. "An Interview with Mondale," *Time*, August 25, 1980.

18. Lou Cannon, "Reagan: 'Peace Through Strength,'" *Washington Post*, August 19, 1980, A1.

19. Frank Reynolds, *World News Tonight*, ABC News Transcripts, August 18, 1980; Associated Press, "Reagan Calls Vietnam War a 'Noble Cause,'" *Los Angeles Times*, August 18, 1980, A2.

20. Martin Schram, Lou Cannon, Robert G. Kaiser, Edward Walsh, and Maralee Schwartz, "Post-Convention Surge," *Washington Post*, August 20, 1980, A1.

21. Ibid.

22. Lou Cannon, "Reagan Asserts U.S. Security Is in Jeopardy," *Washington Post*, August 21, 1980, A2.

23. Thomas J. Foley and Stewart Powell, "Could Anderson Be President?" *U.S. News & World Report*, August 11, 1980, 25.

24. "Candidates Battle Over Defense Policy," Associated Press, August 19, 1980.

25. David S. Broder and Robert G. Kaiser, "Anderson Close to Selecting Wisconsin Democrat Lucey," *Washington Post*, August 22, 1980, A1.

26. Associated Press, "Reagan and Bush to Stump in New Jersey Over Holiday," *New York Times*, August 29, 1980, A14.

27. Jeremiah O'Leary, "Carter Picks in Picnic in South for 1980 Campaign Kickoff," *Washington Star*, August 24, 1980, A3.

28. United Press International, "Bush to Open Campaign with Portland, Me., Rally," *New York Times*, August 26, 1980, B7.

29. O'Leary, "Carter Picks Picnic in South for 1980 Campaign Kickoff."

30. Howell Raines, "Reagan Campaign Runs into Unexpected Obstacles," *New York Times*, August 24, 1980, 28.

31. James J. Kilpatrick, "For Reagan, the Noble Truth Will Serve Well," *Los Angeles Times*, August 29, 1980, F11.

32. Rowland Evans and Robert Novak, "Making Reagan 'Fail-Safe,'" *Washington Post*, August 22, 1980, A15.

33. Henry S. Bradsher, "Muskie Reiterates U.S.'s Mild Response," *Washington Star*, August 23, 1980, A1.

34. Katharine Macdonald, "Reagan Acts to Reassure Peking on Ties," *Washington Post*, August 17, 1980, A4.

35. John Brecher and Melida Liu, "Bush Bombs in Peking," *Newsweek*, September 1, 1980, 33.

36. Jay Mathews, "Chinese Reiterate Attack on Reagan's Taiwan Stand," *Washington Post*, August 23, 1980, A4.

37. Peter Goldman, Gerald C. Lubenow, Thomas M. DeFrank, and Stryker McGuire, "The Battle of the Button," *Newsweek*, September 1, 1980, 18.

38. Lisa Myers, "Reagan Bids for Vote of Evangelicals," *Washington Star*, August 23, 1980, A3.

39. Kathy Sawyer, Lou Cannon, Don Oberdorfer, and Marylou Lawrence, "Reagan Sticks to Stand on Taiwan Ties," *Washington Post*, August 23, 1980, A1.

40. Raines, "Reagan Campaign Runs into Unexpected Obstacles."

41. Myers, "Reagan Bids for Vote of Evangelicals."

42. John F. Stacks, "Going Straight for the Jugular," *Time*, August 25, 1980.

43. Memorandum from Struble to Kraft, "General Election Observations."

44. "An Interview with Mondale."

45. Jim Laurie, *World News Tonight*, ABC News Transcripts, August 21, 1980.

46. Sawyer et al., "Reagan Sticks to Stand on Taiwan Ties."

47. United Press International, "Carter Policy on China Wins Ford's Approval," *New York Times*, September 1, 1980, A7.

48. "Reagan Will Face Press Today," *Los Angeles Times*, August 25, 1980, B12.

49. Jack W. Germond, "Reagan Wants Improved Ties with Taiwan," *Washington Star*, August 26, 1980, A1.

50. Howell Raines, "Reagan, Conceding Misstatements, Abandons Plan on Taiwan Office," *New York Times*, August 26, 1980, A1.

51. Howell Raines, "Reagan Campaign Problems," *New York Times*, August 27, 1980, A17.

52. Jack W. Germond and Jules Witcover, "Reagan Forgets China Policy Is Unneeded Issue," *Washington Star*, August 26, 1980, A3.

53. David Wood, "Lucey Makes It Official: He's on Anderson Ticket," *Washington Star*, August 26, 1980, A3.

54. Lisa Myers, "Kennedy to Support Entire Ticket 'Actively,'" *Washington Star*, August 26, 1980, A3.

55. Lee Byrd, "Anderson Finds His Stretch for the Stretch Drive a Painful One," Associated Press, August 29, 1980.

56. Donald M. Rothberg, "Reagan Would Debate Carter If Anderson Included," Associated Press, August 27, 1980.

57. Dan Carmichael, "Washington News," United Press International, September 26, 1987.

58. Richard Bergholz, "Reagan Says Carter Has Created a 'Severe Depression,'" *Los Angeles Times*, August 28, 1980, B11.

59. Jack W. Germond, "Reagan Labels Carter Cause of 'Depression,'" *Washington Star*, August 27, 1980, A3.

60. Gerald F. Seib, "Reagan Sees U.S. in 'Severe Depression,' 'Molded by Carter,' but Word Stirs Debate," *Wall Street Journal*, August 28, 1980, 2.

61. Steven Rattner, "Bid to Widen Voter Support," *New York Times*, August 29, 1980, 1.

62. Jimmy Carter, in discussion with the author, July 11, 2006.

63. "Reagan Sees Flaws in Carter's Program," *New York Times*, August 29, 1980, D13.

64. Mike Causey, "The Federal Diary," *Washington Post*, August 28, 1980, B2.

65. Richard Bergholz, "Reagan Calls Carter Program 'Quick Fix,'" *Los Angeles Times*, August 29, 1980, B4.

66. John Anderson, in discussion with the author, December 10, 2007.

67. David Wood, "Anderson Shakes Up Staff, Giving Garth Total Control," *Washington Star*, August 29, 1980, A3.

68. Jack W. Germond, "Reagan Seeks to Get Campaign on Track," *Washington Star*, August 29, 1980, A3.

69. Stuart Spencer, in discussion with the author, September 28, 2006.

70. Germond, "Reagan Seeks to Get Campaign on Track."

71. Barry Serafin, *World News Tonight*, ABC News Transcripts, August 29, 1980.

72. Ken Khachigian, in discussion with the author, May 2007.

73. Mary Thornton, "Carter, Reagan Neck and Neck in Roper Survey," *Washington Star*, August 30, 1980, A3.

74. Germond, "Reagan Seeks to Get Campaign on Track."

75. Timothy D. Schellhardt, "President to Stress His Wide Differences with Reagan During Bid for Reelection," *Wall Street Journal*, August 29, 1980, 4.

CHAPTER 30: SLOUCHING TOWARDS NOVEMBER

1. Associated Press, "Out of Mental Hospital, Candidate Maps Campaign," *New York Times*, September 6, 1980, 8.

2. John W. Mashek, "Campaign Kickoff; Has Reagan Dropped the Ball?" *U.S. News & World Report*, September 8, 1980, 20.

3. Richard Bergholz, "Reagan Deplores Economy; Carter Seeks to Hold Dixie," *Los Angeles Times*, September 2, 1980, B1.

4. Steven R. Weisman, "President Denounces the Klan," *New York Times*, September 2, 1980, A1.

5. Bergholz, "Reagan Deplores Economy."

6. Edward Walsh, "Carter to Return to 'Peace or War' Issue," *Washington Post*, September 28, 1980, A2.

7. Carla Hall, "Liberty and Unions Forever," *Washington Post*, September 2, 1980, B1.

8. Timothy D. Schellhardt, "Carter Strikes Hard at Reagan, by Name, Claiming Nuclear Arms Race Threatened," *Wall Street Journal*, September 3, 1980, 4.

9. Walter R. Mears, "Reagan's Pitch Suffers from Throwaways," Associated Press, September 3, 1980; "Reagan Klan Remark Stirs Furor," *Facts on File World News Digest*, September 5, 1980.

10. Schellhardt, "Carter Strikes Hard at Reagan."

11. Lou Cannon, *Reagan* (New York: G. P. Putnam's Sons, 1982), 274.

12. Martin Schram, Lou Cannon, Edward Walsh, and Valarie Thomas, "Reagan Beats a Retreat on Klan Remark," *Washington Post*, September 3, 1980, A1.

13. Michele Davis, in discussion with the author, March 14, 2008.

14. Andrew Young, "Chilling Words in Neshoba County," *Washington Post*, August 11, 1980, A19.

15. Schellhardt, "Carter Strikes Hard at Reagan."

16. David Treadwell, "Democrats Mobilize to Register Blacks," *Los Angeles Times*, September 4, 1980, B15.

17. Hamilton Jordan, *Crisis: The Last Year of the Carter Presidency* (New York: G. P. Putnam's Sons, 1982), 339.

18. Rowland Evans and Robert Novak, "Carter's Resurgence," *Washington Post*, September 5, 1980, A11.

19. James R. Dickenson, "Reagan Issues Apology for Klan Remarks," *Washington Star*, September 3, 1980, A1.

20. John F. Stacks, "Going Straight for the Jugular," *Time*, August 25, 1980.

21. Memorandum from Karl Struble to Tim Kraft, "General Election Observations," May 12, 1980, Carter/Mondale Presidential Committee, Jimmy Carter Presidential Library, Atlanta, GA.

22. Edward Walsh, "'Serious Threat' to Peace Seen," *Washington Post*, September 3, 1980, A1.

23. Richard Bergholz, "President Invokes Truman Aura as He Attacks Reagan," *Los Angeles Times*, September 3, 1980, B15.

24. Walsh, "'Serious Threat' to Peace Seen."

25. Bergholz, "President Invokes Truman Aura as He Attacks Reagan."

26. Roger Stone, in discussion with the author.

27. Memorandum, unsigned, "Governor Reagan's Visit to Liberty State Park, NJ," August 31, 1980, Colin Clark Archives Collection.

28. Lou Cannon, "Reagan; Castigating the 'Betrayal' of Workers' Aspirations," *Washington Post*, September 2, 1980, A1.

29. Howell Raines, "Republican Stresses Economy," *New York Times*, September 2, 1980, A1.

30. Cannon, "Reagan; Castigating the 'Betrayal' of Workers' Aspirations."

31. Ibid.

32. Lou Cannon and David S. Broder, "Reagan Vows to Try to Halt 'Deluge' of Japanese Autos," *Washington Post*, September 3, 1980, A2.

33. Douglas E. Kneeland, "Reagan Accuses Carter of Breaking Faith with Israel," *New York Times*, September 4, 1980, A1; Steven V. Roberts, "Jews at B'nai B'rith Parley Voice Disappointment in Carter," *New York Times*, September 6, 1980, A8.

34. "Reagan Says Carter Has Undermined Security of Israel," *Wall Street Journal*, September 4, 1980, 18.

35. Lou Cannon, John M. Goshko, and Martin Schram, "Reagan: Carter Imperils Israel," *Washington Post*, September 4, 1980, A1.

36. Roberts, "Jews at B'nai B'rith Parley Voice Disappointment in Carter."

37. W. Dale Nelson, "Pro-Reagan Group Attacks Democratic Broadcast Move," Associated Press, September 10, 1980.

38. Myra MacPherson, "The New Right Brigade," *Washington Post*, August 10, 1980, F1.

39. Bill Peterson, "FEC Rules Anderson Eligible for Funds," *Washington Post*, September 5, 1980, A3.

40. Richard Bergholz, "Carter Woos Pennsylvania Ethnic Votes, Hits Reagan Remarks on Social Security," *Los Angeles Times*, September 4, 1980, A16.

41. Brooks Jackson, "Reagan Vows to Defend Social Security in Rejoinder to Carter Campaign Attack," *Wall Street Journal*, September 8, 1980, 7.

42. Bergholz, "Carter Woos Pennsylvania Ethnic Votes."

43. Jackson, "Reagan Vows to Defend Social Security in Rejoinder to Carter Campaign Attack."

44. Douglas E. Kneeland, "Reagan Vows to Support Social Security Program," *New York Times*, September 8, 1980, B10.

45. "What's News," *Wall Street Journal*, September 4, 1980, 1.

46. Allan J. Mayer, Eleanor Clift, and Thomas M. DeFrank, "Oh, I'll Take the Low Road," *Newsweek*, September 29, 1980, 22.

47. Peter Goldman, Eleanor Clift, Thomas M. DeFank, James Doyle, John Walcott, and Howard Fineman, "Now for the Hard Part," *Newsweek*, August 25, 1980, 18.

48. Albert R. Hunt, "Reagan Accuses White House of Leaking U.S. Security Data for Political Purposes," *Wall Street Journal*, September 5, 1980, 6.

49. Jeremiah O'Leary and John J. Fialka, "White House Calls Reagan Charge False," *Washington Star*, September 6, 1980, A1.

50. Douglas E. Kneeland, "Kissinger Backs Reagan on Secret Plane Charge," *New York Times*, September 6, 1980, A8; Lawrence L. Knutson, "Reagan Defense Aides Rap Disclosure," Associated Press, September 10, 1980.

51. Douglas E. Kneeland, "Reagan Assails Carter Over Disclosure of Secret Plane," *New York Times*, September 5, 1980, A19.

52. Paul Blustein, "How a Sick Ronald Reagan Rumor Sent Shiver Down Investors' Spines," *Wall Street Journal*, September 5, 1980, 17.

53. Martin Schram, "Reagan's Problems Like Carter's in '76," *Washington Post*, September 7, 1980, A1.

54. Cristine Russell, "Aquarian Reagan Reassures the Scientists," *Washington Star*, September 5, 1980, A4.

55. Allan J. Mayer, Thomas DeFrank, Gloria Borger, and Gerald C. Lubenow, "A Debate Over the Debates," *Newsweek*, September 8, 1980, 18.

56. Ibid.

57. Tom Morganthau and Richard Manning, "John Anderson's Troubles," *Newsweek*, September 1, 1980, 24.

58. Mayer et al., "A Debate Over the Debates."

59. James R. Dickenson, "Reagan Charges Carter Revealed Secrets on 'Stealth' to Boost Re-election Chances," *Washington Star*, September 5, 1980.

60. Roberta Hornig and Phil Galley, "Libya Money Described as 'Gift' to Billy," *Washington Star*, September 5, 1980, A1.

61. United Press International, "Reagan Campaign Chief Says Civiletti Ought to Leave Post," *Washington Star*, September 5, 1980, A4.

62. Hedrick Smith, "Reagan Given an Edge in 'Big 9' Battleground States," *New York Times*, September 14, 1980, 32; Anthony Lewis, "The Anderson Difference," *New York Times*, September 11, 1980, A18; United Press International, "Connecticut," *Washington Star*, September 2, 1980, A3.

63. Hedrick Smith, "Decision Day for Participation in the Presidential Debates," *New York Times*, September 9, 1980, D18.

64. Maurice Carroll, "Javits Campaign Aides Call a Low Turnout Chief Fear," *New York Times*, September 1, 1980, B1.

65. Smith, "Decision Day for Participation in the Presidential Debates."

66. Hedrick Smith, "Carter Declines to Debate After Anderson Is Invited," *New York Times*, September 10, 1980, A1.

67. Bernard Weinraub, "Carter's New TV Ads Stress Complexity of His Job," *New York Times*, September 7, 1980, A33.

68. Robert G. Kaiser, "Candidates on TV: Reagan Goes Low-Key, Carter Goes Dramatic," *Washington Post*, September 9, 1980, A2.

69. Francis X. Clines, "Time for the Song and 'Nuance Man,'" *New York Times*, September 25, 1980, B10.

70. "Campaign Notes," *Washington Post*, September 8, 1980, A4.

71. John Herbers, "Nixon Views Carter: 'Shrewd' with 'Ruthless' Staff," *New York Times*, September 8, 1980, B7.

72. James David Barber, "Worrying About Reagan," *New York Times*, September 8, 1980, A19.

73. Douglas E. Kneeland, "Reagan Offers Plan to Cut Taxes, Balance Budget, Restore Defenses," *New York Times*, September 10, 1980, A1.

74. "Anderson Feels He Can Retrieve White House for GOP," Associated Press, January 9, 1980.

75. Kneeland, "Reagan Offers Plan to Cut Taxes, Balance Budget, Restore Defenses."

76. Lou Cannon, "Reagan Scales Down Plan for Patching Up Economy," *Washington Post*, September 10, 1980, A1.

77. Kneeland, "Reagan Offers Plan to Cut Taxes, Balance Budget, Restore Defenses."

78. Jonathan Fuerbringer, "Key Groups Call Policy 'Disastrous,'" *Washington Star*, September 10, 1980, A1.

79. Allan J. Mayer and Rich Thomas, "Reaganomics, New Version," *Newsweek*, September 22, 1980, 27.

80. Terence Smith, "Mondale, Ending 2-Day Tour, Is Pressed to Defend Carter's Stand on Debates," *New York Times*, September 11, 1980, D18.

81. Douglas E. Kneeland, "Reagan Presses Carter on Charge of Misleading Nation on Energy," *New York Times*, September 12, 1980, D14.

82. Howell Raines, "Reporter's Notebook: Reagan Gropes for Old 'Magic' to Reawaken Crowds," *New York Times*, September 15, 1980, B12.

83. Judy Bachrach, "Cocaine Adds an Unpleasant Political Twist," *Washington Star*, September 29, 1980, A4.

84. Ibid.

85. Hedrick Smith, "Reagan's Packagers Worry Over Loose Ends," *New York Times*, September 7, 1980, E2.

86. Albert R. Hunt, "Reagan Drive Wobbles as Nominee Misspeaks and His Advisers Feud," *Wall Street Journal*, September 4, 1980, 1.

87. Jay Perkins, "Bush Says Democrats Trying to Hide Their Record," Associated Press, September 4, 1980.

88. Robert Shogan, "Reagan Supporters Believe Blunders Can Be Remedied," *Los Angeles Times*, September 7, 1980, A16.

89. Jordan, *Crisis*, 339.

90. Barry Sussman and Paul Ferber, "Economic Prospects Give Carter Edge," *Washington Post*, September 14, 1980, A1.

CHAPTER 31: THE TORRENTS OF AUTUMN

1. James R. Dickenson, "Reagan Assures Aged He Backs Social Security," *Washington Star*, September 8, 1980, A4.

2. Jeremiah O'Leary, "Carter Warns Aides of GOP 'Distortions,'" *Washington Star*, September 13, 1980, A3.

3. "Politicians Rate Reagan Ahead in Electoral Battle," *Washington Star*, September 11, 1980.

4. Douglas Brew, "Bush Says Foes Deal in 'Innuendo,'" *Washington Star*, September 12, 1980.

5. Howell Raines, "Lyn Nofziger: Barometer in Reagan Strategy Shift," *New York Times*, September 28, 1980, 36.

6. T. R. Reid, "'Bowling,' Candy Part of Ritual on Reagan Campaign Plane," *Washington Post*, September 20, 1980, A3.

7. Bill Prochnau, "'Feeding the Animals,'" *Washington Post*, September 30, 1980, A1.

8. Donald P. Baker, "TV Reporters with Vice President Seldom Appear on the News Shows," *Washington Post*, September 30, 1980, A2.

9. Bill Lauderback, in discussion with the author, August 2, 2006; Gary Hoitsma, in discussion with the author, July 24, 2006.

10. Terence Smith, "Carter Declares Reagan Is 'Muzzled' by Advisers," *New York Times*, September 16, 1980, B4.

11. Associated Press, September 10, 1980.

12. Bernard Gwertzman, "Muskie Discourages Hope That Hostages Will Be Freed Soon," *New York Times*, September 16, 1980, A1.

13. Jimmy Carter, in discussion with the author, July 11, 2006.

14. Martin Tolchin, "Reagan and Others in GOP Vow to Be Unified If They Control Congress," *New York Times*, September 16, 1980, B4.

15. Barry Serafin, *World News Tonight Sunday*, ABC News Transcripts, September 15, 1980.

16. Newt Gingrich, in discussion with the author, May 21, 2006.

17. Dennis Farney, "'New Right' Adherents in Congress Now Play Mainly Defensive Role," *Wall Street Journal*, September 16, 1980, 1.

18. James Mann and Sarah A. Peterson, "Preachers in Politics: Decisive Force in '80?" *U.S. News & World Report*, September 15, 1980, 24.

19. George Skelton, "Reagan Gains with Some Evangelicals," *Los Angeles Times*, September 17, 1980, B4.

20. Pat Robertson, "Preachers in Politics," *U.S. News & World Report*, September 29, 1980, 3.

21. "Christian Right Equated with Iran's Mullahs," *Washington Star*, September 24, 1980, A4.

22. Mann and Peterson, "Preachers in Politics."

23. Adam Clymer, "Reagan Viewed in Poll as Leader; Carter Cited on Concern for People," *New York Times*, September 17, 1980, A1.

24. Martin Schram, "President Voices Optimism, Muskie Wary on Hostages," *Washington Post*, September 16, 1980, A1.

25. Francis X. Clines, "Carter Suggests Turn to Racism in Reagan Views," *New York Times*, September 17, 1980, B10.

26. Lyn Nofziger, in discussion with the author.

27. Michael K. Deaver, *A Different Drummer: My Thirty Years with Ronald Reagan* (New York: HarperCollins, 2001), 186.

28. Martin Schram, "Carter Says Reagan Injects Racism: President Says Reagan Has Injected Hatred and Racism into Campaign," *Washington Post*, September 17, 1980, A1.

29. United Press International, "Carter Gets Tip from an Old Foe of Reagan," *Washington Star*, September 15, 1980, A3.

30. Eleanor Randolph, "Carter Says Reagan Abets Racial Unrest," *Los Angeles Times*, September 17, 1980, B19.

31. Howell Raines, "Reagan Woos the Mexican-Americans," *New York Times*, September 17, 1980, B10.

32. Gregory Nokes, "Bush Hits Carter's Comments on Reagan's Civil Rights Record," Associated Press, September 17, 1980; Steven R. Weisman, "Bush Assails Carter on 'Ugly Insinuations' of Racism," *New York Times*, September 18, 1980, B10.

33. Harry F. Rosenthal, "Ford Assails Carter Campaign Rhetoric," Associated Press, September 18, 1980.

34. Mary McGrory, "Character Isn't Carter's Issue in This Campaign," *Washington Star*, September 26, 1980, A4.

35. Hamilton Jordan, *Crisis: The Last Year of the Carter Presidency* (New York: G. P. Putnam's Sons, 1982), 343.

36. T. R. Reid, "Reagan Chastises Carter for No-Show in 1st Debate," *Washington Post*, September 18, 1980, A5.

37. "Transcript of the President's News Conference on Foreign and Domestic Matters," *New York Times*, September 19, 1980, B5.

38. Terence Smith, "Carter Says He Isn't Terming Reagan Racist," *New York Times*, September 19, 1980, B4.

39. Eleanor Randolph and Richard Bergholz, "Carter Denies Suggesting That Reagan Is a Racist," *Los Angeles Times*, September 19, 1980, B1.

40. Smith, "Carter Says He Isn't Terming Reagan Racist."

41. Randolph and Bergholz, "Carter Denies Suggesting That Reagan Is a Racist."

42. Lisa Myers, "President Backs Off 'Racism,'" *Washington Star*, September 19, 1980, A1.

43. Associated Press, "Reagan Camp Objects," *Washington Star*, September 19, 1980.

44. Lance Gay, "New Carter Ad Campaign Raises Race Charge Again," *Washington Star*, September 20, 1980, A1.

45. Adam Clymer, "Carter Campaign Ad Attacked as a 'Smear,'" *New York Times*, September 21, 1980, 34.

46. Patrick Caddell, in discussion with the author, May 13, 2009.

47. Editorial, "Running Mean," *Washington Post*, September 18, 1980, A18.

48. James Reston, "What Ails Carter?" *New York Times*, September 21, 1980, E19.

49. Jack W. Germond and Jules Witcover, "Racism Charge Is Risky Ground for President," *Washington Star*, September 17, 1980, A3.

50. Reston, "What Ails Carter?"

51. Hugh Sidey, "More Than a Candidate," *Time*, September 29, 1980,

52. Clymer, "Carter Campaign Ad Attacked as a 'Smear.'"

53. John H. Averill, "Reagan Accuses Carter of Trying to Hide '81 Deficit," *Los Angeles Times*, September 20, 1980, A28.

54. United Press International, "Reagan Aide Hits Carter 'Mudthrowing,'" *Washington Post*, September 20, 1980, A4.

55. "Laxalt Calls Carter Hypocrite on Rights," *Washington Star*, September 20, 1980, A3.

56. David M. Alpern, Eleanor Clift, Gloria Borger, Thomas M. DeFrank, "And Then There Were Two," *Newsweek*, September 22, 1980, 22.

57. Jack Nelson, "Reagan Backs Legalizing Mexican Aliens, Letting Them Stay as Long as They Want," *Los Angeles Times*, September 17, 1980, B20.

58. Howell Raines, "League Eliminates Chair from Debate," *New York Times*, September 18, 1980, B10.

59. Felicity Barringer and Dale Russakoff, "Baltimore's 2 Faces: A Stage for the Great Debate, Rubble and Renovation," *Washington Post*, September 22, 1980, A10.

60. United Press International, "Public Limited to 100 Seats," *New York Times*, September 18, 1980, B10.

61. Associated Press, "Moyers to Be Moderator for First Campaign Debate," *New York Times*, September 19, 1980, B4.

62. Jules Witcover, "Two Candidates Differ on Most Issues in Debate," *Washington Star*, September 22, 1980, A1.

63. "Transcript of Campaign's First Presidential Debate, with Reagan vs. Anderson," *New York Times*, September 22, 1980, B6.

64. David S. Broder, Lou Cannon, Bill Peterson, and Maralee Schwartz, "Debate Shows Rivals' Wide Differences," *Washington Post*, September 22, 1980, A1.

65. United Press International, September 27, 1980.

66. Walter Isaacson, Christopher Ogden, and Douglas Brew, "Throwing High and Inside," *Time*, September 29, 1980,

67. Phil Gailey, "New Carter Remarks Keep the Issue Alive," *Washington Star*, September 24, 1980, A1.

68. "What's News," *Wall Street Journal*, September 24, 1980, 1.

69. Lisa Myers, "Reagan Describes Carter as Liberal 'McGovernite,'" *Washington Star*, September 23, 1980, A1.

70. Edward Walsh and Lou Cannon, "Carter Assailed for Depicting a Warlike Reagan," *Washington Post*, September 24, 1980, A1.

71. Jack Nelson, "Reagan Upset, Says Carter Implies He's a Warmonger," *Los Angeles Times*, September 24, 1980, B1.

72. Walsh and Cannon, "Carter Assailed for Depicting a Warlike Reagan."

73. Ibid.

74. Lisa Myers, "'Beneath Decency' Challenger Cries," *Washington Star*, September 24, 1980, A1.

75. Associated Press, "Reagan Links Iran-Iraq War to Vacillation by Carter," *New York Times*, September 25, 1980, B11.

76. Ibid.

77. Jack W. Germond and Jules Witcover, "Perhaps Carter Should Leave Reagan Alone," *Washington Star*, September 24, 1980, A3.

78. McGrory, "Character Isn't Carter's Issue in This Campaign."

79. Adam Clymer, "Hostage Issue: The Incumbent's Advantage," *New York Times*, September 25, 1980, B10.

80. United Press International, September 28, 1980.

81. Jordan, *Crisis*, 345.

82. Donald M. Rothberg, "Reagan Uses Carter 'Family Suffering Index,'" Associated Press, September 22, 1980.

83. Lisa Myers, "Reagan Vetoes 2d Debate for Anderson, Hits Carter," *Washington Star*, September 22, 1980, A4.

84. United Press International, "Candidate Ronald Reagan Autographs a Cast for a Fan During a Campaign Appearance at Springfield, Mo.," *Washington Star*, September 25, 1980, A3.

85. "Reagan the Man Is Easy to Read; the Record Is Not," *Washington Star*, September 29, 1980, A5.

86. Alpern et al., "And Then There Were Two."

87. William Endicott, "Reagan Rejects One-on-One Debate with Carter," *Los Angeles Times*, September 26, 1980, B8.

88. Mike Feinsilber, "League Appealing for Candidates to Agree on Debates," Associated Press, September 27, 1980.

89. United Press International, "Bush Accepts Challenge for Debate with Mondale," *New York Times*, July 23, 1980, A14.

90. George H. W. Bush, in discussion with the author, February 16, 2007; Walter Mondale, in discussion with the author, February 28, 2007.

91. William Endicott, "Rep. McCloskey Endorses Reagan," *Los Angeles Times*, September 26, 1980, B9.

92. Lisa Myers, "Reagan, McCloskey Hold Unity Show in California," *Washington Star*, September 26, 1980, A3.

93. David S. Broder, "Ford Is Campaigning with a Vengeance—Against Carter," *Washington Post*, September 26, 1980, A4.

94. Associated Press, "Reagan Judged Best to Handle U.S. Economy," *Washington Star*, September 27, 1980, A3.

95. Raines, "Lyn Nofziger."

96. Hedrick Smith, "Poll Finds Reagan Leads After Debate," *New York Times*, September 28, 1980, 1; William Endicott, "Reagan Would Be Happy If There Were No More Debates Unless He Slips in Polls," *Los Angeles Times*, September 27, 1980, A28.

CHAPTER 32: MISSION FROM GOD

1. Walter R. Mears, "Reagan Rated Ahead in Presidential Race with Month to Go," Associated Press, October 4, 1980.

2. Barry Sussman and David S. Broder, "Carter, Reagan Close in 7 Key States," *Washington Post*, October 12, 1980, A1.

3. Jeffrey Bell, in discussion with the author.

4. Gene I. Maeroff, "In Spotlight, Reagan's School Is Wary," *New York Times*, September 23, 1980, C1.

5. Advertisement, *New York Times*, September 28, 1980, 56.

6. Bernard Weinraub, "TV Battlefield Tests Presidential Strategies," *New York Times*, October 8, 1980, B8.

7. Robert G. Kaiser, "Carter and Reagan Media Strategies," *Washington Post*, October 12, 1980, A2.

8. Edward Walsh and David S. Border, "Carter Camp Sees Anderson 'Decline,'" *Washington Post*, October 1, 1980, A3.

9. Steven R. Weisman, "Carter Campaign Says Attack Strategy Is Working," *New York Times*, September 26, 1980, A18.

10. Tom Wicker, "A Calculated Contempt," *New York Times*, September 28, 1980, E21.

11. Memorandum from Karl Struble to Tim Kraft, "General Election Observations," May 12, 1980, Carter/Mondale Presidential Committee, Jimmy Carter Presidential Library, Atlanta, GA.

12. "Reagan Accused of 'Duplicity,'" *New York Times*, September 27, 1980, 8.

13. Howell Raines, "Reagan Backs Cautious Advisers in Split on a Debate with Carter," *New York Times*, September 23, 1980, B8.

14. Edward Cowan, "GOP Senators Lose in Bid to Bring Up Tax Cut Legislation," *New York Times*, September 26, 1980, A1.

15. Warren Weaver Jr., "Anderson Assails President for Implying Only He Can Keep World Peace," *New York Times*, September 24, 1980, A26.

16. Warren Weaver Jr., "Anderson Says Carter and Reagan Have 'Folly' Alliance on Atom War," *New York Times*, September 25, 1980, B10.

17. Howell Raines, "Reagan Presses 'High Road' Response," *New York Times*, September 24, 1980, A26.

18. Ibid.

19. Associated Press, "Bush Faults Carter on Foreign Policy," *New York Times*, September 26, 1980, A19.

20. "UPI Survey Shows Reagan Way Ahead," United Press International, October 11, 1980.

21. Jeff Prugh, "The South: It May Not Rise So Solidly Again for Carter," *Los Angeles Times*, October 11, 1980, A1.

22. Howell Raines, "Reagan Is Balancing 2 Different Stances," *New York Times*, October 4, 1980, 9.

23. Hedrick Smith, "Democrats in Jersey Fear Loss of Blue-Collar Vote," *New York Times*, September 26, 1980, A18.

24. Richard Bergholz, "Reagan Renews Call for Parochial-School Tax Credits," *Los Angeles Times*, October 2, 1980, B20.

25. Lou Cannon, "Reagan, Echoing 'New Deal,' Woos Hard-Hats," *Washington Post*, October 2, 1980, A4.

26. James R. Dickenson, "Reagan Claims Carter Copied His Steel Plan," *Washington Star*, October 2, 1980, A3.

27. Robert Shogan, "Carter Assails Reagan on Arms Treaty, Warns of Nuclear Race," *Los Angeles Times*, October 3, 1980, 6.

28. Edward Walsh, "Carter Chides Reagan on Debate Issue," *Washington Post*, October 1, 1980, A2.

29. Robert Shrum, in discussion with the author, March 19, 2008.

30. Sheilah Kast, "Unemployment Declines; Producer Prices Take a Dip," *Washington Star*, October 3, 1980, A1.

31. Edward Walsh, "Carter Loads the Guns of Incumbency," *Washington Post*, October 5, 1980, A1.

32. David Wood, "House Ousts Myers on 376–30 Vote," *Washington Star*, October 3, 1980, A1.

33. Kenneth R. Walker and Adrienne Washington, "Past Bauman Encounters Cited by FBI," *Washington Star*, October 4, 1980, A1.

34. Saundra Saperstein and Donald P. Baker, "Bauman in the Balance," *Washington Post*, October 26, 1980, A1.

35. Judy Bachrach, "Reagan Tries Hard to Avoid Communicating," *Washington Star*, October 3, 1980, A4.

36. Beverly Beyette, "NOW Assails Reagan's 'Medieval Stance on Women,' Withholds Support for Carter," *Los Angeles Times*, October 6, 1980, B8.

37. Wayne Slater, "Mondale Criticizes Reagan on SALT," Associated Press, October 11, 1980.

38. Jan Carroll, "Muskie Assails Reagan as Warmonger," Associated Press, October 11, 1980.

39. B. Drummond Ayres Jr., "Barbs and Gossamer Line First Lady's Political Trail," *New York Times*, October 12, 1980, 34.

40. Philip Shabecoff, "Labor Political Action Groups Mobilize in Bid to Defeat Reagan in Pennsylvania," *New York Times*, October 8, 1980, B6.

41. Steven Rattner, "Rating Carter on the Economy," *New York Times*, October 8, 1980, D1.

42. Clay F. Richards, United Press International, October 6, 1980.

43. Norman C. Miller, "Perspective on Politics," *Wall Street Journal*, October 9, 1980, 28.

44. Richard L. Madden, "Anderson Accuses 2 Foes of 'Low-Level' Politics," *New York Times*, October 8, 1980, B6.

45. Douglas E. Kneeland, "Reagan Declares Carter Is at 'a Point of Hysteria,'" *New York Times*, October 8, 1980, B6.

46. Steven R. Weisman, "Carter Plans Shift in Campaign Tactics," *New York Times*, October 9, 1980, B8.

47. William J. Eaton, "Carter Says He Erred in Sharply Assailing Reagan," *Los Angeles Times*, October 9, 1980, B1.

48. Michele Davis, "1980 Diary," October 8, 1980, Michele Davis Archives Collection.

49. Eaton, "Carter Says He Erred in Sharply Assailing Reagan."

50. Terence Smith, "But President Still Attacks," *New York Times*, October 10, 1980, A1.

51. Eaton, "Carter Says He Erred in Sharply Assailing Reagan."

52. James Gerstenzang, Associated Press, October 8, 1980.

53. Richard L. Madden, "Anderson, in Manhattan, Says Rivals Flip-Flopped," *New York Times*, October 10, 1980, A1.

54. Smith, "But President Still Attacks."

55. Jimmy Carter, *Keeping Faith: Memoirs of a President* (New York: Bantam Books, 1982), 561.

56. Howell Raines, "In Move to the Center, Reagan Plans to Alter 2 Antiunion Positions," *New York Times*, October 9, 1980, A1.

57. Timothy D. Schellhardt, "Scratch One Carter Election Tactic, Courtesy of a Prescient Gov. Reagan," *Wall Street Journal*, October 9, 1980, 31.

58. Raines, "In Move to the Center, Reagan Plans to Alter 2 Antiunion Positions."

59. Joanne Omang, "Reagan Criticizes Clean Air Laws and EPA as Obstacles to Growth," *Washington Post*, October 9, 1980, A2.

60. Winston Williams, "Ohio: The Beat of the Heartland," *New York Times*, October 12, 1980, F1.

61. Lisa Myers, in discussion with the author.

62. Bill Prochnau, "Reagan Endorsement Flouts Union Chief," *Washington Post*, October 11, 1980, A4.

63. United Press International, "Teamster Executive Board Unanimously Backs Reagan," *New York Times*, October 9, 1980, B8.

64. Myron Mintz, in discussion with the author.

65. F. C. Duke Zeller, *Devil's Pact: Inside the World of the Teamsters Union* (Secaucus, NJ: Birch Lane Press, 1996), 47.

66. Mintz, in discussion with the author.

67. Lawrence Martin, "On the Campaign Trail: From Turkeys to Trees to Longshots," *Globe and Mail* (Toronto), October 31, 1980.

68. Lou Cannon, *Governor Reagan: His Rise to Power* (New York: PublicAffairs, 2003), 308.

69. Michele Davis, "1980 Diary," October 7, 1980, Michele Davis Archives Collection.

70. Jack Nelson, "Reagan Denies, Then Affirms Pollution Remark," *Los Angeles Times*, October 10, 1980, 1.

71. Eleanor Randolph, "Reagan Rally in Northridge Draws Backers," *Los Angeles Times*, October 11, 1980, C1.

72. Terence Smith, "Carter Asserts Reagan Presidency Would Be 'Bad Thing' for Country," *New York Times*, October 11, 1980, 8.

73. Ibid.

74. Howell Raines, "Reagan's Camp Sees Carter as His Own Worst Enemy," *New York Times*, October 12, 1980, 32.

75. Patrick Caddell, in discussion with the author, May 13, 2009.

76. Lee Lescaze, "Reagan, a Promising Campaigner, Makes Another One in Florida," *Washington Post*, October 11, 1980, A2.

77. Douglas E. Kneeland, "Reagan Seeks Halt to an Income Curb," *New York Times*, October 11, 1980, 8.

Chapter 33: Stalled

1. Mary Thornton, "Carter, Reagan Rated Even in Texas Survey," *Washington Star*, October 9, 1980, A6.

2. Laurence I. Barrett, Edwin Warner, and Christopher Ogden, "The Jackpot States," *Time*, October 13, 1980.

3. Bill Lauderback, in discussion with the author, August 2, 2006.

4. Owen Ullmann, "Carter Administration Announces More Help for Auto Industry," Associated Press, October 14, 1980.

5. Peter Goldman, James Doyle, Eleanor Clift, Thomas M. DeFrank, Martin Kasindorf, and John Walcott, "The Electoral Numbers Game," Newsweek, October 13, 1980, 38.

6. "Campaign Notes," Washington Post, October 21, 1980, A3.

7. Winston Williams, "Ohio: The Beat of the Heartland," New York Times, October 12, 1980, F1.

8. Adam Clymer, "Ohio Race Expected to Be Close as Labor Mobilizes for President," New York Times, October 16, 1980, A1.

9. Barrett et al., "The Jackpot States."

10. Ibid.

11. Martin Schram, "Solid Edge Seen in Florida, Texas," Washington Post, October 22, 1980, A1.

12. Robert Shrum, in discussion with the author, March 19, 2008.

13. Bernard Weinraub, "Carter and Reagan Ads Try to Hit Right Negative Note," New York Times, October 28, 1980, A26.

14. Jimmy Carter, in discussion with the author, July 11, 2006.

15. David S. Broder, "Reagan's a Fat Target—but He Goes Unpunctured," Los Angeles Times, October 13, 1980, C7.

16. Joseph F. Sullivan, "Reagan, Campaigning in New Jersey, Receives an Unexpected Endorsement From a Mayor," New York Times, October 7, 1980, D21.

17. Martin Schram, "An Optimistic Camp: 'Jimmy Carter Always Comes Back,'" Washington Post, September 16, 1980, A2.

18. Albert R. Hunt and James M. Perry, "Reagan's Momentum Is Slowing in States He Needs for Election," Wall Street Journal, October 16, 1980, 1.

19. James Doyle, "The Boys in the Back Room," Newsweek, October 6, 1980, 45.

20. Hedrick Smith, "Jersey Appears to Support Reagan; Carter Strives to Overcome Apathy," New York Times, October 17, 1980, 1.

21. Owen Ullmann, "Confidential AFL-CIO Poll Shows Union Members Back Conservative Stands," Associated Press, October 15, 1980.

22. Memorandum by Timothy L. Roper.

23. "Poll Shows Democrats Lead in Fight for House Control," New York Times, October 13, 1980, B5.

24. Steven R. Weisman, "Carter Says His Programs Can Lead U.S. to an 'Economic Renaissance,'" New York Times, October 13, 1980, B5.

25. Marjorie Hunter, "Mondale Stressing Reagan 'Flip-Flops,'" New York Times, October 13, 1980, B6.

26. Terence Smith, "White House Repudiates Andrew Young Remarks," New York Times, October 16, 1980, B6.

27. "GOP Candidate Gets Treed by the Wags in California," Washington Post, October 15, 1980, A4.

28. Lou Cannon and Katharine MacDonald, "Reagan's California Swing Evokes the Clashes of 1966," Washington Post, October 14, 1980, A5; Lisa Myers, "Reagan Assails Carter's Failure to Condemn Attacks on Jews; Says President Did Not Speak Out on the Issue," Washington Star, October 14, 1980, A1.

29. Howell Raines, "Reagan Reiterates Warning on Schools," New York Times, October 14, 1980, D22.

30. Jerry Hicks, "Orange County Rallies; 13,000 Flock to Hear Reagan," Los Angeles Times, October 14, 1980, 1.

31. Richard Bergholz, "Reagan Defends His Views; Carter Vows Aid to Israel," Los Angeles Times, October 14, 1980, B1.

32. Myers, "Reagan Assails Carter's Failure to Condemn Attacks on Jews."

33. Terence Hunt, "Reagan Promises to Name Woman to Supreme Court," Associated Press, October 14, 1980.

34. Edward Walsh, "Reagan Is Still the Women's Second Choice," Washington Post, October 16, 1980, A1.

35. "Reagan Vows to Appoint Woman to Highest Court," Wall Street Journal, October 15, 1980, 35.

36. Paul Conrad, Washington Post, October 18, 1980, A2.

37. Jerry Adler, Jane Whitmore, Phyllis Malamud, William D. Marbach, and Nancy Stadtman, "The Finer Art of Politics," Newsweek, October 13, 1980, 74.

38. Michael Coakley, "Carter Pledges a Coal Empire," *Chicago Tribune*, October 14, 1980, 8.

39. James R. Dickenson, "Carter Gets His Act Together, Woos Disaffected Party Members," *Washington Star*, October 19, 1980, A1.

40. Robert McG. Thomas Jr., "Reagan, Briefed by Koch, Demurs on Welfare Help," *New York Times*, October 18, 1980, 1.

41. Douglas E. Kneeland, "Reagan Opposes a City Aid Curb," *New York Times*, September 28, 1980, 1.

42. Hunt and Perry, "Reagan's Momentum Is Slowing in States He Needs for Election."

43. Martin Schram and Lou Cannon, "Key Is Voters League Decision on Anderson," *Washington Post*, October 16, 1980, A1.

44. United Press International, "Reagan Electoral-Vote Lead Is Slipping, Survey Shows," *New York Times*, October 19, 1980, 38.

45. Adam Clymer, "President Is in the Lead, Especially in the City—Anderson Slide Noted," *New York Times*, October 21, 1980, A1.

46. Warren Weaver Jr., "Anderson's Campaign Style Gains as He Loses Ground," *New York Times*, October 17, 1980, 24.

47. Douglas E. Kneeland, "Reagan, in Michigan, Focuses on Economy," *New York Times*, October 16, 1980, B6.

48. Douglas E. Kneeland, "Reagan Is Endorsed by 2 Black Leaders," *New York Times*, October 17, 1980, 1.

49. Patrick Caddell, in discussion with the author, May 13, 2009.

50. "Carter Renews Debate Challenge," *New York Times*, October 16, 1980, B8.

51. Schram and Cannon, "Key Is Voters League Decision on Anderson."

52. Howell Raines, "Reagan Backs Cautious Advisers in Split on a Debate with Carter," *New York Times*, September 23, 1980, B8.

53. Schram and Cannon, "Key Is Voters League Decision on Anderson."

54. "Survey Shows 221 Dailies for Reagan, 59 for Carter," Associated Press, October 16, 1980.

55. Michael Putzel, "Reagan Agrees to Debate Carter," Associated Press, October 17, 1980.

56. "Business Digest: The Economy," *New York Times*, October 17, 1980, D1.

57. Edward Walsh and Lou Cannon, "Reagan and Carter Finally Brought Together," *Washington Post*, October 17, 1980, A4.

58. Terence Smith, "Carter and Reagan Trade Quips on Same Dais at Al Smith Dinner," *New York Times*, October 17, 1980, 22.

59. Walsh and Cannon, "Reagan and Carter Finally Brought Together."

60. James R. Dickenson, "Carter and Reagan Parry Politely at an Al Smith Dinner Encounter," *Washington Star*, October 17, 1980, A1.

61. Walsh and Cannon, "Reagan and Carter Finally Brought Together."

62. Ed Magnuson, Laurence I. Barrett, Christopher Ogden, "Building to a Climax," *Time*, October 27, 1980.

63. Lyn Nofziger, *Nofziger* (Washington, DC: Regnery Gateway, 1992), 260.

64. Edward Walsh and Lou Cannon, "Reagan, Carter Plan Debate," *Washington Post*, October 18, 1980, A1.

65. Hedrick Smith, "Lead Slipping, a New Reagan Suits Up for the Big Debate," *New York Times*, October 19, 1980, E1.

66. Bernard Weinraub, "Carter and Reagan Go on Attack in Ads," *New York Times*, October 19, 1980, 38.

67. Lisa Myers, "GOP's Challenger Wants New Treaty," *Washington Star*, October 20, A1.

68. Peter Hannaford, *The Reagans: A Political Portrait* (New York: Coward-McCann, 1983), 294.

69. Steven R. Weisman, "President Suggests Reagan's Policy Could Lead to a 'Nuclear Precipice,'" *New York Times*, October 20, 1980, A1; Jeremiah O'Leary and Alison Muscatine, "Carter Assails Reagan Plan to Scrap SALT II as 'Naïve,'" *Washington Star*, October 20, 1980, A1.

70. Howell Raines, "Reagan, in Speeches, Doesn't Let the Facts Spoil a Good Anecdote or Effective Symbol," *New York Times*, October 19, 1980, 38.

71. Goldman et al., "The Electoral Numbers Game."

72. Eugene Robinson, "Kennedy, Mindful of Future, Is Going All-Out for Carter," *Washington Post*, October 12, 1980, A1.

73. Jack W. Germond and Jules Witcover, "Arkansas Bares Weak Spot in Carter's Base," *Washington Star*, October 15, 1980, A3.

74. Donald M. Rothberg, "Anderson Slide in Polls Set Stage for League Debate," Associated Press, October 22, 1980.

75. Alison Muscatine, "Top Reagan Aide Urges Debate Be Held the Night Before Election," *Washington Star*, October 20, 1980, A1.

76. Terence Smith, "Presidential Debate Format Set; Camps Differ on Time and Place," *New York Times*, October 21, 1980, A1.

77. Alison Muscatine, "Agreement Is Expected on Debate," *Washington Star*, October 21, 1980, A1.

78. James Baker, in discussion with the author, September 6, 2006.

79. Jody Powell, in discussion with the author, April 10, 2006.

80. Muscatine, "Top Reagan Aide Urges Debate Be Held the Night Before Election."

81. Douglas E. Kneeland, "Reagan Tour Rolls Through Illinois," *New York Times*, October 19, 1980, 42.

82. Hannaford, *The Reagans*, 296.

83. Stuart Spencer, in discussion with the author.

CHAPTER 34: ON DECK

1. James Baker, in discussion with the author.

2. James Baker, in discussion with the author, September 6, 2006.

3. Ibid.

4. Stuart Spencer, in discussion with the author, September 28, 2006.

5. Baker, in discussion with the author, September 6, 2006.

6. Ibid.

7. House Committee on Post Office and Civil Service, Subcommittee on Human Resources, *Unauthorized Transfers of Nonpublic Information During the 1980 Presidential Election*, 98th Cong., 2d sess., 1984, Committee Print 98–12, 114. Hereinafter cited as House Committee report.

8. Memorandum from Patrick H. Caddell to the President, "Where We Go from Here—How to Win," August 18, 1980, Jimmy Carter Presidential Library, Atlanta, GA.

9. Tom Wicker, "All Stops Out in Texas," *New York Times*, October 26, 1980, E19.

10. Robert Pear, "Drought Aid to Jersey Authorized by Carter; U.S. to Build Pipeline," *New York Times*, October 20, 1980, A1.

11. Jeremiah O'Leary, "Carter Will Deny Saudis F-15 Gear," *Washington Star*, October 26, 1980, A1.

12. Dick Kirschten, "Cabinet Government Really Does Work—on the Presidential Campaign Trail," *National Journal*, October 25, 1980, 1800.

13. Lou Cannon, "Reagan Raises Hostage Issue in Campaign," *Washington Post*, October 21, 1980, A1.

14. Brooks Jackson, "Reagan Puts Increasing Stress on Theme That Carter Is a Dangerous Incompetent," *Wall Street Journal*, October 24, 1980, 16.

15. Richard Bergholz, "Reagan Blames President for Hostage Tieup," *Los Angeles Times*, October 22, 1980, B1.

16. "Quotations of the Day," *New York Times*, October 22, 1980, B1.

17. Terence Smith, "President Critical," *New York Times*, October 22, 1980, A1.

18. Lou Cannon, "Political Dueling on Hostage Issue," *Washington Post*, October 22, 1980, A1.

19. Edward Walsh, "In Texas, Carter Sounds Hawkish Note and Derides Reagan on Hostage Issue," *Washington Post*, October 23, 1980, A4.

20. Peter A. Brown, United Press International, October 23, 1980.

21. Jack Nelson, "Carter Alludes to His Calm in Crisis," *Los Angeles Times*, October 22, 1980, B16.

22. "Criticism of President by Governor of Texas Stirs a Political Furor," *New York Times*, October 26, 1980, 41.

23. Smith, "President Critical."

24. Letter from American Indian Party to Senator S. I. Hayakawa, July 29, 1980, FBI, Box 2, Ronald Reagan Presidential Library, Simi Valley, CA.

25. Letter to Reagan for President, April 14, 1980, FBI, Box 2, Ronald Reagan Presidential Library, Simi Valley, CA.

26. Dudley Clendinen, "Campaign Report," *New York Times*, October 21, 1980, B6.

27. Dudley Clendinen, "Campaign Report," *New York Times*, October 25, 1980, 8.

28. Hedrick Smith, "Poll Shows President Has Pulled to Even Position with Reagan," *New York Times*, October 23, 1980, A1.

29. Clendinen, "Campaign Report," October 25, 1980.

30. Michele Davis, in discussion with the author, March 14, 2008.

31. Dick Wirthlin, in discussion with the author.

32. Smith, "Poll Shows President Has Pulled to Even Position with Reagan."

33. Adam Clymer, "Carter Found Far Behind '76 Pace in Jewish Support," *New York Times*, October 25, 1980, 8.

34. United Press International, "McCarthy Is Said to Back Reagan," *New York Times*, October 22, 1980, A25.

35. "Clean Gene Is at It Again," *Time*, November 14, 1988.

36. Don Shannon, "Reagan Gets Backing of Former Sen. McCarthy," *Los Angeles Times*, October 24, 1980, B15.

37. Jackson, "Reagan Puts Increasing Stress on Theme That Carter Is a Dangerous Incompetent."

38. United Press International, "Reagan Preparing for Debate," *New York Times*, October 26, 1980, 41.

39. Editorial, "At the End of the Alley," *New York Times*, October 26, 1980, E18.

40. Mike Causey, "Reagan Is Endorsed by PATCO's Board," *Washington Post*, October 24, 1980, C2.

41. Joseph E. Persico, *Casey: From the OSS to the CIA* (New York: Viking, 1990), 194.

42. Lou Cannon, "Reagan's Team Perplexed by Uncontrollable Events," *Washington Post*, October 24, 1980, A1.

43. Persico, *Casey*, 195.

44. William K. Stevens, "Kennedy Rouses Mexican-Americans to Aid Carter's Drive to Win Texas," *New York Times*, October 23, 1980, B12.

45. Gregory Nokes, "Reagan Raps Carter Economic Record of 'Misery, Despair,'" Associated Press, October 23, 1980.

46. "Business Digest: Markets," *New York Times*, October 24, 1980, D1.

47. Clyde H. Farnsworth, "Consumer Prices Up by 1% in September and 12.7% in a Year," *New York Times*, October 25, 1980, 1.

48. Steven R. Weisman, "Californian's Plan Attacked," *New York Times*, October 25, 1980, 1.

49. William J. Eaton, "Reagan Says Carter May Rig Report on Price Index," *Los Angeles Times*, October 24, 1980, B16.

50. Terence Smith, "Carter Gets Rights Leader's Pledge and Seeks Help of Black Ministers," *New York Times*, October 24, 1980, A16.

51. Jackson, "Reagan Puts Increasing Stress on Theme That Carter Is a Dangerous Incompetent."

52. Clay F. Richardson, "Carter, Reagan Prepare for Crucial Debate," United Press International, October 27, 1980.

53. House Committee report, 110.

54. "Excerpts From Reagan TV Address on the Economy," *New York Times*, October 25, 1980, 10.

55. Ibid.

56. Ibid.

57. Ibid.

58. Gregory Nokes, "Reagan Says Carter's Spending, Tax Policies Caused Inflation," Associated Press, October 25, 1980.

59. Jackson, "Reagan Puts Increasing Stress on Theme That Carter Is a Dangerous Incompetent."

60. *U.S. News & World Report*, October 20, 1980, 18.

61. Richard Halloran, "Libyans Are Challenging U.S. Forces in War of Nerves," *New York Times*, October 24, 1980, A8.

62. Howell Raines, "Reagan Focus Is on Carter Competence as Key Issue," *New York Times*, October 24, 1980, A16.

63. Steven R. Weisman, "Carter Asserts Reagan Shifted on Embargo," *New York Times*, October 26, 1980, 41.

64. "Today's News," *Washington Star*, October 24, 1980, A1.

65. Weisman, "Carter Asserts Reagan Shifted on Embargo."

66. Patrick Caddell, in discussion with the author, May 13, 2009.

67. Jody Powell, in discussion with the author, April 10, 2006.

68. Rich Jaroslovsky, "Carter, Reagan Teams Sketch Game Plan for Face-Off Tentatively Set for Oct. 28," *Wall Street Journal*, October 20, 1980, 4.

Chapter 35: Cleveland

1. Arthur M. Schlesinger Jr., *Journals: 1952–2000* (New York: Penguin Press, 2007), 504.

2. Elizabeth Drew, *Portrait of an Election: The 1980 Presidential Campaign* (New York: Simon & Schuster, 1981), 307.

3. Martin Schram, "Carter Goes into Debate with Lead in New Poll," *Washington Post*, October 28, 1980, A1.

4. "Campaign Notes," *Washington Post*, October 25, 1980, A6.

5. John F. Stacks, "Right Now: a Dead Heat," *Time*, November 3, 1980.

6. "A Slugfest in the Midwest; Third in a Series of Regional Surveys," *U.S. News & World Report*, October 20, 1980, 22.

7. "Survey Finds Missouri Race Nearly Even," *Washington Star*, October 24, 1980, A6.

8. "Carter, Reagan—How They Rate," *U.S. News & World Report*, October 20, 1980, 11.

9. Howell Raines, "Reporter's Notebook: Tension Grips Gipper's Camp," *New York Times*, October 27, 1980, B6.

10. Ken Khachigian, in discussion with the author, May 2007.

11. Thomas M. DeFrank, *Write It When I'm Gone: Remarkable Off-the-Record Conversations with Gerald R. Ford* (New York: G. P. Putnam's Sons, 2007), 113.

12. Alison Muscatine, "Carter Might Make 'Political' Deal for Hostages' Release, Ford Says," *Washington Star*, October 20, 1980, A3.

13. Richard Allen, in discussion with the author, April 12, 2008.

14. Michael Putzel, "Carter Aide Calls Ford Charge on Hostages 'Trash,'" Associated Press, October 28, 1980.

15. Ellen Hume, "Civil Rights Leader Calls Reagan a Racist," *Los Angeles Times*, October 28, 1980, B15.

16. Associated Press, "Birch Society Narrows Comments on Reagan," *New York Times*, October 30, 1980, B19.

17. Allan J. Mayer, Gerald C. Lubenow, Gloria Borger, and Diane Camper, "Beyond the Melting Pot," *Newsweek*, October 20, 1980, 29.

18. David Bird, "George Scott Is Chary of Giving Political Advice," *New York Times*, October 27, 1980, A21.

19. "Newspapers Make Endorsements," *New York Times*, October 27, 1980, B8.

20. Editorial, "Ronald Reagan for President," *Chicago Tribune*, October 26, 1980, A4.

21. "Newspapers Make Endorsements."

22. House Committee on Post Office and Civil Service, Subcommittee on Human Resources, *Unauthorized Transfers of Nonpublic Information During the 1980 Presidential Election*, 98th Cong., 2d sess., 1984, Committee Print 98–12, 111.

23. Marc Rotterman, in discussion with the author, March 15, 2007.

24. Michael Putzel, Associated Press, September 26, 1984.

25. Robert G. Kaiser, "Grueling Prep Work Precedes Critical Clash," *Washington Post*, September 26, 2008, A6.

26. Memorandum from Anthony R. Dolan to Ed Meese, "Debates," September 1980, Box 139, Ronald Reagan Presidential Library, Simi Valley, CA.

27. Dudley Clendinen, "Campaign Report," *New York Times*, October 28, 1980, A24.

28. Eleanor Randolph, "On Eve of Debate, Carter Accuses Reagan of Switching Roles," *Los Angeles Times*, October 28, 1980, B16.

29. Jody Powell, in discussion with the author, April 10, 2006; United Press International, October 26, 1980.

30. Memorandum from Martin D. Franks, "Memorandum on the Reagan Book," September 10, 1980, Carter/Mondale Re-Election Committee, Jimmy Carter Presidential Library, Atlanta, GA.

31. United Press International, October 28, 1980.

32. Schram, "Carter Goes into Debate with Lead in New Poll."

33. James A. Baker III and Steve Fiffer, *Work Hard, Study . . . and Keep Out of Politics!* (New York: G. P. Putnam's Sons, 2006), 108.

34. "Horoscope; Tuesday, October 28," *Chicago Tribune*, October 28, 1980, E6.

35. Rebecca Donatelli, in discussion with the author, July 14, 2006.

36. Memorandum from Paul Manafort to RPDSs, State Chairmen, Executive Directors, and Campaign Directors, "Debate Consequences and Considerations," October 18, 1980.

37. John J. O'Connor, "TV: Instant Poll Steals Past-Debate Scene," *New York Times*, October 30, 1980, C26.

38. Michael K. Deaver with Mickey Herskowitz, *Behind the Scenes: In Which the Author Talks About Ronald and Nancy Reagan . . . and Himself* (New York: William Morrow, 1987), 98.

39. Walter Mondale, in discussion with the author, February 28, 2007.

40. Peter G. Bourne, *Jimmy Carter: A Comprehensive Biography from Plains to Postpresidency* (New York: Scribner, 1997), 471.

41. Walter R. Mears, "Reagan Would Pull SALT from Senate," Associated Press, October 1, 1980.

42. Hamilton Jordan, *Crisis: The Last Year of the Carter Presidency* (New York: G. P. Putnam's Sons, 1982), 302.

43. Walter R. Mears, Associated Press, October 28, 1980.

44. "Transcript of the Presidential Debate Between Carter and Reagan in Cleveland," *New York Times*, October 29, 1980, A26.

45. Ibid.

46. Ibid.

47. Ibid.

48. Robert A. Rosenblatt, "Carter, Reagan Agree Oil Prices Must Increase," *Los Angeles Times*, October 27, 1980, B8.

49. "Transcript of the Presidential Debate Between Carter and Reagan in Cleveland."

50. George H. W. Bush, in discussion with the author, February 16, 2007.

51. "Transcript of the Presidential Debate Between Carter and Reagan in Cleveland."

52. Ibid.

53. Ibid.

54. Walter Isaacson, Laurence I. Barrett, and Christopher Ogden, "Now, a Few Words in Closing," *Time*, November 10, 1980.

55. "Transcript of the Presidential Debate Between Carter and Reagan in Cleveland."

56. Ibid.

57. Ibid.

58. Ibid.

59. Ibid.

60. Ibid.

61. Ibid.

62. Ibid.

63. Ibid.

64. Ibid.

65. Ibid.

66. Ibid.

67. Ibid.

68. Ibid.

69. Ibid.

70. Ibid.

71. Ibid.

72. Ibid.

73. Ibid.

74. Ibid.

75. Ibid.

76. Ibid.

77. Ibid.

78. Ibid.

79. Ibid.

80. Ibid.

81. Ibid.

82. Ibid.

83. Ibid.

84. Ibid.

85. Ibid.

86. Ibid.

87. Brad Knickerbocker, "A Governor's Report Card," *Christian Science Monitor*, October 1, 1980, 13.

88. "Transcript of President's State of the Union Message to Nation," *New York Times*, January 27, 1982, A16.

89. "Transcript of the Presidential Debate Between Carter and Reagan in Cleveland."

CHAPTER 36: MELTDOWN

1. Lou Cannon, *Reagan* (New York: G. P. Putnam's Sons, 1982), 294.

2. Hedrick Smith, "Carter and Reagan Voicing Confidence on Debate Showing," *New York Times*, October 30, 1980, A1.

3. Walter R. Mears, Associated Press, October 29, 1980.

4. Jimmy Carter, *Keeping Faith: Memoirs of a President* (New York: Bantam Books, 1982), 565.

5. Memorandum from Gerald M. Rafshoon to the President, "1980 General Election Themes," July 3, 1980, Rafshoon Communications, Susan Clough Files, Box 5, Jimmy Carter Presidential Library, Atlanta, GA.

6. "Both Sides Claim Their Man Won the Debate," *Los Angeles Times*, October 29, 1980, B2.

7. Jimmy Carter, in discussion with the author, July 11, 2006.

8. Peter Goldman, James Doyle, Martin Kasindorf, Eleanor Clift, and Thomas M. DeFrank, "The Great Homestretch Debate," *Newsweek*, November 10, 1980, 34.

9. Memorandum from Rafshoon to the President, "1980 General Election Themes," July 3, 1980.

10. "Full Transcript of Debate Between Reagan and Carter," *Washington Star*, October 29, 1980, A4.

11. Hans Christian Andersen, *The Emperor's New Clothes*, illus. by Virginia Lee Burton (Boston, MA: Houghton Mifflin Harcourt, 2004), 11.

12. Jack W. Germond and Jules Witcover, "Debate Offers No Real 'Hook' for Undecided," *Washington Star*, October 29, 1980, A1.

13. Robert G. Kaiser, "Looking for Old Ghosts," *Washington Post*, October 30, 1980, A1.

14. David S. Broder, "Carter on Points, but No KO," *Washington Post*, October 29, 1980, A1.

15. Tom Shales, "Live, from Cleveland, It's . . . Debatable!" *Washington Post*, October 29, 1980, B1.

16. Mary McGrory, "No Surprises, but Both Men Debated Well," *Washington Star*, October 29, 1980, A4.

17. Fred Barnes, in discussion with the author, September 29, 2008.

18. Bernard Weinraub, "Area Panel's Scorecard on the Debate: Reagan Won It by a Wide Margin," *New York Times*, October 30, 1980, B20.

19. "Both Sides Claim Their Man Won the Debate," *Los Angeles Times*.

20. R. Emmett Tyrrell Jr., "The Wise and the Wisenheimers," *Washington Post*, November 3, 1980, A21.

21. Mary McGrory, "Big Debate Failed to Sway Undecideds," *Washington Star*, October 31, 1980, A4.

22. Sam Donaldson, in discussion with the author.

23. Robert Shrum, in discussion with the author, March 19, 2008.

24. Kaiser, "Looking for Old Ghosts."

25. Dick Wirthlin, in discussion with the author.

26. "CBS Poll on the Carter-Reagan Debate," *Washington Star*, October 30, 1980, A4.

27. Dudley Clendinen, "Campaign Report," *New York Times*, October 30, 1980, B14.

28. Editorial, "The Choice for President," *Washington Post*, October 31, 1980, A14.

29. "Endorsements," *Washington Star*, October 31, 1980, A4.

30. Fay Willey, "Carter Blasts Rupert Murdoch," *Newsweek*, October 27, 1980, 33.

31. James R. Dickenson, "President Hammers at Rival's Image," *Washington Star*, October 30, 1980, A1.

32. Jules Witcover, "Carter's Hopes in West Are Necessarily Modest," *Washington Star*, October 30, 1980, A1.

33. Kenneth Reich, "Carter, Reagan to Contest California to the End," *Los Angeles Times*, October 30, 1980, 5.

34. Steven R. Weisman, "Carter Intensifies Criticisms of Reagan," *New York Times*, October 31, 1980, 16.

35. Carter, *Keeping Faith*, 565.

36. David S. Broder, Maralee Schwartz, and Chris Colford, "Reagan Is in the Driver's Seat," *Washington Post*, November 2, 1980, A1.

37. Donald Totten, in discussion with the author, January 4, 2008.

38. United Press International, "Blacks," *Washington Star*, October 31, 1980, A3.

39. Warren Weaver Jr., "Anderson Charges Democratic 'Lie' for Black Vote," *New York Times*, November 1, 1980, 8.

40. Don Oberdorfer, "From U.S. Officials, Denials and Uncertainty," *Washington Post*, November 1, 1980, A1.

41. Walter Mondale, in discussion with the author, February 28, 2007.

42. Howard Rosenberg, "'Presidential' Debate: And the Winner Is . . . ," *Los Angeles Times*, October 30, 1980, H1.

43. Lance Gay, "ABC's Experimental Poll After Debate Was Marred by Technological Foul-Ups," *Washington Star*, October 30, 1980, A4.

44. Tony Schwartz, "Pollsters Denounce ABC's Debate Survey," *New York Times*, October 30, 1980, B19.

45. "ABC, AP Monitor Viewer Reaction," *Washington Star*, October 29, 1980, A1.

46. Gay, "ABC's Experimental Poll After Debate Was Marred by Technological Foul-Ups."

47. Schwartz, "Pollsters Denounce ABC's Debate Survey."

48. Gay, "ABC's Experimental Poll After Debate Was Marred by Technological Foul-Ups."

49. Bill Timmons, in discussion with the author.

50. Editorial, "Words, and Music, in the Debate," *New York Times*, October 30, 1980, A26.

51. Schwartz, "Pollsters Denounce ABC's Debate Survey."

52. Ibid.

53. Jonathan Friendly, "Columnist Helped Reagan on Debate," *New York Times*, July 9, 1983, 12; Sydney H. Schanberg, "Crossing the Line," *New York Times*, July 26, 1983; Joyce Purnick, "Survey of Newspapers Finds Support for Column by Will," *New York Times*, July 11, 1983.

54. Edward Cowan, "U.S. Budget Deficit of $59 Billion for 1980 Is the Second Biggest Ever," *New York Times*, October 30, 1980, A1.

55. Douglas E. Kneeland, "White House Is Accused of Not Cooperating in Justice Dept. Inquiry," *New York Times*, November 1, 1980, 1; Lou Cannon, "Reagan Campaigns Like a Man Who's Won," *Washington Post*, November 1, 1980, A4.

56. Leslie Maitland, "Williams Is Indicted with 3 for Bribery in New Abscam Case," *New York Times*, October 31, 1980, 1.

57. Wendell Rawls Jr., "Jenrette, in an Uphill Battle, Calls Abscam the Only Issue," *New York Times*, October 31, 1980, 18.

58. Howell Raines, "Reagan Stresses Economic Issue Anew," *New York Times*, October 30, 1980, A1.

59. Douglas E. Kneeland, "Reagan Steps Up Attack on Carter's Performance," *New York Times*, October 31, 1980, A16.

60. United Press International, "Nancy," *Washington Star*, October 31, 1980, A4.

61. Francis X. Clines, "About Politics; Calling the Tune to Call Democrats," *New York Times*, October 31, 1980, 18.

62. Ibid.

63. Kneeland, "Reagan Steps Up Attack on Carter's Performance."

64. Jonathan Kwitny, "Richard V. Allen Used White House Prestige Freely in Nixon Years," *Wall Street Journal*, October 28, 1980, 1.

65. "Reagan Adviser Drops Out of Campaign Because of Reports on Business Activities," *Wall Street Journal*, October 31, 1980, 3.

66. Howell Raines, "Reporter's Notebook: Tension Grips Gipper's Camp," *New York Times*, October 27, 1980, B6.

67. Kneeland, "Reagan Steps Up Attack on Carter's Performance."

68. Cannon, "Reagan Campaigns Like a Man Who's Won."

69. Michele Davis, "1980 Diary," October 30, 1980, Michele Davis Archives Collection.

70. Michele Davis, "1980 Diary," October 31, 1980, Michele Davis Archives Collection.

71. Judy Bachrach, "It's Not Like Taking Candy from a Baby," *Washington Star*, October 20, 1980, A5.

72. Memorandum from Jim Purks, Media Liaison to Dick Moe, "Thoughts on Last Three Weeks," October 10, 1980, Box 8, Jimmy Carter Presidential Library, Atlanta, GA.

73. Edward Walsh, "Concerned Carter Pleads for Help from South," *Washington Post*, November 1, 1980, A5.

74. Martin Schram, "After the Debate, the Pollsters Scramble," *Washington Post*, October 30, 1980, A1.

75. Elizabeth Drew, *Portrait of an Election: The 1980 Presidential Campaign* (New York: Simon & Schuster, 1981), 334.

76. Walsh, "Concerned Carter Pleads for Help from South."

77. Walter Mondale, in discussion with the author, February 28, 2007.

78. Lisa Myers, "Reagan Criticizes President's Ability," *Washington Star*, October 31, 1980, A1.

79. Mary McGrory, "Reagan Senses That His Goal Is in Reach," *Washington Star*, November 3, 1980, A4.

80. Cannon, "Reagan Campaigns Like a Man Who's Won."

81. Lisa Myers, "Confidence Reigns in GOP Camp," *Washington Star*, November 1, 1980, A1.

82. Lou Cannon, "GOP Challenger," *Washington Post*, November 2, 1980, A17.

83. Tim Ahern, "Candidates Pushing as Campaign Nears End," Associated Press, November 1, 1980.

84. United Press International, "Staubach Out of Bounds?" *New York Times*, November 4, 1980, B14.

85. Fay Willey, "A Reagan Boost from Betty Ford," *Newsweek*, October 27, 1980, 33.

86. John Herbers, "Worried Democrats in the South Battle to Hold Region for Carter," *New York Times*, November 1, 1980, 1.

87. Hedrick Smith, "Survey Indicates Reagan Is Holding Lead in Battle for Electoral Votes," *New York Times*, November 2, 1980, 1.

88. Mark Shields, "Behind Closed Curtains," *Washington Post*, October 31, 1980, A15.

89. Tom Shales, "The Harassment of Ronald Reagan," *Washington Post*, October 31, 1980, C1.

90. Lisa Myers, "Reagan, Ford Rip President in Michigan," *Washington Star*, November 2, 1980, A1.

91. Cannon, "GOP Challenger."

92. Myers, "Reagan, Ford Rip President in Michigan."

93. Howell Raines, "Reagan Prepares an Attack on Carter If 52 Are Freed," *New York Times*, November 2, 1980, 36.

94. Karlyn Barker, "Bush: Partnership with Reagan Is Flowering on the Campaign Trail," *Washington Post*, November 1, 1980, A3.

95. Cannon, "Reagan Campaigns Like a Man Who's Won."

96. Dudley Clendinen, "Campaign Report," *New York Times*, October 31, 1980, A16.

97. *U.S. News & World Report*, October 27, 1980, 18.

98. Smith, "Survey Indicates Reagan Is Holding Lead in Battle for Electoral Votes."

99. "A Look Ahead from the Nation's Capital," *U.S. News & World Report*, November 3, 1980, 15.

100. Edward Walsh, "Carter Acknowledges Some Failings; Reagan Courts Michigan Voters," *Washington Post*, November 2, 1980, A17.

101. Michele Davis, "1980 Diary," November 1, 1980, Michele Davis Archives Collection.

102. Drew, *Portrait of an Election*, 18.

103. Cannon, "GOP Challenger."

CHAPTER 37: ENTRANCE, STAGE LEFT

1. George J. Church, Christopher Ogden, and Laurence I. Barrett, "Nation: Reagan Coast-to-Coast," *Time*, November 17, 1980.

2. Hedrick Smith, "President Concedes," *New York Times*, November 5, 1980, A1.

3. Jeremiah O'Leary and James R. Dickenson, "Carter Predicts Long Night Before Results Are Known," *Washington Star*, November 4, 1980, A1.

4. Sam Donaldson, *World News Tonight*, ABC News Transcripts, November 4, 1980.

5. O'Leary and Dickenson, "Carter Predicts Long Night Before Results Are Known."

6. Bill Stall and William J. Eaton, "Reagan Goes from Ballot to Barber to Bigger Things," *Los Angeles Times*, November 5, 1980, B1.

7. Douglas E. Kneeland, "Reagan Vows to Do His Best to Justify Hopes of Backers," *New York Times*, November 5, 1980, A22.

8. Lou Cannon, "Reagan Promises to Heal and Unify," *Washington Post*, November 5, 1980, A17.

9. Kneeland, "Reagan Vows to Do His Best to Justify Hopes of Backers."

10. Nancy Reagan with William Novak, *My Turn: The Memoirs of Nancy Reagan* (New York: Random House, 1989), 220.

11. Barry Serafin, *World News Tonight*, ABC News Transcripts, November 4, 1980.

12. Kneeland, "Reagan Vows to Do His Best to Justify Hopes of Backers."

13. Adam Clymer, "Carter and Reagan Make Final Appeals Before Vote Today," *New York Times*, November 4, 1980, A1; "The Final Round," *U.S. News & World Report*, November 3, 1980, 22.

14. "The General Election Day," *New York Times*, November 3, 1878, 6; Andreas Teuber, "Elections of Yore," *New York Times*, November 4, 1980, A19.

15. Jody Powell, in discussion with the author, April 10, 2006; Martin Schram, "At White House: Setting the Stage," *Washington Post*, November 3, 1980, A1.

16. Schram, "At White House: Setting the Stage."

17. Martin Schram, "Nation's Longest Campaign Comes to an End," *Washington Post*, November 4, 1980, A1.

18. Hedrick Smith, "Campaign Tightrope," *New York Times*, November 3, 1980, A15.

19. Schram, "At White House: Setting the Stage."

20. Jimmy Carter, in discussion with the author, July 11, 2006.

21. Bruce Langdon, in discussion with the author.

22. Lisa Myers, "Confidence Reigns in GOP Camp," *Washington Star*, November 1, 1980, A1.

23. Ibid.

24. Terence Hunt, "Reagan in Last Push in Illinois, Oregon, and California," Associated Press, November 3, 1980.

25. George J. Church, Evan Thomas, and Douglas Brew, "Nation: A Determined Second Fiddle," *Time*, November 17, 1980.

26. Harry F. Rosenthal, "Reagan and Bush Making Final Pitch to Voters," Associated Press, November 3, 1980.

27. Howell Raines, "Reagan Attacks President on Economy and Defense," *New York Times*, November 4, 1980, B5.

28. Terence Smith, "Carter Makes an Appeal to Backers of Anderson," *New York Times*, November 4, 1980, B5.

29. Bill Peterson, "Anderson Brings 'Most Exhilarating Experience' to a Poetic Close," *Washington Post*, November 4, 1980, A11.

30. Bill Peterson, "John Anderson's 'Unlikely' Campaign an Air of Unreality at the End," *Washington Post*, November 3, 1980, A6.

31. Warren Weaver Jr., "Anderson Campaign Finishing with Upbeat Feeling," *New York Times*, November 3, 1980, D13.

32. Ronald Reagan, "Election Eve Address 'A Vision for America,'" University of Texas, http://www.reagan.utexas.edu/archives/reference/11.3.80.html.

33. John W. Mashek, "Massive Shift to Right Story of '80 Elections," *U.S. News & World Report*, November 17, 1980, 26.

34. Lisa Myers, "Confident Reagan Uses Words of John Wayne," *Washington Star*, November 4, 1980, A1.

35. Raines, "Reagan Attacks President on Economy and Defense."

36. Church et al., "Nation: Reagan Coast-to-Coast."

37. Stuart Spencer, in discussion with the author, September 28, 2006.

38. Ken Khachigian, in discussion with the author, August 29, 2008.

39. United Press International, "Reagan Wins Dixville Notch," *Washington Star*, November 4, 1980, A5.

40. Jerry Harkavy, "First Voters in New Hampshire Primary Cast Their Ballots," Associated Press, February 26, 1980.

41. Kenny Klinge, in discussion with the author, July 12, 2006.

42. Jody Powell, in discussion with the author, April 10, 2006.

43. James R. Dickenson and Jeremiah O'Leary, "On His Final Campaign Swing, Carter Learned It Was All Over," *Washington Star*, November 6, 1980, A1.

44. Jody Powell, in discussion with the author, April 10, 2006.

45. Dickenson and O'Leary, "On His Final Campaign Swing, Carter Learned It Was All Over."

46. Jody Powell, in discussion with the author, April 10, 2006.

47. Dickenson and O'Leary, "On His Final Campaign Swing, Carter Learned It Was All Over."

48. Jody Powell, in discussion with the author, April 10, 2006.

49. Dickenson and O'Leary, "On His Final Campaign Swing, Carter Learned It Was All Over."

50. Jody Powell, in discussion with the author, April 10, 2006.

51. A. O. Sulzberger Jr., "Bush, in Victory Talk, Says Reagan Will Lead U.S. 'Back to Greatness,'" *New York Times*, November 5, 1980, A21.

52. "Mondale Votes in Minnesota in 'Tight' Election," Associated Press, November 4, 1980.

53. Walter Mondale, in discussion with the author, February 28, 2007.

54. Jimmy Carter, in discussion with the author, July 11, 2006.

55. James R. Dickenson and Jeremiah O'Leary, "Carter Defends His Leadership," *Washington Star*, November 5, 1980, A3.

56. Church et al., "Nation: Reagan Coast-to-Coast."

57. Dickenson and O'Leary, "On His Final Campaign Swing, Carter Learned It Was All Over."

58. Sam Donaldson, *World News Tonight*, ABC News Transcripts, November 3, 1980.

59. Patrick Caddell, in discussion with the author.

60. Jerry Adler, Gerald C. Lubenow, and Martin Kasindorf, "Reagan: Easy Rider," *Newsweek*, November 17, 1980, 30; Stall and Eaton, "Reagan Goes from Ballot to Barber to Bigger Things."

61. Ken Khachigian, in discussion with the author, May 2007.

62. James M. Perry and Albert R. Hunt, "Reagan Buries Carter in Roaring Landslide Throughout Country," *Wall Street Journal*, November 5, 1980, 1.

63. Bernard Weinraub, "The Election on TV: Networks Gearing Up," *New York Times*, November 4, 1980, B5.

64. Ibid.

65. Harry F. Waters and George Hackett, "Peacock's Night to Crow," *Newsweek*, November 17, 1980, 82.

66. Dom Bonafede, "The Press Does Some Soul Searching in Reviewing Its Campaign Coverage," *National Journal*, November 29, 1980, 2032.

67. Janice Castro and Elizabeth Rudulph, "Press: Like a Suburban Swimming Pool," *Time*, November 17, 1980.

68. D'Vera Cohn, "Election Fizzles as Cliff-Hanger," United Press International, November 5, 1980.

69. Barbara Walters, *World News Tonight*, ABC News, November 4, 1980.

70. Frank Reynolds and Ted Koppel, *World News Tonight*, ABC News, November 4, 1980.

71. Perry and Hunt, "Reagan Buries Carter in Roaring Landslide Throughout Country."

72. Terence Smith, "Carter, Saying Defeat 'Hurt,' Pledges Fullest Cooperation," *New York Times*, November 5, 1980, A19.

73. John Chancellor, *Decision '80*, NBC, November 4, 1980.

74. Nancy Reagan, *I Love You, Ronnie: The Letters of Ronald Reagan to Nancy Reagan* (New York: Random House, 2000), 135.

75. Ibid.

76. Perry and Hunt, "Reagan Buries Carter in Roaring Landslide Throughout Country."

77. Dickenson and O'Leary, "On His Final Campaign Swing, Carter Learned It Was All Over."

78. Walter Cronkite, *Election Night*, CBS News, November 4, 1980.

79. Donnie Radcliffe, "The Democrats," *Washington Post*, November 5, 1980, E3.

80. "Plains Truth," *Time*, April 30, 1984.

81. "Transcript of the President's Concession Statement," *New York Times*, November 5, 1980, A19.

82. Walter Cronkite, *Election Night*, CBS News, November 4, 1980.

83. "Transcript of the President's Concession Statement."

84. Dick West, United Press International, November 5, 1980.

85. Tip O'Neill with William Novak, *Man of the House: The Life and Political Memoirs of Speaker Tip O'Neill* (New York: Random House, 1987), 328–29.

86. Ibid., 329.

87. Smith, "President Concedes."

88. Bill Peterson, "Anderson Is Upbeat and Philosophical," *Washington Post*, November 5, 1980, A17.

89. Adler et al., "Reagan: Easy Rider."

90. United Press International, "Reagan's Former Wife Is Happy Over Victory," *New York Times*, November 6, 1980, A26.

91. Lisa Myers, "Reagan Finds His Victory 'Humbling,'" *Washington Star*, November 5, 1980, A3.

92. Doug Bandow, in discussion with the author, October 10, 2006.

93. Barry Serafin, *World News Tonight*, ABC News, November 4, 1980.

94. Frank Reynolds, *World News Tonight*, ABC News, November 4, 1980.

95. Stuart Spencer, in discussion with the author, September 28, 2006.

96. Kathleen Kennedy Townsend, in discussion with the author, December 18, 2007.

97. Arthur M. Schlesinger Jr., *Journals: 1952–2000* (New York: Penguin Press, 2007), 506.

98. David Keene, in discussion with the author, October 10, 2006.

99. Jimmy Carter, in discussion with the author, July 11, 2006.

100. Muriel Coleman, in discussion with the author, May 2, 2007.

101. Elisabeth Bumiller, "The Harrimans' Party for the Party That Was," *Washington Post*, November 5, 1980, E1.

102. "Facts That Help Put Election in Focus," *U.S. News & World Report*, November 17, 1980, 38; Mashek, "Massive Shift to Right Story of '80 Elections."

103. Warren Weaver Jr., "Anderson Says He Feels No Bitterness and That He Might Consider 1984 Run," *New York Times*, November 6, 1980, A27.

104. "Carter's Collapse: The Anatomy of Reagan's Victory," *National Journal*, November 8, 1980, 1878.

105. Allan J. Mayer, Thomas M. DeFrank, Eleanor Clift, and Henry W. Hubbard, "Carter: A Long Day's Night," *Newsweek*, November 17, 1980, 29.

106. "A Friendlier Congress for Ronald Reagan," *U.S. News & World Report*, November 17, 1980, 31.

107. Edward Walsh, "Bill Brock: Architect of Republican Revival," *Washington Post*, November 20, 1980, A21; "Election '80—New Faces in the House," *Washington Post*, November 23, 1980, A15.

108. Associated Press, "White Upsets Clinton in Arkansas," November 5, 1980.

109. Ken Khachigian, in discussion with the author, May 2007.

110. "Transcript of Reagan's Remarks," *New York Times*, November 5, 1980, A22.

111. Church et al., "Nation: Reagan Coast-to-Coast."

112. "Transcript of Reagan's Remarks."

Epilogue: Destiny

1. William Safire, *Safire's Political Dictionary* (New York: Oxford University Press, 2008), 154.

2. *A Time for Choosing: The Speeches of Ronald Reagan, 1961–1982* (Chicago: Regnery Gateway, 1983), 189.

3. Helene Von Damm, *At Reagan's Side: Twenty Years in the Political Mainstream* (New York: Doubleday, 1988), 119.

4. Aleksandr Solzhenitsyn, "A Special Message," *National Review*, June 28, 2004, 26.

5. Michael T. Kaufman, "Solzhenitsyn, Literary Giant Who Defied Soviets, Dies at 89," *New York Times*, August 4, 2008, A1.

6. "Detente Comes Down to Earth," *Economist*, July 26, 1976, 55.

7. Michael Waldman, ed., *My Fellow Americans: The Most Important Speeches of America's Presidents, from George Washington to George W. Bush* (Naperville, IL: Sourcebooks, 2003), 253.

8. Jay Nordlinger, "Being Sharansky—On Russia, Israel, 'Reaganite Readings' . . . ," *National Review*, July 4, 2005.

9. Nicole Hoplin, "Cold War–Era European Leaders Reflect on Reagan and the Impact of Freedom," *Libertas*, 30, no. 1.

10. *A Time for Choosing*, 186.

11. Karl Vick, "U.S., Soviet Diplomatic License Plates Retain Cold War Symbolism," *St. Petersburg Times*, December 19, 1987, 8A.

12. Christopher Andrew and Vasili Mitrokhin, *The Sword and the Shield: The Mitrokhin Archive and the Secret History of the KGB* (New York: Basic Books, 2000), 242.

13. Newt Gingrich, in discussion with the author, May 21, 2006.

14. George Will, in discussion with the author.

15. R. Emmett Tyrrell Jr., "Mr. Can-Do Versus Mr. Can't," *Washington Post*, September 15, 1980, A21.

16. Peter B. Sperry, "The Real Reagan Economic Record: Responsible and Successful Fiscal Policy," Heritage Foundation, March 1, 2001, http://www.heritage.org/research/taxes/bg1414.cfm.

17. Peter Goldman, "The Republican Landslide," *Newsweek*, November 17, 1980, 27

18. Richard Wirthlin, "Reagan for President Campaign Plan," June 29, 1980, Richard Wirthlin Archives Collection.

19. Stanley Greenberg, *Middle Class Dreams: The Politics and Power of the New American Majority* (New Haven: Yale University Press, 1996).

20. George J. Church, Christopher Ogden, and Laurence I. Barrett, "Nation: Reagan Coast-to-Coast," *Time*, November 17, 1980.

21. Peter J. Wallison, "Reagan Co-opted," *American Spectator*, July–August 2007; James MacGregor Burns, "Risks of the Middle," *Washington Post*, October 24, 1999, B7.

22. Edward Kennedy, "Reagan Brought 'A Special Grace,'" *Boston Irish Reporter*, July 31, 2004.

23. Adam Miller, "Wyman Hails Her Great Ex," *New York Post*, June 12, 2004, 13.

24. Theodore H. White, "The Small-Town Boys Who Seek to Govern," *Washington Star*, September 29, 1980, A1.

25. Lou Cannon, *President Reagan: The Role of a Lifetime* (New York: Norton, 2000), 113.

26. Lou Cannon, "Role of a Lifetime," *Newsweek*, October 4, 1999, 31.

27. Gerald C. Lubenow, Martin Kasindorf, Frank Maier, and James Doyle, "Ronald Reagan Up Close," *Newsweek*, July 21, 1980, 25.

28. Ralph Z. Hallow, "A Not-So-Mellow Skeptic Sees a GOP with No Focus," *Washington Times*, November 23, 2005, A1.

29. Phil Alexander, in discussion with the author.

30. Steven V. Roberts, "Reagan's Final Rating Is Best of Any President Since '40s," *New York Times*, January 18, 1989, A1.

31. John McConnell, in discussion with the author, March 30, 2006.

32. Grover Norquist, in discussion with the author, March 21, 2006.

33. Newt Gingrich, in discussion with the author, May 21, 2006.

34. William F. Buckley Jr., in discussion with the author.

35. Ron Robinson, in discussion with the author; "Commencement Address," University of Notre Dame, May 17, 1981; Ronald Reagan, "Remarks and a Question-and-Answer Session with the Students and Faculty," Moscow State University, May 31, 1988.

36. Karen Spencer, in discussion with the author, December 20, 2006.

37. Newt Gingrich, "What Would Lincoln Say to Us Today?" *Newsmax*, February 2009, 62.

38. Ed Blakely, in discussion with the author, April 17, 2007.

39. Richard Cheney, in discussion with the author, March 19, 2007.

40. Philip Kennicott, "Reagan's Legacy, Where 'Angels' Dares to Tread," *Washington Post*, December 21, 2003, N2.

41. Steve Neal, "Scripts Have Changed, but Reagan Remains a Star," *Chicago Tribune*, March 7, 1980, 1.

42. Melinda Beck, Mary Lord, Gloria Borger, Martin Kasindorf, and Jerry Buckley, "A Star-Studded Inaugural," *Newsweek*, January 26, 1981, 32.

43. Tip O'Neill with William Novak, *Man of the House: The Life and Political Memoirs of Speaker Tip O'Neill* (New York: Random House, 1987), 360.

44. David S. Broder, "When Partisan Venom Didn't Rule," *Washington Post*, January 29, 2006, B7.

45. Ronald Reagan, *An American Life: The Autobiography* (New York: Simon & Schuster, 1990), 215; Nancy Reagan with William Novak, *My Turn: The Memoirs of Nancy Reagan* (New York: Random House, 1989), 212–213.

46. Arlie Schardt, Lucy Howard, George Hackett, Eric Gelman, and Renee Michael, "TV's Rush to Judgment," *Newsweek*, July 28, 1980, 72.

47. Veronique de Rugy and Tad DeHaven, "On Spending, Reagan Is No Bush," *Cato Institute Tax and Budget Bulletin*, August 2003, no. 15; Chris Edwards, "Number of Federal Subsidy Programs Tops 1800," *Cato Institute Tax and Budget Bulletin*, April 2009, no. 56.

48. Office of the Clerk of the House of Representatives, "Presidential Vetoes," http://clerk.house.gov/art_history/house_history/vetoes.html.

49. Paul Krugman, *The Conscience of a Liberal* (New York: W. W. Norton & Co., 2007), 178.

50. Robert Shrum, in discussion with the author, March 19, 2008.

51. Peter Hannaford, in discussion with the author; Ken Khachigian, in discussion with the author.

52. David E. Rosenbaum, "The Gridiron: Bush and Quayle Join in an Evening's Ribbing," *New York Times*, April 3, 1989, A18.

53. John Sears, "Reagan: How He Decides," *Washington Post*, July 16, 1980, A19.

54. Wallace Turner, "Anti-Reagan Protests Continue for 3d Day on California Campus," *New York Times*, November 7, 1980, 16.

55. Anthony Lewis, "The Tidal Wave," *New York Times*, November 6, 1980, A35.

56. Wesley G. Pippert, United Press International, October 19, 1980.

57. Judy Bachrach, "Reagan Tries Hard to Avoid Communicating," *Washington Star*, October 3, 1980, A4.

58. Walter Wisniewski, "Soviets Warn Reagan They Will Not Lose Arms Race," United Press International, November 7, 1980; "World News Summary," United Press International, November 7, 1980.

59. Michele Davis, "1980 Diary," November 6 and 7, 1980, Michele Davis Archives Collection.

60. "Job Seekers Take Notice," *Human Events*, November 22, 1980, 4.

61. Douglas Brinkley, *The Unfinished Presidency: Jimmy Carter's Quest for Global Peace* (New York: Viking, 1998), 3.

62. Chet Currier, "Markets Surge on GOP Victory," Associated Press, November 5, 1980.

63. John Tierney, "A Cold Morning in Vermont," *New York Times*, June 13, 2004, 38.

64. Muriel Coleman, in discussion with the author, May 2, 2007.

65. Jeb Bush, in discussion with the author, August 22, 2006.

66. Adam Clymer, "'Minority Party' Strives for a Wider Appeal," *New York Times*, July 14, 1980, A9.

67. Lou Cannon, *Governor Reagan: His Rise to Power* (New York: PublicAffairs, 2003), 97–98.

68. Ronald Reagan, "Homosexual Rights: Policy Statement," April 1, 1980, Box 371, Ronald Reagan Presidential Library, Simi Valley, CA.

69. *A Time for Choosing*, 199.

70. Ronald Reagan, First Inaugural Address, January 20, 1981, http://www.bartleby.com/124/pres61.html.

71. Jack Diggins, in discussion with the author, August 4, 2006.

72. Roberts, "Reagan's Final Rating Is Best of Any President Since '40s."

73. George F. Will, "The Candidates at Bay," *Newsweek*, October 22, 1984; George F. Will, "'Fresh Start'?" *Washington Post*, October 31, 1985; George F. Will, "Bad Advice from Washington," *Washington Post*, July 7, 1991; George F. Will, "The Limits of Sunniness," *Washington Post*, February 11, 2007; George F. Will, "The Cosmopolitan," *Washington Post*, August 3, 2008.

74. Neil Reynolds, "Freed Poles Build One for the Gipper," *Globe and Mail* (Toronto), July 4, 2007, B2.

75. Edward Crane, "The Rise and Fall of the GOP," *Cato Policy Report*, November/December 2003, 2.

76. "Transcript of Reagan's Farewell Address to American People," *New York Times*, January 12, 1989, B8.

77. James Rosen, "Tom Wolfe's Washington Post," *Washington Post*, July 2, 2006, B5.

78. Crane, "The Rise and Fall of the GOP."

79. Al Neuharth, "Two 'Iron Ladies' at Reagan's Funeral," *USA Today*, June 11, 2004, 13A.

80. Parke May, "A National Farewell for a Beloved Leader," *Washington Times*, June 19, 2004, B6; Evan Thomas and Eleanor Clift, "As the Shadows Fell," *Newsweek*, June 21, 2004, 22.

81. James Stockdale, in discussion with the author, February 15, 2007.

82. Ibid.

83. Tarron Lively and Jeffrey Sparshott, "Funeral Procession Fuels Record Usage of Metro," *Washington Times*, June 11, 2004, A12.

84. "Cashing in on Reagan Funeral," *The Hill*, June 22, 2004, 10.

85. Confidential interview with the author.

86. Julie Mason, "Friends Travel to D.C. to Reminisce," *Houston Chronicle*, June 11, 2004, 17.

87. Colleen McCain Nelson, "Visitors Passing on Presidential Libraries," *Dallas Morning News*, March 24, 2006, 1A; Carl Schoettler and Seth Michelson, "They Provide Stamps of Approval," *Baltimore Sun*, April 6, 1997, 3J.

88. Mark Steyn, "The Joke's on Them," *National Review*, June 28, 2004, 56.

89. "The Week," *National Review*, June 28, 2004.

90. Adrian Wooldridge, "The Great Delegator," *New York Times*, January 29, 2006, 11.

91. Bill Carter, "Shifting 'Reagans' to Cable Has CBS Facing New Critics," *New York Times*, November 5, 2003, 1

92. James Reston, "The Evils of 2 Lessers," *New York Times*, September 28, 1980, E21.

93. Nancy Reynolds, in discussion with the author, October 3, 2006.

94. Lubenow et al., "Ronald Reagan Up Close."

95. John F. Stacks, *Watershed: The Campaign for the Presidency, 1980* (New York: Times Books, 1981), 13–14.

96. William F. Buckley Jr., in discussion with the author.

Bibliography

Books

A Time for Choosing: The Speeches of Ronald Reagan, 1961–1982. Chicago: Regnery Gateway, 1983.

Abramson, Paul R., John H. Aldrich, and David W. Rohde. *Change and Continuity in the 1980 Elections.* Washington, DC: Congressional Quarterly Press, 1982.

Adams, William C., ed. *Television Coverage of the 1980 Presidential Campaign.* Norwood, NJ: ABLEX Publishing, 1983.

Adler, Bill, with Bill Adler Jr., eds. *The Reagan Wit.* Aurora, IL: Caroline House Publishers, 1981.

Agnew, Spiro T. *Go Quietly . . . or Else.* New York: William Morrow, 1980.

Aikman, Lonnelle. *The Living White House.* Washington, DC: White House Historical Association/National Geographic Society, 1982.

Alexander, Herbert E. *Financing the 1980 Election.* Lexington, MA: Lexington Books, 1983.

American Enterprise Institute. *The Candidates 1980: Where They Stand.* Washington, DC: AEI, 1980.

Andersen, Hans Christian. *The Emperor's New Clothes.* Boston: Houghton Mifflin Harcourt, 2004.

Anderson, Martin. *Revolution.* New York: Harcourt Brace Jovanovich, 1988.

Anderson, Patrick. *Electing Jimmy Carter: The Campaign of 1976.* Baton Rouge, LA: Louisiana State University Press, 1994.

Andrew, Christopher, and Vasili Mitrokhin. *The Sword and the Shield: The Mitrokhin Archive and the Secret History of the KGB.* New York: Basic Books, 1999.

Andrew, Christopher, and Vasili Mitrokhin. *The World Was Going Our Way: The KGB and the Battle for the Third World.* New York: Basic Books, 2005.

Andrew, John A., III. *The Other Side of the Sixties: Young Americans for Freedom and the Rise of Conservative Politics.* New Brunswick, NJ: Rutgers University Press, 1997.

Bailey, Thomas A. *Democrats vs. Republicans: The Continuing Clash.* New York: Meredith Press, 1968.

Baker, James A., III, with Steve Fiffer. *"Work Hard, Study . . . and Keep Out of Politics!": Adventures and Lessons from an Unexpected Public Life.* New York: G. P. Putnam's Sons, 2006.

Bakshian, Aram, Jr. *The Candidates—1980: A Professional Handicaps the Presidential Derby.* New Rochelle, NY: Arlington House, 1980.

Barletta, John R., and Rochelle Schweizer. *Riding with Reagan: From the White House to the Ranch.* New York: Citadel Press, 2005.

Barone, Michael. *Our Country: The Shaping of America from Roosevelt to Reagan*. New York: Free Press, 1990.

Barrett, Laurence I. *Gambling with History: Ronald Reagan in the White House*. New York: Penguin Books, 1984.

Barron, John. *KGB Today: The Hidden Hand*. New York: Reader's Digest Press, 1983.

Bell, Jack. *Mr. Conservative: Barry Goldwater*. New York: Doubleday, 1962.

Billingsley, Kenneth Lloyd. *Hollywood Party: How Communism Seduced the American Film Industry in the 1930s and 1940s*. Rocklin, CA: Forum, 1998.

Black, Earl, and Merle Black. *The Rise of Southern Republicans*. Cambridge, MA: Belknap Press, 2002.

Black, Earl, and Merle Black. *The Vital South: How Presidents Are Elected*. Cambridge, MA: Harvard University Press, 1992.

Boller, Paul F., Jr. *Presidential Anecdotes*. New York: Penguin Books, 1981.

Boller, Paul F., Jr. *Presidential Campaigns*. New York: Oxford University Press, 1984.

Bourne, Peter J. *Jimmy Carter: A Comprehensive Biography from Plains to Postpresidency*. New York: Scribner, 1997.

Boyarsky, Bill. *Ronald Reagan: His Life and Rise to the Presidency*. New York: Random House, 1981.

Boyarsky, Bill. *The Rise of Ronald Reagan*. New York: Random House, 1967.

Bradlee, Ben. *A Good Life: Newspapering and Other Adventures*. New York: Touchstone, 1995.

Brinkley, Douglas, ed. *The Reagan Diaries*. New York: HarperCollins, 2007.

Brinkley, Douglas. *Gerald R. Ford*. New York: Times Books, 2007.

Brinkley, Douglas. *The Unfinished Presidency: Jimmy Carter's Journey Beyond the White House*. New York: Penguin Books, 1998.

Broder, David S. *The Party's Over: The Failure of Politics in America*. New York: Harper & Row, 1972.

Brookhiser, Richard. *The Outside Story: How Democrats and Republicans Re-elected Reagan*. Garden City, NY: Doubleday, 1986.

Buckley, William F., Jr. *God and Man at Yale: The Superstitions of "Academic Freedom."* Washington, DC: Regnery Gateway, 1986.

Buckley, William F., Jr. *On the Firing Line: The Public Life of Our Public Figures*. New York: Random House, 1989.

Buckley, William F., Jr. *The Reagan I Knew*. New York: Basic Books, 2008.

Buckley, William F., Jr. *Up from Liberalism*. New York: Bantam Books, 1968.

Buckley, Priscilla L. *Living It Up with National Review: A Memoir*. Dallas, TX: Spence Publishing Company, 2005.

Bunzel, John H., ed. *Political Passages: Journeys of Change Through Two Decades, 1968–1988*. New York: Free Press, 1988.

Busch, Andrew E. *Reagan's Victory: The Presidential Election of 1980 and the Rise of the Right*. Lawrence, KS: University Press of Kansas, 2005.

Bush, Barbara. *A Memoir*. New York: A Lisa Drew Book/Scribner, 1994.

Bush, George, with Victor Gold. *Looking Forward: An Autobiography*. New York: Doubleday, 1987.

Bush, Gregory, ed. *Campaign Speeches of American Presidential Candidates, 1948–1984*. New York: Frederick Ungar Publishing, 1985.

Cannon, Lou. *Governor Reagan: His Rise to Power*. New York: PublicAffairs, 2003.

Cannon, Lou. *President Reagan: The Role of a Lifetime*. New York: PublicAffairs, 2000.

Cannon, Lou. *Reagan*. New York: G. P. Putnam's Sons, 1982.

Carroll, Peter N. *It Seemed Like Nothing Happened: America in the 1970s*. New Brunswick, NJ: Rutgers University Press, 2000.

Carter, Hodding, III. *The South Strikes Back: The Citizens' Council in Mississippi Leads the Area-Wide Resistance to Integration*. Garden City, NY: Doubleday, 1959.

Carter, Jimmy. *Keeping Faith: Memoirs of a President*. New York: Bantam Books, 1982.

Carter, Rosalynn. *First Lady from Plains*. Fayetteville, AR: University of Arkansas Press, 1994.

Cash, Kevin. *Who the Hell Is William Loeb?* Manchester, NH: Amoskeag Press, 1975.

Cassell, Clark, ed. *President Reagan's Quotations*. Washington, DC: Braddock Publications, 1984.

Clymer, Adam. *Edward M. Kennedy: A Biography*. New York: William Morrow, 1999.

Cohen, Richard M., and Jules Witcover. *A Heartbeat Away: The Investigation and Resignation of Vice President Spiro T. Agnew.* New York: Viking Press, 1974.

Colacello, Bob. *Ronnie & Nancy: Their Path to the White House, 1911 to 1980.* New York: Warner Books, 2004.

Costikyan, Edward N. *How to Win Votes: The Politics of 1980.* New York: Harcourt Brace Jovanovich, 1980.

Couch, Ernie, ed. *Presidential Trivia.* Nashville, TN: Rutledge Hill Press, 1996.

Coy, Walter Theron, Sr. *My Uncle Sam Don't Like Me.* New York: Vantage Press, 1980.

Crane, Philip M. *Surrender in Panama: The Case Against the Treaty.* Ottawa, IL: Green Hill, 1978.

Crane, Philip M. *The Sum of Good Government.* Ottawa, IL: Green Hill, 1976.

Crawford, Alan. *Thunder on the Right: The "New Right" and the Politics of Resentment.* New York: Pantheon Books, 1980.

Crouse, Timothy. *The Boys on the Bus.* New York: Random House, 1973.

Dallek, Matthew. *The Right Moment: Ronald Reagan's First Victory and the Decisive Turning Point in American Politics.* New York: Oxford University Press, 2004.

Dallek, Robert. *Ronald Reagan: The Politics of Symbolism.* Cambridge, MA: Harvard University Press, 1999.

David, Paul T., and David H. Everson, eds. *The Presidential Election and Transition 1980–1981.* Carbondale, IL: Southern Illinois University Press, 1983.

Davis, Patti. *The Way I See It: An Autobiography.* New York: G. P. Putnam's Sons, 1992.

Deaver, Michael K. *A Different Drummer: My Thirty Years with Ronald Reagan.* New York: HarperCollins, 2001.

Deaver, Michael K. *Nancy: A Portrait of My Years with Nancy Reagan.* New York: William Morrow, 2004.

Deaver, Michael K., with Mickey Herskowitz. *Behind the Scenes: In Which the Author Talks About Ronald and Nancy Reagan . . . and Himself.* New York: William Morrow, 1987.

DeFrank, Thomas M. *Write It When I'm Gone: Remarkable Off-the-Record Conversations with Gerald R. Ford.* New York: G. P. Putnam's Sons, 2007.

Dervin, Daniel. *Bernard Shaw: A Psychological Study.* Lewisburg, PA: Bucknell University Press, 1975.

Devine, Donald J. *Reagan Electionomics: How Reagan Ambushed the Pollsters.* Ottawa, IL: Green Hill, 1983.

Dickson, Paul, ed. *The Dickson Baseball Dictionary.* New York: Avon Books, 1989.

Diggins, John Patrick. *Ronald Reagan: Fate, Freedom, and the Making of History.* New York: W. W. Norton & Company, 2007.

Donovan, Robert J. *The Future of the Republican Party.* New York: NAL-World, 1964.

Drew, Elizabeth. *Portrait of an Election: The 1980 Presidential Campaign.* New York: Simon & Schuster, 1981.

Drosnin, Michael. *Citizen Hughes.* New York: Holt, Rinehart and Winston, 1985.

D'Souza, Dinesh. *Ronald Reagan: How an Ordinary Man Became an Extraordinary Leader.* New York: Free Press, 1997.

Dugger, Ronnie. *On Reagan: The Man & His Presidency.* New York: McGraw-Hill, 1983.

Duignan, Peter, and Alvin Rabushka. *The United States in the 1980s.* Stanford, CA: Hoover Institution, 1980.

East, John P. *The American Conservative Movement: The Philosophical Founders.* Washington, DC: Regnery Gateway, 1986.

Edsall, Thomas B. *Building Red America: The New Conservative Coalition and the Drive for Permanent Power.* New York: Basic Books, 2006.

Edwards, Anne. *Early Reagan: The Rise to Power.* New York: William Morrow, 1987.

Edwards, Anne. *The Reagans: Portrait of a Marriage.* New York: St. Martin's Press, 2003.

Edwards, Lee. *Goldwater: The Man Who Made a Revolution.* Washington, DC: Regnery Gateway, 1995.

Edwards, Lee. *Ronald Reagan: A Political Biography.* Houston TX: Nordland Publishing International, 1981.

Edwards, Lee. *The Conservative Revolution: The Movement That Remade America.* New York: Free Press, 1999.

Edwards, Lee. *The Essential Ronald Reagan: A Profile in Courage, Justice, and Wisdom.* Lanham, MD: Rowman & Littlefield, 2005.

Eigen, Lewis D. and Jonathan P. Siegel. *The Macmillan Dictionary of Political Quotations.* New York: Macmillan, 1993.

Ericson, Edward E., Jr., and Daniel J. Mahoney. *The Solzhenitsyn Reader: New and Essential Writings 1947–2005.* Wilmington, DE: ISI Books, 2006.

Evans, M. Stanton. *The Future of Conservatism.* Garden City, NY: Anchor Books, 1969.

Evans, M. Stanton. *The Theme Is Freedom: Religion, Politics, and the American Tradition.* Washington, DC: Regnery Gateway, 1994.

Evans, Rod L., and Irwin M. Berent. *The Quotable Conservative: The Giants of Conservatism on Liberty, Freedom, Individual. Responsibility, and Traditional Virtues.* Holbrook, MA: Adams Publishing, 1995.

Evans, Rowland, and Robert Novak. *The Reagan Revolution.* New York: E. P. Dutton, 1981.

Evans, Thomas W. *The Education of Ronald Reagan: The General Electric Years and the Untold Story of His Conversion to Conservatism.* New York: The Mentor Center, 2006.

Ferguson, Thomas, and Joel Rogers, eds. *The Hidden Election: Politics and Economics in the 1980 Presidential Campaign.* New York: Pantheon Books, 1981.

Feulner, Edwin J., and Doug Wilson. *Getting America Right: The True Conservative Values Our Nation Needs Today.* New York: Crown Forum, 2006.

Ford, Gerald R. *A Time to Heal: The Autobiography of Gerald R. Ford.* New York: Harper & Row, 1979.

Franke, David, ed. *Quotations from Chairman Bill: The Best of William F. Buckley, Jr.* New York: Pocket Books, 1971.

Freeman, Joe. *At Berkeley in the Sixties: The Education of an Activist, 1961–1965.* Bloomington, IN: Indiana University Press, 2004.

Frohnen, Bruce, Jeremy Beer, and Jeffrey O. Nelson, eds. *American Conservatism: An Encyclopedia.* Wilmington, DE: ISI Books, 2006.

Frum, David. *Dead Right.* New York: Basic Books, 1994.

Frum, David. *How We Got Here: The 70's—The Decade that Brought You Modern Life (For Better or Worse).* New York: Basic Books, 2000.

Garment, Leonard. *In Search of Deep Throat: The Greatest Political Mystery of Our Time.* New York: Basic Books, 2000.

Gelb, Norman. *The Berlin Wall: Kennedy, Khrushchev, and a Showdown in the Heart of Europe.* New York: Simon & Schuster, 1986.

Germond, Jack W., and Jules Witcover, *Blue Smoke and Mirrors: How Reagan Won and Why Carter Lost the Election of 1980.* New York: Viking Press, 1981.

Goldwater, Barry M., with Jack Casserly. *Goldwater.* New York: Doubleday, 1988.

Goldwater, Barry. *The Conscience of a Conservative.* New York: Hillman Books, 1960.

Gould, Lewis L. *Grand Old Party: A History of the Republicans.* New York: Random House, 2003.

Green, Fitzhugh. *George Bush: An Intimate Portrait.* New York: Hippocrene Books, 1989.

Green, Mark, and Gail MacColl. *There He Goes Again: Ronald Reagan's Reign of Error.* New York: Pantheon Books, 1983.

Greenberg, Stanley B. *Middle Class Dreams: The Politics and Power of the New American Majority.* New Haven, CT: Yale University Press, 1995.

Greenfield, Jeff. *The Real Campaign: How the Media Missed the Story of the 1980 Campaign.* New York: Summit Books, 1982.

Greenstein, Fred I. *The Presidential Difference: Leadership Style from FDR to George W. Bush. Second Edition.* Princeton, NJ: Princeton University Press, 2004.

Halberstam, David. *The Powers That Be.* Chicago: University of Illinois Press, 2000.

Hannaford, Peter, ed. *Recollections of Reagan: A Portrait of Ronald Reagan.* New York: William Morrow, 1997.

Hannaford, Peter. *The Reagans: A Political Portrait.* New York: Coward-McCann, 1983.

Harwood, Richard, ed. *The Pursuit of the Presidency 1980.* New York: Berkley Books, 1980.

Hatfield, Mark, O. with the Senate Historical Office. *Vice Presidents of the United States, 1789–1993.* Washington: U.S. Government Printing Office, 1997.

Hayward, Steven F. *Greatness: Reagan, Churchill, and the Making of Extraordinary Leaders.* New York: Crown Forum, 2005.

Hayward, Steven F. *The Age of Reagan: The Fall of the Old Liberal Order, 1964–1980.* Roseville, CA: Forum, 2001.

Hayward, Steven F. *The Real Jimmy Carter: How Our Worst Ex-President Undermines American Foreign Policy, Coddles Dictators, and Created the Party of Clinton and Kerry.* Washington, DC: Regnery Gateway, 2004.

Helms, Jesse. *Here's Where I Stand: A Memoir.* New York: Random House, 2005.

Hersh, Seymour M. *The Dark Side of Camelot.* New York: Little, Brown and Co., 1997.

Hess, Stephen, and David S. Broder. *The Republican Establishment: The Present and Future of the GOP.* New York: Harper & Row, 1967.

Hofstadter, Richard. *The American Political Tradition: And the Men Who Made It.* New York: Vintage Books, 1974.

Holmes, Joseph R., ed. *The Quotable Ronald Reagan: The Common Sense and Straight Talk of Former California Governor Ronald Reagan.* San Diego: JRH & Associates, 1975.

Honegger, Barbara. *October Surprise: Did the Reagan-Bush Election Campaign Sabotage President Carter's Attempts to Free the American Hostages in Iran?* New York: Tudor, 1989.

Jamieson, Kathleen Hall. *Everything You Think You Know About Politics . . . and Why You're Wrong.* New York: New Republic, 2000.

Johnson, Haynes. *Sleepwalking Through History: America in the Reagan Years.* New York: Anchor Books, 1992.

Jones, Charles O. *The Trusteeship Presidency: Jimmy Carter and the United States Congress.* Baton Rouge, LA: Louisiana State University Press, 1988.

Jones, Charles O., ed. *The Reagan Legacy: Promise and Performance.* Chatham, NJ: Chatham House, 1988.

Jordan, Hamilton. *Crisis: The Last Year of the Carter Presidency.* New York: G. P. Putnam's Sons, 1982.

Jowett, John, ed. *William Shakespeare: The Tragedy of King Richard III.* Oxford, UK: Oxford University Press, 2000.

Kaiser, Charles. *1968 in America: Music, Politics, Chaos, Counterculture, and the Shaping of a Generation.* New York: Weidenfeld and Nicolson, 1988.

Kaufman, Burton I. *The Presidency of James Earl Carter, Jr.* Lawrence, KS: University Press of Kansas, 1993.

Kelley, Kitty. *Nancy Reagan: The Unauthorized Biography.* New York: Pocket Star Books, 1991.

Kelley, Kitty. *The Family: The Real Story of the Bush Dynasty.* New York: Doubleday, 2004.

Kemp, Jack. *An American Renaissance: A Strategy for the 1980s.* New York: Harper & Row, 1979.

Kengor, Paul, and Patricia Clarke Doerner. *The Judge: William P. Clark, Ronald Reagan's Top Hand.* San Francisco: Ignatius Press, 2007.

Kengor, Paul. *God and Ronald Reagan: A Spiritual Life.* New York: Regan Books, 2004.

Kengor, Paul. *The Crusader: Ronald Reagan and the Fall of Communism.* New York: Regan Books, 2006.

Kessler, Ronald. *Inside the White House: The Hidden Lives of the Modern Presidents and the Secrets of the World's Most Powerful Institution.* New York: Pocket Books, 1995.

Kilian, Pamela. *Barbara Bush: A Biography.* New York: St. Martin's Press, 1992.

King, Nicholas. *George Bush: A Biography.* New York: Dodd, Mead & Company, 1980.

Kirk, Russell. *The Roots of American Order.* Washington, DC: Regnery Gateway, 1991.

Kirkpatrick, Jeane J. *The Reagan Phenomenon and Other Speeches on Foreign Policy.* Washington, DC: American Enterprise Institute, 1983.

Kissinger, Henry. *The White House Years.* Boston: Little, Brown and Co., 1979.

Klein, Joe. *Politics Lost: How American Democracy Was Trivialized by People Who Think You're Stupid.* New York: Doubleday, 2006.

Krugman, Paul. *The Conscience of a Liberal.* New York: W. W. Norton & Co., 2007.

Kuttner, Robert. *Revolt of the Haves: Tax Rebellions and Hard Times.* New York: Simon & Schuster, 1980.

Laxalt, Paul. *Nevada's Paul Laxalt: A Memoir.* Reno, NV: Jack Bacon & Company, 2000.

Laxalt, Paul. *The Nominating of a President: The Three Nominations of Ronald Reagan as Republican Candidate for the Presidency.* Reno, NV: Native Nevadan Publications, 1985.

Leighton, Frances Spatz. *The Search for the Real Nancy Reagan.* New York: Macmillan, 1987,

Link, William A. *Righteous Warrior: Jesse Helms and the Rise of Modern Conservatism.* New York: St. Martin's Press, 2008.

MacDougall, Malcolm D. *We Almost Made It.* New York: Crown Publishers, 1977.

Marlin, George J. *Fighting the Good Fight: A History of the New York Conservative Party.* South Bend, IN: St. Augustine's Press. 2002.

Marton, Kati. *Hidden Power: Presidential Marriages That Shaped Our Recent History.* New York: Pantheon Books, 2001.

Mayer, Jane, and Doyle McManus. *Landslide: The Unmaking of the President, 1984–1988.* Boston: Houghton Mifflin, 1988.

McClelland, Doug. *Hollywood on Ronald Reagan: Friends and Enemies Discuss Our President, the Actor.* Winchester, MA: Faber and Faber, 1983.

McGrath, Jim, ed. *Heartbeat: George Bush in His Own Words.* New York: A Lisa Drew Book/Scribner, 2001.

McLuhan Marshall. *Understanding Media: The Extensions of Man.* New York: A Mentor Book, 1964.

McWilliams, Wilson Carey. *Beyond the Politics of Disappointment? American Elections 1980–1998.* New York: Chatham House, 2000.

Meese, Edwin, III. *With Reagan.* Washington, DC: Regnery Gateway, 1992.

Melder, Keith. *Hail to the Candidate: Presidential Campaigns from Banners to Broadcasts.* Washington, DC: Smithsonian Institution Press, 1992.

Micklethwait, John, and Adrian Wooldridge. *The Right Nation: Conservative Power in America.* New York: Penguin Books, 2004.

Middendorf, J. William, II. *A Glorious Disaster: Barry Goldwater's Presidential Campaign and the Origins of the Conservative Movement.* New York: Basic Books, 2006.

Miers, Earl Schenck. *The White House and the Presidency.* New York: Wonder Books, 1965.

Minutaglio, Bill. *First Son: George W. Bush and the Bush Family Dynasty.* New York: Times Books, 1999.

Moore, Jonathan, ed. *The Campaign for President: 1980 In Retrospect.* Cambridge, MA: Ballinger Publishing Company, 1981.

Moos, Malcolm, ed. *H. L. Mencken: On Politics: A Carnival of Buncombe.* New York: Vintage Books, 1960.

Morris, Edmund. *Dutch: A Memoir of Ronald Reagan,* New York: Random House, 1999.

Morris, Kenneth E. *Jimmy Carter: American Moralist.* Athens, GA: University of Georgia Press, 1996.

Mounger, William D., with Joseph L. Maxwell III. *Amidst the Fray: My Life in Politics, Culture, and Mississippi.* Brandon, MS: Quail Ridge Press, 2006.

Muir, William Ker. *The Bully Pulpit: The Presidential Leadership of Ronald Reagan.* San Francisco: ICS Press, 1992.

Murray, Charles. *Losing Ground: American Social Policy, 1950–1980.* New York: Basic Books, 1984.

Nash, George H. *The Conservative Intellectual Movement in America Since 1945.* Wilmington, DE: ISI Books, 1998.

Neustadt, Richard E. *Presidential Power and the Modern Presidents: The Politics of Leadership from Roosevelt to Reagan.* New York: Free Press, 1991.

Nofziger, Lyn. *Nofziger.* Washington, DC: Regnery Gateway, 1992.

Novak, Robert D. *The Prince of Darkness: 50 Years Reporting in Washington.* New York: Crown Forum, 2007.

O'Brien, Cormac. *Secret Lives of the U.S. Presidents: What Your Teachers Never Told You About the Men of the White House.* Philadelphia: Quirk Books, 2004.

O'Neill, Tip, with William Novak. *Man of the House: The Life and Political Memoirs of Speaker Tip O'Neill.* New York: Random House, 1987.

Osborne, John. *White House Watch: The Ford Years.* Washington, DC: New Republic Books, 1977.

O'Sullivan, John. *The President, the Pope, and the Prime Minister: Three Who Changed the World.* Washington, DC: Regnery Publishing, 2006.

Palmer, John L., and Isabel V. Sawhill, eds. *The Reagan Record: An Assessment of America's Changing Domestic Priorities.* Cambridge, MA: Ballinger Publishing Company, 1984.

Parmet, Herbert S. *George Bush: The Life of a Lone Star Yankee.* New York: A Lisa Drew Book/Scribner, 1997.

Pemberton, William E. *Exit with Honor: The Life and Presidency of Ronald Reagan*. Armonk, NY: M. E. Sharpe, 1998

Perlstein, Rick. *Before the Storm: Barry Goldwater and the Unmaking of the American Consensus*. New York: Hill and Wang, 2001.

Perry, Roland. *Hidden Power: The Programming of the President*. New York: Beaufort Books, 1984.

Persico, Joseph E. *Casey: From the OSS to the CIA*. New York: Viking Press, 1990.

Peters, Charles. *Five Days in Philadelphia*. New York: PublicAffairs, 2005.

Phillips, Howard, ed. *The New Right at Harvard*. Vienna, VA: Conservative Caucus, 1983.

Podhoretz, John. *Hell of a Ride: Backstage at the White House Follies, 1989–1993*. New York: Simon & Schuster, 1993.

Polsby, Nelson W., and Aaron Wildavsky. *Presidential Elections: Contemporary Strategies of American Electoral Politics*. New York: Free Press, 1991.

Polsby, Nelson W., and Aaron Wildavsky. *Presidential Elections: Strategies of American Electoral Politics*. New York: Charles Scribner's Sons, 1984.

Pomper, Gerald, et al. *The Election of 1980: Reports and Interpretations*. Chatham, NJ: Chatham House, 1981.

Post, Robert C., ed. *Every Four Years: The American Presidency*. Washington, DC: Smithsonian Exposition Books, 1980.

Powell, Jody. *The Other Side of the Story*. New York: William Morrow, 1984.

Powell, S. Steven. *Covert Cadre: Inside the Institute for Policy Studies*. Ottawa, IL: Green Hill Publishers, 1987.

Presidential Inaugural Committee. *A Great New Beginning—The 1981 Inaugural Story*. Washington, DC: 1981.

Radcliffe, Donnie. *Simply Barbara Bush: A Portrait of America's Candid First Lady*. New York: Warner Books, 1989.

Ranney, Austin, ed. *The American Elections of 1980*. Washington, DC: American Enterprise Institute, 1981.

Reagan, Maureen. *First Father, First Daughter: A Memoir*. Boston: Little, Brown and Co., 1989.

Reagan, Michael, with Joe Hyams. *On the Outside Looking In*. New York: Zebra Books, 1988.

Reagan, Michael. *In the Words of Ronald Reagan: The Wit, Wisdom, and Eternal Optimism of America's 40th President*. Nashville, TN: Thomas Nelson, 2004.

Reagan, Nancy, with William Novak. *My Turn: The Memoirs of Nancy Reagan*. New York: Random House, 1989.

Reagan, Nancy. *I Love You, Ronnie: The Letters of Ronald Reagan to Nancy Reagan*. New York: Random House, 2000.

Reagan, Ronald. *An American Life: The Autobiography*. New York: Simon & Schuster, 1990.

Reagan, Ronald. *Speaking My Mind: Selected Speeches*. New York: Simon & Schuster, 1989.

Reagan, Ronald, with Charles D. Hobbs. *Ronald Reagan's Call to Action*. New York: Warner Books, 1976.

Reagan, Ronald, and Richard G. Hubler. *Where's the Rest of Me? The Autobiography of Ronald Reagan*. New York: Karz Publishers, 1981.

Reed, Thomas C. *At the Abyss: An Insider's History of the Cold War*. New York: Presidio Press, 2004.

Reeves, Richard. *Convention*. New York: Harcourt Brace Jovanovich, 1977.

Reeves, Richard. *President Reagan: The Triumph of Imagination*. New York: Simon & Schuster, 2005.

Reeves, Richard. *The Reagan Detour*. New York: Simon & Schuster, 1985.

Regnery, Alfred S. *Upstream: The Ascendance of American Conservatism*. New York: Threshold Editions, 2007.

Reshetar, John S., Jr. *The Soviet Polity: Government and Politics in the U.S.S.R.* New York: Harper & Row, 1978.

Reston, James, Jr. *The Lone Star: The Life of John Connally*. New York: Harper & Row, 1989.

Revel, Jean-Francois, with Branko Lazitch. *How Democracies Perish*. New York: Harper & Row, 1983.

Revel, Jean-Francois. *The Totalitarian Temptation*. Garden City, NY: Doubleday, 1977.

Rhatican, Bill, ed. *The Constitution: Written in Sand or Etched in Stone?* Bloomington, IN: Author House, 2006.

Rhatican, Bill, ed. *White House Under Fire*. Bloomington, IN: Author House, 2005.

Roberts, James C. *The Conservative Decade: Emerging Leaders of the 1980s*. Westport, CT: Arlington House, 1980.

Roberts, James C., ed. *A City Upon A Hill: Speeches by Ronald Reagan Before the Conservative Political Action Conference, 1974–1988*. Washington, DC: American Studies Center, 1989.

Robinson, Michael J., and Margaret A. Sheehan. *Over the Wire and on TV: CBS and UPI in Campaign '80*. New York: Russell Sage Foundation, 1983.

Rollins, Ed, with Tom DeFrank. *Bare Knuckles and Back Rooms: My Life in American Politics*. New York: Broadway Books, 1996.

Rusher, William A. *The Making of the New Majority Party*. Ottawa, IL: Green Hill, 1975.

Rusher, William A. *The Rise of the Right*. New York: William Morrow, 1984.

Sabato, Larry J. *The Rise of Political Consultants: New Ways of Winning Elections*. New York: Basic Books, 1981.

Safire, William. *Lend Me Your Ears: Great Speeches in History*. New York: W. W. Norton & Company, 1992.

Safire, William. *Safire's Political Dictionary*. New York: Oxford University Press, 2008.

Sager, Ryan. *The Elephant in the Room: Evangelicals, Libertarians, and the Battle to Control the Republican Party*. Hoboken, NJ: John Wiley and Sons, 2006.

Sandoz, Ellis, and Cecil V. Crabb Jr., eds. *A Tide of Discontent: The 1980 Elections and Their Meaning*. Washington, DC: Congressional Quarterly Press, 1980.

Sargent, L. T. *Contemporary Political Ideologies*. Homewood, IL: Dorsey Press, 1972.

Schlafly, Phyllis. *A Choice, Not An Echo*. Alton, IL: Pere Marquette Press, 1964.

Schlesinger, Arthur M., Jr. *Journals: 1952–2000*. New York: Penguin Books, 2007.

Schlesinger, Arthur M., Jr. *Robert Kennedy and His Times*. Boston: Mariner Books, 2002.

Schlesinger, Arthur M., Jr. *The Cycles of American History*. Boston: Mariner Books, 1999.

Schneider, Gregory L., ed. *Conservatism in America Since 1930: A Reader*. New York: New York University Press, 2003.

Schulman, Bruce J. *The Seventies: The Great Shift in American Culture, Society, and Politics*. Cambridge, MA: Da Capo Press, 2001.

Schweizer, Peter. *Reagan's War: The Epic Story of His Forty-Year Struggle and Final Triumph Over Communism*. New York: Doubleday, 2002.

Schweizer, Peter. *Victory: The Reagan Administration's Secret Strategy That Hastened the Collapse of the Soviet Union*. New York: Atlantic Monthly Press, 1994.

Schweizer, Peter, and Rochelle Schweizer. *The Bushes: Portrait of a Dynasty*. New York: Doubleday, 2004.

Shadegg, Stephen. *What Happened to Goldwater? The Inside Story of the 1964 Republican Campaign*. New York: Holt, Rinehart and Winston, 1965.

Shakespeare, William. *The Complete Works of William Shakespeare: Illustrated*. New York: Avenel Books, 1975.

Shesol, Jeff. *Mutual Contempt: Lyndon Johnson, Robert Kennedy, and the Feud That Defined a Decade*. New York: W. W. Norton & Company, 1997.

Shirley, Craig. *Reagan's Revolution: The Untold Story of the Campaign That Started it All*. Nashville, TN: Nelson Current, 2005.

Shogan, Robert. *None of the Above: Why Presidents Fail—and What Can be Done About It*. New York: A Mentor Book, 1982.

Shrum, Robert. *No Excuses: Concessions of a Serial Campaigner*. New York: Simon & Schuster, 2007.

Sick, Gary. *October Surprise: America's Hostages in Iran and the Election of Ronald Reagan*. New York: Times Books, 1991.

Simon, William E. *A Time for Truth*. New York: Berkley Books, 1979.

Skinner, Kiron K., Annelise Anderson, and Martin Anderson, eds. *Reagan's Path to Victory: The Shaping of Ronald Reagan's Vision: Selected Writings*. New York: Free Press, 2004.

Skinner, Kiron K., Annelise Anderson, and Martin Anderson, eds. *Reagan, In His Own Hand: The Writings of Ronald Reagan That Reveal His Revolutionary Vision for America*. New York: Free Press, 2001.

Skinner, Kiron K., Annelise Anderson, and Martin Anderson, eds. *Reagan: A Life in Letters*. New York: Free Press, 2003.

Skinner, Kiron K., Serhiy Kudelia, Bruce Bueno de Mesquita, and Condoleezza Rice. *The Strategy of Campaigning: Lessons from Ronald Reagan & Boris Yeltsin*. Ann Arbor, MI: University of Michigan Press, 2007.

Smith, Geoffrey. *Reagan and Thatcher*. New York: W. W. Norton & Company, 1991.

Smith, Hedrick, Adam Clymer, Leonard Silk, Robert Lindsey, and Richard Burt. *Reagan the Man, the President*. New York: Macmillan, 1980.

Spada, James. *Ronald Reagan: His Life in Pictures*. New York: St. Martin's Press, 2000.

Stacks, John F. *Watershed: The Campaign for the Presidency, 1980*. New York: Times Books, 1981.

Stockman, David A. *The Triumph of Politics: How the Reagan Revolution Failed*. New York: Harper & Row, 1986.

Strober, Deborah Hart, and Gerald S. Strober. *Reagan: The Man and His Presidency*. Boston: Houghton Mifflin, 1998.

Strock, James M. *Reagan on Leadership: Executive Lessons from the Great Communicator*. Rocklin, CA: Forum, 1998.

Stroud, Kandy. *How Jimmy Won: The Victory Campaign from Plains to the White House*. New York: William Morrow, 1977.

Thomas, Tony. *The Films of Ronald Reagan*. Secaucus, NJ: Citadel Press, 1980.

Treen, David C., ed. *Can You Afford This House?* Edison, NJ: Green Hill Publishers, 1978.

Trilling, Lionel. *The Liberal Imagination: Essays on Literature and Society*. New York: Viking Press, 1950.

Trippi, Joe. *The Revolution Will Not Be Televised: Democracy, the Internet, and the Overthrow of Everything*. New York: Regan Books, 2004.

Troy, Gil. *Morning in America: How Ronald Reagan Invented the 1980s*. Princeton, NJ: Princeton University Press, 2005.

United States Congress. *Ronald Reagan: Late a President of the United States*. Washington, DC: U.S. Government Printing Office, 2005.

Van der Linden, Frank. *The Real Reagan: What He Believes, What He Has Accomplished, What We Can Expect from Him*. New York: William Morrow, 1981.

Viereck, Peter, with Claes G. Ryn. *Conservatism Revisited: The Revolt Against Ideology*. New Brunswick, NJ: Transaction Publishers, 2005.

Viguerie, Richard A., and David Franke. *America's Right Turn: How Conservatives Used New and Alternative Media to Take Power*. Chicago: Bonus Books, 2004.

Viguerie, Richard A. *The New Right: We're Ready to Lead*. Falls Church, VA: Viguerie Company, 1980.

Von Damm, Helene, ed. *Sincerely, Ronald Reagan*. New York: Berkley Books, 1980.

Von Damm, Helene. *At Reagan's Side*. New York: Doubleday, 1989.

Wallison, Peter J. *Ronald Reagan: The Power of Conviction and the Success of His Presidency*. Boulder, CO: Westview Press, 2004.

Warren, Donald J. *The Radical Center: Middle Americans and the Politics of Alienation*. Notre Dame, IN: University of Notre Dame Press, 1976.

Watson, Richard A. *The Presidential Contest: With a Guide to the 1980 Race*. New York: John Wiley & Sons, 1980.

Wattenberg, Ben J. *The Real America: A Surprising Examination of the State of the Union*. New York: Capricorn Books, 1976.

Wead, Doug, and Bill Wead. *Reagan: In Pursuit of the Presidency—1980*. Plainfield, NJ: Haven Books, 1980.

Welch, Robert H. W., Jr. *Life of John Birch*. Boston: Western Islands Publishers, 1954.

West, Darrell M. *Air Wars: Television Advertising in Election Campaigns, 1952–2000*. Washington, DC: CQ Press, 2001.

Whitaker, Robert W., ed. *The New Right Papers*. New York: St. Martin's Press, 1982.

White, F. Clifton, and William J. Gill. *Why Reagan Won: A Narrative History of the Conservative Movement, 1964–1981*. Chicago: Regnery Gateway, 1981.

White, F. Clifton. *Politics as a Noble Calling: The Memoirs of F. Clifton White*. Ottawa, IL: Jameson Books, 1994.

White, Theodore H. *America in Search of Itself: The Making of the President, 1956–1980*. New York: Harper & Row, 1982.

White, Theodore H. *The Making of the President, 1960*. New York: Atheneum, 1961.

White, Theodore H. *The Making of the President, 1968*. New York: Atheneum, 1969.

White, Theodore H. *The Making of the President, 1964*. New York: Atheneum, 1965.

Wilentz, Sean. *The Age of Reagan: A History 1974–2008*. New York: HarperCollins, 2008.

Wirthlin, Dick, and Wynton C. Hall. *The Greatest Communicator: What Ronald Reagan Taught Me about Politics, Leadership, and Life*. Hoboken, NJ: John Wiley and Sons, 2004.

Witcover, Jules. *Crapshoot: Rolling the Dice on the Vice Presidency*. New York: Crown Publishers, 1992.

Witcover, Jules. *Marathon: The Pursuit of the Presidency 1972–1976*. New York: Viking Press, 1977.

Woodward, Bob, and Carl Bernstein. *The Final Days*. New York: Simon & Schuster, 1976.

Woodward, Bob. *Shadow: Five Presidents and the Legacy of Watergate*. New York: Simon & Schuster, 1999.

Yager, Edward M. *Ronald Reagan's Journey: Democrat to Republican*. New York: Rowman & Littlefield, 2006.

Zak, Michael. *Back to Basics for the Republican Party*. Chicago: Thiessen Printing & Graphics, 2000.

Zeiger, Hans. *Reagan's Children: Taking Back the City on the Hill*. Nashville, TN: Broadman and Holman, 2006.

Zeller, F. C. Duke, *Devil's Pact: Inside the World of the Teamsters Union*. Secaucus, NJ: A Birch Lane Press Book, 1996.

PERIODICALS

Atlanta Journal Constitution

Austin (TX) American-Statesman

Baltimore Sun

Boston Globe

Boston Irish Reporter

Buffalo News

Burlington (VT) Free Press

Capital Times (WI)

Cato Institute Tax and Budget Bulletin

Cato Policy Report

Chicago Daily Herald

Chicago Tribune

Christian Science Monitor

Citizens for the Republic Newsletter

Concord (NH) Monitor

Courier-Journal (KY)

Dallas Morning News

Detroit News

Economist

Evans–Novak Political Report

Globe and Mail (Toronto)

Hartford (CT) Courant

Houston Chronicle

Human Events

Idaho Statesman

Indianapolis Star

Kansas City Times

Libertas

Los Angeles Times

Manchester (NH) Union-Leader

Melrose Mirror

Miami Herald

Milwaukee Journal
Montgomery (AL) *Advertiser*
N.H. Business Review
Nashua (NH) *Telegraph*
Nashville Tennessean
National Journal
National Review
New York Post
New York Times Magazine
New York Times
Newark (NJ) *Star-Ledger*
News and Observer (NC)
Newsmax
Newsweek
Philadelphia Inquirer
Plain Dealer (OH)
Providence (RI) *Journal*
Sacramento Bee
San Juan (PR) *Star*
Sioux Falls (SD) *Argus Leader*
State (SC)
Time
Times-Picayune (LA)
U.S. News & World Report
USA Today
Wall Street Journal
Washington Post
Washington Star
Washington Times
Washingtonian
Wisconsin State Journal

NEWS WIRES

Associated Press
Newhouse News Service
United Press International

ELECTRONIC MEDIA

ABC News
ATV-10 (Melbourne)
CBS News
CNN
MSNBC
NBC News

OTHER MATERIALS

Archived Collection, *American Spectator*
Archived Collection, Hoover Institution
Archived Collection, *Human Events*
Archived Collection, John M. Ashbrook Center for Public Affairs
Archived Collection, Media Research Center Archives
Archived Collection, The Robert J. Dole Institute of Politics

Archived Collection, Young America's Foundation
Arizona State University Libraries
Brigham Young University
Cornell University
Federal Bureau of Investigation Archives
Georgetown University Library
Presidential records, Franklin D. Roosevelt Presidential Library and Museum
Presidential records, George Bush Presidential Library and Museum
Presidential records, Gerald R. Ford Presidential Library and Museum
Presidential records, Jimmy Carter Presidential Library and Museum
Presidential records, John F. Kennedy Presidential Library and Museum
Presidential records, Lyndon Baines Johnson Library and Museum
Presidential records, Ronald Reagan Presidential Foundation and Library
Presidential Ratings, Roper Center for Public Opinion Research
Private Archives Collection of Bill Hecht
Private Archives Collection of Bruce Eberle
Private Archives Collection of Gary Maloney
Private Archives Collection of Ken Khachigian
Private Archives Collection of Kenny Klinge
Private Archives Collection of Michele Davis
Private Archives Collection of Paul Russo
Private Archives Collection of Richard Bond
Private Archives Collection of Richard Greenfield
Private Archives Collection of Robert Novak
Private Archives Collection of Ron Robinson
Private Archives Collection of Richard Viguerie
Private Archives Collection of Richard Wirthlin
St. John's University Library
U.S. Army Center for Military History
U.S. Department of State
University of Connecticut
University of Oklahoma Political Communications
University of Texas
Video Material, Miller Center of Public Affairs
Walter Reed Medical Center
Washington Post Writers Group

INTERVIEWS

Ahearn, Rick. Interview by Craig Shirley. Tape recording. February 4, 2009.
Albosta, Don. Interview by Craig Shirley. Tape recording. January 5, 2007.
Allen, George. Interview by Craig Shirley. 2006.
Allen, Richard. Interview by Craig Shirley. April 12, 2008.
Allen, Richard. Interview by Craig Shirley. Tape recording. June 14, 2006.
Anderson, John. Interview by Craig Shirley. Tape recording. December 10, 2007.
Anderson, Marty. Interview by Craig Shirley. Tape recording. May, 2007.
Angelo, Ernest. Interview by Craig Shirley. Tape recording. November 13, 2006.
Baker, James. Interview by Craig Shirley. Tape recording. September 6, 2006.
Bandow, Doug. Interview by Craig Shirley. Tape recording. October 10, 2006.
Barnes, Fred. Interview by Craig Shirley. September 29, 2008.
Barone, Michael. Interview by Craig Shirley. Tape recording. December 14, 2007.
Bartlett, Charlie. Interview by Craig Shirley. Tape recording. November 4, 2007.
Bell, Jeff. Interview by Craig Shirley. Tape recording. June 27, 2006.
Black, Charles. Interview by Craig Shirley. January 16, 2007.

Black, Charles. Interview by Craig Shirley. Tape recording. March 20, 2006.

Blackwell, Morton. Interview by Craig Shirley. Tape recording. February 28, 2007.

Blakely, Ed. Interview by Craig Shirley. Tape recording. April 17, 2007.

Bond, Richard. Interview by Craig Shirley. Tape recording. October 4, 2006.

Boone, Pat. Interview by Craig Shirley. Tape recording. September 7, 2006.

Bozell, Brent. Interview by Craig Shirley. Tape recording. January 4, 2007.

Brady, John. Interview by Craig Shirley. Tape recording. March 10, 2006.

Brock, Bill. Interview by Craig Shirley. Tape recording. October 15, 2006.

Broder, David S. Interview by Craig Shirley. Tape recording. June 23, 2006.

Brokaw, Tom. Interview by Craig Shirley. Tape recording. September 19, 2006.

Buchanan, Bay. Interview by Craig Shirley. Tape recording. July 19, 2006.

Buckley, William F., Jr. Interview by Craig Shirley. Tape recording. July 27, 2006.

Bufkin, Dave. Interview by Craig Shirley. Tape recording. March 14, 2006.

Burnley, Jim. Interview by Craig Shirley. Tape recording. April 17, 2007.

Bush, George H. W. Interview by Craig Shirley. February 16, 2007.

Bush, Jeb. Interview by Craig Shirley. Tape recording. August 22, 2006.

Caddell, Patrick. Interview by Craig Shirley. Tape recording. May 13, 2009.

Campo, Terry. Interview by Craig Shirley. Tape recording. February 7, 2007.

Cannon, Lou. Interview by Craig Shirley. Tape recording. December 5, 2006.

Cannon, Lou. Interview by Craig Shirley. Tape recording. June 6, 2006.

Carmen, Gerald. Interview by Craig Shirley. Tape recording. July 25, 2006.

Carmen, Gerald. Interview by Craig Shirley. Tape recording. June 18, 2007.

Carney, David. Interview by Craig Shirley. Tape recording. April, 12, 2007.

Carter, Jimmy. Interview by Craig Shirley. Tape recording. July 11, 2006.

Chavez, Linda. Interview by Craig Shirley. Tape recording. February 16, 2007.

Cheney, Richard. Interview by Craig Shirley. Tape recording. June 9, 2004.

Cheney, Richard. Interview by Craig Shirley. Tape recording. March 19, 2007.

Clark, Colin. Interview by Craig Shirley. Tape recording. September 22, 2006.

Coleman, Muriel. Interview by Craig Shirley. Tape recording. May 2, 2007.

Corbin, Darlene. Interview by Craig Shirley. Tape recording. December 11, 2007.

Davis, Michele. Interview by Craig Shirley. Tape recording. March 14, 2008.

Deaver, Mike. Interview by Craig Shirley. Tape recording. October 18, 2006

Devine, Don. Interview by Craig Shirley. Tape recording. September 14, 2006.

Diggins, Jack. Interview by Craig Shirley. August 4, 2006.

Doherty, Eileen. Interview by Craig Shirley. Tape recording. April 11, 2007.

Donaldson, Sam. Interview by Craig Shirley. Tape recording. December 12, 2007.

Donatelli, Frank J. Interview by Craig Shirley. Tape recording. July 14, 2006.

Donatelli, Frank J. Interview by Craig Shirley. Tape recording. July 26, 2006.

Donatelli, Rebecca R. Interview by Craig Shirley. Tape recording. July 14, 2006.

Dunn, Robert. Interview by Craig Shirley. Tape recording. June 23, 2009.

Duvall, Dale C. Interview by Craig Shirley. Tape recording. November 6, 2006.

Eberle, Bruce. Interview by Craig Shirley. Tape recording. March 4, 2007.

Edwards, Lee. Interview by Craig Shirley. Tape recording. April 11, 2007.

Ellis, Tom. Interview by Craig Shirley. Tape recording. May 10, 2004.

Evans, Stan. Interview by Craig Shirley. Tape recording. February 25, 2004.

Fabrizio, Tony. Interview by Craig Shirley. Tape recording. April 6, 2007.

Finkelstein, Arthur. Interview by Craig Shirley. Tape recording. 2007.

Fund, John. Interview by Craig Shirley. Tape recording. April 12, 2007.

Gingrich, Newt. Interview by Craig Shirley. Tape recording. May 21, 2006.

Gold, Victor. Interview by Craig Shirley. December 19, 2007.

Gold, Victor. Interview by Craig Shirley. Tape recording. April 16, 2007.

Gold, Victor. Interview by Craig Shirley. Tape recording. April 5, 2007.

Gold, Victor. Interview by Craig Shirley. Tape recording. March 27, 2006.

Halper, Stefan. Interview by Craig Shirley. Tape recording. March 20, 2007.

Hannaford, Peter. Interview by Craig Shirley. June 25, 2009.

Hannaford, Peter. Interview by Craig Shirley. June 30, 2009.

Hannaford, Peter. Interview by Craig Shirley. March 4, 2008.

Hannaford, Peter. Interview by Craig Shirley. Tape recording. March 24, 2006.

Hecht, Bill. Interview by Craig Shirley. Tape recording. September 28, 2006.

Heckman, Bob. Interview by Craig Shirley. 2007.

Herring, Joanne. Interview by Craig Shirley. Tape recording. 2007.

Hillyer, Quin. Interview by Craig Shirley. Tape recording. May 5, 2006.

Hoitsma, Gary. Interview by Craig Shirley. Tape recording. July 24, 2006.

Hooley, Jim. Interview by Craig Shirley. Tape recording. February 4, 2009.

Hume, Brit. Interview by Craig Shirley. Tape recording. December 19, 2007.

Kaufman, Ron. Interview by Craig Shirley. Tape recording. August 25, 2006.

Keene, David. Interview by Craig Shirley. May 12, 2009.

Keene, David. Interview by Craig Shirley. Tape recording. March 17, 2006.

Keene, David. Interview by Craig Shirley. Tape recording. November 18, 2007.

Keene, David. Interview by Craig Shirley. Tape recording. October 10, 2006.

Kemp, Jack. Interview by Craig Shirley. Tape recording. November 15, 2006.

Kennedy Townsend, Kathleen. Interview by Craig Shirley. Tape recording. December 18, 2007.

Khachigian, Ken. Interview by Craig Shirley. August 29, 2008.

Khachigian, Ken. Interview by Craig Shirley. Tape recording. May 2007.

Kinder, Lorelei. Interview by Craig Shirley. Tape recording. July 12, 2007.

Klinge, Ken. Interview by Craig Shirley. Tape recording. July 12, 2006.

Klinge, Ken. Interview by Craig Shirley. Tape recording. June 27, 2006.

Kudlow, Larry. Interview by Craig Shirley. Tape recording. March 8, 2004.

Lacy, Bill. Interview by Craig Shirley. Tape recording. March 23, 2006.

Laffer, Arthur. Interview by Craig Shirley. Tape recording. January 18, 2007.

Lake, Jim. Interview by Craig Shirley. Tape recording. January 16, 2004.

Lake, Jim. Interview by Craig Shirley. Tape recording. September 19, 2006.

Lambro, Don. Interview by Craig Shirley. Tape recording. January 24, 2007.

Langdon, Bruce. Interview by Craig Shirley. Tape recording. 2006.

Lauderback, Bill. Interview by Craig Shirley. Tape recording. August 2, 2006.

Laxalt, Paul. Interview by Craig Shirley. Tape recording. July 31, 2006.

Leonard, Tish. Interview by Craig Shirley. Tape recording. September 12, 2006.

Levin, Mark. Interview by Craig Shirley. Tape recording. March 14, 2006.

Lewis, Marrin. Interview by Craig Shirley. September 6, 2006.

Livingston, Bob. Interview by Craig Shirley. Tape recording. April 19, 2007.

Long, Mike. Interview by Craig Shirley. Tape recording. April 19, 2007.

Lucey, David. Interview by Craig Shirley. Tape recording. December 8, 2006.

Lucey, Laurel. Interview by Craig Shirley. Tape recording. January 4, 2009.

Lucey, Pat. Interview by Craig Shirley. Tape recording. December 5, 2006.

Mahe, Eddie. Interview by Craig Shirley. Tape recording. May 12, 2006.

Maloney, Gary. Interview by Craig Shirley. Tape recording. 2006.

Maxwell, John. Interview by Craig Shirley. Tape recording. July 20, 2006.

McConnell, John. Interview by Craig Shirley. Tape recording. March 30, 2006.

McInturff, Bill. Interview by Craig Shirley. Tape recording. 2007.

McPherson, Peter. Interview by Craig Shirley. Tape recording. April 25, 2007.

McShane, Michael. Interview by Craig Shirley. Tape recording. 2007.

Meese, Edwin. Interview by Craig Shirley. Tape recording. May 6, 2006

Minnick, Brad. Interview by Craig Shirley. Tape recording. March 5, 2007.

Mintz, Myron. Interview by Craig Shirley. Tape recording. June 8, 2008.

Mondale, Walter. Interview by Craig Shirley. Tape recording. February 28, 2007.

Morris, Brent. Interview by Craig Shirley. Tape recording. May 15, 2006.

Morrison, Susan. Interview by Craig Shirley.

Mounger, William D. Interview by Craig Shirley. Tape recording. April 16, 2007.

Murphy, Jim. Interview by Craig Shirley. Tape recording. April 5, 2006.

Myers, Lisa. Interview by Craig Shirley. Tape recording. June 9, 2008.

Nolan, Pat. Interview by Craig Shirley. Tape recording. August 1, 2006.

Norquist, Grover. Interview by Craig Shirley. Tape recording. March 21, 2006.

Novak, Robert. Interview by Craig Shirley. Tape recording. December 11, 2007.

Peden, Neal. Interview by Craig Shirley. Tape recording. July 6, 2006.

Pickering, Charles. Interview by Craig Shirley. Tape recording. 2006.

Pinkerton, Jim. Interview by Craig Shirley. Tape recording. November 2, 2006.

Plissner, Marty. Interview by Craig Shirley. Tape recording. August 4, 2008.

Powell, Jody. Interview by Craig Shirley. Tape recording. April 10, 2006.

Rafshoon, Gerald. Interview by Craig Shirley. Tape recording. June 1, 2009.

Rafshoon, Gerald. Interview by Craig Shirley. Tape recording. March 20, 2008.

Reagan, Michael. Interview by Craig Shirley. Tape recording. July 2, 2004.

Reed, Clarke. Interview by Craig Shirley. Tape recording. 2006.

Reed, Rick. Interview by Craig Shirley. 2007.

Reynolds, Nancy. Interview by Craig Shirley. Tape recording. October 3, 2006.

Roberts, Jim. Interview by Craig Shirley. Tape recording. July 20, 2006.

Robinson, Ron. Interview by Craig Shirley. Tape recording. March 22, 2007.

Roper, Tim. Interview by Craig Shirley. 2007.

Rotterman, Marc. Interview by Craig Shirley. Tape recording. March 15, 2007.

Russo, Paul. Interview by Craig Shirley. Tape recording. September 8, 2006.

Ryan, Fred. Interview by Craig Shirley.

Schulz, Bill. Interview by Craig Shirley. Tape recording. January 23, 2007.

Schweiker, Richard. Interview by Craig Shirley. Tape recording. November 6, 2006.

Sears, John. Interview by Craig Shirley. Tape recording. July 26, 2006.

Sears, John. Interview by Craig Shirley. Tape recording. March 18, 2004.

Seigenthaler, John. Interview by Craig Shirley. Tape recording. March 25, 2008.

Seigenthaler, John. Interview by Craig Shirley. Tape recording. November 15, 2007.

Shankman, Frida. Interview by Craig Shirley. Tape recording. 2007.

Shelby, Rick. Interview by Craig Shirley. Tape recording. September 12, 2006.

Shrum, Robert. Interview by Craig Shirley. Tape recording. March 19, 2008.

Sinnott, Nancy. Interview by Craig Shirley. Tape recording. March 29, 2007.

Smick, David. Interview by Craig Shirley. Tape recording. October 18, 2006.

Smith, Rodney. Interview by Craig Shirley. Tape recording. September 7, 2006.

Spencer, Karen. Interview by Craig Shirley. Tape recording. December 20, 2006.

Spencer, Stuart. Interview by Craig Shirley. Tape recording. June 21, 2004.

Spencer, Stuart. Interview by Craig Shirley. Tape recording. September 28, 2006.

Spencer, Stuart. Interview by Craig Shirley. Tape recording. September 29, 2006.

Stockdale, James. Interview by Craig Shirley. Tape recording. February 15, 2007.

Stone, Ann. Interview by Craig Shirley. Tape recording. December 18, 2007.

Stone, Roger. Interview by Craig Shirley. Tape recording. April 10, 2006.

Sweat, Joseph. Interview by Craig Shirley. Tape recording. February 12, 2007.

Tapscott Canevaro, Cindy. Interview by Craig Shirley. Tape recording. November 3, 2006.

Tapscott, Mark. Interview by Craig Shirley. Tape recording. January 1, 2008.

Teague, Randal C. Interview by Craig Shirley. Tape recording. August 22, 2006.

Thomasson, Ray. Interview by Craig Shirley. Tape recording. February 12, 2007.

Timmons, Bill. Interview by Craig Shirley. March 10, 2008.

Timmons, Bill. Interview by Craig Shirley. Tape recording. September 6, 2006.

Totten, Don. Interview by Craig Shirley. Tape recording. January 4, 2008.

Tucker, Bill. Interview by Craig Shirley. Tape recording. September 11, 2006.

Tutwiler, Margaret. Interview by Craig Shirley. Tape recording. December 1, 2006.

Valis, Wayne. Interview by Craig Shirley. Tape recording. March 27, 2008.

Viguerie, Richard A. Interview by Craig Shirley. Tape recording. December 6, 2006.

Von Damm, Helene. Interview by Craig Shirley. Tape recording. May 17, 2006.

Walinsky, Adam. Interview by Craig Shirley. Tape recording. June 10, 2005.

Whitfield, Dennis. Interview by Craig Shirley. Tape recording. June 29, 2006.

Wirthlin, Dick. Interview by Craig Shirley. Tape recording. November 8, 2006.

Wren, Carter. Interview by Craig Shirley. Tape recording. October 23, 2006.

ACKNOWLEDGMENTS

People live and people die.

In the three-plus years since I began work on *Rendezvous with Destiny*, many of the players in this compelling drama have passed on, including a number of friends. Bill Buckley, Jack Kemp, Jude Wanniski, Lyn Nofziger, Mary Dent Crisp, Jeane Kirkpatrick, Bob Teeter, Jesse Helms, Guy Vander Jagt, Jennifer Dunn, Jerry Falwell, Hamilton Jordan, Michael A. W. Evans, Bob Novak, Hugh Sidey, Dennis Warren, Mike Deaver, Paul Weyrich, Ted Kennedy, Jody Powell, Caspar Weinberger, and others who played roles in the 1980 campaign have, in the words of Ronald Reagan, "gone home," as we all must someday. Still, I was able to interview some of these individuals among the hundred-plus people I spoke with, and thus to preserve their recollections. To all, I am beholden.

I am also deeply indebted to Ken Cribb and ISI Books for their faith and confidence in this project. Ken is not only a dear friend but also one of the most influential men in the American conservative movement today. Conversations with him remind one of the phrase "the pleasure of his company."

Also to Jed Donahue, editor in chief of ISI Books. Though a young man, he nearly had a heart attack when I turned in a 1,700-page draft. But as George Will, Fred Barnes, and Michael Barone can attest, and as I now know, Jed is one of the best, most patient, and most understanding editors in America. And to Doug Mills, Spencer Masloff, Jennifer Connolly, Chris Michalski, Christian Tappe, Jeremy Beer, Doug Schneider, and all the other fine people at ISI and ISI Books, thank you.

Special thanks go to Mrs. Ronald Reagan, Joanne Drake, and Fred Ryan of the Reagan Library for their support and assistance in the writing and research of *Rendez-*

vous with Destiny. Files long sealed at the Reagan Library were made exclusively available to me because of the kindness of Mrs. Reagan, Joanne, and Fred, and with the special assistance of Reagan Library senior archivist Jennifer Mandel. Their help is a debt I can never repay. More half a million documents were made available for review, and we selected five hundred of the most useful for this project.

I had less luck with the George Bush Presidential Library. The former president's 1980 papers are not accessible even to the archivists there. According to my researcher, Andi Hedberg Maloni, they require a "deed of gift" from Bush himself, since the files are considered private. This he has refused to grant. The commonly held view among Bush's former staff and other knowledgeable individuals is that these files contain memos and notations critical of his 1980 opponents, including Reagan. We were, however, able to review the 68,000 papers contained in the Robert M. Teeter Papers stored at the Bush Library. Thanks go to Doug Campbell for his help there.

Thanks also to President Jimmy Carter for agreeing to an interview. Although nearly thirty years had passed, it was evident that the president still had strong feelings about the election of 1980. Carter's presidential library has not yet processed the 1980 campaign documents, but I was allowed to review other files in which campaign documents resided, including the personal papers of many Carter White House aides and 1980 campaign aides. I am grateful to Mary Ann McSweeney, archives specialist at the Carter Library.

I am also grateful to Richard Cheney, Walter Mondale, James A. Baker III, John Sears, Brit Hume, Tom Brokaw, David Broder, John Anderson, Pat Boone, Newt Gingrich, Art Laffer, Bruce Langdon, Pat Lucey, Bill Brock, Michael Barone, Dick Schweiker, Lou Cannon, Sam Donaldson, Larry Kudlow, Lisa Myers, Dick Wirthlin, Stu Spencer, Richard Viguerie, Jody Powell, Pat Caddell, Jerry Rafshoon, Kathleen Kennedy Townsend, Ed Meese, Adam Walinsky, and so many others for taking time out of their busy schedules to sit down and speak with me.

Vice President Mondale was an utter joy to talk to, garrulous and full of pep. He told me of going out to California before running against Reagan in 1984 to meet with Jesse "Big Daddy" Unruh, Democratic speaker of the state house. Unruh was an unreconstructed liberal and thus he and Reagan battled mightily over the years. Mondale asked Unruh how he could beat Reagan. The blunt reply was: "You can't." Big Daddy expanded, "You won't know what hit you. . . . This guy's got some kind of magic. He has some kind of touch with the public that [is] phenomenal." Then he warned the Minnesotan, "I figure that you're going to find out about it."

Mondale himself was not immune to Reagan's charms, telling me, "I opposed him as hard as I could, but I still liked the guy."

Only four people I sought out I was not able to interview. David Stockman was at the time under indictment; Ted Kennedy was under a physician's care; Karl Rove would not give a reason. The fourth, rocker Alice Cooper, a Reagan supporter in 1980, had a unique reason for begging off. In an e-mail to Hayley McConnell, a research assistant on this book, an aide to Cooper wrote, "I am not sure [Cooper] remembers much about 1980 as he was drunk the entire time. Well, most of the time from 1969 through 1982 actually."

I also had a sneaking suspicion that Kennedy may not have wanted to address the issue of whether he really wanted Carter to win in November 1980. Jody Powell told me he always "felt . . . that Kennedy did not want Carter to win that election." It may be, too, that Kennedy did not want to relive that painful campaign, having been ahead of everybody by miles, only to lose ignominiously to Carter. It was evident in my interview with President Carter that he bears no good wishes for Ted Kennedy; I would have liked to ask Kennedy whether they had spoken since 1980.

Extraordinary special thanks go to my principle research aide, Borko Komnenovic, for his years, months, weeks, days, and hours of extraordinary work. Borko is an émigré from the former Communist Yugoslavia, where he grew up under the mailed fist of dictator Marshal Tito's regime. "Growing up . . . Ronald Reagan to me was the face of America," Borko wrote. "One of the first passages I read in my entire life was a short article about Ronald Reagan. It was about how Reagan spent his holy days at his Santa Barbara ranch." One of Borko's neighbors, who had once been imprisoned by Tito, told the young man, "There is no joke with this Reagan. He is the one who is going to finally destroy this evil."

Borko concluded, "Reagan's philosophy, accentuated by his always forceful articulation, awoke the inner American in my heart. I wholeheartedly believe that I speak for countless millions who lived beneath the dark cloud of Communism when I say that those longing for freedom had no better friend than Ronald Reagan. There is no doubt in my mind that if Reagan had been born Serbian Orthodox, he would not be referred by many merely as President Reagan, but as Saint Reagan."

Special thanks are also owed to Sean Kennedy for all of his fine work, especially his diligence in the chapter on Paul Corbin; Andi Hedberg Maloni for her adroit research work at the Reagan, Bush, Ford, and Carter presidential libraries, the Hoover Institution, and the Robert J. Dole Institute of Politics; Erica Hare for tracking down local newspapers from the 1980 campaign; and Seaton Motley, Stephen Saunders, Maggie Lyons, Kyra-Verena Sendt, and Andreja Komnenovic for their tireless work. And to Bob Clark of the Franklin D. Roosevelt Presidential Library; Jean Bischoff, Bob Clark, and Bill Lacy of the Dole Institute; Carol Leadenham and Kiz Konzak of the Hoover Institution; Marv Krinsky and David Roepke of the John M. Ashbrook Center for Public Affairs; the University of Oklahoma Department of

Political Communications; and the Media Research Center. Also, thanks to Gary Johnson of the Library of Congress, Debbie Lopez of the FBI's Freedom of Information Act division, David M. Hardy of the FBI, Doris M. Lama and Lori Twardzik of the Department of the Navy, and Margaret Grafeld of the State Department for their assistance in tracking down government documents on Paul Corbin. And to Charles Brock and Paul Nielsen of The DesignWorks Group, who did such a masterful job for the dust jacket of this book, as well as to Cheryl Hendrick, formerly of The DesignWorks Group, for my previous book.

Of course, none of this would have been possible without the friendship, kind assistance, and patience of my business partner and friend, Diana Banister, to whom I am deeply indebted. And to the staff at Shirley & Banister Public Affairs, including Kevin McVicker, Meghan Snyder, Amy Haas, Dan Wilson, Hayley McConnell, Katelyn Gimbel, and others, for their support and patience over the past three years.

Before turning the manuscript over to Jed Donahue's warm though necessarily ruthless edits, I first carefully chose three men—all professional editors—to help me along the way. Again, as with so many others, I am in their debt.

Peter Hannaford helped immensely in the factual accounting of this story. He wrote so many of Reagan's speeches, op-eds, radio commentaries, and the like and simply knew the man's mind as well as anyone. He was at Reagan's side constantly during the tumultuous years from 1976 through 1980. And of course he knew all of the other key players involved for many years.

Quin Hillyer, a conservative columnist of long standing for the *American Spectator*, the *Washington Examiner*, and the *Washington Times*, argued with me, cajoled me, pushed me, always in search of the same goal: a book that would stand the test of time.

John Persinos is not a commonly known writer, but he can turn a phrase as well as anyone. And because John's politics are decidedly liberal, I deliberately sought him out in an effort to drain any overt bias out of this book. I simply wanted to report the facts, whether they favored Reagan or not, and John came through like a champ.

Thanks to the following for allowing me to review their private papers covering the election of 1980. Among them are Ken Khachigian, Allan Ryskind, Tim Roper, Dr. Richard Wirthlin, J. Kenneth Klinge, Ron Robinson, Gary Maloney, Rich Bond, N. Richard Greenfield, Bruce Eberle, Richard Viguerie, Robert Novak, Michele Davis, Colin Clark, and Paul Russo. And thanks to my friend David Doll for undertaking research on James Baker at Princeton University.

Sadly, the documents for Citizens for the Republic, the National Conservative Political Action Committee, the Fund for a Conservative Majority, and the Congressional Club were destroyed after the demise of each. Thanks, however, to Brigham Young University, where the papers of the American Conservative Union are stored.

Some close friends over the past three years gave me advice and encouragement, read chapters, and generally put up with me, and they, too, are owed a large measure of gratitude. In no particular order, Bill Schulz, Fred Barnes, Tony Fabrizio, Becky Norton Dunlop and George Dunlop, Marc and Karen Rotterman, Dick Allen, Mark Tapscott, Ralph and Millie Hallow, Jim Pinkerton, Jim Burnley, Al Regnery, Bob Tyrrell, Newt and Callista Gingrich, Frank and Becki Donatelli, George and Susan Allen, Fred Eckert, Brad O'Leary, Bill Hecht, Jerry Eckert, Rich Bond, Tom and Lyn Finnigan, Michele Davis, Richard Viguerie, Kenny and Jean Klinge, Colin Clark, Paul Russo, Sara Davis, Dave Keene, Fred Barbash, Tom Edsall, Michael and Susan McShane, Brent and Norma Bozell, Christian Josi, Tish Leonard, Stephen Moore, Bill Timmons, Vic and Dale Gold, Pat and M. J. Pizzella, Jim Ragonnet, Ed Meese, Ron Robinson, Michelle Easton, Bruce and Kathy Eberle, Carl Cannon, Don Devine, Nancy Reynolds, Karen Spencer, Muriel Coleman, Doug Bandow, Lou Cannon, Sara Davis, Frank and Ann Lavin, Tom Winter, Allan Ryskind, Kevin and Chris Kabanuk, Floyd Brown, Howard Fineman, Dick Allen, Tom Edsall, Bill Clark, Mike Reagan, Joanne Herring, Tom Loringer, Paul Laxalt, Roger Stone, Eric Dezenhall, Chuck DeFeo, Chris Ruddy, Charles Pratt, Roshan and Perin Bhappu, Ross and Candy Bhappu, Dan and Soona Jacob, Manek Bhappu, and Ellen, Nathan, Eric, and Todd Shirley

And special thanks to George F. Will, for agreeing to write the foreword to this book.

Finally, I am most deeply indebted to my beloved wife, Zorine—"Reggie"—who so patiently read, edited, listened, and made superior suggestions over the past several years. For much of the time, I labored in a tiny den at home, crammed with books, interview transcripts, DVDs, CDs, newspapers, magazines, presidential library material, and other source material. So concerned was I about losing anything, no one was allowed into my *sanctum sanctorum* with the exception of Zorine. I understand that Mark Twain operated in much the same fashion, allowing only his beloved Olivia, "Liv Darling," to cross a chalk line he'd drawn across the floor. This system seemed to work for us as well, but as dust gathered and I fulminated, Zorine's fortitude never wavered.

Our four children also helped along the way, from Mitchell reviewing videotapes to Matt and Andrew (who often worked into the wee hours of the morning) and Taylor reading manuscripts, fact-checking, and offering advice to their old man.

Thank you all.

Craig Shirley
Alexandria, Virginia

INDEX

Communist Party USA, 422, 426, 430, 436
Conconi, Chuck, 418–19
Concord Monitor, 131
Congressional Club, 212
Connally, John, 125, 212, 221, 229, 243, 390, 391; 1980 Republican convention and, 344; 1980 Republican presidential nomination and, 36, 38, 72; abortion and, 58; age issue and, 72; announcement of candidacy of, 38; Arkansas and, 117–18; Bush and, 56–59, 92; campaign finance and, 51, 87–88, 114; conservatism and, 58; ERA and, 58; fundraising and, 87–88; health of, 140; HUAC and, 435–36; Indiana and, 69; Iowa and, 70, 91, 98, 102; military service of, 57; Mississippi and, 134; New Hampshire and, 57, 91, 110, 126, 147, 148, 157; party-switching of, 38, 58, 86; Reagan, attacks on by, 58, 72, 86; Reagan, endorsement of by, 271; Republican Party and, 18; SALT II and, 58; South Carolina and, 92, 100, 111, 178–79, 189–90, 197–99; strategy of, 91; withdrawal of, 198–99
Connally, John, III, 178, 189
Connecticut: 1980 Democratic presidential nomination and, 190, 223–24, 228–30; 1980 presidential election and, 391; 1980 Republican presidential nomination and, 121, 134–35, 221–22, 230
conservatism: 1980 presidential election and, xii; Buckley and, 339–40; Bush and, 48–49, 58, 261; change and, 2; Cold War, 58; compassionate, 596; Connally and, 58; Dole and, 49; Goldwater and, 18; grassroots, 36, 68; liberalism vs., 21; media and, 24; *National Review* and, 339–40; neo-, 597, 602; Panama Canal treaties and, 26; Reagan and, 2, 8–9, 13, 15, 18, 21–23, 54, 92, 94, 107, 119, 128, 138, 173, 191, 194, 261, 336, 403, 450, 595–97, 602; religious, 254–56; Republican Party and, 19, 21–23, 339; rise of, 4, 339–40, 602; Roosevelt and, 2; social, 21, 52; South

and, 392; Sun Belt, 18. *See also* conservative movement
Conservative Digest, 329
conservative movement: Christian Right and, 340; Cold Warriors and, 68; growth of, 22–23, 32; importance of, 25; New Right and, 23–25; Nofziger and, 174; Reagan and, 2, 9; Republican Party and, 25. *See also* conservatism
Conservative Political Action Conference (CPAC), 8, 21–23, 151, 585
Constitution, U.S., 185, 291, 327, 354, 542; Bill of Rights, 597; First Amendment, 403; Tenth Amendment, 403; Twelfth Amendment, 291, 351
Conte, Silvio, 352
Coolidge, Calvin, 215
"co-presidency," 3, 349–69, 371, 373, 376, 393, 591
Corbin, Darlene, 424, 609
Corbin, Gertrude, 429
Corbin, Paul, 429; 1960 presidential election and, 237; 1980 presidential election and, 416; background of, 420–21; Carter, undermining of and, 413, 416; Carter briefing books and, 420, 435, 437–41, 516, 529, 607–9; Catholic conversion of, 429–30; Communist affiliations of, 422–23, 426–27, 430, 435–36; death of, 419; DNC and, 428–29, 430, 431, 432; FBI and, 419, 421, 423, 426, 428, 430–31, 432; FBI file on, 418; HUAC and, 422, 430–31; Kennedy, Edward "Ted," and, 429; Kennedy, John F., and, 428–29; Kennedy, Robert F., and, 103, 418, 424–30, 431, 432, 433; labor unions and, 419, 421–22, 436; Lucey and, 425, 433, 434–35, 436–37; marriages of, 421, 426
Corbin, Seena, 421
Corcoran, Tommy "The Cork," 8
Cotten, Ben, 296, 314
Council on Foreign Relations, 177, 215
Coyne, Jim, 249
CPAC. *See* Conservative Political Action Conference
Crane, Arlene, 47, 90
Crane, Philip M., 58, 125, 376, 596; 1980 Republican presi-

dential nomination and, 32–33, 47, 560–61; campaign finance and, 51, 90, 205; Illinois and, 206; Iowa and, 40, 111; New Hampshire and, 68, 126, 147, 153, 154; Reagan and, 47–48; withdrawal of, 227
Criscom, Tommy, 147
Crisp, Mary Dent, 296, 314, 327–28, 413
Cronkite, Walter, 149, 171–72, 270, 357, 359, 361, 367, 531, 546, 570, 573
C-SPAN, 572
Cuba, 114, 117, 186, 265, 338, 398, 586
Culture of Narcissism, The (Lasch), 47
Culver, John, 581
Curson, Elliott, 139, 213
Cutler, Lloyd, 550

Dailey, Peter, 308, 315, 331, 377, 390, 465, 524
Daley, Richard, 211
Dalton, John, 203
D'Amato, Alfonse, 464–65
Dart, Justin, 308
Davis, Dr. and Mrs. Loyal, 36
Davis, Michele, 339, 350, 391, 492, 554, 558, 593
Davis, Patti, 318, 343, 363, 581–82
Dawson, Robert, 184
Dear, Ron, 65
Deardourff, John, 196
Deaver, Carolyn, 83
Deaver, Michael, 23, 113, 308, 313, 332, 390; 1976 Republican presidential nomination and, 14; 1980 presidential election and, 55, 72, 81–84, 453; 1980 Republican presidential nomination and, 34; CFTR and, 19; Cleveland debate and, 532; Election Day 1980 and, 579; Iowa and, 111; Keene and, 39; Reagan running mate choice and, 360; Reagan-Ford relationship and, 17; Sears and, 36, 40, 65, 66, 136–37, 166, 169, 180
Debategate, 420, 435, 437–41, 515–16, 529, 607–12
defense, 32, 114, 396, 397, 458–59, 479, 592
Dellums, Ron, 403
Democratic National Committee (DNC), 224; Anderson and,